D1273490

Social Psychology Through Symbolic Interaction

Gregory P. Stone
UNIVERSITY OF MINNESOTA

Harvey A. Farberman
STATE UNIVERSITY OF NEW YORK AT STONY BROOK

SOCIAL PSYCHOLOGY THROUGH SYMBOLIC INTERACTION

Ginn–Blaisdell A XEROX COMPANY

WALTHAM, MASSACHUSETTS · TORONTO · LONDON

To Herbert Blumer, teacher and scholar, who has kept the perspective of symbolic interaction alive and lively in the continuing dialogue that we call social psychology.

CONSULTING EDITORS

Kurt Lang *State University of New York at Stony Brook*
Gladys Engel Lang *Center for Urban Education, New York City*

Preface

People transform themselves and their worlds as they engage in social dialogue. This theme is rendered in many variations throughout this volume, hopefully to strike responsive chords in different audiences. There are uncluttered presentations for liberal arts undergraduates, technical expositions for pre-professional and professional trainees, and more than an occasional original research piece for those who practice the craft.

In our selection of material, we have made a determined effort (1) to present materials, whenever possible, in their actual historical sequence so as to underline the cumulative development of knowledge and technique; (2) to go beyond the bounds of social psychology proper into such areas as the sociology of knowledge, anthropology, linguistics, philosophy, and literature to illustrate the applicability of symbolic interactionist principles; and (3) to conclude each part of the volume with materials that are, in the editors' opinions, as close to the cutting edge of the field as possible. Needless to say, we have not, with any great consistency, achieved these goals.

Above and beyond our criteria of selection, the critical reader may find us vulnerable on other counts. For a variety of reasons outlined in the Introduction, our volume is concerned singularly with symbolic interaction; other perspectives do not receive their due. Even within this perspective, however, we may be challenged. We have, for example, omitted areas of conceptual focus such as "reference group" and "role." They have been so absorbed into current thinking that to separate them out for individual treatment seems superfluous. Moreover, from time to time, especially in our introductory and interstitial materials, we have raised questions, made criticisms, and offered leads for new directions in research with which others might well take issue. We hope they do.

So far as the logic of presentation is concerned, we have placed into Part One, under the heading "Symbolic Interaction: Perspective and Directions," those pieces that set the perspective in its larger philosophical and historical tradition, outline its major assumptions, and stake out those problem areas that have been and will be of considerable concern. In Part Two, entitled "Social Process As Symbolic Transformation," we emphasize man's capacity for creating and altering meaning, but pay special attention to those factors that condition this process, such as the collective nature of consensus, the underlying logic of linguistic systems, social position, and cultural epoch. Parts Three and Four, "The Definition of the Situation" and "Situations and Social Worlds," elaborate the theme first by presenting the progressive conceptual development of "The Definition of the Situation" as an analytic tool, and then by presenting different social worlds in which people construct definitions and act upon them.

Although Part Five carries the neutral title "Interaction Processes," its thrust lifts into relief relationships among the personal purposes one brings to a situation, those forms of dramatic presentation used to realize them, and the effect of such strategies on others' interpretive processes. In effect, Blumer's idea that we *construct* lines of action is fleshed out a bit.

In Part Six, "The Self," we present the major formulations of James, Cooley, Mead, and Sullivan in order to show the successive refinement and development of "self" as a concept, and conclude with an empirically grounded analytic model by Stone that builds on the earlier formulations. "Tests of the Perspective," Part Seven, offers some empirical support for many of the assertions about "self" made in the previous section. In addition, a critical methodological review of the very research strategies that generate this support culminates with some recommendations that might help to offset the more obvious defects. The general notion is that methodological techniques should not contravene theoretical assumptions.

Part Eight deals with how self keeps going in society. Entitled "Motives and Motivation," it presents a strictly sociological framework that sets the whole problem of motivation in the context of interpersonal control, deviant behavior, and the negotiation of identity and credibility. Part Nine, "Socialization as a Life Process," again emphasizes the continuous nature of self and identity transformation, especially as it continues beyond the early stages of childhood development. We conclude with Part Ten, "The Making and Breaking of Deviants," which builds on the premise that deviance does not inhere in an act, but is conferred upon it and oftimes by the judgment of a coalition of reality makers whose own sense of normality and sanity may be somewhat impoverished. In sum, we have made an effort to codify and extend a body of ideas that apprehends and analyzes man as a locus of purpose and power.

Finally, we wish to thank our friends and colleagues for the valuable criticism they gave us at various stages in the preparation of the manuscript—Donald W. Ball, Judith D. Bennet, Stephen D. Berger, Sherri Cavan, Norman K. Denzin, Eric Dunning, Harold Finestone, John Gagnon, Michael Gillespie, Erich Goode, Norman Goodman, James R. Hudson, Elias S. Mahigel, Donald G. McTavish, Peter McHugh, Marvin B. Scott, Thomas J. Scheff, Gladys I. Stone, and Eugene A. Weinstein.

G.P.S.
H.A.F.

Contents

INTRODUCTION   1

Part One: *Symbolic Interaction: Perspective and Directions*   11

1. Functional Analysis: A Statement of Problems   21
   Marvin B. Scott

2. The Oversocialized Conception of Man in Modern Sociology   29
   Dennis H. Wrong

3. On Psychology   40
   Benjamin Lee Whorf

4. Social Psychology: Model For Liberals   42
   C. Wright Mills

5. The Position of George Herbert Mead   55
   William H. Desmonde

6. Some Neglected Problems in Social Psychology   63
   Leonard S. Cottrell, Jr.

7. Major Trends in Symbolic Interaction Theory in the Past
   Twenty-five Years   70
   Manford H. Kuhn

Part Two: *Social Process as Symbolic Transformation*   89

8. That Powerful Drop   93
   Langston Hughes

9. The Stolen Base as a Social Object   93
   George J. McCall and J. L. Simmons

10. From Animal to Human Reactivity   95
    Ernest Becker

11. On the Edge of Rapprochement: Was Durkheim Moving Toward the
    Perspective of Symbolic Interaction?   100
    Gregory P. Stone and Harvey A. Farberman

12. Science and Linguistics   112
    Benjamin Lee Whorf

13. A Chinese Philosopher's Theory of Knowledge   121
    Chang Tung-Sun

14. On Relativism and Relationism   140
    Karl Mannheim

Part Three: *The Definition of the Situation*   147

15. Situations Defined as Real Are Real in Their Consequences   154
    William I. and Dorothy Swaine Thomas

16. On the Humanistic Coefficient   156
    Helena Znaniecki Lopata

17. The Context of Situation   158
    Bronislaw Malinowski

18. The Name of the Situation as Affecting Behavior   160
    Benjamin Lee Whorf

19. The Definition of the Situation   162
    Willard Waller

20. Embarrassment and the Analysis of Role Requirements   174
    Edward Gross and Gregory P. Stone

21. Making the Scene   190
    David J. and Judith D. Bennett

22. An Abortion Clinic Ethnography   196
    Donald W. Ball

Part Four: *Situations and Social Worlds*   207

23. On Crying and Mourning   213
    Meyer Fortes

24. Territoriality: A Neglected Sociological Dimension   214
    Stanford M. Lyman and Marvin B. Scott

25. Sex and Age as Universes of Appearance   227
    Gregory P. Stone

26. Who's Passing for Who?   237
    Langston Hughes

27. Reciprocal Exploitation in an Indian-White Community   240
    Niels Winther Braroe

28. The Circumstance and Situation of Social Status   250
    Gregory P. Stone

29. On Locals and Cosmopolitans   259
    Gerald Thielbar

Part Five: *Interaction Processes*   277

30. Sociological Implications of the Thought of George Herbert Mead   282
    Herbert Blumer

31. The Social Act: Re-examination of a Concept   293
    S. Frank Miyamoto

32. On Visual Interaction   300
    Georg Simmel

33. Classification of the Phenomena of Fellow-Feeling   303
    Max Scheler

34. Sarcasm as Sociation: The Rhetoric of Interaction   312
    Donald W. Ball

35. Love   319
    Nelson N. Foote

36. Some Dimensions of Altercasting   327
    Eugene A. Weinstein and Paul Deutschberger

37. Awareness Contexts and Social Interaction   336
    Barney G. Glaser and Anselm L. Strauss

38. Toward a Sociological Model of Consensus   348
    Thomas J. Scheff

Part Six: *The Self*   367

39. The Social Self   373
    William James

40. Self as Sentiment and Reflection   377
    Charles H. Cooley

41. Self as Social Object   383
    George Herbert Mead

42. Self as Concept and Illusion   386
    Harry Stack Sullivan

43. Appearance and the Self   394
    Gregory P. Stone

Part Seven: *Tests of the Perspective*   415

44. A Test of Interactionist Hypotheses of Self-Conception   419
    S. Frank Miyamoto and Sanford M. Dornbusch

45. Self-Attitudes by Age, Sex, and Professional Training   424
    Manford H. Kuhn

46. Self-Conceptions and Others: A Further Test of Meadian Hypotheses   436
    E. L. Quarantelli and Joseph Cooper

47. The Methodologies of Symbolic Interaction: A Critical Review
    of Research Techniques   447
    Norman K. Denzin

Part Eight: *Motives and Motivation*   467

48. On Motive   471
    John Dewey

49. Situated Actions and Vocabularies of Motive   472
    C. Wright Mills

50. Identification as the Basis for a Theory of Motivation   480
    Nelson N. Foote

51. Accounts   489
    Marvin B. Scott and Stanford M. Lyman

Part Nine: *Socialization*   511

52. Infant Training and the Personality of the Child   521
    William H. Sewell

53. The Rules of the Game   532
    Jean Piaget

54. Development of the Self Through Play and Games   537
    George Herbert Mead

55. The Play of Little Children   545
    Gregory P. Stone

56. The Etiquette of Youth   554
    Sherri Cavan

57. Some Recent Developments in Socialization Theory and Research   566
    William H. Sewell

58. Personal Change in Adult Life   583
    Howard S. Becker

59. Alternation and Conversion as Qualitatively Different Transformations   594
    Richard V. Travisano

60. Adjustments to Conflicting Expectations in the Development
    of Identification with an Occupation   606
    James W. Carper and Howard S. Becker

61. Changes in Status and Age Identification   613
    Zena Smith Blau

Part Ten: *The Making and Breaking of Deviants*   621

62. The Insanity Bit   626
    Seymour Krim

63. The Myth of Mental Illness   637
    Thomas S. Szasz

64. Mental Illness as Residual Deviance   645
    Thomas J. Scheff

65. Paranoia and the Dynamics of Exclusion   652
    Edwin M. Lemert

66. The Moral Career of the Mental Patient   667
    Erving Goffman

67. Life as Theater: Some Notes on the Dramaturgic Approach to Social Reality   689
    Sheldon L. Messinger with Harold Sampson and Robert D. Towne

68. Social Disintegration as a Requisite of Resocialization   699
    Peter McHugh

69. The Sociology of Deviance   709
    Kai T. Erikson

APPENDIX   717

    The Effects of Psychotherapy   718
    Hans J. Eysenck

INDEX
                                                                                      771

Social Psychology Through Symbolic Interaction

Introduction

A distinctive mark of all science is the persistence of problems and the obsolescence of theories.[1] Important problems persist; theories die. In fact, the history of any science can be looked upon as a graveyard of theories. In sociology, the paradox of society's persistence and the individual's uniqueness continues to mobilize scientific inquiry. Kant's formulation of man's "asocial sociability" captured this paradox, and theories of social psychology have long addressed themselves to this problem. How can we explain how men are held together and, at the same time, set apart? The science of social psychology can be viewed as a continuing disciplined dialogue focused upon this question. By and large, the dialogue has singled out either the bonds that tie men together or the variables that presumably account for individual differences. What is emphasized in this book is that the very fact of man's sociability is a basis for his uniqueness, and that his uniqueness is a basis for his sociability.

For us, the perduring question is: What is the meaning of the personal life? Observations of reflex (as opposed to reflective) behavior, conditioned (as opposed to interpretive) behavior, bodies (as opposed to persons) simply have no general *relevance* for our conversation. Herbert Blumer made the point when he frequently raised this question in his lectures on social psychology: "What is the difference between the accounts of a physicist observing a falling object and those of a social psychologist observing two people falling in love?"[2] By raising this question, Blumer was suggesting that there is a multifaceted set of transactions established between the social psychological observer and the objects of his inquiry. This is fundamentally different from the interaction established between the physicist and his objects of inquiry. People think; particles don't. For us, *six questions demarcate the field of social psychology from the standpoint of symbolic interaction:*

1. What is meaning?
2. How does the personal life take on meaning?
3. How does the meaning persist?
4. How is the meaning transformed?
5. How is the meaning lost?
6. How is meaning regained?

[1] See the preliminary remarks of Dennis H. Wrong, "The Oversocialized Conception of Man in Modern Sociology," reprinted in Part One of this volume.
[2] The question obviously implies something other than the "principle of indeterminacy" in physics, something other than the fact that the measurement of an object in one dimension, for example velocity, distorts measurements accomplished in another dimension, for example location, and vice versa. Cf. R. Rosenthal, *Experimenter Effects in Behavioral Research* (New York: Appleton-Century-Crofts, 1966). See also Marvin B. Scott, "Functional Analysis: A Statement of Problems," particularly the section on "Social Action and Functionalism," in Part One of this volume.

In asking such questions, we eschew the notion that meaning is preeminently a philosophical or speculative matter. We shall regard meaning as *objective* or *behavioral* after the fashion of George H. Mead. Specifically, the problem of *personal meaning* lies in the forefront of our conversation and gives it its relevance. *Meaning*, however, *can only be established in communication.* Should the reader deny this, quite clearly we cannot discuss it!

Underlying our emphasis is the matter of *metaphors*—images of man, society, communication, and their interrelations. For social psychology, the image of man is of crucial importance. Two fundamentally disparate images persist. First, man is conceived as a passive neutral agent buffeted about by stimuli that impinge upon his nerve endings. These stimuli may be *external*—reifications of society, culture, physical environment, or words and other symbols. They may be *internal*—instincts, needs, or drives—or they may be some combination of external and internal forces. Second, and in direct contrast, man is viewed as an active agent, selecting out those stimuli or objects to which he shall respond, accomplishing his selections in the matrix of communication, and transforming his society or his social world in the process. Embracing one or the other of these metaphors will determine the kinds of questions the social psychologist raises about human conduct. *The question establishes the relevance of his observations.* Frequently relevance has been confused with *validity* in social psychology.

Relevance

An extreme example of this confusion may be found in an early effort by Floyd H. Allport to demonstrate that such concepts as "group" and "institution" did not permit explicit denotation.[3] In effect, Allport argued, were a physicist, a physiologist, and a behavioral psychologist to come across a prostrate man during a nocturnal stroll, each would "stumble over," "see," and perhaps initiate a natural science investigation of the event. A sociologist, looking for a group, "would never encounter him at all."[4] Such a position incensed many sociologists. Louis Wirth, in his lectures at the University of Chicago, railed at Allport's contention, observing that only a sociologist would have made valid observations in the situation. Realizing that the prostrate man was preeminently a member of social groups, Wirth argued that a sociologist would recognize immediately that the man carried a wallet containing a record of many of his group affiliations, would notify those close to him of his condition and, if necessary, contact the appropriate religious representatives, etc. In addition, the sociologist would know that groups existed precisely to cope with such emergencies. He would call the police, a hospital, or whatever agency was appropriate to the situation. (Undoubtedly he would not call a specific individual policeman or doctor.) In fact, Wirth defined sociology as the study of what is unique about man by virtue of the fact that everywhere and

---

[3] Floyd H. Allport, " 'Group' and 'Institution' as Concepts in a Natural Science of Social Phenomena," in Ernest W. Burgess (ed.) *Personality and the Social Group* (Chicago: University of Chicago Press, 1929), pp. 162–80. Allport has since revised his argument, but the original statement carries with it the rhetorical advantage of clarifying the distinction between relevance and validity.

[4] *Ibid.*, p. 168. Allport presumed a "kickable" world. First, he missed the perspectival differences of physics, physiology, and behavioral psychology—the three people would ask different questions of the prostrate body. Second, and more important, he assumed that all objects are "kickable." On the fallacy of this point, see Simmons and McCall, "The Stolen Base as a Social Object," in Part Two of this reader.

at all times he has lived in social groups. A more succinct definition of the situation is: to be social is to be human.

In such a way, the argument between psychologists and sociologists about the place of social psychology in the social sciences became polarized, and the argument persists today. Note well that the argument is not at all centered on the matter of *validity*, but on that of *relevance*. Neither Allport nor Wirth were correct, for the physicist, the physiologist, the behavioral psychologist, *and* the sociologist all would have been able to formulate statements about the prostrate figure. Each would have asked different questions. Talcott Parsons illustrated this nicely long ago:

> . . . the velocity of a man falling off a bridge, as he is about to strike the water is a physical fact. But if the person in question is a suicide it is certainly not proved by the statement of the fact that all the antecedents of which this velocity is a consequence can be explained in terms of the theory of mechanics. Similarly, if there has been a great rise in the price of wheat in the first few days of war, there is no proof that this fact . . . a fact relevant to the descriptive and analytic schemata of economics, can be satisfactorily explained in terms of the factors formulated in economic theory.[5]

Parsons' point was that any "piece of reality" is differentially relevant for different inquirers—a point reminiscent of the old tale about the encounter of blind men with an elephant. As Florian Znaniecki has written somewhere, concrete reality is inexhaustible. Indeed, our very formulated questions *bring* objects of inquiry into our disciplined conversation. It is simply not the other way around. Even in everyday conversation this is the case. Of course, the carrying on of a conversation requires that we know who one another *are*—a point not made in the tale of the elephant and the blind men.

Suppose a close friend were to call some Friday night and ask whether you were available for a blind date on the weekend. Some desperate readers might accept outright; others might be a bit more circumspect and ask who their friend had in mind. Suppose, then, the friend replied, "It's a member of the human species." Now, this statement conveys a fantastic amount of *valid* information (check any reference on human anatomy or physiology). Again, for some readers this amount of information may be adequate for arriving at their decisions about the weekend; others may still insist on circumspection. Questions about age, education, occupation, and other characteristics of the species member undoubtedly would be raised during the telephone conversation. (Questions about sex are seldom asked!) The *meaning* of the potential blind date will be established only in the telephone conversation prior to the decision to accept or reject that particular future. Thereafter, the meaning may well be altered, but only in the communication that ensues with the blind date.

Or consider another apparently simple matter—the description of a room. Some time ago one of us carried out a demonstration (by no means an experiment!) of the point. At the outset of a course in social psychology, the students (about sixty) were asked to imagine that they were writing letters to friends and, for whatever reason, to list the three most important features of their classroom. Three weeks later, they were asked to imagine that they were social psychologists (admittedly difficult for some) and were writing letters to some other social psychologist. Here,

[5] Talcott Parsons, *The Structure of Social Action* (Glencoe, Illinois: The Free Press, 1949), p. 29.

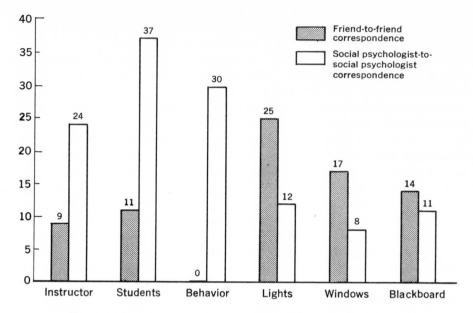

FIGURE 1.   Perceptions of a room from different perspectives.

again, for whatever reason, they were asked to list the three most important features of their classroom. Figure 1 presents the most outstanding differences in the listings. Clearly, the *objects* of observation changed emphatically in the three-week interim, although the room presumably remained much the same. The instructor and the students were regarded by some as features of the room at the outset, but their prominence had increased two- or three-fold in the second trial. References to physical features, such as lights and windows, decreased by half over the time period. Mentions of the blackboard (a means of communication as well as a "physical" object) decreased less in frequency. Most striking was that "behavior" was not considered part of the room by any student during the first trial, but was viewed in that manner by half the students in the second.[6]

In addition to the specific changes illustrated in Figure 1, the number of categories in terms of which the students' reports were classified decreased between the first and second trials. (In classifying the students' responses, an attempt was made to remain as true or close to their written materials as possible.) Features of the room listed by students writing to friends *as* friends generated forty descriptive categories. This number decreased to twenty-nine in the classification of descriptions made by students writing to social psychologists *as* social psychologists. Intimate communication undertaken on a first-name basis, as in the case of the communication between friends, expands, in a sense, the world of objects established by the communication. Less personal communication undertaken by those sharing the same titles or categories, as in the communication between social psychologists, constricts the world of objects established by the communication to the extent an analytical vocabulary is introduced that alters one's standpoint.

But, to constrict the world of objects in communication enables a sharper focus, a deeper inquiry, and often a tighter analysis. In this respect, Veblen has spoken of the *trained incapacities* of those socialized into occupational identities and role

---

[6] The importance of staging and defining situations is anticipated by this demonstration. These things will be taken up in more detail in Part Three of this volume.

performances ("seeing" is always simultaneously "not seeing"), while Dewey has conveyed the same notion with the phrase "occupational psychosis."

Validity

Now, the point is that observations may be relevant but not valid, or valid but not relevant, in addition to the other evident combinations of these distinctions. Our contention is that the argument between sociologists and psychologists about the proper place of social psychology has centered around two assertions: (1) that irrelevant observations are invalid; and (2) that valid observations are relevant. When we express our disagreement with such assertions, we must obviously turn to the matter of validity. This is the house of *method* or, better, *techniques of investigation*. Criteria of validity lend discipline to the social psychological conversation about the meaning of the personal life. Three criteria of validity are conventionally proposed: universal applicability of statements, logical coherence of statements, and the consensus that such statements may be able to mobilize among competent observers.[7]

Universality. The criterion of universality asks that statements about whatever observation hold (established by replication) no matter the time or the place in which the observation has been made. Presumably, then, in social psychology our statements about the meaning of the personal life ought to apply historically and cross-culturally. The latter stipulation seems rather easy to meet in these days of the Human Relations Area Files, Inc., but there are difficulties. First, as we have implied in our discussion of relevance, many cross-cultural studies have been conducted asking questions that are, at best, only peripherally relevant to social psychology. This is particularly the case because such questions about the meaning of the personal life have been generated by Freudian theory.[8] Our view of meaningful human conduct considerably transcends that of Freud. As we see it, Freud has made one seminal contribution to the study of meaningful human conduct: *Any instance of human conduct may be construed as symbolically significant.* If, as we shall see in this volume, the meaning of an object or an event is established in the mutual transactive responses of persons, then there is no call to single out sexual response as determinative of the meaning of the personal life.[9] Besides, the notion of mutual response or communication implies a universe of discourse—an ongoing relationship of common meanings or mutually adaptive responses. Freud, or more especially the Freudians, focus upon the family as a universe of discourse, particularly child-parent relations. Our view conceives the meaning of the personal life as established in any number of a wide variety of relationships that include the family but reach out into the world of work, politics, the peer group, the church, the circles of the elderly, the insane, and the whole variety of social worlds that, taken together, comprise what we so glibly call society. Because so many cross-cultural studies have been conducted within the more restrictive *Freudian* perspective, it is difficult at this time to test out our statements cross-culturally. Second, there is again the relation between the social psychological observer and the persons observed. Sardonically, Louis Wirth used to say in his lectures,

---

[7] Lectures by Louis Wirth at the University of Chicago during the mid-forties.
[8] See Parts Nine, Ten, and the Appendix of this volume.
[9] Freud's *Psychopathology of Everyday Life* goes beyond this limitation on the analysis of meaning and comes close to the perspective we have adopted. Probably Freud, following the pattern of Marx, would have said, "As for me, I am not a Freudian."

Margaret Mead has visited all the primitive societies, and they aren't primitive any more.

Nevertheless, while barriers to the universal applicability of statements in space might well be overcome (as social psychologists carry relevant questions to distant places and begin to solve the problem of the interaction between the social psychologist and his subject), the former stipulation, that our statements about human conduct apply historically, seems not at all capable of being met. There are at least two barriers in this regard that will probably never be overcome. First, the further we go back in history, the more specialized are the accounts of human conduct. This is the case simply because literacy is restricted to higher status segments of populations in past centuries, and the other artifacts and relics available to us from archeology permit few inferences about social psychological problems. Second, and more important, the meaning of the personal life changes drastically from historical epoch to historical epoch. How, for example, can we arrive at historically universal generalizations about the socialization of children, when, in fact, there is evidence to indicate that the social identity, Child, did not emerge in recent European history until the seventeenth century? [10] Are we not deluding ourselves when we draw upon twentieth-century vocabularies of motive to "explain" the conduct of a Moses or a Leonardo? [11]

That the criterion of universality will likely never be met does not mean that it ought to be dismissed out of hand. In our view, it is best maintained as an ideal toward which the serious social psychologist ought to strive, knowing that the ideal can never be achieved. Embracing such an ideal will encourage historical and cross-cultural study and, at least, enlarge the universe of human conduct within which our statements can apply. It will also encourage replication of observations, a most important content of the scientific dialogue.

Logical coherence. This criterion of validity rests upon a trust or faith in the rules of syntax or grammar. If statements do not contradict one another or if statements are "logically," that is, grammatically or syntactically, derivative from one another, then we may acknowledge their validity. It is from such notions that *truth tables* are built in conventional courses of logic. Yet, we know that this criterion is not often met in the physical sciences and very seldom met in the social sciences. Writers of texts in the social sciences have frequently grasped at this fact to excuse themselves from the disciplined requirements of science. They appeal to the criterion of *eclecticism.*

Eclecticism is defined in the dictionary as the use of a method that proceeds by:

> Selecting; choosing from various sources; not following any one system . . . but selecting and appropriating whatever is considered best in all systems; also, made up of what is selected from diverse sources; also, broad in acceptance of ideas, etc., from other sources.[12]

Those who adopt such a perspective adhere to the naive faith that the more diverse points of view presented in the examination of an event, the nearer to the whole truth the examination will arrive. Thus, textbook writers provide books written on the assumption that all points of view must be presented in their texts. In so doing, they neglect the problem of relevance and assume that "reality" is somehow

[10] See Philippe Ariès, *Centuries of Childhood*, translated by Robert Baldick (New York: Alfred A. Knopf, Inc., 1962).
[11] See C. Wright Mills, "Situated Actions and Vocabularies of Motive," reprinted in Part Eight of this volume.
[12] *The New Century Dictionary* (New York: D. Appleton-Century Company, 1946).

all of one piece, so that, if we fit all the pieces together, we shall come eventually to understand the "laws" that govern, in this case, the matter of human conduct. Obviously, in this book of readings, we reject the approach of naive eclecticism. We agree that *concrete reality is really inexhaustible;* that the question is at the center of our inquiries; that different accounts of human conduct are generated by the different questions that are asked. We abjure naive eclecticism.

Scientists, however, must be *reluctantly eclectic.* At this writing, physicists have yet to decide whether wavular or particular models can answer the questions they are directing toward the "nature" of light. Right now, the evidence seems to favor the particular model, but some observations remain that can only be accounted for in terms of a wavular model. What is needed is some kind of *crucial experiment.* Physics has not yet been able to design such an experiment. Social psychology is in a much less desirable position—the crucial alternatives have not yet been specified. For example, most social psychologists assert that early childhood experiences have an extreme influence upon subsequent adult conduct. We shall present evidence in this volume that challenges that assertion.[13] However, for us, the evidence itself rests upon an unacceptable holistic view of both personality and early childhood experiences. In the face of such evidence, we cannot reject the original assertion out of hand. Our guess is that early childhood experience must be taken into account insofar as it is relevant to adult conduct. Sexuality and ethnicity insofar as they remain problematic throughout the life cycle must be considered. Until such crucial distinctions are made and incorporated into research designs, we can neither reject nor accept conventional social psychological hypotheses. In arriving at this position, we would say that we are reluctantly eclectic.

Once having arrived at such a position, we must admit our misgivings about the fact that our very conceptions of logic are totally ethnocentric. Conventional logic (the logic that social psychologists know best) is merely a formalization of Greek grammar.[14] Why, then, should Greek grammar be accepted as a criterion of validity when there are so many other grammars at our disposal? Greek grammar breaks down the world as a number of objects acting upon other objects to bring about certain observed results or consequences. From our earliest childhood we are constrained to parse sentences in terms of subjects (active agents), predicates (processes exerted upon some object), and objects (the agents acted upon). We see the world as an outcome of things acting upon other things. Consequently we look to *things* (independent variables) as acting upon other *things* (dependent variables) to bring about our observations (associations, correlations, etc.). We miss the processes that may well alter the very identity of things we have observed. In this presentation, we can only ask—supposing we were to adopt another grammar, let us say Turkish—and state: "I will go to Turkey." The student can parse the complete sentence for himself, but in Turkish the statement would read *Türkiyeye gideceğim,* literally "Turkey-to my-going-in-the-future." In this case, the subject is conceived as literally caught up in the process of "going-to-Turkey," or "going-to-Turkey" is *his* process. Greek grammar emphasizes things; Turkish grammar, processes.

In social psychology, we are very much concerned with the matter of process,

---

[13] See William H. Sewell, "Infant Training and the Personality of the Child," reprinted in Part Nine of this volume.
[14] See Benjamin Lee Whorf, "Science and Linguistics," and Chang Tung-Sun, "A Chinese Philosopher's Theory of Knowledge," reprinted in Part Two of this volume.

and the English language is ill-equipped to talk about it. Why, then, ought we to rely on a logical criterion of validity that contravenes the processes we are trying to discuss? Whether mathematical sociology can provide an escape is moot. To date, mathematical sociology explores trite problems couched in the grammar of the Greeks. Apparently, some mathematical sociologists are already disenchanted. Unless some mathematical breakthroughs are made, as may be possible through the application of Markov chains to sociological analysis, the criterion of logical coherence seems not to be very compelling. This, of course, is not to say that social psychological statements ought to fly in the face of logic!

Consensus of the competent. If, following Mannheim,[15] we adopt a relational, rather than an absolutistic or relativistic conception of truth, the criterion of the consensus or agreement maintained by competent, i.e. skilled and trained, observers with reference to the validity of our social psychological statements seems to be the most basic. In social psychology, however, there are various perspectives concerning how human conduct must be interpreted. Consequently, there is no overriding consensus among social psychologists about the validity of statements. Indeed, some pools of consensus, for example those bounded by orthodox psychoanalysts, seem to be circumscribed by wishes, beliefs, and assertions that eschew the ideals of universality and logic in complete ignorance of the impress of history or the variety of syntax in the human world.

Those who find themselves swimming in such pools of consensus, if they are creative at all, are seldom content with agreements commonly held, and they intrude upon other areas of commonly held "knowledge" to inform and reshape their own notions about the validity of their statements concerning human conduct. George Herbert Mead was such a person, moving from a concern with physical science to a concern with the behavioral components of meaningful human conduct. Harry Stack Sullivan sought to throw off the constraints of psychoanalytic theory by investigating the promise of social science. We could name others—William I. Thomas, Ernest W. Burgess, Benjamin Whorf, Edward Sapir—each of whom penetrated beyond his own particular circle of consensus, his own particular universe of discourse, to call into question truths commonly held and maintained. This is the way science progresses. Consensus, then, is always a dynamic, shifting, never realizable agreement among those who are competent to pass judgment upon observations or statements.

Consensus is always momentary. It is never fixed. If this is the case, then there is a political dimension to truth. Consensus is something that must be, if only for the moment, won or lost. It is a consequence of struggle. One offers up his statements in the arena of the competent and waits on their decision. There are two implications of this fact. First, the arena of the competent is structured. Judgments of competence parallel the ranking of universities—a skilled and trained social psychologist, ensconced in a Harvard, Columbia, Chicago, or Berkeley chair, carries more weight in his judgment of the validity of a statement than a skilled and trained social psychologist at, let us say, Valley State Teachers College in North Dakota. Second, the social psychologist is constrained to employ *rhetoric* [16] to have his statements heard in the arena of the competent, that is, to get pub-

---

[15] *Cf.* Karl Mannheim, "On Relativism and Relationism," reprinted in Part Two of this volume.

[16] The term is used in the sense employed by Kenneth Burke: ". . . . a symbolic means of inducing cooperation in beings that by nature respond to symbols." See his *Rhetoric of Motives* (New York: Prentice-Hall, Inc., 1950), p. 43.

lished. The rhetoric employed may often belie his mode of data gathering and presentation, but it is nevertheless of predominant concern.[17] What is valid, then, depends upon the political structuring of the discipline, the willingness of scientists to challenge consensual conceptions of truth, and the effectiveness of the rhetoric they employ. All this goes on within the constraints of a larger society, but this is a point that must be skirted in this book.

Conclusions

What we have maintained in the preceding pages is that questions of validity lead us into the realm of method, and that rhetoric is an important method that has long been ignored in social psychology, above all, in the sciences. The question of relevance seems to us to be the more fundamental, establishing, as it does, the problems of a discipline. In reviews of the development of any scientific discipline, we find that problems live and theories die. The questions are important in that they mobilize and focus the continuing disciplined dialogue that we call science. Moreover, questions always imply metaphors, that is, ways of picturing objects of inquiry. In social psychology, as construed, we ask questions about the meaning of the personal life, and we assert that such meaning can never be established outside the matrix of communication. Any attempt to understand personal conduct outside such a matrix we think of as a "psychologistic fallacy."

---

[17] One of us submitted an article to the *American Sociological Review* some years ago. It was rejected because of a lack of "empirical" evidence. The author looked about and found a statistical table that had a very peripheral bearing upon the statements in question and inserted the table in a footnote. The article was then published. Both editors of this volume agree that rhetoric should be included as a basic area of methods.

PART ONE
SYMBOLIC INTERACTION: PERSPECTIVE AND DIRECTIONS

It is fitting that we begin our delimitation of the social psychological perspective called "symbolic interaction" with a statement of what it is not. For, as Kenneth Burke has shown, man, the namer or definer, is always confronted with a *paradox of substance:* ultimately he must define objects in terms that pertain to their opposites.[1] Clearly, structural-functionalism is the major alternative to symbolic interaction among those social psychological orientations most appealing to sociologists. The article by Marvin B. Scott tells us why the larger conceptions proposed by structural-functionalism, as well as those conceptualizations of persons and their conduct, cannot answer the basic questions of symbolic interaction. These center on *meaningful* human *process.*

As with all general perspectives in sociology, structural-functionalism has not provided us with any unitary body of logically compendent propositions. Indeed, within that perspective or "body of ideas," the range includes the quite different observations of Robert K. Merton and Talcott Parsons. Moreover, there is conflict in the house, as functionalist$_1$ (Lewis Coser) hurls barbs at functionalist$_2$ (Talcott Parsons). Yet, certain assumptions are held in common (not always explicitly) by most self-designated structural-functionalists, and these assumptions do violence to the symbolic interactionist view of social life.

First, change is located *within* larger organizational units and is conventionally construed as a circulation of persons among those positions whose integrated interdependence presumably gives the organization its unitary systemic character. At times, such an internal circulation of personnel may eventuate in maldistributions,

---

[1] Kenneth Burke, *A Grammar of Motives* (New York: Prentice-Hall, Inc., 1945), p. 23, but see the entire chapter.

throwing the system temporarily off balance. There are, of course, other sources of systemic imbalance, but systems are viewed as perpetually (we might well say "teleologically") operating or functioning to retain or regain balance. Social systems are conceived as moving equilibria. When larger historical changes are considered, the idea of "progress" is resurrected from the graveyards of sociological theory, particularly some aspects of Herbert Spencer's work. Scott cites Alvin W. Gouldner's apt phrase, "the Pollyanna fallacy": "every day in every way we are becoming better and better integrated." Note well, in neither the idea of a moving equilibrium nor the idea of progress, is there any way of explaining *transformations in the identities of larger social organizations.* For example, the transformation of the Russian Empire to the Union of Soviet Socialist Republics was a vital change in the identity of a nation. Such revolutionary changes escape the functionalist perspective. On the personal side, consider the names, nicknames, and titles Malcolm Little, El-Hajj Malik El-Shabazz, Mascot, Detroit Red, Satan, and Minister. All were appropriated by Malcolm X at different times of his life.[2] Were these the same selves? Can functionalism explain these changes?

According to Scott, functionalists invoke *dei ex machina*, such notions as conflict and deviance, to explain such critical changes. But these invocations are tautological, for these "gods of the machine" dwell in some heaven outside the green pastures of functionalism. They must be determined or detected empirically. They are not theoretically derived. "Because deviance . . . [and conflict are] . . . endemic feature[s] of society, the functionalist is assured of success before he undertakes his analysis." There is always some body of behavior around that can be labeled as deviant and invoked to "explain" social change.[3] In his criticisms, Scott lays bare one of the continuing and basic fallacies of social psychology—the *fallacy of tautology*—a fallacy that ensnares scholars and students alike. "Need psychology" provides many excellent examples. To commit such a fallacy is to make an observation, rename it, and attribute the cause of the observation to the new name. Reducing the idea to the absurd, we observe an electric bulb glowing. We assert that the bulb has a need to glow. Ergo, the need to glow causes the glowing of the bulb. Latent structure analysis runs the same risks, as does the imputation of unconscious motives. Latent structures are in the eye or the words of the beholder, just as one's unconsciousness is in the consciousness of another.

Second, Scott claims that functionalists eschew the meaningful character of personal conduct. Persons, when they are studied, are torn from the context of their conversations. Scott seizes upon this observation to reformulate Talcott Parsons' well-known definition of a fact. *Social facts* are statements about phenomena, in terms of a conceptual scheme, that take as their topic conceptual schemes in operation. While this approach carries with it dangers, as when we naively regard other people's statements as really real,[4] we have often been tempted to define social psychology as a disciplined conversation about other people's conversations. Yet, we are just beginning to see how nonverbal communications affect what people talk about.[5]

---

[2] We are indebted to a paper by Arthur Manousos, "The Education of Malcolm Little: A Study in Transformations of Identity and Motivations," prepared for a course in social psychology at the University of Minnesota, 1966, for this example.

[3] See Kai Erikson, "The Sociology of Deviance," reprinted in Part Ten of this volume.

[4] See the review by James S. Coleman of Harold Garfinkel, *Studies in Ethnomethodology* (Englewood Cliffs: Prentice-Hall, Inc., 1967) in the *American Sociological Review*, XXX (February 1968), pp. 126–30, especially pp. 128–29.

[5] See Parts Three and Four of this volume.

Dennis H. Wrong narrows his criticism of functionalism by focusing on its view of man as oversocialized, although he observes in passing that the conception of an overintegrated society, presumed by many functionalists, may also be seriously questioned. Such dubious views of man and society, Wrong argues, have emerged because sociologists have lost sight of questions in their preoccupation with answers. Probing questions about society were raised long ago, for example Hobbes' inquiry into the "problem of order," and answers have been adduced over the centuries; and, in the dialogue that has pitted this against that set of answers —one theory against another—the basic questions have been lost. Many early answers to important questions, as that posed by Georg Simmel— "What makes society possible?"—established dialectic alternatives. Simmel's proposal of sociation and individuation as fundamental social processes; Hobbes' contrast between "Leviathan," or the highly organized state, and the *bellum omnium in omnes,* or chaos; and Ferdinand Tönnies' *Gemeinschaft* and *Gesellschaft,* built on the psychological antinomy between *Wesenswille* (existential will), or passion and *Kürwille* (optative will), or reason, serve as examples. At any rate, dialectic conceptions do not permit mutually exclusive distinctions. At the height of furious passion, pressures for sweet reasonableness arise; and the coldest calculating reason cries out for the comforting warmth of passion. Cooley pointed out long ago that one's individuality can only be realized in contrast. Individuality demands the presence of others, or society, just as society can never exist without individuals. At one time, Carl Sandburg asked the question, "What did the last man on earth say?" He answered his own question, "The last man on earth said, 'Where is everybody?'" Sociology has ignored the mutual determinativeness of the varieties of personal conduct and has probed, for example, matters of conformity *or* deviance. Why is it, sociologists have asked, that so many conform, while so few deviate? Their answers, for the most part, have extensively searched the matter of conforming behavior, often treating deviance as residual, usually to be explained in terms of aberrations of individual experience.

Conformity has been accounted for in two broad ways. First, given the shifting Durkheimian view of the nature of constraints (from extra-individual to personally internalized),[6] coupled with the Freudian formulation of the superego as internalized social rules, sociologists have interpreted conformity as a consequence of socialization (usually childhood socialization)[7]—the internalization of norms. Guilt operates to maintain personal conformity and minimize deviance. Second, man is construed as involved in a continuous quest for social acceptance. Here, anxiety operates to maintain conformity and minimize deviance. Wrong astutely links these interpretations to David Riesman's historically emergent character types—inner direction and other direction—but notes that Riesman, despite these depictions, insists on the tension between the individual and society. Riesman would agree with the sense of Freud: Man is social, but never completely socialized.

It seems to us that Wrong raised two basic objections to these conceptions of man as oversocialized. First, sociologists tend to grasp one or the other of the alternatives sketched above. In so doing, they miss the potential for insight that the rejected alternative provides. Specifically, one finds few references to anxiety in

---

[6] See Gregory P. Stone and Harvey A. Farberman, "On the Edge of Rapprochement: Was Durkheim Moving Toward the Perspective of Symbolic Interaction?" reprinted in Part Two of this volume.

[7] See Part Nine of this volume, particularly William H. Sewell, "Infant Training and the Personality of the Child," and the Appendix for evidence that casts serious doubt on this notion.

the writings of structural-functionalists, but many references to the superego, the prick of conscience, or the constraining effects of guilt. And the one person who has placed greatest emphasis upon anxiety as a basis of motivation, Harry Stack Sullivan, has written:

> I shall not attempt to express . . . [the expansion of the self-dynamism and the simplification of living] . . . in terms of the Ego and the Superego. I have not found these conceptions useful in formulating problems.[8]

Wrong, then, adopts the position of the reluctant eclecticist: Both guilt and anxiety, normative internalization and acceptance seeking, must be considered in the explanation of conformity.

Second, Wrong is concerned with the battle between the individual and society. Does not, he seems to ask, the individual *always* seek to preserve a part of himself from the intrusions of society? Is there anyone who has not felt guilty because of his very conformity? We add: Is there anyone who has not felt anxiety about his very acceptance by significant others? Of course, these are rhetorical questions, but, as such, they do demand research—research that would, indeed, refresh the entire field of social psychology.

Wrong grasps at Freud's conception of the id to secure this principle of the separability of the individual from the demands of his society. In fact, he seems ambivalently enamoured of Freud. We are not even that much enamoured. There are at least four sources of separability alternative to the Freudian conception of the id: (1) Mead's formulation of the "I"—experience or the continuing phase of man's activity; (2) the matter of human intention and value; (3) Sullivan's conception of parataxic distortion; [9] and (4) role distance—a concept introduced by Erving Goffman at about the same time Wrong's critique was published.[10]

In delimiting the perspective of symbolic interaction, it is not enough to confine the alternatives within the walls of sociology. Social psychology inhabits a ground contested by psychology and sociology, and the contest has continued since the nearly simultaneous publications (in 1908) of William McDougall's *Social Psychology* (on the psychological side) and Edward A. Ross's *Social Psychology* (on the sociological side). Benjamin Whorf's brief paper succinctly presents the rationale for our rejection of alternative perspectives from psychology. Although it was written in 1927, this critique of psychological approaches remains relevant. Much of psychology today is a special area of physiology, and the relation between neurological findings and variations in personal conduct has yet to be established except in very extreme instances. "Mentally retarded" persons, for example, comprise a numerically small, nevertheless socially significant, proportion of the population, but of these, the most generous estimate is that 15 per cent can be accounted for on physiological grounds. Moreover, some "retardates" once thought to have been physiologically doomed, for example hydrocephalics, have shown a remarkable capacity for rational human conduct. As a matter of fact, a whole new horizon is opening up for social psychology. It centers on the question of how retardates become so labeled when the vast majority have no physiological incapacities capable of being diagnosed. Even so, the species traits that qualify

---

[8] Harry Stack Sullivan, *Conceptions of Modern Psychiatry* (New York: W. W. Norton and Co., Inc., 1953), p. 98.

[9] Sullivan clearly indicates that this process is not a stage of development, as some social psychologists would have it, but a process that continues throughout the personal life. See his *The Psychiatric Interview* (New York: W. W. Norton and Co., Inc., 1954), pp. 25–26.

[10] Erving Goffman, *Encounters* (Indianapolis: The Bobbs-Merrill Co., Inc., 1961), pp. 85–152.

us as human beings have little relevance (as opposed to validity) in accounting
for the varieties of meaningful human interaction.

Nor are we inert objects that must be pushed this way or that to set us into motion. Whorf consequently rejects psychological behaviorism and its usual explanation of conduct, conditioning. (We might observe, at this juncture, that Pavlov's dog never ate the bell!) But some branches of psychology continue apace in
this vein. For example, Guthrie, in his attempts to formulate "contiguity theory,"
complains that the poor record of predictability established by S–R theory might
well be due to the fact that the "slices" of examined human conduct have not been
cut thin enough. "Operant conditioning theory" is currently enjoying some vogue
in mental therapy.

Gestalt psychologists claim, however, that the basic tenets of psychological behaviorism are empirically indefensible. People, they say, do not respond to discrete stimuli, but to their configurations of the world. Their argument carries no
little weight. Suppose we were confronted with the following five items:

FIGURE 1.

Their arrangement certainly affects our conceptions of item "e," and we would
undoubtedly act differently toward "e" in the first Gestalt than we would toward
that same item in the second.

Gestalt psychology comes close to the symbolic interactionist concept "definition of the situation," but places the mechanisms of definition "in the head."
Quite obviously, one can arrange the components of a situation, as we have done
in the diagrams above, so that the "mental Gestalt" is emphatically altered. Indeed, the clever definer of the situation manipulates and arranges symbols in such
a way that the meaning of the "same" situation may be established in different
ways. Psychoanalysis misses this point, because, as Whorf observes, it concentrates on the abnormal—relatively meaningless conduct. Yet, most psychologistic
schemes that have been formulated for the study of human conduct do just this.
They study meaningless behavior—from the learning of nonsense syllables to the
presumably insignificant meanderings of psychotics. They seem to studiously ignore the communicative matrix of human conduct. This studied ignorance we
call *the psychologistic fallacy.* The emergence of pragmatism in American thought
constitutes a revolutionary mode of interpreting human conduct. It has carried social psychology away from the psychologistc fallacy.

C. Wright Mills anchors the rise of pragmatism, particularly the contributions
of John Dewey, in the great debate that has been raging for almost three hundred
years in the political arena of Western Civilization. The debate has been carried

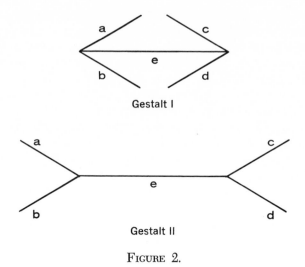

Gestalt I

Gestalt II

FIGURE 2.

on between conservatives, who posit an unchangeable human nature rooted in the species characteristics of man, and the "short cut revolutionists" or reformers, who view man's conduct as eminently plastic by virtue of his characteristic rationality. Dewey, Mills maintains, has built a middle ground or a "mediatory conception" of change. What seems to be the source of constancy in human conduct is not rooted in physiology, but in customs and institutions. Instinctual responses are altered easily in contrast to the inertia of custom. This inertia is due to intellect, the individual phase of mind; yet mind is preeminently social. The minded person is one who participates in the communicative processes of the larger society and can propose alternative lines of action for himself, when habits have been blocked and impulses, consequently, released. Thus, education is of overriding importance. It brings man into communication or mind, permitting the possibility of continued growth—the persistent sensitivity to and ability to act upon alternative lines of action. Both Mead and Dewey were very much concerned with education as a source of social change. And, if one views the development of Mead's writings chronologically, it is clear that his participation in educational programs (quite probably because of Dewey's influence when they were together at the University of Chicago at the turn of the century) accounts for his progressively lessened interest in the philosophy of science and his increasing concern with the problems of social psychology.[11] Mills concludes, in his postscript, that no account of the development of pragmatism can be complete without a thorough consideration of the work of George H. Mead.

In our view, the best concise summary of Mead's social psychology is that by William H. Desmonde. This writer was attempting to provide an argument for the integration of Mead's views with those of Sigmund Freud—an attempt that we regard as highly forced, although we readily admit that subsequent psychiatric views, particularly those of Harry Stack Sullivan and Ernest Becker, are quite compatible with those of Mead, if not so compatible with those of Freud. Accordingly, we have deleted the references to Freud in that selection.

[11] This transition in Mead's intellectual concerns has been ably documented in a paper, presented to a seminar in the Principles of Sociology by Penelope Baron at the University of Minnesota, 1967.

While Mills linked social Darwinism and "instinctive psychology" as constituting the conservative influence against which pragmatism argued in its emergence as a powerful strain of sociological thought, Desmonde observes that Mead and Dewey were quite positively influenced by Darwin. For Mead, the attraction was Darwin's emphasis upon process. Indeed, he ignored the *laissez-faire* implications of Darwinism and seized the basic theoretical import: *the same process gives rise to different forms.* Social psychology must focus its inquiries on process, specifically the process of communication. Different selves (forms) emerge from differential participation in the general and universal process of communication.

Mead, therefore, turned his attention to significant communication. This process transforms those who are caught up in it, as well as the world within which their communication takes place. There is, then, no demarcation between mind and body, nor is there any meaningful demarcation between body and environment. Such conventional distinctions disappear in the process of communication. At the same time, those engaged in communication can transform the quality of the process, either as individuals or in concerted conduct. There is a fundamental distinction between the "nonsignificant" gestures of dogs engaged in the "conversation" of a dog fight and the "significant" gestures of socialized persons engaged in mutual talk. The latter envision futures and take one another's future conduct into account in their present actions. One regulates what he is doing at the time in terms of his anticipations of the other's proposed actions and vice versa. Here is the nexus of significance or meaning. The guarantee of such mutually anticipated and proposed acts is language—common symbols or universals (Mead pays little attention to the matter of rules of syntax or grammar). One's use of language requires that he take two roles at once—his own and that of the other. Although Desmonde does not mention this, he implies an essential fact of human conduct: *no socialized person ever does one thing at a time* (he smokes a cigarette and talks, he talks and paces, he appears and talks)—another aspect of conduct that most of the metaphors of psychology fail to take into account.

One cannot engage in symbolic communication until he has formed a conception of self. He must conceive that he is different from but related to others. This conception emerges as one takes over others' reactions toward himself in the form of a "me." The "me" is given full expression when one takes over the attitude of the "generalized other," the community, or a social world, and regulates his own conduct in terms of such organized expectations. One becomes something. Yet, there is always process. One acts against, or in dialogue with, these other attitudes. Because these attitudes have been incorporated, the "I" is engaged in constant conversation with the "me"—the internalized attitudes of others. One *thinks,* and thought is an internalized forum—an ongoing conversation between the "I" and the "me"—between experience and conceptualization.

As we have said earlier, the phenomenon of process, given our language and the crudity of our research techniques, is terribly difficult to apprehend, designate, and analyze. Leonard S. Cottrell, Jr., in his presidential address to the American Sociological Society almost twenty years ago, listed the principal neglected problem areas in social psychology: (1) the empathic processes; (2) the self; (3) the situation; and (4) motivation. That these problems persist today is evident from the fact that four parts of this volume are exclusively devoted to each of these areas. It is not as though there has been no advance.

Cottrell was ambivalent about the matter of empathy—Is it an "ability," or a situationally variable phenomenon? His guess favors the latter, although he persists in using the term, "empathic ability." One can readily comprehend the ambivalence by contrasting the first problem he poses under the category of "empathic processes" with the third, "the situation." Ultimately, Cottrell identifies empathy with prediction, but, again, he is ambivalent. He knows that actuarial predictions are not empathic. Sheldon Stryker has shed considerable light on this matter,[12] and so has Scheff in Part Five of this volume. Scheff distinguishes agreement from understanding and realization. There remains the matter of *sympathy*—of sharing the other's feelings and sentiments. Cooley, of course, made much of this. Still, we must look to the past—to Scheler—and to distant places—Ball and Foote (see Part Five of this volume)—to find bare beginnings of inquiry into this area. In addition, studies of empathy confuse *identification of* (knowing who the other is or what he believes) with *identification with* (understanding or realizing the other). In our view, the empathic processes refer to the latter, but research on empathy has focused on the former.

Cottrell's second neglected problem area is that of the self. We shall see in Kuhn's article that this problem has not been so much neglected in recent symbolic interaction research. However, little attention has been given to Cottrell's plea that we distinguish persistent and latent selves from those that are relatively easily abandoned. Why can we readily adopt and cast aside some selves, but not other selves? This question remains in the forefront of symbolic interactionist inquiry.

The third and fourth areas of investigation that Cottrell proposes—the situation and motivation—have engaged many researchers since the appearance of his article. As far as the situation is concerned, we can say that it is defined, in great part, by staging.[13] But the boundaries of the situation remain vague, and routine assumptions patrol those vague boundaries.[14] The problem remains: What are the spatial and temporal boundaries of situations? Referring to the matter of motivation, Cottrell relies on Foote's paper (reprinted in Part Eight of this volume). Since the appearance of Foote's contribution, considerable advance has been made on this problem, notably by Howard S. Becker, R. S. Peters, and Marvin B. Scott and Stanford M. Lyman.[15]

Symbolic interactionists repudiate the notion that man is a passive, neutral agent, pushed one way or another by external or internal forces. Man is *both* actor (the "I") and acted upon (the "me"), both subject and object. Moreover, having formulated an objective conception of self, man can act to influence that conception. Manford Kuhn establishes one of the basic weaknesses in symbolic interactionist research. One dimension of its view of man assumes the determinacy of his conduct; the other singles out indeterminacy. Current conceptions of method proceed best on the former assumption, but those conceptions are left floundering, if they must come to grips with the study of human indeterminacy.

---

[12] Sheldon Stryker, "Conditions for Accurate Role-Taking: A Test of Mead's Theory," in Arnold Rose (ed.), *Human Behavior and Social Processes* (Boston: Houghton-Mifflin Company, 1962), pp. 41–62.

[13] See Part Three of this volume.

[14] See Harold Garfinkel, "Studies of the Routine Grounds of Everyday Activities," *Social Problems*, XI (Winter 1964), pp. 225–50.

[15] Scott and Lyman provide their observations on motive in Part Eight of this volume. But see also Howard S. Becker, "Notes on the Concept of Commitment," *American Journal of Sociology*, LXVI (July 1960), pp. 32–40, and R. S. Peters, *The Concept of Motivation* (London: Routledge and Kegan Paul, 1958).

Undoubtedly, the disparity can be traced to the fact that sociological techniques of investigation and analysis are rooted in Greek grammar. On the determinant side of symbolic interaction, methods of study and analysis have been profusely generated, and the knowledge generated by the application of these methods is not particularly impressive. On the indeterminate side, profound insights abound, but methods for their test are scarce and presently unavailable. Kuhn emphasizes the fact that Clyde Kluckhohn termed the Sapir-Whorf hypothesis (that grammar determines notions of causality and conceptions of the world) untestable.

Narrowing down his concern with the directions research in symbolic interaction has taken, Kuhn notes that research focusing on the determinacy of the self has concentrated on linguistic evidence (we would say naively), and has emphasized the concept of role. In contrast, if the self is construed as an initiator of action, constituting its own realities, two important questions are posed: (1) Is this self an antecedent variable, establishing paths of personal action, or can other variables predict the constitution of the self? (2) If the latter, are such variables remote in time, that is, operant in childhood; or immediate, that is, situational? To these questions a variety of answers has been proposed. Above all, the matter of which self we are speaking is overriding: Are we speaking of the public, or the private self? We would note that a purely private self could never be known by researchers, for the very observation of it would amount to publication.[16] The difference, then, is in the extent of the audience that lends validation to the self, rather than in some presumed intrinsic character of the self. As a matter of fact, Kuhn, in his discussion, often removes the self from its "culture" (in the biological sense) of communication.

Even so, Kuhn notes well that emphases on the determinacy of the self, although highly proliferated, are suspect. *Role theory* has focused on conforming behavior with some refreshing exceptions (Sarbin and Turner). Moreover, the contrasts of role and role performance have seldom been explicated. *Reference group theory* has had a considerable empirical development, but, Kuhn asks, have the methods of such studies seriously taken theories into account? Studies of *social and person perception*, for the most part, have been accomplished by those unacquainted with symbolic interaction, and they have usually sought the shelter of the Freudian umbrella to protect their conclusions. We would argue that the researches to which Kuhn refers are *conceptually* and not *theoretically* oriented. "Role" and "reference group" are concepts, not theories.

Observations that take into account the indeterminacy of the self and human conduct have recently emerged on the social psychological scene. Kuhn cites the dramaturgical approach of Erving Goffman, "interpersonal theory," the studies of Everett C. Hughes and Howard S. Becker on later socialization and careers, and studies of the interaction between language and culture. But the problem of operationalizing and generalizing such perspectives is a formidable one.

Kuhn concludes by specifying neglected problems in social psychology. Just what is a reference group? How do self conceptions change? Are some dimensions of the self stable and others volatile? If so, which dimensions and why? These are very important questions, but, in our view, as well as that of Kuhn, such questions will not be answered outside the perspective of symbolic interaction. We agree with Kuhn: Symbolic interaction will emerge as the dominant perspec-

---

[16] See Harry Stack Sullivan, "The Illusion of Personal Individuality," part of which appears in Part Six of this volume, under the title, "Self as Concept and Illusion."

tive of the future. Psychoanalysis, learning theory, and field theory will ultimately be laid to rest in the vast graveyard of social science theory.

Suggested Readings

BERGER, PETER L. *Invitation to Sociology*. New York: Doubleday Anchor, 1963.

BROWN, ROGER. *Social Psychology*. New York: The Free Press, 1965.

DEUTSCH, MORTON, and ROBERT M. KRAUSS. *Theories in Social Psychology*. New York: Basic Books, Inc., 1965.

DUNCAN, HUGH D. *Symbols in Society*. New York: Oxford University Press, 1968.

HOROWITZ, I. L. (ed.). *The New Sociology*. New York: Oxford University Press, 1964.

LINDESMITH, ALFRED, and ANSELM STRAUSS. *Social Psychology*, 3rd edition. New York: Dryden Press, 1968.

LINDZEY, GARDINER, and ELLIOT ARONSON (eds.). *The Handbook of Social Psychology*, 2nd edition. Reading, Mass.: Addison-Wesley Publishing Co., 1968.

MANIS, JEROME G., and BERNARD N. MELTZER (eds.). *Symbolic Interaction*. Boston: Allyn and Bacon, 1967.

ROSE, ARNOLD M. (ed.). *Human Behavior and Social Process*. Boston: Houghton Mifflin, 1962.

SHIBUTANI, TAMOTSU. *Society and Personality*. Englewood Cliffs, N.J.: Prentice-Hall, 1961.

STOODLEY, BARTLETT H. (ed.). *Society and Self*. New York: The Free Press, 1962.

1 Functional Analysis: A Statement of Problems

● MARVIN B. SCOTT

Wittgenstein, the greatest linguistic philosopher of the twentieth century, once remarked that if you wrap the furniture of the world with enough toilet paper—everything looks round. What Wittgenstein had in mind is that certain terms, having a history of various shades of meaning, are wrapped in so many tissues of ambiguities that they have lost their connotative shape. "Functionalism" is such a shapeless term.

While to some analysts functionalism is a theory for all seasons, to others—and here I include some of its leading practitioners—it is a theory having few if any consensual characteristics, and not deserving of a distinctive name.[1] To avoid semantic disputes, we might say that "functional analysis" or "structural-functional analysis" is a body of ideas that are explicitly rooted in the writings of Durkheim,[2] Malinowski,[3] and Radcliffe-Brown,[4] and refined by Merton,[5] Parsons,[6] and Davis.[7] These names, of course, constitute only a small fragment of a list of precursors and contemporaries who have contributed to what is still the predominant mode of sociological theorizing.[8] Moreover, criticisms that might be relevant to, say, Mertonian functionalism may not hold with the same degree of validity with respect to Parsonian functionalism, and vice versa.

My purpose here is not to parade the dead horses of functionalism and submit them to still another public flogging (though such practices may have an occasional pedagogic value), but to pinpoint with perhaps exaggerative clarity the problems of functionalism and to suggest, by implication, an alternative formulation for the analysis of social life. My strategy, then, is to suggest the viability of an alternative conceptual framework by highlighting those alleged characteristics of functionalism with which this alternative framework is in polemical opposition. This alternative, which may be called "social behaviorism," consists of a synthesis

SOURCE: Marvin B. Scott, "Functional Analysis: A Statement of Problems," original paper prepared especially for this volume.

[1] Kingsley Davis, "The Myth of Functional Analysis," *American Sociological Review,* 24 (December 1959), 757–72.
[2] Emile Durkheim, *The Rules of Sociological Method,* Glencoe: The Free Press, 1938, esp. 89–97.
[3] Bronislaw Malinowski, "Anthropology," *Encyclopedia Britannica,* First Supplementary Volume, London and New York, 1926, 132–39.
[4] A. R. Radcliffe-Brown, "On the Concept of Function in Social Science," in *Structure and Function in Primitive Society,* Glencoe: The Free Press, 1952.
[5] Robert K. Merton, "Manifest and Latent Functions," in *Social Theory and Social Structure,* Glencoe: The Free Press, 1957.
[6] Talcott Parsons, *The Social System,* Glencoe: The Free Press, 1951.
[7] K. Davis, *op. cit.*
[8] For a critical historical summary of functional analysis see Walter Buckley, "Structural-Functional Analysis in Modern Sociology," in Howard Becker and Alvin Beskoff, eds., *Modern Sociological Theory in Continuity and Change,* New York: Holt, Rinehart and Winston, 1957, 236–59. For a useful compendium of contemporary writers on functionalism, both pro and con, see N. J. Demerath and Richard A. Peterson, eds., *System, Change, and Conflict,* New York: The Free Press, 1967.

of G. H. Mead's symbolic interactionism,[9] Weber's action orientation,[10] and Alfred Schutz's phenomenology.[11] At the very least, the work of these men—either singularly or in combination—succeeds in transcending the foibles of functionalism.

The foibles of functionalism are best highlighted by considering two problem areas, namely, social change and social action.

Problems in the Study of Social Change

Taunted by adversaries [12] to cope with social change, functionalists have rushed in where a Malinowski feared to tread. As an upshot of this intellectual martyrdom, they have—in their study of change—continued to commit the sins of evolutionism plus the sins that functionalism is allegedly heir to.

Theories of social change have a disturbingly unchanging quality. Some thirty years ago Talcott Parsons pronounced Spencer dead.[13] Nevertheless, Spencer's ghost haunts the theoretical edifice built along functional design. That is to say, with reference to social change functionalists often fall into the same traps, commit the same sins and repeat the same errors as the evolutionary thinkers they have so successfully attacked in the past.

The first "evolutionary hangover" is *functional ahistoricism.* Hallmark of evolutionary thinking—exemplified in the writings of Spencer, Tyler, and Comte—was a general disregard for the historical record. For these thinkers "a scientific study of man could never rest upon a consideration of particular events, persons, and peoples in specific time and place situations." [14] To circumvent the difficulties involved in a detailed account of the historical record, the evolutionists used the "comparative method." Briefly, this method proceeds by taking a spatial sequence and treating it as a temporal sequence. Evolutionists, for example, observed that axes in country Z were more advanced than in country Y, which in turn were more advanced than in country X. Conclusion: the evolution of the ax followed the temporal sequence of XYZ.

Because it emphasizes the study of society in the present, functionalism is particularly prone to use the comparative method. For example, to account for social changes in underdeveloped countries under the impact of industrialization, a functionalist might proceed as follows. He would note that underdeveloped country X has characteristics of particularism, diffuseness, and affectivity.[15] He would note further that industrialized country Y has characteristics of universalism, specificity, and neutrality. On the basis of these observations he concludes that, under industrialization, a society changes from one type of pattern variable profile to another; and, further, industrialization can take place only in the presence of these values.

Although such conclusions have a spurious ring of truth to them, the reasoning

---

[9] G. H. Mead, *Mind, Self and Society,* Chicago: University of Chicago, 1934.

[10] Max Weber, *The Theory of Social and Economic Organization,* trans. by A. M. Henderson and T. Parsons, Glencoe: The Free Press, 1947.

[11] Alfred Schutz, *Collected Papers,* Vol. I, edited by Maurice Natanson, The Hague: Martinus Nijhoff, 1962.

[12] See, e.g., Ralph Dahrendorf, "Out of Utopia," *American Journal of Sociology,* 64 (September 1958), 115–27; and David Lockwood, "Some Remarks on 'The Social System,'" *British Journal of Sociology,* 7 (June 1956), 134–46.

[13] T. Parsons, *The Structure of Social Action,* Glencoe: Free Press, 1949, 3.

[14] Kenneth E. Bock, "Evolution and Historical Process," *American Anthropologist,* 54 (October-December 1952), 489.

[15] These are Parsons' terms, discussed in his various explanations of his concept of "pattern variable." See, for instance, *The Social System, op. cit.*

is patently circular. For example: the pattern variables of universalism and specificity are said to be generated by industrialization—but industrialization is in turn
advanced as the manifestation of the pattern variables! Clearly, under such reasoning the pattern variables are empty as explanatory concepts, resembling the
explanation of Molière's medico who accounted for the dormative power of opium
by its sleep-inducing qualities.

The logic of functional practitioners is not the point at issue, however. Rather,
I wish to emphasize here that functional theory—by viewing various aspects of society with reference to a system in equilibrium having mutually determining parts
—tends to restrict explanations to the present. The notion that explanations should
be sought in the present vitiates the functionalist position at the outset. For how
does functionalism explain itself?

Kingsley Davis attempted to free functionalism from such pitfalls. He has asserted that the core of functionalism rests in two essential tasks: "to relate the
parts of society to the whole, and to relate one part to another." [16] If functionalism
is essentially concerned with "interrelatedness" then Davis' thesis that functionalism is not a special type of analysis, but *is* sociological analysis, must go unquestioned, and the errors attributed to functionalism are simply the errors of individual sociologists. However, in another statement that purportedly touches on the
core of functionalism, Davis writes:

> It is only in terms of equilibrium that most sociological concepts make sense.
> Either tacitly or explicitly anyone who thinks about society tends to use the
> notion. The functional-structural approach to sociological analysis is basically an
> equilibrium theory.[17]

Hence, it is the notion of equilibrium theory that identifies functionalism as a distinctive mode of analysis. It seems, then, that while all sociologists are functionalists, some are more functional than others.[18]

Dahrendorf has argued that equilibrium theory makes functional analysis inherently incapable of studying change.[19] The target of Dahrendorf's volleys is not sociologists concerned with interrelatedness, but those who emphasize an equilibrium model. Anticipating such criticisms of the equilibrium model, Davis states
that while the functional approach "is usually phrased in static terms, as soon as
the element of time is added it alludes to a *moving* equilibrium." [20]

As conceived by Parsons, the "moving equilibrium" illustrates the orderly process of change whereby a society retains the "conditions of disturbance . . . *within*
its boundaries over against its environment." [21] Thus equilibrium theory accounts
for change—but change *within* the social system. Herein lies the rub and the nub
of functional ahistoricism.

The connection between analysis of change *within* a system and a general disregard for the historical record is made by Nisbet, who points out that "the chief
danger of contemporary functional approaches [toward change] seems . . . to lie
in the search for causes *within the social system,* as though the social system were,

[16] Davis, *op. cit.,* 757.
[17] K. Davis, *Human Society,* New York: Macmillan, 1948, 634.
[18] That functionalist$_1$ is not functionalist$_2$ is evident in Coser's (functionalist$_1$) vitriolic attack
on Parsons (functionalist$_2$). See Lewis Coser, *The Functions of Social Conflict,* Glencoe:
Free Press, 1956.
[19] Dahrendorf, *op. cit.*
[20] Davis, *Human Society, op. cit.,* 634.
[21] T. Parsons, *The Social System, op. cit.,* 36.

like a biological entity, governed by autonomous inner drives toward cumulative change." He emphasizes that the search for causes of change in allegedly autonomous mechanisms within the structure—instead of dealing with the problem of structural change in *historical* terms—is at best "a dubious procedure." Social change, he continues, "is always historical in inception, it cannot be detached from initiating contexts of cultural intrusion, impact, and conflict which only the historical record will reveal." [22]

In still another way do the evolutionary ghosts stir in functional theory. Besides ahistoricism, functional analyses of change disclose a *commitment to progress*. After the French Revolution, writes Bury, the immense significance of the idea of progress "was apprehended and a search began for a general law which would define and establish it." [23] The founders of sociology, some of whom narrowly escaped the guillotine, had reason for optimism. In the hands of Saint-Simon and Comte the rising science of sociology was hitched to the rising star of universal progress. Down the sociological ranks passed the notion of universal progress, known to functionalists today as "structural differentiation."

As first used by Durkheim, structural differentiation is "any adaptive response to increased competition: by specializing in different activities the units no longer come in conflict." [24] Arguing that functional analysis from its inception was concerned with history and social change, Bellah points to structural differentiation as a major aspect of societal evolution.

The specific connection between the idea of progress and the functional analysis of change is clearly seen when we understand the underlying principle of structural differentiation:

> Namely, that when in the course of differentiation a unit appears to lose important functions, it is not necessarily a weakened version of its former self; it may be a new, more specialized unit, fulfilling important functions at a new level of complexity in the larger system.[25]

To this way of thinking, the loss of traditional functions of (say) the family is an indicator of good tidings: now the family can better perform its *real* function (which, alas, is real by heuristic assumption).[26] Such optimistic apologetics assume the workings of an invisible hand of progress: dissatisfaction of alienated groups, for instance, is viewed as a temporary condition resulting from increasing differentiation. Structural differentiation illustrates what Gouldner has called the "Pollyanna fallacy," [27] which proclaims that every day in every way we are becoming better and better integrated.

The conservative bias that functionalism is often charged with is rooted in its emphasis on slow, orderly change; conflict and deviance are regarded as pathological tendencies disturbing the social equilibrium. And yet, consistent with their taste for irony, functional analysts find the source of social change in deviance. The problem, however, is that functionalists have no systematic theory of deviance to account for change. This in part is Lockwood's criticism of the functional the-

---

[22] Robert Nisbet, "Social Structure and Social Change," *Research Studies of the State College of Washington*, 20 (June 1952), 76.
[23] J. B. Bury, *The Idea of Progress*, New York: Dover, 1955, 334.
[24] Robert Bellah, "Durkheim and History," *American Sociological Review*, 24 (1959), 452.
[25] *Ibid.*, 453.
[26] See, for instance, T. Parsons *et al.*, *Family*, Glencoe: Free Press, 1955.
[27] Alvin W. Gouldner, "The Norm of Reciprocity," *American Sociological Review*, 25 (April 1960), 164.

ory of change. "Pressures making for deviance," he writes, "are regarded as being a matter for investigation in each empirical situation as it arises. In general, there are no social processes, corresponding to these stabilizing mechanisms . . . which systematically make for deviance and social change." [28] The absence of a systematic theory of deviance tends to lead toward circular reasoning. Thus the functionalist first documents that change has taken place; then he turns to the sources of change, presumed to lie in deviance. Because deviance must be empirically determined in each case, and because deviance is an endemic feature of society, the functionalist is assured of success before he undertakes his analysis. The rabbit, so to speak, is already in the hat.

Social Action and Functionalism

A kind of intellectual schizophrenia characterizes much contemporary sociology. This schizophrenia centers around the nature of social action. Functionalists, on the one hand, accept—or at least pay lip service to—one conception of social action. When they turn to undertake empirical studies or construct theoretical systems, however, they adopt another and opposing conception.

The writings of Max Weber and George H. Mead have converged to give us a picture of social action that represents one of the solid foundations of the sociological discipline. According to Weber, "action" involves all behavior to which the actor attaches a subjective meaning; social action involves all action that takes account of the behavior of others by virtue of the meaning the actor attaches to it. [29] Along the same lines as Weber, Mead pointed out that man has the capacity for symbolic representations. He remembers the past, anticipates the future, and, on the basis of these memories and aspirations, brings meaning to his actions in the present. The actor is not buffeted about by social organization, social systems, and social stratification; these structural features of his environment set conditions for action—they do not determine action. [30]

While paying lip service to this account of social action, most functionalists in practice have implied an entirely different view—a view that divorces human action from the very process (i.e., the "interpretive process") that gives it definition. According to this view, the actor is a creature susceptible to the tugging of forces by stimuli of any kind and group, by the injunction of social norms, his social class, and so on. This conception of action likens man to a slot machine. Here the sociologist feeds in *variables*, cranks the lever, and awaits a mechanical response.

For the functional analyst, then, human behavior is an expression of the bombardment of forces upon the individual. [31] In this way of thinking the actors are not important, but the *categories*—such as "religion" and "social class"—that bombard the actors. Following this conception of action, the study of social phenomena (when it becomes quantitative) often takes the form of counting plumbing fixtures and telephone lines [32] and leads to the tendency described by Morris Cohen

---

[28] Lockwood, *op. cit.*, 135.

[29] Weber, *op. cit.*, 9, 18, 22, 90 and *passim*.

[30] For an elaboration of this point, see Herbert Blumer, "Society as Symbolic Interaction," in *Human Behavior and Social Processes*, Arnold Rose, ed., Boston: Houghton Mifflin, 1962.

[31] H. Blumer, "Sociological Analysis and the Variable," *American Sociological Review*, 21 (December 1956), 683–90.

[32] Alan Gewirth, "Subjectivism and Objectivism in Social Science," *Philosophy of Science*, 21 (April 1954), 157–63.

"to rush off to measure something without considering what it is we are measuring," and in this respect the findings of such studies "are of the same logical type as Plato's determination that a just ruler is 729 times as happy as an unjust one."[33]

What makes such measurement spurious is the lack of respect for the nature of the subject matter under study. Such respect can only be manifested by taking into account the fundamental importance of the interpretive process. Rather than respecting his subject matter—which is the first commandment of all science[34]— the functional analyst substitutes instead an emphasis on method, a method borrowed (an "illegitimate diffusion," in Dewey's phrase) from the physical sciences.

This method follows what may be called the "methodological postulate of objectivism." (The postulate is in accord with the principle advanced by Durkheim that social life is to be explained not by the meanings of those who participate in it, but by causes unperceived by consciousness.[35])

Two major pitfalls await the analyst committed to the postulate of objectivism. First, the abandonment of all hope of *understanding* social action; and second, the risk of smuggling in one's own subjective responses and imputing them to the actor.

Why do I say that, if we follow the postulate of objectivism, we must abandon all hope of understanding social action? Consider the argument of Alfred Schutz.[36] Schutz has reminded us that in science there are two meanings of "understanding." In the first sense, to "understand" is to reduce facts to other facts. To "understand," for example, why mercury rises in a thermometer, we refer to other facts such as molecular movement and capillary action. But there is a second sense to "understanding"—and this is peculiar to the subject matter of sociology. To "understand" human action, one cannot reduce it to other facts, but must refer to human motives. As Schutz pointed out, one cannot "understand a tool without knowing the purpose for which it was designed" or an institution without knowing what it means to the actors involved.

It should be clear, then, that the objects of sociological investigation are fundamentally different from those of the natural scientist. The objects investigated by the methods of the natural scientist are "first order constructs," i.e., objects for his observation. The social scientist, on the other hand, must face a qualitatively different situation. His objects are not only objects for his observation—they are beings who have preinterpreted the world. That is, a series of constructs have already interpreted reality. These "objects" are what Schutz has called "second order constructs."[37]

The distinction between first and second order constructs forces us to revise Par-

---

[33] Quoted by F. A. Hayek, *The Counter-Revolution of Science*, Glencoe: Free Press, 1952, 51.
[34] On this point see the important but neglected work by Kurt Riezler, *Man: Mutable and Immutable*, Chicago: Henry Regnery, 1951, 287. Riezler echoes Weber's attack on positivism when he writes: "Science aims at 'laws'—constant relations between variables, which enable us to draw conclusions from the known to the unknown. The science of man, however, has not yet discovered universal variables that belong to every and any human society, let alone constant relations. Since its variables are not universal, their relations not constant, its laws are not laws and change as societies change." (p. 286).
[35] Durkheim, *op. cit.* For a persuasive argument that Durkheim in his later years shifted his position, resulting in a convergence with symbolic interactionism, see Gregory P. Stone and Harvey A. Farberman, "On the Edge of Rapprochement: Was Durkheim Moving Toward the Perspective of Symbolic Interaction?" *Sociological Quarterly*, VIII (Spring 1967), 149–64. Reprinted in Part Two of this volume.
[36] Schutz, *op. cit.*, ch. 1.
[37] *Loc. cit.*

sons' definition of a fact. This definition, first offered by Parsons in 1937, is *inappropriate* for the study of social action. In *The Structure of Social Action*, Parsons defines a fact as a "statement about phenomena in terms of a conceptual scheme." [38] But the events of social action will not fit this definition, for the world has already been preinterpreted by the actors. Thus we may revise Parsons' definition and say that *a social fact is a statement about phenomena in terms of a conceptual scheme that takes as its topic conceptual schemes in operation.* The definition is here awkwardly stated, but it emphasizes that social facts, unlike physical facts, are "second order" constructs. Consequently, we cannot deal with phenomena in the social world as we do with phenomena belonging to the natural sphere. In short, we can *understand* social phenomena only in terms of human ends and human planning—that is, in terms of the categories of human action.

I turn now to the second pitfall of objectivism: imputing the observer's meaning to the actor.

Because social action must be understood in terms of the meaning actors attach to the social world rather than an objectively defined set of conditions, one cannot be certain that a particular event will have a given meaning to the actor. By ascribing meaning to the actor, we are creating our own mythical world—and this is the greatest risk of social science research. We say, for instance, that the modern college girl confuses career and marriage, being pushed in opposite directions as a result of an unintegrated set of norms. In other words, the analyst following the principle of objectivism assumes that what he sees as a source of confusion in the culture is a source of confusion in the life of the actor. But this cannot be validated without also determining the meaning the actors attach to the situation. Unless this is done, the objectivist approach leads to the worst kind of subjectivism by smuggling in one's own surmises of the meaning actors are giving to the situation. [39]

By ignoring the actor's meanings, the investigator commits the very error he wishes to avoid: wanting to be objective, he ends up imputing his own meaning to the actors. He naively accepts the social world with all its institutions and deems as his only task to describe and explain his experiences; he doesn't think it necessary to go back to subjective activities to give a description of the facts of the social world. But such description presupposes criteria that enable one to determine whether two observations of some social event are the same sort of thing, i.e., whether they can be coded as instances of the same category. To code our data we must make reference to a set of criteria that lay down what is to be regarded as a relevant basis for description. Two instances of, say, religion will count as religion only relative to certain criteria for identifying religion. Otherwise put, "different objects mean the same thing to different people and different people mean the same thing by different acts." [40] Thus *it is necessary to understand the meaning people give to objects before one can classify an instance of a concept.*

A problem arises, for instance, when we are called upon to classify a tribal ritual as an instance of "religion" or "magic." Underlying our choice of vocabulary is a theoretical presupposition. This presupposition is that categories of the natural language, which the sociologist shares with the objects of his study, may serve as

---

38 T. Parsons, *op. cit.*, 41.
39 Blumer, "Society as Symbolic Interaction," *op. cit.*, 188.
40 Hayek, *op. cit.*, 43.

conceptual tools for analysis.[41] But that's the rub. For description in sociology must depend even for its vocabulary on first determining the meaning individuals attach to these concepts. In other words, commonsense concepts—such as "religion," "magic," "suicide"—cannot be used as tools of sociological analysis until they first become the *subject matter* of sociological analysis. Unless that is done we, as observers, run the risk of attaching to these concepts our own commonsense meanings.[42]

Such, then, are the two pitfalls of following the postulate of objectivism, which is so fundamentally characteristic of functional analysis. This leads to a final word about the stuff that societies are made of, namely, persons.

In quest of theoretical consistency functionalists have advanced a conceptual framework of the personality system isomorphic with the social system. What emerged from this effort is the oversocialized conception of man. Functionalists, writes Dennis Wrong, "have appropriated the super-ego concept, but have separated it from an equivalent of the Freudian id."[43] In the language of Mead, they have retained the "Me" but not the "I." Hence there are no surprises or disappointments in conduct. According to Wrong this view of man serves "as a kind of *ad hoc* social psychology, easily adaptable to particular sociological purposes."[44] The oversocialized conception of man has a goodness of fit with the stable equilibrium model of functionalism. The problem with this model of man becomes obvious in explanations of social change.

Blumer has remarked that the "outstanding consequence" of the functional assumptions about the character of human nature is the tendency to overlook the part played by cognition; for human action is necessarily mediated by interpretation on the part of the people caught up in social life.[45] The oversocialized man of functionalism is not equipped with the natural interpretive process that involves dynamic assessments of self and situation.

In the functional portrayal of man, the human comedy has become a comedy of insects.

---

[41] The problem of natural language and its relation to concept formation is a central issue in the monumental work of Ludwig Wittgenstein. The problem of concept formation in the social sciences is also dealt with in Stuart Hampshire's *Thought and Action,* London: Chatte and Windus, 1959; and Peter Winch's *The Idea of a Social Science,* London: Routledge, 1958. Both Hampshire and Winch—under the influence of Wittgenstein—present a picture of social action that is, from a logical point of view, the only one possible—a view substantially in accord with the Mead-Weber-Schutz conception presented here.

[42] For a discussion of these and related problems, see Harold Garfinkel, *Studies in Ethnomethodology,* Englewood Cliffs, N.J.: Prentice-Hall, Inc., 1967.

[43] Dennis H. Wrong, "The Oversocialized Conception of Man," *American Sociological Review,* 26 (April 1961) 18. Reprinted in Part One of this volume.

[44] *Ibid.,* 190.

[45] H. Blumer, "Society as Symbolic Interaction," *op. cit.,* 191.

2   The Oversocialized Conception of Man in Modern Sociology

● DENNIS H. WRONG

Gertrude Stein, bed-ridden with a fatal illness, is reported to have suddenly muttered, "What, then, is the answer?" Pausing, she raised her head, murmured, "But what is the question?" and died. Miss Stein presumably was pondering the ultimate meaning of human life, but her brief final soliloquy has a broader and humbler relevance. Its point is that answers are meaningless apart from questions. If we forget the questions, even while remembering the answers, our knowledge of them will subtly deteriorate, becoming rigid, formal, and catechistic as the sense of indeterminacy, of rival possibilities, implied by the very putting of a question is lost.

Social theory must be seen primarily as a set of answers to questions we ask of social reality. If the initiating questions are forgotten, we readily misconstrue the task of theory and the answers previous thinkers have given become narrowly confining conceptual prisons, degenerating into little more than a special, professional vocabulary applied to situations and events that can be described with equal or greater precision in ordinary language. Forgetfulness of the questions that are the starting points of inquiry leads us to ignore the substantive assumptions "buried" in our concepts and commits us to a one-sided view of reality.

Perhaps this is simply an elaborate way of saying that sociological theory can never afford to lose what is usually called a "sense of significance"; or, as it is sometimes put, that sociological theory must be "problem-conscious." I choose instead to speak of theory as a set of answers to questions because reference to "problems" may seem to suggest too close a linkage with social criticism or reform. My primary reason for insisting on the necessity of holding constantly in mind the questions that our concepts and theories are designed to answer is to preclude defining the goal of sociological theory as the creation of a formal body of knowledge satisfying the logical criteria of scientific theory set up by philosophers and methodologists of natural science. Needless to say, this is the way theory is often defined by contemporary sociologists.

Yet to speak of theory as interrogatory may suggest too self-sufficiently intellectual an enterprise. Cannot questions be unsatisfactorily answered and then forgotten, the answers becoming the assumptions from which we start in framing new questions? It may convey my view of theory more adequately to say that sociological theory concerns itself with questions arising out of problems that are inherent in the very existence of human societies and that cannot therefore be finally "solved" in the way that particular social problems perhaps can be. The "problems" theory concerns itself with are problems *for* human societies which, because of their universality, become intellectually problematic for sociological theorists.

Essentially, the historicist conception of sociological knowledge that is central to the thought of Max Weber and has recently been ably restated by Barrington Moore, Jr. and C. Wright Mills [1] is a sound one. The most fruitful questions for

SOURCE: Dennis H. Wrong, in *American Sociological Review*, XXVI (April 1961), pp. 183–193.

[1] Barrington Moore, Jr., *Political Power and Social Theory*, Cambridge: Harvard University Press, 1958; C. Wright Mills, *The Sociological Imagination*, New York: Oxford University Press, 1959.

sociology are always questions referring to the realities of a particular historical situation. Yet both of these writers, especially Mills, have a tendency to under-emphasize the degree to which we genuinely wish and seek answers to trans-his-torical and universal questions about the nature of man and society. I do not, let it be clear, have in mind the formalistic quest for social "laws" or "universal prop-ositions," nor the even more formalistic effort to construct all-encompassing "con-ceptual schemes." Moore and Mills are rightly critical of such efforts. I am think-ing of such questions as, "How are men capable of uniting to form enduring societies in the first place?"; "Why and to what degree is change inherent in hu-man societies and what are the sources of change?"; "How is man's animal nature domesticated by society?"

Questions:

Such questions—and they are existential as well as intellectual questions—are the *raison d'être* of social theory. They were asked by men long before the rise of sociology. Sociology itself is an effort, under new and unprecedented historical conditions, to find novel answers to them. They are not questions which lend themselves to successively more precise answers as a result of cumulative empiri-cal research, for they remain eternally problematic. Social theory is necessarily an interminable dialogue. "True understanding," Hannah Arendt has written, "does not tire of interminable dialogue and 'vicious circles' because it trusts that imag-ination will eventually catch at least a glimpse of the always frightening light of truth." [2]

I wish briefly to review the answers modern sociological theory offers to one such question, or rather to one aspect of one question. The question may be vari-ously phrased as, "What are the sources of social cohesion?"; or, "How is social order possible?"; or, stated in social-psychological terms, "How is it that man be-comes tractable to social discipline?" I shall call this question in its social-psycho-logical aspect the "Hobbesian question" and in its more strictly sociological aspect the "Marxist question." The Hobbesian question asks how men are capable of the guidance by social norms and goals that makes possible an enduring society, while the Marxist question asks how, assuming this capability, complex societies manage to regulate and restrain destructive conflicts between groups. Much of our current theory offers an oversocialized view of man in answering the Hobbesian question and an overintegrated view of society in answering the Marxist question.

Hobbes
ques.

Marx's ques.

A number of writers have recently challenged the overintegrated view of soci-ety in contemporary theory. In addition to Moore and Mills, the names of Bendix, Coser, Dahrendorf, and Lockwood come to mind. [3] My intention, therefore, is to concentrate on the answers to the Hobbesian question in an effort to disclose the oversocialized view of man which they seem to imply.

Since my view of theory is obviously very different from that of Talcott Parsons and has, in fact, been developed in opposition to his, let me pay tribute to his rec-

[2] Hannah Arendt, "Understanding and Politics," *Partisan Review*, 20 (July–August, 1953), p. 392. For a view of social theory close to the one adumbrated in the present paper, see Theo-dore Abel, "The Present Status of Social Theory," *American Sociological Review*, 17 (April, 1952), pp. 156–164.

[3] Reinhard Bendix and Bennett Berger, "Images of Society and Problems of Concept Forma-tion in Sociology," in Llewellyn Gross, editor, *Symposium on Sociological Theory*, Evanston, Ill.: Row, Peterson & Co., 1959, pp. 92–118; Lewis A. Coser, *The Functions of Social Con-flict*, Glencoe, Ill.: The Free Press, 1956, Ralf Dahrendorf, "Out of Utopia: Towards a Re-Orientation of Sociological Analysis," *American Journal of Sociology*, 64 (September, 1958), pp. 115–127; and *Class and Class Conflict in Industrial Society*, Stanford, Calif.: Stanford Uni-versity Press, 1959; David Lockwood, "Some Remarks on 'The Social System,'" *British Journal of Sociology*, 7 (June, 1956), pp. 134–146.

ognition of the importance of the Hobbesian question—the "problem of order," as he calls it—at the very beginning of his first book, *The Structure of Social Action.*[4] Parsons correctly credits Hobbes with being the first thinker to see the necessity of explaining why human society is not a "war of all against all"; why, if man is simply a gifted animal, men refrain from unlimited resort to fraud and violence in pursuit of their ends and maintain a stable society at all. There is even a sense in which, as Coser and Mills have both noted,[5] Parsons' entire work represents an effort to solve the Hobbesian problem of order. His solution, however, has tended to become precisely the kind of elaboration of a set of answers in abstraction from questions that is so characteristic of contemporary sociological theory.

We need not be greatly concerned with Hobbes' own solution to the problem of order he saw with such unsurpassed clarity. Whatever interest his famous theory of the origin of the state may still hold for political scientists, it is clearly inadequate as an explanation of the origin of society. Yet the pattern as opposed to the details of Hobbes' thought bears closer examination.

The polar terms in Hobbes' theory are the state of nature, where the war of all against all prevails, and the authority of Leviathan, created by social contract. But the war of all against all is not simply effaced with the creation of political authority: it remains an ever-present potentiality in human society, at times quiescent, at times erupting into open violence. Whether Hobbes believed that the state of nature and the social contract were ever historical realities—and there is evidence that he was not that simple-minded and unsociological, even in the seventeenth century—is unimportant; the whole tenor of his thought is to see the war of all against all and Leviathan dialectically, as coexisting and interacting opposites.[6] As R. G. Collingwood has observed, "According to Hobbes . . . *a body politic is a dialectical thing*, a Heraclitean world in which at any given time there is a negative element."[7] The first secular social theorist in the history of Western thought, and one of the first clearly to discern and define the problem of order in human society long before Darwinism made awareness of it a commonplace, Hobbes was a dialectical thinker who refused to separate answers from questions, solutions to society's enduring problems from the conditions creating the problems.

What is the answer of contemporary sociological theory to the Hobbesian question? There are two main answers, each of which has come to be understood in a way that denies the reality and meaningfulness of the question. Together they constitute a model of human nature, sometimes clearly stated, more often implicit in accepted concepts, that pervades modern sociology. The first answer is summed up in the notion of the "internalization of social norms." The second, more commonly employed or assumed in empirical research, is the view that man is essentially motivated by the desire to achieve a positive image of self by winning acceptance or status in the eyes of others.

---

[4] Talcott Parsons, *The Structure of Social Action*, New York: McGraw-Hill Book Co., 1937, pp. 89–94.

[5] Coser, *op. cit.*, p. 21; Mills, *op. cit.*, p. 44.

[6] A recent critic of Parsons follows Hobbes in seeing the relation between the normative order in society and what he calls "the sub-stratum of social action" and other sociologists have called the "factual order" as similar to the relation between the war of all against all and the authority of the state. David Lockwood writes: "The existence of the normative order . . . is in one very important sense inextricably bound up with potential conflicts of interest over scarce resources . . . ; the very existence of a normative order mirrors the continual potentiality of conflict." Lockwood, *op. cit.*, p. 137.

[7] R. G. Collingwood, *The New Leviathan*, Oxford: The Clarendon Press, 1942, p. 183.

The following statement represents, briefly and broadly, what is probably the most influential contemporary sociological conception—and dismissal—of the Hobbesian problem: "To a modern sociologist imbued with the conception that action follows institutionalized patterns, opposition of individual and common interests has only a very limited relevance or is thoroughly unsound." [8] From this writer's perspective, the problem is an unreal one: human conduct is totally shaped by common norms or "institutionalized patterns." Sheer ignorance must have led people who were unfortunate enough not to be modern sociologists to ask, "How is order possible?" A thoughtful bee or ant would never inquire, "How is the social order of the hive or anthill possible?" for the opposite of that order is unimaginable when the instinctive endowment of the insects ensures its stability and built-in harmony between "individual and common interests." Human society, we are assured, is not essentially different, although conformity and stability are there maintained by non-instinctive processes. Modern sociologists believe that they have understood these processes and that they have not merely answered but disposed of the Hobbesian question, showing that, far from expressing a valid intimation of the tensions and possibilities of social life, it can only be asked out of ignorance.

It would be hard to find a better illustration of what Collingwood, following Plato, calls *eristical* as opposed to dialectical thinking: [9] the answer destroys the question, or rather destroys the awareness of rival possibilities suggested by the question which accounts for its having been asked in the first place. A reversal of perspective now takes place and we are moved to ask the opposite question: "How is it that violence, conflict, revolution, and the individual's sense of coercion by society manage to exist at all, if this view is correct?" [10] Whenever a one-sided answer to a question compels us to raise the opposite question, we are caught up in a dialectic of concepts which reflects a dialectic in things. But let us examine the particular processes sociologists appeal to in order to account for the elimination from human society of the war of all against all.

The Changing Meaning of Internalization

A well-known section of *The Structure of Social Action*, devoted to the interpretation of Durkheim's thought, is entitled "The Changing Meaning of Constraint." [11] Parsons argues that Durkheim originally conceived of society as controlling the individual from the outside by imposing constraints on him through sanctions, best illustrated by codes of law. But in Durkheim's later work he began

[8] Francis X. Sutton and others, *The American Business Creed*, Cambridge: Harvard University Press, 1956, p. 304. I have cited this study and, on several occasions, textbooks and fugitive articles rather than better-known and directly theoretical writings because I am just as concerned with what sociological concepts and theories are taken to mean when they are actually used in research, teaching, and introductory exposition as with their elaboration in more self-conscious and explicitly theoretical discourse. Since the model of human nature I am criticizing is partially implicit and "buried" in our concepts, cruder and less qualified illustrations are as relevant as the formulations of leading theorists. I am also aware that some older theorists, notably Cooley and MacIver, were shrewd and worldly-wise enough to reject the implication that man is ever fully socialized. Yet they failed to develop competing images of man which were concise and systematic enough to counter the appeal of the oversocialized models.
[9] Collingwood, *op. cit.*, pp. 181–182.
[10] *Cf.* Mills, *op. cit.*, pp. 32–33, 42. While Mills does not discuss the use of the concept of internalization by Parsonian theorists, I have argued elsewhere that his view of the relation between power and values is insufficiently dialectical. See Dennis H. Wrong, "The Failure of American Sociology," *Commentary*, 28 (November, 1959), p. 378.
[11] Parsons, *op. cit.*, pp. 378–390.

to see that social rules do not "merely regulate 'externally' . . . they enter directly into the constitution of the actors' ends themselves." [12] Constraint, therefore, is more than an environmental obstacle which the actor must take into account in pursuit of his goals in the same way that he takes into account physical laws: it becomes internal, psychological, and self-imposed as well. Parsons developed this view that social norms are constitutive rather than merely regulative of human nature before he was influenced by psychoanalytic theory, but Freud's theory of the superego has become the source and model for the conception of the internalization of social norms that today plays so important a part in sociological thinking. The use some sociologists have made of Freud's idea, however, might well inspire an essay entitled, "The Changing Meaning of Internalization," although, in contrast to the shift in Durkheim's view of constraint, this change has been a change for the worse.

What has happened is that internalization has imperceptibly been equated with "learning," or even with "habit-formation" in the simplest sense. Thus when a norm is said to have been "internalized" by an individual, what is frequently meant is that he habitually both affirms it and conforms to it in his conduct. The whole stress on inner conflict, on the tension between powerful impulses and superego controls the behavioral outcome of which cannot be prejudged, drops out of the picture. And it is this that is central to Freud's view, for in psychoanalytic terms to say that a norm has been internalized, or introjected to become part of the superego, is to say no more than that a person will suffer guilt-feelings if he fails to live up to it, not that he will in fact live up to it in his behavior.

The relation between internalization and conformity assumed by most sociologists is suggested by the following passage from a recent, highly-praised advanced textbook: "Conformity to institutionalized norms is, of course, 'normal.' The actor, having internalized the norms, feels something like a need to conform. His conscience would bother him if he did not." [13] What is overlooked here is that the person who conforms may be even more "bothered," that is, subject to guilt and neurosis, than the person who violates what are not only society's norms but his own as well. To Freud, it is precisely the man with the strictest superego, he who has most thoroughly internalized and conformed to the norms of his society, who is most wracked with guilt and anxiety.[14]

Paul Kecskemeti, to whose discussion I owe initial recognition of the erroneous view of internalization held by sociologists, argues that the relations between social norms, the individual's selection from them, his conduct, and his feelings about his conduct are far from self-evident. "It is by no means true," he writes, "to say that acting counter to one's own norms always or almost always leads to neurosis. One might assume that neurosis develops even more easily in persons who *never* violate the moral code they recognize as valid but repress and frustrate some strong instinctual motive. A person who 'succumbs to temptation,' feels guilt, and then 'purges himself' of his guilt in some reliable way (e.g., by confession) may achieve in this way a better balance, and be less neurotic, than a person who never violates his 'norms' and never feels conscious guilt." [15]

[12] *Ibid.*, p. 382.
[13] Harry M. Johnson, *Sociology: A Systematic Introduction*, New York: Harcourt, Brace and Co., 1960, p. 22.
[14] Sigmund Freud, *Civilization and Its Discontents*, New York: Doubleday Anchor Books, 1958, pp. 80–81.
[15] Paul Kecskemeti, *Meaning, Communication, and Value*, Chicago: University of Chicago Press, 1952, pp 244–245.

Recent discussions of "deviant behavior" have been compelled to recognize these distinctions between social demands, personal attitudes towards them, and actual conduct, although they have done so in a laboriously taxonomic fashion.[16] They represent, however, largely the rediscovery of what was always central to the Freudian concept of the superego. The main explanatory function of the concept is to show how people repress themselves, imposing checks on their own desires and thus turning the inner life into a battlefield of conflicting motives, no matter which side "wins," by successfully dictating overt action. So far as behavior is concerned, the psychoanalytic view of man is less deterministic than the sociological. For psychoanalysis is primarily concerned with the inner life, not with overt behavior, and its most fundamental insight is that the wish, the emotion, and the fantasy are as important as the act in man's experience.

Sociologists have appropriated the superego concept, but have separated it from any equivalent of the Freudian id. So long as most individuals are "socialized," that is, internalize the norms and conform to them in conduct, the Hobbesian problem is not even perceived as a latent reality. Deviant behavior is accounted for by special circumstances: ambiguous norms, anomie, role conflict, or greater cultural stress on valued goals than on the approved means for attaining them. Tendencies to deviant behavior are not seen as dialectically related to conformity. The presence in man of motivational forces bucking against the hold social discipline has over him is denied.

Nor does the assumption that internalization of norms and roles is the essence of socialization allow for a sufficient range of motives underlying conformity. It fails to allow for variable "tonicity of the superego," in Kardiner's phrase.[17] The degree to which conformity is frequently the result of coercion rather than conviction is minimized.[18] Either someone has internalized the norms, or he is "unsocialized," a feral or socially isolated child, or a psychopath. Yet Freud recognized that many people, conceivably a majority, fail to acquire superegos. "Such people," he wrote, "habitually permit themselves to do any bad deed that procures them something they want, if only they are sure that no authority will discover it or make them suffer for it; their anxiety relates only to the possibility of detection. Present-day society has to take into account the prevalence of this state of mind."[19] The last sentence suggests that Freud was aware of the decline of "inner-direction," of the Protestant conscience, about which we have heard so much lately. So let us turn to the other elements of human nature that sociologists appeal to in order to explain, or rather explain away, the Hobbesian problem.

Man the Acceptance-Seeker[20]

The superego concept is too inflexible, too bound to the past and to individual biography, to be of service in relating conduct to the pressures of the immediate

[16] Robert Dubin, "Deviant Behavior and Social Structure: Continuities in Social Theory," *American Sociological Review*, 24 (April, 1959), pp. 147–164; Robert K. Merton, "Social Conformity, Deviation, and Opportunity Structures: A Comment on the Contributions of Dubin and Cloward," *Ibid.*, pp. 178–189.

[17] Abraham Kardiner, *The Individual and His Society*, New York: Columbia University Press, 1939, pp. 65, 72–75.

[18] Mills, *op. cit.*, pp. 39–41; Dahrendorf, *Class and Class Conflict in Industrial Society*, pp. 157–165.

[19] Freud, *op. cit.*, pp. 78–79.

[20] In many ways I should prefer to use the neater, more alliterative phrase "status-seeker."

situation in which it takes place. Sociologists rely more heavily therefore on an alternative notion, here stated—or, to be fair, overstated—in its baldest form: "People are so profoundly sensitive to the expectations of others that all action is inevitably guided by these expectations." [21]

Parsons' model of the "complementarity of expectations," the view that in social interaction men mutually seek approval from one another by conforming to shared norms, is a formalized version of what has tended to become a distinctive sociological perspective on human motivation. Ralph Linton states it in explicit psychological terms: "The need for eliciting favorable responses from others is an almost constant component of [personality]. Indeed, it is not too much to say that there is very little organized human behavior which is not directed toward its satisfaction in at least some degree." [22]

The insistence of sociologists on the importance of "social factors" easily leads them to stress the priority of such socialized or socializing motives in human behavior. [23] It is frequently the task of the sociologist to call attention to the inten-

However, it has acquired a narrower meaning than I intend, particularly since Vance Packard appropriated it, suggesting primarily efforts, which are often consciously deceptive, to give the appearance of personal achievements or qualities worthy of deference. "Status-seeking" in this sense is, as Veblen perceived, necessarily confined to relatively impersonal and segmental social relationships. "Acceptance" or "approval" convey more adequately what all men are held to seek in both intimate and impersonal relations according to the conception of the self and of motivation dominating contemporary sociology and social psychology. I have, nevertheless, been unable to resist the occasional temptation to use the term "status" in this broader sense.

[21] Sutton and others, op. cit., p. 264. Robert Cooley Angell, in Free Society and Moral Crisis, Ann Arbor: University of Michigan Press, 1958, p. 34, points out the ambiguity of the term "expectations." It is used, he notes, to mean both a factual prediction and a moral imperative, e.g. "England expects every man to do his duty." But this very ambiguity is instructive, for it suggests the process by which behavior that is non-normative and perhaps even "deviant" but nevertheless "expected" in the sense of being predictable, acquires over time a normative aura and becomes "expected" in the second sense of being socially approved or demanded. Thus Parsons' "interaction paradigm" provides leads to the understanding of social change and need not be confined, as in his use of it, to the explanation of conformity and stability. But this is the subject of another paper I hope to complete shortly.

[22] Ralph Linton, The Cultural Background of Personality, New York: Appleton-Century Co., 1945, p. 91.

[23] When values are "inferred" from this emphasis and then popularized, it becomes the basis of the ideology of "groupism" extolling the virtues of "togetherness" and "belongingness" that have been attacked and satirized so savagely in recent social criticism. David Riesman and W. H. Whyte, the pioneers of this current of criticism in its contemporary guise, are both aware, as their imitators and epigoni usually are not, of the extent to which the social phenomenon they have described is the result of the diffusion and popularization of sociology itself. See on this point Robert Gutman and Dennis H. Wrong, "Riesman's Typology of character" (forthcoming in a symposium on Riesman's work to be edited by Leo Lowenthal and Seymour Martin Lipset), and William H. Whyte, The Organization Man, New York: Simon and Schuster, 1956, Chapters 3–5. As a matter of fact, Riesman's "inner-direction" and "other-direction" correspond rather closely to the notions of "internalization" and "acceptance-seeking" in contemporary sociology as I have described them. Riesman even refers to his concepts initially as characterizations of "modes of conformity," although he then makes the mistake, as Robert Gutman and I have argued, of calling them character types. But his view that all men are to some degree both inner-directed and other-directed, a qualification that has been somewhat neglected by critics who have understandably concentrated on his empirical and historical use of his typology, suggests the more generalized conception of forces making for conformity found in current theory. See David Riesman, Nathan Glazer, and Reuel Denny, The Lonely Crowd, New York: Doubleday Anchor Books, 1953, pp. 17 ff. However, as Gutman and I have observed: "In some respects Riesman's conception of character is Freudian rather than neo-Freudian: character is defined by superego mechanisms and, like Freud in Civilization and Its Discontents, the socialized individual is defined by what is forbidden him rather than by what society stimulates him to do. Thus in spite of Riesman's generally sanguine attitude towards modern America, implicit in his typology is a view of society as the enemy both of individuality and of basic drive gratification, a view that contrasts with the at least

sity with which men desire and strive for the good opinion of their immediate associates in a variety of situations, particularly those where received theories or ideologies have unduly emphasized other motives such as financial gain, commitment to ideals, or the effects on energies and aspirations of arduous physical conditions. Thus sociologists have shown that factory workers are more sensitive to the attitudes of their fellow-workers than to purely economic incentives; that voters are more influenced by the preferences of their relatives and friends than by campaign debates on the "issues"; that soldiers, whatever their ideological commitment to their nation's cause, fight more bravely when their platoons are intact and they stand side by side with their "buddies."

It is certainly not my intention to criticize the findings of such studies. My objection is that their particular selective emphasis is generalized—explicitly or, more often, implicitly—to provide apparent empirical support for an extremely one-sided view of human nature. Although sociologists have criticized past efforts to single out one fundamental motive in human conduct, the desire to achieve a favorable self-image by winning approval from others frequently occupies such a position in their own thinking. The following "theorem" has been, in fact, openly put forward by Hans Zetterberg as "a strong contender for the position as the major Motivational Theorem in sociology": [24]

An actor's actions have a tendency to become dispositions that are related to the occurence [sic] of favored uniform evaluations of the actor and-or his actions in his action system.[25]

Now Zetterberg is not necessarily maintaining that this theorem is an accurate factual statement of the basic psychological roots of social behavior. He is, characteristically, far too self-conscious about the logic of theorizing and "concept formation" for that. He goes on to remark that "the maximization of favorable attitudes from others would thus be the counterpart in sociological theory to the maximization of profit in economic theory."[26] If by this it is meant that the theorem is to be understood as a heuristic rather than an empirical assumption, that sociology has a selective point of view which is just as abstract and partial as that of economics and the other social sciences, and if his view of theory as a set of logically connected formal propositions is granted provisional acceptance, I am in agreement. (Actually, the view of theory suggested at the beginning of this paper is a quite different one.)

But there is a further point to be made. Ralf Dahrendorf has observed that structural-functional theorists do not "claim that order *is based on* a general consensus of values, but that it *can be conceived of in terms of* such consensus and that, if it is conceived of in these terms, certain propositions follow which are subject to the test of specific observations."[27] The same may be said of the assumption that people seek to maximize favorable evaluations by others; indeed this assumption has already fathered such additional concepts as "reference group"

potentially benign role assigned it by neo-Freudian thinkers like Fromm and Horney." Gutman and Wrong, "Riesman's Typology of Character," p. 4 (typescript).

[24] Hans L. Zetterberg, "Compliant Actions," *Acta Sociologica*, 2 (1957), p. 189.
[25] *Ibid.*, p. 188.
[26] *Ibid.*, p. 189.
[27] Dahrendorf, *Class and Class Conflict in Industrial Society*, p. 158.

and "circle of significant others." Yet the question must be raised as to whether we really wish to, in effect, define sociology by such partial perspectives. The assumption of the maximization of approval from others is the psychological complement to the sociological assumption of a general value consensus. And the former is as selective and one-sided a way of looking at motivation as Dahrendorf and others have argued the latter to be when it determines our way of looking at social structure. The oversocialized view of man of the one is a counterpart to the overintegrated view of society of the other.

Modern sociology, after all, originated as a protest against the partial views of man contained in such doctrines as utilitarianism, classical economics, social Darwinism, and vulgar Marxism. All of the great nineteenth and early twentieth century sociologists [28] saw it as one of their major tasks to expose the unreality of such abstractions as economic man, the gain-seeker of the classical economists; political man, the power-seeker of the Machiavellian tradition in political science; self-preserving man, the security-seeker of Hobbes and Darwin; sexual or libidinal man, the pleasure-seeker of doctrinaire Freudianism; and even religious man, the God-seeker of the theologians. It would be ironical if it should turn out that they have merely contributed to the creation of yet another reified abstraction in socialized man, the status-seeker of our contemporary sociologists.

Of course, such an image of man is, like all the others mentioned, valuable for limited purposes so long as it is not taken for the whole truth. What are some of its deficiencies? To begin with, it neglects the other half of the model of human nature presupposed by current theory: moral man, guided by his built-in superego and beckoning ego-ideal.[29] In recent years sociologists have been less interested than they once were in culture and national character as backgrounds to conduct, partly because stress on the concept of "role" as the crucial link between the individual and the social structure has directed their attention to the immediate situation in which social interaction takes place. Man is increasingly seen as a "role-playing" creature, responding eagerly or anxiously to the expectations of other role-players in the multiple group settings in which he finds himself. Such an approach, while valuable in helping us grasp the complexity of a highly differentiated social structure such as our own, is far too often generalized to serve as a kind of *ad hoc* social psychology, easily adaptable to particular sociological purposes.

But it is not enough to concede that men often pursue "internalized values"

---

[28] Much of the work of Thorstein Veblen, now generally regarded as a sociologist (perhaps the greatest America has yet produced), was, of course, a polemic against the rational, calculating *homo economicus* of classical economics and a documentation of the importance in economic life of the quest for status measured by conformity to arbitrary and shifting conventional standards. Early in his first and most famous book Veblen made an observation on human nature resembling that which looms so large in contemporary sociological thinking: "The usual basis of self-respect," he wrote, "is the respect accorded by one's neighbors. Only individuals with an aberrant temperament can in the long run retain their self-esteem in the face of the disesteem of their fellows." *The Theory of the Leisure Class,* New York: Mentor Books, 1953, p. 38. Whatever the inadequacies of his psychological assumptions, Veblen did not, however, overlook other motivations to which he frequently gave equal or greater weight.

[29] Robin M. Williams, Jr. writes: "At the present time, the literature of sociology and social psychology contains many references to 'Conformity'—conforming to norms, 'yielding to social pressure' or 'adjusting to the requirements of the reference group.' . . . ; the implication is easily drawn that the actors in question are *motivated* solely in terms of conformity or nonconformity, rather than in terms of 'expressing' or 'affirming' internalized values . . ." (his italics). "Continuity and Change in Sociological Study," *American Sociological Review,* 23 (December, 1958), p. 630.

remaining indifferent to what others think of them particularly when, as I have previously argued, the idea of internalization has been "hollowed out" to make it more useful as an explanation of conformity. What of desire for material and sensual satisfactions? Can we really dispense with the venerable notion of material "interests" and invariably replace it with the blander, more integrative "social values"? And what of striving for power, not necessarily for its own sake—that may be rare and pathological—but as a means by which men are able to *impose* a normative definition of reality on others? That material interests, sexual drives, and the quest for power have often been over-estimated as human motives is no reason to deny their reality. To do so is to suppress one term of the dialectic between conformity and rebellion, social norms and their violation, man and social order, as completely as the other term is suppressed by those who deny the reality of man's "normative orientation" or reduce it to the effect of coercion, rational calculation, or mechanical conditioning.

The view that man is invariably pushed by internalized norms or pulled by the lure of self-validation by others ignores—to speak archaically for a moment—both the highest and the lowest, both beast and angel, in his nature. Durkheim, from whom so much of the modern sociological point of view derives, recognized that the very existence of a social norm implies and even creates the possibility of its violation. This is the meaning of his famous dictum that crime is a "normal phenomenon." He maintained that "for the originality of the idealist whose dreams transcend his century to find expression, it is necessary that the originality of the criminal, who is below the level of his time, shall also be possible. One does not occur without the other." [30] Yet Durkheim lacked an adequate psychology and formulated his insight in terms of the actor's cognitive awareness rather than in motivational terms. We do not have Durkheim's excuse for falling back on what Homans has called a "social mold theory" of human nature. [31]

Social But Not Entirely Socialized — Freud

I have referred to forces in man that are resistant to socialization. It is not my purpose to explore the nature of these forces or to suggest how we ought best conceive of them as sociologists—that would be a most ambitious undertaking. A few remarks will have to suffice. I think we must start with the recognition that *in the beginning there is the body.* As soon as the body is mentioned the specter of "biological determinism" raises its head and sociologists draw back in fright. And certainly their view of man is sufficiently disembodied and non-materialistic to satisfy Bishop Berkeley, as well as being de-sexualized enough to please Mrs. Grundy.

Am I, then, urging us to return to the older view of a human nature divided between a "social man" and a "natural man" who is either benevolent, Rousseau's Noble Savage, or sinister and destructive, as Hobbes regarded him? Freud is usually represented, or misrepresented, as the chief modern proponent of this dualistic conception which assigns to the social order the purely negative role of blocking

---

[30] Emile Durkheim, *The Rules of Sociological Method,* Chicago: University of Chicago Press, 1938, p. 71.
[31] George C. Homans, *The Human Group,* New York: Harcourt, Brace and Company, 1950, pp. 317–319.

and re-directing man's "imperious biological drives." [32] I say "misrepresented" because, although Freud often said things supporting such an interpretation, other and more fundamental strains in his thinking suggest a different conclusion. John Dollard, certainly not a writer who is oblivious to social and cultural "factors," saw this twenty-five years ago: "It is quite clear," he wrote, ". . . that he (Freud) does not regard the instincts as having a fixed social goal; rather, indeed, in the case of the sexual instinct he has stressed the vague but powerful and impulsive nature of the drive and has emphasized that its proper social object is not picked out in advance. His seems to be a drive concept which is not at variance with our knowledge from comparative cultural studies, since his theory does not demand that the 'instinct' work itself out with mechanical certainty alike in every varying culture." [33]

So much for Freud's "imperious biological drives!" When Freud defined psychoanalysis as the study of the "vicissitudes of the instincts," he was confirming, not denying, the "plasticity" of human nature insisted on by social scientists. The drives or "instincts" of psychoanalysis, far from being fixed dispositions to behave in a particular way, are utterly subject to social channelling and transformation and could not even reveal themselves in behavior without social molding any more than our vocal chords can produce articulate speech if we have not learned a language. To psychoanalysis man is indeed a social animal; his social nature is profoundly reflected in his bodily structure. [34]

But there is a difference between the Freudian view on the one hand and both sociological and neo-Freudian conceptions of man on the other. To Freud man is a *social* animal without being entirely a *socialized* animal. His very social nature is the source of conflicts and antagonisms that create resistance to socialization by the norms of any of the societies which have existed in the course of human history. "Socialization" may mean two quite distinct things; when they are confused an oversocialized view of man is the result. On the one hand socialization means the "transmission of the culture," the particular culture of the society an individual enters at birth; on the other hand the term is used to mean the "process of becoming human," of acquiring uniquely human attributes from interaction with others. [35] All men are socialized in the latter sense, but this does not mean that they have been completely molded by the particular norms and values of their culture. All cultures, as Freud contended, do violence to man's socialized bodily drives, but this in no sense means that men could possibly exist without culture or independ-

---

[32] Robert K. Merton, *Social Theory and Social Structure*, Revised and Enlarged Edition, Glencoe, Ill.: The Free Press, 1957, p. 131. Merton's view is representative of that of most contemporary sociologists. See also Hans Gerth and C. Wright Mills, *Character and Social Structure*, New York: Harcourt, Brace and Company, 1953, pp. 112–113. For a similar view by a "neo-Freudian," see Erich Fromm, *The Sane Society*, New York: Rinehart and Company, 1955, pp. 74–77.

[33] John Dollard, *Criteria for the Life History*, New Haven: Yale University Press, 1935, p. 120. This valuable book has been neglected, presumably because it appears to be a purely methodological effort to set up standards for judging the adequacy of biographical and autobiographical data. Actually, the standards serve as well to evaluate the adequacy of general theories of personality or human nature and even to prescribe in part what a sound theory ought to include.

[34] One of the few attempts by a social scientist to relate systematically man's anatomical structure and biological history to his social nature and his unique cultural creativity is Weston La Barre's *The Human Animal*, Chicago: University of Chicago Press, 1954. See especially Chapters 4–6, but the entire book is relevant. It is one of the few exceptions to Paul Goodman's observation that anthropologists nowadays "commence with a chapter on Physical Anthropology and then forget the whole topic and go on to Culture." See his "Growing up Absurd," *Dissent*, 7 (Spring, 1960), p. 121.

[35] Paul Goodman has developed a similar distinction. *Op. cit.*, pp. 123–125.

ently of society.[36] From such a standpoint, man may properly be called as Norman Brown has called him, the "neurotic" or the "discontented" animal and repression may be seen as the main characteristic of human nature as we have known it in history.[37]

But isn't this psychology and haven't sociologists been taught to foreswear psychology, to look with suspicion on what are called "psychological variables" in contradistinction to the institutional and historical forces with which they are properly concerned? There is, indeed, as recent critics have complained, too much "psychologism" in contemporary sociology, largely, I think, because of the bias inherent in our favored research techniques. But I do not see how, at the level of theory, sociologists can fail to make assumptions about human nature.[38] If our assumptions are left implicit, we will inevitably presuppose a view of man that is tailor-made to our special needs; when our sociological theory over-stresses the stability and integration of society we will end up imagining that man is the disembodied, conscience-driven, status-seeking phantom of current theory. We must do better if we really wish to win credit outside of our ranks for special understanding of man, that plausible creature [39] whose wagging tongue so often hides the despair and darkness in his heart.

3   On Psychology

● BENJAMIN LEE WHORF

Psychology has developed a field of research that may no doubt be useful or valuable in itself, but it throws little or no light on problems of the normal human mind or soul. The person who wishes to understand more fully the laws and, so to speak, topography, of the inner or mental life is as much thrown back on his own difficultly acquired store of wisdom and his native judgments, intuitions, sympathies, and common sense as though the science of psychology did not exist. Such a one, for instance, is the teacher, educator, sociologist, anthropologist, trainer, coach, salesman, preacher, manager, diplomat, executive: anyone who must deal

---

[36] Whether it might be possible to create a society that does not repress the bodily drives is a separate question. See Herbert Marcuse, *Eros and Civilization*, Boston: The Beacon Press, 1955; and Norman O. Brown, *Life Against Death*, New York: Random House, Modern Library Paperbacks, 1960. Neither Marcuse nor Brown are guilty in their brilliant, provocative, and visionary books of assuming a "natural man" who awaits liberation from social bonds. They differ from such sociological Utopians as Fromm, *op. cit.*, in their lack of sympathy for the de-sexualized man of the neo-Freudians. For the more traditional Freudian view, see Walter A. Weisskopf, "The 'Socialization' of Psychoanalysis in Contemporary America," in Benjamin Nelson, editor, *Psychoanalysis and the Future*, New York: National Psychological Association For Psychoanalysis, 1957, pp. 51–56; Hans Meyerhoff, "Freud and the Ambiguity of Culture," *Partisan Review*, 24 (Winter, 1957), pp. 117–130.
[37] Brown, *op. cit.*, pp. 3–19.
[38] "I would assert that very little sociological analysis is ever done without using at least an implicit psychological theory." Alex Inkeles, "Personality and Social Structure," in Robert K. Merton and others, editors, *Sociology Today*, New York: Basic Books, 1959, p. 250.
[39] Harry Stack Sullivan once remarked that the most outstanding characteristic of human beings was their "plausibility."

SOURCE: Benjamin Lee Whorf, in his *Language, Thought and Reality* (Cambridge: M.I.T. Press, 1956), pp. 40–42.

with human intangibles, especially the man concerned in leadership of any sort. If he seeks aid from books, he will get far more information about this field from literature not intended to be scientific, that is, from the best works of the novelists, playwrights, and poets, than he will from any textbook of psychology. There are certain courses that psychology has elected to follow that have estranged it, perhaps permanently, from the truly mental field.

First, the "old school" of experimental laboratory psychology has rather definitely assumed the character of a branch of physiology. Its findings and their value all redound back to physiology. It is undoubtedly valuable to the student of mental phenomena to know the mechanisms of the body, but rather in the character of auxiliary information than anything else; and knowledge about the oxidation of the blood and the details of brain and nerve responses, sense perceptions, and association times are equally of this character. Moreover, one is impressed (and depressed) by the appalling sterility of the vast mass of minutiae that this science accumulates, and the dearth of integrating principles.

Second, the school of behaviorism has begun to appear in its true character as simply the old experimental psychology over again in a more pick-and-shovel aspect. That it is in many ways an improvement on the old school and has enlarged our understanding in certain fields I personally believe. It has been of service by teaching us to think more in terms of behavior, but, when all is said and done, it can teach us little that is new. It has shown us how behavior may be conditioned by physical means, but along much the same lines that we already knew although they have been more systematically explained. It has become apparent that we may "condition" either with or against the cooperation of truly psychic considerations. This we already knew, but we are particularly interested in "conditioning" WITH the cooperation of and in accordance with the particular laws of the psychic. No doubt the same process of stimulus and response "conditions" a man into being a scientist or a maniac, a leader of men or a nervous wreck, a good workman or one who cannot hold a job, an inspiring helper or a resentful cog in the machine; but behaviorism does not show us which lines to work upon in order to be really in accord with human intangibles, except by way of announcing in behavioristic terms things already obvious to common sense.

Gestalt psychology does seem to me to have discovered an important truth about mind, the importance of configurations in the mental domain. At the same time the Gestalt psychologists have their hands full with the manifold mechanical, experimental, and personal data required to develop this large subject, most of which data are chiefly valid on the animal level. When we attempt to apply the configurative principle to the understanding of human life, we immediately strike the cultural and the linguistic (part of the cultural), especially the latter, as the great field par excellence of the configurative on the human level. Here the Gestalt psychologists let the matter drop. They have neither the time nor the linguistic training required to penetrate this field; moreover their ideas and terminology inherited from the old laboratory psychology are a liability rather than an asset.

Psychoanalysis is the one school that really deals with mental material, and it sometimes gets results, but it works only in the sphere of the abnormal and the deranged, and it is becoming evident that the abnormal is not the key to the normal. Moreover, it is so resolute in its determination to deal with intangibles that it shows almost a contempt for the external world and strays continually into the realms of phantasm. It is too heavily stamped with the signature of its founder,

Freud, an erratic genius with a faculty of apperceiving deep but obscure truths, and is notion-obsessed and cluttered with weird dogma. As an empirical tool for the clinic it may serve for a while, but I do not see how it can possibly be a means for the careful scientific scrutiny of the normal mind.

All the schools then have been surveyed and found wanting, and the seeker for knowledge about the human mind is forced to fall back on the long-collected mass of empirical observations sometimes called "the wisdom of the ages," on the works of keenly intuitive authors, on his own insight, and on what few general truths he can cull here and there from all the above schools.

One fact that stands out to a detached viewpoint, but is not stressed by any of the schools, is the great and perhaps basic importance of the principle we denote by the word "meaning." Meaning will be found to be intimately connected with the linguistic: its principle is symbolism, but language is the great symbolism from which other symbolisms take their cue.

4   Social Psychology: Model for Liberals

● C. WRIGHT MILLS

"Social Darwinism" and instinctivist psychology were a thorn in the political flesh of liberalism. Both these inferences from evolution fitted a laissez-faire faith and a traditional policy of individualism. The neo-Comteanism of Ward—its utilitarian view of science, its social meliorism and telesis of progress, its foresight formulation, and its faith in education—all these were anti-Spencerian, anti-laissez-faire.[1]

Now there were two features of the general instinctivist view which liberals wished to overcome or to replace: they wanted to give mind, rationality, a place in nature and in the psychology of human affairs; and they wanted to see human nature as modifiable through the reconstruction of the social "environment." They wanted substantive rationality to prevail and to be diffused by mass education, but they wanted to deny the political implications of historical individualism.[2] It is between these two poles that the social psychological tradition of pragmatism is worked out.[3] In William James the substantive rationality is so played up and so

SOURCE: C. Wright Mills, in his *Sociology and Pragmatism*, edited by Irving Louis Horowitz (New York: Oxford University Press, 1966), pp. 447–463.

[1] *Dynamic Sociology.* Many passages of this book could almost have been written by John Dewey.

[2] In this connection, *see* Baldwin's blast, *Social and Ethical Interpretations in Mental Development,* p. 96 f.

[3] The structure in Mead's conceptual apparatus is clearly a bridge of this tension: Specifically, the "I" of a liberal individual and the "me" of a sociologized conscience. In terms of this tension between rationality and individuality Mead would stand opposite James, for Mead would seat rationality itself in the social process; for him mind became a little parliament, or an "inner forum." Both celebrate the self. But Mead's celebration of the self is a social fiesta, James' is the celebration of a man alone. Mead's "me" is closest approximated in James by "habit" which although socially acquired is a very definite possession of the individual. For James, society is held together by habituated individuals; for Mead, individuals are held together by the social process. "Habit," wrote James, "is thus the enormous fly wheel of society." *Principles of Psychology,* Vol. I, 21. However, *see* James' discussion of the "social self" which is tied *organically* at all points. It should also be kept in mind that for James the self is "the sum total of all that he [the individual] can call his." *Ibid.,* Vol. I, p. 291.

wedded to individualism that the "social" in the psychology suffers badly, and his political views are not as "social" as are Dewey's.

Dewey is entirely too "generous" when he writes:

"The objective biological approach to the Jamesian psychology led straight to the perception of the importance of distinctive social categories, especially communication and participation. It is my conviction that a great deal of our philosophizing needs to be done over again from this point of view, and that there will ultimately result an integrated synthesis in a philosophy congruous with modern science and related to actual needs in education, morals, and religion." [4]

Dewey could see this "led straight" only because his social slant and motives refracted his understanding of James so as to stress the plasticity in the view and lead to recognition of the social to an extent which James would never have accepted.

Now it is precisely the importance of the accomplishment of Dewey, and in this connection even more so of G. H. Mead, that the *social* angle is intrinsically knit to the *rational:* the answer to the tension is a *social* theory of *mind.* And this is the mudsill of the liberal psychology of Dewey. With this recognition of *social* influences as molding the person, the fate of the individual who must carry the *rationality* is jeopardized. That is why this tradition from Ward, through Dewey, to W. I. Thomas and Mead has gone in for education. For this tension between the substantive rationality of an individual and the "anti-individualist" orientation and implication of social influences makes a social education of the individual come squarely to the front. *Biological individualism,* classically put in modern times by instinctivism, is replaced by *sociological* rationality: by a perspective which makes rational mind, individuality itself, strongly dependent upon social "education." [5]

If mind [Dewey writes] in any definitely concrete sense of that word, is an offspring of the life of association, intercourse, transmission, and accumulation rather than a ready-made antecedent cause of these things, then the attitude of polite aloofness of condescending justification as to social institutions has its nerve cut, and with this the intellectual resources of sanctified conservatism disappear. [Mind is a product of the] shared life of the place and time, [and the kind of mind that develops] depends upon the kind of objects of attention and affection which the specific social conditions supply.[6]

That answered both a biological determinism and a laissez-faire type of calculating individualism. No wonder that Dewey has said that his philosophy was best expressed for a long time by his educational writings, which are, of course, strongly imprinted by social psychological views.

In England, Graham Wallas [7] retreated from an earlier instinctivism in the name of its anti-intellectuality; he wanted a view of "thinking" that is no "mere servant of the lower passions." He refused to polarize and separate "instinct" and "intelligence," preferring a hyphenated form, "instinct-intelligence." Thus intelligence itself becomes "elemental," biologized as it were, and thought is reinstated in the range of man's actions. Hobhouse also wishes to "effect a complete revolution in

---

[4] "From Absolutism to Experimentalism," pp. 25–26.
[5] ". . . 'mind' . . . represents something acquired . . . It is a formation, not a datum; a product, and a cause only after it has been produced." *Psychology Rev.,* Vol. 24, p. 271.
[6] *Ibid.,* p. 274.
[7] *The Great Society,* pp. 39, 42–43, 53.

the position" assigned to "mind." [8] Both of these English liberals made an effective challenge to Spencer, and they did so in terms of the Darwinian model. But Dewey and the other pragmatists exceeded them.

That Dewey's social psychology is conceived as a contribution to morals in the eighteenth century sense is an important fact in grasping this social psychology and, indeed, of Dewey's larger style of reasoning. [9] The stated point of view is the Humean one:

> . . . that a knowledge of human nature provides a map or chart of all humane and social subjects, and that with this chart in our possession we can find our way intelligently about through all the complexities of the phenomena of economics, politics, religious beliefs, etc.

To Hume's angle is added the recognition of "the pervasive and powerful influence of what anthropologists call culture in shaping the concrete manifestations of every human nature subject to its influence."

In a 1929 preface Dewey brings to the fore the nature-nurture controversy: he states that he wants "to keep the two forces in balance." And then, very significantly:

> There is, I hope, due emphasis upon the power of cultural habitude and trend in diversifying the forms assumed by human nature. But there is also an attempt to make clear that there are always intrinsic forces of a common human nature at work; forces which are sometimes stifled by the encompassing social medium but which also in the long course of history are always striving to liberate themselves and to make over social institutions so that the latter may form a freer, more transparent and more congenial medium for their operation. "Morals" in its broad sense is a function of the interaction of these two forces.

We can formulate a socially oriented principle which underlies all that Dewey says on this issue. With it we can explain and predict what he will say on given issues. It is this: *he will always take a view that leaves man's biologized nature plastic enough to make social reforms possible, but he will try to keep it unitary enough to be the seat and anchor and implicit standard of certain colors.* He will deny fixed "instincts," but keep modifiable "impulses," and thus steer clear of determinism on either side and allow for freedom. In the last analysis, human nature will be good if it is left alone, but to be good it must have a good society. A good society is one "congenial" to the "potentiality," "growth," the workings of human nature. Again, he will not lose the individual, the center of "intelligence" and the agent of social change, but the individual will not become a passionate, instinctive animal. He will be a "social" creature, and in this sociality will reside some of his goodness and his rationality. He will avoid social determinism of man and of morals, because this would mean "the level of colorless conformity"; it would mean loss of individuality and loss of a "standard" rooted at least loosely in man. Yet, on the other hand, he does not "romantically glorify" individuality: for, "subjection to passion" is not "a manifestation of freedom."

Each of the key concepts of the statement serves a definite function in presenting and sustaining the orientation of these underlying propositions.

The political slant of liberalism overtly crosses the psychological when "two

---

[8] *Development and Purpose*, pp. 10–12.
[9] *Human Nature and Conduct* (Mod. Lib. ed.), Preface. This is the source for the following quotations. These pages correspond to the paginations in the order given: vi, vii, viii, viii–ix, 5–6, 7, 9, 10, 11, 106, 106–107, 108, 109, 111, 115, 115, 115, 125, 125, 41.

schools of social reform" are set forth and a third, a mediatory conception, is advanced by Dewey: on the one hand we have a:

> . . . notion of a morality which springs from an inner freedom, something mysteriously cooped up within personality. It asserts that the only way to change institutions is for men to purify their own hearts, and that when this has been accomplished, change of institutions will follow of itself. The other school denies the existence of any such inner power, and in so doing conceives that it has denied all moral freedom. It says that men are made what they are by the forces of the environment, that human nature is purely malleable, and that till institutions are changed, nothing can be done.

But Dewey finds the way out by the concept "interaction":

> . . . all conduct is *interaction* between elements of human nature and the environment, natural and social. Then we shall see that progress proceeds in two ways, and that freedom is found in that kind of interaction which maintains an environment in which human desire and choice count for something. There are in truth forces in man as well as without him. While they are infinitely frail in comparison with exterior forces, yet they may have the support of a foreseeing and contriving intelligence. When we look at the problem as one of an adjustment to be intelligently attained, the issue shifts from within personality to an engineering issue, the establishment of arts of education and social guidance.

This passage seems quite significant, for:

(i) it permits "intelligence" to save the individual, while at the same time it recognizes "environmental" forces.

(ii) Because of the latter recognition, it shifts the issue to a technological level. It is an "engineering issue." This, of course, opens a space for the appeal to science. Notice in the following the biological conception of this science in a moral posture:

> Each sign of disregard for the moral potentialities of physical science drafts the conscience of mankind away from concern with the interactions of man and nature which must be mastered if freedom is to be a reality.

The same strategy, moving from the nature-nurture issue to the liberal and engineering standpoint is evidenced in later chapters of *Human Nature and Conduct*. In his more extended treatment of the plasticity of "human nature," we recognize the basic dialectic of Dewey's style of reasoning, culminating in a liberal mediation of "extremes." On the one hand, John Locke and other "early reformers" were:

> . . . inclined to minimize the significance of native activities, and to emphasize the possibilities inherent in practice and habit-acquisition. There was a political slant to this denial of the native and a priori, this magnifying of the accomplishments of acquired experience. It held out a prospect of continuous development, of improvement without end.

On the other hand, the conservative:

> . . . has thought to find in the doctrine of native instincts a scientific support for asserting the practical unalterability of human nature. Circumstances may change, but human nature remains from age to age the same. Heredity is more potent than environment, and human heredity is untouched by human intent. Effort for a serious alteration of human institutions is utopian.

Dewey accepts neither. For:

> . . . the radical reformer rests his contention in behalf of easy and rapid change upon the psychology of habits, of institutions in shaping raw nature, and the conservative grounds his counter-assertion upon the psychology of instincts. As a matter of fact, it is precisely custom which has greatest inertia, which is least susceptible of alteration; while instincts are most readily modifiable through use, most subject to educative direction.

Both the shortcut revolutionist and the die-hard conservative are mistaken in their views of human nature and *therefore* in the tempo and possibilities of human change which they respectively envision. For "actual social change is never so great as is apparent change." Then Dewey proceeds to take the question of historical change out of the content of psychology *per se:* to locate it in "customs."

> Those who argue that social and moral reform is impossible on the ground that the Old Adam of human nature remains forever the same, attribute however to native activities the permanence and inertia that in truth belong only to acquired customs.

He then goes into a social and pluralist view of history and institutions. And the problem is again seated within "interactions."

> Pugnacity and fear are no more native than are pity and sympathy. The important thing morally is the way these native tendencies interact, for their interaction may give a chemical transformation not a mechanical combination.

After indicating that war is not rooted in any one or even two "instincts," but is "a function of social institutions" he cites James' essay on war approvingly and states: "A general social re-organization is needed which will redistribute forces, immunize, divert and nullify." It should be noticed here that his own analysis leads him away from a specification of the locus of war-making forces. He is pushed upon a high and general level of abstraction, a level incommensurate with his epistemological exhortations.

> History does not prove the inevitability of war, but it does prove that customs and institutions which organize native powers into certain patterns in politics and economics will also generate the war-pattern. The problem of war is difficult because it is serious. It is none other than the wider problem of the effective moralizing or humanizing of native impulses in times of peace.

Dewey's larger model in terms of which "social problems" are conceived is (a) on the *social* plane, that is, he rejects a psychological definition via instincts, *e.g.,* and more precisely, on this social plane difficulties are defined in terms of:
(b) the "lag" of habits in the face of change, more especially, technological change. This leads to a "truer psychology" for "the trouble lies in the inertness of established habit."

In putting the problem on a social plane he gets away from the conservative who would seal the status quo in the nature of man. In recognizing the force of habit and custom he avoids the "shortcut revolutionary" who would urge a change of conditions very quickly. For, writes Dewey, "Man is a creature of habit, not of reason nor yet of instinct."

The conception of habit, which is one of the three key terms of Dewey's psychology, is ideally calculated to mediate the instinctivist with a conservative political implication, and extreme environmentalism with its revolutionary import, "Habit" could almost have been deduced by Dewey to fulfill this mediation.

Habit is *acquired* and it is *not* merely "repetition." Dewey wants to keep man modifiable; even from the "acquired" side he wants no ball-and-chain conceptions.[10] He wants to make habit a lag which sets problems (and hence constitutes a limen for intelligence), and, at the same time, he wants adaptability to be a feature of human nature. The meaning of habit is shaped by these two motives.

In order to avoid the "repetition" meaning of habit Dewey bends over backwards to make it dynamic: "habit means will." [11] It is a motivational affair as well as a stabilizer, for, taken consecutively, one's habits form one's character. There are several meanings given to habit, as G. W. Allport has noted, there are no criteria advanced by Dewey for distinguishing between habit as motivational and dynamic, and habit as a lagging repetition.[12] We are, however, not surprised to realize that Dewey's concepts can deal better with adaptive shifts and changes in personality than with its more stable aspects.

This seating of motivation within the ambivalence of the conception of habit gets Dewey away from the wild animal man of James, with his uncontrollable passions. It makes easier, as we shall see, a view of man's rationality and, more importantly, it definitely implements a Socratic ethic. For if Dewey's account of habit is accepted, it becomes more difficult to raise the question of motivation for acting upon the good after it is discerned. Indeed, we are further along than that. It tends to seat the good in the easy workings of released impulses controlled by intelligently composed habits.

> The word habit may seem twisted somewhat from its customary use when employed as we have been using it. But we need a word to express that kind of human activity which is influenced by prior activity and in that sense acquired; which contains within itself a certain ordering or systematization of minor elements of action; which is projective, dynamic in quality, ready for overt manifestation; and which is operative in some subdued subordinate form even when not obviously dominating activity. Habit even in its ordinary usage comes nearer to denoting these facts than any other word.[13]

Given this action of habit (which is identified with "attitude" and "predisposition") what is then needed is only a release of "positive forms of action" (*i.e.*, good ones).

> If we perceive that they [attitude and disposition] denote positive forms of action which are released merely through removal of some counteracting "inhibitory" tendency, and then become overt, we may employ them instead of the word habit to denote subdued, non-patent forms of the latter.[14]

The tacit assumption underlying these passages and forming the perspective in which they are to be understood is that "human nature" is good. It is a literal faith in man's goodness if "he" is let alone to grow under proper community conditions. This assumption is again evident in the conception of "growth" which is used as a norm within educational theory.

All orientations and tensions in the social psychology have their reflexes, at least, in the educational context.

First, of course, is the fact that this psychology's stress on the modifiability of human nature opens wide the possibility of improvement by means of the educa-

---

[10] See G. W. Allport in *Philosophy of John Dewey*, p. 270.
[11] *Human Nature and Conduct*, p. 41.
[12] *Philosophy of John Dewey*, p. 275.
[13] *Human Nature and Conduct*, pp. 40–41.
[14] *Ibid.*, p. 41.

tional enterprise. The classification of "psychology" into *physiological* or *social* obviously suits the stress on modifiability, indeed, it opens the way for a *social* theory of mind, which is at once the chief outcome of Dewey's social psychology and which is slanted specifically to *educational* endeavors. It is significant that Dewey credits Mrs. Young, with whom he was associated primarily in an educational context, with inspiring this view: "I owe chiefly to association with Mrs. Young the depth of my conviction that all psychology that isn't physiological is social." [15]

This educational wish to see man as modifiable has its implication for the focus of Dewey, his selective omission of certain topics. Despite the fact that educators have been absorbed in capacity testing, Dewey has never been interested in I.Q. tests. *Anyone* is capable of thinking, of securing his adaptation. "Barring physical defect or disease, slowness and dullness in all directions are comparatively rare." [16]

In more technical debates concerning choice of curricula, it should be recalled that "faculty psychology" buttressed the discipline idea of certain formal subjects. The shift in occupational structure within which educational institutions are anchored was antagonistic to these subjects, clamored for a different set. In going against faculty types of psychology and the theories of mind underpinning them, Dewey was, therefore, aiding the newer occupational imperatives for education.

The modifiability of man is a leverage precisely for reform and "universal education" becomes thereby a psychologically possible and portentous ideal. The psychology of habits thus connects with an education interest.

> . . . the cold fact of the situation is that the chief means of continuous, graded, economical improvement and social rectification lies in utilizing the opportunities of educating the young to modify prevailing types of thought and desire. The young are not as yet as subject to the full impact of established customs.[17]

But the matter does not end here, for this focus upon the young makes possible the tacit anchorage of *values* in the child. The fact of the modifiability of the young is construed as a source of potential social value.

> The combined effect of love of power, timidity in the face of the novel and a self-admiring complacency has been too strong to permit immature impulse to exercise its reorganizing potentialities. The younger generation has hardly even knocked frankly at the door of adult customs, much less been invited in to rectify through better education the brutalities and inequities established in adult habits.

Thus:

> Original modifiability has not been given a fair chance to act as a trustee for a better human life. It has been loaded with convention, biased by adult convenience. It has been practically rendered into an equivalent of non-assertion of originality, a pliant accommodation to the embodied opinions of others.

And the character of this value inherent in modifiability is independent individuality: "That the most precious part of plasticity consists in ability to form habits of independent judgment and of inventive initiation has been ignored." In the

---

[15] McManus, *E. F. Young*, p. 121.
[16] *How We Think*, p. 35. G. W. Allport has noted Dewey's lack of interest in any "capacity psychology." "Dewey's Individual and Social Psychology," *The Philosophy of John Dewey*, P. A. Schilpp. Ed., p. 277.
[17] *Human Nature and Conduct*, p. 127. The quotations which follow are from this source and correspond to its pagination in the following order: 96, 97, 97, 127, 128.

following, read the plus-adjectives of Dewey's vocabulary as used in his "description" of a child's life.

> Yet [even adults] wish a different life for the generation to come. In order to realize that wish they may create a special environment whose main function is education. In order that education of the young be efficacious in inducing an improved society, it is not necessary for adults to have a formulated definite ideal of some better state. An educational enterprise conducted in this spirit would probably end merely in substituting one rigidity for another. What is necessary is that habits be formed which are more intelligent, more sensitively percipient, more informed with foresight, more aware of what they are about, more direct and sincere, more flexibly responsive than those now current. Then they will meet their own problems and propose their own improvements.

Here the notion of habit as dynamic, plus the values implicitly seated in the nature of the child, again makes less possible the raising of the moral question as to what values we are to "teach" in educational enterprises. This item comes out more explicitly in the concept of "growth," which operates as a norm under the guise of a description. For the:

> . . . aim of education is to enable individuals to continue their education [or] . . . the object and reward of learning is continued capacity for growth. Now this idea cannot be applied to *all* the members of a society except where intercourse of man with man is mutual, and except where there is adequate provision for the reconstruction of social habits and institutions by means of wide stimulation arising from equitably distributed interests. And this means a democratic society. In our search for aims in education, we are not concerned, therefore, with finding an end outside of the educative process to which education is subordinate. Our whole conception forbids.[18]
>
> Education is thus a fostering, a nurturing, a cultivating, process. All of these words mean that it implies attention to the *conditions of growth* . . . the ideal of growth results in the conception that education is a constant reorganizing or reconstructing of experience. It has all the time an immediate end, and so far as activity is educative, it reaches that end—the direct transformation of the quality of experience.[19]

When "growth" is defined, Dewey gets very formal. The possibility of "good growth" and "bad growth" is not entertained, nor does "educational growth" tell us how to decide between them.

> Our net conclusion is that life is development, and that developing, growing, is life. Translated into its educational equivalents, this means (i) that the educational process has no end beyond itself; it is its own end; and that (ii) the educational process is one of continual reorganizing, reconstructing, transforming . . . Growth is regarded as *having* an end, instead of *being an end* . . . Since in reality there is nothing to which growth is relative save more growth, there is nothing to which education is subordinate save more education.[20]

Dewey repudiates the notion of education as "unfolding," or as "preparation." Either view would lead to questions of goal setting. But education as growth is calculated to avoid just such questions. The same strain has Rousseauian political

---

[18] *Democracy and Education*, p. 117.
[19] *Ibid.*, p. 12, 89.
[20] *Ibid.*, pp. 59–60.

eventuations. What he stands for, liberalism, here consists in "the development of the inherent capacities of individuals. . . ." [21] He cites Emerson approvingly:

> Respect the child. But not too much his parents . . . Also respect yourself . . . The two points in a boy's training are, to keep his *nature* and train off all but that; to keep his *nature*, but stop off his uproar, fooling, and horseplay; keep his nature and *arm it with knowledge in the very direction* it points.[22]

Throughout Chapter IV of *Democracy and Education* he underplays the degree to which the adult sets the child's learning. For this purpose, the concept of "growth" is useful. All of his concepts in this chapter are positive: "immaturity" is the "ability" or "power" to "develop" or to "grow." "Dependence" means "interdependence"; it also means "plasticity" which does not signify "putty," but "power to develop dispositions." Again, "habits" are not mechanical but, in this context, become "expressions of growth." A habit is "a form of executive skill, of efficiency in doing . . . and ability to use natural conditions as means to ends." [23] This conception aids in keeping the child as a center of Deweyan social change. He wants *not* to throw educational issues upon the moral, political plane where decisions between adults must be made. He wants to root change as well as its directions in the child. Seeing the child as "social" implements this motive, as does Dewey's seating of "social control" in "the situation." Indeed, Dewey thinks it might be well if adults would or could get back to the child's world in certain moral and intellectual matters: they "must become as little children." [24]

Lastly, it should be noted that the educational and psychological concepts of Dewey mutually buttress one another in the conception of the place of intelligence. For since intelligence plays a dynamic, yet mediatory, role in the changing social situations, there is a still firmer basis for a faith in education which will foster the growth of intelligence. Morally and politically, intelligence is enough, and education builds it.

The three central categories of Dewey's psychology are habit, impulse, and intellect. Each of these categories stands in a definite relation with each of the others. In the most general way, the schema runs like this: action runs along on habit, some obstacle blocks the action, impulse arises and tries to make its way to action. Prior habit and now impulse are in conflict. A problem then exists. Enter intelligence, which mediates between impulse and habit, thus facilitating the release of action, which will be a projection of existent habits newly combined so as to satisfy the stymied impulse. Several other relations between habit, impulse, and intelligence are possible, but they are to be scorned. Impulse may not get to "useful production" and this, in the Puritanical conception of the place of such things, is not so good: "Castles in the air like art have their source in a turning of impulse away from useful production . . . fancy remains an end in itself." [25]

Habits are necessary for thought; they restrict its reach, "fix its boundaries" but they are also "positive agencies"; "formed in . . . exercising biological aptitudes" they are agents of "observation, collection, foresight and judgment . . ." Although they do not "know" the obstacles they override, "we may . . . be said to *know how* by means of our habits." [26]

---

[21] *Liberalism and Social Action*, p. 32.
[22] *Democracy and Education*, p. 62.
[23] *Ibid.*, p. 55.
[24] *Ibid.*, p. 50; *see* also p. 58.
[25] *Human Nature and Conduct*, pp. 163–64.
[26] *Ibid.*, pp. 172, 175, 176, 177.

What is Dewey doing here? He is seating rational processes in biology. On the one hand, we have the eighteenth century "man is a rational creature"; on the other, we have the nineteenth century, "man is animal." But Dewey would have man rational, or at the very least would make for the possibility of man as rational *because* he is an animal. Conscious rationality is not operative in habitual behavior no matter how "rational" habits grounded in biological aptitudes may be. A "disturbed adjustment of organism and environment" must come about before an "old habit and the new impulse" can come to terms.[27]

Impulse is seated in an individual. It is this impulse which "determines the direction of movement"; it "defines the peering, the search, the inquiry" which will release it by that reconstructing of habit and impulse known as intelligence. In this deliberation we dramatically rehearse (in imagination) "various competing possible lines of action." "Choice" consists in "hitting in imagination upon the object which furnishes an adequate stimulus to the recovery of overt action." Mind is then "unified." Again the side workings of the scheme which have been pointed out are avoided:

> We may not look far enough ahead because we are hurried into action by stress of impulse; but we may also become overinterested in the delights of reflection; we become afraid of assuming the responsibilities of decisive choice and action, and in general be sicklied over by a pale cast of thought. We may become so curious about remote and abstract matters that we give only a begrudged, impatient attention to the things right about us. We may fancy we are glorifying the love of truth for its own sake when we are only indulging a pet occupation and slighting demands of the immediate situation.[28]

We are "irrational" if either habit or impulse wins out. And "end" should not be "so fixed, a passion . . . so absorbing, that the foresight of consequences is warped to include only what furthers execution of its predetermined bias." We are "rational" if by deliberation "old aims and habits" are remade, and thus a "love of new ends and acts" is instituted.

In this biologized and Puritanic schema of the place and meaning of rational thought the adjustment of man to nature is reproduced in microcosm of the rational individual. The political controls which operate on this statement are constant:

> The oscillation between impulse arrested and frozen in rigid custom and impulse isolated and undirected is seen most conspicuously when epochs of conservatism and revolutionary ardor alternate. But the same phenomenon is repeated on a smaller scale in individuals.

It is also true that this statement is so made as to give foundation for a moral theory which will break down the distinction between the expedient and the moral.[29] "Morality," writes Dewey, "is an endeavor to find for the manifestation of impulse in special situations an office of refreshment and renewal. The endeavor is not easy of accomplishment." [30]

However, intelligence, and intelligence alone, can accomplish it:

---

[27] *Ibid.*, p. 179.
[28] *Ibid.*, pp. 190, 192 and 197–98.
[29] *Ibid.*, pp. 98, 169–70, *See* page 210.
[30] *Ibid.*, p. 169. The quotations which follow are from this source, in the following order: 210, 211, 227.

> There is but one issue involved in all reflection upon conduct: The rectifying of present troubles, the harmonizing of present incompatibilities by projecting a course of action which gathers into itself the meaning of them all. The recognition of the psychology also reveals to us the nature of good or satisfaction. Good consists in the meaning that is experienced to belong to an activity when conflict and entanglement of various incompatible impulses and habits terminate in a unified orderly release in action. This human good, . . . [is] a fulfillment, conditioned upon thought . . .

With "rigid habits" and traditions there is no meaning at all. And since the world changes, they will plunge us in "disaster." Again, when the ends of impulse are "frozen and isolated" they cannot operate in the quest for good. That the moral issue is loaded with assumptions is clear by the very definition of intelligence. For instance it is interesting to see "business calculation" ruled out [31] because it is:

> . . . obviously of the kind where the end is taken for granted and does not enter into deliberation. It resembles the case in which a man has already made his final decision . . . . His end-in-view already exists; it is not questioned . . . Deliberation *is* not free but occurs within the limits of a decision reached by some prior deliberation or else fixed by unthinking routine.[32]

And hence:

> A radical distinction thus exists between deliberation where the only question is whether to invest money in this bond or that stock, and deliberation where the primary decision is as to the *kind* of activity which is to be engaged in.

Morally, this is:

> . . . the substantial fact: Ends are foreseen consequences which arise in the course of activity and which are employed to give activity added meaning and to direct its further course. They are in no sense ends *of* action. In being ends of *deliberation* they are redirecting pivots *in* action.[33]

And thus, the "categorical imperative" does "so act as to increase the meaning of present experience." [34] The moral ideal is, therefore, the thoughtful life in Dewey's special meaning of thoughtful as the intelligent. We thus end, as we began, with a view of intelligence as central precisely because its statement is shaped to fit the moral, educational, and political values of Dewey's style of liberalism.

Postscript: Some Last Reflections on Pragmatism

It would surely signify either ignorance or hypocrisy to consider this endeavor to be a complete sociological account of pragmatism. It is perhaps the major fragment of such a task. I do not wish to apologize for this acknowledged incompleteness, but for future reference what is lacking must be recorded. To supply these deficiencies is, I have felt in the process of the work, beyond the confines of the usual expectations of a single book. The sociological account of American prag-

---

[31] Yet note the ambivalence: "A businessman proceeds by comparing today's liabilities and assets with yesterday's, and projects plans for tomorrow by a study of the movement thus indicated in conjunction with study of the conditions of the environment now existing. It is not otherwise with the business of living.

[32] *Ibid.*, p. 215.

[33] *Ibid.*, pp. 217 and 225.

[34] *Ibid.*, p. 283.

matism is most likely a good two-volume opportunity. What must be made is a brief anticipatory statement of the outlines of this task and of what it will require. If it should be somewhat personal in nature, that is due to my desire for self-clarification concerning future work.

1. An account of George H. Mead must be included. It is true that many features of Mead's thought are treated by the consideration given to the work of John Dewey. However, in view of the course of the pragmatic movement and of Dewey's differential evaluation of Mead and James, the inclusion of James and the omission of Mead is an unrepresentative act that is intellectually unwarranted.

2. This specific omission is linked with an equally important, though more diffuse, inadequacy: the architecture of the entire presentation as it now stands. There is needed a more concise *phraseology and development statement* of the course of the movement as a whole as it lies within a changing social structure. This omission involves three considerations: (a) it must, of course, wait upon the account of Mead. (b) It will require a *larger* conception of the course of the entire movement of pragmatism from Peirce to Mead than I have here permitted myself. (c) This entire matter must wait upon an increase of the writer's knowledge of the political, economic, and social history of the United States since the Civil War as it may bear upon the conditions of the total intellectual life. The sort of knowledge really required can only come with a constant working of the facts over a considerable period and from many detailed studies. The lack of this sort of knowledge is a major reason for such deficiencies as these materials may have. It is because of this personal deficiency, which can only be remedied by work in time, and because of the omission of Mead, that I have refrained from an attempted over-all reconstruction of "pragmatism" in a concise field at this time. Within the limits of such scholarly conscience as I possess, I cannot now undertake such an attempt. I thought it wiser, first, to focus upon detailed statements of each major pragmatist tied down as closely as possible to their actual texts. Only after this should one attempt to formulate the developmental phases of the movement as a whole and to state the commonalities and variations in foci, style, and result of respective pragmatists.

3. Such an overview and total grasp of the movement also waits upon at least three specialized inquiries, aspects of which have certainly been touched upon in the above, but which require systematic and more thorough consideration. (a) One is what might be called the regional or "the frontier hypothesis of pragmatism." The reader will realize from what has already been written that I am not prepared lightly to accept this so far unverified theory. It is, however, believed that the matter is capable of a refined statement, one that will permit detailed and empirical, rather than rhetorical and romantic, testing. Indeed, such a statement and test is required. This task involves a sociological portrayal of the St. Louis school. (b) Another over-all hypothesis, suggested by Mannheim and others, although not established by anyone as yet, conceives "pragmatism" as representing a "democratization" of criteria. (c) There is the often carelessly made imputation of pragmatism as a rationale of a crude commercialization of American cultural life. As is the case with (a) and (b) this matter is believed capable of yielding its full fruit only after it has been restated in terms of concrete data and connective mechanisms. These matters may be conceived as portions of the job of systematizing and stating the "friendly" explanations of pragmatism given by such men as Sidney Hook, Horace Kallen, and, above all, G. H. Mead.

4. There is also required more definitive data upon the extraction and general social composition of the academic personnel of philosophy (and of certain non-academic intellectuals) since the Civil War. This lack, as well as the omission of an account of Mead, is primarily due to the fact that research funds are needed to obtain required data.

5. A broader matter of at present unknown importance must be examined: the relations, if any, and their character, between pragmatic elements of thought and the New Deal government, especially its earlier phases. Certain important actors in the New Deal, such as Henry A. Wallace and Rexford Tugwell, have been influenced by Dewey's writings. At the same time it would seem that those so placed have also been close readers of Thorstein Veblen and that this has influenced their understanding of Dewey. To get at the bottom of this problem, one must ascertain more precisely the influence of Charles Peirce on the young Veblen and the influence of Veblen upon Dewey. Veblen heard Peirce lecture at Johns Hopkins, and Dewey was in at least reading contact with Veblen at Chicago. An important clue to the matter resides in what I have termed technologic meanings in Peirce, which became one facet of Dewey's theory of meaning. Sociologically, the problem can most easily be approached by direct interviews with the relevant men of the early New Deal government.

6. The major critics at various stages in the development of pragmatism should be considered in a systematic and sociological way. The correct performance of this task, which at a minimum should include Bertrand Russell, Carl Schurz, A. E. Murphy, Lewis Mumford, Waldo Frank, as well as those who so valiantly fought by Dewey's students and colleagues, waits upon a more detailed understanding such as is indicated. It would culminate in a more explicit and close account on the competition of ideas throughout the period.

7. It is also the opinion of the writer that such an endeavor as the present one should by all means be accompanied, when completed, with detailed methodological self-reflections. In the present stage of research in sociology of knowledge there is a need for every substantive attempt to be accompanied by *explicit* self-awareness both of detailed procedure and of larger epistemological concerns. Advance in sociology of knowledge will not follow from substantive work alone, for every such piece of work involves methodological issues, whether we endeavor to hide them or whether we take the risk of crossing intellectually outmoded academic fences. I am by no means satisfied with the methodological basis and rationale of such concrete work in sociology of knowledge as lies within my awareness. The writer has not been unaware of these problems and has, indeed, filled many margins of pages with such reflections. Their omission in the present work is in large part due to irrelevant considerations for this statement.

8. It is perhaps not indispensable, but it would certainly be interesting and in all probability revealing, to examine the non-American refractions and criticisms of pragmatism. In Italy, especially, as well as in England, France, and Germany, there has developed, since the time of William James, a literature on this topic. In this connection it would be significant to trace the receptions of Dewey's work in the hands of Orientals and scholars of non- or only semi-industrialized countries, especially those of China and India, as well as of Mexico and Turkey.

9. There remains the present situation of pragmatism in America. Perhaps never before in its eighty years' existence has this style of thinking been so under attack as it has since the world crises which came to fruition in the late thirties.

The attack has been in "spiritual" or "religious" terms and also on "political" grounds. No volume that in any sense could be called major has as yet resulted from these reactions. The personal and political reasons for such a course of events must be examined from a standpoint as removed from these reasons as is possible. To so examine it would offer the possibility of a fundamental understanding of the conditions for the future development of philosophy in the United States.

5   The Position of George Herbert Mead

● WILLIAM H. DESMONDE

George Herbert Mead (1863–1931) is now esteemed as one of the most creative thinkers in the pragmatist movement of the twentieth century. In the view of Charles W. Morris, an outstanding disciple, "the analytical depth and scientific precision he gave to the naturalistic theory of personality" entitles Mead to a permanent place among the founders of social psychology. Though to date, Mead's work has exerted greater influence on psychologists and sociologists than on philosophers, he has been acclaimed a creative mind of the first rank by such writers as John Dewey and Alfred North Whitehead.[1] . . .

The Influence of Darwin

Mead was a contemporary and close friend of the sociologist Charles Horton Cooley [2] and the philosopher, John Dewey. Like . . . Dewey, Mead derived his basic orientation from the impact of Darwin's theory upon nineteenth-century thought. Darwin's indications that man is an organism functioning in accordance with natural laws gave a fresh impetus to the scientific investigation of the determinants of human behavior. It was confidently anticipated by many people all over the world that the application of scientific method of human phenomena would bring about the solution of numerous age-old problems in social relations. . . . Mead [was born] four years after the publication (1859) of Darwin's *Origin of Species.* . . .

As for the influence of Darwin upon George Herbert Mead, Charles W. Morris wrote:

> It has been the philosophical task of pragmatism to reinterpret the concepts of mind and intelligence in the biological, psychological, and sociological terms which post-Darwinian currents of thought have made prominent, and to reconsider the

---

SOURCE: William H. Desmonde, from "G. H. Mead and Freud: American Social Psychology and Psychoanalysis," in *Psychoanalysis and the Future,* edited by Benjamin Nelson (New York: National Psychological Association for Psychoanalysis, Inc., 1957), pp. 31–50.

[1] For an evaluation of Mead's work and excerpts from his key writings, see now: *The Social Psychology of George Herbert Mead,* ed. Anselm Strauss (Chicago: University of Chicago Press, 1956), esp. pp. ix–xvi (in introduction); also, Grace C. Lee, *George Herbert Mead: Philosopher of the Social Individual* (New York: King's Crown Press, 1945).

[2] Cooley's development is described and appraised in Edward C. Jandy, *Charles Horton Cooley* (New York: Dryden Press, 1942).

problems and task of philosophy from this new standpoint . . . the outlines of an empirical naturalism based on biological, psychological, and sociological data and attitudes are clearly discerned, a naturalism which sees thinking men in nature, and which aims to avoid the inherited dualism of mind and matter, experience and nature, philosophy and science, teleology and mechanism, theory and practice. It is a philosophy which, in terms used by Mead, opposes "the otherworldliness of the reason . . . of ancient philosophy, the otherworldliness of soul . . . of Christian doctrine, and the otherworldliness of the mind . . . of the Renaissance dualisms." [3]

Not only did Darwin's theory enable man to regard himself scientifically, but it emphasized the concept of process in the consideration of personality. It is difficult for us to appreciate today the extent to which the concept of process was neglected in thought prior to the time of Darwin. Nature was regarded as consisting of fixed, unalterable substances which existed independently of one another. These substances or essences possessed static forms which did not undergo transformations in time, but were eternal. If the recently deceased pioneer social psychologist, Kurt Lewin, is to be believed, the Aristotelian world-view which Western civilization had inherited divided the world into classifications which were unchangeable and immutable:

> In modern quantitative physics dichotomous classifications have been entirely replaced by continuous gradations. Substantial concepts have been replaced by functional concepts.
>
> Here also it is not difficult to point out the analogous stage of development in contemporary psychology. The separation of intelligence, memory, and impulse bears throughout the characteristic stamp of Aristotelian classification; and in some fields, for example, in the analysis of feelings (pleasantness and unpleasantness) or of temperaments, or of drives, such dichotomous classifications as Aristotle's are even today of great significance. Only gradually do these classifications lose their importance and yield to a conception which seeks to derive the same laws for all these fields, and to classify the whole field on the basis of other, essentially functional, differences.[4]

Darwin demolished this conception of fixed species; his work led to the acceptance of the notion of process. Nature was now viewed as a continuum, and all natural objects, including organisms, were part of an eternally changing, ceaselessly dynamic matrix. Psychic phenomena, too, were part of this process. It was no longer possible to regard men as possessing fixed, unalterable attributes or "traits." Instead, the mind was to be viewed as arising developmentally. . . . Mead . . . started from the assumption that psychic phenomena are evolutionary emergents subject to causal laws. . . .

If man is to be conceived as a natural, determined phenomenon, the problem arises of fitting the organism into the universal causal nexus. Mead fought against any type of artificial dualism between organism and environment. An "organism" must be conceived as a temporary equilibrium within a field of force, an equilibratory state which comes into existence, maintains itself in a position of relative stability for a period of time, then literally disintegrates back into the nexus from which it emerged. Organism and environment, Mead wrote, are mutually determinate; each is in a continual state of reciprocal reconstruction. . . .

---

[3] In his introduction to George Herbert Mead's *Mind, Self, and Society* (Chicago: The University of Chicago Press, 1934), p. x.
[4] Kurt Lewin, *A Dynamic Theory of Personality* (New York: McGraw-Hill, 1935), p. 4.

Abandoning the conception of personality as a fixed, unchanging set of pre-ordained faculties, [Mead] sought to show the emergence of complex psychic phenomena from an environmental matrix.

Mead's "Social Behaviorism"

By destroying the mind-body dualism, Darwin's theory gave impetus to those philosophies which regarded mind and body as parts of a natural process. It was now contended that all psychic phenomena could be observed and understood in the same manner as other natural processes, with the aid of measuring instruments and laboratory controls. The influential American school of behaviorism constituted one such effort to make psychology a natural science. George Herbert Mead's "social behaviorism" was an attempt to correct many of the crudities of early behavioristic psychology.

Mead's criticisms began with an objection to the dismissal of introspection by many of the objective psychologists. By rejecting introspection as a methodological tool, the behaviorists tended to regard it as a non-existent phenomenon. *Mead, however, believed that the scope of behaviorism could be extended to include the neglected introspective phenomena.*

Furthermore, Mead stated that the behaviorists' description of the organism was based on an abstraction of the individual from the social process in which actions occur. The consequences of this artificial abstracting was a conception of individuals acting and reacting to each other, on the causal model of billiard balls. It was Mead's contention that the behaviorists were merely considering the external aspect of the total behavior of the organism. Actually, stimulus and response are meaningful only when viewed as part of a complete communicative situation.

Mead also rejected the notion that organisms passively respond to stimuli. He contended that the organism dynamically selects its stimuli; it does not react to perceptions. The organism to a great extent determines its environment.

> . . . attention enables us to organize the field in which we are going to act. Here we have the organism as acting and determining the environment. It is not simply a set of passive senses played upon by the stimuli that come from without.[5]

Mead thus opposed the British associationist school, in regarding the organism as a dynamic, forceful agent molding the world around it, rather than existing as a mute receptacle for stimuli which are later associated.

Mead began the construction of his "social behaviorism" by considering the function of gestures in social acts. An "idea," he stated, is the early, unobservable stage in an ongoing act directed toward an environmental goal. Before an organism makes any overt movements, an inner mobilization of energy takes place, which no other organisms (except with special instruments) can observe. The mistake of the early behaviorists was to study merely one part of the complete act —the last, overt stages—thereby ignoring the initial stages, which occur behind the organism's epidermis. Ideas, therefore, are attitudes: the internal organization and preparation for the developing act. Hence, if we regard ideas as "inner" or "private" phases in ongoing acts, it becomes possible to construct a naturalistic theory of introspection.

Some of the early stages in an ongoing act are objectively observable. The initial

---

[5] *Mind, Self, and Society,* p. 24.

aspect of the overt phase of an action indicates to other organisms the direction and goal of the progressing movement. These initial actions, said Mead, borrowing from Wundt, are gestures.

> The term "gesture" may be identified with these beginnings of social acts which are stimuli for the response of other forms.[6]

For example, when a person draws back his arm and clenches his fist, this indicates to the other organisms that the former is going through the initial phase of a striking movement. Similarly, the roar of a lion is a gesture which displays readiness to attack. The gesture of "A" is a sign to "B" of "A's" complete act. It is through such observed preparatory movements that an organism's intentions become known to other individuals.

However, gestures are usually part of a complex social situation. The social situation in its simplest form consists, for Mead, in the "conversation of gestures," in which a gesture on the part of one individual evokes a preparatory movement on the part of the second person, and this gesture on the part of the second calls out a response in the former, and so on. For example, dog "A" makes a preparatory action towards springing at the throat of dog "B"; this gesture causes "B" to spring back; and this springing-back action of "B" is in turn a stimulus to "A."

But as yet, according to Mead, no communication need have taken place between the dogs—the gestures are *non-significant,* in that neither organism is aware of the effect of its gestures upon the other. In order for communication to take place, each organism must obtain cognition of the reaction of the other individual to his own behavior. This involves a temporal organization of the act, whereby the consequences of actions are already present while the behavior develops.

> The later stages of the act are present in the early stages—not simply in the sense that they are all ready to go off, but in the sense that they serve to control the process itself. They determine how we are going to approach the object, and the steps in our early manipulation of it.[7]

That is to say, when we stretch out our hand to pick up a book, the neural process that will activate the later clenching reaction has been already initiated before the clenching occurs; these processes exert an influence upon the phases of action which are already in progress. Mead cites the phenomenon of the hurdle runner. Several seconds before he jumps the hurdle, and while he is rapidly running toward it, the runner is timing himself so that he will be in the proper position to leap over the hurdle when he finally reaches it.

On the basis of such phenomena, Mead assumed that the central nervous system provides a mechanism whereby our behavior is organized with reference to the future. In so doing, he explained the determination of the present by the future, without resorting to obsolete versions of teleological concepts.

Furthermore, the capacity of the later phases of an act to control the earlier stages makes the organism an intelligent being, rather than a mere automaton acting on the basis of conditioned reflexes, as was the crude belief of the early behaviorists.

Now before any given act is completed, there are a number of alternative ways of carrying out the movement. Since the later stages of the developing action determine the earlier phases, it is possible for the organism to select one of these al-

---

[6] *Ibid.,* p. 43.
[7] *Ibid.,* p. 11.

ternative ways of completing the motion. In this manner, rational conduct is possible, as over against behavior which is determined in advance by instincts, as in the lower forms of life.

> It is the entrance of the alternative possibilities of future response into the determination of present conduct . . . which decisively contrasts intelligent conduct or behavior with reflex, instinctive, and habitual conduct. . . .[8]
> Rational conduct always involves a reflexive reference to self, that is, an indication to the individual of the significance which his actions and gestures have for other individuals.[9]

The temporal organization of the act provides a necessary condition for the existence of communication. Effective sociality requires that organism "A" be capable of responding to its own response in the same way as does organism "B," the other participant in the social situation. But Mead rejects Tarde's conception of a "faculty" of imitation, and isolates the mechanism whereby symbols achieve significance.

The first condition for the existence of significant symbols is that organism "A" have present within it the same possibilities for response as has organism "B." The second condition is that organism "A" be capable of responding to its own responses, through the use of some sense-modality, in the same way as would "B."

Language meets these conditions, for we can hear what we are saying, and thus evoke in ourselves the same ideas (preparations to act) as are evoked in the other organism. Thus, by means of the verbal response, we can simultaneously respond as would the other, while at the same time evoking the other's response by our action. Hence, in advance of our completion of a social action, we can already anticipate the response of the other. And, since our behavior is temporally organized, this anticipation works back on the ongoing act, and may cause the selection of a different alternative course of action than we originally intended.

In general, then, whenever organism "A" makes a gesture of any sort, to which "A" can at the same time respond in the same way as would "B," then "A" is making a significant gesture. And only when organisms can employ significant gestures does sociality exist.[10]

Through its capacity to use significant symbols, a given organism can take two or more roles simultaneously. The other's point of view is called out along with the given organism's perspective. For Mead, "mind" is the ability of an organism to take the role of the other toward its developing action. Mind emerges in the social act when the person is able to obtain cognition of the perspective of the other individual, and hence is able to modify his original response in the light of his knowledge of how the other may react to that response.

> Mind arises in the social process only when that process as a whole enters into or is present in the experience of any one of the given individuals involved in that process. . . . It is by means of reflexiveness—the turning-back of the experience of the individual upon himself—that the whole social process is thus brought into the experience of the individuals involved in it; it is by such means, which enable

---

[8] *Ibid.,* p. 98.
[9] *Ibid.,* p. 122.
[10] It is interesting to compare Mead's "significant symbol" with Max Weber's definition of sociality: "Action is social in so far as, by virtue of the subjective meaning attached to it by the acting individual, it takes account of the behavior of others and is thereby oriented in its course." Talcott Parsons, *Max Weber: The Theory of Social and Economic Organization* (New York: Oxford University Press, 1947), p. 88.

the individual to take the attitude of the other toward himself, that the individual is able consciously to adjust himself to that process, and to modify the resultant of that process in any given social act in terms of his adjustment to it. Reflexiveness, then, is the essential condition, within the social process, for the development of mind.[11]

Once reflexivity comes to exist, the entire social act is imported within the individual. Society is internalized, and serves to alter the original developing acts of the person. A complete social act can thus be internally carried out within the organism, without any overt movements necessarily taking place. This inner rehearsal of projected actions constitutes introspection.

That is to say, communication exists because organisms are capable of responding to their own response in the same manner as the other. The individual thus can, at the same time, take the role of the other, as well as act out its own role. Through this mechanism the unification of roles or perspectives occurs, and common viewpoints become possible.

By being able to take the role of the other, the organism becomes capable of looking at itself and observing itself as do other organisms. And taking the role of the other toward the beginnings of an act can occur even if the other organism is not in the field of perception. Thus, the social act is internalized.

The "I" and the "Me"

As a result of the internalization of the social act, the "inner forum" comes into being. The organism rehearses internally various types of possible social relations. Mead denotes the internalized role of the other towards the beginnings of a response the "me." That is to say, the "me" is the other person's reaction, implanted within the organism, toward the initial stages of the given organism's developing actions. It is in this manner that it is possible for other people to influence permanently our lives. A person who is important to us is internalized in the form of a "me" which modifies the course of our ongoing behavior. The altered, or adjusted, response of the organism to the imported reaction of the other is termed by Mead the "I."

> The "I" is the response of the organism to the attitudes of the others; the "me" is the organized set of attitudes of others which one himself assumes.[12]

Personality is the resultant of the interaction between the "I" and the "me"; the organism is perpetually beginning acts, then taking the attitude of the other toward this act, and finally readjusting the ongoing behavior in accordance with the anticipated reactions of the other.

> Now this is the highest expression of sociality, because the organism not only passes from one attitude to another, by means of a phase which is a part of all these attitudes, but also comes back on itself in the process and responds to this phase. It must get out of itself in the passage and react to this factor in the passage.[13]

---

[11] *Mind, Self, and Society*, p. 134.
[12] *Ibid.*, p. 175.
[13] George Herbert Mead, *The Philosophy of the Present* (Chicago: Open Court Publishing Co., 1932), p. 86.

Through man's capacity to readjust his developing acts to his anticipations of the future, he achieves freedom. The knowledge of what is necessary enables us to make an appropriate adjustment to that reality when it eventuates. We are not bound by the past, but can utilize the past to prepare for the future.

As Patrick Mullahy has pointed out,[14] the fact that society is imported within us is not incompatible with the uniqueness of each individual. According to Mead, innovation always can arise through the readjustment of the original ongoing act to the "me." The "I" is the source of all novelty and individuality, for by this readjustment new social forms come into being. We do not passively adapt ourselves to the reactions of others, but we actively create new relationships to other individuals. Because of the "I," we live in a constant state of growth, in which fresh perspectives are continually being created.

> By its own struggles with its insistent difficulties, the human mind is constantly emerging from one chrysalis after another into constantly new worlds which it could not possibly previse.[15]

The world of interpersonal relations is in a continual state of flux, for each individual is occupied in reconstructing the social group, by means of the "inner forum"—the interaction between the "I" and the "me."

> [It is the possession of] . . . mind or powers of thinking which enables human individuals to turn back critically, as it were, upon the organized social structure of the society to which they belong, and to reorganize or reconstruct or modify that social structure.[16]

One of Mead's most fruitful concepts is the "generalized other," which is the importation of the social organization within the individual. In group situations, such as games, the individual must adjust his actions, not merely to one other person (the "me"), but to the entire community. In a baseball game, for example, a person must act in accordance with the organized roles of every other member of the group.

> . . . in a game where a number of individuals are involved, then the child taking one role must be ready to take the role of everyone else. If he gets in a ball nine he must have the responses of each position involved in his own position. He must know what everyone else is going to do in order to carry out his own play. He has to take all of these roles.[17]

It is through the internalization of the organized attitudes of the entire group that the individual develops a complete self, according to Mead. The manifold functions of a society, its cooperative processes and institutions, are possible only insofar as the individual can carry within himself the numerous roles of the other people involved in group situations, and can extend these group attitudes to larger social organizations.

> It is in the form of the generalized other that the social process influences the behavior of the individuals involved in it and carrying it on, i.e., that the community exercises control over the conduct of its individual members; for it is in this

---

[14] "A Philosophy of Personality," *Psychiatry*, XIII (1950), p. 436.
[15] George Herbert Mead, "Scientific Method and the Moral Sciences," *International Journal of Ethics*, XXXIII (1923), 33: p. 246.
[16] *Mind, Self, and Society*, p. 308.
[17] *Ibid.*, p. 151.

form that the social process or community enters as a determinative factor into the individual's thinking.[18]

In the mature individual, the "inner forum" becomes more than an inner conversation with one other person; it becomes an imaginative discourse with a large group of other individuals who are organized into a cooperative enterprise.[19] And, just as in the case of the "me," the adjustment of the organism to the role of the generalized other causes the creation of new social forms.

There are certain occasions, Mead wrote, when all of the members of the group achieve a very close relationship, because of some common venture in which all are engaged. In such situations, each person has a feeling of being identified with the other members of the group. Inspired by this sense of closeness or identity, a sense of exaltation develops. This feeling is at the core of all religious experiences, according to Mead.

> In a situation where persons are all trying to save someone from drowning, there is a sense of common effort in which one is stimulated by the others to do the same thing they are doing. . . . In the case of team work, there is an identification of the individual with the group; but in that case one is doing something different from the others, even though what the others do determines what he is to do. If things move smoothly enough, there may be something of the same exaltation as in the other situation. There is still the sense of directed control.[20]

This phenomenon is found mainly in religion, patriotism, and team work; it consists of a fusion of the "I" and the "me." That is to say, the internalized response of the other toward the given organism's ongoing act is such as to permit a harmonious merging of the two components. In these situations, there is agreement between the "I" and the "me" in the inner forum, and there results, according to Mead, "a peculiarly precious experience," which involves "the successful completion of the social process." [21]

> The self under these circumstances is the action of the "I" in harmony with the taking of the role of the others in the "me." [22]

In the fusion of the "I" and the "me," it may be said that Mead terminates his task of expressing psychic phenomena in terms of "social behaviorism." For here the dualism of environment and organism against which he fought is finally destroyed, and the mutual interdetermination of these two aspects of nature is clarified. . . .

---

[18] *Ibid.*, p. 155.
[19] Mead's "generalized other" is remarkably similar to Emile Durkheim's conception of the "collective representation." See for example, Durkheim's *The Elementary Forms of the Religious Life* (New York: Macmillan, 1915), p. 271.
[20] *Mind, Self, and Society*, p. 273.
[21] *Ibid.*, p. 275.
[22] *Ibid.*, p. 277.

6   Some Neglected Problems in Social Psychology

● LEONARD S. COTTRELL, JR.

. . . I could not, time and your patience permitted, cover the entire range of important problems confronting social psychology in the next phase of its development. My efforts shall be limited to brief citations of a few rather specific problems which, in my opinion, are characterized by the fact (1) that they have not yet received adequate systematic attention; and (2) that direct and indirect results of intensive attack upon them would greatly strengthen our theory and method for the responsibilities social psychology is now expected to assume.

I. The Empathic Responses

Social psychologists in this country have thus far succeeded in ignoring almost completely what, in my opinion, is one of the most fascinating and challenging as well as one of the most critical processes in the whole range of phenomena with which they are concerned. I refer to the empathic responses.

Many of you have sought to understand the processes involved in such phenomena as the development of a conception of self, in acquiring a role, in the emergence of insight, in communication, in the integration of a group, in the internalization of social norms, or have at least studied the work of those who have made major contributions to our understanding of these processes—for example, G. H. Mead, C. H. Cooley, Sigmund Freud, H. S. Sullivan. You must, therefore, share with me the recognition that in most current theory regarding human interaction there is the basic assumption that as the individual reacts in his various life situations he not only develops those responses appropriate to his own part in the relationships but also incorporates in his reactive system the responses of the others in the situation. Only as this takes place, we say, can the individual acquire a system of significant symbols by means of which true communication takes place, or can he acquire a mind or a social self, or can collectivities achieve a consensus upon which must rest their capacity to function as integrated units. Under such terms as internalization, identification, taking the role of the other, empathic response, social psychologists have recognized the universality and central importance of this process.

If the empathic phenomena are so crucial in human interaction, it is indeed surprising that they have not been subject to intensive research. This lack may be due in part to the fact that these responses are so much a part of our taken-for-granted experience that they have failed to challenge interest and attention. I suspect, however, that a large part of the failure to tackle problems in this area stems from the nature of the phenomena which makes them very difficult to study with available techniques. But whatever the reasons for this lack of research on empathic phenomena, it is my conviction that a vigorous effort in this direction is a prime need now.

This field is teeming with problems that challenge interest and skill. Take, for

SOURCE: Leonard S. Cottrell, Jr., from "Some Neglected Problems in Social Psychology," *American Sociological Review*, XV, No. 6 (December 1950), pp. 705–712.

example, the problem of variability both among individuals and in the same individual in different situations. Preliminary explorations of these questions which we have undertaken at Cornell [1] indicate that tests of relative empathic responsiveness which will discriminate reasonably well are feasible and that such tests will show wide variability among individuals. Results also suggest that the empathic responsiveness of a given individual will vary with the situational context. Moreover, it seemed clear that our subjects who were consistently high in empathic performance and those who were low differed rather markedly in developmental histories, personal characteristics, social insight, and relations with others.

With nothing more than this modest amount of exploration one becomes aware of a substantial list of questions and problems that press for serious attention. Only a few may be noted here.

There is the obvious task of developing a reliable and sensitive index of the empathic ability which will permit appropriate rankings of individuals and the detection of changes in individuals under varying conditions. Equipped with such an index we may then undertake through descriptive and experimental procedures to answer the following questions:

1. Is this a general capacity or is it specific to situations?
2. What types of early formative social relations are associated with varying levels of empathic responsiveness? in general? in specified types of situations?
3. What types of social situations heighten and depress empathic responsiveness?
4. What kinds of social relations and adjustments are made by persons of varying empathic capacity?
5. Is it possible to modify empathic responsiveness by deliberate training?
6. If so, are solutions to certain problems in human relations facilitated by increasing or decreasing the level of responsiveness?
7. Are there optimal levels of empathic responsiveness for the various social roles called for in our society?

And so we could continue this list indefinitely. It is generally recognized, I believe, that a fool can ask more questions in five minutes than a wise man can answer in a lifetime. But sometimes the wise man finds one or two of the fools' questions worth, if not a lifetime, then at least six months.

But before we leave the subject of empathy, I should like to touch briefly upon two other matters which appear to me to merit some attention by members of our craft. One has to do with a deliberate use of empathic responses for conscious investigative purposes. We have long used the participant observer technique in the social sciences, but in much of the use of this technique I doubt that the user knew what was taking place and hence did not use himself as an instrument of observation as effectively as might be. It appears to me on the basis of as yet very informal and unsystematically gathered evidence that the perception of social situations under observation is greatly sharpened when the participant observer is aware of his covert role-taking and deliberately stimulates himself to do it systematically. Just the simple device of saying to himself, "Now I am X facing this situation and having to deal with this problem," seems to enhance the observer's comprehension of

---

[1] See Rosalind Dymond, "Empathic Ability: An Exploratory Study." An unpublished Ph.D. thesis written under my direction, Cornell University, 1949. See also an article by the same author, "A Scale for the Measurement of Empathic Ability," *Journal of Consulting Psychology,* 13 (1949), 127–133.

the perspectives, attitudes, and overt behavior of his subject. Deliberate role-taking practice also seems to increase these observational skills. Harry Stack Sullivan came closer than anyone in the clinical field in explicit recognition of the deliberate use of empathic methods in analysis and therapy and made it a part of the training he gave to those who studied under him. All of this leads me to suggest as a very promising field the systematic study of the devices and operations used by clinicians and research workers to empathize with their subjects. I have no illusions about the difficulties involved, for many of the operations are covert and unconscious; but at least we can begin by finding out what the good operators report they do. Such information should at least be of some help in answering our tougher minded students when they ask us just what one does when he takes the role of another in participant observation.

This leads me to my second observation, namely, that we must undertake to state more explicitly than we have thus far the operations we refer to when we use such terms as empathic response or taking the role of the other. Certainly we have no wish to leave these terms in the realm of mysticism nor are we satisfied with circular definitions. At present the nearest we can come to an operational statement of empathy is to say that an empathic response of individual A to individual B is that response of A to B assumed to take place whereby A is able to correctly predict B's response to a specified situation. But this merely sets up correct prediction as a way of testing the degree to which A has taken B's role. It says nothing about the nature of this response. However, we can at least go as far as we can with this criterion and hope to make more explicit what does take place which makes possible these predictions which we are constantly making not only in our professional studies of behavior but in all of our social interaction.

In this connection it should be noted that prediction is not necessarily based upon the kind of knowledge and understanding which comes from an alleged empathic response. Actuarial knowledge provides the basis for prediction without the kind of understanding which we assume results from empathy.

We have by no means exhausted the important and interesting problems having to do with empathic processes. But enough has been said to indicate an extensive and almost untouched field in which we may expect some significant research in the near future.

Let me turn, then, to another not unrelated category of problems.

II. The Self

It may seem a bit presumptuous on my part to point to the self as a neglected problem for research in view of the increasing attention the concept has received during the past several years, culminating in the recognition given the problem by Professor Hilgard [in his presidential address to the American Psychological Association (1949)]. However, it might be noted that Hilgard's paper is chiefly devoted to pointing out the failures of psychologists to make any significant progress in research on this problem and to suggesting the directions which he thinks an appropriate program of research should take. Moreover, I think it fair to say that with a few exceptions the research reported and the general discussions of the self still suffer from a failure to profit fully by the insights and formulations contributed by G. H. Mead, H. S. Sullivan and others of their general orientation. Our thinking and our formulation of research problems with reference to the self lack clarity because so few workers use the term self with the sophistication, say of Lindesmith and Strauss. I quote from their recent text: [2]

> The use of such expressions as "awareness of self" and "selfconsciousness" naturally leads to the question of what the "self" is. Since the term "self" is used as a noun, the existence of a corresponding entity or object seems to be implied. This, however, is an erroneous conception—as erroneous as it would be to think of "speed" in the same manner. Both terms refer to events and relationships, rather than to entities having a definite location in space. It is for reasons of this kind that the self or ego has been described as a "grammatical illusion."
>
> The concept of self, if it is to be useful and valid, must be formulated as an organization of activity. More specifically, it refers to (a) a set of responses which (b) exercise a regulatory function over other responses of the same organism. This is equivalent to saying in another way what we have already noted: that the behavior of the child is first controlled and guided by the responses of others, but in time these responses become internalized so that the person himself controls and guides his own behavior.
>
> It is both convenient and necessary to use a term like "self" to refer to this relationship of response systems within the same person. . . . When an individual assumes the roles of others toward himself, he begins to evaluate and thereby to regulate his own behavior in terms of those assumed roles of other persons. The term "self" may be applied to this organization of the responses of an individual to his own behavior. One's self is, therefore, indissolubly linked with participation in groups, since the way in which one responds to himself is a partial reflection of the way other persons respond to him.

In my opinion the unsatisfactory state of our knowledge about self phenomena and the very hazy notions of the directions present research should take is due largely to the fact that we have not followed out the concrete research implications of the view of the self expressed by the authors just cited. This theoretical position has been in our sociological literature a long time now, but we have not sufficiently exploited it in systematic empirical research.

What are some of the research problems implicit in this theory of self? Certainly a general implication is that the focus of attention be shifted away from a search for attributes of an entity or for an intrinsic complex of reified motive patterns to an analysis of interaction in an explicitly described context of relations. More specifically we should devote systematic effort to such problems and questions as the following:

1. What patterns of self conception emerge from what types of interactional contexts in the early social experiences of the individual? By self conception I mean the individual's characteristic pattern of expected response from others and his assumption as to what response others expect from him in given types of situations. The nature of the self conception can be inferred partly through the individual's own communication and partly through interpretation of his behavior. While new research with this explicit frame of reference should be undertaken, it should also be remembered that already existing clinical and observational records, although gathered with a different frame of reference and interpreted differently, are a rich source for investigation of this problem.

---

[2] A. R. Lindesmith and A. L. Strauss, *Social Psychology*, New York: Dryden Press, 1949, pp. 100–201.

2. What accounts for persistence of a given self-other organization? Unfortunately the vast amount of work on learning has been so preoccupied with rote learning in molecular problems that their results are of little help here. It is to be hoped that substantial effort in learning research can be directed to this problem. One important line of investigation would be to study the extent to which self conceptions persist as a result of the stability of situational contexts rather than as an intrinsic perseveration. This leads into such interesting questions as to the tendency of a self conception to select or actually contrive and create those social contexts which confirm and support its patterns of self-other expectations. This is a particularly interesting problem when it involves self conceptions involving what to an outsider appear to be negative and punishing expectations.

3. Closely related to the problem of persistence is that of change. How do self-other organizations change? We need here to have intensive studies of the impact of changes in the social context as well as changes in the perceptive structuring of the context by the individual.

4. When the individual manifests a change in his self-other pattern, what happens to the previous pattern? If we interpret within our present frame of reference the clinical findings made by Freudians, hypnotists, and others using "depth" techniques, we are led to suspect that previous self-other patterns remain more or less intact and sometimes are rather active and troublesome inhabitants of the personality. A very important problem is the determination of the conditions under which earlier self-other patterns disintegrate or are integrated into new patterns and those under which they seem to remain as relatively separate organizations which either press for overt expression or simply remain as latent but available for appropriate situational conditions.

5. The foregoing readily leads into the much more generally recognized problem of multiple selves, and the question of the unity of the personality. Here again I feel that in searching for some intrinsic principle of unity and integration (which is entirely proper) we have neglected to study the phenomena of unity and integration in terms of the nature of the life situations of the individual and his roles in them to determine the extent to which his experience of a unified self is based on the integration and consistency of his life situations.

6. Another question on which we need more explicit theory and empirical study is: What are the determinants of identity? The problem can be stated concretely somewhat as follows: As the child develops he is faced with competing definitions of himself by his various social contexts. In any context one of these definitions is accepted by him and becomes his self-concept while the other possible selves are not accepted. Moreover, as the person develops further he accepts certain significant members of his social contexts as identification models and not others. As he moves into contexts involving group symbols he identifies with some and not with others. Now, in social interaction the roles of all components of the field are assumed here to be incorporated in some measure in the reactive systems of each participant. But fortunately for order and stability most of us are reasonably clear most of the time as to what our roles of identity are. How and why we embraced these rather than others is not so clear. Of course we make *post hoc* interpretations of great plausibility and no doubt of genuine validity. But we are as yet quite lost when called upon to state, for example, the conditions under which a child's major identification model will be that of his father or his mother.

7. And while we are discussing what determines selection of group symbols of

identification we should also list the neglected problem of how the individual manages an identification with a group symbol. That something of this sort happens we are certain, but the processes by which it happens are very obscure. Terms like "taking the role of the generalized other" and "ego-involvement" are useful up to a point in suggesting what may be taking place, but they are far from adequate to our present need for precise description. This problem of course has more significance than merely tidying up our descriptions. It leads us into the question of how separate individuals integrate their separate goals and actions into a collective unity; how that unity is maintained; how it disintegrates. These are questions of utmost relevance to a society facing the testing we are bound to undergo in our long struggle ahead for a democratic world community.

8. The group self or the self-other pattern in which the other is a generalized other confronts us with another important but neglected problem. This problem has to do with what might be called a role taking or empathic range of which individuals are capable. Human beings *can* be integrated by controls over them by which they are directed in the performance of their parts without any awareness of the total process. Authoritarian systems rest heavily on such controls. But a sounder social order and one which democratic values call for is based upon maximum participation in the total process. This participation depends upon the role-taking processes so that each member of the social action is able to some extent at least to incorporate the social act in himself and to conceive his own activity in relation to the whole. Now it is relatively easy for this to happen in the smaller life situations of which we are a part, but as the dimensions of the situational field expand the role-taking process may become quite attenuated. The problem, therefore, in building and maintaining a real and genuinely experienced consensus is in part at least one of the role-taking or empathic capacities of human beings plus means of communication which fully utilize these capacities. This obviously opens up an extensive area for research (a) in empathic capacity as we have noted before, and (b) in methods and techniques of communication by which role-taking processes are facilitated and maximized in situations of secondary contact. It might be noted that as yet little if any of the research in communication is formulated properly to explore this field.

I shall not tax your patience with further discussions of needed research on the self. There are many other problems, but these have impressed me as having special interest and importance for social psychologists at the present time.

III. The Situation

One can hardly have an ordinary conversation without making frequent use of the word situation. Such popularity must be deserved, and I have little doubt that its function in communication is important, though I sometimes suspect its utility is quite as great in preserving an illusion of understanding as it is in conveying genuine comprehension.

When we move over into the more technical conversations, we also find the term widely used by students of social behavior. Indeed, sociology can be thought of as a discipline devoted to the analysis of social situations. Here again, however, it must be said that in the ready use of this term we do not always find the ends of precise communication well served.

A social psychologist of my orientation would, of course, be quite lost if you deprived him of the word situation or situational field. But, in spite of the embarrassment it would cause me I must confess that the use of the word in social psychology is almost as vague as it is in general conversation. This is as true among those who aspire to a rigorous experimentation as it is among those who operate with less refined research procedures.

The neglected question is essentially one of how we can precisely define the situations to which we refer the behavior of individuals or groups which we happen to be studying. Now all of us—at least in the social behavior fields—have gotten away from the naive effort to study behavior as though it related to single isolated stimuli. We know that social behavior takes place and can be understood only as a part of a complex process of interaction among the component parts of an identifiable situational field. But when we try to state the composition and boundaries of a particular situation we discover that our conceptual and methodological tools are inadequate. We are quite certain that individuals and groups react to their own definitions of situations and that we must understand these definitions in order to understand their reactions, but we are very uncertain in describing these defined unities for ourselves or for others. At my own institution we are finding situational analysis a highly promising approach to social behavior, but we are also finding it extremely awkward to identify precisely and describe the situations we seem to be studying. If you think this is a pedantic or irrelevant problem, try it yourself some time.

Various suggestions of solutions have been proposed which if followed out systematically should yield a convergence of knowledge and experience out of which an adequate answer will emerge. According to Mead the dynamic field is structured by the social act.[3] Dewey's emphasis on the problematic situation adds greatly to the value of Mead's conception.[4] Lewin integrates the field by a structure of goals, vectors, barriers and pathways.[5] Newcomb proposes to use a "motive pattern" to integrate a field.[6] Kretch and Crutchfield emphasize perceptual structuring.[7] I have suggested the expected responses of self and of others aroused by the initiation of an act as a way of defining the situational field.[8] None of these is sufficient but they all suggest research of a type which should yield results relevant to a solution.

One dimension usually neglected in the analysis of situational contexts is that of time. Harold Lasswell, fifteen years ago, pointed out this gap in the analysis of political behavior,[9] but we still fail to give this dimension adequate recognition, to say nothing of developing a way of describing it precisely.

If our theory and method for determination of the boundaries and structures of situations, including the time dimension, were developed satisfactorily, we should then be in position to provide a more adequate analysis of the phenomena of overlapping and conflicting situations and their resolutions. One need not dwell on the practical importance of this particular problem in a world as full of conflict as ours.

---

[3] G. H. Mead, *Mind, Self and Society,* University of Chicago Press, 1934.
[4] J. Dewey, *Human Nature and Conduct,* New York: Henry Holt & Co., 1922.
[5] K. Lewin, "Field Theory and Experiment in Social Psychology: Concepts and Methods," *American Journal of Sociology,* 44 (1939), 868–896.
[6] T. M. Newcomb, *Social Psychology,* Dryden Press, 1950, pp. 98–106.
[7] D. Kretch and R. S. Crutchfield, *Theory and Problems of Social Psychology,* McGraw-Hill, 1948, Chaps. 3 and 4.
[8] L. S. Cottrell, Jr., "Analysis of Situational Fields in Social Psychology," *American Sociological Review,* 7 (1942), 370–382.
[9] H. D. Lasswell, *World Politics and Personal Insecurity,* McGraw-Hill, 1935, Chap. I.

IV. *Motivation*

It is fortunately not necessary for me to discuss in any detail here the neglected problems of research on motivation with a situational rather than an individual orientation. My colleague, Mr. Nelson Foote, will present a paper on this problem in one of the section meetings of this Society.[10] I shall merely note the following general observations. Motivation is, of course, not a neglected field of research, but we are still handicapped by our distorted emphasis on seeking for motive categories as intrinsic attributes of individuals. What we need to fructify our present knowledge is a frankly avowed situational approach to the problem. I hope Mr. Foote's paper will give us a good start in this direction. Current discussions and research in motivation still fail to relate satisfactorily individual motives and social values.

Had we time to discuss matters tonight, I am quite sure we would find some disagreement as to whether or not I have picked for mention problems of importance, but I am confident that, with certain qualifications I have noted, there would be substantial agreement that they are neglected problems. However, I should be prepared to argue that they are not only neglected but are of basic importance. The empathic processes are crucial in social integration; the self organization is the most important resultant of these processes; the concept of the situational field is fundamental to all modern social psychology. The solutions of these three problems together with a suitably consistent theory of motivation without question will form the core of a matured social psychology able to undertake its obligations and responsibilities as the basic social science.

---

7   Major Trends in Symbolic Interaction Theory in the Past Twenty-five Years

● MANFORD H. KUHN

Ordinarily an anniversary occasions the reification of an artificial period. In this case however, there is a certain juncture in the history of the point of view which makes of the past quarter-century something worthy of consideration for symbolic interactionism as well as for our celebration of the founding of the Midwest Sociological Society.

The year 1937 lies virtually in the middle of a four-year period which saw the publication of *Mind, Self, and Society, Movements of Thought in the Nineteenth Century,* and *The Philosophy of the Act.*[1] It would represent the greatest naiveté to suggest that thus the year 1937 represented the introduction of symbolic interactionism. We are all aware of the long development: from James, Baldwin, and Cooley to Thomas, Faris, Dewey, Blumer, and Young. Even the

---

[10] Reprinted in Part Eight of this volume.

SOURCE: Manford H. Kuhn, *Sociological Quarterly,* V (Winter 1964), pp. 61–84.

[1] George H. Mead, *Mind, Self, and Society,* ed. with an Introduction by Charles W. Morris (Chicago: Univ. of Chicago Press, 1934); *Movements of Thought in the Nineteenth Century,* ed. by Merritt H. Moore (Chicago: Univ. of Chicago Press, 1936); *The Philosophy of the Act,* ed. by Charles W. Morris (Chicago: Univ. of Chicago Press, 1938).

Tardean imitation and suggestion which underlay Ross's *Social Psychology* [2] contributed a good deal ordinarily not credited to him in the development of interaction theory. Nor is it the fact that Mead represents the fullest development of the orientation that makes so significant the posthumous publication of his works (for which we may conveniently take 1937 as an anchoring point). Mead's ideas had been known for a very long time. He had taught University of Chicago students from 1893 to 1931. His notions were bruited about in classes and seminars wherever there were professors conducting them who had studied at the University of Chicago—not least in the great heartland included in the Midwest of our Society. Some of Mead's students had published their versions of his ideas or quotations from some of his philosophical papers—Kimball Young's *Source Book for Social Psychology* of a decade earlier contained a paper by Mead, and his *Social Psychology* bore the strong imprint of Meadian interactionism. [3]

No, the significance of the publication of Mead's books is that it ended what must be termed the long era of the "oral tradition," the era in which most of the germinating ideas had been passed about by word of mouth. (It should be noted parenthetically that Mead had published earlier a considerable number of papers, but they were mainly in journals devoted to philosophy and ethics, journals not likely to be read by sociologists or social psychologists. His only paper in a sociological journal—of which I am aware—was his assessment of Cooley's theories.) [4]

The oral tradition, it must be noted, has some generic peculiarities which are evidenced equally by primitive myth and by unpublished intellectual orientation: there tends to be much (almost ritual) repetition; there is a strain to "get it right," that is, to be correct; there is much debate over orthodoxy, and whatever intellectual powers there may be, are more devoted to casuistry and criticism than to inquiry and creativity. The mnemic effort freed from its task of remembering "how it goes" is somehow transformed into energy for imagination on the one hand and for the drudgery of testing and justification on the other. This is what was made possible by the belated publication of the three books by Mead.

Mead had not been the only one of the symbolic interactionists who had failed to publish. The year 1937 was the one in which some of the papers of Ellsworth Faris appeared under the title, *The Nature of Human Nature.* [5] Here, too, was a belated publication which, in its sprinkling and scatter, speaks more for what Faris never published—a rounded theoretical conception of his social psychology. Thomas' *theoretical* formulations were similarly scarce, scattered and incomplete—however influential. While Dewey published voluminously, his chief

[2] Edward Alsworth Ross, *Social Psychology* (New York, 1908).

[3] George H. Mead, "Thought, Symbols, and Language," in Kimball Young (ed.), *Source Book for Social Psychology* (New York: Alfred A. Knopf, 1928), pp. 341–46, reprinted from "The Behavioristic Account of the Significant Symbol," *Journal of Philosophy,* 19:159–63 (1922). Kimball Young, *Social Psychology: An Analysis of Social Behavior* (New York: F. S. Crofts, 1930).

[4] [Kuhn is referring to George H. Mead, "Cooley's Contribution to American Social Thought," *American Journal of Sociology,* 35:693–706 (Mar., 1930). The same journal did in fact publish two earlier papers by Mead: "The Working Hypothesis in Social Reform," *American Journal of Sociology,* 5:367–71 (Nov., 1899); "The Psychology of Punitive Justice," *ibid.,* 23:577–602 (Mar., 1918).—The Editors].

[5] Ellsworth Faris, *The Nature of Human Nature and Other Essays in Social Psychology* (New York and London: McGraw-Hill, 1937).

formulation of symbolic interaction theory is, in my view, his *Experience and Nature* which did not appear until late and which is written in such a forbidding Germanic version of the English language that many sociologists and social psychologists have not read it even yet.[6] Blumer, the young and promising heir apparent, has published relatively little and has nowhere gathered together a rounded version of his point of view.

But even though the oral tradition has some tendency to continue in symbolic interactionism, the past twenty-five years have seen a marked increase in all kinds of activity involving the published symbol: three textbooks on "our side of the social psychological fence"—that by R. E. L. Faris, that by Lindesmith and Strauss (now in its second edition) and the very recent one by Shibutani;[7] a sizable fraction of Newcomb's text [8] and lesser amounts of others on the "other side"; a considerable number of monographs, and into the hundreds of journal articles.

Basically the past twenty-five years have constituted, in contrast to the preceding era, the *age of inquiry* in symbolic interactionism.

But while it has been an era of inquiry, the inquiry has been directed at the testing and developing of what amounts almost to a welter of subtheories going by a variety of names other than symbolic interactionism. This spawning of smaller, less inclusive theories has been due, in my opinion, neither to the propensity of scholars to attempt to make names for themselves by renaming what has already been proposed, nor to their having modified or augmented symbolic interaction in significant measures. This development of sub- or related orientations has stemmed from the essential ambiguities and contradictions in the Meadian statement—ambiguities and contradictions which were generally interpreted to be dark, inscrutable complexities too difficult to understand as long as the orientation remained largely in the oral tradition. Much of this confusion and contradiction may be summed up—but only in a vastly oversimplifying way and for purposes limited to immediate ones I hope here to expound—as a contradiction between *determinacy* and *indeterminacy* in Mead's over-all point of view.

It is apparent that Mead took the view that the individual is initially dependent on the antecedent existence of a social system, specifically as it exists in the ongoing process of a functioning language, for the means wherewith to engage in experience or to take any kind of self-conscious and self-directed action. This internalization of language and the concomitant internalization of the role of the other has, in the Meadian description, nothing in it inconsistent with strict regularity or determinism.[9] Yet, as Mead proposed the *I* and the *Me* as the internal conversationalists constituting in their conversion the self, he indicated that the *I* is impulsive and essentially unpredictable—and furthermore that the *I* is the initiating, acting aspect of the self. It is never completely clear whether he meant only that the *I* is *subjectively* unpredictable or that it is indeterminate in a scientific sense.

---

[6] John Dewey, *Experience and Nature* (Chicago: Open Court Publishing Company, 1925).
[7] Robert E. L. Faris, *Social Psychology* (New York: The Ronald Press, 1953); Alfred R. Lindesmith and Anselm L. Strauss, *Social Psychology* (New York: The Dryden Press, 1949: rev. ed., 1956); Tamotsu Shibutani, *Society and Personality: An Interactionist Approach to Social Psychology* (Englewood Cliffs, N.J.: Prentice-Hall, 1961).
[8] Theodore M. Newcomb, *Social Psychology* (New York: The Dryden Press, 1950).
[9] "Mead's account [of conduct] . . . is not opposed, in principle, to a deterministic view of behavior."—Guy E. Swanson, "Mead and Freud, Their Relevance for Social Psychology," *Sociometry* 24:327 (Dec., 1961).

Furthermore, it seems apparent that there was a basic initiative attributed to the self in the whole process of role-taking, at any rate after the early learning of language and probably even during that process as well. Mead, after all, insisted that the self constitutes its own environment, its own reality. Furthermore, there is the implicit possibility of indeterminacy in the whole conversation between the *I* and the *Me*. And, finally, it is possible to see in Mead's notion of the self such an antithesis to structure, such a dynamically volatile process of shifting self-indications that, whatever the *theoretical* view of determinacy *vs.* indeterminacy in any of the attributes of the self, the whole matter is so evanescent and shifting that it is obviously a practical impossibility to obtain access to any—possibly determinate—antecedents in time to make usable or testable predictions.

We may sum up this set of ambiguities about determinism as follows: The notion that the *I* is indeterminate but the *Me's* are determinate; the notion that both the *I* and the *Me's* are indeterminate; the notion that whereas both the *I* and *Me's* are determinate results of identifiable events, the interaction (conversation) between the two is somehow itself indeterminate or emergent.

But this is a preliminary view and does not cover the varieties of ways in which symbolic interactionism may be structured and, for that matter, has been structured by those proposing inquiry under its aegis. The two most frequently complicating considerations are: (1) the question whether the self is conceived, for research purposes, as the antecedent variable with criterion events (especially behaviors) as consequent variables, or conversely whether antecedent variables (ascribed identities, affiliations, associations, or communication variables and other events) are conceived to predict—that is, to exist in regularity with—consequent self variations; and (2) the question whether the relevant antecedent variables are conceived to be *immediate* or *remote* in time with respect to the events thought of as consequent.

This set of questions and ambiguities in symbolic interaction theory has led to a variety of answers. One answer structures human behavior deterministically by conceiving antecedent, causal variables to be contemporaneous social ones with the consequent ones having to do with the nature or structure of the self (either as a whole or of the elements seen to constitute the whole).

A second answer conceives the antecedent variables to be historical or developmental, thus possibly quite temporally remote from the consequent variables which are, as in the first answer, taken to be the nature or structure of the self, either holistically or elementally constituted.

A third answer conceives the antecedent variables to be the self, either as a whole or elementally, and the consequent variables to be those of overt behavior.

A fourth answer conceives the antecedent variables to be self variables which among themselves produce consequent, novel, but determinate self-attributes.

A similar variety of *indeterminate* answers has been given to the questions raised by ambiguities and inconsistencies in symbolic interaction orientation:

One answer appears to see virtually all significant attributes of behavior to be internal choices and other self-indications, all of which are conceived to be emergent, with no observable, regular antecedent.

Another is similar to this view but sees antecedents to these internal events in experiences lost, or partially lost, in the antiquity of the individual's early biography, and without too close a dependence on, or regularity with, such early happenings.

A third sees the significant variables as external behaviors which are either un-related to the self, or deviously related, or only loosely related, to the self. Such is often the kind of orientation held by those who see a sharp disjunction be-tween public and private selves, where the private self is the true self with un-searchable antecedents, and where the public self is the social self, both in that it relates to observable behaviors and in that it has social antecedents.

A fourth conceives external events to be shaped more or less unpredictably by self-activities which in turn are "self-developed," *i.e.*, indeterminate in any test-able way.

Types of Symbolic Interaction Theory

Presupposing determinacy   *Presupposing indeterminacy*

(1) Soc $A_1 \longrightarrow$ Beh C

$$(6) \qquad A \qquad\qquad \overset{*}{Ch} \\ \qquad\qquad\qquad\qquad Ind$$

(2) Soc $A_1 \longrightarrow$ Self C

$$(7) \qquad A_2 \dashrightarrow \overset{*}{\;} \overset{*}{Ch} \\ \qquad\qquad\qquad\qquad Ind$$

(3) Soc $A_2 \longrightarrow$ Self C

$$(8) \ Self_{pr}\ A \dashrightarrow \overset{*}{\;} \overset{*}{\to Self_{pub}}$$

(4) Self A $\longrightarrow$ Beh C
(5) Self A $\longrightarrow$ Self C

$$(9)\ Self_{pr}\ \overset{*}{A} \dashrightarrow \overset{*}{\to} Beh\ C$$

Where Soc refers to social variable
  Self refers to self variable, either holistic or elementalistic
  $Self_{pr}$ refers to "private self"
  $Self_{pub}$ refers to "public self"
  A indicates antecedent variable
  A_1 indicates immediately antecedent variable
  A_2 indicates antecedent but temporarily distal variable
  C indicates consequent variable
  Beh indicates overt behavioral variable
  Ch indicates internal choice-making
  Ind indicates internal (self) indications
  Em indicates an emergent (I or Me)
  Det indicates a determinate (I or Me)
  Solid arrow indicates a determinate, causal process
  Broken arrow indicates an indeterminate, emergent process
  Asterisk (*) indicates the locus of indeterminacy; this may lie in the nexus between
    antecedent and consequent variables as well as in any of the following internal
    aspects of the self:

(a) $A \longrightarrow (I_{Em} \dashrightarrow Me_{Det}) \dashrightarrow Beh\ C$
(b) $A \longrightarrow (I_{Em} \dashrightarrow Me_{Em}) \dashrightarrow Beh\ C$
(c) $A \longrightarrow (I_{Det} \dashrightarrow Me_{Det}) \dashrightarrow Beh\ C$

If one were to arrogate to oneself the privilege of deciding these issues and others raised essentially by the ambiguities in symbolic interaction orientation, one could sharply narrow the task surveying the major trends in this theory in the past twenty-five years. This, however, I deem to be neither proper nor useful. Similarly, if symbolic interactionists had their own professional organization, their own journal or journals, their own pontifical leader or tight-knit little clique of leaders clearly assigned the role of determining the "correct" view among competing doctrinal differences, the survey of the fruits of orthodoxy might be simple. Instead, however, we have none of these things, and for the most part we wish none of them. But the consequences are that there is a welter of partial orientations which bear varying relationships to the general point of view.

There is, for example, *role theory*. Role theory has many intellectual antecedents other than those in Cooley, Dewey, Thomas, Faris, and Mead. There are debts, for instance, to Linton, to Moreno, to Parsons; there are often overtones of one or another of the learning theories. These are but a few of the strands of thought in role theory. Yet role theory is not sharply distinguishable—if at all—from symbolic interactionism. The *emphasis* in role theory is on overt role playing and on the researchable relation between role expectations and role performances; the emphasis is either less, or altogether lacking, on role-taking, on the interior processes of the self, and what Shibutani calls the sentiments are often ignored. Thus role theory tends toward what Turner wishes to call the processes of conformity.[10]

Yet I must underscore the word *emphasis*, for in Sarbin's useful chapter in the *Handbook of Social Psychology*, there is no ignoring of self nor of empathy, nor is there in his own research (of which there is a fine example indicating a positive relation between role-taking ability on the one hand and degree of malleability of self-conception on the other).[11] But on the whole, role theory has implied determinacy of Type 1.

Among the important contributions of the quarter-century under the general aegis of role theory have been the preliminary systematization provided in the early part of Gross, Mason, and McEachern's *Explorations in Role Analysis*, and Turner's paper in Rose's *Human Behavior and Social Processes*, in which issues of determinacy *vs.* indeterminacy of the sort here proposed for all of symbolic interactionism are made with respect specifically to role theory.[12] Role theory has engendered a great deal of research; in fact, it is as much to role theory as to any other development that I point when I have designated this period under scrutiny as the era of inquiry. This is no place in which to attempt to summarize this research. By and large we can say it has underscored Thomas' dictum that "people tend to play the roles assigned to them." There is by no means any strong evidence that there is a completely determinate relation between role expectations or recipes on the one hand and role performance on the other. On the other hand, there is a growing mountain of evidence that with "known" or public role recipes in hand we can make very useful probabilistic predictions with respect to subsequent behaviors, not alone those representing the answering role performances but even those which are but logically related and ancillary behaviors.

10 [Cf. Shibutani, *op. cit.*, pp. 323 ff., 548 ff. *et passim*; Ralph H. Turner, "Role-Taking: Process Versus Conformity," in *Human Behavior and Social Processes: An Interactionist Approach*, Arnold M. Rose, ed. (Boston: Houghton Mifflin, 1962), pp. 20–40:—The Editor].

11 Theodore R. Sarbin, "Role Theory," in *Handbook of Social Psychology*, ed. by Gardner Lindzey (Cambridge, Mass.: Addison-Wesley Publishing Company, 1954), 1:223–58. [The example of Sarbin's own research that Kuhn probably had in mind is Theodore R. Sarbin and Norman L. Farberow, "Contributions to Role-Taking Theory: A Clinical Study of Self and Role," *Journal of Abnormal and Social Psychology*, 47:117–25 (Jan., 1952).—The Editor].

12 Neal Gross, Ward S. Mason, and Alexander W. McEachern, *Explorations in Role Analysis: Studies of the School Superintendency Role* (New York: John Wiley, 1958); Ralph H. Turner, "Role-Taking: Process Versus Conformity," *op. cit.*

Much of the utility of role theory has been demonstrated thus far in the study of internalized role conflicts and contradictions. This study has ranged from the imaginative employment of personal documents and interviews by Mirra Komarovsky in her study of the conflicts surrounding the role of young women in college [13] to the construction of fairly precise and rigorous scales in the measure of such role conflict in the work of Stouffer and Toby. Even in such studies which imply internalization and thus the interposition of intermediate or intervening variables into our Type 1 determinacy pattern, such intervening variables are basically unnecessary even in the operations by Komarovsky; for although they involved reports of subjective valuations, these reports could have been replaced by direct observations of communications applying the opposing pressures—it was simply inconvenient to do so.

Another equally salient development has been that of *reference group* theory, so-named, of course, by Hyman [14] but getting much of the attention it has received from the concept of relative deprivation as employed by Stouffer in *The American Soldier* and as reworked in the well-known chapter on reference group theory by Merton and Kitt.[15] There have been a number of useful theoretical critiques as well as creative employments of reference group theory, notable among them those of Kelley, Shibutani, Turner, Neweomb, and Sherif. The notion of reference group is obviously closely related to the whole problem of the other as dealt with by Mead and Sullivan on the one hand, and to that of the primary group as described by Cooley and Faris on the other. Much of the employment of this new theory has been so far to provide *ex post* or circular explanation (explanation by naming). Controversy abounds, to be sure, over the meaning of the term *reference group* itself—whether it refers to a normative or to an evaluative function; whether it must point to groups, to categories or both; whether it may best refer to relationships, as Rose suggests, or whether we may better use it to refer to derivative orientations, as Shibutani indicates. May we use the term to refer to empirically identifiable attitudes, expectations, and norms of existent *others,* or must we limit ourselves to such matters only after they have been transmuted to the images in the imagination of the *actors* themselves, to which Cooley referred as the "solid facts" of social life?

The classification of reference group theory is difficult, for in the theoretical statements of it, indeterminate model 7 fits, but in the actual application of the theory, determinate models 1 through 4 have been variously employed. The contradictions between theoretical statements and operational implications in reference group theory are one of the most unhappy aspects of symbolic interactionism today, in this author's opinion.

Next consider the related development of points of view known as *social perception* and *person perception.* If we regard the ancient dicta "We see things not as they are but as we are," and "We do not first see and then define; we define first and then see," as intimately involved in the point of view of symbolic interactionism, we may properly claim at least a strong interest in the develop-

[13] Mirra Komarovsky, *Women in the Modern World: Their Education and Their Dilemmas* (Boston: Little, Brown, 1953).
[14] H. Hyman, *The Psychology of Status* (Archives of Psychology, vol. 38, no. 269, June 1942).
[15] Robert K. Merton and Alice S. Kitt, "Contributions to the Theory of Reference Group Behavior," in *Continuities in Social Research: Studies in the Scope and Method of "The American Soldier,"* ed. by Robert K. Merton and Paul F. Lazarsfeld (Glencoe, Illinois: The Free Press, 1950): reprinted in Robert K. Merton, *Social Theory and Social Structure,* revised and enlarged edition (Glencoe, Ill.: Free Press, 1957), pp. 225–80.

ment of these interrelated schools. The researches contained in the volume edited by Petrullo and Tagiuri, for example, bear in many instances on hypotheses generated by symbolic interactionism.[16] On the other hand, this research movement is led by men relatively unacquainted with "our" literature. Consequently our own reaction to any one piece of research such as is contained in Petrullo and Tagiuri's volume is that it is in one or more respects naive: in its lack of sophistication about the function of language in interaction, in its failure to employ a concept equivalent to social act or social object or significant other, etc. etc.

Jerome Bruner, whose own experimental work on the differential perception of the size of coins by subjects of different income levels is a classic study in the field of social perception, has admirably stated in summary form the general position of these schools in "Social Psychology and Perception," in the third edition of *Readings in Social Psychology* edited by Maccoby, Newcomb, and Hartley.[17] His summary is such that the symbolic interactionist can easily deduce for himself the common ground this position shares with symbolic interaction theory; I am therefore spared this task by citing this article. I would only object that the Bruner paper misleads somewhat in failing to indicate the degree to which "perceptual set" as a key concept central to this school has come to serve as umbrella for Freudian rather than symbolic interaction variables, and for implying, on the other hand, that social perception treats what people are doing as central to the nature of what they perceive (for this is not borne out by their experimental designs).

The models on which social and person perception theory rest appear to be types 1 and 4. That is, they are determinate and tend to designate either immediate or temporally distal antecedent social variables and consequent behavioral variables. Had symbolic interactionists initiated the exploration of this field, they would have emphasized the ways in which the individual conceives himself as antecedent and the manner he perceives other objects including persons as consequent, with probably some attention to designs in which these types of variables are reversed in time.

So far, we have dealt with subtheories which have had very ambiguous boundaries. The same thing is certainly true of *self* theory with which I have identified my own research activities. It was my intention in 1946 or 1947 to employ a term which would not so much differentiate an emerging point of view from the more or less orthodox ideas of symbolic interaction as it would enable, on the other hand, a distinction between a body of conjectural and deductive orientation—as represented by Cooley, Dewey, and Mead—and a derivative but developing set of generalizations, tested by empirical research. I found later that, at about the same time, Carol Rogers had also termed as self theory his notions in clinical psychology having to do with the varying discrepancies between the actual or perceived self and the ideal self. Since then the term has been variously employed, often as an umbrella word, to cover several or all of the subtheories here under consideration.

The work undertaken by students of symbolic interaction at the State Uni-

[16] *Person Perception and Interpersonal Behavior*, ed. by Renato Tagiuri and Luigi Petrullo (Stanford, Calif.: Stanford University Press, 1958).
[17] Jerome Bruner, "Social Psychology and Perception," in *Readings in Social Psychology*, 3d ed., Editorial Committee: Eleanor E. Maccoley, Theodore M. Newcomb, Eugene L. Hartley (New York: Henry Holt, 1958), pp. 85–94.

versity of Iowa followed in several respects the programmatic proposals of the
summary monograph on social psychology in the 1930's by Leonard Cottrell and
Ruth Gallagher and of Cottrell's later presidential address before the American
Sociological Society: that is to say, there has been considerable attention to the
self itself and to role-taking.[18] McPartland [19] pioneered in his study relating differential nexi-to-social-structure to the differential characteristics of the self.
Later he has studied the relations among self, social strata, and the differential
syndromes of mental-emotional disturbance. Fred Waisanen [20] explored relations between self characteristics and prejudice. Stewart [21] demonstrated the
often alleged relation of the self to a system of objects, as did Carl Waisanen [22]
and Wynona Garretson [23] in other ways. Maranell [24] studied relations between
self and role-taking and began the exploration of transparency, the obverse of
empathy. Rogler [25] established that there is a direct relation between role-taking
and access to a communication system. The validation and extension of symbolic interaction ideas represented in these researches is for the most part preliminary and one must assess it as modest. Perhaps the most significant contribution of the Iowa research is simply that in which it joins the research of Miyamoto and Dornbusch, Deutsch and Solomon, Dick, Dinitz and Mangus, McKee
and Sherriffs, Stryker, Videbeck and Bates, and many others in demonstrating to
some degree at least that the key ideas of symbolic interactionism could be operationalized and utilized successfully in empirical research.[26]

Self theory of this variety has implied one or another of the five determinate
models in our diagram, although this point is implicit rather than explicit, and
never a salient issue. The general attempt rests on the notion that there is among
the several important matters a process considered nomothetic or genotypical
by the symbolic interaction orientation.

Among the subtheories that seem to imply indeterminacy—phenomenological
theory, the study of careers, language, and culture of Sapir and Whorf, the interpersonal theory of H. S. Sullivan, the self-constancy and self-actualizing theories of such men as Stegner and Maslow—one seems to stand out as just a shade
more radical and eye-catching than the rest: *the dramaturgical school* of Ken-

---

[18] Leonard S. Cottrell, Jr., and Ruth Gallagher, *Developments in Social Psychology, 1930–
1940* (New York: Beacon Press, 1941); Leonard S. Cottrell, Jr., "Some Neglected Problems in
Social Psychology, *American Sociological Review*, 15:705–12 (Dec., 1950). Reprinted in Part
One of this volume.
[19] Thomas S. McPartland, "The Self and Social Structure," unpublished doctoral dissertation,
State University of Iowa, 1953; "Self Conception, Social Class, and Mental Health," *Human
Organization*, 17:24–29 (1958); T. S. McPartland, John H. Cumming, and Wyonna S. Garretson, "Self-Conception and Ward Behavior in Two Psychiatric Hospitals," *Sociometry*, 24:11–24
(June, 1961).
[20] F. B. Waisanen, "The Prejudice Variable: A Social Psychological and Methodological Study,"
unpublished doctoral dissertation, State University of Iowa, 1954.
[21] Robert L. Stewart, "The Self and Other Objects: Their Measurement and Interrelationship,"
unpublished doctoral dissertation, State University of Iowa, 1955.
[22] Carl E. Waisanen, "Preference Aspects of Self-Attitudes," unpublished doctoral dissertation,
State University of Iowa, 1957.
[23] Wynona Smutz Garretson, "College as Social Object: A Study in Consensus," unpublished
doctoral dissertation, State University of Iowa, 1961; "The Consensual Definition of Social Objects," *Sociological Quarterly*, 3:107–13 (Apr., 1962).
[24] Gary M. Maranell, "Role-Taking: Empathy and Transparency," unpublished doctoral dissertation, State University of Iowa, 1959.
[25] Lloyd H. Rogler, "An Experimental Study of the Relationship between Structured Behavior
Patterns and Accuracy of Social Sensitivity," unpublished doctoral dissertation, State University of Iowa, 1957.
[26] See the appended bibliography.

neth Burke, Erving Goffman, and possibly Nelson Foote and Gregory Stone. The most significant alteration made by this school is the general transmutation of the social act from what in traditional symbolic interactionism had continued to be paradoxically an individual model (triggered by organic tensions and impulses and following through the course of the action with reference to the single—almost feral—man to equilibrium, restitution of tensionlessness in the organism) to the team-of-players model which implies that social agenda rather than tissue conditions serve to initiate the act and to cue its end as well. This, of course, is but one of the extremely provocative aspects of dramaturgical theory, especially as initiated by Burke and developed by Goffman.

The difficulties with this subtheory are, in the main, those of deriving from it any testable generalizations. One must be tentative about this, it seems to me, for this was exactly the complaint lodged against the whole of symbolic interaction orientation in its early years. It may well be that ingenious solutions will be found to the problems of operationalizing the basic conceptions of this orientation.

Of the models we suggest diagrammatically, numbers 8 and 9 seem to be the ones most frequently implied in dramaturgical theory, although the team characteristics of Goffman's units appear to imply models indicating team rather than individual conduct.

The longitudinal study of socialization and especially of career trajectories, best indicated in the work of E. C. Hughes and Howard S. Becker, seems also to lie on the indeterminacy side. The work of these two men is virtually as imaginative and as creative as that of Burke and of Goffman. There is, in the literature, no more insightful account of the relation of the actor to a social object through the processes of communication and of self-definition, than Becker's account of becoming a marijuana user.[27] Hughes's sensitivity to lingual indicators of status is wonderfully revealed in his well-known and fundamental essay, "Work and the Self." [28] In it he presents a modern-age social psychological interpretation of "what the social classes owe to each other."

Again, the difficulties with this approach seem to lie in operationalization. It is most difficult to establish generalizations valid for human behavior without methods wherewith to make precise checks on intersubjective perceptions of events such as are involved in witnessing transitional stages in a socialization process or rites of passage in the trajectory of a career.

The indeterminate model on which this approach seems to rest is our type no. 7; that is, the antecedent variables, temporarily distal, are loosely (indeterminately) related to the processes of choice and self-indication which constitute the self.

The *interpersonal theory* of psychiatry proposed by Harry Stack Sullivan was constructed early in this quarter-century period.[29] It has been almost ubiquitously incorporated into the general body of symbolic interaction orientation, or perhaps the verb should be "reincorporated" since Sullivan had been well introduced to Meadian theory in the 1920's and had built the interpersonal theory in

[27] Howard S. Becker, "Becoming a Marihuana User," *American Journal of Sociology*, 59:235–42 (Nov., 1953). [Cf. Howard S. Becker, *Outsiders: Studies in the Sociology of Deviance* (New York: Free Press of Glencoe, 1963.)—The Editor].

[28] Everett C. Hughes, "Work and the Self," in *Social Psychology at the Crossroads: The University of Oklahoma Lectures in Social Psychology*, ed. by John H. Rohrer and Muzafer Sherif (New York: Harper and Brothers, 1951), pp. 313–23.

[29] See the appended bibliography.

significant part out of elements provided by Mead on the one hand and by Freud on the other. The theory is distinctive for the unique way in which it manages a synthesis of Meadian and Freudian viewpoints without admitting any of the Freudian nonsense about phylogenetic inheritance of unconscious sense of guilt, the early Oedipus notion, the nature of man pitted against society, etc., while utilizing to the full the power of Freudian explanation of interpersonal rivalry and of distortions in communication—down to the utilization of the concept of self-derogation and self-rejection and repression (the not-me)—concepts hinging on interpersonal relations (reflected appraisals by others) rather than on thwarted instincts and biological drives as Freud had it.

Unfortunately, the Sullivan interpersonal theory is quite disjoined from ideas of culture and of formal social organization. This has led Shibutani to set up disjunctive self components: Those derived from conventional role-playing and those derived as sentiments from the kinds of interpersonal processes Sullivan described, completely divorced from culture and organized systems. It is also unfortunate that the interpersonal theory suffers from the same difficulties as the other indeterminate theories: inability to apply the usual scientific methods in order to build increasingly supported, dependable generalizations. The Sullivan model appears to rest on a combination of models, 7, 8, and 9, thus indicating looseness between antecedent, intervening and consequent variables, plus the possibility for further emergence in the interior processes of the self. The specific temporally distal, antecedent variables on which the theory rests are those having to do with what Sullivan calls the *parataxic* and *prototaxic* stages in what is essentially the preverbal period. In these, there is no real opportunity conceived for direct empirical observation, and thus there is further indeterminacy beyond the posited looseness between these stages and later self-attributes.

One more indeterminate subtheory is the Sapir-Whorf-Cassirer *language and culture orientation*.[30] This is truly a theory behind a theory, for it tends to be presumed by symbolic interactionists as being preliminary even to a consideration of the basic assumptions of the theory under review. The language and culture point of view is surely so familiar as not to need much description. It points to the basic proposition that a language consists of a very finite and limited number of concepts out of an unlimited set of possibilities. Furthermore it underscores the fact that even the ultimate and basic concepts—which we in our society think of as those dealing with time, motion, matter and space—are themselves lingually variable and relative. And, perhaps even more important, it takes the position that the very grammar of a language is based on an unspoken, taken-for-granted logic which determines how people in that society think about anything. Thus it must follow that the categorization of one's self and his attributes, as well as of his others, and of the significant non-human objects in his system of objects is entirely dependent on the language of his group. He cannot think of himself or his experiences, or of his relationships, except in the arbitrary conceptualizations provided him in his language.

This is an indeterminate theory in so far as the individual person's behavior is concerned, for the language only sets the basic framework for his thought and the

---

[30] [See, *e.g.*, Edward Sapir, *Language: An Introduction to the Study of Speech* (New York: Harcourt, Brace, 1921); Benjamin L. Whorf, *Language, Thought, and Reality: Selected Writings* edited by John B. Carroll (Technology Press of Massachusetts Institute of Technology, 1956); Ernest Cassirer, *The Philosophy of Symbolic Forms*, 2 vols. (New Haven: Yale Univ. Press, 1953–1955).—The Editor].

outer limits, beyond which he cannot conceive of things. Within these limits, and around this framework, there is a looseness of connection. No determinate statements are suggested. However, attached as a preliminary set of assumptions to any of the previously examined determinate sub-theories, this point of view removes it from determinacy only in the sense that, as is pointed out posthumously in the *American Anthropologist* by the late Clyde Kluckhohn, the Whorf-Sapir-Cassirer notions are basically untestable.[31]

There are a number of other subtheories which have had their development during these past twenty-five years and which are related in one or several respects to symbolic interactionism, and which serve, if nothing else, to suggest extensions or amendments to the orientation. These include such points of view as cognitive theory, field theory, phenomenology, the developmental notions of Piaget, the current scrutiny of identity which bears strong overtones of ego psychology, the self-constancy theory of Stager and others, and the self-actualizing theory of Maslow, in addition to which there is the self theory of Carl Rogers, already mentioned. Many of those theories were developed by students in the field of psychology. Few indicate acquaintance with the intellectual stream to which symbolic interactionism belongs. The line I have drawn, excluding these from consideration but including the ones I have discussed, is highly arbitrary and may not be defensible in any other sense than that time places limitations even upon the most condensed of discussions.

Applications

So far we have considered the development of amplifications, sub-theories, and operationalizations of symbolic interaction theory. We cannot conclude without considering the promising starts made in applying the orientation to problem areas. There is the much neglected book by Lemert, *Social Pathology*,[32] which should have been called *A Social Psychology of Deviants*, in which the author makes the interesting proposal that a fundamental distinction exists in the behaviors of those whose deviation is accompanied by no corresponding self-definition and those whose deviation is so accompanied—he refers to the difference as secondary differentiation.

Much of the application of symbolic interaction theory has been made by students of crime and delinquency—notably Cressey, Glaser and Reckless. Of the Iowa students, Nardini in the field of the criminal,[33] Mulford in the area of the alcoholic,[34] Hurlburt in the area of family adjustment,[35] and Nass in the field of driver safety records,[36] have made application of self-dimensions as antecedent

[31] Clyde Kluckhohn, "Notes on Some Anthropological Aspects of Communication," *American Anthropologist* 63:895–910 (Oct., 1961).

[32] Edwin M. Lemert, *Social Pathology: Approach to the Theory of Sociopathic Behavior* (New York: McGraw-Hill, 1951).

[33] William Nardini, "Criminal Self-Conceptions in the Penal Community: An Empirical Study," unpublished doctoral dissertation, State University of Iowa, 1959.

[34] Harold A. Mulford, Jr., "Toward an Instrument to Identify and Measure the Self, Significant Others, and Alcohol in the Symbolic Environment: An Empirical Study," unpublished doctoral dissertation, State University of Iowa, 1955.

[35] Julia Knaff Hurlburt, "Role Expectations and the Self: An Empirical Study of Their Relationship to Marital Adjustment," unpublished doctoral dissertation, State University of Iowa, 1960.

[36] Gilbert D. Nass, "A Study of the Teen-Age Driver, His Self-Definition, and Definition of the Driving Situation," unpublished Master's thesis, State University of Iowa, 1958.

variables in promising endeavors to understand consequent variable behavior in problem fields. The new compilation edited by Rose already referred to, *Human Behavior and Social Processes,* contains as its third and final section a set of papers on the relation of interaction theory to social problem areas. Notable is Rose's own paper presenting his social-psychological theory of neurosis, which has a number of parallels with Sullivan's theory, but is distinctive in most respects for its general application of the symbolic interaction orientation.[37]

Neglected Problems

I cannot leave the consideration of the development of symbolic interactionism in the past twenty-five years without reconsidering the title of Cottrell's presidential address—the question of "neglected problems." Many of the problems which he found to be neglected are still neglected, while others—such as role-taking, on which his own student, R. F. Dymond, made such a notable start [38]—are beginning to be studied with more and more sophistication.

There is no time here to make a thorough canvass of neglected problems, but I should like to mention two. One is the failure to make appropriate conceptualization of the varieties of functional relations that regularly occur between self and other. At present we appear to be in that rather foolish and useless situation in which we debate what a reference group really is. Most of the suggestions point to varieties of functional relations between self and groups or categories of others. The question ought not to be which of these is really a reference group, but rather, what special term shall we agree to use for each particular relation? [39] Having reached a consensus on a constructed vocabulary with which to refer to these functional relationships between self and other, we need then to consider the serious questions of operationalization. What kinds of questions must be asked to discover the nature of the particular relationship under inquiry?

A second pressing question implied in much of this paper has to do with the process by which self-conceptions change. Some theorists, notably those who lean toward the indeterminate side, discuss self-change as if it were most volatile and evanescent; the self shifts with each new indication one makes to himself, and these indications are the constant accompaniments of experience. Others see in the self the more or less stable, continuous, organizing principle for the personality, offering the only constant, non-shifting anchorage for the perception of other objects. We have arrived at the point in sharpening of the tools by which we may identify self-attributes and measure them and compare them with those of others, where we may treat this issue as a researchable question. As we attempt to measure the relative stability of the self, we need to study the con-

[37] Arnold M. Rose, "A Social-Psychological Theory of Neurosis," in *Human Behavior and Social Processes.*

[38] [See Rosalind F. Dymond, "A Preliminary Investigation of the Relation of Insight and Empathy," *Journal of Consulting Psychology,* 12:228–33 (1948); "A Scale for the Measurement of Empathic Ability," *Journal of Consulting Psychology,* 13:127–33 (1949), reprinted in *Small Groups: Studies in Social Interaction,* ed. by A. Paul Hare, Edgar F. Borgatta, and Robert F. Bales (New York: Alfred A. Knopf, 1955), pp. 226–35. See also Rosalind F. Dymond, Anne S. Hughes, and Virginia L. Raabe, "Measurable Changes in Empathy with Age," *Journal of Consulting Psychology,* 16:202–6 (1952); Rosalind Dymond Cartwright, Julius Seeman, and Donald L. Grummon, "Patterns of Perceived Interpersonal Relations," *Sociometry* 19:166–77 (Sept., 1956).—The Editor].

[39] [Cf. Manford H. Kuhn, "The Reference Group Reconsidered," in *The Sociolgical Quarterly,* V (Winter 1964).

comitants of self-attitude change. It may be argued that the self, like any attitude, may be usefully treated as an hypothesis which the individual holds about himself, and with respect to which he holds certain notions about testing for validity. We need to study in short what correlates of self-attitude stability are phenomenal and which are non-conscious and outside self-directed control.

If I may be permitted a brief look at the crystal ball, I would see in it for the next twenty-five years of symbolic interaction theory an accelerated development of research techniques on the one hand, and a coalescing of most of the separate subtheories under consideration in this paper on the other. I have a basic confidence that symbolic interactionism will hold its own and gain against the competition of such major theories as psychoanalysis, the learning theories, and field theory. The reason I am confident is that I believe that of these major theories only symbolic interactionism is logically consistent with the basic propositions of the social sciences: the psychic unity of man (Boas); the extreme cultural variability of man; the creativity of man; the continual socializability and modifiability of man; the ability of man to feed back complex correctives to his behavior without engaging in trial and error, or conditioning, learning.

Bibliography

APPLE, D. "Learning Theory and Socializations," *American Sociological Review*, 16:23–27 (Feb., 1951). Comment by J. Gillin, *American Sociological Review*, 16:384 (June 1951).

ARGYRIS, C. "The Fusion of an Individual with the Organization," *American Sociological Review*, 19:267–72 (June 1954).

BECKER, ERNEST. "Socialization, Command of Performance, and Mental Illness," *American Journal of Sociology*, 67:484–501 (Mar. 1952).

BECKER, HOWARD S. "Problems of Inference and Proof in Participant Observation," *American Sociological Review*, 23:652–60 (Dec. 1958).

BECKER, HOWARD S., and CARPER, JAMES. "The Elements of Identification with an Occupation," *American Sociological Review*, 21:341–48 (June 1956).

BECKER, HOWARD S., and GEER, BLANCHE. "The Fate of Idealism in Medical School," *American Sociological Review*, 23:50–56 (Feb. 1958).

BLAU, ZENA SMITH. "Changes in Status and Age Identification," *American Sociological Review*, 21:198–203 (Apr. 1956).

BLUMER, HERBERT. "Sociological Analysis and the 'Variable,'" *American Sociological Review*, 21:683–90 (Dec. 1956).

BOGGS, STEPHEN T. "An Interactional Study of Ojibwa Socialization," *American Sociological Review*, 21:191–98 (Apr. 1956).

BORDUA, DAVID J. "Authoritarianism and Intolerance of Nonconformists," *Sociometry*, 24:198–216 (June 1961).

BRIM, ORVILLE J., JR. "Family Structure and Sex Role Learning by Children: A Further Analysis of Helen Koch's Data," *Sociometry*, 21:1–16 (Mar. 1958).

BROWN, J. C. "An Experiment in Role-taking," *American Sociological Review* 17:587–97 (Oct. 1952).

BUCHER, RUE, and STRAUSS, ANSELM. "Professions in Process," *American Journal of Sociology*, 66:325–34 (Jan. 1961).

BURKE, KENNETH. *A Grammar of Motives*. New York: Prentice-Hall, 1945.

————. *A Rhetoric of Motives*. New York: Prentice-Hall, 1950.

CAMERON, NORMAN. *The Psychology of Behavior Disorders*. Boston: Houghton Mifflin Co., 1947.

CARTWRIGHT, ROSALIND DYMOND, SEEMAN, JULIUS, and GRUMMON, DONALD L. "Patterns of Perceived Interpersonal Relations," *Sociometry*, 19:166–77 (Sept. 1956).

CLARK, JOHN P. "Measuring Alienation Within a Social System," *American Sociological Review*, 24:849–52 (Dec. 1959).

COATES, CHAS. H., and PELLEGRIN, ROLAND J. "Executives and Supervisors: Contracting Self-Conceptions and Conceptions of Each Other," *American Sociological Review* 22:217–20 (Apr. 1957).

CORWIN, RONALD G. "A Study of Identity in Nursing," *Sociological Quarterly*, 2:69–86 (Apr. 1961).

COUCH, CARL J. "Self-Attitudes and Degree of Agreement with Immediate Others," *American Journal of Sociology*, 63:491–96 (Mar. 1958).

————. "Family Role Specialization and Self-Attitudes in Children," *Sociological Quarterly*, 3:115–21 (Apr. 1962).

COTTRELL, L. A., JR. "The Adjustment of the Individual to His Age and Sex Roles," *American Sociological Review*, 7:617–20 (Oct. 1942).

————. "The Analysis of Situational Fields in Social Psychology," *American Sociological Review*, 7:370–82 (June 1942).

————. "Some Neglected Problems in Social Psychology," *American Sociological Review*, 15:705–12 (Dec. 1950).

COUTU, WALTER. *Emergent Human Nature*. New York: Knopf, 1949.

————. "Role-Playing *vs.* Role-Taking: An Appeal for Clarification," *American Sociological Review*, 16:180–87 (Apr. 1951). Comment by J. L. Moreno, *ibid.*, 16:550–51 (Aug. 1951).

DAI, B. "A Socio-Psychiatric Approach to Personality Organization," *American Sociological Review*, 17:44–49 (Feb. 1952).

————. "Personality Problems in Chinese Culture," *American Sociological Review*, 6:688–90 (Oct. 1941).

DAVIS, JAMES A. "A Formal Interpretation of the Theory of Relative Deprivation," *Sociometry*, 22:280–96 (Dec. 1959).

DEUTSCH, MORTON, and SOLOMON, LEONARD. "Reactions to Evaluations by Others as Influenced by Self-Evaluations," *Sociometry*, 22:93–112 (June 1959).

DICK, HARRY B. "The Office Worker: Attitudes toward Self, Labor and Management," *Sociological Quarterly*, 3:45–56 (Jan. 1962).

DINITZ, SIMON, MANGUS, A. R., and PASSAMANICK, BENJAMIN. "Integration and Conflict in Self-Other Conceptions as Factors in Mental Illness," *Sociometry*, 22:44–55 (Mar. 1959).

FARIS, R. E. L. *Social Psychology*. New York: Ronald Press, 1952.

————. "Sociological Causes of Genius," *American Sociological Review*, 5:689–99 (Oct. 1940).

FOOTE, NELSON N. "Anachronism and Synchronism in Sociology," *Sociometry*, 21:17–29 (Mar. 1958).

————. "Identification as a Basis for a Theory of Motivation," *American Sociological Review*, 16:14–21 (Feb. 1951). Comment by R. Bendix, *ibid.*, 16:22 (Feb. 1951).

GARRETSON, WYNONA SMUTZ. "The Consensual Definition of Social Objects," *Sociological Quarterly*, 3:107–13 (Apr. 1952).

GERTH, HANS, and MILLS, C. WRIGHT. *Character and Social Structure*. New York: Harcourt Brace and Co., 1953.

GETZELS, J. W., and GUBA, E. G. "Role, Role Conflict and Effectiveness: An Empirical Study," *American Sociological Review*, 19:164–75 (Apr. 1954).

GLASER, DANIEL. "Criminality Theories and Behavioral Images," *American Journal of Sociology*, 61:433–44 (Mar. 1956).

GOFFMAN, ERVING. *The Presentation of Self in Everyday Life*. Garden City, N.Y.: Doubleday Anchor, 1959.

GOLDHAMER, H. "Recent Developments in Personality Studies," *American Sociological Review*, 13:355–65 (Oct. 1948).

GOUGH, H. G. "A New Dimension of Status: I. Development of a Personality Scale," *American Sociological Review*, 13:401–9 (Aug. 1948).

GROSS, NEAL, MASON, WARD S., and McEACHERN, ALEXANDER W. *Explorations in Role Analysis: Studies of the School Superintendent Role*. New York: Wiley, 1958.

HALBWACHS, M. "Individual Psychology and Collective Psychology," *American Sociological Review*, 3:615–23 (Oct. 1938).

HEIDER, FRITZ. *The Psychology of Interpersonal Relations*. New York: Wiley, 1958.

HYMAN, H. *The Psychology of Status* (Archives of Psychology, 38, no. 269, 1942).

ICHHEISER, G. "Structure and Dynamics of Interpersonal Relations," *American Sociological Review*, 8:302–5 (June 1943).

JACKSON, JAY. "Reference Group Processes in a Formal Organization," *Sociometry*, 22:307–27 (Dec. 1959).

KOHN, MELVIN L. "Social Class and the Exercise of Parental Authority," *American Sociological Review*, 24:352–66 (June 1959).

KOHN, A. ROBERT, and FIEDLER, FRED E. "Age and Sex Differences in the Perceptions of Persons," *Sociometry*, 24:157–64 (June 1961).

KUENZLI, ALFRED E. (ed.). *The Phenomenological Problem*. New York: Harper, 1959. Papers by Combs, Snygg, McLeod, Brewster, Smith, Jessor, *et al.*

LEMERT, EDWIN M. *Social Pathology*. New York: McGraw Hill, 1951.

LINDESMITH, A. R. "The Drug Addict as a Psychopath," *American Sociological Review*, 5:914–20 (Dec. 1940).

LITTMAN, RICHARD A., MOORE, ROBERT C. A., and JONES, JOHN PIERCE. "Social Class Differences in Child Rearing: A Third Community for Comparison with Chicago and Newton," *American Sociological Review*, 22:694–704 (Dec. 1957).

LUNDY, RICHARD M. "Self Perceptions and Descriptions of Opposite Sex Sociometric Choices," *Sociometry*, 19:272–77 (Dec. 1956).

———. "Self Perceptions Regarding M-F and Descriptions Same and Opposite Sex Sociometric Choices," *Sociometry*, 21:238–46 (Sept. 1958).

McKEE, JOHN P., and SHERRIFFS, ALEX C. "Men's and Women's Beliefs, Ideals, and Self-Concepts," *American Journal of Sociology*, 64:356–63 (Jan. 1959).

McPARTLAND, T. S., CUMMING, JOHN M., and GARRETSON, WYNONA S. "Self-Conception and Ward Behavior in Two Psychiatric Hospitals," *Sociometry*, 24:111–24 (June 1961).

MEAD, GEORGE HERBERT. *Mind, Self, and Society*. Chicago: University of Chicago Press, 1934.

———. *Movements of Thought in the Nineteenth Century*. Chicago: University of Chicago Press, 1936.

———. *The Philosophy of the Act*. Chicago: University of Chicago Press, 1938.

MERRILL, FRANCIS. "Stendhal and the Self: A Study in the Sociology of Literature," *American Journal of Sociology*, 66:446–53 (Mar. 1961).

MERTON, ROBERT K., and KITT, ALICE S. "Contributions to the Theory of Reference Group Behavior," in R. K. Merton and P. F. Lazarsfeld (eds.), *Continuities in Social Research: Studies in the Scope and Method of "The American Soldier."* Glencoe, Ill.: The Free Press, 1950.

MILLS, C. WRIGHT. "Language, Logic and Culture," *American Sociological Review*, 4:670–80 (Oct. 1939).

———. "Situated Actions and Vocabularies of Motive," *American Sociological Review*, 5:904–13 (Dec. 1940).

MIYAMOTO, S. FRANK, and DORNBUSCH, SANFORD M. "A Test of Interactionist Hypotheses of Self-Conception," *American Journal of Sociology*, 61:399–403 (Mar. 1956).

Motz, A. B. "The Role Conception Inventory: A Tool for Research in Social Psychology," *American Sociological Review*, 17:465–71 (Aug. 1952).

Mullahy, Patrick. *The Contributions of Harry Stack Sullivan*. New York: Hermitage House, 1952.

Nathanson, Maurice. *The Social Dynamics of George H. Mead*. Washington, D.C.: Public Affairs Press, 1956.

Pfuetze, Paul E. *The Social Self*. New York: Bookman Associates, 1954.

Phillips, Bernard S. "A Role Theory Approach to Adjustment in Old Age," *American Sociological Review*, 22:212–17 (Apr. 1957).

Reckless, Walter C., Dinitz, Simon, and Murray, Ellen. "Self Concept as an Insulator Against Delinquency," *American Sociological Review*, 21:744–46 (Dec. 1956).

Reckless, Walter C., Dinitz, Simon, and Kay, Barbara. "The Self Component in Potential Delinquency and Potential Non-Delinquency," *American Sociological Review*, 22:566–70 (Oct. 1957).

Rose, Arnold (ed.). *Human Behavior and Social Processes*. Boston: Houghton Mifflin Co., 1962.

Rosengren, William R. "The Self in the Emotionally Disturbed," *American Journal of Sociology*, 66:454–62 (Mar. 1961).

Sarbin, Theodore, "Role Theory," in Gardner Lindzey (ed.), *Handbook of Social Psychology* (Cambridge, Mass.: Addison-Wesley Publ. Co., 1945), 1, ch. 6, pp. 223–58.

Schuessler, K. F. and Strauss, A. "A Study of Concept Learning by Scale Analysis," *American Sociological Review*, 15:752–62 (Dec. 1950).

Shibutani, Tamotsu. *Society and Personality*. Englewood Cliffs, N.J.: Prentice-Hall, 1961.

Simpson, Richard L., and Simpson, Ida Harper. "The Psychiatric Attendant: Development of an Occupational Self-Image in a Low-Status Occupation," *American Sociological Review*, 24:389–92 (June 1959).

Slater, Philip E. "Parental Role Differentiation," *American Journal of Sociology*, 67:296–311 (Nov. 1961).

Strauss, Anselm. *Mirrors and Masks: The Search for Identity*. Glencoe, Ill.: The Free Press, 1959.

Stryker, Sheldon. "Role-Taking Accuracy and Adjustment," *Sociometry*, 20:286–96 (Dec. 1957).

Sullivan, Harry Stack. "A Note on the Implications of Psychiatry. The Study of Interpersonal Relations for Investigations in the Social Sciences," *American Journal of Sociology*, 42:846–61 (May 1937).

———. "Conceptions of Modern Psychiatry," *Psychiatry*, 3:1–117 (1940).

———. *Conceptions of Modern Psychiatry*. Washington: Wm. A. White Psychiatric Foundation, 1947.

———. *The Interpersonal Theory of Psychiatry*. New York: Norton, 1953.

Swanson, Guy E. "Mead and Freud: Their Relevance for Social Psychology," *Sociometry*, 24:319–39 (Dec. 1961).

Tagiuri, Renato, and Petrullo, Luigi (eds.). *Person Perception and Interpersonal Behavior*. Stanford, Calif.: Stanford University Press, 1958.

Tremmel, Wm. C. *The Social Concepts of George Herbert Mead*. Emporia State Research Studies, Kansas State Teachers College, vol. 5, no. 4 (June 1957).

Troyer, W. L. "Mead's Social and Functional Theory of Mind," *American Sociological Review*, 11:198–202 (Apr. 1946).

Turner, R. H. "Moral Judgment: A Study in Roles," *American Sociological Review*, 17:70–77 (Feb. 1952).

———. "Self and Other in Moral Judgment," *American Sociological Review*, 19:249–59 (June 1954).

VIDEBECK, RICHARD. "Self-Conception and the Reactions of Others," *Sociometry*, 23:351–59 (Dec. 1960).

VIDEBECK, RICHARD, and BATES, ALAN P. "An Experimental Study of Conformity to Role Expectations," *Sociometry*, 22:1–11 (Mar. 1959).

WATSON, JEANNE. "A Formal Analysis of Sociable Interaction," *Sociometry*, 21:269–80 (Dec. 1958).

WHITE, L. A. "Culturological *vs.* Psychological Interpretations of Human Behavior," *American Sociological Review*, 12:688–98 (Dec. 1947).

WHORF, BENNJAMIN LEE. *Language, Thought and Reality.* New York: Wiley and the Technology Press of MIT, 1956.

WYLIE, RUTH. *The Self Concept: A Critical Survey of Pertinent Research Literature.* Lincoln: University of Nebraska Press, 1961.

PART TWO
SOCIAL PROCESS AS SYMBOLIC TRANSFORMATION

If the articles in the previous section have worked their magic, the reader should have more than a vague suspicion that man is front stage center. Inherently the universe is meaningless and totally indifferent to the existence of man. While it *conditions*, it does not determine. Indeed, the universe presents itself as an occasion for man's creative capacities. *It is there.* It awaits his investiture of identity, meaning, value, sentiments, and rules. It is a convertible commodity—a taken, not a given; a concept, not a datum. Witness the history of thought in Western civilization as its basic paradigm of natural order is transformed radically by the genius of Ptolemy, Copernicus, Newton, and Einstein. At this very writing even the Einsteinian conception is being questioned by some physicists. For better or for worse, man is the locus of purpose and power. He is the reality maker and the reality breaker. He alone is engaged in the "politics of reality." Should it be asked: "Whose definition of reality shall prevail?" no easy answer can be given, except to say that it is a matter of "negotiation" that can range from arbitrary imposition through reasonable dialogue to uncritical acceptance. But no matter what, it will be man who creates, sustains, and changes meaning. In this section, we wish to focus on several aspects of the development of meaning, namely, consensus, the underlying logic of linguistic systems, social position, and cultural milieu.

That man creates meaning is obvious: Consider the fact that a red, white, and blue cloth, which has no inherent meaning, takes on enormous meaning when arranged in a configuration of stars and stripes. Obviously, multicolored cloth can be transformed into a socially meaningful object that symbolically represents the United States of America. Though the decorated cloth is an arbitrary designation and might well have been substituted for by something else—say, a totem pole—we have endowed it so with value and sentiment that any desecration of the transformed cloth is interpreted as an assault upon the nation for which it stands.

While the relationship between an object and its representative designation is arbitrary, it is, nevertheless, established and maintained through consensus. The power of consensus is such that man can transform the essence of that which exists, even at the expense of denying the obvious, such as labeling a white man nonwhite, as depicted in the selection by Langston Hughes; or he can bring into essence that which has no "kickable" existence, for example Santa Claus, Easter bunnies, and, as McCall and Simmons suggest, "stolen bases."

Lest the point be missed, the creation and alteration of meaning requires the participation of all those concerned. It takes eleven men, all playing under a set of rules, to create such things as stolen bases. If the reader alone insisted that every October 22, since 1939 A.D., little green men have emerged from the depths of the earth to help in the celebration of damn-it-all-to-hell day, he would not be long deprived of more secluded surroundings.

Now the capacity to create meaning is unique to man and contingent on the quality of his mind, or on what Becker calls his "style of reactivity." Man's particular style of reactivity is qualitatively different from that of lower forms. Only man reaches the stage of actual symbolic behavior where he gains freedom from the intrinsic properties of the universe. The point is reached in symbolic behavior where individuals respond to arbitrary designations of their own creation that *stand for* things but bear no intrinsic relationship to them—such as the American flag, and the American Republic.

Although the creation of meaning requires a certain quality of mind, which is a personal characteristic, and consensus, which is a collective characteristic, this is not to imply that individuals do not introduce new meanings that play back on the universe of collectively established meanings. Stone and Farberman focus on this point in their analysis of Durkheim's conception of the collective representation and Mead's conception of the significant symbol. In each case, shared meaning is seen as the objectification and universalization of particular experiences. These experiences synthesize into an emergent universe of discourse that is ever changing and ever becoming. It constitutes an objective phase of experience, prior, external, and constraining on the individual but which is, nonetheless, sensitive to new meaningful distinctions that arise from his experience.

Although the power of collective definition and meaning is enormous, let there be no confusion: No amount of collective definition or consensus can wish away the reality of a brick wall. As with all things that object, walls offer a resistance, through which we may not walk. Just such resistance, however, offers up the occasion for the creation of meaning. The meaning of a wall would be quite different were we to play handball against it, or execute by firing squad someone standing in front of it. Using the wall as a means toward an end establishes or alters its meaning. The meaning of the wall is in the response made to it. As a mere datum, the wall awaits an action that will interpret it to mean one thing rather than another.

Perhaps the most dramatic example of the operation of consensus or collective definitions appears in the work of Benjamin Lee Whorf. Traditionally most people believed thinking to be independent of language, and that no matter what one spoke, he would arrive at universal meanings. When comparisons among different linguistic systems are made, the realization occurs that such systems codify, in their very categories of analysis, the consensual definitions arrived at by people as they go about solving the problems of collective existence. These codifications become embedded in the grammar of the system and influence subsequent thought. As a result, linguistic systems do not merely reflect thought. They shape it. Formulation of ideas is therefore part and parcel of a particular grammar. Since linguistic systems grow out of the collective life of a specific people and provide categories relative to that collectivity, "no individual is free to describe nature with absolute impartiality but is constrained to certain modes of interpretation." Even such fundamental categories as time, space, and substance are rendered relative to culture.

Just this point is emphasized by Chang Tung-Sun in his essay on the theory of knowledge. Indeed, all of Western philosophy is called to task for not realizing that its basic categories of analysis are quite relative to its underlying logic and grammar. For example, traditional Aristotelian logic, which operates with subject-predicate propositions, invites the notion of substratum and substance. In the sentence, "This is yellow and hard," the characteristics yellowness and hardness are attributed to whatever "this" stands for. The "this" becomes a substratum that has certain recognizable attributes. Subject in language calls forth the notion of substratum or more generally substance in thought. Accordingly, central to Western thought is the notion that something underlies whatever appears.

Sun contends that Chinese does not have a subject-predicate construction and thus is incompatible with Aristotelian logic. In contradistinction, Chinese can be described as based on a dialectical, or correlative, logic that emphasizes the relational significance of phenomena. Phenomena implicate one another such as above-below, positive-negative. The principle is one of relation of opposites or antonyms, rather than of identity and exclusion. Such logic encourages a search for interconnection and comparison among phenomena rather than for an underlying base upon which to set phenomena. In consequence, the apprehension and creation of meaningful distinctions will follow quite different lines when pursued in Chinese as opposed to English.

In addition to the categorical constraints on thought or symbolization imposed by logic or grammar, Mannheim shows how social position and the vested interests associated with it constrain thought content, while participation in a particular cultural-historical epoch conditions the very form of mentality.

Constraint on thought content is referred to as the particular conception of ideology, while constraint on the categorical apparatus of mentality is referred to as the total conception. Both modes of ideology discount the face value of what an adversary professes by assuming that what is asserted is a function of the structural conditions under which it appears. In both cases, an assumption is made concerning the conditional influence on representation of either life situation or historical situation. However, in the former, we are interested only in discovering the presumably disguised self-interest of the opponent. In the latter, we are interested in the total formation of the mental structure on the assumption that it is influenced by the collective matrix from which it emerges. Accordingly, the particularistic conception invites a purely psychological analysis, which demands the imputation of motives and the understanding that, even if the opponent is lying, we can uncover the lie on the basis of some common criterion. Though our interests are different, we express them within a shared theoretical framework. This is not the case with regard to the total conception. Here the theoretical frameworks themselves are divergent, and there is no common criterion for discerning validity. As do Whorf and Sun, Mannheim concludes that to the extent our mental frameworks themselves arise out of different collective matrices, the very "categories" of thought are different.

Given this predicament, the usual conclusion is that all thought is hopelessly relative. The usual conclusion, however, presupposes the usual premise that any thought or knowledge that depends on the subjective standpoint and social situation of the individual is *ipso facto* biased. To the contrary, Mannheim argues that a new conception of knowledge is required whose first premise must recognize that there are certain spheres of thought where truth value cannot be conceived apart from the values and social context of the individual. Such knowledge is relational, and its validity is established only in the clashing of points of view where error, bias, or partiality are exorcised. Right- and left-handed electrons could probably never have been conceived in China or in the United States. It required the relational knowledge of the two nations to win a Nobel Prize for Yang and Lee.

Suggested Readings

BECKER, ERNEST. *The Birth and Death of Meaning.* New York: The Free Press of Glencoe, 1962.

————. *The Revolution in Psychiatry.* New York: The Free Press, 1964.

BERGER, PETER L., and THOMAS LUCKMAN. *The Social Construction of Reality.* Garden City: Anchor Books, Doubleday and Co., 1967.

CASSIRER, ERNST. *An Essay on Man.* New Haven and London: Yale University Press, 1944.

DEWEY, JOHN. *Experience and Nature.* New York: W. W. Norton, 1925.

DEWEY, JOHN, and ARTHUR F. BENTLY. *Knowing and the Known.* Boston: Beacon Press, 1949.

DUNCAN, HUGH D. *Communication and the Social Order.* New York: Bedminster Press, 1962.

————. *Symbols in Society.* New York: Oxford University Press, 1968.

HOIJER, HARRY (ed.). *Language in Culture.* Chicago: University of Chicago Press, 1954.

LANGER, SUZANNE K. *Philosophy in a New Key.* New York: Penguin Books, Inc., 1948.

MEAD, GEORGE H. *Mind, Self, and Society.* Chicago: University of Chicago Press, 1934.

RIEZLER, KURT. *Man: Mutable and Immutable.* Chicago: Regnery, 1950.

SAPIR, EDWARD. *Language.* New York: Harcourt, Brace and Co., 1921.

WHORF, BENJAMIN LEE. *Language, Thought, and Reality* (ed.) John B. Carroll. Cambridge: Technology Press of Massachusetts Institute of Technology, 1956.

8   That Powerful Drop

● LANGSTON HUGHES

Leaning on the lamp post in front of the barber shop, Simple was holding up a copy of the *Chicago Defender* and reading about how a man who looks white had just been declared officially colored by an Alabama court.

"It's powerful," he said.

"What?"

"That one drop of Negro blood—because just *one* drop of black blood makes a man colored. *One* drop—you are a Negro! Now, why is that? Why is Negro blood so much more powerful than any other kind of blood in the world? If a man has Irish blood in him, people will say, 'He's *part* Irish.' If he has a little Jewish blood, they'll say, 'He's *half Jewish*.' But if he has just a small bit of colored blood in him, BAM!—'He's *a Negro!*' Not, 'He's *part* Negro.' No, be it ever so little, if that blood is black, 'He's *a Negro!*' Now, that is what I do not understand—why our *one* drop is so powerful. Take paint—white will not make black *white*. But black will make white *black*. One drop of black in white paint —and the white ain't white no more! Black is powerful. You can have ninety-nine drops of white blood in your veins down South—but if that other *one* drop is black, shame on you! Even if you look white, you're black. That drop is really powerful. Explain it to me. You're colleged."

"It has no basis in science," I said, "so there's no logical explanation." . . .

SOURCE: Langston Hughes, in *The Langston Hughes Reader* (New York: George Braziller, 1958). Reprinted by permission of Harold Ober Associates, Inc., 1958. Copyright 1953 by Langston Hughes.

9   The Stolen Base as a Social Object

● GEORGE J. MC CALL AND J. L. SIMMONS

. . . Mead was perfectly aware that *things*—the bundles of stimuli the animal encounters—exist prior to and independent of the animal. Mead was simply drawing a distinction between such "things" and what he called *objects*, which exist only in relation to acts. In brief, "things" are converted to "objects" through acts.

Perhaps the best way to wrestle with this point is by example. What is the object of a given act? Let us take eating. The object of the act of eating is *nutrition*. Therefore, if one is hungry (has an impulse to eat), he seeks out stimuli

SOURCE: George J. McCall and J. L. Simmons, from their "Social Acts and Social Objects," in *Identities and Interaction*. Reprinted with permission of The Macmillan Company. Copyright by The Free Press, a Division of The Macmillan Company 1966, pp. 51–52.

that will release the act of eating. If, in this seeking, he comes across a tomato, he picks it up, puts it in his mouth, chews it, and swallows it. The object of this act is nutrition.

But if he has a different impulse—if he is angry at someone nearby—and he comes across that same tomato, he may suddenly snatch it up and throw it at his tormentor. And what is the object of that act? Expression of his anger.

Really to grasp Mead's concept of objects, we have to play on his *double-entendre*. Let us take our tomato, which is simply a red, leathery firmly soft, juicy spheroid with a mildly pungent smell and a slightly acid taste. This same bundle of stimuli, this one "thing," releases two very different acts (eating and throwing) with two very different objects (nutrition and expression of anger). Now, this tomato *serves* as both of these objects of acts. It is nutrition when eaten, and it is an expression of anger when hurled at someone. A thing thus *becomes* an object, through the completion of an act. The tomato is not nutrition until it is eaten, nor is it an expression of anger until it is thrown.

Thus, in Mead's theory, "things" are made to serve as various "objects" (in an enriched sense of that word), objects of acts—that is, the *consummations* of those acts.[1]

But this usage is somewhat confusing as long as we confine ourselves to what we ordinarily think of as *physical* objects. The strength of Mead's notion is more apparent when we consider *social objects*, which are the objects of *social acts* (acts involving the coordinated activity of a plurality of persons).[2] Let us consider one admittedly bizarre act. A rather young man, in a park in the Bronx, is standing quietly but very alertly in the afternoon sun. Suddenly he tenses and scurries a few tentative steps to his right, still rather frozen, his gaze locked on a man only a few feet away. This other man makes a sudden movement with his right arm, and the first fellow breaks into sudden flight. Twenty or thirty yards away, still another fellow starts to run to cut him off, and the first man falls flat on his face, skidding and bouncing roughly along the ground for several feet as a result of his great momentum.

What object has this act created? What was the object of the act? Male readers, at least, may have recognized this common social object for what it is, a "stolen base." It has no physical structure but is simply a social object, a symbolic structure generated by a cooperative social act. A stolen base cannot be touched, smelled, or tasted, but it does exist, through the joint efforts of human actors. No one person can create a stolen base all by himself. It takes at least eleven men, laboring together under a common rule, to do so.

Such social objects are insubstantial, but they are extremely abundant and important. Most of the things we officially strive for—marriage, academic degrees, occupational positions, grades—do not exist in nature but are created jointly by the persons involved. Perhaps the reader has never pondered the metaphysical status of these social objects, but it is sobering to do so, and it raises profound theoretical questions as to why we should be so exclusively oriented to such "insubstantial" objects. . . .

---

[1] Mead, *The Philosophy of the Present,* Chicago: Open Court, 1932, pp. 190 ff.
[2] *Ibid.,* pp. 180, 185.

10   From Animal to Human Reactivity

● ERNEST BECKER

The development of the brain to its present size and complexity in man is a prodigious evolutionary feat. It represents a sensitivity to the environment unique in the animal kingdom. But this sensitivity was once the simple irritability that is characteristic of all of life: when an organism ceases to respond to stimuli we usually judge it dead.

The type of response that can be made to a stimulus varies considerably between organisms. The style of reaction to a given range of stimuli creates the world of experience of a given form. From a behaviorist point of view, "mind" is merely the style of reaction of an organism to the environment. Sherrington observed on the reactivity of the amoeba that if it were the size of a dog we should have to grant it a mind; it does act purposively in relation to various stimuli. The world of meaning is created for an animal out of the range and subtlety of its reactivity; Leslie White used the apt term "reactivity meaning" to describe the emergence of types of sensitivity in evolution. Paying attention to the world with a capacity to react to it in a certain way is "mind" on its most direct level: "minding." Jakob von Uexküll used "Umwelt" to refer to the world an animal is equipped to pay attention to. The "Umwelt" of a fly, for example, would hardly contain a distinction between a rug and slippers; that of a dog would. And Madison Avenue is sensitized to subtle differences in cigarette filters beyond the reactivity of most consumers.

The progressive development of animal reactivity is easy to trace. Let us employ a simplified concept of stimulus, and follow the changes by means of the four diagrams in the text. On its simplest level (Figure 1),* the organism re-

$$O \text{———} S$$

FIGURE 1. Type 1 reactivity. Simplest type of reactivity: Organism (O) responds directly to stimulus (S).

sponds to a stimulus by a direct reflex. If the stimulus emanates from something edible, the organism ingests the particle it encounters; if inedible, it recoils or ignores the particle. The relationship between the organism and the thing in its field seems to be determined by intrinsic properties. In this kind of direct stimulus-response relationship, the organism is then a slave, so to speak, to the properties of the object itself.

A real liberation took place when the conditioned reflex made its appearance (Figure 2). Remember Pavlov's classic experiment with the salivating dog. At first, the dog salivates in response to food. Then, food and another stimulus, a

SOURCE: Ernest Becker, in his *The Birth and Death of Meaning*. Reprinted with permission of The Macmillan Company. Copyright by The Free Press of Glencoe, 1962, pp. 15–22.

* The figures in this article are taken from Leslie A. White, "Four Stages in the Evolution of Minding," in *The Evolution of Man: Man, Culture, and Society*, Vol. 2 of *Evolution After Darwin*, edited by Sol Tax (Chicago: University of Chicago Press, 1960). The explanatory text also is adapted from this source.

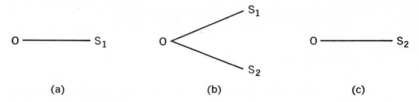

FIGURE 2.   Type 2 reactivity. The conditioned response. In (a), organism responds to food. In (b), food and another stimulus are presented simultaneously, and animal learns to associate the two. So that, in (c), the animal can make the same response to the substitute stimulus that he had previously made to the food.

bell, are presented simultaneously, so that the animal grows accustomed to associating one with the other. Finally, the food is omitted and only the bell presented, but the animal, having associated his gratification with the bell, salivates when it is rung.

The liberation here is fundamental: the animal reacts to a stimulus *whose intrinsic property is of no immediate interest to him.* The dog has little interest in the bell, but since it has now become a sign of something else, it becomes part of his reactive world. Consider how fortunate an animal is to be able to make chance associations and become easily conditioned to them. It is then free from abject dependence upon the stimulus itself. For example, an animal who can associate the sound of a gun with the death of one of the herd can flee immediately at the sound of the gun, knowing what is inevitably to follow. (But this example is not the best: animals don't usually make this correlation; the intelligent elephant remains unconcerned as members of his herd are shot down around him.) On the human level, the conditioning of the individual to the equation smoke = fire can lead to an instant mobilization of energy, with only the faintest stimulus to the nostrils.

A third type of reactivity (Figure 3) is even more advanced than the conditioned reflex. The best example of it is the chimp who uses a stick to knock down a banana, suspended out of reach. He sees a relationship between two objects in his visual field, and swings the stick to bring down the banana. The crucial difference between this behavior and that of Pavlov's dog is that, for the chimp, the relationship between banana and stick is something he establishes himself. It results from an alertness to a problem situation. The equation is not built into the chimp by an experimenter, in step-by-step fashion. There is some

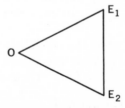

FIGURE 3.   Type 3 reactivity. The chimpanzee is O; E_1 is a banana; E_2 is a stick. Unlike the conditioned response, both stimuli are present in the field from start to finish of the problem. Also, the organism, and not an experimenter or a chance association, determines the relationship between the stick and the banana.

masterful autonomy here that is absent in the simple conditioned reflex. It is not easy for an animal to relate itself to two or more things in the environment. A dog, for example, seeing food through a picket fence, will detour to a gate twenty feet down the fence to get to the food on the other side. He has seen a relationship between the open gate and getting the food. But a hen, seeing the same food and the gate as well, does not establish any relationship, and runs helplessly back and forth directly in front of the food, watching it through the pickets.

The final type of reactivity-meaning is what we are accustomed to calling symbolic behavior. It is given only to man, the symbolic animal, to enjoy the freedom and powerful mastery of this type of reaction potential. In symbol behavior, the human animal responds to an arbitrary designation for an object, a

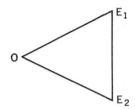

FIGURE 4.   Type 4 reactivity. The human organism is O; E_1 is a house; E_2 is the *word* "house." Again, as in Figure 3, there is a continuous relationship between the organism and both objects in his visual field. The crucial difference in this type of reactivity is that the word "house" is fabricated by the organism itself. The organism not only perceives the relationship between two objects in its field but also creates the relationship by coining the word "house." The symbol creates a world of reference that may or may not be present originally in the perceptual field.

designation coined by him alone, that stands for the object. The word "house," for example, has no intrinsic qualities within itself that would connect it with an object, since someone else may use "casa" or "maison" or "dom." Unlike Pavlov's dog, man *creates* the relationship between stimuli. But unlike the chimp reaching with a firm pole for a banana, the shadowy word "house" has nothing intrinsic in it that would connect it with the object it stands for. Symbolic behavior depends, of course, upon the ability to create identifiable word sounds that become object representations of infinite degrees of subtlety—from "minnow hook" to "minestrone."

These four types of behavior are curious from one point of view: while they are evolutionary, they do not seem to be *degrees* of difference in minding the environment, but rather actually *kinds* of behavior. An organism can either be conditioned or it cannot; it can correlate two or more objects in its environment or it cannot. Figure 5 is striking. There seems to be a series which is cumulative: Man can respond to all four types of stimulus, but the lowest forms can respond to the simple stimulus or tropism only. Furthermore, at the top of the pyramid, man is by himself in an exclusive club, not only looking down at the lower animals but also, by arbitrarily coining words, assigning the very meaning to the universe.

The development of mind, then, is a progressive freedom of reactivity. The reactive process which is inherent in the organism not only gradually arrives at freedom from the intrinsic properties of things but also proceeds from there to

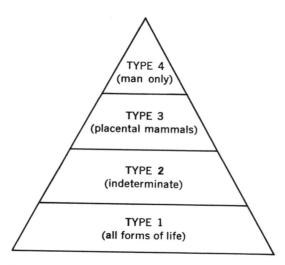

FIGURE 5.   As we progress up the pyramid, the number of species capable of a given type of behavior diminishes. Also, those at the top can exercise the entire range of reactivity.

assign *its own stimulus meanings*. Mind culminates in the organism's ability to *choose* what it will react to. White calls this a "traffic in non-sensory meanings." Nature provided all of life with H_2O, but only man could create a world in which "holy" water generates a special stimulus.

There has always been some confusion in distinguishing a sign from a pure symbol. A sign is characterized by the fact that its meaning is identified with its physical form, and may be grasped via the senses. Dark clouds, for example, are a sign of rain; a yellow flag signals quarantine. But the matter is not quite that simple. Actually, the phonetic form of a word symbol, like "holy water," enters our reactivity consciousness through our ears and is grasped by the senses. As soon as we react to the immediate stimulus property of a thing, we are reacting in a conditioned-reflex manner, and sign and symbol become confused. Even though we *assign* meaning to a thing via symbols, once the reaction becomes a habit we may respond unhesitatingly, as though the meaning were inherent in the thing itself. Thus, symbolism represents a form of flexible power over things that is lost when our response to them becomes habitually binding. We may react involuntarily to "holy water" long after we've been converted to another religion, for example. The body remains, in W. H. Gantt's beautiful phrase, "a museum of conditioned reflex antiquities." This is one reason why psychotherapy, for instance, is a long and wearisome, frustrating experience: the individual must patiently unlearn old unquestioning habitual responses, and come to assign new meanings of his own. To control the symbolic meaning of a stimulus is a power that not everyone enjoys to the same degree. An object may obtrude its concrete immediateness despite our best efforts to maintain a symbolic distance. This is one explanation for the unusual feeling of power and delight that comes with manipulating "four-letter words." We seem to be transacting with the stark objects themselves rather than with their shadowy word representations. The confusion of the concrete and the symbolic can have a less fortunate issue: one patient in a mental hospital could not look at numbers without seeing copulating figures.

A word, of course, is a social object. We learn all our symbols from others in the long, patient acquisition of language. Then, if we wish, we can spend the rest of our lives talking to ourselves. But initially, at least two people had to agree on a word before it became a social symbol. Something had to be expressed *to* someone in order to be communicated. Some schizophrenics are irritating only because so much of their language is not comprehensible to their interlocutor. That they seem to know what they mean is not enough. The private experience has to be conveyed with word signs that are intelligible to others.

Keenly aware of our powers of speech, we look with pity upon our friends "the dumb animals." Often they seem to have something to say but have not learned words for it. The reader may object that animals can't have thoughts unless they have words in which to formulate them; therefore it would be idle to assume that they have anything to say. But the matter is not that simple. Hallowell thinks there is good evidence for what he calls "intrinsic symbolic processes" on the subhuman level. An animal may privately produce memory representations of objects that are not present in the immediate visual field. After all, an ape's, dog's, or cat's senses are highly developed, and there is no reason to assume that images of remembered striking events do not pop into consciousness. An ape's 450-cubic-centimeter brain is of considerable size, and could conceivably permit imaginary picturing of past or even of potential events. Meredith Crawford observed that chimps were able to learn a gestural form of communication, gentle taps on the shoulder by means of which they could summon one another. Viki the chimpanzee seems to have played sometimes with an imaginary toy on an imaginary string, which she pulled around behind her.

But intrinsic symbolization is not enough. In order to become a social act, the symbol must be joined to some extrinsic mode; there must exist an external graphic mode to convey what the individual has to express. The chimp's gentle taps on the shoulder were already a cue which anticipated a social response. If the response did not come, he would pull forcibly to involve the other chimp in his laboratory task, or continue at it alone. This is a striking example of the developed mammalian intersensitivity, of which we spoke earlier. But it also shows how separate are the worlds we live in, unless we join our inner apprehensions to those of others by means of socially agreed symbols.

Thus, freedom to react to the environment is in its highest degree a social affair. No matter how acute, an animal's capacity to react to stimuli cannot reach a symbolic form until this reaction becomes a mutually shared venture. The helpless postnatal dependence of the mammals laid the basis for a heightened consciousness of an organic environment inhabited by creatures similar in form and function to oneself. But the meaning that man assigns to his world via symbols, as well as the consequent power that he has over it, is not due to his mammalian heritage alone. Helpless young in need of suck came upon the evolutionary scene over seventy million years ago. Paleolithic cave art is only forty thousand years old—the first evidence we have of true extrinsic symbolization. Reactive power over the immediate sensory bondage to the environment had to wait until one animal could intricately link his reaction sensitivity to that of another, by means of extrinsic symbolic modes. The popular "Two heads are better than one," might better be changed: "Two heads are needed for one."

11   On the Edge of Rapprochement: Was Durkheim Moving Toward the Perspective of Symbolic Interaction?

• GREGORY P. STONE AND HARVEY A. FARBERMAN

After the publication in 1912 of *The Elementary Forms of the Religious Life,* Emile Durkheim turned almost at once to the epistemological problems raised by that work in a series of lectures on "Pragmatism and Sociology," delivered at the Sorbonne in 1913 and 1914.[1] Durkheim's concern with pragmatism (especially the work of Charles Peirce, William James, and John Dewey) shortly before his death in 1917 is almost patent evidence of the direction his theoretical development was taking at the culmination of his sociological inquiries.[2] However, he was unable to make the full transition which, indeed, would have required a revolutionary transformation of his ontological position.

This article will focus on the development of Durkheim's thought in the direction of symbolic interaction. In addition, some attention will be paid to objective and metaphorical barriers blocking the transition. In accomplishing these things, the notion of metaphor will be central to our argument.[3] Moreover, we shall not be concerned here with any substantive exegesis of Durkheim's works. We presume substantive knowledge on the part of the reader.

Every sociological theory or perspective implies some image of man, communication, society, and their interrelations. Our contention is that the development of Durkheim's sociological thought was marked by significant metaphorical changes, particularly in respect to the image of man. Two additional metaphors proved less yielding and provided powerful obstacles to thoroughgoing theoretical reformulation: first, the image of communication as interaction or action in parallel;[4] second, the image of society as a container of communication and individual contents.

Metaphorical Development of Durkheim's Theory

To deal with the metaphors of man, society, and communication which are presupposed by any sociological theory is to carry critical analysis into a highly de-

SOURCE: Gregory P. Stone and Harvey A. Farberman, *Sociological Quarterly,* VIII (Spring 1967), pp. 149–164.

[1] The first five and the thirteenth and fourteenth lectures, reconstructed from student notes, have been translated by Charles Blend in Kurt H. Wolff (ed.), *Essays on Sociology and Philosophy by Emile Durkheim, et al.* (New York): Harper and Row, 1964), pp. 386–436.

[2] The *account* of Durkheim's theoretical development in Talcott Parsons, *Structure of Social Action* (Glencoe, Ill.: The Free Press, 1949), pp. 301–470 remains the best exegetic treatment available. Obviously we question Parsons' interpretation of the development as moving inexorably toward an impasse with idealism. In all fairness, it should be noted that *Pragmatisme et sociologie* did not appear until 1955, eighteen years after Parsons had completed his study.

[3] On metaphor, see *inter alia* Kenneth Burke, *Permanence and Change* (Indianapolis. Ind.: Bobbs-Merrill, 1965), pp. 94–96.

[4] On this view, "symbolic *interaction*" is a misnomer, and we would prefer to return to Mead's original designation of the perspective as "social behaviorism." However, since the former phrase has so much currency in sociological circles, we will use it, explicitly recognizing its inadequacies. On the distinctions among "self action," "interaction," and "transaction," see John Dewey and Arthur F. Bentley, *Knowing and the Known* (Boston: Beacon Press, 1960), pp. 103–43.

batable area. For metaphors are frequently implicit in theory, and, in the final analysis, implications are always made by the critic. Confronted by the explication of his presuppositions, the theorist may well deny them, or, acknowledging them, may alter his theoretical statement in a fundamental way so that they no longer obtain. In Durkheim's case, metaphors became more explicit as his thought developed, until, in *The Elementary Forms of the Religious Life*, critical confrontation with the presuppositions underlying his thought produced a crucial philosophical impasse. Our treatment of the metaphorical development in Durkheim's theory, then, is a kind of *tour de force* and necessarily oversimplified. Questions will undoubtedly be raised by the reader, but, hopefully, this will lead to a necessary re-examination of Durkheim's contributions by symbolic interactionists.

A further caveat must be entered before our treatment begins. To assert that some image of *man* is presumed by a sociological theory is not to assert that individual *men* are the theorist's central objects of inquiry. Durkheim was always centrally concerned with the nature of society or the nature of the social bond. Yet, the implicit view of man and its progressive alteration had a critical impact on his conceptualization and study of society. The more Durkheim began to understand that the fabric of society—collective representations—was a creation of man, the more he altered his image of man and, consequently, his image of society.

The development of Durkheim's thought can be interpreted as an elaboration on the mechanistic metaphor, changing from a view of man as a moving particle, to a conductor of societal energy, to a transformer of society itself. Until the very end of this development, society is seen as a container and energizer of these individual particles. It is a reality *sui generis* and made up of materials distinctively its own, collective representations or social facts exterior to and constraining of its individual contents. So is any container distinguished from the things it contains.

The Division of Labor. Key terms in this work—density, volume, and dynamic or moral density—suggest the metaphorical raiment which cloaks and disguises genuinely social phenomena in a vocabulary more appropriate to physical energy systems. If a bounded area (the container) is overpopulated in such a way that the enclosed moving particles cannot avoid colliding with one another, something must give—some new process must be set in motion. What occurs is a progressive differentiation of the particles and their movements in an increasing division of labor. At one time (under conditions of mechanical solidarity) particles are alike, their movements relatively undifferentiated, and they have access to all "corners" of the container's space. They collide relatively infrequently with one another, given their small numbers and the relatively large volume of the container. With increasing numbers and density, the container, in a metaphorical sense, must expand and develop internal compartments to minimize collisions and facilitate the "existence" of the whole.[5]

---

[5] This image of society persists through the *Elementary Forms*, e.g., "Society supposes a self-conscious organization which is nothing other than a classification. . . . To avoid all collisions, it is necessary that each particular group have a determined portion of space assigned to it: in other terms, it is necessary that space in general be divided, differentiated, arranged, and that these divisions and arrangements be known to everybody." Emile Durkheim, *The Elementary Forms of the Religious Life*, translated by Joseph Ward Swain (New York: Collier Books, 1961), p. 492 (hereafter cited as *Elementary Forms*). Yet, on the very next page, Durkheim writes: "Consequently things can no longer be contained in the social moulds according to

To be sure, mere material density is not enough. The concentrated population must engage in communication as well as collision. Density, therefore, has a moral or social dimension, and Durkheim recognizes that "there are particular, exceptional cases . . . where material and moral density are *perhaps* not entirely in accord." [6] Nevertheless, the moral dimension of density is decidedly underplayed when Durkheim states his central proposition in the main text of the *Division of Labor:* [7]

> The division of labor varies in direct ratio with the volume and density of societies, and, if it progresses in a continuous manner in the course of development, it is because societies become regularly denser and generally more voluminous.

The image of man as a particle persists, as individuality, *per se*, becomes merged with the changing character of the container induced by the progressive differentiation of the contents. Thus, "individuality is something which the society possesses." [8] Later, discussing the weakening of the collective *conscience* (the "walls" of the container) brought on by the emergence of organic solidarity, Durkheim observed: [9]

> This is not to say that the [collective *conscience*] is threatened with total disappearance. . . . There is even a place where it is strengthened and made more precise: that is the way in which it regards the individual. As all the other beliefs and all the other practices take on a character less and less religious, the individual becomes the object of a sort of religion. We erect a cult in behalf of personal dignity which, as every strong cult, already has its superstitions.

Even as man approaches a condition where he can feel more actor than acted upon, he reaches that condition precisely by being acted upon by external and constraining forces.

If in the *Division of Labor* Durkheim maintained a consistent image of man, his conception of society must be said to have vacillated. In explaining the transition to organic solidarity, the moral dimension of society was de-emphasized. Yet, at the end of this major work, Durkheim turned to the "abortive" forms of the division of labor. This led him once again to a consideration of variations in containers—the moral dimension. Compartmentalization may proceed in a disjointed way, as in the anomic division of labor. Compartments may be sealed too tightly as in caste societies. Finally, the container may become overcompartmentalized so that *particular* motion is so severely constricted that it may be brought to a standstill.

The Rules. Reconsidering his magnificent effort in the *Division of Labor,* Durkheim emerged filled with unbounded enthusiasm and perhaps somewhat

---

which they were primitively classified; they must be organized according to *principles which are their own,* so logical organization differentiates itself from the social organization and becomes autonomous." *Ibid.,* p. 493. Italics ours. Here our main point is anticipated. It becomes increasingly difficult for Durkheim to maintain his image of society as a container. As most readers will know, Hughes has also seen the problems posed by Durkheim's metaphor, or "mechanistic vocabulary." However, Hughes, like Parsons, sees these difficulties leading Durkheim into an idealism. This, of course, is farthest from our mind, and, we think, Durkheim's. See H. Stuart Hughes, *Consciousness and Society* (New York: Vintage Books, 1958), pp. 278–87.

[6] Emile Durkheim, *The Division of Labor in Society,* translated by George Simpson (Glencoe, Ill.: The Free Press, 1947), p. 260, note 11. Italics ours.

[7] *Ibid.,* p. 262.

[8] *Ibid.,* p. 130.

[9] *Ibid.,* p. 172.

starry-eyed. He had discovered what social facts *were* and felt he had a firm grasp on their method of study. Sociology as a science could at last be clearly distinguished from philosophical speculation.

His conception of social facts as exterior to and constraining of individual conduct led him back to a reconsideration of societal variation—the moral dimension. Moral density, as "dynamic density," had replaced material density in Durkheim's conceptualization of the necessary conditions for the proliferation of the division of labor.[10] He specifically acknowledged his error: "We made the mistake, in our *Division du travail*, of presenting material density too much as the exact expression of dynamic density."[11] Durkheim, thus, was led to a recasting of the metaphor of society as a generalized container—a return to the moral dimension. There were many societies; many varieties of containers. Individual acts, however, remained irrelevant—constrained by the character of the container: "When . . . the sociologist undertakes the investigation of some order of social facts, he must consider them . . . independent of their individual manifestations."[12] What better test, then, of sociological method than to investigate the "ultimate" individual act—the suicide?

Suicide. In *Suicide*, Durkheim's view shifts from a conception of man as the thing contained, the moving particle, to man as a conductor. Society is no longer seen as purely a container, but as an energizer of individual conduct. Different societies "energize" man in different ways.[13]

Subsequently, communication is viewed by Durkheim as exchange: ". . . conversation and all intellectual communication between men is an exchange of concepts."[14] On this view also, man may be seen as a kind of conductor of the energy generated by society. Pushing the metaphor almost to the absurd—absolutely rhetorically—we might conceive egoistic suicide as a consequence of "overloading" the conductor; altruistic suicide as implying a short circuit—the faulty conductor must be replaced in the interest of maintaining an efficient generator. Anomic suicide is the mark of a defect in the generator. With no more current, the conductor atrophies, rusts, or otherwise falls into disuse.

But not all individuals in societies or social segments characterized by faulty circuits or power-losses commit suicide. Durkheim, then, reviews the extreme position he assumed in *The Rules*. In the Preface to the second edition, written in 1901, four years after the publication of *Le suicide*, he observed:[15]

> Because beliefs and social practices thus come to us from without, it does not follow that we receive them passively or without modification. In reflecting on collective institutions and assimilating them for ourselves, we individualize them and impart to them more or less personal characteristics. Similarly, in reflecting on the physical world, each of us colors it after his own fashion, and different

---

[10] Emile Durkheim, *The Rules of Sociological Method*, translated by Sarah A. Solovay and John H. Mueller and edited by George E. G. Catlin (Chicago: Univ. of Chicago Press, 1938), pp. 113–15.

[11] *Ibid.*, p. 115, note 22.

[12] *Ibid.*, p. 45.

[13] Parsons' interpretation is quite compatible on this point: "Instead of the *conscience collective* being contrasted with organic solidarity, there now are two types of influence of the *conscience collective,* and set over against both of them the state where its disciplining influence is weak, at the polar extreme altogether absent. In so far as this weakening of discipline is present, the state of *anomie* exists." Parsons, *op. cit.*, p. 336.

[14] *Elementary Forms*, p. 482.

[15] Durkheim, *The Rules of Sociological Method*, pp. lvi–lvii, note 7. Italics ours.

individuals adapt themselves differently to the same physical environment. It is for this reason that each one of us creates, in a measure, his own morality, religion, and mode of life. There is no conformity to social convention that does not comprise an entire range of individual shades. It is nonetheless true that this field of variation is a limited one. It *verges on non-existence.* . . .

Although he tried, Durkheim could not wish the individual away. The stage, at last, was set for him explicitly and directly to confront his formerly implicit views of man, society, and communication.

The Elementary Forms. In the concluding section of *The Elementary Forms of the Religious Life,* when Durkheim attempts to secure the foundation of religious experience in society, the culmination and subsequent erosion of the mechanistic metaphor occur. Man is seen as a transformer of reality,[16] for Durkheim notes clearly that, with respect to religious experience, "it does not follow that the reality which is its foundation conforms *objectively* to the idea which believers have of it."[17] From this point on, the metaphor of society as a container cannot be maintained, for Durkheim begins to see the contained as the creator of the container. The force of collective definition, when universalized and objectified *through symbolization,* comes to the fore. The collective representation, itself, even though it is impersonal and exterior and may take a religious form, is a precipitate of collective action and *formulation.*[18] Indeed, the religious cosmos is no more than a magnified, transformed, and dramatized image of ordinary life. As Durkheim suggests, "Men alone have the faculty of conceiving the ideal, of *adding something* to the real."[19] Why does man idealize the real? Because, in the throes of religious passion, "man does not recognize himself; he feels transformed and consequently he transforms the environment which surrounds him."[20]

We find that Durkheim's metaphor of man has shifted from that of a particle-in-motion to a conductor, to a particle physiochemically transformed and transforming, to a creative human transformer of the world around him. Man has, in his collective existence, become the source of reality. The consequences for this sociological epistemology seem bold and clear to us, and Durkheim asks the pertinent question, "what has been able to make social life so important a source for the logical life?"[21] The answer focuses on the development of concepts in society. Concepts are depicted as impersonal, fixed, and immutable—

---

[16] In his preface to the second edition of *The Rules,* Durkheim specifically recognizes the transforming character of human association: "Whenever certain elements combine and thereby produce, by the fact of their combination, new phenomena, it is plain that these new phenomena reside not in the original elements, but in the totality formed by their union. . . . What we say of life could be repeated for all possible compounds. The hardness of bronze is not in the copper, the tin, or the lead, which are its ingredients and which are soft and malleable bodies; it is in their mixture. The fluidity of water and its nutritional and other properties are not to be found in the two gases of which it is composed but in the complex substance which they form by their association. Let us apply this principle to sociology." *The Rules of Sociological Method,* pp. xlvii–xviii. However, the transformation remains physical–biological and chemical. In *The Elementary Forms,* Durkheim's view of the transforming function of communication undergoes a profound change.

[17] *Elementary Forms,* p. 465. Italics ours.

[18] As Durkheim says, "This is because society cannot make its influence felt unless it is in action, and it is not in action unless the individuals who compose it are assembled together and act in common." *Ibid.,* p. 465. Note the persistent conception of "communication" as parallel action and not transaction.

[19] *Ibid.,* p. 469. Italics ours.

[20] *Ibid.*

[21] *Ibid.,* p. 480.

of themselves, static. If a concept changes, "it is not because it is its nature to do so, but because *we* have discovered some imperfection in it; it is because it had to be rectified." [22] By implication, the collective representation is becoming the internalized concept rather than the exterior and constraining social fact. It becomes part of the content of society rather than the material from which the "walls" of society are constructed. This signals a fundamental change in Durkheim's conception of society, but the reformulation is given no definitive statement. The concept is seen as a tool of collective existence—if it is imperfect or not useful, *we* change it.[23] It is only by thinking with concepts, moreover, that the realm of impersonal and stable ideas is reached—the realm of truth. Once man becomes conscious of this realm of ideas,[24]

> . . . and, in so far as he believes that he has discovered their causes, he undertakes to put these causes into action for himself, in order that he may draw from them by his own force the effects which they produce; that is to say, he attributes to himself the right of making concepts.

So man does more than formulate concepts; he passes collective judgment on their acceptability: [25]

> It is not enough that they be true to be believed. If they are not in harmony with the other beliefs and opinions, or, in a word, with the mass of the other collective representations, they will be denied: minds will be closed to them; consequently it will be as though they did not exist.

Although Durkheim saw truth as characterized by "stability" and "impersonality," he could not but acknowledge that it was a collective formulation, hence, temporally and societally specific. "To be sure," he writes, "we cannot insist too much upon the different characteristics which logic presents at different periods in history; it develops like the societies themselves." [26] In his statement on the method he used for investigating religion, he writes, "social facts vary with the social system of which they form a part; they cannot be understood when detached from it." [27] Clearly Durkheim has apprehended the temporal and locational relativity of truth. Thus, we are not surprised when he muses: [28]

> In a word, the old gods are growing old or already dead, and others are not yet born. . . . There are no gospels which are immortal, but neither is there any reason for believing that humanity is incapable of inventing new ones.

Obviously Durkheim has placed the realm of the gospel (or truth) squarely within the domain of human intervention. The metaphor of society as a container is no longer compatible with the main thrust of Durkheim's intellectual thought.

---

[22] *Ibid.*, p. 481. Italics ours.
[23] At this point, Durkheim falls squarely in the camp of *social* pragmatism, as opposed to the *subjective* pragmatism of James and, occasionally, Dewey. This is a major distinction to which we shall return.
[24] *Ibid.*, p. 485.
[25] *Ibid.*, p. 486.
[26] *Ibid.*, p. 487.
[27] *Ibid.*, p. 113.
[28] *Ibid.*, pp. 475–76. It is difficult to refrain from the observation that, today, more than a half century after Durkheim made these remarks, some segments of Christianity seem to be catching up with the past. We refer to the "Is God Dead?" controversy.

The Problem of Truth

In what may be his most radical statement, Durkheim analyzes the rhetorical power of both science and religion down to the base of collective faith. In effect, the truth value of a concept is guaranteed less by its objective reference than by the faith that it mobilizes: [29]

> Today it is generally sufficient that [concepts] bear the stamp of science to re-ceive a sort of privileged credit, because we have faith in science. But this faith does not differ essentially from religious faith. . . . science continues to be de-pendent upon opinion at the very moment when it seems to be making its laws; for, as we have already shown, it is from opinion that it holds the force necessary to act upon opinion.

There can be no doubt then that Durkheim apprehended truth as a function of a larger consensus. In his opinion the ultimate insurance against irrational ele-ments in truth was the emergence of a new form of inter-societal, cosmopolitan life. Much in the way Mannheim's relational conception of truth rested on the surmounting of barriers by divergent groups in communication, so Durkheim saw the depreciating importance of the social segment and the concomitant up-surge of the transnational life as a filter for the elimination of "bias." [30] The greater its dispersion in collective opinion, the more autonomous the development of truth; or the wider the societal base of truth, the less is the emergence of truth inhibited by society. But, alas, the flow of humanity is the flaw of tragedy: "Really and truly human thought is not a primitive fact; it is the product of his-tory; it is the ideal limit towards which we are constantly approaching, but which in all probability we shall never succeed in reaching." [31] As Mead might well have said, we premise our acts on a future of which we are certainly un-certain.

Given the general direction of his statements at the conclusion of the *Ele-mentary Forms*, it is not surprising that Durkheim turned immediately to a consideration of the pragmatic reaction against the classical conceptions of truth, mind, and reality. He had already consulted and cited James's *Varieties of Re-ligious Experience* and *Principles of Psychology* in the concluding sections of the *Elementary Forms*.

Truth and Pragmatism

In his lectures on pragmatism and sociology, Durkheim had arrived at the seminal insight that "today's truth is tomorrow's error" [32]—a proposition which

---

[29] *Ibid.*, pp. 486–87. The reader ought really to compare this conception of science with the conception stated in *The Rules*. For Durkheim, science, just as religion, develops as a cult based on faith. We cannot help but observe at this time that the "new left" is precisely a cult without faith, and, if we may, we hope wistfully that science will be *a* faith without cults.

[30] It seems almost unnecessary to point out Mannheim's profound distinction between relativis-tic and relationistic conceptions of truth. See Karl Mannheim, *Ideology and Utopia*, translated by Louis Wirth and Edward Shils (New York: Harcourt, Brace, and World, 1963), pp. 78–80. Mannheim's epistemology is premised on a dialectic, and this is precisely the process that Durk-heim misses. For Durkheim, cosmopolitanism is accomplished when collective representations "spill over the walls" of the container and engulf the world at large. Suddenly, the fabric of the "walls of the container" becomes its content. This is an additional flaw in the transition of Durkheim's metaphor that ought, one day, be examined by the critical theorist.

[31] *Ibid.*, p. 493.

[32] Emile Durkheim, "Pragmatism and Sociology," in Wolff (ed.), *op. cit.*, p. 409.

confounded most of the assumptions of nineteenth-century European philosophy and which forced him to look elsewhere for an epistemology consonant with his theoretical advances in sociology. He turned to pragmatism. Not only was Durkheim already familiar with the work of James, but James had a spokesman and critic who had the ear of European intellectuals, namely the Englishman, F. C. S. Schiller. Moreover, both Durkheim and James were influenced, if in different ways, by Charles Bernard Renouvier—Durkheim as a student and James through careful reading of Renouvier's works. Each must have been impressed with Renouvier's rejection of the Kantian dichotomy between noumena and phenomena—James settling on the notion of truth as experiential, Durkheim on the notion of "presentations" as facts.

In his review of pragmatism, Durkheim observed that Peirce, James, Schiller, and Dewey were in agreement: no exterior, impersonal, and complete truth, irrespective of its source (intellection or sensory perception) could be a living and compelling truth without taking the realm of goals, means, and choices (the realm of human purpose) into account. In fact, to conceive truth as "given," i.e., "out there," divorces it from human life and action.

Any conception which makes truth independent of the intervention of man, as the argument goes, implies a theory of mind (and reality) which eliminates man as an agent of influence on truth. For, if the best that mind can do is merely to describe the out-there-given truth, then man becomes a passive recorder of an established and impinging universe. This image is, of course, unacceptable to pragmatism which postulates the inextricable connection of thinking and living or of mind and existence. Hence, in the early statements of James, truth must be conceived as having a "personal character," and this conception persists throughout the work of James.

To root truth in existence, is to place it in the realm of means, ends, and choices. From this perspective, truth is seen as a matter of *efficacious* choice with respect to an end-in-view which itself is dictated by human interest. Truth, then, devolves around the matter of assessing the efficacy of means, and its detection requires an examination of consequences. More important to our argument is the fact that, for James, the detection of truth *also* requires an examination of the personal psychology of any individual who asserts the truth value of his statements. Truth becomes a very personal and, by implication, pluralistic affair. There is the further implication that, to the degree individual interest (or consciousness) lends relevance (for the individual) to certain aspects of reality by bringing them into a means-end schema, mind must be conceived as an additive principle. In searching for solutions, mind converts unformulated sensuous experience into formulated reality, but, for James, reality is *personally* formulated.[33] It was against such a position, no doubt, that Bertrand Russell was

---

[33] Durkheim clearly understood the fundamental distinction between experience and formulated reality: "Sensual representations are in a perpetual flux; they come after each other like the waves of a river, and even during the time that they last, they do not remain the same thing. . . . We are never sure of again finding a perception such as we experience it the first time; for if the thing perceived has not changed, it is we who are no longer the same. On the contrary, the concept is, as it were, outside of time and change; it is in the depths below all this agitation; it might be said that it is in a different portion of the mind, which is serener and calmer. . . . It is a manner of thinking that, at every moment of time, is fixed and crystallized." See *Elementary Forms*, p. 481. It is at this point that Durkheim cites James. However, as we shall see, Durkheim could never conceptualize the concept as personal. The distinction, of course, persists in pragmatism and has received its most extensive formulation in Dewey's *Experience and Nature*. For a fundamental reformulation that brings the distinction squarely into

reacting when he proclaimed that, at least James's work "is only [another] form of the subjective madness which is characteristic of most modern philosophy." [34]

Russell's criticism, however, echoed a far earlier one; for, after considering the major alternatives offered by the pragmatists in opposition to the classical position, Durkheim said rather decisively, "Pragmatism . . . claims to explain truth psychologically and subjectively." He went on to argue in the same passage: [35]

> . . . the nature of the individual is too limited to explain by itself alone all things human. Therefore, if we envisage individual elements alone, we are led to underestimate the amplitude of the effects that we have to account for. . . . But men have always recognized in truth something that in certain respects imposes itself on us, something that is independent of the facts of sensitivity and individual impulse.

What Durkheim was reacting to in the pragmatic resolution was the persistent strain of subjective nominalism embodied in a psychological, as opposed to a sociological, conception of mind. With a purely individualistic theory of mentality, one could hardly arrive at a phenomenon "that is independent of the facts of sensitivity and individual impulse." And this is precisely the position that Durkheim had already developed in his extensive analyses of collective representations. A purely psychologistic perspective could never account for a collectively established universal. Hence, while Durkheim appears extremely sympathetic to the pragmatic rejection of the classical views and, indeed, seems to resonate, if ambivalently, not only with the notion of a living truth but also with an instrumentalistic formulation of mind as well as an emergent conception of reality, he could not resonate with an atomistic or elementaristic psychology. He was literally forced to reject the subjective pragmatism of James.

Durkheim required a *social* theory of mind which could be built on a conception of society as a "synthesis of human consciousness." [36] Such a theory would apprehend concepts as collectively established representations somewhat free from, but not insensitive to, the fact of individual percipience. Truth, in this way, while neither a detached given nor a simple consequence of individual adjustment, could be conceived as an emergent collective reconstruction.

Possibilities of Convergence with Symbolic Interaction

The social theory of mind which Durkheim was on the edge of discerning, but for which no support was forthcoming in the subjective pragmatism available to him at the time, appears full blown in the work of George Herbert Mead. In Mead's work, we find a *social* pragmatism based on a conceptualization of mind which accounts, by way of a theory of significant symbols, for the linkage between any particular communicative act and universal meaning. The heart of Mead's work rests on the proposition that mind develops out of and sustains it-

the perspective of symbolic interaction, see Harry Stack Sullivan, "The Illusion of Personal Individuality," in Helen Swick Perry, Mary Ladd Gawel, and Martha Gibbon (eds.), *The Collected Works of Harry Stack Sullivan*, II (New York: W. W. Norton, 1964), pp. 198–226, especially p. 214.

[34] Bertrand Russell, *A History of Western Philosophy* (New York: Simon and Schuster, 1954), p. 818.
[35] Durkheim, "Pragmatism and Sociology," in Wolff (ed.), *op. cit.*, pp. 429–30.
[36] *Elementary Forms*, p. 479.

self within an objective phase of experience. This objective phase of experience is, of course, what is captured in Mead's concept of the significant symbol or universal and Durkheim's concept of a collective representation.[37] In each case the symbol (or representation) is an objectification and universalization of particular experiences. Neither Mead nor Durkheim confused the universality of the symbol with its generality. For each, the objective meaning of the symbol is universal in the sense that it has currency within some social circle. As Durkheim put it: [38]

> This universality of the concept should not be confused with its generality: they are very different things. What we mean by universality is the property which the concept has of being communicable to a number of minds, and in principle, to all minds; but this communicability is wholly independent of the degree of its extension. A concept which is applied to only one object, and whose extension is consequently at the minimum, can be the same for everybody. . . .

This idea is pervasive in Mead, and it seems unnecessary to provide cited examples of the distinction.

Although Durkheim speaks of the *property* of concepts as being communicable, the main force of his argument leads him away from this conception. In the first place, while any particular symbol objectifies experience, it may be replaced by any other symbol in that more than one symbol may evoke the objectified experience: [39]

> . . . as far as religious thought is concerned, the part is equal to the whole, it has the same powers, the same efficacy. The debris of a relic has the same virtue as a relic in good condition. The smallest drop of blood contains the same active principle as the whole thing.

More important, the symbol, *per se*, is irrelevant. "Surely," Durkheim writes, "the soldier who falls while defending his flag does not believe that he sacrifices himself for a bit of cloth." [40] And Mead also insists on the irrelevancy of the concrete symbol or object: [41]

> . . . one has a nail to drive, he reaches for the hammer and finds it gone, and he does not stop to look for it, but reaches for something else he can use, a brick or a stone, anything having the necessary weight to give momentum to the blow. Anything that he can get hold of that will serve the purpose will be a hammer. That sort of response which involves the grasping of a heavy object is a universal.

In short, the meaning or relevance of symbols for both Mead and Durkheim was not in the character of the symbols themselves but in the responses that they mobilized.

On this point, Durkheim becomes explicit: [42]

---

[37] Roscoe C. Hinkle, Jr., has incisively established the relationship between the significant symbol of Mead and the collective representation of Durkheim. See his, "Durkheim in American Sociology," in Wolff (ed.), *op. cit.*, pp. 278–79.
[38] *Elementary Forms*, p. 482, note 9. Here Durkheim remains attached to the metaphor of the symbol, or collective representation, as a *thing*. On this point, he vacillates, and the vacillation is never resolved.
[39] *Ibid.*, p. 261. Although he was speaking of religion, as we have shown earlier (pp. 104–5), we may generalize the implication to all knowledge.
[40] *Ibid.*, p. 260.
[41] George Herbert Mead, *Mind, Self, and Society* (Chicago: University of Chicago Press, 1934), p. 83.
[42] *Elementary Forms*, pp. 481–82.

The concept is universal, or at least capable of becoming so. A concept is not my concept: I hold it in common with other men, or, in any case can communicate it to them. It is impossible to make a sensation pass from my consciousness into that of another; it holds closely to my organism and personality and cannot be detached from them. All that I can do is to invite others to place themselves before the same object as myself and leave themselves to its action.

Here, we see that Durkheim is, indeed, on the edge of apprehending Mead's profound conceptualization of a universe of discourse: [43]

This universe of discourse is constituted by a group of individuals carrying on and participating in a common social process of experience and behavior, within which all these gestures or symbols have the same or common meanings for all members of that group, whether they make them to other individuals, or whether they overtly respond to them as made or addressed to them by other individuals. A universe of discourse is simply a system of common or social meanings.

And for Mead, the meaning of the "hammer" is in its use, or the meaning of the symbol in the response that is made to it.

In such a way, Durkheim comes to the very edge of conceiving society as a universe of discourse, but he can not move over that edge. He holds up the symbol and awaits the action of others, and their action is construed as common or parallel. Above all, he does not inquire into his own action—how he might respond to the symbol he holds up as he waits on the action of others. Durkheim has no notion of concert, transaction, or role-taking.

Obstacles to Convergence

Although James asserted, in effect, that we have as many selves as we have group affiliations, this statement seems not to have influenced his psychologistic conception of mind. Consciousness, for James, was instrumental for bringing the *individual* into a more serene adjustment to the problematics of his existence. Thought was an instrument of individual existence. James did not speak of maintaining concerted, ongoing transactions. In other words, the means-end schema was not anchored in the transactive context. To repeat, this subjective pragmatism was unacceptable to Durkheim. It is our contention that he could easily have accepted Mead's *social* pragmatism, had it been made explicit to him at the time. Social pragmatism conceives consciousness as instrumental for the maintenance of concerted conduct. Mind is social, shared, and objective. It acts to bring individuals into a more serene adjustment to the problematics of *their* existence. But mind, for Mead, is never epiphenomenal. It is a *conversation* rooted in action. Thus, the pragmatic truth is the *conception* that keeps the conversation going or permits the conversation to overcome temporary interruptions. Even pragmatic truth for the person emerges from the dialogue—the dialogue between experience and formulation, or, as Mead would have it, the dialogue between the "I" and the "me."

In the final stages of his sociological inquiry, Durkheim would almost assuredly have accepted the position of social pragmatism, even down to the rooting of personal truth, *or faith*, in the internalized conversation between the "I" and the "me." How else could he have secured the foundation of scientific

---

[43] Mead, *op. cit.*, pp. 89–90.

knowledge in the bedrock of faith? [44] Such a conception of truth transcends the subjective perspective. This transcendence, however, can never be detached from the individual response, for the representative symbol or the objective phase of experience is established ultimately in the concerted response in which the individual, of course, plays a part. As Durkheim barely hinted in his discussion of the genesis of concepts: "The general only exists in the particular; it is the particular simplified and impoverished." [45] This is a formulation of the universal which Mead elaborates in his discussion of meaning: [46]

> Meaning is that which can be indicated to others while it is by the same process indicated to the indicating individual. In so far as the individual indicates it to himself in the role of the other, he is occupying his perspective, and as he is indicating it to the other from his own perspective, and as that which is so indicated is identical, it must be that which can be in different perspectives. It must therefore be a universal, at least in the identity which belongs to the different perspectives which are organized into the single perspective. . . .

Hence, the universal is not in the stimulus but in the collective response. As soon as we consider the response, however, we are in a position to see the essential difference between Mead and Durkheim.

As a social psychologist concerned primarily with the emergence of mind and self, Mead began from a *process orientation;* as a worried sociologist concerned with explaining solidarity or the moral value of social life, Durkheim worked from an *entity orientation.* For Durkheim a collective representation was a social "fact"—a *thing*—which in its symbolic form existed outside of man and constrained him into using it, like money or language. While it is true that it emerges out of collective life, any given individual is constrained by it. Mead, however, looks at symbols rather than the language that they comprise. Such symbols are implemented in an ongoing conversation and may be altered—indeed, they are always in the process of becoming—as responses are played back upon them by individuals. This implies that the individual is entirely capable of transforming the collective dialogue by making crucial unanticipated responses to symbols that have become conventionally established. Such unanticipated responses arise out of the individual's self-indicative or interpretive capacities.

Although Durkheim also allows for modification of the collective representation, such changes are seen as nonprocessual or mechanistic. Durkheim notes that in assimilating (not producing!) concepts, one must [47]

> . . . assimilate them to himself, for he must have them to hold intercourse with others; but the assimilation is always imperfect. Each of us sees them after his own fashion. There are some which escape us completely and remain outside of our circle of vision; there are others of which we perceive certain aspects only. There are even a great many which we pervert in holding, for as they are collective by nature, they cannot become individualized without being retouched, modified, and consequently falsified. Hence comes the great trouble we have in understanding each other. . . .

---

[44] See p. 106, above. Durkheim speaks of "collective faith," but the conversation between the "I" and the "me" is precisely one's participation in a collective dialogue. Any resolution of the dialogue places one in a universe of discourse—a social circle.

[45] *Elementary Forms,* p. 480. Again, this marks a transformation of Durkheim's metaphorical view of the individual, since he speaks of the concept "impoverishing" individual experience. Literally, Durkheim has "discovered" the individual and doesn't know what to do with him!

[46] Mead, *op. cit.,* p. 89.

[47] *Elementary Forms,* p. 484.

What Durkheim is referring to are sources of ambiguity. Notice that these sources have a spatial and locational tone which removes them from the social process. Mead takes the opposite tack. Ambiguity, for him, is part and parcel of the social process. Individuals because of their *interpretative* capacities may misformulate the conceptual meaning of any given symbol. More important is Mead's core distinction between the "I" and the "me." This distinction takes into account the fact that an individual can never be certain of his own next action. If the "I" is interpreted as a principle of pure, hence meaningless, experience, an individual can not know what he is doing until he has done it. In other words, one must have an experience before one can formulate it by referring it back to a conceptual framework—a universe of discourse or the collective *conscience*. If every activity sequence contains an element of uncertainty, or unpredictability, then each act, whether in mental, verbal, or physical form, becomes a source of change. The ongoing conversation is always in motion.

Now Durkheim could not comprehend such an ontology. For him, as we have shown, "communication" was either collision, chemical synthesis, or action-in-parallel. Durkheim never grasped the essence of communication as conversation or transaction. Moreover, society was implicitly viewed as a constraining container of its individual human particles. The walls were made of collective representations, symbols, or social facts. Men might be variously attached to them, energized by them, or cement them more firmly together as they exchanged them. When Durkheim finally came to see that the particles made the symbols or that the symbols themselves were the "things contained" and threatened to spill out over the walls that had been built by the symbols, he was confounded and groped for a new epistemology and, implicitly, a new ontology. The classical European solutions had already been transcended, and the new American pragmatism had not been fully enough developed to provide him convincing solutions—solutions in which he could have faith. He was certainly on the edge of symbolic interactionism, but he died in 1917, perhaps disenchanted by the death of his only son in World War I. At any rate, all the essentials were there, and he could not grasp them. In our view no social theorist had ever come farther over the course of his lifetime.

12   Science and Linguistics

● BENJAMIN LEE WHORF

Every normal person in the world, past infancy in years, can and does talk. By virtue of that fact, every person—civilized or uncivilized—carries through life certain naïve but deeply rooted ideas about talking and its relation to thinking. Because of their firm connection with speech habits that have become unconscious and automatic, these notions tend to be rather intolerant of opposition. They are by no means entirely personal and haphazard; their basis is definitely systematic, so that we are justified in calling them a system of natural logic—a

SOURCE: Benjamin Lee Whorf, in his *Language, Thought and Reality* (Cambridge: M.I.T. Press, 1956), pp. 207–219.

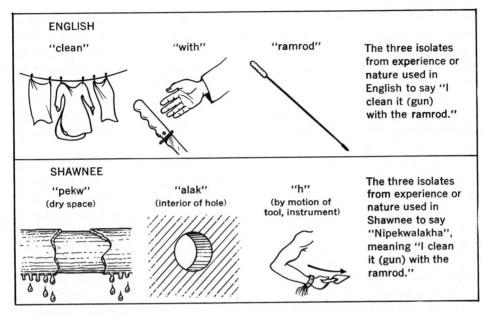

FIGURE 1.   Languages dissect nature differently. Different isolates of meaning (thoughts) are used by English and Shawnee in reporting the same experience, that of cleaning a gun by running the ramrod through it. The pronouns 'I' and 'it' are not shown by symbols, as they have the same meaning
in each language. In Shawnee, ni- equals 'I'; -a equals 'it.'

term that seems to me preferable to the term common sense, often used for the
same thing.

According to natural logic, the fact that every person has talked fluently since
infancy makes every man his own authority on the process by which he formulates and communicates. He has merely to consult a common substratum of
logic or reason which he and everyone else are supposed to possess. Natural logic
says that talking is merely an incidental process concerned strictly with communication, not with formulation of ideas. Talking, or the use of language, is
supposed only to "express" what is essentially already formulated nonlinguisti-
cally. Formulation is an independent process, called thought or thinking, and is
supposed to be largely indifferent to the nature of particular languages. Languages have grammars, which are assumed to be merely norms of conventional
and social correctness, but the use of language is supposed to be guided not so
much by them as by correct, rational, or intelligent THINKING.

Thought, in this view, does not depend on grammar but on laws of logic or
reason which are supposed to be the same for all observers of the universe—to
represent a rationale in the universe that can be "found" independently by all
intelligent observers, whether they speak Chinese or Choctaw. In our own culture, the formulations of mathematics and of formal logic have acquired the reputation of dealing with this order of things: i.e., with the realm and laws of pure
thought. Natural logic holds that different languages are essentially parallel
methods for expressing this one-and-the-same rationale of thought and, hence,
differ really in but minor ways which may seem important only because they
are seen at close range. It holds that mathematics, symbolic logic, philosophy,
and so on are systems contrasted with language which deal directly with this

realm of thought, not that they are themselves specialized extensions of language. The attitude of natural logic is well shown in an old quip about a German grammarian who devoted his whole life to the study of the dative case. From the point of view of natural logic, the dative case and grammar in general are an extremely minor issue. A different attitude is said to have been held by the ancient Arabians: Two princes, so the story goes, quarreled over the honor of putting on the shoes of the most learned grammarian of the realm; whereupon their father, the caliph, is said to have remarked that it was the glory of his kingdom that great grammarians were honored even above kings.

The familiar saying that the exception proves the rule contains a good deal of wisdom, though from the standpoint of formal logic it became an absurdity as soon as "prove" no longer meant "put on trial." The old saw began to be profound psychology from the time it ceased to have standing in logic. What it might well suggest to us today is that, if a rule has absolutely no exceptions, it is not recognized as a rule or as anything else; it is then part of the background of experience of which we tend to remain unconscious. Never having experienced anything in contrast to it, we cannot isolate it and formulate it as a rule until we so enlarge our experience and expand our base of reference that we encounter an interruption of its regularity. The situation is somewhat analogous to that of not missing the water till the well runs dry, or not realizing that we need air till we are choking.

For instance, if a race of people had the physiological defect of being able to see only the color blue, they would hardly be able to formulate the rule that they saw only blue. The term blue would convey no meaning to them, their language would lack color terms, and their words denoting their various sensations of blue would answer to, and translate, our words "light, dark, white, black," and so on, not our word "blue." In order to formulate the rule or norm of seeing only blue, they would need exceptional moments in which they saw other colors. The phenomenon of gravitation forms a rule without exceptions; needless to say, the untutored person is utterly unaware of any law of gravitation, for it would never enter his head to conceive of a universe in which bodies behaved otherwise than they do at the earth's surface. Like the color blue with our hypothetical race, the law of gravitation is a part of the untutored individual's background, not something he isolates from that background. The law could not be formulated until bodies that always fell were seen in terms of a wider astronomical world in which bodies moved in orbits or went this way and that.

Similarly, whenever we turn our heads, the image of the scene passes across our retinas exactly as it would if the scene turned around us. But this effect is background, and we do not recognize it; we do not see a room turn around us but are conscious only of having turned our heads in a stationary room. If we observe critically while turning the head or eyes quickly, we shall see no motion, it is true, yet a blurring of the scene between two clear views. Normally we are quite unconscious of this continual blurring but seem to be looking about in an unblurred world. Whenever we walk past a tree or house, its image on the retina changes just as if the tree or house were turning on an axis; yet we do not see trees or houses turn as we travel about at ordinary speeds. Sometimes ill-fitting glasses will reveal queer movements in the scene as we look about, but normally we do not see the relative motion of the environment when we move;

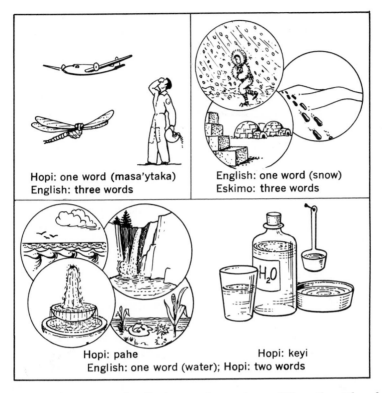

Hopi: one word (masa'ytaka)
English: three words

English: one word (snow)
Eskimo: three words

Hopi: pahe

Hopi: keyi

English: one word (water); Hopi: two words

FIGURE 2.   Languages classify items of experience differently. The class corresponding to one word and one thought in language A may be regarded by language B as two or more classes corresponding to two or more words and thoughts.

our psychic makeup is somehow adjusted to disregard whole realms of phenomena that are so all-pervasive as to be irrelevant to our daily lives and needs.

Natural logic contains two fallacies: First, it does not see that the phenomena of a language are to its own speakers largely of a background character and so are outside the critical consciousness and control of the speaker who is expounding natural logic. Hence, when anyone, as a natural logician, is talking about reason, logic, and the laws of correct thinking, he is apt to be simply marching in step with purely grammatical facts that have somewhat of a background character in his own language or family of languages but are by no means universal in all languages and in no sense a common substratum of reason. Second, natural logic confuses agreement about subject matter, attained through use of language, with knowledge of the linguistic process by which agreement is attained: i.e., with the province of the despised (and to its notion superfluous) grammarian. Two fluent speakers, of English let us say, quickly reach a point of assent about the subject matter of their speech; they agree about what their language refers to. One of them, A, can give directions that will be carried out by the other, B, to A's complete satisfaction. Because they thus understand each other so perfectly A and B, as natural logicians, suppose they must of course know how it is all done. They think, e.g., that it is simply a matter of choosing words to express thoughts. If you ask A to explain how he got *B*'s agreement so readily, he will simply repeat to you, with more or less elaboration or abbreviation, what he said to *B*. He has no notion of the process involved. The amazingly complex system of linguistic patterns and classifications, which *A* and *B* must have in common before they can adjust to each other at all, is all background to *A* and *B*.

These background phenomena are the province of the grammarian—or of the linguist, to give him his more modern name as a scientist. The word linguist in common, and especially newspaper, parlance means something entirely different, namely, a person who can quickly attain agreement about subject matter with different people speaking a number of different languages. Such a person is better termed a polyglot or a multilingual. Scientific linguists have long understood that ability to speak a language fluently does not necessarily confer a linguistic knowledge of it, i.e., understanding of its background phenomena and its systematic processes and structure, any more than ability to play a good game of billiards confers or requires any knowledge of the laws of mechanics that operate upon the billiard table.

The situation here is not unlike that in any other field of science. All real scientists have their eyes primarily on background phenomena that cut very little ice, as such, in our daily lives; and yet their studies have a way of bringing out a close relation between these unsuspected realms of fact and such decidedly foreground activities as transporting goods, preparing food, treating the sick, or growing potatoes, which in time may become very much modified, simply because of pure scientific investigation in no way concerned with these brute matters themselves. Linguistics presents a quite similar case; the background phenomena with which it deals are involved in all our foreground activities of talking and of reaching agreement, in all reasoning and arguing of cases, in all law, arbitration, conciliation, contracts, treaties, public opinion, weighing of scientific theories, formulation of scientific results. Whenever agreement or assent is arrived at in human affairs, and whether or not mathematics or other specialized symbolisms are made part of the procedure, THIS AGREEMENT IS REACHED BY LINGUISTIC PROCESSES, OR ELSE IT IS NOT REACHED.

As we have seen, an overt knowledge of the linguistic processes by which agreement is attained is not necessary to reaching some sort of agreement, but it is certainly no bar thereto; the more complicated and difficult the matter, the more such knowledge is a distinct aid, till the point may be reached—I suspect the modern world has about arrived at it—when the knowledge becomes not only an aid but a necessity. The situation may be likened to that of navigation. Every boat that sails is in the lap of planetary forces; yet a boy can pilot his small craft around a harbor without benefit of geography, astronomy, mathematics, or international politics. To the captain of an ocean liner, however, some knowledge of all these subjects is essential.

When linguists became able to examine critically and scientifically a large number of languages of widely different patterns, their base of reference was expanded; they experienced an interruption of phenomena hitherto held universal, and a whole new order of significances came into their ken. It was found that the background linguistic system (in other words, the grammar) of each language is not merely a reproducing instrument for voicing ideas but rather is itself the shaper of ideas, the program and guide for the individual's mental activity, for his analysis of impressions, for his synthesis of his mental stock in

OBJECTIVE FIELD	SPEAKER (SENDER)	HEARER (RECEIVER)	HANDLING OF TOPIC, RUNNING OF THIRD PERSON
Situation 1a.			English . . . "He is running" Hopi . . . "wari" (running, statement of fact)
Situation 1b. Objective field blank devoid of running			English . . . "He ran" Hopi . . . "wari" (running, statement of fact)
Situation 2			English . . . "He is running" Hopi . . . "wari" (running, statement of fact)
Situation 3 Objective field blank			English . . . "He ran" Hopi . . . "Era wari" (running, statement of fact from memory)
Situation 4 Objective field blank			English . . . "He will run" Hopi . . . "Warikni" (running, statement of expectation)
Situation 5 Objective field blank			English . . . "He runs" (e.g. on the track team) Hopi . . . "Warikngwe" (running, statement of law)

FIGURE 3. Contrast between a "temporal" language (English) and a "timeless" language (Hopi). What are to English differences of time are to Hopi differences in the kind of validity.

trade. Formulation of ideas is not an independent process, strictly rational in the old sense, but is part of a particular grammar, and differs, from slightly to greatly, between different grammars. We dissect nature along lines laid down by our native languages. The categories and types that we isolate from the world of phenomena we do not find there because they stare every observer in the face; on the contrary, the world is presented in a kaleidoscopic flux of impressions which has to be organized by our minds—and this means largely by the linguistic systems in our minds. We cut nature up, organize it into concepts, and ascribe significances as we do, largely because we are parties to an agreement to organize it in this way—an agreement that holds throughout our speech community and is codified in the patterns of our language. The agreement is, of course, an implicit and unstated one, BUT ITS TERMS ARE ABSOLUTELY OBLIGATORY; we cannot talk at all except by subscribing to the organization and classification of data which the agreement decrees.

This fact is very significant for modern science, for it means that no individual is free to describe nature with absolute impartiality but is constrained to certain modes of interpretation even while he thinks himself most free. The person most nearly free in such respects would be a linguist familiar with very many widely different linguistic systems. As yet no linguist is in any such position. We are thus introduced to a new principle of relativity, which holds that all observers are not led by the same physical evidence to the same picture of the universe, unless their linguistic backgrounds are similar, or can in some way be calibrated.

This rather startling conclusion is not so apparent if we compare only our modern European languages, with perhaps Latin and Greek thrown in for good measure. Among these tongues there is a unanimity of major pattern which at first seems to bear out natural logic. But this unanimity exists only because these tongues are all Indo-European dialects cut to the same basic plan, being historically transmitted from what was long ago one speech community; because the modern dialects have long shared in building up a common culture; and because much of this culture, on the more intellectual side, is derived from the linguistic backgrounds of Latin and Greek. Thus this group of languages satisfies the special case of the clause beginning "unless" in the statement of the linguistic relativity principle at the end of the preceding paragraph. From this condition follows the unanimity of description of the world in the community of modern scientists. But it must be emphasized that "all modern Indo-European-speaking observers" is not the same thing as "all observers." That modern Chinese or Turkish scientists describe the world in the same terms as Western scientists means, of course, only that they have taken over bodily the entire Western system of rationalizations, not that they have corroborated that system from their native posts of observation.

When Semitic, Chinese, Tibetan, or African languages are contrasted with our own, the divergence in analysis of the world becomes more apparent; and, when we bring in the native languages of the Americas where speech communities from many millenniums have gone their ways independently of each other and of the Old World, the fact that languages dissect nature in many different ways becomes patent. The relativity of all conceptual systems, ours included, and their dependence upon language stand revealed. That American Indians speaking only their native tongues are never called upon to act as scientific observers is in no wise to the point. To exclude the evidence which their languages offer as to what the human mind can do is like expecting botanists to study nothing but food plants and hothouse roses and then tell us what the plant world is like!

Let us consider a few examples. In English we divide most of our words into two classes, which have different grammatical and logical properties. Class 1 we call nouns, e.g., 'house, man'; class 2, verbs, e.g., 'hit, run.' Many words of one class can act secondarily as of the other class, e.g., 'a hit, a run,' or 'to man (the boat),' but, on the primary level, the division between the classes is absolute. Our language thus gives us a bipolar division of nature. But nature herself is not thus polarized. If it be said that 'strike, turn, run,' are verbs because they denote temporary or short-lasting events, i.e., actions, why then is 'fist' a noun? It also is a temporary event. Why are 'lightning, spark, wave, eddy, pulsation, flame, storm, phase, cycle, spasm, noise, emotion' nouns? They are temporary events. If 'man' and 'house' are nouns because they are long-lasting and stable events, i.e., things, what then are 'keep, adhere, extend, project, continue, persist, grow, dwell,' and so on doing among the verbs? If it be objected that 'possess, adhere' are verbs because they are stable relationships rather than stable percepts, why then should 'equilibrium, pressure, current, peace, group, nation, society, tribe, sister,' or any kinship term be among the nouns? It will be found that an "event" to us means "what our language classes as a verb" or something analogized therefrom. And it will be found that it is not possible to define 'event, thing, object, relationship,' and so on, from nature, but that to define them always involves a circuitous return to the grammatical categories of the definer's language.

In the Hopi language, 'lightning, wave, flame, meteor, puff of smoke, pulsation' are verbs—events of necessarily brief duration cannot be anything but verbs. 'Cloud' and 'storm' are at about the lower limit of duration for nouns. Hopi, you see, actually has a classification of events (or linguistic isolates) by duration type, something strange to our modes of thought. On the other hand, in Nootka, a language of Vancouver Island, all words seem to us to be verbs, but really there are no classes 1 and 2; we have, as it were, a monistic view of nature that gives us only one class of word for all kinds of events. 'A house occurs' or 'it houses' is the way of saying 'house,' exactly like 'a flame occurs' or 'it burns.' These terms seem to us like verbs because they are inflected for durational and temporal nuances, so that the suffixes of the word for house event make it mean long-lasting house, temporary house, future house, house that used to be, what started out to be a house, and so on.

Hopi has one noun that covers every thing or being that flies, with the exception of birds, which class is denoted by another noun. The former noun may be said to denote the class (FC–B)—flying class minus bird. The Hopi actually call insect, airplane, and aviator all by the same word, and feel no difficulty about it. The situation, of course, decides any possible confusion among very disparate members of a broad linguistic class, such as this class (FC–B). This class seems to us too large and inclusive, but so would our class 'snow' to an Eskimo. We have the same word for falling snow, snow on the ground, snow packed hard like ice, slushy snow, wind-driven flying snow—whatever the situation may be. To an Eskimo, this all-inclusive word would be almost unthinkable; he would say that falling snow, slushy snow, and so on, are sensuously and operationally different, different things to contend with; he uses different words for them and for other kinds of snow. The Aztecs go even farther than we in the opposite direction, with 'cold,' 'ice,' and 'snow' all represented by the same basic word with different terminations; 'ice' is the noun form; 'cold,' the adjectival form; and for 'snow,' "ice mist."

What surprises most is to find that various grand generalizations of the Western world, such as time, velocity, and matter, are not essential to the construction of a consistent picture of the universe. The psychic experiences that we class under these headings are, of course, not destroyed; rather, categories derived from other kinds of experiences take over the rulership of the cosmology and seem to function just as well. Hopi may be called a timeless language. It recognizes psychological time, which is much like Bergson's "duration," but this "time" is quite unlike the mathematical time, T, used by our physicists. Among the peculiar properties of Hopi time are that it varies with each observer, does not permit of simultaneity, and has zero dimensions; i.e., it cannot be given a number greater than one. The Hopi do not say, "I stayed five days," but "I left on the fifth day." A word referring to this kind of time, like the word day, can have no plural. The puzzle picture (Fig. 3, page 117) will give mental exercise to anyone who would like to figure out how the Hopi verb gets along without tenses. Actually, the only practical use of our tenses, in one-verb sentences, is to distinguish among five typical situations, which are symbolized in the picture. The timeless Hopi verb does not distinguish between the present, past, and future of the event itself but must always indicate what type of validity the SPEAKER intends the statement to have: (a) report of an event (situations 1, 2, 3 in the picture); (b) expectation of an event (situation 4); (c) generalization or law about events (situation 5). Situation 1, where the speaker and listener are in contact with the same objective field, is divided by our language into the two conditions, 1a and 1b, which it calls present and past, respectively. This division is unnecessary for a language which assures one that the statement is a report.

Hopi grammar, by means of its forms called aspects and modes, also makes it easy to distinguish among momentary, continued, and repeated occurrences, and to indicate the actual sequence of reported events. Thus the universe can be described without recourse to a concept of dimensional time. How would a physics constructed along these lines work, with no T (time) in its equations? Perfectly, as far as I can see, though of course it would require different ideology and perhaps different mathematics. Of course V (velocity) would have to go too. The Hopi language has no word really equivalent to our 'speed' or 'rapid.' What translates these terms is usually a word meaning intense or very, accompanying any verb of motion. Here is a clue to the nature of our new physics. We may have to introduce a new term I, intensity. Every thing and event will have an I, whether we regard the thing or event as moving or as just enduring or being. Perhaps the I of an electric charge will turn out to be its voltage, or potential. We shall use clocks to measure some intensities, or, rather, some RELATIVE intensities, for the absolute intensity of anything will be meaningless. Our old friend acceleration will still be there but doubtless under a new name. We shall perhaps call it V, meaning not velocity but variation. Perhaps all growths and accumulations will be regarded as V's. We should not have the concept of rate in the temporal sense, since, like velocity, rate introduces a mathematical and linguistic time. Of course we know that all measurements are ratios, but the measurements of intensities made by comparison with the standard intensity of a clock or a planet we do not treat as ratios, any more than we so treat a distance made by comparison with a yardstick.

A scientist from another culture that used time and velocity would have great difficulty in getting us to understand these concepts. We should talk about the intensity of a chemical reaction; he would speak of its velocity or its rate, which words we should at first think were simply words for intensity in his language. Likewise, he at first would think that intensity was simply our own word for velocity. At first we should agree, later we should begin to disagree, and it might dawn upon both sides that different systems of rationalization were being used. He would find it very hard to make us understand what he really meant by velocity of a chemical reaction. We should have no words that would fit. He would try to explain it by likening it to a running horse, to the difference between a good horse and a lazy horse. We should try to show him, with a superior laugh, that his analogy also was a matter of different intensities, aside from which there was little similarity between a horse and a chemical reaction in a beaker. We should point out that a running horse is moving relative to the ground, whereas the material in the beaker is at rest.

One significant contribution to science from the linguistic point of view may be the greater development of our sense of perspective. We shall no longer be able to see a few recent dialects of the Indo-European family, and the rationalizing techniques elaborated from their patterns, as the apex of the evolution of the human mind, nor their present wide spread as due to any survival from fitness or to anything but a few events of history—events that could be called fortunate only from the parochial point of view of the favored parties. They, and our own thought processes with them, can no longer be envisioned as spanning the gamut of reason and knowledge but only as one constellation in a galactic expanse. A fair realization of the incredible degree of diversity of linguistic system that ranges over the globe leaves one with an inescapable feeling that the human spirit is inconceivably old; that the few thousand years of history covered by our written records are no more than the thickness of a pencil mark on the scale that measures our past experience on this planet; that the events of these recent millenniums spell nothing in any evolutionary wise, that the race has taken no sudden spurt, achieved no commanding synthesis during recent millenniums, but has only played a little with a few of the linguistic formulations and views of nature bequeathed from an inexpressibly longer past. Yet neither this feeling nor the sense of precarious dependence of all we know upon linguistic tools which themselves are largely unknown need be discouraging to science but should, rather, foster that humility which accompanies the true scientific spirit, and thus forbid that arrogance of the mind which hinders real scientific curiosity and detachment.

13   A Chinese Philosopher's Theory of Knowledge

● CHANG TUNG-SUN

I

In this essay an attempt will be made to deal with theoretical knowledge in a more or less comprehensive way. It is an attempt at a theory of knowledge. For quite a number of years, the writer has had in mind the idea of elaborating more satisfactorily a hint given him in the discovery that Western philosophical problems are not exactly similar to those which were in the minds of Chinese philosophers. There seems to be some difference between the Western and Chinese intellectual processes. With this in mind, it is desirable to have our view of the Western theory of knowledge somewhat clarified. For the Western theory of

SOURCE: Chang Tung-Sun, in ETC: A Review of General Semantics. Reprinted by permission from ETC: A Review of General Semantics, IX, No. 3, pp. 203–226; copyright 1952, by the International Society for General Semantics.

This article appeared originally in the Yenching Journal of Social Studies, Vol. I, No. 2, 1939 (Peking). It is a translation, by Mr. Li An-che, of Chang Tung-Sun's original paper in Chinese which appeared in the Sociological World, Vol. X, June 1938, under the title, "Thought, Language and Culture."

knowledge has taken knowledge as the *universal* knowledge of mankind. As a matter of fact, however, it is only one kind of knowledge, other kinds being present in other cultures. Support for the view that knowledge can be studied sociologically or culturally came recently in Karl Mannheim's *Ideology and Utopia: An Introduction to the Sociology of Knowledge*. Nevertheless, there are points of difference between Mannheim and the present writer.

The sociology of knowledge, historically, has merged with Marxism. But the Marxian interpretation of society is different from the point of view to be elaborated here in that it laid its emphasis on the antagonism of economic classes. Its sociology of knowledge is, therefore, characterized by class interests. In other words, it is nothing but an attempt to give knowledge its background in class struggles. This theory of knowledge cannot be properly called a sociological theory of knowledge but rather a class interpretation of knowledge. It is evident that the influence of social relations upon thought will not be adequately accounted for merely in terms of economic interests. Mannheim's merit lies in the fact that he has transcended this limit. Still there is much to be desired in his work, because it has been entirely in the field of concrete thought, or the prevalent thought of a given time, such as particular "isms" and theories. It is legitimate, of course, to analyze the social relations underlying such thought, but we must realize that in concrete social thought, there are also categories employed, and these categories themselves can also be analyzed from the sociological point of view. The attempt of this essay is primarily concerned with the latter, that is, the categories used in social thought. In other words, our interest here lies more in the structures underlying thought than in concrete thought as such.

By the nature of the problem our approach should be similar to that of Kant. The Kantian type of interest in knowledge is concerned with the fundamental conditions of knowledge, and to this extent the Kantian theory of knowledge seems to be acceptable, for a theory of knowledge should be a study of the forms of knowledge without touching upon its contents. But a sociological theory of knowledge will inevitably go beyond Kant, for Kant himself thought that he was treating the universal categories employed in the thinking process of all mankind, while as a matter of fact he has treated the forms of thought characteristic only of Western culture. Yet it is not to be taken to mean that it is not possible to have universal categories applying to human thought in general, or that only ethnically and culturally determined forms of thought are possible. Universal categories for human thought may be recognized, but not those defined by Kant. The Kantian theory of knowledge is within the limits of the Western type of knowledge; he attempted to establish a foundation for the great tradition of the West. He himself, of course, was influenced by his time and the culture of the Western tradition. He attempted to use the problem of knowledge to make a new approach to metaphysics in order to revive it. In his view, should he succeed in establishing the non-empirical aspect of human *understanding*, his metaphysics, as a prelude to the philosophy of life, would be on solid ground. Our problem today does not seem to be parallel with his.

We are in need of a theory of knowledge, but its use is not for the support of metaphysics. Our attitude, therefore, is different from that of Kant. It is nearer to that of Spengler. Following the latter, we may attribute the genesis and differences of the categories of thought to cultural differences. A given culture must have a given set of categories. This does not mean that a given culture is derived from a given set of categories, or that a given set of categories gives birth to a given culture. It means that the establishment of culture and categories is one and the same thing. The formation of a given culture lies in the use of a given set of categories, but the relation between them is not in terms of cause and effect. They are two aspects of the same entity.

Being a philosopher and not a student of cultural anthropology or any other social science, the writer's treatment of knowledge from the cultural point of view may not necessarily be in agreement with that of the cultural and social scientists. The point of view expounded here arises from the findings of the history of philosophy. It is for the social scientist to revise or modify this contribution if necessary.

To recapitulate thus far: firstly, a theory of knowledge and cultural history must be treated simultaneously; secondly, not only does concrete social thought have its social background but logical forms and theoretical categories also have their cultural determinants; thirdly, the difference between Western and Eastern thought can be explained from this point of view; fourthly, from this we may understand that Western philosophy is nothing but a particular form of knowledge characteristic of and for the use of Western culture. All these points will be further elaborated in the following pages in which an attempt will be made to establish a new theory of knowledge.

II

Before proceeding further, it is well to distinguish the various types of knowledge. Generally speaking, there are two kinds of knowledge, the perceptual and the conceptual. Take a table or a chair for instance. It can be touched and perceived directly. This is perceptual knowledge. The uniformity of nature and the idea of a Supreme Being, on the other hand, cannot be verified by the senses, and causality, teleology, and the like are also conceptual in nature. It may be noted that perceptual knowledge cannot be outside the conceptual, nor can conceptual knowledge be separated from the perceptual. As a matter of fact, any conceptual knowledge contains perceptual elements and vice versa. The differentiation between the two is always for the mere convenience of discussion. They do not exist separately.

The kind of knowledge treated in this essay, it will be seen, is not perceptual but conceptual knowledge. In so far as the conceptual guides the perceptual, the importance of the former surpasses that of the latter. This point is often neglected by the empiricists, but from the standpoint of cultural history it is desirable to have it emphasized.

Conceptual knowledge is also interpretative in nature. By interpretation we understand the manipulation of concepts and the employment of categories. For instance the apprehension of a flower is a perception, but it is an interpretation to say that flowers are derived from leaves, or that the formation of the flower is for the purpose of reproduction. In an interpretation of this kind at least the following concepts are being used: any event must have its antecedent; each change must have its cause; and, the final result in a concept of evolution is so much the more derived from interpretation. Therefore, interpretative knowledge, because it contains concepts and results in concepts, is conceptual knowledge.[1] The manipulation of concepts is for the purpose of interpreting perceived facts. Thus, it is evident that conceptual knowledge is interpretative knowledge, and interpretative knowledge is theoretical knowledge.

At this point we may mention the thesis of Pareto,[2] the Italian sociologist, for purposes of comparison. According to him, theoretical knowledge has very mixed elements: descriptive elements, axiomatic elements, concrete elements, and imaginary elements, in addition to those appealing to sentiments and beliefs. He also classifies theoretical knowledge into two kinds: the experimental and the non-experimental. And, with these two as *matter* he has as *nexus* the logical and the non-logical. Thus there are four classes, the logico-experimental, the non-logico-experimental, the logico-non-experimental, and the non-logico-non-experimental. In this connection we are not interested in developing his theory, but merely in pointing out that his experimental knowledge is outside the theoretical knowledge discussed herewith.

His distinction between the logical and the non-logical indicates that the non-logical is not very important, but the term "the logical" itself seems very ambiguous. The thought of man may not necessarily be in agreement with formal logic, but it cannot be otherwise than in agreement with *a* logic. We are treating, therefore, not formal logic but real logic. The type of logic used by Chinese philosophers is different from that of the West, while the Hindus may have a logic different from both the Chinese and the Western. Logic follows the trend of culture. Western scholars often mistake their logic for the universal logic of mankind, as we have seen in the case of Kant. We will have more to say on this point later. It suffices here to say that the distinction between the logical and the non-logical is of no particular importance, because there is no theoretical knowledge which does not imply real logic. It sounds like nonsense to speak of non-logical theoretical knowledge. Pareto has made a real point in saying that approval and disapproval of non-experimental knowledge depends upon sentiment, and thereby speaks of the "logic of sentiment." But from the logic of sentiment we must exclude experimental knowledge before we can go any further. What we are interested in here is a kind of knowledge which is both interpretative and conceptual and outside the experimental.

The newly arisen Vienna school has noted this point. Carnap, for example, has made a distinction between the problems of facts and the problems of logic.[3] The former are those arising from facts while the latter are problems of words symbolizing things, and of the judgments which are made about things. This distinction may be of use by bringing before us the fact that much of our knowledge is not directly related to things, but merely to views about things. This kind of knowledge has a great place in human life. In our discussion we are dealing with this kind of knowledge which in concrete cases is comprised of political thought, social thought, philosophical thought, and moral points of view, as well as the theoretical part of religious beliefs. Scientific knowledge, apart from its experimental elements, belongs here also in the form of interpretative theory.

It is worthwhile to note that experimental knowledge is guided by conceptual

---

[1] [Compare Charles Morris's discussion of "post-language signs" in his "Comments on Mysticism and Its Language," *ETC.*, 9:3–8, Autumn, 1951. Ed.]
[2] Vilfredo Pareto, *The Mind and Society*, tr. Andrew Bongiorno and Arthur Livingston (New York 1935), I, 8 ff.
[3] Rudolf Carnap, *The Logical Syntax of Language* (London 1937), 277.

knowledge. Whitehead is very clear on this point.[4] According to him, science is a synthesis of two kinds of knowledge, one direct observation, the other interpretation. Thus he speaks of "observational order" and "conceptual order." The former is explained as well as supplemented by the latter. Points of view among scholars may differ as to the priority of the two, but since the emergence of higher animal forms, both of them have co-existed. New observations may modify original concepts while new concepts may lead to new points of observation. We may take the evolution of physics as an example. Newtonian physics starts with matter in the form of concrete things. Hence the conceptions of absolute motion, and absolute space and time. But modern physics takes cognizance of concrete matter only as a point in the framework of time and space. Hence, what Whitehead calls "simple location" is discarded. From this it may be seen that the development of physics follows the conceptual scheme which is employed in it. In addition to Whitehead, V. F. Lenzen, the American physicist, in his *The Nature of Physical Theory* has illustrated the changes and developments of physical concepts in relation to physics. In the field of biology, Woodger in his recent book, *The Axiomatic Method in Biology,* has also demonstrated very clearly that categories have guided observation. All these examples show that experimental knowledge is perceptually derived knowledge which is guided and influenced by underlying non-experimental knowledge or conceptual knowledge. It is easy to see that experimental knowledge can modify conceptual knowledge, while it is not so obvious to many people that conceptual knowledge may be underlying and guiding the perceptual knowledge.

Another point to be made concerns the social nature of conceptual knowledge. All experimental knowledge is derived from the senses, and thus is individual and private, in other words, non-social. Consequently, perceptual knowledge can hardly be social knowledge. Yet no knowledge can do away with its social content, the emergence and existence of which occur only in the field of interpretative knowledge. S. Alexander [5] has pointed out that the problem of valuation has a social nature, and that without presupposing society we cannot speak of value. It is needless to say that valuation is possible only in the field of interpretative knowledge. So far as perceptual knowledge is concerned, by the nature of the fact that it is private and individual, there is no problem of objective valuation. The importance of perceptual knowledge is self-evident, while non-experimental knowledge is apparently unimportant because its importance is not so evident, though nevertheless real.

III

The reason for the social nature of theoretical knowledge is not far to seek; it is that it is thinking expressed in terms of language, which in scientific terminology is called "linguistic thinking." It is needless to say that language is a social product. Although the child's language has a stage of monologue, it is self-evident that language implies or presupposes an audience. Primitive man, we are told, often takes language as a concrete entity. The lower the culture, the greater the power of words. In primitive society language has magical power, therefore there is a direct connection between language and thought. If a

4 Alfred North Whitehead, *Adventures in Ideas* (New York 1933), ch. 9.
5 Samuel Alexander, *Space, Time and Deity* (London 1920).

primitive man is accused of being a thief, he most certainly becomes angry. But in modern society a sophisticated person can turn aside this accusation by a smile, provided he is innocent. We may take the degree of the power of words as a gauge to measure the development of an ethnic intellectual development. This point has been sufficiently demonstrated by modern students of child psychology and "primitive mentality," so we do not need to dwell upon it any further.

The arguments thus far seem to reveal the discrepancy between language and things, and thus to advocate the emancipation of thought from language. Almost all the philosophers, from remote times to our own, have been aware of the limitations imposed by language, with the implication that real thinking cannot be clothed in language. The ordinary view is something like this: thought is primary, and with new terms thought has a better chance for expression. But this argument does not necessarily reveal the nature of the development of human thought. As a matter of fact, it is better to say that language has been a contributing factor rather than an obstacle to the development of thought. Viewing human history as a whole, any new creation in language, e.g., new terminology, represents a development of thought along a new line. Language and thought are fundamentally indivisible. Any thought can only be articulated through language or symbol. That which cannot be thus articulated most likely will not be counted as thought. Although language and thought cannot be absolutely identified, they cannot be separated. It is not that language limits thought or hinders it, but rather that language creates thought and develops it. Should we consider the two points together, namely, that thought develops with language and that language is a form of social behavior, it will be clear that apart from the experimental elements all knowledge is social.

With the cognizance of the determination of thought by social conditions, there develops the sociology of knowledge. But the sociology of knowledge has shown only that human thought is determined by socially visible or invisible forces without realizing that apart from all these immediate concrete forces there are underlying social forces of a remote nature. We may identify these remote forces with cultural relations. All thought, in addition to being influenced by our immediate social environment, is also moulded by our remote cultural heritage. The immediate forces determine the trend of our thought, while the remote cultural heritage determines the forms in which thought is made possible. All these forces help to determine interpretative knowledge. With different interpretations come different cultures. And, being born into different cultures people learn to interpret differently: Thus we may use culture to explain categories, and categories to explain mental differences, e.g., those between the West and the East.

IV

With regard to types of language, a distinction may be observed between "emotive language" and "referential language." The first is used to arouse, with necessary gestures and appropriate sounds, the corresponding gestures or mental attitudes in the person to whom they are addressed. The latter is used to refer to things and ideas about things, largely in terms of organized symbols or articulate language. According to Darwin, the animal expressions in the form of singing and roaring may be taken as the precursors of human language. Thus emotive language is nearer to elemental expressions and more concerned with mental attitudes while referential language, being nearer to abstract thinking, is more concerned with grammatical constructions than mere changes in sounds.

With grammar and sentence-structure comes logic, and in this connection we have to deal for a moment with the nature of logic. Western logicians take it for granted that the object of logic is rules of human reasoning. This assumption, however, is not quite justified. Take aristotelian logic, for example, which is evidently based on Greek grammar. The differences between Latin, French, English, and German grammatical forms do not result in any difference between aristotelian logic and their respective rules of reasoning, because they belong to the same Indo-European linguistic family. Should this logic be applied to Chinese thought, it will prove inappropriate. This fact shows that aristotelian logic is based on the structure of the Western system of language. Therefore, we should not follow Western logicians in taking for granted that their logic is the universal rule of human reasoning.[6]

In so far as the object of logic lies in the rules of reasoning implied in language, the expression of reasoning must be implicitly influenced by language-structure, and different languages will have more or less different forms of logic. Hence the difference between Chinese logic and aristotelian logic. The traditional type of subject-predicate proposition is absent in Chinese logic. According to the usage of Western logic, in such a sentence as "A relates to B" the form is not a subject-predicate proposition but a relational proposition. Another sentence like "A is related to B" is in the form in question, because there is the distinction between the subject and predicate. For both forms, however, there is in literary Chinese only one, that is, *chia lien yi* 甲 連 乙 . Although we may say colloquially *chia shih lien yi* 甲 是 連 乙, the function of the *shih* is that of the so-called "empty words" 虛 字, which are used only for emphasis or intonation, without any grammatical function. Both of these Chinese propositions mean the same thing, without grammatical distinction except that the latter is more emphatic. Neither is a subject-predicate proposition. *Lien* relates the two terms *chia* and *yi* but it is not a copula.

Regarding the "empty words" such as *che* 者 , *yeh* 也 , *hu* 乎 , *tsai* 哉 , *yi* 矣 , *wei* 爲 , and so forth, they were not primarily so, their original meaning having been lost. Their function is based on their sounds. As such sounds do not have proper characters, they are represented by characters of similar sounds, which are called "borrowed" 假 借 words. Such a "borrowed" use denotes only the sound without any implications as to meaning. The original characters had their own meaning. For example, the *wei* 爲 mentioned a moment ago originally meant *hou* 猴 or "apes." It is the sound, not the meaning of the original which is borrowed. In the formula ". . . *che* 者 . . . *yeh* 也 ," *che* serves the function of a comma and *yeh* that of a full stop. According to the types of language mentioned above, the referential and the emotive, the Chinese "empty words" are emotive words. These empty-emotive words are closely related to the ideographic nature of Chinese characters, on which we will have more to say later. Now it suffices to say that aristotelian logic is based on the sentence structure characterized by the subject-predicate form. Should we alter the sentence structure, the validity of the traditional aristotelian logic may be questioned. With these preliminary remarks we may proceed to a discussion of the differences between the Western linguistic family and the Chinese language, and their respective influences on logic.

---

6 [See S. I. Hayakawa, "What is Meant by Aristotelian Structure of Language?" *ETC*. 5:225–230, Summer 1948. Ed.]

V

Western thought is in the last analysis confined to aristotelian logic although later developments in logic have gone beyond the aristotelian type. Modern mathematical logic, for example, is only an extension of formal logic. In no way can it unify all the forms of logic. The reason why Bertrand Russell is opposed to the idea of substance lies entirely in the fact that he has discovered a new logic not based upon the form of subject-predicate proposition. As a matter of fact, however, this new system of logic applies, apart from mathematics, only to the physical sciences. It is not applicable to the social sciences. Therefore, traditional logic is still the "living logic" in the mind of Western thinkers. Now it can be shown that the "ten categories" and the later modified "five predicables" in aristotelian logic are based on Greek grammar. And so long as definition and division are derived from the "ten categories" and the "five predicables" they in their turn are limited by Greek grammar. The "fallacies" pointed out by Aristotle are essentially those found in the Greek language.

Apart from the obvious examples mentioned above, the basis of aristotelian logic may be seen definitely to lie in the subject-predicate form of language structure. It is seen in the English sentence "it is," which means "it exists." The verb "to be" has the meaning of existence, and Western logic is closely related to the verb "to be" in Western languages. It must have occurred to the readers of Plato that the verb "to be" is quite rich in meaning. Many philosophical problems come from it. Because the verb "to be" has the meaning of existence, the "law of identity" is inherent in Western logic; without it there can be no logical inference. Western logic, therefore, may be called "identity-logic."

The law of identity does not merely control logical operations such as deductions and inferences but also influences concepts of thought. As we know, Aristotle's philosophy was made possible entirely by the use of "identity-logic." For him the substance is merely derived from the subject and the verb "to be." From the latter, because its implication of existence leads naturally to the idea of "being," and from the former because in a subject-predicate proposition the subject cannot be eliminated. From the indispensability of the subject in a sentence, only a short step leads to the necessity for a "substratum" in thought. For example, when we say, "this is yellow and hard," yellowness and hardness are the so-called "attributes" which are attributed to something, the something in this case being "this." The "something" in general is the substratum. With a substratum emerges the idea of "substance." The idea of substance is indeed a foundation or fountainhead for all other philosophical developments. If there is any description, it becomes an attribute. An attribute must be attributed to a substance, thus the idea of substance is absolutely necessary in thought in the same way as the subject is absolutely necessary in language. This is the reason why in the history of Western philosophy, no matter how different the arguments may be, pro or con, about the idea of substance, it is the idea of substance which itself constitutes the central problem.[7]

The English word "it" also has its own peculiarities. It is a non-definitive. It denotes *something*, but not what. Once the *what* is stated there develop the

7 [On subject-predicate structure, see A. Korzybski, *Science and Sanity: An Introduction to Non-Aristotelian Systems and General Semantics* (Lancaster, Pa. 1933), pp. 62, 85, 92, 131, 189, 190, 224, 306, 371. On "substance," see A. J. Ayer, *Language, Truth and Logic* (New York 1936), pp. 28, 32–3, 50, 195. Ed.]

subject and predicate, or in other words, the substance is characterized by its attributes and the attributes are attributed to the substance. Thus, the separation between existence and whatness was the fundamental condition under which the concept of the substance was born. And this condition is expressed only in Western language-structure. It may be agreed then, after considering the peculiarities of the verb "to be" and the word "it," that many philosophical problems are merely problems of language.[8]

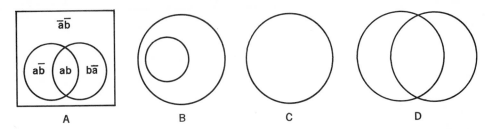

The Chinese language has its own peculiarities. First, it is not essential for a Chinese sentence to have a subject. It is often understood. In a sentence like *hsueh erh shih hsi chih pu yi yueh hu* 學而時習之, 不亦悅乎 ("When we study and constantly review it, is it not pleasant?"), or *kou chih yu jen yi wu o yeh* 苟志於仁矣, 無惡也 ("If there is devotion to benevolence, there is no evil"), the subject is eliminated. Examples of this kind are too numerous to mention. The above two are random examples from the *Analects*. Secondly, in Chinese there is no verb "to be" comparable to the English form. The colloquial *shih* 是 does not convey the idea of existence. The literary *wei* 為 on the other hand conveys an idea of *ch'eng* 成 which means "to become." But in English "becoming" is exactly opposite to "being." Such a formula as ". . . *che* 者 . . . *yeh* 也 " does not mean anything identical, and consequently does not constitute a logical proposition in the Western sense. If we say *"jen che jen yeh"* 仁者人也, we cannot say the first 仁 is the subject and the second 人 the predicate. In such a sentence the idea cannot be expressed diagrammatically, as is often used in Figure A in the case of Western logic.

The other figures B, C, D cannot convey the exact idea of the sentence. It may be either of the three, or it may be in between the three. This is the best proof of the absence of the word "to be" in Chinese.

VI

We have seen above that Western logic is essentially based upon the law of identity.[9] Division, definition, syllogism, and even conversion and opposition are based upon it. All these are correlated and constitute a system. The basic structure of Chinese thought is different from this system. The Chinese system of logic, *if we may call it a system, is not based upon the law of identity.*

---

[8] This view differs from that of the Vienna school in that, according to that school, once language is clearly defined, some problems will cease to exist. But it seems to me that there are problems arising from language which indicate emotive drives which cannot be eliminated.
[9] The rules of "contradiction" and "excluded middle" are simply corollaries of the law of identity.

Let us begin with Western logical division. As it is based on the law of identity, it must be dichotomous in such forms as "A and not-A," "literary books and non-literary books." Cases like "A and B" or "Good and Evil" are not dichotomous in form because besides A and B there may be C and besides Good and Evil there may be Not-Good and Not-Evil. Thus, there is the need in classification for the rule of exclusiveness. But Chinese thought puts no emphasis on exclusiveness, rather it emphasizes the relational quality between above and below, good and evil, something and nothing. All these relatives are supposed to be interdependent. In a sentence like *yu wu hsiang sheng, nan i hsiang ch'eng, ch'ang tuan hsiang chiao, ch'ien hou hsiang sui* 有 無 相 生 , 難 易 相 成, 長 短 相 較, 前 後 相 隨 ("Something and nothing are mutually generative; the difficult and the easy are mutually complementary; the long and short are mutually relative; the front and the rear are mutually accompanying"), we have a logic of a quite different nature.

Next we come to the discussion of definition. In Western logical definition it is necessary to make the sign of equation between the "definiendum" and the "definiens." For example, "a triangle is a portion of a plane bounded by three straight lines." But in Chinese thought the problem of equation between the two is never thought of. For example, "wife" is denoted as "a woman who has a husband."

This cannot constitute a definition in Western logic, in which it must be condemned as a fallacy, or as begging the question, but it is characteristic of Chinese logic. *Chuan chu* 轉 註 or the "inverted use of a word" in classical commentaries belongs to the same category. So also the "metaphoric" use or *chiâ chieh* 假 借 . The most important concept in ancient China might be said to be concerned with "heaven" (*t'ien* 天), but according to the definition in the *Shuo Wen* 說 文 , *t'ien* means the "human head" or that which is above the head 天 者 顛 也 . It is evident that that which is above the head may not necessarily be "heaven. There may be many other things such as clouds, wind, the moon, birds, and what not. This "indicative" method of definition 指 事 的 訓 詁 is quite different from the Western type. Examples of this sort of definition, such as 仁 者 人 也, 義 者 宜 也 are too numerous in the Chinese Classics to need mention here. It suffices here to point out that in addition to its difference from the Western type of definition, a Chinese term may also be explained or indicated by another term similar in sound and associated in meaning. To explain a term by means of others of similar sound is inconceivable in Western logic, for Western logic always aspires to be detached from language, and the explanation by means of sound is merely linguistic, it contains no logical implications. In short, it may even be safe to say that ancient Chinese literature contains no such method of definition as that found in the West.

It may be well at this juncture to discuss the Chinese characters *fei* 非 and *pu* 不 . In an English sentence like "A is not-B" or "A is not B" the affirmative or negative nature is easily determined. But if in Chinese we say *chia fei yi* 甲 非 乙 , it may mean either the first or the second. The difficulty is not so apparent in this simple proposition, but it is clear that conversion is unnecessary and opposition impossible. In the nature of the case it is, therefore, evident that Chinese thought cannot be placed in the Western logical framework. We must give it an independent name.

It may be proposed to call this type of logic "correlation-logic" or "the logic of correlative duality." This type of logic emphasizes the relational significance between something and nothing, between above and below, and so on. It is expressed sufficiently in the *Book of Changes* 周易. Although modern archaeologists may not accept the *Book of Changes* as one of the earliest records, we cannot say that it does not contain the traditional thought of China. The most dominant note here is the so-called *i yin i yang chih wei tao* 一陰一陽之爲道 ("The positive and negative principles constitute what is called *tao* or nature"). With *yang* 陽 or the positive principle we presuppose the *yin* 陰 or the negative principle, and with the *yin* we presuppose the *yang*. Each is dependent upon the other for its completion. Other examples like *kang* 剛 and *jou* 柔, *chin* 進 and *t'ui* 退, and *chi* 吉 and *hsiung* 凶 are exactly similar.[10] Should we wish to adopt a terminology much in vogue, we might call this way of thinking an illustration of "dialectical logic." But this term is very ambiguous, and its historical allusions do not allow it to be adopted in this connection. We will have to be content with noticing that Chinese ways of thinking are different from those characterized by the use of the law of identity. Without defining the different terms used, it is impossible to speak intelligibly in the West. But the Chinese language, which is characterized by the use of correlation-logic, has nothing to do with identification. Rather it uses antonyms to make an idea complete.

Opposition as a means of expression is not only used in propositions like "death without passing away," "a great sound but scarcely audible," "the greatest omen without being visible," "non-resistance means strength," or "the most fluent speech seems to stutter," but it is also used to denote a single term. In the *Shuo Wen*, for example, "outgoing" 出 means "incoming" 進 and "disorder" 亂 means "order" 治. In this case, it is better not to consider the words as having contradictory meanings, because it is the meaning, not the word, which awaits its opposite for a complete illustration of the connotation. For example, *ch'u* 出 must wait for *chin* 進 ("incoming"). Without *chin* there cannot be *ch'u*. Other examples such as *luan* 亂 ("disorder") and *chih* 治 ("order"), and *kung* 貢 ("tribute") and *tz'u* 賜 ("grants") are similar in nature. The explanation of the word "to sell" is also given by means of its opposite "to buy." "To sell" and "to buy" in contrast to each other become clearer, because buying and selling constitute the same transaction when viewed from the different standpoints of the buyer and seller. From this it is seen that Chinese thought is not based upon the law of identity, but takes as its starting point relative orientation or rather the relation of opposites. This type of thought evidently constitutes a different system. This system is probably related to the nature of Chinese characters. Being ideographic 象形 Chinese characters put emphasis on the signs or symbols of objects. The Chinese are merely interested in the inter-relations between the different signs, without being bothered by the substance underlying them. Hence the relational or correlational consideration.

VII

The ideographic nature of Chinese characters influences not only the structure of the Chinese language but also the thought or philosophy of the people as well. The *Book of Changes* may be taken as the best example. Most probably words were originally coined as token-symbols. Thus, it is said "the sage

---

[10] Emotive and phlegmatic, assertive and resigned, lucky and unlucky.

arranged diagrams 卦 in order to see the significance of any sign 象 ." Although we are not quite justified in saying that the diagrams are the original Chinese characters, it may at least be granted that they are similar in nature to Chinese characters. The creation of the diagrams served the purpose of divination, but there must have been previously arranged limits of possible combinations for the purpose of divination. Each combination is a possible sign. "Heaven indicates good and bad fortune by signs which are signified by the sages." The "sages" must have been such heroes of cultural history as Pao Hsi Shih 包犧氏, to whom the discovery of the diagrams was attributed. It may be said that the signs do not merely symbolize something external but also indicate possible changes. For example, it was from the *yi* 益 diagram that farming implements 耜耒 were invented, and from the *li* 離 diagram that fishing nets 網罟 were invented. Dr. Hu Shih has well said, "Confucius was of the opinion that with the genesis of the signs there come things. The signs are the primeval archetypes after which things are modeled."

According to ancient Chinese thought, first came the signs then the development of things. This assertion is quite different from that of the West. Although platonic ideas have a superficial resemblance, it must be remembered that Plato's "ideas" are self-existent, which is not true in the case of the eight diagrams. As we have seen, Western thought is consistently based on the idea of substance. Consequently there is the need for a substratum, and the final result of this trend of thought gives rise to the idea of "pure matter." It is characteristic of Western philosophy to penetrate into the background of a thing, while the characteristic of Chinese thought lies in exclusive attention to the correlational implications between different signs, such as *yin* and *yang*, *ho* 圖 ("involution") and *p'i* 闢 ("evolution"). It is also because of this fact that there is no trace of the idea of substance in Chinese thought. It should be noted that the presence of an idea gives rise to word-forms with which to express it. In China there is no such word as substance. Such words as *t'i* 體 ("body") and *yung* 用 ("function"), *neng* 能 ("knowing") and *so* 所 ("known") in their function of expressing subject and object came from the translation of the Buddhistic scriptures. It makes no difference to the Chinese mind, whether or not there is any ultimate substratum underlying all things. Because the Chinese characters are ideographic, Chinese thought takes cognizance only of the signs and the relations between them.

It must be evident thus far that there is not only a close relation between logic and language, but that a logical system must presuppose a philosophy, that is, cosmology and the philosophy of life. Chinese cosmology may be called "significism" 唯象論 or "omenism." The Chinese character *hsiang* 象 which we have translated as "sign" has all the meanings of the English words phenomenon, symbol, and omen, but it must be noted that behind the *hsiang* no concrete things are implied. Its signification is only concerned with human affairs. Thus a sign is for the purpose of giving lessons to the people, and consequently, all the heavenly phenomena such as stars and comets were taken as evil omens. The Chinese cosmogony characterized by omenism is essentially a practical guide to human life. In this point it also differs from the West. It may be true that in Western philosophy, cosomology is a preliminary step to the philosophy of life, but the two cannot be confused. Chinese thought, on the contrary, does not make any distinction between the cosmos and all the problems of human life.

According to Western tradition philosophy may be classified into ontology, cosmology, and the philosophy of life. In China there are only cosmogony and the philosophy of life, without any ontology or cosmology proper, and even cosmogony is absorbed into the philosophy of life. The reason for this lies in the neglect of the law of identity on the part of Chinese thinkers. Even such expressions in the *Lao Tzu* 老子 as 天地根 "*t'ien ti ken*" and 道紀 "*tao chi*" are only concerned with the origin of the universe. In spite of the fact that the later development in the *Chuang Tzu* 莊子 , in such a sentence as "whether an object is made or unmade it remains same thing," is often alleged to be similar to Western substance, the aim of *Chuang Tzu* is only "the proper degree of adjustment." Consequently, his identification of the cosmos with the self is only a sort of mystic experience. In other words, he is concerned with "participation" or "transduction" [11] rather than with the problem of existence. The book *Chuang Tzu* has a mixed origin. It is doubtful whether there may not have been insertions and alterations on the part of the Wei and Chin scholars, but it is evident that the author's ideas are more or less similar to those of the Hindus.

The later cognizance of the problem of substance on the part of the Chinese is due to the influence of India. The ethical systems of the Sung and Ming dynasties are merely reactions against Buddhism. It is often said that Western philosophy began with the idea of substance and later got rid of it, and that China originally did not have it—but later acquired it. She acquired it through cultural contact, a fact which raises problems which cannot be discussed here. Our problem is whether or not there are original forces which still underlie Chinese thought, whether, for example, the Chinese mind is still characterized by neglect of the idea of substance. The weight of evidence, in spite of abundant Western influence, is that it is.

VIII

Because the idea of substance is related to the idea of causality most of the sciences are still determined by the concept of causality. At this point it may be said that Kant was the first to reveal the mystery of Western thought. He is not surpassed by anyone, even today. He puts the idea of reciprocity between the ideas of substance and causality in order to make the three interdependent. Consequently, wherever there is causality there must be reciprocity, and wherever there is reciprocity there must be substance. No one of the three is dispensable. From this we may learn that the idea of causality is derived from that of substance. That causality is later combined with substance gives rise to the idea of the atom. On this ground is based our thesis that in Western thought religion, science, and materialism are interdependent, a position which is not taken by recent Chinese scholars.

Roughly speaking, there are two forms of religion in the West, the early Greek type and the Christian type. The first is neither monopolized by the Greeks nor is it exclusively Western. It is similar to that of the early Chinese life. It should be remembered in this connection that in Greek mythology there are potentialities of materialism. And the early religion of China, as of all early societies, was close to Nature. But when theology developed it had to be based

---

[11] These terms are borrowed from Jean Piaget, *The Child's Conception of the World* (New York and London, 1929).

upon the idea of substance. The idea of the Supreme Being or a Creator is closely correlated with the idea of Substance. Furthermore, it is also closely connected with the idea of identity. Metaphysics, which is based on substance, is religion. An Ultimate Reality is in essence God. Thus it may be maintained that metaphysical or ontological philosophy is a type of religious thought. The logic characterized by the law of identity underlies this type of religious thinking. Finally, it may be said that ontology in philosophy, the idea of God in religion, and the law of identity in logic are in essence one and the same thing.

Spengler [12] has shown that "there is no natural Science without a precedent Religion." Whitehead also maintains that the development of modern science was closely related to the religious beliefs of the medieval ages. So long as science is related to religion it is to be understood that in Western culture the two are but different streams from the same fountainhead. They are not so much opposed as ordinarily assumed. But this should not be understood in causal terms; the one does not determine the other, they are both parallel developments from a common origin. Thus although science and religion are opposed to each other on the surface, they are not opposed in their innermost nature.

Furthermore, Spengler has informed us that Catholic cosmology and materialism are not different things, but the same thing expressed in different terminology. Leaving aside Catholicism, we may say that materialistic thought is based on the idea of atoms, and the idea of atoms is related to the ideas of substance and causality. We may maintain that there are three fundamental categories in Western thought, substance, causality, and atoms. Religion has a foundation in substance. With causality science is developed, and from atoms materialism is derived. Behind these three categories there is another to string them together, namely, that of identity. The French philosopher Meyerson has done a service in pointing out that all scientific theories and quests are concerned with identity.[13] It may be easily seen that with identity there must be substance; with substance there must be causality; and the atom is between the two. Thus Western thought is essentially based on these four categories. Without understanding the importance and priority of these categories, we cannot thoroughly understand Western culture and thought.

Chinese culture, on the other hand, has no relation whatsoever to the above-mentioned categories. Let us begin with early religious life in China. The Chinese religious life is not very unlike that of the Greeks. Yet religious ideas in China were not associated with the rituals of worship and the institution of official temples. It is not certain whether there were any other deities before the concept of Heaven arose. But so far as Heaven 天 and God 帝 are concerned, the Chinese have never been concerned with them primarily. When we speak of Heaven we have in mind only Providence 天意, which is merely a manifestation of Heaven. In other words the Chinese are concerned with the will of Heaven without being too particular about Heaven itself, because according to the Chinese point of view the will of Heaven is Heaven itself, and to inquire into Heaven without paying attention to its will is logically inconceivable in China. Heaven and the will of Heaven are the same thing. There is not first Heaven and later the manifestation of its will. Because Heaven and its will are identical, the Chinese have never considered Heaven as an entity, and so long as it is not an entity it is not a sub-

---

[12] Oswald Spengler, *The Decline of the West* (London 1926–28), I, 380.
[13] Emile Meyerson, *Identity and Reality* (New York 1930).

stance. Thus the Chinese Heaven has no relation whatsoever to the Western substance . . . Through divination the gap between man and Heaven is bridged. The Chinese are only interested in knowing the will of Heaven in order to seek good fortune and to avoid misfortune. As to the nature of Heaven as such they are indifferent. This fact shows that the Chinese have not applied the category of substance to the idea of Heaven and have not taken Heaven as the ultimate stuff of the universe.

Another point of interest is the fact that most of the statements concerning the will of Heaven in the *Shang Shu* 尚 書 indicate only the transfer of political power among different dynasties or from one dynasty to another. Political power was alienated in China in two ways, the hereditary and the revolutionary. When hereditary rule was abused it gave rise to revolution. No trouble arose in the case of the hereditary transfer, but there had to be a justification for a revolution, and the justification was found in the will of Heaven. Such a revolutionary transfer has great political and social consequences. That this is attributed to the will of Heaven is evidence that all great changes are beyond the control of the human will, and that the will of Heaven is only manifested in politics and social life. This is just the reverse of the case in the West in which the concept of substance was taken as the basis for its emphasis on religious thought.

In this connection something might be said about the changes and influences of religious life in China and the West. In the West the Greek type of religious life ended by the time of the unification of the Roman Empire, but the new form of religion survived the decay of feudalism. Consequently, Western religion and politics are dual currents. Chinese religious life, which bore many resemblances to that of Greece, was a powerful support of Chinese feudalism, which was similar to the European. In the time of the *Ch'un-Ch'iu* feudalism was shaken and the thought of the people was no doubt affected. Hence such statements as "the Heavenly path is far and the human path near," and "What has Heaven said? Yet the four seasons are functioning regularly." Confucianism, without having done away with the doctrine of Heaven, pushed it beyond human affairs. This type of thought had a tendency to make religious belief less influential in China, and later there was only politics and no religion. The same trend is manifested in thought, and we may recapitulate by saying that the law of identity in logic, the subject-predicate proposition in sentence structure, and the category of substance in philosophy all have religious thought as a background. This is characteristic of Western culture. Correlation-logic, non-exclusive classification, analogical definition, all have political thought as a background. This is characteristic of Chinese culture.

IX

These two types of thought differ not only in their categories and their basic rules of logic but also in their attitudes. In putting a question about anything, it is characteristic of Western mentality to ask "What is it?" and then later "How should one react to it?" The Chinese mentality does not emphasize the "what" but rather the "how." Western thought is characterized by the "what-priority attitude," Chinese by the "how-priority attitude." In other words, Western people use the "what" to embody and absorb the "how." The "how" is to be determined by the "what." The Chinese on the other hand use the "how" to imply the "what." The "what" type of thought may develop through religion to science. This is one of the characteristics of scientific thought. The type of thought characterized by emphasis on the "how" can develop only in the socio-political sphere, especially in connection with the problem of ethics. Neglect of the "what" accounts for the neglect or absence of epistemology in China.

That Chinese thought always centers on human affairs while neglecting nature may thus be accounted for. It is often alleged that in Chinese philosophy there are disputes between nominalism and realism and the problem of the relation between Man and Nature, thus implying that Chinese philosophy is similar to Western philosophy. In fact, it is not so. The Chinese interest in the problem of nominalism and realism, as well as in the problem of the relation between Man and Nature, is concerned with socio-political thought and the philosophy of life.

Chinese and Western thought differ also on the question of inference. The syllogism, which is based on the law of identity, is the form of inference in Western logic, while the Chinese use analogy instead of inference. The formula mentioned above, *jen che jen yeh* 仁者人也 is a type of analogical thinking. Other examples from Mencius are more to the point, for example, "the goodness of human nature is like the downward tendency of water" and "Does not life mean nature just as white means white? Does not the whiteness of a white feather mean the whiteness of white snow, and the whiteness of snow mean the whiteness of white jade? . . . if so, then is the nature of the dog similar to that of man?" Such examples in Mencius are too numerous to need further quotation. I. A. Richards in his *Mencius on the Mind* contrasted this type of argument with the Western type. The former may be called the "logic of analogy." This logic, as a matter of fact, though it cannot be appropriately applied to scientific thought is what is largely used in socio-political arguments. Analogical argument indeed is one of the characteristics of political thought. Marxism may be taken as one of the best examples. The formula, Thesis-Antithesis-Synthesis, which is to be applied by any historical process, is analogical in nature. In the same way we may consider the transformation of seeds into trees, as the antithesis of the seeds. So also the theory of the class struggle is argument by analogy. Without criticising the fallacy implied in Marxism it may be profitably observed that the Marxian philosophy is political in nature.

X

The type of thought primarily interested in politics may also have some connections with language. Thus, Confucius was for the "rectification of names" or *cheng ming* 正名. The rectification of names was not advocated by Confucius for the sake of logic but rather as the means by which the order of society was to be maintained. Hence the saying "If names be not correct, language is not in accordance with the truth of things. If language be not in accordance with the truth of things, affairs cannot be carried on to success. When affairs cannot be carried on to success, proprieties and music will not flourish." The function of the rectification of names lies in the discernment between what is above and what is below, the determination of the superior and the inferior and the distinction between good and evil. Its aim lies in human affairs rather than in logic. For example, to kill a king is called murder or *shih* 弒, implying that this involves a violation of the superior by the inferior. The killing of an inferior by a superior is called execution or *chan* 斬, implying that the executed is justifiably punished according to law. For the emperor to travel is called *hsing* 幸 or "to favor." To "come directly" is called *lai* 來 and "to come to settle" *lai kuei* 來 歸 . To go from the local districts to the central government is "to go up" or *shang* 上 as in the expression "to go up west" 西 上 and "to go up north" 北 上 . And to go from the central government to the local regions is to "go down" or *hsia* 下, such as to "go down south" 南 下, to "go down east" 東 下. There are similar distinctions in English as seen already in these translations, but their emphasis is not so obvious and systematic. Dr. Hu Shih considers all these distinctions merely those of parts of speech with grammatical functions. He further remarks "Confucius by rectifying the names is the first logician in China." But such, as we have seen, is not the case.

Further proof may be found in a comparison with Western grammatical changes. Take the English word "sense" for instance. Its changes may take the following forms: senses, sensation, sensational, sensible, sensibility, sensum (sensa), sensationalism, senseless, sensitive, sensitivity, sensibly, sensory, sensorium, etc. All these forms are derived from the same root. Because of the use of inflections, cases, or other grammatical forms the "form" is an essential element in Western thought. In spite of the fact that the aristotelian idea about "form" may be different from that of Bacon and the Baconian "form" from that of Kant, it may be observed that among all of them there is something basic and uniform, namely, the emphasis on the idea or "form." The Chinese characters are ideographic; though they have radicals or *p'ien p'ang* 偏 旁 they do not have roots. The radicals are used merely for the purposes of classification, for example, certain words belong to the realm of water and others to the realm of plants. Whenever there is a new idea a new word must be invented, a new word not derived simply from a root. Chinese ideographs are not subject to grammatical changes; there is no inflection, declension or conjugation.

As the creation of new words must be based upon the needs of society, it is interesting to note that the most numerous terms in China come from two realms; the one, kinship, illustrated by *po* 伯 or father's elder brother, *shu* 叔 or father's younger brother, *t'ang* 堂 or paternal cousin, *piao* 表 and *yi* 怀 or other forms of cousins; the other from the realm of ethics, illustrated by *chung* 忠 or loyalty, *hsiao* 孝 or filial piety, *lien* 廉 or frugality in taking and *chien* 儉 or frugality in spending. All the fine shadings in Chinese terminology in these two fields may be lumped together in such English terms as brothers, uncles, cousins, frugality. Such a lumping together is justifiable in the West, but in China all the differences must be preserved owing to their social significance, and we may attribute such fine shadings in Chinese terminology to the rectification of names.

It should be explained also why the type of thought which is interested in politics values more highly the logic of correlation. The reason lies in the fact that in social phenomena anything may be considered in terms of correlations, such as male and female, husband and wife, father and son, the ruling and the ruled, the civil and military, and so forth. It is but a short step from this realm to that of cosmology. For example, we say, "with Heaven being superior and the Earth inferior the universe is fixed." Furthermore political affairs may have cosmological implications; for example, from the positive 陽 and negative 陰 principles in the cosmos we may derive the principle of evolution 闢 and involution 闔 underlying the universe and human affairs, finally to be developed into such concepts as proper rule 治 or disorder 亂 in political affairs. It should be remembered that this type of thinking is characteristic of political and social thinking.

Even in this, however, there is a difference between China and the West. It is true that Marxism has done away with the law of identity, and has advocated the law of opposition in thinking, being essentially a philosophy concerned with political and social affairs. But its difference from Chinese thought lies in the fact that while Marxism puts emphasis on opposition and thus class struggle, Chinese thought puts emphasis on the result or adjustment of such an opposition. When Mencius said "mental laborers rule while manual laborers are ruled," the emphasis is on the division of labor, and mutual aid as conceived by him is thus made possible. In contradistinction to the Chinese logic of correlation, the Marxian type of logic may be called the "logic of opposition."

XI

Now we are in a position to discuss the relation between logical categories on the one hand and human nature on the other. With a given event, we may have different interpretations. For example, sunset is an observed phenomenon concerning which there may be different interpretations, such as, the sun goes beneath the earth westward, or, the earth turns eastward. It is therefore that identity, substance, and causality are all interpretations, or concepts employed in the act of interpretation, and these concepts themselves are interpretative in nature.

But it may be asked, from what do these interpretations arise and how do they become valid? We may borrow the terms from Pareto without following him in their further implications. According to him there are "residues" and "derivations." The first are the emotional drives, and the latter, outward manifestations or rationalizations. A distinction may be made between two kinds of residues, namely, the "residue of persistence" and the "residue of dominance." From the "residue of persistence" develops religious thought; and the category of substance, the subject-predicate proposition, the logic characterized by the law of identity, and the concept of causality developed thereby are its derivations. From the "residue of dominance" comes all social thought, political theories, and the concrete institutions developed thereby. All the derivations are derived from residues which are rooted in emotional drives. In order to express these emotional drives there are all the religious and political developments or derivations. Students of culture cannot afford to forget that these residues, persistence and dominance, are universal traits of man. And, it must be granted that it is not only in the social and political fields but also in the linguistic and mental fields we can see the universal traits of man. The reason why there are cultural differences between China and the West seems to lie simply in the development and underdevelopment of the derivations along certain lines. It is not that the Chinese do not have the "residue of persistence," but in their original culture or derivations it is not developed. But once in contact with India, the Chinese gave a warm reception to its religion, because Buddhism aroused the "residue of persistence" dormant in the Chinese nature. Chinese culture being underdeveloped in this respect, Buddhism found in China a second home.

Neither is it that the Western people do not have the residue of dominance. Western philosophy is certainly a transformation of religion. Kant, as we have known, in his study of knowledge has given a theoretical justification for the existence of substance. But his *Critique of Pure Reason* has left room for his *Critique of Practical Reason*. If in knowledge the substance is not revealed, it is certainly in conduct that it is realized. In these respects Kant, although trying to analyze

Western thought, is limited by it. His attitude, it must be remembered, is the traditional Western attitude, namely, that of using religion as an indirect means for approaching society and politics. From this it may be observed that all Western metaphysics is essentially socio-political in nature. But the relation between the two is not so obvious. It is to the credit of Marxism that this point is clearly grasped. It is a pity however that it has too narrow a conception, in taking classes for society. Metaphysics was taken as merely a rationalization of social and political thought. The pure theoretical aspect of Western philosophy is nothing but a disguised form of socio-political thought. This observation may seem to be exaggerated, but as a matter of fact, philosophy is part of culture and culture always constitutes a total configuration. Politics, society, and human life cannot be divorced from philosophy. It is often alleged that philosophy is primarily concerned with the unraveling of the secrets of the universe, but this view seems very superficial. Two attitudes are usually taken towards the social and political problems of the present. The one attitude seeks to conserve, the other to change conditions. Marxism may have gone too far in identifying idealism with conservatism and materialism with revolutionism, but the fact remains that idealism and materialism are related to society and politics.

It is on this ground that the views of the Vienna school, for example those of Carnap, should be reconsidered. Carnap considers all philosophical propositions as "nonsense" because they are not verifiable. He needs hardly be reminded that there is much in human knowledge that cannot be verified; and we cannot say that anything that is not verifiable is not true. Rousseau's famous sentence "man is born free" cannot be verified. Yet it helped in contributing towards American Independence and the French Revolution. Social thought is not concerned with verification. It is *unverifiable* but *realizable*. This is the basis for the Determination of Man to combat Nature, as we say in China. Western metaphysical thought is nothing but socio-political theory in another form. And consequently, philosophy has this unverifiable but realizable nature.

Before concluding this essay, my own theory of knowledge may be briefly formulated. It seems to me that human knowledge may be considered in four groups, each penetrating into and dependent upon the others. The first is the external "structure," which accounts for immediate sensation. The external world being merely "structure," we can only know its "mathematical properties," to borrow a term from Russell. As to its qualitative nature, we know nothing. But it must be pointed out that these mathematical properties are not static and rigid, but flexible and changeable. The second group is the "sensa," to use the terminology of neo-realism. Our sensation is a curious thing. Although externally aroused, it is different from the external world in nature. There may be said to be correspondence and not identity between the two. Sensation by its nature is something independent. The third group consists of "constructions." The ordinarily perceived tables, chairs, houses, friends, and what not, are "constructions." These constructions are often taken naively as independent self-existent things. But as a matter of fact, these things are constructed through the perceptions of the observer. The fourth group is what we have already discussed as "interpretation." These four groups are interdependent.[14] Comparatively speaking, the first two are more closely related to the external world and, therefore, more objective, while the last two are more closely related to the inner world and, therefore, more subjective.

---

[14] [Compare Korzybski, *op. cit.*, Chapter XIV, "On Abstracting." Ed.]

The process from the last two to the first two may be called the process of "attachment," while the reverse may be called that of "detachment." Theoretical knowledge is a process of detachment. After detachment theoretical knowledge still invisibly underlies positivistic knowledge. The problem of validity occurs only after the process of detachment. Because of the fact that there may be different interpretations, the problem arises as to which is right and which is wrong, or which is reasonable and which is not. (As a matter of fact, from the cultural point of view there is only difference, and no correctness or incorrectness.) And this is characteristic of theoretical knowledge to which philosophy, social thought, political theories and religious beliefs all belong.

In conclusion, we may say we have discussed the following points in order to show that human culture [15] constitutes a whole. First, what is Western philosophy? Second, what is the relation between language and thought? Third, what is the relation between logic and philosophy? Fourth, what is the relation between philosophy, society, politics, and religion? Fifth, what is the relation between theoretical knowledge and perceptual knowledge? Sixth, what is the relation between human nature and culture (between "residues" and "derivations")? Seventh, what is the difference between Chinese and Western thinking processes? All these points have been discussed from the point of view of philosophy; if they have any bearing on sociology, evaluation and criticism must be left to the sociologists.

Should the reader have had the patience to follow through all the discussion, it may have seemed to him that the writer has been guilty of eclecticism. But there is eclecticism and eclecticism. Should eclecticism prove useful in offering a more synthetic view of all the related problems, it does not need too much apology.

14   On Relativism and Relationism

● KARL MANNHEIM

In order to understand the present situation of thought, it is necessary to start with the problems of "ideology." For most people, the term "ideology" is closely bound up with Marxism, and their reactions to the term are largely determined by the association. It is therefore first necessary to state that although Marxism contributed a great deal to the original statement of the problem, both the word and its meaning go farther back in history than Marxism, and ever since its time new meanings of the word have emerged, which have taken shape independently of it.

There is no better introduction to the problem than the analysis of the meaning of the term "ideology" . . . in general there are two distinct and separable meanings . . . .—the particular and the total.

---

[15] Culture in our discussion is confined to the mental aspect. Its material aspect being outside the scope of the essay, this is not discussed. This should not however be taken as implying that culture has no material aspects.

SOURCE: Karl Mannheim, from his *Ideology and Utopia,* translated by Louis Wirth and Edward Shils (Harcourt, Brace and World, Inc., and Routledge, and Kegan Paul Ltd.), pp. 56–58; 76–83. Reprinted by permission of Harcourt, Brace and World, Inc.

The particular conception of ideology is implied when the term denotes that we are skeptical of the ideas and representations advanced by our opponent. They are regarded as more or less conscious disguises of the real nature of a situation, the true recognition of which would not be in accord with his interests. These distortions range all the way from conscious lies to half-conscious and unwitting disguises; from calculated attempts to dupe others to self-deception. This conception of ideology, which has only gradually become differentiated from the common-sense notion of the lie is particular in several senses. Its particularity becomes evident when it is contrasted with the more inclusive total conception of ideology. Here we refer to the ideology of an age or of a concrete historico-social group, e.g. of a class, when we are concerned with the characteristics and composition of the total structure of the mind of this epoch or of this group.

The common as well as the distinctive elements of the two concepts are readily evident. The common element in these two conceptions seems to consist in the fact that neither relies solely on what is actually said by the opponent in order to reach an understanding of his real meaning and intention.[1] Both fall back on the subject, whether individual or group, proceeding to an understanding of what is said by the indirect method of analysing the social conditions of the individual or his group. The ideas expressed by the subject are thus regarded as functions of his existence. This means that opinions, statements, propositions, and systems of ideas are not taken at their face value but are interpreted in the light of the life-situation of the one who expresses them. It signifies further that the specific character and life-situation of the subject influence his opinions, perceptions, and interpretations.

Both these conceptions of ideology, accordingly, make these so-called "ideas" a function of him who holds them, and of his position in his social milieu. Although they have something in common, there are also significant differences between them. Of the latter we mention merely the most important:—

(a) Whereas the particular conception of ideology designates only a part of the opponent's assertions as ideologies—and this only with reference to their content, the total conception calls into question the opponent's total *Weltanschauung* (including his conceptual apparatus), and attempts to understand these concepts as an outgrowth of the collective life of which he partakes.

(b) The particular conception of "ideology" makes its analysis of ideas on a purely psychological level. If it is claimed for instance that an adversary is lying, or that he is concealing or distorting a given factual situation, it is still nevertheless assumed that both parties share common criteria of validity—it is still assumed that it is possible to refute lies and eradicate sources of error by referring to accepted criteria of objective validity common to both parties. The suspicion that one's opponent is the victim of an ideology does not go so far as to exclude him from discussion on the basis of a common theoretical frame of reference. The case is different with the total conception of ideology. When we attribute to one historical epoch one intellectual world and to ourselves another one, or if a certain historically determined social stratum thinks in categories other than our own, we

---

[1] If the interpretation relies solely upon that which is actually said we shall speak of an "immanent interpretation": if it transcends these data, implying thereby an analysis of the subject's life-situation, we shall speak of a "transcendental interpretation." A typology of these various forms of interpretation is to be found in the author's "Ideologische und soziologische Interpretation der geistigen Gebilde," *Jahrbuch für Soziologie,* vol. ii (Karlsruhe, 1926), p. 424 ff.

refer not to the isolated cases of thought-content, but to fundamentally divergent thought-systems and to widely differing modes of experience and interpretation. We touch upon the theoretical or noological level whenever we consider not merely the content but also the form, and even the conceptual framework of a mode of thought as a function of the life-situation of a thinker. "The economic categories are only the theoretical expressions, the abstractions, of the social relations of production. . . . The same men who establish social relations conformably with their material productivity, produce also the principles, the ideas, the categories, conformably with their social relations." (Karl Marx, *The Poverty of Philosophy*, being a translation of *Misère de la Philosophie*, with a preface by Frederick Engels, translated by H. Quelch, Chicago, 1910, p. 119.) These are the two ways of analysing statements as functions of their social background; the first operates only on the psychological, the second on the noological level.

(c) Corresponding to this difference, the particular conception of ideology operates primarily with a psychology of interests, while the total conception uses a more formal functional analysis, without any reference to motivations, confining itself to an objective description of the structural differences in minds operating in different social settings. The former assumes that this or that interest is the cause of a given lie or deception. The latter presupposes simply that there is a correspondence between a given social situation and a given perspective, point of view, or apperception mass. In this case, while an analysis of constellations of interests may often be necessary it is not to establish causal connections but to characterize the total situation. Thus interest psychology tends to be displaced by an analysis of the correspondence between the situation to be known and the forms of knowledge. . . .

. . . We have already traced the development from the particular to the total conception. This tendency is constantly being intensified. Instead of being content with showing that the adversary suffers from illusions or distortions on a psychological or experiential plane, the tendency now is to subject his total structure of consciousness and thought to a thoroughgoing sociological analysis.[2]

As long as one does not call his own position into question but regards it as absolute, while interpreting his opponent's ideas as a mere function of the social positions they occupy, the decisive step forward has not yet been taken. It is true, of course, that in such a case the total conception of ideology is being used, since one is interested in analysing the structure of the mind of one's opponent in its totality, and is not merely singling out a few isolated propositions. But since, in such an instance, one is interested merely in a sociological analysis of the opponent's idea, one never gets beyond a highly restricted, or what I should like to call a special, formulation of the theory. In contrast to this special formulation, the general [3] form of the total conception of ideology is being used by the analyst when he has the courage to subject not just the adversary's point of view but all points of view, including his own, to the ideological analysis.

---

[2] This is not meant to imply that for certain aspects of the struggles of everyday life the particular conception of ideology is inapplicable.

[3] We add here another distinction of our earlier one of "particular and total," namely that of "special and general." While the first distinction concerns the question as to whether single isolated ideas or the entire mind is to be seen as ideological, and whether the social situation conditions merely the psychological manifestations of concepts, or whether it even penetrates to the noological meanings in the distinction of special *versus* general, the decisive question is whether the thought of all groups (including our own) or only that of our adversaries is recognized as socially determined.

At the present stage of our understanding it is hardly possible to avoid this general formulation of the total conception of ideology, according to which the thought of all parties in all epochs is of an ideological character. There is scarcely a single intellectual position, and Marxism furnishes no exception to this rule, which has not changed through history and which even in the present does not appear in many forms. Marxism, too, has taken on many diverse appearances. It should not be too difficult for a Marxist to recognize their social basis.

With the emergence of the general formulation of the total conception of ideology, the simple theory of ideology develops into the sociology of knowledge. What was once the intellectual armament [4] of a party is transformed into a method of research in social and intellectual history generally. To begin with, a given social group discovers the "situational determination" (*Seinsgebundenheit*) of its opponents' ideas. Subsequently the recognition of this fact is elaborated into an all-inclusive principle according to which the thought of every group is seen as arising out of its life conditions.[5] Thus, it becomes the task of the sociological history of thought to analyse without regard for party biases all the factors in the actually existing social situation which may influence thought. This sociologically oriented history of ideas is destined to provide modern men with a revised view of the whole historical process.

It is clear, then, that in this connection the conception of ideology takes on a new meaning. Out of this meaning two alternative approaches to ideological investigation arise. The first is to confine oneself to showing everywhere the interrelationships between the intellectual point of view held and the social position occupied. This involves the renunciation of every intention to expose or unmask those views with which one is in disagreement.

In attempting to expose the views of another, one is forced to make one's own view appear infallible and absolute, which is a procedure altogether to be avoided if one is making a specifically non-evaluative investigation. The second possible approach is nevertheless to combine such a non-evaluative analysis with a definite epistemology. Viewed from the angle of this second approach there are two separate and distinct solutions to the problem of what constitutes reliable knowledge—the one solution may be termed *relationism*, and the other *relativism*.

Relativism is a product of the modern historical-sociological procedure which is based on the recognition that all historical thinking is bound up with the concrete position in life of the thinker (*Standortsgebundenheit des Denkers*). But relativism combines this historical-sociological insight with an older theory of knowledge which was as yet unaware of the interplay between conditions of existence and modes of thought, and which modelled its knowledge after static prototypes such as might be exemplified by the proposition $2 \times 2 = 4$. This older type of thought, which regarded such examples as the model of all thought, was necessarily led to the rejection of all those forms of knowledge which were dependent upon the subjective standpoint and the social situation of the knower, and which were, hence, merely "relative." Relativism, then, owes its existence to the discrepancy between this newly won insight into the actual processes of thought and a theory of knowledge which had not yet taken account of this new insight.

If we wish to emancipate ourselves from this relativism we must seek to understand with the aid of the sociology of knowledge that it is not epistemology in any

---

[4] Cf. the Marxist expression "To forge the intellectual weapons of the proletariat."
[5] By the term "situational determination of knowledge" I am seeking to differentiate the propagandistic from the scientific sociological content of the ideological concept.

absolute sense but rather a certain historically transitory type of epistemology which is in conflict with the type of thought oriented to the social situation. Actually, epistemology is as intimately enmeshed in the social process as is the totality of our thinking, and it will make progress to the extent that it can master the complications arising out of the changing structure of thought.

A modern theory of knowledge which takes account of the relational as distinct from the merely relative character of all historical knowledge must start with the assumption that there are spheres of thought in which it is impossible to conceive of absolute truth existing independently of the values and position of the subject and unrelated to the social context. Even a god could not formulate a proposition on historical subjects like $2 \times 2 = 4$, for what is intelligible in history can be formulated only with reference to problems and conceptual constructions which themselves arise in the flux of historical experience.

Once we recognize that all historical knowledge is relational knowledge, and can only be formulated with reference to the position of the observer, we are faced, once more, with the task of discriminating between what is true and what is false in such knowledge. The question then arises: which social standpoint *vis-à-vis* of history offers the best chance for reaching an optimum of truth? In any case, at this stage the vain hope of discovering truth in a form which is independent of an historically and socially determined set of meanings will have to be given up. The problem is by no means solved when we have arrived at this conclusion, but we are, at least, in a better position to state the actual problems which arise in a more unrestricted manner. In the following we have to distinguish two types of approach to ideological inquiry arising upon the level of the general-total conception of ideology: first, the approach characterized by freedom from value-judgments and, second, the epistemological and metaphysically oriented normative approach. For the time being we shall not raise the question of whether in the latter approach we are dealing with relativism or relationism.

The non-evaluative general total conception of ideology is to be found primarily in those historical investigations, where, provisionally and for the sake of the simplification of the problem, no judgments are pronounced as to the correctness of the ideas to be treated. This approach confines itself to discovering the relations between certain mental structures and the life-situations in which they exist. We must constantly ask ourselves how it comes about that a given type of social situation gives rise to given interpretation. Thus the ideological element in human thought, viewed at this level, is always bound up with the existing life-situation of the thinker. According to this view human thought arises, and operates, not in a social vacuum but in a definite social milieu.

We need not regard it as a source of error that all thought is so rooted. Just as the individual who participates in a complex of vital social relations with other men thereby enjoys a chance of obtaining a more precise and penetrating insight into his fellows, so a given point of view and a given set of concepts, because they are bound up with and grow out of a certain social reality, offer, through intimate contact with this reality, a greater chance of revealing their meaning. (The example cited earlier showed that the proletarian-socialistic point of view was in a particularly favourable position to discover the ideological elements in its adversaries' thought.) The circumstance, however, that thought is bound by the social- and life-situation in which it arises creates handicaps as well as opportunities. It is clearly impossible to obtain an inclusive insight into problems if the observer or thinker is confined to a given place in society. For instance, as has already been pointed out, it was not possible for the socialist idea of ideology to have developed of itself into the sociology of knowledge. It seems inherent in the historical process itself that the narrowness and the limitations which restrict one point of view tend to be corrected by clashing with the opposite points of view. The task of a study of ideology, which tries to be free from value-judgments, is to understand the narrowness of each individual point of view and the interplay between these distinctive attitudes in the total social process. We are here confronted with an inexhaustible theme. The problem is to show how, in the whole history of thought, certain intellectual standpoints are connected with certain forms of experience, and to trace the intimate interaction between the two in the course of social and intellectual change. In the domain of morals, for instance, it is necessary to show not only the continuous changes in human conduct but the constantly altering norms by which this conduct is judged. Deeper insight into the problem is reached if we are able to show that morality and ethics themselves are conditioned by certain definite situations, and that such fundamental concepts as duty, transgression, and sin have not always existed but have made their appearance as correlatives of distinct social situations.[6] The prevailing philosophic view which cautiously admits that the content of conduct has been historically determined, but which at the same time insists upon the retention of eternal forms of value and of a formal set of categories, is no longer tenable. The fact that the distinction between the content and the forms of conduct was made and recognized is an important concession to the historical-sociological approach which makes it increasingly difficult to set up contemporary values as absolutes.

Having arrived at this recognition it becomes necessary also to remember that the fact that we speak about social and cultural life in terms of values is itself an attitude peculiar to our time. The notion of "value" arose and was diffused from economics, where the conscious choice between values was the starting-point of theory. This idea of value was later transferred to the ethical, aesthetic, and religious spheres, which brought about a distortion in the description of the real behaviour of the human being in these spheres. Nothing could be more wrong than to describe the real attitude of the individual when enjoying a work of art quite unreflectively, or when acting according to ethical patterns inculcated in him since childhood, in terms of conscious choice between values.

The view which holds that all cultural life is an orientation toward objective values is just one more illustration of a typically modern rationalistic disregard for the basic irrational mechanisms which govern man's relation to his world. Far from being permanently valid the interpretation of culture in terms of objective values is really a peculiar characteristic of the thought of our own time. But even granting for the moment that this conception had some merit, the existence of certain formal realms of values and their specific structure would be intelligible only with reference to the concrete situations to which they have relevance and in which they are valid.[7] There is, then, no norm which can lay claim to formal validity and which can be abstracted as a constant universal formal element from its historically changing content.

---

6 Cf. Max Weber, *Wirtschaft und Gesellschaft, Grundriss der Sozialökonomik*, Part iii, p. 794, dealing with the social conditions which are requisite to the genesis of the moral.

7 Cf. E. Lask, *Die Logik der Philosophie und die Kategorienlehre* (Tübingen, 1911), uses the term *hingelten* in order to explain that categorical forms are not valid in themselves but only with reference to their always changing content which inevitably reacts upon their nature.

To-day we have arrived at the point where we can see clearly that there are differences in modes of thought, not only in different historical periods but also in
different cultures. Slowly it dawns upon us that not only does the content of
thought change but also its categorical structure. Only very recently has it become possible to investigate the hypothesis that, in the past as well as in the present, the dominant modes of thought are supplanted by new categories when the
social basis of the group, of which these thought-forms are characteristic, disintegrates or is transformed under the impact of social change.

Research in the sociology of knowledge promises to reach a stage of exactness if
only because nowhere else in the realm of culture is the interdependence in the
shifts of meaning and emphasis so clearly evident and precisely determinable as
in thought itself. For thought is a particularly sensitive index of social and cultural change. The variation in the meaning of words and the multiple connotations
of every concept reflect polarities of mutually antagonistic schemes of life implicit
in these nuances of meaning.[8] . . .

---

[8] For this reason the sociological analysis of meanings will play a significant role in the following studies. We may suggest here that such an analysis might be developed into a sympto-
matology based upon the principle that in the social realm, if we can learn to observe carefully,
we can see that each element of the situation which we are analysing contains and throws
light upon the whole.

PART THREE
THE DEFINITION OF THE SITUATION

There is now general agreement in sociology that definitions of situations are necessary conditions of human *conduct*. In their absence, human *behavior* may be paralyzed or so disoriented that what is often called panic ensues. For example, in a study of responses to a devastating tornado, fewer instances of panic behavior were found among those who experienced the catastrophe in assembled family units, even though injury and, at times, death had occurred in the family. Panic behavior occurred most frequently among those who were not with their families at the time of the disaster. Once the family situation was defined, panic behavior was reduced and ordered human conduct was resumed.[1]

This notion of the definition of the situation has been progressively defined and operationalized since its original statement by William I. Thomas in 1923.[2] In the early development of the concept, the definition of the situation was apprehended *either* as a *mentalistic* (subjective) *or* as a *culturological* phenomenon. This distinction is possibly a consequence of the incipient formulation found in Thomas' and Znaniecki's differentiation of attitude and value in their seminal study, *The Polish Peasant in Europe and America.* The distinction persists today in the adoption of phenomenology by ethnomethodologists who rally behind the ideas of Harold Garfinkel and the notion of pattern variables insisted upon by Talcott Parsons. Earlier examples of the mentalistic-culturological dichotomy can be found in the concept "dynamic assessment" propounded by MacIver,[3] and the idea of the "humanistic coefficient" set forth by Florian Znaniecki. This latter notion, as

---

[1] William H. Form and Sigmund Nosow, *Community in Disaster* (New York: Harper and Brothers, 1958), especially pp. 85–90. The entire matter of panic behavior in disaster, however, is much more complicated than this. We intend the point to be illustrative.

[2] See his *The Unadjusted Girl* (Boston: Little, Brown, and Co., 1923), pp. 41–50.

[3] See Robert M. MacIver, *Social Causation* (New York: Ginn and Co., 1942), pp. 291–350.

the readings in this section indicate, was ultimately apprehended as a consequence of "cultural conditioning."

There has always been the problem in the study of human conduct of locating the source of symbolic transformation, and we have already seen that man responds not to some objectively-given environment, but instead to a symbolic transformation of that environment. This transformation can only be accomplished by man's use of symbols, for most of which he is not himself responsible, but which he must implement in his definitions of situations. Symbols are nothing without man. Man is nothing without symbols. The very fact that man must use symbols to define the situations in which he conducts himself implies communication, since those very definitions require the meaningful responses of others.

W. I. and Dorothy Swaine Thomas establish this point in the excerpt reprinted here. They are concerned with the importance of documents in the study of the personal life. One's own account of the world seriously modifies his response to it (the case of the prisoner from Dannemora). However, the Thomases are not naive. The accounts of one's "significant others" (they cite the family) and "disinterested others" (they cite social workers' reports) must be included in the sociologist's assessments of situations. We have already shown that ethnomethodologists may circumvent the importance of this rounded view, but this is also true of culturologists, for example, Merton in his well known paradigm for the study of anomie.[4] The Thomases root the definition of the situation in interaction or communication. In doing this, we can say they were ahead of their time. They show how this is particularly important for psychiatry and criminology in the study of deviant behavior. While the definition of the situation is real for some, it may not be for others, and there may be serious consequences for those caught up in the incongruities. We can see the beginnings of "labeling theory"[5] in this short excerpt.

Although the Thomases' contributions chronologically preceded those of Znaniecki, logically and methodologically they carried the concept much closer to the present perspective of symbolic interaction. To place definitions of situations in some hypostatized culture, as Znaniecki ultimately did, is to run the risks of a too-tight tautology: Definitions of the situations are a part of culture, therefore culture causes (or "conditions") definitions of the situation. This, of course, is reasoning in too tight a circle.

Almost at the same time (1923) that Thomas had introduced the concept, the anthropologist Bronislaw Malinowski was stressing the significance of the *context of situation* for the interpretation of words. In particular he noted the difference in interpretation formulated by philologists, most of whom had studied dead languages bereft of social, communicative, cultural, or environmental context, and interpretations of ethnographers who necessarily made their interpretations in the context of actual encounters. He deplored the fact that the analysis of meaning was most often carried on after the fashion of the philologists who conceived meaning as somehow rooted in the word, most often its referent—that which is designated in "nature"—and, we would add, less often

---

[4] Robert K. Merton, *Social Theory and Social Structure* (Glencoe, Ill.: The Free Press, 1957), pp. 131–94. See also his "The Self-Fulfilling Prophecy," *ibid.*, pp. 421–36, for a contrasting view.

[5] For what has come to be called "labeling theory," see, *inter alia*, Howard S. Becker, *The Outsiders* (New York: The Free Press of Glencoe, 1963).

in its connotation—that "state of mind" aroused by the word in the user *or* the audience—rather than in the mutual responses of communicator *and* audience *by* the word.

This naive approach persists today in most survey methodology. Interviewers (particularly pollsters) are instructed to direct questions to each subject precisely as each question reads without regard to the situation in which the question is posed. But the meaning of any given word varies between the sexes, among age groups, status groupings, the so-called ethnic or racial groups, regions within nations, and all the divisions of society. Consider the word "family." In the higher status circles of the United States, the term most frequently refers to lineage. In the lower status circles, the term usually refers to the presence of children and the harmonious and viable integration of the household. Among men, the phrase "S.O.B." varies in its meaning from an extremely derogatory appellation to a highly affectionate one; and, we suspect, among women the term "deary" can have the same variation in meaning. Words, then, must be interpreted in transactive situations—as *situated conduct*—for it is in concerted response that they find their meaning. Words are vehicles for establishing meanings in communication. Less often it may be the other way around. But, to interpret a word outside the context of situation is, as Malinowski put it, "nothing short of preposterous."

This is not to say that words have no influence on human conduct. Benjamin Lee Whorf points out that some words may be regarded as shorthand terms for situations.[6] *Empty* containers are often considered harmless; *stone* is construed to be non-combustible; spatially *remote things* are apprehended as causally insulated. The consequences of such names for situations may at times be devastating. As a matter of fact, just because of this increased capacity for error, Suzanne Langer has distinguished the symbolic responses of human beings from the signal responses of other animals.[7] The awareness of error is the beginning of truth, Langer states, but we would observe that it is also the beginning of the "con game." The other animals may act in error, but, so far as we know, this is seldom, if ever, taken into mutual account in their signal communications. The con game is not carried off by any animal except man—certainly not the "long con" (where the "mark" must leave the scene, collect the money, and bring it back to the scene). Not only is this because signal communications are anchored in the time and space within which they are accomplished—the here and now—while symbolic communications enable us to transcend temporal and spacial barriers, but because situations are *given* for the other animals and *constructed* by man. Thus, children can fill the family sugar bowl with salt on April Fool's Day, and parents can get needed rest on Christmas Eve by assuring their children that Santa Claus will only visit the household when everyone is asleep, or at least in bed and quiet.

Situations, in other words, are *staged*. By this we mean that the elements of a situation are typically assembled, arranged, manipulated, and controlled by human beings so that the vast range of the possibilities of human conduct is

---

[6] On the motivational implications (as opposed to causative forces) of words, the best statement is to be found in Kenneth Burke, *Permanence and Change* (New York: New Republic, 1936)—since published in various editions—p. 45: "Our introspective words for motives are rough shorthand descriptions for certain typical patterns of discrepant and conflicting stimuli."
[7] Suzanne Langer, *Philosophy in a New Key* (New York: Penguin Books, Inc., 1948), pp. 22–26.

circumscribed, once other humans enter the constructed situational scene. All this is accomplished, of course, within the context of history, but this is one of the most difficult facts that situational analysts must contend with. Willard Waller, so far as we know, was the first sociologist to make an analysis of this basic process of staging. He investigated the classroom situation in detail and began his observations with the axiom: *The definition of the situation is a process.* In proposing this axiom, and with no little difficulty, Waller removed the concept from its formulation as either culturally given or mentalistically adduced. *Man creates definitions of the situation*—"one person defines a situation for another." This should not be taken to mean that each situation is defined *de novo.* For many situations of human life are conventionally defined as is their staging. The elements persist — Christmas trees, fireworks, Easter eggs, flags, altars, churches, courthouses, classroom, etc. Thus, there is a continuity of situational elements—collective representations—and the mode of their arrangement may be thought of as a kind of grammar, a set of rules regulating how such elements should be assembled, arranged, manipulated, and controlled.

Yet, Waller points out, persons do not passively accept the definitions of situations that others make for them. "There is . . . a place for self-activity." Confronted with a constructed situation, the person, by virtue of his intelligence, "enters into the process, and there ensues a dynamic reorganization of the parts of the situation into a pattern." Indeed, a mark of intelligence is "the ability to blast the units of configurations loose from their context and to recombine them in different patterns." The intelligent man is difficult to con!

In such a "dynamic assessment" of the situation, as MacIver would have called it—whether intelligent or not—attitudes or incipient acts are established or built up.[8] Assessing the constructed situation, one can decide the role he will perform—what his future in that situation will probably become.[9] Here Waller relies very much on principles of Gestalt psychology (mentalistic, for example, "the social role appears in the mind by a sudden *Einschnappen*"). Nevertheless, the bulk of the excerpt is given over to the active and objective staging of the classroom situation and its maintenance over time. The consequences for variations in situated conduct are clearly limned, as well as the ambivalent value Waller holds toward the extremes of the range—rigid versus pliable definitions. Finally, Waller shows how definitions of situations in one area of life spill over into other situations that may not be formally linked, for example, classroom encounters and personal sexual encounters. We invite the reader to employ this discussion as an analogue for the analysis of other situated conduct in seemingly unrelated social gatherings—at parties, in churches, in elevators—wherever people come together in one another's presence.

Gross and Stone have made a preliminary attempt to conceptualize some of

---

[8] Waller's notion of attitude is remarkably similar to that of George H. Mead and may reflect his study at the University of Chicago in the '20's. However, there is no evidence that Waller ever studied under Mead. William J. Goode has explained this to us in personal correspondence: "I suspect, as is true now, *that* was 'Philosophy,' and not many outsiders came." Our guess is that some osmosis was pervading the graduate student membrane. At any rate, Waller left Chicago and continued his graduate studies at the University of Pennsylvania in 1926. We are very much indebted to Goode for this information.
[9] Goode has also told us that Waller frequently tested definitions of the situation by repudiating implied role performances. This is a tactic that has most notably been employed since that time by Erving Goffman and Harold Garfinkel. By breaking what he surmises the rules are, the sociologist can determine the rules, for sanctions will be applied if the infraction bears upon the regulated conduct that the definition of the situation has established.

the elements of situations that must be assembled, arranged, manipulated, and controlled in the staging process by examining instances of embarrassment—instances where role performances are rendered difficult, if not impossible, because elements of situations have not been assembled correctly, have been disarranged, fumbled, or otherwise have escaped control. They show how closely role performances and definitions of the situation are linked. In an inadequately defined situation or an inappropriate situation, an identity may be lost or become meaningless, and one may find oneself without poise, future, or role—consensual attitudes (incipient acts) mobilized by an announced and ratified identity in a specified social situation. Identity and poise are not sufficient to account for human conduct without reference to situation. *There is no role—of mother, father, child, teacher, student, or whatever—without reference to the situation in which that role is to be performed.* Not only do mothers behave differently, let us say, with other mothers than they do with sons and fathers, but mothers behave differently *as* mothers and *with* mothers at picnics and at Kaffee-Klatsches. Similarly, teachers behave differently with students in the classroom, in the office, and in the home. One must not know merely who he is to perform a role or conduct himself; he must know or define the situation in which who he is has relevance.[10] This definition is typically made for him by others, by him for others, or jointly constructed in gestural and verbal dialogue.

Staging the definition of a situation requires that at least five elements be assembled, arranged, manipulated, and controlled: (1) spaces; (2) props; (3) equipment; (4) clothing; and (5) bodies.[11] This operation may be as or more important than the employment of linguistic symbols, although it must ultimately be interpreted linguistically. What permits such staging to be carried off lies outside, beyond, or under the staging process. It is a matter of taken-for-granted rules—what Garfinkel calls "routine grounds";[12] Goffman, "working consensus";[13] and Gross and Stone, "performance norms." Such common assumptions allow for flexibility in role performance and give the other fellow the benefit of the doubt. Again, these assumptions permit the distinctively human con, but, we must add, some delight and surprise in human encounters. When performance norms do not permit such flexibility, as in some bureaucracies, encounters may be fraught with disappointment.

Notwithstanding these assumptions, there is something about spaces, particularly enclosed spaces, that requires further investigation. The enclosure itself, modified by lighting, sound, color, odor, temperature, and humidity, affects the character of the interaction carried on inside. Variations in any or all of these elements can noticeably affect the mood of the interaction, as the article by David J. and Judith D. Bennett asserts. Such concrete alterations of settings have not been systematically investigated by sociologists. Nevertheless, imagine

---

[10] See Merton's notion of "role-set." Robert K. Merton, *op. cit.*, pp. 368–80. Merton's analysis suffers from a failure to consider situational dimensions of role-sets. This is a general shortcoming of sociologists who emphasize structure.

[11] At the time of publication the authors had extended their list to forty such "elements." Subsequently, the list was expanded to more than fifty. At that point, obviously, the simple enumeration of such elements was seen clearly to violate the law of parsimony, and some mode of conceptualization is still sought. The contribution by David J. and Judith D. Bennett in this section represents a preliminary attempt in this direction.

[12] Harold Garfinkel, "Studies of the Routine Grounds of Everyday Activities," *Social Problems*, XI (Winter 1964), pp. 225–50.

[13] Erving Goffman, *The Presentation of Self in Everyday Life*, Monograph No. 2 (Edinburgh: University of Edinburgh Social Sciences Research Centre, 1956), pp. 4–5.

the consequences for conduct of two social occasions, each with the same people meeting in the same place. First, the host, dressed in a suit, shirt, and tie, meets the guests at the door and seats them in the living room. The lights are turned up—not brilliant—and Bach is playing on the hi-fi. The host asks the guests what they prefer to drink and serves them. In the second scene, the host meets the guests at the door dressed in a sport shirt and slacks. He greets them heartily and says, "The drinks are in the kitchen—help yourselves." Francis Albert Sinatra, or Nancy, or Frank, Jr., or some current jazz group is playing on the hi-fi. The lights are turned down in the living room (which has become a dancing chamber). Obviously, the design and management of each occasion will culminate in different social outcomes, despite the "personalities" involved.

Such staging of situations may well be considered a rhetoric in the sense used in our introductory chapter: ". . . a symbolic means of inducing cooperation in beings that by nature respond to symbols." [14] Donald W. Ball provides an excellent example of such a technique in his ethnographic analysis of an abortion clinic. Abortion is thought of in the middle strata of our society as a deviant act. From the successful abortionist's point of view, the question is how such a deviant act may be neutralized—staged, or defined—so that the act might be accepted by the participant as legitimate and not at odds with conventional expectations. The success of the rhetoric obviously depends on the social world of the clientele. In this case, the clients are drawn from the middle or upper-middle stratum of our society. Thus, the "scene is made" a setting of luxury and medical practice. The former impression is established by the sunken waiting room, deep carpeting, and appropriate decor; the latter, by the clothing of the personnel, the quasi-bureaucratic recording of case histories, and the vocabulary—"abortion" is never mentioned; the treatment is a matter of "D & C" (dilation and curettage).

Ball seeks to establish the rhetorical nature of such staging by pointing out discrepancies between the staging and "reality." He singles out pesudo-sterility practices, lack of privacy, and the contrast between the car that brings the "patient" to the clinic and the one that takes her away. In doing so, he raises a Pirandello-like question: Whose reality is he talking about and, more important, what is reality? These are questions we shall take up in the next section. They are not easy, and they raise the matter of boundaries of social worlds. Indeed, if the client of the abortion clinic did not accept the rhetoric, the entire procedure would falter and fail. Undoubtedly, this is the case with the abortionist himself. Reality rests upon consensus, and consensus is always negotiated, deliberately or not.

Suggested Readings

BERREMAN, GERALD D. *Behind Many Masks*. The Society for Applied Anthropology Monograph No. 4, 1962.

FIREY, WALTER. *Land Values in Central Boston*. Cambridge: Harvard University Press, 1945.

GOFFMAN, ERVING. *The Presentation of Self in Everyday Life*. Garden City: Doubleday, 1959.

————. *Behavior in Public Places*. New York: The Free Press of Glencoe, 1963.

[14] Kenneth Burke, *Rhetoric of Motives* (New York: Prentice-Hall, Inc., 1950), p. 43.

HALL, EDWARD T. *The Hidden Dimension.* Garden City: Doubleday, 1966.

————. *The Silent Language.* Greenwich, Conn.: Fawcett Publications, 1964.

McHUGH, PETER. *Definition of the Situation.* Indianapolis, Ind.: Bobbs-Merrill, 1968.

MERTON, ROBERT K. "The Self-Fulfilling Prophecy," *Social Theory and Social Structure.* Glencoe, Ill.: The Free Press, Rev. ed., 1957, 421–436.

PIRANDELLO, LUIGI. *Naked Masks,* (ed.) Eric Bently. New York: Dutton, 1952.

SCHEFF, THOMAS J. "Negotiating Reality: Notes on Power in the Assessment of Responsibility," *Social Problems,* 16 (Summer 1968), 3–17.

STEBBINS, ROBERT A. "A Theory of the Definition of the Situation," *The Canadian Review of Sociology and Anthropology,* 4 (August, 1967), 148–164.

15   Situations Defined as Real are Real in Their Consequences

● WILLIAM I. AND DOROTHY SWAINE THOMAS

. . . The behavior document (case study, life-record, psychoanalytic confession) represents a continuity of experience in life situations. In a good record of this kind we are able to view the behavior reactions in the various situations, the emergence of personality traits, the determination of concrete acts and the formation of life policies, in their evolution. Perhaps the greatest importance of the behavior document is the opportunity it affords to observe the attitudes of other persons as behavior-forming influences, since the most important situations in the development of personality are the attitudes and values of other persons. . . . [B]ehavior [is determined] partly by institutions, taken as situation, and partly by behavior of others, taken as situation.

It has been strongly objected, especially by the adherents of the school of "behaviorism," that this introspective method has no objectivity or validity. What they mean is that these records will not reveal the mechanisms of behavior, the process of consciousness, what is going on inside of us when we think and act, and with this we are in agreement. But the unique value of the document is its revelation of the situations which have conditioned the behavior, and concerning this there can be no doubt.

There may be, and is, doubt as to the objectivity and veracity of the record, but even the highly subjective record has a value for behavior study. A document prepared by one compensating for a feeling of inferiority or elaborating a delusion of persecution is as far as possible from objective reality, but the subject's view of the situation, how he regards it, may be the most important element for interpretation. For his immediate behavior is closely related to his definition of the situation, which may be in terms of objective reality or in terms of a subjective appreciation—"as if" it were so. Very often it is the wide discrepancy between the situation as it seems to others and the situation as it seems to the individual that brings about the overt behavior difficulty. To take an extreme example, the warden of Dannemora prison recently refused to honor the order of the court to send an inmate outside the prison walls for some specific purpose. He excused himself on the ground that the man was too dangerous. He had killed several persons who had the unfortunate habit of talking to themselves on the street. From the movement of their lips he imagined that they were calling him vile names, and he behaved as if this were true. If men define situations as real, they are real in their consequences.

The total situation will always contain more and less subjective factors, and the behavior reaction can be studied only in connection with the whole context, i.e., the situation as it exists in verifiable, objective terms, and as it has seemed to

SOURCE: William and Dorothy Swaine Thomas, from *The Child in America* (New York: Alfred A. Knopf, Inc., 1928), pp. 571–573 and 575. Copyright 1928 by Alfred A. Knopf, Inc., copyright renewal 1956 by William and Dorothy Swaine Thomas. Reprinted by permission of the publisher.

154

exist in terms of the interested persons. Thus, the behavior records of the child clinics are contributing important data by including the child's account of the difficult situation, the often conflicting definitions of this situation given by parents, teachers, etc., and the recording of such facts as can be verified about the situation by disinterested investigators.

In the field of psychiatry the context becomes particularly significant, and it is desirable to have here a multiplication of records showing how situations are appreciated and motivate behavior, but the records should be made not without regard to the factual elements in the situation. To the degree that the psychiatric cases are approached from the standpoint of the total situation it will appear that the problems of behavior taken all together assume an aspect of totality. The unfortunate separation of the "abnormal" from the "normal" in behavior studies will disappear, and the abnormal, pathological and criminal behavior reactions will appear not as "disease" but as socially (and individually) undesirable behavior reactions in given situations, and from this standpoint they will lend themselves more readily to study from the behavioristic standpoint. . . .

With the progress of our studies of the various behavior-forming situations we may hope to approach the still more obscure problem of mass behavior— the participation of whole populations in common sentiments and actions. This is represented by fashions of dress, mob action, war hysteria, the gang spirit, mafia, omertà, fascism, popularity of this or that cigarette or tooth paste, the quick fame and quick infamy of political personalities, etc. We are unable to define this total situation satisfactorily, but it involves the interaction of language and gesture and gossip and print and symbols and slogans and propaganda and imitation, and seems, more than anything else, the process eventuating in the formation of the distinctive character of communities, nationalities and races. The process itself may be described as a series of definitions of situations whereby behavior norms are established.

In the same connection (while we do not advocate anthropological and historical studies as remunerative behavioristic studies in themselves and are of the opinion that the past contains no models on which we may build in the present) it would be useful to extend our studies of this situational character to the large cultural areas, to the contemporaneous races and nationalities, in order to understand the formation of behavior patterns comparatively, in their most general and particular expressions, and appreciate the capacity of human nature to work under various and widely contrasted habit systems. Furthermore, behavior studies within these wide limits may be expected to reveal comparatively and in the most general way the situations within which particular maladjustments (delinquency, crime, the psychoneuroses) tend to appear, and the situations and habit systems unfavorable to their appearance, or, more positively, the situations within which the activities are integrated about particular interests, leading to pursuits, roles and careers.

16   On the Humanistic Coefficient

● HELENA ZNANIECKI LOPATA

Although prior work in Polish had already stressed the importance of studying social systems from the point of view of those involved in them, Florian Znaniecki's conceptualization of the humanistic coefficient first appeared in English in his *The Method of Sociology*. The significance of such an approach was explained in a chapter of that book, entitled, "The Principles of Selection of Cultural Data": [1]

> Generally speaking, every cultural system is found by the investigator to exist for certain conscious and active historical subjects, i.e., within the sphere of experience and activity of some particular people, individuals and collectivities, living in a certain part of the human world during a certain historical period. Consequently, for the scientist this cultural system is really and objectively as it was (or is) given to those historical subjects themselves when they were (or are) experiencing it and actively dealing with it. In a word, the data of the cultural student are always "somebody's," never "nobody's" data. This essential character of cultural data we call the *humanistic coefficient,* because such data, as objects of the student's theoretic reflection, already belong to somebody else's active experience and are such as this active experience makes them.
>
> If the humanistic coefficient were withdrawn and the scientist attempted to study the cultural system as he studies a natural system, i.e., as if it existed independently of human experience and activity, the system would disappear and in its stead he would find a disjointed mass of natural things and processes, without any similarity to the reality he started to investigate.

The concept of humanistic coefficient remained an important part of Znaniecki's work, and *The Social Role of the Man of Knowledge,* contains an elaboration of it: [2]

> . . . an objective investigation of systems of knowledge in their composition, structure, and relationships must take fully into consideration that which is an essential characteristic of every system of knowledge: its claim to be true, that is, objectively valid. The sociologist, however, is not entitled to make any judgments concerning the validity of any systems of knowledge except sociological systems. He meets systems of knowledge in the course of his investigation only when he finds that certain persons or groups that he studies are actively interested in them, that they construct, improve, supplement, reproduce, defend, or popularize systems which they regard as true or else reject, oppose, criticize, or interfere with the propagation of systems which they consider untrue. In every such case the sociologist is bound to abide by whatever standards of validity these individuals or groups apply to the knowledge in which they take an active share. For, as an observer of cultural life, he can understand the data he observes only if he takes them with the "humanistic coefficient," only if he does not limit his observation to

SOURCE: Helena Znaniecki Lopata, "On the Humanistic Coefficient," original paper prepared especially for this volume.

[1] Florian W. Znaniecki, *The Method of Sociology* (New York: Rinehart and Company, 1934), pp. 36–37.
[2] Florian W. Znaniecki, *The Social Role of the Man of Knowledge* (New York: Columbia University Press, 1940), p. 5.

his own direct experience of the data but reconstructs the experience of the men who are dealing with them actively.

Znaniecki, prior to his death, had conceived a "magnum opus"—*Systematic Sociology*—and the presumed introduction to that work became a volume in its own right. *Cultural Sciences* was entirely devoted to the analysis of the subject matter and methods of sociology and the related sciences. Published in 1952, it included an extensive discussion of the humanistic coefficient: [3]

> In contrast with the natural scientist, who seeks to discover an order among empirical data entirely independent of conscious agents, the student of culture seeks to discover any order among empirical data which depends upon conscious human agents, is produced, and is maintained by them. To perform this task he takes every empirical datum which he investigates with what we have called its humanistic coefficient, i.e., as it appears to those human individuals who experience it and use it. He can apply this coefficient both to data which natural scientists include in the physical world—a star, a mountain, a plant, an animal—and to those which they exclude from it—a religious myth, the fictional plot of a novel, an ethical ideal. Furthermore, in applying the humanistic coefficient, an inductive student of culture does not accept the doctrine that his own active experience constitutes the main and most reliable source of knowledge about the data which he experiences.

Znaniecki had hoped to include in his *Systematic Sociology* considerations of social relations and social roles, social groups, and societies. However, he was only able to complete the study of the former. In his *Social Relations and Social Roles,* the notion of the humanistic coefficient found its final form in a chapter entitled, "The Humanistic versus Naturalistic Approach to Sociological Fields." Published posthumously in 1965, this chapter focussed first on the nature of naturalistic observation: [4]

> A study limited to these (physical) data is strictly objective, in the sense that its results, such as they are, seem entirely independent of all subjective ideas, beliefs, attitudes, and tendencies of the people who compose a collectivity.
> But this is precisely the fundamental weakness of the naturalistic approach. For the people who participate in a human collectivity are not only biological organisms: They are also conscious thinkers and agents, just like the observer himself. It is impossible to explain what they are doing or to predict what they will do without taking fully into consideration their ideas, beliefs, attitudes, and active tendencies. Almost all the data which the investigator experiences are also experienced by them, indeed, were probably experienced by them long before he arrived. This includes the area which they inhabit, its topography, its climate, all the objects, animate and inanimate, in this area, their bodies, everything they may consume and produce, and all the tools they use. Whatever these data may be to the observer as a natural scientist, to them practically they are meaningful *values:* and how they treat these values depends not on what he thinks, but on what they think about them.

Znaniecki, then, drew a sharp distinction: [5]

---

[3] Florian W. Znaniecki, *Cultural Sciences* (Urbana: University of Illinois Press, 1952), p. 132.
[4] Florian W. Znaniecki, *Social Relations and Social Roles* (San Francisco: Chandler Publishing Co., 1965), pp. 49–50.
[5] *Ibid.,* p. 50.

Consequently, through his study the investigator must always try to discover how anything he observes within his field of research is experienced and evaluated by those human agents who are actively interested in it. We call this the *humanistic approach*. And in the course of this approach, he will find that the valuations and actions of conscious human agents are not naturally determined but culturally conditioned.

Thus, Florian Znaniecki gradually modified the original concept of humanistic coefficient as a subjective datum which the method of sociology must investigate into a cultural datum, or a total *humanistic approach to sociological fields*.

17   The Context of Situation

● BRONISLAW MALINOWSKI

. . . It needs no special stressing that in a primitive language the meaning of any single word is to a very high degree dependent on its context. The words 'wood,' 'paddle,' 'place' had to be retranslated in the free interpretation in order to show what is their real meaning, conveyed to a native by the context in which they appear. Again, it is equally clear that the meaning of the expression 'we arrive near the village (of our destination)' literally: 'we paddle in place,' is determined only by taking it in the context of the whole utterance. This latter again, becomes only intelligible when it is placed within its *context of situation*, if I may be allowed to coin an expression which indicates on the one hand that the conception of *context* has to be broadened and on the other that the *situation* in which words are uttered can never be passed over as irrelevant to the linguistic expression. We see how the conception of context must be substantially widened, if it is to furnish us with its full utility. In fact it must burst the bonds of mere linguistics and be carried over into the analysis of the general conditions under which a language is spoken. Thus, starting from the wider idea of context, we arrive once more at the results of the foregoing section, namely that the study of any language, spoken by a people who live under conditions different from our own and possess a different culture, must be carried out in conjunction with the study of their culture and of their environment.

But the widened conception of *context of situation* yields more than that. It makes clear the difference in scope and method between the linguistics of dead and of living languages. The material on which almost all our linguistic study has been done so far belongs to dead languages. It is present in the form of written documents, naturally isolated, torn out of any *context of situation*. In fact, written statements are set down with the purpose of being self-contained and self-explanatory. A mortuary inscription, a fragment of primeval laws or precepts, a chapter or statement in a sacred book, or to take a more modern example, a passage from a Greek or Latin philosopher, historian or poet—one and all of these were composed with the purpose of bringing their message to posterity unaided, and they had to contain this message within their own bounds.

SOURCE: Bronislaw Malinowski, from C. K. Ogden and I. A. Richards, *The Meaning of Meaning* (New York: Harcourt, Brace, and World, Inc., 1923), pp. 306–309. Reprinted by permission of the publisher.

To take the clearest case, that of a modern scientific book, the writer of it sets out to address every individual reader who will peruse the book and has the necessary scientific training. He tries to influence his reader's mind in certain directions. With the printed text of the book before him, the reader, at the writer's bidding, undergoes a series of processes—he reasons, reflects, remembers, imagines. The book by itself is sufficient to direct the reader's mind to its meaning; and we might be tempted to say metaphorically that the meaning is wholly contained in or carried by the book.

But when we pass from a modern civilized language, of which we think mostly in terms of written records, or from a dead one which survives only in inscription, to a primitive tongue, never used in writing, where all the material lives only in winged words, passing from man to man—there it should be clear at once that the conception of meaning as *contained* in an utterance is false and futile. A statement, spoken in real life, is never detached from the situation in which it has been uttered. For each verbal statement by a human being has the aim and function of expressing some thought or feeling actual at that moment and in that situation, and necessary for some reason or other to be made known to another person or persons—in order either to serve purposes of common action, or to establish ties of purely social communion, or else to deliver the speaker of violent feelings or passions. Without some imperative stimulus of the moment, there can be no spoken statement. In each case, therefore, utterance and situation are bound up inextricably with each other and the context of situation is indispensable for the understanding of the words. Exactly as in the reality of spoken or written languages, a word without *linguistic context* is a mere figment and stands for nothing by itself, so in the reality of a spoken living tongue, the utterance has no meaning except in the *context of situation*.

It will be quite clear now that the point of view of the Philologist, who deals only with remnants of dead languages, must differ from that of the Ethnographer, who, deprived of the ossified, fixed data of inscriptions, has to rely on the living reality of spoken language *in fluxu*. The former has to reconstruct the general situation—*i.e.*, the culture of a past people—from the extant statements, the latter can study directly the conditions and situations characteristic of a culture and interpret the statements through them. Now I claim that the Ethnographer's perspective is the one relevant and real for the formation of fundamental linguistic conceptions and for the study of the life of languages, whereas the Philologist's point of view is fictitious and irrelevant. For language in its origins has been merely the free, spoken *sum total* of utterances such as we find now in a savage tongue. All the foundations and fundamental characteristics of human speech have received their shape and character in the stage of development proper to Ethnographic study and not in the Philologist's domain. To define Meaning, to explain the essential grammatical and lexical characters of language on the material furnished by the study of dead languages, is nothing short of preposterous in the light of our argument. Yet it would be hardly an exaggeration to say that 99 per cent of all linguistic work has been inspired by the study of dead languages or at best of written records torn completely out of any context of situation. That the Ethnographer's perspective can yield not only generalities but positive, concrete conclusions I shall indicate. . . .

[The] attitude in which the word is regarded as a real entity, containing its meaning as a Soul-box contains the spiritual part of a person or thing, is shown to be derived from the primitive, magical uses of language and to reach right into the most important and influential systems of metaphysics. Meaning, the real 'essence' of a word, achieves thus Real Existence in Plato's realm of Ideas; and it becomes the Universal, actually existing, of mediæval Realists. The misuse of words, based always on a false analysis of their Semantic function, leads to all the ontological morass in philosophy, where truth is found by spinning out meaning from the word, its assumed receptacle. . . .

The clear realization of the intimate connection between linguistic interpretation and the analysis of the culture to which the language belongs shows convincingly that neither a Word nor its Meaning has an independent and self-sufficient existence. The Ethnographic view of language proves the principle of Symbolic Relativity as it might be called, that is that words must be treated only as symbols and that a psychology of symbolic reference must serve as the basis for all science of language. Since the whole world of 'things-to be-expressed' changes with the level of culture, with geographical, social and economic conditions, the consequence is that the meaning of a word must be always gathered, not from a passive contemplation of this word, but from an analysis of its functions, with reference to the given culture. Each primitive or barbarous tribe, as well as each type of civilization, has its world of meanings and the whole linguistic apparatus of this people—their store of words and their type of grammar—can only be explained in connection with their mental requirements. . . .

18   The Name of the Situation as Affecting Behavior

● BENJAMIN LEE WHORF

. . . In the course of my professional work for a fire insurance company, . . . I undertook the task of analyzing many hundreds of reports of circumstances surrounding the start of fires, and in some cases, of explosions. My analysis was directed toward purely physical conditions, such as defective wiring, presence or lack of air spaces between metal flues and woodwork, etc., and the results were presented in these terms. Indeed it was undertaken with no thought that any other significances would or could be revealed. But in due course it became evident that not only a physical situation *qua* physics, but the meaning of that situation to people, was sometimes a factor, through the behavior of the people, in the start of the fire. And this factor of meaning was clearest when it was a LINGUISTIC MEANING, residing in the name or the linguistic description commonly applied to the situation. Thus, around a storage of what are called "gasoline drums," behavior will tend to a certain type, that is, great care will be exercised; while around a storage of what are called "empty gasoline drums," it will tend to be different—careless, with little repression of smoking or of tossing cigarette stubs about. Yet the "empty" drums are perhaps the more dangerous, since they

SOURCE: Benjamin Lee Whorf, in his *Language, Thought and Reality* (Cambridge: M.I.T. Press, 1956), pp. 135–137.

contain explosive vapor. Physically the situation is hazardous, but the linguistic analysis according to regular analogy must employ the word 'empty,' which inevitably suggests lack of hazard. The word 'empty' is used in two linguistic patterns: (1) as a virtual synonym for 'null and void, negative, inert,' (2) applied in analysis of physical situations without regard to, e.g., vapor, liquid vestiges, or stray rubbish, in the container. The situation is named in one pattern (2) and the name is then "acted out" or "lived up to" in another (1), this being a general formula for the linguistic conditioning of behavior into hazardous forms.

In a wood distillation plant the metal stills were insulated with a composition prepared from limestone and called at the plant "spun limestone." No attempt was made to protect this covering from excessive heat or the contact of flame. After a period of use, the fire below one of the stills spread to the "limestone," which to everyone's great surprise burned vigorously. Exposure to acetic acid fumes from the stills had converted part of the limestone (calcium carbonate) to calcium acetate. This when heated in a fire decomposes, forming inflammable acetone. Behavior that tolerated fire close to the covering was induced by use of the name "limestone," which because it ends in "-stone" implies noncombustibility.

A huge iron kettle of boiling varnish was observed to be overheated, nearing the temperature at which it would ignite. The operator moved it off the fire and ran it on its wheels to a distance, but did not cover it. In a minute or so the varnish ignited. Here the linguistic influence is more complex; it is due to the metaphorical objectifying . . . of "cause" as contact or the spatial juxtaposition of "things"—to analyzing the situation as 'on' versus 'off' the fire. In reality, the stage when the external fire was the main factor had passed; the overheating was now an internal process of convection in the varnish from the intensely heated kettle, and still continued when 'off' the fire.

An electric glow heater on the wall was little used, and for one workman had the meaning of a convenient coathanger. At night a watchman entered and snapped a switch, which action he verbalized as 'turning on the light.' No light appeared, and this result he verbalized as 'light is burned out.' He could not see the glow of the heater because of the old coat hung on it. Soon the heater ignited the coat, which set fire to the building.

A tannery discharged waste water containing animal matter into an outdoor settling basin partly roofed with wood and partly open. This situation is one that ordinarily would be verbalized as 'pool of water.' A workman had occasion to light a blowtorch near by, and threw his match into the water. But the decomposing waste matter was evolving gas under the wood cover, so that the setup was the reverse of 'watery.' An instant flare of flame ignited the woodwork, and the fire quickly spread into the adjoining building.

A drying room for hides was arranged with a blower at one end to make a current of air along the room and thence outdoors through a vent at the other end. Fire started at a hot bearing on the blower, which blew the flames directly into the hides and fanned them along the room, destroying the entire stock. This hazardous setup followed naturally from the term 'blower' with its linguistic equivalence to 'that which blows,' implying that its function necessarily is to 'blow.' Also its function is verbalized as 'blowing air for drying,' overlooking that it can blow other things, e.g., flames and sparks. In reality, a blower simply makes a current of air and can exhaust as well as blow. It should have been installed at the vent end to DRAW the air over the hides, then through the hazard (its own casing and bearings), and thence outdoors.

Beside a coal-fired melting pot for lead reclaiming was dumped a pile of "scrap lead"—a misleading verbalization, for it consisted of the lead sheets of old radio condensers, which still had paraffin paper between them. Soon the paraffin blazed up and fired the roof, half of which was burned off.

Such examples, which could be greatly multiplied, will suffice to show how the cue to a certain line of behavior is often given by the analogies of the linguistic formula in which the situation is spoken of, and by which to some degree it is analyzed, classified, and allotted its place in that world which is "to a large extent unconsciously built up on the language habits of the group." And we always assume that the linguistic analysis made by our group reflects reality better than it does.

19   The Definition of the Situation

● WILLARD WALLER

One of the sociological concepts most useful for the understanding of the life of human beings in and about the school is that of the definition of the situation. This concept we owe to W. I. Thomas. Although loosely defined, it is a valuable concept because it designates certain real aspects of psychic and social life, and explains phenomena otherwise without significance.

Strictly speaking, the definition of the situation is a process. It is the process in which the individual explores the behavior possibilities of a situation, marking out particularly the limitations which the situation imposes upon his behavior, with the final result that the individual forms an attitude toward the situation, or, more exactly, in the situation. In another sense, however, we use the phrase, *the definition of the situation,* to denote the actual concrete situation as it has been defined, or to denote certain psychic products of group life which are left as residua from the definition of many situations. Many persons living together in a common group life for many overlapping generations have mapped out clearly the limitations of behavior inherent in the social situations most common in their culture. From their experience has arisen a consensus concerning what is and what is not thinkable in those situations. From these situations as they have been defined have been generalized certain group products which have in turn become important conditions of life in that group. We may refer to these group products as definitions of situations. When we take an abstracting attitude toward these group products we may think of them as folkways, mores, taboos, collective representations, group attitudes, laws, etc. But all these things affect the individual only as they are incorporated into the situations of his life; they affect him by virtue of the fact that while he is working out his attitude toward the situations of his own life he is influenced by certain preexisting

SOURCE: Willard Waller, from his *The Sociology of Teaching* (New York: John Wiley & Sons, Inc., 1961).

definitions of situations; they affect him only in so far as he becomes aware of and assimilates those preexisting definitions of situations. Those group products that we know as folkways, mores, etc., are preconditions and necessary elements of the definition of the situation which the individual works out for himself.

From a slightly different point of view further looseness of expression appears. Actually the definition of the situation, as a process by which the individual explores and feels out through behavior and thought the behavior possibilities of a situation, is a process most intimately subjective, and one that must be worked out anew in the mind of every human being. But because one person can greatly affect the definition of the situation which another arrives at, we are accustomed to say that one person defines a situation for another. The attitudes of others are in fact the most important limitations upon the behavior of any one person, and they are also the most important inducements to any particular action. The attitudes of others are dynamic elements in the undefined situation which presents itself to any individual, and as a result of those attitudes the individual may come to define the situation in one way and not in another. Therefore we may say that one person defines a situation for another.

Before proceeding further with our elaboration of this concept we turn to Thomas for a statement of his views: [1]

> Preliminary to any self-determined act of behavior there is always a stage of examination and deliberation which we may call *the definition of the situation.* And actually not only concrete acts are dependent upon the definition of the situation, but gradually a whole life-policy and the personality of the individual himself follow from a series of such definitions. . . .
>
> The family is the smallest social unit and the primary defining agency. As soon as the child has free motion and begins to pull, tear, meddle, and prowl, the parents begin to define the situation through speech and other signs and pressures: "Be quiet," "Sit up straight," "Blow your nose," "Mind your mother," "Be kind to sister," etc. This is the real significance of Wordsworth's phrase, "Shades of the prison house begin to close upon the growing child." His wishes and activities begin to be inhibited, and gradually, by definitions within the family, by playmates, in the school, in the Sunday School, in the community, through reading, by formal instruction, by informal signs of approval and disapproval, the growing member learns the code of his society.

This behavioristic account of the process of the definition of the situation seems essentially correct. One might venture to change its emphasis in two ways: (1) by substituting for its atomistic conception a more explicit statement of the fact that every situation affecting the individual is organized into some kind of totality, usually a wholly unambiguous totality, and (2) by allowing for the self-activity, often the intelligent self-activity, of the individual who is learning the definition of a situation.

There is, indeed, a place for self-activity in a possible behavioristic account of the definition of the situation. The individual facing a situation with a relatively rigid social framework makes a large number of incipient attempts to adjust; those not adapted to his purpose fail and are eliminated; those which are adapted persist and are at length assembled into the individual's final adjustment. But it is submitted that this is not an altogether truthful account of the

---

[1] Thomas, W. I., *The Unadjusted Girl*, pp. 42 ff. (Reprinted by permission of Little, Brown, & Company.)

manner in which a definition of a situation is arrived at; intelligence enters into the process, and there ensues a dynamic reorganization of the parts of the situation into a pattern. In short, it is submitted that a Gestaltist account of the process of the definition of the situation is in some respects superior to the behavioristic account.

It is clear that the definitions of situations which the child must learn are in fact a part of culture, and are carried by the group and imposed upon the child through group activity. When we turn our attention more narrowly to the subjective activity of the individual who is working out a definition of a situation, or, if one prefers, is assimilating the definition of a situation which his group is imposing upon him, we find that the process resolves itself into certain other elements. Elements implicit in the process of the definition of the situation are:

1. The configuration in which it is perceived.
2. The aspect of the situation toward which action is directed.
3. The attitude or activity which comes out of the interaction between individual and situation and the organization of himself which the individual effects with regard to the situation.

Much of the importance of the definition of the situation in human affairs arises from the configurational element involved in the process. When a situation has once been seen in a particular configuration, it tends to be seen in that configuration ever after, and it is very difficult to see it in any other. The configuration first established may be said to inhibit the formation of other configurations. The changelessness of custom arises in part from the fact that we cannot see those alternatives of behavior which are contrary to the folkways of our group; we have organized the situation, and ourselves with reference to it, in another configuration. As configurations differ in their stability, we find some definitions of situations which are easily resolved, whereas others are stubborn and resistant to change. The extraordinary rigidity of certain cultures may thus arise from the fact that they are organized into stable configurations. Further, as an important element of intelligence is the ability to blast the units of configurations loose from their context and to recombine them in different patterns, we find the intelligent ever the (relatively) emancipated. From this configurational element, too, arises in part our well-known lack of ability to discover many things which are close to us; the things we do not see appear in our vision, but with the arrangement of foreground and background or of wholes and subwholes such that they do not take shape as definite entities.

The aspect of the situation toward which action is directed is also a factor of importance. We direct our attention toward that which is in the foreground, and we overlook that which is in the background of the situation as it is organized into a particular configuration. The foreground tends to be, in a configuration which makes up the definition of a situation, the point of least resistance. We direct our attention and our action toward that which can be changed, and we do not attempt to alter changeless things. Only so, of course, can we realize ourselves at all, and that law of attention is also a law of mental hygiene. The attitude or activity which comes out of the situation is the third element which we have noted. We think of the attitude as behavior or incipient behavior resulting from the organization of the situation in the individual's mind and the concurrent organization of the individual with reference to the situation.

The process by which the individual works out a definition of the situation, or an attitude toward a situation, seems to conform closely to Kohler's concept of closure, which is defined as follows: "In every process which issues at all in an end-situation, independent of time (although it is possible to apply this to events occurring in time), the mode of distribution [of energy] shifts in the direction of a minimum of configurative energy." [2] The attitude inheres in the definition of the situation as "the answer sticks in the question." "Questions demanding thought arouse configurational processes which are incomplete and call for closure. The answer thus 'sticks' in the question. A good question and a good answer are not matters of chance: they fit each other as the key and the lock. Once the form suggested by the question is apprehended, there is a sudden *Einschnappen;* the inner bond appears, baring the structure, and the configuration is completed." [3] In a manner exactly analogous the attitude is interlocked with the definition of the situation.

The social rôle, like the definition of the situation, appears in the mind by a sudden Einschnappen. In a simple society, one always prays, or one always gets drunk on certain occasions, but it sometimes happens in our more complicated life that an individual enters a new group quite uncertain as to which of these he will be called upon to do. Who has not, when faced with a novel situation, felt an unease and a sensation of gawky discomfort, and who has not felt these suddenly dissipated by a flashing awareness of his rôle? The problem of social adjustment is the problem of finding a rôle. The definition of the situation determines one's rôle and sets up the delimitations of his self-feelings. The rôle appears in the social situation, as the attitude in any situation, in accordance with configurational processes conforming to the concept of closure.

Personality develops through the growth of adaptations to a finely graded series of definitions of situations. (From discontinuity and discordance in the definitions of situations presented to the individual arise most of our mental conflicts.) The evolution of situations, and of definitions of situations, goes from simple to complex, with occasional breakdowns (in which complex wholes, of which the structure may or may not have been perceived at one time, break up into simpler units) apparently determined by the laws of attention. Within existing situations, too, there may be a growth of structure attended by a corresponding refinement of adaptation. In accordance with general principles of configurational change, human situations advance from chaotic and confused groups of elements with a minimum of structuration to more and more complex and clearly organized structures.

Without embarking upon any more extended discussion of the concept of the definition of the situation as an important bit of social theory, we may remark that this concept becomes important in our interpretation of the social life of the school in a number of different ways. First, the school may be viewed as an agency for imposing preformed definitions of situations. Education, as has been truly said, is the art of imposing upon the young; it is the art of imposing upon the young the definitions of situations current and accepted in the group which maintains the schools. The school is thus a gigantic agency of social control. It is part of its function to transmit to the young the attitudes of the elders, which it does by presenting to them social situations as the elders have defined them.

---

[2] Quoted by Helson, Harry, *The Psychlogy of Gestalt*, p. 45.
[3] Helson, *op. cit.*, p. 54.

Again, and this is our major concern at this point, the social life of the schools may be seen as a mass of situations to be defined by or for the persons involved in them. The many and various social situations of school life may be defined, as it seems, in three ways:

1. Spontaneously by students or teachers, or by students and teachers.
2. By teachers, chiefly with reference to standards current in society outside the school or current in the teacher group.
3. By students, chiefly with reference to standards current outside the school.

From the fact that situations may be defined in different ways and by different groups arises a conflict of definitions of situations, and we may see the whole process of personal and group conflict which centers about the school as a conflict of contradictory definitions of situations. The fundamental problem of school discipline may be stated as the struggle of students and teachers to establish their own definitions of situations in the life of the school.

We see many undefined situations confronting the individual in the school. The new teacher confronts a situation wholly undefined, and he has very little idea as to the details of the definition that would be desirable from his own point of view. The experienced teacher who faces a new class faces an undefined situation, and it is part of his job to impose his definition of the situation upon the class quickly, before any alternatives have had an opportunity to be considered. The child in school for the first time also faces a situation with whose definition he is not familiar, and it is sometimes long before he can understand what is expected of him in school.

It may be well to consider in detail the process by which some of these persons work out satisfactory definitions of school situations, impose those definitions upon others, or adjust to the definitions put forward by others. Many teachers have learned that it pays to spare themselves no unpleasantness in order to establish and make secure their dominance in the first few days and weeks of school. They exert themselves particularly to define the situation as one in which the teacher is dominant. Until this definition of the situation is accepted, there will be some conflict between teacher and student, and some hostility of students toward the teacher; the problem will be more severe in a school that has previously been poorly disciplined. Until his definition of the situation is thoroughly established in the minds of his students, the teacher cannot relax. After the first few weeks in which conflict over the definition of the situation has been severe, the hostility toward the teacher dies down; this is in most cases owing to the operation of two factors: use and acceptance of the situation makes teacher domination bearable to the students, and the teacher relaxes his grip slightly, just enough to give friendly attitudes a chance to spring up within the situation. But these friendly attitudes must always spring up within the situation as defined in terms of teacher domination; if they spring up outside it, they conflict with it and operate to overthrow the so painfully established social order. . . .

It is axiomatic among school men that the first day of school, or the first meeting of a class, is all-important in determining the success or failure of the school year. A realization of this fact has led certain school men to lay down rigid rules for the conduct of classes on the first day of school. Bagley, whose work along this line is classic, has given us a set of directions for the first day, which, if closely followed, will present the child with a situation whose boundaries are quite clearly indicated and quite firmly held, so that acceptance of the teacher's definition of the situation is almost inevitable. . . .

Since nearly all his suggestions have some implications as to the relationship established between the teacher and his students, they will be quoted *in extenso*.

1. Be on hand early.
2. See that the classroom is in good condition; floors clean, desks dusted, wardrobes ready for use. Do not complain to principal or janitor unless conditions are intolerable. Remedy matters yourself.
3. See that the chalk and erasers are distributed at the blackboard, or in readiness for distribution by monitors to be appointed. In any case, be sure that these necessary materials are on hand and in condition to be used— chalk boxes open, erasers cleaned, etc.
4. Place upon the blackboard whatever work you have provided for your earliest classes. Your program will doubtless indicate arithmetic as one of the earliest forms of seat work. Have examples upon the blackboard in sufficient number to provide arithmetic for all classes.
5. Pupils who arrive early should be greeted pleasantly and directed to take seats. Many successful teachers require pupils arriving before the "first bell" to observe the same decorum that they would observe during the regular session, so long as they remain in the school room rather than upon the playground. Whether you adopt this policy or not, it is well on the first morning to check any tendency to run about the room or to pass from seat to seat.
6. It is good policy always to enlist the aid of pupils in helping you about the routine preparatory to the real school work. On the first morning, they may, at your direction, distribute the chalk and erasers, slips of paper for the names of the pupils, the pencils, etc.
7. Everything should be in readiness when the bell rings and the lines come in. The teacher should direct the pupils to take seats regularly in the different rows in the order of their entering the room. After this preliminary seating, changes may be immediately made if desired. If there are two classes, and if one has already been in the room—as will be the case wherever the promotions are semi-annual—let the older pupils take the seats occupied the preceding term. If all or most of the pupils are new, let them take seats as suggested as speedily as possible, making temporary changes where necessary to accommodate pupils to different sizes of seats and desks. This should occupy but a brief period.
8. Place into immediate application your prearranged plan for disposing of the hats and wraps. If they are to be collected, appoint the first or the last pupil in each row as a monitor for this purpose. Give clear, distinct directions, and enforce these directions rigidly from the outset. If the wraps are to be left in the wardrobe as the pupils pass in, have the lines file out and return to the room according to your plan, depositing their wraps as they pass. The manner in which you handle this, the very first bit of routine, will have a large share in determining the first impression that you leave with your students.
9. When this has been accomplished, the time is opportune for your opening remarks, if you wish to make any. Let these be brief, clear-cut, and devoid of threats, cant, or platitudes. Especially guard against "soft-soapiness."

A song is also in place if you can select one which is familiar to all the pupils, and lead it well yourself. Devotional exercises are in place unless prohibited by law, ruling, or public sentiment.

10. After these preliminaries direct each pupil to write his name upon the slip of paper handed to him. Have the first pupil in each row collect the slips, placing his own at the bottom of the bundle, and the others in order. As the slips of each row are brought to you, place a rubber-band about them and then arrange the bundles across your desk in the order of the rows. You will then be able, with a minimum of trouble, to find the name of any pupil by reference to the slips belonging to his row.

11. All this should occupy but a brief period of time—certainly not more than twenty minutes—and from this time on, in a two-class or three-class room, the regular program should be adhered to. Assign work to the more advanced class, if there are two, or to all but the lowest class, if there are more than two. The first recitation should begin with this. If the pupils are to come forward to occupy a recitation bench, give explicit directions for the passing of lines, and explain the signals that you propose to use. It will probably be necessary to give two or three drills upon this before the movement to the bench and back to the seats satisfies you. The first day's work may very well be devoted in part to such drills, but always save time for some serious work. If the class passes to the blackboard, drill it several times in the prearranged movement of lines.

12. [Relates to classification of ungraded schools.]

13. Stop all work a few minutes before recess time to drill pupils upon the passing of lines. In a large graded school it will be necessary to know how all the lines pass to the playground in order that you may assemble your pupils in the proper place. This should be one of the matters learned beforehand by consultation with the principal or with other teachers.

14. Appoint monitors to distribute pens, tablets, copy-books, etc., just prior to the first periods when these materials are used. Distribute the monitorial functions among as many pupils as possible, holding each strictly responsible from the first for the efficiency of his service. Devote some time during the first day to drilling the monitors in these duties. Let them pass and collect the materials again and again, until they can do the work with celerity, dispatch, and good order. If you propose to use this monitorial service as a reward of good standing, let the pupils know this at the start, stating that changes will be made at the beginning of the second week or month, as the case may be.[4]

Perhaps the thing which most impresses one who is familiar with a different philosophy of school management is the extreme rigidity of the social order which Bagley would see fit to set up in the schools. But one is struck, too, with the extreme practicality of the discussion, and this impression is increased by the reflection that thousands of teachers and prospective teachers have profited in the past from a study of Bagley. Bagley has stated clearly and succinctly the rules of thumb which school men have worked out for the starting procedure

---

[4] Bagley, W. C., *Classroom Management*, pp. 25–28. Reprinted by permission of The Macmillan Company.

in schools of the more rigid sort. These rules of thumb are correct as far as they go, and Bagley's remains the classic statement of them. They have more meaning, however, when we think of them as going together to make up a procedure for the definition of the social situation in the school, a procedure for working out and imposing upon students a particular definition of the situation in which the student does almost nothing on his own initiative and in which the teacher is completely dominant. . . .

Particular rules are perhaps deserving of further comment. The meaning of the suggestions concerning preparation of the school room on the physical side, and the assembling of materials for school work, is plainly to prevent improvisation by students, which is not regarded as desirable. It is suggested that many teachers require pupils arriving before the first bell to take their seats at once and to observe school-room decorum, and that those who consider this excessively stern should at any rate check any tendency to run about the room or to pass from seat to seat. This prevents the spontaneous definition of the situation which children might work out on the spur of the moment from becoming established before school opens. The drill upon routine matters serves two purposes: it impresses the school situation, with its rules and its restrictions and its mechanized routine, firmly upon the student's mind; and it gives the teacher an opportunity to establish his domination by giving directions about matters over which conflict is not likely to arise. The monitorial system which Bagley recommends has another function, that of aligning certain students favorably with respect to the teacher; the drill upon the functions of the monitors is again a means of impressing the teacher's definition of the situation upon the student's mind. (As we have elsewhere noted, the use of monitors allows the teacher to remain immobile, and therefore to remain in command of the situation more easily.)

In certain places in the discussion quoted above, the attitudes of the professional teacher crop out undisguised. ". . . the time is opportune for your opening remarks, if you wish to make any. Let these be brief, clear-cut, and devoid of threats, cant, or platitudes. Especially guard against *soft-soapiness*." There speaks the teacher! Intercourse between teacher and student must be limited to the matter in hand; the teacher must not say anything which would involve him in a human interaction with his pupils. Bagley here demonstrates his thorough understanding of life within the institution of the school; it is better if the teacher takes the classroom situation for granted and defines the situation from that standpoint by words and deeds relevant to that orientation; and a verbalization of any of the principles upon which the classroom rapport is based would be very difficult and dangerous; a correct statement would antagonize students unduly, and a faulty statement would set up a conflicting definition of the situation. Undoubtedly this is excellent advice for one who wishes to keep a well-regimented school room, but one feels that it is the sort of advice which ought to be given regretfully. To the professional teacher, there is no occasion for regret in the fact that neither teacher nor pupil can express his whole self in the classroom; it is all to the good that teachers speak little, crisply, and without tenderness. But from the larger point of view this may have regrettable consequences for teachers and students alike.

Bagley would probably be the first to admit that all definite rules have limited utility. Teachers differ, and the sort of rapport which one finds workable may be quite impossible for another. The teacher who regiments his students in the older way might not make a good Morrison plan teacher, nor should a teacher whose effectiveness depends upon good nature and stability ever attempt to increase his effectiveness by adding to his accomplishments the fault-finding technique. Better, then, than to suggest specific techniques as always useful, and better than to attempt to develop like character traits in all teachers, would it be to attempt to give teachers a complete understanding of the social processes centering about school life, and to leave to each one the task of working out that technique which will help him most in carrying on the particular sort of education which he considers desirable.

But it is never enough to define the situation clearly on the first day of school. If the teacher is to retain control of the school-room social life, he must renew his definition of the situation from moment to moment and adapt his technique to the developing occasion. Bagley, in common with many other writers, suggests that as much of this school-room activity as possible should be routinized and mechanized. According to this theory, the teacher must so order the first day that everything goes as he has planned and no opportunity is given for even a moment of spontaneous life in which a definition of the situation contrary to that of the teacher can be worked out, and thereafter he must crystallize as much of this procedure as possible into routine. Thus from one year to the next the teacher maintains his absolute unvarying control and children never slip from his fingers.

It never happens, however, that the situation can be so clearly defined and classroom procedure so rigidly routinized that no disorder, that is, no definition of the situation spontaneously arrived at by students in opposition to the definition of the situation put forward by the teacher, can ever arise. Life has a way of finding breaches in the fences that we put around it (and this is one of the arguments for a more plastic technique of maintaining discipline). When these conflicting definitions of the situation confront the teacher, the teacher must consistently renew his own definition of the situation, using whatever technique he has found most satisfactory for himself. The conflict of definitions of situation may involve the teacher in personal conflict, or it may be resolved in other ways. Bagley, discussing the quality of persistence as an attribute of the teacher, has incidentally described the technique by which the stern disciplinarian maintains his initial definition of the situation. It is a technique of persistence, consistency, and persistence with redoubled effort. (All of these depend upon an initial stability of character.) . . .

We become aware how far we have travelled along the road toward the humanization of education when we contrast the arbitrary mode of maintaining the definition of the situation described by Bagley with the one which would be recommended on the basis of modern psychology and the experience of the more advanced modern schools. The stern disciplinarian knew only one tune; he played it softly at first and then he played it more loudly; we know some variations now. Nor are we quite so sure as Bagley was that the character training which is always one of the aims of education is to be effected by denial of choice and the imposition of good habits from without. We should pin our faith to that subtler control which comes from insight into the character of the person to be controlled, and should try to inculcate in him desirable general attitudes rather than specific habits. Nor do we think, now, that the "acme of good discipline is attained when the conditions of order are preserved automatically, without thought or judgment on the pupil's part." When we did think that, persistence with redoubled effort was the keynote of school policy; now the cardinal point of policy is persistence with an effort revised and corrected by growing understanding and insight. And though good order might well be habitual and largely unconscious we should not want good order attained without thought or judgment on the pupil's part.

The newer order of school discipline, still rare, it should be said, makes greater demands upon the teacher than did the old. It requires a greater imagination, a greater understanding, and a more fluid and adaptable technique. To be sure, the demands of enlightened discipline may cost the teacher less than it would cost her to maintain a Prussian organization; the teacher's personality was warped under the old system as thoroughly as the student's, the strong teacher's character no less, though differently, than that of the weak teacher who broke her heart trying to maintain an order that was, for her, impossible. But whereas a simple technique for defining the situation was sufficient for the highly regimented school, a complicated technique is required for a school that tries to maintain a more flexible life. . . .

Whatever the type of discipline which he tries to build up, and whatever the sort of social order which the teacher tries to establish in the school, the teacher has need of a number of techniques for defining the situation. The same techniques, with different emphases, are apparently used by all kinds of teachers. Some of the more important devices for defining the situation or maintaining an existent definition are the following; routinization, punishment, express statement, ritual, personal influence resulting from the involvement of the teacher in classroom situations, and personal influence derived from understanding and the use of psychological mechanisms. Routinization has already been discussed.

The favorite device of the teacher attempting to maintain strict discipline in the older sense is punishment. Punishment separates out certain kinds of behavior as reprehensible, and imposes certain unpleasantnesses upon those guilty of such behavior. When punishment is successful, it defines the situation by imposing a taboo upon certain aberrant behavior. The empirical psychologists who conduct the schools think of punishment as a deterrent to undesirable behavior on a hedonistic basis. The penalty, as in the old criminology, must be made just sufficient to outweigh any pleasure which those to be controlled might take in tabooed behavior. It would be possible to work out a theoretical justification of punishment in terms of behavioristic psychology as negative conditioning. The difficulty here, as in the hedonistic theory of behavior and its control, is that the behavior itself often springs from attitudes which are not affected by punishment. There is a further difficulty, too, in that punishment often gives rise to countervailing attitudes which more than outweigh the punishment itself as a determinant of behavior. Experienced teachers, however, know that punishment does sometimes work, that it is called for in the dynamic social situation of the school. The value which it has seems to arise from the fact that it marks out certain behavior as taboo.

Another technique by which the situation is often defined is that of express statement. The teacher says, "We do this in our school," or "We do not do that in our class." This technique often suffices for the verbal imposition of a taboo or to mark out a change in the situation. Almost every teacher who has to succeed some weak or easy-going or popular teacher in the control of a school or class finds that he has to resort to some such device as this to make clear the transition from the control of the other person to his own domination. Students say, "But Mr. So-an-so let us keep our books open in class," and the teacher replies, "It's not old Man Nelson you are dealing with this year. It's Old Smith, and that's another story altogether."

Ritual is often used as a means of establishing a definition of the situation and keeping it established without change. Thus certain formalities in the relation of student and teacher are ritualized in order that no variants in those formalities may arise and in order that the attitudinal sets involved in the formalities may be carried over into other aspects of the relationship. This is one of the benefits of that mechanization of routine which Bagley advocates. In another use of ritual, formalized attitudes are taken or expressed with the hope that they may become internal. . . .

When the teacher becomes identified with the formal social organization of the school, his personal influence is likely to be almost wholly directed at the maintenance of that social order. The social order of the school has become a part of the teacher's expanded social self, and he lives and breathes in and through it. Thus it may happen that all the teacher's personal influence, composed of all the subtle and unconsidered personal emanations and psychic irradiations that come from him, his earnestness, his character, and his personal force, seems to be concerned with the maintenance of the teacher's definition of the situation. The temper of the teacher, to be specific, is nearly always metamorphosed into an instrument for maintaining teacher domination. As the new teacher becomes familiar with all the intricacies of the social situation of the classroom as students and teachers come to define it, he learns to become angry when any action of a student gives the slightest indication that the student is trying to define the situation in an unorthodox manner. This is the institutionalized temper.

In our discussion of the techniques used by teachers for defining the situation we should not fail to reckon with the possibility of a technique based upon a different kind of personal influence. This would be a technique not based upon the earnestness with which the teacher identifies himself with the moral order of the school room but upon his personal qualities plus an understanding of the social process in the school and of the characterological trends of his students. It is a technique already practiced in its simpler forms by teachers who have a high common-sense knowledge of human nature, and with more sophistication but perhaps less judgment by those teachers whose psychological and psychiatric training has made them aware of suggestion mechanisms and inferiority complexes.

We have already indicated that students become aware of many of the definitions of situations current in their culture as a direct or indirect result of their social experience in the schools. We have implied, as well, that one of the most important functions of the school is to transmit to young persons an awareness of these definitions of situations. That is, indeed, the central task of character education—to lead the young so to perceive and so to range themselves for action with reference to the social situations current in our culture that the result will be in accord with social policy. This is a task for which the actual social situations of school life should be utilized, for it is difficult to impose definitions of situations at long range through either the assigning of lessons or the reading of lectures. The social life of children has been utilized all too little, school authorities preferring to suppress that social life as frivolous or worse and to impose character traits by exhortation or other sleight of hand. Certain definitions of situations, however, do become clear to the child while he is in school, and it is perhaps worth while to consider these briefly.

The definition of the situation which teachers are at most pains to impose is that concerning the school life of the child, especially so far as it concerns his relation to his teachers. Since we have discussed this at such length, we shall say no more about it here except to state that this definition of the situation, so laboriously built up by teachers and so deeply impressed upon the child, is one which rarely finds a parallel in adult life, and that it is therefore wasted as a training for life. Subordination to the teacher does not prepare the child for anything, because there will be no teachers where he is going.

A type of definition of the situation which grows more spontaneously out of the life of children, and which therefore more often has a parallel in life outside the institution, concerns sportsmanship and fair play. The spirit of fair play or sportsmanship is often quite strongly inculcated in children who play competitive games. Perhaps it is the result of those endless arguments and interminable joukings of young boys who are learning to play games. It is a very limited spirit of fair play which boys develop in the unguided interaction of the play group. It is a fair play, usually, which does not necessarily apply to an individual who is not a member of the group; it does not hold for a member of another gang or for a teacher or a member of the opposite sex. It is an honesty which does not condemn a sharp trick. But, within its limitations, this is a definition of the situation concerning which the boy's attitude is sharp and clear. With boys in a private school, or in some other groups where much is made of competitive athletics, sportsmanship comes to be something of a religion; it is the one moral principle which boys can understand.

Since the most important value in our culture is property, it is only natural that the school child should absorb certain taboos concerning property and its use while yet in school. It is one of the situations most sharply defined for the child. One of the few situations (perhaps the only one) in which students and teachers can cooperate whole-heartedly in defense of the social order is that created by the presence of a thief in their midst. Much more rarely, and always more uncertainly, students work out certain taboos concerning personal honesty. There are in fact many features of school life which make rather for the development of personal dishonesty. There is the school situation which calls for a respect to the teacher which is quite contrary, often, to the child's actual feeling and to the attitudes which he expresses outside of school. There is the rigid marking system, with its emphasis on grades and its invitation to cheat, and this feature of the situation is made worse by the enemy morality which holds between teachers and students. Under such circumstances, cheating can come to be a fascinating game, and one which the student loses no status by playing; it often happens that students do not outgrow this conception even when they enter college. When the main thing is the amassing of a certain number of meaningless credits, what does it matter, after all, by what method they are acquired? There is, too, a deep-lying discrepancy between the precepts which teachers give out to students and the ingrowing personal dishonesty of teachers who say things for hire that they do not believe.

Certain definitions of the situation with regard to sexual functions are very much a part of school life. One of the definitions which it is most important to impose upon children is the heterosexual definition of the situation. This is sometimes done, and in a natural and spontaneous way. Teachers who arrange for a cross sex interchange of valentines on Valentine Day are thus doing something to manipulate the social process in the correct direction. In a monosexual group, it is sometimes necessary to impose taboos in a drastic manner. When certain definitely sexual ties began to appear in a group of boys as a result of the assumption of feminine rôles by some of them in a minstrel show, a virile man teacher was able by means of a downright speech to define clearly what expressions of affection were and what were not proper in a group of boys, with the result that the homosexual interchange became much less open and in most cases disappeared entirely. Teachers are also concerned with imposing the taboos of conventional morality upon their charges. The taboo of chastity is imposed upon girls with unrelenting severity. There is evidence that the virginity of their female charges is a matter over which women teachers exercise themselves greatly.[5] As a result partly of this feeling, and partly of the feeling that "puppy-love" is a silly and bootless emotion, and one not in accord with the ideal of academic achievement, many teachers ridicule or punish all students who take an obvious interest in members of the opposite sex.

20   Embarrassment and the Analysis of Role Requirements

● EDWARD GROSS AND GREGORY P. STONE

Attitudes, in the view of George Herbert Mead, are incipient acts. Meaningful discourse requires that discussants take one another's attitudes—incorporate one another's incipient activities—in their conversation. Since all social transactions are marked by meaningful communication, discursive or not, whenever people come together, they bring futures into one another's presence. They are ready, balanced, *poised* for the upcoming discussion. The discussion, of course, remands futures to a momentary present, where they are always somewhat inexactly realized, and relegates them in their altered form to the collective past we call memory. New futures are constantly built up in discussions. Indeed, they must be, else the discussion is over and the transaction is ended. Without a future, there is nothing else to be done, nothing left to say. Every social transaction, therefore, requires that the participants be poised at the outset and that

---

[5] Of a group of about seventy-five short papers written by women teachers upon subjects to be chosen by themselves, about one quarter concerned the experiences of some girl who departed from the conventional morality. This would seem to be a strong indication that this is, for women teachers, one of the central problems of school life.

SOURCE: Edward Gross and Gregory P. Stone, *The American Journal of Sociology*, LXX (July 1964), pp. 1–15. Reprinted by permission of the University of Chicago Press.

poise be maintained as the transaction unfolds, until there is an accord that each can turn to other things and carry other futures away to other circles.

Poise is not enough. The futures that are presented, imperfectly realized, and re-established must be relevant. Relevance is achieved by establishing the *identities* of those who are caught up in the transaction. Futures or attitudes are anchored in identities. We speak of *role* as consensual attitudes mobilized by an announced and ratified identity. In social transactions, then, persons must announce who they are to enable each one to ready himself with reference to appropriate futures, providing attitudes which others may take or assume. Often announced identities are complementary, establishing the transaction as a social relationship, for many identities presuppose counteridentities. Whether or not this is the case, the maintenance of one's identity assists the maintenance of the other.[1]

Furthermore, all transactions are transactions through time. It is not enough that identity and poise be established. They must be continuously reaffirmed, maintained, and provisions made for their repair in case of breakdown. Role performers count on this. We attempt here to limn the structure of transactions by examining instances where identities have been misplaced or forgotten, where poise has been lost or destroyed, or where, for any reason, confidence that identities and poise will be maintained has been undermined. We have in mind instances of embarrassment, whether or not deliberately perpetrated.

Embarrassment and the Analysis of Role Requirements

Embarrassment exaggerates the core dimensions of social transactions, bringing them to the eye of the observer in an almost naked state. Embarrassment occurs whenever some *central* assumption in a transaction has been *unexpectedly* and unqualifiedly discredited for at least one participant. The result is that he is incapacitated for continued role performance.[2] Moreover, embarrassment is infectious. It may spread out, incapacitating others not previously incapacitated. It is destructive dis-ease. In the wreckage left by embarrassment lie the broken foundations of social transactions. By examining such ruins, the investigator can reconstruct the architecture they represent.

To explore this idea, recollections of embarrassment were expressly solicited from two groups of subjects: (1) approximately 800 students enrolled in introductory sociology courses; and (2) about 80 students enrolled in an evening extension class. Not solicited, but gratefully received, were many examples volunteered by colleagues and friends who had heard of our interest in the subject. Finally we drew upon many recollections of embarrassment we had experienced ourselves. Through these means at least one thousand specimens of embarrassment were secured.

---

[1] Alfred R. Lindesmith and Anselm L. Strauss assert that *every* role presupposes a counter-role. There is a sense in which the assertion is correct, as in Kenneth Burke's "paradox of substance," but it may also be somewhat misleading in sociological analysis. Specifically, there is a role of cigarette smoker, but the role is not really dependent for its establishment on the counter-role of non-smoker in the sense that the parental role is dependent upon child roles and vice versa. Thus, in some social transactions the establishment and maintenance of one identity may be very helpful for the establishment and maintenance of a counter-identity; in other transactions, this may not be the case at all (see Lindesmith and Strauss, *Social Psychology* [New York: Dryden Press, 1956], pp. 379–80; and Kenneth Burke, *A Grammar of Motives* [New York: Prentice-Hall, 1945], pp. 21–58).

[2] Not all incapacitated persons are always embarrassed or embarrassing, because others have come to expect their *incapacities* and are consequently prepared for them.

We found that embarrassments frequently occurred in situations requiring continuous and co-ordinated role performance—speeches, ceremonies, processions, or working concerts. In such situations embarrassment is particularly noticeable because it is so devastating. Forgetting one's lines, forgetting the wedding ring, stumbling in a cafeteria line, or handing a colleague the wrong tool, when these things occur without qualification, bring the performance to an obviously premature and unexpected halt. At the same time, manifestations of the embarrassment—blushing, fumbling, stuttering, sweating [3]—coerce awareness of the social damage and the need for immediate repair. In some instances, the damage may be potentially so great that embarrassment cannot be allowed to spread among the role performers. The incapacity may be qualified, totally ignored, or pretended out of existence.[4] For example, a minister, noting the best man's frantic search for an absent wedding ring, whispers to him to ignore it, and all conspire to continue the drama with an imaginary ring. Such rescues are not always possible. Hence we suggest that every enduring social relation will provide means of preventing embarrassment, so that the entire transaction will not collapse when embarrassment occurs. A second general observation would take into account that some stages in the life cycle, for example, adolescence in our society, generate more frequent embarrassments than others. These are points to which we shall return.

To get at the content of embarrassment, we classified the instances in categories that remained as close to the specimens as possible. A total of seventy-four such categories were developed, some of which were forced choices between friends, public mistakes, exposure of false front, being caught in a cover story, misnaming, forgetting names, slips of the tongue, body exposure, invasions of others' back regions, uncontrollable laughter, drunkenness in the presence of sobriety (or vice versa), loss of visceral control, and the sudden recognition of wounds or other stigmata. Further inspection of these categories disclosed that most could be included in three general areas: (1) inappropriate identity; (2) loss of poise; (3) disturbance of the assumptions persons make about one another in social transactions.

Since embarrassment always incapacitates persons for role performance (to embarrass is, literally, to bar or stop), a close analysis of the conditions under which it occurs is especially fruitful in the revelation of the requirements *necessary* for role-playing, role-taking, role-making, and role performance in general. These role requirements are thus seen to include the establishment of identity, poise, and valid assumptions about one another among all the parties of a social transaction. We turn now to the analysis of those role requirements.

Identity and Poise

In every social transaction, selves must be established, defined, and accepted by the parties. Every person in the company of others is, in a sense, obligated to bring his best self forward to meet the selves of others also presumably best fitted to the occasion. When one is "not himself" in the presence of others who

---

[3] Erving Goffman, in "Embarrassment and Social Organization," *American Journal of Sociology*, LXII (November, 1956), 264–71, describes these manifestations vividly.

[4] A more general discussion of this phenomenon, under the rubric civil inattention, is provided in Erving Goffman, *Behavior in Public Places* (New York: Free Press of Glencoe, 1963), pp. 83–88 and *passim*.

expect him to be just that, as in cases where his mood carries him away either by spontaneous seizure (uncontrollable laughter or tears) or by induced seizure (drunkenness), embarrassment ensues. Similarly, when one is "shown up" to other parties to the transaction by the exposure of unacceptable moral qualifications or inappropriate motives, embarrassment sets in all around. However, the concept, self, is a rather gross concept, and we wish to single out two phases that frequently provided focal points for embarrassment—identity and poise.[5]

Identity.—Identity is the substantive dimension of the self.[6]

> Almost all writers using the term imply that identity establishes what and where the person is in social terms. It is not a substitute word for "self." Instead, when one has identity, he is *situated*—that is, cast in the shape of a social object by the acknowledgement of his participation or membership in social relations. One's identity is established when others *place* him as a social object by assigning the same words of identity that he appropriates for himself or *announces*. It is in the coincidence of placements and announcements that identity becomes a meaning of the self.

Moreover, as we have already pointed out, identity stands at the base of role. When inappropriate identities are established or appropriate identities are lost, role performance is impossible.

If identity *locates* the person in social terms, it follows that locations or spaces emerge as symbols of identity, since social relations are spatially distributed. Moreover, as Goffman has remarked,[7] there must be a certain coherence between one's personal appearance and the setting in which he appears. Otherwise embarrassment may ensue with the resulting incapacitation for role performance. Sexual identity is pervasively established by personal appearance, and a frequent source of embarrassment among our subjects was the presence of one sex in a setting reserved for the other. Both men and women reported inadvertent invasions of spaces set aside for the other sex with consequent embarrassment and humiliation. The implication of such inadvertent invasions is, of course, that one literally does not know where one is, that one literally has no identity in the situation, or that the identity one is putting forward is so absurd as to render the proposed role performance totally irrelevant. Everyone is embarrassed, and such manifestations as, for example, cries and screams, heighten the dis-ease. In such situations, laughter cannot be enjoined to reduce the seriousness of the unexpected collapse of the encounter, and only flight can insure that one will not be buried in the wreckage.

To establish *what* he is in social terms, each person assembles a set of apparent [8] symbols which he carries about as he moves from transaction to transaction. Such symbols include the shaping of the hair, painting of the face, clothing, cards of identity, other contents of wallets and purses, and sundry additional marks and ornaments. The items in the set must cohere, and the set must be

---

5 Other dimensions of the self—value and mood—will be taken up in subsequent publications.
6 Gregory P. Stone, "Appearance and the Self," in Arnold Rose (ed.), *Human Behavior and Social Processes* (Boston: Houghton Mifflin, 1962), p. 93. Reprinted in Part Six of this volume.
7 Erving Goffman, *The Presentation of Self in Everyday Life* (New York: Doubleday Anchor Books, 1959), p. 25.
8 We use the term "appearance" to designate that dimension of a social transaction given over to identifications of the participants. Apparent symbols are those symbols used to communicate such identifications. They are often non-verbal. Appearance seems, to us, a more useful term than Goffman's "front" (*ibid.*), which in everyday speech connotes misrepresentation.

complete. Taken together, these apparent symbols have been called *identity documents,*[9] in that they enable others to validate announced identities. Embarrassment often resulted when our subjects made personal appearances with either invalid or incomplete identity documents. It was embarrassing for many, for example, to announce their identities as customers at restaurants or stores, perform the customer role and then, when the crucial validation of this identity was requested—the payoff—to discover that the wallet had been left at home.

Because the social participation of men in American society is relatively more frequently caught up in the central structures, for example, the structure of work, than is the social participation of women who are relatively more immersed in interpersonal relations, the identities put forward by men are often *titles;* by women, often *names.* Except for very unusual titles,[10] such identities are shared, and their presentation has the consequence of bringing people together. Names, on the other hand, mark people off from one another. So it is that a frequent source of embarrassment for women in our society occurs when they appear together in precisely the same dress. Their identity documents are invalidated. The embarrassment may be minimized, however, if the space in which they make their personal appearance is large enough. In one instance, both women met the situation by spending an entire evening on different sides of the ballroom in which their embarrassing confrontation occurred, attempting to secure validation from social circles with minimal intersection, or, at least, where intersection was temporally attenuated. Men, on the other hand, will be embarrassed if their clothing does not resemble the dress of the other men present in public and official encounters. Except for "the old school tie" their neckties seem to serve as numbers on a uniform, marking each man off from every other. Out of uniform, their structural membership cannot be visibly established, and role performance is rendered extremely difficult, if not impossible.[11]

Not only are identities undocumented, they are also misplaced, as in misnaming or forgetting, or other incomplete placements. One relatively frequent source of embarrassment we categorized as "damaging someone's personal representation." This included cases of ethnically colored sneers in the presence of one who, in fact, belonged to the deprecated ethnic group but did not put that identity forward, or behind-the-back slurs about a woman who turned out to be the listener's wife. The victim of such misplacement, however inadvertent, will find it difficult to continue the transaction or to present the relevant identity to the perpetrators of the embarrassment in the future. The awkwardness is reflexive. Those who are responsible for the misplacement will experience the same difficulties and dis-ease.

Other sources of embarrassment anchored in identity suggest a basic characteristic of all human transactions, which, as Strauss puts it, are "carried on in

---

[9] Erving Goffman, *Stigma* (Englewood Cliffs, N.J.: Prentice-Hall, 1963), pp. 59–62. Goffman confines the concept to personal identity, but his own discussion extends it to include matters of social identity.

[10] For example, the title, "honorary citizen of the United States," which was conferred on Winston Churchill, served the function of a name, since Churchill was the only living recipient of the title. Compare the titles, "professor," "manager," "punch-press operator," and the like.

[11] The implication of the discussion is that structured activities are uniformed, while interpersonal activities emphasize individuation in dress. Erving Goffman suggests, in correspondence, that what may be reflected here is the company people keep in their transactions. The work of men in our society is ordinarily teamwork, and teams are uniformed, but housework performed by a wife is solitary work and does not require a uniformed appearance, though the "housedress" might be so regarded.

thickly peopled and complexly imaged contexts." [12] One always brings to transactions more identities than are necessary for his role performance. As a consequence, two or more roles are usually performed at once by each participant.[13]

If we designate the relevant roles in transactions as *dominant roles* [14] then we
may note that *adjunct roles*—a type of side involvement, as Goffman would have
it,[15] or better, a type of side *activity*—are usually performed in parallel with
dominant role performance. Specifically, a lecturer may smoke cigarettes or a
pipe while carrying out the dominant performance, or one may carry on a heated
conversation with a passenger while operating a motor vehicle. Moreover, symbols of *reserve identities* are often carried into social transactions. Ordinarily,
they are concealed, as when a court judge wears his golfing clothes beneath his
robes. Finally, symbols of abandoned or *relict identities* may persist in settings
where they have no relevance for dominant role performances.[16] For example,
photographs of the performer as an infant may be thrust into a transaction by a
doting mother or wife, or one's newly constituted household may still contain
the symbols of a previous marriage.

In these respects, the probability of avoiding embarrassment is a function of
at least two factors: (1) the extent to which adjunct roles, reserve identities and
relict identities are not incongruent with the dominant role performance; [17] and
(2) the allocation of prime attention to the dominant role performance so that
less attention is directed toward adjunct role performance, reserve identities, and
relict identities. Thus the professor risks embarrassment should the performance of his sex role appear to be the main activity in transactions with female
students where the professorial role is dominant—for example, if the student
pulls her skirt over her knees with clearly more force than necessary. The judge
may not enter the courtroom in a golf cap, nor may the husband dwell on the
symbols of a past marriage in the presence of a new wife while entertaining

---

[12] Anselm L. Strauss, *Mirrors and Masks* (Glencoe, Ill.: Free Press, 1959), p. 57.
[13] This observation and the ensuing discussion constitute a contribution to and extension of
present perspectives on role conflict. Most discussions conceive of such conflict as internalized contradictory obligations. They do not consider simultaneous multiple-role performances. An exception is Everett C. Hughes' discussion of the Negro physician innocently sum-
moned to attend a prejudiced emergency case in "Dilemmas and Contradictions in Status,"
American Journal of Sociology, L (March, 1945), pp. 353–59.
[14] We have rewritten this discussion to relate to Goffman's classification which came to our
attention after we had prepared an earlier version of this article. Goffman distinguishes between
what people do in transactions and what the situation calls for. He recognizes that people do
many things at once in their encounters and distinguishes those activities that command most
of their attention and energies from those which are less demanding of energy and time. Here,
the distinction is made between *main* and *side involvements*. On the other hand, situations often
call for multiple activities. Those which are central to the situation, Goffman speaks of as
dominant involvements; others are called *subordinate involvements.* Dominant roles, therefore,
are those that are central to the transactional situation—what the participants have come together to do (see Goffman, *Behavior in Public Places*, pp. 43–59).
[15] Adjunct roles are one type of side involvement or activity. We focus on them because we
are concerned here with identity difficulties. There are other side *activities* which are *not* necessarily adjunct *roles*, namely, sporadic nosepicking, scratching, coughing, sneezing, or stomach
growling, which are relevant to matters of embarrassment, but not to the conceptualization of
the problem in these terms. Of course, such activities, insofar as they are consistently proposed
and anticipated, may become incorporated in the *personal role* (always an adjunct in official
transactions), as in the case of Billy Gilbert, the fabulous sneezer.
[16] This phenomenon provides the main theme and source of horror and mystery in Daphne du
Maurier's now classic *Rebecca.*
[17] Adjunct roles reserve identities, and relict identities need not cohere with the dominant role;
they simply must not clash so that the attention of participants in a transaction is not completely
diverted from the dominant role performance.

guests in his home. Similarly, should adjunct role performance prove inept, as when the smoking lecturer ignites the contents of a wastebasket or the argumentative driver fails to observe the car in front in time to avert a collision, attention is diverted from the dominant role performance. Even without the golf cap, should the judge's robe be caught so that his golfing attire is suddenly revealed in the courtroom, the transactions of the court will be disturbed. Fetishistic devotion to the symbols of relict identities by bereaved persons is embarrassing even to well-meaning visitors.

However, the matter of avoiding incongruence and allocating attention appropriately among the several identities a performer brings to a transaction verges very closely on matters of poise, as we shall see. Matters of poise converge on the necessity of controlling representations of the self, and identity-symbols are important self-representations.

Personal poise.—Presentation of the self in social transactions extends considerably beyond making the appropriate personal appearance. It includes the presentation of an entire situation. Components of situations, however, are often representations of self, and in this sense self and situation are two sides of the same coin. Personal poise refers to the performer's control over self and situation, and whatever disturbs that control, depriving the transaction, as we have said before, of any relevant future, is incapacitating and consequently embarrassing.

Loss of poise was a major dimension in our scrutiny of embarrassment, and its analysis can do much to shed light on the components of social situations—a necessary task, because the concept, "situation," is quite difficult to specify and operationalize. Working from the outside in, so to speak, we wish to single out five [18] elements of self and situation with reference to which loss of control gave rise to considerable embarrassment.

First, *spaces* must be so arranged and maintained that they are role-enabling. This is sometimes difficult to control, since people appear in spaces that belong to others, over which they exercise no authority and for which they are not responsible. Students, invited to faculty parties where faculty members behave like faculty members, will "tighten up" to the extent that the students' role performance is seriously impeded. To avoid embarrassment, people will go to great lengths to insure their appearance in appropriate places, and to some to be deprived of access to a particular setting is to limit performance drastically.

Spaces are often fixed in location and have boundaries. As such they may partake of the character of territories or domains: a particular person (or persons) is "in command" (it is "his" domain) and most familiar with it, and the territory is in continual danger of being invaded (deliberately or inadvertently). Embarrassments were reported for both of these features of space. Being "in command" and familiar with an area means knowing where the back regions are and having the right of access to them. The host at a party in his own home, however much he may be vanishing,[19] is at least the person in whose territory the gathering takes place. Should a guest spill food on his clothes, he has no choice but to suffer embarrassment for the remainder of the party. The host, by contrast, can retire to his bedroom and change his clothes quickly, often be-

[18] The five components to be discussed—spaces, props, equipment, clothing, and the body—are not offered as an exhaustive list. We have been able to distinguish close to forty such elements.
[19] David Riesman, Robert J. Potter, and Jeanne Watson, "The Vanishing Host," *Human Organization,* XIX (Spring, 1960), 17–21.

fore the momentary loss of poise becomes known. A striking case of the man "in command" of a territory is the person delivering a speech to a fixed audience in a closed room. In being presented to the audience, he may even be told, "The floor is yours." To underline his exclusive domain, the speaker may wait until waiters clear the last table of cups and saucers and the doors are closed. In such a setting, where the audience is not free to leave, the speaker is now in great danger of embarrassing his audience unless his speech is such that the audience is not let down. Should he show lack of poise, the audience will feel embarrassed for him, yet be unable to escape, for that would further embarrass him. Hence they will suffer silently, hoping for a short speech.

In a situation reported to us, the discussant at a professional meeting was able to save the situation. The speaker was a man of national reputation—one of the pillars of his discipline. To everyone's dismay and embarrassment, he proceeded to give a pedestrian address of the caliber of an undergraduate term essay. Everyone hoped the discussant would save them, and he did. His tactic was to make clear to the audience that the identity presented by the speaker was not his real identity. This result he accomplished by reminding the audience of the major contributions of the speaker, by claiming the paper presented must be interpreted as evidence that the speaker was still productive, and that all could expect even more important contributions in the future. When the audience thundered applause, they were not simply expressing their agreement with the discussant's appraisal of the speaker: they were also thanking him for saving them all from embarrassment by putting the speaker back in command of the territory.

We have already touched upon problems presented by invasions of spaces, and little more need be said. Persons lose poise when they discover they are in places forbidden to them, for the proscription itself means they have no identity there and hence cannot act. They can do little except withdraw quickly. It is interesting that children are continually invading the territories of others—who can control the course of a sharply hit baseball?—and part of the process of socialization consists of indications of the importance of boundaries. Whether territories are crescive or contrived affects the possibility of invasion. When they are contrived and boundaries are marked, the invader knows he has crossed the boundary and is embarrassed if caught. With crescive territories inadvertent invasions occur, as when a tourist reports discovery of a "quaint" area of the city only to be met with the sly smiles of those who know that the area is the local prostitution region.

Such considerations raise questions concerning both how boundaries are defined and how boundary violations may be prevented. Walls provide physical limits, but do not necessarily prevent communications from passing through.[20] Hence walls work best when there is also tacit agreement to ignore audible communication on the other side of the wall. Embarrassment frequently occurs when persons on one side of the wall learn that intimate matters have been communicated to persons on the other side. A common protective device is for the captive listeners to become very quiet so that their receipt of the communication will not be discovered by the unsuspecting intimates. When no physical boundaries are present, a group gathered in one section of a room may have developed a common mood which is bounded by a certain space that defines the

---

[20] See Erving Goffman, *Behavior in Public Places*, pp. 151–52.

limits of their engagement to one another. The entry of someone new may be followed by an embarrassed hush. It is not necessary that the group should have been talking about that person. Rather, since moods take time to build up, it will take time for the newcomer to "get with it" and it may not be worth the group's trouble to "fill him in." However unintentionally, he has destroyed a mood that took some effort to build up and he will suffer for it, if only by being stared at or by an obvious change of subject. In some cases, when the mood is partially sustained by alcohol, one can prepare the newcomer immediately for the mood by loud shouts that the group is "three drinks ahead" of him and by thrusting a drink into his hand without delay. So, too, a function of foyers, halls, anterooms, and other buffer zones or decompression chambers around settings is to prepare such newcomers and hence reduce the likelihood of their embarrassing both themselves and those inside.

Spaces, then, include bounded areas within which transactions go on. The boundaries may be more or less sharply defined, that is, walled in or marked off by the distances that separate one encounter from another. Overstepping the bounds is a source of embarrassment, signaling a loss of poise. Consequently, the boundaries are usually controlled and patrolled and come to represent the selves of those who are authorized to cross them.

A second component of self and situation that must be controlled to maintain poise is here designated *props*. Props are arranged around settings in an orderly manner commonly called décor. Ordinarily they are not moved about during a transaction, except as emergencies arise, to facilitate the movement of people about the setting and to protect the props from damage. In some cases, their adherence to settings is guaranteed by law. Wall-to-wall carpeting, mirrors attached to walls, and curtain fixtures, for example, may not be removed from houses, even though ownership of such domestic settings may change hands. The arrangement of less adhesive props within a setting may mark off or suggest (as in the case of "room dividers") smaller subsettings facilitating the division of large assemblies into more intimate circles. Moreover, although props are ordinarily not moved about *during* transactions, they are typically rearranged or replaced between major changes of scene, marking off changes in life situations.[21]

Perhaps just because of their intimate connection with the life situations of those who control them,[22] loss of control over props is a more frequent (though usually milder) source of embarrassment than the violation of boundaries. When one stumbles over his own furniture or slips on his own throw rug, doubt may be cast on the extent to which such props represent, in fact, the self and situation of the person or team members who have arranged them. Gifts of props are frequently embarrassing to the recipients. Thus an artist (or would-be

---

[21] David Riesman and Howard Rosenborough, in a discussion of family careers, indicate the linkage between the rearrangement of props and the rearrangement of life situations: "One of our Kansas City respondents, whose existence had been wrapped up in her daughters' social life, when asked what she did when the daughters married and moved away, said that she slept more—and redecorated the living room. Still another became more active in church work—and redecorated the vestry" ("Careers and Consumer Behavior" in Lincoln Clark [ed.], *Consumer Behavior*, Vol. II: *The Life Cycle and Consumer Behavior* [New York: New York University Press, 1955], p. 14).

[22] Striking examples are provided by Harvey W. Zorbaugh in Ernest W. Burgess (ed.), *The Urban Community* (Chicago: University of Chicago Press, 1926), pp. 103–4; and in Anonymous, *Street-Walker* (New York: Gramercy Publishing Co., 1962), pp. 46–48.

artist) may foist a painting on a friend without recognizing that the painting is contrary to the recipient's aesthetic taste. Moreover, the artist may expect that his work will be given a prominent display commensurate with his investment. A conflict is immediately established between loyalty to the artist-friend and loyalty to the recipient's self. A way out is to include the prop in question only in those situations where the donor is present, but this may become tedious, depending on the frequency and scheduling of visiting. A classic case is the wealthy relative's gift of a self-photograph, which must be dragged out of the closet for display when the relative visits.

Clashing differences in domestic décor will usually terminate or restrict house-to-house visiting. Because of this, many wartime friendships have been abruptly ended shortly after the cessation of hostilities and demobilization. In a common military setting, servicemen would meet and become close friends, sometimes building up life-and-death obligations to one another. They would eagerly anticipate extending their hard-won intimacy into the workaday world of peacetime. Then, when they met in one or the other's home, the glaring incompatibility in décor would silently signal an incompatibility in life situation. Such embarrassing confrontations would be covered over with empty promises and futile vows to meet again, and the former friends would part as embarrassed strangers. If incompatibilities in décor can bring about the estrangement of friends who owe their lives to one another, we can see how props and their arrangement become powerful guaranties of the exclusiveness of social circles and status strata.

Much of our earlier discussion of adjunct roles, reserve identities, and relict identities applies to props. The porcelain dinnerware may always be kept visibly in reserve for special guests, and this very fact may be embarrassing to some dinner guests who are reminded that they are not so special after all, while, for other guests, anything but the everyday props would be embarrassing. Relict props also present a potential for embarrassment, persisting as they do when one's new life-situation has made them obsolete. The table at which a woman used to sit while dining with a former husband is obviously still quite serviceable, but it is probably best to buy another.

Third, every social transaction requires the manipulation of *equipment*. If props are ordinarily stationary during encounters, equipment is typically moved about, handled, or touched.[23] Equipment can range from words to physical objects, and a loss of control over such equipment is a frequent source of embarrassment. Here are included slips of the tongue, sudden dumbness when speech is called for, stalling cars in traffic, dropping bowling balls, spilling food, and tool failures. Equipment appearances that cast doubt on the adequacy of control are illustrated by the clanking motor, the match burning down to the

---

[23] Whether objects in a situation are meant to be moved, manipulated, or taken up provides an important differentiating dimension between equipment on the one hand and props (as well as clothing, to be discussed shortly) on the other. Equipment is meant to be moved, manipulated, or taken up *during* a social transaction whereas clothing and props are expected to remain unchanged during a social transaction but will be moved, manipulated, or taken up *between* social transactions. To change props, as in burning the portrait of an old girl friend (or to change clothes, as in taking off a necktie), signals a change in the situation. The special case of the strip-tease dancer is no exception, for her act transforms clothes into equipment. The reference above to the "stickiness" of props may now be seen as another way of describing the fact that they are not moved, manipulated, or taken up during transactions, but remain unchanged for the course of the transaction. Clothing is equally sticky but the object to which it sticks differs. Clothing sticks to the body; props stick to the settings.

fingers, tarnished silverware, or rusty work tools. Equipment sometimes extends beyond what is actually handled in the transaction to include the stage props. Indeed, items of equipment in disuse, reserve equipment, often become props—the Cadillac in the driveway or the silver service on the shelf—and there is a point at which the objects used or scheduled for use in a situation are both equipment and props. At one instant, the items of a table setting lie immobile as props; at the next, they are taken up and transformed into equipment. The close linkage of equipment and props may be responsible for the fact that *embarrassment* at times not only *infects* the participants in the transaction but the *objects* as well. For example, at a formal dinner, a speaker was discovered with his fly zipper undone. On being informed of this embarrassing oversight after he was reseated, he proceeded to make the requisite adjustment, unknowingly catching the table cloth in his trousers. When obliged to rise again at the close of the proceedings, he took the stage props with him and of course scattered the dinner tools about the setting in such a way that others were forced to doubt his control. His poise was lost in the situation.

Just as props may be adjunct to the dominant role performance, held in reserve, or relict, so may equipment. Indeed, as we have said, reserve equipment is often an important part of décor.

Fourth, *clothing* must be maintained, controlled, and coherently arranged. Its very appearance must communicate this. Torn clothing, frayed cuffs, stained neckties, and unpolished shoes are felt as embarrassing in situations where they are expected to be untorn, neat, clean, and polished. Clothing is of special importance since, as William James observed,[24] it is as much a part of the self as the body—a part of what he called the "material me." Moreover, since it is so close to the body, it conveys the impression of body maintenance, paradoxically, by concealing body-maintenance activities.[25] Hence, the double wrap—outer clothes and underclothes. Underclothes bear the marks of body maintenance and tonic state, and their unexpected exposure is a frequent source of embarrassment. The broken brassière strap sometimes produces a shift in appearance that few women (or men, for that matter) will fail to perceive as embarrassing.

Fifth, the *body* must always be in a state of readiness to act, and its appearance must make this clear. Hence any evidence of unreadiness or clumsiness is embarrassing. Examples include loss of whole body control (stumbling, trembling, or fainting), loss of visceral control (flatulence, involuntary urination, or drooling), and the communication of other "signs of the animal." The actress who is photographed from her "bad side" loses poise, for it shakes the foundation on which her fame rests. So does the person who is embarrassed about pimples, warts, or missing limbs, as well as those embarrassed in his presence.

Ordinarily, persons will avoid recognizing such stigmata, turn their eyes away, and pretend them out of existence, but on occasion stigmata will obtrude upon the situation causing embarrassment all around. A case in point was a minor flirtation reported by one of our students. Seated in a library a short distance from a beautiful girl, the student began the requisite gestural invitation to a more intimate conversation. The girl turned, smiling, to acknowledge the bid, revealing an amputated left arm. Our student's gestural line was brought to a crashing

[24] William James, *Psychology* (New York: Henry Holt & Co., 1892), pp. 177–78.
[25] A complete exposition of the body-maintenance function of clothing is set forth in an advertisement for Jockey briefs, entitled: "A Frank Discussion: What Wives Should Know about Male Support," *Good Housekeeping*, May, 1963, p. 237.

halt. Embarrassed, he abandoned the role he was building even before the foundation was laid, pretending that his inviting gestures were directed toward some imaginary audience suggested by his reading. Such stigmata publicize body-maintenance activities, and, when they are established in social transactions, interfere with role performances. The pimples on the face of the job applicant cast doubt on his maturity, and, consequently, on his qualifications for any job requiring such maturity.

All this is to say that self and situation must be in a perpetual condition of poise or readiness, adequately maintained, and in good repair. Such maintenance and the keeping of self in a state of good repair obviously require energy and time. While engaged in maintenance or repair, the person is, for that time, unable to play the role. Hence we may expect that persons will, in order to avoid casting doubt on their ability to play a role, deliberately play down or conceal maintenance and repair activity. Speakers know that spontaneity cannot be left to chance but must be prepared for, even rehearsed. Yet obviously information on the amount of preparation it took to be spontaneous would destroy the audience's belief in the spontaneity. Outer clothes require underclothes, as social life requires an underlife (which is, of course, also social).[26]

Maintenance of Confidence

When identities have been validated and persons poised, interaction may begin. Its continuation, however, requires that a scaffolding be erected and that attention be given to preventing this scaffolding from collapsing. The scaffold develops as the relationship becomes stabilized. In time persons come to expect that the way they place the other is the way the other announces himself, and that poise will continue to be maintained. Persons now begin to count on these expectations and to have confidence in them. But at any time they may be violated. It was such violations of confidence that made up the greatest single source of embarrassment in our examples. Perhaps this is only an acknowledgment that the parties to every transaction must always maintain themselves *in role* to permit the requisite role-taking, or that identity-switching ought not be accomplished so abruptly that others are left floundering in the encounter as they grope for the new futures that the new identity implies.

This is all the more important in situations where roles are tightly linked together as in situations involving a division of labor. In one instance, a group of social scientists was presenting a progress report of research to a representative of the client subsidizing the research. The principal investigator's presentation was filled out by comments from the other researchers, his professional peers. Negatively critical comments were held to a bare minimum. Suddenly the principal investigator overstepped the bounds. He made a claim that they were well on the road to confirming a hypothesis which, if confirmed, would represent a

---

[26] Consider the fact that the physician often needs time and opportunity to consult medical books and colleagues before he can render an authoritative medical diagnosis. A structural assurance is provided by his having been taught to make diagnoses slowly. Through time thus gained, he takes advantage of informal encounters with colleagues and spare moments between patients when he can consult medical books. A direct revelation of his need for such aids and his rather unsystematic way of getting them would be embarrassing. Yet it is in the patient's best interest that they be kept secret from him, otherwise the patient would be in the position of having to pass judgment on a professional practice when he is, in fact, too involved to render an objective judgment.

major contribution. Actually, his colleagues (our informant was one of them) knew that they were very far indeed from confirming the hypothesis. They first sought to catch the leader's eye to look for a hidden message. Receiving none, they lowered their eyes to the table, bit their lips, and fell silent. In the presence of the client's representative, they felt they could not "call" their leader for that would be embarrassing, but they did seek him out immediately afterward for an explanation. The leader agreed that they were right, but said his claim was politic, that new data might well turn up, and that it was clearly too late to remedy the situation.

Careful examination of this case reveals a more basic reason for the researchers' hesitance to embarrass the leader before the client's representative. If their leader were revealed to be the kind of person who goes beyond the data (or to be a plain liar), serious question could have been raised about the kind of men who willingly work with such a person. Thus they found themselves coerced into unwilling collusion. It was not simply that their jobs depended on continued satisfaction of the client. Rather they were unwilling to say to themselves and to the client's representative that they were the kind of researchers who would be party to a fraud. To embarrass the leader, then, would have meant embarrassing themselves by casting serious question upon their identities as researchers. Indeed, it was their desire to cling to their identities that led, not long afterward (and after several other similar experiences), to the breakup of the research team.

Just as, in time, an identity may be discredited, so too may poise be upset. Should this occur, each must be able to assume that the other will render assistance if he gets into such control trouble, and each must be secure in the knowledge that the assumption is tenable. Persons will be alert for incipient signs of such trouble—irrelevant attitudes—and attempt to avert the consequences. Goffman has provided many examples in his discussion of dramaturgical loyalty, discipline, and circumspection in the presentation of the self, pointing out protective practices that are employed, such as clearing one's throat before interrupting a conversation, knocking on doors before entering an occupied room, or begging the other's pardon before an intrusion.[27]

The danger that one's confidence in the other's continued identity or his ability to maintain his poise may be destroyed leads to the generation of a set of *performance norms*. These are social protections against embarrassment.[28] If persons adhere to them, the probability of embarrassment is reduced. We discovered two major performance norms.

First, *standards of role performance almost always allow for flexibility and tolerance*. One is rarely, if ever, totally in role (an exception might be highly ritualized performances, where to acknowledge breaches of expectation is devastatingly embarrassing).[29] To illustrate, we expect one another to give attention to what is going on in our transactions, but the attention we anticipate is always *optimal*, never total. To lock the other person completely in one's glance and refuse to let go is very embarrassing. A rigid attention is coerced eventuating in a loss of poise. One is rapt in the other's future and deprived of control almost

---

[27] Goffman, *The Presentation of Self in Everyday Life*, pp. 212–33.
[28] Implicit in Georg Simmel, *The Sociology of Georg Simmel*, trans. Kurt H. Wolff (Glencoe, Ill.: Free Press, 1950), p. 308.
[29] See the discussion of "role distance" in Erving Goffman, *Encounters* (Indianapolis, Ind.: Bobbs-Merrill Co., 1961), pp. 105–52.

like the hypnotist's subject. Similarly, never to give one's attention to the other is role-incapacitating. If one focuses his gaze not on the other's eyes, but on his forehead, let us say, the encounter is visibly disturbed.[30] Norms allowing for flexibility and tolerance permit the parties to social transactions ordinarily to assume that they will not be held to rigid standards of conduct and that temporary lapses will be overlooked. The norm is respected by drinking companions who both understand how it is to have had a drop too much and who can also be counted on not to hold another to everything he says, does, or suggests. So, too, colleagues are persons who know enough to embarrass one another but can ordinarily be trusted not to do so. The exclusiveness of colleague groups can be seen, therefore, as a collective defense against embarrassment.

The second performance norm was that of *giving the other fellow the benefit of the doubt*. For the transaction to go on at all, one has at least to give the other fellow a *chance* to play the role he seeks to play. Clearly, if everyone went around watching for chances to embarrass others, so many would be incapacitated for role performance that society would collapse. Such considerate behavior is probably characteristic of all human society, because of the dependence of social relations on role performance. A part of socialization, therefore, must deal with the prevention of embarrassment by the teaching of tact. People must learn not only not to embarrass others, but to ignore the lapses that can be embarrassing whenever they occur. In addition, people must learn to *cope* with embarrassment. Consequently, embarrassment will occasionally be deliberately perpetrated to ready people for role incapacitation when it occurs.

Deliberate Embarrassment

Although we have emphasized up to this point instances of embarrassment which arise from wholly unexpected acts and revelations, the unexpected is often deliberately perpetrated. Examples are practical jokes, teasing, initiation into secret societies, puncturing false fronts, and public degradation. Since embarrassment appears to represent social damage that is not at all easily repaired, we might well ask why the condition may be deliberately established. The embarrassed person stands exposed as incapable of continued role performance—a person who cannot be depended upon. In his presence, all must pause and review their assessments and expectations. Whatever they decide, the transaction is halted, and those dependent upon it are deprived of the realization of the futures that they have entrusted to others.

Embarrassments, therefore, always have careers. One person embarrasses others whose hurried attempts to salvage the situation merely call further attention to the embarrassment. A point may be reached where no repair is possible —the embarrassed person breaks into tears, flees, or, in the classic case, commits suicide—not to save face, but because face has been destroyed beyond repair.[31] Other terminations are possible, as we have shown. The embarrassing situation may be transformed by humor—laughed off—to define it as unserious and to invite others to symbolize their solidarity with the embarrassed person by join-

---

[30] Here we are speaking of what Edward T. Hall calls the "gaze line." He points out there are cultural variations in this phenomenon. See his "A System for the Notation of Proxemic Behavior," *American Anthropologist*, LXV (October, 1963), 1012–14.

[31] Goffman, "On Face-Work," *Psychiatry*, XVIII (August, 1955), 213–31.

ing in the laughter.[32] Blame may be diverted away from the transaction and placed on others on the outside. The embarrassed one may fall sick. There are numerous outcomes, and, while some are less drastic than others, none is completely devoid of risk. Why is it, then, that embarrassment may be deliberately perpetrated? There are at least three reasons or social functions that may be attributed to deliberate embarrassment.

First, since embarrassing situations are inevitable in social life, persons must be schooled to maintain poise when poise is threatened, to maintain the identities they have established in social situations in the face of discreditation, and to sustain the confidence others have built up about such matters. Deliberate embarrassment acts to socialize young people with these skills. Consequently, all young children trip one another, push, disarrange one another's clothing and other items of personal appearance. Besides being fun, such play [33] socializes the child in the maintenance of poise despite direct physical attacks on his "balance." Indeed, young children will spin about, inducing dizziness as they unknowingly test their ability to handle the imbalance in the play that Roger Caillois speaks of as *ilinx* or *vertigo*.[34] But socialization continues throughout life, and adult men, for example, test who can maintain poise in the face of the other's loss by playing at "drinking the other under the table." The roller coaster and tilt-a-whirl, and less upsetting machines like the merry-go-round and ferris wheel can be interpreted as a technology available to test poise.[35] Almost by definition, every game is a test of poise, but some sports place particular emphasis upon such tests—ski-jumping and gymnastics.[36] Announced identities are also challenged and impugned in play, as in "name-calling," and such teasing often reaches out to call into question everything one seeks to establish about himself in social encounters:

> Shame! Shame! Double shame!
> Everybody knows your name!

The child, of course, learns the institutionalized replies to such tests of identity and self-confidence which throw the challenge back:

> My name, my name is Puddin' Tame.
> Ask me again and I'll tell you the same!

As others have noted, the challenges and responses inherent in such tests of poise, identity, and self-confidence often assume a pattern of interactive insult. The classic case is "playing the dozens." [37]

---

[32] See Ruth Laub Coser, "Some Social Functions of Laughter: A Study of Humor in a Hospital Setting," *Human Relations*, XII (May, 1959), 171–82.

[33] Careful attention must be given to all phases of children's play, which includes very much more than the anticipatory and fantastic dramas emphasized by George H. Mead.

[34] "The Structure and Classification of Games," *Diogenes*, No. 12 (Winter, 1955), pp. 62–75.

[35] A definite age-grading of the technology may be noticed in our society. The mildest test of poise is provided for the very young—the merry-go-round—and the devilish devices seem to be reserved for the middle and late teen-agers.

[36] Poise is an essential part of the commercialized tumbling exhibitions we call wrestling. Interviews with professional wrestlers by one of the writers establish that the most feared "opponent" is not at all the most fierce, but the neophyte, upon whose poise the established professional cannot rely.

[37] This game, found most commonly among American Negroes, is never carried on between two isolated antagonists, but requires the physical presence of peers who evaluate each insult and goad the players to heightened performances. The antagonists and their peers are usually

If one function of deliberate embarrassment is socialization, we would guess that such tests would be concentrated in the formative years and in other periods of major status passage. Our survey of adults in the evening extension class showed this to be true. When we asked them to recall the time of their lives when they were frequently embarrassed, the adolescent years were most commonly mentioned. Instances of deliberate embarrassment also included hazings and the humiliation which accompanied socialization into the armed forces. It may well be that every move into an established social world—every major *rite de passage*—is facilitated by the deliberate perpetration of embarrassing tests of poise, identity, and self-knowledge.[38]

Second, embarrassment is deliberately perpetrated as a negative sanction as in "calling" the one who is giving an undesirable performance. Since embarrassment does incapacitate the person from performing his role, it can clearly be used to stop someone from playing a role that might discredit a collectivity. Empirical categories include public reprimands, exposure of false fronts, open gossip and cattiness, or embarrassment perpetrated as a retaliation for an earlier embarrassment. In some of these cases, a person is exposed as having no right to play the role he has laid claim to, because the identity in which his role is anchored is invalid. In others, the person is punished by terminating his role performance so that he can no longer enjoy its perquisites.

A third function of deliberate embarrassment is the establishment and maintenance of power. The technique here is rather more subtle than those we have discussed. Specifically, the scene may be laid for embarrassment so that only by following the line established by the one who sets the scene may embarrassment be avoided. In this case, one assures himself that his decision will carry the day by guaranteeing that any alternative will result in irreparable damage to the whole collectivity. Organizational policy changes, for example, may be accomplished by cloaking them in a cover story impregnated with the organizational ideology. To resist the proposed changes, consequently, risks the discreditation of the entire organization. Another example is to be found in "kicking an official upstairs." The decision will be reached in a policy-making discussion where the official in question may be present. In the discussion, emphasis will be given to the official's qualifications for the new post so that the "stage manager" leads a new self forward to replace the old self of the official in question. Discreditation of the new self, particularly in the official's presence, would wreak such damage on the transaction that it must be foregone and the "manager's" decision conceded.[39]

---

members of the same in-group, again emphasizing the socializing function of the play. As the insults become more and more acrid, one antagonist may "break down" (lose poise) and suggest fighting. That person is perceived as having failed the test and the group then moves to prevent a fight from actually occurring. For Negroes, the ability to take insults without breaking down is clearly functional for survival in Negro-white interaction (see John Dollard, "The Dozens: Dialectic of Insult," *The American Image*, I [November, 1939], 3–25; Ralph E. Berdie, "'Playing the Dozens,'" *Journal of Abnormal and Social Psychology*, XLII [January, 1947], 120–21; and Cornelius L. Golightly and Israel Scheffler, "'Playing the Dozens': A Research Note," *Journal of Abnormal and Social Psychology*, XLIII [January, 1948], 104–5).

[38] An interesting comment on this point was made by Erving Goffman in a personal communication: "Since the theater is *the* place for the issue of poise, could our extensive high-school theatrical movement then be part of the socialization you speak of?"

[39] Erving Goffman describes a similar process by which persons are channeled through a "betrayal funnel" into a mental hospital (see "The Moral Career of the Mental Patient," *Psychiatry*, XXII [May, 1959], 123–42. Reprinted in Part Ten of this volume.

Conclusion

In this paper, we have inquired into the conditions necessary for role performance. Embarrassment has been employed as a sensitive indicator of those conditions, for that which embarrasses incapacitates role performance. Our data have led us to describe the conditions for role performance in terms of identity, poise, and sustained confidence in one another. When these become disturbed and discredited, role performance cannot continue. Consequently, provisions for the avoidance or prevention of embarrassment, or quick recovery from embarrassment when it does occur, are of key importance to any society or social transaction, and devices to insure the avoidance and minimization of embarrassment will be part of every persisting social relationship. Specifically, tests of identity, poise, and self-knowledge will be institutionalized in every society. Such devices, like all mechanisms of social control, are capable of manipulation and may well be exploited to establish and maintain power in social transactions. Yet, deliberate or not, embarrassment is as general a sociological concept as is role.

21   Making the Scene

● DAVID J. BENNETT AND JUDITH D. BENNETT

All social interaction is affected by the physical container within which it occurs. The various elements of the container establish a world of meaning through the arrangement of non-verbal symbolism. For this reason, the common practice in the social sciences of focusing on behavior without reference to the physical setting would seem to ignore an important dimension of the total picture of interaction.

As in the case of spoken language and even gestural conduct, there must be a consensus upon meaning for this symbolism to play a relevant part in social situations. The container imposes both physical and symbolic limitations upon behavior. Its sheer physical dimension limits the range of possible movement. We do not neck in the back of churches; we do in movie theatres.

Recently, some work has been done in exploring the relation between the physical and interactional worlds of human beings. The more obvious effects of the physical setting as the background against which interaction takes place have been dealt with as "regions" by Erving Goffman;[1] the physical territory as a generator of behavior has been hypothesized by Robert Ardrey;[2] the physical container as a variable matrix of interaction within different cultural frameworks

SOURCE: David J. Bennett and Judith D. Bennett, "Making the Scene," original paper prepared especially for this volume.

[1] Erving Goffman, *The Presentation of Self in Everyday Life* (Garden City: Doubleday Anchor Books, 1959), and his *Behavior in Public Places* (New York: The Free Press, A Division of The Macmillan Company, 1963).
[2] Robert Ardrey, *The Territorial Imperative* (New York: Dell Publishing Co., 1966).

has been studied by Edward T. Hall;[3] others[4] have concerned themselves with the variable effects of physical containers. However, with the possible exception of Hall, this area has not been dealt with systematically.

While very few systematic studies exist, the practice of dealing with the physical environment by deliberately manipulating it and its constituent parts and dimensions to secure some desired social effect has long been a practice of those professions concerned with environmental design: architects, planners, industrial designers, interior decorators, stage managers, and others. These people, however, have not developed quantitative techniques for analyzing physical settings as symbolic frameworks within which social interaction proceeds. Rather, their work is guided by tradition, "common sense," and accumulated, but unsystematized, experience. They assume causal relationships between certain physical arrangements and specific social "end results."[5] Whether these assumed relationships are valid has yet to be determined. Yet, there are some physical arrangements that have occurred with remarkable consistency around the world throughout human history.

The physical building or space which forms the symbolic edifice of super-human power, whether God, Hero, or State, seems to have the following universal characteristics: (1) tremendous size in relation to other buildings, or, when diminutive in actual size, as in the case of some shrines in both Oriental and Occidental civilizations, a scale, i.e., a relation of the elements of the object to the whole, which suggests tremendous size; (2) an expression of great stability, durability, and immutability, often achieved by symmetry, and, when not, by a highly stylized arrangement of objects or parts of the whole; (3) a carefully organized progression of spaces (be it the entrance to an ancient Egyptian royal tomb, the path through the Acropolis at Athens, the forecourt to a Shinto shrine, the road to Versailles, or the monumental steps up to almost any seat of judgment of any time or place in the Western world) arranged so that they are experienced as a linear sequence of events invested with awesome meaning. Similarly, other symbolic-physical arrangements seemingly have the same cross-cultural uniformity. Authority is usually physically elevated.

Components and Dimensions of the Scene

In order to analyze the specific relationships which obtain between physical environment and social behavior, it is necessary to establish precisely which elements of the environment or scene may affect human conduct. Such elements may have isolated effects or may affect human conduct in interaction with

---

[3] Edward T. Hall, *The Hidden Dimension* (Garden City: Doubleday and Co., 1966).
[4] In searching the literature for studies and discussions of how the physical container affects social behavior, we find two areas which are indirectly related to our problem. The first of these is the work of the transactional psychologists concerned with the nature of perception. See, for example, Franklin P. Kilpatrick (ed.), *Exploration in Transactional Psychology* (New York: New York University Press, 1961). Many of the studies in this collection deal with the ways in which the perception of objects occurs. In addition, there is an excellent bibliography in that volume. From the developmental perspective, Piaget has dealt with the problem of how children learn to organize external reality. See Jean Piaget, *The Construction of Reality in the Child* (New York: Basic Books, 1954).
[5] Note well that the process of assuming a causal relationship between physical form and meaning may act to bring about that very relationship. Thus, the recurring use of great scale (monumental buildings) to symbolize super-human authority finally dictates that, if one wishes to symbolize super-human authority, he must use great scale.

one another. We have made a preliminary attempt to list such elements, and our attempt has generated the following six components or dimensions of any scene:

1. The *container*—the fixed external enclosure of human interaction.
2. The *props*—physical objects which adhere to persons in the enclosure or to the enclosure itself, including dress and furnishings.
3. The *actors*—persons involved in, peripheral to, or spectators to the transactions carried on in the enclosure.

These components have been dealt with, one way or another, in the works we have cited earlier. Taken together, they are what most social psychologists have considered when they have included aspects of the scene in their analysis of social interaction. The following three elements have seldom been considered in such analyses:

4. The *modifiers*—elements of light, sound, color, texture, odor, temperature, and humidity which serve to affect the emotional tone or mood of the interaction.
5. *Duration*—the objective time in measurable units (minutes, hours, etc.) during which the interaction occurs, as well as the anticipated time the interaction will require.
6. *Progression*—the order of events which precede and follow, or are expected to follow, the interaction and have some bearing upon it.

These latter three terms, as can be seen, do not deal with objects, but with action or modifiers of action. In most European grammars, as Whorf noted, these are verbs or adverbs in the object-action conception of reality demanded by the rules of syntax.[6] As such, they add a critical dimension to the enclosure within which interaction transpires, but, more important, they lend the interaction a certain affect or mood. We can understand such affects by imagining four situations occurring within enclosures, each of identical dimensions, with three constant props and the same number of actors.

Behavioral Consequences of Scenes

The scene is a room only large enough to accommodate one table with sufficient space to move around it. Two men are seated at opposite sides of the table. Without changing the arrangement of the men, the chairs, and the table, let us show how the entire context of interaction—its symbolic significance—can be altered by manipulating other components and dimensions of the scene.

SITUATION ONE: The walls, floor, and ceiling of the room are concrete and plaster, unpainted and bare of any decoration. There is a single bare, bright electric bulb suspended above the table as the only source of light. The table and chairs are wood, bare, hard, and smooth. The temperature is relatively low (say 60 degrees Fahrenheit), and the relative humidity is high, making the room chilly and damp. There is a slight odor of mildew. The predominant colors are gray and white.

---

[6] Benjamin Lee Whorf, *Language, Thought, and Reality* (New York: John Wiley and Sons, Inc., 1959), pp. 207–219; 233–245.

SITUATION TWO: Now the walls are hung with dark red drapes. The floor is thickly carpeted, and the ceiling painted a soft off-white. The light source is a light cove around the ceiling which gives off a soft, diffuse, dim light. The table is covered with a white cloth and the chairs are upholstered with a nappy material. The temperature and humidity are a little above the American Standard Engineering "Comfort Range" (68 degrees Fahrenheit and 45% relative humidity), making the room feel a little warm and humid. There is a slightly "stuffy" odor in the room. The predominant colors are dark red, off-white, and a muted gold.

SITUATION THREE: The ceiling is a luminous fluorescent ceiling such as may be found in many contemporary office buildings. Three of the walls are smooth white plaster; the fourth, a chromatic blue. The floor is covered with a dark gray carpet. The table is very low, its top no more than sixteen inches above the floor. Its base is polished steel, its top is glass.   The chairs are polished steel frames fitted with black leather cushions. The room is cool and dry and, for all intents and purposes, "odorless."

SITUATION FOUR: The ceiling is an off-white plaster. The walls, also plaster, are painted beige. The floor is a vinyl asbestos tile of a light brown color with a green oval woven area rug. The light source is a floor-to-ceiling pole light with three shaded fixtures. The table is a dark grained wood, and the chairs are wood frame with green upholstered seats and backs. The temperature and relative humidity are within the "comfort range." There is no discernible odor.

What is significant about the four situations presented above is not that a precise description of their meaning can be made—it cannot—but they are presented in the expectation that the reader will respond to each one of them differently despite the fact that: (1) the dimension of the enclosure, the arrangement of people and objects (although the appearance of chairs and tables are modified) remain unchanged; (2) the reader knows nothing specific about either the people or the nature of the interaction; (3) the description of the situations is incomplete, having not included the elements of sound (although the quality of sound is implied), duration, or progression. Also, the situations, each a carefully contrived ensemble of mutually reinforcing conventionalized elements in conventionalized combinations, probably will evoke grossly predictable responses from specific audiences, presuming cultural, age, and socio-economic homogeneity.

We may describe these four situations as settings for the following interactions. The reader, although he will be able to supply alternatives, will find it difficult to reject these possibilities.

Situation One—an interrogation
Situation Two—a social conversation
Situation Three—an interview
Situation Four—indeterminate (could be any one of the above)

All of these interpretations apply, remember, to the same enclosure, the same number of objects, and the same number of people. The fourth scene is indeterminate, we would assert, because of the relative neutrality, in symbolic terms, of the modifying elements which ordinarily enhance mood or affect. That the

reader may be able to supply alternative interpretations of the interaction taking place in any of the situations we have presented is not an indication of the
symbolic imprecision, in any absolute sense, of our descriptions. In fact, the
situations are of a generalized type. Each can accommodate a number—but a
finite number—of different interactions in the context of our culture. It is important to note that, whatever number of events may occur in each of these
situations, that number could probably be counted or estimated while the number which could *not* occur is probably beyond measure or estimate. We have
mentioned that, among other elements of the situation, we have ignored matters
of duration and progression. These seem to us to be of seminal importance, and
we wish now to speculate about their possible impact on these situated interactions.

Duration. The expected duration of an interrogation has no objective time
unit. Instead, it is a function of the relative definitions of the situation formulated by the interrogated and the interrogator. Both may, for separate reasons,
want it over "quickly" (a subjective time unit). However, if the interrogated's
aim is resistance, he may wish to extend it indefinitely, while the interrogator's
desire may be a rapid termination of the encounter. The opposite may also be
the case. In any event, the interrogation is a situation in which the duration of
the situation is highly significant for the actor's conception of its meaning, even
without some prior established expectation about the objective time of duration.
For the interrogated, this is part of the terror.

In contrast, a social conversation or an interview present situations in which
actors usually have distinct and mutual expectations about how long the encounter will last, and they are prepared to engage one another for that length
of time. The job interviewer who conducts an interview with, let us say, a potential secretary over a four-hour period will be violating a norm so flagrantly
that the applicant may well redefine the situation as an interrogation.[7] In other
words, time can affect the definition, including the mood of the situation.

We enter a situation with a learned expectation of its duration and are prepared to participate for that length of time. If that expectation is not met, our
definition of the situation will be altered, and our ability to sustain the appropriate mood of the encounter will be seriously tested. As Hall observed, our
expectations in this regard vary widely from one culture to the next. In the unitary linear treatment of time which characterizes the "American Way of Life"
time units, in discrete segments and in highly conventionalized sequences, are
a salient feature of the way we give form and meaning to the sensational chaos
of experience.

Progression. Like duration, progression is another dimension of the meaning
of a situation. Having acquired expectations about the sequence of events both
in space (one expects the invisible part of a road around a curve to *be there*, if
one can see the continuation of the road in the distance and, often, if one cannot) and in time, we extend the isolated scene into a sequential pattern in order
to increase our understanding of its scope. Progression, as sequence, affects
both the meaning of the scope of the interaction and the interaction itself. To
descend into a shaft in the earth and then step through an opening into outer

---

7 Edward T. Hall, *The Silent Language* (New York: Doubleday, Inc., 1959), has discussed at
length cultural differences in the perception and meaning of time.

space constitutes a break in environmental sequence for which our original definitions of that situation have left us unprepared. Kafka's *The Trial* achieves its sense of strangeness and distortion in part from the deliberate deletion of key transitional scenes so that both the protagonist and the audience—the observers and vicarious actors—lose confidence in their ability to predict what will happen next. Here, the factor of continuity emphasizes the overriding importance progression has in establishing the meaning of a situation.[8] Progression, therefore, is an ordered sequence of events within an ordered sequence of scenes which is related to learned expectations, i.e., the taken-for-granted dimensions of everyday conduct.

Social interaction, then, takes place in a physical world full of objects, their modifiers, movement, and change—not in a vacuum. What is more, this physical world, differentially arranged and modified, is not so ambiguous in its relation to social interaction that its effects cannot be measured or estimated by analytical inquiry. Nor is this world so incidental that it can continue to be ignored.

A Paradigm for the Analysis of the Components and Dimensions of Scenes

Although this treatment of the subject has been necessarily brief and tentative, too exploratory to establish a comprehensive scheme which will embrace all alternative possibilities, we can propose the following paradigm as a point of departure for the initial investigation of those effects on social interaction perpetrated by the scene:

The Setting

Basic Physical Container as It Might Affect Social Interaction	*Number and Arrangement of Props and Persons in the Encounter*
1. Natural, man-made, or both.	1. Physical objects which are not part of the space, but are in it and are taken into account in the interaction, e.g., furniture, automobiles, etc.
2. Interior, exterior, or both.	2. Number of people who act as participants and their measurable spatial relation to each other.
3. Meaningful size in relation to type of interaction (too large? too small? not culturally significant?).	3. Number of people who act as spectators and their spatial relation to the other participants and to each other.
4. Single or multiple spaces.	4. Number of people who are neither participants nor observers, but who occupy the same significant area and who, by being present, affect interaction.
5. Connected or disconnected.	

---

[8] One reason that a film like *Last Year at Marienbad* is so disorienting is that it violates our expectations of progression. By externalizing the random order of events which we have learned to accept as the unique characteristic of thought, memory, and imagination and making them appear to be happening "out there," the hermetic seal between internal and external experience is broken and our ability to predict within our conventionalized framework is destroyed.

Basic Physical Container as It Might Affect Social Interaction	Number and Arrangement of Props and Persons in the Encounter
6. Relative proximity (measured in real time, subjective time, means of locomotion).	
7. Salient features, scale, size, multiple levels, etc.	

Modifiers					
Light	Sound	Color	Texture	Odor	Relative Temperature and Humidity
Source(s)	Volume	Hues	Location	Source(s)	
Intensity	Pitch	Location	Mixture	Mixture	
Direction	Intensity	Mixture		Permanence	
Color	Duration	Chromatic			
	Source	intensities			
	Direction				

Duration
Objective time span measured against conventional and/or subjective expectations.

Progression
The actual sequence of events implied by the scene and considered significant by those persons encountering one another on the scene.

From this rough diagram a list of questions may be drawn which adds another dimension to the existing set of questions about the meaning of behavior. Obviously, as the questions are asked and a body of quantitative information is assembled, an assessment can be made of what is or is not significant about physical environment as it applies to social interaction, and a more comprehensive and sophisticated scheme will evolve. Until such time, this scheme, or one like it, can serve as a point of departure from which an initial investigation can be made into the unexplored dimensions of non-verbal, non-gestural, symbolic reality.

22   An Abortion Clinic Ethnography

● DONALD W. BALL

. . . What follows is an effort to describe ethnographically certain aspects of a particular abortion clinic, especially as such data may illuminate the presentational strategies employed by an habitually deviant establishment in its dealing with a situationally deviant clientele.

SOURCE: Donald W. Ball, *Social Problems* (The Society for the Study of Social Problems), XIV, No. 3, pp. 293–301. I am grateful to Stanford Lyman for his critical comments on an earlier draft of this paper, to Theodore Ravetz for help at various stages of the project, and to Carma Westrum Coon for clerical assistance. I cannot adequately express my debt of gratitude to the anonymous contacts and informants who made this study possible. Portions of this material were presented to the panel on Medical Sociology, Pacific Sociological Association meetings, Vancouver, British Columbia, April 7, 1966.

For the clinic's staff, participation in an action legally defined as deviant, i.e. criminal abortion, is habitual; that is to say, it is regularly repeated on a routine, business-like basis. For patrons, however, participation is occasional, irregular, and frequently a once-in-a-lifetime engagement in this form of deviance. Most of them are members of otherwise law abiding cultures. Unlike the staff, their involvement in this deviant setting is not an aspect of a career, but an accidental consequence of an unwanted pregnancy.

In the context of the clinic, therefore, the deviant transaction ordinarily is enacted by two kinds of actors: those habitually involved in such exchanges, i.e. the staff; and those only situationally deviant, the otherwise conventional actors in their clinic-related roles as patrons. It becomes of some interest, then, to consider how the clinic manages and fosters impressions for this audience constituted of actors drawn from outside its habitually deviant, abortion-oriented sub-culture, and some of the characteristics of such strategies. Put another way, the focus herein will be upon techniques used by the clinic to key itself to the demands and expectations of a patronage drawn from the conventional culture.

Suffice to say, strictures of confidence prevent any elaborate discussion of method, problems of access, etc. Let it be noted, however, that the materials reported and interpreted herein are based upon: 1) sufficiently lengthy observation of a clinic's routine (exclusive of specifically medical procedures, which are not strictly relevant to the problem) to establish the patterns of its everyday functioning; 2) extensive interviews with a necessarily small number of patrons, some of whom were also observed within the clinic; and 3) limited discussions with some of the clinic's non-medical staff. Additionally, supplementary and confirmatory data have been drawn from interviews with individuals who have utilized other, similar facilities. Unfortunately, any more detailed methodological description would, not surprisingly, violate promises of anonymity guaranteed to the subjects involved; for similar reasons, no direct quotations will be presented.[1]

Background

The clinic studied is located, along with several like establishments, in a border town along the California-Mexico line. Its staff includes two practitioners or abortionists, ostensibly physicians, the younger of whom is in an apprentice relationship to the senior man; a practical nurse; a receptionist-bookkeeper; a combination janitress and custodian; a chauffeur-errand boy; and a telephone-appointments secretary.

As costs for such procedures go, the clinic is a relatively expensive one, with fees averaging $500 per abortion. The rate is somewhat less for other medical personnel and students, who are eligible for a discount; and more for persons desiring post-operative overnight observation, or else beyond the tenth week of pregnancy. In terms of finances, the clinic studied is probably representative of others catering to a middle and upper-middle class clientele.

In order to obtain a better picture of the establishment, a brief natural

---

[1] For those interested in procedural minutiae as criteria of validity, the only answer can be: Go out and replicate using your own design. Though precise comparisons would not be possible, such confirmation or refutation would be most desirable.

history of a typical involvement between clinic and patron is useful at this point.

Preliminarily, it should be recognized that the ideal-typical practitioner-patient model is not appropriate for the analysis of abortion. Like veterinarians and pediatricians, abortionists frequently have patients for whom financial, if not moral, responsibility is an aspect of the role of some other person, i.e., a client. For abortionists such clients include boyfriends, husbands, and parents. Along with persons such as accompanying friends, they comprise for the patient what might be classified as *supportive others:* persons attending the clinic along with the patient in order to provide psychological support and reinforcement in this crisis situation. Not surprisingly, it is rare for a patient to go to the clinic completely alone, without some morally supportive other. Thus, within the context of abortion, the typical practitioner-patient dyad usually becomes a triad, comprising practitioner, patient, and supportive other.[2]

After referral, usually by a physician, less often by friend or acquaintance, the patron makes original contact with the clinic by telephone. The typically tentative, noncommital, but implicitly urgent communication of the patron is immediately treated in a matter-of-fact manner by the telephone girl. In appropriate middle class speech patterns she asks the length of the pregnancy, extolls the skill of the staff, sets up a tentative appointment, and discusses the fee and its mode of payment. Treating as routine the patron's problem helps minimize anxiety inherent in such situations. Parallel to this is a "medicalization" of the situation, also helping to disarm the patron vis-à-vis the deviant nature of the proposed transaction; at all times, the terminology is that of conventional medicine and surgery. Later, ordinarily two or three days prior to the appointment, the patron again calls the clinic, this time to get confirmation of date and time.

Usually patrons spend the night before their appointment at a hotel or motel near the clinic. Early in the morning of the scheduled date they call the clinic once again, this time to get directions to the only then revealed place of rendezvous where they are picked up and transported to the clinic by one of the staff members in a large, late model station wagon.

It is at this time that patrons find that they are not alone in their dilemma as there are also several others picked up at the same time, filling the station wagon to capacity. Although propinquity might argue for it, there is little deliberate interaction among the patrons during the ride to the clinic, uncertainty effectively immobilizing them in this ambiguous situation.

Upon arrival at the clinic site, where the wagon and all related cars of the staff are hidden from street view, the patrons are ushered into a large, well furnished waiting room. The clinic itself resembles a roomy private home, both externally and internally in its non-medical areas, and is located in a prestigious residential neighborhood.

Once in, the patrons find seats for themselves and settle into a waiting period of hushed expectancy. Conversation is limited to patients and their respective supportive others, i.e., to those previously known to one another. After a short interval of perhaps five minutes, the receptionist appears and calls out the name

---

[2] In this discussion the general label patron will be used in reference to patients, clients, and supportive others, unless reference is specifically limited to one of the roles in this category.

of the first patient. The pair, patient and receptionist, then retire out of sight of the remaining patrons and into the medical wing of the clinic.

The first stop in the medical wing is an office. After first explaining the procedure in explicitly medical terminology, the receptionist shifts to her book-keeper role and requests the fee (in cash or traveler's checks) from the patient, frequently finding that it is being held by an accompanying supportive other still in the waiting room. Following this discussion and collection of the fee, the patient is then sent to a bathroom, well appointed in terms of luxury rather than gynecology, to remove her street clothes and put on a surgical gown. Once gowned, the patient is directed to the room where the actual abortion will take place.

Those specifically involved in the procedure include, in addition to the patient, the two practitioners, senior and apprentice, and a practical nurse. Although an anesthetic is administered, at no time is the patient allowed to lose consciousness; a necessity born of the possible need for quick removal in the event of visitation by legal agents. Immediately upon completion of the procedure the patient leaves the table and is sent to another room to rest for fifteen minutes to an hour and a half. Finally, after receiving medication and instruction regarding post-operative care from the receptionist, the patient and any supportive others are returned to the site of the original rendezvous and thus to their conventional worlds.

Analysis

With this brief, oversimplified picture it is now possible to turn to more specifically sociological concerns: the aforementioned presentational strategies which make up what may be called, for the clinic, a *rhetoric of legitimization*.

Sociologically, a rhetoric is a vocabulary of limited purpose; that is to say, it is a set of symbols functioning to communicate a particular set of meanings, directed and organized toward the representation of a specific image or impression. Such vocabularies are not only verbal but also include visual symbols such as objects, gestures, emblems, etc.[3]

In the case of the clinic the rhetoric operates to subvert the conventional world's view of abortion, and to generate a picture of legitimate activity. Fundamentally, the question thus becomes: What techniques are utilized via this rhetoric to *neutralize* the context of deviance in which the clinic operates, so as to enhance parallels with conventional medical and social situations and thus derive a kind of "rightness" or legitimization?[4] How, in other words, are the

---

[3] The concept of rhetoric as used herein is similar to but independent of the work of Kenneth Burke. As a theoretical point it should be noted that rhetorics are not necessarily the same thing as ideologies, although this may empirically be the case. The conceptual difference between the two is that rhetoric speaks to communication, both style and content, while ideology refers to perception and justification in terms of the ideologue's conception of the relevant portions of the world. It is quite conceivable that individual actors will utilize a rhetoric without any ideological convictions as regards its validity, but with a recognition of its pragmatic efficacy; and similarly, that ideological dedication does not automatically assume any developed rhetoric to attempt its maintenance or furtherance.

[4] Compare Gresham M. Sykes and David Matza, "Techniques of Neutralization: A Theory of Delinquency," *American Sociological Review*, 22 (December, 1957), pp. 664–670, where the analysis is individual rather than institutional; also Matza, *Delinquency and Drift*, New York: John Wiley and Sons, 1964.

setting and actions *qua* impressions manipulated to maximize the clinic's image over and above successful performance of its task and contradict the stereotypic stigma of deviance? Specifically, how does the clinic 1) minimize the possibilities of trouble with frightened or recalcitrant patrons; 2) generate the patron satisfaction necessary for referral system maintenance; and 3) present an image which will provide the most favorable self image or identity for the actors involved, whether patron or staff? [5]

For conceptual purposes, the clinic's rhetoric of legitimization may be treated by employing Goffman's delineation of *front* and its constituents of setting, appearance, and manner; [6] originally a framework for analyzing the presentation of self, it seems extendible to the strategies of establishments and institutions as well.

Essentially, front consists of those communications which serve to define the situation or performance for the audience; standardized expressive equipment including *setting*, the spatial/physical background items of scenery in the immediate area of the interaction; *appearance*, the sign-vehicles expressing the performer's social status or type; and those expressions which warn of a performer's demeanor, mood, etc., i.e., *manner*.

Examining each of these elements for evidence of how they are manipulated to make up a rhetoric will show the central themes and dimensions of the clinic's presentational strategies. Although the combination of the conceptions of rhetoric, neutralization, and front produces an admittedly loose theoretical scheme, the character of the data does not suggest the need for further rigor.

Setting. A paramount feature of the clinic's rhetoric is its physical and spatial characteristics. Especially important for patrons generally is the stereotype-contradicting waiting room, the first impression of the clinic itself—and the dominant one for supportive others. The waiting room is likely to be the only room in which the supportive others will be present during their entire visit to the clinic, save the possibility of a short interval in the office if they happen to be holding the fee, a frequent occurrence, especially if the other is also a client.

Spatially, the waiting room is L-shaped and extremely large; approximately 75 feet long and 50 feet wide at the base leg. Its size is accentuated by the fact that most of the room is sunken about three feet below other floor levels. Fully and deeply carpeted, well furnished with several couches, arm chairs, large lamps, and tables, the room speaks of luxury and patron consideration, also implied by the presence of a television set, a small bar, and a phonograph, in addition to the usual magazines present in waiting room situations.

Both the size of the room and the placement of the furniture function to provide private islands which need not be shared; space is structured so as to create withdrawal niches for each set of patrons. Couches and chairs are arranged along the walls of the room, maximizing distance between groupings and mini-

---

[5] The second and third problems are, in effect, special cases of the first. Minimization of trouble is not motivated by fear of patron complaints to legal agents, which would involve the complainants in admitting complicity, but by desire to maintain referrals and enhance self images. Additionally, such minimization produces a smoother, easier work-flow for the staff; and similar rationale in conventional medical settings sometimes dictates the use of general anesthetics when, in terms of patient pain, locals would be adequate.

[6] Erving Goffman, *The Presentation of Self in Everyday Life*, Garden City, N.Y.: Doubleday Anchor, 1959, pp. 22–30. This scheme formed the observational framework for data collection as well as a perspective for preparing the data.

mizing the possibilities of direct, inter-group eye-contact between the various patron-sets who, despite their shared problem and the recently experienced forced propinquity of the ride to the clinic, tend to keep their anxieties private. Thus, interaction among patrons in the waiting room is closed, confined to patients and their own accompanying supportive others only.

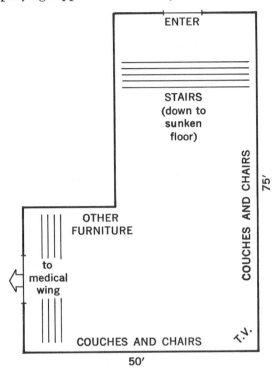

FIGURE 1.   The ecology of the clinic's waiting room.

Turning to the medical wing: The picture is a far cry from the shabby and sordid image of "kitchen table abortion" drawn in the popular press; it is one of modern scientific medicine, and with it comes assurance to the patient. Once the patient has donned a gown, her next stop is the operating room, a designation used without exception by the staff. In addition to a gynecological table, the room contains familiar (to the lay patient) medical paraphernalia: surgical tools, hypodermic syringes, stainless steel pans and trays, bottles and vials enclosing various colored liquids, capsules, pills, etc.—props effectively neutralizing the negative stereotypes associated with abortion as portrayed in the mass media.

After the procedure has been completed, the patient is moved from the scientific arena of the operating room and back again into luxury. As is the waiting room, the rooms in which the patients spend their short period of post-operative rest are expensively furnished.

Ultimately, after resting, the patient returns to the waiting room and, for most, to supportive others, and receives a final post-operative briefing before being returned to the rendezvous site. Parenthetically it may be noted that throughout the entire episode piped-in music has pervaded every room in which patrons are present.

In terms of setting, the clinic presents itself as not unlike a small hospital albeit with a decorator-designed interior. For patient and supportive others the scenery and props have functioned to communicate an image of assurance and protection through the devices of cost and luxury along with scientific medicine, to minimize the deviant nature of the transaction, and to emphasize positive cultural values, thus efficiently counteracting the stereotypic image.

Appearance and Manner. A widespread device for visibly differentiating various social categories or types is clothing.[7] Items of dress may function as insignia or uniforms to label the persons so garbed as members of particular social groups, occupations, etc. Such institutionalized symbols act as both identifiers and identities; to be attired in certain ways is to be a certain kind of person, not only in the eyes of the audience, but also in terms of the actor's perception of himself. Dress is an integral aspect of social identity.

So it is with the staff of the clinic: practitioners, patient, nurse—all wear the appropriate symbols, from the layman's point of view, of dress for surgically centered roles. White tunics are worn by the practitioners; the patient is surgically gowned; the nurse and even the janitress wear white uniform dresses. This element of the rhetoric is highlighted at the beginning of the procedure when both practitioners ostentatiously don surgical gloves, visibly emphasizing their, and the clinic's, concern with the necessities of asepsis. This ritualistic activity also serves to forcefully identify these actors in their roles as defined by the rhetoric.

The medical model is further underscored by the pre-operative medical history which is taken and recorded upon a standard, multi-carboned form (the destiny of these duplicate copies is unknown). Actions such as this, along with dress, provide major modes of stressing the medical legitimacy of the clinic, its staff and its task.

From the receptionist on up through the clinic's hierarchy, behavior, particularly verbal, emphasizes medical and professional aspects of the clinic's operation. Nowhere is this more apparent than in the area of vocabulary; it is strictly medical, with no effort either made or implied to speak down to the less knowledgeable lay patron. It is also noteworthy that at no time is the word abortion used in the presence of a patron; rather, it is referred to as the operation, the procedure, or as a D and C (dilation and curettage). Similarly, as noted above, the room in which the procedure takes place is at all times designated by the staff as the operating room.

Other elements of staff behavior which further the medical impression are 1) the post-operative consultation and medication which effectively contrast with the popular view of abortion as an "off-the-table-and-out" procedure, and 2) the presence of an apprentice practitioner and its obvious analogy, at least to the medically sophisticated, with a teaching hospital. For the patient, the teaching aspects of the senior practitioner's role help to generate confidence in his skill, a matter which is verbally reinforced by other staff members in their interactions with the patrons.

As with appearance, the manner of the staff is essentially directed toward the medical elements of the clinic's rhetoric; their demeanor is professional at all times, with one exception. This exception is the receptionist-bookkeeper, whose

---

[7] Mary Ellen Roach and Joanne Bubolz Eicher (eds.), *Dress, Adornment, and the Social Order,* New York: John Wiley and Sons, 1965.

role is, by definition, outside the strictly medical aspects of the clinic. As a result, freed of the obligations of professional mien, the receptionist is able to interact with patrons in a reassuring and supportive manner; in effect, her presentation of the rhetoric is through expressive strategies, while the manner of other staff members is more instrumentally oriented.[8]

Before turning to the central themes engendered among the patrons by the clinic's rhetorical strategies, it may be well to at least take note of some flaws in the presentation, even though they may escape the usual patron's attention. These may be considered under the general rubrics of pseudo-sterility and miscellaneous delicts.

Pseudo-Sterility. Although ostentation is the rule as regards the emphasis of aseptic and antiseptic precautions, there are also omissions less readily obvious. It will be recalled that measures apparently designed to minimize infection and also at the same time maximize parallels with legitimate medicine included the wearing of tunics by the practitioners, their donning of surgical gloves prior to the procedure, and the display of the tools and paraphernalia of medicine and surgery in the operating room.

It should be pointed out that, aseptically, tunics are no substitute for full surgical gowns, that full precautionary tactics would also include items such as face masks, caps, etc.; and that it is highly irregular for an operating room to lack an autoclave (for the sterilization of instruments) and changeable covering for the table, and for surgical instruments to stand on display, exposed to the air for long periods of time. Additionally, it may be noted that the portion of the preoperative medical history which is taken by the senior practitioner is recorded by him after his elaborate display of putting on the surgical gloves—a less than ideal practice for sterility.

These breaches of standard procedure suggest that much of what is passed to the lay patron as concern with aseptic and antiseptic practices is actually rhetoric, designed to communicate to the audience a standard of medical rigor which does not in fact exist.

Miscellaneous Delicts. Within this category are included additional practices at variance with the fostered impression.

Perhaps the most glaring of these is the lack of privacy afforded the patient in comparison with more conventional medical settings. The fact that patients are handled in groups, and moved and serviced in what in comparison with a hospital is a small and not systematically designed space, leads to a good deal of enforced contact between patients and staff involved in various stages of the process. Of necessity this leads to invasions of privacy, at least as perceived by patients accustomed to more traditional medical situations. Thus, for instance, the room used as an office also doubles as a resting room, and a patient lying there for postoperative rest may suddenly find herself witness to a financial transaction as a later-scheduled patron pays the fee; the resting patient is thus treated, in effect, as an object, becoming, in Goffman's phrase, a non-person,[9] i.e., an actor not accorded the usual deferences given as minimal acknowledgements of a person's moral worth simply by virtue of that person's being human.

---

[8] Excluded from this consideration is the telephone girl who is never in face-to-face interaction with the patrons but is also supportive in her demeanor.
[9] Goffman, *The Presentation of Self, op. cit.,* pp. 151–152.

Also of interest is the function of the music, piped into every room including the one for the procedure. When the patrons first arrive at the clinic the music is quiet, soothing, and relaxing in style; but with the entrance of the first patient into the medical wing, the tempo and timbre increase. The volume of the music then operates to drown out any untoward sounds which might emanate from the medical wing and alarm those patrons still in the waiting room.

Another delict involves the marked contrast in vehicles used in picking up and returning patrons to the rendezvous. In keeping with the symbolism of cost and luxury presented to the prospective patrons, the station wagon which brings them to the clinic is an expensive late model. By contrast, for the return to the rendez-vous, which is not done en masse as is the initial pick up, and by which time presentational strategies are less necessary, the car driven by the chauffeur-errand boy is an old, rather decrepit foreign sedan of low cost and questionable re-liability.

Another item at variance with traditional medical procedures is the emphasis, especially by the practitioners, on the necessity of the patient's cooperation to as-sure the procedure's success. The patient is in effect invited, if not commanded, to become an active participant in the ongoing activity.[10] She is told, for instance, of the desirability of her concentrating on other matters, e.g., "think of something else and all will go smoothly and rapidly." This assigning an active role to the patient stands in marked contradiction to her objectification as regards matters of privacy, and implies expediency as a more central concern of the clinic's operation than is patient welfare.

Finally, it may be noted that though the practitioners are verbally represented by others on the staff as physicians, gynecologists in fact, no evidence of medi-cal training in the form of certificates or diplomas is available for patron scrutiny.

Discussion

From this selective ethnographic description of various aspects of the clinic's front, two broad dimensions appear essential to its rhetoric of legitimization: 1) luxury and cost, and 2) conventional medical practices and procedures. It is these two themes which are emphasized in the clinic's efforts to neutralize its aura of habitual deviance before an audience of situationally deviant patrons drawn from the world of conventional culture. Thus, the rhetoric draws its vo-cabulary from meaningful and positive values of the patron's culture.

Within these two valued themes, four elements may be specified as contribut-ing to the two broader dimensions of luxury and cost and conventional medicine: cleanliness, competence, conventionality, and concern for the patron.

Cleanliness and competence are both elements of the instrumental aspects of medicine. Albeit with significant flaws, unrecognized by most lay patrons any-way, the clinic's presentational strategies enhance these impressions, if not to the same extent their actualities. The obvious symbols of dress and equipment

10 See the discussion of the patient as basically helpless and passive in Talcott Parsons, *The Social System*, Glencoe, Ill.: The Free Press, 1951, pp. 439–447. An alternative approach is indicated in Robert Leonard's work. See his several papers in James Skipper, Jr. and Robert Leonard (eds.) *Social Interaction and Patient Care*, Philadelphia: J. P. Lippincott, 1965.

are presented to the patient in the medical wing of the clinic where anxiety and uncertainty are high. The symbols are readily recognizable and imply the conventionality of the situation; they provide, in effect, a set of familiar expectations drawn from past experience with legitimate medicine. In a similar allaying manner, the practitioner's skill and competence is repeatedly voiced by the staff from the time of the initial telephone contact until the beginning of the actual abortive procedure itself.

Conventionality here means a realization of the middle class values of most patrons. One of these values is, of course, a positive view of professional medicine, a view which the clinic attempts to exploit. Throughout the patron's experience with the clinic, parallels with this model are highlighted; but it is in another area that this element of the rhetoric functions most effectively.

This is the waiting room setting. The obvious expense, comfort, and general decor of this room are such as to disarm all but the most fearful and suspicious patron. This room and the first impressions it presents are such as to immediately link the clinic to the safe, known world of respectable middle class conventionality. In the process of this linkage, the clinic is, in the patron's perception, divorced from the usually illicit image conjured by abortion; if not rendered totally respectable, the clinic is at least brought within the context of the definitions and expectations of mundane, everyday experience. Because of its crucial location in the process, being the patron's first direct exposure to the clinic milieu, it is fair to say that this room is the most successful presentational strategy in the clinic's legitimizing rhetoric.

The comfort of the waiting room is but one of the forms of expression of concern for the patron which help to create a legitimitizing presentation. Other strategies include the telephone girl's supportive routinization of the patron's problem at the time of the initial contact; the similarly solicitous demeanor of the receptionist; and the post-operative consultation. This involves not only the dispensing of drugs to facilitate the patient's convalescence, but also a brochure specifically detailing an expected course of progress and steps to be taken in case of complications.

By demonstrating concern, the clinic affirms its subscription to the values of its patrons, and thus asserts its basically conventional nature, i.e. the congruence of its operation with the norms of those upon whom its income relies.

All of these factors combine to help construct a rhetoric of legitimacy: a set of presentational strategies which allows the clinic to minimize problems inherent in typically anxious and fearful patrons, and thus to function more effectively; and in addition to generate the reputation necessary for an establishment of its kind, dependent upon referrals from physicians.

Additionally, whether manifest or latent, the rhetoric also has consequences for the identities of the actors involved. Both habitual deviants, the staff, and situational deviants, the patrons, are able to partake of the rhetoric so as to enhance their own self images. The rhetoric helps the staff define their participation in the clinic's habitually deviant activities, despite the occasional flaws, as involvement in a professionally operating establishment with the trappings of conventional medicine. For patrons, though they too are admittedly involved in a deviant situation, the rhetoric blunts this hard truth. By accepting the presentational strategies as part of the clinic's image, the patron is allowed to define the situation through the symbols drawn from his conventional everyday experience. Thus, for both patron and staff alike, the rhetoric allows for a minimization of the threat to identity which is built into their illicit transaction.

Unfortunately, the confidential nature of this research does not allow one of the usual canons of science to be met, i.e. that regarding exact replication; and no claim regarding the typicality of the clinic described herein can be made. Hopefully, however, the materials have shed some light on a relatively little known area of social behavior. Given the incidence of abortion, it may be hoped that similar analyses can be conducted by others.[11] Additionally, it may be suggested that the concept of rhetoric provides a useful tool for examining the dramas of social life, whether deviant or conventional, spontaneous or routine, unusual or mundane.

----

[11] A step in this direction is the dissertation (in progress) of Nancy L. Howell, "Information Channels and Informal Networks in the Distribution of Source Information," Department of Social Relations, Harvard University.

PART FOUR:
SITUATIONS AND SOCIAL WORLDS

In the preceding section on the definition of the situation, we raised the question of reality—what it is and to whom it belongs.[1] Here we find one of the most difficult questions of social psychology, for the social psychologist must always locate his subject in that subject's *real* world to achieve even a beginning explanation of his conduct. As George H. Mead stated so well:

> Social psychology . . . presupposes an approach to experience from the standpoint of the individual, but undertakes to determine in particular that which belongs to this experience because the individual himself belongs to a social structure, a social order.[2]

The study of society necessarily precedes the study of personal conduct. Social matrices of individual activity must first be determined before that activity can be interpreted.

The importance of these assertions is conveyed vividly by the brief account of a Tallensi mourning procession observed by Meyer Fortes. Suddenly, as the procession crosses some boundary invisible to the observer, the interaction shifts from joking and laughter to wailing and tears. Indeed, we are reminded of our own attendance at such grave ceremonies as funerals or weddings. There is always some point in time and space where our demeanor undergoes drastic change. It is reflected in our conversation, its pitch and intensity, and our bearing. Our very

---

[1] For a provoking discussion of the problem, see Peter L. Berger and Thomas Luckmann, *The Social Construction of Reality* (Garden City: Anchor Books, Doubleday and Co., Inc., 1967). Frequently these authors confuse knowledge and reality. In spite of this confusion the study remains a valuable one.

[2] George Herbert Mead, *Mind, Self and Society* (Chicago: University of Chicago Press, 1934), p. 1.

selves are transformed. Fortes reports the questions of the mourners: "Are there not appropriate times, places and occasions for people to act in . . . customary ways . . . ?" He notes that occasions evoke and confer roles. Roles cannot be interpreted outside the context of situation. As a consequence, we offer a definition of *role—those expectations mobilized by an identity through verbal and nonverbal communication in a specified social situation.* Role performance, or personal conduct, obviously takes established roles into account, though never completely. In any case, the situation must be specified. At first glance this seems a simple matter and leads us into the problem of territories.

Lyman and Scott consider this problem. Implicitly, they raise the yet-unsolved question concerning the boundaries of situations. The question also applies to Gestalt psychology: Where does the field end? In discussions of situations, *Gestalten,* or fields, the center is always more readily ascertained than are the edges. Lyman and Scott begin their endeavor by proposing a typology of territories ranging from open or public places to highly personalized places, for example, those felt somehow to belong to the body. In this latter respect, the *sense* of territory is very difficult to distinguish from territory itself. Undoubtedly this is the case because the boundaries of public places are ordinarily more clearly demarcated in space than more personal territories. Thus, interactional territories are said to be set off by "invisible boundaries"—social membranes and rules, understood but not officially promulgated, that govern access to and egress from the interaction. Interactional territories may, in addition, be mobile through space, as in walking conversations, and body territories are probably more often in motion than at rest. Moreover, territories typified in this manner are characterized by mutual transformations. Groupings may convert public places, like bars, into home territories. Marriage or love may convert the body into interactional territory, or make the other's body one's home base.

Some light is shed on the question of boundaries when encroachments and reactions to them are viewed. Territories may be violated (often unknowingly), invaded deliberately, or contaminated. Such encroachments result in a tightening and clarification of boundaries by aggressive defenses of "turf," or by setting up defense perimeters, by insulation—throwing up barricades, uniforming those who are granted access to the violated space, or sealing off interaction by developing a gestural code of secret handclasps, and other gestural countersigns. Closely akin to such gestural insulation is linguistic collusion whereby a distinctive argot is employed or developed by insiders, effectively barring outsiders from interaction.[3] These reactions to encroachment, since they tighten territorial boundaries, have the consequence of restricting freedom—of fencing people in. Hemmed-in groupings may cope with such restrictions by carving out public space for themselves or by expressively manipulating and adorning body territories. They may also enlarge personal territories "internally" by "expanding consciousness" or removing their *selves* from the scene, while leaving their *bodies* behind.

People *appear* to belong in one "place" or another. These appropriate appearances are demarcated by a vast number of *apparent symbols,* often nonverbal,

---

[3] An excellent example is provided by black professional baseball players, who share many of the same spaces with whites but effectively seal themselves off from social interaction not relating specifically to the performance of the sport. See Robert H. Boyle, *Sport—Mirror of American Life* (Boston: Little, Brown and Co., 1963), pp. 100–134. The linguistic devices detailed there are profuse and certainly collusive. Some nicknames used within black circles are still not revealed to outsiders, though their general existence is admitted.

which are interpreted conventionally by those who display them and by those for whom they are displayed. Such displays literally embed persons in social worlds, and these worlds have been interpreted by Stone as universes of appearance. In the socialization process one enters (or is inducted into) universes of appearance as well as those universes of discourse emphasized so strongly by George H. Mead. One must learn to appear to be what he is or has become perhaps even more importantly than to talk that way. In this sense and only this, the medium may be the message.

We can understand this best when we examine the worlds of the sexes. One's appearance announces his sex, and people seldom inquire into the sex or gender of one another. Sexual appearances, moreover, are buttressed by a host of moral justifications, ranging from religious beliefs, through law, to assertions of genetic destiny (men are not *meant* to wear dresses). In addition, concern with clothes is differentially attributed to the sexes. Women are expected to cultivate and diversify their personal appearances; men are expected to play down such concerns (above some vaguely specified minimal point). Even so, sexual barriers demarcated by personal appearance are being penetrated as women move into those orders of society previously reserved for men, for example, occupational worlds. The appropriation of quasi-male appearances by women encounters less resistance—and hostility—than the opposite.

With age, it is another matter. As Stone suggests, it may well be fruitful for sociologists to distinguish *circumstances* from *situations*. Circumstances may be said to envelop acts:

> . . . the acting one is trapped, ensnared, fated. On this view sex is a circumstance for most people. . . . In some societies, age is also a circumstance, but in our own it increasingly becomes a situation, eminently capable of redefinition, a situation from which escape is encouraged on a large scale.

Indeed, fifty-year-olds are spoken of as "boys" or "girls." Collective misrepresentations—the hair dyes, wigs, face-lifts, cosmetics, and such instruments as corsets and "falsies"—enable the chronologically old to appear socially young. They may as a consequence *act* younger. As one of Stone's respondents says, "If I look older, I'll act older." Children, in contrast, can appear as young men or women, though they may not as often act that way. More and more in our society the appearances of age seem only to distinguish the very old from the very young.

Now, reminding the reader of Mead's notion that social psychology studies individual experience in the context of social organization, we see that fundamental questions are raised here concerning the interpretations of personal conduct. Sex and age have been employed conventionally as "independent variables" in the analysis of opinion and behavior in social psychological research. However, even sex differences in opinion and behavior, while they are consistently revealed in research, are never absolute. Researchers fail to take into account the permeability of social worlds—if you like, the difference between circumstance and situation. In his presidential address to the American Sociological Society in September 1956, Herbert Blumer captured the essence of the problem: [4]

> In my judgment, the crucial limit to the successful application of variable analysis to human group life is set by the process of interpretation or definition that goes

---

[4] Herbert Blumer, "Sociological Analysis and the 'Variable,'" *American Sociological Review*, XXI (December 1956), p. 685.

on in human groups. This process, which I believe to be the core of human action, gives a character to human group life that seems to be at variance with the logical premises of variable analysis.

Race or ethnicity is another "independent variable" that is employed to explain personal conduct, but race also rests on interpretation and definition as it is taken into account in human interaction. Even seemingly visible "variables" or boundaries of color rest on consensual meaning.

Langston Hughes' account of a "racial encounter" in a Harlem night club and, subsequently, in a restaurant provides an excellent demonstration of the permeability of racial boundaries as well as their impenetrability. A white man ceases his defense of an apparently white woman attacked by her apparently black husband when he learns that she is—perhaps in fact—a light-colored Negro. Matters of race, in his mind, predominate over matters of sexual propriety. Defining the blonde as black, the white man refuses to intrude into that black racial world and leaves the scene. Afterwards, the remaining "white" couple acknowledge their "blackness," are accepted into that black racial world, but, at the end of the evening, imply that they are, in fact, "white." The entire encounter has a Pirandello-like quality.[5] No one *really* knows who the other one is in racial terms. Each accepts social definitions, and conduct is severely altered by virtue of those definitions. Again the "variable" depends on its interpretation. Hughes reminds us that a distinctive mark of interaction is the "con."

"Con games" may become mutually supportive, and this also affects the penetrability of social worlds. The "mark," precisely by performing the role of a mark, may elevate himself into the position of conning the con man. This is well documented by Niels Braroe's account of reciprocal exploitation by whites and Indians living in close physical proximity. Both whites and Indans know they are exploiting or conning one another, yet neither can acknowledge this awareness, else their game is destroyed. Braroe cites Goffman: [6]

> Any event which demonstrates that someone has made a false claim, defining himself as something which he is not, tends to destroy him.

Who is destroyed—the falsified claimant, or the audience? Braroe indicates neither. A "working consensus" protects falsifier and audience alike. We deal here with the interaction of two social worlds—whites and Indians—involved in a mutual, tacitly agreed upon, con game. Openly to admit the falsification *that each is aware of* destroys the interaction. Whites view Indians as childish and irresponsible. They view themselves as responsible, independent, and self-sufficient. Thus, when Indians dupe whites by painting fence posts with laundry bluing rather than a legitimate preservative, the "mark" can chalk up the ruse to Indian childish irresponsibility, which he must accept and tolerate as his own presumed adult responsibility dictates. Whites *expect* to be conned! Thereby, their image of the Indian is validated, their own exploitation of the Indian is justified (they pay!), and the Indians behave so that the white image is validated. Backstage, on the reservation, the assumed front is dropped, but no matter: "Indian-ness" cannot

---

[5] The play that best makes this point is "It *Is* So! (If You Think So)," in Eric Bentley (ed.), *Naked Masks—Five Plays by Luigi Pirandello* (New York: E. P. DuHar and Co., Inc., 1952), pp. 61–138.

[6] Erving Goffman, "On Cooling the Mark Out," reprinted in Arnold M. Rose, *Human Behavior and Social Processes* (Boston: Houghton Mifflin, 1962), p. 500.

be employed as an explanatory variable without reference to this interactive pattern. When social worlds come together, each modifies the other and complicates the explanation of human conduct.

Socio-economic status is also a conventionally employed "variable" adduced by social psychologists in the explanation of human conduct. The selection by Stone points to the same permeability of status lines that characterize the age grades. Although status may be more of a circumstance for those "in" the lower socio-economic levels, where money is not available to enlarge their repertoire of apparent symbols, this is not always precisely so—for example, the shipping foreman and the freight hand. In general, social status is less often a circumstance and more often a manipulable situation, the higher the socio-economic level, but even this does not hold for everyone. Contrast the impression management of "Mrs. Cavendish" with the entrapment of "Mrs. Branchwood." Social controls, such as police intervention, ostracism, and obvious "noticing," however, do maintain lines of status as the boundaries of social worlds at least *within* the small town. Some people can escape the boundaries of the town itself and move out into the world at large where they define, for themselves and others, status situations that have no place in the small local community.

And this is a matter that complicates the worlds of status. Gerald Thielbar singles out the prime foci of complications in his essay on "locals" and "cosmopolitans." In the first place, he observes that physical and social distance are seldom isomorphic—a point that calls into question not only Goffman's frequent emphasis upon physical space as a container of social situations, but also the earlier stress by Lyman and Scott on territories. There, however, they anticipate these difficulties by merging the *sense of territory* with the *notion of physical boundaries.* Thielbar points out that there is an emerging horizontal differentiation of life styles that escapes the more conventional vertical dimensions of socio-economic status. People may live *in* but not be *of* the spatial locales of their residence. Cosmopolitanism emerges as a life style that is not rooted in any particular home ground. When persons embrace such a life style, there is little that can be predicted of their conduct by geographical location or by ranking them on some scale of socio-economic status.

But the matter is even more complex. Cities themselves are more or less cosmopolitan, as are institutions. Thus, the personal cosmopolite or localite will undoubtedly conduct himself differently depending on whether he finds himself in a local or cosmopolitan community and/or institution. We can diagram the possibilities. There are at least eight.

INSTITUTION	COMMUNITY			
	LOCAL		COSMOPOLITAN	
	Personal Local	*Personal Cosmopolitan*	*Personal Local*	*Personal Cosmopolitan*
Local				
Cosmopolitan				

It is understandable, then, why Gouldner, in his groundbreaking study of localism and cosmopolitanism,[7] found that cosmopolites were characterized by a high mobility potential. What cosmopolite in his "right mind" would not want to leave Yellow Springs, Ohio? In Washington, D.C., San Francisco, or New York, his spacial mobility aspirations might be considerably lessened. When we introduce to the dimensions in the above diagram conventional measures of social status, we can see how explanation is made considerably more difficult. And we shall not mention matters of sex, age, and ethnicity or race.

All this is to say that there are social worlds of sex, age, ethnicity, and status, but that these worlds are variously permeable and are undergoing transformations over historical time. Consequently conventional variable analysis may not be the most appropriate model to use in social psychological study. The outstanding problem of interpretation now seems to narrow on the situation as distinguished from circumstance. The matter of boundaries—their formulation, maintenance, change, loss, and reconstitution—is of overriding importance. In stating this, very little has been said about temporal boundaries set by history—epochs, periods of war and peace, prosperity and depression, and periods marked off by notable shifts in fashion. Here we reach the limits of current knowledge. Clearly this is an area in which much work remains to be done by social psychologists.

Suggested Readings

BALZTELL, DIGBY. *An American Business Aristocracy.* New York: Collier Books, 1962.

GANS, HERBERT J. *The Urban Villagers.* New York: The Free Press, 1962.

GLAZER, NATHAN, and DANIEL PATRICK MOYNIHAN. *Beyond the Melting Pot.* Cambridge, Mass.: The M.I.T. Press, 1963.

HOOKER, EVELYN. "The Homosexual Community," Proceedings of the XIVth International Congress of Applied Psychology. *Personality Research,* Vol. 2, Copenhagen, Munksgaard, 1962.

HUGHES, HELEN MacGILL (ed.). *The Fantastic Lodge.* Boston: Houghton Mifflin, 1961.

LEWIS, OSCAR. *La Vida.* New York: Vintage Books, 1968.

LIEBOW, ELLIOT. *Tally's Corner.* Boston, Toronto: Little, Brown and Co., 1967.

POLSKY, NED. *Hustlers, Beats, and Others.* Chicago: Aldine, 1968.

SHOSTAK, ARTHUR B., and WILLIAM GOMBERG (eds.). *Blue Collar World.* Englewood Cliffs, N.J.: Prentice-Hall, 1964.

SUTTLER, GERALD D. *The Social Order of the Slums.* Chicago: University of Chicago Press, 1968.

WIRTH, LOUIS. *The Ghetto.* Chicago: Phoenix Books, 1956.

---

[7] Alvin W. Gouldner, "Cosmopolitans and Locals: Toward an Analysis of Latent Social Rôles," *Administrative Science Quarterly,* II (December 1957 and March 1958), pp. 281–306; 444–480.

23 On Crying and Mourning

● MEYER FORTES

I remember the first time I saw a procession of mourners on their way to a funeral among the Tallensi. They included both men and women, dressed in gala clothes and carrying condolence gifts of guinea corn and chickens. A drummer and a fiddler escorted them. As they hove in sight, they were carrying on an animated conversation, laughing and joking. A bystander praised their admirable turnout. This, he said, was the proper way to attend the funeral of your father-in-law. All of a sudden the procession halted. Then, as it began to move forward again, a heart-rending wail broke forth. It came from the women. Tears were now streaming down their cheeks; and, as their wailing swelled, the men joined in with a melancholy dirge. In this way they arrived at the house of the bereaved family. What was the meaning of this transformation of mien and mood? Was it sincere or were the players simply putting on an act for which they were cast in their capacity as the kinsfolk of a son-in-law fulfilling a kinship obligation? I often discussed this question with Tallensi. Invariably they insisted that the wailing and the dirges expressed sincere grief. This, they insisted, is the customary mode of expressing condolence by a son-in-law's kin. How else could the mourners have shown their grief? Are there not, they went on, appropriate times, places and occasions for people to act in the customary ways that show the world that one is a kinsman or an affine or just a good friend? Mourners attending an in-law's funeral do not give vent to grief in their own home settlements. The appropriate place is the bereaved clan settlement.

Here we see how occasions evoke, and thus confer roles, according to standard patterns. But this occurrence is fully intelligible only if we take into account the whole context of status relationships implicit in it. A man has unrestricted rights over his wife's reproductive capacity in virtue of the bride-price he has paid to her father. But she never wholly forfeits her status as her father's daughter. This gives her residual claims on her father's protection and him a lien on her. If her marriage is unsuccessful she can, with her father's support, escape from it. A son-in-law is therefore in the perpetual debt of his father-in-law, being dependent on his goodwill, first for the original gift of his daughter, later for backing in maintaining the marriage. To mourn for his father-in-law is one of a number of customary demonstrations of respect he is obliged to make throughout his married life. If he inexcusably neglects these duties his wife's paternal kin may assert their rights and take her away. Jural right is here backed by moral justification. For people will say: how can a man be so callous towards his wife's feelings or so deficient in a sense of duty and propriety as wilfully to fail in his affinal obligations? The status of son-in-law carries with it not only rights and duties but also attitudes and sentiments, as shown, *inter alia*, by the appropriate mourning behaviour

SOURCE: Meyer Fortes, from his "Ritual and Office," in *Essays on the Ritual of Social Relations,* edited by Max Gluckman (Manchester: Manchester University Press, 1962), pp. 62–64.

for an affine. We should note that a respectable son-in-law takes pride in this. It reaffirms the affinal relations created by his marriage and this is tantamount to advertising the rights he holds and making acknowledgement of the obligations incurred.

Let me state the conclusion prompted by this example in what might be thought to be somewhat far-fetched terms; but I think it will help to advance the discussion. Firstly, roles, even transient ones, are only evoked in persons who may legitimately exercise them—nay must, in certain circumstances, do so; and secondly, roles are performed not automatically, but in response to social controls that emanate from the relationships in which the roles emerge.[1] For what, in fact, is the capacity to take on a role other than the manifestation of engagement in social relations? If role is status in action then status is shorthand for everything that is required of a person or permitted to him in virtue of a specified field of social relations in which he is involved. . . .

24   Territoriality: A Neglected Sociological Dimension

● STANFORD M. LYMAN AND MARVIN B. SCOTT

All living organisms observe some sense of territoriality,[1] that is, some sense—whether learned or instinctive to their species—in which control over space is

---

[1] As Parsons fully explains in *The Social System* (1951).

SOURCE: Stanford M. Lyman and Marvin B. Scott, in *Social Problems* 15, No. 2 (Fall 1967), pp. 236–249. Permission to reprint granted by The Society for the Study of Social Problems.
    We are grateful to Donald Ball and Edwin Lemert for their critical reading of the manuscript.

---

[1] The concept of territoriality was introduced into sociological analysis in the twenties under the label of "the ecological school." For an early statement see Robert E. Park, Ernest W. Burgess, and R. D. McKenzie, *The City*, Chicago: University of Chicago Press, 1925. For a summary and bibliography of the school see Milla Aissa Alihan, *Social Ecology*, N.Y.: Columbia University Press, 1938. An updated version of this school is found in James A. Quinn, *Human Ecology*, N.Y.: Prentice-Hall, 1950, and Amos H. Hawley, *Human Ecology, A Theory of Community Structures*, N.Y.: The Ronald Press, 1950.

Originating in animal studies, "territoriality" still looms large as an organizing concept in ethology. For a summary statement see C. R. Carpenter, "Territoriality: A Review of Concepts and Problems," in A. Roe and G. Simpson, editors, *Behavior and Evolution*, New Haven: Yale University Press, 1958, pp. 224–250.

For a challenging argument that sociological investigation can fruitfully employ the techniques of comparative ethology—especially to such subjects as territoriality—see Lionel Tiger and Robin Fox, "The Zoological Perspective in Social Science," *Man*, I., 1, (March, 1966), esp. p. 80.

Only very recently have sociologists revived ecological thinking to include a truly *interactional* dimension. The outstanding contributor is, of course, Edward T. Hall. See his *The Silent Language*, Garden City, N.Y.: Doubleday and Co., 1959, and *The Hidden Dimension*, Garden City, N.Y.: Doubleday and Co., 1966. For a masterful application of the concept of territoriality in interactional terms see Erving Goffman, *Asylums*, Garden City, N.Y.: Doubleday and Co., Anchor Books, 1961, pp. 227–248. In a slightly different vein see the interesting efforts of Robert Sommer, "Studies in Personal Space," *Sociometry*, 22 (September, 1959), pp. 247–260, and the writings of Roger Barker, especially his "Roles, Ecological Niches, and the Psychology of the Absent Organism," paper presented to the conference on the Propositional Structure of Role Theory, University of Missouri, 1962.

deemed central for survival.[2] Although man's domination over space is potentially unlimited, in contemporary society it appears that men acknowledge increasingly few *free* territories for themselves.[3]

Free territory is carved out of space and affords opportunities for idiosyncrasy and identity. Central to the manifestation of these opportunities are boundary creation and enclosure. This is so because activities that run counter to expected norms need seclusion or invisibility to permit unsanctioned performance, and because peculiar identities are sometimes impossible to realize in the absence of an appropriate setting.[4] Thus the opportunities for freedom of action—with respect to normatively discrepant behavior and maintenance of specific identities—are intimately connected with the ability to attach boundaries to space and command access to or exclusion from territories.

In American society where territorial encroachment affects nearly all members of society, certain segments of the population are particularly deprived, namely, Negroes, women, youth, and inmates of various kinds. With these categories in mind, this paper re-introduces a neglected dimension of social analysis important to understanding deprived groups.

Our strategy is twofold: first, to bring together under a new set of organizing concepts the notions of types of territory, types of territorial encroachment, and types of responses to encroachment; and second, to specify the reactions of spatially deprived groups.

The Types of Territories

We can distinguish four kinds of territories, namely, *public territories, home territories, interactional territories* and *body territories.*

PUBLIC TERRITORIES

Public territories are those areas where the individual has freedom of access, but not necessarily of action, by virtue of his claim to citizenship.[5] These territories are officially open to all, but certain images and expectations of appropriate behavior and of the categories of individuals who are normally perceived as using these territories modify freedom. First, it is commonly expected that illegal activities and impermissible behavior will not occur in public places. Since public territories are vulnerable to violation in both respects, however, policemen are charged with the task of removing lawbreakers from the scene of their activities and restricting behavior in public places.[6]

Second, certain categories of persons are accorded only limited access to and

---

[2] For the argument that human territoriality is a natural rather than a cultural phenomenon see Robert Ardrey, *The Territorial Imperative*, New York: Atheneum, 1966, pp. 3–41.

[3] The idea of "free territory" is derived from Goffman, *loc. cit.*

[4] See Erving Goffman, *The Presentation of Self in Everyday Life*, Garden City, N.Y.: Doubleday Anchor Books, 1959, p. 22.

[5] The term "citizenship" is used in a sense similar to that employed by T. H. Marshall in *Class, Citizenship and Social Development*, Garden City, N.Y.: Doubleday Anchor Books, 1965, esp. pp. 71–134.

[6] See Harvey Sacks, "Methods in Use for the Production of a Social Order: A Method for Warrantably Informing Moral Character," Center for the Study of Law and Society, University of California, Berkeley, 1962; and Aaron Cicourel, *The Social Organization of Juvenile Justice,* unpublished manuscript.

restricted activity in public places. It is expected, for instance, that children will not be playing in public playgrounds after midnight; that lower-class citizens will not live—although they might work—in areas of middle-class residence; and that Negroes will not be found leisurely strolling on the sidewalks of white neighborhoods, though they might be found laying the sewer pipe under the streets.

Since the rights of such discrepant groups to use these territories as citizens sometimes contradicts the privileges accorded them as persons, such territories are not infrequently the testing grounds of challenges to authority. The wave of sit-ins, wade-ins, and demonstrations in racially segregated restaurants, public beaches, and schools constitutes an outstanding recent example. Informal restrictions on access to public territories often violate unenforced or as yet untested rights of citizens. Since the informal delineation of some of these territories implies the absence of certain persons, their presence stands out. Policemen frequently become allies of locals in restricting citizenship rights when they remove unseemly persons from territories which they do not regularly habituate or when they restrict certain categories of persons to specific areas.[7]

Public territories are thus ambiguous with respect to accorded freedoms. First, the official rights of access may be regularly violated by local custom. Second, status discrepancy may modify activity and entrance rights. For example, the ambiguity in the distinction between minors and adults is a source of confusion and concern in the regulation of temporal and access rights to those whose status is unclear. Finally, activities once forbidden in public may be declared permissible, thus enlarging the freedom of the territory; or activities once licit may be proscribed, thus restricting it. Hence display of female breasts is now permitted in San Francisco nightclubs, but not on the streets or before children. Nude swimming enjoys police protection at certain designated beaches, but watching nude swimmers at these same beaches is forbidden to those who are attired.

HOME TERRITORIES

Home territories are areas where the regular participants have a relative freedom of behavior and a sense of intimacy and control over the area. Examples include makeshift clubhouses of children, hobo jungles, and homosexual bars. Home and public territories may be easily confused. In fact "the areas of public places and the areas of home territories are not always clearly differentiated in the social world and what may be defined and used as a public place by some may be defined and used as a home territory by others."[8] Thus, a home territory that also may be used as a public one is defined by its regular use by specific persons or categories of persons and by the particular "territorial stakes" or "identity pegs" that are found in such places. The style of dress and language among the patrons at a bar may immediately communicate to a homosexual that he has arrived in home territory, while a heterosexual passerby who pauses for a drink may be astonished or outraged when he is accosted for sexual favors from the stranger seated next to him. Large-scale clandestine brotherhoods indoctrinate their members in secret codes of dress and demeanor so that regardless of their later travels they can unobtrusively communicate their fraternal identity and ask for assistance

---

[7] See Jerome Skolnick, *Justice Without Trial,* New York: John Wiley, 1966, pp. 96–111 *et passim;* and Sacks, *op. cit.*

[8] Sherri Cavan, "Interaction in Home Territories," *Berkeley Journal of Sociology,* 5 (1963), p. 18.

from one another in otherwise public places. Home territories sometimes enjoy a proactive status, beyond the presence of their inhabitants, in the form of reserved chairs, drinking mugs, signs or memorabilia that serve to indicate special and reserved distinctions.

Home territories may be established by "sponsorship" or "colonization." An example of the former is found in the merchant emigrants from China who established caravansaries in certain quarters of Occidental cities which served as public trading establishments but also as living quarters, employment agencies, meeting places, and courts for their *Landsmänner*.[9] Colonization occurs when a person or group lays claim to a formally free territory by virtue of discovery, regular usage, or peculiar relationship. Thus certain restaurants become home territories to those who are impressed with their first meal there; to those who eat there on specific occasions, such as luncheons, birthdays, or after sporting events; and to those who are intimate with the waitress.

Loss of home status may be occasioned by the death or resignation of a sponsor, by violation of the previously established usages, by rejection, or by conquest. Erstwhile "regulars" at a bar may discover they are no longer warmly greeted nor eligible for a free drink when the proprietor dies or when their patronage becomes irregular. Homosexuals may desert a "queer bar" when it becomes a place which heterosexuals frequent to observe deviant behavior.

It is precisely because of their officially open condition that public areas are vulnerable to conversion into home territories. The rules of openness are sufficiently broad and ambiguous so that restrictions on time, place, and manner are difficult to promulgate and nearly impossible to enforce. Armed with a piece of chalk children can change the public sidewalk into a gameboard blocking pedestrian traffic. Despite building codes and parental admonitions youngsters convert abandoned buildings or newly begun sites into forts, clubs, and hideaways.[10]

But children are not the only colonizers on the public lands. Beggars and hawkers will stake out a "territory" on the sidewalks or among the blocks and occupy it sometimes to the exclusion of all others similarly employed. The idle and unemployed will loiter on certain streetcorners, monopolizing the space, and frightening off certain respectable types with their loud, boisterous, or obscene language, cruel jests, and suggestive leers. Members of racial and ethnic groups colonize a portion of the city and adorn it with their peculiar institutions, language, and rules of conduct.[11] Ethnic enclaves, like certain notorious homosexual bars and prisons on open-house day, are often "on display" to non-ethnics who thus grant legitimacy to the colony's claim for territorial identity.

---

9 See Stanford, M. Lyman, *The Structure of Chinese Society in Nineteenth-Century America*, unpublished, Ph.D. dissertation, Berkeley: University of California, 1961.

10 Indeed, children are among the most regular and innovative creators of home territories from the space and material available to the public in general. Speaking of their peculiar tendency to violate the rules governing trespass, William Prosser has aptly observed, "Children, as is well known to anyone who has been a child, are by nature unreliable and irresponsible people, who are quite likely to do almost anything. In particular, they have a deplorable tendency to stray upon land which does not belong to them, and to meddle with what they find there." "Trespassing Children," *California Law Review*, (August, 1959), p. 427.

11 Ethnic groups in the process of assimilation sometimes discover to their astonishment that the isolated slum wherein they have traditionally and unwillingly dwelt is in fact a home territory possessed of cherished values and irreplaceable sentiments. A militant Negro thus writes: "For as my son, Chuck, wrote me after exposure to the Negro community of Washington: 'I suddenly realized that the Negro ghetto is not a ghetto. It is home.'" John Oliver Killens, *Black Man's Burden*, New York: Trident Press, 1965, p. 94.

Among the most interesting examples of colonizing on the public lands are those attempts by youths to stake out streets as home territories open only to members of their own clique and defended against invasion by rival groups. Subject always to official harassment by police and interference by other adults who claim the streets as public territories, youths resolve the dilemma by redefining adults as non-persons whose seemingly violative presence on the youth's "turf" does not challenge the latter's proprietorship. Streets are most vulnerable to colonizing in this manner and indeed, as the early studies of the Chicago sociologists illustrated so well, streets and knots of juxtaposed streets become unofficial home areas to all those groups who require relatively secluded yet open space in which to pursue their interests or maintain their identities.[12]

INTERACTIONAL TERRITORIES

Interactional territories refer to any area where a social gathering may occur. Surrounding any interaction is an invisible boundary, a kind of social membrane.[13] A party is an interactional territory, as are the several knots of people who form clusters at parties. Every interactional territory implicitly makes a claim of boundary maintenance for the duration of the interaction. Thus access and egress are governed by rules understood, though not officially promulgated, by the members.

Interactional territories are characteristically mobile and fragile. Participants in a conversation may remain in one place, stroll along, or move periodically or erratically. They may interrupt only to resume it at a later time without permanently breaking the boundary or disintegrating the group. Even where "settings" are required for the interaction, mobility need not be dysfunctional if the items appropriate to the setting are movable. Thus chemists may not be able to complete a discussion without the assistance of a laboratory, but chess players may assemble or disassemble the game quite readily and in the most cramped quarters. Similarly, so long as Negroes were chattel slaves slaveholders might move them anywhere where their services or appearance were needed.

The fragility of interactional territories is constantly being tested by parvenus and newcomers. The latter, even when they possess credentials entitling them to entrance into the interactional circle, break down ongoing interaction and threaten it by requiring all to start over again, end it instead, and begin a new subject of common interest, or disintegrate.[14] Parvenus are a greater threat since their presence breaks the boundaries of the interaction and challenges the exclusiveness of the group. They may be repulsed, or accepted fully, though the latter is less likely than the granting of a "temporary visa," i.e., rights to interact for the instant occasion with no promise of equal rights in the future.

BODY TERRITORIES

Finally, there are body territories which include the space encompassed by the human body and the anatomical space of the body. The latter is, at least theoreti-

---

[12] Harvey W. Zorbaugh, *The Gold Coast and the Slum*, Chicago: University of Chicago Press, 1929. See also Jane Jacobs, *The Death and Life of Great American Cities*, N.Y.: Vintage Books, 1961, pp. 29–142.

[13] See Erving Goffman, *Behavior in Public Places*, N.Y.: The Free Press of Glencoe, 1963, pp. 151–165 *et passim*.

[14] An excellent illustration of the several facets of this process and attendant issues in social gatherings is found in David Riesman, *et al.*, "The Vanishing Host," *Human Organization* (Spring, 1960), pp. 17–27.

cally, the most private and inviolate of territories belonging to an individual. The rights to view and touch the body are of a sacred nature, subject to great restriction. For instance, a person's rights to his own body space are restricted where norms govern masturbation, or the appearance and decoration of skin. Moreover, rights of others to touch one's body are everywhere regulated, though perhaps modern societies impose greater restrictions than others.[15]

Body territory is also convertible into home territory. The most common method is marriage in a monogamous society in which sexual access to the female is deemed the exclusive right of the husband so long as he exercises propriety with respect to his status. Ownership, however, is not necessarily or always coterminous with possession, so that sexual rivalry might continue illegitimately after a marital choice has been made and erupt in trespass on the husband's sexual property.[16] Under situations where women are scarce, such as nineteenth-century overseas Chinese communities in the United States, sexual property was institutionalized through organized prostitution, and the few Chinese wives among the homeless men were carefully secluded.[17]

Body space is, however, subject to creative innovation, idiosyncrasy, and destruction. First, the body may be marked or marred by scars, cuts, burns, and tattoos. In addition, certain of its parts may be inhibited or removed without its complete loss of function. These markings have a meaning beyond the purely anatomical. They are among the indicators of status or stigma. They can be signs of bravado as was the dueling scar among German students, or of criminality as is a similar scar on Italians and Negroes in America. Loss of an eye may prevent one's entrance into dental school, but at least one clothing manufacturer regards one-eyed men as status symbols for starched shirts. Tattoos may memorialize one's mother or sweetheart as well as indicate one's seafaring occupation.

The human organism exercises extraterritorial rights over both internal and external space. In the latter instance the space immediately surrounding a person is also inviolate.[18] Thus conversations among friends are ecologically distinguishable from those between acquaintances or strangers. A person who persists in violating the extraterritorial space of another of the same sex may be accused of tactlessness

---

15 Talcott Parsons notes that "the very fact that affectionate bodily contact is almost completely taboo among men in American society is probably indicative of [the limited nature of intra-sex friendship] since it strongly limits affective attachment." *The Social System*, Glencoe: Free Press, 1951, p. 189. For an empirical study and analysis of touching relations see Erving Goffman, "The Nature of Deference and Demeanor," *American Anthropologist*, 58 (June, 1956), pp. 473–502.

16 See Kingsley Davis, *Human Society*, New York: Macmillan, 1948, pp. 175–193.

17 Lyman, *op. cit.*, pp. 97–111.

18 The perceptions of Simmel on this subject surpass all others and we are indebted to his work. Thus Simmel has noted: "In regard to the 'significant' [i.e., "great"] man, there is an inner compulsion which tells one to keep at a distance and which does not disappear even in intimate relations with him. The only type for whom such distance does not exist is the individual who has no organ for perceiving distance. . . . The individual who fails to keep his distance from a great person does not esteem him highly, much less too highly (as might superficially appear to be the case); but, on the contrary, his importune behavior reveals lack of proper respect. . . . The same sort of circle which surrounds a man—although it is value-accentuated in a very different sense—is filled out by his affairs and by his characteristics. To penetrate this circle by taking notice constitutes a violation of personality. Just as material property is, so to speak, an extension of the ego, there is also an intellectual private property, whose violation effects a lesion of the ego in its very center." Georg Simmel, "Secrecy and Group Communication," reprinted in T. Parsons, *et al.*, *Theories of Society*, New York: The Free Press of Glencoe, 1961, p. 320. For an updated statement of Simmel's point see Goffman, *Behavior in Public Places, op. cit.*

and suspected of homosexuality, while uninvited intersex invasion may indicate unwarranted familiarity.[19] Moreover, eye contact and visual persistence can be a measure of external space. Thus two strangers may look one another over at the proper distance, but as they near one another, propriety requires that they treat one another as non-persons unless a direct contact is going to be made.[20]

Control over "inner space" is the quintessence of individuality and freedom. Violations of "inner space" are carried out by domination, ranging in intensity from perception of more than is voluntarily revealed to persuasion and ultimately hypnosis.[21] Demonstration of idiosyncrasy with respect to "inner space" is exemplified by the modifications possible in the presentation of self through the uses of the several stimulants and depressants.

Territorial Encroachment

We can distinguish three forms of territorial encroachment: violation, invasion, and contamination.

Violation of a territory is unwarranted use of it. Violators are those who have repulsed or circumvented those who would deny them access. Violators are also, by virtue of their acts, claimants in some sense to the territory they have violated. Their claim, however, may vary in scope, intensity, and objective. Children may violate the graves of the dead by digging "for treasure" in the cemetery, but unlike ghouls, they are not seeking to remove the bodies for illicit purposes. Some territories may be violated, however, merely by unwarranted entrance into them. Among these are all those territories commonly restricted to categorical groups such as toilets, harems, nunneries, and public baths—areas commonly restricted according to sex. Other territories may not be necessarily violated by presence but only by innovative or prohibited use. Thus some parents regard family-wide nudity as permissible, but hold that sexual interest or intercourse among any but the married pair is forbidden. Interactional territories are violated when one or more of the legitimate interactants behaves out of character.[22]

Invasion of a territory occurs when those not entitled to entrance or use nevertheless cross the boundaries and interrupt, halt, take over, or change the social meaning of the territory. Such invasions, then, may be temporary or enduring.

---

[19] An interesting dilemma in this respect arises for the deaf and myopic. In attempting to appear as "normals" they may overstep another's territorial space and thus call attention to the very stigma they wish to conceal. On the problems of these who are stigmatized see Goffman, *Stigma*, Englewood Cliffs, New Jersey: Prentice-Hall, 1963.

[20] Goffman refers to this as "civil inattention." See *Behavior in Public Places, op. cit.*

[21] Compare the remarks by Simmel, *op. cit.*, p. 321. "In the interest of interaction and social cohesion, the individual *must* know certain things about the other person. Nor does the other have the right to oppose this knowledge from a moral standpoint, by demanding the discretion of the first: he cannot claim the entirely undisturbed possession of his own being and consciousness, since this discretion might harm the interests of his society. . . . But even in subtler and less unambiguous forms, in fragmentary beginnings and unexpressed notions, all of human intercourse rests on the fact that everybody knows somewhat more about the other than the other voluntarily reveals to him; and those things he knows are frequently matters whose knowledge the other person (were he aware of it) would find undesirable." See also Goffman, *The Presentation Of Self in Everyday Life, op. cit.*, pp. 1–16.

[22] The structural properties and parameters of interactional territories in unserious gatherings have been admirably presented by Georg Simmel. See his "The Sociology of Sociability," *American Journal of Sociology IV* (November, 1949), pp. 254–261. Reprinted in Parsons, et al., *Theories of Society I, op. cit.*, pp. 157–163.

Contamination of a territory requires that it be rendered impure with respect to its definition and usage. Cholera may require that a portion of the city be quarantined. In a racial caste society the sidewalks may be contaminated by low caste persons walking upon them. Home territories may be contaminated by pollution or destruction of the "home" symbols. Orthodox Jews may destroy their dinnerware when an unwary maid has accidentally mixed the milk and meat dishes. Heterosexuals who regularly congregate at a bar sometimes discontinue their patronage when known homosexuals begin frequenting the bar. (This example illustrates a continuum in the process of territorial encroachment from invasion to contamination.) Interactional territories may be contaminated by sudden odors, especially if they emanate from one of the interactants, or by indiscreet language, e.g., obscenity, among those for whom identification with such language constitutes a loss of face or a reduction in status.[23]

Contamination of bodily territories occurs whenever the immediate space of or around the body is polluted. The removal by bathing of material involuntarily attached to the skin constitutes a ritualized purification rite of considerable importance in industrial societies.[24] However, body space may be contaminated in many ways, by smell, look, touch, and by proximity to contaminated persons or things. The sensitivity with respect to touch illustrates the complex nature of this contamination and also its peculiarly social character. The rules regarding touch are highly developed in American society and are clear indicators of social distance between individuals and groups.[25] Typically, older people can touch younger ones, but suspicions of sexual immorality modify such contacts. Women who are friends or relatives may greet one another with a light kiss (commonly called a "peck") on the cheek, but not on the lips. Men who are long absent may be greeted by male friends and relatives with a hearty embrace and a touching of the cheeks, but the embrace must not be overlong or tender. Indeed, "roughhousing," mock-fighting, and pseudo-hostility are commonly employed in masculine affective relationships. Touch which would otherwise be contaminating is exempt from such designation when it takes place in situations of intense social action, e.g., on a dance floor, or in situations where the actors are not privileged to interact, e.g., crowded buses. At other times bodies contaminated by impermissible contacts are restored to their pure state by apologies.

Body space may be contaminated by a kind of negative charismatic contact whereby objects which, though neutral in themselves, carry contaminating effect when transferred directly to the body. Thus a comb or toothbrush may not be lent or borrowed in certain circles since to use someone else's tools of personal hygiene is to contaminate oneself. Typically, when clothing, especially clothing that will directly touch the skin, is lent, it is proper for the lender to assure the borrower that the apparel is clean, and that it has not been worn by anyone since its

---

[23] Here perhaps it is worth noting that language has a "tactile" dimension, in the sense that to be "touched" audially by certain terms is to be elevated or reduced in status. For Southern Negroes to be publicly addressed as "Mr.," "Miss," and "Mrs.," and by last names is considered so relevant for removal of caste barriers that legal action to require these usages has been undertaken. We may also note that genteel persons are polluted by audial contact with slang, obscenity, and, on occasion, idiomatic expression.

[24] See Horace Miner, "Body Ritual Among the Nacirema," *American Anthropologist,* 55, No. 3, 1956.

[25] Note such phrases as "I wouldn't touch him with a ten-foot pole"; "she's under my skin"; "he's a pain in the neck," and "Look, but don't touch." For the rules regarding touch see Erving Goffman, "The Nature of Deference and Demeanor," *op. cit.*

last cleaning.[26] A more striking example involves the rule of some shops forbidding Negroes from trying on clothes—their skin being regarded as a source of pollution. Similarly, drinking from the same glass as another is discouraged as a matter of hygiene among the middle class and as a source of pollution if it occurs among persons of different races or castes.

Reaction to Encroachment

We have already suggested that something of a reciprocal relation exists between the territorial types. For example, a public swimming pool—while officially open to all persons—might be conceived by certain regular users as an exclusive area. Strangers seeking access by virtue of their diffuse civic rights might be challenged by those whose sense of peculiar propriety is thus violated. Such a confrontation (sometimes called "when push meets shove") could result in retreat on the part of the party seeking admittance, flight on the part of those favoring denial, or strategy and tactics on the part of the contending parties to expand the area of legitimate access on the one hand, and withhold entirely or restrict the meaning of entry on the other.

Of course, the occupants of a territory may extend its use to others whose presence is not regarded as a threat. The most common situation is that in which common usage will not destroy or alter the value of the territory.[27] When public territories have been colonized by users who do not fully monopolize the space, who embroider it by their presence, or whose occupancy still allows for other public and colonizing usages, the colonists will not be seriously opposed. Delinquent gangs who often define the streets of a neighborhood as a home territory do not usually regard the presence of local adults and children as an encroachment on their own occupancy. Unwarranted intrusion on interactional territories may be countenanced if the unwelcome guest indicates his willingness to be present on this occasion alone with no future rights of reentry or to listen only and not to interrupt the proceedings. Bodies usually invulnerable to feel and probe by strangers may be violated if circumstances render the act physically safe, socially irrelevant, or emotionally neutral. Thus female nurses may massage their male patients with mutual impunity, and striptease dancers may perform unclothed upon a raised stage out of reach of the audience.[28] However, all such contacts will tend to be defined as territorial encroachment when the claimants threaten obliteration, monopoly, or fundamental alteration of a territory. Under these conditions, the holders of territory are likely to react to unwelcome claimants in terms of *turf defense, insulation*, or *linguistic collusion*.

---

[26] Robin Williams has shown that one test of social distance among the races in America is their unwillingness to try on clothing at an apparel shop when they have witnessed that clothing tried on and rejected by members of another—and supposedly inferior—race. Robin Williams, *Strangers Next Door*, Englewood Cliffs: Prentice-Hall, 1964, pp. 125–130.

[27] Our usage is similar to that employed in describing the relationships in plant-communities. "The majority of individuals of a plant-community are linked by bonds other than those mentioned—bonds that are best described as *commensal*. The term commensalism is due to Van Beneden, who wrote 'Le commensal est simplement un compagnon de table'; but we employ it in a somewhat different sense to denote the relationship subsisting between species which share with one another the supply of food-material contained in soil and air, and thus feed at the same table." Robert E. Park and Ernest W. Burgess, *Introduction to the Science of Sociology*, Chicago: University of Chicago Press, 1921, p. 175. (Adapted from Eugenius Warming, *Oecology of Plants*, London: Oxford University Press, 1909, pp. 12–13, 91–95.)

[28] Ann Terry D'Andre, "An Occupational Study of the Strip-Dancer Career," paper delivered at the annual meetings of the Pacific Sociological Association, Salt Lake City, Utah, 1965.

TURF DEFENSE

Turf defense is a response necessitated when the intruder cannot be tolerated. The animal world provides a multitude of examples which are instructive with respect to the human situation.[29] Here we may be content, however, to confine ourselves to the human scene. When Chinese merchants sought "colonizing" rights among the urban merchants of San Francisco, they were welcomed and honored. A few years later, however, the appearance of Chinese miners in the white Americans' cherished gold fields called forth violent altercations and forced removals.[30] In contemporary American cities delinquent gangs arm themselves with rocks, knives, tire irons, and zip guns to repel invaders from other streets.[31] Among the "primitive" Kagoro the choice of weapons is escalated in accordance with the social distance of the combatants; poison spears and stratagems are employed exclusively against hostile strangers and invaders.[32]

Turf defense is an ultimate response, however. Other more subtle repulsions or restrictions are available to proprietors wishing to maintain territorial control.

INSULATION

Insulation is the placement of some sort of barrier between the occupants of a territory and potential invaders. The narrow streets, steep staircases, and regularized use of Cantonese dialects in Chinatowns serve notice on tourists that they may look over the external trappings of Chinese life in the Occidental city but not easily penetrate its inner workings. Distinct uniforms distinguishing status, rights, and prerogatives serve to protect military officers from the importunities of enlisted men, professors from students, and doctors from patients.[33] Bodily insulation characteristically takes the form of civil inattention and may be occasioned by a subordinate's inability to repel invasion directly. Another common form of insulation involves use of body and facial idiom to indicate impenetrability. It may be effected by the use of sunglasses,[34] or attained accidentally, by dint of culturally distinct perceptions of facial gestures, as, for example, often happens to orientals in Western settings.[35] It can also be attained by conscious efforts in the management and control of the mouth, nostrils, and especially the eyes.[36]

---

[29] See Ardrey, *op. cit.*, p. 210, who writes: "Biology as a whole asks but one question of a territory: is it defended? Defense defines it. Variability becomes the final description." See also Konrad Lorenz, *On Aggression*, New York: Harcourt, Brace and World, 1966, pp. 33–38 *et passim*.

[30] See Mary Coolidge, *Chinese Immigration*, New York: Henry Holt, 1909, pp. 15–26, 255–256.

[31] See Lewis Yablonsky, *The Violent Gang*, New York: Macmillan, 1962, pp. 29–100 for a good ethnography of urban gangs. For an analytical treatment see Frederic M. Thrasher, *The Gang*; Chicago: University of Chicago Press, 1927, pp. 97–100, 116–129.

[32] See M. G. Smith, "Kagoro Political Development," *Human Organization* (Fall, 1960), pp. 137–149.

[33] It is now a commonplace of sociological irony that persons thus insulated are vulnerable once the insulating material is removed or ubiquitously available. Thus non-coms will insult officers in clubs when both are out of uniform, psychiatrists will be mistaken for patients at dances held in the recreation room of an insane asylum, and students will adopt an inappropriate familiarity with professors not wearing a coat and tie.

[34] See Goffman, *Behavior in Public Places, op. cit.*, p. 85 for a succinct account of the elements of this process as a form of civil inattention.

[35] Kathleen Tamagawa, *Holy Prayers in a Horse's Ear*, New York: Long, Smith, Inc., 1932, pp. 144–151 *et passim*. Andre M. Tao-Kim-Hai, "Orientals are Stoic," in F. C. MacGregor, *Social Science in Nursing*, New York: Russell Sage, 1960, pp. 313–326.

[36] See Georg Simmel, "The Aesthetic Significance of the Face," in Kurt H. Wolff, editor, *Georg Simmel 1858–1918*, Columbus: Ohio State University Press, 1959, pp. 280–281.

LINGUISTIC COLLUSION

Linguistic collusion involves a complex set of processes by which the territorial integrity of the group is reaffirmed and the intruder is labelled as an outsider. For example, the defending interactants may engage one another in conversation and gestures designed to so confuse the invader that he responds in a manner automatically labelling him eligible for either exclusion from the group or shameful status diminution. In one typical strategy the defending interactants will speak to one another in a language unfamiliar to the invader. Ethnic enclaves provide numerous examples. Jewish and Chinese storekeepers will speak Yiddish and Cantonese respectively to their clerks when discussing prices, bargaining rights, and product quality in the presence of alien customers. Negroes may engage one another in a game of "the dozens" in the presence of intruding whites, causing the latter considerable consternation and mystification.[37] And teenagers develop a peer group argot (frequently borrowed from Negro and jazz musician usages) which sets them apart from both children and adults, and which, incidentally, is most frequently cited as proof for the claim that a distinctive youth culture does exist in the United States.

In another recognizable strategy, the participants continue to engage in the same behavior but in a more exaggerated and "staged" manner. Mood and tone of the voice are sometimes regulated to achieve this effect. Thus persons engaged in conversation may intensify their tone and include more intra-group gestures when an outsider enters the area. Professors may escalate the use of jargon and "academese" in conversations in the presence of uninvited students or other "inferiors." Homosexuals engaged in flirtations in a "gay" bar may exaggerate their femininity when heterosexuals enter the establishment. Such staged displays call attention to the exclusive culture of the interactants and suggest to the outsider that he is bereft of the cards of identity necessary to participate.

Reaction to the Absence of Free Space

There are some segments of society that are systematically denied free territories. One outstanding example is that of lower-class urban Negro youth. Their homes are small, cramped, and cluttered and also serve as specialized areas of action for adults; their meeting places are constantly under surveillance by the agents of law enforcement and social workers; and, when in clusters on the street, they are often stopped for questioning and booked "on suspicion" by the seemingly ever-present police.[38]

What is the condition of Negro youth in particular appears to be an exaggerated instance of the trend with respect to denial of freedom among youth in general. Thus it has been suggested that youth are adrift somewhere between humanism and fatalism, i.e., between situations in which they feel they have lost control over their destinies and those in which such control is in the hands of forces outside youth's individual direction and influence.[39] In such a situation one response is to

---

[37] The usual situation is quite the reverse, however. The "dozens" and other verbal contest forms are most frequently used by Negroes within the ethnic enclave out of earshot and view of whites. See Roger D. Abrahams, *Deep Down in the Jungle*, Hatboro, Penn.: Folklore Associates, esp. pp. 41–64.

[38] See Carl Werthman, *Delinquency and Authority*, M.A. Thesis, University of California, Berkeley, 1964.

[39] David Matza, *Delinquency and Drift*, New York: John Wiley, 1964.

seek to maximize the area of freedom, the situations in which one can exercise liberty and license, the times one can be cause rather than effect. Among lower-class youth the carving of home territories out of the space provided as public ones is common and has already been noted. Note also, however, the frequency with which youth-created home territories are subject to invasion, violation, and contamination and the relative vulnerability of youth home territories to such encroachments.

Exercising freedom over body territory provides a more fruitful approach to those for whom public territories are denied and home territories difficult or impossible to maintain. The body and its attendant inner and external space have an aura of ownership and control about them that is impressed upon the incumbent. The hypothesis we wish to suggest here is that as other forms of free territory are perceived to be foreclosed by certain segments of the society, these segments, or at least those elements of the segments not constrained by other compelling forces, will utilize more frequently and intensively the area of the body space as a free territory. Three forms of such utilization are prominent: *manipulation, adornment* and *penetration.*

Manipulation rests upon the fact that the body is adjustable in a greater number of ways than are positively sanctioned and that by modifying the appearance of the self one can establish identity, and flaunt convention with both ease and relative impunity. Thus children, separated from one another for being naughty and enjoined from conversation, may sit and "make faces" at one another, conforming to the letter of their punishment but violating its principle. Teenagers, denied approval for the very sexual activity for which they are biologically prepared, and also enclosed more and more from private usage of public territories for such purposes, have developed dance forms which involve little or no body contact but are nevertheless suggestive of the most intimate and forbidden forms of erotic interaction. Further, male youth—enjoined from verbal scatological forms by customs and by rules of propriety—have developed a gesture language by which they can communicate the desired obscenity without uttering it.

Adornment of the body is another response.[40] By covering, uncovering, marking, and disfiguring the body individuals can at least partly overcome whatever loss of freedom they suffer from encroachments. Both the French "bohemians" of the nineteenth century and the disaffected American Negro youths of the twentieth have exhibited themselves as "dandies," [41] while the ascetic Doukhobors of British Columbia disrobe entirely and in public when challenged by authority.[42] Body space may also be attended by filling in the apertures in nose, mouth and ears by rings, bones, and other emblematic artifacts; by marking upon the skin with inks and tattoos; and by disfigurements, scars, and severance of non-vital members. An alternative mode of adornment, that appears to be directed definitely against elements of the core culture, is the refusal to use instruments of personal hygiene. We have already noted how these instruments acquire a peculiar aspect of the personal charisma of the user so that people do not customarily borrow the comb, toothbrush, and razor of another unless the contamination that

---

[40] Many suggestive essays on this subject can be found in *Dress, Adornment, and the Social Order,* in M. E. Roach and J. B. Eicher, editors, N.Y.: John Wiley, 1965.
[41] See Cesar Grana, *Bohemian vs. Bourgeois,* New York: Basic Books, 1964, and Harold Finestone, "Cats, Kicks, and Color," *Social Problems* 5, 1 (1957) pp. 3–13.
[42] See Harry B. Hawthorn, editor, *The Doukhobors of British Columbia,* Vancouver, B. C.: The University of British Columbia and Dent & Sons, 1955.

occurs thereby is neutralized. Here, however, adornment occurs by simply *not* washing, combing, shaving, cutting the hair, etc. Like public nudity this form of assertiveness and reaction to oppression has the advantage of inhibiting a like response among those who are offended by the appearance created thereby, but, unlike stripping in public, has the added advantage of being legal.

Penetration refers to the exploitation and modification of inner space in the search for free territory. One might hypothesize that the greater the sense of unfreedom, the greater the exercise of body liberty so that penetration is an escalated aspect of manipulation and adornment. There is, as it were, a series of increasing gradations of body space. The ultimate effort is to gain freedom by changing one's internal environment. The simplest form of this is cultivating a vicarious sense of being away, of transporting the self out of its existential environment by musing, daydreaming, or relapsing into a reverie.[43] However, voluntary reorganization of the inner environment can be assisted by alcohol and drugs. Contemporary college youth sometimes partake of hallucinogenic and psychedelic drugs in order to make an inner migration (or "take a trip" as the popular idiom has it).

Conclusion

The concept of territoriality offers a fruitful approach for the analysis of freedom and situated action. Although the early school of ecology in American sociology provided a possible avenue for this kind of exploration, its practitioners appear to have eschewed the interactionist and phenomenological aspects of the subject in favor of the economic and the biotic. Nevertheless, much of their work needs to be examined afresh for the clues it provides for understanding the nature and function of space and the organization of territories. Similarly the work done by the students of non-human animal association provides clues to concept formation and suggestions for research. Here we may mention several potentially fruitful areas. The first involves cross-cultural studies of territoriality. Such studies would attempt to describe in greater specificity the constituent features of types of territoriality, the ways in which they vary, and their interrelationships. Using a cross-cultural perspective would also serve to specify generic forms of reactions to territorial encroachment and to establish how certain contexts predispose one type of response rather than another. A second area of research would focus on a variety of deviant behaviors (e.g., crime, juvenile delinquency, drug addiction) with the purpose of understanding the part the territorial variable plays in the etiology of such behaviors. Finally, we may suggest that micro-sociological studies of territoriality—which are perhaps more amenable to rigorous research design—may be extrapolated to an analysis of macro-sociological inquiries, especially in the realm of international affairs.

[43] Goffman, *Behavior in Public Places, op. cit.*, pp. 69–75.

25 Sex and Age as Universes of Appearance

● GREGORY P. STONE

As the world changes, so does one's apparel, and, as has been so often ignored in the literature, a change of dress may change one's very world. George Orwell, that meticulous student of appearance, noted in his *Homage to Catalonia* the details of his wardrobe as he arrived in Spain to offer his personal support to the Loyalists —a heroic gesture that seems pitifully quaint in these times. After the failure of his cause, the disappointment of his hope, and the betrayal of his convictions, Orwell fled Spain with the others—frightened, sick at heart, bewildered. The world had changed, and, to guarantee the empty success of his flight—indeed, to insure his very life—Orwell adopted a different dress, rhetorically inducing the enemy, who was everywhere, to ignore his passage.[1]

Earlier, in London, Orwell's world had also collapsed about him. At that time, the collapse was temporary, but the reconstruction was fully visible in an imagined future. Unable to continue his work as a *plongeur* in a Paris restaurant, he secured the promise of a job from a friend in London. On his arrival there he learned that his prospective employer was out of the country and would not return for a month. Orwell was without money and without the "indecency" to ask his friend for a loan at that time. He decided to live in "some hole-and-corner way" for as much of the month's time as he could endure. His world had changed. He exchanged his second-best suit for some rags and a shilling:

> The clothes were a coat, once dark brown, a pair of black dungaree trousers, a scarf and a cloth cap; I had kept my own shirt, socks and boots, and I had a comb and razor in my pocket. It gives one a very strange feeling to be wearing such clothes. I had worn bad enough things before, but nothing at all like these; they were not merely dirty and shapeless, they had—how is one to express it?—a patina of antique filth, quite different from mere shabbiness. They were the sort of clothes you see on a bootlace seller, or a tramp. An hour later, in Lambeth, I saw a hand-dog man, obviously a tramp, coming towards me, and when I looked again it was myself, reflected in a shop window. The dirt was plastering my face already. Dirt is a great respecter of persons; it lets you alone when you are well dressed, but as soon as your collar is gone it flies toward you from all directions.
>
> I stayed in the streets till late at night, keeping on the move all the time. Dressed as I was, I was half afraid that the police might arrest me as a vagabond, and I dared not speak to anyone, imagining that they must notice a disparity between my accent and my clothes. (Later I discovered that this never happened.) *My new clothes had put me instantly into a new world.* Everyone's demeanour seemed to have changed abruptly. I helped a hawker pick up a barrow that he had upset. "Thanks, mate," he said with a grin. No one had called me mate before in my life—it was the clothes that had done it. For the first time I noticed, too, how the attitude of women varies with a man's clothes. When a badly dressed man passes them they shudder away from him with a quite frank movement of disgust, as though he were a dead cat. Clothes are powerful things. Dressed in a tramp's

SOURCE: "Sex and Age as Universes of Appearance," original paper prepared especially for this volume.

[1] George Orwell, *Homage to Catalonia* (London: Secker and Warburg, 1938), pp. 4, 8–9, 306, and especially 309.

clothes, it is very difficult, at any rate the first day, not to feel that you are genuinely degraded. You might feel the same shame, irrational but very real, your first
night in prison.[2]

If we look upon meaning as response, we note that dressing may itself be viewed
as meaning. The defeat of the Loyalists *meant* a change of dress for Orwell as did
his temporary poverty in London. There is also the meaning of dress that is provided by the responses made to it. In response to his altered appearance in the
flight from Spain, the enemy ignored his passage. In response to the ragged appearance in London, Orwell *expressed* his strange feeling and his fear of the police; the hawker *placed* him as a "mate," *appreciating* his assistance with a grin;
and women *appreciated* his appearance with shudders, *expressing* their disgust.
The strange mood, the fear, the grin, the shuddering, and the disgust, involving
him as a "mate" of the hawker, in fact, defined Orwell's *new world.* We will regard a *universe of appearance* in this behavioral sense. Such behaviors or acts
may be either the appearances mobilized by events or the events mobilized by appearances. The universe of appearance, then, is not some ill-defined *Gestalt* or
"field." It is a very *real* behavioral matrix of meaning—a social world.[3]

Within such worlds, because of common apparent meanings, discourse is more
readily accomplished than among such worlds. As Orwell said in effect, differences in discourse are lost among those who belong to a common universe of appearance. The accent went unnoticed by the members of Orwell's new world.

Moreover, without symbols, social sentiments could have only a precarious existence. Though very strong as long as men are together and influence each other
reciprocally, they exist only in the form of recollections after the assembly has
ended, and when left to themselves, these become feebler and feebler; for since the
group is now no longer present and active, individual temperaments easily regain
the upper hand. The violent passions which may have been released in the heart of
a crowd fall away and are extinguished when this is dissolved, and men ask themselves with astonishment how they could ever have been so carried away from their
normal character. But if the movements by which these sentiments are expressed
are connected with something that endures, the sentiments themselves become
more durable. These other things are constantly bringing them to mind and arousing them; it is as though the cause which excited them in the first place continued to act. Thus these systems of emblems, which are necessary if society is to
become conscious of itself, are no less indispensable for assuring the continuation of
this consciousness.

*So we must refrain from regarding these symbols as simple artifices, as sort of
labels attached to representations already made, in order to make them more
manageable: they are an integral part of them.* Even the fact that collective sentiments are thus attached to things completely foreign to them is not purely conventional: it illustrates under a conventional form a real characteristic of social facts,
that is, their transcendence over individual minds. In fact, it is known that social
phenomena are born, not in individuals, but in the group. Whatever part we may
take in their origin, each of us receives them from without. So when we represent
them to ourselves as emanating from a material object, we do not completely misunderstand their nature. Of course, they do not come from the specific thing to
which we connect them, but nevertheless, it is true that their origin is outside of us.

---

[2] George Orwell, *Down and Out in Paris and London* (New York: Avon Publications, Inc.,
no date), pp. 114–15. Italics mine.
[3] For specifications of such terms as "placed," "appreciation," and "expression," see Gregory P. Stone, "Appearance and the Self," reprinted in Part Six of this volume.

If the moral force sustaining the believer does not come from the idol he adores or the emblem he venerates, still it is from outside of him, as he is well aware. The objectivity of its symbol only translates its externalness.

Thus social life, in all its aspects and in every period of its history, is made possible only by a vast symbolism. The material emblems and figurative representatives with which we are more especially concerned in our present study, are one form of this: but there are many others.[4]

Durkheim put dress as an "integral part" of the symbolism that we are examining. Sex and age are conceived as mobilizing the dress behavior of the sexes and age groupings, and dress is conceived as mobilizing the placements of those who *review* the sex and age of the wearers. Moreover, dress facilitates the formulation and maintenance of the *programs* of the wearers.[5] By dressing, they are themselves reminded of their sex and age. The mobilization of all these responses may be thought of as a universe of appearance, *vis à vis* the worlds of sex and age, giving to dress a universal character, as the universality of the word depends upon the responses it elicits in its production.

The Concept: Universe of Appearance

In a review of C. Willet Cunnington's *English Women's Clothing in the Nineteenth Century*, Elizabeth Bowen insisted that: [6]

To present an appearance, a whole, that shall be not only pleasing but significant (which is, after all, the aim, however imperfectly realized, of the woman buying a hat or a man buying a tie) is at least as difficult technically, requires as close a grip by the imagination, as disabused an attitude, as the writing of a book that should be fit to be published, or the painting of a picture that is to be seen.

Although I would not make a similar distinction between significance and pleasure (which can, of course, be significant), Miss Bowen's insistence upon the matter of making a *significant* or *meaningful* appearance captures the core of my main line of argument. Moreover, the analogy of appearance and writing a book or painting a picture is apt. Writing a book, a discursive production, poses precisely the problem of meaningful communication with some audience, and the meaning of the book lies in the coincident lines of response called out in the writer and his audience. It is, as Mead put it, in the universe of discourse of the writer and the readers.

I shall fashion the concept, universe of appearance, on the leads provided by Mead in his discussions of universal discourse. Thus, I would remind the reader: [7]

The significant gesture or symbol always presupposes for its significance the social process of experience and behavior in which it arises; or, as the logicians say, a universe of discourse is always implied as the context in terms of which, or as the field within which, significant gestures or symbols do in fact have significance. This universe of discourse is constituted by a group of individuals carrying on and participating in a common social process of experience and behavior, within which

---

[4] Emile Durkheim, *The Elementary Forms of the Religious Life* (Glencoe: The Free Press, 1947), pp. 231–32. Italics mine.
[5] For the meaning of "program" and "review," see Gregory P. Stone, *op. cit.*
[6] Elizabeth Bowen, *Collected Impressions* (New York: Knopf, 1950), p. 112. I am grateful to Erving Goffman for recommending this particular discussion of dress.
[7] George Herbert Mead, *Mind, Self, and Society* (Chicago: University of Chicago Press, 1934), pp. 89–90.

these gestures or symbols have the same or common meanings for all members of that group, whether they make them or address them to other individuals, or whether they overtly respond to them as made or addressed to them by other individuals. A universe of discourse is simply a system of common or social meanings.

In its most extensive sense, the universe of discourse was held by Mead to be the community, but the community, in turn, is viewed as a set of continuing differentiated relations or less extensive and more specialized "sub-universes" of discourse. The political party is one example:

> In politics, for example, the individual identifies himself with an entire political party and takes the organized attitudes of that entire party toward the rest of the given social community and toward the problems which confront the party within the given social situation; and he consequently reacts or responds in terms of the organized attitudes of the party as a whole. He thus enters into a special set of social relations with all the other individuals who belong to that political party; and, in the same way, he enters into various other special sets of social relations with various other classes of individuals respectively, the individuals of each of these classes being the other members of some one of the particular organized subgroups (determined in socially functional terms) of which he himself is a member within the entire given society or social community.[8]

From the standpoint of the individual participating in the ongoing communication, he is at once brought together with the other members of the community and set apart from them. Consequently, the behavior of the individual is never a simple reproduction of community response.

> In other words, the organized structure of every individual self within the human social process of experience and behavior reflects, and is constituted by, the organized relational pattern of that process as a whole; but each individual self-structure reflects, and is constituted by, a different aspect or perspective of this relational pattern, because each reflects this relational pattern from its own unique standpoint; so that the common social origin and constitution of individual selves and their structure does not preclude wide individual differences and variations among them, or contradict the peculiar and more or less distinctive individuality which each of them in fact possesses. Every individual self within a given society or social community reflects in its organized structure the whole relational pattern of organized social behavior which that society or community exhibits or is carrying on, and its organized structure is constituted by this pattern; but since each of these individual selves reflects a uniquely different aspect or perspective of this pattern in its structure, from its own particular and unique place or standpoint within the whole process of organized social behavior which exhibits this pattern—since, that is, each is differently or uniquely related to that whole process, and occupies its own essentially unique focus of relations therein—the structure of each is differently constituted by this pattern from the way in which the structure of any other is so constituted.[9]

Now, although the members of different political parties may dress differently and respond to dress differently as the members of some religious sects—the Amish, the Quakers, the brothers of the House of David, or the members of Students for a Democratic Society—most certainly do, I do not wish to single out these aspects of social organization, for the communicative lives of everyone are not caught up

---

[8] *Ibid.*, pp. 156–57.
[9] *Ibid.*, pp. 201–02.

in such distinctions or subgroups. With sex and age it is a different matter. These are sets of social relations that seem persistently to differentiate the conduct of all members of whatever community, within which significant discourse is indeed different.

However, the difference in the discourse among members of different social relations rests upon the universal acknowledgment of their membership in those different social relations. This is a point which Mead did not systematically explore, perhaps thinking (rightly enough) that the style of discourse—the discursive appearance—provided an adequate enough basis for the identification of the different social relations in which the members of the community were engaged. Yet, there seems to be an order of symbolism or a phase of symbolism—apparent symbolism—to which clothing belongs that has its significance precisely in the identification of the relations in which the members of any community are engaged. Clothing has its significance in the recognition, differentiation, and *rapprochement* of people. Coincident lines of identification-of-one-another mobilized by apparent symbols are what we subsume under the concept of universe of appearance. The universe of appearance may, in fact, be regarded as the guarantee, foundation, or substrate of the universe of discourse.

Sex

On January 28, 1955, the following AP news dispatch, datelined Ann Arbor, Michigan, appeared in the Lansing *State Journal:*

> A 34-year-old man, disguised as a woman, was thrown out of the Washtenaw county circuit court Thursday when he appeared for sentencing with long curly hair and tight fitting dress.
> Circuit Judge R. Breakey told Dale Upton, alias Dale Sexton, to return at 3:30 P.M. with his hair shorn and in men's clothes.
> Upton pleaded guilty to a charge of uttering and publishing after he was arrested by Texas police and returned to Ann Arbor.
> Texas authorities arrested Upton in female attire at his job as a waitress in a drive-in restaurant. Returning to Ann Arbor, Upton told police he had worked as a waitress in South Lyon and Whitmore Lake and that his female dress made it easier to pass bad checks.

The motives of transvestitism are diverse and fascinating (the subject begs extensive exploration by sociologists), but the consequences seem always in this country, except in certain circumstances, to be dire. As naive as our transvestite's rationalization may appear to the uninformed, there can be little doubt that the donning of female apparel by a man *in the course of daily work* is more acceptably explained to most police authorities in this country as a means of facilitating a "con game" (asexual) than by the frank acknowledgment that it represents a repudiation of one's sexual identity. The law guarantees that men will appear as men (especially at work). With women, the law is less exacting. I have attempted to explore these matters with interviews of over 200 married men and women living in a Midwestern community of 10,000 population. I shall call this community, "Vansburg."

Such guarantees of the distinctive dress of the sexes were discovered by some of our respondents as inhering in obedience to the will of God, or, at least, as a matter of genetic destiny. Thus, the wife of the foreman of a local manufacturing plant said she didn't like to see men in shorts, adding, "I think the same thing is true of men as women. God gave them clothing and intended them to be clothed." The wife of a molder agreed that she didn't like to see men in shorts, and explained:

> Shorts are disgraceful. Women were born to wear dresses. They banned slacks and shorts at the lodges here in town. I feel women should wear what they are supposed to. Of course, for fishing and hunting, a woman should wear slacks so that she can move around. That's different.

The roots of sexually distinctive dress lie deep in the sentiments of many people. Others did not, however, appeal to the will of God or the destiny of birth in insisting that the sexes maintain a distinctive dress. For a clothing salesman, it was a matter of liking and disliking: "It's just the difference between the masculine and the feminine. In my opinion, a woman should look feminine. A man doesn't like to have a woman dress as a man." For the wife of a custodial supervisor in a State Training School, the idea of a man in a woman's dress was a surprise so incongruous as to provoke laughter and start a humorous, somewhat irrelevant fantasy. When asked what kind of clothes men should not wear, she replied:

> Dresses. I don't know what to say. Women wear pants. Men ought to start wearing dresses. (Laughter and giggling.) I'd like to see that! Oh! Did you put that down? (Gales of laughter.) (Persistently, the interviewer asks whether the informant has any particular reason in mind for suggesting that men should not wear dresses.) Oh, it don't look very masculine. Women can get away with it.

There is considerable evidence that such differences get established early. Among some people they are established in an atmosphere of suspicion and distrust. A cook in a local restaurant maintained that women should not wear "some of these shorts and halters." When asked why, she replied:

> On the little young girls, they're O.K., but, for young married women who have children, you feel as though they should really know better—to set a good example to little young girls. There's a waitress I know who has a girl thirteen or fourteen and a son eight or nine. The little son notices too many things. When she and the little girl sit in a chair, they're careful to pull down their dress. When you have children, you have to set a good example, if you want 'em to grow up to be good. 'Course, you shouldn't go to extremes either.

These differences in the dress of the genders are undoubtedly becoming less evident, as women become more involved with "male activities"—work and play. There is some evidence, too, to show that the differences in dress are not as sharply maintained among younger people. Although there are efforts to encourage men to adopt more "feminine" styles (fashion designers are relentless in their attempts to catch men up in the fashion cycle), the breakdown in apparent differentiation seems, even among the young, to be accomplished more by the girls who are adopting the dress of the boys. A teacher in junior high school digressed in the interview to observe:

> My impression is that the girls are more particular than the boys. (Interviewer: Boys?) Jackets and overall pants and blue jeans. Perhaps the most luxurious things they wear are their shoes. They spend more for their shoes than the rest of their outfit. (Interviewer: What about the girls?) Some of them wear dresses, and some of them I don't think I've ever seen in a dress. They wear blue jeans. They don't wear silk hose. They all wear pretty nice coats—fluffy, wool type coats. They

don't take care of their clothes—leave them all around. The clothing—boys' cloth-ing—the likeness is so alike that they get their jackets mixed up. The confusion is great because of the similarities in pattern.

The wife of an "old retailer" has accepted the adolescent adoption of male dress by girls:

> Jeans, slacks, and shorts are all right on young girls, but they better leave them off when they get to be women. They'd be monstrosities. (Interviewer: What would others do, if you went shopping dressed like that?) They would probably gasp.

Despite the exceptions, the differences in the dress of the sexes are maintained, but the universe of sexual appearance has contracted somewhat. When women enter the occupations and preoccupations of men, they undoubtedly lose something of their femininity—an identity now acquired somewhat later in life than it was at an earlier time. Russell Lynes, wondering what has happened to the popular con-ception of a lady, concluded that a woman is a lady when she makes a man behave like a gentleman.[10] In the work place and on the sporting fields, she is losing that quality.

In spite of the penetrations women are making of the apparent sexual barriers, people generally assign to women a distinctive interest in clothing. The resigna-tion on the part of men to this interest and the appropriation on the part of women of this interest serves as a further guarantee of sexual differentiation. When asked whether he thought the people he worked with noticed his way of dressing on the job, an accountant replied:

> If they did, I'd be unhappy about it. (Interviewer: Why is that?) Well, maybe it's because I feel if a man dresses so it's noticeable, it's wrong. . . . Every six months we have a service rating. We're rated on appearance. If it wasn't all right, I'd have heard about it.

Later, when he said that he thought about his wife's clothes more than about the clothes of any other member of his family, he explained:

> It is more of a catastrophe if the woman isn't dressed just right. A woman is judged much more severely by her clothes. If a woman wears a suit a few times in a row, there are comments.

A weighmaster estimated that his daughter was more interested in clothes than any other member of his family, elucidating:

> My daughter—she's fifteen years old. You know what public school is. You don't send your daughter to school with a gingham gown on. That's one instance where you have to keep up with the Jones's. The children of the banker go to school, and he thinks nothing of peeling off one hundred and fifty bucks for a dress, where fifty bucks to me is a lot of money. Then, she's inherited a desire for out of the ordinary clothes from her mother.

He believed that his son was least interested in clothing:

> My son at Michigan State—he's a two-fisted individual. He doesn't want to call attention to himself as a panty-waist. He doesn't care about a white shirt. Then, there's the younger son—he's the outdoor type—wears overalls a lot of the time.

---

[10] Russell Lynes, *A Surfeit of Honey* (New York: Harper and Brothers, 1957), p. 104, but see the entire discussion, pp. 86–104.

Occasionally, he's the sheik—there's a young woman in his life—but that's under protest. He's a characteristic American boy.

The wife of a local printer echoed some of the sentiments of the weighmaster, when she also acknowledged that her teen-age daughter was the most interested member of the family as far as clothing was concerned:

> Girls have to have so many more things, because they are in high school—the boys— and the style standards at high school are high. I've known girls who quit school, because they couldn't get the clothes.

The wife of a custodial supervisor asserted:

> Women need more clothes than men. A man can wear a suit all the time, but, if a woman tries to wear the same dress all the time, people say that's all you have. . . . I guess it's just instinct in a woman that she wants nice clothes, if she can have them.

Her husband had learned the vocabulary of motives well, replying *independently* in response to the same question, "Women need more clothes than men." Our conception of meaning was captured nicely, in this respect, by the wife of a foundry laborer who said, "I think clothes mean more to a girl than a boy. They're noticed more."

The knowing of the other's gender is known silently. Seldom, upon meeting a stranger, do we inquire concerning the stranger's sex, although we may ask age and initiate some circumlocutions in the effort to place and appraise his social status.

A few excerpts from interview materials bear on the point. Various aspects of dress may be viewed as sexual representations. A furniture salesman reminded us of the traditional color distinctions:

> When I was selling furniture, I had to know what colors would go with the rest of the room. I do the same with my clothes. I always say that the color of the clothes you wear fits the personality. Know what I mean? Like the color, blue, for a boy and otherwise for a girl.

A doctor's wife seemed to be having difficulty representing her sex to herself, and, perhaps significantly, was being conspicuously shunned by her husband. Her remarks are pertinent:

> I'd love to wear frilly and very feminine things. . . . I thought I'd like to wear ruffles and organdy, and more feminine things. I tried to, but I swing back. . . . My husband likes earrings, and I have to force myself to wear them.

An oil salesman, when asked whose opinion about clothing mattered most to him, said:

> The women. (Interviewer: Any particular ones?) All of 'em—old and young. (Interviewer: Any particular reason?) Aw, hell! I don't know. I dress for 'em in the first place.

Selection of the opposite sex as a significant audience for his dress reminds him, perhaps, of his maleness. *Vive la différence!*

These materials suggest, then, that sex is, in fact, a universe of appearance. Adopting sexually distinctive dress commits one to a social world, and the commitment is enforced by law, God, birth, and social expectations. However, men and women seem to be involved differently in that world.

Age

One day it may be well for sociologists—as the anthropologist Linton has distinguished among universals, particulars, and specialties—to propose distinctions along the dimension of, let us say, *circumstance* and *situation*. The circumstance may be said to envelop the act. For whatever reason, escape from or a redefinition of the circumstance lies outside the range of possibility. From the standpoint of the observer, the acting one is trapped, ensnared, fated. On this view, sex is a circumstance for most people, although there are rare and occasional possibilities of escape or redefinition.[11] Play is one of the more common. Serious redefinitions provide headlines for the tabloids. In some societies, age is also a circumstance, but, in our own, it increasingly becomes a situation, eminently capable of redefinition, a situation from which escape is encouraged on a large scale. Not only the ad men—Veblen's "creative psychiatrists"—lure us away from the situation of age, but also most of the columnists in the mass media, popular counselors, and the high priests of physique—the doctors. Thus, age categories, as universes of appearance, are even more riddled than sex categories, as youth spills over into old age, and old age takes on the appearance of youth.

For some, like Judge Hancock in our sample, the scene is viewed with ill-disguised disdain. Aware that people dress in different ways for different reasons, Judge Hancock singled out "old cougars or duffers trying to look young." For others, like the wife of the teacher in a State Training School, the possibilities are examined with a studied concern:

> I have to watch what I wear. I have a square figure and not everything looks well on me. Since I'm prematurely gray, people think that I'm a lot older than I am. I don't want to look older, or I'll feel older. If I feel older, I'll act older! I have to watch what I wear.

For still others, like the wife of a local theater manager, a part-time nurse, the situational character of age was reported matter-of-factly. Asked in what respects she dressed differently from other people in town, the woman replied:

> I don't know as I dress differently from my friends. However I do dress a little younger than many of them. I have daughters in school and often interchange with them.

She was forty-three years old at the time of the interview; her children in their early teens. For her, this "homogenization of the age grades" seems almost circumstantial. Explaining why she used to dress up in her mother's clothes as a child, she said, "Children like to look older and appear grown up . Then, when they get older, they want to look younger."

Although age undoubtedly lends itself more to manipulation through the rhetorical possibilities of appearance than does sex, age differences have not been completely lost in some large formless sartorial olio. People of different ages still dress differently in Vansburg. There is still a broad distinction between the very young and the old. The manager of a state–operated store, maintaining that he seldom thought about his young son's clothing, explained, "His clothing is a regulation children's clothing." Moreover, he expressed a wish for "better quality" clothing, saying, "They can be made to fit better a person of my age." The wife

---

[11] For an account of such an escape, see Harold Garfinkel, *Studies in Ethnomethodology* (Englewood Cliffs: Prentice-Hall, 1967), pp. 116–185.

of a gas station owner averred, "If you were a young gal, you might wear an extra supply of jewelry." A telephone repairman, identifying shorts with the knee-pants of his childhood, opined, "Men shouldn't wear knee pants. They look too much like a little boy." Later, asked what kind of clothes should not be worn by a person of his age, he replied, "You shouldn't look too young." Queried about the kind of clothes proscribed by his body build, he said, "Knee pants. Too much like a boy." The wife of the grocery store owner explained that her wardrobe did not include formal gowns: "There are no formal gowns. We don't go out too much any more. We're getting in the older class." Differences in the dress of the age groups persist, but are not enforced by law, the will of God, or the teleology of birth.

Instead, the enforcement of age distinctions in dress is a matter of informal social control not too firmly anchored in institutionalized vocabularies of motive. Such controls may be barely perceptible, exercised by mere *notice* and subtly indicating to the noticed one that the dress is out of place. The wife of a policeman, for example, "notices" manipulations of the age situation, ". . . sometimes, when I see an older woman who is dressing in clothes a younger woman should wear." As an "interest" in clothing is generally ascribed to and appropriated by women, so may such "interests" be ascribed to people of a particular age, often adolescents. An elementary school teacher thought most about the clothing of her children, as compared to other family members: "I like to see them dressed as well as we can afford to dress them, because they're at an age when clothes are important." At some unascertainable earlier age, the importance of clothing is denied the child. A gas station owner felt that his children were least interested in clothing among the members of his family, saying, "They are too young to comprehend the meaning of clothes." The wife of a foreman in a local manufacturing plant provided a nice contrast between the expectations of the young and the expectations of the old with respect to dress. Asked whose clothes, among the members of her family, she thought about most, she singled out her daughter:

> She's young, and I feel she's more the center of attraction. She's young and it means more to her than an older person.

She acknowledged that she, herself, was the family member whose clothing was considered least often:

> I think that they [her daughter] are in the limelight more than we who are older. They are more dependent upon clothes. They feel left out, if they have no clothes. I used to feel that way. When you get old, you lose that perspective.

These remarks, made by a woman forty-four years old, might well be compared with the remarks made by the wife of the theater manager, cited earlier, at the age of forty-three.

Occasionally the controls exerted may take a more positive turn and be more rigorously applied than has been indicated by the exercise of noticing or the assignment of interest and meaning to those of particular age grades. This is suggested by the imaginative reconstructions of the wife of an assistant cashier in the local bank. She reported that shorts should not be worn by women while shopping:

> It's all right for young girls, but I can't stand heavyset women in shorts. (Interviewer: What would happen if you were to wear shorts shopping?) I can imagine!

They would tell me to go home and get a dress on, and I wouldn't blame them. I wouldn't do it anyway.

A retired machine operator in a cement factory recounted an even more positive mode of re-enforcing age norms with respect to dress. Asked, "If you could have worn any kind of clothes that you wanted on the job, what would you suggest?", he replied:

> I would have liked to have worn something different than overalls. (Interviewer: What did you have in mind?) Work pants—gabardine—and a matching shirt. (Interviewer: How would the others you worked with feel about that?) I think they would have gone along. (Interviewer: What others do you have in mind?) The younger men. There was older men there who didn't care at all. They had no pride, you'd say. You meet them anywhere. There was one old fellow—I won't mention his name—we got together and bought him an outfit. There's a saying "You dress 'em in silk, and they wouldn't look dressed." He was one of those.

But this man is undoubtedly speaking of a time thirty or forty years before the interview took place. The guarantees of age-distinctive dress, while present, seem no longer so effective.

While the age of the stranger is a more fitting subject of inquiry in establishing an acquaintance than is the stranger's sex (which would only be impugned, if questioned), it is a topic that must be approached with circumspection. Indeed, women have recently been given some legal assistance in carrying off the subterfuge of disguising their age. They need not betray their age to certain official enumerators.

On the basis of these illustrative materials, then, it seems reasonable to assert that sex and age constitute universes of appearance. However, the limitations upon the representation of age by dress are not so stringent as those placed upon the representation of sex. Age provides, in fact, a more permeable world. Thus, age differences in the meaning assigned to dress are not so consistent, nor so clear-cut, as sex differences.

26   Who's passing for Who?

● LANGSTON HUGHES

One of the great difficulties about being a member of a minority race is that so many kindhearted, well-meaning bores gather around to help. Usually, to tell the truth, they have nothing to help with, except their company—which is often appallingly dull.

Some members of the Negro race seem very well able to put up with it, though, in these uplifting years. Such was Caleb Johnson, colored social worker, who was always dragging around with him some nondescript white person or two, inviting them to dinner, showing them Harlem, ending up at the Savoy—much to

SOURCE: Langston Hughes, in *The Langston Hughes Reader* (New York: George Braziller, Inc., 1958), pp. 30–33. Reprinted by permission of Harold Ober Associates, Inc. Copyright 1952 by Langston Hughes.

the displeasure of whatever friends of his might be out that evening for fun, not sociology.

Friends are friends and, unfortunately, overearnest uplifters are uplifters—no matter what color they may be. If it were the white race that was ground down instead of Negroes, Caleb Johnson would be one of the first to offer Nordics the sympathy of his utterly inane society, under the impression that somehow he would be doing them a great deal of good.

You see, Caleb, and his white friends, too, were all bores. Or so we, who lived in Harlem's literary bohemia during the "Negro Renaissance" thought. We literary ones considered ourselves too broad-minded to be bothered with questions of color. We liked people of any race who smoked incessantly, drank liberally, wore complexion and morality as loose garments, and made fun of anyone who didn't do likewise. We snubbed and high-hatted any Negro or white luckless enough not to understand Gertrude Stein, Ulysses, Man Ray, the theremin, Jean Toomer, or George Antheil. By the end of the 1920's Caleb was just catching up to Dos Passos. He thought H. G. Wells good.

We met Caleb one night in Small's. He had three assorted white folks in tow. We would have passed him by with but a nod had he not hailed us enthusiastically, risen, and introduced us with great acclaim to his friends who turned out to be schoolteachers from Iowa, a woman and two men. They appeared amazed and delighted to meet all at once two Negro writers and a black painter in the flesh. They invited us to have a drink with them. Money being scarce with us, we deigned to sit down at their table.

The white lady said, "I've never met a Negro writer before."

The two men added, "Neither have we."

"Why, we know any number of *white* writers," we three dark bohemians declared with bored nonchalance.

"But Negro writers are much more rare," said the lady.

"There are plenty in Harlem," we said.

"But not in Iowa," said one of the men, shaking his mop of red hair.

"There are no good *white* writers in Iowa either, are there?" we asked superciliously.

"Oh, yes, Ruth Suckow came from there."

Whereupon we proceeded to light in upon Ruth Suckow as old hat and to annihilate her in favor of Kay Boyle. The way we flung names around seemed to impress both Caleb and his white guests. This, of course, delighted us, though we were too young and too proud to admit it.

The drinks came and everything was going well, all of us drinking, and we three showing off in a high-brow manner, when suddenly at the table just behind us a man got up and knocked down a woman. He was a brownskin man. The woman was blonde. As she rose he knocked her down again. Then the red-haired man from Iowa got up and knocked the colored man down.

He said, "Keep your hands off that white woman."

The man got up and said, "She's not a white woman. She's my wife."

One of the waiters added, "She's not white, sir, she's colored."

Whereupon the man from Iowa looked puzzled, dropped his fists, and said, "I'm sorry."

The colored man said, "What are you doing up here in Harlem anyway, interfering with my family affairs?"

The white man said, "I thought she was a white woman."

The woman who had been on the floor rose and said, "Well, I'm not a white woman, I'm colored, and you leave my husband alone."

Then they both lit on the gentleman from Iowa. It took all of us and several waiters, too, to separate them. When it was over the manager requested us to kindly pay our bill and get out. He said we were disturbing the peace. So we all left. We went to a fish restaurant down the street. Caleb was terribly apologetic to his white friends. We artists were both mad and amused.

"Why did you say you were sorry," said the colored painter to the visitor from Iowa, "after you'd hit that man—and then found out it wasn't a white woman you were defending, but merely a light colored woman who looked white?"

"Well," answered the red-haired Iowan, "I didn't mean to be butting in if they were all the same race."

"Don't you think a woman needs defending from a brute, no matter what race she may be?" asked the painter.

"Yes, but I think it's up to you to defend your own women."

"Oh, so you'd divide up a brawl according to races, no matter who was right?"

"Well, I wouldn't say that."

"You mean you wouldn't defend a colored woman whose husband was knocking her down?" asked the poet.

Before the visitor had time to answer, the painter said, "No! You just got mad because you thought a black man was hitting a *white* woman."

"But she *looked* like a white woman," countered the man.

"Maybe she was just passing for colored," I said.

"Like some Negroes pass for white," Caleb interposed.

"Anyhow, I don't like it," said the colored painter, "the way you stopped defending her when you found out she wasn't white."

"No, we don't like it," we all agreed except Caleb.

Caleb said in extenuation, "But Mr. Stubblefield is new to Harlem."

The red-haired white man said, "Yes, it's my first time here."

"Maybe Mr. Stubblefield ought to stay out of Harlem," we observed.

"I agree," Mr. Stubblefield said. "Good night."

He got up then and there and left the café. He stalked as he walked. His red head disappeared into the night.

"Oh, that's too bad," said the white couple who remained. "Stubby's temper just got the best of him. But explain to us, are many colored folks really as fair as that woman?"

"Sure, lots of them have more white blood than colored, and pass for white."

"Do they?" said the lady and gentleman from Iowa.

"You never read Nella Larsen?" we asked.

"She writes novels," Caleb explained. "She's part white herself."

"Read her," we advised. "Also read the *Autobiography of an Ex-colored Man.*" Not that we had read it ourselves—because we paid but little attention to the older colored writers—but we knew it was about passing for white.

We all ordered fish and settled down comfortably to shocking our white friends with tales about how many Negroes there were passing for white all over America. We were determined to *épater le bourgeois* real good via this white couple we had cornered, when the woman leaned over the table in the midst of our dissertations and said, "Listen, gentlemen, you needn't spread the word, but me and my husband aren't white either. We've just been *passing* for white for the last fifteen years."

"What?"

"We're colored, too, just like you," said the husband. "But it's better passing for white because we make more money."

Well, that took the wind out of us. It took the wind out of Caleb, too. He thought all the time he was showing some fine white folks Harlem—and they were as colored as he was!

Caleb almost never cursed. But this time he said, "I'll be damned!"

Then everybody laughed. And laughed! We almost had hysterics. All at once we dropped our professionally selfconscious "Negro" manners, became natural, ate fish, and talked and kidded freely like colored folks do when there are no white folks around. We really had fun then, joking about that red-haired guy who mistook a fair colored woman for white. After the fish we went to two or three more night spots and drank until five o'clock in the morning.

Finally we put the light-colored people in a taxi heading downtown. They turned to shout a last good-by. The cab was just about to move off, when the woman called to the driver to stop.

She leaned out the window and said with a grin, "Listen, boys! I hate to confuse you again. But, to tell the truth, my husband and I aren't really colored at all. We're white. We just thought we'd kid you by passing for colored a little while— just as you said Negroes sometimes pass for white."

She laughed as they sped off toward Central Park, waving, "Good-by!"

We didn't say a thing. We just stood there on the corner in Harlem dumbfounded—not knowing now *which* way we'd been fooled. Were they really white —passing for colored? Or colored—passing for white?

Whatever race they were, they had had too much fun at our expense—even if they did pay for the drinks.

27   Reciprocal Exploitation in an Indian-White Community

● NIELS WINTHER BRAROE

In this paper I shall examine the manner in which conceptions of self and other held by Indians and whites contribute stability to a community structure of roles and values which is riddled with apparent inconsistency and contradiction. As a point of departure, I shall focus on a recurrent type of behavior: the practice by Indians and whites alike of "victimizing" one another, of misrepresenting the self and self-motivations in social and economic transactions. The insight gleaned from consideration of these performances will be offered in support of the hy-

SOURCE: Niels Winther Braroe, in the *Southwestern Journal of Anthropology*, XXI (Summer 1965), pp. 166–178.

The research upon which this paper is based was done in the summer of 1963, and was supported by the University of Illinois and in part by the Saskatchewan Cultural Ecology Research Program, NSF Grant G23815, administered by the Social Science Institute of Washington University, and directed by John W. Bennett. I am indebted to Edward M. Bruner, Joseph R. Gusfield and George L. Hicks for critical comments and suggestions.

pothesis that these misrepresentations allow both Indians and whites to resolve value and role contradictions which might otherwise engender social conflict or personal disorganization.

I

The perspective adopted in this paper draws on the work of Rose, Goffman, Berreman and others relating to the nature of the self and human interaction. Human beings are categorized according to the major roles they enact in society, roles being a "cluster of related meanings and values that guide and direct an individual's behavior in a given social setting . . ." (Rose, 1962, p. 10). Roles and the self are seen as growing out of continuous social symbolic interaction in which individuals present and express themselves in ways intended to influence a shared definition of the situation. A large portion of this interaction is concerned with crediting or discrediting the selves thus presented: "this imputation—this self—is a *product* of the scene that comes off . . ." (Goffman, 1959, p. 252).

Two aspects of this perspective are prominent in the following pages. The first deals with the tendency of the participants in a community or a social setting to arrive at a working consensus, an agreement about how they will behave toward one another and upon the symbols and meanings which will guide this action. Secondly, people generally work to support consensus and devise means of avoiding its disintegration and the associated failure of self-validations.

A person is an individual who becomes involved in a value of some kind . . . and then makes a public claim that he is to be defined and treated as someone who possesses the value or property in question. The limits to his claims, and hence the limits to his self, are primarily determined by the objective facts of his social life and secondarily determined by the degree to which a sympathetic interpretation of these facts can bend them in his favor. Any event which demonstrates that someone has made a false claim, defining himself as something which he is not, tends to destroy him (Goffman, 1962, p. 500).

This paper explores self and other images of white and Indian persons vis-à-vis one another. Attention is directed to the ways in which each credits or validates the roles and self of the other in the context of a community "working consensus" that provides the framework of day-to-day interaction. One question is central to this discussion: how do Indians adapt to circumstances of economic and social deprivation? How do they adapt to membership in the lowest category of a rigidly hierarchical status system?

II

Jasper is a town of about 2400 persons on the western prairie of Saskatchewan.[1] Small-scale cattle ranching and mixed farming are the predominant economic activities of whites in this region; they come to Jasper for goods and services, and often move there after retirement. In Jasper there are two general stores, a movie theatre, two small hotels, a pub, three Chinese-owned restaurants, several auto and farm equipment stores and so on. The town, however, is no longer the isolated focus of patterns of leisure and consumption, as area residents now make frequent trips to a shopping center in a small city about sixty miles away.

---

[1] The name Jasper, and the names of all informants mentioned in this paper, are pseudonyms.

Twenty miles from town is a small non-treaty Indian reserve which is the home of about a hundred and ten Plains Cree. The Indians make their living by the sale of poplar posts to ranchers and to the lumber yard in town, and by seasonal agricultural labor. All receive government relief, their most stable source of income. Jasper Indians do not identify with whites to the extent that white cultural goals and values are outwardly accepted and Indian ones entirely rejected. They revere generosity and sharing, for example, and ridicule white ideas about the dignity of work, the accumulation of material goods, punctuality and the like. The fact that so few of them are acculturated—that is, display their selves as white—is not difficult to understand given the nature of their relations with the dominant society; these relations impede the communication of white culture and limit the participation of Indians in white institutional activities. Until six years ago there was no school for Indian children; even now their school is segregated on the reserve. Since most parents do not value education, class attendance is poor. Children do not learn to speak English until they are six or seven years old. Jasper Indians uniformly profess belief in "Indian" religion and emphatically call attention to their participation in it. None of the Indians are even nominally Christian, and there is no record of any effort in the past generation to convert them. No one among them has ever served in the military.

While Indians go to town frequently, even in the worst weather, the reserve itself is isolated. Whites seldom visit it and never live there. A policeman said, "We don't really know what goes on up there, and don't really care as long as they don't make trouble in town." Lacking electricity, reserve Indians have no radios or television sets, and hence are further isolated by minimal exposure to mass media.[2] Occupational opportunities in town do not exist. None of the merchants or businessmen questioned said that they were willing to hire Indians, even for the most menial tasks.

Similarly, the legal status of Indians and their dependence on paternalistic government relief are important factors in their marginal involvement in the local economy. They do not have the capital resources to increase the income from communally-owned reserve holdings. They have not learned skills that would bring them regular employment in the Jasper community or allow them to emigrate to a more favorable urban location.[3]

Attitudes of whites toward Indians are obstacles to Indian assimilation. The common denominator of nearly all of these attitudes is that Indians are childish and irresponsible. For some, such as the man to whom Indians bring their dilapidated cars for repair, this is mixed with pity. He knows that his work will likely go unpaid, but he says, "They can't help it, they're just kids with money. They got nothing, and whenever they do get a little money they can't wait to spend it." At the other extreme there are people who share this appraisal of Indian character as child-like, but who express a spare-the-rod-spoil-the-child opinion. They insist that Indians should be compelled to behave responsibly and that they ought to be given no social privileges or aid until they do so. Others, including many ranchers, think that the Indians should be allowed to rot. "I can make a living off this land," they say, "why can't they? It's because we help them so much that they're so lazy."

---

[2] Several families have quite recently acquired small transistor radios.

[3] One family of Jasper Indians does travel to Alberta each summer to work on the beet farms there. They return at the end of each season to spend the winter on the reserve.

Jasper whites not only consider Indians to be irresponsible, but speak of them as worthless. Some see them circumstantially so, others consider Indians worthless as human beings. For the latter, Indians are innately without value, and no amount of "help" by white society will ever make Indians self-sufficient. They are regarded as parasites, a liability inherited from the past. Few whites, however, display active hostility toward Indians, not excluding those who consider them little more than superfluous appendages to white society. The absence of malice on the part of whites is one of the most remarkable aspects of Indian-white relations. Even those white men who have been involved in brawls with Indians do not bear animosity toward them. In fact, both Indians and whites describe these events with the greatest amusement.

The conception which whites have of Indians differs dramatically from whites' image of themselves. They extol responsibility, independence and self-sufficiency. The residents of Jasper and its surroundings feel themselves close to the western frontier era—indeed this part of North America was the scene of the closing days of the "Old West" (Stegner, 1955, pp. 127–138). A sentiment commonly expressed by Jasper whites is one of confidence in the face of adversity, of dauntlessness in the confrontation of nature. Town-dwelling men speak with pride of the ability to "take care of myself." Only Indians go on relief. The image of the strong, silent cowboy is taken seriously in Jasper. With it go the attributes of unwavering integrity, fairness and helpfulness. Jasper is a particularistic community, where people applaud the man who is willing to help others without demanding repayment; but they believe that a man must not accept a hand unless he intends to reciprocate someday. These values pervade the complex, reticulate cooperative work groups among ranchers.

III

The whites' emphasis upon the values of integrity and charity are often not discernible in their day-to-day behavior toward Indians. Indians who have cut and cured poplar posts near the reserve, and who do not have trucks, persuade whites to haul the posts to town. For his small investment of time, the white charges as much as 25 percent of the load's value; customarily he goes into the lumber yard office to collect his money from the manager while the Indian unloads the posts in the yard. Whites say that one has to pocket one's money before the Indian "gets his hands on it," or risk never being paid. Again, whites frequently take advantage of the restrictions placed upon Indians in disposing of reserve resources. The law forbids Indians to sell cattle or hay without permission from the Indian agent, and the money from such sales is supposed to go to a common reserve fund rather than to individaul Indians. To circumvent this, Indians sell these things to whites, but for only a fraction of their value.[4] Similarly, a few ranchers take advantage of the Indians' desire for spending money, by arranging to place cattle on reserve pasture for much less than it would cost if legal channels were used. In this way a small "grazing fee" is collected by an Indian who needs money for a trip to a Sun Dance on another reserve, and the white is enabled to feed his cattle for a pittance. Indians are overcharged for merchandise and services in town,

---

[4] Six years ago, the Indian Affairs Branch supplied reserve families with a total of about seventy cows: today there are only about twenty-five. They have been sold (illegally), eaten and allowed to starve or freeze to death.

and they are paid less for their labor than a white man would be. Indian women are not infrequently objects of white sexual gratification.

White belief in the irresponsibility of Indians is demonstrated continuously. For example, at the suggestion of some Jasper residents, the Indian Department no longer gives relief money directly to the Indians. Instead, a local general store receives these funds, which are credited to Indian families to whom supplies of food and clothing are doled out on a weekly basis.

While not all whites engage in these practices, those who do are neither publicly nor privately censured by those who do not have such dealings with Indians. Neither do white members of the Jasper community comment upon the less direct deprivation of Indians. The legal and political status of Indians is, of course, a matter of national governmental policy. But whites make no effort to bring about policy changes which might lead to Indian self-sufficiency, nor do they take action at the local community level to provide Indians with occupational skills or agricultural training which would improve Indian standards of living.

In a particularistic community where standards of honesty and humaneness are prized, the exploitation and deprivation of a segment of that community stands out as a manifest anomaly. It is not out of place to ask how the conceptions of self which incorporate these values also incorporate behavior and attitudes which contradict them. One way to minimize this conflict is to insist upon maintaining social distance between whites and Indians. This amounts to ignoring that a conflict exists. To a certain extent, the white members of the Jasper community take this solution. For instance, an examination of back issues of the weekly Jasper newspaper for its sixty year history revealed that, apart from mentions of Indians in the "Police Court" column, there has been no recognition that an Indian reserve exists near Jasper. Not even editorial notice has been taken of the Indian members of the community.

It is impossible, nonetheless, for Jasper whites always to ignore the presence and condition of Indians. There are other features of white deportment toward Indians which lend understanding of how apparent value contradictions are resolved. To identify these, it is useful to consider some of the ways that Indians, in turn, "con" white men.

Jasper Indians find one source of income in the poplar posts which they cut from reserve lands and (illegally) from the nearby forest preserve. Ordinarily, these are soaked in a "bluestone" preservative for about a day. Sometimes an impatient Indian will paint the posts with laundry bluing instead and then sell them to an unsuspecting white man. Another quick way of getting money is to sell a quantity of posts sight unseen, telling the buyer that they are stacked at some spot on the reserve. When the white man returns later, having found no posts, the Indian innocently conjectures that "somebody musta stole 'em." Again, Indians are able to stack posts for white buyers in such a way that there appear to be more than there actually are.

The "con game" played by Indians against whites is often carried out in the context of enduring relationships. For example, one Indian, John Sweet Grass, receives a monthly disability check from the government for about seventy dollars. Each month, he takes part of it to the owner of an appliance store in Jasper to "hold" for him, with the understanding that he may request small amounts of it at any time. By the end of every month John has overdrawn his allowance, and the financial state of affairs between him and his "banker" is hopelessly confused, as it has been for years. In effect, John has a reliable, permanent source of spending money. The storekeeper laments, "I really don't know anymore *how* much he owes me, I probably never will. What can I do? If I don't take care of him, he'll probably starve."

At every turn, Indians act the part of con artists in their dealings with whites. An Indian will call at the home of an absent white man and tell his wife that her husband instructed him to get from her several dollars due him for some work done. When the husband returns, his wife discovers that the payment was for an imaginary task—*he* hasn't seen this Indian in weeks.

Incidents of Indians duping whites occur with persistent, almost monotonous regularity: an Indian persuades a white to transport him and his family home from town in sub-zero weather for some agreed-upon price. When they arrive at the reserve, the Indian proclaims that he "hasn't got the money now, but I'll pay you later," which means never. A common way for Indians to borrow money is to offer some useless, worthless item as security—a piece of clothing or household utensil—and then never return to claim it, nor to pay the debt.

One of the most celebrated recent coups concerned the illegal sale of a water pump and windmill by several Indians to a neighboring rancher. This man paid for the machinery and steel tower on which it was mounted without a permit from the Indian agent, whose office is more than a hundred miles from Jasper. The rancher and his son disassembled the purchase and took it home. That night, the same Indians collected the tower and pump, hauled it into town, and resold it the next day to a junk dealer. In these transactions, whites do not hold Indians guilty for their behavior. They do not complain to the police when they suffer losses, even in cases where there is proof that Indians are the malefactors. A rancher, from whom Indians regularly poach chickens, says, "They know that all they have to do is ask me for 'em if they were really hungry, but they'd rather steal 'em."

Why, one may ask, does a white man, whom we should expect to know better, buy a pig-in-a-poke? Why, in their relations with Indians, do whites keep coming back for more? Why is an Indian lent money when all past experience must teach that it probably will never be returned? One outcome of the usual sequence of events in a con is that the "mark" learns his lesson; he is presumably a poorer but a more cautious man. We must look elsewhere for the source of white gullibility than in some sort of "mass stupidity" or failure to learn from experience. In fact, Jasper whites *expect* to be conned by Indians; storekeepers extend credit to Indians knowing that the accounts will never be settled.[5] It may be suggested that whites allow Indians to con them in order that Indian irresponsibility and childishness may be demonstrated and confirmed. A rancher pays an Indian in advance for his labor in stacking bales of hay. When the Indian does not show up to fulfill his part of the bargain, the rancher's image of the Indian as irresponsible is validated. His tolerance of the social deprivation of Indians can then be justified: "They *are* children and irresponsible. They are not really men, so they cannot be expected to participate in the adult world." Similarly, those whites who directly exploit Indians are provided a means of preserving a defensible image

---

[5] White residents of Jasper, especially those who have fewest contacts with Indians, and who are the most literate members of the community, point to a novel as an accurate portrayal of Indian character. *Stay Away, Joe*, by Dan Cushman, describes the slapstick adventures of a young Indian in his con game with white society. "If you want to know what Indians are *really* like," they advise, "read that book, it's a scream."

of self: "Sure, he takes advantage of me, but then, that is to be expected of children. I graze my cattle on the reserve, but then I'm the one who takes care of him, who gives him money, and sees that he does not starve." Not a few whites are persuaded that Indians have no desire to adopt white roles. A veterinarian claimed, "The last thing they want is to live like white men—they're no more than unemployed buffalo hunters, and happy just like they are."

IV

Looking at these transactions from an Indian point of view, an arresting feature is disclosed. Most Indians do not accept white judgments of their role, their self or their personal worth. Still, they seldom openly dispute white conceptions of Indian character—in fact, as we have seen, they behave in such a way to validate the white image of themselves.

Indians do not regard themselves as foolish children; on the contrary they consider themselves rather artful and successful exploiters of white men. What they do is to represent themselves to white audiences as the sort of persons whites take them to be, and represent themselves to other Indians as something different. In their performances before whites, Indians acknowledge irresponsibility, but they perform for a dual audience; to other Indians they are seen as turning to account (mistaken) white imputations of themselves.

Backstage, in Goffman's terminology, Indians "drop the front." In this region, "the impression fostered by the performance is knowingly contradicted as a matter of course" (Goffman, 1959, p. 112). Jokes are made about the stupidity of whites and the ease with which they are taken in. Fine points of strategy are discussed. "The way to get off easy," according to one informant, "is to act like a dumb Indian in front of the magistrate." This way, the punishment for being drunk and disorderly will be lighter than a white man would receive, and "credit" can even be arranged—the magistrate will give the guilty Indian months to pay his fine.

Much of this backstage activity resembles that reported by Berreman for the Aleut. Aleuts, though they identify with whites as a *valuation group*, respond to the denial of entrance into white institutional activities by valuation group alienation. They have come to look more appreciatively at white society, but, deprived of acceptance by whites, they orient themselves negatively toward those people toward whose cultural values and goals they are drawn. "Role segregation" and "role-distance" are two of the means Aleuts employ to cope with their ambivalence (Berreman, 1964, p. 235).

Earlier, we observed that Jasper Indians are excluded from playing white roles, and that structural barriers prevent Indian participation in the larger society. It was noted that, to a greater or lesser extent, most Jasper Indians do not perform in the presence of a white audience in a fashion which suggests that they embrace white cultural goals. The impression of them was that they are relatively "unacculturated." Nevertheless, it is evident that Jasper Indians too have begun to identify positively with white culture. In spite of the barriers to acculturation, they show signs of having recognized the taking of white roles as desirable. Perhaps one of the facilitating circumstances of this process has been the similarity between some of the principal values of traditional Plains Indian culture and those of the Anglo-American Jasper community. Standards of masculinity, competitiveness, a dual standard of sex behavior, qualities of leadership and the like are features of value orientations among Jasper whites which are remarkably like value orientations of the formerly more autonomous Plains Cree. We may expect that a group of one cultural heritage will identify with a group of another with greater ease when their conceptions of the male role contain analogous properties.

Many aspects of the structural relations between whites and Indians have worked toward acceptance by Indians of white cultural goals and meanings. For one, the extermination of the buffalo and the demise of the traditional pattern of Plains subsistence forced Indians to search elsewhere for means of livelihood. Formerly, Indians were spatially less isolated from whites than today: in the last ten years all of the white families but one which lived in the hills near the reserve have moved away because of the cold, lonely winters. Today also, with modern mechanized agriculture, the demand for Indian labor has declined. In the early reserve period, after the turn of the century, it was common for Indian families to live for long periods on the property of ranchers for whom they worked. Some Jasper adults, in fact, were born on ranches where their parents lived permanently, in familiar interaction with their white employers.

Indians have other opportunities for exposure to white culture. All Indian women now go to the hospital in Jasper to have their children. Indian men mix with whites in the pub; Indian children now have a white schoolteacher; Jasper Indians maintain close relations with members of other reserves who are more acculturated than they.

Continuous face to face interaction over generations leads to some consensual definition of the situation, and it is reasonable to expect that the subordinate Indians should have incorporated into their conceptions of self some of the content of white roles. One piece of evidence indicating that Indians have come to regard whites as a positive reference group is that they frequently judge their own behavior by white standards. It is not uncommon for Indians to show remorse about excessive drinking, for example. Most Indians express a desire to be self-supporting, and to own land and cattle the same as their white neighbors. An excerpt from the author's field diary is illustrative:

> Saturday nite: Charlie Running Calf, his wife and I strolled around town this evening. Charlie, who had been hauling bales on Newcomb's ranch for the past two days, had just come from the pub and was a little tight. We passed Roger Mc-Dougal. Charlie said, "Hiya Roger, how you been," in an expansive tone. Charlie's wife said, *"Charlie,* you can't talk to those people like that." He replied, "Whatdya mean, I'm a *workin'* man, ain't I?"

However much Indians embrace white culture, they are refused the privilege of playing white roles. They cannot go into business for themselves, as has been indicated, because their legal status prohibits the accumulation of the capital necessary to engage in full-scale farming or ranching. Nor have they skills which would allow wage employment off the reserve. Consequently, Jasper Indians are alienated from their valuation group just as Berreman's Aleuts were. If they cannot be white, however, it is necessary for them to define the self ". . . along defensible lines" (Goffman, 1962, p. 493). This must furthermore be done in a way that permits validation of this self by whites. To the Indian, then, his "irresponsible" performances declare: "Because I can trick white men so easily, they are not as smart as they think they are. *I'm* the one who's taking advantage of them. I can make a living by my wits."

V

We have looked at some of the ways whites and Indians in a small community portray the self in the ordinary course of daily life. We have seen also how the actions of each group validate the claims of the other. Indians and whites successfully predict one another's behavior, in a manner which mutually credits images of Indian and white selves. Among the consequences of this exchange, two are selected here for discussion.

In his article, "On Cooling the Mark Out," Erving Goffman (1962, pp. 482–505) addresses himself to the problem of adaptations which people make to failure, to the ways that individuals deal with repudiations of the self which are implied by the unsuccessful fulfillment of some role. It often becomes necessary that a person whose self has suffered failure be "consoled" by some other person. He is helped to adjust to his loss, he is "cooled out." This is particularly important when a person is deeply engaged in this self, and where its loss reflects upon him negatively. It sometimes occurs, Goffman adds, that the various participants in a network of interaction take measures to avoid altogether the troublesome procedure of cooling out; they attempt to cover up the fact that a person has failed or that his value as an individual is negligible.

Such processes may be recognized in transactions between Jasper whites and Indians. Indians do not have the liberty of playing white roles, but at the same time they increasingly identify with these roles and with white cultural values. They are accordingly in the plight of people whose worth is denied. Indians cannot salvage much of their value in the estimation of whites, but they do have means of saving face in the eyes of other Indians. This is accomplished, we have noted, when the Indian sub-community observes one of its members making a fool of a white man, bringing off some deception with impunity. In effect, the validation of this transaction by whites serves to "cool out" Indians. Now, few Jasper Indians show evidence of serious personal disorganization, a consequence, it is proposed, of whites and Indians having found a way of avoiding a confrontation. Whites, at the same time, are spared the malaise of recognizing moral inconsistency in their own behavior.

Routines of self-presentation and identification in Jasper have consequences for stability at the structural as well as at the personal level.[6] The successful cooling out of a failure means that he will be less likely to protest or to threaten the established system of social relationships. The position of Indians in Jasper is one of subordination and deprivation. The social-psychological dynamics of role-playing and identification take place in a manner which contributes to the perpetuation of a caste-like status system. Indians are provided an "out," entailing adjustment to a place in their social environment which would otherwise be intolerable. The alternative to acquiescence, of course, would be for Indians to try to alter their environment, to challenge white superordination. Support for this assertion can be found in historical data, and in the examination of instances where the customary validations of Indian and white images of self fail.

Nearly a hundred years ago, not far from Jasper, a group of white traders "massacred" a small band of Indian horse-thieves (Cf. Sharp, 1955, pp. 55–77). The

---

[6] Both Indians and whites are, of course, largely unaware of the social and personal consequences of their behavior. It is likely that this ignorance is requisite to the achievement of these results. See Schneider (1962:494–495) for a discussion of the *structured* necessity for keeping "failures" ignorant of their status.

expedition was organized by a white man whose horse had been stolen by an Indian, sold back to him, and then stolen again by the same Indian; the whites attacked a camp where they believed the culprit was hiding. The significant aspect of white ideas about Indians at that time was that they were held responsible for their behavior and punishable for their deceptions. In this and numerous other instances, whites were not indulgently disposed to treat Indians as irresponsible, and the outcome was frequently violent.

Today, when representations of Indian and white selves fail, persons are embarrassed, insulted or provoked. An Indian, for example, inopportunely asked a white man in town for several dollars. He was refused, and told that he was a worthless beggar, incapable of properly supporting his wife and children. The Indian was affronted, enraged, and the two men exchanged blows in the street. It was not so much the refusal that brought violence, as the white's rejection of the self presented by the Indian. The normal course of interaction was disrupted when the white man withheld agreement to a definition of the situation including an image of the Indian as uncommitted to white values and unobligated by white standards of responsibility.

In this paper, I have described something of the tenor of Indian-white interaction, employing the social-psychological perspective which stresses role-taking, performances and the self. It was suggested that a social structure including the superordination of whites over Indians is supported through a consensual definition of the situation embodying images of self which Indians and whites present to one another. The analysis was not exclusively concerned with the *results* of acculturation, or the extent to which Indians overtly embrace white values, but considered as well the kinds of involvement of these values in selves identified with whites and Indians vis-à-vis one another. In other words, the emphasis has been on the *mechanisms* of acculturative processes rather than upon the conditions of culture contact or the larger, more abstract, results of contact. As much space has been devoted to the "how" of persistence of Indian segregation—the complimentary presentation of diverse self images—as to the "why."

A final comment is in order. Looking at the results of acculturation rather than at the daily interplay between whites and Indians, one might conclude that differences in cultural values expressed in the different presentations of self represent points of tension or potential conflict between whites and Indians. The evidence presented above suggests that such a view is not entirely accurate. The different sets of values embodied in Indian and white roles constitute an accommodation or a *solution* to certain conflicts and not merely a source of them. It is, in fact, because of the contrasting images of Indian and white man that interaction proceeds with as little conflict as actually occurs.

Bibliography

BERREMAN, GERALD D. "Aleut Reference Group Alienation, Mobility, and Acculturation." *American Anthropologist* 66, 1964, pp. 231–250.

CUSHMAN, DAN. *Stay Away, Joe.* New York: Viking Press, 1953.

GOFFMAN, ERVING. *The Presentation of Self in Everyday Life.* New York: Doubleday, 1959.

———. "On Cooling the Mark Out," in *Human Behavior and Social Processes,* ed. by A. M. Rose. Boston: Houghton Mifflin, 1962, pp. 482–505.

ROSE, ARNOLD M. "A Systematic Summary of Symbolic Interaction Theory," in *Human*

Behavior and Social Processes, ed. by A. M. Rose. Boston: Houghton Mifflin, 1962, pp. 3–19.

SCHNEIDER, LOUIS. "The Role of the Category of Ignorance in Sociological Theory: an Exploratory Statement." *American Sociological Review* 27, 1962, pp. 492–508.

SHARP, PAUL F. *Whoop-Up Country.* Minneapolis: University of Minnesota Press, 1955.

STENGER, WALLACE. *Wolf-Willow: A History, A Story, and A Memory of the Last Plains Frontier.* New York: Viking Press, 1955.

28   The Circumstance and Situation of Social Status

● GREGORY P. STONE

A frequently echoed argument against generalizing about social stratification in the society at large from observations made in the context of local community organization asserts that the "upper class" person in the small town is not "upper class" in the large city. I must reject this line of reasoning. Status is a *circumstantial* fact for some people, a network of life fate, but, for others, status is a *situational* phenomenon, eminently capable of manipulation and established by one's self or one's social circle by the artful staging of appearances. To say that "upper class" people living in small towns are, *de facto,* not "upper class" in large cities is to emphasize the circumstantial aspects of status to the neglect of its situational character and to assume that one's personal horizons of experience are circumscribed by local community boundaries. However, not all the residents *in* local communities are *of* those communities, nor are all people whom the sociologist may place *in* status categories *of* those categories.

Some are. For such people, the manipulation of status is outside the realm of possibility. They are existentially committed to their status circumstances. Thus, when asked what kind of clothes should not be worn by persons in the respondent's social position, a truckdriver replied, "I wouldn't have any use for a tuxedo or things like that. . . . I'd just be out of my class wearing evening clothes and morning clothes." A part-time housewife, working in a local restaurant, replied, "Some of these nice, fancy, expensive furs. They wouldn't fit me—real expensive, kinda high-tone clothes. Them and I wouldn't mix. It would be someone tryin' to overdo, and make people think they're higher than they are." [1] The operator of a small body-repair shop echoed the same sentiments:

> Anyone who is in this category of business should not be outstanding. It looks like you're trying to step out of your class a little bit, go too far in your dress. You should be conservative.

Similar thoughts were provided in responses to other questions. For example, when a household domestic was asked whether or not she would like to dress like

SOURCE: "The Circumstance and Situation of Social Status," original paper prepared especially for this volume.

This article continues the argument presented in "Sex and Age as Universes of Appearance," reprinted in this section. The data are based on a study of a small (10,000 population) Midwestern community.

[1] Note the conception of *fit.*

some of the better dressed people in town, she answered, "I couldn't afford to. If I could, I would be out of place."

This circumstantial quality of appearance—one dresses as he does, because he is what he is—does seem to be generally (but, as we shall see, not exclusively) typical of life in the lower ranges of socio-economic status. For one thing, of course, the range of apparent symbols is sharply restricted for these people. Apparent symbols cost money. Also contributing to the matter of "apparent circumstance" is the restricted exposure on the part of those in the lower socio-economic levels to the range of apparent symbols. Asked whether she could tell social differences among people by the clothes they wear, the wife of a core-maker in the local foundry said:

> You probably could. Now we don't go to the Country Club, 'cause we don't belong. They might dress better, but we don't see them, but, when you go uptown, they are all dressed about the same.

Significantly, in an analysis of clothing shopping, questions asking the day of the week and the time of the day preferred for clothing shopping in town revealed that housewives at the extremes of the socio-economic scale could seldom, if ever, meet one another while shopping for clothing. Typically, higher status women shopped early in the day and week and lower status women shopped late in the week. The probability is that the people seen by the wife of the core-maker are dressed the same, because they are "the same" in status terms.[2]

On special occasions, the circumstances of appearance may cause minor discomfort and embarrassment, but lack of facility with impression management is only underscored. A carpenter's wife put it this way:

> Sometimes when you go to a party, you wish you'd worn a little better dress, after you see what they've got on. Sometimes I go to Bible Study in a cotton dress, and the others are more dressed up. Then, I'll go more dressed up, and all they'll have on is cotton dresses.

Or lack of facility with the staging of appearance may prevent the consolidation of social mobility. A former molder in a local foundry had managed to set enough aside to establish his own small aluminum foundry in partnership with another man. The small foundry was quite successful, but the former molder had not consolidated the "move" with the appropriate apparent symbolism. In fact, he *could not*, so immersed was he in the circumstances of his former status. A typical work day still sees him "in the shop" from 7:00 A.M. until 5:00 P.M. Under the protection of night, he goes to the office. When asked what kind of clothes he would suggest for his kind of work, he replied:

> You might say just for comfort—sport clothes, maybe—to meet the public. That doesn't go over too good sometimes. I've worked in the foundry all my life. I don't belong to the executive class; I'm not a white collar man.

Later, "I don't like office work. I'm not cut out for it. I liked molding, when I was able to do it." His response to this aspect of life is comprised by a fatalistic "philosophy" documented by legend:

---

2 Gregory P. Stone and William H. Form, *The Local Community Clothing Market: A Study of the Social and Social Psychological Contexts of Shopping* (East Lansing, Michigan: State University Agricultural Experiment Station Technical Bulletin 262, November, 1957), pp. 21–24. I might add, "It's *really* a small world!"

If you can put up a front, you can get by for a while, but eventually it seems to catch up with you. That reminds me of some boys I grew up with. Their father was a plain everyday man. He founded the business. When he'd go out of town on a business trip, he'd maybe go on some side street and get a good meal, but, when the boys went out, they had to stay at the best hotels and get expensive dinners. They were just putting up a front. It didn't mean anything. They could go any place, and they were the life of the party. There were four of them—two younger than me and two older. They inherited a good business and, in a few years, went bankrupt. A man came in and straightened the business out from the creditors, and they got back on their feet. But the boys were very much putting up a front.

Yet, in the lower socio-economic levels, there are occasional signs of ambivalence leading to embryonic attempts to manipulate appearance. A shipping foreman in the stock room of a local manufacturing plant, for example, permitted himself the hope of mobility. He mentioned "businessmen" and "party-goers" as the best dressed people in town, and, asked whether he would like to dress as they do, he replied, "I have hopes of being able to." He has, in fact, attempted to manage his impressions. Thinking that clothing does influence one's chances on the job, he says, "I buy my clothes purposely for work." Yet, in conjunction with this question, the foreman observes, "Well, your dressing brings out your character." (The "character" is there to begin with!) Asked later what clothes should not be worn by those in his social position, the foreman responded:

> They shouldn't wear expensive or flashy clothes. [Interviewer: Why not?] Because they can't afford expensive clothes. [Interviewer: Why shouldn't they wear flashy clothes?] It builds bad character, because you're trying to attract attention by other than your social position. [Interviewer: Would you explain that a little more?] Well, if you can't have the friends or the attention of people by your social position, it seems false to get it by the clothes you wear.

The foreman, cautiously aspiring, may be moving out of the circumstance of the working class.

A freight hand and trucker's helper had also begun to question the fated character of his appearance. We can see this in his response to the question: "Do you think the way you dress on the job makes any difference in your job opportunities or advancement?"

> Yes and no. It's possible that you could get a better job, if you dressed different, but I don't know. It's possible, but I wouldn't want to say either way. [Interviewer: How is it possible?] In contacting people—different stores and different customers. [Interviewer: Do you do anything about this in planning what you wear on the job?] I've thought some I'd change to a wool dress pant, but I like a good overall. It's comfortable. You're not all bundled up.

But the circumstances of work and the controls exerted by his social circle provide imposing obstacles to the manipulation of his appearance:

> The truckers dress like I do in the summer time. In the winter, they're inside and those truck heaters keep them warm. Me and the other fellows are outside most of the time.

Asked what should not be worn by people in his social position, the freight hand replied:

You should wear clothing that fits the occasion. [Interviewer: Why?] Well, I could dress real fancy at some occasion, if I wanted to, but, where I am socially, my kind would start talking about you quite easily, and that's one thing I can't stand at all.

Moreover, one's dress may not gibe with his discursive appearance. As a doctor's wife put it:

Some gals who make their own clothes and have little social prestige, you meet downtown, might fool you for a while. But I say it would be something they do or say that would give them away rather than clothes.

Although there are instances, here and there, of a manipulative or rhetorical orientation to the apparent representation of status by the selection of clothes among those in the lower ranges of socio-economic status, seldom are there instances of the use of dress to maintain and define situations which can parallel the case of a seventy-year-old wife of a retired cigar manufacturer. Her facility with dress is wonderfully exemplified in the following remark:

I knew I would look bigger in that coral suit, but . . . [it would] . . . bring out the color in my face. That would offset making my hips look larger.

The same acuity in contriving appearance is manifested in her comments on dressing up:

I never go out without dressing up. I don't feel right. I think there are certain kinds of clothes to be worn outside the home, a kind for inside the home on an afternoon, and a thing to scrub—when you wear any old thing. In Florida, at Gulfport, you'd never wear a formal. You never see a formal there. At the Moonlight Club, where we go every Wednesday night, you wouldn't think of going without a formal. You'd keep trying to pull your skirt down longer, if you did. Only people who are tourists—just there for a couple of weeks—could go like that. If they were just there for a couple of weeks and didn't bring many clothes, that would be all right. I'm not self-conscious. There are just standards that you should abide by.

Her staging of appearance at the Moonlight Club, however, is not simply a matter of immediate response to standards of propriety. Appearance is a product of collective staging undertaken jointly by herself and her husband:

When we're going to a dance, I ask what he's going to wear. Then, we dress in harmony so the colors won't clash. When he's going out, I ask what he's going to wear, so I'll know it's suitable and wear the same thing.

This collective staging of appearance extends to her larger social circle and reflects the conscious maintenance of status enforced by informal controls. Asked what others in her social position should not wear, the lady replied:

You must dress well. [Interviewer: Why is that?] You're kinda looked at as an example or pattern, and, if you go around looking sloppy, you're taboo. [Interviewer: Who would you be a pattern to?] My associates—the same as I use them as a pattern—not that we keep up with the Joneses. They'd say, "See Patricia!! Can't imagine what's got into her. Never saw her look that way before."

Still, the circumstantial character of status does not exclusively typify the lower levels of socio-economic status. Interesting contrast is provided by the response of Mrs. Branchwood to the "invasion of the cosmopolitans,"[3] and the response of Mrs. Cavendish. Both belong to the "old families" of Vansburg, the first to an "old retailing family" and the second to a "local manufacturing family." Mrs. Branchwood, like members of many other old families, has "retired" from the competition for status:

> I know, before the war, we used to dress up in formals for dinner parties and dances. Now we don't dress up. In fact, we don't have much in the social life way.

Mrs. Cavendish presented a "double face" to the world—one for the benefit of the local community audience, the other for the benefit of the world at large, represented locally by the "cosmopolite set."

> A lot of people feel they have to have the latest style—a lot of older people especially. You have to grow old graciously. To me a mink coat is lovely no matter the style. The things can be changed a little. Once a year I get the fashions from Paris and look them over. The people in New York dress entirely different from the people in the Middle West. Everyone downtown will tell you that I don't care what I wear. But I was trained to teach art, and I'm always looking at design— not so much for the style. When I dress to go out, I dress. The dinner gowns I wear in New York are considered conservative there, but I wouldn't dare wear them here.

Asked whether she preferred to shop for clothes in chain stores or local independent stores, Mrs. Cavendish replied, "Well, we don't think the chain stores give to the community. I certainly give my home merchants the chance." In contrast: "I don't mind shopping in New York. They know me and what I want. . . . I have ten or twelve pairs of kid gloves that I send to New York at one time to be cleaned."

Such impression management requires extremely careful definitions of situations. Mrs. Cavendish was careful to note, "Some people who have come from New York dress as though they are still there. They are overdressed." By artfully employing dress, however, she could adapt herself to varying status situation:

> Naturally I'd dress differently in the Chateau-Frontenac in Quebec or in the Ambassador Hotel in New York. . . . I do most of my buying in New York, and I dress differently when I am there. . . . When I'm around here, I dress differently from when I'm away. I'm apt to wear medium-priced garments so I won't be overdressed.

On the other hand, Mrs. Branchwood seemed unable to rise above the circumstances of status:

> When I was in Florida, I was invited to a luncheon. We didn't know what to wear —hats or gloves. When we got there, everyone else was wearing gloves and hats.

The two present an interesting contrast, indeed. Both were the same age (50 and 51 years old), both were members of "old families" in town, both were rated as "upper class," but their status worlds were different. Mrs. Branchwood seemed somehow ensnared by the circumstances of her status; Mrs. Cavendish looked

---

[3] A point discussed extensively in William H. Form and Gregory P. Stone, "Instabilities in Status: The Problem of Hierarchy in the Community Study of Status Arrangements," *American Sociological Review*, XVIII (April, 1953), pp. 149–162. On cosmopolitans see Gerald Thielbar, "On Locals and Cosmopolitans," immediately following in this section.

upon status as a situation to be defined and redefined by dress as she moved back and forth between town and metropolis.

Status, like age, presents a permeable world, but, in a sense, it is a less permeable world for some. Penetration of status barriers and the misrepresentation of the self require anonymity—the kind that is afforded by the metropolis and to residents of Vansburg whose visits away from town are frequent—but within the town itself, knowledge of one another, at times unexpectedly intimate, precludes extensive manipulations of the status world. If one stays *in* town and becomes *of* the town, status is circumstantial, but frequent movement out of town loosens local status controls.

If we are to establish social stratification as a universe of appearance, we must first establish that people in different strata dress differently. Of course, the demonstration seems unnecessary, since all studies of dress show income and status differences, but the point may be emphasized by referring to a few selected interview materials. Listen to the spate of remarks volunteered to an interviewer by a local furniture salesman before the matter of status had been introduced in the interview:

> You'll find that, generally speaking, the crowd we run with are conservative. I travel with the conservative crowd. We don't try to outdo each other. Associations have some effect on everything you do. They have money, but it doesn't show much. They are all business and professional folks, but nobody can crap anybody. You can look 'em up in D and B. There is no object to foolin' around. [Interviewer: Who does "fool around"?] The "tin-horn millionaire" crowd—they dress to beat hell. They owe about three-quarters of the amount for their clothes. They have everything but the money. They aren't crapping anyone but themselves and some half-ass people. A lot of 'em have minor administrative jobs in the plants. You don't find many professional people in that group. That crowd spends a lot of time at the Elks. They hate to go to the Chamber of Commerce, but they do. They do more partying; we spend more time at home. They go to the dance halls and taverns. Their organizations are the Elks, the Country Club, the Lions, and the Rotary. Ours are Kiwanis—there's not so much money there as in the Rotary, but they're all swell—the Masons rather than the Elks, because it's not a drinking crowd, and the Chamber of Commerce. Most of my gang are too old for the Junior Chamber of Commerce. Now we are in the Chamber of Commerce.
>
> It shows up in clothes and clubs. We go to good shows and good places to eat. They go to burlesques. There is no clash between the two, but they are two different types. I can figure a guy fairly good. You take solid people. They are straight down the line. . . . There have to be a few lines drawn. You can't help it. It's just normal that you have to associate with people in your station. You don't go out and eat with them. You can call them by name, but you go to associate with people you eat with.

Status was this man's circumstance:

> I remember the time I pulled into the Palmer House [in Chicago] with no coat. They asked me to leave. I was griped. I went down to Walgreens.

And the principal cleavage he perceived as differentiating the dress of people in different walks of life seems to have been the cleavages between those who dressed to meet their status and those who, from his standpoint, sought to have their status meet their dress.

Other respondents presented more conventional pictures of different dress in different statuses. An accountant at the State Training School, when asked to enumerate the "social classes" in Vansburg, said:

> You'll find three groups. There's not much difference in what they do, except that they do it by themselves. First, a low income group—$3,000 and less; second, the average—from $3000 to $6,000; and, third, a small group above $6,000.[4] Then there are sub-groups. They are the first to adopt new fads. They gamble for higher stakes more flamboyantly. Finally, the element that's always being the newest thing. They will follow the trend of the above group, if they are buying something that's worth the money or the trouble.

Still, the cleavage between those who "dress in" and those who "dress out"—the conservatives and the Country Club group—persists. A radio repairman and bill collector missed the cleavage completely and commented upon the different dress of three strata:

> I wouldn't say that I dress any differently from other people, except maybe the foundry workers or the so-called 400's that are going out to the Country Club. In a small town, you dress more informally in work clothes or business clothes and then change. And then there are those that stay continually dressed up. They don't work. They just change clothes several times a day.

Most respondents, however, observed differences in dress only among extreme groups. A funeral director's wife observed, "The *Gute Freunden* [a high status club] may look frumpy. The Grange group are lovely people, but they dress differently." A weighmaster singled out:

> The "codfish aristocracy"—they may be the luminaries of a lodge gathering who spend all their dough treating everybody and feeding the slot machines. They want to impress everybody that they have the dough.

His wife echoed his words: "The 'codfish aristocracy.' They have a different pair of shoes to go with every gown and a purse and all that." A carpenter and mason commented on the different dress of those in the lower reaches of socio-economic status:

> Most of 'em all have pants and shirt alike, unless you get into dirty work; then they wear overalls. There's some don't dress as good as I do even when they're working. A lot of 'em drink it all up instead of puttin' clothes on their body. I know two or three guys who drink up their pay check as soon as they get it. Monday morning they're wearing the same old pants and shirt.

An osteopath, whose clientele are drawn from the lower socio-economic levels, observed:

> Well, you know, some of the people I visit—I wish you could go with me on my calls. There's one family. They sleep in an attic. They have to climb a ladder to get up. If you gave them my clothes or your clothes, in one week they'd be filthy and ragged. They just wouldn't know what to do with them.

The osteopath expounded at length on the importance of knowing how to wear clothes. Ambitious and aspiring, incidentally, he was caught in an interesting dilemma. To maintain his clientele (his source of wealth), he had to speak the language of his lower status patients. This adversely affected his own speech *vis à vis* his acceptance in the social circle to which he aspired.

---

[4] Interview taken in the early '50's.

Differences in dress among the different levels of socio-economic status are, of course, maintained by present-day counselors, not only of beauty, but of occupation. A sales manager for a local foundry talked at length upon the importance of matching occupation and clothing, concluding:

> I helped and made a fellow quite a success in Chicago in a clothes bureau. He charged ten dollars to interview people and tell them how to dress. First question he asked them was, "What is your position?" Then he asked them, "What is your work?"

Those in different status levels dress distinctively. The wife of the sales manager, just cited, observed:

> Clothes and speech. I can tell the minute a person comes through the door what kind of person they are and what their home surroundings are like. Speech is a very important factor. Those things tell class, too.

A hotel clerk assigned "social classes" on the basis of dress. Asked to enumerate the different social classes in Vansburg, she replied:

> Oh, I don't know. There would be the "butterfly type"—you know—just a bit on the overdressed order. Second, the conservative type. Then, the lower class, of course, who try, but get their clothing from Wards, Sears, or Spiegels, who get their clothing without trying it on to see if it suits their personality.

A nurse noted, "It's either the very wealthy or the lower class who get themselves decked out. You expect it with the wealthy." An oil salesman's wife said, "Millionaires dress better. There's no place in this town for that. That's why they look peculiar to us." The wife of an accounting supervisor asserted, "People of higher class wear clothes of better quality."

Interview excerpts also provide some evidence for the contention that different dress, construed as a variable symbol of status, does in fact mobilize the responses of different people. Consider the remarks of Elmer Olds—one of the "dirty Oldses" —a conspicuous "lower-lower" family. Asked, "What happens to people around here when they don't dress right?" Elmer replied:

> I don't know. [Interviewer: Are there any people around here who don't dress right?] A lot of 'em don't. [Interviewer: Well, what happens?] They get in for vagrancy mostly. They think they're from out of town. There is a place for 'em, but I don't know what they do with 'em. Around here they don't bother 'em too much.

Now consider the remarks of a local policeman in response to the same question:

> Most of them are fellows that we have trouble with at the office. They wear anything that someone else throws away. [Interviewer: Why is that?] Mostly because they don't want to work.

I think these remarks can be construed as rather plausible evidence that the dress of those of very low status in Vansburg mobilized a particular response from a particular group—the police—that such dress is not calculated to arouse within the social circles of those manifesting very low status.

Sometimes one's dress culminates in a somewhat more subtle response than that of police arrest—social ostracism. Asked what might happen to her should she appear on the streets in a ragged and torn housedress, a carpenter's wife replied:

They'd probably stick up their noses at you and say, "Funny she comes uptown dressed that way." [Interviewer: What people did you have in mind?] There are some people that go around with their noses up in the air. If you're all dressed up, they'll pass the time of day with you. If you're not, they won't speak to you. They're the snobbish people.

Others provided evidence of similar consequences for the person who does not keep up his appearance according to local standards. In response to the question: "What happens to people around here when they don't dress right?" a woman employed as an assembler at Amalgamated Chieftain, a national corporation which had recently established an assembly and packaging plant in Vansburg, replied:

They're generally shoved off to the side. With me, I don't shove them off to the side. I can speak to someone in overalls as well as someone in furs. If we'd all dress in overalls, we'd be better off.

Yet, not everyone dresses in overalls, as a livestock broker observed, and these variations in dress mobilize different people as members of continuing social circles:

I usually go with people according to the way they dress. Groups dress about the same. If they don't dress right, they'd probably go with another group of people.

His wife validates her husband's comments:

Nothing happens to them. [Interviewer: You mean socially?] Yes. They wouldn't associate with them. [Interviewer: Who?] The people in their social class.

In a more direct manner, the differential mobilization of audience and dress was captured by the terse remark of an oil salesman: "Now, when you go to the Elks, you got to dress up, but not at the Eagles." Or, an iron molder, admitting that he is more careful with his clothes when he appears in some groups rather than others, explained:

'Cause I was going out, and, if somebody thought they was a little better than I was, I'd dress a little better. If I was among my friends, I wouldn't. [Interviewer: What do you mean—a little better than you?] There's a certain group in town. They don't make any more money than you do, but they think they're better — "nickel millionaires"—you know what I mean.

A local nurse, wife of a civil employee, explained her early wishes for clothing in much the same way:

We were thrown together with a group of girls, various types, various classes: I wanted to be well dressed. In groups like that, there's a class distinction, and you want to be dressed nice.

This perceived relation between audience, symbol, and self facilitated for some a "full-blown" rhetoric:

You can do well, if you're judicious and far-sighted, too. It pays to look smart and have a good appearance. When I was in school, my sister and I associated with people who had more money than we did, but nobody knew, because my mother planned well for me. I was afraid to join a sorority because many of the girls used to take thousand-dollar summer vacations and had plenty. I was afraid I couldn't keep up with the Joneses. But my mother said that, as long as I could pay the dues and not be any more shabbily dressed than the others, that I would make out all right.

Others somehow merely *experience* the audience response and never quite manage to anticipate it. For them, status is their circumstance. Asked to recall an early unpleasant experience with clothing, a carpenter's wife remembered:

> We was going to children's exercises, and we put on the best we had, and we went up there, and the woman who was in charge asked us if we were going home and change our dresses.

Such entrapment is frequently economic, as the wife of a weight-shifter in one of the foundries put it, when she was asked whether she would like to dress like some of the salesclerks she saw in the clothing stores:

> Yes. So I'd look nice on the street, and people wouldn't talk about you. I try to look as nice as I can, but, if you haven't got the money to buy the clothes, you have to do something else.

These data suggest that the situations and circumstances of social status are perhaps more sharply distinguished by the residents of Vansburg than are the situations and circumstances of age. Perhaps for this reason, the universes of appearance mobilized around problems of status—its conferral, appropriation, and maintenance—are revealed more by the responses the residents of the town make to one another's clothed appearances, than in gross variations of meaning dress may be said to have for people of differing socio-economic ratings. The comprehension of one's status as a situation to be defined *for* as well as *by* others would, indeed, sensitize one to the status-meanings of dress. It is the very situational character that status has for some people that enables them to "escape" the limits of status "objectively" imposed upon them by their work by manipulating the apparent symbols available on the consumer market.

29   On Locals and Cosmopolitans

● GERALD THIELBAR

This essay explores social relations and their analysis in terms of a local–cosmopolitan distinction. Several questions are posed. In what ways has the local–cosmopolitan distinction been used? What are its empirical referents? What contribution can be made through this conceptualization to the theory and investigation of complex society?

Erving Goffman has observed that American society is complex in part because multiple social transactions are carried on within shared physical space, and frequently endure as stable relationships, with little mutual interference and disruption.[1] Under conditions of industrial society, group boundaries often are not geographical boundaries and communication networks frequently are not discovered

SOURCE: Gerald Thielbar, "On Locals and Cosmopolitans," original paper prepared especially for this volume.

[1] Erving Goffman, *The Presentation of Self in Everyday Life* (Garden City: Doubleday, 1959), *passim*.

through a principle of territoriality. These conditions are implicitly recognized by sociologists who use space and distance as metaphorical terms.[2] Social space is a useful concept in many sociological contexts and is a metaphor through which the local–cosmopolitan distinction may be apprehended. Persons who share physical space are not necessarily intimate. Conversely, when persons are spatially separated, they are not necessarily distant in a metaphorical sense. In describing association between persons who are socially intimate but separated geographically, the concept of reference relationships is useful. For example, in complex societies social mobility requires only membership change, and, although geographical and social mobility often are concomitant, they need not be. Here membership becomes a matter of concern *because* geographical location is an inadequate indicator of a person's affiliations. Where affiliations or reference relationships are altered frequently, and alternatives are many, it is inevitable that persons learn to discriminate among others within proximity. As frequently occurs, those who are closest in physical space are those who matter least socially. Selective attending to persons and events that are physically distant may be more important to understanding and predicting behavior than social stimuli that impinge upon persons by virtue of their physical presence. Selectivity is accomplished through (symbolic) memory and is greatly reinforced through communications technology.

The term reference relationship, as usually employed to describe this discrimination of stimuli, connotes intimacy with or imitation of significant others characteristic of primary interaction. Modification of this usage is required for present purposes. Cosmopolitanism, in terms of space and distance, means the extent to which space is occupied and distance traversed. Howard Becker used the term "mental mobility" to characterize persons who extend their horizons beyond the realm of physical occupancy.[3] Robert Merton has observed that some persons live in the larger society in contrast to others whose social participation takes their thoughts no farther than the city limits.[4] Cosmopolitanism, as a reference relationship, is not attachment to a significant few intimates but orientation toward the larger social world—events and processes in society writ large. Localism, in contrast, means limitation of attention to a small social space, to the personal, the familiar, and, at least sometimes, to a geographically bounded locality.

Approximate to localism–cosmopolitanism, distinctions have been drawn between the parochial and the ecumenical, the provincial and the urbane, the naive and the sophisticated. These characterizations, regarded as either definitive or descriptive of localism and cosmopolitanism, have gained some support in both ethnographic and more rigorous research. Since the distinction was introduced, it has continued to appear in the literature, at first as a general sensitizing concept, then as an *ad hoc* interpretation of research findings, and finally as a focus of more refined investigation. As the distinction has gained in usage, it has sometimes gained in rigor and clarity.

[2] Conceptions of space and distance underlie explanations of such diverse social events as change of job and treatment of Negroes. From the latter context comes a hypothesis that ecological segregation is in many instances established only as a last-ditch defense when ritual patterns of avoidance are disrupted. Edward T. Hall has established social distance as a universal phenomenon within cultures and a universal problem between them. Cf. Edward T. Hall, *The Silent Language* (Garden City: Doubleday, 1959).

[3] Howard Becker, *Man in Reciprocity: Introductory Lectures on Culture, Society and Personality* (New York: F. A. Praeger, 1956), p. 396.

[4] Robert K. Merton, *Social Theory and Social Structure* (Glencoe: Free Press, 1957), pp. 387–420.

The Study of Locals and Cosmopolitans

An early discussion of "cosmopolitanism" is contained in an article by that title in the *Encyclopedia of the Social Sciences*.[5] Max Boehm described the modern world as becoming less provincial as a result of deracination from native soil and loss of permanent domicile, which are produced in turn by industrialization, urbanization, and their concomitants. Travel and interaction with representatives of diverse cultures bring into perspective a larger community of men. The breakdown of parochial communities frees some people from a taken-for-granted microcosmic world. The cosmopolitan is a person who is alienated from primary communal relationships and the parochial communities in which these inhere. A cosmopolitan is inclined toward intellectual pursuits and social perspectives that never penetrate the boundaries of local parochial communities. As Boehm suggests, problems may arise for cosmopolitans as a result of their tendency toward ideologically structured affiliations. Fanaticism and cultish commitment to ideologies may develop among persons released from participation in the immediate struggle for existence and from direct social responsibility. Cosmopolitanism, according to this account, is a form of social participation that leads to internationalism and revolutionary tendencies.

Along similar lines is Karl Mannheim's discussion of the *"freischwebende Intelligenz,"* a classless group of intellectuals that exists in modern as well as traditional societies.[6] Writers, artists, and others who constitute this group are described as unattached to local communities, and in association with others from the whole range of strata in society. Robert Bierstedt, taking his lead from Mannheim, viewed academicians as a highly (geographically) mobile group of persons, who, as a consequence, do not strive to conform to the class criteria of their local communities of residence and employment.[7] Academicians, and others whose careers follow a similar pattern of mobility and participation in nationally and internationally based organizations, are disposed toward more ecumenical social concerns. An academic discipline is both a national association and part of a larger community of science and scholarship in which persons may seek to gain recognition as an alternative to pursuit of status conferred within local communities. A key characteristic of cosmopolitans identified by Boehm, Mannheim, and Bierstedt is status involvement that transcends the boundaries of a local community.

A distinction between localism and cosmopolitanism is implicit in many discussions of industrialization, urbanization, and modernization, and is anticipated in typology construction in line with Tönnies' *Gemeinschaft* and *Gesellschaft*. In 1938, Carle Zimmerman used the local–cosmopolitan distinction to analyze rural communities.[8] The meaning of the distinction in this context is close to what Tönnies appears to have intended, i.e., an antinomy of extremes in social relations as they tend toward intimacy or formality.

It was Robert K. Merton, who first established the usage of localism and cosmopolitanism as alternative personal styles.[9] Merton distinguished between two

---

[5] Max Hildebert Boehm, "Cosmopolitanism," in *Encyclopaedia of the Social Sciences*, Edwin R. A. Seligman (ed.) (New York: Macmillan, 1931), pp. 457–461.

[6] Karl Mannheim, *Ideology and Utopia* (New York: Harcourt-Brace, 1936), pp. 136–146, *passim.*

[7] Robert Bierstedt, *The Social Order* (New York: McGraw-Hill, 1963), p. 463 *et seq.*

[8] Carle Zimmerman, *The Changing Community* (New York: Harpers, 1938).

[9] Merton, *loc. cit.*

patterns of influence he observed in a study of a small Eastern seaboard city. Merton's 1942 study identified one basis of influence in intimate knowledge of fellow residents of "Rovere." The local influentials' understanding and involvement with local issues and people were extensive. According to Merton, however, local influentials tended to confine their interests to the local community, which for them established boundaries of the social world. The cosmopolitan influentials, in contrast, were regarded not for the number of people they knew but the *kinds* of people they knew. Their contacts tended to be extra-local as were the issues on which they exercised influence.

A local–cosmopolitan pattern was for Merton a serendipitous discovery. Before applying this distinction, participation in voluntary associations, interaction patterns, and geographic mobility appeared unrelated. Under the rubric of this conceptual distinction, they could be seen as expressions of a more encompassing pattern of social participation. Holding educational level and occupational status constant, the local–cosmopolitan pattern of difference persisted. Merton concluded that alternative styles of utilizing status, not status *per se*, distinguished local and cosmopolitan influentials.

In the early 1950's, Gregory P. Stone and William Form conducted a study of status arrangements within a small Michigan town (population 10,000).[10] Their findings demonstrated that cosmopolitan influence may disrupt and complicate a local status order. The pattern of cosmopolitanism reported in their "Vansburg" study was sufficiently encompassing to be conceptualized by Stone as a life-style differentiating dimension.[11] The investigation in Vansburg was conducted at a time when the social order of the town was altered by the establishment of a branch plant of a national firm. In addition, the local newspaper editorship was assumed by a "cosmopolite." These events produced a status struggle between the local elite and the invading "outsiders." The effect on the local status structure was a bifurcation at the top. The established local upper class was threatened by the presence of "organization men" and their wives, who either ignored or challenged the status claims of leading indigenous residents. Townspeople were faced with alternative models of status and style. Within a short time after their arrival, the cosmopolitan invaders became an object of emulation and respect for at least a minority of the town's residents. The urbane ways of the cosmopolitan invaders gained greatest following among teenagers and young adults who apparently found the newly visible cosmopolitan life-style a marked improvement over the provincial and prudish style of local notables.

These newcomers to Vansburg, Stone reported, dressed in conformity to national and international styles rather than local patterns of dress, tended to drink alcoholic beverages publicly, rather than privately as the locals did, and formed social relationships that did not conform to the preexisting local status order. These traits marked them as *stylistically* different from localities. This type, moreover, could be distinguished on the basis of broader perspective, e.g., preference for newspaper coverage of national and international rather than local news. Ultimate victory of the status competition was not determined by the time the Vans-

---

[10] Gregory P. Stone and William H. Form, "Instabilities in Status: The Problem of Hierarchy in the Study of Status Arrangements," *American Sociological Review*, 17 (1953), pp. 149–162.

[11] Gregory P. Stone, "Comments on Careers and Consumer Behavior," in Lincoln H. Clark (ed.), *Consumer Behavior: The Life Cycle and Consumer Behavior,* II (New York: New York University Press, 1955), pp. 21–27.

burg study was terminated. The cosmopolitans, however, clearly were the more powerful group, representing corporate interests that controlled the jobs of some localities and affected significantly the economy of the town, which in turn affected nearly everyone. C. Wright Mills has predicted the outcome of such status struggles in his *White Collar*.[12] As power becomes more centralized, so also does status. The cosmopolitans in Vansburg had their status grounded in power with which the locals could not compete.

In a reanalysis of his Vansburg data, Stone found both status and localism–cosmopolitanism are related to life style differentiation. Local status placement of all respondents was established through use of Warner's Index of Status Characteristics.[13] Drinking clubs were stratified within the local status order and ranged from upper class to lower class. Only when interviewees identified as cosmopolitan were removed from the total sample was status a good predictor of participation in drinking clubs, i.e., there was congruence between the clubs' status and the status of their participants.[14] Cosmopolitans, however, tended to affiliate with respect to local status. I.S.C. scores for cosmopolitans showed them to be poor status matches to their club affiliations. Two things become clear from Stone's studies: First, some people were constrained by the local status order and others were not. Hierarchical differentiation within a local community is only one dimension of which life-style variation is a function. In moving beyond conventional hierarchical conceptions of social structure, a dimension of local–cosmopolitan differentiation of life-styles emerges as significant. Second, the local population was not a homogeneous consensual validator of status. Physical presence within a local place is no guarantee of perceptual attendance to its collective representations, its norms, or its status bestowals.

Stone proposed that localism–cosmopolitanism be viewed as a *horizontal* dimension of life-style differentiation. Although stylistically different, locals and cosmopolitans are regarded as members of the same stratum when placed either in a local status order or a national socio-economic order. A cross-cutting local–cosmopolitan variable can be added as a potentially explanatory variable in accounting for specific or patterned behavioral differences. Cosmopolitans may be thought of as participants in national or international status aggregates rather than local status groups.[15] Nationally shared life-styles develop and diffuse through the mass media, but their distribution is variable rather than uniform. Thus, localism–cosmopolitanism may be regarded as a differentiating dimension rather than a homogenizing trend toward a "middle majority life-style." The latter suggestion is made explicit by Riesman and Rosenborough, but is a commonplace notion found in both sociological and popular literature.[16]

Approximately at the time of Stone and Form's study, Gresham Sykes, in an investigation of the distribution of community knowledge, found that the proportion

[12] C. Wright Mills, *White Collar* (New York: Oxford University Press, 1956), p. 48, *passim*. Another insightful analysis of the rising new middle class is that of William H. Whyte, Jr., *The Organization Man* (Garden City: Doubleday, 1956), p. 307, *passim*.
[13] Cf. W. Lloyd Warner, *et al.*, *Social Class in America* (Chicago: Science Research Associates, 1949).
[14] Gregory P. Stone, "Drinking Styles and Status Arrangements," in David J. Pittman and Charles R. Snyder (eds.), *Society, Culture, and Drinking Patterns* (New York: Wiley, 1962), pp. 121–140.
[15] The concepts, "status group" and "status aggregate" are differentiated by Stone and Form in, "Instabilities in Status," *op. cit.*
[16] David Riesman, *Abundance for What? and Other Essays* (Garden City: Doubleday, 1964), pp. 113–137.

of persons in his sample scoring high in community knowledge increased with educational attainment through the high school graduate level.[17] Sykes found a tendency for the highest educational level (college and beyond) to include persons whose orientation was toward the social world beyond the local community. Their knowledge of community affairs was less than that of those just below them in educational attainment. William Dobriner, in a study of suburban Huntington, Long Island, found a similar pattern of extra-local orientation, that failed to disappear when controls were applied for age, sex, and income.[18] Greater duration of residence was found to be associated with localistic orientation. Geographical immobility disposes persons toward provincialism of life-style and perspective, but whether geographical mobility so readily results in "mental mobility" is not determined by these and similar local community case studies.

A more specialized usage of localism–cosmopolitanism is provided by Alvin Gouldner's study of academicians, as they participate in their hiring organization and academic associations.[19] Gouldner conceptualized localism and cosmopolitanism as latent organizational identities which dispose academicians toward different patterns of participation in a local college where they are employed. In his study of Antioch College, Gouldner distinguished two subtypes of cosmopolitans and four subtypes of locals. The cosmopolitans were classified as "outsiders" and "empire builders." Among the locals were the "dedicated," "bureaucrats," "homeguard," and "elders." Local types were distinguished from cosmopolitan types in terms of (i) greater loyalty to their hiring organization, (ii) less commitment to professional skills, and (iii) reference group orientation within rather than outside of the college community. Local–cosmopolitan identification was found to be predictive of (i) influence patterns, (ii) participation in the college, (iii) propensity to accept or reject organizational rules, and (iv) informal associations. Some of the locals were more committed to the community of residence than the organization of employment, and were willing to subvert organizational goals in an effort to accommodate to community pressures. Other locals confined their interest to the college. Cosmopolitans, in contrast, were primarily oriented to the goals of research and scholarship fostered by their larger academic and scientific communities.

Cosmopolitans were in a situation of stress. The organization did not support but competed with their scholarly-scientific ambitions and commitments. Gouldner's study characterized the problem of a cosmopolitan within a provincial locality, and raised some problems of conceptualization and measurement. His indicators of cosmopolitanism were appropriate to his data, but not necessarily useful in differentiating locals from cosmopolitans within a cosmopolitan social milieu. A recent study by Barney Glazer is relevant to the problem of conceptualization and measurement.[20] From his study of research scientists in a "high prestige re-

---

[17] Gresham M. Sykes, "The Differential Distribution of Community Knowledge," *Social Forces,* 29 (1951), pp. 376–382.
[18] William M. Dobriner, "Local and Cosmopolitan as Contemporary Suburban Character Types," in William M. Dobriner (ed.), *The Suburban Community,* (New York: G. P. Putnam, 1958), pp. 132–143.
[19] Alvin W. Gouldner, "Cosmopolitans and Locals: Toward An Analysis of Latent Social Roles," *Administrative Science Quarterly,* 2 (1957–1958), pp. 281–306, 444–448. See also Louis C. Goldberg, Frank Baker, and Arthur H. Rubenstein, "Local–Cosmopolitan: Unidimensional or Multidimensional?" *American Journal of Sociology,* 70 (May 1965), pp. 704–710.
[20] Barney G. Glazer, *Organizational Scientists: Their Professional Careers* (Indianapolis: Bobbs-Merrill, 1964), p. 121.

search organization," Glazer concluded that cosmopolitanism and localism are, for highly motivated scientists, dual orientations that vary independently. A local–cosmopolitan conflict derives from a conflict between the goals of science and the goals of the organization in which scientists are employed. There need be personal conflict only so long as there is goal conflict; but it is possible, as Glazer's data demonstrate, for the local organization to support and share in the goals of science.

Glazer is correct in his assertion that local and cosmopolitan commitments may vary independently. The reason is that places and organizations as well as individuals vary on a local–cosmopolitan continuum. Independent variation of organizational commitment and academic commitment does not mean that a person ceases to be cosmopolitan when he moves from a provincial to a cosmopolitan organizational milieu. He continues to be cosmopolitan in orientation and style. Cosmopolitan proclivities may become accentuated where they are reinforced with appreciation and approval. Localites, or more specifically social structures of localites, vary in their propensity to foster provincialism. Variation of organizations and other social structures in cosmopolitanism, however, has been obscured by the frequent use of a case study method.

Some Assessments and Observations

Alternative modes of participating in a complex social world are contrasted in the terms local and cosmopolitan. This was implied by Robert Merton's use of the terms to describe influentials, who act in some cases as intermediaries and interpreters of a larger human community to fellow residents of their town. Gresham Sykes and others substantiate Merton's observation that persons who sink their roots into a community may come to disregard the society beyond. Sykes explained an apparent anomaly that the best educated are not the best informed of local affairs by pointing to their extra-local social participation. Events in the microcosm are of less interest to some persons than events in the larger social world.

Gouldner's analysis of latent organizational identities demonstrates that place of work as well as place of residence may become a focus of attachment. Affiliations in this context readily may be examined in terms of the scale of the social environment with which persons identify and in terms of which they identify themselves.[21] The boundaries of any social unit whether household, neighborhood, organization, city, or society may serve to mark the limit to which the mental horizons of its members extend. This procedure identifies locals and cosmopolitans only very imperfectly. Cosmopolitanism is better established through delineating a boundary of social space that marks minimal scope regarded as cosmopolitan. For this reason I take the national community rather than a local community as a point of reference, and arbitrarily consider cosmopolitan orientation as attending to events and processes of at least national scope. To do otherwise misses certain types of parochialism completely.

Mobility and migration, it seems, do not always serve to broaden horizons. One parochial type, whose mobility is *only* geographical, can be termed the "mobile local." He may be an organization man of commerce and industry or a career

---

[21] Thomas R. Dye, "The Local–Cosmopolitan Dimension and the Study of Urban Politics," *Social Forces*, 42 (March, 1963), p. 239. See also Daniel J. Elazer and Douglas St. Angelo, "Cosmopolitans and Locals in Contemporary Politics," *Proceedings*, Minnesota Academy of Science, 31 (1964), pp. 171–178.

military man, whose career takes him from one local outpost of his organizational community to another. His interaction pattern, regardless of where he is stationed geographically, hardly varies, and he may never acquire the broader orientation thought of as cosmopolitan. A second parochial type, the "global local," is exceedingly mobile. He may be exemplified by the sectarian missionary who is an international traveler but symbolically never leaves the confines of the sect. His community defies precise geographical delimitation, although he and his sectarian group are parochial in the extreme. A third type of local, who is missed in case studies of small communities in which outside orientation is equated with cosmopolitan organization, is the "other local." The other local's roots are attached to a distinct locality, "back home." He may reside in Chicago but never sever his ties with Peoria, which he identifies as his hometown when the question is put to him. This reference relationship may become somewhat mythical over a period of time, but it is never abandoned. The other local may be forced to spend his life away from home, but in the end he may arrange to be buried there. In his place of residence, which is never his hometown, he assumes the stance of a "colonizer" toward an outpost of civilization. He depends upon his ties with home to comfort and sustain him in a hostile environment. Yet another type of local is the "neolocal," whose ties with a community of orientation are temporary. He becomes convinced after a period of time that the new neighbors, the new P.T.A., and so forth are superior to the old. He shifts his allegiance and becomes converted in his orientation from one microcosm to another. These types are familiar but easily can be obscured in equating localism with attachment to a particular locality and cosmopolitanism with its absence.

Not all outsiders are cosmopolitan and not all insiders are local. Whether membership status with regard to a particular group constitutes localism or cosmopolitanism is entirely dependent upon the character of that group. The meaning of affiliation with *any* group, whether geographically dispersed or locally specific, must be sought in terms of that group's variably local or cosmopolitan character. Investigation of local–cosmopolitan differentiation must take account simultaneously of variation in the individual's breadth of perspective and the variation in scope and style of the social milieux in which he is located.

Because studies of localism–cosmopolitanism have been limited to specific localities and to specific behavior patterns, a compilation of empirical findings fails to answer a fundamental question: Is the broad range of behavior which has been analyzed in local–cosmopolitan terms a general life-style difference or a specific behavior pattern which has little or no relevance beyond the scope in which it is reported? It is useful to discover, for example, whether persons who are cosmopolitan by virtue of their professional-occupational participation are also cosmopolitan with regards to consumption patterns—tastes and preferences popularly regarded as *avant garde*. Is cosmopolitanism–localism a life-style differentiating dimension on a horizontal axis, as suggested by Stone, or a term that obscures more specific variables whose empirical referents should be made more specific?

Some Findings from a Study of Academicians

Here some findings are reported in order to further specify answers to general questions raised in the preceding discussion. These questions concern use of the polarity and its empirical referents, i.e., whether localism–cosmopolitanism constitutes a general dimension of life-style differentiation or several more specific dimensions of variation. Questionnaire data were obtained from a sample of academicians from each of four liberal arts colleges and a large public university. The hiring organizations were selected in order to capture variation of organizational milieux in terms of the local cosmopolitan polarity.

Colleges are identified as Colleges A, B, C, and D, from most to least provincial. The milieu of College A is especially provincial. It is sect-controlled and sectarian oriented. College B is church-affiliated but considerably less parochial. It recently has become more secular and heterogeneous in student and faculty composition. College C is less provincial than either A or B, but less cosmopolitan than College D. College D most closely approximates the cosmopolitan university. Assessment of the colleges initially was based on general impression and two objective measures which corroborate this impression. The more cosmopolitan the college, the greater the proportion of its faculty with Ph.D. degrees, and the less the proportion of its faculty who are graduates and former students. This may be seen in Table 1.

TABLE 1   Sample Characteristics

	College [b]				
	A	B	C	D	University
Student enrollment [a]	966	2,300	1,250	1,770	36,000
Faculty size [a]	84	125	88	167	2,486
Proportion Ph.D.[a]	23%	26%	26%	42%	65%
Proportion of own grads on faculty [a]	18%	32%	36%	14%	———[c]
Location	Midwest	Pac. Coast	Midwest	Midwest	Midwest
Data collection	Mailed	Personal interview	Personal interview	Personal interview	Mailed
Proportion sampled	100%	100%	100%	50% [d]	15% [e]
Proportion returned	64%	70%	84%	73%	62%
Proportion of universe returned	64%	70%	84%	38%	11%

[a] Source of data: organizational publications.
[b] Order of organizations from College A to University represents variation from most local to most cosmopolitan.
[c] Data were not available.
[d] Quota sample.
[e] Probability sample.

Faculty members at each of the hiring organizations were administered three scales designed to measure localism–cosmopolitanism. The first, the life-style and perspective (LSP) index, is composed of 25 statements expressing tastes, preferences, values, and beliefs, determined by a preliminary item analysis to differentiate persons who are stylistically cosmopolitan from those who stylistically are local.[22] The following statements constitute the LSP index. C and L designate cosmopolitan and local proclivities respectively.

1. I am opposed to censoring books and plays. (C)
2. The United States should stop giving money to countries which don't outlaw Communism. (L)

22 Gerald Thielbar, "Localism–Cosmopolitanism: Social Differentiation in Mass Society," unpublished Ph.D. dissertation, University of Minnesota, 1966.

3. I would like to live in Paris for two or three years. (C)
4. Above everything else, friendly neighbors make a good town. (L)
5. I wish we could teach the American Way of Life to all of the underprivileged people of the world so they would be more like us. (L)
6. There is a case for legalized prostitution. (C)
7. It's nicer to live in a small town than a big city. (L)
8. Nice ladies never smoke on the street. (L)
9. These days it makes more sense to think of yourself as a citizen of the world rather than a citizen of the country. (C)
10. Some of the immoral movies around here should never be shown. (L)
11. The national debt is similar to the individual's personal debt and should be paid off as soon as possible. (L)
12. I prefer a newspaper that has lots of local news items. (L)
13. I feel it's all right for Christians and Jews to intermarry. (C)
14. We ought to put a stop to the teaching of radical and irreligious ideas on University campuses. (L)
15. I make (or serve) a good dry martini. (C)
16. I wish there were an authentic Siamese or Thai restaurant in town so I could try it. (C)
17. Homosexuals are a menace to society. (L)
18. I like to have wine with my dinner. (C)
19. I think universities *are* more important than churches in setting the pattern of city life. (C)
20. I like foreign movies. (C)
21. Most of the problems of this country would be solved if people would only turn to religion. (L)
22. I have either eaten snails or I would like to try them. (C)
23. There ought to be a law against nudists. (L)
24. I like popular music played on the electric organ. (L)
25. I prefer homeowners to apartment dwellers. (L)

The second measure, the Community Reference (CR) index, purports to measure directly the scale of the social world to which people are oriented, i.e., the local community versus some larger community.[23] The third measure, the organizational reference (OR) index, is based on an assumption of competing commitments to hiring organization or profession and was adapted from Alvin Gouldner's factor analytic study of organizational localism–cosmopolitanism.[24] A comparison

---

[23] Dye, *op. cit.*, p. 241. The CR index statements are as follows:
  1. The most rewarding organizations a person can belong to are local clubs and associations rather than large nation-wide organizations.
  2. Despite all the newspaper and TV coverage, national and international happenings rarely seem as interesting as events that occur right in the local community in which one lives.
  3. No doubt many newcomers in the community are capable people, but when it comes to choosing a person for a responsible position in the community, I prefer a man whose family is well established in the community.
  4. Big cities may have their place but the local community is the backbone of America.
  5. I have greater respect for a man who is well established in the local community than for a man who is widely known in his field but has no local roots.
[24] Gouldner, *op. cit.*, pp. 444–448. The OR index statements are as follows:
  1. It is unfortunate but true that there are very few people around here with whom one can share his professional interests.

of mean scores on these measures for the five samples, shown in Table 2, demonstrated that the more cosmopolitan the hiring organization, the more cosmopolitan are its employees in terms of community reference, life-style and perspective.

TABLE 2   *Local–Cosmopolitan Organizational Variation*

Organization	LSP		CR		OR	
	$\overline{X}$	S.D.	$\overline{X}$	S.D.	$\overline{X}$	S.D.
University (n = 122)	119.1	18.8	25.6	5.4	39.5	5.8
College D (n = 62)	118.6	16.7	25.4	4.4	38.0	6.0
College C (n = 74)	108.6	17.8	23.6	4.1	38.3	5.7
College B (n = 86)	97.9	18.9	22.8	4.6	40.2	5.9
College A (n = 54)	97.7	18.3	22.4	4.8	38.3	6.1
F Ratio: [a]	26.96		7.94		2.12	
	$p < .001$		$p < .001$		$p > .10$ (N.S.)	

[a] All findings are assessed in terms of a .10 level of statistical significance. It is unwise to reject potentially fruitful theory on the basis of too rigorous criteria. Conversely, it makes good sense to grant tentative acceptance liberally to propositions that subsequently may be researched. I.e., this procedure avoids rejecting "true" hypotheses, a strategy appropriate to the initial phases of inquiry.

The occupational reference index deviated from the general pattern established by the other two measures. Both variation between samples and direct correlation with other measures of localism–cosmopolitanism give an impression that the Gouldnerian conception of professional cosmopolitanism is independent of cosmopolitan life-style or community reference. That this impression is false is demonstrated in Table 3. There is a tendency for the OR index to correlate more highly with the other two measures of localism–cosmopolitanism for the samples drawn at the more provincial organizations. For the university sample, there appears to be a low positive correlation between organizational localism and a more broadly conceived cosmopolitanism. The reason for this becomes clear in examining the relationship between cosmopolitanism and mobility orientation, as shown in Table 4. Cosmopolitans employed by a cosmopolitan university are less likely to entertain the idea of changing jobs than are their local colleagues. Cosmopolitans are especially mobility-oriented when employed by provincial organizations where

2. Students (at College X) should take a bit more interest in course content and somewhat less interest in its application to their personal problems.
3. A satisfying academic job provides time for personal research and scholarship.
4. Faculty members (at College X) should have their loads lightened in order to make more time available for research.
5. There is no need for a chapter of the American Association of University Professors (AAUP) at X College.
6. Although there are probably reasons for it, it is too bad that faculty salaries here at X College are so low.
7. One of the important ways people are kept in line around here is through gossip.
8. After all, since X College is an educational institution, more of the decision making should rest with the teaching faculty.
9. Even though they are competent, somehow or other one gets little intellectual stimulation from one's colleagues here.

TABLE 3   *Correlation Coefficients Measuring the Relationships Among Community Reference, Life-Style and Perspective, and Occupational Reference*

Sample	CR/LSP	LSP/OR	CR/OR
College A	.66	.26	.14 *
College B	.71	.62	.48
College C	.55	.32	.21
College D	.70	.26	.32
University	.68	−.06 *	−.08 *
Combined samples	.69	.29	.17

* r is not significant at .10 level.

it is the locals who want to remain. Cosmopolitans, it appears, are likely to establish friendship ties with organizational colleagues if those colleagues are like themselves in life-style. Cosmopolitans are likely to establish bonds with their organizations of employment if the organizational milieux are congenial to their own personal life-style and perspective.

TABLE 4   *Associations Among LSP, CR, and Mobility Orientation* *

Sample	LSP	CR
College A	+	+
College B	.54	.46
	.10 > p < .01	.10 > p < .01
College C ᵃ	+	.24
		.30 > p > .10
University	.17 **	.05 **
	.30 > p > .10	.30 > p > .20

* Chi-square computations, unless otherwise indicated, are based on 2 by 3 tables. Categories of response: Agree, Don't Know, Disagree, in response to, "Barring unforeseen changes, I will remain at my present position permanently."
ᵃ "Don't know" and "Disagree" combined.
** Reverse direction.

These findings demonstrate a tendency toward a selective process in which cosmopolitan persons find their way to cosmopolitan organizational milieux, while the locals do the reverse. Or alternatively, persons may be "converted" by their situations and bring their orientations into line with their surroundings. Organizations of employment, because recruitment and selection of employees are selective processes, may create dominantly local or cosmopolitan milieux. Cosmopolitan organizations become arenas of interaction for cosmopolitans just as cosmopolitan places that provide amenities of cosmopolitan life-style become such arenas of interaction.[25] Both organizations and places may become dominantly local or cosmopolitan, but organizations because of the control which they exercise over personnel recruitment may more effectively manipulate their own milieux. In addition a certain amount of inter-organizational movement is self-selective. Universities, like cities, establish reputations as provincial or cosmopolitan. There seems

[25] In an unreported study, the writer in collaboration with Gregory P. Stone, used the following magazines as indicators of cosmopolitanism: *Saturday Review, The New Yorker, The New Republic,* and *Playboy.* The forty most populous metropolitan areas in the U.S. were ranked in terms of cosmopolitanism based on the *per capita* circulation rates of these magazines. Washington, D.C., New York, and San Francisco were shown to be the most cosmopolitan.

to be a self-selection of migrants to places such as the San Francisco Bay area. People attracted by its cosmopolitan reputation reinforce its cosmopolitanism if only by virtue of a self-fulfilling prophecy. The same process appears to operate among academic hiring organizations.

These findings demonstrate what was suspected, i.e., both persons and places vary in localism–cosmopolitanism. Moreover, support was found for the interpretation that localism–cosmopolitanism represents an encompassing dimension of life-style differentiation. Those persons who are cosmopolitan by virtue of their style of consumption and conduct, e.g., in preference for wine with dinner and tolerance for deviants, are cosmopolitan in their professional orientation. Those persons who drink and serve a good dry martini tend to be the same persons who are academically productive. We see this in Table 5.

TABLE 5   *Cosmopolitanism Associated with Academic Productivity and Expected Productivity* [a]

Total and Sub-samples	Number of Papers Presented or Published [b]		Expected Future Academic Productivity [c]	
	LSP	CR	LSP	CR
Combined samples [d]	.20	+	.36	.24
	$.10 > p > .05$		$.10 > p < .001$	$.10 > p < .001$
College A	+	−	+	+
College B	−	−	+	+
College C [e]	.30	.22	.35	+
	$.10 > p < .05$	$.30 > p > .10$	$.10 > p < .02$	
College D [e]	.33	.36	+	.39
	$.10 > p < .05$	$.10 > p > .01$		$.10 > p < .05$
University	.24	+	.45	.14
	$.10 > p > .05$		$.10 > p < .001$	$.30 > p > .10$
Men	.17	+	.37	.26
	$.10 > p < .05$		$.10 > p < .01$	$.10 > p < .01$
Women	.14	+	.30	.26
	$.30 > p > .20$		$.10 > p < .02$	$.10 > p < .02$
Ages:				
20–35	.20	+	.32	.22
	$.10 > p < .05$		$.10 > p < .01$	$.10 > p < .05$
36–50	+	+	.26	.24
			$.10 > p < .05$	$.10 > p < .05$
Over 50	.42	.33	.46	.40
	$.10 > p < .001$	$.10 > p < .01$	$.10 > p < .001$	$.10 > p < .001$

[a] Coefficients reported are Cramer's V, based on chi–square. Cf. Hubert Blalock, *Social Statistics* (New York: McGraw-Hill, 1960), p. 230.
[b] Unless otherwise indicated, chi–square computations are based on 2 by 3 tables; number of papers categorized as none, one or two, 3 or more.
[c] Unless otherwise indicated, chi–square computations are based on 2 by 3 tables; expected productivity categorized as none or very little, moderate amount, a good deal.
[d] Number of papers categorized as none, 1–2, 3–4, 5 or more.
[e] Moderate amount and good deal combined.

Cosmopolitanism, data from this investigation show, varies somewhat according to age but not according to sex. There is an indication that older persons are somewhat less cosmopolitan than younger persons. The peak of cosmopolitanism occurs in the age range twenty to thirty-five. This pattern may be related to both changes in career and family patterns. Family and job ties, it is hypothesized, may both strengthen local ties for persons at approximately age thirty-five. It can be seen from these data, however, that local–cosmopolitan differentiation occurs for persons of all ages represented by respondents. In some cases the concomitants of this variation are especially marked for older persons. This can be seen in the case of academic productivity. It is persons over fifty for whom greatest difference between locals and cosmopolitans was found in expectation of future publication.

Differences were observed in localism–cosmopolitanism according to academic discipline of respondents. Cosmopolitans are concentrated most heavily in the social sciences, followed by the humanities. Among the strictly academic disciplines, "hard science" disciplines and mathematics are most local, while persons in less academic disciplines such as home economics and physical education are least cosmopolitan of all. It appears that some fields develop cosmopolitan academic associations that attract cosmopolitans or socialize their members to become cosmopolitan.

Support was generally found for the hypothesis that local and cosmopolitan organizational identities occur within academic organizations. Locals and cosmopolitans differ in productivity and commitment to professional skills. When a qualification is added that cosmopolitans seek to leave local organizations and locals seek to leave cosmopolitan organizations, there is difference in mobility orientation as well. Evidence provided by the life-style and perspective index, however, indicates that localism–cosmopolitanism extends beyond the work place. Cosmopolitanism encompasses professional orientation, community reference, and life-style and perspective. Localism and cosmopolitanism are broad social orientations that have ramifications for a wide range of activities.

Concomitant with variation in these three aspects of cosmopolitanism, viz., professional orientation, greater interest and involvement in national and international affairs, and urbane tastes and consumption patterns are other ramifications which were explored. Findings support a conclusion that localism and cosmopolitanism constitute social orientations or belief systems. Among the attitudinal correlates of localism is authoritarianism. Localism, in addition, is positively associated with religious belief, conventional morality, and alienation from the larger social world.[26]

Association between localism and alienation from the larger social world may seem almost tautological. One may sensibly ask if these are not alternative conceptualizations of the same phenomenon. The answer, of course, depends upon conceptualization and measurement. Logically, estrangement from something is different both from involvement with it and a condition of neither estrangement nor involvement. Thus persons who confine their participation to a small social space are not necessarily estranged from the larger social world. They may merely disregard it. Evidence indicates, however, that this is not the case.

The larger social world is not ignored by locals but their interpretation of it is strikingly different from that of cosmopolitans. Locals tend to personalize the impersonal, e.g., structured institutionalized processes and intergroup relations. For locals, the national debt is similar to the individual's personal debt, international relations tend to be interpreted as interpersonal relations, and so forth. They in-

---

[26] Pearsonian r between cosmopolitanism and authoritarianism is −.69 for the College B sample to which F Scale items were administered. Correlation between religious belief and cosmopolitanism for the combined five samples is −.42. Association between localism and conventional morality is .59 (Cramer's V based on chi-square for a two by two table).

dicate bad government is a matter of personal responsibility and that individuals are able to do a good deal to improve world opinion of the United States. That the locals' personalized view of the larger social world is not satisfactory for them is evidenced in their tendency to find international relations confusing and to feel "helpless in the face of what is happening in the world today." [27]

Cosmopolitans seem to be both more comfortable and more realistic in their approach to the larger social world. They are less optimistic than locals concerning personal political effectiveness, but appear to be neither apathetic nor estranged. Locals, perhaps, are not secure in their provincialism. Cosmopolitans, on the contrary, seem to be oriented to a world of "structural" relations and to feel at home in such a context. The local's pattern of social participation is confined to primary interpersonal relations and he may rely almost exclusively on interpersonal norms in his interpretation of society. A logical analysis of alienation indicates that cosmopolitans as well as locals may be alienated or anomic. They may be alienated from primary social ties and suffer an interpersonal normlessness, along lines suggested by Durkheim.[28] Some evidence is found for this both in the alienation scale and on an anomie measure which was administered.[29] Although the anomie scale is constructed so that these two forms of anomie are indistinguishable, an item analysis permitted separation of these, i.e., alienation from the larger social world and primary social ties.

The anomie scale shows locals to be anomic with regard to their orientation to the larger social world, but indicates, as well, that cosmopolitans experience anomie. Although cosmopolitans tend to reject an idea that people were better off in the old days when people knew just how to act, they are more inclined than locals to admit sometimes feeling awkward and out-of-place. Their mode of social participation may provide more occasion for dis-ease and awkwardness. Moreover, cosmopolitans more frequently than locals agree that other persons find it easier to decide what is right than they. Interpersonal relations are viewed by the extreme local in terms of a conventional morality that defines them as black or white. The cosmopolitan has rejected traditional morality and has no ready-made code to define his interpersonal relations. A profile of the cosmopolitan emerges as a person who is secular, tolerant, and *avant garde*, identified with a new morality and a new moral order. The local is conventional, moralistic, a personalizer, intolerant, and committed to a passing moral order.[30] Correlations of alienation and authoritarianism with localism show the local to be frustrated and apathetic with regard to the larger social world but finding security in the *Gemeinschaft*.

---

[27] This interpretation is based on an item analysis of items composing two scales, alienation and anomie. The alienation scale items were developed by Arthur C. Neal and Solomon Rettig, "Dimensions of Alienation Among Manual and Non-Manual Workers," *American Sociological Review*, 28 (1963), pp. 559–608. Anomie items were developed by Herbert McClosky and John H. Schaar, "Psychological Dimensions of Anomy," *American Sociological Review*, 30 (1965), pp. 14–40.

[28] Emile Durkheim, *Suicide* (Glencoe: Free Press, 1951).

[29] See footnote 27 above.

[30] My assessment that cosmopolitan values are on the ascendance is based on several observations: increased discussion and published debate regarding a "new morality," growth of science and secularism at the expense of religious dogma, and the observation that these trends particularly influence younger people who almost take cosmopolitan tolerance and internationalism for granted. Cosmopolitan culture may eventually become absorbed into the microcosm. The diffusion of cosmopolitan culture does not necessarily imply that everyone who is influenced by it becomes cosmopolitan.

Explanation of Localism–Cosmopolitanism

Localism–cosmopolitanism is not readily explained in terms of structural conditions. The academicians studied have available to them avenues of social participation in the social world beyond their community of residence and employment. Some of them take advantage of these and others do not. External barriers do not seem to account adequately for the pattern of provincialism observed. It is tempting then to invent psychologistic explanations, such as authoritarian personalities become locals. Explanation of localism–cosmopolitanism as a function of cognitive structure is tautological and based on an unwarranted assumption that behavior is the discharge of internal forces, drives, or motives.

A more thorough study of local–cosmopolitan differentiation may uncover structural conditions which dispose persons toward either local or cosmopolitan social participation. Locals and cosmopolitans are not randomly distributed but are linked by associational ties that have social location. Locals associate with locals and cosmopolitans with cosmopolitans, even though cosmopolitans sometimes pay additional costs in order to overcome propinquitous tendencies and sustain social relations with colleagues at a physical distance. These interactive networks sustain local and cosmopolitan patterns. Induction into these networks may best be studied by a longitudinal investigation which traces the careers of individuals. Currently the genesis of localism and cosmopolitanism as modes of social participation is somewhat obscure. Explanation is limited to identifying the covariation of behavior patterns, i.e., specific manifestations of localism such as intolerance are made more comprehensible by linking them with a more general pattern of which they are a part. In this sense anomie or authoritarianism is explained as a response pattern of persons with a local mode of social participation. Conversely, tolerance for deviations from conventional morality is explained as a characteristic of cosmopolitan social participation. The local–cosmopolitan pattern of differentiation itself becomes an explanation of behavioral variations just as stratification may be used to explain specific behavioral differences.

Conclusion

In their effort to apprehend life-style differentiations within complex society, sociologists have most frequently appealed to the principle of hierarchy, seeking to delineate a vertical ordering of social positions. Irrefutable evidence has established the principle of vertical ordering, although the application of this principle to complex society remains problematic. Status stratification occurs within social orders or interactive networks. Interactive networks which give rise to status stratification are multiple, and boundaries are not always clear. Some status communities are provincial and locality bound, others are dispersed or global. In this complex situation, some persons limit their participation to microcosmic status orders and others extend their social participation beyond them to larger social spheres. A local–cosmopolitan conceptualization of horizontal differentiation orders this complexity. Status involvements of at least national scope are shown to be anchored in a pattern of life-style and perspective that is distinct from and, in some respects, the polar opposite of the life-style and perspective of persons with more limited status involvements. The major conclusion here is that localism–cosmopolitanism is a life-style differentiating dimension. The local communtiy and the larger social world provide alternative foci of social involvement. Local and cosmopolitan modes of social participation come to be anchored in contrasting modes of life-style and perspective.

Qualification or extension of this conceptual framework awaits further investigation. Indications are, from the review of a range of investigations, that the conceptual scheme will prove to be useful for the analysis of social participation in complex society. Research implications include the study of family units as well as individuals, and cities as well as organizations. This line of investigation follows from a more general commitment that complex societies are structured according to links of communication and interaction. It is the structuring of these that gives rise to life-style variation, and it is the investigation of these patterns which will provide better understanding of social life in a complex industrial society.

PART FIVE
INTERACTION PROCESSES

We have seen that interpretation is the core process of interaction. As Blumer so often has noted, we do not respond automatically to stimuli, but rather cogitate, analyze, judge, and then react. The stimulus can be an idea, thing, or individual; no matter what, we come to some kind of decision regarding its possible meaning for us before we assume a posture toward it.

Lest we imagine, however, that interpretation is an abstract, detached process, we should remember that it occurs within particular joint acts. Interpretation is as much embedded in acts of mutual aggression, sarcasm, and hatred, as in acts of agreement, friendship, and love. Moreover, each kind of joint act probably affects the process and outcome of interpretation differently; exactly how is in question. Any answer presupposes the ability to identify the properties of the different forms of action.

There is little doubt that different forms of action contain different recognizable dispositional qualities that are invariant and convey the actors' intention or purpose. For example, as Miyamoto notes, hardly anyone would confuse very hostile from very friendly communicative acts. But what is it about these types of acts that allows us to interpret them and respond to them appropriately? Is it possible that hostile and friendly communicative acts are based on completely different vocabularies, vocal intonations, rhythmic patterns, breathing phrases, body gestures, eye movements, or whatever?

How do we know, for example, when to take someone seriously or humorously? When do pejorative epithets indicate friendship, as opposed to antagonism? Successful analysis of this sort may well allow us to generate a typology of acts based on their formal invariant properties. To insure the relevance of such a classificatory scheme, it probably should be based on action forms recognized in everyday interaction and related to particular social settings so that inferences concerning their function would be easier to make.

To be sure, we react to *how* something is presented to us. Moreover, our re-action probably occurs along both cognitive and affective lines. None will deny, for example, Simmel's contention that there is a discernible relationship between the sound of a voice and the meaning of an utterance. We feel ripples of excita-tion or rubbery limbs as we react to the tone of someone's voice. Or again, who can describe adequately those moments of transcendent ecstasy, when time and place fall away, as one looks deeply and searchingly into the eyes of his love? We reach into the soul of the other as we give up our own in the exchange of glances. But who among us would rush in to decipher, in cognitive terms, the meaning, value, and sentiment of such ecstasy?

Indeed, the area of fellow-feeling, which bridges both affective and cognitive dimensions, crosscuts the process of interpretation. As another example, consider Scheler's typology of fellow-feeling, which describes the different ways individ-uals resonate in terms of emotions and moods. For example, *feeling in common* —a mother and father come together and share the anguish of burying their dead child; *feeling about something*—a close friend of the aggrieved parents commiser-ates with them; *mere emotional infection*—one enters a situation that is overcast with solemnity and tears and finds himself becoming depressed; and, finally, in the case of true *emotional identification*—we become one with the other and feel his feelings as our own.

The interpretation going on among the participants surely is influenced by factors of mood and emotion. We have already shown in Part Three how verbal, nonverbal, or contextual elements establish such dimensions. Consideration of factors that induce affect, and tend to qualify or even establish the substantive or cognitive aspects of interaction, leads to the fair assumption that, in many situations, our own *personal* purposes or intentions incline us to present stimuli in the most dramatic and compelling form possible in order to realize our own ends.

For example, if our intention is to shut someone out of a circle of conversa-tion, we might employ a sarcastic form of presentation. Although, as Ball con-tends, no communications are inherently sarcastic, most can be made to be sar-castic. A statement, joke, gesture, or allusion can be transformed from a mere communication into a sarcastic transaction by the parties involved, namely the producer, the target, and the audience. The actual use of sarcasm is restricted to higher status levels, where verbal facility is well developed and symbolic aggres-sion replaces physical assault; it is always used to control others through isola-tion, and the person isolated is not left in doubt as to how the interaction should be interpreted. By way of contrast, love may be considered a form of dramatic presentation aimed at including another over a long period of time without vio-lating his autonomy. According to Foote, love may be defined as that relation-ship between one person and another that is conducive to the optimal develop-ment of both. Optimal development means ever-increasing competence in inter-personal relations or the ability to respect and understand the other person enough to allow him to become what he can be. For the loved one to realize his potential, a critical but appreciative audience, comparatively equal in status and open for reciprocity, is ideal. The audience should be able to view the loved one as *ultimately incommensurable with any other,* thus able to take him on his own terms.

Whether our form of dramatic presentation be cutting with sarcasm or tender with love, the purpose is to let the other know just how he should interpret our communication. In large measure, just as our interpretation of the meaning, value, and sentiment brought into the interaction by the other will take into account the dramatic form in which it is presented, our definition for the other of the meaning, value, and sentiment brought by us will be conveyed, in part, by the form of our presentation.

In focusing on the forms of social acts, and their effects on the interpretation of the meanings of acts, we are beginning to probe into the methodology of communication. We are exploring strategies and tactics required to socialize our intentions and purposes in order to commit others to them. In this sense, forms of dramatic presentation and/or provocation may be considered tactics of appeal used in interpersonal control. The implied proposition is: People bring personal purposes into interaction, which they attempt to realize in lines of action, and employ particular forms of dramatic presentation to do so—that is, people *construct* lines of action.

Empirical investigation along these general lines comes from Weinstein and Deutschberger, who hypothesize that lines of action, which are meant to realize intentions or personal purposes and are thereby goal-directed, are "capable of being stated in terms of some response from other participants." To get others to behave as we wish requires casting them into particular identities that compel them into the desired lines of action. In their experimental approach to the dynamics of altercasting, the investigators tack down empirically some of the more abstract theorizing on the "self-indicating" individual so prominent in the work of Mead and Blumer.

Glaser and Strauss also deal with strategies and tactics of interaction in their examination of the relationship between awareness contexts and identity. Regardless of situation, the participants to an interaction sequence have more or less information about each other's identity. This information serves as a context that can be manipulated strategically. Four types of awareness contexts are discussed. An *open,* as opposed to a *closed,* context is one in which each participant is aware of the other's true identity, as well as his own identity from the other's point of view. A *suspicion* context prevails when one party suspects the identity of the other, and a *pretense* context occurs when both know each other's identity but pretend they do not. During the span of an interaction sequence, any context can be transformed into any other, depending on the information acquired.

Glaser and Strauss report on the manipulation of awareness contexts in the hospital situation. Patients for whom death is imminent may not be advised of the fact, because the hospital staff may believe that the patient is thereby spared stressful emotional scenes with friends and relatives. Accordingly, the manipulation of contexts points toward a more general proposition: by offering up (or withholding) information concerning possible future identities, control is gained over present conduct. Deliberate manipulation of awareness contexts may be seen, therefore, as a device for gaining control over interaction.

Now it should be made clear that interpretation is co-orientational. We take our *interpretation* of others' presentations into account before we resolve upon a line of action for ourselves. It is perfectly possible, therefore, that *our interpretation* of the meaning, value, and sentiment of the other's presentation is in error. We might very well undertake a line of action based on a false or unwarranted premise. Scheff considers this point when he probes into the theoretical possibilities of consensus, and finds it to be more complex than mere coordination of values.

Two approaches are identified: individual agreement and coordination. Scheff dismisses the individual agreement approach, for if consensus was the result of individuals actually agreeing on something, how could we explain the phenomenon of pluralistic ignorance? Here no one really agrees with a certain view, but everyone thinks that everyone else agrees, and behaves as though there were consensus. True agreement is lacking, but everyone thinks it obtains, and, in terms of effect, it does. The problem of "perceived consensus" underlines the mutual or interactive nature of consensus. Our own orientation to a view is conditioned by our *interpretation* of how others are oriented to it; accordingly, consensus is a matter of coorientation.

This insight opens up an exciting line of inquiry concerned with levels or *orders* of coorientation. Reference to the work of Schelling on bargaining situations, Durkheim on collective representations, and Garfinkel on background understanding, illustrates how the process of reciprocal reflection can generate emergent realities that may be construed as external and constraining on individuals. Scheff considers an interesting attempt by Laing, Phillipson, and Lee to operationalize levels of coorientation into agreement, understanding, and realization. If A and B independently give identical answers to the same question, there is *agreement*. If each is asked how the other would answer, and the answers turn out to be correct, there is *understanding*. Finally, if A is asked how B thinks A will have answered, and the correct answer is given, *realization* has occurred. With some modifications Scheff extrapolates the technique from the inter-individual level to the group level, and adduces a typology for the study of consensus in collectivities.

Although Scheff does not deal with the strategic implications of orders of coorientation for interpersonal control, his own analysis, when considered together with Glaser and Strauss' notion of awareness contexts, might lead to a very fruitful inquiry into the strategic implications of levels of exchange awareness for the establishment of consensus or dissensus. In any event, it is a fair expectation that future research will establish a firm relationship between personal purposes, forms of dramatic presentation, levels of exchange awareness, and the process of interpretation.

Suggested Readings

COUTU, WALTER. "Role-Playing vs. Role-Taking: An Appeal for Clarification." *American Sociological Review*, 16, 1951.

GOFFMAN, ERVING. "Role Distance" in his *Encounters*. Indianapolis: Bobbs-Merrill, 1961.

GUMPERY, J. J., and D. HYMES (eds.). *The Ethnography of Communication*. Special Publication of *The American Anthropologist*, 66, No. 4, Part 2, 1964.

JONES, EDWARD E. *Ingratiation*. New York: Appleton-Century-Crofts, 1964.

JONES, EDWARD E., KENNETH J. GERGEN, PETER GUMPERT, and JOHN W. THIBAUT. "Some Conditions Affecting the Use of Ingratiation to Influence Performance Evaluation." *Journal of Personality and Social Psychology*, I (June 1965), 613–625.

KELLEY, HAROLD H. "Experimental Studies of Threat in Interpersonal Negotiations." *Journal of Conflict Resolutions*, 9 (March 1965), 79–105.

STRYKER, SHELDON. "Conditions of Accurate Role-Taking: A Test of Mead's Theory." Arnold M. Rose (ed.), *Human Behavior and Social Process*. Boston: Houghton Mifflin, 1962, 41–62.

TURNER, RALPH. "Role-Taking: Process Versus Conformity" in Arnold M. Rose (ed.), *Human Behavior and Social Process*. Boston: Houghton Mifflin, 1962, 20–40.

30 Sociological Implications of the Thought of George Herbert Mead

● HERBERT BLUMER

My purpose is to depict the nature of human society when seen from the point of view of George Herbert Mead. While Mead gave human society a position of paramount importance in his scheme of thought he did little to outline its character. His central concern was with cardinal problems of philosophy. The development of his ideas of human society was largely limited to handling these problems. His treatment took the form of showing that human group life was the essential condition for the emergence of consciousness, the mind, a world of objects, human beings as organisms possessing selves, and human conduct in the form of constructed acts. He reversed the traditional assumptions underlying philosophical, psychological, and sociological thought to the effect that human beings possess minds and consciousness as original "givens," that they live in worlds of pre-existing and self-constituted objects, that their behavior consists of responses to such objects, and that group life consists of the association of such reacting human organisms. In making his brilliant contributions along this line he did not map out a theoretical scheme of human society. However, such a scheme is implicit in his work. It has to be constructed by tracing the implications of the central matters which he analyzed. This is what I propose to do. The central matters I shall consider are (1) the self, (2) the act, (3) social interaction, (4) objects, and (5) joint action.

The Self

Mead's picture of the human being as an actor differs radically from the conception of man that dominates current psychological and social science. He saw the human being as an organism having a self. The possession of a self converts the human being into a special kind of actor, transforms his relation to the world, and gives his action a unique character. In asserting that the human being has a self, Mead simply meant that the human being is an object to himself. The human being may perceive himself, have conceptions of himself, communicate with himself, and act toward himself. As these types of behavior imply, the human being may become the object of his own action. This gives him the means of interacting with himself—addressing himself, responding to the address, and addressing himself anew. Such self-interaction takes the form of making indications to himself and meeting these indications by making further indications. The human being can designate things to himself—his wants, his pains, his goals, objects around him, the presence of others, their actions, their expected actions,

SOURCE: Herbert Blumer, in *The American Journal of Sociology*, LXXI (March 1966), pp. 535–544. Reprinted by permission of the University of Chicago Press.

or whatnot. Through further interaction with himself, he may judge, analyze, and evaluate the things he has designated to himself. And by continuing to interact with himself he may plan and organize his action with regard to what he has designated and evaluated. In short, the possession of a self provides the human being with a mechanism of self-interaction with which to meet the world— a mechanism that is used in forming and guiding his conduct.

I wish to stress that Mead saw the self as a process and not as a structure. Here Mead clearly parts company with the great bulk of students who seek to bring a self into the human being by identifying it with some kind of organization or structure. All of us are familiar with this practice because it is all around us in the literature. Thus, we see scholars who identify the self with the "ego," or who regard the self as an organized body of needs or motives, or who think of it as an organization of attitudes, or who treat it as a structure of internalized norms and values. Such schemes which seek to lodge the self in a structure make no sense since they miss the reflexive process which alone can yield and constitute a self. For any posited structure to be a self, it would have to act upon and respond to itself—otherwise, it is merely an organization awaiting activation and release without exercising any effect on itself or on its operation. This marks the crucial weakness or inadequacy of the many schemes such as referred to above, which misguidingly associate the self with some kind of psychological or personality structure. For example, the ego, as such, is not a self; it would be a self only by becoming reflexive, that is to say, acting toward or on itself. And the same thing is true of any other posited psychological structure. Yet, such reflexive action changes both the status and the character of the structure and elevates the process of self-interaction to the position of major importance.

We can see this in the case of the reflexive process that Mead has isolated in the human being. As mentioned, this reflexive process takes the form of the person making indications to himself, that is to say, noting things and determining their significance for his line of action. To indicate something is to stand over against it and to put oneself in the position of acting toward it instead of automatically responding to it. In the face of something which one indicates, one can withhold action toward it, inspect it, judge it, ascertain its meaning, determine its possibilities, and direct one's action with regard to it. With the mechanism of self-interaction the human being ceases to be a responding organism whose behavior is a product of what plays upon him from the outside, the inside, or both. Instead, he acts toward his world, interpreting what confronts him and organizing his action on the basis of the interpretation. To illustrate: a pain one identifies and interprets is very different from a mere organic feeling and lays the basis for doing something about it instead of merely responding organically to it; to note and interpret the activity of another person is very different from having a response released by that activity; to be aware that one is hungry is very different from merely being hungry; to perceive one's "ego" puts one in the position of doing something with regard to it instead of merely giving expression to the ego. As these illustrations show, the process of self-interaction puts the human being over against his world instead of merely in it, requires him to meet and handle his world through a defining process insead of merely responding to it, and forces him to construct his action instead of merely releasing it. This is the kind of acting organism that Mead sees man to be as a result of having a self.[1]

The Act

Human action acquires a radically different character as a result of being formed through a process of self-interaction. Action is built up in coping with the world instead of merely being released from a pre-existing psychological structure by factors playing on that structure. By making indications to himself and by interpreting what he indicates, the human being has to forge or piece together a line of action. In order to act the individual has to identify what he wants, establish an objective or goal, map out a prospective line of behavior, note and interpret the actions of others, size up his situation, check himself at this or that point, figure out what to do at other points, and frequently spur himself on in the face of dragging dispositions or discouraging settings. The fact that the human act is self-directed or built up means in no sense that the actor necessarily exercises excellence in its construction. Indeed, he may do a very poor job in constructing his act. He may fail to note things of which he should be aware, he may misinterpret things that he notes, he may exercise poor judgment, he may be faulty in mapping out prospective lines of conduct, and he may be half-hearted in contending with recalcitrant dispositions. Such deficiencies in the construction of his acts do not belie the fact that his acts are still constructed by him out of what he takes into account. What he takes into account are the things that he indicates to himself. They cover such matters as his wants, his feelings, his goals, the actions of others, the expectations and demands of others, the rules of his group, his situation, his conceptions of himself, his recollections, and his images of prospective lines of conduct. He is not in the mere recipient position of responding to such matters; he stands over against them and has to handle them. He has to organize or cut out his lines of conduct on the basis of how he does handle them.

This way of viewing human action is directly opposite to that which dominates psychological and social sciences. In these sciences human action is seen as a product of factors that play upon or through the human actor. Depending on the preference of the scholar, such determining factors may be physiological stimulations, organic drives, needs, feelings, unconscious motives, conscious motives, sentiments, ideas, attitudes, norms, values, role requirements, status demands, cultural prescriptions, institutional pressures, or social-system requirements. Regardless of which factors are chosen, either singly or in combination, action is regarded as their product and hence is explained in their terms. The formula is simple: Given factors play on the human being to produce given types of behavior. The formula is frequently amplified so as to read: Under specified conditions, given factors playing on a given organization of the human being will produce a given type of behavior. The formula, in either its simple or amplified form, represents the way in which human action is seen in theory and research.

---

[1] The self, or indeed human being, is not brought into the picture merely by introducing psychological elements, such as motives and interests, alongside of societal elements. Such additions merely compound the error of the omission. This is the flaw in George Homan's presidential address on "Bringing Man Back In" (*American Sociological Review*, XXIX, No. 6, 809–18).

Under the formula the human being becomes a mere medium or forum for the operation of the factors that produce the behavior. Mead's scheme is fundamentally different from this formula. In place of being a mere medium for operation of determining factors that play upon him, the human being is seen as an active organism in his own right, facing, dealing with, and acting toward the objects he indicates. Action is seen as conduct which is constructed by the actor instead of response elicited from some kind of preformed organization in him. We can say that the traditional formula of human action fails to recognize that the human being is a self. Mead's scheme, in contrast, is based on this recognition.

Social Interaction

I can give here only a very brief sketch of Mead's highly illuminating analysis of social interaction. He identified two forms or levels—non-symbolic interaction and symbolic interaction. In non-symbolic interaction human beings respond directly to one another's gestures or actions; in symbolic interaction they interpret each other's gestures and act on the basis of the meaning yielded by the interpretation. An unwitting response to the tone of another's voice illustrates non-symbolic interaction. Interpreting the shaking of a fist as signifying that a person is preparing to attack illustrates symbolic interaction. Mead's concern was predominantly with symbolic interaction. Symbolic interaction involves *interpretation*, or ascertaining the meaning of the actions or remarks of the other person, and *definition*, or conveying indications to another person as to how he is to act. Human association consists of a process of such interpretation and definition. Through this process the participants fit their own acts to the ongoing acts of one another and guide others in doing so.

Several important matters need to be noted in the case of symbolic interaction. First, it is a formative process in its own right. The prevailing practice of psychology and sociology is to treat social interaction as a neutral medium, as a mere forum for the operation of outside factors. Thus psychologists are led to account for the behavior of people in interaction by resorting to elements of the psychological equipment of the participants—such elements as motives, feelings, attitudes, or personality organization. Sociologists do the same sort of thing by resorting to societal factors, such as cultural prescriptions, values, social roles, or structural pressures. Both miss the central point that human interaction is a positive shaping process in its own right. The participants in it have to build up their respective lines of conduct by constant interpretation of each other's ongoing lines of action. As participants take account of each other's ongoing acts, they have to arrest, reorganize, or adjust their own intentions, wishes, feelings, and attitudes; similarly, they have to judge the fitness of norms, values, and group prescriptions for the situation being formed by the acts of others. Factors of psychological equipment and social organization are not substitutes for the interpretative process; they are admissible only in terms of how they are handled in the interpretative process. Symbolic interaction has to be seen and studied in its own right.

Symbolic interaction is noteworthy in a second way. Because of it human group life takes on the character of an ongoing process—a continuing matter of fitting developing lines of conduct to one another. The fitting together of the lines of conduct is done through the dual process of definition and interpretation. This dual process operates both to sustain established patterns of joint conduct and to open them to transformation. Established patterns of group life exist and persist only through the continued use of the same schemes of interpretation; and such schemes of interpretation are maintained only through their continued confirmation by the defining acts of others. It is highly important to recognize that the established patterns of group life just do not carry on by themselves but are dependent for their continuity on recurrent affirmative definition. Let the interpretations that sustain them be undermined or disrupted by changed definitions from others and the patterns can quickly collapse. This dependency of interpretations on the defining acts of others also explains why symbolic interaction conduces so markedly to the transformation of the forms of joint activity that make up group life. In the flow of group life there are innumerable points at which the participants are *re*defining each other's acts. Such redefinition is very common in adversary relations, it is frequent in group discussion, and it is essentially intrinsic to dealing with problems. (And I may remark here that no human group is free of problems.) Redefinition imparts a formative character to human interaction, giving rise at this or that point to new objects, new conceptions, new relations, and new types of behavior. In short, the reliance on symbolic interaction makes human group life a developing process instead of a mere issue or product of psychological or social structure.

There is a third aspect of symbolic interaction which is important to note. In making the process of interpretation and definition of one another's acts central in human interaction, symbolic interaction is able to cover the full range of the generic forms of human association. It embraces equally well such relationships as cooperation, conflict, domination, exploitation, consensus, disagreement, closely knit identification, and indifferent concern for one another. The participants in each of such relations have the same common task of constructing their acts by interpreting and defining the acts of each other. The significance of this simple observation becomes evident in contrasting symbolic interaction with the various schemes of human interaction that are to be found in the literature. Almost always such schemes construct a general model of human interaction or society on the basis of a particular type of human relationship. An outstanding contemporary instance is Talcott Parsons' scheme which presumes and asserts that the primordial and generic form of human interaction is the "complementarity of expectations." Other schemes depict the basic and generic model of human interaction as being "conflict," others assert it to be "identity through common sentiments," and still others that it is agreement in the form of "consensus." Such schemes are parochial. Their great danger lies in imposing on the breadth of human interaction an image derived from the study of only one form of interaction. Thus, in different hands, human society is said to be fundamentally a sharing of common values; or, conversely, a struggle for power; or, still differently, the exercise of consensus; and so on. The simple point implicit in Mead's analysis of symbolic interaction is that human beings, in interpreting and defining one another's acts, can and do meet each other in the full range of human relations. Proposed schemes of human society should respect this simple point.

Objects

The concept of object is another fundamental pillar in Mead's scheme of analysis. Human beings live in a world or environment of objects, and their activities are formed around objects. This bland statement becomes very significant when it is realized that for Mead objects are human constructs and not self-existing entities with intrinsic natures. Their nature is dependent on the orientation and action of people toward them. Let me spell this out. For Mead, an object is anything that can be designated or referred to. It may be physical as a chair or imaginary as a ghost, natural as a cloud in the sky or man-made as an automobile, material as the Empire State Building or abstract as the concept of liberty, animate as an elephant or inanimate as a vein of coal, inclusive of a class of people as politicians or restricted to a specific person as President de Gaulle, definite as a multiplication table or vague as a philosophical doctrine. In short, objects consist of whatever people indicate or refer to.

There are several important points in this analysis of objects. First, the nature of an object is constituted by the meaning it has for the person or persons for whom it is an object. Second, this meaning is not intrinsic to the object but arises from how the person is initially prepared to act toward it. Readiness to use a chair as something in which to sit gives it the meaning of a chair; to one with no experience with the use of chairs the object would appear with a different meaning, such as a strange weapon. It follows that objects vary in their meaning. A tree is not the same object to a lumberman, a botanist, or a poet; a star is a different object to a modern astronomer than it was to a sheepherder of antiquity; communism is a different object to a Soviet patriot than it is to a Wall Street broker. Third, objects—all objects—are social products in that they are formed and transformed by the defining process that takes place in social interaction. The meaning of the objects—chairs, trees, stars, prostitutes, saints, communism, public education, or whatnot—is formed from the ways in which others refer to such objects or act toward them. Fourth, people are prepared or set to act toward objects on the basis of the meaning of the objects for them. In a genuine sense the organization of a human being consists of his objects, that is, his tendencies to act on the basis of their meanings. Fifth, just because an object is something that is designated, one can organize one's action toward it instead of responding immediately to it; one can inspect the object, think about it, work out a plan of action toward it, or decide whether or not to act toward it. In standing over against the object in both a logical and psychological sense, one is freed from coercive response to it. In this profound sense an object is different from a stimulus as ordinarily conceived.

This analysis of objects puts human group life into a new and interesting perspective. Human beings are seen as living in a world of meaningful objects—not in an environment of stimuli or self-constituted entities. This world is socially produced in that the meanings are fabricated through the process of social interaction. Thus, different groups come to develop different worlds—and these worlds change as the objects that compose them change in meaning. Since people are set to act in terms of the meanings of their objects, the world of objects of a group represents in a genuine sense its action organization. To identify and understand the life of a group it is necessary to identify its world of objects; this identification has to be in terms of the meanings objects have for the members of the group. Finally, people are not locked to their objects; they may check action toward objects and indeed work out new lines of conduct toward them. This condition introduces into human group life an indigenous source of transformation.

Joint Action

I use the term "joint action" in place of Mead's term "social act." It refers to the larger collective form of action that is constituted by the fitting together of the lines of behavior of the separate participants. Illustrations of joint action are a trading transaction, a family dinner, a marriage ceremony, a shopping expedition, a game, a convivial party, a debate, a court trial, or a war. We note in each instance an identifiable and distinctive form of joint action, comprised by an articulation of the acts of the participants. Joint actions range from a simple collaboration of two individuals to a complex alignment of the acts of huge organizations or institutions. Everywhere we look in a human society we see people engaging in forms of joint action. Indeed, the totality of such instances—in all of their multitudinous variety, their variable connections, and their complex networks—constitutes the life of a society. It is easy to understand from these remarks why Mead saw joint action, or the social act, as the distinguishing characteristic of society. For him, the social act was the fundamental unit of society. Its analysis, accordingly, lays bare the generic nature of society.

To begin with, a joint action cannot be resolved into a common or same type of behavior on the part of the participants. Each participant necessarily occupies a different position, acts from that position, and engages in a separate and distinctive act. It is the fitting together of these acts and not their commonality that constitutes joint action. How do these separate acts come to fit together in the case of human society? Their alignment does not occur through sheer mechanical juggling, as in the shaking of walnuts in a jar or through unwitting adaptation, as in an ecological arrangement in a plant community. Instead, the participants fit their acts together, first, by identifying the social act in which they are about to engage and, second, by interpreting and defining each other's acts in forming the joint act. By identifying the social act or joint action the participant is able to orient himself; he has a key to interpreting the acts of others and a guide for directing his action with regard to them. Thus, to act appropriately, the participant has to identify a marriage ceremony as a marriage ceremony, a holdup as a holdup, a debate as a debate, a war as a war, and so forth. But, even though this identification be made, the participants in the joint action that is being formed still find it necessary to interpret and define one another's ongoing acts. They have to ascertain what the others are doing and plan to do and make indications to one another of what to do.

This brief analysis of joint action enables us to note several matters of distinct importance. It calls attention, first, to the fact that the essence of society lies in an ongoing process of action—not in a posited structure of relations. Without action, any structure of relations between people is meaningless. To be understood, a society must be seen and grasped in terms of the action that comprises it. Next, such action has to be seen and treated, not by tracing the separate lines of action of the participants—whether the participants be single individuals, collectivities, or organizations—but in terms of the joint action into which the separate lines of action fit and merge. Few students of human society have fully grasped this point or its implications. Third, just because it is built up over time by the fitting together of acts, each joint action must be seen as having a career or a history. In having a career, its course and fate are contingent on what happens during its formation. Fourth, this career is generally orderly, fixed and repetitious by virtue of a common identification or definition of the joint action that is made by its participants. The common definition supplies each participant with decisive guidance in directing his own act so as to fit into the acts of the others. Such common definitions serve, above everything else, to account for the regularity, stability, and repetitiveness of joint action in vast areas of group life; they are the source of the established and regulated social behavior that is envisioned in the concept of culture. Fifth, however, the career of joint actions also must be seen as open to many possibilities of uncertainty. Let me specify the more important of these possibilities. One, joint actions have to be initiated —and they may not be. Two, once started a joint action may be interrupted, abandoned, or transformed. Three, the participants may not make a common definition of the joint action into which they are thrown and hence may orient their acts on different premises. Four, a common definition of a joint action may still allow wide differences in the direction of the separate lines of action and hence in the course taken by the joint action; a war is a good example. Five, new situations may arise calling for hitherto unexisting types of joint action, leading to confused exploratory efforts to work out a fitting together of acts. And, six, even in the context of a commonly defined joint action, participants may be led to rely on other considerations in interpreting and defining each other's lines of action. Time does not allow me to spell out and illustrate the importance of these possibilities. To mention them should be sufficient, however, to show that uncertainty, contingency, and transformation are part and parcel of the process of joint action. To assume that the diversified joint actions which comprise a human society are set to follow fixed and established channels is a sheer gratuitous assumption.

From the foregoing discussion of the self, the act, social interaction, objects, and joint action we can sketch a picture of human society. The picture is composed in terms of action. A society is seen as people meeting the varieties of situations that are thrust on them by their conditions of life. These situations are met by working out joint actions in which participants have to align their acts to one another. Each participant does so by interpreting the acts of others and, in turn, by making indications to others as to how they should act. By virtue of this process of interpretation and definition joint actions are built up; they have careers. Usually, the course of a joint action is outlined in advance by the fact that the participants make a common identification of it; this makes for regularity, stability, and repetitiveness in the joint action. However, there are many joint actions that encounter obstructions, that have no pre-established pathways, and that have to be constructed along new lines. Mead saw human society in this way—as a diversified social process in which people were engaged in forming joint actions to deal with situations confronting them.

This picture of society stands in significant contrast to the dominant views of society in the social and psychological sciences—even to those that pretend to view society as action. To point out the major differences in the contrast is the best way of specifying the sociological implications of Mead's scheme of thought.

The chief difference is that the dominant views in sociology and psychology fail, alike, to see human beings as organisms having selves. Instead, they regard human beings as merely responding organisms and, accordingly, treat action as mere response to factors playing on human beings. This is exemplified in the efforts to account for human behavior by such factors as motives, ego demands, attitudes, role requirements, values, status expectations, and structural stresses. In such approaches the human being becomes a mere medium through which such initiating factors operate to produce given actions. From Mead's point of view such a conception grossly misrepresents the nature of human beings and human action. Mead's scheme interposes a process of self-interaction between initiating factors and the action that may follow in their wake. By virtue of self-interaction the human being becomes an acting organism coping with situations in place of being an organism merely responding to the play of factors. And his action becomes something he constructs and directs to meet the situations in place of an unrolling of reactions evoked from him. In introducing the self, Mead's position focuses on how human beings handle and fashion their world, not on disparate responses to imputed factors.

If human beings are, indeed, organisms with selves, and if their action is, indeed, an outcome of a process of self-interaction, schemes that purport to study and explain social action should respect and accommodate these features. To do so, current schemes in sociology and psychology would have to undergo radical revision. They would have to shift from a preoccupation with initiating factor and terminal result to a preoccupation with a process of formation. They would have to view action as something constructed by the actor instead of something evoked from him. They would have to depict the milieu of action in terms of how the milieu appears to the actor in place of how it appears to the outside student. They would have to incorporate the interpretive process which at present they scarcely deign to touch. They would have to recognize that any given act has a career in which it is constructed but in which it may be interrupted, held in abeyance, abandoned, or recast.

On the methodological or research side the study of action would have to be made from the position of the actor. Since action is forged by the actor out of what he perceives, interprets, and judges, one would have to see the operating situation as the actor sees it, perceive objects as the actor perceives them, ascertain their meaning in terms of the meaning they have for the actor, and follow the actor's line of conduct as the actor organizes it—in short, one would have to take the role of the actor and see his world from his standpoint. This methodological approach stands in contrast to the so-called objective approach so dominant today, namely, that of viewing the actor and his action from the perspective of an outside, detached observer. The "objective" approach holds the danger of the observer substituting his view of the field of action for the view held by the actor. It is unnecessary to add that the actor acts toward his world on the basis of how he sees it and not on the basis of how that world appears to the outside observer.

In continuing the discussion of this matter, I wish to consider especially what we might term the structural conception of human society. This conception views society as established organization, familiar to us in the use of such terms as social structure, social system, status position, social role, social stratification, institutional structure, cultural pattern, social codes, social norms, and social values.

The conception presumes that a human society is structured with regard to (a) the social positions occupied by the people in it and with regard to (b) the patterns of behavior in which they engage. It is presumed further that this inter-linked structure of social positions and behavior patterns is the over-all determinant of social action; this is evidenced, of course, in the practice of explaining conduct by such structural concepts as role requirements, status demands, strata differences, cultural prescriptions, values, and norms. Social action falls into two general categories: conformity, marked by adherence to the structure, and deviance, marked by departure from it. Because of the central and determinative position into which it is elevated, structure becomes necessarily the encompassing object of sociological study and analysis—epitomized by the well-nigh universal assertion that a human group or society is a "social system." It is perhaps unnecessary to observe that the conception of human society as structure or organization is ingrained in the very marrow of contemporary sociology.

Mead's scheme definitely challenges this conception. It sees human society not as an established structure but as people meeting their conditions of life; it sees social action not as an emanation of societal structure but as a formation made by human actors; it sees this formation of action not as societal factors coming to expression through the medium of human organisms but as constructions made by actors out of what they take into account; it sees group life not as a release or expression of established structure but as a process of building up joint actions; it sees social actions as having variable careers and not as confined to the alternatives of conformity to or deviation from the dictates of established structure; it sees the so-called interaction between parts of a society not as a direct exercising of influence by one part on another but as mediated throughout by interpretations made by people; accordingly, it sees society not as a system, whether in the form of a static, moving or whatever kind of equilibrium, but as a vast number of occurring joint actions, many closely linked, many not linked at all, many prefigured and repetitious, others being carved out in new directions, and all being pursued to serve the purposes of the participants and not the requirements of a system. I have said enough, I think, to point out the drastic differences between the Meadian conception of society and the widespread sociological conceptions of it as structure.

The differences do not mean, incidentally, that Mead's view rejects the existence of structure in human society. Such a position would be ridiculous. There are such matters as social roles, status positions, rank orders, bureaucratic organizations, relations between institutions, differential authority arrangements, social codes, norms, values, and the like. And they are very important. But their importance does not lie in an alleged determination of action nor in all alleged existence as parts of a self-operating societal system. Instead, they are important only as they enter into the process of interpretation and definition out of which joint actions are formed. The manner and extent to which they enter may vary greatly from situation to situation, depending on what people take into account and how they assess what they take account of. Let me give one brief illustration. It is ridiculous, for instance, to assert, as a number of eminent sociologists have done, that social interaction is an interaction between social roles. Social interaction is obviously an interaction between *people* and not between roles; the needs of the participants are to interpret and handle what confronts them—such as a topic of conversation or a problem—and not to give expression to their roles. It is only in highly ritualistic relations that the direction and content of conduct can be explained by roles. Usually, the direction and content are fashioned out of what people in interaction have to deal with. That roles affect in varying degree phases of the direction and content of action is true but is a matter of determination in given cases. This is a far cry from asserting action to be a product of roles. The observation I have made in this brief discussion of social roles applies with equal validity to all other structural matters.

Another significant implication of Mead's scheme of thought refers to the question of what holds a human society together. As we know, this question is converted by sociologists into a problem of unity, stability, and orderliness. And, as we know further, the typical answer given by sociologists is that unity, stability, and orderliness come from a sharing in common of certain basic matters, such as codes, sentiments, and, above all, values. Thus, the disposition is to regard common values as the glue that holds a society together, as the controlling regulator that brings and keeps the activities in a society in orderly relationship, and as the force that preserves stability in a society. Conversely, it is held that conflict between values or the disintegration of values creates disunity, disorder, and instability. This conception of human society becomes subject to great modification if we think of society as consisting of the fitting together of acts to form joint action. Such alignment may take place for any number of reasons, depending on the situations calling for joint action, and need not involve, or spring from, the sharing of common values. The participants may fit their acts to one another in orderly joint actions on the basis of compromise, out of duress, because they may use one another in achieving their respective ends, because it is the sensible thing to do, or out of sheer necessity. This is particularly likely to be true in our modern complex societies with their great diversity in composition, in lines of interest, and in their respective worlds of concern. In very large measure, society becomes the formation of workable relations. To seek to encompass, analyze, and understand the life of a society on the assumption that the existence of a society necessarily depends on the sharing of values can lead to strained treatment, gross misrepresentation, and faulty lines of interpretation. I believe that the Meadian perspective, in posing the question of how people are led to align their acts in different situations in place of presuming that this necessarily requires and stems from a sharing of common values, is a more salutary and realistic approach.

There are many other significant sociological implications in Mead's scheme of thought which, under the limit of space, I can do no more than mention. Socialization shifts its character from being an effective internalization of norms and values to a cultivated capacity to take the roles of others effectively. Social control becomes fundamentally and necessarily a matter of self-control. Social change becomes a continuous indigenous process in human group life instead of an episodic result of extraneous factors playing on established structure. Human group life is seen as always incomplete and undergoing development instead of jumping from one completed state to another. Social disorganization is seen not as a breakdown of existing structure but as an inability to mobilize action effectively in the face of a given situation. Social action, since it has a career, is recognized as having a historical dimension which has to be taken into account in order to be adequately understood.

In closing I wish to say that my presentation has necessarily skipped much in

Mead's scheme that is of great significance. Further, I have not sought to demonstrate the validity of his analyses. However, I have tried to suggest the freshness, the fecundity, and the revolutionary implications of his point of view.

31   The Social Act: Re-examination of a Concept

● S. FRANK MIYAMOTO

The interactionist point of view in social psychology was for some time mainly a framework of suggestive concepts, but as a result of recent studies of status and roles, the self, interpersonal perception, communication, and consensus, the framework is now acquiring the kind of connective tissue that was long wanting. While these studies have brought notable advances and their continuation should yield important consequences for social psychology, it is a curious fact that current investigations tend to ignore the concept which originally was considered the keystone of the interactionist approach. I wish to clarify what I consider this lacuna to be.

Although the exaggeration does some injustice, one is tempted to say that much of current research in this area is less concerned with social interaction itself than with the components of interaction, or with its consequences. Furthermore, in those studies which focus upon interaction, the process tends to be conceived as a mechanistic interplay of actions, selves, roles, and norms, thus eliminating the need to consider the meaningful context of interaction.

For the earlier writers who were largely responsible for initiating the interactionist view, however, the socially meaningful context of interaction was of primary significance and was, indeed, the foundation idea upon which their analyses were constructed. Thus, W. I. Thomas clearly implied that the *definition of the situation* provides the frame of reference of social interaction, and that organized social relations presuppose the existence of a body of common definitions among the group members. Park and Burgess referred to the cooperative (that is, corporate) nature of social relations within which individual behavior is implicated. Finally, G. H. Mead repeatedly emphasized that the interactional processes with which he was concerned occur within the context of the social act, that is, within the context of a goal-oriented, organized group action.

Mention of this classical background may cause you to wonder "what all the shooting is about" for no one to my knowledge questions the import of the concepts referred to, and a generation of social psychologists has been trained to think in these terms. The concern here, however, is with the gap between theory and research, with the fact that what is explicit in the theoretical statement is reduced to the status of the implicit in empirical research. The latter assertion is again an exaggeration for a few have attempted to deal explicitly with the context of interaction as a variable. Leonard Cottrell, in particular, has stressed *the*

SOURCE: S. Frank Miyamoto, *Pacific Sociological Review*, II (Fall 1959), pp. 51–55.
Presidential address read at the annual meeting of the Pacific Sociological Society, April 1959.

situation as a neglected area of interaction studies.[1] In a series of publications he and his students have foreshadowed many of the ideas offered here, so much so that I may often be dangerously close to plagiarism. The justification for this presentation is the hope that, as in musical composition, a variation on a theme may be considered provocative and as offering new meanings.

Although a number of different concepts with similar meanings have been used in reference to the aspect of the social process under discussion, for reasons I shall clarify later, special attention is given to Mead's notion of the social act. The latter term is familiar to many, but to make sure that our ideas about it correspond, a little space is devoted to its explication.

The Social Act

The term "social act" has been used with two different meanings. Loosely employed, it refers to any act occurring in a social context; that is, any act having a social object as referent. In Mead's usage, however, it refers to a group action; specifically, to an organized action of two or more individuals that is directed toward some common goal. It is the latter meaning with which we are concerned.

Virtually all meaningful human behavior is implicated within social acts. As I sit in my office writing this paper, I am implicated in that social act called the annual meeting of the Pacific Sociological Society. The annual meeting is in fact a social act that covers a rather long time span, and is composed of those manifold coordinated actions of many persons which occur in the planning, preparation, and carrying out of the meeting. My writing is interrupted by a student who wishes to discuss some problems related to my course which he is taking, and now I am implicated in a social act that represents a segment of the academic process. Even with regard to that self-destructive behavior of stopping to smoke a cigarette, a case can be made out for its implication within a social act.

Illustrations are readily offered, but the attempt to define the concept technically reveals its ambiguities. Ignoring the ambiguities for the moment, however, some of the general features of the social act may be indicated. First, the concept refers to an abstraction from a continuous social process. Most social acts are intricately interwoven with many other acts and it is only by abstraction that a given instance may be singled out for observation. Second, a social act is conceived as having a beginning and ending even though it is difficult to define these boundaries in specific cases. Third, social acts may be subsumed within larger social acts and in certain respects it is arbitrary as to which segment one chooses to give attention.

Fourth and most important is the assumption that the social act is goal-directed or functional for the group and that individual acts will tend to be coordinated toward the fulfillment of the function. It is further assumed that people are capable of recognizing the social act which each situation implies as well as their respective role in each act. Alternatively, it is assumed that if the definition of the social act is not pre-established, but interaction continues, the participants will seek to define the social act. Viewed in this way, the social process is con-

---

[1] Leonard S. Cottrell, Jr., "The Analysis of Situational Fields in Social Psychology," *American Sociological Review*, 7 (June, 1942), pp. 370–382; and his, "Some Neglected Problems in Social Psychology," *American Sociological Review*, 15 (December, 1950), pp. 705–712. Reprinted in Part One of this volume.

stituted not of a network of individual behaviors but of a network of social acts
within which individual behaviors are organized.

Beyond these basic notions there are some important variations of conception.
Mead said little or nothing about changes in the social act which may be induced
by the accompanying social interaction, assuming rather its prior organization in
a relatively stable form. By contrast, it seems clear that Blumer regards social
acts as representing highly fluid situations in which the coordination of action
is something attained rather than something given.[2] A distinction thus arises
between the structured as opposed to fluid conception of social acts.

In discussing these same problems, Cottrell has expressed a preference for the
concept of *the situation* over that of the social act,[3] perhaps because the former
is more general in meaning covering all the variations that may come to mind.
There are two reasons why we have reversed the choice. The problems which
we find interesting concern those interpersonal relations in which the participants adapt, or attempt to adapt, their behavior to each other in an effort to
move along some directionally oriented course. The concept of the situation fails
to suggest the idea of joint action and is also a more diffuse reference that may
imply non-social as well as social situations. On the other hand, the social act,
as an analogy to the idea of the individual act, implies both motivation and coordination of group action. Second, if the concept of the social act is often unsatisfactory because of its ambiguities, one may solve the problem by wielding
Occam's Razor. There are many social acts which are relatively well organized
and stable, and where the ambiguities of definition are minimal. Initially, observation may be restricted to these relatively clearly defined instances. Social
psychology may perhaps first learn to walk by solving interaction problems in
these relatively uncomplex settings, and later learn to run.

Implications

The question of why anyone should interest himself in the concept still remains
for consideration. Three examples are cited of how this way of viewing interaction problems may yield interesting consequences.

If the assumption is accepted that socially meaningful relations generally take
place within the context of social acts, it would seem that such processes as self-
conceptualization, role definition, and definition of expectations, which are usually considered significant aspects of interactional processes, must be affected by
the specific social acts within which these defining processes occur. There is, in
fact, one area of social psychological research in which the latter view has come
to be accepted. Leadership studies of an earlier day concentrated on generalized
personal traits or personality types which might be found associated with leadership. The inconclusive findings of these studies, plus the impact of other investigations which showed that a leader in one situation might turn out a non-
leader in another, has led to the currently accepted proposition that leadership is
a function of the situation.[4] Probably a better formulation of the proposition

---

[2] See, for example, Herbert Blumer, "Psychological Import of the Human Group," in Muzafer
Sherif and M. O. Wilson (eds.), *Group Relations at the Crossroads*, New York: Harpers and
Brothers, 1953, pp. 193–197.
[3] Cottrell, "Some Neglected Problems in Social Psychology," *op. cit.*, p. 711 f.
[4] Cecil A. Gibb, "Leadership," in Gardner Lindzey (ed.), *Handbook of Social Psychology*,
Vol. II, Cambridge, Mass.: Addison-Wesley Publishing Co., 1954, especially pp. 913–917.

remains to be stated. Nevertheless, there appears to be a fair amount of validity to the proposition that, to put the matter in our terms, leadership is functionally related to the social act.

This kind of interpretation, however, has to date made relatively little impress upon other areas of interaction research. For example, Gough in his use of the adjective check-list for defining the self-concept takes account of situational variations in self-definition, but the primary aim of his research seems directed toward determining the generalized self-conception of each of his subjects.[5] Similarly, Dymond in her study of empathic ability implies a generalized empathic ability,[6] but the example of an American trying to empathize with a Chinese in Peiping should suggest the element of situational specificity in empathic ability. That is, to my knowledge there is at present no widely held view that self-conception, empathic ability, role definitions, and other components of social interaction are functions of the situation. Indeed, the research evidence with which to accept or reject such a proposition is lacking. If the proposition is true, however, it may account for a good deal of the unexplained variance often found in correlations between self-concept or empathic ability and certain criterion variables. Our suggestion is that the problem of the generalized as opposed to the situationally specific aspects of the self-concept, roles, and norms may be solved by research on these phenomena within the context of defined social acts.

Research on the social act should also illuminate a type of problem to which Theodore Newcomb has given attention in his article "The Communicative Act." [7] Using a communication model involving two persons, A and B, and an object of reference, X, Newcomb derives an hypothesis such as the following: [8]

> The stronger the forces toward A's co-orientation in respect to B and X, (a) the greater A's strain toward symmetry with B in respect to X; and (b) the greater the likelihood of increased symmetry as a consequence of one or more communicative acts.

The proposition is difficult to express more simply, for the term "co-orientation" is not clearly defined. Symmetry may be translated readily to mean agreement, but co-orientation refers to some meaning such as interdependence. Hence, the proposition may be interpreted to mean that the greater the interdependence between A, B, and X, the greater the strain toward agreement between A and B with respect to X, where communication occurs. Newcomb's main concern is to derive other hypotheses regarding symmetry from this basic postulate.

Newcomb seems fully aware that the concept of co-orientation is necessary to his model, yet he remains inordinately vague regarding the meaning of the term. We would suggest that the most significant way in which co-orientation occurs is by the joint definition by a number of persons of a social act situation. When people participate in a social act there is interdependence of the members as well as pressure to communicate, both of which are implied in the idea of co-

[5] Harrison G. Gough, *Reference Handbook for the Gough Adjective Check-list*, Berkeley: The University of California Institute of Personality Assessment and Research (Mimeographed), April, 1955.

[6] Rosalind F. Dymond, "A Scale for the Measurement of Empathic Ability," *Journal of Consulting Psychology*, 13 (April, 1949), pp. 127–133.

[7] Theodore M. Newcomb, "An Approach to the Study of Communicative Acts," *Psychological Review*, 60 (November, 1953), pp. 393–404.

[8] *Ibid.*, p. 396.

orientation. Furthermore, where Newcomb speaks of the "forces toward co-orientation" we might substitute the idea of forces toward participating in given social acts. If a typology of social acts can be established, it would be possible to determine for a given group those social acts in which the forces for participation are strong and those for which the forces are weak. In short, it seems possible to reduce the vagaries of Newcomb's model by specifying social acts as the context of communicative acts.

Finally, with regard to social organization, the central subject matter of sociology, one could elaborate at length on a conception of social organization as a network of social acts. However, I prefer to devote the limited space to a quick look at the related topic of social disorganization. In the framework of the present discussion, the obvious conception of social disorganization that comes to mind is that of a situation in which a group of people are unable to carry out social acts; that is, there is insufficient coordination of action to maintain organized social relations. For example, we speak of mental disorder and alcoholism as disorganizing in a family because they interfere with the coordination of member actions for the fulfilment of normal family expectations. Social disorganization may also be viewed in another way. The non-social and erratic behavior of the mentally disordered and the alcoholic are often the products of an organized social process. That is, there are social acts by which people become intoxicated and there are others by which people become personally disorganized. There are also those intriguing instances of social acts called intergroup conflict in which the actions of one group produce predictable and, in a sense, coordinate but opposed responses on the part of the other. One suspects that the appropriate formulation of disorganization problems in terms of social acts may lead to added understanding of the organized processes which yield some disorganization.

Some Problems for Investigation

If social acts are to be studied profitably, it will be necessary to have some method of identifying them and an appropriate conceptual scheme for their analysis. Unfortunately, I have no ready-made scheme to offer. My purpose, therefore, will be to indicate some of the directions in which I believe the answers are to be found.

The basic assumption regarding social acts is that they represent organized social processes with respect to which people orient their behavior and coordinate their actions. This leads us to assume, further, that people must be able to arrive at common definitions of social acts.

The assumption of common definitions of situations, however, seems contradicted by the studies of perception variability and particularly by the findings in the recent study of role consensus by Gross, McEachern, and Mason.[9] In their study of role definitions among school superintendents and school board members in Massachusetts, the authors emphasize the variability of role definitions which occur within each group as well as between them. That variability of situational definitions occurs seems undeniable. It is consistent with the present argument to expect differences of definitions as situations vary. However, these studies do not exclude the possibility that in the organized relations of people

---

[9] Neal Gross, Ward S. Mason, and Alexander McEachern, *Explorations in Role Analysis: Studies of the School Superintendency Role,* New York: John Wiley & Sons, 1957.

certain common perceptions and common definitions will be found present. Reversing the problem of variability of consensus posed by Gross and associates, we ask whether a minimal consensual basis will be found wherever people are engaged in a social act.

Fritz Heider in his recent work, *The Psychology of Interpersonal Relations*, deals with problems which, although primarily psychological in formulation, bear directly on these issues.[10] Heider, whose forte is perception psychology, begins by pointing to the fact of perception constancy. He would say, for example, that this sheet of paper which I hold before you is seen by you as a rectangular sheet, $8\frac{1}{2}$ by 11 inches in size, but that if you were responding only to the light stimuli reaching you at your respective positions most of you could not possibly see it as a rectangle nor as anything so large. That is, psychologically we impose invariances upon the variability of stimuli which reach us, and those attributes of objects which dispose them to manifest themselves as invariant and predictable he calls "psychological dispositional properties." Size, shape and color are among the invariant properties of physical objects. Heider's concern in this work is to ascertain the psychological dispositional properties in interpersonal relations. Using common-sense psychology for data and what Newcomb calls "a cultivated naivete," Heider searches out the psychological dispositional properties of such everyday concepts as *can, trying, wanting, suffering, sentiment, belonging,* and *ought.*

The cultivated naivete of Heider's work is too sophisticated for summary presentation here, but the implications of his study for our discussion may be obvious. Social acts are historical events and as with history we might say that "a social act never repeats itself." Moreover, a social act may possess incredible complexity and variability. Nevertheless, people are able to coordinate action in even very complex social acts. We assume that this is possible because of a sufficient consensual basis for joint action. We further assume that the sufficient consensual basis will be found in the dispositional properties of social acts and of interpersonal relations.

Heider, unfortunately, deliberately set aside consideration of sociological problems and therefore provides no blueprint of the dispositional properties of social acts. His method, however, may be directly applicable to our problem. He took common-sense words, grammatical structure, and ways of thinking as primary data, and then looked for invariant properties among them. Similarly, social acts may perhaps be studied by examining the common sense verbal identifications which are made of them and by searching for the psychological dispositional properties (or perhaps we should say "sociological dispositional properties") to be found in the verbal characterizations of social acts.

To take a simple illustration, we generally have little difficulty distinguishing between communicative acts which are very hostile from those which are friendly. We should like to know what the psychological dispositional properties are by which these two situations are distinguished.

The obvious answer may be that communications which are very hostile employ entirely different words from those used in friendly social relations and that the difference of meaning is readily apprehended. There are occasions of social conversation, however, when people jokingly speak and act as if they were

---

[10] Fritz Heider, *The Psychology of Interpersonal Relations,* New York: John Wiley & Sons, 1958.

very hostile, but despite the antagonistic format of the communicated matter, there may be no doubt that the statement is made as a friendly gesture. Pursuing this line of inquiry, one would be led into a Heiderian type of analysis with regard to the psychological dispositional properties in the intentions of communicators, the segment of life space which the act occupies, the sentiments and values expressed, and so on. What may result from such a mode of analysis cannot be foreseen, but one suspects that by treating social acts as perceptual objects in the common-sense field, a fruitful application may be made of Heider's method.[11]

If it is possible to identify social acts we should then be able to solve another problem, namely, the typing of social acts. The idea of typologizing social acts and identifying their invariant properties is not at all new. Some years ago La-Piere in his *Collective Behavior* devoted major attention to classifying and describing the basic characteristics of the cultural, recreational, control, and escape types of social interaction and their subtypes.[12] His work still remains the most comprehensive treatment of the subject.

Typologies, however, prove sterile when their relevance for problems fails to be demonstrated. To help insure relevance, two things might be done. First, instead of employing any objectively derived scheme of classification, types recognized in common sense might be used. Second, the typology of social acts should be developed with respect to defined social settings, such as the family, industry, or any setting in which fairly definite group objectives may occur. It then becomes meaningful to ask what function each type of social act serves. For example, although the typology developed by Slater[13] distinguishing the "idea men" and "best-liked men" in small group relations has more to do with the differentiation of roles than of social acts, his study suggests analogically that social acts of the task variety as opposed to those emphasizing socio-emotional reactions may serve related but different functions within a given social process. Typologies of this type may be limited but they have the virtue of relevance in research and should in time provide the basis for more inclusive schemes.

Finally, the main purpose in studying social acts is to permit a less segmented approach to the study of social interaction. The basic idea underlying this paper is the belief that when social acts are identified as distinct entities the accompanying interaction then can be carefully observed from beginning to end, as Bales has done. Unlike Bales, however, it would be necessary to inquire how the participants defined the situation and to inquire further how this perception affects their action in the given context.

In addition, instead of studying self-conceptions, role definitions, and empathizing in the abstract, they would be investigated in their native habitat, within the social act. In particular, inquiry would be directed at the question of how these components are affected by the particular kind of social act within which they occur. Nor would the approach preclude the possibility that generalized

---

[11] For examples of work in this direction see Roger G. Barker and Herbert F. Wright, *Midwest and Its Children*, Evanston, Ill.: Row, Peterson and Co., 1955, and Nelson Foote, "Concept and Method in the Study of Human Development," in Muzafer Sherif and M. O. Wilson (eds.), *Emerging Problems in Social Psychology*, Norman, Oklahoma: Institute of Group Relations, University of Oklahoma, 1957, pp. 29–49.

[12] Richard T. LaPiere, *Collective Behavior*, New York: McGraw-Hill Book Co., 1938.

[13] Philip E. Slater, "Role Differentiation in Small Groups," *American Sociological Review*, 20 (June, 1955), pp. 303–310.

aspects of self-conception, role definitions, and the like might be uncovered, but the generalization would not be brought into existence by fiat and the generalized conception would have a known relationship to the situationally specific aspects of these components.

The suggested approach should be acceptable even for those who emphasize, as does Nelson Foote, "The uncertainty of every outcome . . . (the) exploratory, formulative, creative in every observable episode." [14] Even highly fluid social acts must be held together by some bonds and our guess is that these bonds have their basis in the invariant properties which we have hypothesized. The question then concerns the relationship between the invariant properties and the variable conditions.

Summary

The modest aim of this paper has been to emphasize again the need for research on the organized character of the interactional process. It has suggested that the social process can, with some arbitrariness to be sure, be divided into definable units which some have called "interaction episodes." More than this, however, this paper urges the development of methods by which to identify the definitions of social acts which we assume occur phenomenally in people. It then should be possible to determine how such definitions affect, or fail to affect, roles, self-concept, and other apparatus of interaction; and this kind of knowledge, it would seem, might give us some fairly basic understanding of organized social process.

It will be obvious to you that the ideas expressed here are extremely traditional. What is suggested, however, is that a number of lines of thinking—including those of Leonard Cottrell, Nelson Foote, R. E. L. Faris, Robert F. Bales, Theodore Newcomb, Fritz Heider, and Barker and Wright—appear to be converging again upon this traditional problem. There is this difference, however, that in the intervening period since the classical writings a slow but certain accumulation of social psychological knowledge has taken place that provides us with new ideas and instruments with which to explore the area. One wonders if the time may not be ripe to launch a thorough re-exploration of this traditional problem.

32   On Visual Interaction

● GEORG SIMMEL

It is through the medium of the senses that we perceive our fellow-men. This fact has two aspects of fundamental sociological significance: (a) that of appreciation, and (b) that of comprehension.

---

[14] Foote, op. cit., p. 36.

SOURCE: Georg Simmel, in Robert E. Park and Ernest W. Burgess, *Introduction to the Science of Sociology* (Chicago: University of Chicago Press, 1924), pp. 356–361. Reprinted by permission of University of Chicago Press.

Translated and adapted from Georg Simmel, *Soziologie*, pp. 646–665. (Leipzig: Duncker and Humbolt, 1908).

a) *Appreciation*—Sense-impressions may induce in us affective responses of pleasure or pain, of excitement or calm, of tension or relaxation, produced by the features of a person, or by the tone of his voice, or by his mere physical presence in the same room. These affective responses, however, do not enable us to understand or to define the other person. Our emotional response to the sense-image of the other leaves his real self outside.

b) *Comprehension*—The sense-impression of the other person may develop in the opposite direction when it becomes the medium for understanding the other. What I see, hear, feel of him is only the bridge over which I reach his real self. The sound of the voice and its meaning, perhaps, present the clearest illustration. The speech, quite as much as the appearance, of a person, may be immediately either attractive or repulsive. On the other hand, what he says enables us to understand not only his momentary thoughts but also his inner self. The same principle applies to all sense-impressions.

The sense-impressions of any object produce in us not only emotional and aesthetic attitudes toward it but also an understanding of it. In the case of reaction to non-human objects, these two responses are, in general, widely separated. We may appreciate the emotional value of any sense-impression of an object. The fragrance of a rose, the charm of a tone, the grace of a bough swaying the wind, is experienced as a joy engendered within the soul. On the other hand, we may desire to understand and to comprehend the rose, or the tone, or the bough. In the latter case we respond in an entirely different way, often with conscious endeavor. These two diverse reactions which are independent of each other are with human beings generally integrated into a unified response. Theoretically, our sense-impressions of a person may be directed on the one hand to an appreciation of his emotional value, or on the other to an impulsive or deliberate understanding of him. Actually, these two reactions are coexistent and inextricably interwoven as the basis of our relation to him. Of course, appreciation and comprehension develop in quite different degrees. These two diverse responses—to the tone of voice and to the meaning of the utterance; to the appearance of a person and to his individuality; to the attraction or repulsion of his personality and to the impulsive judgment upon his character as well as many times upon his grade of culture—are present in any perception in very different degrees and combinations.

Of the special sense-organs, the eye has a uniquely sociological function. The union and interaction of individuals is based upon mutual glances. This is perhaps the most direct and purest reciprocity which exists anywhere. The highest psychic reaction, however, in which the glances of eye to eye unite men, crystallizes into no objective structure; the unity which momentarily arises between two persons is present in the occasion and is dissolved in the function. So tenacious and subtle is this union that it can only be maintained by the shortest and straightest line between the eyes, and the smallest deviation from it, the slightest glance aside, completely destroys the unique character of this union. No objective trace of this relationship is left behind, as is universally found, directly or indirectly, in all other types of associations between men, as, for example, in interchange of words. The interaction of eye and eye dies in the moment in which the directness of the function is lost. But the totality of social relations of human beings, their self-assertion and self-abnegation, their intimacies and estrangements, would be changed in unpredictable ways if there occurred no glance of eye to eye. This mutual glance between persons, in distinction from the simple sight or observation of the other, signifies a wholly new and unique union between them.

The limits of this relation are to be determined by the significant fact that the glance by which the one seeks to perceive the other is itself expressive. By the glance which reveals the other, one discloses himself. By the same act in which the observer seeks to know the observed, he surrenders himself to be understood by the observer. The eye cannot take unless at the same time it gives. The eye of a person discloses his own soul when he seeks to uncover that of another. What occurs in this direct mutual glance represents the most perfect reciprocity in the entire field of human relationships.

Shame causes a person to look at the ground to avoid the glance of the other. The reason for this is certainly not only because he is thus spared the visible evidence of the way in which the other regards his painful situation, but the deeper reason is that the lowering of his glance to a certain degree prevents the other from comprehending the extent of his confusion. The glance in the eye of the other serves not only for me to know the other but also enables him to know me. Upon the line which unites the two eyes, it conveys to the other the real personality, the real attitude, and the real impulse. The "ostrich policy" has in this explanation a real justification: who does not see the other actually conceals himself in part from the observer. A person is not at all completely present to another, when the latter sees him, but only when he also sees the other.

The sociological significance of the eye has special reference to the expression of the face as the first object of vision between man and man. It is seldom clearly understood to what an extent even our practical relations depend upon mutual recognition, not only in the sense of all external characteristics, as the momentary appearance and attitude of the other, but what we know or intuitively perceive of his life, of his inner nature, of the immutability of his being, all of which colors unavoidably both our transient and our permanent relations with him. The face is the geometric chart of all these experiences. It is the symbol of all that which the individual has brought with him as the pre-condition of his life. In the face is deposited what has been precipitated from past experience as the substratum of his life, which has become crystallized into the permanent features of his face. To the extent to which we thus perceive the face of a person, there enters into social relations, in so far as it serves practical purposes, a super-practical element. It follows that a man is first known by his countenance, not by his acts. The face as a medium of expression is entirely a theoretical ogan; it does not act, as the hand, the foot, the whole body; it transacts none of the internal or practical relations of the man, it only tells about him. The peculiar and important sociological art of "knowing" transmitted by the eye is determined by the fact that the countenance is the essential object of the inter-individual sight. This knowing is still somewhat different from understanding. To a certain extent, and in a highly variable degree, we know at first glance with whom we have to do. Our unconsciousness of this knowledge and its fundamental significance lies in the fact that we direct our attention from this self-evident intuition to an understanding of special features which determine our practical relations to a particular individual. But if we become conscious of this self-evident fact, then we are amazed how much we know about a person in the first glance at him. We do not obtain meaning from his expression, susceptible to analysis into individual traits. We cannot unqualifiedly say whether he is clever or stupid, good- or ill-natured, temperamental or phlegmatic. All these traits are general characteristics which he shares with unnumbered others. But what this first glance at him transmits to us cannot be analyzed or appraised into any such conceptual and expressive elements. Yet our initial impression remains ever the keynote of all later knowledge of him; it is the direct perception of his individuality which his appearance, and especially his face, discloses to our glance.

The sociological attitude of the blind is entirely different from that of the deaf-mute. For the blind, the other person is actually present only in the alternating periods of his utterance. The expression of the anxiety and unrest, the traces of all past events, exposed to view in the faces of men, escape the blind, and that may be the reason for the peaceful and calm disposition, and the unconcern toward their surroundings, which is so often observed in the blind. Indeed, the majority of the stimuli which the face presents are often puzzling; in general, what we see of a man will be interpreted by what we hear from him, while the opposite is more unusual. Therefore the one who sees, without hearing, is much more perplexed, puzzled, and worried, than the one who hears without seeing. This principle is of great importance in understanding the sociology of the modern city.

Social life in the large city as compared with the towns shows a great preponderance of occasions to *see* rather than to *hear* people. One explanation lies in the fact that the person in the town is acquainted with nearly all the people he meets. With these he exchanges a word or a glance, and their countenance represents to him not merely the visible but indeed the entire personality. Another reason of especial significance is the development of public means of transportation. Before the appearance of omnibuses, railroads, and street cars in the nineteenth century, men were not in a situation where for periods of minutes or hours they could or must look at each other without talking to one another. Modern social life increases in ever growng degree the rôle of mere visual impression which always characterizes the preponderant part of all sense relationship between man and man, and must place social attitudes and feelings upon an entirely changed basis. The greater perplexity which characterizes the person who only sees, as contrasted with the one who only hears, brings us to the problems of the emotions of modern life: the lack of orientation in the collective life, the sense of utter lonesomeness, and the feeling that the individual is surrounded on all sides by closed doors.

33   Classification of the Phenomena of Fellow-Feeling

● MAX SCHELER

We must first distinguish from true fellow-feeling all such attitudes as merely contribute to our *apprehending, understanding,* and, in general, *reproducing* (emotionally) the experiences of others, including their states of feeling. Such acts have often, and quite mistakenly, been assimilated to fellow-feeling. This has come about chiefly through the theory of projective 'empathy' which attempted to explain both at the same time.

SOURCE: Max Scheler, from his *The Nature of Sympathy*, translated by Peter Heath (London: Routledge and Kegan Paul, Ltd., 1954), pp. 8–36.

But it should be clear (before we even begin to consider this class of acts), that any kind of rejoicing or pity *presupposes,* in principle, some sort of *knowledge* of the fact, nature and quality of experience in other people, just as the possibility of such knowledge presupposes, as its condition, the existence of other conscious beings. It is not *through* pity in the first place that I learn of someone's being in pain, for the latter must already *be given* in some form, if I am to notice and then *share* it. One may look at the face of a yelling child as a merely physical object, or one may look at it (in the normal way) as an expression of pain, hunger, etc., though without therefore pitying the child; the two things are utterly different. Thus experiences of pity and fellow-feeling are always additional to an experience in the other which is already grasped and understood. The givenness of these experiences (and naturally, their value) is not based, in the first instance, on sympathy or fellow-feeling—still less is the existence of other selves so established (as W. K. Clifford held).[1] Nor does this apply merely to the knowledge given in the proposition: 'X is in pain' (for I can also be informed of this), nor to the factual judgement 'that X is suffering'—the other person's experience may also be completely realized in the peculiar form of 'reproduced' experience *without* any sort of fellow-feeling being entailed thereby. It is perfectly meaningful to say: 'I can quite visualize your feelings, but I have no pity for you.' Such 'visualized' feeling remains within the cognitive sphere, and is not a morally relevant act. The historian of motives, the novelist, the exponent of the dramatic arts, must all possess in high degree the gift of visualizing the feelings of others, but there is not the slightest need for them to share the feelings of their subjects and personages.

The reproduction of feeling or experience must therefore be sharply distinguished from fellow-feeling. It is indeed a case of feeling the other's feeling, not just knowing of it, nor judging that the other has it; but it is not the same as going through the experience itself. In reproduced feeling we sense the *quality* of the other's feeling, without it being transmitted to us, or evoking a similar real emotion in us.[2] The other's feeling is given exactly like a landscape which we 'see' subjectively in memory, or a melody which we 'hear' in similar fashion— a state of affairs quite different from the fact that we remember the landscape or the melody (possibly with an accompanying recollection of the fact 'that it was seen, or heard'). In the present case there is a real seeing or hearing, yet without the object seen or heard being perceived and accepted as really present; the past is simply 'represented.' Equally little does the reproduction of feeling or experience imply any sort of 'participation' in the other's experience. Throughout our visualizing of the experience we can remain quite indifferent to whatever has evoked it.

We shall not, at present, give any very detailed account of those acts which serve to establish the existence of other people and their experiences.[3] It only needs to be emphasized that this acceptance and understanding does not come

---

[1] A. Riehl has followed him in this. *Vide Principles of Critical Philosophy* (tr. by Arthur Fairbanks, 1894). Part II, p. 160. Cf. W. K. Clifford, *Seeing and Thinking,* London, Macmillan, 1879; O. Külpe's criticism of Clifford's and Riehl's assertions, partly pertinent and partly beside the mark, in his book, *Die Realisierung,* Leipzig, 1920; and also the last chapter of this book.
[2] We feel the quality of the other's sorrow without suffering with him, the quality of his joy without ourselves rejoicing with him. On this, cf. Edith Stein: 'Neues zum Problem der Einfühlung'; Dissertation, Freiburg, 1917.
[3] Cf. Part III.

about as the conclusion to an 'argument from analogy,' nor by any protective *'empathy'* or 'mimetic impulse' (Lipps).[4] That we cannot be aware of an experience without being aware of a self is something which is directly based upon the intuitable intrinsic connection between individual and experience; there is no need of empathy on the part of the percipient. That is why we can also have it given to us that the other has an individual self distinct from our own, and that we can never fully comprehend this individual self, steeped as it is in its own psychic experience, but only our own view of it as an individual, conditioned as this is by our own individual nature. It is a corollary of this that the other person has— like ourselves—a sphere of absolute personal privacy, which can never be given to us. But that 'experiences' occur there is given for us *in* expressive phenomena —again, not by inference, but directly, as a sort of primary 'perception.' It is *in* the blush that we perceive shame, *in* the laughter joy. To say that 'our only initial datum is the body' is completely erroneous. This is true only for the doctor or the scientist, i.e. for man in so far as he abstracts *artificially* from the expressive phenomena, which have an altogether primary givenness. It is rather that the same basic sense-data which go to make up the body for outward perception, can also construe, for the act of insight, the expressive phenomena which then appear, so to speak, as the 'outcome' of experiences within. For the relation here referred to is a *symbolic,* not a causal one.[5] We can thus have insight into others, in so far as we treat their bodies as a *field of expression* for their experiences. In the sight of clasped hands, for example, the 'please' is given exactly as the physical object is—for the latter is assuredly *given* as an object (including the fact that it has a back and an inside), in the visual phenomenon. However, the qualities (i.e. the character) of expressive phenomena and those of experiences exhibit connections of a unique kind, which do not depend at all on previous acquaintance with real experiences of our own, plus the other's expressive phenomena, such that a tendency to *imitate* the movements of the gesture seen would first have to reproduce our own earlier experiences. On the contrary, imitation, even as a mere 'tendency,' already presupposes some kind of acquaintance with the other's experience, and therefore cannot explain what it is here supposed to do. For instance, if we (involuntarily) imitate a gesture of fear or joy, the imitation is never called forth simply by the visual image of the gesture; the impulse to imitate only arises when we have already apprehended the gesture *as* an expression of fear or joy. If this apprehension itself were only made possible (as Theodor Lipps believes), by a tendency to imitate and by the *reproduction,* thus evoked, of a previously experienced joy or fear (*plus* an empathic projection of what is reproduced into the other person), we should obviously be moving in a circle. And this applies also to the 'involuntary' imitation of gestures. It already presupposes an imitation of the inner intention of action, which could be realized by quite different bodily movements.[6] We do not imitate the same or similar bodily movements in observed connections of the inorganic, e.g. in inani-

---

[4] Cf. Theodor Lipps: 'Das Wissen von fremden Ichen,' in *Psychologische Untersuchungen,* Bd. I, Heft 4, 1905.

[5] We might also say that it is not the mere relation of a 'sign' to the presence of 'something,' whereby the latter is subsequently inferred; it refers to a genuine, irreducible property of the sign itself.

[6] On the distinction between imitation of action and imitation of movement, cf. K. Koffka: *The Growth of the Mind* (tr. by R. M. Ogden), Kegan Paul, 1924.

mate nature, where they cannot be phenomena expressive of psychic experience. Further evidence against Lipps' theory of imitation lies in the fact that we can understand the experience of animals, though even in 'tendency' we cannot imitate their manner of expression; for instance when a dog expresses its joy by barking and wagging its tail, or a bird by twittering. The relationships between expression and experience have a *fundamental* basis of connection, which is independent of our specifically human gestures of expression. We have here, as it were, a *universal grammar*, valid for all languages of expression, and the ultimate basis of understanding for all forms of mime and pantomime among living creatures. Only so are we able to perceive the *inadequacy* of a person's gesture to his experience, and even the contradiction between what the gesture expresses and what it is meant to express. But apart from all this, the imitation of another person's expressive gestures certainly cannot explain the act of *understanding* his inner life. The only way of explaining imitation, and the reproduction of a personal experience similar to that underlying a perceived expressive gesture, is that through this a genuine experience takes place in me, objectively *similar* to that which occurs in the other person whose expression I imitate. For such objective similarity of experience, however, there need be no present consciousness of the similarity, still less an intentionally directed act of 'understanding' or a reproduction of feeling or experience. For my having an experience *similar* to someone else's has nothing whatever to do with understanding him. Besides, such a reproduction in one's experience would require the 'understanding' of another's experience to be preceded in the participant, by a similar *real* experience (however brief); i.e. in the case of feelings, a reproduction of feeling, which would always be itself an actual feeling. But one who 'understands' the mortal terror of a drowning man has no need at all to *undergo* such terror, in a real, if weakened form. This theory therefore contradicts the observable fact that in the process of understanding the thing understood is in no way experienced as real.

It also seems clear that what this theory could explain for us is the very opposite of genuine 'understanding.' This opposite is that *infection* by others' emotions, which occurs in its most elementary form in the behaviour of herds and crowds. Here there is actually a common making of expressive gestures in the first instance, which has the secondary effect of producing similar emotions, efforts and purposes among the people or animals concerned; thus, for instance, a herd takes fright on seeing signs of alarm in its leader, and so too in human affairs. But it is characteristic of the situation that there is a complete lack of mutual 'understanding.' Indeed, the purer the case, inasmuch as a rudimentary act of understanding plays little or no part in it, the more clearly do its peculiar features emerge, namely that the participant takes the experience arising in him owing to his participation to be his *own* original experience, so that he is quite unconscious of the contagion to which he succumbs. This resembles those post-hypnotically suggested acts of will which are carried out without awareness of suggestion (unlike the obeying of commands, where one remains consciously aware that the other's will is not one's own); such acts, indeed, are characteristically regarded by the agent as being his *own*, and so too the experiences arising through participation in a common gesture of expression are ascribed, not to others, but to *oneself*. For this reason, even in daily life, we distinguish between merely aping someone ('taking him off,' for instance) and really understanding him, and point the contrast between them.

Thus neither 'projective empathy' nor 'imitation' is necessary in order to explain the primary components of fellow-feeling, viz. understanding, and the vicarious reproduction of feeling or experience. Indeed so far as the first-mentioned acts come into it, it is not understanding they produce, but the possibility of *delusive* understanding.

Let us now turn to *fellow-feeling*, which is primarily based upon . . . 'vicarious' understanding. . . . Here there are *four* quite different relationships to be distinguished. I call them:

1. Immediate community of feeling, e.g. of one and the same sorrow, 'with someone.'
2. Fellow-feeling 'about something'; rejoicing in his joy and commiseration with his sorrow.
3. Mere emotional infection.
4. True emotional identification.

(1) *Community of Feeling*

Two parents stand beside the dead body of a beloved child. They feel in common the 'same' sorrow, the 'same' anguish. It is not that A feels this sorrow and B feels it also, and moreover that they both know they are feeling it. No, it is a *feeling-in-common*. A's sorrow is in no way an 'external' matter for B here, as it is, e.g. for their friend C, who joins them, and commiserates 'with them' or 'upon their sorrow.' On the contrary, they feel it together, in the sense that they feel and experience in common, not only the self-same value-situation, but also the same keenness of emotion in regard to it. The sorrow, as value-content, and the grief, as characterizing the functional relation thereto, are here *one and identical*. It will be evident that we can only feel mental suffering in this fashion, not physical pain or sensory feelings. There is no such thing as a 'common pain.' Sensory types of feeling ('feeling-sensations' as Stumpf calls them), are by nature not susceptible of this highest form of fellow-feeling. They are inevitably 'external' to us in some respect, inspiring only commiseration 'with' and 'upon' the suffering of pain by the other person. By the same token, there is certainly such a thing as rejoicing *at* another's sensory pleasure, but never mutual enjoyment of it (as a common feeling-sensation). It may, however, be the case that A first feels sorrow by himself and is then joined by B in a common feeling. But this, as will be seen, presupposes the higher emotion of love.

(2) *Fellow-feeling*

The second case is quite different. Here also, the one person's sorrow is not simply the motivating cause of the other's. *All* fellow-feeling involves *intentional reference* of the feeling of joy or sorrow to the other person's experience. It points this way simply *qua* feeling—there is no need of any prior judgement or intimation 'that the other person is in trouble'; nor does it arise only upon sight of the other's grief, for it can also 'envisage' such grief, and does so, indeed, in its very capacity *as* a feeling.[7] But here A's suffering is first presented *as* A's in an act of understanding or 'vicarious' feeling experienced as such, and it is to this material that B's primary commiseration is directed. That is, *my* commiseration and *his* suffering are phenomenologically *two different facts,* not *one* fact, as in the first case. While in the first case the functions of vicarious experience and feeling are so interwoven with the very fellow-feeling itself as to be indistinguishable from it, in the second case the two functions are plainly distinguished even *while* experiencing them. Fellow-feeling proper, actual 'participation,' presents itself in the very phenomenon as a *re-action* to the state and value of the other's feelings— as these are 'visualized' in vicarious feeling. Thus in this case the two functions of *vicariously visualized* feeling, and *participation* in feeling are separately given and must be sharply distinguished. Very many descriptions of fellow-feeling suffer from failure to make this distinction.[8]

Nothing shows the fundamental diversity of the two functions more plainly, than the fact that the first of them can not only be given without the second, but is also present as a basis for the very *opposite* of an (associated) act of fellow-feeling. This happens, for instance, where there is specific pleasure in cruelty, and to a lesser extent in brutality. The *cruel* man owes his awareness of the pain or sorrow he causes entirely to a capacity for visualizing feeling! His joy lies in 'torturing' and in the agony of his victim. As he feels, vicariously, the increasing pain or suffering of his victim, so his own primary pleasure and enjoyment at the other's pain also increase. Cruelty consists not at all in the cruel man's being simply 'insensitive' to other peoples' suffering. Such 'insensitivity' is therefore a quite different defect in man to lack of fellow-feeling. It is chiefly found in pathological cases [9] (e.g. in melancholia), where it arises as a result of the patient's exclusive preoccupation in his own feelings, which altogether prevents him from giving emotional acceptance to the experience of other people. In contrast to cruelty, *'brutality'* is merely a disregard of other peoples' experience, despite the apprehension of it in feeling. Thus, to regard a human being as a mere log of wood and to treat the object accordingly, is not to be 'brutal' towards him. On the other hand, it is characteristic of brutality, that, given merely a sense of life, undifferentiated, as yet, into separate experiences, given even the fact of an enhanced appearance of life or a tendency towards it, any violent interruption of this tendency (as in vandalism towards plants and trees, to which one cannot be 'cruel'), is enough to mark it as brutal.

(3) *Emotional Infection*

Quite different again from these, is the case where there is no true appearance of fellow-feeling at all, although it is very frequently confused with this. Such confusion has given rise to the mistaken theories of positivism concerning the

---

[7] In *Zur psychologischen Analyse der ästhetischen Anschauung* Witasek defends the view that what we have called 'understanding' and 'vicarious feeling' is only an 'intuitive presentation of the experience in question.' This contention is decisively refuted by Edith Stein, op. cit., § 4: 'Der Streit zwischen Vorstellungs und Qualitätsansicht,' p. 19.

[8] In particular the theory of projective empathy, developed by Theodor Lipps.

[9] From the psychopathological side, Kurt Schneider's valuable work, *Pathopsychologische Beiträge zur psychologischen Phänomenologie von Liebe und Hass* is in part a verification, in other respects an elaboration and extension, of the phenomenology of sympathetic experience set out in the text (Cologne, Dissertation, 1921). Also in *Zeitschrift für die ges. Neurol. u. Psychiatrie,* Bd. 65, 1921.

evolution of fellow-feeling (Herbert Spencer) and, moreover, to a quite false appreciation of values, particularly in connection with pity. I have in mind the case of mere *emotional infection*. We all know how the cheerful atmosphere in a 'pub' or at a party may 'infect' the newcomers, who may even have been depressed beforehand, so that they are 'swept up' into the prevailing gaiety. Of course such people are equally remote from a rejoicing of either the first or the second type. It is the same when laughter proves 'catching,' as can happen especially with children, and to a still greater extent among girls, who have less sensitivity, but react more readily. The same thing occurs when a group is infected by the mournful tone of one of its members, as so often happens among old women, where one recounts her woes, while the others grow more and more tearful. Naturally, this has nothing whatever to do with pity. Here there is neither a *directing* of feeling towards the other's joy or suffering, nor any participation in her experience. On the contrary, it is characteristic of emotional infection that it occurs only as a transference of the *state* of feeling, and does *not* presuppose any sort of *knowledge* of the joy which others feel. Thus one may only notice afterwards that a mournful feeling, encountered in oneself, is traceable to infection from a group one has visited some hours before. There is nothing in the mournful feeling itself to point to this origin; only by inference from causal considerations does it become clear where it came from. For such contagion it is by no means necessary that any *emotional* experiences should have occurred in the other person. Even the *objective* aspects of such feelings, which attach to natural objects, or are discerned in an 'atmosphere'—such as the serenity of a spring landscape, the melancholy of a rainy day, the wretchedness of a room—can work infectiously in this way on the state of our emotions.[10]

The process of infection is an involuntary one. Especially characteristic is its tendency to return to its point of departure, so that the feelings concerned *gather momentum* like an avalanche. The emotion caused by infection reproduces itself *again* by means of expression and imitation, so that the infectious emotion increases, again reproduces itself, and so on. In all mass-excitement, even in the formation of 'public opinion,' it is above all this *reciprocal effect* of a self-generating infection which leads to the uprush of a common surge of emotion, and to the characteristic feature of a crowd in action, that it is so easily carried beyond the intentions of every one of its members, and does things for which no one acknowledges either the will or the responsibility. It is, in fact, the infective process itself, which generates purposes beyond the designs of any single individual.[11]

---

[10] This shows that the process of infection does *not* lie in the imitation of others' expressed experiences, even though these may actually bring it about, where it is a case of infection through experiences undergone by animals or other human beings.

[11] I refrain here from describing the immense part which infection plays in the historical evolution of whole systems of morality, in the genesis of psychopathic group-movements (from *folie à deux* to the emergence of enduring pathological customs and usages on a national scale), in the onset of panics, and particularly within all revolutionary mass-movements. Cf. Gustave Le Bon, *The Crowd: a Study of the Popular Mind*, Unwin, 1896, and *L'Ame Révolutionnaire;* see also Tarde: *Les lois de l'imitation;* and Sigmund Freud: *Group Psychology and the Analysis of the Ego,* who there observes:

'Psycho-analytic research, which has already occasionally attacked the more difficult problems of the psychoses, has also been able to show identification as present in some other cases which are not immediately comprehensible. I shall treat two of these cases in detail as material for our further consideration.

'The genesis of male homosexuality in a large class of cases is as follows. A young man has been unusually long and intensely fixated upon his mother in the sense of the Œdipus complex.

Although these processes of infection are not merely involuntary but operate 'unconsciously' (however conspicuous they may be), in the sense that we 'get into' these states without realizing that this is how it comes about, the process itself can again become an instrument of conscious volition. This occurs, for instance, in the search for 'distraction,' when we go into gay company, or attend a party, not because we are in festive mood, but simply in order to find distraction; here we anticipate that we shall be infected and 'caught up' in the prevailing gaiety. When someone says that he wants 'to see cheerful faces around him,' it is perfectly clear that he does not mean to rejoice with them, but is simply hoping for infection as a means to his *own* pleasure. Conversely, an awareness of possible infection can also create a peculiar *dread* of it, as is found wherever a person shuns melancholy places or avoids the *appearance* of suffering (not the suffering itself), by trying to banish this image from the field of his experience.

That this form of emotional infection also has nothing whatever to do with genuine fellow-feeling should be too obvious for any need of emphasis. And yet the aberrations of some most weighty authors make this emphasis necessary. Thus virtually the whole extent of Herbert Spencer's treatment of the emergence of fellow-feeling (and Darwin's also, to some extent), is no more than a persistent *confusion* of fellow-feeling with emotional infection. This confusion is dominant, especially, in the ever-recurring error of these writers, whereby they seek to derive fellow-feeling from the herd-consciousness and herd-behaviour of the higher animals. An entire trend of thought having thus gone astray, it is no wonder that, in presupposing this false conception of fellow-feeling, Friedrich Nietzsche, for his part, should have arrived at a completely *misguided evaluation* of fellow-feeling, and especially of pity. I select one passage—among many—from his outbursts against pity: 'Through pity, suffering itself becomes infectious; in certain circumstances it may lead to a total loss of life and vital energy which is absurdly out of proportion to the magnitude of the cause (—the case of the death of the Nazarene). This depressing and infectious instinct thwarts those in-

---

But at last, after the end of his puberty, the time comes for exchanging his mother for some other sexual object. Things take a sudden turn: the young man does not abandon his mother: he transforms himself into her, and now looks about for objects which can replace his ego for him, and on which he can bestow such love and care as he has experienced from his mother. This is a frequent process, which can be confirmed as often as one likes, and which is naturally quite independent of any hypothesis which may be made as to the organic driving force and motives of the sudden transformation. A striking thing about this identification is its ample scale; it remoulds the ego in one of its important features—in its sexual character—upon the model of what has hitherto been the object. In this process the object itself is renounced— whether entirely or in the sense of being preserved only in the unconscious is a question outside the present discussion. Identification with an object that is renounced or lost as a substitute for it, introjection of this object into the ego, is indeed no novelty to us. A process of the kind may sometimes be directly observed in small children. A short time ago an observation of this sort was published in the *Internationale Zeitschrift für Psychoanalyse*. A child who was unhappy over the loss of a kitten declared straight out that now he himself was the kitten, and accordingly crawled about on all fours, would not eat at table, etc. (Marcuszewicz: 'Beitrag zum autistischen Denken bei Kindern,' *Internationale Zeitschrift für Psychoanalyse*, 1920, Bd. VI).

'Another such instance of introjection of the object has been provided by the analysis of melancholia, an affection which counts among the most noteworthy of its exciting causes the real or emotional loss of a loved object. A leading characteristic of these cases is a cruel self-depreciation of the ego combined with relentless self-criticism and bitter self-reproaches. Analyses have shown that this disparagement and these reproaches apply at bottom to the object and represent the ego's revenge upon it. The shadow of the object has fallen upon the ego, as I have said elsewhere. The introjection of the object is here unmistakably clear,' p. 66 (tr. by James Strachey, International Psycho-analytical Library, No. 6, 1922).

stincts which aim at the preservation and enhancement of the value of life; by *multiplying* misery quite as much as by preserving all that is miserable, it is the principal agent in promoting decadence' (*Anti-Christ*, pp. 131 and 134).[12] It is obvious that here, as in all similar passages, pity is confused with emotional infection. Suffering itself does *not* become infectious through pity. Indeed, it is just where suffering is infectious that pity is completely excluded; for to that extent I no longer view it as the *other's* suffering, but as my *own*, which I try to get rid of, by putting the notion of suffering out of mind. Indeed it is just where infection *does* occur via suffering, that pity for the other person's sufferings, as being *his*, can stay the infection itself; just as the emotional re-living of an earlier painful experience, which still weighs heavy upon the present, can take this weight off one's mind.[13] Pity would be a 'multiplier of misery' only if it were identical with emotional infection. For only the latter—as we have seen—can produce in others a real suffering, a state of feeling akin to the infectious one. But such real suffering does not occur, however, in *true* fellow-feeling.

(4) *Emotional Identification*

The true *sense of emotional unity*, the act of identifying one's own self with that of another, is only a heightened form, a limiting case as it were, of infection. It represents a limit in that here it is not only the separate process of feeling in another that is unconsciously taken as one's own, but his self (in all its basic attitudes), that is identified with one's own self. Here too, the identification is as involuntary as it is unconscious. Lipps has wrongly sought to construe this as a case of æsthetic empathy. Thus, according to him, the absorbed spectator of an acrobat in a circus turn identifies himself with the performer, whose movements he reproduces within himself, in the character of an acrobat. Lipps believes that only the spectator's real self remains distinct here, his conscious self having sunk itself completely in that of the acrobat. Edith Stein has interposed a just criticism on this point.[14] 'I am not,' she says, ' "one with" the acrobat; I am only "with" him. The correlated motor-impulses and tendencies are carried out here by a fictional "I," which remains recognizably distinct as a phenomenon from my individual self; it is simply that my attention is passively fixed throughout on the fictional "I," and by way of this, on the acrobat.'

There are other cases, however, insufficiently recognized either by Theodor Lipps or Edith Stein, in which such identification is undoubtedly complete; which do not merely exemplify a moment of true 'ecstasy,' but may be of long duration, and can even become habitual throughout whole phases of life. They are of two opposite kinds: the *idiopathic* and the *heteropathic*. Thus identification can come about in *one* way through the total eclipse and absorption of another self by one's own, it being thus, as it were, completely dispossessed and deprived of all rights in its conscious existence and character. It can also come about the other way, where 'I' (the formal subject) am so overwhelmed and hypnotically bound and fettered by the other 'I' (the concrete individual), that my formal status as a

---

[12] [Translated by A. M. Ludovici, London, T. N. Foulis, 1911.]
[13] It is not the mere reconstruction of repressed memories, nor yet the abreaction from them, but this *reliving* of them, that underlies whatever therapeutic efficacy psycho-analysis may possess.
[14] Op. cit.

subject is usurped by the other's personality, with all *its* characteristic aspects; in such a case, I live, not in 'myself,' but entirely in 'him,' the other person—(in and through him, as it were).

Such paradigm-cases of identification, either by way of an all-inclusive propensity to infect, or as a state of complete and total infection of the very roots of individuality, I find exemplified in very different kinds of experience. . . .

34   Sarcasm as Sociation: The Rhetoric of Interaction

● DONALD W. BALL

Like conflict, authority, and many other sociological concepts, sarcasm may profitably be viewed, in Simmel's famous phrase, as a societal form irrespective of content.[1] To use Simmel's terminology again, sarcasm is a sociation,[2] a kind of interaction appearing in the diverse natural settings and situations of face-to-face social behaviour. Social scientists studying interaction have, in general, focused upon rather more abstracted analytical dimensions such as cohesion, differentiation, dominance and subordination, complementarity, and so on. Valuable as their studies are, they ignore the common-sense constructs prevalent in the everyday life of the mundane world where people meet, talk, visit, chat, argue, and so forth.

To the extent that participants implicitly or explicitly analyse the qualities of such sociations, it is not in terms dear to experiment-oriented students of small group interaction, but rather at a different (and not necessarily internally consistent) level: the level of typifications of the everyday world.[3] These common-sense constructs embrace terms of description and evaluation such as strained, friendly, brusque, humorous, pleasant, dull, or sarcastic; assessments of the interaction, or the actors, or both. They constitute what might be called the *rhetoric of interaction,* standing well below the level of abstraction characteristic of the usual dimensions of behavioural analysis.

It is a rhetoric of common-sense constructs, sarcasm and its derivatives among them, which helps to provide vocabularies of motives and evaluations for actors involved in the dramas of everyday interaction in natural settings. Of course, this rhetoric may itself be described in more conventional social scientific terms, and should be subjected to such analysis. Such an effort involves creating, in Schutz's

SOURCE: Donald W. Ball, in *Canadian Review of Sociology and Anthropology*, II (November 1965), pp. 190–198.

Outgrowth of an earlier paper, read at the West Coast Conference for Small Group Research, Salt Lake City, 1965, "Sarcasm as Sociation: Suggestions for Small Group Theory and Research."

[1] *The Sociology of Georg Simmel,* trans. K. Wolff (Glencoe, 1950), 21–23, 40–43.
[2] *Ibid.,* 43–57; also Georg Simmel, "The Sociology of Sociability," trans. E. Hughes, *American Journal of Sociology,* LV, November, 1949, 254–261.
[3] A. Schutz, "Common Sense and Scientific Interpretation of Human Action," *Collected Papers* (The Hague, 1962), I, 3–47; C. Shepherd, *Small Groups* (San Francisco, 1964), 9–14. One exception among social scientists has been Tom Burns. See for instance his consideration of banter and irony in "Friends, Enemies, and the Polite Fiction," *American Sociological Review,* XVIII, December, 1953, 654–63. Like the work of Burns, the following will attempt to view the rhetoric of interaction in other than what are considered socio-linguistic terms.

terms, typifications of typifications, that is, second-order constructs based upon the common-sense categories of everyday experience.[4]

Almost intuitively it can be asserted that, though the rhetoric of interaction is highly evocative, it may be subject to serious methodological problems, especially in regard to operationalization. This difficulty will be discussed below; it is argued, however, that the constructs and terminology of the rhetoric of interaction, including sarcasm, are worthy of social scientific consideration.

As a preliminary to such an examination, it may be useful to consider some forms and functions of sarcasm and a few of its possible structural correlates. Such a consideration may shed light upon such questions as: What are typical forms of sarcasm as sociation? What elements or roles or both are involved? What social functions are performed by sarcasm? For or upon whom are these functions performed, or, in other words, where in the social structure is the phenomenon most probable and prevalent? These questions and the following discussion are not meant to be exhaustive. Rather it should be emphasized that the discussion is suggestive and exploratory and highly tentative in speaking to, and about, some of the problems relating to sociological analysis of sarcasm. Perhaps it should also be noted that illustrative examples are deliberately avoided. This is because of the character of sarcasm, as sketched below, and, equally important, because of the tendency towards cuteness inherent in such a subject. If the present treatment seems somewhat ponderous, it is due at least in part to the latter consideration.

Form

By form is meant a "grammar,"[5] concerned with the generalized social elements of sarcasm, not specific instances of its occurrence, foscusing on abstractions rather than particulars.

Sarcasm is, of course, a common everyday linguistic form of biting communication, especially, it would seem, an oral one, with its locus in intimate settings. This follows from the relatively "flat" character of the written as compared to the more readily dramatized spoken word.[6] Most generally, it is probably true that sarcasm requires not only a set of appropriate words, sharply and uniquely relevant to the particular situation, but also a presentation context which allows the use of such other arts of communication as inflection and intonation, gesture, timing, and facial and postural expression.[7]

Ordinarily it is not enough that the proper potentially sarcastic words and phrases be presented; they must also be accompanied by ancillary elements of communication which summon up a sarcastic totality, that is, by the over- and under-emphasis of key symbols involving not only words, but also tone and

---

[4] See Schutz, "Common Sense and Scientific Interpretation of Human Action." Although the following is informed by Schultz's methodological perspective, it should not be construed as an attempt systematically to emulate it. Rather, its exploratory nature leads to a method utilizing observation, deduction, and, at times, hopefully well-grounded speculation.

[5] Compare K. Burke, *A Grammar of Motives* (Cleveland, 1962), xviii.

[6] See E. Goffman, *The Presentation of Self in Everyday Life* (Garden City, 1959). Carol Virak has pointed out that sarcasm may occur entirely without words, e.g., in offering a handkerchief as a "crying towel."

[7] *Ibid.* It is this characteristic of sarcasm that allows it to be, in Goffman's words, strategically disattended, i.e., its form may be ignored. For similar reasons, it can also easily be denied by the originator.

expression. In many cases whether or not a given phrase is sarcastic is entirely a function of these other elements; words of commendation may be so presented as to become what is typically considered sarcasm. The meaning of the words "nice job" for instance, remains obscure without additional information; it may be high praise or low criticism, depending upon other contextual communicative techniques as they are defined by the interactants' culture. It is in small natural groups with their enlarged private vocabularies, transcending the strictly verbal, that such consensually held definitions, and thus sarcasm, are likely to be highest.

As a form involving a network of roles, sarcasm is analytically at least a triadic relationship, although empirically fewer units may be involved. Minimally, a creator of sarcasm, a *sarcaster*, is necessary, along with an *object* and an *audience* to receive the sarcastic communication. The object is frequently combined with or resides in one of the other two units, so that empirically sarcasm can often be considered as either a self-directed or an other-directed dyad.[8] In self-direction the sarcaster communicates about himself as object to his audience. From a strictly sociological perspective, however, it is the case where audience and object are one and the same which is perhaps most frequently of interest. As an other-directed form, sarcasm is a mechanism frequently used in the application of the informal social controls necessary to give shape and order to interaction in the small groups and encounters of everyday social intercourse.[9]

So far no formal definition of sarcasm has been suggested; this has been deliberate. Though sarcasm is often humorous, humour is not a necessary condition and, like humour,[10] sarcasm is difficult, if not impossible, to define precisely and operationally from an external-observational perspective. Etymologically, sarcasm is derived from the Greek *sarkazein,* to speak bitterly [11]—literally, to tear flesh. This is suggestive of the flavour, but only suggestive. To some literary scholars (to whom social scientists, by default, have left such study) sarcasm is a form of verbal irony,[12] but this definition also is imprecise. Like irony, sarcasm conveys more than its obvious overt meaning. But sarcasm seems, much more than simple irony, to imply a social-purposive, functional use of communication. Where irony has to do with content, the thrust of sarcasm is in terms of social function, that is, the meaning of the early Greek stem refers not so much to what is said as to its consequences. Obviously, this is not to deny the ironic content of much that is deemed sarcastic, nor the sarcastic form of much that is deemed ironic.

None of this seems to lend itself to the operationalization typical of contemporary methodology: a series of words to identify sarcasm having their referents in still other words and intuitions, *ad infinitum.*[13] This is not, however, an insoluble

---

[8] Even talking to one's self is dyadic in so far as the actor is playing the two roles of communicator and audience simultaneously. An anonymous reader has suggested that self-directed sarcasm is actually sardonicism.

[9] See E. Goffman, *Behavior in Public Places* (New York, 1963). Note that while the roles of sarcaster and audience are conceived of as social, such a conception vis-à-vis the object is problematic, since this unit may or may not be human, e.g., possibly an element of the physical-spatial-temporal environment. Such an object may have social meaning, but lacks the dynamic *human* interaction potential.

[10] J. Flügel, "Humor and Laughter," in G. Lindzey, ed., *Handbook of Social Psychology* (Reading, 1964), II, 709; M. Eastman, *Enjoyment of Laughter* (New York, 1936).

[11] This root suggests the not always humorous vein in sarcasm.

[12] Thrall and A. Hibbard, *A Handbook to Literature* (New York, 1960), 435. This is not to suggest sociological poaching, but an alternative and complementary focus.

[13] G. Homans, *The Human Group* (New York and Burlingame, 1950), 24.

problem for, as may be inferred from the above, that which is crucial to sarcasm is its phenomenology, its existence and apprehension in direct, naïve experience. What is important is that a given message is defined as sarcastic by one or more of the parties involved, the sarcaster, his object, and his audience. The perception and definition of sarcasm as such by at least one of these three are the momentous elements.[14] Sarcasm *per se* is not inherent in a combination of communicative elements, but is relative, existing only in the socially structured perceptions and definitions common to the interactants' culture. When such perception and definition take place, sarcasm is seen as rising out of and becoming a sociation—a kind of interaction—not a communication.

Here Simmel's conceptualization of societal forms as sociations independent of their more specific contents may be applied.[15] Regardless of content—the particular words, phrases, expressions, gestures, and emphases—sarcasm ultimately rests upon its apprehension as such by relevant parties. Any given content may or may not be defined as sarcastic depending upon various situational and personal variables. Unless the sarcaster, audience, object, or some combination thereof defines a message as sarcastic, the content is irrelevant. Which party (or parties) makes such a definition will have important functional implications.

Thus, it makes little theoretical sense to think of sarcasm as an always hostile, alienated form of communication. Sarcasm is as much a function of its reception as of its inception.[16] It is a truism of daily interaction that the intent of a given communication does not necessarily equal or even resemble its ultimate perception by the audience. To conceive of sarcasm only in terms of initiations is to over-simplify and even distort empirical reality, to ignore the emergent and reflexive nature of human conduct, especially as it is influenced in the interactions of everyday life.

Social Functions

A major instrumental function of sarcasm, as noted above, is in terms of its utility for social control: what might be termed part of the politics of sarcasm. This is particularly true where the setting is a small, intimate, primary group. In such groups there are few if any legitimized formal sanctions readily available to encourage consistency of interactional-behaviour. At the same time, the problem exists, whether it is conscious and explicit among the members or not, of maintaining some minimal degree of social order, some base line of conformity to expectations.[17] Given the high degree of mutual awareness among members of such groups, the use of sarcasm becomes particularly appropriate as a mechanism of social control because of the lack of social distance between the members.

It is within intimate natural groups that the desire and regard for the social

---

[14] To paraphrase the Thomas dictum: "If things are defined as real, their consequences are real." W. I. Thomas, as quoted in R. Merton, *Social Theory and Social Structure* (Glencoe, 1957), 421. Also Schutz, "Common Sense and the Scientific Interpretation of Human Action."
[15] Simmel, "The Sociology of Sociability." This is, of course, not to deny the possibility of institutionalization, leading to the automatic cognition of a given set of communicative elements as being a case of sarcasm; but again, such a response is based socially, not on inherent characteristics.
[16] Thomas, in Merton, *Social Theory and Social Structure*.
[17] On functional analysis, see Merton, *ibid.*, esp. 19–84. On informal social control, for much of the recent small group research on cohesion, conformity, etc., see e.g., D. Cartwright and A. Zander, *Group Dynamics* (Evanston, 1960), 69–341; also M. Sherif, *The Psychology of Social Norms* (New York, 1936).

approval of other members is usually assumed by social scientists to be strongest.[18] To be the sarcaster's object before such an audience is to suffer loss of social approval, and thus be discouraged from future departures from behavioural expectations. Furthermore, in these small groups there is the probability that in the object's mind sarcasm will be imagined as but the first in a series of sanctions of increasing severity, ultimately leading to degradation, ostracism, and expulsion, should deviation persist. In this way the effectiveness of sarcasm, like that of many other informal sanctions, lies in its imagined consequences.

Sarcasm as control is not empirically limited to closed forms of the small group: for example, the object may be external to the sarcaster's immediate audience, but at the same time a "potential" member, whose circumspect receipt of the communication is desired; such a relationship is overtly dyadic but covertly triadic. Other instances of control can be imagined which are overtly triadic and covertly dyadic, as when the object is wholly external to both the sarcaster and the audience. In this situation the control dimension would come into play only if the object had a contextually meaningful symbolic relationship to the audience.

Conversely, sarcasm may also be utilized as a technique for impairing or destroying control and stability, by deflating or debasing the controller or in some other way encouraging a state of disequilibrium. Thus, sarcasm as control may be a two-edged sword, at the disposal of the controlled as well as the controllers. There the strategies of Potter's gamesmanship seem especially relevant.

Another element in the politics of sarcasm is its utilization in boundary-maintenance. In such cases sarcasm may function to include or exclude, or to do both simultaneously. Fowler's observation, made originally about irony, describes such cases when sarcasm "postulates a double audience" of initiatives and naïves, a double circle of knowing "ins" and unaware "outs." [19] For the "ins" such communication serves not only to maintain the boundaries of group exclusiveness, but also promotes or reinforces solidarity in much the same way as a shared joke.

Yet another political function of sarcasm is as a sharpened and pointed form of communication, achieving emphasis through style rather than content, as in sarcastic understatement. Here sarcasm may serve as a functional surrogate for more literal communication such as direct attack upon the object. Thus the sarcaster may select his form as a deliberate political strategy, especially if alternative modes might lead to reprisals or excessive situational disruption. In such instances sarcasm is clearly instrumental. Paradoxically, sarcasm may be chosen as a vehicle of praise if it is desired to inhibit response or put the object at ease or both.[20]

---

[18] R. LaPiere, *A Theory of Social Control* (New York, 1954). As a sanction, sarcasm has the functional virtue of having relatively low group disruption potential as compared with many other control techniques involving the manipulation of diminished or denied social approval, without the more unbalancing and sometimes long range effects of these other sanctions, e.g., physical restraint and coercion or violence. Thus the costs are relatively small. See A. R. Radcliffe-Brown on the joking relationship, *Structure and Function in Primitive Society* (Glencoe, 1952), ch. 4. It should also be apparent that to the extent that group stability is valued by its members sarcasm as control functions positively at the individual expressive level. This may even include deviant objects who share the stability value (regardless of whether or not this is to be defined a false-consciousness).

[19] H. Fowler, *A Dictionary of Modern English Usage* (London, 1927), 295–296.

[20] It should be remembered that not all sarcasm is verbal abuse; such a technique would seem especially likely where the sarcaster and the object are in a superordinate-subordinate relationship respectively, and the dissemination of praise is incongruent with the role definition of the former *vis-à-vis* the latter, and vice-versa. On superordinate-subordinate relationships, see *The Sociology of Georg Simmel*, 181–303. For hierarchical aspects of sarcasm, see structural correlates, below.

Expressively, sarcasm may function as a means of tension management or re-lease for the sarcaster and his audience, even while operating instrumentally as control or in emphatic communication. Tension control without an instrumental function is probably more frequent than the reverse, however, and is probably the most common function of sarcasm.[21] It should be noted that this function may appear at either the group or the individual level or simultaneously at both.

Finally, a way in which sarcasm may function both instrumentally and expres-sively at one and the same time may be noted, the explication of which may add to the understanding of a facet of classical sociological theory. In this case per-sons are subject to the social psychological condition conceptualized by Max Scheler as *ressentiment*.[22] In such situations persons who are the lower members of a status-discrepant relationship are hypothesized to experience feelings of hos-tility which, because of their positional disadvantage, they are unable to express openly. According to Scheler, their hostility will work itself out through the covert inversion and debasement of the superior's values, even while they osten-sibly confirm these same values. When such a condition is operative, sarcasm becomes particularly appropriate; it seems especially fitted for debasing and in-verting the superior object's values, even if the sarcaster alone provides the audi-ence. Such a utilization of sarcasm, if subtle enough in execution, may avoid actual detection if not suspicion by the object or other audience, and thus avoid possible retaliation. In such a situation, sarcasm is instrumental in venting hos-tility "safely" while the sarcaster at the same time enjoys the release.

Needless to say, the foregoing does not exhaust the functions of sarcasm or the analytic possibilities of sociological examination of it. More specifically, it ignores psychological aspects of sarcasm although they may obviously have social conse-quences. It does, however, suggest the relevance of some conventional theoretical axes as they relate to the investigation of sarcasm, such as instrumental-expressive and group-individual. The specification of others awaits systematic research and further theorization.

Structural Correlates

Any discussion of structural correlates must, of course, be highly speculative. Still, given certain rather generally accepted propositions about social structure, some "educated guesses" may be hazarded.

For one thing, it is probable that in terms of class or status, that is, as regards external attributes achieved or ascribed outside the setting (which may of course carry over into the internal situation), sarcasm is a relatively high status phenom-enon. This seems probable because of the sheer verbal ability necessary, such ability being to a great extent dependent upon education, in turn closely corre-lated with status.[23] Also, given the tendency of people of higher status to express aggression verbally, it would seem logical that such persons would utilize sar-casm; [24] it is an effective weapon in intellectual attack, being at once more subtle,

---

[21] This is probably the case even ignoring the biologically oriented tension-reduction theories of behaviour.

[22] M. Scheler, *Ressentiment*, ed. L. Coser, trans. H. Holdheim (New York, 1961); D. Ball, "Covert Political Rebellion as *Ressentiment*," *Social Forces*, XLVIII, October, 1964, 93–101.

[23] This hypothesis deliberately ignores "wit," the measurement of which may be even more culture-bound than intelligence, and thus, like education, related to education and social rank.

[24] A. Cohen, *Delinquent Boys* (Glencoe, 1955); Ball, "Covert Political Rebellion as *Ressenti-ment*," in D. G. McKinley (ed.), *Social Class and Family Life* (New York, 1964), 51–62.

sophisticated, and pointed than the more direct expressions of aggression and hostility.[25]

For internal aspects of stratification, that is, the hierarchical differentiation of those involved, it is probable that sarcasm most frequently involves unequals: either subordinates engaging in a covert aggression which can be denied, or superordinates exercising social power and control in cases where less temperate communication is undesirable. Interestingly, both situations involve techniques whereby the sarcaster utilizes ambiguity to provide a potential strategic withdrawal. Relationally, such cases involve superordinates and subordinates within a division of labour; situationally, the ups-men and downs-men of Potter's manuals;[26] culturally, actors subject to invidious definition and differentiation and their more favourably evaluated colleagues.

Another place in the social structure where sarcasm would seem highly probable is within those groups where the costs of open internal conflict are likely to be excessive but where institutionalized procedures for containing conflict are lacking, as in the family, friendship groups, gangs,[27] and so on. Whether deliberate or not, sarcasm in these groups would be politically strategic, reducing the possibilities of disruptive cleavage at least temporarily.

Yet another structural correlate, in another context mentioned above, would be those structural relationships characterized by inequality which generate *ressentiment*. Relationships like father and son, powerful or important parishioner and clergyman, daughter-in-law and mother-in-law, are all examples of the types of case referred to by Scheler where the latter partner is constrained against the overt expression of hostility towards the former because of that person's status definition and concomitant rights and power.

Again, the above are merely suggestions and in no way a complete listing of the possibilities. They do, however, suggest starting points for the empirical investigation of sarcasm in terms of locations in behavioural space as they may relate to social structures and processes.[28]

Research

Given a substantially phenomenological conception of sarcasm, it follows that research must take the common-sense constructs and perceptions of the mundane world as its point of departure. A vital first step, prior to the actual study of sarcasm in social settings, would be to map these common-sense constructs which

---

[25] On this type of hostility and aggression, see E. Goffman, "On Face-Work: An Analysis of Ritual Elements and Social Interaction," excerpted in W. Bennis, E. Schein, D. Berlew, and F. Steele (eds.), *Interpersonal Dynamics* (Homewood, 1964), 226–249, esp. 240–241. For a more general analysis, derived from Simmel, see L. Coser, *The Functions of Social Conflict* (New York, 1964).

[26] The situational inequality does not deny the possibility of a more generalized equality within the relationship, broadly conceived. It seems, in fact, quite probable in equalitarian friendship groups, where activities which temporarily put a participant at a disadvantage, i.e., momentarily declass him, serve to trigger the opportunity for sarcasm by others not so indicted. See S. Potter, *The Theory and Practise of Gamesmanship* and *One-Upmanship* (New York, 1948 and 1952).

[27] See F. Thrasher, *The Gang*, abridged (Chicago, 1963), 204–205; also Coser, *The Functions of Social Conflict*.

[28] One possibility is shown in Goffman's discussion of how role incumbents attempt to express their lack of total absorption in the role they are playing. See "Role Distance," in *Encounters* (Indianapolis, 1961).

provide the contextual background for sarcasm-oriented behaviour. Here the survey analyst and his techniques of questionnaire and interview can be of much aid. Once preliminary mapping has been accomplished, investigations more directly relevant to the specific social and cultural context in which sarcasm occurs can begin.

Because of sarcasm's presupposition of shared meanings, the purposes of research in this area would seem to be served best by the use of natural, rather than experimentally created groups. Future research should, then, make a genuine effort to relate its theories, constructs, concepts, and research more directly to the natural contexts of interaction in the mundane world. Sarcasm is but one example of the forms of sociation which make up a rhetoric of interaction in everyday life. Existing approaches to the small group are useful, of course, but a broader view, even at the expense of methodological rigour, is desirable. The insidious influence of procedural or technological feasibility upon theory and problem selection is well known. Ultimately, the value of any research must be assessed in terms of its ability to aid in describing and making predictions about life outside its own limited setting.

In brief, then, investigation of sarcasm as a social phenomenon and development of a sociology of sarcasm must bear upon the interrelated structures of personality, group, and culture, examining forms and styles, norms and values,[29] and other factors governing probabilities and establishing qualities of the definition and location of sarcasm within the various social orders of the mundane world of everyday life.

35   Love

● NELSON N. FOOTE

The title of this paper has provoked comments from friends and acquaintances ever since it was publicly announced. If those comments are classified according to the attitudes they express, they appear to fall into four rough categories: *cynical, joking, sentimental,* and *matter-of-fact.* Comments falling into the fourth category were least frequent, totaling three cases out of perhaps twenty. Of these three persons, two pointed out to me that love is not considered a proper subject for academic discourse: one claimed that the title would draw only a group of moralistic or sentimental listeners, lacking in scientific motive; the other claimed that the regular academics would be scornful unless I devised a more pompous and wordy title. The third merely made the cryptic remark that it takes courage to speak on this subject. This paper is aimed at drawing scientific attention to a matter-of-fact attitude toward love. Serious matter-of-factness toward love is a minority point of view even among professed social scientists. Indeed, one gains

---

[29] A pilot study touching upon this and several other areas is currently in progress by the author.

SOURCE: Nelson N. Foote, in *Psychiatry,* XVI (1953), pp. 245–251. Reprinted by special permission of The William Alanson White Psychiatric Foundation, Inc., copyright owners.

some introductory illumination of the subject from recognizing that the first three categories of comments are far more representative of the common approach to love.

Ambivalence

Cynicism, joking, and sentimentality alike bespeak a fundamental ambivalence toward love. Cynicism is the attitude of a person who is afraid that he will become the victim of illusions—illusions which he believes exist, entrap others, and are dangerous to himself. He hungers and thirsts for beliefs he can trust, but he never finds any that he can trust. Joking is the classical symptom by which the field ethnologist identifies status relationships that evoke conflicting emotions. And sentimentality is of course the lavish counterfeiting of genuine emotion that occurs when genuine emotion is deemed appropriate in a particular social situation but is not forthcoming spontaneously.

Freud believed that ambivalence was characteristic of all human love, and he also appeared to believe that the characteristic complement of love was hate. There is much truth in what he says, but at the present time some refinement and qualification are required. In general, the appearance of ambivalence in love relationships is probably peculiar to our own highly competitive society and may not be characteristic of other times and places. To suggest that it may happily be made to disappear in our own time is the only preachment I would proffer in this paper.

To understand how ambivalence toward love may diminish and disappear requires more precise analysis than is implied by the simple concept of ambivalence as the concurrence of love and hate. In a competitive society, as Bacon long ago pointed out, "he that hath wife and children hath given hostages to fortune." One who entrusts himself fully to another may find his credulity and kindness exploited. His love may be rejected or betrayed. To expose oneself to another is to run the risk of getting hurt. It may take only foolhardiness, among specialists in human development, to talk about love, but it does take courage to love in a society like our own. Many dare not try; they fear involvement. In short, fear rather than hate appears to be the original rival of love in the ambivalent situations that one encounters daily.

To be sure, when the fear seems justified by some act of the other, then the sense of betrayal is keen, and hostility is at once engendered. Several years ago I formed a habit of collecting clippings about domestic crimes in which wives, husbands, and children burned, poisoned, shot, and butchered each other. These clippings mounted so fast that I soon had a manila folder full of them. I was very glad to terminate the habit by donating the whole batch to Robert Hess of the Committee on Human Development, who has been doing a study of aggression in families for the United States Public Health Service. Aggression against the other is always potential in love relationships, but it forms a secondary and conditional phase; the fear of being hurt oneself is primary and continuous. Yet to the extent that one is withheld from entering into love relationships by fear of being hurt, he is deprived of love and may crave it all the more.

This unrequited craving for love, in a society which demands the seal of love upon most interpersonal relations, leads not only to the characteristic expressions of cynicism, joking, and sentimentality, but also to a kind of self-renewing vicious circle. The signs of love are demanded, disbelieved, and demanded again. The oftener they are required, the oftener they are simulated; the more often they are distrusted, the more often further reassurance is demanded—until it is a wonder that any sound currency for conducting valid exchanges remains in use at all. The inflation of amatory declaration in the country has regularly puzzled foreign visitors. Fortunately some Americans do develop a keen and insistent ear for the real article, whereby they can detect it beneath the babble of spurious affirmations. The honored heroes of our best fiction are those who can with relentless accuracy distinguish true from false in this shadowy realm; they are sparing in terms of endearment to the point of taciturnity.

Competence

A matter-of-fact approach to the study of love requires a redefinition and even some reconceptualization of its nature. Some would doubt that anything new could be said on a subject that has been popular for so many thousands of years. Can contemporary social scientists, for instance, improve upon the old Greek distinction between *eros* and *agape,* the sexual and nonsexual types of love? Did Freud really add something to modern knowledge and insight by his many assertions that *eros* really underlies the expressions of *agape?* In attempting to answer these challenges, it may be helpful strategy to pick out the most basic innovation of modern social science and proceed from that to an appropriately contemporary redefinition of love.

The most basic finding of recent social science is undoubtedly the novel proposition that human nature, conceived in terms of personality, is a cultural product, subject to a continuous process of re-creation and development. This concept is not to be found in the Greeks or the Scholastics or even, in its present form, in the philosophers of the Enlightenment, though these last certainly turned scientific attention to processes of history, change, and progress. As late as Darwin, the notion that personality is biologically given still had sway. The evolutionary model of thought, however, with its emphasis upon continuous creation, eventually became the basis for overthrowing so-called Social Darwinism (approximately in the 1930's in this country if we count in terms of majority sentiment). Even so, we still have with us those who fear that national intelligence is declining because the Ph.D.'s have so few children.

There is a growing number of scholars nowadays who conceive that not only personality in general but intelligence in particular are modifiable and develop differently in both kind and degree as social and cultural conditions are varied. In fact, it seems possible that purposive development of personality along optimal lines may soon become an objective of public policy. The recent report of the Midcentury White House Conference on Children and Youth carries a title, *Personality in the Making,*[1] which almost any previous decade would have found revolutionary.

In a recent article entitled "The Role of Love in Human Development," Daniel Prescott attempted to arrive at a satisfactory definition of love in order to explore its implications for human development.[2] He reviewed critically the conceptions

---

[1] Helen Leland Witmer and Ruth Kotinsky (eds.), *Personality in the Making: The Fact-finding Report of the Midcentury White House Conference on Children and Youth;* New York, Harper, 1952.
[2] Daniel A. Prescott, "The Role of Love in Human Development," *J. Home Economics* (1952) 44:173–176.

of love mentioned by the standard writers of the standard textbooks on child de-velopment, and also those set forth by such psychiatric thinkers as James Plant, Erich Fromm, and Harry Stack Sullivan.[3] The results of his library search are in-teresting, but it seems more illuminating to pursue his quest in the opposite direc-tion. That is, it may be better to define love in terms of human development, as follows: *Love is that relationship between one person and another which is most conducive to the optimal development of both.* This optimal development is to be measured practically in the growth of competence in interpersonal relations.

Sullivan's definition is a helpful beginning: "When the satisfaction or the se-curity of another person becomes as significant to one as is one's own satisfaction or security, then the state of love exists."[4] But his approximation is static, uni-lateral, and still tinged with the Christian morality which honors sacrifice of one-self to another as an ultimate good, though it may thwart the development of both. Erich Fromm's notion of productive love, and his insistence upon the le-gitimacy of self-love, appear more analytically precise and valid: ". . . love is an activity and not a passion . . . the essence of love is to 'labor' for something and 'to make something grow.' . . . To love a person productively implies to care and to feel responsible for his life, not only for his physical existence but for the growth and development of all his human powers . . . without *respect* for and *knowledge* of the beloved person, love deteriorates into domination and posses-siveness."[5]

Fromm might well have gone further than he did to exclude other kinds of behavior as not coming within a definition of love which emphasizes mutual de-velopment—for example, dependency, conceit, and mere tribal identification with kindred. The director of a child care agency told me recently that her agency had come to recognize that the best mother for a child was not the one who re-garded the child as an extension of the parent, but the one who could regard the child as *another person,* to be respected, responded to, and understood for his own sake.

If by definition we love most those to whose development we contribute most, whether wittingly or unwittingly, such a definition has specific virtues over the popular conception of love as a fluctuating emotion which can only to a degree be stabilized by ritual or pretense. Rather, love is to be known by its works. The familiar emotions may be evoked intermittently by the works of love; there is nothing drab about the joys of receiving the actual evidence of love as against merely its verbal affirmation; but the more important point is that the growth of love can thus be charted as a developing process, progressive fruition of which is more to be desired than attainment and fixation of a particular state of emo-tional response. From this viewpoint, one values another not only for what he is at the moment but for his potentialities of development, and these are necessarily assessed longitudinally and not by comparison shopping. One commits himself to another not on the basis of romantic, forced illusions, but of real possibilities which can emerge with proper cultivation. Trust and appreciation accumulate through proven results as indexed in mutual personal development.

---

[3] James Plant, *The Envelope;* New York, Commonwealth Fund, 1950. Erich Fromm, *Man for Himself: An Inquiry into the Psychology of Ethics;* New York, Rinehart, 1947. Harry Stack Sullivan, *Conceptions of Modern Psychiatry;* Washington, D. C., William Alanson White Psy-chiatric Foundation, 1947.

[4] Sullivan, reference footnote 3: p. 20.

[5] Fromm, reference footnote 3: pp. 98–101.

Audience

I want to turn now to the question of the precise delineation of the relationship of lover to loved one—parent and child, husband and wife, friend and friend—which is most conducive to the optimal development of each. A beginning toward the precise characterization of the ideal form of this relationship can be made by likening it to the relationship of artist and audience. There are of course all kinds of artists and all kinds of audiences. But almost every artist is acutely conscious of the bearing of his audience upon his performance and development as an artist. To attain an audience that is critical but appreciative, objective but hopeful, and neither patronizing nor condemnatory nor sentimentally adulatory, is the ideal his experience leads him toward. This ideal audience expects from him a performance as good or better than he has given before; it expects him to work hard for it. But it is identified with the artist, and sympathetic in an informed, understanding way. Thus it never unrealistically demands that he exceed his powers, achieve a result he never aimed for, or be something he is not. Best of all is the audience that clearly differentiates between the artist and the work of art, judging the latter as a finished product but the former as a never-fully-disclosed realm of potential productivity. Such an audience is only disappointed when its favored artist does less than his best.

Everyone knows the prodigies of creativity which are occasionally unleashed when a person discovers and is discovered by the perfect critic. Many a person can look back upon an incident in his school career when a sensitive teacher recognized at the critical moment an emerging talent and thereby permanently exalted his conception of himself and his capabilities. These are the moments of love in its sublime power to move. Such incidents are the imputed reference when a husband speaks of his wife as his "best friend and critic," although the phrase has become shopworn through sentimental usage. To be critical is thus to be neither hypercritical nor hypocritical. To achieve the delicate adjustment which is required means that criticism itself must become almost an art. Many a great artist has been intimately associated with a great critic.

The ideal audience, however, is often found among those with whom the artist tends to compare himself in measuring his own worth, as in the case of his fellow students. For it is never quite as positive a stimulus for the artist to have his creative productions praised by a teacher or master, as it is for him to have them praised by those who are themselves his potential emulators and who know intimately what these creative productions cost the artist.

Thus the relationship most conducive to development may be further described as one of social equality and of reciprocity. It cannot be a relationship of superiority and subordination. Nor can it even be the relationship of counselor and client, contrary to some present-day currents of thought, for even the most nondirective counselor-client relationship is unequal and unilateral. It is worth while to glance still more closely at what social equality and reciprocity mean between two persons.

Somewhere Durkheim contends that equality is indispensable if genuine discussion is to occur between persons; Simmel has made the same point with reference to the occurrence of sociability.[6] Discussion and sociability are two of the

---

[6] Kurt H. Wolff (ed.), *The Sociology of Georg Simmel;* Glencoe, Ill., Free Press, 1950; pp. 47–49.

activities indispensable to carrying on the dialectic of creation and criticism from which comes personal development. By equality, however, is not meant sameness; quite the contrary. Let us take parents and children as the most obvious case where the persons involved are never—unless perhaps in the case of twins—of the same age or powers. The practice of equality may be exhibited by sharing alike in certain valued experiences and by such devices as taking turns—things that are familiar to everyone who ever had brothers or sisters. But obviously it would be ruinous for parents to insist that each child reach the same standard of performance. Rather, each is expected by a loving parent to move toward a standard which is reasonable for a person of his capacities. Moreover, the most important expression of the kind of equality I am defining lies in the conception of each child as *ultimately incommensurable with any other.* He may be compared quantitatively to another child in this or that respect, but as a whole person he is unique. Also, as a whole person he is such a pregnant complex, such a rich array of potentialities, that the loving parent can always find some respects in which each child does excel. By developing these special talents or virtues, each child can outshine the others on his own grounds; the competition which is so threatening and destructive when all are judged by a single standard loses its force when each child is judged by his own.

The parent does not have to determine arbitrarily the line of development for which each child is best disposed; he has only to observe attentively the outcome of the child's own search for the notion of his particular talents which is most satisfying and promising, and then to ratify, as only a sympathetic audience can, the correctness of the discovery made. To do otherwise is to be as disruptive of orderly and optimal development as is the patron who tells the artist what he is to create. Wholeness and individuality, integrity and autonomy, are inseparable.

Reciprocity is perhaps a peculiar kind of equality, but so peculiar that it needs careful analysis. Malinowski [7] has analyzed its ubiquitous function in regulating primitive social organization. Someone of equal genius, I hope, will someday set forth in full the way it works throughout interpersonal relations. In the many books and articles on child development, reciprocity rarely gets the attention due it in terms of the scope of its influence. The child who is denied the opportunity to reciprocate according to his powers the favors conferred upon him by his parents is thwarted in the growth of those powers. Many people have no doubt witnessed the crushing effect upon a child of having a parent ignore or disparage a gift which the child has made and tendered him. Conversely, when a child has labored unstintingly to produce some offering and the parent accepts it with honest gratitude and praise, the delight of the child is sometimes almost physically convulsive.

I cannot resist mentioning the first party which my seven-year-old daughter threw for her parents. It consisted only of two pieces of pastry taken secretly from the refrigerator, a small table cloth and napkins spread carefully on her own little table, two cups of milk, and of course two chairs. It was entirely her own idea, and from a realistic point of view it was rather inappropriate, since we had only finished dinner half an hour before. She did not sit down with us after inviting our presence, but stood there giggling and squirming in ecstasy as we thanked her and praised her cooking. She has already learned the role of hostess and fancies grander successes in the future.

---

[7] Bronislaw Malinowski, *Argonauts of the Western Pacific,* New York, Dutton, 1950.

To deny a person opportunities for reciprocating is to forestall his respect for himself, to keep him dependent and inferior. This is one point where resentment of do-gooders arises. A person may garner flattery by surrounding himself with dependents, but flattery can hardly match the satisfaction of contributing to the growth of others by stimulating their achievement of autonomy and equality. In fact, the person who insists upon the expression of affection from dependents whom he cannot let go may not be autonomous himself—as in the case of over-protective parents. On the other hand, the encouragement of reciprocation by those of lesser powers is about as strong a medicine for stimulating their growth as is likely to be found. In competition, as studies on recreation show, stimulation is maximal when rivals are equally matched. Equality and reciprocity are not static concepts; it is hierarchy and unilateralism which are static and which hinder development.

Self-transcendence

Any present-day scholar would be loathe to say that the impulse to explore and develop individuality is natural, in the sense of being an inborn imperative. On the other hand, it is certainly an almost universal discovery that development of one's powers is the primary value in life, since these powers are the instruments which provide access to all other values. If a person is permitted freedom to play and is stimulated by a loving audience, he moves on not merely from one requisite developmental task to another, but toward self-chosen goals which are not requisite but are autonomously affirmed.

No one has quite as well described as has James Mark Baldwin [8]—the father of genetic psychology—the dialectic of personal growth in all its intricacy and cumulative onwardness, whether vicious or benevolent in trend. It is very significant that Baldwin encouraged his wife to translate the two classical treatises on the psychology of play by Karl Groos,[9] for these works stress the importance of play as a kind of practice for the tasks of reality. Some students of human development have lately taken up where Groos left off, and in a few years may go far beyond him. It is nonetheless regrettable for progress in the discipline of human development that there was a fifty-year lapse in serious scientific analysis of the consequences of play.

Art, however, is not play, any more than it is work. It is an activity of intense seriousness and concentration, although it excites joy of a kind and degree which is neither an illusion nor a joking matter nor a hypocrisy. Perhaps art could be called the serious form of play. Both work and play at their best become art. In the best art, the artist performs at the limit of his capacities. By performing at the limit of his capacities, he continually transcends the limits of those capacities. That is, he goes beyond the point he had previously reached in the development of his capacities.

It is at this point that it may be appropriate to mention that at the Family Study Center we are engaged in working out a theory of human development based upon a concept of self-transcendence. I might stick my neck out further and add that this theory in its embryonic form is one of self-transcendence

---

[8] James Mark Baldwin, *Social and Ethical Interpretations in Mental Development;* New York, Macmillan, 1809.
[9] Karl Groos: *The Play of Animals;* New York, D. Appleton & Co., 1911. *The Play of Man;* New York, D. Appleton & Co., 1912.

through love. By self-transcendence we have in mind an entirely secular and matter-of-fact approach.

To review briefly some ideas which are by now commonplace: Human beings, as human beings, are among other features distinguished by the acquisition of selves through experience. The self, however, is a symbolic construct postulated for certain kinds of behavior not otherwise explainable. This self develops in terms of abilities to perform various kinds of behavior. There are a number of definable abilities, growth in which may properly be taken as the measures of human development. The process by which these abilities increase always occurs and is exhibited within a matrix of interpersonal relations.

The Family Study Center is engaged in a series of studies in the measurement and experimental development of a number of these abilities, which we designate jointly as interpersonal competence. The three we are doing research upon are empathy, autonomy, and creativity, but there are others. In order to generate desired movement in these respects, our staff has been devising a number of very specific hypotheses as to the reproducible conditions under which measurable change in the optimal direction regularly occurs. Once these conditions for the growth of interpersonal competence can be validly stated, we shall have the full description of what I have been speaking of as the relationship of love. Love so defined *is* enough.[10]

This conception of love as [those] interpersonal conditions optimal for self-transcendence is a hard doctrine from which many will shrink, because it puts the claim of love to the test of the results produced. It should have a cauterizing effect upon the sentimentality and falsehood by which a parent can protest that he loves a child while frustrating his development. Likewise it implies a conception of marriage, in which the success of the marriage is judged by the degree to which each partner contributes reciprocally to the continuous development of the other.

The dialectical transactions between artist and audience to which we have referred need not be limited to two persons, though it is convenient to analyze them in this manner. At one time, a child may be considered as a work of art produced by the mother, with the father as audience; at another, by the father, with the mother as audience; and at a third, as himself an aspiring artist engaged in producing some piece of work, with both parents as his audience. Most importantly, as the child increases in interpersonal competence, he becomes a successful artist in evoking desired behavior from his parents—ideally, their delight rather than their dismay.

Professor Frank H. Knight at the University of Chicago has written profoundly about the matter of love. I would particularly recommend his long essay on "Ethics and Economic Reform." [11] He has been heard to declare that if Western civilization succeeds in developing a workable society on a secular basis, it will be for the first time in history. I believe that the effort to advance human development through a matter-of-fact investigation of the relationships most conducive to self-transcendence is a reasonable and even promising experiment. And I would go further to predict that the proven attainment of desired results in this

---

[10] Cf., Bruno Bettelheim, *Love Is Not Enough: The Treatment of Emotionally Disturbed Children;* Glencoe, Ill., Free Press, 1950.
[11] Frank H. Knight, *Freedom and Reform: Essays in Economics and Social Philosophy;* New York, Harper, 1947; pp. 45–128.

direction will be a more substantial and enduring source of joy than all the pretended ecstasies of those who still put their hope in nonrational wish-fulfillment.

It now seems in order to take another look at Freud's statement that erotic motivation underlies all other expressions of human ties. If one speaks of humans as selves, it is at least equally as plausible that *eros* is the symbol and *agape* the substance. In an age in which the substance is lacking, people in their loneliness grasp feverishly but vainly for the symbol. If by the progressive restoration of trust through proving the consequence of love in action, we are able to diminish the fear of each other which makes our love so ambivalent, then *eros* as the symbol of love becomes no longer counterfeit, and no longer properly regarded with cynicism, joking, or sentimentality.

36   Some Dimensions of Altercasting

● EUGENE A. WEINSTEIN AND PAUL DEUTSCHBERGER

Among the most venerable notions in social psychology is the assumption that human behavior is goal directed. It is implicit in Plato and Aristotle, and explicit in the hedonistic calculus of Bentham, in motivational theory, and in psychoanalytic theory.[1] Yet the implications of this assumption for the analysis of social interaction have not been given a central place in sociologically oriented theories. It is only recently, in what might be termed a "new look" in role theory, that greater recognition has been given to the idea that people bring personal purposes into interaction.[2] The pursuit of these purposes rather than the automatic unfolding of role reciprocity according to a normatively written script is seen as the underlying texture of interaction.[3]

If we accept the postulate that human behavior is goal directed, then the goal of any actor in a social encounter is capable of being stated in terms of some response from other participants in that encounter. For the purposes of this paper (and following what has become institutionalized form in these matters), the actor shall henceforth be designated "Ego," and the other, whose response is the goal, as "Alter." All of Ego's behavior directed toward Alter shall be called "lines

SOURCE: Eugene Weinstein and Paul Deutschberger, from *Sociometry*, XXVI, #4 (December 1963), pp. 454–466. Reprinted by permission of The American Sociological Association.

Revised version of paper read at 1962 meetings of The American Sociological Association, Washington, D. C.

[1] Gordon W. Allport, "The Historical Background of Modern Social Psychology," in Gardner Lindzey, ed., *Handbook of Social Psychology*, Cambridge: Addison Wesley, 1954.
[2] Samuel A. Stouffer, "An Analysis of Conflicting Social Norms," *American Sociological Review*, 24 (December, 1949), pp. 707–717; George C. Homans, "Social Behavior as Exchange," *American Journal of Sociology*, 63 (May, 1958), pp. 597–606; Howard S. Becker, "Notes on the Concept of Commitment," *American Journal of Sociology*, 66 (July, 1960), pp. 32–40; William J. Goode, "A Theory of Role Strain," *American Sociological Review*, 25 (August, 1960), pp. 483–496.
[3] William J. Goode, "Norm Commitment and Conformity to Role-Status Obligations," *American Journal of Sociology*, 66 (November, 1960), pp. 246–258; Ralph Turner, "Role-Taking, Process Versus Conformity," *Human Behavior and Social Processes*, Arnold M. Rose, ed., Boston: Houghton-Mifflin, 1962.

of action." The response of Alter they are intended to elicit will be termed "the interpersonal task."

Developing a typology of interpersonal tasks might prove a rewarding effort in itself. Tasks can differ in the direction of Alter's response—toward Ego ("Lend me five dollars") or toward some third party or object ("Stop beating your dog"). They can vary in the amount of effort required of Alter in making the response, in the overtness of the response, or in the degree to which the response is an end in itself or a means to evoke other responses more crucial to Ego. But whatever the task may be, the question must be raised: how are lines of action selected and elaborated in Ego's expressive behavior in order to elicit the desired response? We have brought *Homo Economicus* to the bargaining table of inter-action.[4] Now just how does he go about the business of getting others to feel or to do what he wants them to feel or do?

One important step toward dealing with this problem was taken by Goffman in his "dramaturgical analysis of encounters."[5] For Goffman the critical intervening variable is the actor's definition of the situation. If we relate this concept spe-cifically to the personal purposes of the actor, to define a situation is to take into account the symbolic cues present in a social encounter, to integrate them, and from this process to draw inferences about the interpersonal tasks that may be pursued and about the lines of action appropriate to these tasks. Similarly, roles become purposive as well as normative. In our terms a role is defined as a reper-toire of lines of action structured around a specifiable set of interpersonal tasks. From the definition of the situation comes the decision-making process as to which role to play. To affect Alter's behavior in the desired direction, Ego must manip-ulate the cues in the encounter in order to influence selectively Alter's definition of the situation. If this process is effective, what is a task response for Ego will become a line of action for Alter.

In Goffman's analysis, the focus of the problem of influencing Alter's defini-tion of the situation is Ego's presentation of himself. If Ego successfully presents the correct identity, Alter, in his responsive lines of action, will be obligated to deal with Ego as persons with such an identity have a right to expect. The source of Alter's obligation and Ego's right are unclear in Goffman's analysis. He makes the implicit assumption that they are functionally necessary for the maintenance of social encounters (and hence for the larger social system of which any encounter is a concrete expression). Presumably the constraints are normative, although the term "norm" is conspicuous by its rarity in his work.

Goffman goes on to concentrate on techniques and problems of self presenta-tion. Little more is done with Alter's responses beyond indicating that they can-not explicitly reject Ego's projected identity if the interaction is to be long main-tained. This tacit acceptance of Ego's projected identity (and Alter's as well) constitute what he terms a "working consensus." A working consensus, then, is a tacit agreement as to the roles the several participants will play out in the en-counter.

But the tasks that can be pursued as well as the lines of action used to pursue them within the boundaries of a given working consensus will be many. How does

[4] John W. Thibaut and Harold H. Kelley, *The Social Psychology of Groups*, New York: Wiley, 1959; George C. Homans, *Social Behavior: Its Elementary Forms*, New York: Harcourt, Brace, and World, 1961.

[5] Erving Goffman, *The Presentation of Self in Everyday Life*, Garden City: Doubleday, 1959.

Ego attempt to narrow down Alter's choice of roles and Alter's responsive lines of action within the repertoire of a given role? Self-presentation is one approach. But it might be equally fruitful to concentrate more directly on the implications of Ego's behavior for Alter's definition of the situation. Instead of looking at Ego's actions on the basis of the identity they create for him (self-presentation), it might be better to look at them on the basis of the identity they create for Alter. This latter perspective is termed *altercasting*—casting Alter into a particular identity or role type.

It is our contention that altercasting is a basic technique of interpersonal control. Goffman has remarked that Ego may be much more involved in his own projected image than in alter's identity. Although a successful projection may be an end in itself, in many instances self-presentation can be regarded as a special case of altercasting. "Coming on strong" in a particular identity may point out to Alter restrictions on the identities he can assume and still maintain a working consensus. However, the process of altercasting can be a good deal more direct. Ego may make explicit the identity he wishes Alter to assume and overtly make the task response an integral part of that identity ("Now, Joe, as a good friend of mine, I know you would . . ."). Less direct, but still more closely related to altercasting than to self-presenting, are the multiform gestures of approval and disapproval Ego makes to Alter's responsive lines of action, which serve as signposts for the route he wishes Alter to take. Whether direct or indirect, altercasting should supply a useful perspective for research, since it builds interaction directly into the analysis.

Dimensions of Altercasting

The first question to be asked in trying to evolve measures of altercasting is, what are the important dimensions of the role into which Alter is being cast? Six such dimensions were formulated on the basis of theoretical considerations and holistic analysis of a series of role playing scenes. These dimensions, described below, are by no means exhaustive. They are defined without overlap, but their distinctness requires empirical investigation. For each, a seven point rating scale was developed. Student volunteers role-played three types of situations: establishment of a relationship; maintenance of a relationship under external threat; and maintenance of a relationship under internal strain.

1. *Structural Distance*—the position of relative authority Ego is directing Alter to play out in the current encounter. The qualification, "in the encounter," is important since there may be a number of positions Alter occupies vis-a-vis Ego. Moreover, as Anselm Strauss points out in his discussion of *status forcing*, Ego may attempt to switch Alter from one position to another in mid-encounter.[6] A rating of 7 on this dimension indicated maximum authority ceded by Ego to Alter with a rating of 4 as structural parity.

2. *Evaluative Distance*—the relative evaluative status of Ego and Alter as presented selves, independent of the structural distance involved. One can be in a subordinate position and still, through skillful playing, cast Alter into a "one down" identity, making it clear that Alter is not as superior, holy or infallible as his position might imply. On the other hand, girls, starting from structural parity, have been known to cast their male Alters into near reverential identities. It is to this dimension that ploys and flattery, deference and derogation, are relevant.

---

6 Anselm Strauss, *Mirrors and Masks*, Glencoe, Ill.: Free Press, 1959, pp. 76–84.

A rating of 7 indicates maximum worth ceded by Ego to Alter; a rating of 4, evaluative parity.

3. *Emotional Distance*—the "primariness" or "secondariness" of Alter's relationship with Ego as projected by Ego. To what extent is Alter cast into a role in which he is presumed to be involved with Ego's feelings, needs, and everyday concerns? One's awareness of this dimension tends to be evoked when there is dissonance. Someone is perceived as "coming too close" when he casts you into the undesired role of intimate or confidant, reveals intimate information about himself, seeks it from you, or simply affirms the strength of emotional ties which are actually unilateral at best. A rating of 1 indicates maximum involvement or intimacy.

4. *Support vs. Support Seeking*—Ego's indications to Alter that Alter is in an identity requiring Ego's help or assistance (a rating of 1) or, at the other extreme, being required to give aid and comfort to Ego (a rating of 7). Self-presentation and altercasting clearly merge on this dimension. Casting one's self in a succorant role tends automatically to place Alter in the nurturant reciprocal. The simple affirmation that one is in difficulty acts as a demand upon Alter without the necessity of a specific request for assistance from him. (Sometimes the request is vehemently denied by Ego.) The reverse, while not as apparent, also holds. Witness the discomfiture we feel when approached by another who "comes on" full of unrequested assistance, conveying, by implication, a picture of ourselves as incapable of dealing with the business at hand.

5. *Interdependence vs. Autonomy*—the extent to which Ego projects Alter as being tied to him by bonds of common fate, perspective, or concurrence of interests. A rating of 1 indicates complete identity, a rating of 7 complete separateness.

6. *Degree of Freedom Allowed Alter*—the range of behavior Ego allows Alter within the encounter. Strictly speaking, this dimension does not characterize Alter's role but the altercasting process itself. Of course, all lines of action are ultimately directed at narrowing Alter's choice of responses so as to increase the probability of eliciting the task response. However, the strength of the constraints placed on Alter to assume the projected role as well as the techniques used for constraining can vary a great deal.

One approach to restricting Alter's degree of freedom is to communicate that certain of one's own responses (presumably desired by him) are contingent upon his assuming the identity projected for him. In the more coercive forms of altercasting, the relationship between Ego and Alter may be "laid on the line." Other approaches focus not on Ego's evaluation of Alter but on Alter's self evaluation. Ego may project a representation of Alter with which the desired behavior would be consonant. Often, this role is framed in symbols Alter is felt to value. Thus Alter, if he rejects the role, is put in the position of also rejecting or being inconsistent with his ideal conception of himself. A rating of 7 on this dimension indicates maximum range given Alter by Ego, while a rating of 1 would be indicative of extreme coercion.

The Pilot Experiment

In order to explore the usefulness of this approach for analyzing interaction, a pilot experiment was undertaken. It was designed to investigate the effects of two situational variables on Ego's altercasting activity. The first was the role he was formally assigned to play. The second was the feedback he received from Alter (i.e., Alter's Altercasting).

Students in a class in Introductory Sociology were told they would be participating in a class project investigating campus attitudes toward various minority groups. The grade each was to receive on this project was to constitute ten per cent of his final grade for the course. Eighteen randomly selected students in the class (the experimental subjects) were told they would be working on questionnaire construction. The questionnaire was to consist of three parts: one each on attitudes toward Negroes, Chinese, and Jews. Appointments for three work sessions of one half hour each were then made for each subject. When the subject arrived he was introduced to his work partner (in each case another student who was a trained confederate of the experimenter). The pair was told that they would be working together this session on attitudes toward Negroes, but in subsequent sessions would be working on different attitude areas with different partners.

In order to vary assigned role, the subject was told in one session that he was appointed group leader and had final authority regarding any issues of wording or item inclusion. He was responsible for seeing that the job was done. In another session the confederate was appointed group leader, and in another session no appointment of a group leader was made. In all sessions the pair was informed that they would both be graded on their joint product.

The confederates provided the feedback variation. In one session the subject received feedback from a confederate instructed to give responses which consistently attacked the subject's suggestions and ability; in one session consistently supportive feedback was given; and in one session mixed supportive and attacking feedback was given.

Confederates were also trained to maintain their assigned roles and not to use the words "we" or "us." In the earlier work, we had noted that "we" tends to be one of the most seductive of English words. Its appearance almost automatically heralds a relationship structured in terms of mutuality and interdependence. The feedback and role conditions were ordered according to a Latin Square such that each subject received each assigned role and each type of feedback once. The design was replicated for each sex, with order of role and feedback combinations and sex of alter also systematically varied to produce the complete design.

Work sessions took place in the office of the instructor while he was absent. The sessions were tape recorded with a concealed recorder and microphone. The altercasting ratings were made directly from tapes.

This study is not designed to test whether altercasting takes place, nor is any attempt made to dissociate altercasting from self presentation or similar interpersonal processes. It is assumed that altercasting is taking place; that Ego's actions are casting Alter into some desired identity. This assumption is then incorporated directly into the ratings. Thus the ratings involve the rater in a role-taking process, and it is Alter's role that is being taken. The perspective taken by the rater is: "If I were Alter, what kinds of responses do Ego's acts seem to be directing me to make?" "Kinds of responses" are then summarily described by ratings on the first five dimensions; the heaviness of Ego's direction on the sixth. The procedure is admittedly crude, and a good deal is dependent on the sensitivity of the rater. On the other hand, if coherent results are found, further refinement would be encouraged.

Except for twelve tapes used in training sessions, the ratings were made independently by two persons. The first was second author, the second a graduate student from another department who had not been previously exposed to the theoretical perspective and who was not aware of the purpose of the experiment or that situational conditions were being experimentally varied. His ratings provided the basis for assessing inter-rater agreement and for avoiding contamination of the ratings by knowledge of the experimental conditions in each case. They are the ones incorporated into all subsequent analyses.

In addition to the altercasting ratings, the tapes were used to derive pronoun counts. These provided us with a less "subjective" measure of the subject's behavior in each session. The pronouns "I," "We," and "You," and their respective possessives were tabulated for each subject in each session. To eliminate the effect of variability in total verbal productivity each frequency was expressed as a proportion of the total pronoun usage. Correlations with the altercasting ratings were computed in order to test three specific hypotheses. Relative frequency of "I" was expected to be high when Alter was cast into a subordinate role (low score on Structural Distance). "We" was predicted to be relatively frequent in altercasting of interdependence, and "You" was expected to be preponderant in cases in which heavy constraints were placed on Alter (a low Degree of Freedom rating).

To test the reliability of confederate performance, and of the feedback differentials as experienced by the subject, at the end of the experiment the subjects were asked to rate their partners (on a five point scale) for each session, on "cooperativeness" and "likeability," and to grade the adequacy of their own performance for each session.

Findings

Altercasting ratings—One of the experiment's purposes was to evaluate the altercasting ratings themselves. Inter-rater reliability was estimated by having a sample of 30 sessions rated independently by two raters working directly from the tapes. Each taped session was rated on all six dimensions, and product moment correlations computed for each of the six sets. These appear in the diagonal of Table 1. They are not comfortably high, averaging about .70, but compare favorably with global ratings found in the literature.

Our main concern in examining the intercorrelations among the ratings was the possibility of "halo effect." The ratings show some overlap, but in only one

TABLE 1   *Intercorrelations among Altercasting Dimensions,[a] and Inter-rater Reliabilities* [b]

Dimensions	1	2	3	4	5	6
1. Structural distance	(.84) [c]					
2. Evaluative distance	.60	(.73)				
3. Emotional distance	.14	.01	(.66)			
4. Support-support seeking	.31	.43	.12	(.73)		
5. Interdependence-autonomy	.02	−.04	.47	.21	(.73)	
6. Degrees of freedom	−.10	.13	−.29	−.10	−.08	(.64)

[a] $n = 54$, $r(.05) = .27$.
[b] $n = 30$, $r(.05) = .36$.
[c] Inter-rater correlations on the diagonal.

case is the existence of separate dimensions questionable. Casting Alter into a superordinate role goes hand in hand with according him higher status in the encounter.

The other statistically significant correlations make interpretive sense if we view them simply as a model of the rater's judgmental processes rather than assuming that they reflect real relationships present in the observed interaction. Structuring the relationship along secondary lines should be associated with the projection of greater autonomy. It is also associated with placing heavier constraints upon Alter. Finally, it is reasonable that seeking support from Alter should go along with ceding superordination and evaluative worth to him.

TABLE 2   Correlations between Relative Frequency of Pronoun Usage and Altercasting Dimensions

Dimension	I	We	You
Structural distance	.06	.03	−.01
Evaluative distance	−.03	.12	−.02
Emotional distance	−.19	.17	.39
Support-support seeking	−.07	−.06	.12
Autonomy-interdependence	−.05	−.36	.32
Degrees of freedom	.28	.19	−.74

$r(.05) = .27$.

Table 2 contains the correlations between relative frequency of pronoun usage and the altercasting ratings. The prediction that high frequency of "I's" would be related to claiming superordinate status was not borne out. The other two hypotheses were confirmed. "We" was associated with greater projection of interdependence. The correlation between frequent usage of "you" and attempting to impose greater restrictions on Alter's responsive behavior exceeded our expectations. Even when allowance is made for the possibility that the correlation is in part an artifact of the rating process, "you" appears to be an oft-used tool for those who would "muscle" social relationships.

Treatment differentials—Assigned role and feedback were the two main experimental variables to be related to altercasting. Before proceeding with a discussion of these findings, however, it is important to estimate the degree to which we were successful in securing adequate differentials in treatment levels. Analyses of variance for responses to the post-experimental questionnaire are summarized in Table 3. The subjects made significant discriminations in grading their partners on cooperativeness and likeability, and grading themselves on adequacy of performance according to the assigned feedback stance of those

TABLE 3   Subjects' Judgments of Alter's Cooperativeness, Likeability, and Their Own Adequacy of Performance, by Assigned Feedback Stance of Alter

Mean Score On:	Feedback Stance			P
	Attack	Mixed	Support	
1. Cooperativeness	2.58	4.06	4.61	.01
2. Likeability	2.56	3.92	4.19	.01
3. Own Adequacy	3.00	3.94	4.39	.01

partners. Thus, it may be safely assumed that the necessary differentials in feedback were represented in the experiment.[7]

An analysis of the cooperation, likeability, and adequacy of own performance scores by assigned role revealed no statistically significant differences, raising the question of just how seriously the subjects took their assigned roles. Yet, there is some evidence (to be discussed later) that role differentials were experienced as such by the subjects.

TABLE 4   *Sample Analysis of Variance for "Degree of Freedom" Dimension*

Source	Sum of Squares	df	Mean Square	F	P
Between Subjects	40.6	17			
Sex	7.4	1	7.40	3.43	<.10
Groups	5.3	2	2.65	1.23	——
Sex x Groups	2.0	2	1.00	.46	——
Subjects within groups	25.9	12	2.16		
Within Subjects					
Role	7.4	2	3.70	2.14	——
Feedback	10.1	2	5.05	2.91	<.10
Role x Feedback	8.3	2	4.15	2.40	——
Sex x Role (w)	1.2	2	.60	.35	——
Sex x Feedback (w)	0.5	2	.25	.14	——
Sex x Role x Feedback	10.5	2	5.25	3.03	<.10
Error (within)	41.4	24	1.73		

Sex—To test the role, feedback, and sex of subject main effects, an analysis of variance was performed on the subjects' scores on each of the six dimensions. A sample of this procedure is given in Table 5. In addition, the relationship of order

TABLE 5   *Probability Levels of Results for Sex, Role and Feedback Main Effects*

Experimental Variable	Dimension					
	Structural Distance	Evaluative Distance	Emotional Distance	Support-Support Seeking	Inter-dependence Autonomy	Degree of Freedom
Sex	——	——	<.10	——	——	<.10
Role	——	——	——	——	<.01	——
Feedback	<.01	<.10	——	——	<.001	<.10

of experimental conditions, sex of Alter, and the sex composition of the dyad to each of the altercasting dimensions was explored in separate analyses.

In no case was there a significant order effect. Furthermore, in no case did sex of Alter or sex composition of the dyad have a significant effect, nor were there significant interactions of these variables with other situational conditions.

However, as can be seen from Table 5, the sex of subject effect approached significance in two instances. Boys tended to structure the relationship in more primary terms. This went so far, in one instance, as attempting to suggest an

---

[7] Further analysis revealed, however, that one of the confederates (responsible for nine sessions of mixed feedback) apparently did not meet the specifications for performance, weighting the entire experiment in the direction of supportive feedback conditions at the cost of beclouding the effects of mixed feedback on altercasting behavior.

even closer relationship to a female confederate who was giving supportive feed-back on the attitude items. It may be of some practical interest to know that the female side-stepped the offer neatly.

Girls tended to place heavier constraints on the relationship. This tendency seemed to come less from active manipulation than from a kind of aggressive passivity. It would be interesting to know whether this is a general tendency for middle class girls. They are more normatively limited than boys in the range of roles they are allowed to play and are made conscious, during socialization, of being held accountable for the kinds of relationships they do enter. Perhaps, in turn, they are more limiting in their interaction.

Role—Findings for the principal effects are found in Table 5. One noteworthy pattern is the failure of assigned role as an important situational variable in this experiment. This finding could be interpreted as the failure of the experimenter to altercast the subject into the experimentally desired role. In retrospect, the explanation appears simple. First, the altercasting of the experimenter was di-rected at the role the subject was to assume toward a third party, and was on a "one shot" rather than a continuous basis. Furthermore, superordination over one's fellow students, whether delegated from on high or not, is foreign to the stu-dent culture. The results for Structural Distance show that where role differences should have been built in by the experimenter's instructions, it was feedback rather than assigned role that was the critical variable.

On only one dimension did the assigned role have a significant effect. When the confederate was in a superordinate position, his altercasting ran counter to normal undergraduate expectations. The subjects coped with this behavior in-geniously, not by challenging the authority of the confederate, but by emphasiz-ing the mutual interdependence between them. Here we have an extension of the theory of coalitions in the triad.[8] Offers of coalitions should come most fre-quently from those with least power. Subjects were quite inventive in finding someone against whom to form a dyadic coalition. "He" (the experimenter) or "they" (the student who would be taking the questionnaire) were the usual foils for the subject's proposed "we."

Feedback—The most striking results are found for feedback. In four of the six cases, feedback differentials achieved or approached statistical significance. In each case, the main contrast was between wholly supportive feedback and any negative feedback (either mixed or consistently attacking). Students working on a joint task are not apt to expect open criticism, certainly not without some sugar coating. The negative elements in mixed feedback are likely to have stood out in the subject's perception, so that he experienced this condition as attack.

The feedback results form a consistent pattern. Regardless of assigned role, subjects under attack cast their Alter into positions of subordinate responsibility. They accord Alter evaluative superiority in the task at hand, and project a picture of the relationship in which Alter's desires, rather than cooperation and mutual involvement, are primary. Furthermore, they tend to constrain their Alters to play this and no other role. Under attack, the main thrust of Ego's acts is to tell Alter, "You take over."

---

[8] Theodore M. Mills, "Power Relations in Three-Person Groups," *American Sociological Re-view*, 18 (August, 1953), pp. 351–357.

Conclusions

Accounting for the processes involved in interpersonal control is basic to under-standing interaction. We have attempted to deal with this problem by assuming that control is carried out through altercasting—creating an identity for the other congruent with one's goals. The research undertaken had two main purposes. The first was to test the feasibility of this approach; the second, to test its utility in yielding theoretically meaningful results.

The methodological findings were promising in relation to the first purpose. The reliability coefficients indicate the possibility of close agreement among in-dependent observers and suggest that the rating techniques are readily commu-nicable. Intercorrelations among the dimensions reveal little "halo effect," with one possible exception, and the pronoun count correlations show that the ratings are significantly related to a more "objective" behavioral index.

Although it is safe to assume that the necessary feedback differentials were se-cured for the experiment as a whole, no such assumption can be made about role assignment. The evidence from the post-experimental questionnaire seems to in-dicate that assigned role carried little saliency for the subjects. However, the finding that offers of coalition were initiated almost exclusively by subordinates makes little sense unless the subjects were aware of their positions in the encoun-ters and were acting on the basis of that awareness.

The research turned up findings of substantive interest. The typical response to attack in a peer relationship was to place the mantle of responsibility on the other's shoulders. It would be interesting to know how situationally general this tendency is. The same question may be asked concerning the observed sex differ-ences in altercasting patterns.

In sum, this maiden voyage shows some promise for the interpersonal task ap-proach. In this approach, acts are analyzed on the basis of their potential conse-quences for limiting others' responsive lines of action. This pilot study represents a beginning toward operationalizing functionalism in social psychology.

37   Awareness Contexts and Social Interaction

● BARNEY G. GLASER AND ANSELM L. STRAUSS

When men confront each other, each cannot always be certain—even when given seemingly trustworthy guarantees—that he knows either the other's identity or his own identity in the eyes of the other. An honest citizen may be taken in by a

SOURCE: Barney G. Glaser and Anselm L. Strauss, in the *American Sociological Review*, XXIX (October 1967), pp. 669–679. Reprinted by permission of The American Sociological Associa-tion.

Many of the examples used in this paper are taken from the authors' study of Hospital Person-nel, Nursing Care and Dying Patients, supported by National Institutes of Health, Grant GN9077. For a full discussion of awareness contexts related to social interaction in the hospital dying situation, see our book, *Awareness of Dying: A Study of Social Interaction* (Chicago: Aldine Press, 1967). Jeanne Quint, a member of our project team, has worked closely with us on these data. We are indebted to Howard S. Becker, Fred Davis, Erving Goffman, Sheldon Messinger, and Melvin Sabshin for their helpful comments on this volume.

confidence man, a government official by a foreign spy passing as his secretary, or a dying patient by his doctor. But the confidence man's mark may actually be from the local detective squad; the official, suspecting undercover play, may be pretending innocence while spilling the secretary false documents; and the dying patient may suspect his true condition but not reveal his suspicion to the physician. Thus, who is really being "taken in" is a matter of the awareness of both parties to the situation.

The phenomenon of awareness—which is central to the study of interaction—can be quite complex for at least two reasons. First, interaction may involve not merely two persons, but a third or quite a few more. For instance, when a homosexual flashes cues to another homosexual in the presence of many straight people, some may not notice and others may misread the cues, while others might be aware of their intended meaning. The identity of the homosexual is, therefore, unknown or suspect to some straights and known to still others. Conversely, a homosexual cannot always be certain who suspects or who is or is not aware of his true identity. Second, each person involved may be the representative of a system with specific requirements for, and perhaps a high stake in, how the person manages his own and the other's identity. Spies and counterspies are linked to such systems as often as are doctors and nurses.

These considerations highlight important features of the relation between interaction and awareness. To establish our basic notions, however, we shall content ourselves in this paper with the least complex situation: two interactants (whether persons or groups) who face the dual problem of being certain about both their identity in the other's eyes and the other's identity.

Contexts of Awareness

By the term *awareness context* we mean the total combination of what each interactant in a situation knows about the identity of the other and his own identity in the eyes of the other.[1] This total awareness is the context within which are guided successive interactions between the two persons over periods of time—long or short. Empirically the question of true identity may focus only on that of one of the two persons (the dying patient) or on that of both persons (spy and counter-spy).

We have singled out four types of awareness context for special consideration since they have proved useful in accounting for different types of interaction. An *open* awareness context obtains when each interactant is aware of the other's true identity and his own identity in the eyes of the other. A *closed* awareness context obtains when one interactant does not know either the other's identity or

[1] The concept of awareness context is a structural unit, not a property of one of the standard structural units such as group, organization, community, role, position, etc. By "context" we mean it is a structural unit of an encompassing order larger than the other unit under focus: interaction. Thus, an awareness context surrounds and affects the interaction. Much as one might say that the interaction of staff with dying patients occurs within the context of a cancer ward or a veteran's hospital, one can also say that this interaction occurs within a type of awareness context. Note that ward or hospital are concrete, conventional social units, while awareness context is an analytic social unit, constructed to account for similarities in interaction in many diverse conventional units.

A more general definition of awareness context is the total combination of what specific people, groups, organizations, communities or nations know what about a specific issue. Thus, this structural concept can be used for the study of virtually any problem entailing awareness at any structural level of analysis.

the other's view of his identity. A *suspicion* awareness context is a modification of the closed one: one interactant suspects the true identity of the other or the other's view of his own identity, or both. A *pretense* awareness context is a modification of the open one: both interactants are fully aware but pretend not to be.

These types illustrate how the sociologist's total picture may differ from that held by each interactant, no matter how well informed or expert. For example, a doctor may state that a patient does not yet know that he is dying (his identity in the eyes of the doctor) while the patient may very well suspect the physician's definition. Thus, the doctor believes that closed awareness obtains when actually there is a suspicion context within which the patient is testing his suspicions. If the doctor recognizes those suspicions he may attempt to parry them. If the doctor believes himself successful, he may only report to the sociologist that as yet the patient is unaware, neglecting to mention the patient's suspicions. Therefore, delimiting an awareness context requires always that the sociologist ascertain independently the awareness of each interactant. The safest method is to obtain data, through observation or interview, from each interactant on his own state of awareness. To accept the word of only one informant is risky, even perhaps for the open awareness context.

The successive interactions occurring within each type of context tend to transform the context. As yet it is an empirical question as to the direction in which a change in one context will lead, or what are some patterns of successive transformations. Thus, a closed context can be shattered by arousing suspicions; but if suspicions are quelled, the closed context is reinstituted. If suspicions are validated, the context may change to either pretense or open awareness. With a change in identity of one interactant in the eyes of the other, an open context can easily become either closed or pretense. For instance, the government official who suspects that his secretary is a spy must now check his suspicions. If he discovers that she is a spy but does not reveal his knowledge, then she in turn misreads his view of her identity. Thus, a closed context now obtains! If she in turn surreptitiously learns of his new view of her but says nothing, the context is again closed. But if he unmasks her spying, then the context now becomes open, since each now fully acknowledges the other's true identity.

How long each context will last before it is transformed is also an empirical question. In the abstract none is inherently less stable than another; although within a given substantive area, differential degrees of stability may become apparent. For dying patients, a suspicion context is probably the least stable, becoming resolved by successive interactions with staff which confirm the patient's suspicions.

A Paradigm for the Study of Awareness Contexts

To organize a study of interaction within different awareness contexts, we have developed a paradigm or set of directives. These directives focus on the study of developmental interaction process—interaction that changes as it continues—as distinct from the relatively static study of the rules that govern interaction.[2]

The component parts of the paradigm are as follows: (1) a description of the given type of awareness context; (2) the structural conditions under which the

---

[2] Cf. Erving Goffman, *Behavior in Public Places*, New York: Free Press of Glencoe, 1963.

awareness context exists;[3] (3) the consequent interaction; (4) changes of inter-action that occasion transformations of context, along with the structural condi-tions for the transformations; (5) the tactics of various interactants as they at-tempt to manage changes of awareness context; and (6) some consequences of the initial awareness context, its transformation and associated interactions—for interactants and for the organizations or institutions notably affected.

To illustrate the use of this paradigm, we briefly sketch the closed awareness context surrounding dying patients.

(1) Hospitalized patients frequently do not recognize their impending death while staff does.[4] Thus interaction between staff and patient occurs within a closed awareness context about the patient's true identity.

(2) At least four major structural conditions determine this closed awareness context. First, most patients are not especially experienced at recognizing the signs of impending death. Second, the hospital is magnificently organized, both by accident and design, for hiding the medical truth from the patient. Records are kept out of reach. Staff is skilled at withholding information from him. Med-ical talk about him occurs generally in far-removed places. Also, the staff is trained or accustomed to act collusively around patients so as not to disclose medical secrets. Third, physicians are supported in their withholding of informa-tion by professional rationales: "Why deny them all hope by telling them they are dying?" Fourth, ordinarily the patient has no allies who can help him discover the staff's secret: even his family or other patients will withhold such information if privy to it.

(3) To prevent the patient's comprehension of the truth, the personnel utilize a number of "situation as normal" interaction tactics. They seek to act in his presence as if he were not dying but only ill. They talk to him as if he were going to live. They converse about his future, thus enhancing his belief that he will re-gain his health. They tell him stories about others (including themselves) who have recovered from similar or worse illnesses. By such indirect signaling they offer him a false biography. Of course, they may directly assure him that he will live, lying with a clear purpose.

To supplement these tactics the staff members use additional ones to guard against disclosure. They carefully guard against the patient's overhearing any con-versation about his real condition. They engage also in careful management of expressions, controlling their facial and other gestures so as not to give the show away:[5] they must control the expression of any sadness they experience over the patient's approaching death. Almost inevitably they attempt, not always con-sciously, to reduce the number of potentially disclosing cues by reducing time spent with the patient or by restricting their conversations with him.

---

[3] We use the phrase "structural conditions" to emphasize that the conditions are conceived of as properties of social structural units. These units may vary from the smallest (such as role, status, or relationship) to the largest (such as organization, community, nation or society) and may be either larger or smaller than the unit of discussion. Usually they are larger contextual units. Structural conditions tend to have a determining or guiding effect on the unit of dis-cussion. Since structural conditions are the tools-in-trade of most sociologists, this footnote is not meant for them. The structural conditions under which interaction takes place, however, are not typically included in the work of social psychologists, especially those trained in de-partments of psychology.

[4] We shall assume that the staff members all share the same awareness and that the staff's definition of a patient's identity (dying) is correct.

[5] Erving Goffman, *The Presentation of Self in Everyday Life*, Edinburgh, Scotland: University of Edinburgh, 1956; see also the Doubleday-Anchor Book edition.

(4) In such collusive games, the teamwork can be phenomenal but the dangers of disclosure to the patient are very great. Unless the patient dies quickly or becomes permanently comatose, the patient tends to suspect or even clearly understand how others identify him. Patients do overhear occasional conversations about themselves. Personnel unwittingly may flash cues or make conversational errors, which arouse the patient's suspicions. Day and night staff may give him contradictory information or divergent clues. The frequent practice of rotating personnel through the hospital services, or adding new personnel, may add to the danger of disclosure. The patient himself may become more knowledgeable about what is going on around him after some days in the hospital, or after repeated hospitalizations. Eventually he may also understand that the hospital is organized not to give him all the information about his condition but rather to withhold most information. He therefore takes what is told him with a grain of salt and some distrust of its accuracy. In short, the original structural conditions that sustain closed awareness begin to disappear, or are counteracted by new structural conditions that make for suspicion or open awareness. This is true even when the patient's symptoms do not badly worsen, but when he does turn worse this may cause him to ask new questions about his illness, which staff members need to handle cannily to keep from him their knowledge that he is dying.

(5) Some interactants may wish to move him along into other types of awareness context. If so, they can employ certain interactional tactics which are, for the most part, merely the opposites of the non-disclosure tactics. Intentionally, a staff member may give the show away wholly or partly, by improper management of face, by carefully oblique phrasing of words, by merely failing to reassure the patient sufficiently about a hopeful prognosis, by changing all talk about the future into concentration upon the present, or by increasing avoidance both of conversation and the patient himself. Of course, personnel occasionally may just plain tell him that he is dying.

(6) The closed awareness that "surrounds" the dying patient has many significant consequences for patient and staff. The patient, unaware of the other's view of his identity, cannot act as if he were aware of dying. Thus he cannot talk to close kin about his fate. He cannot assuage their grief. Nor can he act toward himself as if he were dying, by facing his expected death gracefully—or with panic and hysteria.

The kinsmen and hospital personnel are saved from certain stressful scenes that accompany open awareness about death, but they are also blocked from participating in various satisfying rituals of passage to death. Wives cannot openly take farewells of husbands; personnel cannot share the patient's sometimes ennobling acceptance of death. A profound consequence for the hospital itself, as well as for staff, of the closed awareness context is an interesting division of labor wherein nurses carry the brunt of stressful verbal interaction during which dying and death talk must be avoided. The physicians escape much of this stress since only brief visits are required for patients seemingly on the mend, hence talk is held to a minimum. Moreover, the climate of certain hospital services would be quite different (usually less oppressive) if closed awareness contexts were completely absent—as they are on certain special types of hospital wards.[6]

---

[6] Cf. Renée Fox, *Experiment Perilous*, Glencoe, Ill.: The Free Press, 1959.

Previous Analyses of Interaction

The notion of awareness context is useful for understanding other theoretical approaches to awareness as it relates to social interaction. Our paradigm for the study of interaction within awareness contexts may be used to locate, in a single scheme, the diverse aspects of awareness and social interaction attended to in sociological writings. To illustrate this application of both concept and paradigm, we shall discuss the theoretical work of George H. Mead and Erving Goffman as well as the researches of Donald Roy and Fred Davis. Rather than assess their work *per se,* we shall discuss the writings of these men as good examples of the current state of theory and research about social interaction.

GEORGE H. MEAD

Mead's concern with social interaction was secondary to a lifetime preoccupation with the problems of social order and its orderly change. We interpret his analysis of interaction—also his writing about communication and thought—as bearing principally on an open awareness context. In a well known passage he wrote that: "In short, the conscious or significant conversation of gestures is a much more adequate and effective mechanism of mutual adjustment within the social act—involving, as it does, the taking, by each of the individuals carrying it on, the attitudes of the others toward himself—than is the unconscious or non-significant conversation of gestures." [7] For Mead, "awareness" was essentially an *accurate* awareness of how one's own gesture (vocal or otherwise) was being defined by others, followed by further action based on that awareness. Thus: "That process . . . of responding to one's self as another responds to it, taking part in one's own conversations with others, being aware of what one is saying to determine what one is going to say thereafter—that is a process with which we are all familiar" (p. 217). This perceptive social philosopher gave his readers a rich but highly generalized analysis of that universal situation in which men genuinely and openly communicate.

Mead was not always consistently concerned with shared communication but —as the preceding quotations suggest—also with how one guesses the other's perception of his behavior so as further to direct that behavior oneself. Whether on the basis of these guesses one then misleads the other or plays the game honestly is left ambiguous. Presumably Mead meant the ensuing interaction to be genuinely open and cooperative.[8] The full force of our commentary on this aspect of his work is best demonstrated by an unusual passage wherein Mead raises and dismisses those aspects of interaction that do not involve shared symbolization. He remarks:

> There is, of course, a great deal in one's conversation with others that does not arouse in one's self the same response it arouses in others. That is particularly true in the case of emotional attitudes. One tries to bully somebody else; he is not trying to bully himself. . . . We do at times act and consider just what the effect of

[7] Anselm Strauss (ed.), *The Social Psychology of George Herbert Mead,* Chicago: University of Chicago Press, 1956, p. 173. All references are to this volume.

[8] Herbert Blumer, in pointing to the great value of Mead's approach, has also emphasized concerted action, whether accomplished or developed. See Blumer's "Society as Symbolic Interaction" in Arnold Rose (ed.), *Human Behavior and Social Processes,* Boston: Houghton Mifflin, 1962, esp. pp. 187–188.

our attitude is going to be, and we may deliberately use a certain tone of voice to bring about a certain result. Such a tone arouses the same response in ourselves that we want to arouse in somebody else. But a very large part of what goes on in speech has not this . . . status.

It is the task not only of the actor but of the artist as well to find the sort of expression that will arouse in others what is going on in himself . . . the stimulus calls out in the artist that which it calls out in the other, but this is not the natural function of language. . . . (pp. 224–226).

And what is the natural function of language? "What is essential to communication is that the symbol should arouse in one's self what it arouses in the other individual." Mead seems here to touch on interaction based on something different from open awareness and genuine communication. In deliberate bullying, for example, one's activity may frighten the other but does not frighten oneself. In writing poetry, one finds the means to arouse responses in others what one finds in himself (and Mead remarks that Wordsworth took some years to turn those immediate responses into poetry). And in this same passage, Mead notes that "we do not assume that the person who is angry is calling out the fear in himself that he is calling out in someone else"; that is, in this spontaneous expression of feeling, actor and audience do not respond identically. We should not be surprised to find, sandwiched within this passage, Mead's laconic comment that though we can act—quite like the actor does—"It is not a natural situation; one is not an actor all of the time." Of course no one is! But what about the times when we do act?

Mead's analysis is especially pertinent to this paper because it emphasizes a property of interaction so often absent in other men's work: the developmental properties of interaction. In Mead's writing the concept of significant symbol not only underscores the consensual character of social order but also shows how social order is changed—how social objects are formed and transformed during the course of constructed acts. In current reading of Mead, this developmental aspect tends to be overlooked; so does his processual, rather than substantial, treatment of the self. The self as process insures that interaction is usually not static or merely repetitive. In Mead's world, acts are open-ended, frequently surprising to the actors themselves. And in some of his finest writings Mead emphasizes how even past events are reconstructed, powerfully influencing the directions taken by present events. In short, interaction always tends to go somewhere, but exactly where is not always known for certain by the interactants.

ERVING GOFFMAN

Erving Goffman's work is probably the most influential among current theoretical analyses of interaction. If he does not stand at an opposite pole from Mead, he surely stands far removed—in style, temperament, theoretical perspective, and above all in his focus on the interplay of people. In his first book, *The Presentation of Self in Everyday Life*,[9] one can easily follow his detailed, central analysis of interaction.

From the beginning, Goffman emphasizes an audience's need to define an individual's identity. "When an individual enters the presence of others, they commonly seek to acquire information about him or to bring into play information

---

[9] All references are to the original Edinburgh edition.

about him already possessed" (p. 2). Whether or not an actor wishes, his actions yield impressions of him to his audiences. Therefore, people most frequently "devote their efforts to the creation of desired impressions" rather than act completely without guile or contrivance. "Engineering a convincing impression" is an inescapable fact (p. 162). It is a way for each interactant "to control the conduct of others" (p. 2).

Because of such impression management, "events may occur within the interaction which contradict, discredit, or otherwise throw doubt upon the actor's projection of himself." Much of Goffman's book turns around the confusion or embarrassment that occurs when interaction is thus disrupted. He analyzes extensively the "preventive practices" consequent upon disruptions: "defensively by the actor himself, and protectively when the audience strives to save the definition of the situation projected by another" (p. 7).

In all of this, Goffman focuses on closed awareness. He has a section on "team collusion" (pp. 112–120), and another on the "maintenance of expressive control" (pp. 33–37). Second, he explicitly treats pretense awareness contexts. For instance, "each team tends to suppress its candid view of itself and of the other team, projecting a conception of self and a conception of other that is relatively acceptable to the other. And to insure that communication will follow established, narrow channels, each team is prepared to assist the other team, tacitly and tactfully, in maintaining the impression it is attempting to foster" (p. 107).[10] In general, Goffman, at least in this volume, is uninterested in open awareness contexts; and though he touches on contexts where audiences are suspicious of the actor's projected definition, he does not go into the ways in which the suspicion gradually grows and then is validated.

But whether pretense or closed awareness is at issue, Goffman's principal focus is on how the interaction is kept going, or if disrupted, how interactants manage to get it going again. He has little interest in awareness contexts that are transformed through the deliberate operations of the interactants or through the continued course of the interaction itself. Indeed, his analysis is geared to episodic or repeated interactions rather than to sustained interplay. Consistently with this non-developmental focus, his dramaturgical model refers to the *team* of stage actors who night after night seek to create an acceptable illusion, rather than to the *drama* itself, with its plot line and evolving, relatively unpredictable, sequence of transactions.[11] Particularly it is worth underscoring that the identity of Goffman's actor is rarely problematical to himself, but only and always to his audience.[12]

In this book Goffman tends to leave implicit the structural conditions imposed by the larger social unit. Rather, he focuses mainly on situational conditions such as setting and front and back regions. Of course, most interaction in *The Presentation of Self* occurs in establishments containing service personnel and clients, insiders and outsiders; that is, persons who are either relatively unknown to each other or respectively withhold significant aspects of their private lives from each

---

[10] This passage is a pretty fair description of the situation in which a dying patient and his nurses both engage in pretense by delicately avoiding talk about the patient's impending death.

[11] Many readers seemed to have missed this point. Cf. a similar comment in Sheldon Messinger, Harold Sampson and Robert Towne, "Life as Theater: Some Notes on the Dramaturgic Approach to Social Reality," *Sociometry*, 25 (March, 1962), p. 108. Reprinted in Part Ten of this volume.

[12] To Goffman, surprise means potential disruption of interaction—as compared with Mead's notion of the creative and surprising impulsivity of the "I."

other. Goffman leaves to his readers the task of considering what kinds of structural conditions might lead to interactions quite different from those described. For example, his discussion of impression management might have been very different had he studied neighborhood blocks, small towns, or families, where participants are relatively well known to each other. Similarly, he is not much concerned with systematically tracing various consequences of the interaction (especially for large social units); although for interactants, of course, consequences are noted in terms of specific linkages with the disruption or smooth continuance of encounters.

Aside from its restricted range of awareness contexts, Goffman's world of interaction is non-developmental and rather static. In other writings, he is concerned with interaction of considerable duration, but characteristically his interest is in the rules that govern that interaction. Often interaction proceeds to its termination almost as inexorably as a Greek tragedy.[13] For these aspects, however, his analysis is a considerable advance beyond those of his predecessors.

Next we re-examine two useful papers, our aim being first, to locate the reported research within our awareness paradigm; second, to assess its contribution to interactional analysis; and third, to suggest what might be added to that analysis if one were now to undertake such research.

DONALD ROY

In his "Efficiency and 'The Fix': Informal Intergroup Relations in a Piecework Machine Shop, [14] Roy is interested in demonstrating "that the interaction of two groups in an industrial organization takes place within and is conditioned by a larger intergroup network of reciprocal influences." The interaction is a contest between management and the workers. The latter adroitly scheme, connive and invent methods for attaining quotas set by management; while management attempts to minimize the success of these "black arts of 'making out.'" These arts "were not only responses to challenge from management but also stimulations, in circular interaction, to the development of more effective countermagic in the timing process" established by management's time-checkers. An important segment of Roy's discussion deals with "intergroup collusion" among workers from other departments, who become allies in this unending contest with management.

Where shall we locate Roy's research in our awareness context paradigm? From Roy's description, the awareness contexts are not entirely clear since we do not always know the extent to which management was aware of what was going on among the workers. But in general, workers' attempts to keep closed awareness about their specific collusive games seem to have alternated with management's periodic awareness of such games. Whether this periodic awareness of management transformed the closed context temporarily into pretense or open awareness is difficult to determine. Roy does, however, clearly give the structural conditions that permit both the closed awareness context and its periodic, temporary transformation to pretense or open before the workers reinstitute the closed context with a new collusive game.

Roy describes in great detail the interactional tactics of both sets of players which maintain, transform and reinstitute closed awareness. Teamwork on the

---

[13] Cf. Messinger, et al., op. cit.
[14] American Journal of Sociology, 60 (November, 1954), pp. 255–266.

worker's side is exceptionally well sketched. Managerial tactics, however, are described principally from "below," for two reasons. First, Roy was doing field work as an industrial worker, and could scarcely be privy to management's specific perspectives and decisions. Second, he did not need to scrutinize management's views because his research was designed to explore how workers organized their work.

In spite of the fact that Roy describes the phases through which the contest, and hence the awareness context, oscillates, true temporal development is lacking. This is because he conceives of the interaction as unendingly the same. Apparently the limits of the interaction were set by the time period devoted to the research itself. As Roy himself notes in passing: "How far the beginning of the series [of new rules] antedated the writer's arrival is not known. Old-timers spoke of a 'Golden Age' enjoyed before the installation of the 'Booth System' of production control." An interest in interactional process must raise these questions: from what situation did the interaction phases develop, where did they end, and what happened if someone attempted to bring the collusive interaction out into the open?

The consequences of the interaction are noted sporadically—mainly in terms of work blockages and cumulative inefficiency—but again we might wish to know much more, especially about diverse consequences for the functioning of the organization at large.

FRED DAVIS

A very different presentation of interaction is Fred Davis' "Deviance Disavowal: The Management of Strained Interaction by the Visibly Handicapped." [15] The sub-title accurately describes what this paper is all about. The visible stigma of the handicapped person presents a threat to sociability which "is, at minimum, fourfold: its tendency to become an exclusive focal point of the interaction, its potential for inundating expressive boundaries, its discordance with other attributes of the person and, finally, its ambiguity as a predicator of joint activity." These are "contextual emergents which, depending on the particular situation, serve singly or in combination to strain the framework of normative rules and assumptions in which sociability develops."

After a discussion of these various emergents, which constitute a grave threat to interaction, we are shown "how socially adept handicapped persons cope with it so as to either keep it at bay, dissipate it or lessen its impact upon the interaction." The analysis is aimed at delineating "in transactional terms the stages through which a social relationship with a normal typically passes." The stages are: (1) fictional acceptance, (2) "breaking through" or facilitating normalized role-taking, and (3) institutionalization of the normalized relationship. From the viewpoint of the handicapped person, the "unfolding" of the stages represents deviance disavowal; from that of the normal person it is normalization. For each stage in the process, a certain number of interactional tactics are noted, though Davis is more interested in interactional stages than in the "tremendous variety of specific approaches, ploys and stratagems that the visibly handicapped employ in social situations."

[15] *Social Problems*, 9 (Winter, 1961), pp. 120–132.

This research deals with the transformation of pretense awareness ("fictional acceptance") to open awareness ("institutionalization of the normalized relationship"), chiefly but not solely under the control of transforming operations by the handicapped. As Davis describes it, the handicapped person attempts first to keep interaction in the fictional mode (both interactants mutually aware of his stigma but neither acting as though it existed); then, gradually, the handicapped person engineers matters to a final phase where it is openly "fitting and safe to admit to certain incidental capacities, limits, and needs"—that is, where both parties may openly refer to the stigma of the handicapped person.

Davis' discussion is additionally rich because he makes some very explicit remarks about how difficult the open awareness (normalization) phase is for either party to maintain. For instance: "to integrate effectively a major claim to 'normalcy' with numerous minor waivers of the same claim is a tricky feat and one which exposes the relationship to the many situational and psychic hazards of apparent duplicity. . . ." By implication, this relationship between the two parties has a future: because it is difficult to maintain, it cannot remain at a standstill. We say "by implication" because Davis is content to carry the story only to where something like normal sociability can take place. Said another way, Davis actually is analyzing a developmental—not merely an engineered—interaction situation. "As against the simplistic model of a compulsive deviant and a futile normalizer we would propose one in which it is postulated that both are likely to become engaged in making corrective interactional efforts toward healing the breach." Precisely because *both* are likely to make those correctional efforts, this is a developmental relationship. Our paradigm helps raise the questions of where the relationship is going and what further transformations, under what conditions, may occur.

Our paradigm also suggests focusing on both parties to the interplay even when it is relatively adeptly controlled by one, since our understanding of the relationship's developmental aspects necessarily requires knowledge of the actions and awareness of both parties. Thus, how does the normal interactant see the handicapped, and the interaction, at various phases of the interaction—and what is he doing, or deciding to do, about it? What will his tactics be, whether occasional or continual? Davis also assumes that the handicapped person has often been through this type of interaction—hence has evolved tactics for handling it—while the normal person is a novice. This may be so, but in actual life both players may have had similar experiences.

Lastly, Davis attempts to specify one class of structural conditions that permit the handicapped person to manage strained interaction. He begins his paper by referring to "that genre of everyday intercourse" which is characteristically face-to-face, not too prolonged but not too fleeting either, with a certain degree of intimacy, and "ritualized to the extent that all know in general what to expect but not so ritualized as to preclude spontaneity and the slightly novel turns of events." This explicit detailing is not a mere backdrop but an intrinsic part of the analysis of interaction in the presence of physical stigma. The consequences of interaction (e.g., the satisfaction of both parties and the possibility of a continuing relationship) are left mainly implicit.

General Implications of Paradigm

Our examination of these four writers indicates that future research and theory on interactional problems should encompass a far broader range of phenomena than heretofore. Of course, one need not do everything demanded by the paradigm. But it guides the researcher in exploring and perhaps extending the limits of his data, and in stating clearly what was done and left undone, perhaps adding why and why not. The paradigm helps the theorist achieve greater clarity, integration, and depth of analysis by encouraging reflection upon what he has chosen *not* to make explicit. It also raises questions about development and structure that a straight factor approach to the study of interaction typically does not: [16] how does one type of context lead to another; what are the structural conditions —including rules—in the relevant institutions that facilitate or impede existence of a context, and changes in it; what are the effects of a changing awareness context on the identity of a participant; why does one party wish to change a context while another wishes to maintain it or reinstate it; what are the various interactional tactics used to maintain or reinstate change; and what are the consequences for each party, as well as for sustaining institutional conditions?

This developmental focus helps to eliminate the static quality and restricted boundaries for analysis that are characteristic of the factor approach. The factor approach is useful only when the analyst is conscious of the location of his conceptual boundaries within a larger developmental, substantive scheme, and can thereby explain their relevance to his readers, rather than implicitly declaring all other substantive factors out of bounds. Only then is it sensible to leave out so much that other sociologists, in the light of present theory and knowledge, recognize as relevant to the area under consideration.

The focus on structural conditions increases the likelihood that the microscopic analysis of interaction will take into account the nature of the larger social structure within which it occurs. The usual structural approach in sociology tends to neglect microscopic analysis of interaction and also inhibits attention to its developmental character. Our paradigm encompasses in one developmental scheme the twin, but often divorced, sociological concerns with social structure and social interaction. Neither need be slighted, or forgotten, for a focus on the other.

Our discussion has touched on only four possible types of awareness contexts: open, closed, pretense and suspicion. These four types are generated by the substantively relevant combinations of four variables found in our study of the literature and in our data on awareness of identity and interaction. We have considered two variables as dichotomous—*two interactants; acknowledgment of awareness* (pretense or no pretense)—and two as trichotomous—*degree of awareness* (aware, suspicious and unaware); and *identity* (other's identity, own identity, and own identity in the eyes of the other). Logical combination of these variables would yield 36 possible types, but to start research with all the logical combinations of these variables would be an unnecessarily complex task, considering that many or most types are empirically non-existent. Therefore, the procedure used to develop awareness context types related to interaction was first, to search data for

---

[16] The factor approach is a standard one in sociology: it is legitimated by the notion that one can only consider so much at one time with precision and clarity, and therefore boundaries must be chosen, usually according to one's interests, provided they are theoretically relevant. For a discussion of "simultaneous *versus* sequential" factor models, see Howard S. Becker, *Outsiders,* New York: The Free Press, 1963, pp. 22–25.

relevant types; second, to logically substruct the variables involved; and third, on the basis of these variables to judge whether other possible types would be useful or necessary for handling the data.

Presumably, more empirically relevant types can be found by scrutinizing the sociological literature, one's own data, and one's own life.[17] Another implication of the present analysis is that increasingly complex types of awareness contexts and their distinctive consequences should be systematically sought. We recommend our procedure for evolving types, as opposed to starting out with the full set of logical combinations, each of which must then be screened for empirical relevance.

We suggested, at the beginning of the paper, two factors that further complicate awareness contexts: additional people, and people representing organized systems with a stake in certain types of awareness context. Certain types of social phenomena are probably stategic for extending our knowledge of awareness contexts: for example, research discoveries in science and in industry, spy systems, deviant communities whose actions may be visible to "squares," types of bargaining before audiences, such as occurs in diplomatic negotiations, and unofficial reward systems like those depicted by Melville Dalton and Alvin Gouldner.[18]

38   Toward a Sociological Model of Consensus

● THOMAS J. SCHEFF

The importance of the concept of consensus for sociological theory has been stated eloquently and often. Park and Burgess used it as the central concept in their textbook in 1921, and Wirth made an impassioned plea for the study of consensus in 1948. More recently, Gross *et al.* have argued (in the context of their study of roles) that sociologists should not merely postulate consensus, but should transform the concept into a variable, in order to be able to study the degree to which it occurs.[1] Klapp, most recently, has reaffirmed the importance of the concept, and strongly urged its further development: [2]

---

[17] We are working with the "unawareness" context, in which neither party knows the identity of the other or his identity in the other's eyes. This is illustrated by strangers meeting or passing each other on a dark street. If they stop to talk, the first task they are likely to engage in is to transform the "unawareness" context to facilitate interaction.

[18] *Men Who Manage,* New York: Wiley, 1959; and *Patterns of Industrial Bureaucracy,* Glencoe, Ill.: The Free Press. 1954, respectively.

SOURCE: Thomas J. Scheff, in the *American Sociological Review,* XXXII, #1 (February 1967), pp. 32–46. Reprinted by permission of The American Sociological Association.

Written with the financial support of the Research Committee of the University of California, Santa Barbara, and the Social Science Research Council. The author wishes to acknowledge the helpful comments by Milton Bloombaum, Herbert Costner, and my colleagues in the Department of Sociology, University of California, Santa Barbara.

---

[1] Neal Gross *et al., Explorations in Role Analysis,* New York: Wiley, 1958.
[2] Orrin E. Klapp, "The Concept of Consensus and its Importance," *Sociology and Social Research,* 41 (1957), pp. 336–342.

. . . consensus should have an importance in sociology comparable to that of energy in physics—namely, as a unifying concept, an abstraction that will include and relate more specific concepts and data. Light, heat, sound, and electromagnetism are forms of energy; so, I think, culture, structure, norm, role, symbol, and so on, should be treated as forms of consensus.

Klapp goes on to suggest the need for analytic formulations which give a common theoretical base to concepts such as: [3]

. . . nationalism, class and race consciousness, culture, norm, status, system, morale, solidarity, integration, and *anomie*. For example, I believe that consensus should be considered as a dimension and measure of integration, and inversely of *anomie;* that morale should not refer to solidarity as a whole but a kind of consensus relating to tasks and goals; and that solidarity is a loose term that should be specified as to whether consensus or integration or something else is meant. The idea of social function, too, I believe should be defined to mean a contribution to consensus, hence, to organization.

These earlier discussions make clear the continuing need for rigorous conceptual and operational definitions of the concept of consensus. These definitions are necessary not only for research which is directed toward consensus itself, such as small group and public opinion research, but also, more widely, in the most diverse kinds of analysis in sociology, anthropology, and social psychology, on norms, roles, institutions, group goals, and culture.

The purpose of this paper is to formulate a conceptual and an operational definition of degree of consensus, which may provide a basis for a more precise and extensive theory. These definitions are used to formulate a series of propositions which relate *degree of consensus* in a group to the *degree of coordination* between members of the group, when communication is held constant. Some dimensions of type of coordination (formalization, complexity, and pay-off) and sub-dimensions of each of these in turn, are also delineated. Finally, applications to three problems are discussed: a test of the interactionist theory of consensus, the study of social integration, and studies of leadership and political representation. The discussion begins with a review of the literature on consensus.

There are two main traditions in the study of consensus. The majority of investigators have taken an informal, commonsense approach to the concept. For researchers in this tradition, consensus on an issue appears to be taken to mean simply agreement in a group. The degree of consensus with respect to a statement X, by this definition, would simply be the extent to which individuals in the group state their agreement with X. We may call this definition of consensus the *individual agreement* definition. Research which appears to have been based on this definition has been reported by Riley, Riley and Toby, Bales and Slater, Gross, Mason, and McEachern, and E. Gross to mention just a few such studies.[4] In theoretical work, the individual agreement definition is implicit in formal discussion of social

---

[3] *Ibid.*
[4] Matilda W. Riley, John W. Riley, and Marcia L. Toby, "The Measurement of Consensus," *Social Forces*, 31 (1952), pp. 97–106; Robert F. Bales and Philip E. Slater, "Role Differentiation in Small Decision-Making Groups," in Talcott Parsons and Robert F. Bales (eds.), *Family Socialization and Interaction Process*, Glencoe, Illinois: The Free Press, 1955, pp. 274–296; Neal Gross *et al., op. cit.,* Edward Gross, "Symbiosis and Consensus as Integrative Factors in Small Groups," *American Sociological Review*, 21 (1956), pp. 174–179.

norms (Morris, Blake and Davis, Gibbs, and Clark and Gibbs), roles (Gross *et al.*), public opinion, and theory (Parsons and Shils).[5]

The other major tradition stems from the interactionist social psychology of Dewey and Mead, and stresses the *co-orientation* of individuals in a group toward a statement, rather than the individual orientations of the members of the group. The most widely known use of this tradition in current theory and research is found in the work of Newcomb, whose ABX model of co-orientation and whose empirical work on the estimation of group attitudes is related to the approach that will be taken here.[6] Implicit in the co-orientation approach is a social-systemic model of consensus, rather than an individual-systemic model as assumed by the agreement definition.

Perhaps the major difficulty with the individual agreement definition is found in the paradox of pluralistic ignorance. If we postulate that consensus affects behavior, which is the usual assumption, it is not difficult to find situations which violate this assumption, when consensus is taken to mean agreement. If no one in a community agrees with a view, but everyone thinks that everyone else does, the effect on behavior is sometimes the same as if everyone actually agreed. By the agreement definition of consensus, the norm should not be in effect, since no one agrees. But actually, since everyone thinks that everyone else agrees (each person thinks of himself as the only exception), the norm might be as operative as it would be if everyone did agree, to take an extreme example. Even allowing that such extreme situations rarely occur, the objection is not met. The agreement definition of consensus makes no provision for perceptions of agreement, which may be independent of actual agreement, and affect behavior. We need a modification of the commonsense definition which would meet this objection.

Not all work on consensus has been based on the agreement definition. For example, the question which forms the basis for the North-Hatt scale of occupational prestige is:

> Which statement . . . best gives your own personal opinion of the *general standing* of a (specific occupation)?[7]

---

[5] Richard T. Morris, "A Typology of Norms," *American Sociological Review*, 21 (1956), pp. 610–613; Judith Blake and Kingsley Davis, "Norms, Values and Sanctions," in *The Handbook of Modern Sociology*, Robert E. L. Faris (ed.), Chicago: Rand McNally, 1964, pp. 456–484; Jack P. Gibbs, "Norms: The Problem of Definition and Classification," *American Journal of Sociology*, 70 (1965), pp. 586–594; Alexander L. Clark and Jack P. Gibbs, "Social Control: A Reformulation," *Social Problems*, 12 (1965), pp. 398–414; Neal Gross, *op. cit.*, pp. 11–79; Talcott Parsons and Edward A. Shils (eds.), *Toward a General Theory of Action*, Cambridge, Massachusetts: Harvard University Press, 1951, pp. 193–194. A dissenting opinion on public opinion as agreement is found in Kurt Riezler, "What Is Public Opinion?" *Social Research*, 11 (1944), pp. 397–428. Riezler appears to argue that public opinion is a social system, although his meaning is not always clear.

[6] Theodore M. Newcomb, "An Approach to the Study of Communicative Acts," *Psychological Review*, 60 (1953), pp. 393–404; Mary Monk and Theodore M. Newcomb, "Perceived Consensus Within and Among Occupational Classes," *American Sociological Review*, 21 (1956), pp. 71–79; Kamla Chowdry and Theodore M. Newcomb, "The Relative Abilities of Leaders and Non-Leaders to Estimate Opinions of Their Own Groups," *Journal of Abnormal and Social Psychology*, 47 (1952), pp. 51–57.

[7] Albert J. Reiss, *Occupations and Social Status*, New York: Free Press, 1961, p. 19. Reiss is also critical:

> The criteria that respondents used in rating the "general standing" of an occupation were not standardized, but left to each respondent to define for himself . . . Is it a community content? How do other people view it? How do you view it? (p. 22).

Although the juxtaposition of the phrases "your own personal opinion" and "general standing" might be expected to cause respondents some confusion, it is clear that the intent of the question is to obtain not the respondent's personal opinion as to the prestige of an occupation, but his perception of other's opinions.

In the study of occupational prestige, the investigator wishes to get at the individual's perception of group opinion, but the results are probably confounded by those individuals who misinterpret this intent, and express their personal opinion, rather than their judgment of the opinion of others. In the question of Social Desirability, just the opposite problem arises. The psychological tests are intended to tap the individual's own personal beliefs and his actual behavior, but, as has been pointed out, this personal information tends to be contaminated with answers which reflect the individual's judgment of what the tester or the community would consider desirable or acceptable answers.[8]

Perhaps one way out of both of these difficulties is to ask both types of question. This would certainly clarify the respondent's task for him, and might give the investigator the kind of data which would allow him to build a more complex, and perhaps therefore a more adequate scale of occupational prestige, or of individual attitude or behavior. We suspect that the relationship between individual and group attitudes is often an intimate one. The model of consensus discussed below could provide an avenue for exploring and representing the joint effect of personal and group attitudes.

As stated, Newcomb has sought to develop a concept of consensus more differentiated than the agreement model. His separation of "homogeneity of orientation" and "perceived consensus" as two analytically distinct group properties was one step in this direction. Another has been the development of a model of co-orientation, the ABX model. In this work, Newcomb has constructed a scheme for showing the ramifications of co-orientation between individuals A and B, toward an object X. Since Newcomb has stressed that this model is based on the co-orientation of A and B toward X, and not just on their individual orientations, and he has explicitly linked this model to the study of consensus, his work must be taken as a major departure from the traditional approach.[9]

Communication and Consensus

The interactionist social psychologists describe communication and consensus as a collective process, rather than as an aggregate of individual processes. This distinction can be exemplified by comparing Dewey's discussion of communication with the model proposed by Lasswell. For Lasswell, communication could be represented by the formula, "Who says what in which channel to whom with what effect?" Communication is seen as the transmission of a message by the sender to the receiver, with the sender and receiver considered to be independent agents. The model would work as well for a mechanical system: the sender could be an oscillator and the receiver a tape-recorder.

For Dewey, however, the sender and the receiver were not considered to be

---

[8] Allen L. Edwards, *The Social Desirability Dimension in Personality Assessment and Research*, New York: Dryden Press, 1957.

[9] Theodore M. Newcomb, "The Study of Consensus," in *Sociology Today*, Merton, Broom, and Cottrell (eds.), New York: Basic Books, 1959, pp. 277–292. See also the treatment of social norms in Newcomb *et al.*, *Social Psychology*, New York: Holt, Rinehart and Winston, 1965, Chap. 8.

separate systems; for human communication to occur, they must be at least temporarily joined together into a single system. Dewey considered communication to be the interpenetration of perspectives: the communicating individuals actually share, at least for the moment, some of each other's point of view. Communication might be deemed, therefore, a type of "mind reading." Each person knows what the other is thinking; they are engaged in joint thought about an object.[10]

Using the concept of role-taking, Mead suggested how such mind reading might take place. As described by Mead, role-taking is a sequential, self-correcting process through which one individual can experience another's subjective state to any required degree of approximation.[11] The sequence starts with the projection of some of one's own experience onto the other, hypothesizing what gestures one would use that would correspond with this experience, perceiving the gestures of the other that actually occur, reformulating the hypothesized experience to project, searching again for the corresponding gestures, reformulation of the second hypothesis on the basis of the actual gestures perceived, and so on indefinitely in a cycle of hypothesis-checking which allows for the successive approximation of the other's experience.

Corresponding closely to the Mead-Dewey formulation of consensus and communication is the Schutz-Scheler concept of intersubjectivity: the joint consciousness of communicating individuals.[12] Also related is Durkheim's concept of the collective consciousness, which will be discussed further after we have introduced the idea of tacit coordination.[13]

Schelling's work on tacit coordination will be discussed as a final example of the tradition of co-orientation in the study of consensus.[14] The basic proposition in this tradition is that the necessity of social coordination gives rise to the seeking of consensus, and that consensus, in turn, is a product of communication.

Implicit in this tradition is a theory of social coordination. Flexible coordination (coordination in situations in which there are no rigid rules which allow for the fitting together of individual lines of action into a collective act) is made possible by consensus, which in turn is made possible by communication.[15] One serious limitation of this theory is that it assumes that actors *want* to coordinate their lines of activity, and that the only obstacle is the problem of articulating their actions with others. In other words, the interactionist social psychologists (and most other sociological theorists, as well) have dealt only with the case where *motivation* for coordination is high. The theory fails to deal with situations where motivation is low or absent. It also does not deal with another important contingency. Even if motivation is high, it may be high because of threat of punishment, i.e., the motivation may not be intrinsic to the goal of the transaction, but based on the superior

[10] John Dewey, *Experience and Nature*, New York: Dover, 1958, Chapter 5. A recent illustration of the process of "mind reading" can be found on pp. 227–228 in Harold Garfinkel, "Studies of the Routine Grounds of Everyday Activities," *Social Problems*, 11 (1964), pp. 225–250.
[11] George Herbert Mead, *Mind, Self and Society*, Chicago: University of Chicago Press, 1934.
[12] A discussion of Scheler's concept of intersubjectivity is found in Alfred Schutz, *Collected Papers*, M. Natanson (ed.), The Hague: Martinus Nijhoff, 1962.
[13] Emile Durkheim, *Sociology and Philosophy*, in George Simpson, *Emile Durkheim*, New York: Thomas Y. Crowell, 1963, pp. 18–21.
[14] Thomas C. Schelling, *The Strategy of Conflict*, New York: Oxford University Press, 1963, pp. 54–67.
[15] For a consideration of this theory, see the author's paper "A Theory of Coordination Applicable to Experimental Games" (in press).

power of the other.[16] A general theory of coordination must deal not only with the situation in which the motivation to coordinate is high and intrinsic but also with the situations in which motivation is low or absent, and/or based on threat of punishment.[17] The limitation of this paper to intrinsically motivated social situations should be kept in mind.

The conjunction of coordination, consensus, and communication is neatly caught in Schelling's consideration of tacit coordination. A person in a position in which he must coordinate his own line of activity with another will engage in attempts to read the other's mind by interpreting communicative acts. At times, Schelling argues, such processes are successful; co-orientation may occur even if there is no direct communication. There is instead a "conversation of gestures":

> If the Yalu River is to be viewed as a limit in the Korean War that was recognized on both sides, its force and authority is to be analysed not in terms of the joint unilateral recognition of it by both sides of the conflict—not as something that we and the Chinese recognized unilaterally and simultaneously—but as something that we "mutually recognized." It was not just that we recognized it and they recognized it, but that we recognized that they recognized it, they recognized that we recognized it, we recognized that they recognized that we recognized it, and so on. It was a shared expectation. To that extent, it was a somewhat undeniable expectation. If it commands our attention, then we expect it to be observed and we expect the Chinese to expect us to observe it. We cannot unilaterally detach our expectations from it. In that sense limits and precedents and traditions of this kind have an authority that is not exactly granted to them voluntarily by the participants in a conflict. They acquire magnetism or focal power of their own.[18]

What is particularly instructive about this example is that it suggests higher orders of co-orientation than the simple perception of the other's feelings.[19] If we call agreement the zero level of co-orientation, then perception of the other's feeling ("we recognized that they recognized it") is first-level co-orientation, and perception of the other's perception ("we recognized that they recognized that we recognized it") is the second-level of co-orientation.

Having introduced the higher orders of co-orientation, we may now return to Durkheim. For Durkheim, collective representations were the fundamental building blocks of society. Yet there is a paradox in his formulations.

> Collective representations are exterior to individual minds . . . they do not derive from them as such, but from the association of minds, which is a very different thing.

He goes on to say:

> Once a basic number of representations has been thus created, they become . . . partially autonomous realities, with their own way of life.

---

[16] Cf. I. L. Horowitz, "Consensus, Conflict, and Cooperation: A Sociological Inventory." *Social Forces*, 41 (1962), pp. 177–188.

[17] For further development of this problem, see the author's "A Theory of Social Order," (in preparation).

[18] Thomas C. Schelling, *Toward a Theory of Strategy for International Conflict*, Rand Publication P-1648, pp. 40–41. Schelling develops further the idea of tacit coordination in *The Strategy of Conflict*, op. cit., especially chap. 4.

[19] For a discussion of the process of reflected, reciprocating attribution, see P. H. Maucorps and Rene Bassoul, "Jeux de Miroir et Sociologie de la Connaissance D'Autrui," (The Mirror Game and the Sociology of Knowledge of the Other) *Cahiers Internationaux Sociologie*, 32 (1962), pp. 43–60. Arturo Biblarz called this paper to my attention.

Durkheim insists that collective consciousness is more than the sum of individual consciousnesses, that it has a life of its own, yet he gives no explanation of how individual consciousnesses (in "association") become group consciousness. Durkheim leaves us not with a theory but an enigma.

It is possible that the example that Schelling uses will allow us to resolve Durkheim's paradox. Note that Schelling allows for still higher orders of mutual understanding ("and so on"). This allowance gives Durkheimian force to Schelling's final sentences.

> In that sense limits and precedents and traditions of this kind have an authority that is not exactly granted to them voluntarily by the participants in a conflict. They acquire magnetism or focal power of their own.

It seems that this is just the sense that Durkheim intended for his statement about the exteriority and constraint of social facts. The collective representations are felt as powerful exterior constraints because each individual agrees, recognizes that his neighbors agree, that they each recognize that he agrees, that he recognizes they recognize, and so on indefinitely. Although he agrees (or disagrees) with the sentiment, it is also something beyond his power to change, or even completely explore. The potentially endless mirror reflections of each of the others' recognitions is felt as something utterly final. From this formulation it follows that each actor feels the presence of the collective representation with a sense of exteriority and constraint, even if he, as an individual, is himself wholeheartedly dedicated or opposed to the representation.

A process similar to the mirroring discussed above is suggested by Schutz's concept of "the reciprocity of perspectives." [20] The similarity is clearly seen in Garfinkel's explication of the concept of "background understandings."

> According to Schutz, the person assumes, assumes that the other person assumes as well, and assumes that as he assumes it of the other person the other person assumes the same for him.[21]

The paper from which the quotation is taken is concerned, for the most part, with reporting studies which illustrate background understandings in ordinary social transactions. The concept of background understandings would appear to correspond to what is referred to in this paper as the *issue* (X) about which consensus may occur. The first three levels of co-orientations are explicit in Garfinkel's description of background understandings. The present formulation differs from his description in that it posits still higher orders.

It is not necessary for the actor to actually explore the degrees of co-orientation higher than the second or third to be aware of the massiveness of a collective representation. Just as in the endless chain of reflections in two opposing mirrors, the details that are reflected coalesce, after a few reflections, into a formless blur, so the actor can feel the weight of the collective representation, without necessarily making a detailed, level-by-level examination of its form and extent.

This discussion leads us finally to a formal definition of a social system model of consensus: complete consensus on an issue exists in a group when there is an infinite series of reciprocating understandings between the members of the group concerning the issue. I know that you know that I know, and so on. This is the definition of *complete* consensus. In actual research, one might find it difficult to

[20] Schutz, *op. cit.*, pp. 11–13.
[21] Garfinkel, *op. cit.*, p. 237.

locate a single example of such complete consensus, and of demonstrating that it occurred if one did find it. For actual situations, one can derive various degrees of partial consensus, depending upon the level of co-orientation achieved. The zero level would represent agreement, but not consensus. The first level (New-comb's *perceived consensus*), would be a first degree consensus, the second level (we recognized that they recognized that we recognized) a second degree consensus, and so on.

If we accept this definition of consensus, if only for discussion, the next problem is to operationalize it. Very suggestive for this purpose is the work of Laing, Phillipson and Lee. They have developed a technique for measuring three levels of co-orientation between marital couples, which they call agreement, understanding, and realization.[22] At the first level the pair, interviewed separately, simply give the same response to an issue. For example, the issue may be the following statement: "Mary is dependent on John." If Mary and John express agreement with this statement independently, they *agree*. The second question is to ask each how the other would answer the question. If John answers that Mary will agree, and in fact she does agree, John *understands* Mary on this issue. If John's guess does not agree with Mary's actual answer, then he *misunderstands* Mary. The third and final level is called realization. The operational index of realization (for John) is contained in the question: How will Mary think you will have answered this question? If John correctly judged how Mary thinks he has answered the question, then John *realizes* that he is understood by Mary. If he does not, he *fails to realize* that he is understood.

Laing, Phillipson and Lee use a shorthand notation for characterizing the profile of mutuality between the marital pair. Allow A to stand for agreement, D for disagreement, U for understanding, M for misunderstanding, R for realization, and F for failure to realize, then the profile (R U A U R) means that the husband and the wife agree and that each understands and realizes that he is understood. Similarly, (F M D M F) means that husband and wife disagree and each misunderstands and fails to realize that he is misunderstood. The profile, husband (F M A U R), wife, is indicative of unilateral understanding. The husband and the wife agree, but the husband thinks that they disagree and fails to realize that he is understood. The wife, however, understands that they agree, and realizes that she is misunderstood. The Laing technique may be used as a basis for the study of consensus by generalizing it to groups of any size, and to co-orientation at any desired level. Two somewhat different techniques are relevant to this task: the measurement of accuracy of role-taking developed by Stryker, and the measurement of perceived consensus, as used by Newcomb.[23] Stryker's technique is the more elegant of the two, and will be discussed first.

Stryker measured the amount of first level co-orientation among persons in eight statuses in the extended family: son, daughter, father, mother, son-in-law, daughter-in-law, father-in-law, and mother-in-law. He asked each person to judge the answers given by two other persons in his family to a twenty-item questionnaire on family ideology. The statuses of the target persons are randomly changed and an analysis of variance design is used. Since Stryker asked his respondents to judge

22 Ronald Laing, H. Phillipson, and A. Russell Lee, *Interpersonal Perception: A Theory and a Method of Research*, New York: Springer, 1966, Chapter 5.
23 Sheldon Stryker, "Conditions for Accurate Role-Taking: A Test of Mead's Theory," in Arnold Rose (ed.), *Human Behavior and Social Processes*, Boston: Houghton-Mifflin, 1962, pp. 41–62; Monk and Newcomb, *op. cit.*, and Chowdry and Newcomb, *op. cit.*

the answers of *particular* other people (for example, a respondent's wife and father-in-law), the Laing technique is directly applicable. If we measured the first three levels of co-orientation using the Stryker design, the results would be profiles of *inter-status* consensus in the family, similar to those obtained by Laing on *inter-person* consensus. What makes Stryker's design promising is that it enables the researcher to make a variable of *relationships* between persons. For example, one could compare the amount of consensus existing between spouses, as against the amount of consensus existing between parents and children. The significance of this kind of comparison will be discussed below.

The other technique, similar to that used by Newcomb in his studies of perceived consensus, is to ask the respondents to judge the opinion not of particular persons but of particular groups. In order to utilize the Laing technique, it is necessary to decide at what level of plurality an opinion will be designated as characteristic of the group. Previous writers have been reluctant to set some specific level of agreement as an index of normative consensus. Although there appears to be agreement that this level should fall somewhere between (or including) a simple majority, at the one extreme, and complete unanimity, at the other, fixing a definite index presents some difficulty. A simple majority means one thing, for example, when there is a large unified minority, and another when the minority is composed of a set of competing opinions and/or apathetic responses. The level of two-thirds would have little support other than American legislative practice. Unanimity would appear to be too stringent a requirement.

Perhaps a successful resolution of the problem of the index level for consensus requires two or more dimensions, rather than the single dimension of size of plurality. It would seem logical to include both the number and the size of modes in the distribution of opinion in a refined index of consensus.

Since the definition suggested here involves some complexity even with a single dimension of agreement based on proportion alone, the question of further dimensions of the agreement index will be postponed. For the present, to advance the argument, I would like to designate the index level as the majority. Choosing the majority as indicative of agreement is not a completely arbitrary decision because it represents the situation in which the actor will be right more times than he is wrong in acting on the basis of his expectations.

To use a simplified example to illustrate this approach, suppose in a survey we ask two questions: (1) Do you agree or disagree with the following statement, "There is a God"? (2) How will the average person answer this question? The results can be most easily visualized in a four-fold table.

TABLE 1

| | Majority | |
Majority	Understands	Misunderstands
Agrees (with the statement X)	UA Monolithic consensus (1st degree)	MA Pluralistic ignorance
Does not agree	UD Dissensus (1st degree)	MD False consensus

At this point it may be useful to introduce a slight change in the Laing procedure concerning the meaning of *agreement*, as noted in Table 1. For Laing, agreement means simply similarity of response. It has therefore a double meaning: either that both parties agree with the symbolic statement X, or that both disagree. For the purposes of this paper, however, we will take agreement to have a single meaning: that both parties *endorse* the statement X. Since we wish to talk about conscious agreement and shared experience, it is important to avoid mere similarity of response in our conception of consensus. For example, one reason that respondents do not agree with a given statement may be that they do not understand it, i.e., it is not meaningful to them. Yet if the majority responded in this way, scoring mere similarity of response in the way Laing does would indicate consensus exists, which is far from our intention. For convenience, we will retain Laing's notation of (R U A), and so on. It should be noted, however, that the D, which in Laing's usage stands for disagreement, will mean non-agreement in this discussion.

There is *monolithic consensus* if the majority agrees and understands that there is agreement; there is *pluralistic ignorance* if the majority agrees but thinks that there is disagreement; there is *dissensus* if the majority does not agree and understands that they do not agree. And there is *false consensus* if the majority does not agree and thinks that they agree. This example uses only the first two levels of mutuality. If the third level is added, that of realization, the table becomes eight-fold and the conceptual and operational difficulty of the approach is increased greatly.

Conceptually it is very difficult to conceive of partial consensus, say of the type (R M D)—realization of misunderstanding about not agreeing. Operationally it becomes necessary to ask respondents questions such as: "How would the average person think that the average person will have answered?"

Perhaps a less awkward approach to the higher levels of consensus would be a question such as: "Now pretend you are the average person in this community. How would he answer the question? How would he think that you have answered it?" This form or its equivalent might facilitate gathering of what is admittedly an intricate and (for the respondent) confusing type of information.

Introducing the third level of mutuality, realization, generates a property space with eight cells as follows and is depicted in Table 2.

TABLE 2

	Majority Realization		Failure to Realize	
	Understands	Misunderstands	Understands	Misunderstands
Agrees (with the statement X)	RUA(UR) Monolithic consensus (2nd degree)	RMA(MR) Realized pluralistic ignorance	FUA(UF) Monolithic consensus (1st degree)	FMA(MF) Pluralistic ignorance
Does not agree (with the statement X)	RUD(UR) Dissensus (2nd degree)	RMD(MR) Realized false consensus	FUD(UF) Dissensus (1st degree)	FMD(MF) False consensus

The difficulty of visualizing a profile such as (R M A)—a majority of the group agree, but a majority misunderstands that there is agreement, yet a majority realize that there is misunderstanding—makes it necessary to adopt an artifice. Suppose we divide the group, at random, into two sub-groups, and then consider the responses of the majority in each sub-group, as if each were considering the responses of the other. Using this device, the profile becomes similar to the Laing model, but considering two majorities, rather than two persons. Then (R M A) becomes: Sub-group 1 (R M A M R) Sub-group 2, a majority in each group agrees but a majority in each misunderstands that there is agreement, i.e., a majority in each sub-group thinks that a majority in the other sub-group does not agree, yet, a majority in each sub-group realizes that it is misunderstood by the other sub-group. (F U A U F) is the situation in which the majority is in agreement, understands that there is agreement, but fails to realize that it is understood. That is to say the majority is unaware that others are aware that there is agreement. Similarly, (F U D U F) is the situation in which the majority does not agree, understands that there is not agreement, but fails to realize that it is understood.

Such a typology of consensual structures should allow a first approximation of the complex process of inter-subjectivity. It is not intended actually to represent this process, but only to provide a static and finite index of the reciprocating, inter-acting experiences of the members of a group.

It should be noted that there is an extensive literature which is relevant to the operational definition of consensus: the critiques of methodology in studies of empathy.[24] This literature points to the necessity of introducing experimental or statistical controls for extraneous variables. For example, Hill, Stycos, and Back sought to determine the role that empathy between husband and wife (what we have called first level co-orientation) played in contraception.[25] Since they did not, however, control for other variables, such as agreement or amount of communication, they were unable to discern unambiguously the effects of empathy on behavior. A study of three levels of co-orientation of the kind suggested here would require either elaborate experimental controls, or the large number of cases that would allow for partialling, in order to avoid this difficulty.

Causes and Consequences of Consensus

So far we have outlined conceptual and operational definitions of consensus. These definitions generate a series of possible consensual structures in groups: partial consensuses of various degrees, and non-consensual structures such as false consensus and pluralistic ignorance. We now turn to a brief consideration of the dynamics of consensus—how these structures are effects of various antecedent conditions, and are in turn the causes of certain consequences.

Newcomb's discussion of the ABX model suggests both causes and consequences of consensus. He uses causal variables such as:

1. The attraction of A to B;
2. Frequency of communication between A and B;
3. Intensity of A's feeling about X;
4. Degree of differentiation of A's and B's roles.

Newcomb goes on to link the antecedent variables to a consequent variable, "desire to communicate." The basic premise in all of his propositions is that of balance: he thinks that there is a "strain toward symmetry" (i.e. co-orientation). The

[24] For a recent review of this literature, see Victor B. Cline, "Interpersonal Perception," in Brendon A. Maher, *Progress in Experimental Personality Research*, V. 1, New York: Academic Press, 1964, pp. 221–284.
[25] Reuben Hill, J. Mayone Stycos, and Kurt W. Back, *The Family and Population Control*, Chapel Hill: The University of North Carolina Press, 1959, pp. 152–160, and 316–321.

postulate of the strain toward symmetry generates a whole series of propositions about the conditions under which asymmetry (non-consensual structures) will lead to further attempts at communication.

1. The stronger the forces toward A's co-orientation in respect to B and X:
   (a) the greater A's strain toward symmetry with B in respect to X
   (b) the greater the likelihood of increased symmetry as a consequence of one or more communicative acts.
2. The less the attraction between A and B, the more nearly strain toward symmetry is limited to those particular X's, coordination toward which is required by the conditions of association.[26]

I think that Newcomb overstates the strain toward symmetry, because he underestimates the importance of the underlying variable of the degree and extent of *coordination* required by different kinds of relationships (see below). Nevertheless, his postulates generate useful propositions.

Dimensions of Coordination

One difficulty with the propositions stated by Newcomb is that each in itself appears meaningful, but as a group they lack coherence and completeness. Ultimately one would like to be able to list the determinants and consequences of consensus in such a way that the items in each set would be mutually exclusive and exhaustive. In Newcomb's approach, personal, interpersonal and social variables are mixed together. In the following discussion, as one step toward a theory of consensus, we will limit our concern to a single sociological variable, the type of coordination required by a social relationship.

This variable is suggested by Newcomb's second hypothesis, above, which concerns issues in which coordination is required by the "conditions of association." Some types of relationship involve little coordination and therefore do not require consensus, except in very limited areas. One doesn't need to know the bartender's political opinions in order to get a drink. On the other hand, the confidence man seeks a high degree of consensus—to be sure, a unilateral consensus: confidence man—(R U D M F)—victim.

The following proposition is suggested: *The type and extent of consensus is dependent on the type and extent of coordination required between the members of the group.* This proposition leads us back to the social-psychological bases of coordination, which are communication and consensus.

What is needed for the further exploration of this proposition is the conceptual refinement of the variable of coordination. Coordination is an extremely abstract concept covering an enormous span of behaviors, from an event as simple as shaking hands to a sequence of events as intricate as international trade. Let us consider, for illustrative purposes, just three dimensions of coordination, one antecedent, one concomitant, and one consequent. Other things being equal we would expect that the higher the degree of formalization, the more complex and the more cooperative (rather than competitive) the pay-off of the coordinated activity, and the greater the consensus between the participants. Since degree of formalization, complexity, and type of pay-off are still quite abstract, we can break each of these down into sub-dimensions, beginning with formalization.

---

[26] Newcomb, "An Approach to the Study of Communicative Acts," *op. cit.*

One important component of formalization is the degree to which the transaction is scripted: symphonic music, with the exception of an occasional cadenza in concerti, is almost completely scripted; some kinds of jazz have little if any script. This is the dimension pointed to in Park's distinction between elementary and conventional collective behavior. A second component of formalization is the extent to which control is vested in a special office: the symphony orchestra has a director; the jam session may not. A third component is obligatoriness; a fourth is preemptiveness. Usually, but not always, the more formalized the transaction, the more obligatory and preemptive. Finally, degree of anonymity is related to formalization: the more formal the transaction, the more fully the participant is identified.

With respect to the complexity of the coordinated act, there are many dimensions that could be considered. For purposes of illustration, only six dimensions will be introduced. A dimension of precision would seem to be of primary importance: some kinds of transaction can occur if the participants' actions are only very loosely coordinated; others have only a very low tolerance or leeway in performance. When an infirm person is helped across the street by another person, there is some coordination involved, but the leeway in the timing and positioning of the two participants is broad. With trapeze artists, on the other hand, one would need quite precise instruments to detect the range of variation in timing and positioning.

Other components of complexity of a transaction are *duration, repetitiveness, symmetry, cumulativeness,* and *uniqueness.* Duration and repetitiveness are self-explanatory; symmetry refers to the degree to which there is division of labor among the coparticipants in the transaction; cumulativeness refers to the degree of ordering in the sequence of acts which make up the transaction; uniqueness refers to the degree to which the participants can call upon analogous experiences in coordinating their actions. In general, the more complex the transaction, the more consensus there must be for coordination to occur. That is to say, the longer, the less repetitive, the less symmetric, the more cumulative, and the more unique the transaction, the more consensus is necessary to bring off the transaction.

The consequent variable, the cooperativeness or competitiveness of the payoff, is also complex. Since this variable has been explored with some diligence, particularly in studies of experimental games, it will not be analyzed into subdimensions here. In "Prisoner's Dilemma," a single dimension, the temptation for each partner to defect, is used. This dimension is constructed from a ratio of the rewards for cooperation, compared to the punishment if caught defecting. Some such index might be constructed for any transaction.

If we wish to analyze systematically any particular type of coordinated activity, the variables of position and timing must be considered in precise detail. Consider, for example, the transaction which occurs on a highway when an automobile passes another, in the presence of an oncoming car. The exact positions and speeds of the three cars become desiderata, if we consider the three drivers to comprise a social group involved in a transaction (one getting past another without colliding). For such an example, it might be helpful to borrow the terminology from the physics of wave phenomena or from ballistics. Each car generates a wave whose front can be considered a certain *distance* from the point of origin. The measured distance from the center of the lane would be the *ampli-*

tude of the wave, the car's speed, its *velocity*. In this case, highway traffic would be analyzed as a pattern of waves, with measurable shapes and configurations. The characteristic patterns would be aperiodic, but with quite similar sizes and shapes. Alternatively, we could consider the trajectories of the vehicles, as in ballistic studies.

In the case of automotive traffic, it would appear that each transaction involving passing of the kind noted above involves a momentary consensual system: each driver subscribes to, and attributes to the other two participants, certain rules of the road, e.g., the car being passed, and the oncoming car, will not increase their speed, one signals and/or checks traffic before changing lanes, and so forth. At the same time, each participant is almost instinctively involved in a complex process of role-taking: he puts himself in the place of the other drivers and makes a judgment on his own future position and speed relative to that of the others. Every such transaction on the highway, whether successful or not, could be analyzed using the wave phenomena or trajectories as a dependent variable, and the consensual processes as independent variables.

Moreover, the same type of analysis could be extended to any kind of coordination. Depending upon the type of coordination, some ingenuity might be necessary in selecting the dimensions of coordination to be measured. In championship chess, for example, a crude measure of amplitude of movement would be of little interest. A more sophisticated series of measurements, such as degree of aggressiveness, obviousness and positional *vs.* exchange strategies might be in order. Nevertheless, the same basic plan of research would be followed: first, the measurement of coordinated actions as interfering waves or trajectories, and second, the determination of the level and type of consensus existing between the participants, with communication held constant.

Discussion

This approach may be relevant to one of the difficulties which Stryker met in his study. Stryker sought to test Mead's hypothesis that role-taking actually occurs. To do this, Stryker developed 15 hypotheses and 147 tests. Having gone through these procedures, however, he reports that the results are ambiguous: [27]

> Of the 147 tests, 57, or 39%, produced results clearly supporting the theory: 90, or 61%, did not. Only one test produced a statistically significant finding contradictory to the hypotheses.

One way of evaluating these results would lead to a quite positive conclusion: where there was a statistically significant relationship, the ratio was 57 to 1 in favor of the theory. On the other hand, Stryker had expected to find such relationships in all 147 tests, but they occurred in only a minority (40%), which might be construed as a setback for the theory.

An even more troublesome problem is connected with the way Stryker's propositions were derived. Except for those hypotheses that are related to Mead's notion of a "common universe of discourse," the relationship between the hypotheses and Mead's theory is not always clear. Even if the empirical findings had been unambiguous, it might not have been clear that Mead's theory had been supported.

---

[27] Stryker, *op. cit.*

If we use the definitions and hypotheses concerning consensus that were discussed above, a different approach to the interpretation of Stryker's findings is
suggested. Since these hypotheses are more closely related to the fundamental
postulates in Mead's theory, less ambiguous findings might ensue. Two hypotheses provide such a test. First, for those issues which are directly related to problems of coordination, the more precise the coordination that is required, the
greater the consensus. For example, on the issue of permissiveness in child-rearing, one would hypothesize that there would be more consensus between spouses
than between the parents and the grandparents (since more coordination is required between the spouses, who actually have the job of child-raising, than the
grandparents, who look on from a distance).

This hypothesis relates amount of consensus to *type* of relationship, and follows
directly from Mead's theory. Since type of relationship is a variable in Stryker's
design, this hypothesis could be tested by classifying the issues and the status relationships with respect to their inter-relation. This classification would obviously
have to be made by independent raters who have no knowledge of the actual
findings.

A second hypothesis would allow a more refined testing of Mead's theory. The
proposition that consensus varies with degree of coordination is not unique to
Mead, but is shared by others interested in consensus. What is unique to the interactionist framework is the insistence on the existence and importance of the
higher orders of co-orientation. The common-sense definition of consensus is in
terms of agreement. From this point of view, the more that coordination is required by a relationship, the more *agreement* there will be. From our discussion
of the interactionist view of consensus, however, we can postulate an alternative
hypothesis: agreement is less important than the higher orders of co-orientation.
*This comparison allows a critical test of the interactionist theory against the com-
mon sense point of view.* If the higher orders of co-orientation predict the degree
of coordination better than simple agreement, the interactionist theory of consensus will have been given very strong support.

The last section of this paper is concerned with two other possible applications
of the model of consensus discussed here. The first, which will be dealt with only
briefly, is the problem of leadership, the second, of social integration. Newcomb
and others have found that leaders are somewhat more perceptive of followers'
views than vice versa.[28] This finding follows from the postulate above: the greater
the need for coordination, the greater the consensus. In the case of leaders, the
situation is asymmetric: it is the leader more often than the follower who faces
problems of coordination. (The follower must coordinate his actions only with
one leader, but the leader must coordinate *his* actions with *all* of the followers.)
Therefore we would expect Newcomb's findings on the superior perceived consensus of leaders.

The study of the representative process is a particularly interesting area for the
study of consensual structures in leader-follower relationships. The degree of
consensus between the representative and his constituency might turn out to be
an extremely strategic variable in explaining the behavior of the representative.
We can visualize situations in which the higher orders of co-orientation are used
routinely by the representative. For example, in planning his campaign strategy,
the representative will wish to select issues, and positions on these issues, which

---

[28] Newcomb, "An Approach to the Study of Communicative Acts," *op. cit.*

will improve his chances of winning the election. In order to do this, he must not only visualize the opinions of his constituency with some accuracy (first level co-orientation), but also perceive what groups in his constituency think *his* position on these issues is (second level co-orientation), so that the representative, by his choice of issues and position, can correct them in order to win.[29] We would also expect that the consensual structures in the representative process would tend to be unilateral, since the views of the constituency are much more fateful for the representative than vice versa.

The second application concerns the measurement of social integration. As Klapp notes (in the excerpt quoted in the beginning of this paper), degree of consensus can be used as an index of degree of social integration. He argues that anomie is the negative pole of the continuum, and (by implication) that complete consensus is the positive pole. His idea that lack of consensus can be used as indicative of anomie seems well served by the model described here: normlessness is not so much the situation that people don't know of *any* rules to fit the situations that confront them, but rather they don't know which rules others share; normlessness is the absence of *shared* rules.

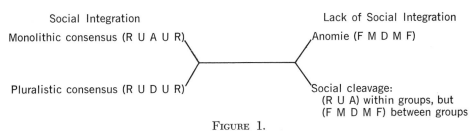

Social Integration   Lack of Social Integration

Monolithic consensus (R U A U R)   Anomie (F M D M F)

Pluralistic consensus (R U D U R)   Social cleavage:
               (R U A) within groups, but
               (F M D M F) between groups

FIGURE 1.

The model of consensus used here suggests, however, that the dimension of social integration is more complex than the simple continuum suggested by Klapp's remarks. At the negative pole, a possible alternative to the state of social anomie is the condition of cleavage. Looking at the views of the population as a whole, it might seem that individuals' estimations of the others' views are no better than chance. However, if the population is partitioned by the right variable, e.g., Moslems and Hindus in pre-partition India, the level of consensus is very high within the sub-groups and very low between them. Thus what might look like a state of anomie to the outside observer could be re-interpreted to show that a split of the larger social group into two or more smaller social groups has occurred; the larger group has disintegrated, but there is high social integration in the new groups it has spawned.

At the positive pole of integration, there is also a consensual structure alternative to complete consensus. In a highly integrated pluralist society, one might find sub-groups, but there are groups which have agreed to disagree, e.g., Switzerland, with its French, German, and Italian sub-cultures. Just as consensus based on agreement can be depicted by the profile (R U A) so consensus based on disagreement can be described by the profile (R U D U R). The first structure we might call a monolithic consensus, the second a pluralistic consensus. Using these ideas, the straightline dimension of social integration becomes a continuum with branches at each end.

A further complication is occasioned by the fact that the consensual structure

---

[29] This example was suggested to me by Janet Chewning.

which exists between the subgroups need not be symmetric. Myrdal's discussion of "the rank order of discriminations" is a case in point. With respect to the highest rank—the bar against intermarriage and sexual intercourse involving white women—he states that there is agreement between the two groups. Implicit in his discussion is the suggestion that there is understanding of agreement on the Negro side, but misunderstanding on the white side. Thus he says: [30]

> The writer has observed, however, that the average white man, particularly in the South, does not feel quite convinced of the Negro's acquiescence. In several conversations the same white person in the same breath has assured me on the one hand that the Negroes are perfectly satisfied in their position and would not like to be treated as equals, and on the other hand that the only thing these Negroes long for is to be like white people and marry their daughters.

Using Laing's notation, the profile of intergroup mutuality on this issue, with the white persons on the left, would probably be (F M A U R), that is, agreement on the issue of marital and sexual segregation, with incorrect attribution on the white side (note that Myrdal talks about the average white man), and correct attribution on the Negro side. A similar analysis could be made of the other ranks in the order of discriminations.

In this case the profile (F M A U R) represents an asymmetric consensus based on physical domination. Once again we have a situation in which the structure of consensus derives from the nature of the coordination required: because perception of the white person's views is far more fateful for the Negro than vice versa, the subordinate is more sensitive to the gestures of the superordinate, and co-orientation tends to be unilateral. The author has found what appears to be a similar situation in classroom surveys of male-female differences in opinions on sexual permissiveness. The males tend to agree on a more permissive standard than the girls do, but misunderstand this agreement, each thinking that he is more liberal than his fellows. The girls understand, however. The profile of the intergroup consensus is the same as in the color-line situation described by Myrdal: men (F M D U R) women.

Both of these situations represent a partial consensus, and therefore a middle amount of social integration in the larger community comprised by the two subgroups, the Negroes and the whites, or the men and the women. There is neither complete consensus nor complete lack of consensus, but a partial consensus based upon an asymmetric profile of one-way understanding and realization.

Summary

This discussion began with a comparison of two approaches to consensus: interactionist theory and the common sense approach. From interactionist theory a social-systemic model of consensus has been derived. This model leads to a conceptual definition of consensus as an infinite series of reciprocating understandings between the members of a group. In research, this model would lead us to look for higher orders of co-orientation than the more usual investigations of agreement, or, at best, perceived consensus, which would be represented as consensual structures of the second degree, third degree, and so on, asymptotically nearer to the hypothesized infinite limit.

Utilizing techniques derived from the work of Newcomb, Stryker, and Laing,

---

[30] Gunnar Myrdal, *An American Dilemma,* New York: Harper, 1944, p. 64.

Phillipson and Lee, procedures have been outlined for generalizing these techniques to groups of any size and co-orientation of any degree. The two generalized techniques can be considered to be operational definitions of the concept of consensus for two different problems: the Stryker design allowing the measurement of inter-status consensus through judgments of the orientation of the other person in a pair; the Newcomb technique of judgment of group opinion allowing for the measurement of intra- and inter-group consensus.

Newcomb's propositions concerning causes and consequences of consensus led us to a discussion of an important concomitant of the degree of consensus in a group: the type of coordination. The analysis of type and degree of coordination into various dimensions and sub-dimensions leads to a series of propositions which relate degree of consensus to the type, precision and extent of coordination (with communication held constant). One application of such propositions is suggested by Stryker's attempt to test Mead's theory. A design is formulated which might lead to a less ambiguous test of interactionist theory as over against commonsense notions of consensus.

Finally, two problems are considered: consensual structures in leader-follower relationships, and the measurement of social integration. Several other problems, such as the measurement of occupational prestige, and the social desirability dimension of psychological testing, have been mentioned in passing. The model of the degree of consensus outlined here offers a technique for the systematic exploration of these and similar problems.

Two theoretical problems alluded to in passing seem particularly worthy of further exploration. The first problem follows from Klapp's suggestion that consensus is the common denominator of almost all of the concepts in sociology and cultural anthropology. The definition of consensus developed in this paper might be used as a step first, toward systematizing the various basic concepts, such as norm, role, and institution, and second, toward rigorously defining their interrelationships.

The second problem is the statement of a formal theory of interaction in terms of communication, consensus, and coordination. In the discussion above, it was shown how a set of propositions could be generated from the proposition that the degree of consensus is reciprocally related to the degree of coordination, with degree of communication held constant, by introducing sub-dimensions in the variable of coordination. Using similar techniques, two further sets of propositions could be generated, by partialling the relationship between communication and consensus with coordination held constant, on the one hand, and the relationship between communication and coordination with consensus held constant, on the other. Finally, a fourth set of propositions could be generated by stating the dynamic interrelation of all three variables. These four sets would offer a series of propositions that could lead to empirical testing, and would at the same time be directly articulated with sociological theory.

More generally, the investigation of higher-order co-orientations promises a procedure for unraveling some of the more intricate puzzles in human relationships. For example, it is possible that much of the moral ambiguity facing actors in modern large-scale societies is a product of the multi-group, multi-faceted consensual structures depicted here. Exploration of these patterns could lead, in the long run, to an understanding of the processes which create and terminate consensus, and the consequences of these processes for the actors and their society.

PART SIX
THE SELF

In the preceding section, careful attention was given to interaction processes, and, in their analysis, the centrality of self-indication was established. If self-indication is so central to interaction, meaning, understanding, and realization, we must ask: Just what is this "self" that is indicated and indicates?

There has been a long-standing argument between psychologists and sociologists about the conceptualization of the person. Most psychologists—not all—prefer the term "personality"; most sociologists—not all—prefer the term "self." Obviously, we take the latter position. There are several reasons for this decision.

The meaning of most words or concepts seems to fade [1] over time. As words come into widespread use, their precision ordinarily is blunted. So it is with the term "personality" (and as it may well be for "self" in some ill-defined future). Personality has come to mean all things to all men,[2] and a term that can mean many things at once can come to mean very little indeed.

Yet, it is not for purely semantic reasons that we find the term of relatively little use in our version of social psychology. Usually, in psychology, personality presumes an organized set of persistent and characteristic patterns of individual behavior. Thus situational variations in personal conduct are de-emphasized. We are not suggesting an either-or position here. As a matter of fact, at either extreme we are confronted with personal conduct that usually is labeled pathological:

Total Situational Invariance $\longleftrightarrow$ Total Situational Variance

Advanced Psychosis $\longleftrightarrow$ Extreme Psychopathy

---

[1] The notion of fading is taken from Suzanne K. Langer, *Philosophy in a New Key* (New York: Penguin Books, Inc., 1948), pp. 114 and 229. Her discussion applies to metaphors.

[2] More than thirty years ago, Gordon W. Allport compiled an extensive list of the meanings of the term "personality" employed by psychologists. Even then there were enormous difficulties. See Gordon W. Allport, *Personality: A Psychological Interpretation* (New York: Holt, Rinehart and Winston, Inc., 1937).

Rather, we need a conception that can account at once for the situational continuity *and* variability—a concept that is rooted in the transforming process of communication.

Furthermore, the concept "personality" often presupposes that behavior is consistent and integrated with some presumed "value-attitude system," some "hierarchy of needs," or some differently designated internal system. Quite obviously there is no overriding consistency between what people *want* or *need* to do, and what they actually do. Activities often conflict with goals and needs. We may want very much to give up cigarettes and hold powerful negative attitudes against smoking, but we continue to smoke. Even such tested needs as metabolic requirements may be defied, both in human interaction and by our very biological responses. Thus, we may fast unto death, or decline a well-appointed meal of grasshoppers, ants, or rattlesnakes in the face of starvation (as starving Indian Hindus may decline beef). We are hungry when we do not need food, and "It is reported that after the first few days a person who is starving to death feels little or no hunger." [3] When we find ourselves short of needed oxygen, we enter into a kind of blissful, but ineffectual, dream state—a matter that concerned the United States Air Force in World War II and accounted for strange, apparently untraumatic blackouts by pilots at relatively high altitudes. Thus, inconsistency between wants, needs, and conduct is usual and cannot be adequately explained by invoking some such concept as personality.

The concept "personality" encourages us to look at the individual first and his social relations second in our interpretations of human conduct. Analytical use of this concept has often constrained investigators to look to social relations only when there is something wrong with personal conduct—some breach of expectations—and seldom when there is something right with personal conduct—a meeting of expectations. This mode of analysis is unacceptable to the social psychologist who views conduct from the standpoint of symbolic interaction. *All conduct must be situated in a matrix of communication before analysis and explanation begin.*

Finally, many social psychologists employing the concept "personality" view this *social object* as comprised of "layers" ranging from public to private dimensions, for example, conscious, preconscious, and subconscious or unconscious levels. Often the private or subconscious dimensions are viewed as the "real core" of personality. Now this has considerable rhetorical (and financial) value for the social psychologist, clinical psychologist, psychiatrist, or psychoanalyst. If one can never know who he really is, but the other professes to know, he comes readily under the other's control and becomes, through the process that Kenneth Burke called *secular conversion*,[4] what the other defines him to be—a transaction that often costs him dearly. Our position draws heavily upon that presented by Harry Stack Sullivan in this section. Perhaps there are private meanings that may be construed as personality or individuality, but, once they are communicated, their privacy and individuality are lost. Perhaps there is an unconscious or subconscious, but it is always *known* in another's consciousness! The concept "self" seems less open to the criticisms we have made here, but that concept did not

[3] Alfred R. Lindesmith and Anselm L. Strauss, *Social Psychology*, Third Edition (New York: Holt, Rinehart and Winston, 1968), p. 59.
[4] Kenneth Burke, *Permanence and Change* (Los Altos, California: Hermes Publication, 1954), ch. 5.

make its entry into the field of social psychology without difficulty and controversy.

Although conceptions of the self have been proposed and argued for centuries in the history of Western social thought, it is adequate for our discussion to begin with the statement by William James. Contemporary formulations find their fundamental origins in James' contribution. James immediately establishes the reflexive character of the self—it is apprehended as both Knower and Known, subject and object, "I" and "me." These distinctions are not to be thought of as things or components, but as *discriminated aspects*. Neither aspect can be subjected to fruitful analysis in disregard of the other, and this basic principle persists in the important conceptualizations of the self today. George H. Mead put the point succinctly: "... a 'me' ... is a 'me' which was the 'I' at the earlier time." [5]

A student takes an examination. His answering is his "I." As Mead puts it, "The 'I' is the response of the organism to the attitudes [read "anticipations"—the student's answer is anticipated] of the others." [6] The examination is graded. The student then reflects upon his earlier response in the light of the faculty (or community) response. His conception of self, "me," is altered. Out of the interaction, he views himself as a bit more or less of a student than he was while taking the examination, or he knows a bit more surely that he is the student he thought he was at the time he took the examination. Thus, the "I" pushes into the "me," and the stage is set for further evolving transformations of the self.

But as James points out, *me* is very close to *mine:* "We feel and act about certain things that are ours very much as we feel and act about ourselves." He defines the self-conception, the self as object—the "me"—as "... *the sum total of all that he can call his.*" This encompasses a material "me" (which we have not included in this selection)—one's possessions; a social "me," essentially one's reputation; and a spiritual "me" (also deleted from the selection). Central to our discussion is James' version of the social "me," for in that discussion James' oft-quoted statement is made: "A man has as many selves as there are individuals who recognize him and carry an image of him in their minds." In short, the objective self finds its reality in communication—"[one] ... has as many different social selves as there are distinct groups of persons about whose opinion he cares." Of course this multifaceted character of the self sets up conflicts. Whose opinions do we care about most, and in what situations? How are such decisions made? James singles out the significance of self-esteem and suggests that the maintenance of the *social* self is, in fact, a matter of the maintenance of self-esteem, a ratio between success and aspiration, or what he calls "pretension."

"Me's," then, are sources of the variability of the self as well as its multifaceted character. What, then, is the source of continuity? James turns to the self as Knower, Thinker, or "I." The "I" is the root of identity. Later, George H. Mead echoed the thought of James: "The 'I' is in a certain sense that with which we do identify ourselves." [7] One is asked, "Who is there?" The proper response is, "It is I." The "I" is formulator; the "me," formulated. Formulations change and proliferate, but the process is continuous and universal over the life cycle. There

[5] George Herbert Mead, *Mind, Self, and Society* (Chicago: University of Chicago Press, 1934), p. 174.
[6] *Ibid.*, p. 175.
[7] *Ibid.*, pp. 174–175.

is, of course, a paradox here—a kind of Simmelesque antimony. The "I" is certainly uncertain, momentary, yet continuing, a source of evolving uncertainly certain objective "me's." We live, as Mead puts it, in a "knife-edge present," conjuring up potential future objective selves, some of which remain in the wake of our lives as the "me's" we were in past time.

Cooley, the profound observer if not the trenchant theorist, was obviously impatient with this kind of abstract discussion and attempted to bring the concept of self down to the level of everyday discourse. Observing—but really not incorporating the observation into his explanations—that the "I" always must consider others in any adequate conceptualization, Cooley actually built on one of James' definitions of the self. Cooley added the dimension of feeling, mood, or sentiment. Such a self-feeling may be taken as a definitive "sign and proof" of the self: "The social self is simply any idea, or system of ideas, drawn from the communicative life, that the mind *cherishes* as its own." The cherishing of ideas is rooted in some sense of appropriation that Cooley thought of as instinctive. Hence, the deficiency as a theorist. The explanation becomes tautological, even though the "sense of appropriation" must be developed, refined, and differentiated through communication. One might also query whether such emphasis would be given the appropriative instinct in another world, at a time other than the turn of the century in the United States—a time just beyond the apex of development of industrial capitalism. Nevertheless, the notion of the self as "mine" can generate as fruitful a technique of self-study as the notion of self as object. Kuhn's TST, asking "Who am I?", might well ask, "What is mine?" [8]—at least in the context of those societies that place property in the center of their institutional arrangements.

But for Cooley the self is not merely what one appropriates as his own—cherished ideas. It is composed of imagined reflections. It is an outcome of our own imaginations as to how we appear to others, of their judgments of that imagined appearance, and some resultant self-feeling of pride or mortification. James' conception of self-esteem is retained but is charged with the voltage of affect. Mortification is somehow something other than disesteem. Again the observer, Cooley arrives at this conception of self by carefully noting the development of his children. His explanations seem less than adequate. For example, "The self-feeling had always been there"; the child "studies" the movements of others; etc. What in fact must be explained, is presumed, and Cooley's solipsism is laid bare.[9]

Unlike Cooley, George H. Mead was convinced that such human processes as reason and self were phenomena to be explained rather than presumed. There are many discussions of the self by Mead that we might have presented here, but probably because the methodological remonstrance of Cooley—that we attend to what we can observe—still rings in our ears, we have chosen Mead's treatment of the self as object. Such a self can only emerge in the process of communication, for it is only in communication that one can, figuratively, get outside himself, take the attitude of another or organized others, and gain a reflected view of the self as object from these other standpoints. In particular, reason, thought, and intelligence are merely inner forms of this larger social process, but they are not

---

[8] For a discussion of the TST, see Part Seven of this volume.
[9] See George H. Mead, "Cooley's contribution to American Social Thought," *American Journal of Sociology*, XXXV (March 1930), pp. 693–706.

realizable until the self has first emerged out of significant communication with others. As Mead says, "it is impossible to think of the self arising outside of social experience." Once the self is established, however, one can endure long periods of isolation, because one "has himself as a companion, and is able to think and converse with himself as he had communicated with others." Yet, such a process can continue up to some as yet unspecified point in time. Eventually, one must find validation for his inner conversations in direct conversations with others, else one moves perilously near the point of madness or, as Mead so accurately calls it, dissociation. Perhaps this is one important reason why so many successful film actors seek employment in legitimate theater, accepting severe financial penalties—ultimately, they must confront a living audience.

Sullivan begins his analysis of the emergence of the self at a somewhat different point. While Mead begins with gestural conversation, Sullivan begins with babbling and, unlike others—for example Suzanne K. Langer,[10] who would see in babbling the beginning of symbolization as the expression of a need—he promptly recognizes that the significance of babbling is established by socialized others' responses or intervention. The arousal of significant others' responses by accidental infantile noise may be the origin of a sense of power, consolidated and extended in early socialization as the verbalized "me" is succeeded by the verbalized "I" in statements of personal action—as self-indication makes possible the formulation of self-initiated acts.

Paradoxically, this very incipience of personal power renders irrelevant the sense of uniqueness or autistic experience. The establishment of a noise as a symbol through *consensual validation* carries one's direct experience into the realm of the understood or the conventional, at least insofar as he can represent that experience to himself or others. In entering an ongoing conversation one's uniqueness is lost, but an entire world or universe is won. Sullivan construes this world as the proper unit of inquiry for psychiatry, the study of interpersonal relations.

But conversation is built on the empathic process (see Stone's discussion of meaning and identification). Sullivan singles out empathy as a possible source of disagreeable experience, just as those most often concerned with pathology single out negative aberrant influences on conduct. The empathic processes, notably role-taking and sympathy, of course have their positive consequences for the formulation of the self, as Cooley and Mead so frequently emphasized. Be these things as they may, Sullivan guesses that empathy may be an early source of anxiety for the child, and anxiety is viewed as a powerful "motivating" force accounting for the diversities and variations in the formulation of self. Sullivan says elsewhere that the self is comprised of the reflected appraisals of others, but is also viewed as a formulated way of coping with those appraisals, particularly negative ones, in the very early years. Such negative appraisals are *selectively inattended* and are dissociated from the self (as "not-me"), remaining perhaps as a source of "autonomous" anxiety at a later age. At any rate, even such aberrations cannot be construed as individual in character. Their very selectivity, involving both inattention and attention, are formulations. The self is such a formulation, and, since the formulation is accomplished in symbolic or universal terms, the uniqueness of such experiences is not communicable, consequently not capable of study. In this sense, personal individuality is an illusion.

---

[10] Suzanne K. Langer, *op. cit.*, pp. 85 ff.

Stone has attempted to draw together the observations and conceptualizations of James, Cooley, Mead, and Sullivan in his conceptualization of self, which emphasizes the dimensions of *identity* (James' and Mead's notions of the self as object), *value* (James' idea of esteem, Cooley's emphasis on judgment, and Sullivan's focus on appraisals), *mood* (Cooley's concern with sentiment and feeling, Sullivan's with anxiety), and *attitude* (a concept taken directly from Mead). He places the analysis of self directly in the matrix of communication and meaning, but stresses the importance of nonverbal or apparent symbols in such an analysis. The establishment of such dimensions in human transactions is accomplished by singling out two foci of the self—the program ("I"?) and the review (the response of others). A third focus—the imagined review ("me"?) is omitted from the discussion in the interest of space and parsimony. Appearance is seen as a fundamental communication of self and other, and an attempt is made to link the significance of appearance to the socialization of the self along the lines sketched out by Cooley, Mead, Piaget, and Sullivan.

Were Stone to reconsider this contribution, he would probably opt for a more exact set of terms. For example, the concepts "identification with" and "identification of," although they permit an heuristic play on words, would give way to the more accurate designations—the "empathic processes," and, drawing on Sullivan, "personification," literally "person-building." "Play," as used by Mead, would give way to "drama"—what Mead was really talking about. Play is too general a concept to do the service Mead asked of it, for there are other forms of play, for example, "tests of poise," which are an important part of the socialization process. This is a matter we shall turn to in Part Nine.

Suggested Readings

BALDWIN, JAMES MARK. *Social and Ethical Interpretations in Mental Development.* New York: The Macmillan Company, 1897.

COOLEY, CHARLES H. *Human Nature and the Social Order.* New York: Scribner, 1902.

ERIKSON, ERIK H. "The Problem of Ego Identity." *Psychological Issues: Identity and the Life Cycle.* Vol. I, No. I, 1959.

LYND, HELEN MERRELL. *On Shame and the Search for Identity.* New York: Harcourt, Brace, 1958.

SARBIN, THEODORE R. "A Preface to a Psychological Analysis of the Self." *Psychological Review.* No. 59 (1962), pp. 11–22.

STRAUSS, ANSELM. *Mirrors and Masks.* Glencoe, Ill.: Free Press, 1959.

SULLIVAN, HARRY STACK. *The Interpersonal Theory of Psychiatry.* New York: W. W. Norton and Co., 1933.

39 The Social Self

● WILLIAM JAMES

The Me and the I

Whatever I may be thinking of, I am always at the same time more or less aware of *myself*, of my *personal existence*. At the same time it is *I* who am aware; so that the total self of me, being as it were duplex, partly known and partly knower, partly object and partly subject, must have two aspects discriminated in it, of which for shortness we may call one the *Me* and the other the *I*. I call these "discriminated aspects," and not separate things, because the identity of *I* with *me*, even in the very act of their discrimination, is perhaps the most ineradicable dictum of common-sense, and must not be undermined by our terminology here at the outset, whatever we may come to think of its validity at our inquiry's end.

I shall therefore treat successively of (A) the self as known, or the *me*, the "empirical ego" as it is sometimes called; and of (B) the self as knower, or the I, the "pure ego" of certain authors.

The Self as Known

THE EMPIRICAL SELF OR ME

Between what a man calls *me* and what he simply calls *mine* the line is difficult to draw. We feel and act about certain things that are ours very much as we feel and act about ourselves. Our fame, our children, the work of our hands, may be as dear to us as our bodies are, and arouse the same feelings and the same acts of reprisal if attacked. And our bodies themselves, are they simply ours, or are they *us?* Certainly men have been ready to disown their very bodies and to regard them as mere vestures, or even as prisons of clay from which they should some day be glad to escape.

We see then that we are dealing with a fluctuating material; the same object being sometimes treated as a part of me, at other times as simply mine, and then again as if I had nothing to do with it at all. *In its widest possible sense*, however, *a man's Me is the sum total of all that he* CAN *call his*, not only his body and his psychic powers, but his clothes and his house, his wife and children, his ancestors and friends, his reputation and works, his lands and horses, and yacht and bank-account. All these things give him the same emotions. If they wax and prosper, he feels triumphant; if they dwindle and die away, he feels cast down— not necessarily in the same degree for each thing, but in much the same way for all. . . .

SOURCE: William James in his *Psychology* (New York: Henry Holt and Co., 1892), pp. 189– 226.

THE SOCIAL ME

A man's social me is the recognition which he gets from his mates. We are not only gregarious animals, liking to be in sight of our fellows, but we have an innate propensity to get ourselves noticed, and noticed favorably, by our kind. No more fiendish punishment could be devised, were such a thing physically possible, than that one should be turned loose in society and remain absolutely unnoticed by all the members thereof. If no one turned round when we entered, answered when we spoke, or minded what we did, but if every person we met "cut us dead," and acted as if we were non-existing things, a kind of rage and impotent despair would ere long well up in us, from which the cruellest bodily tortures would be a relief; for these would make us feel that, however bad might be our plight, we had not sunk to such a depth as to be unworthy of attention at all.

Properly speaking, *a man has as many social selves as there are individuals who recognize him* and carry an image of him in their mind. To wound any one of these his images is to wound him. But as the individuals who carry the images fall naturally into two classes, we may practically say that he has as many different social selves as there are distinct *groups* of persons about whose opinion he cares. He generally shows a different side of himself to each of these different groups. Many a youth who is demure enough before his parents and teachers, swears and swaggers like a pirate among his "tough" young friends. We do not show ourselves to our children as to our club-companions, to our customers as to the laborers we employ, to our own masters and employers as to our intimate friends. From this there results what practically is a division of the man into several selves; and this may be a discordant splitting, as where one is afraid to let one set of his acquaintances know him as he is elsewhere; or it may be a perfectly harmonious division of labor, as where one tender to his children is stern to the soldiers or prisoners under his command.

The most peculiar social self which one is apt to have is in the mind of the person one is in love with. The good or bad fortunes of this self cause the most intense elation and dejection—unreasonable enough as measured by every other standard than that of the organic feeling of the individual. To his own consciousness he *is* not, so long as this particular social self fails to get recognition, and when it is recognized his contentment passes all bounds.

A man's *fame*, good or bad, and his *honor* or dishonor are names for one of his social selves. The particular social self of a man called his honor is usually the result of one of those splittings of which we have spoken. It is his image in the eyes of his own "set," which exalts or condemns him as he conforms or not to certain requirements that may not be made of one in another walk of life. Thus a layman may abandon a city infected with cholera; but a priest or a doctor would think such an act incompatible with his honor. A soldier's honor requires him to fight or to die under circumstances where another man can apologize or run away with no stain upon his social self. A judge, a statesman, are in like manner debarred by the honor of their cloth from entering into pecuniary relations perfectly honorable to persons in private life. Nothing is commoner than to hear people discriminate between their different selves of this sort: "As a man I pity you, but as an official I must show you no mercy"; "As a politician I regard him as an ally, but as a moralist I loathe him"; etc., etc. What may be called "club-opinion" is one of the very strongest forces in life. The thief must not steal from other thieves; the gambler must pay his gambling-debts, though he pay no other debts in the world. The code of honor of fashionable society has throughout history been full of permissions as well as of vetoes, the only reason for following either of which is that so we best serve one of our social selves. You must not lie in general, but you may lie as much as you please if asked about your relations with a lady; you must accept a challenge from an equal, but if challenged by an inferior you may laugh him to scorn: these are examples of what is meant. . . .

RIVALRY AND CONFLICT OF THE DIFFERENT ME'S

With most objects of desire, physical nature restricts our choice to but one of many represented goods, and even so it is here. I am often confronted by the necessity of standing by one of my empirical selves and relinquishing the rest. Not that I would not, if I could, be both handsome and fat and well dressed, and a great athlete, and make a million a year, be a wit, a *bon vivant*, and a lady-killer, as well as a philosopher; a philanthropist, statesman, warrior, and African explorer, as well as a "tone-poet" and saint. But the thing is simply impossible. The millionaire's work would run counter to the saint's; the *bon vivant* and the philanthropist would trip each other up; the philosopher and the lady-killer could not well keep house in the same tenement of clay. Such different characters may conceivably at the outset of life be alike *possible* to a man. But to make any one of them actual, the rest must more or less be suppressed. So the seeker of his truest, strongest, deepest self must review the list carefully, and pick out the one on which to stake his salvation. All other selves thereupon become unreal, but the fortunes of this self are real. Its failures are real failures, its triumphs real triumphs, carrying shame and gladness with them. . . . Our thought, incessantly deciding, among many things of a kind, which ones for it shall be realities, here chooses one of many possible selves or characters, and forthwith reckons it no shame to fail in any of those not adopted expressly as its own.

So we have the paradox of a man shamed to death because he is only the second pugilist or the second oarsman in the world. That he is able to beat the whole population of the globe minus one is nothing; he has "pitted" himself to beat that one; and as long as he doesn't do that nothing else counts. He is to his own regard as if he were not, indeed he *is* not. Yonder puny fellow, however, whom every one can beat, suffers no chagrin about it, for he has long ago abandoned the attempt to "carry that line," as the merchants say, of self at all. With no attempt there can be no failure; with no failure, no humiliation. So our self-feeling in this world depends entirely on what we *back* ourselves to be and do. It is determined by the ratio of our actualities to our supposed potentialities; a fraction of which our pretensions are the denominator and the numerator our success: thus,

$$\text{Self-esteem} = \frac{\text{Success}}{\text{Pretensions}}$$

Such a fraction may be increased as well by diminishing the denominator as by increasing the numerator. . . .

The Self as Knower

The I, or "pure ego," is a very much more difficult subject of inquiry than the Me. It is that which at any given moment *is* conscious, whereas the Me is only one of the things which it is conscious *of.* In other words, it is the Thinker; and the question immediately comes up *what* is the thinker? Is it the passing state of consciousness itself, or is it something deeper and less mutable? The passing state . . . [is] the very embodiment of change. . . . Yet each of us spontaneously considers that by "I," he means something always the same. This has led most philosophers to postulate behind the passing state of consciousness a permanent Substance or Agent whose modification or act it is. This Agent is the thinker; the "state" is only its instrument or means. "Soul," "transcendental Ego," "Spirit," are so many names for this more permanent sort of Thinker. . . .

THE SENSE OF PERSONAL IDENTITY

The thoughts which we actually know to exist do not fly about loose, but seem each to belong to some one thinker and not to another. Each thought, out of a multitude of other thoughts of which it may think, is able to distinguish those which belong to it from those which do not. The former have a warmth and intimacy about them of which the latter are completely devoid, and the result is a Me of yesterday, judged to be in some peculiarly subtle sense the *same* with the I who now make the judgment. As a mere subjective phenomena the judgment presents no special mystery. It belongs to the great class of judgments of sameness; and there is nothing more remarkable in making a judgment of sameness in the first person than in the second or the third. The intellectual operations seem essentially alike, whether I say "I am the same as I was," or whether I say "the pen is the same as it was, yesterday." It is as easy to think this as to think the opposite and say "neither of us is the same." The only question which we have to consider is whether it be a right judgment. *Is the sameness predicated really there?*

SAMENESS IN THE SELF AS KNOWN

If in the sentence "I am the same that I was yesterday," we take the "I" broadly, it is evident that in many ways I am *not* the same. As a concrete Me, I am somewhat different from what I was: then hungry, now full; then walking, now at rest; then poorer, now richer; then younger, now older; etc. And yet in other ways I *am* the same, and we may call these the essential ways. My name and profession and relations to the world are identical, my face, my faculties and store of memories, are practically indistinguishable, now and then. Moreover the Me of now and the Me of then are *continuous:* the alterations were gradual and never affected the whole of me at once. So far, then, my personal identity is just like the sameness predicated on any other aggregate thing. It is a conclusion grounded either on the resemblance in essential respects, or on the continuity of the phenomena compared. And it must not be taken to mean more than these grounds warrant, or treated as a sort of metaphysical or absolute Unity in which all differences are overwhelmed. The past and present selves compared are the same just so far as they *are* the same, and no farther. They are the same in *kind.* But this generic sameness coexists with generic differences just as real; and if from the one point of view I am one self, from another I am quite as truly many. Similarly of the attribute of continuity: it gives to the self the unity of mere connectedness, or un-brokenness, a perfectly definite phenomenal thing—but it gives not a jot or tittle more.

SAMENESS IN THE SELF AS KNOWER

But all this is said only of the Me, or Self as known. In the judgment "I am the same," etc., the "I" was taken broadly as the concrete person. Suppose, however, that we take it narrowly, as the *Thinker*, as *"that to which"* all the concrete deter-minations of the Me belong and are known: does there not then appear an abso-lute identity at different times? That something which at every moment goes out and knowingly appropriates the *Me* of the past, and discards the non-me as for-eign, is it not a permanent abiding principle of spiritual activity identical with it-self wherever found?

That it is such a principle is the reigning doctrine both of philosophy and com-mon-sense, and yet reflection finds it difficult to justify the idea. *If there were no passing states of consciousness*, then indeed we might suppose an abiding prin-ciple, absolutely one with itself, to be the ceaseless thinker in each one of us. But if the states of consciousness be accorded as realities, no such "substantial" iden-tity in the thinker need be supposed. Yesterday's and to-day's states of conscious-ness have no *substantial* identity, for when one is here the other is irrevocably dead and gone. But they have a *functional* identity, for both know the same ob-jects, and so far as the by-gone me is one of those objects, they react upon it in an identical way, greeting it and calling it *mine*, and opposing it to all the other things they know. This functional identity seems really the only sort of identity in the thinker which the facts require us to suppose. Successive thinkers, numeri-cally distinct, but all aware of the same past in the same way, form an adequate vehicle for all the experience of personal unity and sameness which we actually have. And just such a train of successive thinkers is the stream of mental states (each with its complex object cognized and emotional and selective reaction there-upon) which psychology treated as a natural science has to assume. . . .

The logical conclusion seems then to be that *the states of consciousness are all that psychology needs to do her work with. Metaphysics or theology may prove the Soul to exist; but for psychology the hypothesis of such a substantial principle of unity is superfluous.*

40   Self as Sentiment and Reflection

● CHARLES H. COOLEY

It is well to say at the outset that by the word "self" in this discussion is meant simply that which is designated in common speech by the pronouns of the first person singular, "I," "me," "my," "mine," and "myself." "Self" and "ego" are used by metaphysicians and moralists in many other senses, more or less remote from the "I" of daily speech and thought, and with these I wish to have as little to do

SOURCE: Charles Horton Cooley, in his *Human Nature and the Social Order* (New York: Charles Scribner's Sons, 1902), pp. 136–167. Reprinted with the permission of Charles Scrib-ner's Sons.

as possible. What is here discussed is what psychologists call the empirical self, the self that can be apprehended or verified by ordinary observation. I qualify it by the word social not as implying the existence of a self that is not social—for I think that the "I" of common language always has more or less distinct reference to other people as well as the speaker—but because I wish to emphasize and dwell upon the social aspect of it.

Although the topic of the self is regarded as an abstruse one this abstruseness belongs chiefly, perhaps, to the metaphysical discussion of the "pure ego"—whatever that may be—while the empirical self should not be very much more difficult to get hold of than other facts of the mind. At any rate, it may be assumed that the pronouns of the first person have a substantial, important, and not very recondite meaning, otherwise they would not be in constant and intelligible use by simple people and young children the world over. And since they have such a meaning why should it not be observed and reflected upon like any other matter of fact? . . .

The distinctive thing in the idea for which the pronouns of the first person are names is apparently a characteristic kind of feeling which may be called the my-feeling or sense of appropriation. Almost any sort of ideas may be associated with this feeling, and so come to be named "I" or "mine," but the feeling, and that alone it would seem, is the determining factor in the matter. As Professor James says in his admirable discussion of the self, the words "me" and "self" designate "all the things which have the power to produce in a stream of consciousness excitement of a certain peculiar sort." [1] . . .

I do not mean that the feeling aspect of the self is necessarily more important than any other, but that it is the immediate and decisive sign and proof of what "I" is; there is no appeal from it; if we go behind it it must be to study its history and conditions, not to question its authority. But, of course, this study of history and conditions may be quite as profitable as the direct contemplation of self-feeling. What I would wish to do is to present each aspect in its proper light.

The emotion or feeling of self may be regarded as instinctive, and was doubtless evolved in connection with its important function in stimulating and unifying the special activities of individuals.[2] It is thus very profoundly rooted in the history of the human race and apparently indispensable to any plan of life at all similar to ours. It seems to exist in a vague though vigorous form at the birth of each individual, and, like other instinctive ideas or germs of ideas, to be defined and developed by experience, becoming associated, or rather incorporated, with muscular, visual, and other sensations; with perceptions, apperceptions, and conceptions of every degree of complexity and of infinite variety of content; and, especially, with personal ideas. Meantime the feeling itself does not remain unaltered, but undergoes differentiation and refinement just as does any other sort of crude in-

---

[1] *"The words* ME, *then, and* SELF, *so far as they arouse feeling and connote emotional worth, are* OBJECTIVE *designations meaning* ALL THE THINGS *which have the power to produce in a stream of consciousness excitement of a certain peculiar sort."* Psychology, i., p. 319. A little earlier he says: "In its widest possible sense, however, a man's self is the sum total of all he CAN call his, not only his body and his psychic powers, but his clothes and his house, his wife and children, his ancestors and friends, his reputation and works, his lands and horses and yacht and bank-account. All these things give him the same emotions." *Idem*, p. 291.

So Wundt says of "Ich": "Es ist ein *Gefühl*, nicht eine Vorstellung, wie es häufig genannt wird." *Grundriss der Psychologie*, 4 Auflage, S. 265.

[2] It is, perhaps, to be thought of as a more general instinct, of which anger, etc., are differentiated forms, rather than as standing by itself.

nate feeling. Thus, while retaining under every phase its characteristic tone or flavor, it breaks up into innumerable self-sentiments. And concrete self-feeling, as it exists in mature persons, is a whole made up of these various sentiments, along with a good deal of primitive emotion not thus broken up. It partakes fully of the general development of the mind, but never loses that peculiar gusto of appropriation that causes us to name a thought with a first-personal pronoun. . . .

The social self is simply any idea, or system of ideas, drawn from the communicative life, that the mind cherishes as its own. Self-feeling has its chief scope *within* the general life, not outside of it; the special endeavor or tendency of which it is the emotional aspect finds its principal field of exercise in a world of personal forces, reflected in the mind by a world of personal impressions. . . .

That the "I" of common speech has a meaning which includes some sort of reference to other persons is involved in the very fact that the word and the ideas it stands for are phenomena of language and the communicative life. It is doubtful whether it is possible to use language at all without thinking more or less distinctly of some one else, and certainly the things to which we give names and which have a large place in reflective thought are almost always those which are impressed upon us by our contact with other people. Where there is no communication there can be no nomenclature and no developed thought. What we call "me," "mine," or "myself" is, then, not something separate from the general life, but the most interesting part of it, a part whose interest arises from the very fact that it is both general and individual. That is, we care for it just because it is that phase of the mind that is living and striving in the common life, trying to impress itself upon the minds of others. "I" is a militant social tendency, working to hold and enlarge its place in the general current of tendencies. So far as it can it waxes, as all life does. To think of it as apart from society is a palpable absurdity of which no one could be guilty who really *saw* it as a fact of life.

> "Der Mensch erkennt sich nur im Menschen, nur
> Das Leben lehrt jedem was er sei." [3]

If a thing has no relations to others of which one is conscious he is unlikely to think of it at all, and if he does think of it he cannot, it seems to me, regard it as emphatically *his*. The appropriative sense is always the shadow, as it were, of the common life, and when we have it we have a sense of the latter in connection with it. Thus, if we think of a secluded part of the woods as "ours," it is because we think, also, that others do not go there. . . .

In a very large and interesting class of cases the social reference takes the form of a somewhat definite imagination of how one's self—that is any idea he appropriates—appears in a particular mind, and the kind of self-feeling one has is determined by the attitude toward this attributed to that other mind. A social self of this sort might be called the reflected or looking-glass self:

> "Each to each a looking-glass
> Reflects the other that doth pass."

As we see our face, figure, and dress in the glass, and are interested in them because they are ours, and pleased or otherwise with them according as they do or do not answer to what we should like them to be; so in imagination we perceive

---

[3] "Only in man does man know himself; life alone teaches each one what he is." — Goethe, *Tasso*, act 2, sc. 3.

in another's mind some thought of our appearance, manners, aims, deeds, character, friends, and so on, and are variously affected by it.

A self-idea of this sort seems to have three principal elements: the imagination of our appearance to the other person; the imagination of his judgment of that appearance, and some sort of self-feeling, such as pride or mortification. The comparison with a looking-glass hardly suggests the second element, the imagined judgment, which is quite essential. The thing that moves us to pride or shame is not the mere mechanical reflection of ourselves, but an imputed sentiment, the imagined effect of this reflection upon another's mind. This is evident from the fact that the character and weight of that other, in whose mind we see ourselves, makes all the difference with our feeling. We are ashamed to seem evasive in the presence of a straightforward man, cowardly in the presence of a brave one, gross in the eyes of a refined one, and so on. We always imagine, and in imagining share, the judgments of the other mind. . . .

The view that "self" and the pronouns of the first person are names which the race has learned to apply to an instinctive attitude of mind, and which each child in turn learns to apply in a similar way, was impressed upon me by observing my child M. at the time when she was learning to use these pronouns. When she was two years and two weeks old I was surprised to discover that she had a clear notion of the first and second persons when used possessively. When asked, "Where is your nose?" she would put her hand upon it and say "my." She also understood that when someone else said "my" and touched an object, it meant something opposite to what was meant when she touched the same object and used the same word. Now, anyone who will exercise his imagination upon the question how this matter must appear to a mind having no means of knowing anything about "I" and "my" except what it learns by hearing them used, will see that it should be very puzzling. Unlike other words, the personal pronouns have, apparently, no uniform meaning, but convey different and even opposite ideas when employed by different persons. It seems remarkable that children should master the problem before they arrive at considerable power of abstract reasoning. How should a little girl of two, not particularly reflective, have discovered that "my" was not the sign of a definite object like other words, but meant something different with each person who used it? And, still more surprising, how should she have achieved the correct use of it with reference to herself which, it would seem, *could not be copied from anyone else*, simply because no one else used it to describe what belonged to her? The meaning of words is learned by associating them with other phenomena. But how is it possible to learn the meaning of one which, as used by others, is never associated with the same phenomenon as when properly used by one's self? Watching her use of the first person, I was at once struck with the fact that she employed it almost wholly in a possessive sense, and that, too, when in an aggressive, self-assertive mood. It was extremely common to see R. tugging at one end of a plaything and M. at the other, screaming, "My, my." "Me" was sometimes nearly equivalent to "my," and was also employed to call attention to herself when she wanted something done for her. Another common use of "my" was to demand something she did not have at all. Thus if R. had something the like of which she wanted, say a cart, she would exclaim, "Where's *my* cart?"

It seemed to me that she might have learned the use of these pronouns about as follows. The self-feeling had always been there. From the first week she had wanted things and cried and fought for them. She had also become familiar by observation and opposition with similar appropriative activities on the part of R. Thus she not only had the feeling herself, but by associating it with its visible expression had probably divined it, sympathized with it, resented it, in others. Grasping, tugging, and screaming would be associated with the feeling in her own case and would recall the feeling when observed in others. They would constitute a language, precedent to the use of first-personal pronouns, to express the self-idea. All was ready, then, for the word to name this experience. She now observed that R., when contentiously appropriating something, frequently exclaimed, *"my," "mine,"* "give it to *me,*" "*I* want it," and the like. Nothing more natural, then, than that she should adopt these words as names for a frequent and vivid experience with which she was already familiar in her own case and had learned to attribute to others. Accordingly it appeared to me, as I recorded in my notes at the time, that " 'my' and 'mine,' are simply names for concrete images of appropriativeness," embracing both the appropriative feeling and its manifestation. If this is true the child does not at first work out the I-and-you idea in an abstract form. The first-personal pronoun is a sign of a concrete thing after all, but that thing is not primarily the child's body, or his muscular sensations as such, but the phenomenon of aggressive appropriation, practised by himself, witnessed in others, and incited and interpreted by a hereditary instinct. This seems to get over the difficulty above mentioned, namely, the seeming lack of a common content between the meaning of "my" when used by another and when used by one's self. This common content is found in the appropriative feeling and the visible and audible signs of that feeling. An element of difference and strife comes in, of course, in the opposite actions or purposes which the "my" of another and one's own "my" are likely to stand for. When another person says "mine" regarding something which I claim, I sympathize with him enough to understand what he means, but it is a hostile sympathy, overpowered by another and more vivid "mine" connected with the idea of drawing the object my way.

In other words, the meaning of "I" and "mine" is learned in the same way that the meanings of hope, regret, chagrin, disgust, and thousands of other words of emotion and sentiment are learned: that is, by having the feeling, imputing it to others in connection with some kind of expression, and hearing the word along with it. As to its communication and growth the self-idea is in no way peculiar that I see, but essentially like other ideas. In its more complex forms, such as are expressed by "I" in conversation and literature, it is a social sentiment, or type of sentiments, defined and developed by intercourse. . . .[4]

I imagine, then, that as a rule the child associates "I" and "me" at first only with those ideas regarding which his appropriative feeling is aroused and defined by opposition. He appropriates his nose, eye, or foot in very much the same way as a plaything—by antithesis to other noses, eyes, and feet, which he cannot control. It is not uncommon to tease little children by proposing to take away one of these organs, and they behave precisely as if the "mine" threatened were a separable object—which it might be for all they know. And, as I have suggested, even in adult life, "I," "me," and "mine" are applied with a strong sense of their meaning only to things distinguished as peculiar to us by some sort of opposition or contrast. They always imply social life and relation to other persons. That which is most distinctively mine is very private, it is true, but it is the part of the private

---

[4] Compare my "Study of the Early Use of Self-Words by a Child," in the *Psychological Review*, vol. 15, p. 339.

which I am cherishing in antithesis to the rest of the world, not the separate but the special. The aggressive self is essentially a militant phase of the mind, having for its apparent function the energizing of peculiar activities, and, although the militancy may not go on in an obvious, external manner, it always exists as a mental attitude. . . .

The process by which self-feeling of the looking-glass sort develops in children may be followed without much difficulty. Studying the movements of others as closely as they do they soon see a connection between their own acts and changes in those movements; that is, they perceive their own influence or power over persons. The child appropriates the visible actions of his parent or nurse, over which he finds he has some control, in quite the same way as he appropriates one of his own members or a plaything, and he will try to do things with this new possession, just as he will with his hand or his rattle. . . .

The young performer soon learns to be different things to different people, showing that he begins to apprehend personality and to foresee its operation. If the mother or nurse is more tender than just she will almost certainly be "worked" by systematic weeping. It is a matter of common observation that children often behave worse with their mother than with other and less sympathetic people. Of the new persons that a child sees it is evident that some make a strong impression and awaken a desire to interest and please them, while others are indifferent or repugnant. Sometimes the reason can be perceived or guessed, sometimes not; but the fact of selective interest, admiration, prestige, is obvious before the end of the second year. By that time a child already cares much for the reflection of himself upon one personality and little for that upon another. Moreover, he soon claims intimate and tractable persons as *mine*, classes them among his other possessions, and maintains his ownership against all comers. M., at three years of age, vigorously resented R.'s claim upon their mother. The latter was "*my* mamma," whenever the point was raised.

Strong joy and grief depend upon the treatment this rudimentary social self receives. In the case of M. I noticed as early as the fourth month a "hurt" way of crying which seemed to indicate a sense of personal slight. It was quite different from the cry of pain or that of anger, but seemed about the same as the cry of fright. The slightest tone of reproof would produce it. On the other hand, if people took notice and laughed and encouraged, she was hilarious. At about fifteen months old she had become "a perfect little actress," seeming to live largely in imaginations of her effect upon other people. She constantly and obviously laid traps for attention, and looked abashed or wept at any signs of disapproval or indifference. At times it would seem as if she could not get over these repulses, but would cry long in a grieved way, refusing to be comforted. If she hit upon any little trick that made people laugh she would be sure to repeat it, laughing loudly and affectedly in imitation. She had quite a repertory of these small performances, which she would display to a sympathetic audience, or even try upon strangers. I have seen her at sixteen months, when R. refused to give her the scissors, sit down and make-believe cry, putting up her under lip and snuffling, meanwhile looking up now and then to see what effect she was producing.

In such phenomena we have plainly enough, it seems to me, the germ of personal ambition of every sort. Imagination co-operating with instinctive self-feeling has already created a social "I," and this has become a principal object of interest and endeavor.

41   Self as Social Object

● GEORGE HERBERT MEAD

It is the characteristic of the self as an object to itself that I want to bring out. This characteristic is represented in the word "self," which is a reflexive, and indicates that which can be both subject and object. This type of object is essentially different from other objects, and in the past it has been distinguished as conscious, a term which indicates an experience with, an experience of, one's self. *object* It was assumed that consciousness in some way carried this capacity of being an object to itself. In giving a behavioristic statement of consciousness we have to look for some sort of experience in which the physical organism can become an object to itself.[1]

. . . How can an individual get outside himself (experientially) in such a way as to become an object to himself? This is the essential psychological problem of selfhood or of self-consciousness; and its solution is to be found by referring to the process of social conduct or activity in which the given person or individual is implicated. The apparatus of reason would not be complete unless it swept itself into its own analysis of the field of experience; or unless the individual brought himself into the same experiential field as that of the other individual selves in relation to whom he acts in any given social situation. Reason cannot become impersonal unless it takes an objective, non-affective attitude toward itself; otherwise we have just consciousness, not *self*-consciousness. And it is necessary to rational conduct that the individual should thus take an objective, impersonal attitude toward himself, that he should become an object to himself. For the individual organism is obviously an essential and important fact or constituent element of the empirical situation in which it acts; and without taking objective account of itself as such, it cannot act intelligently, or rationally.

The individual experiences himself as such, not directly, but only indirectly, from the particular standpoints of other individual members of the same social group, or from the generalized standpoint of the social group as a whole to which he belongs. For he enters his own experience as a self or individual, not directly or immediately, not by becoming a subject to himself, but only in so far as he first becomes an object to himself just as other individuals are objects to him or in his experience; and he becomes an object to himself only by taking the attitudes of other individuals toward himself within a social environment or context of experience and behavior in which both he and they are involved.

The importance of what we term "communication" lies in the fact that it provides a form of behavior in which the organism or the individual may become an object to himself. It is that sort of communication which we have been discussing

SOURCE: George Herbert Mead, in his *Mind, Self, and Society* (Chicago: University of Chicago Press, 1934), pp. 136–144. Reprinted by permission of The University of Chicago Press.

[1] Man's behavior is such in his social group that he is able to become an object to himself, a fact which constitutes him a more advanced product of evolutionary development than are the lower animals. Fundamentally it is this social fact—and not his alleged possession of a soul or mind with which he, as an individual, has been mysteriously and supernaturally endowed, and with which the lower animals have not been endowed—that differentiates him from them.

—not communication in the sense of the cluck of the hen to the chickens, or the bark of a wolf to the pack, or the lowing of a cow, but communication in the sense of significant symbols, communication which is directed not only to others but also to the individual himself. So far as that type of communication is a part of behavior it at least introduces a self. Of course, one may hear without listening; one may see things that he does not realize; do things that he is not really aware of. But it is where one does respond to that which he addresses to another and where that response of his own becomes a part of his conduct, where he not only hears himself but responds to himself, talks and replies to himself as truly as the other person replies to him, that we have behavior in which the individuals become objects to themselves. . . .

The self, as that which can be an object to itself, is essentially a social structure, and it arises in social experience. After a self has arisen, it in a certain sense provides for itself its social experiences, and so we can conceive of an absolutely solitary self. But it is impossible to conceive of a self arising outside of social experience. When it has arisen we can think of a person in solitary confinement for the rest of his life, but who still has himself as a companion, and is able to think and to converse with himself as he had communicated with others. That process to which I have just referred, of responding to one's self as another responds to it, taking part in one's own conversation with others, being aware of what one is saying and using that awareness of what one is saying to determine what one is going to say thereafter—that is a process with which we are all familiar. We are continually following up our own address to other persons by an understanding of what we are saying, and using that understanding in the direction of our continued speech. We are finding out what we are going to say, what we are going to do, by saying and doing, and in the process we are continually controlling the process itself. In the conversation of gestures what we say calls out a certain response in another and that in turn changes our own action, so that we shift from what we started to do because of the reply the other makes. The conversation of gestures is the beginning of communication. The individual comes to carry on a conversation of gestures with himself. He says something, and that calls out a certain reply in himself which makes him change what he was going to say. One starts to say something, we will presume an unpleasant something, but when he starts to say it he realizes it is cruel. The effect on himself of what he is saying checks him; there is here a conversation of gestures between the individual and himself. We mean by significant speech that the action is one that affects the individual himself, and that the effect upon the individual himself is part of the intelligent carrying-out of the conversation with others. Now we, so to speak, amputate that social phase and dispense with it for the time being, so that one is talking to one's self as one would talk to another person.[2]

[2] It is generally recognized that the specifically social expressions of intelligence, or the exercise of what is often called "social intelligence," depend upon the given individual's ability to take the rôles of, or "put himself in the place of," the other individuals implicated with him in given social situations; and upon his consequent sensitivity to their attitudes toward himself and toward one another. These specifically social expressions of intelligence, of course, acquire unique significance in terms of our view that the whole nature of intelligence is social to the very core—that this putting of one's self in the places of others, this taking by one's self of their rôles or attitudes, is not merely one of the various aspects or expressions of intelligence or of intelligent behavior, but is the very essence of its character. Spearman's "X factor" in intelligence—the unknown factor which, according to him, intelligence contains—is simply (if our social theory of intelligence is correct) this ability of the intelligent individual to take the attitude of the other, or the attitudes of others, thus realizing the significations or grasping

This process of abstraction cannot be carried on indefinitely. One inevitably seeks an audience, has to pour himself out to somebody. In reflective intelligence one thinks to act, and to act solely so that this action remains a part of a social process. Thinking becomes preparatory to social action. The very process of thinking is, of course, simply an inner conversation that goes on, but it is a conversation of gestures which in its completion implies the expression of that which one thinks to an audience. One separates the significance of what he is saying to others from the actual speech and gets it ready before saying it. He thinks it out, and perhaps writes it in the form of a book; but it is still a part of social intercourse in which one is addressing other persons and at the same time addressing one's self, and in which one controls the address to other persons by the response made to one's own gesture. That the person should be responding to himself is necessary to the self, and it is this sort of social conduct which provides behavior within which that self appears. I know of no other form of behavior than the linguistic in which the individual is an object to himself, and, so far as I can see, the individual is not a self in the reflexive sense unless he is an object to himself. It is this fact that gives a critical importance to communication, since this is a type of behavior in which the individual does so respond to himself.

We realize in everyday conduct and experience that an individual does not mean a great deal of what he is doing and saying. We frequently say that such an individual is not himself. We come away from an interview with a realization that we have left out important things, that there are parts of the self that did not get into what was said. What determines the amount of the self that gets into communication is the social experience itself. Of course, a good deal of the self does not need to get expression. We carry on a whole series of different relationships to different people. We are one thing to one man and another thing to another. There are parts of the self which exist only for the self in relationship to itself. We divide ourselves up in all sorts of different selves with reference to our acquaintances. We discuss politics with one and religion with another. There are all sorts of different selves answering to all sorts of different social reactions. It is the social process itself that is responsible for the appearance of the self; it is not there as a self apart from this type of experience.

A multiple personality is in a certain sense normal, as I have just pointed out. There is usually an organization of the whole self with reference to the community to which we belong, and the situation in which we find ourselves. What the society is, whether we are living with people of the present, people of our own imaginations, people of the past, varies, of course, with different individuals. Normally, within the sort of community as a whole to which we belong, there is a unified self, but that may be broken up. To a person who is somewhat unstable nervously and in whom there is a line of cleavage, certain activities become impossible, and that set of activities may separate and evolve another self. Two separate "me's" and "I's," two different selves, result, and that is the condition under which there is a tendency to break up the personality There is an account of a professor of education who disappeared, was lost to the community, and later turned up in a logging camp in the West. He freed himself of his occupation and turned to the woods where he felt, if you like, more at home. The

the meanings of the symbols or gestures in terms of which thinking proceeds; and thus being able to carry on with himself the internal conversation with these symbols or gestures which thinking involves.

pathological side of it was the forgetting, the leaving out of the rest of the self. This result involved getting rid of certain bodily memories which would identify the individual to himself. We often recognize the lines of cleavage that run through us. We would be glad to forget certain things, get rid of things the self is bound up with in past experiences. What we have here is a situation in which there can be different selves, and it is dependent upon the set of social reactions that is involved as to which self we are going to be. . . .

The unity and structure of the complete self reflects the unity and structure of the social process as a whole; and each of the elementary selves of which it is composed reflects the unity and structure of one of the various aspects of that process in which the individual is implicated. In other words, the various elementary selves which constitute, or are organized into, a complete self are the various aspects of the structure of that complete self answering to the various aspects of the structure of the social process as a whole; the structure of the complete self is thus a reflection of the complete social process. The organization and unification of a social group is identical with the organization and unification of any one of the selves arising within the social process in which that group is engaged, or which it is carrying on.

The phenomenon of dissociation of personality is caused by a breaking up of the complete, unitary self into the component selves of which it is composed, and which respectively correspond to different aspects of the social process in which the person is involved, and within which his complete or unitary self has arisen; these aspects being the different social groups to which he belongs within that process.

42   Self as Concept and Illusion

• HARRY STACK SULLIVAN

Now, let me run over briefly this . . . general process of becoming a human being, which is manifested in the early years of life: The transfer from the manifestations of potentialities to learn phonemes and words, and even rough grammatical structures, to the capacity to use language to communicate information and misinformation. All children and for that matter, I believe, all the young of all the species on the face of the earth enjoy, whatever that means, playing with their abilities. As the young mature, these abilities become manifest in play-activities and are obviously pleasant to manifest in that way. And so, before it is possible for a child to articulate syllables, there is a playing with the phonemal stations which the child has finally been able to hit on in the babbling and cooing business. There follows the picking up of some syllables, and sooner or later every child falls upon the syllable "ma." If there is a slight tendency to perseveration

SOURCE: Harry Stack Sullivan, in "The Illusion of Personal Individuality." Reprinted from *The Fusion of Psychiatry and Social Science*, with Introduction and Commentaries by Helen Swick Perry (New York: W. W. Norton & Company, Inc., 1964), pp. 211–228. By permission of W. W. Norton & Company, Inc. Copyright 1964 by The William Alanson White Psychiatric Foundation.

so that it becomes "ma-ma," then truly the child discovers that there is something that he had not previously suspected: namely, magic in this noise-making apparatus of his, because very significant people begin to rally around and do things, and they don't hurt—quite the contrary, they are pleasant. I suppose that that little experience is the beginning of what to most people seems to be a lifelong feeling that there is nothing about them that is as powerful as the noises they make with their mouths. But anyway, it will not be very long before this child has a whole flock of articulate noises more or less strung together as words; and those words, which will be the delight of grandma and the satisfaction of mama, and perhaps even a source of mild satisfaction to papa, will have very little to do indeed with those words as they will be in that person ten years later. The words as they originally come along are happy accidents of maturation and combination of hearing and motor impulse—and vast bunches of potentialities that I couldn't name if I had time to. Especially we see in the case of "ma-ma"—where almost anything might have been said but that happened to be and it causes commotion among the great significant environment—that this obviously represents some personal power. This is one of the most remarkable performances thus far observed. And so "ma-ma" is of course not the name of a creature that runs around offering breasts and rattles: "ma-ma" pertains much more to the general feeling of force, magic, and so on. And I suppose it comes to everyone as a little bit of a letdown to discover that "ma-ma" is the thing that this creature [the mother] feels is its proper appellation, and it is only because the creature responds to that name that all this wonderful appearance of magic was called out.

The transfer from the feeling of power in this combination of noise to the realization that it is a pet name for the maternal relative is a transfer from the realm of the autistic or wholly personal, almost animal meaning, to the impersonal, social, conventional, or, as we like to say, *consensually validated* meaning of the word, and to the realm of scientific discourse, and I hope often to the realm of common speech. One's experience in using words has been observed with such care that one has finally learned how to create in the hearer's mind something remotely resembling what one hoped he would think of. Now, that takes a lot of experimenting, a great deal of observation, many corrections, solemn exhortations, rewards and punishments, and, as can be demonstrated in the case of almost everyone, applies only to a large working vocabulary. In addition to that, there is perhaps twice as large a collection of words in an additional vocabulary that isn't used very much, the meanings of which would come as a mild shock to a lexicographer, and a few words in a very personal vocabulary which are definitely retained in an autistic state—they are a secret language which will be expressed only obscurely in a very intimate relationship. Now, so far as there remain autistic words, those words would be fragments of the culture, torn from it, and kept as magic possessions of, let us say, an animal, and that is not what I am dealing with. In so far as a great deal of consensual validation has gone on and one can make noises which are more or less exactly communicative to a hearer who knows the language, the words have been stripped of as much as possible of the accidents of their personal history in you, and it is by that process that they come to be so peculiarly impersonal, just as if, you see, you hadn't learned them with the greatest care, having a wealth of meaning to your original words, and gradually sorting out that which was relevant from that which was irrelevant to the purposes of verbal communication.

A great deal of life runs through this process. It starts out defined by the more or less accidental occurrence of something. One experiences, observes, formulates —after perhaps naming, symbolizing—and subsequently thinks about, that is, analyzes, and perhaps finally gets insight into or thoroughly understands the relationship of various parts of this complex experience, has information about it; but it is more or less a unique performance. And then, because of the way we live, the equipment we have, the tendencies we mature, and so on, and perhaps the necessities to which we are subjected by others, we want to talk about this; and as we first discuss anything new in our experience—as you may be able to observe from day to day, however mature you are—we don't make awfully good sense; and now and then we have the unpleasant experience in the act of telling somebody about it of discovering that we don't know what we are talking about, even though it is our experience.

The point is that the process of consensual validation running here before our eyes calls in an illusion, an illusory person, in the sense of a critic, more or less like what we think the hearer is. We observe what goes on in him when we make this string of words or say this sentence, and it isn't satisfactory; and so, we feel that it is an inadequate statement, and therefore, of course, it doesn't communicate, even to us as hearers, what we are trying to say. So we look again at our experience, and we consider, from the standpoint of illusory critics, and so on: How can the thing be made to communicate? How can I tell somebody about this? And we finally, if we are fairly clever, get the answer. Once we have got that, the unique individuality of the experience begins to shrink, it becomes part of the general structure of life, we forget how strikingly novel the experience was and how peculiarly it had fringes which apply only to us—we lose all that in the process of validation.

You might feel that we were impoverished of much of the original richness of life in the process; maybe we are, but we get great richness from social intercourse, the sharing of experience, the growth of understanding, and the benefits of other people's more or less parallel experience, and so on. In fact, the whole richness of civilization is largely due to this very sort of thing. We can't be alone in things and be very clear on what happened *to* us, and we, as I have said already, can't be alone and be very clear even on what is happening *in* us very long —excepting that it gets simpler and simpler, and more primitive and more primitive, and less and less socially acceptable.

In all this process of being socialized and particularly of developing the ability to communicate by verbal behavior, quite a time after little Willie has gotten to talk about "me wanting" bread and jam, little Willie begins to talk about "I"; and when little Willie gets to talking about "I," just the same as when you hear other people talking about "I," you will notice that something is going on that wasn't there when it was "me" that wanted bread; and it is really much more important than when he finally gets around to saying that he is Willie Brown, or something like that. The coming of "I," as a term, is great stuff.

I have now to refer to a type of experience which may or may not exist—I wouldn't know. I believe it exists, but no one seems to have any time to make many observations; and so since it is more or less important from my way of explaining things and since I know that no one can now controvert the idea, I will present it to you for what it is worth. Some way or other—and the less said about that the better—there is a certain direct contagion of disagreeable experience from significant adults to very young children; in fact this continues in some cases far into life and is part of the paraphernalia that is so puzzling about certain medium-istic and certain hypnotic performances. A simple way of referring to this is *em-pathy*.[1] Whether empathy exists or not—as I say, take it or leave it—it is demon-strable that there are feeding difficulties when mother is made apprehensive by a telegram, and that it is not communicated by the tone of her voice; so since it oc-curs and is often noticed by pediatricians, I guess maybe I am in a moderately defensible position. And, the encouragement of the sublimation by the rote learn-ing of a vast part of the social heritage in the very young is by way of approval and disapproval. Approval, so far as I know, very early in life has almost no ef-fect, but in that case no effect is very welcome. You know that a very young child sleeps as much as possible, and so if there is no disturbance, well, I think it is do-ing what it wants to do. Disapproval, on the other hand, insofar as there is em-pathic linkage between the young and significant older people, is unpleasant, lowers the euphoria, the sense of well-being, interferes with the ease of falling asleep, the ease of taking nourishment, and so forth.

All this type of interference is originally profoundly unconscious in that it is in no sense a pure content of consciousness made up of sensations, conceptions, de-ductions, and inferences; but it does come ultimately to be clearly connected with disapproving attitudes on the part of others, with other people not being pleased with what we are doing, or not being satisfied with our performances. This early experience is the beginning of what goes on through life as a uniquely significant emotional experience, called by the name of a profoundly important concept in social study and psychiatry—the conception of *anxiety*. Anxiety begins that way —it is always that way, the product of a great many people who have disapproved. It comes to be represented by abstractions—by imaginary people that one carries around with one, some of them in the shape of ideal statements, some of them ac-tually as almost phenomenologically evident people who disapprove. The disap-proval and its effect get to be so subtly effective that a great deal of anxiety which shoos us this way and that, from this and that feeling, emotion, impulse, comes fi-nally to be so smooth-running that very few people have the foggiest notion of what a vast part of their life is influenced by anxiety.

Anxiety is what keeps us from noticing things which would lead us to correct our faults. Anxiety is the thing that makes us hesitate before we spoil our stand-ing with the stranger. Anxiety when it does not work so suavely becomes a psy-chiatric problem, because then it hashes our most polite utterances to the prospec-tive boss, and causes us to tremble at the most inopportune times. So you see it is only reasonable and very much in keeping with an enormously capable organiza-tion, such as the human being, that anxiety becomes a problem only when it doesn't work smoothly, and that the anxiety which has had to be grasped as a fun-damental factor in understanding interpersonal relations is by no means an anxi-ety attack, a hollow feeling in the stomach, and so on. Much, much more fre-quently it manifests as what I have called *selective inattention*, by which I mean you just miss all sorts of things which would cause you embarrassment, or in many

---

[1 Since Sullivan's paper was first presented, empathy has become a field for research. See, for instance, Leonard S. Cottrell, Jr. and Rosalind F. Dymond, "The Empathic Responses: A Neg-lected Field for Research," *Psychiatry* (1949) 12:355–359. The authors note in this article that Mead accepted empathic reactions as given, which was essentially Sullivan's position; nei-ther of course found a way to 'prove' it. H.S.P.]

cases, great profit to notice. It is the means by which you stay as you are, in spite of the efforts of worthy psychiatrists, clergymen, and others to help you mend your ways. You don't hear, you don't see, you don't feel, you don't observe, you don't think, you don't this, and you don't that, all by the very suave manipulation of the contents of consciousness by anxiety—or, if you must, . . . by the threat of anxiety, which still is anxiety. This very great extent of the effects of disapproval and the disturbance of euphoria by the significant people in early life—the people who are tremendously interested in getting you socialized—is what makes the concept of anxiety so crucially important in understanding all sorts of things.

The part of the personality [2] which is central in the experience of anxiety we call the "self." It is concerned with avoiding the supposedly distressing—which is often illuminating—with the exclusion from awareness of certain types of very humiliating recollections, and correspondingly the failure of the development of insight from experience. It maintains selective inattention.

Now the "self" is not coterminous with the ego of the old ego-psychologist, or the ego of Freud, or the superego of Freud, or anything except what I will say it is—which incidentally I believe is a very simple statement of practically universal experience: *The self is the content of consciousness at all times when one is thoroughly comfortable about one's self-respect, the prestige that one enjoys among one's fellows, and the respect and deference which they pay one.* Under those estimable circumstances there is no anxiety; the self is the whole works; everything else in life runs smoothly without disturbing us the least bit. And it is when any of these things begin to go a little haywire, when we tend to remember a humiliating experience which would disturb our self-esteem, when somebody says something derogatory about us in our hearing or to our face, when somebody snubs us, showing the very antithesis of deference, and when somebody shows up our stupidities, thereby impairing our prestige—it is at those times that anxiety is very apt to manifest itself; but, again, it is apt to be overlooked because it is so generally followed by anger. Anger is much more comfortable to experience than anxiety and, in fact, has much the relation of "I" to "me"; anger is much more powerful and reassuring than anxiety, which is the antithesis of power, which is threat and danger. Anger, however, is supposed to intimidate the other fellow, and at least it obscures the damage to our self-esteem, at least temporarily. And so we say that the self is a system within a personality, built up from innumerable experiences from early life, the central notion of which is that we satisfy the people that matter to us and therefore satisfy ourselves, and are spared the experience of anxiety.

We can say that the operations by which all these things are done—in contradistinction to taking food, getting sexual satisfaction, and sleep, and other delightful things—the operations which maintain our prestige and self-respect, which are dependent upon the respect of others for us and the deference they pay us, are *security operations.* Security operations are things which we might say are herded down a narrow path by selective inattention. In other words, we don't learn them as fast as we might; we never seem to learn how unimportant they are in many

---

[2] When I speak of "parts of personality," it must be understood that "personality" is a hypothesis, so this is a hypothetical part of a hypothesis.

[The importance of the explicit recognition of the pyramiding of hypotheses was continually emphasized by Sullivan. In writing about personality, it is particularly easy—and common—to conceal the pyramiding of hypotheses by the facile use of terms of common speech, the ambiguity or hypothetical nature of which is not obvious because of their familiarity. H.S.P.]

circumstances and where they get in our way. They are the things that always have the inside track with denizens of this best of possible variants on the Western culture, the most insecure culture I know—our American people. Well, security operations are the things that don't change much, that have the focus of attention, in and out of season, if there is the least chance of feeling anxious. And the security operations are in many cases assertive, starting out with "I"—and "I" in its most powerful fashion. Sometimes the security operations are more subtle— in fact there are always quite subtle security operations in a person of [at least] ordinary abilities—but they interfere with all sorts of grasps on the universe, grasps which would in essence show that the regard in which a person holds us is defined by the past experience of that person and his actual capacity to know what we were doing, which in some cases is very low. [We often fail to grasp] that the prestige we did or did not get had little bearing on the prestige which we might get for this particular act six weeks later; that all this vast to-do which in early childhood and the juvenile era is practically necessary to survive the distress of the parents is mostly ancient baggage that could very well be replaced with a few streamlined pieces that make a great deal of sense in the interpersonal world in which we have our being.

As I say, the self does not "learn" very readily because anxiety is just so busy and so effective at choking off inquiries where there is any little risk of loss of face with one's self or others. And the operations to maintain this prestige and feeling of security, freedom from anxiety, are of such crucial importance from the cradle on—I mean actually from the very early months of childhood, somewhere around two months onward—that the content of consciousness pertaining to the pursuit of satisfaction and the enjoyment of life is at best marginal. It is one's prestige, one's status, the importance which people feel one is entitled to, the respect that one can expect from people—and even their envy, which becomes precious in that it gives a certain illusion that one has prestige—that dominate awareness. *These things are so focal in interpersonal relations of our day and age that the almost unassailable conviction develops, partly based on the lack of information of our parents and others, that each of us, as defined by the animal organism that we were at birth, are unique, isolated individuals in the human world,* as our bodies are—very figuratively—unique and individual in the biological world.

Now I started out by suggesting that the interrelations, interdependence, interpenetration, and so on, of the biological world are very striking. Yet, no one will quarrel with the separation as an instrument for study, for thought, and so on, of organism and environment. And if you are human biologists, I am perfectly willing for you to talk about individual specimens of man. And in so far as you see material objects, I am perfectly willing to agree that you see people walking around individually, moving from hither to yon in geography, and even persisting from now to then in duration; but that does not explain much of anything about the distinctively human. It doesn't even explain very much about the performance of my thoroughly domesticated cocker spaniels. What the biological organism does is interesting and wonderful. What the personality does, which can be observed and studied only in relations between personalities or among personalities, is truly and terribly marvelous, and is human, and is the function of creatures living in indissoluble contact with the world of culture and of people. In that field it is preposterous to talk about individuals and to go on deceiving oneself with the idea of uniqueness, of single entity, of simple, central being.

So it has come about that there has developed this conception of interpersonal relations as the field of study of those parts of the social sciences concerned with the behavior of people and as the field of study of psychiatry. In so far as difficulties in living are the subject of psychiatry, we must study the processes of living in which the difficulties are manifested, since otherwise we can't really sort out what is "difficulty" and what is perhaps novel genius; we really do have to study interpersonal relations to know what we are talking about when we talk about difficulties in living. As I say, the conceptual system has grown up which finds its subject matter not in the study of personality, which is beyond reach, but in the study of that which can be observed; namely, interpersonal relations. And when that viewpoint is applied, then one of the greatest difficulties encountered in bringing about favorable change is this almost inescapable illusion that there is a perduring, unique, simple existent self, called variously "me" or "I," and in some strange fashion, the patient's, or the subject person's, private property.

Progress begins, life unfolds, and interpersonal relations improve—life can become simple and delightful only at the expense of this deeply ingrained illusion and the parallel conviction that that which has sensations must under all conceivable circumstances be the "same" as that which has tenderness and love—tenderness and love being as obviously communal, involving two personalities, as anything known to man can be.

And so let me say very simply that in so far as you will care to check over these various incomplete sketches that I have made on a vast field and will not dismiss what you heard me say as a misunderstanding, you will find that it makes no sense to think of ourselves as "individual," "separate," capable of anything like definitive description in isolation, that the notation is just beside the point. No great progress in this field of study can be made until it is realized that the field of observation is what people do with each other, what they can communicate to each other about what they do with each other. When that is done, no such thing as the durable, unique, individual personality is ever clearly justified. For all I know every human being has as many personalities as he has interpersonal relations; and as a great many of our interpersonal relations are actual operations with imaginary people—that is, in-no-sense-materially-embodied people—and as they may have the same or greater validity and importance in life as have our operations with many materially-embodied people like the clerks in the corner store, you can see that even though "the illusion of personal individuality" sounds quite lunatic when first heard, there is at least food for thought in it.

Discussion [3]

. . . (*In answer to a question asking, in effect, Can we not say that there is a justifiably characterizable self in each person we deal with, which might be called the "real" self?*)

It is, I believe, a statistically demonstrable fact that the interpersonal relations of any person, even though he feels very full of the conviction of his individuality, are under ordinary circumstances rather strikingly restricted in variety, freedom you might say. Such a person is very much more apt to do the same sort of thing with a number of people than to do very different things with each one of that

---

[3 In the recordings from which this lecture was taken, there are gaps in which questions from the audience can be faintly heard. I have tried to indicate the nature of these questions. H.S.P.]

number. Furthermore, even more striking are the observable performances in which he will persistently misfunction with certain people in characterizable ways, despite the most incongruous objective data—of which, of course, *he* is unaware. It is a notorious fact about personality problems that people act *as if* someone else were present when he is not—as the result of interpersonal configurations which are irrelevant to the other person's concern—and do this in a recurrent fashion without any great difference in pattern. These various factors are so striking, in interpersonal relations, that it is perfectly easy and for many purposes very practical to speak of the structure of the character of the person.

All these are, I believe, correct statements of observable data. But when it comes to attempting to form a general theory on which to approach explanations of everything that happens to one in one's intercourse with others, and all the variety of things that occur in particularly-purposed interpersonal relations such as the psychotherapeutic situation, then it is just as easy to notice that the person maintains quite as many of what you ordinarily call imaginary relationships as he does of those that have the peculiar virtue of objective reference. A person, for example, may be said, with considerable justification, to act towards his wife as he did towards his mother. Now it is true that there are many differences in detail, but the general patterns of emotional relationship of conscious versus unnoticed motivation, of intended versus experienced acts, are very much those that the person first developed in manifest behavior with his mother; and it is quite useful to think of his experience of that mother as interpenetrating the experience of the wife and, in fact, frequently completely suppressing any individualization of or any attention to the characterization of the wife. That is the more difficult part of this conception, but it is quite useful in the sense that it can be made to make sense in many of the maneuvers of interpersonal relations that have effect; whereas operations on any other set of assumptions that explains the same phenomena raise very considerable theoretical difficulties. In other words, it is a matter of what is most generally useful as a theoretical point of departure.

And now to come to the more specific question: Are we not entirely justified—however much we have respect for the fictions which masquerade as human individuals—in realizing that there is a justifiably characterizable self in each person that we deal with?

I, myself, have come gradually to find that unnecessary, whether that be some serious misunderstanding of mine or an insight remains, of course, for others to determine. You know that is true of the evolution of most hypotheses.

One listens, for example, in psychotherapy to a great number of revealing communications, hoping and generally finding finally that the thing has been reviewed very simply in a very small context; and then you run up the flag of hope, and so on, and go hammer and tongs to seeing what can be made of this very simple series of statements which the other fellow won't forget while you are trying to make your point clear. Now, it is decidedly easier to explain this great difficulty on the, you might say, individual-less type of hypothesis than on any other that I have yet dealt with. . . .

(In answer to a question regarding the permissibility of thinking in terms of the individual:)

We have, thus far, I believe, thought in terms of the individual, which is certainly a demonstration of the possibility. The point, rather, I think, is on the utility. I have been at some pains not to deny you the privilege of going on in your convictions, but to suggest to you that there is another view that may—well, if nothing else—permit considerable technological advance, or technical advance as we call it in psychiatry, and may even be useful as a new orientation for certain types of social investigation. I also tried to say at the beginning that for certain purposes it is certainly very useful to separate organism and environment, particularly for example if one is talking about colonies of paramecia, but I think that perhaps there are biologists who think of the paramecium as a particular part of the world showing certain remarkable features of organization in functional activity, but ceasing very suddenly to manifest those if separated from certain parts of the universe which do not manifest those peculiarities of organization in functional activity. It is all perfectly well, if you wish, to limit your personality to the skin over your bones and adnexa, but my notion is not what can be done or what should be done; it is rather a suggestion of a system of reference which seems to eliminate a great many terms, conceptions, perplexities, and to provide some fairly simple operations that seem to bear up pretty well—and which also is extraordinarily unwelcome from the standpoint of our educational training.

My son has to be to many a mother or father something thoroughly unique, almost pricelessly different from anyone else; and with that background it is not difficult to realize that when everything else fails one, membership in that family, which makes one unique and distinguishes one on the basis of the very early valuation, would be a treasured possession. I am talking not so much as to what we are to deny our fellowmen or our colleagues, but only in favor of a conceptual system which I believe is defensible and useful.

43   Appearance and the Self

● GREGORY P. STONE

A primary tenet of all symbolic interaction theory holds that the self is established, maintained, and altered in and through communication. Seeking to probe this tenet, most investigations have emphasized discourse—or, somewhat inexactly, verbal communication—and have shown that language exerts a very great influence indeed upon the structure and process of the self. The present essay attempts to widen the perspective of symbolic interaction studies by isolating a dimension of communication that has received relatively little attention by sociologists and social psychologists—appearance. Except for psychoanalysts, some psychiatrists, and a few anthropologists, one finds almost no scholars willing to bend their efforts to the study of appearance.[1]

SOURCE: Gregory P. Stone, in Arnold M. Rose (ed.), *Human Behavior and Social Processes* (Boston: Houghton Mifflin Co., 1962), pp. 86–118.

[1] Erving Goffman (Ref. 7) must be exempted from the indictment. Recently he has pushed sociological or social psychological analysis far beyond the conventional limits of a perspective that has restricted the study of social transactions to their linguistic characteristics, conditions, and consequences.

This paper seeks to demonstrate that the perspective of symbolic interaction, as it has been formulated by George H. Mead, requires (indeed, *demands*) a consideration of appearance for the adequate interpretation of social transactions as well as the careers of selves in such transactions. Mead's analysis of communication, it is suggested, suffers from what might be called a "discursive bias." [2] Consequently, there are crucial unanswered questions posed by his analysis of communication that can only be answered by extending and refining his perspective. This requires a demonstration that: (1) every social transaction must be broken down into at least two analytic components or processes—appearance and discourse; (2) appearance is at least as important for the establishment and maintenance of the self as is discourse; (3) the study of appearance provides a powerful lever for the formulation of a conception of self capable of embracing the contributions of Cooley and Sullivan as well as Mead; and (4) appearance is of major importance at every stage of the early development of the self. These assertions are all empirically grounded in the author's long-term study of dress as an apparent symbol (Ref. 16).

Appearance, Discourse, and Meaning

According to Mead, meaning is established only when the response elicited by some symbol is the "same" for the one who produces the symbol as for the one who receives it. [3] "Same" appears here in quotation marks, because the responses are *really* never the "same." This is an integral feature of Mead's perspective and calls for some elaboration. The fundamental implication is that *meaning is always a variable.*

We can trace this variable nature of meaning to Mead's conception of the self as process and structure, subject and object, or "I" and "me." The "I" imbues the self with a certain tentativeness—a "certain uncertainty." As a consequence, any future line of action (for example, one's response to one's own symbolic productions) can never be fully anticipated. Mead put it this way:

> So the "I" really appears experientially as a part of the "me." But on the basis of this experience we distinguish that individual who is doing something from the "me" who puts the problem up to him. The response enters into his experience only when it takes place. If he says he knows what he is going to do, even there he may be mistaken. He starts out to do something and something happens to interfere. The resulting actions is always a little different from anything which he could anticipate. . . . The action of the "I" is something the nature of which we cannot tell in advance (14, p. 177).

---

[2] Of course, the gesture is considered at length, and gestures may often be employed to establish appearances, as we shall see. However, Mead views the gesture as incipient discourse, more typical of communication in its rudimentary phases. The aptness of the vocal gesture for explaining the emergence of meaning in sub-social communication may be an important source of Mead's discursive bias. Even more than discourse, appearance presupposes an ongoing social process for its meaning. Apparent symbols are often silent and are best intercepted by mirrors, while one's own ear always intercepts one's own vocal gesture about as it is intercepted by others. But mirrors are not always handy; so it happens that the silent appearance, even more than the vocal utterance, comes to require an audience which can serve as a mirror, reflecting one's appearance back upon himself.

[3] "Response" is usually the production of other symbols. The term is distinguished from "symbol" merely to permit the observer to shift his view as he analyzes what is going on in the social transaction. Actually, all that distinguishes a "response" from any symbol in question is its occurrence later in time. . . .

But the meaning of a symbol, as we have said, is premised upon the notion that the response called out in the other is the *same* as the response called out in the one who produces the symbol—*always a little different from anything which he could anticipate*. Moreover, the other's response has the same characteristically unanticipatable quality.

Meaning, then, is always a variable, ranging between non-sense, on the one hand—the total absence of coincident responses—and what might be called boredom on the other—the total coincidence of such responses. Neither of these terminals can be approached very often in the duration of a transaction, for either can mean its end. It is seldom that we continue to talk non-sense with others, and boredom encourages us to depart from their presence. Thus, meaning is present in communication when the responses that are symbolically mobilized only *more or less* coincide.

This raises the question of *guarantees* for the meaningfulness of social transactions. How can the transaction be prevented from spilling over into non-sense or atrophying into boredom? Because the self is in part an "I"—unpredictable—the risks of boredom are minimized; but, for Mead, the guarantee against non-sense in the transaction is "role-taking," or, more accurately, placing one's self in the attitude of the other. By placing one's self in the attitude or incipient action of the other and representing one's own symbolic production to oneself from that attitude, one guarantees that one's own response will be rather more than less coincident with the response of the other, since the other's incipient actions have become incorporated in the actions of the one producing the symbol. It is here, however, that a gap in Mead's analysis occurs, for a further question arises, and that question was not systematically considered by Mead: if role-taking is the guarantee of meaning, how then is role-taking possible? Obviously, one must apprehend the other's role, the other's attitude—indeed, the other's self—before one can take the other's role or incorporate the other's attitude.

At this point a shift in terminology is required to expedite the analysis of meaning and to provide initial answers to the questions that have been raised. Let us suggest that the guarantee against non-sense in the social transaction is heuristically better conceptualized as *identification*,[4] not role-taking or taking the other's attitude—at best a very partial explanation of how meaning is established in social transactions. The term "identification" subsumes at least two processes: *identification of* and *identification with*. Role-taking is but one variant of the latter process, which must also include sympathy,[5] and there may well be other variants.[6] Nevertheless, the point to be made is this: identifications *with* one another, in whatever mode, cannot be made without identifications *of* one another. Above all, identifications of one another are ordinarily facilitated by appearance and are often accomplished silently or non-verbally. This can be made crystal clear by observing the necessity for and process of establishing gender in social transactions. Everywhere we find vocabularies sexually distinguished: there are languages for males only, languages for females only, and languages employed to communicate across the barriers of gender. Obviously, identifications of the other's gender must be established before the appropriate language can be selected

---

[4] The precedent has been incisively established by Nelson N. Foote (4).
[5] Mead himself distinguishes sympathy as a particular mode of "attitude-taking" in a seldom cited article (13); but for the empirical utility of the distinction, see Sheldon Stryker (17).
[6] An imposing taxonomy has been erected in Howard Becker (1).

for the upcoming discourse. Seldom, upon encountering another, do we inquire concerning the other's gender. Indeed, to do so would be to impugn the very gender that must be established. The knowing of the other's gender is known silently, established by appearances.

Appearance, then, is that phase of the social transaction which establishes identifications of the participants. As such, it may be distinguished from *discourse*, which we conceptualize as the text of the transaction—*what* the parties are discussing. Appearance and discourse are two distinct dimensions of the social transaction. The former seems the more basic. It sets the stage for, permits, sustains, and delimits the possibilities of discourse by underwriting the possibilities of meaningful discussion.

Ordinarily appearance is communicated by such non-verbal symbols as gestures, grooming, clothing, location, and the like discourse, by verbal symbolism. Yet the relationship between the kinds of symbolism and the dimension of the transaction is not at all invariant. Gestures and other non-verbal symbols may be used to talk about things and events, and words may have purely apparent significance. In fact, appearances are often discussed, while discussions often "appear"—that is, serve only to establish the identities of the discussants. In the latter case, the person may seem to be talking about matters other than identifications of self or other, but may actually be speaking only about himself. "Name-dropping" serves as an example. In the former case, which we will term *apparent discourse*, whole transactions may be given over to the discussion of appearances, and this occurs most often when some new turn has been taken by the transaction requiring re-identifications of the parties. Indeed, apparent discourse is often *news* and vice versa.

Appearance and discourse are in fact dialectic processes going on whenever people converse or correspond. They work back and forth on one another, at times shifting, at other times maintaining the direction of the transaction. When the direction of the transaction shifts, appearance is likely to emerge into the discursive phases of the transaction; when the direction is maintained over a relatively long period of time and is uninterrupted, discourse is likely to be submerged in appearances. In all cases, however, discourse is impossible without appearance which permits the requisite identifications with one another by the discussants. One may, nevertheless, appear without entering the discourse. As Veblen suggested, we may escape our discursive obligations, but not our clothed appearances.

Appearance and the Self

Appearance *means* identifications of one another,[7] but the question arises whether such identifications follow any ordered pattern. Mead's perspective insists that we look for the meaning of appearance in the responses that appearances mobilize, and we have examined more than 8,000 such responses supplied by interview materials to discern whether they are consistently patterned. Many responses are, of course, gestural in nature. One's appearance commands the gaze of the audience. An eyebrow is lifted. There is a smile or a frown, an approach or withdrawal. One blushes with shame for the shamelessness of the other's

---

[7] The question of how the meaning of appearance is guaranteed is germane and recognized, but will not be treated here. Aside from the "teamwork" analyzed so carefully by Goffman in his *Presentation of Self in Everyday Life* (7), other guarantees are suggested in his "Symbols of Class Status." (6)

appearance or with embarrassment at one's own. The nature of our data precluded the study of such gestural responses unless they were recorded by the interviewer. Consequently, apparent discourse was examined for the most part—talk about appearance aroused, in particular, by clothing. Over 200 married men and women living in a Midwestern community of 10,000 population supplied the talk. Of the many statements these people made about dress, only statements referring to those who wore the clothing in question were scrutinized. These were construed as identifications of the wearer. Here we shall be concerned for simplicity's sake with only two modes of such responses: (1) responses made about the wearer of clothes by others who, we shall say, *review* his clothing; and (2) responses made about the wearer by the wearer—we shall call these responses *programs*. A third mode of response is relevant, but will not be considered here—the wearer's imagination of others' responses to his dress.

When programs and reviews tend to coincide, the self of the one who appears (the one whose clothing has elicited such responses) is validated or established; when such responses tend toward disparity, the self of the one who appears is challenged, and conduct may be expected to move in the direction of some redefinition of the challenged self. Challenges and validations of the self, therefore, may be regarded as aroused by personal appearance. As a matter of fact, the dimensions of the self emphasized by Mead, Cooley, and Sullivan effectively embrace the content of the responses to clothing we examined in our quest for the meaning of appearance. In response to his clothes, the wearer was cast as a social object—a "me"—or, as we shall say, given some identity. A person's dress also imbued him with attitudes by arousing others' anticipations of his conduct as well as assisting the mobilization of his own activity. In Mead's terms, then, the self as object and attitude is established by appearance. However, the most frequent response to dress was the assignment of value-words to the wearer. One's clothes impart value to the wearer, both in the wearer's own eyes and in the eyes of others. Both Sullivan and Cooley underscore the relevance of value for any adequate conceptualization of the self; Sullivan, by referring to the self as comprised by the "reflected *appraisals* of others," Cooley, by emphasizing "imagined *judgments* of appearance." Finally, Cooley's emphasis upon self-*feeling* or the self as *sentiment* was provided with empirical support by this analysis. A person's clothing often served to establish a mood for himself capable of eliciting validation in the reviews aroused from others. The meaning of appearance, therefore, is the establishment of identity, value, mood, and attitude for the one who appears by the coincident programs and reviews awakened by his appearance. These terms require further discussion.

IDENTITY

It is almost enough to demonstrate the significance of the concept "identity" by referring to the rapidity with which it has caught on in social science. Recently re-introduced to the social sciences by Erik Erikson, the term has provided many new social-psychological insights. Specifically, fruitful inquiries into the sociological implications of the ego have been made possible by releasing the investigator from the commitment to argument and partisanship that alternative concepts such as "personality" demand. Identity, as a concept, is without any history of polemics. However, the impetus to discovery afforded by the term has been so great that its meaning threatens to spill over the bounds of analytic utility. Before its meaning becomes totally lost by awakening every conceivable response in every conceivable investigator (like the term "personality"), the concept must be salvaged.

Almost all writers using the term imply that identity establishes *what* and *where* the person is in social terms. It is not a substitute word for "self." Instead, when one has identity, he is *situated*—that is, cast in the shape of a social object by the acknowledgment of his participation or membership in social relations. One's identity is established when others *place* him as a social object by assigning him the same words of identity that he appropriates for himself or *announces*. It is in the coincidence of placements and announcements that identity becomes a meaning of the self, and often such placements and announcements are aroused by apparet symbols such as uniforms. The policeman's uniform, for example, is an announcement of his identity as policeman and validated by others' placements of him as policeman.

Such a conception of identity is, indeed, close to Mead's conception of the "me," the self as object related to and differentiated from others. To situate the person by establishing some identity for him is, in a sense, to give him position, and a pun permits further elucidation of the concept: identity is established as a consequence of two processes, apposition and opposition, a bringing together and setting apart. To situate the person as a social object is to bring him together with other objects so situated, and, at the same time to set him apart from still other objects. *Identity is intrinsically associated with all the joinings and departures of social life.* To have an identity is to join with some and depart from others, to enter and leave social relations at once.

In fact, the varieties of identity are isomorphic with the varieties of social relations. At least four different types of words were used to place and announce the identities communicated by clothing: (1) universal words designating one's humanity, such as age, gender, and community (we call these "universal" words because people everywhere make such distinctions); (2) names and nicknames; (3) titles, such as occupational and marital titles; (4) "relational categories," such as customer, movie-goer, jazz fan, and the like. Social relations, viewed as ongoing transactions, can be classified according to the identities which must be placed and announced to permit entry into the transaction. Thus, *human relations* are those requiring the placement and announcement of such universal identities as age, gender, or community membership. *Interpersonal relations* are those that may only be entered by an exchange of names or nicknames,[8] while *structural relations* are those that may only be entered by exchanging a name for a title. Finally, we may speak of *masses* as social relations that may be anonymously entered.

The distinction between interpersonal and structural relations seems, at this point, to have the greatest analytical utility. Since one's name ordinarily outlasts one's titles, interpersonal relations probably provide an important social basis for the continuity of identity. Structural relations, on the other hand, are more discontinuous and changing.

We can note how one's name is established by dress if we imagine Teddy Roosevelt without the pince-nez, F. D. R. without the cigarette holder, or Thomas

---

[8] This characterization of interpersonal relations is not reversible. The exchange of names does not guarantee that an interpersonal relationship will always be established.

Dewey without the moustache. One of our informants, a small-time real estate operator, was well aware of the significance of clothing in his attempts to personalize his occupational identity. Asked, "What do your fellow workers say and think when you wear something new for the first time on the job?" he replied:

> Well, I always have a new hat, and I suppose my clientele talks about it. But, you know, I always buy cheap ones and put my name in them. I leave them around in restaurants and places like that intentionally. It has advertising value.

The interviewer asked later, "Would you rather wear a greater variety or a smaller variety of clothes on the job?" and the informant replied:

> A smaller variety so you will look the same everyday. So people will identify you. They look for the same old landmark.

In response to the same question, a working man who had recently opened a small business said:

> A smaller variety for both sales and shop. I think if a person dresses about the same continually, people will get to know you. Even if they don't know your name, you're easier to describe. I knew an insurance man once who used a wheel chair. Everyone knew him because of that chair. It's the same with clothes.

Distinctive, persistent dress may replace the name as well as establish it!

On the other hand, one's career within the structural relation is marked by changes of title, and the change of title demands a change of dress. All of the men in this study were presented with the following story:

> John had an excellent record as foreman in an automobile factory. Eventually, he and two other foremen were promoted to the position of division head. John was happy to get the job, because of the increase in pay. However, he continued to wear his old foreman's vest and work clothes to the office. This went on for several months until the division heads he had been promoted with began to avoid him at lunch and various social gatherings. They had dressed from the beginning in business suits and had mingled more and more with older managerial employees. John found himself without friends in the office.

When asked, "What finally happened to John?" about 80 per cent of the men interviewed predicted termination, demotion, or no further promotion (5, pp. 47–51). One informant, interviewed by the writer, quite seriously suggested that John was a potential suicide.

Appearances, then, are interrupted in social structures as identities are set apart; appearances, so to speak, endure in interpersonal relations where identities are brought into closer proximity. Yet we find that, in the context of structural relations, identities are given a somewhat different cast than in interpersonal relations. In the former, identities are qualified along the axis of value; in the latter, more usually along the axis of mood.

QUALIFICATIONS OF IDENTITY: VALUE AND MOOD

To engage meaningfully in some transactions it is enough to know merely "what" the parties are—to know their identities. This would seem often to be the case in the anonymous transactions of the masses. As Louis Wirth used to tell his students in his elaborations of the "massive" character of urban life, "You go to a bootblack to have your shoes shined; not to save your soul." The implication is, I think, that, when we become concerned with the bootblack's moods or his larger worth in terms of some scheme of value, our relations with him will lose their anonymous character. By so doing, we have, perhaps, disadvantaged ourselves of the freedom the city offers. Ordinarily, however, if transactions persistently engage the same persons or seem likely to continue into an ill-defined future, it is not enough merely to establish identities in the guarantee of meaningful discourse. Thus, when we are introduced to strangers who may become acquaintances or possibly friends, we *express* our pleasure with the introductions, and such expressions are ordinarily *appreciated* by those we have met. Or, meeting an acquaintance on the street, we inquire how he *feels* before the discourse is initiated. In a certain sense, interpersonal relations demand that the *moods* of the participants be established (as well as their names or nicknames) prior to the initiation of discursive phases in the transaction: that "Joe" or "Jane" is mad or sad will have definite consequences for the talk with "Jim" or "Joan."

Ordinarily, also, before a title is bestowed upon us or before we are invested with office, our identities must undergo qualifying scrutiny. In such cases, the qualification does not usually get accomplished in terms of our anger or sadness, but in terms of some assessment of our former careers and future prospects with reference to their *worth*. The tendency is to assess worth in terms of a relatively objective set of standards that can transcend the whim of the assessing one and the whimsy of the one assessed. Upon the initiation of what we have called structural relations, the *values* of the participating persons (as well as their titles) must be established.

Value and mood provide two fundamental axes along which the qualifications of identity are accomplished in *appraising* and *appreciative* responses to appearance. This seems obvious on the face of it: that a teacher is competent has different consequences for faculty-student transactions than that a teacher is a teacher; and that a teacher is temperamental or easy-going presents the possibility of a still different set of consequences for upcoming discussions. The differences between value and mood are suggested by the distinction that Park has made between interests and sentiments, that Helen Lynd has made between guilt and shame, or that Kenneth Burke has made between poetry and pathos (*poiema* and *pathema*). It is the difference between virtue and happiness, and, as we know full well, the virtuous man is not necessarily happy nor the happy man necessarily virtuous. The problem arises when we observe that happiness may be a virtue in some social circles or that one may be happy because he is virtuous (cynics might say "smug"). Value and mood, so patently distinguishable in discourse, merge together inextricably in experience. Can we conceive of feelings of pride without reference to a set of values? I think not, although it does seem possible to conceive of merit without feeling. Yet, in situations that are totally value-relevant, totally given over to matters of appraisal—the courtroom, the examination, the military review—the very constriction of feeling and mood, their suppression, may saturate the situation with a grim somberness that can transform dispassion into passion—as the austerity of the courtroom has provided a curiously fitting context for the impassioned plea; the silence of the examination room is interrupted by nervous laughter; the ordered rhythm of the march engenders song.

As Helen Lynd has written of guilt and shame, so we conceive value and mood:

They are in no sense polar opposites. Both the guilt axis and the shame axis enter into the attitudes and behavior of most people, and often into the same situation. But there are for different persons different balances and stresses between the two, and it does matter whether one lives more in terms of one or the other (11, p. 208).

And we would add that one differentiating condition is the type of social relation that regularly mobilizes the time and attention of the person. Thus, we have found that value has a greater saliency for most men in their conceptions of self and others while, for most women, mood has a greater saliency. This finding is ascribed in part to the American male's more frequent participation and absorption in the structure of work relations, in comparison with the American woman's more frequent preoccupation with the interpersonal relations she carries on with friends and acquaintances.

It is much more difficult to characterize value and mood than it has been to characterize identity. However, the responses to dress that were classified as words of value manifested the following references: (1) to *consensual goals,* such as wealth, prestige, or power; (2) to *achievement standards,* universalistic criteria applied to the assessment of one's proximity to or remoteness from such goals; (3) *norms* or rules regulating the pursuit of consensual goals; and (4) *moral precepts* stipulating valued behavior often employed in the assessment of character (e.g., cleanliness, politeness, thriftiness, and the like). Responses classified as mood-words were even more difficult to order, including references to ease and lack of ease in social transactions, liking, disliking, fearing, and dreading. Anxiety, monotony, rapture, and surprise also were included in the category, as were references to that ill-defined state which the informants called morale.

It may be helpful to borrow again from Helen Lynd, using her technique for contrasting guilt and shame to contrast value and mood. Table 1 attempts to state the social relations for which value and mood *ordinarily* have the greatest saliency, the nature of the criteria which are applied in the establishment of value and mood, the processes by which these qualifications of identity are established, and finally the consequences for the social relationship when identities are qualified along one or the other axis. I wish to emphasize that the summary presentation in Table 1 is in no way meant to be definitive, and that the axes which are characterized as value and mood, although they are set down in a contrasting manner, are not meant to be established as polar opposites. In particular, *sentiments* represent a convergence of the two axes in the qualification of identity. Sentiments are valued feelings or felt values, as for example in Cooley's "looking-glass self"— the sentiments of pride or mortification are *expressive* responses to the judgments or *appraisals* of others.

ACTIVATIONS OF IDENTITY: ATTITUDE

In a brilliant discussion, Kenneth Burke has established the essential ambiguity of the term "attitude": an attitude can be looked upon as a substitute for an act— the "truncated act" of John Dewey—or as an incipient act—a "beginning" from the standpoint of George H. Mead (2, pp. 235–247). The establishment of identity, value, and mood by appearances represents the person as *there, stratified* or assigned a particular distance, and *rapt* or engrossed. There remains the matter of his activation, the assessment of the path along which he has traveled, the path he

TABLE 1   *Value and Mood as Axes Along Which Qualifications of Identity Are Established*

Phases	Value Axis	Mood Axis
Relational Basis	*Structural relations*	*Interpersonal relations*
Criteria	Universalistic Abstract Objective Detachment Poetic (Pious) Neutrality Scalar	Particularistic Concrete Subjective Attachment Pathetic Affectivity Absolute
Establishment	Rationalized Investment Conformity-deviation with respect to universal rules or a social code Future reference Legitimated by appeals to the appraisals of others	Spontaneously communicated Preoccupation or rapture Ease–dis-ease with respect to engagement in social transactions Present reference Legitimated by appeals to the expressions of the self
Relational Consequences	Stratification	Rapport

is traveling, and where he is about to go. These aspects of the person—that he has acted, is acting, and will act further—are also established by appearance. We refer to them as *attitudes*.[9] Attitudes are *anticipated* by the reviewers of an appearance, *proposed* by the one who appears.

Appearance *substitutes* for past and present action and, at the same time, conveys an *incipience* permitting others to anticipate what is about to occur. Specifically, clothing represents our action, past, present, and future, as it is established by the proposals and anticipations that occur in every social transaction. Without further elaboration, I think that this can be clearly seen in the doffing of dress, signaling that an act is done (and another act about to begin), the donning of dress, signaling the initiation of a new act, and the wearing of dress, signaling that action is going on.

APPEARANCE AND THE SELF

The meaning of appearance, therefore, can be studied by examining the responses mobilized by clothes. Such responses take on at least four forms: identities are placed, values appraised, moods appreciated, and attitudes anticipated. Appearance provides the identities, values, moods, and attitudes of the person-in-communication, since it arouses in others the assignment of words embodying these dimensions to the one who appears. As we have noted earlier, this is only one part of the total picture.

---

[9] Of course, the concept "attitude" is of central significance for the social psychology of George Herbert Mead, but, in some ways, it is the least satisfying of the terms we have characterized here. All the meanings of dress or appearance have an attitudinal or "activated" character. In particular, programs and reviews may be conceived as incipient, truncated, or on-going acts. It may be, in fact, that the concept "attitude" is of a different order from the concepts "identity," "value," and "mood," asking the observer to inquire not into the content or structure of the events under scrutiny, but rather to seize those events in their full-blown capacity as processes.

Cooley, Mead, and Harry Stack Sullivan have reminded us often that such responses are reflexive in character, reverberating back upon the one who produces
them and the one toward whom they are directed. In short, identifications of others are always complemented by identifications of the self, in this case, responses
to one's own appearance. In a variety of ways, as a matter of fact, reviews of a
person's appearances are intricately linked with the responses he makes to his own
appearance. We have called the process of making identifications of the one who
appears by that one a *program*. Programmatic responses parallel the responses
that have been called reviews. One appears, reflects upon that appearance, and
appropriates words of identity, value, mood, or attitude for himself in response to
that appearance. By appearing, the person *announces* his identity, *shows* his value,
expresses his mood, or *proposes* his attitude. If the meaning of appearance is "supplied" by the reviews others make of one's appearance, it is established or consensually validated, as Sullivan would have said, by the relative coincidence of
such reviews with the program of the one who appears. In other words, when
one's dress calls out in others the "same" identifications of the wearer as it calls
out in the wearer, we may speak of the appearance as meaningful. It turns out,
in fact, that this is the self, and this may be diagrammed as in Table 2.

TABLE 2   *Schematic Representation of the Meaning of Appearance, Emphasizing the Validation
of Personal Appearance*

Program of Appearance	Review of Appearance			
	Placement	*Appraisal*	*Appreciation*	*Anticipation*
Announcement Show Expression Proposal	Identity	Value	Mood	Attitude

In appearances, then, selves are established and mobilized. As the self is
dressed, it is simultaneously addressed, for, whenever we clothe ourselves, we
dress "toward" or address some audience whose validating responses are essential
to the establishment of our self. Such responses may, of course, also be challenges,
in which case a new program is aroused. This intimate linkage of the self and
clothing was masterfully caricatured by a forty-year-old carpenter's wife who was
herself working in a local factory. Our guess is that a few bottles of beer were
conducive to the spontaneous flow of words, but their import is none the less striking. The woman had interpreted a modified TAT scene as a religious depiction,
and the interviewer asked her, after the completion of the stories, which card she
liked best:

> [Interviewer: Of those three, which did you like best? . . . Oh, that is kinda hard
> for me to do. I like them all. This one here is good, and that one is good, and that
> one is good. I think, of course, religion should come first, but I still think this is
> first right here—of her trying to help this girl. [The card depicts a well-dressed
> woman talking with another woman in rather drab masculine dress.] Looks to me
> like she is just telling her what she should do and how she should dress. Don't
> look very nice. I think that has a lot to do with a person's life afterwards. If they
> can get straightened out on their personal appearance, they can get straightened out
> in their religion a lot quicker. You take personal appearance; goes with their minds.
> Their mind has to work to go with that. They get that straightened out; I think

they can go back to religion and get that straightened out. I don't go to church now, but I used to be, and I am still, and always will be, regardless of what it is I ever do. I smoke a cigarette, drink a bottle of beer. I'm not Catholic. I'm Protestant. Church is my first thing. But this [informant hits the picture] comes first, before church. I don't care what anybody says. Clothes, our personal appearance, and getting our minds settled is how we should do. Some people don't believe that, but I do, 'cause you can go into a church and worship, but that ain't all that makes a go of this world. You have got to have something beside that. I don't care how much you worship. People can laugh at you. When you go into a church, they laugh at a girl dressed like this girl is or this woman is. They'll think she is not all there. But, if she gets herself fixed up, and looks nice, and goes to church like this picture here, they'll think she knows what she's talking about. I've seen too much of that. In other words, *clothes, personal appearance, can make one's life*. [Said slowly, deliberately, with much emphasis.] There is something about it that gives you courage. Some people would call it false courage, but I wouldn't. . . . I think anyone has to have a certain amount of clothes to give them courage. It ain't false courage either or false pride. It's just it. . . . Suppose it was just like it was when I went to that banquet tonight. Everybody told me how nice I looked, but I didn't think so. I had to feel right. . . . when I get the dress I feel right in, I feel like a million dollars. It makes an altogether different person out of me. That's an awful thing to say, but that's true for me.

Similar, but less dramatic, remarks abound in our interview materials. All point to the undeniable and intimate linkage of self and appearance. As a matter of fact, the analysis we have made permits a suggested modification of perhaps the best definition of the self in the social-psychological literature. Lindesmith and Strauss

    . . . think of the self as: (1) a set of more or less consistent and stable responses on a conceptual level, which (2) exercise a regulatory function over other responses of the same organism at lower levels (10, p. 416).

Dispensing with the notion of levels of behavior, which seems unnecessarily misleading (surely the self exercises a regulatory function over discourse—a set of conceptual responses!), we suggest the following definition: *the self is any validated program which exercises a regulatory function over other responses of the same organism, including the formulation of other programs*. What this definition does is spell out the regulatory responses—that is, one's announcements, shows, expressions, or proposals—while linking their consistency to the consensual validations of others. Such selves are established in significant appearances which provide the foundations of significant discourse and which, of course, may be played back upon and altered as the discourse transpires.

Appearance and the Early Emergence of the Self

In explaining the emergence of the self, George H. Mead discusses at length the two stages of "play" and the "game." Prior to entering the stage of play, however, the child must have acquired a rudimentary language at least. We will call this early stage of rudimentary communication "pre-play." For Mead, the emergence of the self in society is inextricably linked to the expansion and consolidation of personal communication as the child participates in and successively generalizes an ever widening universe of discourse—that set of social relations that is mobilized by the symbols the child acquires. We may infer that the type of discourse changes in the different stages of the emergence of the self and shall suggest some possibilities. We shall demonstrate, however, the changing character of appearance in these stages. In particular, we will note how these changing appearances hinder or facilitate the establishment of sexual identity or gender for the child.

PRE-PLAY, INVESTITURE, AND THE UBIQUITOUS MOTHER

It is very difficult to establish in any verifiable way how the child acquires its earliest significant symbols, whether they be gestures or words, because the investigator cannot enter into the rudimentary "prototaxic" communication of the infant. At best, he can observe, make inferences, and check those inferences out against the inferences of family members.

It seems to be the case, however, that some "initiative" is required from the child in this early learning process. Cooley, for example, observed that parents imitate the noises and sounds of their very young children in greater degree than those children imitate the noises and sounds of parents (3, p. 25). These observations have since received further empirical support (12, p. 41). Apparently this phenomenon of "parental imitation" or, more accurately, parental re-presentation is usually linked with the infant's babbling. Through babbling, the child hits upon a word-like sound (often "ma-ma"). This sound is then re-presented to the child as a word, together with the appropriate behavior that is the meaning of the word. Through repetition, the child takes over the response pattern it calls out in the adult, and the sound consequently becomes a significant symbol within the domestic universe of discourse.[10]

Another hypothesis seeking to explain the infant's earliest entrance into communication has been proposed by I. Latif.[11] Initially, the presumed discomfort of the infant is "communicated" by a gross writhing and wriggling of the whole body, setting up a series of responses in the parental person—feeding, cuddling, diaper-changing, and so on. Over time these parental responses become differentiated out as the gross movement of the child is progressively curtailed. Ultimately, the mere beginning of movement can elicit the appropriate parental response. Significant gestures have been established.

The point in all of this is that the child enters discursive communication by, in a sense, "initiating" activity construed as symbolic by parental persons and established as meaningful by their persistent cooperative response. In contrast, the appearance of the infant is imposed. The diaper folded in front *invests* the child with masculinity; in back, with femininity. Or dressing the child in blue invests the child with masculinity; in pink, with femininity. In this way, the responses of the world toward the child are differentially mobilized. The world handles the pink-clad child and the blue-clad child differently. The pink-clad child is *identified* differently. It is "darling," "beautiful," "sweet," or "graceful"; the blue-clad child is "handsome," "strong," or "agile." At a very early age the investiture of the child provides the materials out of which the reflected sexual identity and its

---

[10] There is further probative support for this hypothesis in the research of Omar K. Moore at Yale University, where he is teaching two-and-a-half year old children to read and write. The child is first encouraged to "play" at an IBM typewriter—akin to babbling. An adult responds to the play by re-presenting the letter sound. Eventually the child takes over this response pattern of the adult and "learns" the letters of the keyboard. On this point, see the preceding article by Harry Stack Sullivan, "The Self as Concept and Illusion," in this volume.

[11] Discussed in Lindesmith and Strauss (10, p. 166).

qualifications are formed. And in America the process of investiture is accomplished overwhelmingly by the mother.

One hundred and eighty-five of our informants were asked, "What is the earliest recollection you have of being made to wear particular clothes?" Then we asked, "Who made you wear them?" One hundred and twenty-six provided determinate answers to the question. Of these, 82 per cent named the mother as the "instrument of coercion"; 10 per cent named both parents. For more than 90 per cent of those recalling coercive investitures, the mother was recalled as the agent, usually the sole agent. There were no sex differences in these recollections. She was the sole agent for 83 per cent of the men and for 81 per cent of the women. She acted in conjunction with the father for 13 per cent of the men and for 8 per cent of the women.

It is sociologically significant, of course, that the prime agent of investiture for the men of this Midwestern community was a woman, and no matter how much we might be inclined to disparage Geoffrey Gorer's study of "the American people," these data do suggest that Gorer's "encapsulated mother hypothesis" has some basis in fact (8, pp. 55–68, 124–132).

Because of the ubiquity of the American mother as the prime agent of socialization for the child, it will be recalled, Gorer maintained that the "superego" of the American male was characterized by a significant feminine component manifested in extraordinary anxiety about and fear of homosexuality. We need not accept the entire line of analysis when we recognize, first, that the "significant other" for the male child in our sample has been almost unanimously recalled as the "significant mother," and, second, that the adequate early formulation of a sexual identity may have been impeded among men. Indeed, it may not be a "homosexual anxiety" that typifies American men as much as a generalized "sexual anxiety." If he is represented at all by the men of this Midwestern community, the American male may have found it difficult very early in life to establish who he was in sexual terms. Consequently, an adequate basis in which to "ground" subsequent announcements of maleness may not have been provided. As very young children, most of these men were invested with a program of appearance fashioned exclusively by women. This investiture process persisted beyond infancy, even, in some cases, into relatively late childhood. Their first reflected glimpse of themselves was provided by the eyes of a woman—a woman who, in fact, saw many of those men as girls. Some were dressed as little girls.

A fifty-three year old postal clerk provided a vivid recollection of the early stages in the life cycle as they were represented by dress:

> I can remember back in the South, forty-five years ago, the children—boys—always wore dresses up to the time they were three or four years old. When I was about five, six, seven, or eight, they wore those little Fauntleroy suits. God damn! I hated those. Then knickers came. I wore those until I was about fifteen year old. I was fifteen and a half when I had my first long pants suit.

A sixty-three year old carpenter, born on a Midwestern farm, suggests that the earliest dress of little boys was not restricted to Southern regions:

> Just one thing that always stood out in my mind. I wore dresses until I was six years old, and, as I remember, they were the Mother Hubbard type.

Knee pants, of course, were much more frequently recalled by the men in the sample as early garments in which they were forcibly dressed by the mother, and

these were often interpreted as feminine representations. Asked to state his earliest memory of being forced to wear particular clothing, a twenty-seven year old
oven-tender replied,

> Knee pants. [Interviewer: Who made you wear them?] Mother.
> [Interviewer: How did you feel about that?] I just felt like a girl in them. They
> reminded me so much of a dress.

The revulsion against being a "sissy," recalled by many of the male informants
in the sample, was generally remembered in the context of investiture in short
pants or "fussy" clothing. Again, the investiture was accomplished by the mother,
whose decision they could not appeal.

Investiture takes on even greater significance for the interpretation of the meaning that clothing has for men in our society when we recall our earlier remarks
about the establishment of identity. Identity, as it has been apprehended here, is
only established in the collective or transactive process of announcement and
placement. The knowing of gender is, as we have said, known silently. To appear
in the dress of either sex is to announce one's gender, and the apparent announcement is seldom questioned. The gender is confirmed by ratifying placements.
Dressed as someone he is not, by a ubiquitous mother, in clothing that is employed
arbitrarily by his peers (and himself) to establish who he is, the American male
may, indeed, have been disadvantaged very early with respect to the formulation
of a sense of sexual identity. Advantages, rather, accrued to the female, who from
the earliest age was dressed as she was by a mother from whose perspective she
was provided with an adequate conception of herself in sexual terms.[12]

PLAY, COSTUME, AND DRESSING OUT

In his discussions of the development of the self (more exactly, the development of the "me"), George H. Mead does not concern himself so much with the
establishment of the self *by* others—the phenomenon of investiture—as with the
development of a self-conception *reflected* by the attitudes of others. Such attitudes or roles (Mead uses the terms interchangeably in his discussion of the self)
are at first acted out. By acting out the role of the other, the child develops a
conception of his own attitude or role as differentiated from and related to the
adopted role. The acting out of the other's role is caricatured by the play of the
child in which he amuses himself by acting out the role of the parents, the schoolteacher, the policeman, the cowboy, the Indian, the storekeeper, the customer, and
various other roles that constitute the institutional fabric and legendary *personae*
of the larger community or society. A mere consideration of these roles, incidentally, betrays the fact that at least two kinds of socialization go on in the stage of
play. First, there is a genuine *anticipatory socialization* in which the child acts
out roles that might quite realistically be expected to be adopted or encountered
in later life, such as parental roles, common occupations, or customer. Second,
there is a process of *fantastic socialization* in which the child acts out roles that
can seldom, if ever, be expected to be adopted or encountered in later life—cowboy and Indian, for example. This is a point to which we will return.

Now this phase of play in the development of the self cannot be accomplished

---

[12] There may be a generational problem involved, but we cannot consider that problem in this
place. We are speaking here of those who were adults by 1950, and whose childhoods occurred in the 1930's or earlier.

without costume. Acting out of role implies that one appear out of role. Play demands that the players leave themselves behind, so to speak. The players may do this symbolically by doffing their ordinary dress and donning extraordinary dress so that the play may proceed. Playing the role of the other requires that the player *dress out* of the role or roles that are acknowledged to be his own. Costume, therefore, is a kind of magical instrument. It includes all apparent misrepresentations of the wearer. As such its significance or meaning (the collective response that is mobilized—the coincidence of the wearer's program with the review of the other) is built upon the mutual trust of the one who appears and his audience. Collusion is required to carry off the misrepresentation: the parent, for example, cannot "really" insist that his child is, in fact, not a cowboy or a spaceman. Play is easily transformed into a vast conspiratorial secret, if it has not, in fact, begun secretly. As Huizinga has expressed it:

> The exceptional and special position of play is most tellingly illustrated by the fact that it loves to surround itself with an air of secrecy. Even in early childhood, the charm of play is enhanced by making a "secret" out of it. This is for *us*, not for the "others." . . . The "differentness" and secrecy of play are most vividly expressed in "dressing up." Here the "extraordinary" nature of play reaches perfection. The disguised or masked individual "plays" another part, another being. He *is* another being. The terrors of childhood, open-hearted gaiety, mystic fantasy and sacred awe are all inextricably entangled in this strange business of masks and disguises (9, pp. 12–13).

This element of secrecy would seem to imbue the play of children with sentiment —a nexus of value and mood—establishing for the child *involvements* with the identities that are appropriated in play in addition to the sheer objective *commitments* to such identities, emphasized by Mead. Making the point in another way, it may be that the consequence of childhood play, at least for some children, is not merely the formulation of the self as an object—an identity—differentiated from and related to the objects of play, but the establishment of the self as a sentiment —a base of "show" and expression—as Cooley insisted.

All respondents were asked, "When you were a child, did you ever dress up in anyone else's clothes?" Of the 180 replying to the question, 35 per cent disavowed dressing up in other people's clothing when they were children. The disavowal was predominately male. Fifty-nine per cent of the men replying to the question maintained that they had not dressed up in other people's clothing when they were children, and that figure compares to 14 per cent for the women responding to the question. Again, in a sense, the male child seems to have been "disadvantaged" in the phase of play. The clothing of the others in his earliest social world is not made available to him.

Indeed, one of the still striking features of childhood costume is the fact that boys' costumes are sold in considerably greater quantities than are girls' costumes.[13] Commercial costumes are generally more fantastic than the costumes available from the cast-off clothing of family members. The disavowals of the men do not mean, of course, that the men did not dress out when they were children, but that they did not dress out in clothing ordinarily worn by other people. Assuming that the "dressing out" of men, at least in the higher ranges of the status order, was facilitated by commercial costume and that the "dressing out" of

---

13 The assertion may be verified by telephoning the toy department in any large store. I have not yet found any exceptions to the rule.

women was facilitated by the ordinary dress of others, it may well be that the early conception of self established by men in the phase of play in this country and among the generations interviewed is, in fact, more fantastic than the early conception of self established by women, who can more often reflect upon their own appearance in the dress of and from the standpoint of others who are the *real* population of their social world. But this is a point for which we have no direct evidence.

Of course, the most striking difference between the sexes with respect to the costume of play is, as we have said, found among those who dressed up in other people's clothing at all when they were children. More than half of the men did not, as Table 3 shows, and more than 85 per cent of the women did. Those who did recall dressing up in other people's clothing when they were children were asked whose clothing was worn, and the responses were coded for the person standing in the most "objectively" intimate relationship to the informant. Table 3 shows that the parent of the same sex as the informant was the most frequently mentioned source of childhood costume in play.

TABLE 3   *The Most Intimate Sources of Costume Mentioned by Midwestern Men and Women in Their Recollections of Childhood Play*

Most Intimate Sources of Childhood Costume	Sex of Respondents				Totals	
	Male		Female			
	Number	*Per Cent*	*Number*	*Per Cent*	*Number*	*Per Cent*
None	50	58.8	13	13.7	63	35.0
Parent, same sex	13	15.3	48	50.5	61	33.9
Parent, opposite sex	2	2.4	—	0.0	2	1.1
Sibling, same sex	6	7.1	10	10.5	16	8.9
Sibling, opposite sex	2	2.4	2	2.1	4	2.2
Extended kin	5	5.9	8	8.4	13	7.2
Unrelated adults and peers	7	8.2	14	14.7	21	11.7
Totals	85	100.1	95	99.9	180	100.0

$\chi^2 = 43.791$ *   .05 > p < .001

* The last five rows were combined in the computation of the chi-square, which is for a sixfold table with two degrees of freedom. If the first row is eliminated from the analysis, and the chi-square computed for the second row and the combined remaining rows by sex, then $\chi^2 = 4.432$, and .05 > p > .02.

Yet the male is again "disadvantaged." Even if we exclude from the analysis those informants who could not recall dressing in other's clothing during childhood, men are still significantly underrepresented among those who dressed in the clothing of the father, and women are significantly overrepresented among those who dressed in the clothing of the mother. Childhood play was accomplished by donning the costume of the relevant adult female model—the mother—among the women of the sample, while many men were denied the costume of the relevant adult male model. Among the men who could recall dressing in other's clothing, brothers and extended kin acted as sources of costume in somewhat greater than expected proportions (as did sisters and mothers!—but the numbers there are very small), while, among the women making such recollections, the mother was the sole source of childhood costume noticeably overrepresented. Small wonder that we are tempted to generalize that the men of our sample had a difficult time developing an adequate conception of their sexual identity. The adult models were often not available to them.

It may well be that discourse takes on a characteristic form during the stage of play. For one thing, the speech of the child may be what Piaget has called "egocentric." (15) At least, the child enters the stage of play before his egocentric language dwindles to less than 25 per cent of his discursive communication as recorded by Piaget and his associates. At this point the child is capable of socialized speech. Piaget hypothesizes that this occurs around the age of 7 or 8. On the other hand, the discourse of play is highly suggestive of "parataxic" communication. Sullivan, incidentally, did not restrict the concept to the depiction of psychotic behavior:

> Now let us notice a feature of all interpersonal relations. . . . This is the parataxic, as I call it, concomitant in life. By this I mean that not only are there quite tangible people involved . . . , but also somewhat fantastic constructs of those people are involved. . . . These psychotic elaborations of imaginary people and imaginary performances are spectacular and seem very strange. But the fact is that in a great many relationships of the most commonplace kind—with neighbors, enemies, acquaintances, and even such statistically determined people as the collector and the mailman—variants of such distortions often exist. The characteristics of a person that would be agreed to by a large number of competent observers may not appear to you to be the characteristics of the person toward whom you are making adjustive or maladjustive movements. The *real* characteristics of the other fellow at that time may be of negligible importance to the interpersonal situation. This we call *parataxic distortion* (18, pp. 25–26).

Consider a typical instance of play. The father returns home from work, is ambushed at the door, and "shot" by the young cowboy. The transaction has no "meaning" within the *real* father–son relationship—some psychoanalysts to the contrary notwithstanding! Instead, father and son are "of negligible importance to the interpersonal situation." The "fantastic constructs" of cowboy and Indian or "good guy" and "bad guy" are the relevant personifications or identifications with reference to which the discursive meaning is established. Of course, as *father*, the adult enables the young actor to carry off the performance, imbuing the play, as we have said, with a secrecy shared by *father and son*, charging the play with affect or mood.

THE GAME, THE UNIFORM, AND DRESSING IN

While the costume of play may be construed as any apparent misrepresentation of the self, permitting the wearer to become another, the uniform is precisely any apparent representation of the self, at once reminding the wearer and others of an *appropriate* identity, a *real* identity. The team-player is uniformed; the play-actor is costumed. When we asked our informants their earliest recollections of wanting to wear any particular item of clothing, they responded almost unanimously by recalling their earliest self-conscious appropriations of the dress of their peer groups. In a sense, the earliest items of clothing they wanted comprised the *uniforms* of the peer circle.

Among the men who experienced the wish for particular items of clothing in late childhood, most were concerned with escaping the investitures of the mother. The tenor of their remarks conveyed the undesirability of the clothing they were forced to wear as mother's sons. Thereafter, beginning in early adolescence, their comments focused more and more on the desirability and necessity of conforming to the dress established by their peers or demanded by the dating situation. The women, on the other hand, were concerned from the earliest ages with the desirability of conforming to the dress of peers. Rather than rejecting their early identities as mother's daughters, they began generally to enter the "game of life" at an earlier age than men, and this was represented in part by their self-conscious wishes to don the uniform of their peer circles at earlier ages.

I do not regard these findings as surprising. Indeed, they have been discussed widely by sociologists and social psychologists. It is recognized that women "come of age" more rapidly than men in our society. My only intention here is to frame these data in the perspective of socialization as it concerns the early development of a self-concept in the stages proposed by Mead. Growing up is dressing in. It is signaled by the wish to dress like others who are, in turn, like one's self. The earlier representation of the self is formulated in play which is facilitated by costume. In play one does dress like others, but like others who are, in that case, unlike one's self.

In the stage of the "game," discourse undoubtedly takes on the character of developed speech—what Piaget called "socialized speech" or what Sullivan called "syntaxis." As the game is played, the person becomes an integral part of an ongoing universe of discourse in every sense. The early socialization has been effected; a self has emerged. These stages and processes have been summarized in Table 4.

LATER SOCIALIZATIONS

It may well be the uneasiness attending the American's view of play and the game that inclines him to relegate such matters to the social world of children and disinclines him to acknowledge their central importance in adulthood. However, especially when we employ these processes to caricature socialization, we should not ignore the fact that they occur throughout life. Life must be viewed as a continuous socialization, a series of careers, in which old identities are sacrificed as new identities are appropriated, in which old relations are left behind as new relations are joined. Each critical turning point of life is marked by a change of dress, and, ordinarily, the new upcoming "game" is rehearsed prior to the entry upon the appropriate field of play.

Such rehearsals may be looked upon as the play of the adult. Momentarily the self is misrepresented as the adult plays at the roles he expects to enact in a near future. Particularly for American men, these rehearsals differ from the play of children by virtue of their rather more "realistic" appropriateness. They are much more frequently genuine *anticipatory socializations*. The child plays many more roles than he will enact in later life, while the roles playfully rehearsed by the adult are generally those he firmly expects to enact later on. But his *fantastic socializations* are also different. More often than is the case for the child, they occur in private. In the bathroom, behind closed doors and before a secret mirror, the man may become for an instant a boxer, an Adonis, an operatic virtuoso. The fantastic play of the child occurs in public, usually in areas set aside by the adult community precisely for such fantastic performances. The fact that the play of the adult is more realistic or appropriate, or, if not, more private, does not gainsay its

TABLE 4 *Tentative Model for the Investigation of Processes of Discourse and Appearance in the Early Establishment of the Self*

Stages of Early Socialization	Discursive Processes	Types of Discourse	Apparent Processes	Types of Appearance
Pre-play	1. Parental representation of infant babbling as verbal symbols (Cooley, Markey) 2. Progressive curtailment of whole body movement by parental intervention (Latif)	Conversation of gestures (Mead) Prototaxis (Sullivan) Signal communication, or designation, as in "ma-ma"	Investiture	Representation as infant, young child, and gender
Play	Identification with discrete differentiated others as in role-playing (Mead) 1. Anticipatory socialization 2. Fantastic socialization	Egocentric speech (Piaget) Parataxis (Sullivan)	Dressing out	Misrepresentation of the self Costume
Game	Generalization and consolidation of other roles Taking the role of the "generalized other" or "team"	Socialized speech (Piaget) Syntaxis (Sullivan)	Dressing in	Representation of peer-group affiliation Uniform

significance. The rehearsal is often a dress rehearsal, and the more critical the turning point, the more likely the rehearsal is designed as a full dress affair—leaving school and entering the adult world of work, marriage, baptism, and the institutionalized recognition of death.

More realistic than adult play is the adult game. Indeed, we can conceive of life as a series of games—contests and engagements—that mark the progress of careers, culminating in losses and victories for the participants. Participation in the many "games" of life is, again, always represented by appropriate dress which assists the players in their identifications of one another and helps those on the sidelines—the spectators—to know, in fact, what game they are watching. However, these—the play and games of adults—are matters we must leave for a subsequent analysis in another place.

Summary

In this article, we have attempted to show the importance of appearance for any general theory of communication that is developed in the perspective of symbolic interaction. We have attempted to show also that the self is established, maintained, and altered in social transactions as much by the communication of appearances as by discourse. In this regard, by analyzing many statements evoked by clothed appearances, we have suggested a definition of the self that may have greater empirical utility than existing definitions. Finally, we have staked out the significance of appearance in the early socialization processes. In doing these things, our "real" goal will have been realized if we have encouraged one or two of our colleagues or future colleagues to look at the cloth on which, as Carlyle noted long ago, society may, in fact, be founded.

References

1. BECKER, HOWARD. "Empathy, Sympathy, and Scheler," *International Journal of Sociometry*, Vol. 1 (September 1956), pp. 15–22.
2. BURKE, KENNETH. *A Grammar of Motives*. Englewood Cliffs, N.J.: Prentice-Hall, Inc., 1945.
3. COOLEY, CHARLES H. *Human Nature and the Social Order*. New York: Charles Scribner's Sons, 1902.
4. FOOTE, NELSON N. "Identification as a Basis for a Theory of Motivation," *American Sociological Review*, Vol. 16 (February 1951), pp. 14–21.
5. FORM, WILLIAM H., and GREGORY P. STONE. *The Social Significance of Clothing in Occupational Life*. East Lansing, Mich.: Michigan State University Agricultural Experiment Station Technical Bulletin 262 (November 1957).
6. GOFFMAN, ERVING. "Symbols of Class Status," *British Journal of Sociology*, Vol. 2 (December 1951), pp. 294–304.
7. GOFFMAN, ERVING. *The Presentation of Self in Everyday Life*. Edinburgh: University of Edinburgh Social Science Research Centre Monograph, No. 2, 1956.
8. GORER, GEOFFREY. *The American People*. New York: W. W. Norton & Company, Inc., 1948.
9. HUIZINGA, JAN. *Homo Ludens: A Study of the Play-Element in Culture*. London: Routledge & Kegan Paul, Ltd., 1949.
10. LINDESMITH, ALFRED R., and ANSELM L. STRAUSS. *Social Psychology*. New York: The Dryden Press, 1956.
11. LYND, HELEN MERRELL. *On Shame and the Search for Identity*. New York: Harcourt, Brace and Co., 1958.
12. MARKEY, JOHN F. *The Symbolic Process and Its Integration in Children*. London: Kegan Paul, Trench, Trübner and Co., Ltd., 1928.
13. MEAD, GEORGE H. "Philanthropy from the Point of View of Ethics," in Ellsworth Faris, Ferris Laune, and Arthur J. Fodd (eds.), *Intelligent Philanthropy*. Chicago: The University of Chicago Press, 1930, pp. 133–148.
14. MEAD, GEORGE H. *Mind, Self, and Society*, ed. by Charles W. Morris. Chicago: The University of Chicago Press, 1934.
15. PIAGET, JEAN. *The Language and Thought of the Child*. New York: Meridian Books, 1955.
16. STONE, GREGORY P. "Clothing and Social Relations: A Study of Appearance in the Context of Community Life." Unpublished Ph.D. dissertation, Department of Sociology, University of Chicago, 1959.
17. STRYKER, SHELDON. "Relationships of Married Offspring and Parent: A Test of Mead's Theory," *American Journal of Sociology*, Vol. 62 (November 1956), pp. 308–319.
18. SULLIVAN, HARRY STACK. *The Psychiatric Interview*. New York: W. W. Norton & Company, Inc., 1954.
19. VEBLEN, THORSTEIN. *The Theory of the Leisure Class*. New York: Modern Library, Inc., 1934.

PART SEVEN*

TESTS OF THE PERSPECTIVE

The papers in the following section represent conventional tests of the interaction-ist perspective, in the sense that a variation on the survey method is employed to sound out certain of Mead's key assumptions concerning the self and the significant other. Kuhn's study employs the now famous Twenty Statements Test (TST) to investigate the hypothesis that the self represents a series of attitudes or plans of action the person holds toward himself as a social object. The Quarantelli and Cooper study replicates and extends the earlier research by Miyamoto and Dorn-busch, which suggests that the impact of the significant other on one's self-conception is directly related to one's conception of how the other views him. In effect, we can view the three investigations as building directly on one another, while each derives fundamentally from Mead's view of the self in interaction.

Given this interpretation, what do these studies suggest about the Meadian perspective? And further, what can we say about the use of survey methodology to test interactionist hypotheses?

Kuhn's study points to the necessity of developing a personality test that allows the subject to express his conception of self without prompting or suggestion. His simple test, which asks the respondent to answer the question "Who am I?", achieves precisely this purpose. His earlier studies indicated that the range of self-definitions elicited by this question could be coded into five categories that combined Linton's status-role conception of society with Cooley's hypothesis that the self-concept consists, in part, of self-evaluations. Kuhn's study (reprinted in this section) suggests that as the individual moves through the life cycle of alternative status-role arrangements, his self-conceptions change to reflect these social

---

*Introduction prepared especially for this volume by Norman K. Denzin.

settings. On one level, Kuhn's study supports Mead's hypothesis that the self reflects the social relationships and activities the individual is presently engaged in. On another, it points to the fact that as man moves into a social world in which work arrangements become salient, work itself becomes embedded in the self-concept.

Methodologically, Kuhn's technique represents one of the now classic measures of the self. However, while the TST permits the subject to give his own definitions, it is less than adequate because the self presented is treated as a relatively stable set of attitudes free from situational specification. Further, the temporal-processual features of the self are not reflected in this method. Unless a panel design, with its repeated measures on the same sample of selves, is employed, the test does not measure the self as a set of tentative attitudes that are being continually redefined, tested, and validated.

Miyamoto and Dornbusch provide an alternative approach to the study of the self, since subjects were told to rate their self-concept along the dimensions of intelligence, attractiveness, self-confidence, physical attractiveness, and likableness. Having made these ratings, which only abstrusely bear any resemblance to a traditional interactionist conception of the self, subjects then rated their significant others' (collectively and individually) conception of them along the same dimensions, and significant others made the same ratings on the subjects. This design permitted the investigators to measure the extent of self-other agreement on the self-concept of the focal subjects. Unfortunately, no effort was made to determine whether the others who made the ratings were significant to the subject. Still, partial confirmation was obtained for the hypothesis that there is greater agreement between one's own conception of self and one's perception of others' evaluations than between one's own conception and the actual attitude of others. In addition, this study suggested that persons can more accurately take the role of a generalized other than they can of a specific other—a fact that deserves greater attention in future investigations.

This investigation is extended and replicated by Quarantelli and Cooper, and again confirmation is found for the general hypothesis. However, the latter study is far superior to that of either Kuhn or Miyamoto and Dornbusch, for an attempt is made here to measure the self with the same subjects over a period of time. In addition, role-specific significant others were asked to rate the focal subjects on the same self-concept dimensions. In consequence, a more direct effort at measuring the impact of the other was achieved, since the authors attempted to deduce the total possible range of others that might influence the subject (for example, faculty, classmates, upperclassmen, non-dental school friends, parents, and wives). Given these methodological refinements, Quarantelli and Cooper observe that, over a period of time, the subject's conception of self is more closely linked to "how he thinks" the other feels about him, than to how the other actually regards him.

Taken together, the three investigations indicate that Mead's hypothesis concerning the relationship between the self and its others is valid. Further, it is shown that, with progression through the age cycle, self-conception changes in response to the roles played and the situations confronted. Still, the interactionist must be left with a certain degree of uneasiness regarding these investigations. First, of course, these investigations rely on only one method—the survey—which, as Denzin suggests, is ill-equipped to measure process. Thus, any inference concerning the self as a fluid interactive structure must be made cautiously from these studies. Even Quarantelli and Cooper must be criticized in this respect, as, at best, their measurement of the self over time was a gross one. Second, we find little attempt to investigate taking roles of others or to study the world of self through others' eyes. Kuhn is least prone to this flaw, but we have seen that the TST lacks the situational and temporal specifications necessary to measure the self as a processual set of attitudes. To present the subject categorically with a list of others (after the fashion of Miyamoto and Dornbusch, and Quarantelli and Cooper) neglects the fact that the subject may be carrying on his most crucial interactions with an other who does not, or has never, existed in a co-present interactional sense. Further, to say that the self-concept of a dental student only involves a view of how much one is a dentist at the present time does not capture the complex nature of what it means to view oneself as a *special* dentist with unique qualities and characteristics. Third, there is no attempt to employ a naturalistic methodology that would link man's symbols to his interactions. All these studies demonstrate is some degree of correspondence between one's attitudes and the attitudes one attributes to others—surely we can expect some degree of agreement in this respect. But an interactionist should demand more. He must show that, as man's symbolic constructions change, so do his patterns of interaction. In addition, he must establish the link between man's symbols and the social groups that furnish him with those symbols. In this respect, he can certainly achieve better predictions by allowing his subjects to designate who their significant others are.

An additional confounding error in these investigations is the failure to consider the situated aspects of self and the impact of others. When a respondent is asked to make a self-reference, or to determine the impact of another upon his self, he does so by "situating" that other in a specific time-space locale. That setting may be his home, a local bar, his office, a classroom, or any other of a wide range of interactive settings. The failure to reflect this situated aspect of interactional conduct neglects a fundamental feature of self-conversations with interiorized others and, as such, does not allow us to achieve the kinds of precision Mead's theory specifies.

Denzin's paper offers a set of methodological and theoretical conditions an interactionist methodology must meet. These conditions require a serious re-examination of validity, especially with regard to whether our methods allow us to take the role of the acting other. Moreover, any method must be assessed in terms of its ability to reflect process versus structure through time and across situations. The proper methodology thus becomes one that employs sensitizing concept analysis in conjunction with an attempt to formulate interactive propositions. On nearly all of these counts the empirical investigations reported in this section are weak. The self has not been viewed processually; respondents were not permitted to list their own significant others; and in no case were interactive propositions formulated to describe the fluid nature of self-other interactions.

We are left, then, with a series of unanswered questions that conventional tests of the interactionist perspective are ill-equipped to answer. Process is forsaken for structure, situations are ignored, and significant others are plucked from the imaginations of the investigator. We can conclude only that tests of the interactionist framework that rely on survey methods will, at best, contribute indirectly to the methodological and theoretical refinements of the theory.

Still unanswered are such critical questions as how the self develops and changes over time, how significant others reflect on self-conduct, how situations impinge on ongoing interactions. In short, conventional tests of the perspective at best will capture only the stable, nonreflective aspects of human interaction. What we need are imaginative tests of the perspective that meet our standard criteria of validity, while remaining true to the theory. We need naturalistic methodologies and investigations that capture the complex interpretive elements of human interaction.

Suggested Readings

BLUMER, HERBERT. *An Appraisal of Thomas and Znaniecki's "The Polish Peasant in Europe and America."* New York: Social Science Research Council, Bulletin 44, 1939.

COHEN, MORRIS R. *A Preface to Logic.* New York: Meridian Books, 1956.

DENZIN, NORMAN K. *The Substance of Sociological Theory and Method: An Interactionist Interpretation.* Chicago: Aldine, 1969.

GLASER, BARNEY, and ANSELM L. STRAUSS. *The Discovery of Grounded Theory.* Chicago: Aldine, 1967.

KAPLAN, ABRAHAM. *The Conduct of Inquiry.* San Francisco: Chandler Publishing Co., 1964.

MILLS, C. WRIGHT. *The Sociological Imagination.* New York: Oxford University Press, 1959.

ROSENTHAL, ROBERT. *Experimenter Effects in Behavioral Research.* New York: Appleton-Century-Crofts, 1966.

WEBB, EUGENE, *et al. Unobstrusive Measures: Nonreactive Research in the Social Sciences.* Chicago: Rand-McNally, 1966.

44   A Test of Interactionist Hypotheses of Self-Conception

● S. FRANK MIYAMOTO AND SANFORD M. DORNBUSCH

George Herbert Mead constitutes something of a paradox for modern sociology. His works have been widely acclaimed for their fundamental importance to social-psychological and sociological theory. On the other hand, Mead's admirers have often encountered considerable difficulty in formulating research problems within the framework of his views. True, during the last decade initial advances have been made in the empirical study of roles, role-taking, and role conflicts; however, the notions of self and self-conception—two additional key concepts in his system and the system of Cooley and others within this tradition—remain among the neglected problems of social psychology to which Leonard Cottrell referred.[1]

The aim of this paper is an empirical study of certain basic assumptions in the interactionist view of the self and self-conception. Essentially dynamic, the interactionist theory of the self is not easily translated into research operations. This paper does not study the ongoing process but concentrates instead on static consequences which can reasonably be deduced from Mead. The method here employed is too crude for investigating subtle aspects of Mead's theory, but improvements and refinements of the method are possible. Moreover, many interesting lines of inquiry into the self can be pursued with the method, such as it is.

Our concern is three problems suggested by the interactionist view of the self. First, a basic contribution of Mead and Cooley to the understanding of the self and self-conception lay in their emphasis upon the influence of the responses of others in shaping self-definitions. This principle, once recognized, may appear so self-evident as not to require empirical confirmation. However, it seems of interest to consider any empirical test which will confirm or deny the generalization. Second, although it is Mead's habit to speak of "the response of the other" as providing the key to the definition of the self,[2] the phrase is somewhat ambiguous, for a distinction may be drawn between (a) the actual response of the other and (b) the subject's perception of the response of the other. Mead often does not distinguish between these two; but it is consistent with his view that the perception

SOURCE: S. Frank Miyamoto and Sanford M. Dornbusch, in the *American Journal of Sociology,* LXI (March 1956), pp. 399–403. Reprinted by permission of The University of Chicago Press. This paper reports part of the findings from a study of interpersonal perception, supported by the Agnes Anderson Fund, the Faculty Research Fund of the Graduate School of the University of Washington, and the Center for Advanced Study in the Behavioral Sciences. We are indebted to the following persons who were consulted at various stages of the research project: Charles E. Bowerman, S. Francis Camilleri, Samuel A. Stouffer, Robert E. L. Faris, William H. Sewell, Albert Hastorf, Stephen Richardson, David Gold, and Howard S. Becker. Statistical assistance was provided by Mrs. Joan Carlson, Elizabeth Johnson, John B. Hudson, Gerald Day, and Donald L. Garrity.

[1] Leonard S. Cottrell, Jr., "Some Neglected Problems in Social Psychology," *American Sociological Review,* XV (December, 1950), pp. 708–11. Reprinted in Part One of this volume.
[2] G. H. Mead, *Mind, Self, and Society* (Chicago: University of Chicago Press, 1934), pp. 144–49.

of the other's response is the critical aspect. Will an empirical test support this assumption?

Finally, one of Mead's most illuminating analyses is his account of how the self may take the role of the generalized other. The "generalized other" refers to the individual's conception of the organized social process of which he is a part.[3] This organized social process is composed of numerous specialized roles, and the individual identifies his own role in it and so fulfils his part as to enable the organized process to continue. On the other hand, individuals often enter into social relations wherein the organization of roles is obscure or minimal. In such a case, the individual cannot take the role of the generalized other in Mead's sense; yet, for the individual to act in the situation, some conception of the generalized other may be necessary. What kind of conception of self and others may be employed under these circumstances?

In our research we used social groups whose members were, at best, loosely joined by friendship and had no definite organized group activity within which to identify their respective roles. They were engaged as individuals, at the moment, in making emphatic judgments about one another. It seemed reasonable to assume that the individual might be able to define—and would, in fact, use—a self-conception based on the *typical* attitudes of others toward him. Hence the third problem concerns the relation of self-conceptions to the perception of the typical attitudes of others toward one's self.

Method

Index of self-conception—In recent years, due mainly to the renewed interest of psychologists in the study of the self, a number of methods have been developed for getting self-evaluations from experimental subjects. In one, subjects are requested to give self-characterizations by means of one of the following devices: checking appropriate words on an adjective check list of self-descriptive terms,[4] responding to a standard personality inventory or to some other form of questionnaire that yields self-revealing responses,[5] or writing out self-evaluative autobiographical sketches.[6] These techniques are designed to reveal the content of individual self-conceptions.

A second method requires subjects to indicate their expected score on some test prior to taking the test—usually an aptitude or attitude scale—thus providing a picture of how an individual evaluates himself.[7] Here the unique feature is the objective measure of performance or attitude against which the individual's expectation (self-conception) may be compared.

A third approach that combines features of the previous two requires subjects in a group of limited size to rate themselves on specified personal characteristics, relative to the others. For example, in a study by Calvin and Holtzman, members

---

[3] *Ibid.*, pp. 152–64.

[4] Theodore R. Sarbin, "Role Theory," in *Handbook of Social Psychology*, ed. Gardner Lindzey (Reading, Mass.: Addison-Wesley Publishing Co., 1954), I, 244.

[5] Ely S. Chertok, work in progress for Ph.D. dissertation in department of sociology, University of Washington.

[6] For an interesting variation on the autobiographical method see the W–A–Y technique of J. F. T. Bugental and S. L. Zelen, "Investigation into the Self-concept," *Journal of Personality,* XVIII (1950), 483–98.

[7] E. Paul Torrance, "Rationalizations about Test Performance as a Function of Self-concepts," *Journal of Social Psychology,* XXXIX (1954), 211–17; see also Theodore M. Newcomb, *Personality and Social Change* (New York: Dryden Press, 1943).

of fraternity groups (about twenty members each) ranked all group members, including themselves, on characteristics such as leadership, adjustment, tolerance, drive, and so on.[8] Not only was it possible to use the individuals' self-rankings as a measure of self-concept, but, because each member was rated by all others in the group, it was also possible to derive an average of the others' ratings against which the self-concept could be compared.

For the purpose of investigating interactionist hypotheses of the self, the latter provides the most satisfactory method. In the present study the index of self-conception was derived in the course of investigating a different problem, namely, the measuring of empathic ability, by means of an adaptation of a method developed by Rosalind Dymond and Leonard Cottrell.[9] The Dymond-Cottrell method requires subjects in a group to give self-ratings as well as ratings on every other group member on a short list of specified personal characteristics.

Source of data—Our data were gathered from 195 subjects in ten groups ranging in size from 8 to 48 persons. Four groups, totaling 63 subjects, consisted of volunteering members of two fraternities and two sororities. Each member had lived in his own club's house for at least three months. The other six groups, totaling 132 subjects, were classes in sociology, almost all class members of which participated in the study.

Definition of variables—For convenience in identifying the four variables in this study, labels have been adopted and given specific meanings. Our terminology implies no more than is stated in our definitions.

1. "Self-conception": Each subject was asked to rate himself on a five-point scale for each of the following four characteristics: intelligence, self-confidence, physical attractiveness, and likableness. Subjects were told that the middle of the scale should be regarded as "average for *this* group." The analysis for each characteristic is separate, no summing operations being performed in the four ratings.

2. "Actual response of others": Each member of a group rated every other member of the group on the same four characteristics, using the five-point scale. The mean response to each subject was computed for each of the four characteristics.

The response of others as here defined does not correspond exactly with Mead's meaning of the term; he obviously refers to responses made in direct interpersonal relations, while our reference is to responses on a paper-and-pencil rating scale. It seems reasonable to assume, however, that the rating-scale response would tend to be a condensed symbolic version of real-life responses and that the two would correspond sufficiently for the purposes of this investigation. Mead himself often spoke of "the attitude of the other" interchangeably with the term "the role of the other."

3. "Perceived response of others": Each member of a group predicted how every other member would rate him on the scale. The mean prediction of each subject was found for each of the four characteristics.

4. "The generalized other": Each subject was asked to state, using the same scale, how he perceived *most* persons as viewing him. The specific question was: "How intelligent (self-confident, physically attractive, likable) do most people think you are?"

---

[8] A. D. Calvin and Wayne H. Holtzman, "Adjustment and the Discrepancy between Self-concept and the Inferred Self," *Journal of Consulting Psychology*, XVII (1953), pp. 39–44.
[9] Rosalind F. Dymond, "A Scale for the Measurement of Empathic Ability," *Journal of Consulting Psychology*, XIII (1949), pp. 127–33.

Method of analysis—As in most studies of personal perception, good sampling was not easily achieved. Our sample was larger and more varied than those in most studies of this type, but our findings may not be reliable. Furthermore, data obtained as ours were, are not sufficiently sensitive to allow refined analyses. Because of these limitations in the design, we set restrictions upon our analysis.

First, since the groups are not a random sample from any known universe, statistical tests of significance are not employed, and the data are examined only for consistent tendencies from group to group. Second, we rely for our test upon inspection of gross differences. For each group, on each of the four characteristics, we determine whether the data support or do not support a specific hypothesis. Thus the ten groups and four characteristics yield forty results. If a hypothesis is supported forty times in the forty possible tests, we regard it as receiving perfect support; if the score is only twenty supporting tests out of the possible forty, the hypothesis is regarded as having no more than chance success.

The Findings

Hypothesis 1—According to the interactionist view, the self-conceptions of most persons are likely to be determined by internalization of the behavior of others toward them. If so, those accorded high esteem by others should reflect a higher self-esteem than those poorly regarded. Stating this in the form of a testable hypothesis: *The mean of the actual responses of others to the subject will be higher for those persons with a high self-rating than for those with a low self-rating.* Sorting each group into high and low self-raters and comparing the means of the "actual responses of others" toward the subjects in each subclass, we get the results given in Table 1.

TABLE 1

Characteristic	Hypothesis Supported	Hypothesis Not Supported	Tie
Intelligence	9	0	1
Self-confidence	8	2	0
Physical attractiveness	9	1	0
Likableness	9	1	0
Total	35	4	1

Analysis of the ten groups for all characteristics taken together shows that the hypothesis is supported ten out of ten times.

Hypothesis 2—Earlier it was suggested that it is of interest to evaluate separately the effect on self-conception of the "actual response of other" and the "perceived response of others." As a first step in this analysis, the same procedure applied in the previous test to the "actual responses" may be applied to the "perceived responses." Again, after the high and low self-raters have been sorted, the hypothesis now reads, *The mean of the perceived responses of others will be higher for those persons with a high self-rating than for those with a low self-rating.* The results are shown in Table 2. Ten out of ten groups showed differences in the expected direction.

Hypothesis 3—The next question is the relative effect on self-conception of the perceived response of others as compared to the effect of their actual responses.

TABLE 2

Characteristic	Hypothesis Supported	Hypothesis Not Supported	Tie
Intelligence	10	0	0
Self-confidence	10	0	0
Physical attractiveness	10	0	0
Likableness	10	0	0
Total	40	0	0

Social-psychological theory leads us to believe that the perceived behavior of others toward the self has a more direct influence than their actual behavior. Hence the hypothesis: *Self-conception tends to be closer to the mean perceived response of others to the subject than to the mean actual response of others.* The findings are summarized in Table 3. Of the ten groups, nine showed a tendency to support

TABLE 3

Characteristic	Hypothesis Supported	Hypothesis Not Supported	Tie
Intelligence	8	2	0
Self-confidence	9	0	1
Physical attractiveness	10	0	0
Likableness	7	3	0
Total	34	5	1

the hypothesis, with one class of eleven persons indeterminate, confirming the hypothesis for two characteristics and not confirming for the other two.

Hypothesis 4—It will be remembered that the index of the generalized other was determined by asking each subject, "How intelligent (etc.) do most people think you are?" In effect, the question which was used in testing Hypothesis 2, with respect to specific individuals in a specific group, was broadened to include all other social contacts of our subjects. Hence it is reasonable to assume that the line of thinking employed in developing the earlier hypothesis should apply here. Again using high and low self-raters to provide subclasses with differential self-conception, the following hypothesis is investigated: *Those persons who have high self-ratings on a characteristic will have a higher mean perception of the generalized other than will those with low self-ratings* (Table 4). Once again, all ten groups showed differences as anticipated.

Hypothesis 5—In rating the "perceived responses of others," the subjects considered only those other persons present in the test group. However, self-

TABLE 4

Characteristic	Hypothesis Supported	Hypothesis Not Supported	Tie
Intelligence	9	0	1
Self-confidence	9	1	0
Physical attractiveness	10	0	0
Likableness	10	0	0
Total	38	1	1

conception emerges from interaction in divergent groups. Therefore, it should more closely reflect the way most persons are perceived as viewing the subject than the perception of the responses of any particular group of individuals to the subject. *Accordingly, self-conception should correspond more closely with the generalized other than with the mean of the perceived responses of others.* The results are shown in Table 5. The hypothesis is confirmed for thirty-five out of

TABLE 5

Characteristic	Hypothesis Supported	Hypothesis Not Supported	Tie
Intelligence	10	0	0
Self-confidence	5	4	1
Physical attractiveness	10	0	0
Likableness	10	0	0
Total	35	4	1

forty comparisons. Only for self-confidence is there any tendency to show marked deviations from the expected direction. Analysis of the ten groups shows all ten tending to confirm the hypothesis. A deficiency of the test of Hypothesis 5 is that both self-conception and generalized other are discrete variables, while mean perception is continuous. Essentially, the results show that self-conception and generalized other are usually given the identical rating.

Summary

The results of this research lend empirical support to the symbolic interactionist view of self-conception. Our findings indicate that the response, or at least the attitude, of others is related to self-conception; but they also indicate that the subject's perception of that response is even more closely related. We also find that an individual's self-conception is more closely related to his estimate of the generalized attitude toward him than to the perceived attitude of response of members of a particular group.

These empirical findings do little more than reinforce fundamental notions contained in the interactionist theory of self-conception. Beyond that, however, they suggest possibilities in studying self-conception within the symbolic interactionist framework.

45   Self-Attitudes by Age, Sex, and Professional Training

● MANFORD H. KUHN

Most personality tests consist of several subscales which attempt to cover either the range of areas of adjustment or the varieties of mental-emotional disturbance. Thus the California Test of Personality is composed of two major parts—a test of self-adjustment and one of social adjustment. Each of these is composed of six

SOURCE: Manford H. Kuhn, in the *Sociological Quarterly*, I (January 1960), pp. 39–55.

subsections, the former subsuming Self-Reliance, Sense of Personal Worth, Sense of Personal Freedom, Feeling of Belonging, Withdrawing Tendencies, and Nervous Symptoms: the latter subsuming Social Standards, Social Skills, Anti-Social Tendencies, Family Relations, School Relations, and Community Relations. The respondent simply checks a "yes" or "no" to such questions (*i.e.*, items, of which there are fifteen for each subsection) as "Do you usually do something about it if someone steps in front of you in line?" "Do members of the opposite sex seem to like you?" "Are people frequently so unkind or unfair to you that you feel like crying?" "Do you keep from letting people know when they irritate you?" etc.

The Minnesota Multiphasic Personality Inventory, to take another example, consists of nine clinical scales, a measure of introversion, and four measures of what is called the "test-taking attitude." The 566 items are in the form of statements in the first person. The subject is asked to check "true" or "false" in terms of the application of each item to himself. These characteristics are doubtless familiar to everyone. They are mentioned here in order to highlight the contrasting nature of the Twenty Statements Test of Self-Attitudes.

The TST consists of simply asking the respondent to make twenty different statements in answer to the single question, "Who am I?" addressed to himself. Whatever statements the respondent makes become the items, and whatever scales are possible are those which emerge from a content classification of these items after they have been made.

In responding to this request, respondents tend to give, first, statements which are consensual in nature and which refer to groups and categories with which they feel identified and by which they are identified. Thomas McPartland and I have reported on this characteristic in an earlier article.[1] There we noted the regularity of this—a regularity that is such that it forms a Guttman scale. Furthermore we found that the size of this variable (we called it "locus") is significantly correlated with membership in different kinds of religious groups. It is one of my purposes in this paper to report on the differences in locus scores by age, sex, and professional training.

My major purpose, however, is to report on the range of areas covered by the responses to this test, and of course to make a report on whatever is presently available regarding differences in this range by the three social categories mentioned. In order to provide information of a systematic and inclusive sort, more than two hundred student protocols were content-analyzed by the method of successive combination into more general categories with the following results: five broad categories are sufficient to order *all* the responses made.

These five categories are the following: (1) *social groups and classifications* (such as age, sex, educational level, occupation, marital status, kin relations, socially defined physical characteristics, race, national origin, religious membership, political affiliation, formal and informal group memberships); (2) *ideological beliefs* (including statements of a religious, philosophical, or moral nature); (3) *interests* (including statements relating objects to the self, with either positive or negative affect); (4) *ambitions* (and all anticipated success themata); (5) *self-evaluations* (such as evaluations of mental and physical and other abilities, physique and appearance, relatedness to others, aspirations, persistence, industriousness, emotional balance, material resources, past achievements, habits of neatness,

---

[1] Manford H. Kuhn and Thomas S. McPartland, "An Empirical Investigation of Self Attitudes," *American Sociological Review*, 19:68–76 (1954).

orderliness, and the like, and more comprehensive self-typing in clinical or quasi-clinical terms.

Many of the protocols contain items covering most of the five categories of responses. A good example may be found in Exhibit 1. Others contain items from only one or two categories. Exhibits 2 and 3, for example, seem to specialize in self-derogation. Others, like the respondent whose protocol appears as Exhibit 4, give evidence of wishing to "leave the field" (Lewin).

EXHIBIT 1   *Responses of a University Senior*

I am of the female sex	I am in the Waves Officers School
My age is 20	I attend church
I am from [city and state]	I live a normal life
I have two parents	I am interested in sports
My home is happy	I am a [department] major
I am happy	I am attractive
I have been to 4 colleges	I have high moral standards
I will graduate in [month and year]	I am an adjusted person
I have a brother	I am of the middle class
I am a [sorority name]	

EXHIBIT 2   *Responses of a fourth grade girl. Original spelling retained*

I boss to much	I fidde around
I get mad a my sisters	I am careless at times
I am a show off	I forget
I interupt to much	Sometimes I don't do what mother tells
I talk to much	me to
I wast time	I tattle on my sisters
Sometimes I am a bad sport	Sometimes I am unkind

EXHIBIT 3   *Responses of a high-school senior boy*

I am a human being	thousands of other people
I am a person on this earth	I am just a small thing on earth
I am a nobody to thousands of people	I am a student
I am very small [in] proportion to the	I am a boy

EXHIBIT 4

I am a girl	I am going to take finals soon
I am [name]	I am disgusted with some people
I am an American	I am disgusted with [city]
I am Caucasoid	I am disgusted with the University
I am a student	I am a [department] major
I am going to graduate	I am aware of subtle pressure about me
I am going to work	I am tired of being tied to mother's apron
I am getting married	strings
I am under pressure	I am anxious to get married
I am anxious to get away from [state]	I am anxious to move far from here
I am of average intelligence	

EXHIBIT 5

I am a girl and I wish I were a boy	I am a bitter person at times
I am of an interracial marriage	I am someone trying to find a place in the
I am a senior in high school about to enter	world
college	I am a person fighting uniformity and de-
I am a member of a very independent group	pendence
of brothers and sisters	I am an admirer of beauty in all forms
I am living in a world of wonder and danger	I am not understood by myself
I am a person trying to find truth	I am a person who hates fundamentalism
I am a person finding truth	I am self-centered—I can tell by reaction to
I am a person finding truth not so delightful	situations I face
I am a person who is selfish	I am trying to understand myself and spend
I am a person who wants to "do" instead of	too much time at it
"be" in this world	I am self-conscious, wondering what you'll
I am a solemn person I've been told	make of my case when you read this

EXHIBIT 6   [Responses of a Senior High-School Student]

I am a nursing student	Resident of [county]
I am a [university] student	Resident of [township]
I am a graduate of [name] high school	A farmer's daughter
Daughter of ———	A resident of [dormitory]
Sister of ———	Member of [church choir]
Valedictorian of my high school class	Former president of [church fellowship]
A senior nursing student	Former judiciary chairman for [dormitory]
A senior nursing student in diploma plan	Member of [dormitory chorus]
U.S. citizen	Former member of [dormitory] Council
Member of Presbyterian Church	Member of [nurses' professional organization]

EXHIBIT 7   [Responses of a Male Graduate Student]

I am one who does not know if there is a god	I am one who is partially a hedonist
I am one interested in human beings	I am one who is fairly intelligent
I am one who is searching for values	I am one who has many friends
I am one who is not dominated by parents	I am one who is fairly loyal to friends
I am one who likes human beings	I am one who enjoys "good" literature

The effects of marginality on self-attitudes seem to be plain in the protocol of a senior high school student which appears as Exhibit 5. Exhibit 6, on the other hand, appears to be from a person who is well anchored socially. Such status identities as Exhibit 6 represents stand in sharp contrast to the personality traits and interests which predominate in the protocol of a male graduate student reproduced in Exhibit 7. Concern with personality traits is even more evident in the protocol of a school teacher given here in Exhibit 8. The respondent whose protocol is given as Exhibit 9 appears to be trying to define himself as he thinks a clinician would define him.

The research reported here was carried out on twenty-five 100 per cent groups containing altogether 1185 individuals. Table 1 lists the kinds of groups and the numbers in each case. No pretense is made that the groups involved cover the range of ages in the life trajectory, and only a handful of the professional schools were covered (and only one practicing professional group). The 100 per cent

EXHIBIT 8   [Responses of a Female School Teacher]

I am a serious person	I do not approach others with my views in the right manner
I like to work	I accept what others do, not because of who is doing it but because of what is done
I have ingenuity	
But lack tenacity	
I am loyal to those I don't know as well as those I do know	I like being a woman—there are advantages
I have overcome obstacles	I am afraid of laziness
I am an independent thinker but	Some people don't understand what I say because I'm too brief—don't explain
Need encouragement from some	
I am somewhat bound by group opinions	I feel capable of doing many things
I am not able to take criticism	I do not depend on others for decision
I am not emotionaly stable enough to get respect of others	I don't like unfairness

EXHIBIT 9

I am a male	When I have to act quickly in case of a crisis I seldom tense and think nothing of it afterwards
I am an extrovert	
I am generally optimistic	
Right now when pressed for something to write I become warm all over and slightly tense	As far as sex is concerned I think I am normal
	I do think I day day dream [sic] a little too much
When I become nervous I break out in cold sweat	

TABLE 1   *The Groups Included in This Study*

	Number
Second Grade, University School	28
Fourth Grade, University School	29
Fourth Grade, Grant Wood School	90
Sixth Grade, University School	27
Seventh Grade, University School	31
Eighth Grade, University School	27
Eighth Grade, Wilson Junior High	102
Iowa City High School	89
L'Anse Michigan High School	119
Scattergood School (boarding preparatory)	32
First Year Law (University)	66
Second Year Law	50
First Year Social Work	13
Second Year Social Work	13
Sample Undergraduate Men	65
Sample Undergraduate Women	65
Unitarian Ministers	28
Senior Dentists	48
Freshman Nurses	69
Sophomore Nurses	78
Junior Nurses	79
Senior Nurses (Degree)	17
Senior Nurses (Diploma)	20

groups were used, not because they most adequately provided us with data for the problem at hand, but because they met (in the phrase of my former colleague, Professor Fred Waisanen) "the usual criteria of convenience, co-operation and captivity!"

Changes in Self-Attitudes with Age

McPartland found, in earlier research,[2] a significant association between age and locus scale types for those in a fairly narrow age range (18–24). The present research, dealing with a considerably greater age range, found that locus scores steadily increase from those of seven-year-olds (the youngest thus far tested) with an average locus score of 5.79 through twenty-four-year-olds with an average locus score of 11.03.

This association is what we would expect from the orientation. As the average individual grows from the age of seven to that of twenty-four, he becomes—or so we would suppose—a member of more groups, and his roles are differentiated on the basis of divergent categories. As a consequence he will internalize as a significant part of his self-definition a larger volume of these identifying statuses. There is indication in recent research, not a part of the present study, that as people retire their locus scores—as we would expect—diminish, and diminish more markedly when they are not members of clubs and similar organizations.

The *salience of sex mention* increases with age from the early grades through high school. Counting no mention as rank number 21, the mean rank of sex reference was for the seven-to-ten-year-old group 7.66; for the eleven-to-fourteen-year-old group it was 6.67; for the fifteen-to-eighteen-year-old group it was 5.11. The university undergraduate sample referred to sex in statements having the mean rank of 6.00, but this is probably not so much a reversal as a reflection of the differential selection involved in a university population of those holding the attitudes toward sex described by Kinsey as prevalent in the higher educational level.

In Table 2 are shown *changes in age as an aspect of identity with increasing age.* Only slightly more than a fourth of the nine-year-olds identified themselves

TABLE 2   *Age Reference by Age*

Age	Number	Percentage Who Mention Age	Salience if Mentioned
9	58	27.6	4.75
10	60	35.0	6.75
12	28	46.4	6.85
13	93	74.2	4.93
15–18	179	59.2	4.62
19–22	130	43.1	5.61

by age. This fraction who did identify themselves by age steadily and rapidly increased until nearly three-fourths of the thirteen-year-olds mentioned age in response to the question "Who am I?" Then, reversing direction, the proportion rapidly diminished until, in the sample of university undergraduates, fewer than

[2] Thomas S. McPartland, "The Self and Social Structure: An Empirical Approach," Ph.D. Thesis, University of Iowa Library, 1953. Microfilm. See pp. 96–97.

half identified themselves by age. It would seem that being thirteen is especially significant in our society since one of our major age-grades—the teen age, with its culturally discontinuous role-playing and curiously detached status—begins with this year of age. To enter the teen age therefore is a rite of passage, and it is significant that it is so apparent in the responses to this self-attitudes test.

The mention of age—at any of these ages—appears to be a fairly significant self-reference. Age is mentioned on the average somewhere between the fourth and seventh places in the order of the twenty statements.

Differences in Self-Attitudes by Sex

Probably the most interesting and at the same time the most significant finding of difference in the responses to the Twenty Statements Test by sex is that with respect to the *sex reference* itself. In the grade school years there is no significant difference between the sexes either in the proportion mentioning sex among their self-definitions nor in the salience of sex reference. Beginning with the high school years the proportion of females to males who give sex saliently as one of the twenty statements in answer to the "Who am I?" question increases. Among respondents in the Northern Michigan high school,[3] for example, nearly 78 per cent of the females mention sex first as over against only a little over 64 per cent of the males.

In Table 3, it can be seen that in our undergraduate sample, females were more likely to mention it first, or at least in the first three places. They were also likely to mention sex more than once, for in this sample there were 67 mentions of sex

TABLE 3   *Self-Attitudes by Sex*

Types of Reference	Females		Males		Chi Square	Probability
	Mention	*No Mention*	*Mention*	*No Mention*		
Sex mention by sex (Undergraduate)	57	8	46	19	$\chi^2 = 5.656$	.02 > p > .01
Sex mention in first place	31	34	18	47	$\chi^2 = 5.535$	.02 > p > .01
Sex mention in one of the first three places	54	11	36	29	$\chi^2 = 11.7$	p < .001
Kin reference by sex	49	16	30	35	$\chi^2 = 11.648$	p < .001
Racial identification by sex	6	59	15	50	$\chi^2 = 4.60$	.05 > p > .02
Age reference by sex	32	33	24	41	$\chi^2 = 2.008$	.20 > p > .10

by 65 females, while by the same number of males there were only 46 mentions of sex. The mean salient rank of sex mention (if failure to mention is treated as rank number 21) was 4.1 for females and 7.9 for males. If only those mentioning sex at all are included, then the mean salient rank for females becomes 1.7 and for males 2.5.

Although no rigorous way of verifying this has yet been developed, it is at least a strong impression that those females in this age group who do not give sex as one of their self-definitions (or else give such reference very late, say, somewhere

---

[3] From data collected by Fred Waisanen in connection with his Ph.D. dissertation (Department of Sociology, University of Iowa).

between eighth and twentieth in rank order) give other self-attitudes which indicate that they conceive themselves as either physically unattractive or as having undesirable personality traits. This hypothesis would seem to merit further investigation. It would be useful in exploring the related but possibly more significant hypothesis that the self-definition as sexually unattractive is self-fufilling in that it results in behavior being organized and directed in a sexually neutral or sexually negative way.

From the finding that sex is a more salient self-attitude for females one may argue to a number of other interesting hypotheses. One such hypothesis is that the salience of defining oneself as a woman is related to the status of women as a minority group (sociologically speaking) in our society.[4] We had previously discovered that members of minority groups such as Negroes and Jews are very apt to give such membership saliently in their responses to the Twenty Statements Test. It is apparent, however, that this can be only one of the factors involved in the mention of sex, for males—as we have noted—also define themselves saliently by sex—only less so than do females. Another hypothesis is that disproportionately salient mention of sex by females is greatest during the years of dating and courtship, since it is during this period that females are staking their lifetime status chances on their sexual attractiveness. It would follow from this hypothesis that the larger role of sex in self-definitions for females would tend to decline in middle and old age. It is unfortunate that this research was able to cover only the years of childhood and youth and hence we were not able to test this hypothesis.

Females much more frequently than males defined themselves in terms of their kinship to others. This is evident in Table 3. We would expect women to hold kin membership as a more significant feature of their self-attitudes than do men, both because women are more restricted in their conduct by the rules laid down in the kin and family system and because they are bearers, or at least prospective bearers, of children and are more largely involved in their rearing. Females are more apt to mention kin more than once, for the 65 females in our undergraduate sample mentioned kin relationships 111 times while the same number of males mentioned kin only 62 times. Furthermore, females mentioned kin more saliently. Counting failure to mention as rank number 21, the mean salience of mention [5] of kin was 10.4 for females and as 15.7 for males; including only those who mention kin, the mean salience was 6.9 for females and 9.6 for males.

In Table 3 it is evident that males define themselves in terms of *race* more frequently than do females. Males also mention race, when they do mention it, somewhat more saliently than do the females (7.53 for males as against 8.33 for females). It is unfortunate that we do not have data on the ethnic attitudes of these subjects, for one would certainly hypothesize from the orientation that those who define themselves saliently in terms of race would hold the culturally differentiating (and presumably derogating) attitudes toward those of other racial groups.

If this hypothesis should be supported by empirical data from a representative cross-section of the population, then it would follow that females are less inclined in our society to have race as a social object. This would mesh with Dollard's hypothesis about sexual factors in the relations between the races, and with Myrdal's report on the strongest attitude component toward the Negro on the part of the

---

[4] On women as a minority group, see—*inter alia*—the familiar Appendix 5, "A Parallel to the Negro Problem," in Gunnar Myrdal, *An American Dilemma* (New York, 1944), 2:1073–78.
[5] The rank of the *first* mention was used if more than one reference to kin was made by a single respondent.

white. Unfortunately most studies of ethnic attitudes fail to report sex differentials if any. Persistent trends in findings regarding anti-Semitism indicate females less anti-Semitic than males. Prothro and Jensen in a study of ethnic attitudes among Louisiana college students [6] found women to have a somewhat more favorable attitude toward the Negro and the Jew than did the men. Lundberg and Dickson,[7] on the other hand, found that girls in a high-school population made sociometric choices restricted more frequently to their own ethnic groups than did boys. In any event the present finding that in a sample of undergraduates at the University of Iowa significantly more men than women defined themselves by race raises interesting questions regarding the relations between such self-definitions and interracial attitudes in various social systems.

In the same sample of university undergraduates, women more frequently than men mentioned their *ages*, but this difference was not at the usually acceptable level of significance (see Table 3). It was a difference most of us might expect between the sexes at this age level (18–24). It is probable that the cliché about women being unwilling to tell their ages is one which applies only when age is unfavorable (*i.e.*, older); from the standpoint of our cultural values it is obvious that the best years of a woman's life are the late teens and early twenties.

There was only a slightly greater tendency for males than for females to mention being *U. S. citizens* or *Americans*. It is surprising that so few of these males of draft age made any reference either in this or some other way to this role. Of those students in professional schools who had already served in the army almost all defined themselves as veterans. One might hypothesize that the anticipation of serving in the armed forces is not as pleasurable as the status of having already got it over with.

A final difference between the sexes having to do with self-attitudes is in respect to locus scores. In the grades girls have higher locus scores than boys. The two sexes have mean scale types of about the same order in the high school years. In the undergraduate years the locus scores of men are higher than those of women. This sequential pattern of difference parallels other differences betwen the sexes —in physical size and growth, in language facility, and in sexual maturation. It would be most logical to relate this locus difference to language and accompanying social participation, though in what precise way they are related awaits exploration.

Self-Attitudes by Professional Training

If we may regard statements on the Twenty Statements Test as evidence of interiorized self-definitions, then one of the most significant findings is that the importance of the professional role increases steadily with each year in professional school (see Table 4). This is true whether we measure by presence or absence of mention of it, by the frequency with which profession is mentioned in the first place, or by the salience of mention (rank) by those who mention it. Note, for example, that while only a third of those near the end of their freshman year of nurse's training identify themselves as nurses in one of the first three statements, more than seven in ten do so by the end of their junior year. Whether or not those

[6] "Group Differences in Ethnic Attitudes of Louisiana College Students," *Sociology and Social Research*, 34:252–58 (1950).

[7] "Selective Association among Ethnic Groups in a High School Population," *American Sociological Review*, 17:23–35 (1952).

TABLE 4   *Professional Reference by Year in Professional School*

Group	Percentage who mention in first three	Ave. rank of mention (if mentioned)	Percentage who fail to mention
First-year law students	53.1	3.3	23.4
Second-year law students	59.2	2.8	16.3
First-year nurses	33.3	4.6	18.8
Second-year nurses	65.8	3.6	5.3
Third-year nurses	71.7	3.4	7.0
Fourth-year nurses	70.6	3.7	0.0
First-year social workers	46.2	4.7	7.7
Second-year social workers	84.6	2.5	15.4

who define themselves early and saliently in terms of the professional role for which they are training makes a difference in their performance as students is an intriguing question which awaits further research, but already there are some—albeit slender—shreds of evidence which seem to indicate that there is a relationship here.

It was possible to trace changes in the locus score with increasing years of professional training in only one of the several professional school groups studied—that of nursing. The results may be seen in Table 5, where it is apparent that lo-

TABLE 5   *Mean Locus Scale Type by Year in College of Nursing*

Year	Mean Locus Scale Type
1	9.37
2	9.08
3	10.04
4	11.90

cus score increases with time spent in nurse's training. It is quite possible that the volume of social anchorage does not increase with years spent in every professional school. Graduate study in general, for example, is often characterized by a considerable degree of rootlessness and marginality. The exploration of this problem must await future research.

The results of content analysis of responses to the TST into the five inclusive categories mentioned early in this paper for students in four professional schools and for members of one adult professional group are given in Table 6. Identities in terms of memberships in social groups and categories constituted as few as a third of one group's responses (Unitarian ministers) and as many as approximately three-fourths of another group's responses (senior nurses). On the other hand, as we might expect, the Unitarian ministers made the most statements of an ideological nature—having to do with moral, philosophical, and religious matters, the place of man in the universe, etc. Nearly a third of all their self-statements were of this variety, while senior nurses made almost none. This supports the social interactionist's contention that man is an object to himself—an object whose meaning to himself and others can only be derived from the system of social objects in which he is enmeshed.

Senior dental students made the largest number of statements having to do with

TABLE 6   *Inclusive Content Analysis of TST Protocols from Respondents in Four Professional Schools and One Professional Group (in percentage of total number of responses by each group)*

Themata	Unitarian Ministers	Senior Dentists	Second-Year Law Students	Soc. Wk. Students	Nursing Students	
					2nd Yr.	4th Yr.
1. Social groups and categories	33	35	39	41	66	73
2. Ideological statements	31	5	12	8	4	*
3. Ambition-success themes	4	15	13	10	1	3
4. Interests	17	16	10	10	11	10
5. Self-evaluations	15	29	26	31	18	14
favorable	*8*	*19*	*16*	*16*	*12*	*9*
unfavorable	*7*	*10*	*10*	*5*	*6*	*5*

* Less than 1 per cent

ambition and success, while nursing students made the fewest, closely followed by Unitarian ministers. The dental student protocols indicated they were concerned to make money in a competitive profession, while the nursing student protocols gave no evidence of concern with differential rewards or with competition within the profession once training was completed.

Differences among the groups with respect to the volume of statements made referring to interests (activities, hobbies, possessions, etc.) were small, the two groups making the most being the ministers and the senior dental students.

Statements making explicit self-evaluations constituted only 14 per cent of all self-statements made by senior nurses, and only 15 per cent of those made by Unitarian ministers. At the other extreme they constituted nearly a third of all responses made by students in social work. Furthermore a considerably larger fraction (better than 5 to 1) of these self-evaluative statements made by students of social work were favorable.[8]

Discussion

George Herbert Mead suggested that a person's behavior is a function of his conception of his identity, and further, that his conception of his identity derives from the positions he occupies in society. A self-attitudes test, then, must be constructed in such a manner that it will elicit the person's own conception of his identity.

Ralph Linton in his *The Cultural Background of Personality* suggested that there are five general kinds of statuses to be found in every society: age and sex, specialized occupation, family groups, association groups, and prestige rankings.[9]

---

[8] If this surprises anyone let him consider the fact that training in social work is often focussed on the task of getting the student to know, *evaluate* and *accept himself*. This assertion is not based on impression alone but on empirically gathered data. Second-year social work students were asked to write a characterization of the role of the social worker by answering the question, "What does a social worker do?" Evaluating and accepting oneself were among the major themata of the contents of their replies. On the TST first-year students in social work made a larger proportion of negative self-evaluative statements but a smaller over-all volume of self-evaluative statements, which tends to support the validity of these statements of difference.

[9] See Ralph Linton, *The Cultural Background of Personality* (New York, 1945), pp. 61–62.

If we could rely on the check-list type of attitude-measuring instrument for the identification and measurement of self-attitudes, we could check its logical validity in terms of the relation of the items to social statuses of the kinds to which Linton pointed. As Newcomb indicates, however, if we present ready-made statements to a respondent we can never know whether he would have ever made such statements about himself without such suggestion; it is a reasonable conjecture on the other hand that if he volunteers statements about himself "with a minimum of stimulation"—that is, *saliently*—then these attitudes may be taken to be significant ones.[10] The TST is so designed to get the respondent to volunteer statements about himself. The results which we have surveyed in this paper support the proposition that the test is a valid one; that is, a large fraction of the responses express identity in terms of the very categories Linton listed—age, sex, occupation, kin membership, and other group membership. Furthermore the responses vary in these respects by groups according to the functional relevance of these statuses to the dominant roles.

It will be noted that Linton indicated that some kind of prestige-ranking is pan-human. This is doubtless true. If this is interpreted strictly in terms of *class* consciousness, however, our data include no evidence to support it, at least in the groups which were here under study. From a total of 1185 individuals having a potential total of 22700 responses, only fourteen responses were made which were of a class-designating sort. This evidence carries the argument made by Neal Gross regarding the nonsalience of class attitudes one step further.[11]

Cooley, in a well-known passage, defined the self, additionally, as a kind of *self-feeling*, indicating the ends of a scale of such feelings as may be represented by the words "pride and mortification." Here again the responses to the TST support the contention that it is valid, for from 15 to 30 per cent of the responses are explicitly of a self-evaluational nature. Many of the other responses, explicitly referring to status have an implicit self-evaluational dimension. We are presently exploring a device whereby the respondent is brought to make explicit such implications.

Conclusion

The research on which this paper has been based was designed to carry the logical validation of the Twenty Statements Test of Self-Attitudes further by examining the responses made by members of twenty-five 100-percent-groups to this test in order to discover whether they were logically related to the self as designated by the orientational theory proposed by Cooley, Dewey, Mead and others of the self- and reference-group-theory approach.

1. It was found that locus increased with age; that within the age bracket represented by our groups, sex references increased with age.
2. It was found that females more frequently and saliently than males identified themselves by sex and kin and less frequently by race than did males.
3. Occupational identity increased with years of professional training, and, within one professional school—nursing—locus scores increased with years of training.

---

[10] See Theodore Newcomb, *Social Psychology* (New York, 1950), p. 151.
[11] Neal Gross, "Social Class Identification in the Urban Community," *American Sociological Review*, 18:398–404 (1953).

4. Finally, an over-all content analysis of responses from students in four professional schools and from members of one professional group indicated marked differences in social anchorage, reference to ideology, identity in terms of intention or ambition, and the amount and nature of self-evaluations.

In general the responses were in the direction expected if one argues from the role requirements to the relevant categorical identifications.

46   Self-Conceptions and Others: A Further Test of Meadian Hypotheses

● E. L. QUARANTELLI AND JOSEPH COOPER

In this paper we attempt to do the following with respect to the symbolic interactionist approach to social psychological phenomena: (1) to add to its relatively meager empirical base; (2) to develop a neglected aspect of the position, namely, the time dimension; and (3) to contribute to both the replication and the extension of the limited systematic research which has used this particular framework to focus on the key concept of self.

That the symbolic interactionist approach does not rest on a substantial body of empirical research has been noted by even such a sympathetic critic as Merton.[1] Proponents of the approach have tended to substitute discursive illustrations for hypothesis testing especially when setting forth the ideas of George H. Mead, the major progenitor of the scheme. In fact, some of the major commentators on Mead have at times suggested that his prime contribution is an abstract frame of reference with which an observer can look at behavior rather than a set of specific hypotheses to be tested.[2] We try to show it is possible to test a key Meadian notion on the relationship between self-conception and social others, through an examination of concrete data.

Stryker has noted the general paucity of symbolic interactionist studies which

SOURCE: E. L. Quarantelli and Joseph Cooper, *Sociological Quarterly*, VII (Summer 1966), pp. 281–297. This investigation was supported in part by Public Health Service Research Grant DH–00014–04, The Division of Dental Public Health and Resources. Margaret Helfrich played an important role in gathering a major part of the data used in the analysis. The authors are also indebted to Albert Schwartz for his suggestions and advice on earlier drafts. James Ross helped with some of the data processing.

[1] Robert K. Merton, *Social Theory and Social Structure*, rev. and enlarged (Glencoe, Ill.: Free Press, 1957), p. 239. See also Manford Kuhn, "Major Trends in Symbolic Interaction Theory in the Past Twenty-Five Years," *Sociological Quarterly*, 5:61–64 (Winter, 1964). Reprinted in Part One of this volume.

[2] For example, Strauss once wrote in a preface to a compilation of Mead's work: "The truth of the matter seems to be that Mead offers us not so much specific hypotheses, or even a theory, as a rather abstract frame of reference." See Anselm Strauss (ed.), *The Social Psychology of George Herbert Mead* (Chicago: Univ. of Chicago Press, 1956), p. xvi. These remarks are not in the preface to the 1964 second edition of the same book entitled *George Herbert Mead on Social Psychology*. See also, Guy E. Swanson, "Mead and Freud: Their Relevance for Social Psychology," *Sociometry*, 24:319–39 (Dec., 1961). A somewhat contrasting viewpoint is presented by John Kinch, "A Formalized Theory of the Self Concept," *American Journal of Sociology*, 68:481–86 (Jan., 1963).

systematically deal with the time dimension in the stream of human conduct.[3] This is a telling criticism, since the processual aspects of behavior are central to the interactionist frame of reference. Recent efforts to formulate and test hypotheses based on Mead's view of the self as product of social interaction are cases in point.[4] Although these studies unambiguously view self-conceptions as dynamic consequences of interaction, self-attitudes are typically analyzed either with reference to some static instant or against a time period of short duration.[5] In contrast, our study utilizes data covering time periods of up to two years.

Finally, the symbolic interactionist approach suffers, as does most sociology, from a lack of replication and cumulation. To be sure, findings from innumerable studies can be interpreted in Meadian terms. However, such analyses do not represent any kind of systematic testing of the framework. Even a number of the studies recently brought together by Rose, as being within the symbolic interactionist framework, are neither clearly drawn from the basic propositions in the formulation nor built upon earlier research.[6] This paper instead reports a partial replication of two prior studies specifically testing hypotheses based on Mead's notion of the social origins of the self. It also extends the range of these earlier studies by offering data in support of derived hypotheses which focus on future oriented self-conceptions.

Theoretical Background

As many observers have noted, the dynamic nature of the symbolic interactionist framework has made its empirical test exceedingly difficult. This has been particularly true with respect to a central thesis of the scheme, the view that the self is social in that it is derived from responses of other persons. Nevertheless, some aspects of this particular idea have been investigated, first by Miyamoto and Dornbusch and later by Reeder, Donohue, and Biblarz.[7]

Miyamoto and Dornbusch, using ten somewhat miscellaneous semigroupings from fraternities, sororities, and college sociology classes, ask their respondents to give self-ratings and also to rate every other group member on four specified personal characteristics. They conclude that their findings from 195 individuals not only show the possibility of empirically studying self-conception within the symbolic interactionist framework, but also support three general propositions. First, the response of others is related to self-conceptions; second, the subject's perception of that response is more closely related to self-conception than the actual

---

[3] Sheldon Stryker, "The Interactional and Situational Approaches" in Harold Christensen (ed.), *Handbook of Marriage and the Family* (Chicago: Rand McNally, 1964), p. 162. Neglect of the time dimension in sociological studies has been stressed by Wilbert Moore in his *Man, Time and Society* (New York: Wiley, 1963).

[4] For example, S. Frank Miyamoto and Sanford Dornbusch, "A Test of the Symbolic Interactionist Hypothesis of Self-Conception," *American Journal of Sociology*, 617:399–403 (Mar., 1956); Leo Reeder, George Donohue, and Arturo Biblarz, "Conceptions of Self and Others," *American Journal of Sociology*, 66:153–59 (Sept., 1960); Carl Couch, "Self-Attitude and Degree of Agreement with Immediate Others," *American Journal of Sociology*, 63:491–96 (Mar., 1958); Martin Maehn, Josef Mensing and Samuel Nafager, "Concept of Self and the Reactions of Others," *Sociometry*, 25:353–57 (Dec., 1962); and John J. Sherwood, "Self Identity and Referent Others," *Sociometry*, 28:66–81 (Mar., 1965).

[5] At most the time period is a matter of weeks. For example, a six week period was used by Melvin Manis in "Social Interaction and the Self Concept," *Journal of Abnormal and Social Psychology*, 51:362–70 (Nov., 1955).

[6] Arnold Rose (ed.), *Human Behavior and Social Processes* (Boston: Houghton Mifflin, 1962).

[7] Miyamoto and Dornbusch, *op. cit.;* Reeder, Donohue, and Biblarz, *op. cit.*

response of others; and third, an individual's self-conception is more closely related to his estimate of the generalized attitude toward him than to the perceived responses of members of a particular group.

Reeder, Donohue, and Biblarz are particularly interested in the relation between self-conception and both the actual and the perceived ratings by members of given groups. They report on nine work crews (totaling 54 enlisted men), at a small military base. Each respondent was asked to rank every member of his crew (including himself) in terms of two criteria: best worker and best leader. Further, each respondent was asked to indicate how he thought most of the men in his group would rank him on these dimensions. Reeder and his co-workers find, in general, that the responses of others have "an influence in shaping one's self-definition" and that his self-definition is "derived chiefly from the perception of the generalized other." [8] In essence, the findings parallel those reported by Miyamoto and Dornbusch.

Both sets of authors judge their research as supporting key notions implicit in the Meadian conception of the social nature of the self. Yet both acknowledge the limited conclusions of their studies, while also indicating that future research should go beyond duplicating their own work. Hence our work is not merely a replication of their research on a different and much larger population. More important, we try to develop three lines of new research suggested to us by these previous studies.

First, a better indicator of self-conception is desirable. Miyamoto and Dornbusch use self-ratings of intelligence, self-confidence, physical attractiveness and likeableness as an index of self-conception. But no evidence is presented that any or all of these features were salient in the self-conception of their respondents. While there is no reason to question that some of these characteristics were central to parts of the self-definition of some of their subjects,[9] their centrality to the selves of all of the participants in the study is neither subjectively nor objectively argued or documented. Similarly, Reeder and his co-workers do not particularly justify their use of ranking along the dimensions of best leader and best worker as a valid measure of the individual's self-conception. They simply say that "it is assumed that the self-rank is an expression of the individual's self-conception." [10] An index of self-conception for which a case for saliency in the life of the individual can be made would be more in keeping with Mead's view.

Second, neither of the previous studies takes into account the time dimension in the emergence and maintenance of the self. The questions put to respondents are confined to the instant of questioning. If the Meadian formulation—that the individual learns to define and to identify himself as he begins to perceive (and later to share) the responses of others toward him—is correct, this neglect of time is a serious omission in the research design. There are two ways to remedy this oversight. One way is through a longitudinal study which catches the individual's self-conceptions at two or more points in time. Another way is by having the respondent project his self-conceptions at future times. The latter procedure has the advantage of being less likely to be confused by the attempts of individuals

---

[8] *Ibid.*, p. 158.
[9] Studies that have used the "Who Am I?" instrument would cast some doubt about the saliency of all four characteristics in the self-conceptions of many persons. See Manford Kuhn, "Self-Attitudes by Age, Sex, and Professional Training," *Sociological Quarterly*, 1:40–55 (Jan., 1960). Reprinted in Part Seven of this volume.
[10] Reeder, Donohue, and Biblarz, *op. cit.*, p. 154.

to reconcile what they wish they were with what they perceive themselves to be.

Third, both previous studies struggle to operationalize the somewhat abstract concept of the "generalized other" and seem, in part, to deviate from what its originator had in mind. Miyamoto and Dornbusch take the position that Mead treats the "generalized other" as the individual's conception of the organized social process of which he is a part, and that he sees it "composed of numerous specialized roles." [11] They note, however, that persons often enter into social relationships wherein there is a response to a "generalized other," but where the organization of roles is obscure or minimal. In fact, the Miyamoto and Dornbusch study relies upon social groupings "whose members were, at best, loosely joined by friendships and had no definite organized group activity within which to identify their respective roles." [12] Accordingly, their index of the generalized other is based on the respondent's perception of the *typical* attitudes of others toward him. Operationally, they ask: "How intelligent . . . do most people think you are?" [13]

In other words, Miyamoto and Dornbusch use the term "generalized other" to refer to the nonparticular other taken into account by the individual in situations which are lacking organization for him.[14] This seems a partial, albeit conscious, departure from the Meadian formulation. Mead, in a frequently cited passage, speaks of the generalized other as the process whereby the person "takes the attitudes of the organized social group to which he belongs." [15] As suggested in his account on the game stage in the development of the self, the internalization of the generalized other requires the individual to define and regulate his conduct with regard for the expectations of a complexly organized multiplicity of other actors.

Reeder and his co-workers capture part of this formulation. As an index of the generalized other, they use the participant's "estimated objective group rating." In turn, this rating is based on the respondent's indication of the rank which he thinks most of his work group assign him with respect to two criteria—leadership and workmanship. Unlike the procedure used by Miyamoto and Dornbusch, this technique has the merit of conceiving the generalized other in terms of the attitudes of an organized and on-going group.

Reeder and his co-authors, however, assume "that the individual, in making an estimate of how the group ranks him, is taking the role of the generalized other." [16] In this research the group is treated as the equivalent of the small number of immediately present individuals in any given work crew. This is not inconsistent with one of Mead's two somewhat different uses of the term "organization." In the research of Reeder and his colleagues, the work crews seem analogous to Mead's famous example of the ball team, where the team is seen as the generalized other "insofar as it enters—as an organized process or social activity—into the experience of any one of the individual members." [17] Mead's other use of the term "organization," however, appears to place greater stress on the actor's organizing of attitudes towards himself than on the possibility that these attitudes may be

---

[11] Miyamoto and Dornbusch, *op. cit.*, p. 400. Reprinted in Part Seven of this volume.
[12] *Ibid.*
[13] *Ibid.*, p. 410. There is an interesting assumption here that the "typical" is equivalent to the "most."
[14] *Ibid.*, p. 400.
[15] Charles W. Morris (ed.), *Mind, Self and Society* (Chicago: University of Chicago Press, 1934), p. 155.
[16] Reeder, Donohue, and Biblarz, *op. cit.*, p. 154.
[17] Morris, *op. cit.*, p. 154.

derived from an organized activity. Even while discussing games, it is noted: "We get then an organization of attitudes of those involved in the same process."[18] Clearly the process can extend beyond any group. In fact, most of Mead's discussion of the generalized other is in terms of the socialization of the child. In this context, the child's organization of the attitudes of others is of greater importance than the organized nature of the activity wherein he draws his self-conception.

At still another point, Mead observes that the individual enters into two kinds of social relations: "Some of them are concrete social classes or subgroups. . . . The others are abstract social classes or subgroups . . . in terms of which their individual members are related to one another only more or less indirectly and which only more or less indirectly function as social units. . . ."[19] A research effort centered on the latter formulation seems called for. The generalized other would be viewed as the individual's perception of the responses of others as he sees them with regard to some salient aspect of himself. The perceiving individual and the others whose responses he organizes need not be members of any particular group. They do, however, stand in some role relationship to him (e.g., as friend or teacher). Analysis along these lines emphasizes process rather than structure. Such an analysis proceeds from the actor's point of view and not from the standpoint of an outside observer.

Given these considerations, this study seeks to develop a more salient index of self-conception, to incorporate the temporal aspect of the process of self-identification and to operationalize the generalized other so as to reflect Mead's concern with the self-as-process.

Methods and Techniques

We draw data for this study from a much broader investigation of factors influencing the professionalization of dental students. In the larger effort on career lines, we are following two successive waves of students panel-like from the time of entrance into dental school until graduation. (Two other waves are under study for shorter periods.) This report is based on a small segment of the extensive questionnaire data obtained from all students at the very beginning of each academic year. The larger study is still in progress; but data are available from 600 freshmen (waves 1, 2, 3, 4) and from 450 sophomores (waves 1, 2, 3).[20] No doubt our findings would be strengthened if all the longitudinal data (ultimately to cover the entire four years' experience of 300 dental students) were available. However, the particular hypotheses to be examined are testable just as readily with the information already in hand; that is, with data covering one year's actual experience, as well as a two-year projection of self-ratings.

Among many other questions, we asked each student at the start of every academic year to complete the following professional labeling scale. The line in the diagram represents an arbitrary distance between a dental student and a dentist.

	1	2	3	4	5	6	7	8	9	10	
Dental Student											Dentist

---

18 *Ibid.*, p. 154.
19 *Ibid.*, p. 157.
20 Because of dropouts and failures to answer relevant questions we have data for only 594 freshmen and 432 sophomores.

Using *one* of the whole numbers on this line write in *below:*

A. Where would you place yourself at this time?_____
B. Which point on the line is closest to where you think you will be one year from now?_____
C. In general, where do you think you will be about two years from now, i.e., when you start to work in the clinic?_____
D. Where do you think that the dental faculty now sees you?_____
E. Where do you think that the faculty will expect you to be one year from now?_____
F. Where do you think your parents now see you?_____
G. (*If married*) Where do you think your wife now sees you?_____
H. Where do you think that your non-dental school friends and acquaintances now see you?_____
I. Where do you think that your classmates now see you?_____
J. Where do you think that the advanced dental students now see you?_____

We use the respondent's self-placement on the scale (Item A) as a salient index of self-conception. The student's very presence in a professional school is taken as a firm indication that a dental career is of considerable importance to him. Entering dental school is not only a voluntary act on the part of the student but it also follows upon a series of necessarily rather self-conscious decisions. Even without assuming total or identical commitment to the profession, the embarkation upon a long and expensive educational career argues for the importance of the undertaking to the participant. In this respect the dental student differs from the typical social club member, the student in a sociology class, or the worker on a military crew.

In addition to recording his current location (or actual self-conception) on the professional labeling scale, each respondent projected the locations he expected to occupy in one or two years' time (Items B–C). We discuss these as projected self-ratings or self-conceptions. Further, each respondent noted his perception of current and projected placements by a variety of others: (Items D–J) these we treat as *perceived*—actual or projected—ratings by others. A parallel questionnaire completed by 86 per cent of the dental school's faculty (n–93), provides data on the actual faculty ratings of the students at three points in their academic careers: these data we refer to as the *actual* ratings—current or projected—by others. Table 1 summarizes the data considered in this study. The means of both current and projected ratings at the onset of two academic years are recorded for three analytical categories: self-ratings, perceived ratings by others, and actual ratings by faculty.[21]

We distinguish between particular others and the generalized other. Particular others are specific social alters we assume to be saliently related to our respondents in their role as dental students. Six categories of particular others are used: faculty, classmates, upperclassmen, non-dental school friends, parents, and in appropriate cases, wives. Potentially at least, these categories appear to exhaust the likely sources of major interaction within which the process of self-identification could be developed. Furthermore, and important to our case, we take the perceived responses of these others toward a salient aspect of the student self-conception—his position on the professional labeling scale.

---

[21] We do not have comparable faculty ratings of sophomores.

TABLE 1   *Means of Actual and Projected Ratings by Self and Others*

	Freshmen						Sophomores					
	High		Low		Total		High		Low		Total	
	$\bar{x}$	N	$\bar{x}$	N	$\bar{x}$	N	$\bar{x}$	N	$\bar{x}$	N	$\bar{x}$	N
Self-Ratings												
Current	3.18	91	1.00	503	1.33	594	3.56	214	1.84	218	2.69	432
Projection												
One-Year	4.90	91	2.87	502	3.18	593	6.14	214	4.26	218	5.19	432
Two-Year	6.86	91	5.46	499	5.67	590	—	—	—	—	—	—
Perceived Ratings by Others												
Current												
Faculty	2.12	89	1.04	494	1.21	583	2.94	213	1.78	216	2.36	431
Upperclassmen	2.07	91	1.05	501	1.20	592	3.22	212	1.85	216	2.54	428
Classmates	2.80	91	1.12	492	1.39	583	3.62	210	2.14	214	2.89	424
Non-dental Friends	3.95	91	2.46	501	2.69	592	5.07	425	4.27	217	4.66	425
Parents	4.15	88	2.31	495	2.58	583	5.03	203	4.02	214	4.51	417
Wives	4.60	20	1.88	130	2.25	150	4.73	73	3.00	80	3.81	153
Aggregate *	3.08	—	1.61	—	1.84	—	4.01	—	2.83	—	3.41	—
Aggregate 2 †	3.15	—	1.73	—	1.94	—	4.10	—	2.98	—	3.53	—
Projection												
One-Year Faculty	4.36	91	2.91	502	3.13	593	5.80	213	4.47	216	5.13	429
Actual Ratings by Faculty												
Current	1.71	80	1.71	80	1.71	80	—	—	—	—	—	—
Projection												
One-Year	2.94	80	2.94	80	2.94	80	—	—	—	—	—	—
Two-Year	4.96	80	4.96	80	4.96	80	—	—	—	—	—	—

* Includes classmates.   † Excludes classmates.

We operationally define the generalized other as the aggregate of the student's perceptions of the ratings awarded to him by particular others. This definition of the generalized other differs from the concept as it appears in the work of Miyamoto and Dornbusch and in the paper by Reeder, Donohue, and Biblarz. As noted above, the earlier studies exhibit a partial adherence to the Meadian formulation. The present operationalization, however, has a somewhat different focus. We assume the aggregated data to relate to the respondent's organization of ratings by others of a salient part of himself. We think this is consistent with one reading of the Meadian formulation, and in combination with the time element discussed before, may better capture the processual aspect supposedly involved in the emergence of salient self-conceptions. We claim no more.

Following the analytical lead provided in the two previous studies, we classify (where appropriate) the average ratings of our respondents into "high" and "low." In the case of the freshmen we treat statistical means of one as "low," all others as "high." For sophomores, we classify means of three and over as "high," all below that figure as "low." [22]

---

[22] The rationale for treating sophomores in this fashion is that it gives us an approximate median distribution of the respondents. Unfortunately our data, as was also true in the case of the data obtained by Miyamoto and Dornbusch, and by Reeder and his co-workers, preclude the application of tests of significance. Consequently, as they did, we primarily search for gross differences in examining the validity of the hypotheses.

Hypotheses and Findings

Hypothesis 1. Self-conception is closer to the mean perceived response of others to the actor than to the mean actual response of others.—Drawn directly from Miyamoto and Dornbusch, this hypothesis rests on the assumption that the perceived behavior of others towards the actor has a more direct influence than their actual behavior. For purposes of testing this notion, we match the mean self-rating of freshmen against their perception of faculty rankings, as well as against actual faculty rating of students.

Our data fully support the hypothesis. Freshmen perceive themselves at a mean of 1.33 on the scale; they think the faculty sees them at 1.21; the faculty actually ranks them at 1.71. Thus, there is only a mean difference of .12 (in the direction of a lower estimate) between perceived rating by faculty and self-rating in contrast to a mean difference of .38 between self-rating and actual rating by faculty members.

Although partly dictated by its easier accessability, the choice of data from faculty members to test this hypothesis is also guided by a substantive consideration. In one respect, it seems reasonable to expect that freshmen might be more sensitive to faculty judgments of their relative position on the path to becoming a dentist, than they are to the judgment of most others. The institutional structure is such that, by virtue of the assignment of grades, only faculty members decide whether a freshman can move through the professional school. This is a point sometimes explicitly made by students in personal interviews. Other persons may influence what a student thinks of himself, but only faculty members, particularly in the crucial first year, decide if a freshman can even remain on the path to becoming a dentist. (The poor underestimation by freshmen of how far along faculty members actually see them is of course the kind of finding that would be anticipated by this kind of reasoning.)

Hypothesis 2. The mean of the perceived responses by others is higher for those persons with high self-rating than for those with low self-rating.—This hypothesis is also directly drawn from Miyamoto and Dornbusch.[23] The reasoning here is that if self-conceptions are primarily determined by the perceived responses of others toward the person, those seeing themselves accorded higher ranking should reflect a higher self-evaluation than those visualizing themselves as less highly regarded.

In our examination of this hypothesis, we not only choose to focus on the perceived rather than the actual responses of others, but attempt to strengthen the testing of the hypothesis by taking into account the range of others that could likely by salient to our students. Thus, we examine how both freshmen and sophomores perceive the rating accorded them by faculty members, upperclassmen, classmates, non-dental school friends, parents, wives. Without pretending that all possible others who might be important for every single respondent is included, it seems reasonable to argue that we encompass in our categories most all who would be salient—in the sense of being an "other"—to the mass of our students.

As indicated in Table 1 this hypothesis is supported for each category of others (i.e., faculty, etc.). High self-raters perceive all others as according them a higher rank than do low self-raters. This is equally true for freshmen and

---

[23] Most of the hypotheses said to be set forth by Miyamoto and Dornbusch are more indirectly stated also by Reeder and his co-workers.

sophomore with no mean difference in the twelve comparisons made lower than .80. It is of interest that low self-rates as sophomores perceive themselves ranked higher by only one other category (non-dental school friends), than do high self-raters see others ranking them as freshmen.

Whereas the previous hypotheses were confined to a particular point in time, the following set of hypotheses deals with projections through time.

*Hypothesis 3. Anticipated self-rating is closer to the mean perceived future response of others to the actor than to the mean actual future response of others.—*Of course this is an extension of Hypothesis 1 through time. It assumes that even in future projections, the perceived rather than the actual behavior of others is the more important influence as far as self-conception is concerned.

We again use faculty members as the example of the other in the test of the hypothesis. We contrast the self-ratings which the freshmen project into their sophomore year, first, with their perceptions of the faculty's projected ratings, and second, with the faculty's actual anticipation.

The mean anticipated self-rating is 3.18. The perception of the projected rating by the faculty is 3.13; the actual projected rating is 2.94. Thus, the mean differences between self and perceived projected faculty rating is .05, but it is .24 between self and actual projected faculty rating. Thus, Hypothesis 3 is supported, though perhaps not as strongly as Hypothesis 1.

*Hypothesis 4. The mean of the perceived future responses by others is higher for those persons with high present self-rating than for those with present low self-rating.—*This hypothesis makes the same basic assumption as is made in Hypothesis 2. It differs only in that it involves a projection into the future. The hypothesis assumes that those presently according themselves a high self-rating compared with those who visualize themselves as lower on the scale, will project a higher future self-ranking by others.

We test this hypothesis for both freshmen and sophomores. That is, we examine the freshmen's perceptions of the faculty's projected placement of them as sophomores and the sophomore's perceptions of the faculty's expectations of them as juniors. For this hypothesis, unfortunately, we do not have perceived projections by the students of all possible salient others as we do have for Hypothesis 2.

We find that the high self-raters project a sophomore mean score by others of 4.36 whereas the low self-raters see others as only rating them 2.91. This is a mean difference of 1.45 in the direction of supporting the hypothesis. The same relationship holds for sophomore perceived projections by the faculty into the junior year. The high self-raters project a junior mean score by the faculty of 5.80; the low self-raters see the professional staff as rating them but 4.47. The mean difference here is 1.33. Thus, both sets of data support Hypothesis 4.

*Hypothesis 5. The mean anticipated self-rating is higher for those whose present self-rating is high than for those whose present self-rating is low.—*This hypothesis derives from some of our previous findings. We observe that the anticipated self-conception of our respondents appears to be related to their perception of the future response of others towards them. Likewise, we note that the perceived future responses of others seems to be linked to whether or not the respondent presently rates himself high or low. It follows then that there ought to be some relationship between anticipated self-rating and present high or low self-rating. In the light of Hypothesis 4, the proposition is stated as above.

In testing this hypothesis, we examine the freshman respondents' projected self-ratings as sophomores and as juniors. Present high self-raters project a mean rank of 4.90 as sophomores, whereas low self-raters foresee a mean rank of 2.87: the mean difference of 2.03 is substantial. The mean difference for projected junior ranking is also high, being 1.40. The present high self-raters give themselves an anticipated mean rank of 6.86, but the low self-raters only 5.46. The general hypothesis is thus supported. Similarly, the sophomores who are low self-raters project a self-rating of 4.26 as juniors, while their high self-rating peers anticipate a rating of 6.14. Thus, all comparisons allowed by our data point to a relationship between present self-conception and future oriented self-expectations.

Hypothesis 6. Those persons who have high self-rating have a higher mean perception of the generalized other than those with low self-rating.—Although our formulation of the generalized other is somewhat different from theirs, this hypothesis is also directly drawn from Miyamoto and Dornbusch. Basically, however, the hypothesis tests the notion that self-conception is derived from multiple perspectives, and that persons seeing themselves accorded generally higher ranking should reflect a higher self-evaluation than those visualizing themselves as in general less highly regarded.

We test this hypothesis by comparing summations of the respondents' perceptions of ratings assigned to them by others. In this instance, all other categories are utilized in the analysis of the effects of the generalized other. Both freshman and sophomore data are examined.

The results are clear-cut. The high freshman self-raters have an aggregate mean score of 3.08 while the low self-raters have a score of 1.61. This mean difference of 1.47 compares with a mean difference of 1.18 among the sophomores. In that group, the high self-raters have an aggregate mean score of 4.01 whereas the low self-raters have a mean score of 2.83. Thus both freshman and sophomore high self-raters perceive themselves as being ranked higher from multiple perspectives than to do low self-raters. We thus find support for Hypothesis 6.

Hypothesis 7. Self-conception corresponds more closely to the mean perception of the generalized other than to the mean of the perceived response of particular others.—Again this is a hypothesis derived from Miyamoto and Dornbusch. It rests on the assumption that self-conception as a whole emerges from interaction in divergent relationships. Thus, self-conception should more closely reflect the way most potentially meaningful others are perceived as viewing the subject than the perception of the responses of any particular collection of individuals to the actor.

In testing this hypothesis, we treat the student's classmates as particular others. The rationale for this is that classmates represent those persons with whom the freshman in the dental school has the most social contact, at least in the quantitative sense. (Also, in using this group we have the nearest equivalent in our study to the fraternity, sorority, and school class groupings Miyamoto and Dornbusch used, and the work teams Reeder and his co-workers employed in their study.) For purposes of this analysis, the category of classmates is left out of the aggregated data for the generalized other.

The data do *not* support the hypothesis. Both for freshmen and sophomores the mean perceived response of particular others (i.e., classmates) are closer to the actual self-conception of students than the mean perception of the generalized other. Among freshmen the mean difference between self and particular others is only .06, but it is .61 between self and generalized other. Among sophomores the mean difference between the self and generalized other is .84, whereas it is only .20 between self and particular other. Thus, Hypothesis 7 is not supported.

It is significant that both prior studies of which ours is a partial replication also encountered some unexpected findings in testing variants of this hypothesis. Miyamoto and Dornbusch find that only for the characteristic of self-confidence was there "marked deviations from the expected direction." [24] That is, the findings were not much better than chance when ratings on self-confidence were used to test the hypothesis that self-conceptions should correspond more closely with the generalized other than with the mean of the perceived response of others (i.e., how each individual predicted every other member of his grouping ranked him as to self-confidence). As distinguished from intelligence, physical attractiveness, and likeableness, self-confidence is the one characteristic which most closely approximates the index of self we use in our study—where our subjects rank themselves on a dental student to dentist scale. Hence, the absence of a positive finding along these lines in both studies may be more than a coincidence.

As part of their demonstration of the weight to be given to the perceived response of the generalized other in accounting for self-conception, Reeder and his co-researchers compare subject self-rating with the rankings actually awarded them by work-related others. They find a difference between high and low self-raters. They attribute this difference to the possibility that high self-raters have more reference groups than low self-raters, and thus are less responsive to the actual attitudes of particular others towards the self. (In their study this would be the actual attitudes of the other members of the work crews.)

Following the lead of Reeder and his co-workers, we also examine our data to see if there is a similar high-low self-rating difference. We proceed as in testing Hypothesis 7, except that we divide our subjects into high and low self-raters.

The results are not consistent. For the freshmen we find the same difference found by Reeder and co-workers. That is, the mean self-conception of the low self-raters corresponds more closely to the perceived mean attributed to particular others than to the generalized other. The high self-raters show a reverse pattern. However, the pattern does not hold for the sophomores, where the mean self-conception of the high self-raters corresponds more closely to the perceived mean attributed to particular others than to their perceptions of ratings by the generalized other. The low self-raters among the sophomore students exhibit the same pattern. These findings are not a direct test of the observation by Reeder and his co-workers (i.e., that there is considerable correspondence between self-conception and the actual response of others only for persons who rate themselves low and not for those whose self-rating is high). They, however, do raise questions about its generality.

It is of interest that both prior studies and ours have encountered unhypothesized results when examining roughly the same general proposition. [25] At least it is suggestive of the possibility that the findings are not idiosyncratic to particular pieces of research or specific analytical procedures. It could indicate that something more fundamental may be involved. However, it would probably be most fruitful in future research to attempt to get at the relationship between the generalized other and particular others in still some different way. For instance, it may be that the findings in all three studies are confounded by a research failure to separate the category of significant other from particular others. If this is what

[24] Miyamoto and Dornbusch, op. cit., p. 403.
[25] Vaughan, in a test of three hypotheses which are similar in some respects to the hypothesis in question above, also failed to find anticipated results. See Ted R. Vaughan, "Group Determinants of Self-Conception: An Empirical Assessment of Symbolic Interaction Theory" (Unpublished Ph.D. dissertation, University of Texas, 1964), pp. 102–106.

accounts for the findings, the basic hypothesis may only require modification and may not need a major alteration.

Conclusion

The results of our study reinforce the suggestion of the earlier researchers that it is possible to test and also to find some empirical support for those aspects of the symbolic interactionist framework examined. The posited relationships are clearly supported for six of the seven major hypotheses, even when in our opinion a more rigorous index of self-conception is introduced, when the neglected time dimension is incorporated into some of the data, and when a somewhat different operational measure of the generalized other is utilized.

As did Miyamoto and Dornbusch, we find that it is the perceived rather than the actual response of others that is the more important in the formation of self-conception. Furthermore, this holds true not only for self-conception at a given point in time, but also for anticipated self-rating. It is the same whether a general comparison is made or whether subjects are divided into high and low self-raters. Furthermore, the data indicate that not only is self-definition chiefly derived from the perceived rather than the actual response of others, but that it is also a reflection of the perceived response of the generalized other. The latter statement, however, has to be qualified insofar as the key hypothesis concerning it is not fully supported. Since there have been difficulties with variants of this hypothesis in prior studies, the need for future research to take this as a prime point of attack is obvious.

The possibility of attaining empirical results should be of some comfort to many who, while advocating the symbolic interactionist position, have been bothered with the suspicion that there was no way of either confirming or disproving the basic notions involved. We hope our research, crude and gross as it is, will encourage others towards far more systematic and more rigorous empirical testing not only of the ideas of Mead examined in this paper, but of many others. After all, whether in the course of the development of sociology, Mead is to be eventually ranked with the alchemists or as a Lavoisier is yet to be decided.

47   The Methodologies of Symbolic Interaction: A Critical Review of Research Techniques

● NORMAN K. DENZIN

In his critical assessment of the major trends in symbolic interaction theory since 1937, the late Manford Kuhn suggested that, with the publication of Mead's three major works, interactionism passed from the *oral tradition* into the *age of inquiry*.[1]

SOURCE: Norman K. Denzin, "The Methodologies of Symbolic Interaction: A Critical Review of Research Techniques," original paper prepared especially for this volume.

I am grateful to Gregory P. Stone, Carl J. Couch, and Robert L. Stewart for comments on an earlier version of this paper. For a more complete treatment of the issues contained in this paper see my *The Substance of Sociological Theory and Method: An Interactionist Interpretation* (Chicago: Aldine, 1969).

[1] Manford H. Kuhn, "Major Trends in Symbolic Interaction Theory in the Past Twenty-five Years," *Sociological Quarterly*, 5 (Winter, 1964), pp. 61–84, reprinted in Part One of this volume.

In contrast to the earlier period, with its emphasis on getting the "orthodoxy" right, the age of inquiry brought forth a transformation of creative energies into refinements and proliferations of sub-theories stemming from the framework developed by Mead and others. The present period, then, finds the symbolic interactionist attempting to bring the ephemeral notions of Mead closer to empirical reality.

Still, Kuhn felt that this period, despite its emphasis on research, was plagued by inabilities to:

> . . . close the gaps and distortions that so often lie between the imaginative theoretical model—often consensually shared—and the operations used to investigate the empirical world—often, again, universally shared.[2]

Hence, while the interactionist is told to examine the inter-subjective side of man's social experiences, "we are given few leads as to how to make this subjective life accessible to observation or systematic inquiry." [3]

The present paper builds on Kuhn's assessment of modern interaction theory by arguing that significant advances will not be made until we systematically rethink the methodologies currently available to us as we move from theory to reality. We assume that the contemporary interactionist has at his disposal at least five distinct research methods that can differentially shed light on his theory. These are the experiment, the survey, participant observation, unobtrusive measures, and the life-history. The purpose of the present paper is the serious and critical examination of these research methods from the standpoint of symbolic interaction. We will state the necessary preconditions for their uses, while demonstrating that each fits certain key assumptions of interaction theory. Our central proposition will be, however, that each method represents the sociologist carrying on a different form of symbolic interaction with his environment. Our position holds that research methods are not sterile atheoretical tools. Instead, they are symbolically laden lines of action that represent one or another of the major forms of interaction the sociologist carries on as he moves from theory to reality. All research is a form of symbolic interaction, and, until we recognize this fact and treat our methods in this light, we cannot achieve the necessary empirical links our theory demands.[4]

Sociology's Negotiated Reality

> . . . "Reality" is a social process; it is an orientation that is continuously supported by others. . . . In this sense all knowledge is social. . . . Societies, no matter how stable they may appear, are on-going things. The world is in a state of continuous flux, and as life conditions change, knowledge must keep pace . . . the emergence of new hypotheses and their acceptance as part of a modified outlook is a social process.[5]

Before an interactionist can meaningfully discuss methodological movements from theory to reality, he must first treat the nature of that reality designated by

---

[2] Manford H. Kuhn, "The Reference Group Reconsidered," *Sociological Quarterly*, 5 (Winter, 1964), p. 5.

[3] *Ibid.*, p. 9.

[4] See my *The Substance of Sociological Theory and Method: An Interactionist Interpretation* (Chicago: Aldine, 1969), Chapter 2, where this point is more fully elaborated.

[5] Tamotsu Shibutani, *Improvised News: A Sociological Study of Rumor* (Indianapolis: Bobbs-Merrill, 1966), pp. 170–171, 182.

his theories and research strategies. As the above statement from Shibutani indicates, to speak of a social object called "reality" is to speak of an object that has a negotiated existence—an existence embedded in an ongoing social process. *Reality is that which is perceived and designated by our significant symbols and hence brought into formative lines of action.* Scientists, and sociologists specifically, have tended to ignore this fundamental assertion of symbolic interaction. They accept their theories as flexible, but never doubt the existence of a uniformly perceived empirical world. That this is the case is quickly recognized when we consider the typical impact empirical observations have upon our theories. Disconfirmed hypotheses are seldom sustained in their original form—instead they are reshaped to fit the data. This reshaping process belies a ritualistic belief that empirical reality is always right—our theories may go astray—but never their designated reality.

Belief in an immaculately conceived empirical reality has given rise to a peculiar stance toward sociological theory. The substance of theories becomes the battle-ground for negotiations, political debates, and war-like forays into a theoretical middle ground. Thus we debate the efficacy of Parson's "system theory" as it articulates complex interrelationships between personality, cultural, and social systems—while never once assuming that the reality designated by that theory is quite unique and hence not appropriately open to attack from other perspectives. Interactionists quibble over dramaturgical, deterministic, and indeterministic models of human conduct—forgetting the special reality designated by each formulation.

We are advocating that theoretical, empirical, and methodological realities are realities fraught with conflicting definitions and meanings. As such, the reality of any theory or method is so distinctly unique as to deny complete validation from any other perspective. Indeed, we can never expect more than crude approximations of this negotiated reality. Hence, when we speak in this paper of movements from theory to reality we recognize that each methodology will lead us to a slightly different conception of the world. If, as we state, methodologies represent different lines of action toward our symbolic environment, then we are necessarily led to this conclusion.

The implications of this position are several and complex. The first and most telling consequence suggests that the activities of the scientist are basically no different than those of the actors in the everyday life he studies. Both the scientist and the everyday actor negotiate the definitions, meanings, and lines of action that constitute their relevant symbolic environment. However—

> The main difference between the actor and the actor as a modern researcher is that the latter applies to his research activity a rather rigorous set of rules for the admissibility of evidence and the formulation and transformation of statements. The researcher not only has the problem of getting his questioned activity going again, but he must do so in conformity with these rules.[6]

In this paper the complex nature of these rules is discussed, and their relationship to interaction theory is stressed.

Second, we must realize that different methods will always reveal different aspects of the same process, event, or object. To call for a triangulated methodology in the social sciences is appropriate only when we understand that each of our

---

[6] Robert L. Stewart, in personal communication, April 26, 1968.

triangulated strategies will capture certain unique elements in the research process. The essence of triangulation is this discriminating perception of what researchers hold to be the same object. We strive to discover that which is general and similar about our studied objects across time and situation, and, in this respect, dissimilar research methods aid us immeasurably. But we cannot expect automatic validation by our different methods, even though they focus on the same class of objects. Each research method is a different strategy for reconstructing and making real some designated empirical world.

Third, we will accept findings from divergent methodologies only to the extent that they make this reconstruction process evident and public. Not only will each research method reveal a slightly different aspect of what is presumably the same object, but each investigator who employs that method can be expected to generate slightly different interpretations. Each of us, when he adopts the line of action implied by the experiment, the survey, or participant observation, brings to bear upon that object a special set of definitions and meanings that represents his interpretation of those methods. Hence, we again must expect some degree of non-comparability across investigations, despite the fact that the same strategies may have been employed.

A fourth consequence of our position dictates that, even when the same methods, the same objects, and the same investigators are combined, we can expect different results. This is so, because as Shibutani tells us, the world is in a continual state of flux and change. Every time we dip into that constructed world we can expect different observations and findings to emerge—change, not stability, is the hallmark of this social reality.

Last, our theoretical propositions and methodologies must be flexible enough to grasp this shifting nature of the empirical world. Contingent interactive propositions must be formulated, and not propositions that assume stability and simple causal relationships. Further, our theories, hypotheses, and research strategies must be viewed as elements embedded in an ongoing social process. The social reality of the scientist is a political reality—one in which competing forces, institutions, personal and public careers all combine to forge new definitions and interpretations. Hence, the sources of change in our theories and data derive not only from negative empirical findings—but most importantly from the perspectives of the individual scientists involved in the process of scientifically reconstructing a world that refuses to stand still and arbitrarily accept one interpretation.

The Necessary Preconditions for an Interactionist Methodology

Given the above statements concerning the scientific process, it is appropriate to consider the rules of conduct that make this venture public and hence reproducible by other scientists. We assume that any research methodology must meet the following preconditions before it is acceptable to the interactionist. These may be categorized as conditions stemming from considerations of *validity* and second, from *interaction theory* itself.

CONSIDERATIONS OF VALIDITY

Any research method must first provide answers to the perennial problem of causal inference. It must generate data concerning time order and co-variation between variables, while allowing the investigator to discard rival causal factors and hypotheses. To this end the two categories of *external* and *internal validity* take on central importance for they point to two broad classes of rival hypotheses that can nullify or distort the true causal relationships under analysis.[7]

By *external validity* we refer to the generalizability of findings to other samples and populations. Campbell and Stanley have shown that the following factors may restrict such generalizations. First are restrictions arising from unique respondent characteristics that would set them apart from other respondents in unexamined populations. Second are population instabilities over time. Here the temporal element of human behavior is noted, and the investigator is cautioned to attend to unique events as they occur within specified time periods. Third are population instabilities arising from spacial or geographical differences in samples and populations. In this respect the sociologist must recognize that, while his respondents may not differ on the first two dimensions, they may be unique simply because of their location in a particular social setting.

External validity then refers to one class of variables that can restrict the generalization of findings from any investigation. Generally, two strategies may be employed to counter this problem. The first is to employ some form of statistical sampling model that rigorously insures randomness and the probable representativeness of the sample under study. The second strategy is to employ a theoretical sampling model. In this case, we direct the investigator's attention to the study of social groups and social settings that have high theoretical relevance and value for the problem at hand. This will entail the use of a logic-of-ongoing-inclusion, whereby groups and settings are progressively sampled in the belief that negative comparison groups will be located that disqualify the emergent research propositions and hypotheses.

Whether theoretical or statistical sampling models are employed is irrelevant with respect to the question of external validity. Each method proposes a different solution, but one of these two will be employed.[8]

Internal validity sensitizes the sociologist to the fact that his act of making observations may introduce a series of biasing factors that create the differences he ultimately observes in the sample and setting under study. Seven categories of internal validity may be noted. There are, *first*, historical factors that impinge between the initial and subsequent observations. *Second* is the problem of subject maturation or change between observations. *Third* is subject bias, or the unique features of those studied. *Fourth* is subject mortality. Here we refer to the fact that, in any study over time, some subjects will, for a variety of reasons, leave the research setting. Concern for subject mortality directs attention to the uniqueness of those subjects who remain, in comparison to those who leave. *Fifth* are the reactive effects of the observer in the situation. It is near axiomatic that few natural

---

[7] See Donald T. Campbell and Julian C. Stanley, *Experimental and Quasi-Experimental Designs for Research* (Chicago: Rand-McNally, 1963) for a more complete discussion of these two aspects of validity.

[8] See Denzin, *op. cit.*, Ch. 5, for a review of these two sampling models. In actuality the interactionist should strive for a synthesis of the two approaches. It should not be seen as an either/or decision.

field settings contain a role called sociological observer. In this sense, we can refer to the sociologist as a foreign object in the settings he studies. Any investigation must attend to this potentially reactive effect on those studied.[9] *Sixth* are changes in the observer. During the course of any study, the sociologist will begin to take on new definitions, while discarding old meanings and symbols that refer directly to those he is studying. These changes must continuously be recorded, if this source of internal validity is to be considered. *Seventh* and last are peculiar aspects of the situations in which observations are made. That all of human interaction is situated by time and place is fundamental to the analysis of any observational data. The dynamics of these settings, the rules of etiquette that apply to them, and the varieties of action that transpire within them must be recorded and analyzed. Observations must be gathered that reveal the meanings of situations for the participants studied, and the nature and variety of situations observed must be recorded and analyzed for any biasing factors present.

As we shall see, no single method completely solves the problems of internal and external validity. For example, unobtrusive measures, while removing the reactive observer from the situation, are often ill-equipped to provide data on external validity or on the situational dimensions of internal validity. Similarly, the experiment is well-suited for study of subject maturation, but seldom is conceived so that observer effects can be analyzed. Unfortunately, the present paper will not be able to discuss fully each of these methods in terms of the above dimensions. This has been done elsewhere.[10] However, we do raise one final point of consideration, and this is the fact that, because no single method adequately handles the problems of internal and external validity, it is necessary for the sociologist to *triangulate* his research methods whenever possible. That is, more than one method should be brought to bear upon any research problem. Thus, we will show that participant observation is best viewed as a method that combines survey data and quasi-experimental variations with document analysis and direct observation. Our last criterion under the category of validity is the *triangulation of methodologies*. This, of course, proposes a new line of action as well as a new set of symbolic meanings for the research process generally. We concur with Webb, *et al.*, who argue that in the contemporary age of social research it is no longer appropriate to conceive of *single method investigations*.[11]

To summarize, we have suggested that any research method must first meet the criteria of causal inference and internal and external validity. To this end the standard categories of these factors have been discussed.

METHODOLOGICAL CONSIDERATIONS FROM INTERACTION THEORY

Central to the interactionist's conception of human behavior is the assumption that all behavior is self-directed and hence observable at two distinct levels—the symbolic and the interactional or behavioral.[12] The central keys to understanding

[9] This dimension of internal validity becomes the chief justification for "unobtrusive measures of observation." See Eugene Webb *et al.*, *Unobtrusive Measures: Nonreactive Research in the Social Sciences* (Chicago: Rand-McNally, 1966) for a discussion of this research strategy.
[10] Denzin, *op. cit.*, Ch. 8–12.
[11] Webb *et al.*, *op. cit.*
[12] Herbert Blumer in his "Sociological Implications of George Herbert Mead," *American Journal of Sociology*, 71 (March, 1966), pp. 535–548, provides the main source for the following comments. Reprinted in Part Five of this volume.

human conduct are the range and variety of symbols and symbolic meanings shared, communicated, and manipulated by interacting selves in social situations. Society is viewed as contributing two essential features that reflect directly on concrete interactions. These are, first, the symbols or various languages provided and communicated through the socialization process and, second, the concrete behavioral settings or stages within which behavior occurs.

An interactionist assumes that a complete and meaningful analysis of human conduct will capture the symbolic meanings that emerge over time in interaction. The behaviorism of Mead directs us to link symbols with interaction—hence the term symbolic interaction. The variety of these symbols are manifold and complex, ranging from the verbal to the non-verbal and from the intended to the unintended. The verbal utterance, the non-verbal gesture, the mode of dress, and the style of speech all provide clues to the symbolic meanings that become translated into and emerge out of interaction.

With this set of assumptions we can now discuss the methodological mandates of symbolic interactionism. The most telling is that *both symbols and interaction must be brought together before an investigation is complete.* To focus only on symbols via attitude scales or checklists of beliefs fails to record the emergent and novel relationship these symbols have with observable behavior. Because symbols are forged into meaningful sets of self-definitions, the reflective nature of selfhood must be captured. To this end the investigator is forced to view human conduct from the perspective of those he is studying. He must "take the role of the acting other in concrete situations." Taking the role of the acting other allows the sociologist to escape the often committed *fallacy of objectivism* or the substitution of one's perspectives for those studied. Too often the sociologist enters the field with preconceptions concerning the behavior he is studying and never allows those studied to tell it "as they see it." Adherence to symbolic interaction clearly avoids this fallacy.

Taking the role of the acting other forces the investigator to consider the duality of human existence, which is its simultaneous interrelationship with self-conversations and conversations with the "interiorized" social other or social groupings to which one belongs. In short, man's symbols and conceptions of self reflect his ongoing relationships in social circles. Hence the next mandate from interactionism—*observations must link man's symbols and conceptions of self with the social circles that furnish him with these very symbols and conceptions.* The failure to move beyond individualistic descriptions of isolated actors reduces sociology to an aggregate psychology of the most solipsistic nature. Any method must be capable of moving at both levels—the individualistic and the social.

Research methods must consider the "situated aspects" of human conduct. This dimension was noted in the context of internal validity and reappears at this point, for it flows directly from the interactionist perspective. The specific time-space dimensions of interaction must be recorded by any method, if the complete link between symbols and behavior is to be established.

Conventional tests of the interactionist perspective have often failed to situate respondents. Surveys lend themselves to this flaw and, as a consequence, the situated elements of the self are unanalyzed. The literature does, however, report notable exceptions to this generalization. In a series of interrelated investigations on identification with urban locales, Stone has employed the survey technique in the manner we are suggesting.[13] In a study of housewife shopping patterns and identification with city life, Stone explicitly situated his respondents by asking (depending on a prior choice), "Why would you rather do business with local independent merchants or large chain stores?"[14] This question placed the subject in the setting where she did her shopping and hence permitted a designation and description of relevant activities on that basis. Responses to this question led Stone to the conclusion that urban identification extends beyond occupational affiliation, and may arise any time the person becomes caught up in routinized relationships that are sustained by frequent and regular communication.

Social selves, we have suggested, are situated objects that reflect a person's ongoing definitions of self in the settings at hand. For this reason, both the meanings attached to these situations and the types of selves that emerge within them must be examined. Stone's investigation treats the meanings attached to shopping situations and indirectly infers the types of selves that flow from them.

Our research methods must be capable of capturing the processual elements of human interaction. The emergent relationship between self conceptions, designated meanings, and reflective interaction must be recorded, analyzed, and explained. Methods, such as the survey, which dichotomize all process into past or present, fail to grasp the essential fact that human conduct reflects a world of past, present, and future simultaneously playing upon man's behavior.

The very act of engaging in social research must be seen from the perspective of symbolic interaction. In this vein, the act of being a scientist reflects the continual attempt to lift one's own idiosyncratic experiences to the level of consensual and shared meaning.[15] It is in this context that research method becomes our prime means of both acting on the symbolic environment and making those actions consensual in the broader community of scientists. Our actions are translated into specific methods via lines of action that reflect our very definitions of these methods. At the heart of this interaction are the concept and the clusters of meanings we attempt to formulate with our research methods. The concept and the research method enable the sociologist to carry on an interaction with his environment. We indicate to ourselves what a concept and a method mean and symbolically act toward the designation of that meaning. We are continually reassessing our imputed object meanings—assessing them against their relationships to our theory, their ability to be observed by others, and their ability to generate understanding and explanation in our own symbolic reality. The concept and the method, in combination, act as *sensitizers* of our perception. They open new realms of observation, but concomitantly close others. To conceive and perceive reality from the stance of one method precludes conception from another.

We can argue that all research methods stand in an instrumental relationship to the scientific process. They become plans of actions employed as we move from theory to a constructed reality. They are the major means by which we organize

---

[13] See for example Gregory P. Stone, "Drinking Styles and Status Arrangements," in David J. Pittman and Charles R. Snyder (eds.), *Society, Culture, and Drinking Patterns* (New York: John Wiley and Sons, 1962), pp. 121–40; Joel Smith, William H. Form, and Gregory P. Stone, "Local Intimacy in a Middle-Sized City," *American Journal of Sociology*, 60 (Nov., 1954), pp. 276–284; Gregory P. Stone, "City Shoppers and Urban Identification: Observations on the Social Psychology of City Life," *American Journal of Sociology*, 60 (July, 1954), pp. 36–45.

[14] Stone, "City Shoppers . . . ," *ibid.*, p. 37.

[15] The following draws heavily from Blumer's "Science Without Concepts," *American Journal of Sociology*, 36 (1931), pp. 515–33.

our creative energy or operational activities toward our concepts and our theories. As such they at once release and direct activity. The success of our activities via these means is measured by our ability to satisfy the normal criteria of validity while establishing fruitful ties with our theories.

In the above senses, research methods serve also to provide the scientist with data that later may be placed in deductive schemes of thought. By observing several discrete and separate instances of a concept or a series of concepts, we are able to move above the single instance to the more common problems that transcend immediate perceptions and observations.

And last, we suggest that *from the interactionist's perspective, the proper use of concepts becomes sensitizing,* and not operational. Further, the proper theory becomes formal and not middle range or grand; proper causal propositions become universal and not statistical. These three interrelated notions require explication. By *sensitizing concepts* we refer to concepts that are not immediately transformed into rigid, operational definitions via an attitude scale or check-list.[16] Rather, sensitizing concepts are deliberately left nonoperationalized until the investigator enters the field and learns the specific meanings attached to the processes represented by his concept. Once these meanings are established, multiple research methods are brought to bear upon the concept as it is represented in all its "situated contexts."

Goffman's treatment of stigma provides an excellent example of what we mean by "sensitizing-a-concept."[17] He began with a rather vague and loose definition of stigma, which he claimed was "an attribute that is deeply discrediting."[18] Three types of this attribute were then designated: abominations of the body by physical deformity, blemishes of character (e.g. mental disorder, homosexuality, addiction, alcoholism), and tribal stigmata of race, nation, or religion. Moving past this classification, Goffman then analyzed vast amounts of data collected in such traditionally honored sociological specialties as social problems, ethnic relations, social disorganization, criminology, and deviance. From these areas, relevant commonalities were organized around the theme of stigma. In summarizing this analysis Goffman states:[19]

> I have argued that stigmatized persons have enough of their situations in life in common to warrant classifying all these persons together for purposes of analysis. An extraction has thus been made from the traditional fields of social problems. . . . These commonalities can be organized on the basis of a very few assumptions regarding human nature. What remains in each one of the traditional fields could then be reexamined for whatever is really special to it, thereby beginning analytical coherence to what is now purely historic and fortuitous unity. Knowing what fields like race relations, aging and mental health share, one could then go on to see, analytically, how they differ. Perhaps in each case the choice would be to retain the old substantive areas, but at least it would be clear that each is merely an area to which one should apply several perspectives, and that the development of any one of these coherent analytic perspectives is not likely to come from those who restrict their interest exclusively to one substantive area.

---

[16] See Herbert Blumer, "What Is Wrong with Social Theory," *American Sociological Review,* 14 (February, 1954), pp. 3–10, for a complete discussion of the sensitizing concept.
[17] Erving Goffman, *Stigma: Notes on the Management of Spoiled Identity* (Englewood Cliffs, N. J.: Prentice-Hall, 1963).
[18] *Ibid.,* p. 5.
[19] *Ibid.,* pp. 146–47.

This process of *sensitizing-a-concept* permits the sociologist to discover what is unique about each empirical instance of the concept while he uncovers what it displays in common across many different settings. Such a conception forces (in fact allows) the sociologist to pursue his interactionist view of reality to the empirical extreme.

Our notion of formal, as opposed to grand and middle range theory, relates directly to the assumption that universal explanations of social reality may be discovered.[20] Taking the stance of Simmel, we argue that human conduct presents itself in behavioral *forms* which differ only in their *content*. The job of sociology is to discover these forms which universally display themselves in only slightly different contents. As such, a handful of concepts from the interactionist's perspective are thought to be sufficient to explain the wide range of human behavior whatever the social or cultural context. The proper stance toward theory (and this relates directly to our methods) is the development of formal social theory which relies on multiple methodologies. One formal theory, empirically grounded at all points, is preferred to grand theory with no empirical referents, or a series of middle range theories, each of which has its own method. At the heart of formal theory will be universal propositions that are assumed to apply to all instances of the phenomenon studied—at least until a negative case is discovered. Further, these propositions will be *interactional in nature*. That is they will describe interrelationships between processes that interact, as opposed to propositions that assume linearity or noninteraction between events. If the fact of human behavior is interaction, then our propositions must take an interactional form. Our sixth proposition, to summarize, is that our methods must be constructed so that they contribute to formal theory, while at the same time they allow sensitizing concept analysis and the discovery and verification of universal-interactive propositions.

THE PRECONDITIONS IN REVIEW

We have shown that the symbolic interactionist demands that his methods capture the temporal reflective aspects of self-directed interaction as that interaction relates to the perspectives of social groups. The investigator is forced to take the role of the acting other as he employs any one of several research methods in his interactions on reality. These mandates, coupled with considerations of validity, provide the sociologist with a set of categories by which he can at once evaluate and employ any of the five research methods we now turn to. The general stance in the next section will be critical, in the belief that criticism is better than praise at this point in the methodological development of sociology.

Five Research Methods of the Interactionist

THE EXPERIMENT

In its most generic form the experiment may be defined as a situation in which the investigator controls some and manipulates other variables, thus enabling him to observe and analyze the effects of the manipulated variable(s) upon the de-

[20] Barney G. Glaser and Anselm L. Strauss discuss this view of theorizing in their *The Discovery of Grounded Theory* (Chicago: Aldine, 1967). See also Denzin, *op. cit.*, Ch. 3–4.

pendent variable(s) in a situation in which the operation of other relevant factors is believed to be held constant. The true experimental design contains, at a minimum, two observational groups (e.g., experimental and control). Two sets of observations are made, which introduce the factor of time and change into the design. Two basic types of experiment may be noted: the true experiment and the quasi-experiment. In the latter type, the experiment is moved from the laboratory into a natural field setting although the rigor of the true experiment is approximated as completely as possible. The quasi-experimental design will typically be of the time-series variety, wherein repeated observations are made on either the same or a series of comparable groups through a predesignated time period. In either case two observation groups will be present—thereby maintaining the basic form of the true design.

Given these elements of the experiment, we can see its immediate relevance for the study of face-to-face interaction in a closed behavior setting (e.g., the laboratory). Seldom, however, has it been viewed in this light. We wish to pursue this aspect of the method before turning to its flaws and deficiencies.

Recent observations by Freidman suggest that behavior in the experiment may best be viewed as an encounter in which the experimenter acts more as a participant than an experimenter in the traditional meaning of the word.[21] At every point in the interaction between experimenter and subject we observe the dynamics of face-work Goffman has described as representative of the encounter.[22] In short, we observe an encounter between strangers in a behavior setting that has been given unique cultural meanings by the participants who enter. We observe the transformation of a four-walled room into a setting in which meaningful social conduct occurs. The mechanisms by which selves are defined, projected, and alienated are all present. While the ideal experiment flows from a predetermined script, or plan of action, Friedman has shown that what actually occurs is directly attributable to the presentation of selves of both experimenter and subject.

Rather than viewing the experiment as a sterile method, which approaches methodological perfection, it is suggested that we view it as a behavior setting created by the scientist. It is so unique in its features that we might best study the behavior that occurs within it for what it tells us about symbolic interaction in those behavior settings our culture has labeled experimental laboratories.

Given this interpretation, how have experiments met the interactionist's assumptions? For the most part, not well at all. The role of the acting other is forsaken for an analysis of behavior from the perspective of the experimenter. Symbols are ignored for a behaviorist interpretation, and the situation is ignored because it is assumed to be free of differential meaning. Process is considered, but only as a mediating factor between the first and last observation. Sensitizing concept analysis is not employed. Instead, rigorous operational definitions and indices are formulated, often of the physiological variety.

When matters of causality and validity are raised, the true experimental potential is quite satisfactory. The experimental model of inference, of course, provides the paradigm for all causal analysis. It is irrelevant at this point if it produces only probabilistic statements, for it could quite easily be employed to discover universal causal relationships. On the dimensions of external and internal validity,

---

[21] Neil Freidman, *The Social Nature of Psychological Research* (New York: Basic Books, 1967).
[22] Erving Goffman, *Encounters* (Indianapolis: Bobbs-Merrill, 1961).

Campbell and Stanley have shown that, with certain modifications, the classic before-after design with one control group can be made virtually free of jeopardizing validity factors.

In summary, we have with the experiment, a research method aptly suited to the analysis of certain interactional problems. However, until definitions such as our own are more widely shared, the design of experiments will offer little of theoretical value to the symbolic interactionist.

The Social Survey

As a methodological technique that requires the systematic collection of data from populations or samples through the use of the interview or the self-administered questionnaire, the social survey has traditionally represented one of the most frequently used methods by the symbolic interactionist. That this has been so is curiously paradoxical, given the fact that on nearly every dimension the survey fails to meet even the minimal interactionist's assumptions concerning an adequate methodology. Blumer has suggested that the survey's heavy emphasis on variable, as opposed to sensitizing analysis, precludes the serious study of the interpretive processes contained in symbolic interaction. This factor is compounded when we realize that the typical survey approximates a one-shot case study in which no comparison groups are employed and no before observations are obtained. The survey analyst too often takes a "snapshot" of social behavior at one point in time and relies on his respondent to reconstruct the events preceding the interview. This feature, while correctable through the use of a design that calls for repeated observations, leads the analyst to employ a form of multivariate analysis. While causally acceptable, this mode of causal inference forces him to conceptualize all temporal processes in terms of either past or present events, thereby escaping the fluid temporality of human experience.

The typical survey represents what Gold has termed the observer-as-participant method, in which the investigator presents himself for one short period of time before those studied.[23] No lasting relationship is established. In fact the contact is brief, highly formalized through the use of the questionnaire, and represents no effort on the part of the investigator to form more than a *stranger relationship* with the respondent.

The structured interview and the emphasis on nonsensitizing analytic procedures provide the two key features of the social survey and, as such, point at once to its limitations and its advantages for the symbolic interactionist.

Turning first to limitations, we note that the typical survey never proceeds to establish the social basis of human conduct. Respondents are treated as isolated aggregates, perfectly sampled, but only indirectly related to a social structure. While this atomistic bias can be overcome through the use of a relational or contextual mode of analysis, this variation is infrequently practiced. This feature makes it difficult for the analyst to establish the basis of the symbolic meanings elicited in his interviews, and as such provides valid data only on the individualistic basis of attitudes and social meanings.

Second, because of its emphasis on "respondent reconstruction" of past events and the fact that statements and not ongoing conduct are studied in the interview,

23 Raymond L. Gold, "Roles in Sociological Field Observations," *Social Forces*, 36 (March, 1958), pp. 217–23.

the survey is ill-equipped to relate statements to process. Too many survey ana-lysts assume that the statements they elicit can unequivocally be related to re-spondent reports of past or future behavioral actions. Unfortunately the relation-ship between statements and social acts is not so clear-cut. The very factor of in-teraction leads to, in fact shapes, new and novel attitudes that were not existent before. Persons often go for days without translating a single attitude directly into behavior.

To summarize, we find in the survey a tendency to ignore the role of the acting other by forcing him to respond to a predetermined questionnaire. The situations of interaction are ignored by regarding all of them as equal in meaning. Process is reconstructed, not observed, and variable analysis replaces the sensitizing mode outlined earlier.

Still the emphasis on structure in the questionnaire format points to one of its unique advantages, and that is the fact that the survey method is well suited for the study of stable patterns of interaction. In communities, or social structures where stable patterns of meaning and action are present (e.g., where complex forms of symbolic interaction are absent), the survey is perhaps our best method for discovering and charting these forms of stabilities.

Another unique function of the survey may be noted when we recognize that the interactional situation created by the survey interview represents an encounter between strangers. Conceived in this light, we as sociologists might profitably ex-amine the dynamics of face-work, appearance, mood, gesture, and conversation as they emerge and give shape to the interview encounter.[24] The survey interview can then be seen as a situation in which respondent and interviewer strive for common meaning and consensus as they proceed through a schedule that elicits multiple and conflicting identities, meanings, and symbols. The dynamics of this interactional process thus become one point of study with the survey, for as a method it requires that such encounters be created and played out to successful completion.[25]

In summary, the survey is best seen as a setting for stranger encounters. As a method it is most appropriate for the study of stable forms of interaction. To treat it otherwise (e.g., as a method for studying complex, shifting forms of inter-action) as so many have done is incorrect. The continued use of survey methods to examine the self-concept, social conceptions of deviance, deviant careers, atti-tudes toward social objects, and any other complex forms of symbolic interpreta-tion only drives the wedge in further between symbolic interaction theory and the research findings that flow from the theory.

PARTICIPANT OBSERVATION

In several senses participant observation represents the synthesis of method and theory outlined above. The investigator is directed to take the role of the acting other, to learn his perspectives, and to study his conduct in as many relevant situa-tions as possible. Symbols, action, and the social nexus of meaning are discovered and related by daily participation in the rounds of activity of those studied. Broadly defined, participant observation is a method that simultaneously

---

[24] Herbert H. Hyman in *Interviewing and Social Research* (Chicago: University of Chicago Press, 1954) presents data bearing on this point.
[25] On the problems of these encounters see Denzin, *op. cit.*, Ch. 6.

combines document analysis, respondent and informant interviewing, direct participation, and observation with self-introspection on the part of the investigator. In this respect the method rests fundamentally on triangulation. Survey data will be collected to establish the parameters of the interactants and situations. Document analysis provides historical evidence on events that occurred before the study began, and direct participation and self-introspection provide means of relating symbols to on-going interaction.

The problems of this method are many and arise primarily when the investigator fails to employ triangulated techniques in his fieldwork. This failure leaves the strategy open to criticisms of impressionistic bias and descriptive journalism. However, as Becker and others have shown, qualitative data generated by this method can be converted into quantitative forms that allow more than impressionistic generalizations.[26]

Elsewhere we have shown how problems of internal and external validity may be overcome by careful attention to the reactive influence of the investigator in the field and recurrent measurements of change in those studied.[27] In this respect the participant observer becomes as quantitative as the survey methodologist for he must develop forms and categories to measure his reactive effect.

Many critics have pointed to the masses of data accumulated by the observer method and have suggested that there are no systematic means of assessing final conclusions and generalizations forthcoming from such studies. This criticism disappears when we note that the use of analytic induction, in combination with statistical and theoretical sampling models, provides a rigorous set of standards that must be met before any conclusions can be made. Analytic induction, with its emphasis on discovering negative cases and formulating universal-interactive propositions, provides the main line of action we have proposed for the scientific process.

Lindesmith has provided a model of this scientific process.[28] In a long-term investigation on the dynamics of drug addiction, he combined analytic induction with the formulation of universally applicable propositions concerning the addictive process. In this context we define analytic induction as a method of discovery and proof that directs the investigator to redefining progressively his research problem in the light of contradictory evidence. Each negative case forces a revision of the research hypothesis. The research process does not end until all examined cases can be adequately explained by the theoretical system under development. Lindesmith explains his use of this method as follows:[29]

> The strategy of the present research has been to carve out a limited but specific problem and to analyze it as exhaustively as possible. . . . The principle of limited inquiry was also applied to the definition of the object matter of this study. Opiate addiction was rigorously described as a behavior system characteristic of certain persons in our society. . . .
>
> The advantages of the method [which] require[s] the researcher . . . to formulate propositions that apply to all the instances of the problem without exceptions, are that (1) it makes it possible to disprove theories and to test one

[26] Howard S. Becker, *et al.*, *Boys in White* (Chicago: University of Chicago Press, 1961).
[27] Denzin, *op. cit.*, Ch. 9.
[28] See Alfred R. Lindesmith, *Opiate Addiction* (Bloomington, Ind.: Principia Press, 1947) and his recently revised version of this work, *Addiction and Opiates* (Chicago: Aldine, 1968). Unless otherwise indicated our references to Lindesmith's work are taken from the 1947 edition.
[29] *Ibid.*, pp. 15 and 19.

against another, (2) it provides the possibility of cumulative growth as old theories are revised to take into account new negative evidence, and (3) it makes for close articulation of theory and fact, for whatever a temporary hypothesis may be it must be changed to conform with the evidence it contradicts.

Lindesmith initially began with the hypothesis that "individuals who did not know what drug they were taking would not become addicted." [30] Conversely, it was predicted that persons would become addicted when they knew what they were receiving and had taken it long enough to experience withdrawal distress when they stopped.

This hypothesis was immediately rejected when one of the first addicts interviewed, a doctor, reported that he had once taken morphine for several weeks, was fully aware of this fact but did not become addicted at that time. In light of this evidence, a second hypothesis was formulated which predicted persons would become addicts when they recognized withdrawal symptoms when they ceased to take the drug. This also was revised and the final theory took the following form: [31]

> It has been shown that the opiate habit rests fundamentally upon the effects which follow when the drug is removed rather than upon the positive effects which its presence in the body produces. Addiction occurs only when opiates are used to alleviate withdrawal distress, after this distress has been properly understood or interpreted, that is to say, after it has been represented to the individual in terms of the linguistic symbols and cultural patterns which have grown around the opiate habit. If the individual fails to conceive of his distress as withdrawal distress brought about by the absence of opiates he cannot become addicted, but if he does, addiction is quickly and permanently established through further use of the drug. All of the evidence unequivocally supports this conclusion.

Lindesmith's study thus rests on the assumption that: [32]

> . . . [The analyst] must seek to formulate generalizations which apply to all of the instances of the problem with which he is concerned, rather than to most or some of them only.

The method implied by analytic induction need not be restricted to participant observation. It is appropriate to any research strategy. Surveys, for example, could be designed such that each negative case was either reinterviewed or reanalyzed to fit such contradictions more accurately into emergent explanations.[33] Analytic induction, however, directs attention away from statements of correlation and leads to a focus on all-encompassing propositions. As such, it represents a radical interpretation of the scientific process and implies that true causal analysis applies to all, and not just a significant proportion of the events studied.

The advantages of participant observation are numerous, but derive from the fundamental fact that this is one of the few methods currently available to the sociologist concerned with studying complex forms of symbolic interaction. What better way to study the process of self-hood, of face-work, of emergent group perspectives, of social reactions to deviance, or the interrelated links between formal

---

[30] *Ibid.,* p. 7.
[31] *Ibid.,* p. 165.
[32] *Ibid.,* p. 12.
[33] See, for example, Patricia L. Kendall and Katherine M. Wolf, "The Two Purposes of Deviant Case Analysis," in Paul F. Lazarsfeld and Morris Rosenberg, *The Language of Social Research* (Glencoe, Ill.: The Free Press, 1955), pp. 167–170.

and informal structure in an organization than with a strategy that leads one to observe these events directly as they unfold? The observer method is both our strongest and weakest strategy, for when incorrectly employed, it leads to unfounded, nonreplicable generalizations. But when rigorously practiced, it becomes the one method best suited for the study of symbolic interaction—be it in a formal organization, an informal group, or a primitive community.

THE LIFE-HISTORY METHOD

This method represents an application of participant observation principles to the single case. Its intent, as Park stated, is "obtaining a record of the inner-subjective life of man and relating it to his on-going interactions and social relationships." [34] Life-history materials include any document or record, including case histories of social agencies that throw light on the subjective behavior of individuals. Its basic theme is a record of experiences from the subject's point of view. When fully elaborated, the life-history approach will lead the investigator to share in the activities of those he is studying. In short he acts as a participant observer, except now he is explicitly obtaining subject-reports.

Core sources of data will be letters, personal autobiographies, and observations. The life-history may take any of several forms which include the topical and the comprehensive. In the topical life-history, only a specific phase of the subject's life experiences will be covered, while the comprehensive life-history attempts a total reconstruction.

Letters and personal diaries will be gathered when possible and will usefully complement the subject's own description of his experiences. Direct observation and participation on the part of the analyst represent a means of triangulating the life-history by providing behavioral data that may only be alluded to in the subject's report.

The flaws of this method arise when triangulation is not employed, thereby forcing the investigator to rely totally on what is told him. Further, the user of this method must take care that the single case he selects is typical of the total set of possible cases not studied. [35] He must show that it is a member of that population and, if it differs significantly, this must be established. Conceived in this fashion, the life-history, or case method, becomes a powerful means of studying a total set of events by identifying the generic features and processes representative in a portion of the total set. When analytic induction is employed as a method of proof, the sociologist has at his disposal a means of generating universal propositions that may be tested and expanded in other populations and situations.

Becker has shown that while the single life-history may be inconclusive, when placed beside a series of such studies, a complete picture of the behavior in one broad locale may be derived [36]. Thus the series of life-histories conducted in the city of Chicago in the 1930's and 1940's, taken together, portray the times and conditions of the participants in that city.

Current disfavor for the life-history in contemporary sociology partially reflects

---

[34] Robert E. Park, "The Sociological Methods of William Graham Sumner, and of William I. Thomas and Florian Znaniecki," in Stuart A. Rice (ed.), *Methods in Social Research: A Case Book* (Chicago: University of Chicago Press, 1931), p. 167.

[35] Ernest W. Burgess makes this point in his "Discussion" of Clifford R. Shaw's *The Jack-Roller* (Chicago: University of Chicago Press, 1966), pp. 185–86.

[36] Howard S. Becker, Preface to *The Jack-Roller, op. cit.*

the sociologist's preference for what he feels are more objective and empirical methods (e.g., the survey and the experiment).[37] We have shown that these latter strategies are beset with flaws and of only limited use to the interactionist. The degree of objectivity contained within a method only reflects the extent to which it accurately records the events and processes under study, and, in this respect, the life-history cannot be surpassed.

UNOBTRUSIVE MEASURES OF OBSERVATION

The central feature of this method is the absence of the observer from the social situations he is studying.[38] The reactive effect of a present observer is thereby removed, permitting a noncontaminated description of the events under analysis. Four major forms of this method may be noted. First are the recording of physical traces left by persons as they pass through social situations. These may be *depository* traces (e.g., leaving certain materials) or *erosion* traces (e.g., the selective wear on materials). Second is the analysis of archival records of the public and/or private variety. Newspaper accounts of events, the study of literary forms, and census records all represent public records that are not elicited by the observer which may be analyzed without reactive effect on content. Private archival records include unsolicited letters, memos, diaries, and so on which record behavior on the part of either individuals or organizations. Third are simple behavioral observations in situations where the observer has no control over the behavior or signs in question and plays an unobserved, passive role. Here, study might include: recording nonverbal gestures; variations in dress and adornment in certain situations; the study of body location or the study of language behavior. While the observer is passive and unobtrusive he can obtain valuable information of a behavioristic nature. Last is the use of "contrived hardware" for the study of interaction. Cameras and tape recorders may be employed in an unobtrusive fashion to obtain a complete visual and auditory picture of the behavior in a given setting.

The advantage of these methods is primarily in their nonreactive nature, but secondarily in their ability to provide explicitly focused data on behavioral events of an interactionist variety. Their chief disadvantage lies in the fact that they are behavioristic and hence escape the symbolic elements of interaction. Sheer records of interaction are insufficient. We need methods that combine both the symbolic and the interactional elements. Taken alone, unobtrusive measures are inadequate, but when used in combination with the experiment, the survey, or participant observation, they provide a powerful means of systematically recording patterns of interaction.

THE HISTORICAL PERSPECTIVE

We have suggested that symbolic interactionism requires a longitudinal-historical perspective such that the unfolding trajectories of any set of events are captured and recorded in our investigations. The matter cuts deeper. Not only do social events have histories, but they are also inextricably embedded in specific historical contexts that give them unique meaning and form. As Mills has shown, social events have meaning only within their own reconstructed historical past-

---

[37] *Ibid.*

[38] Webb, *et al., op. cit.,* present the first complete discussion of this method.

presence.[39] The *principle of historical specificity* then must be brought directly into our methodological and theoretical endeavors.[40] We must realize, as Strauss argues, that each generation, each social group, and in fact each social self re-writes its own past. It seems appropriate, on a closing note, to restate Strauss' position that "a social psychology without a full focus upon history is a blind psychology." [41]

It therefore becomes necessary for symbolic interactionists to rethink their positions toward current methodologies so that we begin to investigate systematically the historical dimension of human interaction. Clearly, as we have indicated, this involves two dimensions—the study of man's reconstructed historical past and the examination of events through time. Our methods must capture both dimensions.

Certainly the five methodologies treated in this paper differentially adopt themselves to the historical perspective. The survey, for example, in its most popular forms only indirectly measures events through time. Participant observation, unless documents and interviews are employed, only indirectly reflects past and present history. The life-history method fits the historical model, but again this is limited to single cases.

We need to adopt a stance quite similar to that of the historian who sets for himself the job of faithfully reconstructing historical events. Whether our interest is in broad societal concerns, or with more microcosmic matters such as the analysis of social groups through generations, we must identify the peculiar historical nexus and reconstructed past operative on those events under investigation. In accurately depicting and reconstructing the historical past of any collectivity, our chief sources of data will become public and private archival documents, and to a lesser degree the interview. To analyze these forms of data we must adopt the styles and strategies of the historian so that we become fully conversant with the *historical method*.[42] To this end we will learn to analyze documents and records in terms of their authenticity and intent (e.g., the problem of external criticism) and in terms of their credibility and relationship to emergent hypotheses (e.g., the problem of internal criticism).

It is important in concluding, to remember that the sociologist will differ from the historian by virtue of the comparative method which is central to his models of inference.[43] That is, "the historian is more concerned with detailed descriptions of a particular historical period, while the sociologist looks at different societies or at several periods of history in order to observe what happens under different conditions to a common class of objects." [44]

Summary and Conclusions

I have attempted in this discussion to pursue the problem Kuhn saw confronting the contemporary interactionist (e.g., lack of adequate methodologies). Cen-

[39] C. Wright Mills, *The Sociological Imagination* (New York: Oxford University Press, 1959), Ch. 8. This, of course, is a salient theme in the work of Marx and Weber as well.

[40] Louis Gottschalk, "The Historian and the Historical Document," in Louis Gottschalk, Clyde Kluckhohn, and Robert Angell, *The Use of Personal Documents in History, Anthropology and Sociology* (New York: Social Science Research Council, 1945) Ch. 1.

[41] Anselm Strauss, *Mirrors and Masks* (Glencoe: The Free Press, 1959), p. 173.

[42] Gottschalk, *op. cit.*

[43] This point is made by Joseph R. Gusfield in *Symbolic Crusade* (Urbana, Ill.: University of Illinois Press, 1966), pp. 57–60.

[44] *Ibid.*, p. 58.

tral to our argument was the belief that few advances in theory will occur until we have extracted from symbolic interactionism the necessary preconditions our methods must meet before they can be viewed as appropriate data-generating devices. The continual use of such techniques as the survey to measure central concepts like the self-concept represents confusion on the part of the interactionist, for a method built on principles of stability and structure cannot adequately measure a concept that assumes process and change. We have shown that each of the five methodologies are well-suited for studying certain, but not all, of the key interactionist assumptions. The six methodological assumptions derived from our theory indicate that each method represents a slightly different way of conceiving and hence acting on the empirical world. Our treatment of these methods was meant to indicate new conceptualizations, new problems, and slightly different questions that could be answered by each.

In many respects the present discussion has also built on Blumer's conviction that contemporary sociology needs a naturalistic methodology that accurately reflects the empirical nature of human conduct.[45] We have stated a series of assumptions or preconditions this methodology must meet and have concluded that the method must first be one that satisfies the theoretical dictates of symbolic interactionism. It is our hope that this paper will lead future theorists and investigators to be less parochial in their selection of research strategies so that a fully developed and sophisticated methodological foundation may be built as we continue to develop and refine the theoretical perspective of symbolic interactionism.

----

[45] Blumer, *op. cit.*

PART EIGHT
MOTIVES AND MOTIVATION

The sociological approach to motivation begins with an innocuous-looking proposition: *Man is active naturally*. With this stroke Dewey relegates to the scrap heap of elegant tautology and/or compelling mystery all attempts to explain action by inside urges and outside attractions—pushes and pulls are pre-empted. To some, this unassuming proposition is outrageous, for it discards, out of hand, all attempts to explain *why* man acts in the first place. On the inside, impulsion by instincts, needs, drives, and tension reduction are eliminated, while on the outside, physical, social, cultural, and other such presumed environmental stimuli are neglected. Man simply acts, period!

The sense of Dewey's position, in the selection reprinted here, is that the audience "sees" a given act as displeasing or bad and attempts to get the actor to re-assess his action from its point of view. Presumably the challenging audience (which might be oneself) has some notion of a more acceptable alternative and believes the actor capable of achieving it. If the audience can specify the desirable consequences flowing from the more acceptable alternative, it may well succeed in getting the act redirected. Following Dewey's lead thus shifts the problem of motivation from the strictly psychological to the social psychological by emphasizing the process of interpersonal social control.

For the sociologist, then, motivation is a question of direction, not origination of action. For the sociologist, as with his subjects, the question of motivation does not arise except in those instances where on-going conduct recurrently breaches expectation and mobilizes a control reaction from others. This reaction takes the form of a motivational challenge that asks in effect: "Why are you engaging in a deviation from expectation when you might well be doing what is expected of you?"

Probing the function of motives within situated action, C. W. Mills is concerned particularly with how actors use motives to interpret each other's conduct. Rather than explain action from the standpoint of motives, he sets out to explain motives from the standpoint of action. Specifically, he wants to know:

1. Which action situations require a verbalization of motives?
2. Why are some motives verbalized but not others?
3. How, in fact, are motives linked to action?

Mills' answer to the first question is similar to that implied by Dewey. Un-expected conduct occurs and precipitates crisis. The deviant act is usually chal-lenged in the form of a question. In response to the challenge, a motive is ver-balized. The function of the motive is to satisfy the challenger by giving him a rationale that makes the disputed act intelligible. This rationale usually consists of a reference to the end toward which the disputed conduct was headed. If the challenger can reinterpret the disputed conduct as a means to an end, and if he deems that end worthy, presumably he will rescind his objection.

The answer to Mills' second question hinges on the legitimacy of the end that is presented. Different social circles typically value different ends. For a motive to be efficacious, it had better verbalize an anticipated consequence that the chal-lenger finds credible. Of course, this means an actor may be quite strategic in his selection of motives. He may pick just the right motive with which to interpret his action. The actor may be aware that certain motives have currency in the so-cial circle of the challenger. The general implication here is that certain social circles may have typical vocabularies of motive that may be invoked in certain typical situations. As Mills sees it, a fruitful line of investigation would be the identification of such social circles and their characteristic vocabularies of motive, keeping in mind that at different historical moments and in different societal cir-cumstances what is characteristic will change.

The question that Mills raises but does not answer, concerning the linkage be-tween motives and action, is faced squarely by Foote. To fill the "unanalyzed hiatus between words and acts," Foote introduces the concept of "identification."

First, he declares we ought not talk about "motives" in general, but "motivated acts" in particular. Such acts are characterized by choice, control, and an agenda. Activities that are not so characterized, like habitual behavior and physiological functioning, should not be included in a discussion of motivated acts.

Given choices made in terms of preferred ends-in-view, or in anticipation of specific consummations (agenda), how do we insert this abstract calculus into the activity sequences of concrete human actors? Put another way, why should people undertake certain choices and the actions they imply in order to achieve certain ends when they might well make other choices on the basis of other ends? Foote's answer is that means and ends are chosen by individuals on the basis of the individual's understanding or conception of who he is. If I am so and so, then I will want such and such, and accordingly will do this rather than that.

How, then, do I know who I am? Although Foote does not carry the analysis too far, he does maintain that I can only discover who I am in interaction with other people through the process of mutual categorization or identification. This means that establishing one's own identity as well as that of others is problematic in many situations. If I announce myself to be a social democrat, and my radical friends place me as an establishment lackey, we are going to have identification problems. If I reach the point where I myself am not sure whether I'm the only sane voice left, or, indeed, have sold out the cause, my ability to act with determination may be jeopardized.

Who I can be is contingent, in part, on the willingness of others in the situation to accept me for who I say I am. Accordingly, the alternatives available to me in a situation are coordinated with the range of possibilities others allow me. Where alternative identities, in fact, are available, presumably I will appropriate that identity I value most.

The question of value thus presupposes the appropriation of identity, for it is the decision criterion upon which the choice is made. Foote reminds us that meaningful value is experienced or felt value; it is discovered in one's own concrete experience and is not mere conception. Memory of experienced value becomes advisory to but not determinative of the appropriation of identity. Still, it must be remembered that, by and large, an individual's own felt-value gains advisory capacity if it resonates with the values of the larger social circle.

Scott and Lyman follow this general line of development as they examine more closely the function of motives relative to their currency in particular social circles and in the negotiation of identities. They begin their discussion by introducing the term "account." Accounts presumably supersede the more ambiguous term "motives," but like motives are devices employed to re-integrate disrupted conduct. There are two kinds of accounts: (1) *justifications*, where one assumes responsibility for what he is accused of but sees nothing wrong in what he did and (2) *excuses*, where one refuses to take responsibility.

After adducing a suggestive typology of excuses, which include appeals to accidents, defeasibility, biological drives, and scapegoating, Scott and Lyman contend that certain social circles in dealing with deviation from expectation characteristically invoke certain types of appeal in formulating excuses. For example, Negroes and adolescent delinquents formulate excuses that invoke "fatalism" or lack of control over events. "If forces beyond my control determine how I behave, how can I be blamed for my transgressions?"

Unlike excuses, justifications are efforts to interpret the deviation as an act that should be seen as legitimate so that one ought to be able to claim responsibility for it.

Whether or not accounts will be honored depends on their currency in the social circle in which they are offered. In most circles, there are a set of taken-for-granted accounts that are honored invariably. As an example, "I'm having family problems" generally goes undisputed and may be used in a variety of different situations.

Scott and Lyman next consider challenges and accounts vis-à-vis the negotiation of identities. Often identities must be established as a prerequisite to the exchange of challenges and accounts. Certain identities simply are not open to challenge. Privates do not usually challenge the conduct of generals.

Negotiation of identities can be seen as a power play involving such tactics as mystification, referral, and switching whereby each participant tries to outmaneuver the other—the implication being that the dominant identity controls the flow of motivational challenges and, as such, the establishment of credibility. Generally, who can challenge, who is challenged, and the kinds of accounts presented depends upon the distribution of identities.

In sum, although the sociological approach to motivation is hardly past its inception and cumulative lines of theoretical development are barely visible, certain leads appear promising for research. Certainly, Mills' invitation to identify characteristic vocabularies of motive in relation to typically recurrent situations still stands. In addition, it might be asked whether motivational challenges invariably follow recurrent breaches of expectation. For example, if a close friend recurrently transgresses expectation, would you challenge him and risk losing him as a friend, or would you put up with it? Or, are motivational exchanges always verbal? Can't motives also be *seen* as parts of observable acts rather than heard as parts of verbal acts? A uniformed policeman directing traffic is clothed in motive; a policeman directing traffic out of uniform is in for a challenge. For that matter, who has the right to challenge whom, and why? Indeed, are there any conventions for determining the appropriateness of both challenges and motives? Finally, are there situations in which appeals to mood and emotion are more acceptable than appeals to cognitive values?

We can begin to specify the conditions under which challenges and imputations are made or avoided. A simple 2 x 2 table might force the issue:

	Impute	*Don't impute*
Challenge	1	2
Don't challenge	3	4

When we impute motives but do not challenge behavior (3), as we might in the case of a uniformed policeman directing traffic, aren't we contributing to social stability by assuming we know why that type of person, in that type of situation, is acting as he is? When we neither impute nor challenge (4), aren't we enacting habitual, routine, taken-for-granted behavior? When we don't impute but do challenge (2), aren't we reacting to someone who has us confused as to who he is? And finally, when we both challenge and impute, aren't we being typical Freudians or Marxians who offer the "real" reasons behind offensive behavior? Whatever promise these leads hold, the least we can say is that further inquiry into the relationships between identity, motive, and situation will be exciting and difficult.

Suggested Readings

BURKE, KENNETH. *A Grammar of Motives and a Rhetoric of Motives.* Cleveland and New York: The World Publishing Co., 1962.

————. *Permanence and Change.* Los Altos, California: Hermes Publications, 1954.

CRESSEY, DONALD R. "Role Theory, Differential Association, and Compulsive Crimes," in Arnold M. Rose (ed.), *Human Behavior and Social Process.* Boston: Houghton Mifflin Co., 1962, 443–467.

DEWEY, JOHN. *Human Nature and Conduct.* New York: The Modern Library, 1950.

MacIVER, ROBERT M. *Social Causation.* New York: Ginn and Co., 1942, 203–23.

PETERS, R. S. *The Concept of Motivation.* London: Routledge and Kegan Paul, 1958.

SCHUTZ, ALFRED. "In-Order-To and Because Motive," *Collected Papers I: The Problem of Social Reality.* The Hague: Martinus Nijhoff, 1967, 69–72.

SZASZ, THOMAS. *Law, Liberty and Psychiatry.* New York: Macmillan, 1963.

ZETTERBERG, HANS. "On Motivation," *Sociological Theories in Process I,* Joseph Berger, et al., Boston: Houghton Mifflin Co., 1966, 124–141.

48 On Motive

● JOHN DEWEY

Any one who observes children knows that while periods of rest are natural, laziness is an acquired vice—or virtue. While a man is awake he will do something, if only to build castles in the air. If we like the form of words we may say that a man eats only because he is "moved" by hunger. The statement is nevertheless mere tautology. For what does hunger mean except that one of the things which man does naturally, instinctively, is to search for food—that his activity naturally turns that way? Hunger primarily names an act or active process not a motive to an act. It is an act if we take it grossly, like a babe's blind hunt for the mother's breast; it is an activity if we take it minutely as a chemico-physiological occurrence.

The whole concept of motives is in truth extra-psychological. It is an outcome of the attempt of men to influence human action, first that of others, then of a man to influence his own behavior. No sensible person thinks of attributing the acts of an animal or an idiot to a motive. We call a biting dog ugly, but we don't look for his motive in biting. If however we were able to direct the dog's action by inducing him to reflect upon his acts, we should at once become interested in the dog's motives for acting as he does, and should endeavor to get him interested in the same subject. It is absurd to ask what induces a man to activity generally speaking. He is an active being and that is all there is to be said on that score. But when we want to get him to act in this specific way rather than in that, when we want to direct his activity that is to say in a specified channel, then the question of motive is pertinent. A motive is then that element in the total complex of a man's activity which, if it can be sufficiently stimulated, will result in an act having specified consequences. And part of the process of intensifying (or reducing) certain elements in the total activity and thus regulating actual consequence is to impute these elements to a person as his actuating motives.

A child naturally grabs food. But he does it in our presence. His manner is socially displeasing and we attribute to his act, up to this time wholly innocent, the motive of greed or selfishness. Greediness simply means the quality of his act as socially observed and disapproved. But by attributing it to him as his motive for acting in the disapproved way, we induce him to refrain. We analyze his total act and call his attention to an obnoxious element in its outcome. A child with equal spontaneity, or thoughtlessness, gives way to others. We point out to him with approval that he acted considerately, generously. And this quality of action when noted and encouraged becomes a reinforcing stimulus of that factor which will induce similar acts in the future. An element in an act viewed as a tendency to produce such and such consequences is a motive. A motive does not exist prior to an act and produce it. It is an act *plus* a judgment upon some element of it, the judgment being made in the light of the consequences of the act.

SOURCE: John Dewey, from his *Human Nature and Conduct* (New York: Holt, Rinehart and Winston, Inc., 1922), pp. 119–120. Copyright 1922 by Holt, Rinehart and Winston, Inc. Copyright 1950 by John Dewey. Reprinted by permission of Holt, Rinehart and Winston, Inc.

49   Situated Actions and Vocabularies of Motive

● C. WRIGHT MILLS

The major reorientation of recent theory and observation in sociology of language emerged with the overthrow of the Wundtian notion that language has as its function the "expression" of prior elements within the individual. The postulate underlying modern study of language is the simple one that we must approach linguistic behavior, not by referring it to private states in individuals, but by observing its social function of coordinating diverse action. Rather than expressing something which is prior and in the person, language is taken by other persons as an indicator of future actions.[1]

Within this perspective there are suggestions concerning problems of motivation. It is the purpose of this paper to outline an analytic model for the explanation of motives which is based on a sociological theory of language and a sociological psychology.[2]

As over against the inferential conception of motives as subjective "springs" of action, motives may be considered as typical vocabularies having ascertainable functions in delimited societal situations. Human actors do vocalize and impute motives to themselves and to others. To explain behavior by referring it to an inferred and abstract "motive" is one thing. To analyze the observable lingual mechanisms of motive imputation and avowal as they function in conduct is quite another. Rather than fixed elements "in" an individual, motives are the terms with which interpretation of conduct *by social actors* proceeds. This imputation and avowal of motives by actors are social phenomena to be explained. The differing reasons men give for their actions are not themselves without reasons.

First, we must demarcate the general conditions under which such motive imputation and avowal seem to occur.[3] Next, we must give a characterization of motive in denotable terms and an explanatory paradigm of why certain motives are verbalized rather than others. Then, we must indicate mechanisms of the linkage of vocabularies of motive to systems of action. What we want is an analysis of the integrating, controlling, and specifying function a certain type of speech fulfils in socially situated actions.

The generic situation in which imputation and avowal of motives arise involves, first, the *social* conduct or the (stated) programs of languaged creatures,

SOURCE: C. Wright Mills, in *American Sociological Review*, V (October 1940), pp. 904–13. Copyright 1940 by American Sociological Review. Copyright renewed 1968 by Yaraslava Mills. Reprinted by permission of Brandt & Brandt.

Revision of a paper read to The Society for Social Research, University of Chicago, August 16–17, 1940.

[1] See C. Wright Mills, "Bibliographical Appendices," Section I, 4: "Sociology of Language" in *Contemporary Social Theory*, ed. by Barnes, Becker & Becker, New York, 1940.
[2] See G. H. Mead, "Social Psychology as Counterpart of Physiological Psychology," *Psychol. Bul.*, VI: 401–408, 1909; Karl Mannheim, *Man and Society in an Age of Reconstruction*, New York, 1940; L. V. Wiese-Howard Becker, *Systematic Sociology*, part I, New York, 1932; J. Dewey, "All psychology is either biological or social psychology," *Psychol. Rev.*, vol. 24:276.
[3] The importance of this initial task for research is clear. Most researches on the verbal level merely ask abstract questions of individuals, but if we can tentatively delimit the situations in which certain motives *may* be verbalized, we can use that delimitation in the construction of *situational* questions, and we shall be *testing* deductions from our theory.

i.e., programs and actions oriented with reference to the actions and talk of others; second, the avowal and imputation of motives is concomitant with the speech form known as the "question." Situations back of questions typically involve *alternative* or *unexpected* programs or actions which phases analytically denote "crises." [4] The question is distinguished in that it usually elicits another *verbal* action, not a motor response. The question is an element in *conversation*. Conversation may be concerned with the factual features of a situation as they are seen or believed to be or it may seek to integrate and promote a set of diverse social actions with reference to the situation and its normative pattern of expectations. It is in this latter assent and dissent phase of conversation that persuasive and dissuasive speech and vocabulary arise. For men live in immediate acts of experience and their attentions are directed outside themselves until acts are in some way frustrated. It is then that awareness of self and of motive occur. The "question" is a lingual index of such conditions. The avowal and imputation of motives are features of such conversations as arise in "question" situations.

Motives are imputed or avowed as answers to questions interrupting acts or programs. Motives are words. Generically, to what do they refer? They do not denote any elements "in" individuals. They stand for anticipated situational consequences of questioned conduct. Intention or purpose (stated as a "program") *is* awareness of anticipated consequence; motives are names for consequential situations, and surrogates for actions leading to them. Behind questions are possible alternative actions with their terminal consequences. "Our introspective words for motives are rough, shorthand descriptions for certain typical patterns of discrepant and conflicting stimuli." [5]

The model of purposive conduct associated with Dewey's name may briefly be stated. Individuals confronted with "alternative acts" perform one or the other of them on the basis of the differential consequences which they anticipate. This nakedly utilitarian schema is inadequate because: (a) the "alternative acts" of *social* conduct "appear" most often in lingual form, as a question, stated by one's self or by another; (b) it is more adequate to say that individuals act in terms of anticipation of *named* consequences.

Among such names and in some technologically oriented lines of action there may appear such terms as "useful," "practical," "serviceable," etc., terms so "ultimate" to the pragmatists, and also to certain sectors of the American population in these delimited situations. However, there are other areas of population with different vocabularies of motives. The choice of lines of action is accompanied by representations, and selection among them, of their situational termini. Men discern situations with particular vocabularies, and it is in terms of some delimited vocabulary that they anticipate consequences of conduct.[6] Stable vocabularies of motives link anticipated consequences and specific actions. There is no need to invoke "psychological" terms like "desire" or "wish" as explanatory, since they themselves must be explained socially.[7] Anticipation is a subvocal or overt naming

---

[4] On the "question" and "conversation," see G. A. DeLaguna, *Speech: Its Function and Development*, 37 (and index), New Haven, 1927. For motives in crises, see J. M. Williams, *The Foundations of Social Science*, 435 ff., New York, 1920.

[5] K. Burke, *Permanence and Change*, 45, New York, 1936. I am indebted to this book for several leads which are systematized into the present statement.

[6] See such experiments as C. N. Rexroad's "Verbalization in Multiple Choice Reactions," *Psychol. Rev.*, Vol. 33:458, 1926.

[7] Cf. J. Dewey, "Theory of Valuation," *Int. Ency. of Unified Science*, New York, 1939.

of terminal phases and/or social consequences of conduct. When an individual names consequences, he elicits the behaviors for which the name is a redintegrative cue. In a *societal* situation, implicit in the names of consequences is the social dimension of motives. Through such vocabularies, types of societal controls operate. Also, the terms in which the question is asked often will contain both alternatives: "Love or Duty?", "Business or Pleasure?" Institutionally different situations have different *vocabularies of motive* appropriate to their respective behaviors.

This sociological conception of motives as relatively stable lingual phases of delimited situations is quite consistent with Mead's program to approach conduct socially and from the outside. It keeps clearly in mind that "both motives and actions very often originate not from within but from the situation in which individuals find themselves. . . ." [8] It translates the question of "why" [9] into a "how" that is answerable in terms of a situation and its typal vocabulary of motives, i.e., those which conventionally accompany that type situation and function as cues and justifications for normative actions in it.

It has been indicated that the question is usually an index to the avowal and imputation of motives. Max Weber defines motive as a complex of meaning, which appears to the actor himself or to the observer to be an adequate ground for his conduct.[10] The aspect of motive which this conception grasps is its intrinsically social character. A satisfactory or adequate motive is one that satisfies the questioners of an act or program whether it be the other's or the actor's. As a word, *a motive tends to be one which is to the actor and to the other members of a situation an unquestioned answer to questions concerning social and lingual conduct*. A stable motive is an ultimate in justificatory conversation. The words which in a type situation will fulfil this function are circumscribed by the vocabulary of motives acceptable for such situations. Motives are accepted justifications for present, future, or past programs or acts.

To term them justification is *not* to deny their efficacy. Often anticipations of acceptable justifications will control conduct. ("If I did this, what could I say? What would they say?") Decisions may be, wholly or in part, delimited by answers to such queries.

A man may begin an act for one motive. In the course of it, he may adopt an ancillary motive. This does not mean that the second apologetic motive is inefficacious. The vocalized expectation of an act, its "reason," is not only a mediating condition of the act but it is a proximate and controlling condition for which the term "cause" is not inappropriate. It may strengthen the act of the actor. It may win new allies for his act.

When they appeal to others involved in one's act, motives are strategies of action. In many social actions, others must agree, tacitly or explicitly. Thus, acts often will be abandoned if no reason can be found that others will accept. Diplomacy in choice of motive often controls the diplomat. Diplomatic choice of

---

[8] K. Mannheim, *Man and Society*, 249, London, 1940.
[9] Conventionally answerable by reference to "subjective factors" within individuals. R. M. MacIver, "The Modes of the Question Why," *J. of Soc. Phil.*, April, 1940. Cf. also his "The Imputation of Motives," *Amer. J. Sociol.*, July 1940.
[10] *Wirtschaft und Gesellschaft*, 5, Tubingen, 1922, " 'Motiv' heisst ein Sinnzusammenhang, Welcher dem Handelnden selbst oder dem Beobachtenden als sinnhafter 'Grund' eines Verhaltens in dem Grade heissen, als die Beziehung seiner Bestandteile von uns nach den durchschnittlichen Denk- und Gefühlsgewohnheiten als typischer (wir pflegen in sagen: 'richtiger') Sinzusammenhang bejaht Wird."

motive is part of the attempt to motivate acts for other members in a situation. Such pronounced motives undo snarls and integrate social actions. Such diplomacy does not necessarily imply intentional lies. It merely indicates that an appropriate vocabulary of motives will be utilized—that they are conditions for certain lines of conduct.[11]

When an agent vocalizes or imputes motives, he is not trying to *describe* his experienced social action. He is not merely stating "reasons." He is influencing others—and himself. Often he is finding new "reasons" which will mediate action. Thus, we need not treat an action as discrepant from "its" verbalization, for in many cases, the verbalization is a new act. In such cases, there is not a discrepancy between an act and "its" verbalization, but a difference between two disparate actions, motor-social and verbal.[12] This additional (or "*ex post facto*") lingualization may involve appeal to a vocabulary of motives associated with a norm with which both members of the situation are in agreement. As such, it is an integrative factor in *future* phases of the original social action or in other acts. By resolving conflicts, motives are efficacious. Often, if "reasons" were not given, an act would not occur, nor would diverse actions be integrated. Motives are common grounds for mediated behaviors.

Perry summarily states the Freudian view of motives "as the view that the real motives of conduct are those which we are ashamed to admit either to ourselves or to others." [13] One can cover the facts by merely saying that scruples (i.e., *moral* vocabularies of motive) are often efficacious and that men will alter and deter their acts in terms of such motives. One of the components of a "generalized other," as a mechanism of societal control, is vocabularies of acceptable motives. For example, a businessman joins the Rotary Club and proclaims its public-spirited vocabulary.[14] If this man cannot act out business conduct without so doing, it follows that this vocabulary of motives is an important factor in his behavior.[15] The long acting out of a role, with its appropriate motives, will often induce a man to become what at first he merely sought to appear. Shifts in the vocabularies of motive that are utilized later by an individual disclose an important aspect of various integrations of his actions with concomitantly various groups.

The motives actually used in justifying or criticizing an act definitely link it to situations, integrate one man's action with another's, and line up conduct with norms. The societally sustained motive-surrogates of situations are both constraints and inducements. It is a hypothesis worthy and capable of test that typal vocabularies of motives for different situations are significant determinants of conduct. As lingual segments of social action, motives orient actions by enabling discrimination between their objects. Adjectives such as "good," "pleasant," and

---

[11] Of course, since motives are communicated, they may be lies; but, this must be proved. Verbalizations are not lies merely because they are socially efficacious. I am here concerned more with the social function of pronounced motives, than with the sincerity of those pronouncing them.

[12] See F. Znaniecki, *Social Actions*, 30, New York, 1936.

[13] *General Theory of Value*, 292–93, New York, 1936.

[14] *Ibid.*, 392.

[15] The "profits motive" of classical economics may be treated as an ideal-typical vocabulary of motives for delimited economic situations and behaviors. For late phases of monopolistic and regulated capitalism, this type requires modification; the profit and commercial vocabularies have acquired other ingredients. See N. R. Danielian's *AT & T*, New York, 1940, for a suggestive account of the *noneconomic* behavior and motives of business bureaucrats.

"bad" promote action or deter it. When they constitute components of a vocabulary of motives, i.e., are typical and relatively unquestioned accompaniments of typal situations, such words often function as directives and incentives by virtue of their being the judgments of others as anticipated by the actor. In this sense motives are "social instruments, i.e., data by modifying which the agent will be able to influence [himself or others]." [16] The "control" of others is not usually direct but rather through manipulation of a field of objects. We influence a man by naming his acts or imputing motives to them—or to "him." The motives accompanying institutions of war, e.g., are not "the causes" of war, but they do promote continued integrated participation, and they vary from one war to the next. Working vocabularies of motive have careers that are woven through changing institutional fabrics.

Genetically, motives are imputed by others before they are avowed by self. The mother controls the child: "Do not do that, it is greedy." Not only does the child learn what to do, what not to do, but he is given standardized motives which promote prescribed actions and dissuade those proscribed. Along with rules and norms of action for various situations, we learn vocabularies of motives appropriate to them. These are the motives we shall use, since they are a part of our language and components of our behavior.

The quest for "real motives" supposititiously set over against "mere rationalization" is often informed by a metaphysical view that the "real" motives are in some way biological. Accompanying such quests for something more real and back of rationalization is the view held by many sociologists that language is an external manifestation or concomitant of something prior, more genuine, and "deep" in the individual. "Real attitudes" versus "mere verbalization" or "opinion" implies that at best we only infer from his language what "really" is the individual's attitude or motive.

Now what *could we possibly* so infer? Of precisely *what* is verbalization symptomatic? We cannot *infer* physiological processes from lingual phenomena. All we can infer and empirically check [17] is another verbalization of the agent's which we believe was orienting and controlling behavior at the time the act was performed. The only social items that can "lie deeper" are other lingual forms.[18] The "Real Attitude or Motive" is not something different in kind from the verbalization or the "opinion." They turn out to be only relatively and temporally different.

The phrase "unconscious motive" is also unfortunate. All it can mean is that a motive is not explicitly vocalized, but there is no need to infer unconscious motives from such situations and then posit them in individuals as elements. The phrase is informed by persistence of the unnecessary and unsubstantiated notion that "all action has a motive," and it is promoted by the observation of gaps in the relatively frequent verbalization in everyday situations. The facts to which this phrase is supposedly addressed are covered by the statements that men do not always explicitly articulate motives, and that *all* actions do not pivot around

---

[16] *Social Actions*, 73.

[17] Of course, we could infer or interpret constructs posited in the individual, but these are not easily checked and they are not explanatory.

[18] Which is not to say that, physiologically, there may not be cramps in the stomach wall or adrenalin in the blood, etc., but the character of the "relation" of such items to social action is quite moot.

language. I have already indicated the conditions under which motives are typically avowed and imputed.

Within the perspective under consideration, the verbalized motive is not used as an index of something in the individual but *as a basis of inference for a typical vocabulary of motives of a situated action.* When we ask for the "real attitude" rather than the "opinion," for the "real motive" rather than the "rationalization," all we can meaningfully be asking for is the controlling speech form which was incipiently or overtly presented in the performed act or series of acts. There is no way to plumb behind verbalization into an individual and directly check our motive-mongering, but there is an empirical way in which we can guide and limit, in given historical situations, investigations of motives. That is by the construction of typal vocabularies of motives that are extant in types of situations and actions. Imputation of motives may be controlled by reference to the typical constellation of motives which are observed to be societally linked with classes of situated actions. Some of the "real" motives that have been imputed to actors were not even known to them. As I see it, motives are circumscribed by the vocabulary of the actor. The only source for a terminology of motives is the vocabularies of motives actually and usually verbalized by actors in specific situations.

Individualistic, sexual, hedonistic, and pecuniary vocabularies of motives are apparently now dominant in many sectors of twentieth-century urban America. Under such an ethos, verbalization of alternative conduct in these terms is least likely to be challenged among dominant groups. In this milieu, individuals are skeptical of Rockefeller's avowed religious motives for his business conduct because such motives are not *now* terms of the vocabulary conventionally and prominently accompanying situations of business enterprise. A medieval monk writes that he gave food to a poor but pretty woman because it was "for the glory of God and the eternal salvation of his soul." Why do we tend to question him and impute sexual motives? Because sex is an influential and widespread motive in our society and time. Religious vocabularies of explanation and of motives are now on the wane. In a society in which religious motives have been debunked on a rather wide scale, certain thinkers are skeptical of those who ubiquitously proclaim them. Religious motives have lapsed from selected portions of modern populations and other motives have become "ultimate" and operative. But from the monasteries of medieval Europe we have no evidence that religious vocabularies were not operative in many situations.

A labor leader says he performs a certain act because he wants to get higher standards of living for the workers. A businessman says that this is rationalization, or a lie; that it is really because he wants more money for himself from the workers. A radical says a college professor will not engage in radical movements because he is afraid for his job, and besides, is a "reactionary." The college professor says it is because he just likes to find out how things work. What is reason for one man is rationalization for another. The variable is the accepted vocabulary of motives, the ultimates of discourse, of each man's dominant group about whose opinion he cares. *Determination of such groups, their location and character, would enable delimitation and methodological control of assignment of motives for specific acts.*

Stress on this idea will lead us to investigations of the compartmentalization of operative motives in personalities according to situation and the general types and conditions of vocabularies of motives in various types of societies. The motivational structures of individuals and the patterns of their purposes are relative to societal frames. We might, e.g., study motives along stratified or occupational lines. Max Weber has observed: [19]

> . . . that in a free society the motives which induce people to work vary with . . . different social classes. . . . There is normally a graduated scale of motives by which men from different social classes are driven to work. When a man changes ranks, he switches from one set of motives to another.

The lingual ties which hold them together react on persons to constitute frameworks of disposition and motive. Recently, Talcott Parsons has indicated, by reference to differences in actions in the professions and in business, that one cannot leap from "economic analysis to ultimate motivations; the institutional patterns *always* constitute one crucial element of the problem." [20] It is my suggestion that we may analyze, index, and gauge this element by focusing upon those specific verbal appendages of variant institutionalized actions which have been referred to as vocabularies of motive.

In folk societies, the constellations of motives connected with various sectors of behavior would tend to be typically stable and remain associated only with their sector. In typically primary, sacred, and rural societies, the motives of persons would be regularly compartmentalized. Vocabularies of motives ordered to different situations stabilize and guide behavior and expectation of the reactions of others. In their appropriate situations, verbalized motives are not typically questioned.[21] In secondary, secular, and urban structures, varying and competing vocabularies of motives operate coterminously and the situations to which they are appropriate are not clearly demarcated. Motives once unquestioned for defined situations are now questioned. Various motives can release similar acts in a given situation. Hence, variously situated persons are confused and guess which motive "activated" the person. Such questioning has resulted intellectually in such movements as psychoanalysis with its dogma of rationalization and its systematic motive-mongering. Such intellectual phenomena are underlaid by split and conflicting sections of an individuated society which is characterized by the existence of competing vocabularies of motive. Intricate constellations of motives, for example, are components of business enterprise in America. Such patterns have encroached on the old style vocabulary of the virtuous relation of men and women: duty, love, kindness. Among certain classes, the romantic, virtuous,

---

[19] Paraphrased by K. Mannheim, *op. cit.*, 316–17.
[20] "The Motivation of Economic Activities," 67, in C. W. M. Hart, *Essays in Sociology,* Toronto, 1940.
[21] Among the ethnologists, Ruth Benedict has come up to the edge of a genuinely sociological view of motivation. Her view remains vague because she has not seen clearly the identity of differing "motivations" in differing cultures with the varied extant and approved vocabularies of motive. "The intelligent understanding of the relation of the individual to his society . . . involves always the understanding of the types of human motivations and capacities capitalized in his society . . ." "Configurations of Culture in North America," *Amer. Anthrop.,* 25, Jan.–Mar. 1932; see also: *Patterns of Culture,* 242–43, Boston, 1935. She turns this observation into a quest for the unique "genius" of each culture and stops her research by words like "Apollonian." If she would attempt constructively to observe the vocabularies of motives which precipitate acts to perform, implement programs, and furnish approved motives for them in circumscribed situations, she would be better able to state precise problems and to answer them by further observation.

and pecuniary motives are confused. The asking of the question: "Marriage for love or money?" is significant, for the pecuniary is now a constant and almost ubiquitous motive, a common denominator of many others.[22]

Back of "mixed motives" and "motivational conflicts" are competing or discrepant situational patterns and their respective vocabularies of motive. With shifting and interstitial situations, each of several alternatives may belong to disparate systems of action which have differing vocabularies of motives appropriate to them. Such conflicts manifest vocabulary patterns that have overlapped in a marginal individual and are not easily compartmentalized in clear-cut situations.

Besides giving promise of explaining an area of lingual and societal fact, a further advantage of this view of motives is that with it we should be able to give sociological accounts of other theories (terminologies) of motivation. This is a task for sociology of knowledge. Here I can refer only to a few theories. I have already referred to the Freudian terminology of motives. It is apparent that these motives are those of an upper bourgeois patriarchal group with strong sexual and individualistic orientation. When introspecting on the couches of Freud, patients used the only vocabulary of motives they knew; Freud got his hunch and guided further talk. Mittenzwey has dealt with similar points at length.[23] Widely diffused in a postwar epoch, psychoanalysis was never popular in France where control of sexual behavior is not puritanical.[24] To converted individuals who have become accustomed to the psychoanalytic terminology of motives, all others seem self-deceptive.[25]

In like manner, to many believers in Marxism's terminology of power, struggle, and economic motives, all others, including Freud's, are due to hypocrisy or ignorance. An individual who has assimilated thoroughly only business congeries of motives will attempt to apply these motives to all situations, home and wife included. It should be noted that the business terminology of motives has its intellectual articulation, even as psychoanalysis and Marxism have.

It is significant that since the Socratic period many "theories of motivation" have been linked with ethical and religious terminologies. Motive is that in man which leads him to do good or evil. Under the aegis of religious institutions, men use vocabularies of moral motives: they call acts and programs "good" and "bad," and impute these qualities to the soul. Such lingual behavior is part of the process of social control. Institutional practices and their vocabularies of motive exercise control over delimited ranges of possible situations. One could make a typal catalog of religious motives from widely read religious texts, and test its explanatory power in various denominations and sects.[26]

In many situations of contemporary America, conduct is controlled and integrated by *hedonistic* language. For large population sectors in certain situations, pleasure and pain are now unquestioned motives. For given periods and

---

[22] Also motives acceptably imputed and avowed for one system of action may be diffused into other domains and gradually come to be accepted by some as a comprehensive portrait of *the* motive of men. This happened in the case of the economic man and his motives.

[23] Kuno Mittenzwey, "Zur Sociologie der psychoanalystischer Erkenntnis," in Max Scheler, ed. *Versuche zu einer Sociologie des Wissens*, 365–375, Munich, 1924.

[24] This fact is interpreted by some as supporting Freudian theories. Nevertheless, it can be just as adequately grasped in the scheme here outlined.

[25] See K. Burke's acute discussion of Freud, *op. cit.*, Part I.

[26] Moral vocabularies deserve a special statement. Within the viewpoint herein outlined many snarls concerning "value-judgments," etc., can be cleared up.

societies, these situations should be empirically determined. Pleasure and pain should not be reified and imputed to human nature as underlying principles of all action. Note that hedonism as a psychological and an ethical doctrine gained impetus in the modern world at about the time when older moral-religious motives were being debunked and simply discarded by "middle class" thinkers. Back of the hedonistic terminology lay an emergent social pattern and a new vocabulary of motives. The shift of unchallenged motives which gripped the communities of Europe was climaxed when, in reconciliation, the older religious and the hedonistic terminologies were identified: the "good" is the "pleasant." The conditioning situation was similar in the Hellenistic world with the hedonism of the Cyrenaics and Epicureans.

What is needed is to take all these *terminologies* of motive and locate them as *vocabularies* of motive in historic epochs and specified situations. Motives are of no value apart from the delimited societal situations for which they are the appropriate vocabularies. They must be situated. At best, socially unlocated *terminologies* of motives represent unfinished attempts to block out social areas of motive imputation and avowal. Motives vary in content and character with historical epochs and societal structures.

Rather than interpreting actions and language as external manifestations of subjective and deeper lying elements in individuals, the research task is the locating of particular types of action within typal frames of normative actions and socially situated clusters of motive. There is no explanatory value in subsuming various vocabularies of motives under some terminology or list. Such procedure merely confuses the task of explaining specific cases. The languages of situations as given must be considered a valuable portion of the data to be interpreted and related to their conditions. To simplify these vocabularies of motive into a socially abstracted terminology is to destroy the legitimate use of motive in the explanation of social actions.

50   Identification as the Basis for a Theory of Motivation

● NELSON N. FOOTE

Role theory has suffered since inception from lack of a satisfactory account of motivation. It is all very well as far as it goes to state that a person learns to recognize standard situations and to play expected roles in them according to the status defined for him in each. But this is not enough when the person encounters alternatives and must resolve conflicting definitions of his appropriate behavior.[1] Nor is it enough to account for the emergence of new roles in his conduct, nor for his more or less unique variations upon conventional roles. A strik-

SOURCE: Nelson N. Foote, in *American Sociological Review*, XVI (February 1951), pp. 14–21. Reprinted by permission of the American Sociological Association.

Paper read at the annual meeting of the American Sociological Society held in Denver, September 7–9, 1950.

[1] Leonard S. Cottrell, Jr., "The Adjustment of the Individual to His Age and Sex Roles," *American Sociological Review*, 7 (Dec., 1942).

ing revelation of the need for some theory of motivation to back up situational analysis [2] is disclosed by apathy in the performance of conventional roles, when these are on the verge of abandonment or are accepted only under duress. Roles as such do not provide their own motives.

Most of the recent writers on role theory [3] have recognized this deficiency and have endeavored to make it up through the expedient of eclecticism. Like a Ford car with a Chevrolet motor, each of these "integrators" puts on the road his own model of role theory, one powered by psychic energy, another by a system of tensions or a drive-reduction apparatus, a third by some hierarchy of innate and derived needs. Also, a number of models on the road are said to run through some tendency-to-run established through experiences of the early years, these early years being made to do the work of instincts. Despite the unscientific effort of each writer to achieve uniqueness, their theories all share the postulation of motives as predispositions, purportedly inferred from behavior. As many critics have contended, this either pushes the problem back into an infinite regress or leads circularly to the pseudo-explanation of behavior by inferences from itself.

Only two or three writers, such as Sherif and Cantril [4] or Lindesmith and Strauss [5] come close to dispensing with the effort to sustain a system of predispositions. After much stretching of "frames of reference," however, Sherif and Cantril emerge with an ego consisting of "ego-attitudes," which unlike some other attitudes are not traceable to basic drives, and they promise another work on motivation. Lindesmith and Strauss are far more daring in describing motives, like Mills,[6] as rationalizations of acts, whereby one relates his acts to previous experience and to the values of the groups to which one feels he must justify his behavior. Their analysis correctly calls attention to the function of language in motivation, but leaves the reader with the uncomfortable feeling of an unanalyzed hiatus between words and acts, of mystery as to just how language does in fact motivate. It is this hiatus which the concept of identification seems adequate to fill.

So that we may ignore non-motivated behavior, motivation or motivated behavior has to be defined. We are inclined to scoff at those medieval souls who ascribed purpose to the shape of stones, the falling of water or the absence of beards among women, although remnants of such thinking are common. It is likewise easy to make jokes about Lundberg's assertion that there is no more justification scientifically to seek out the motives of a man who runs down the street than those of a piece of paper which blows down the street, although Lundberg brings strong arguments to support his extreme position. It is far less easy to specify where between these extremes a line can be drawn to differentiate motivated from non-motivated human behavior.

The growing of whiskers we take to be non-motivated; the shaving of them off, motivated. Going to bed is motivated, sleeping is not. Physiological functions

[2] Leonard S. Cottrell, Jr., "The Analysis of Situational Fields in Social Psychology," *American Sociological Review*, 7 (June, 1942).

[3] Walter Coutu, *Emergent Human Nature*, New York: Knopf, 1949; Gardner Murphy, *Personality*, New York: Harper, 1947; Theodore M. Newcomb, *Social Psychology*, New York: Dryden, 1950; S. S. Sargent, *Social Psychology*, New York: Ronald, 1950.

[4] M. Sherif, and H. Cantril, *The Psychology of Ego-Involvements*, New York: Wiley, 1947, pp. 4–8.

[5] A. R. Lindesmith and A. Strauss, *Social Psychology*, New York: Dryden, 1949.

[6] C. W. Mills, "Situated Actions and Vocabularies of Motive," *American Sociological Review*, 5 (December, 1940). Reprinted in Part Eight of this volume.

like growth, digestion, circulation, metabolism, are clearly non-motivated, but there are marginal activities of the organism, like elimination, over which conscious control is only slowly won and may be lost under stress. While we may not gain similar direct control over the former functions, there are almost none which cannot be disrupted by psychic stress or modified by manipulation of their physical conditions.

To approach the dividing line from the opposite side, we go from conscious, rational actions involving choice among alternatives to those which seem compulsive or "unconsciously" motivated, but are not universally so, and thence again to those which seem to be physiologically autonomous.

To generalize, motivated behavior is distinguished by its prospective reference to ends in view, by being more or less subject to conscious control through choice among alternative ends and means. All kinds of human behavior are characterized by direction (or form), intensity, frequency and duration; all literally require expenditure of energy. But only motivated behavior exhibits the fluidity of organization, the paradoxical combinations of phenomenally-experienced choice and compulsion ("I don't want to but I have to because . . ."), the dependence upon learning and the content of previous experience, and, above all, the symbolic structuring which must be taken into account even to begin to understand, for example, the prodigies of effort and self-sacrifice put forth by our representatives in Korea. In a sentence, we take motivation to refer to the degree to which a human being, as a participant in the ongoing social process in which he necessarily finds himself, defines a problematic situation as calling for performance of a particular act, with more or less anticipated consummations and consequences, and *thereby* his organism releases the energy appropriate to performing it. Even the behavior consequent to an irritating organic condition, e.g., heat or hunger, has to be defined according to its meaning in the situation and is so defined, often fallibly. Organic *irritations*, which may or may not be anterior to definition of an act, contrary to some predispositionalists, have no direct and uniform connections with organic *mobilizations*, which are always posterior to definition of an act.

To the extent that we find the term *attitude* useful, it is as a synonym for these mobilizations. Definitions of the situation account for attitudes, not the reverse. And to avoid predispositionalist connotations, we prefer not to speak of particular motives, but only of motivated acts. If we were to speak of motives, it would be as rationalizations of acts, in the sense of Mills and Lindesmith—that is, as symbolic constructs which not only organize these acts in particular situations but make them recognizably recurrent in the life-history of any person or group. This pattern of recurrence constitutes what is often reified as "personality" or "culture." But what is it that makes culture and personality in action different from culture and personality in abstraction? We are back where we began.

Consider the game. For brevity's sake, we must assume reader familiarity with Mead's analysis of play, the game and the generalized "other." Let eighteen strangers, familiar with the rules of baseball and having nothing to do, be told to choose up sides and play a game. At the moment the choosing begins, it makes not the slightest difference to any potential player which side he is on—or which side wins, though if competitively indoctrinated, he might want to be on the winning side. The groups, if such they may be called—the two teams—have no identity. If they could go ahead and play under such conditions—of no identity—the game would be almost pointless. True, people would play the roles appropriate to their positions on the teams, when at bat or in the field, and any physiological needs defined by them as satisfied through exercise might be met. Here would be role theory in action, as Mead left off in describing it [7]—a sort of empty bottle of behavior and formal relations, without motive or incentive save the undifferentiated physiological necessity to dispense energy and kill time. There would be no more reason to obey the rules than to cheat, but the game might proceed by unimaginative observance of them. Since its progress would offer no more interest or involvement to the players than to a spectator ignorant of the rules, it is inconceivable how the observer could ever get them to play it, unless by offering them a reward, such as money, whose value was extraneous to the game itself. Some jobs are like that, but we do not call them games.

Now by contrast consider a ball game like any World Series, when the Mets played the Orioles in 1969. The roles and the statuses are the same, as are the rules of the game. But what a difference! And what is the nature of the difference? It is in the fact that the empty bottle of role and status suddenly has a content. That content is not drives, tensions, energy or needs; it is *identity*. Yet remember that it is still a game; for all the frenzied involvement of players and spectators, of winners and losers, the gain and loss are purely symbolic. Except for the special identity which gives value to their ensuing activity, the behavior of the players would be mere rote—a perfect example of anomie.

As Mead has shown, one learns many more roles than he ever plays overtly. To interact intelligently with another, he must learn correctly to anticipate the responses of that other—that is, to empathize. But implicit role-taking is no metaphysical transmigration of consciousness. It requires playing sub-overtly the role appropriate to the identity of the other in the situation, as accurately as one can read off that identity. In play or in role-playing experiments, a person may disclose the great range of his latent repertoire. The reason he limits his real or realistic behavior to a selected few of all the roles he has learned is that he knows and defines only these certain ones as *his own*. And he can only ascertain which role is his in each situation by knowing *who* he is. Moreover, he must know who he is with considerable conviction and clarity, if his behavior is to exhibit definiteness and force, which is to say, degree of motivation.

All of which thus far may seem so patent as to preclude the raising of more analytical questions about the nature of identity and identification. Is it not altogether obvious that the chairman of this meeting, for instance, is Edward Rose, the one who exists at such and such a time and place and performs largely as others hereabout expect him to? Yet it is just this simple and obvious fact that has to be broken down analytically, like the atom, into its various constituents. And as the analogy suggests, the process of analyzing the self into its parts may go on indefinitely.

Intrusion of the concept of *self* here, however, permits mention of what we take to be the misplaced abstractness of much use of it by social psychologists. Just this wrapping of all the particular constituents of a person's identity into one round bundle and labelling it "the self" have long delayed the analysis of the self and of identity. Too-ready generalization of the identities of any given self into indefinitely extensible statuses has led many social psychologists to feel that they must look "behind" the self for the "underlying" motives of the particular

[7] G. H. Mead, *Mind, Self and Society*, University of Chicago Press, 1934.

kinds of behavior which spring out of it—even to perpetrate such super-generalities as a "drive for self-actualization."

We mean by *identification* appropriation of and commitment to a particular identity or series of identities. As a process, it proceeds by *naming;* its products are ever-evolving self-conceptions—with the emphasis on the *con-*, that is, upon ratification by significant others. If space permitted, it would be valuable to show in detail how much this concept of identification owes to Freud [8]—where it differs from his concept, and where it supplements. Being more psychologist than sociologist, Freud tends to ignore the functions of language; for all his discussion of identification, he never speaks of identity or common identity. We are not concerned here to kick the dead horse of Freudian instinct theory, nor to appreciate the leads he gave to the study of empathy, but only to affirm that his concept of identification is inadequate as a basis for a situational theory of motivation. Neither is it the missing link of social psychology—a description of the specific tie which unites individuals with their fellows. Yet expansion and reinterpretation in interactional terms of his concept of identification provides both.

In surveying the multitude of predispositional theories of motivation which have been set forth, one is struck not only by their regular failure. Equally striking and suggestive is the seductive—not to say sinister, as Burke [9] charges—appeal which is exerted by the hope of reducing human behavior to some permanently definitive order through finding certain elemental imperatives to underly its bewildering variety. Criticism has negated every specific naming of "the mainsprings of human action." If we now boldly draw the indicated conclusion and deny wholesale the *scientific* validity of all such attempts, it remains illuminating to ask why their great continuing appeal in the face of repeated collapse or supersession.

Upon close examination it seems predictable that such attempts will continue, for what is involved is the necessary activity of every social being, and not merely of social psychologists. Every man must categorize his fellows in order to interact with them. We never approach another person purely as a human being or purely as an individual. If a being is human, it shares characteristics with a class of human beings which distinguish them from the non-human. If we ever encountered a creature not identifiable in any other respect than its human-ness, we would be non-plussed. Dewey [10] puts it succinctly:

> We come to know or note not merely this particular which as a particular cannot strictly be known at all (for not being classed it cannot be characterized and identified) but to recognize it as man, tree, stone, leather—an individual of a certain kind, marked by a certain universal form characteristic of a whole species of thing. Along with the development of this common-sense knowledge, there grows up a certain regularity of conduct. The particular incidents fuse, and a *way* of acting which is general, as far as it goes, builds up. . . . This regularity signifies, of course, that the particular case is not treated as an isolated particular, but as one of a kind, which therefore demands a *kind* of action.

Where Dewey's tree, stone or leather is inert and its properties unchanging throughout the known past, his man, however, is not. A rose by any other name

[8] Sigmund Freud, *Group Psychology and the Analysis of the Ego,* London: Hogarth, 1922; *The Ego and the Id,* London: Hogarth, 1927.
[9] Kenneth Burke, *A Grammar of Motives,* New York: Prentice-Hall, 1945.
[10] John Dewey, *Reconstruction in Philosophy,* New York: Holt, 1920, pp. 79–80.

may smell as sweet, but a person by another name will act according to that other name. The regularities in our behavior toward him are necessarily based upon our expectation of regularities in his behavior. The regularities in his behavior toward us are in turn based in the same way upon his sharing our conception of his identity and his expectation that we share his conception of our identity. Naturally there is many a slip!

The common man is always classifying thus. And to make things harder for the social psychologist, his classifications vary with time and place, as identities are elaborated and re-determined. Moreover, the common man assumes that categories applied to his fellows immediately indicate the motives to be imputed to them. "I dislike Communists because I am a Catholic and they are atheistic" is an example of such common-sense explanation (rationalization) of behavior. It is enough for him when imputation suffices for investigation, and extrapolation for prediction—enough, that is, to make possible a more or less orderly social life. Likewise, his identities give common meaning, stability and predictability to his own behavior as long as he clings to them. Possibly the predictions of social scientists will never excel their apprehension of the categories of identity and motive employed among the groups they study; but predictive power is certainly lost when, in place of these, psychologists substitute simpler and less relevant categories of their own—their lists of predispositions.

If the regularities in human behavior are organized responses to situations which have been classified more or less in common by the actors in them, then names motivate behavior. It is by analysis of the function of language, and especially of names ascribed to categories of people, that we can dispense with predispositions and yet maintain a theory of motivation subject to empirical testing—not throwing out baby with bath, as the postivists do.[11]

Establishment of one's own identity to oneself is as important in interaction as to establish it for the other. One's own identity in a situation is not absolutely given but is more or less problematic. Many expositions of interpersonal behavior omit this point, and describe only the process of ascertaining the position of the other, as if that could be read off like a set of labels. Labels are there, to be sure, but the important fact is what these labels mean in a unified definition of the situation embracing both parties. In abstraction one can consider statuses analytically, as the anthropologists do, but in action it is the unique concatenation of relevant statuses at this one time and place—in this *situation*—which constitutes identity.

Social situations always contain standard elements, and always some unique elements, if only a different position in time and space. When one enters a new situation, he attempts to relate it to old ones by familiar signs, and his response may be automatic. Or the preponderance of new elements may make the situation too problematic for a habitual response to be appropriate. For its definition, nonetheless, he must approach it from some fixed point of reference. He must start from what is most definite, find some *given* elements in it. His capacities are given, but they constitute only inert *limits* to his potential behavior, so they are not definitive enough. Although some pressing organic irritation may be quite definite, again his physical condition helps create the situation he confronts, but does not alone dictate what his response will be. The identity of the others involved is dependent upon his own in the familiar reciprocal manner. So inevitably the elements

11 C. L. Stevenson, *Ethics and Language*, New Haven: Yale University Press, 1944.

which have to be "taken as given" are his identities or, more exactly, his special pattern of identity.

In most situations our identity is so completely habitual and taken for granted that we virtually ignore its presence or relevance in our reactions, concentrating only upon the stimulating environment. Researchwise, it is strategic to focus observations upon those situations where identity itself is acutely problematic in order to observe its determining effect upon behavior (although study of the opposite type of situation—the teacher who insists she was cut out only for fifth-grade math, the fifth-grader who insists he was never cut out for it—is also illuminating).[12] When doubt of identity creeps in, action is paralyzed. Only full commitment to one's identity permits a full picture of motivation. Faith in one's conception of one's self is the key which unlocks the physiological resources of the human organism, releases the energy (or capacity, as Dewey would say) to perform the indicated act. Doubt of identity, or confusion, where it does not cause complete disorientation, certainly drains action of its meaning, and thus limits mobilization of the organic correlates of emotion, drive and energy which constitute the introspectively-sensed "push" of motivated action. We are reminded of James Michener's [13] heroes in the South Pacific who were plagued by the question, "What am I doing here?" Also, of William James's contention that only he who has played seriously with the idea of suicide has plumbed the phenomenon of self.

At this moment we can only speculate on how one acquires and gets committed to particular identities. Unless we assume a heaven of unborn souls, the process is obviously a matter of experience. We are limited to the experience available to us from birth, although these limitations become more flexible as we gain in variety of experience. That is, the richer our experience, the more possible it becomes to exercise conscious direction over its further accumulation. Nevertheless, limitations continue, and few persons ever reach the point of considering such a deliberate and drastic shift of identity as to change their names or pass the color line. Primarily then the compulsive effect of identification upon behavior must arise from absence of alternatives, from unquestioned acceptance of the identities cast upon one by circumstances beyond his control (or thought to be). From the point of view of the experiencing individual, however, the process is bound to seem much less like a process of limitation to a few among infinite possibilities than a process of discovery. His accruing conceptions of who he is are usually taken as something verging upon ultimate reality rather than as ultimately arbitrary ascriptions by others. Of course as soon as he encounters alternatives, he is released from such pre-conscious bondage to any particular conception of himself. Thenceforth his identities accrue from more conscious choice and pursuit of the values he has discovered in his experience.

Value, we would insist, is discovered in experience, not conferred upon it from without. The concepts by which we may name our various ends-in-view, and through manipulation of which we are enabled to judge among alternatives, should not—in value theory or motivation theory—be allowed to obscure the concrete consummations to which they refer. Once experienced, these appear permanently registered in the organism. If the concepts have no concrete reference for a person, or if through faulty communication the connection between the abstract values and the actual experience is not made, the abstractions are not mo-

---

[12] Prescott Lecky, *Self-Consistency*, New York: Island Press, 1945.
[13] James Michener, *Tales of the South Pacific*, New York: Pocketbooks, 1948.

tivating *to him,* as every parent finds out daily. Our learning is immensely expedited through being directed by means of these names for experienceable values to undergo and acquire them. Also, if through identification with more experienced mentors upon whose judgment we depend, we hold to the expectation of realizing recommended values eventually, experiential confirmation may remain lacking indefinitely. Nevertheless, all signals pointing to where value may be found in experience probably must be corroborated by its actual discovery, at least by some members of any group which shares them, or these signals become empty shibboleths and lingering memorials of an extinct value community.

If we insist that prior experience is necessary to motivation, however, have we not fallen back once more into predispositional thinking? Not if we are correct in assuming that a predisposition denotes more than a mere statistical tendency, some active thrust which constantly presses like a coiled spring to set off a particular line of action. Metaphorically put, the operation of values in the formulation of responses to situations is advisory, not executive. While we can only mobilize for our next act when it or its elements can be construed as similar to acts which have gone before, the determination of the appropriate act is made in the situation, not prior to it. Experience is continually being recombined in new patterns; and even the most habitual act must be defined as appropriate to its immediate context to be launched overtly. In place of predisposition, therefore, it is necessary and sufficient to put memory (memory plus mobilization equals motivation), by virtue of which we can call up in the present images of past consummations of acts.[14] We set these before us as ideal futures, to be achieved again when we have reconstructed the present situations so as to put us—if this is possible to one of our identity—into an imagined new position where that remembered good will be actually re-experienced. Because we have the capacity through language for conceptualizing these remembered goods as values, and the ingenuity to devise new schemes of relations under which they may be revived in the same or fuller measure, we can invent new roles or deviate from conventional ones. Also, we simultaneously inherit thereby the constant possibility of conflict—both internal and external—which characterizes members of human society.

Because our learning has more often than not been perfected to the point where cognitive judgments in standardized situations are made instantaneously, and the energy for performing the appropriate behavior is released immediately, it has been an easy mistake for many observers to suppose that the organic correlates came first and even account for the definition of the situation, rather than the reverse. Also, it has often led them to ignore or depreciate the long, historical accumulation of experience, organized by our shared conceptual apparatus, which brings our whole past to bear upon our behavior in the momentary present. Yet if past and future did not figure in the determination of the present, would we logically have a phenomenon of motivation or valuation to ponder?

Without the binding thread of identity one could not evaluate the succession of situations. Literally, one could say there would be no value in living, since value only exists or occurs relative to particular identities—at least value as experienced by organisms which do not live in the mere present, as animals presumably do, devoid of self and unaware of impending death. Moreover, it is only through identification as the sharing of identity that individual motives become social values and social values, individual motives.

---

[14] G. H. Mead, *The Philosophy of the Act,* University of Chicago Press, 1938, pp. 23–25.

Fuller recognition of these functions of identity should increase the scope, power and precision of situational analysis in social research, while in turn research oriented to identification should contribute to the elaboration and clarification of its working. It is only because one conceives of himself, via a certain identity, as a member of a class which includes certain others, that he can enjoy or suffer the successes and failures of a group. It is only commitment to his identity which makes him subject without physical compulsion to the control of the groups to which he belongs, or arouses his antagonism to members of a category construed as inimical to his category. In fact, we will carry this so far as to say that only full commitment to identities shared with others makes possible the grand human phenomena of love and grief. This is not tautological, because it calls attention to language in general and names in particular as the mediating links among individuals. It enables us to rephrase such imponderable specula-\ions as "What are the psychological functions of love?" into definitely research-a\ le form, such as "How did this person acquire his identity?" or "How does he get committed to particular identities which tie him constitutionally as a self to other persons?" Also, in reverse, "What kinds of new experience are sufficient to free him from the compulsion of certain old identities?"

This paper must end where it ought to begin. Originally it described some proposals for research on various types of acutely problematic identity, and some suggestions for experimentation with the methods every propagandist—which includes each of us part of the time—uses to motivate others. Space permits only mention of studies of identification among adopted and illegitimate children, the effects of ambiguous identity upon the motivation of "marginal men," the psychological consequences of name-changing, and problems of self-conception among divorced women who keep their husbands' names. Much understanding is already coming from observation of marked effects upon behavior from identification with Alcoholics Anonymous and other therapeutic groups. Regarding the techniques by which the propagandist succeeds in invoking identification of listener with speaker, Kenneth Burke gives the experimenter many leads in his valuable recent book, A Rhetoric of Motives.[15] Would practical successes as a recipe for motivating others be too stringent a test of the validity of a theory of motivation?

We have set forth that (1) role theory needs to be supplemented with an account of motivation consistent with its main premises, (2) a proper definition of motivated and non-motivated behavior makes clear how to avoid both dissolution of the concept of motivation and unchecked imputation of motives, (3) identification is the process whereby individuals are effectively linked with their fellows in groups, (4) predispositional theories, being oblivious to the function of language in motivated behavior, ascribe metaphysical reality to what are actually only the verbal categories whereby human beings regularize their doings, (5) these categorizations of experience motivate behavior through the necessary commitment of individuals to particular concatenations of identity in all situations, (6) commitment to particular identities arises through a limiting and discovering process of acquiring conceptions of self, which are confirmed, revised or elaborated partly by instruction from significant others and partly through direct experience, and (7) the compelling or inhibiting effect of identifications upon the release of varying kinds of behavior can be studied empirically.

In conclusion, let it be emphasized that the title of this paper offered expansion

---

[15] Kenneth Burke, A Rhetoric of Motives, New York: Prentice-Hall, 1950.

of the concept of identification only as the *basis* for a situational theory of motivation, not as a full theory itself, even though it helps dispel certain false theories.
By its use are avoided the fallacies of both biological determinism—the person
impelled from within—and of cultural determinism—the person driven from without. It also avoids the ingenious pretensions by which some theorists, through the
invention of such terms as "bio-social," have resolved a putative opposition between biology and culture which never existed to begin with. When theorists can
do no better in explaining conflict and change than to make the environment the
enemy of the organism, or give no better explanation of personality organization
than as a meeting of protoplasm and society, it is puzzling to note that Cooley
was insisting as early as 1902 that individual and social are two sides of the same
phenomena.[16] They do not have to be joined together by integration in textbooks.
In the concept of identity we can see this clearly: One has no identity apart from
society; one has no individuality apart from identity.[17] Only by making use of this
concept can we account for motivation in terms consistent with the only social
psychology that truly deserves the name "social."

51   Accounts

● MARVIN B. SCOTT AND STANFORD M. LYMAN

From time to time sociologists might well pause from their ongoing pursuits to inquire whether their research interests contribute in any way to the fundamental
question of sociology, namely, the Hobbesian question: How is society possible?
Attempts to answer this question could serve to unite a discipline that may not
yet have forgotten its founders, but may still have forgotten why it was founded.

Our purpose here is not to review the various answers to the Hobbesian question,[1] but rather to suggest that an answer to this macro-sociological problem
might be fruitfully explored in the analysis of the slightest of interpersonal rituals
and the very stuff of which most of those rituals are composed—talk.

Talk, we hold, is the fundamental material of human relations. And though sociologists have not entirely neglected the subject,[2] the sociology of talk has
scarcely been developed. Our concern here is with one feature of talk: Its ability
to shore up the timbers of fractured sociation, its ability to throw bridges between
the promised and the performed, its ability to repair the broken and restore the

---

[16] C. H. Cooley, *Human Nature and the Social Order,* Scribners, 1902.
[17] Kenneth Burke, *A Grammar of Motives,* New York: Prentice-Hall, 1945, pp. 469–470. A
searching criticism of the organism-environment framework.

SOURCE: Marvin B. Scott and Stanford M. Lyman, in *American Sociological Review,* XXXIII
(February 1968), pp. 46–62. Reprinted by permission of the American Sociological Association.

[1] For a now classic statement and analysis of the Hobbesian question, see the discussion by
Talcott Parsons, *The Structure of Social Action,* Glencoe, Ill.: The Free Press, 1949, pp. 89–94.
[2] See, for instance, William Soskin and Vera John, "The Study of Spontaneous Talk," in *The
Stream of Behavior,* edited by Roger Barker, N. Y.: Appleton-Century-Crofts, 1963, pp. 228–
282. Much suggestive material and a complete bibliography can be found in Joyce O. Hertzler,
A Sociology of Language, N. Y.: Random House, 1965.

estranged. This feature of talk involves the giving and receiving of what we shall call *accounts.*

An account is a linguistic device employed whenever an action is subjected to valuative inquiry.[3] Such devices are a crucial element in the social order since they prevent conflicts from arising by verbally bridging the gap between action and expectation.[4] Moreover, accounts are "situated" according to the statuses of the interactants, and are standardized within cultures so that certain accounts are terminologically stabilized and routinely expected when activity falls outside the domain of expectations.

By an account, then, we mean a statement made by a social actor to explain unanticipated or untoward behavior—whether that behavior is his own or that of others, and whether the proximate cause for the statement arises from the actor himself or from someone else.[5] An account is not called for when people engage in routine, common-sense behavior in a cultural environment that recognizes that behavior as such. Thus in American society we do not ordinarily ask why married people engage in sexual intercourse, or why they maintain a home with their children, although the latter question might well be asked if such behavior occurred among the Nayars of Malabar.[6] These questions are not asked because they have been settled in advance in our culture and are indicated by the language itself. We learn the meaning of a "married couple" by indicating that they are two people of opposite sex who have a legitimate right to engage in sexual intercourse and maintain their own children in their own household. When such taken-for-granted phenomena are called into question, the inquirer (if a member of the same culture group) is regarded as "just fooling around," or perhaps as being sick.[7]

To specify our concerns more sharply we should at this point distinguish ac-

---

[3] An account has a family resemblance to the verbal component of a "motive" in Weber's sense of the term. Weber defined a motive as "a complex of subjective meaning which seems to the actor himself or to the observer as an adequate ground for the conduct in question." Max Weber, *Theory of Social and Economic Organization,* translated by Talcott Parsons and A. M. Henderson, Glencoe: The Free Press, 1947, pp. 98–99. Following Weber's definition and building on G. H. Mead's social psychology and the work of Kenneth Burke, C. Wright Mills was among the first to employ the notion of accounts in his much neglected essay, "Situated Action and the Vocabulary of Motives," *American Sociological Review,* 6 (December, 1940), pp. 904–913. Reprinted in Part Eight of this volume. Contemporary British philosophy, following the leads of Ludwig Wittgenstein, has (apparently) independently advanced the idea of a "vocabulary of motives." An exemplary case is R. S. Peters' *The Concept of Motivation,* London: Routledge and Kegan Paul, 1958.

[4] The point is nicely illustrated by Jackson Toby in "Some Variables in Role Conflict Analysis," *Social Forces,* 30 (March, 1952), pp. 323–327.

[5] Thus by an account we include also those non-vocalized but linguistic explanations that arise in an actor's "mind" when he questions his own behavoir. However, our concern is with vocalized accounts and especially those that are given in face-to-face relations.

[6] William J. Goode, *World Revolution and Family Patterns,* New York: The Free Press of Glencoe, 1963, pp. 254–256.

[7] Moreover, common-sense understandings that violate widespread cognitive knowledge, such as are asserted in statements like "The sun rises every morning and sets every night," or avowed in perceptions that a straight stick immersed in water appears bent, are expected to be maintained. Persons who always insist on the astronomically exact statement about the earth's relation to the sun might be considered officious or didactic, while those who "see" a straight stick in a pool might be credited with faulty eyesight. For a relevant discussion of social reactions to inquiries about taken-for-granted phenomena, see Harold Garfinkel, "Studies of the Routine Grounds of Everyday Activities," *Social Problems,* 11 (Winter, 1964), pp. 225–250, and "A Conception of and Experiments with 'Trust' as a Condition of Concerted Action," in *Motivation and Social Interaction,* edited by O. J. Harvey, New York: Ronald Press, 1963, pp. 187–238.

counts from the related phenomenon of "explanations." The latter refers to statements about events where untoward action is not an issue and does not have critical implications for relationship. Much of what is true about accounts will also hold for explanations, but our concern is primarily with linguistic forms that are offered for untoward action. With this qualification to our concern, we may now specify further the nature and types of accounts.

Types of Accounts

There are in general two types of accounts: *excuses* and *justifications*.[8] Either or both are likely to be invoked when a person is accused of having done something that is "bad, wrong, inept, unwelcome, or in some other of the numerous possible ways, untoward."[9] Justifications are accounts in which one accepts responsibility for the act in question, but denies the pejorative quality associated with it. Thus a soldier in combat may admit that he has killed other men, but deny that he did an immoral act since those he killed were members of an enemy group and hence "deserved" their fate. Excuses are accounts in which one admits that the act in question is bad, wrong, or inappropriate but denies full responsibility. Thus our combat soldier could admit the wrongfulness of killing but claim that his acts are not entirely undertaken by volition: he is "under orders" and must obey. With these introductory remarks, we now turn our focus to a more detailed examination of types of justifications and excuses.

Excuses are socially approved vocabularies for mitigating or relieving responsibility when conduct is questioned. We may distinguish initially four modal forms by which excuses are typically formulated: [10] *appeal to accidents, appeal to defeasibilty, appeal to biological drives,* and *scapegoating.*

Excuses claiming *accident* as the source of conduct or its consequences mitigate (if not relieve) responsibility by pointing to the generally recognized hazards in the environment, the understandable inefficiency of the body, and the human incapacity to control all motor responses. The excuse of accident is acceptable precisely because of the irregularity and infrequency of accidents occurring to any single actor. Thus while hazards are numerous and ubiquitous, a particular person is not expected ordinarily to experience the same accident often. In other words, social actors employ a lay version of statistical curves whereby they interpret certain acts as occurring or not occurring by chance alone. When a person conducts himself so that the same type of accident befalls him frequently, he is apt to earn a label—such as "clumsy"—which will operate to stigmatize him and to warn others not to put him and themselves or their property in jeopardy by creating the environment in which he regularly has accidents. When the excuse is rooted in an accident that is unobservable or unable to be investigated—such as blaming one's lateness to work on the heaviness of traffic—frequent pleas of it are likely to be discredited. Excuses based on accidents are thus most likely to be honored precisely because they do not occur all the time or for the most part to the actor in question.[11]

---

[8] We have taken this formulation from J. L. Austin. See his *Philosophical Papers,* London: Oxford University Press, 1961, pp. 123–152.

[9] *Ibid.,* p. 124.

[10] These types of excuses are to be taken as illustrative rather than as an exhaustive listing.

[11] Only where nothing is left to chance—as among the Azande, where particular misfortunes are accounted for by a ubiquitous witchcraft—is the excuse by accident not likely to occur.

Appeals to *defeasibility* [12] are available as a form of excuse because of the wide-spread agreement that all actions contain some "mental element." The components of the mental element are "knowledge" and "will." One defense against an accusation is that a person was not fully informed or that his "will" was not completely "free." Thus an individual might excuse himself from responsibility by claiming that certain information was not available to him, which, if it had been, would have altered his behavior. Further, an individual might claim to have acted in a certain way because of misinformation arising from intentional or innocent misrepresentation of the facts by others. An excuse based on interference with the "free will" of an individual might invoke duress or undue influence. Finally both will and knowledge can be impaired under certain conditions, the invocation of which ordinarily constitutes an adequate mitigation of responsibility—intoxication (whether from alcohol or drugs) and lunacy (whether temporary or permanent) being examples.

In ordinary affairs and in law a person's actions are usually distinguished according to their intent. Further, a person's intentions are distinguished from the consequences of his actions. Under a situation where an action is questioned an actor may claim a lack of intent or a failure to foresee the consequences of his act, or both. If the action in question involves a motor response—such as knocking over a vase—the situation is not very different from that subsumed under the term accident. When actions going beyond motor responses are at issue, the actor's intentions and foresight can be questioned. "Why did you make her cry?" asks the accuser. The presentational strategies in reply to this question allow several modes of defeating the central claim implied in the question, namely, that the actor intended with full knowledge to make the lady weep. The accused may simply deny any intention on his part to have caused the admittedly unfortunate consequence. However, men ordinarily impute to one another some measure of foresight for their actions so that a simple denial of intent may not be believed if it appears that the consequence of the action in question was indeed what another person might expect and therefore what the actor intended.

In addition to his denial of intent an actor may also deny his knowledge of the consequence. The simplest denial is the cognitive disclaimer, "I did not *know* that I would make her cry by what I did." But this complete denial of cognition is often not honored, especially when the interactants know one another well and are expected to have a more complete imagery of the consequences of their acts to guide them. A more complex denial—the gravity disclaimer—includes admitting to the possibility of the outcome in question but suggesting that its probability was incalculable: "I knew matters were serious, but I did not know that telling her would make her weep."

Azande do not assert witchcraft to be the sole cause of phenomena; they have a "practical" and "realistic" approach to events which would enjoy consensual support from Occidental observers. However, Azande account for what Occidentals would call "chance" or "coincidence" by reference to witchcraft. E. E. Evans-Pritchard writes: "We have no explanation of why the two chains of causation [resulting in a catastrophe] intersected at a certain time and in a certain place, for there is no interdependence between them. Azande philosophy can supply the missing link. . . . It is due to witchcraft. . . . Witchcraft explains the coincidence of these two happenings." *Witchcraft, Oracles and Magic Among the Azande,* London: Oxford University Press, 1937, p. 70.

[12] Defeasibility, or the capacity of being voided, is a concept developed by H. L. A. Hart. This section leans heavily on Hart's essay, "The Ascription of Responsibility and Rights," in *Logic and Language, First Series,* edited by Anthony Flew, Oxford: Basil Blackwell, 1960, pp. 145–166.

Still another type of excuse invokes biological drives. This invocation is part of a larger category of "fatalistic" forces which in various cultures are deemed in greater or lesser degree to be controlling of some or all events. Cultures dominated by universalist-achievement orientations [13] tend to give scant and ambiguous support to fatalistic interpretations of events, but rarely disavow them entirely. To account for the whole of one's life in such terms, or to account for events which are conceived by others to be controlled by the actor's conscience, will, and abilities is to lay oneself open to the charge of mental illness or personality disorganization.[14] On the other hand, recent studies have emphasized the situational element in predisposing certain persons and groups in American society to what might be regarded as a "normalized" fatalistic view of their condition. Thus, for example, Negroes [15] and adolescent delinquents [16] are regarded and tend to regard themselves as less in control of the forces that shape their lives than Whites or middle-class adults.

Among the fatalistic items most likely to be invoked as an excuse are the biological drives. Despite the emphasis in Occidental culture since the late nineteenth century on personality and social environment as causal elements in human action, there is still a popular belief in and varied commitment to the efficacy of the body and biological factors in determining human behavior. Such commonplaces as "men are like that" are shorthand phrases invoking belief in sex-linked traits that allegedly govern behavior beyond the will of the actor. Precisely because the body and its biological behavior are always present but not always accounted for in science or society, invocation of the body and its processes is available as an excuse. The body and its inner workings enjoy something of the status of the sociological stranger as conceived by Simmel, namely, they are ever with us but mysterious. Hence, biological drives may be credited with influencing or causing at least some of the behavior for which actors wish to relieve themselves of full responsibility.

The invocation of biological drives is most commonly an appeal to natural but uncontrollable sexual appetite. Among first and second generation Italians in America the recognition and fear of biologically induced sexual intercourse serves men as both an excuse for pre- and extra-marital sexual relations and a justification for not being alone with women ineligible for coitus. Thus one student of Italian-American culture observes:

[13] For a general discussion of cultures in terms of their "fatalistic" orientations or universalist-achievement orientations, see Talcott Parsons, "A Revived Analytical Approach to the Theory of Social Stratification," in *Essays in Sociological Theory*, The Free Press of Glencoe, 1954, pp. 386–439. See also Parsons, *The Social System*, Glencoe: The Free Press, 1951.
[14] Thus, in the most famous study of the psychodynamics of prejudice, one of the characteristics of the intolerant or "authoritarian" personality is "externalization," i.e., the attribution of causality of events believed to be within the actor's power or rational comprehension to uncontrollable forces beyond his influence or understanding. See T. W. Adorno, *et al.*, *The Authoritarian Personality*, N.Y.: Harper & Row, 1950, pp. 474–475. See also Gordon W. Allport, *The Nature of Prejudice*, Garden City: Doubleday Anchor, 1958, p. 379. In a recent study an intermittently employed cab driver's insistence that there would inevitably be a revolution after which the world would be taken over by Negroes and Jews is recalled as one of several early warning cues that he is mentally ill. Marion Radke Yarrow, *et al.*, "The Psychological Meaning of Mental Illness in the Family," in Thomas J. Scheff, *Mental Illness and Social Process*, New York: Harper and Row, 1967, p. 35.
[15] See Horace R. Clayton, "The Psychology of the Negro Under Discrimination," in Arnold Rose, editor, *Race Prejudice and Discrimination*, New York: Alfred Knopf, 1953, pp. 276–280; and Bertram P. Karon, *The Negro Personality*, New York: Springer, 1958, pp. 8–53, 140–160.
[16] David Matza, *Delinquency and Drift*, New York: Wiley, 1964, pp. 88–90, 188–191.

What the men fear is their own ability at self-control. This attitude, strongest among young unmarried people, often carries over into adulthood. The traditional Italian belief—that sexual intercourse is unavoidable when a man and a woman are by themselves—is maintained intact among second-generation Italians, and continues even when sexual interest itself is on the wane. For example, I was told of an older woman whose apartment was adjacent to that of an unmarried male relative. Although they had lived in the same building for almost twenty years and saw each other every day, she had never once been in his apartment because of this belief.[17]

Biological drive may be an expected excuse in some cultures, so that the failure to invoke it, and the use of some other excuse, constitutes an improper account when the appropriate one is available. Oscar Lewis provides such an example in his ethnography of a Mexican family. A cuckolded wife angrily rejects her wayward husband's explanation that the red stains on his shirt are due to paint rubbed off during the course of his work. She strongly suggests, in her retelling of the incident, that she would have accepted an excuse appealing to her husband's basic sex drives: [18]

> And he had me almost believing it was red paint! It was not that I am jealous. I realize a man can never be satisfied with just one woman, but I cannot stand being made a fool of.

Homosexuals frequently account for their deviant sexual desires by invoking the principle of basic biological nature. As one homosexual put it: [19]

> It's part of nature. You can't alter it, no matter how many injections and pills they give you.

Another of the biological elements that can be utilized as an excuse is the shape of the body itself. Body types are not only defined in purely anatomical terms, but also, and perhaps more importantly, in terms of their shared social meanings. Hence fat people can excuse their excessive laughter by appealing to the widely accepted proverb that fat men are jolly. Similarly persons bearing features considered to be stereotypically "criminal" [20] may be exonerated for their impoliteness or small larcenies on the grounds that their looks proved their intentions and thus their victims ought to have been on guard. The phrase, "he looks crooked to me," serves as a warning to others to carefully appraise the character and intentions of the person so designated, since his features bespeak an illegal intent.

The final type of excuse we shall mention is *scapegoating*. Scapegoating is derived from another form of fatalistic reasoning. Using this form a person will allege that his questioned behavior is a response to the behavior or attitudes of another. Certain psychological theory treats this phenomenon as indicative of personality disorder, and, if found in conjunction with certain other characteristic

---

[17] Herbert J. Gans, *The Urban Villagers*, N. Y.: The Free Press, 1962, p. 49. According to another student of Italian-American life, slum-dwelling members of this subculture believe that "a man's health requires sexual intercourse at certain intervals." William F. Whyte, "A Slum Sex Code," *American Journal of Sociology*, 49 (July, 1943), p. 26.

[18] Oscar Lewis, *The Children of Sanchez*, New York: Random House, 1961, p. 475.

[19] Gordon Westwood, *A Minority*, London: Longmans, Green and Co., 1960, p. 46.

[20] For an interesting study showing that criminals believe that a fellow criminal's physical attractiveness will vary with type of crime—robbers are the most attractive, murderers the least; rapists are more attractive than pedophiles, etc.—see Raymond J. Corsini, "Appearance and Criminality," *American Journal of Sociology*, 65 (July, 1959), pp. 49–51.

traits, a signal of authoritarian personality.[21] Our treatment bypasses such clinical and pathological concerns in order to deal with the "normal" situation in which individuals slough off the burden of responsibility for their actions and shift it on to another. In Mexican working-class society, for example, women hold a distinctly secondary position relative to men, marriage causes a loss of status to the latter, and sexual intercourse is regarded ambivalently as healthy and natural, but also as a necessary evil.[22] Such a set of orientations predisposes both men and women to attribute many of their shortcomings to women. An example is found in the autobiography of a Mexican girl: [23]

> I was always getting into fights because some girls are vipers; they get jealous, tell lies about each other, and start trouble.

Similarly, a Mexican youth who tried unsuccessfully to meet a girl by showing off on a bicycle explains: [24]

> She got me into trouble with my father by lying about me. She said I tried to run her down with my bike and that all I did was hang around spying on her.

In another instance the same youth attributes his waywardness to the fact that the girl truly loved was his half-sister and thus unavailable to him for coitus or marriage:

> So, because of Antonia, I began to stay away from home. It was one of the main reasons I started to go on the bum, looking for trouble.[25]

Like excuses, *justifications* are socially approved vocabularies that neutralize an act or its consequences when one or both are called into question. But here is the crucial difference: to *justify* an act is to assert its positive value in the face of a claim to the contrary. Justifications recognize a general sense in which the act in question is impermissible, but claim that the particular occasion permits or requires the very act. The laws governing the taking of life are a case in point. American and English jurisprudence are by no means united on definitions or even on the nature of the acts in question, but in general a man may justify taking the life of another by claiming that he acted in self-defense, in defense of others' lives or property, or in action against a declared enemy of the state.

For a tentative list of types of justifications we may turn to what has been called "techniques of neutralization." [26] Although these techniques have been discussed with respect to accounts offered by juvenile delinquents for untoward action, their wider use has yet to be explored. Relevant to our discussion of justification are the techniques of "denial of injury," "denial of victim," "condemnation of condemners," and "appeal to loyalties." [27]

In *denial of injury* the actor acknowledges that he did a particular act but asserts that it was permissible to do that act since no one was injured by it, or since

[21] Adorno, *op. cit.*, pp. 233, 485; Allport, *op. cit.*, pp. 235–249, suggests the historicity and uniqueness of each instance of scapegoating.
[22] Arturo de Hoyos and Genevieve de Hoyos, "The Amigo System and Alienation of the Wife in the Conjugal Mexican Family," in Bernard Farber, editor, *Kinship and Family Organization*, New York: Wiley, 1966, pp. 102–115, esp., pp. 103–107.
[23] Lewis, *op. cit.*, p. 143.
[24] *Ibid.*, p. 202.
[25] *Ibid.*, p. 86.
[26] Gresham M. Sykes and David Matza, "Techniques of Neutralization," *American Sociological Review*, 22 (December, 1957), pp. 667–669.
[27] One other neutralization technique mentioned by Sykes and Matza, "denial of responsibility," is subsumed in our schema under "appeal to defeasibility."

no one about whom the community need be concerned with was involved, or finally since the act resulted in consequences that were trifling. Note that this justification device can be invoked with respect to both persons and objects. The denial of injury to *persons* suggests that they be viewed as "deserving" in a special sense: that they are oversupplied with the valued things of the world, or that they are "private" persons ("my friends," "my enemies") who have no standing to claim injury in the public, or to be noticed as injured. Denial of injury to *objects* involves redefining the act as not injurious to it but only using it, e.g., car "borrowing" is not theft.

In *denial of the victim* the actor expresses the position that the action was permissible since the victim deserved the injury. Four categories of persons are frequently perceived as deserving injury. First, there are proximate foes, i.e., those who have directly injured the actor; second, incumbents of normatively discrepant roles, e.g., homosexuals, whores, pimps; third, groups with tribal stigmas, e.g., racial and ethnic minorities; and finally, distant foes, that is, incumbents of roles held to be dubious or hurtful, e.g., "Whitey," the "Reds," "politicians." Besides categories of persons, there are categories of objects perceived as deserving of injury. To begin with, the property of any of the above mentioned categories of persons may become a focus of attack, especially if that property is symbolic of the attacked person's status. Thus the clothing of the whore is torn, the gavel of the politician is smashed, and so on. Secondly, there are objects that have a neutral or ambiguous identity with respect to ownership, e.g., a park bench. A final focus of attacked objects are those having a low or polluted value, e.g., junk, or kitsch.

Using the device of *condemnation of the condemners*, the actor admits performing an untoward act but asserts its irrelevancy because others commit these and worse acts, and these others are either not caught, not punished, not condemned, unnoticed, or even praised.

Still another neutralization technique is *appeal to loyalties*. Here the actor asserts that his action was permissible or even right since it served the interests of another to whom he owes an unbreakable allegiance or affection.[28]

Besides these "techniques of neutralization," two other sorts of justification may be mentioned: "sad tales," and "self-fulfillment." The *sad tale* is a selected (often distorted) arrangement of facts that highlight an extremely dismal past, and thus "explain" the individual's present state.[29] For example, a mental patient relates: [30]

---

[28] Note that appeal to loyalties could be an *excuse* if the argument runs that X did to A under the influence of Y's domination or love, or under the coercive influence of Y's injury to him were he not to act, e.g., loss of love, blackmail, etc. In other words, appeal to loyalties is an excuse if X admits it was bad to do A, but refuses to monopolize responsibility for A in himself.

[29] Erving Goffman, *Asylums*, Garden City: Doubleday Anchor, 1961, pp. 150–151. The sad tale involves the most dramatic instance of the general process of reconstructing personal biography whereby—for example—a husband may account for his present divorce by reconstructing the history of earlier events in an ascending scale leading up to the final dissolution. The idea of a reconstruction of biography is a continual theme in the writings of Alfred Schutz. See his *Collected Papers*, Vol. I, edited by Maurice Natanson, The Hague: Martinus Nijhoff, 1962. A short clear summary of Schutz's contribution on the reconstruction of biography is found in Peter L. Berger, *Invitation to Sociology*, Garden City: Doubleday Anchor, 1963, pp. 54–65. Drawing on Schutz, Garfinkel details the concept of reconstruction of biography in a series of experiments on the "retrospective reading" of social action. See his "Common Sense Knowledge of Social Structures," in *Theories of the Mind*, edited by Jordon M. Scher, Glencoe: The Free Press, 1962, pp. 689–712. The empirical use of the concept of retrospective reading of action is nicely illustrated by John I. Kitsuse, "Societal Reaction to Deviant Behavior," in *The Other Side*, edited by Howard S. Becker, New York: The Free Press of Glencoe, 1964, pp. 87–102.

[30] Goffman, *op. cit.*, p. 152.

I was going to night school to get an M.A. degree, and holding down a job in addition, and the load got too much for me.

And a homosexual accounts for his present deviance with this sad tale: [31]

I was in a very sophisticated queer circle at the university. It was queer in a sense that we all camped like mad with "my dear" at the beginning of every sentence, but there was practically no sex, and in my case there was none at all. The break came when I went to a party and flirted with a merchant seaman who took me seriously and cornered me in a bedroom. There was I, the great sophisticate, who, when it came to the point, was quite raw, completely inexperienced; and I might tell you that seaman gave me quite a shock. I can't say I enjoyed it very much but it wasn't long after before I started to dive into bed with anyone.

Finally we may mention a peculiarly modern type of justification, namely, *self-fulfillment*. Interviewing LSD users and homosexuals in the Haight-Ashbury district of San Francisco, we are struck by the prominence of self-fulfillment as the grounds for these activities. Thus, an "acid head" relates: [32]

The whole purpose in taking the stuff is self-development. Acid expands consciousness. Mine eyes have seen the glory—can you say that? I never knew what capacities I had until I went on acid.

And a Lesbian: [33]

Everyone has the right to happiness and love. I was married once. It was hell. But now I feel I have fulfilled myself as a person and as a woman.

We might also note that the drug users and homosexuals interviewed (in San Francisco) who invoked the justification of self-fulfillment did not appear to find anything "wrong" with their behavior. They indicated either a desire to be left alone or to enlighten what they considered to be the unenlightened establishment.

Honoring Accounts, and Background Expectations

Accounts may be honored or not honored. If an account is honored, we may say that it was efficacious and equilibrium is thereby restored in a relationship. The most common situation in which accounts are routinely honored is encounters interrupted by "incidents"—slips, boners, or gaffes which introduce information deleterious to the otherwise smooth conduct of the interactants.[34] Often a simple excuse will suffice, or the other interactants will employ covering devices to restore the *status quo ante*. A related situation is that in which an individual senses that some incident or event has cast doubt on that image of himself which he seeks to present. "At such times," the authority on impression management writes, "the individual is likely to try to integrate the incongruous events by means of apologies, little excuses for self, and disclaimers; through the same acts, incidentally, he also tries to save his face." [35]

One variable governing the honoring of an account is the character of the social circle in which it is introduced. As we pointed out earlier, vocabularies of accounts are likely to be routinized within cultures, subcultures and groups, and some are likely to be exclusive to the circle in which they are employed. A drug addict may be able to justify his conduct to a bohemian world, but not to the

[31] Westwood, *op. cit.,* p. 32.
[32] Tape-recorded interview, May 1967.
[33] Tape-recorded interview, June 1967.
[34] Erving Goffman, *Encounters,* Indianapolis: Bobbs-Merrill, 1961, pp. 45–48.
[35] *Ibid.,* p. 51.

courts. Similarly kin and friends may accept excuses in situations in which strangers would refuse to do so. Finally, while ignorance of the consequences of an act or of its prohibition may exculpate an individual in many different circles, the law explicitly rejects this notion: "Ignorance of the law excuses no man; not that all men know the law but because 'tis an excuse every man will plead, and no man can tell how to confute him." [36]

Both the account offered by *ego* and the honoring or non honoring of the account on the part of *alter* will ultimately depend on the *background expectancies* of the interactants. By background expectancies we refer to those sets of taken-for-granted ideas that permit the interactants to interpret remarks as accounts in the first place.[37] Asked why he is listless and depressed, a person may reply, "I have family troubles." The remark will be taken as an account, and indeed an account that will probably be honored, because "everyone knows" that "family problems" are a cause of depression.

This last illustration suggests that certain accounts can fit a variety of situations. Thus in response to a wide range of questions—Why don't you get married? Why are you in a fit of depression? Why are you drinking so heavily?—the individual can respond with "I'm having family problems." The person offering such an account may not himself regard it as a true one, but invoking it has certain interactional payoffs: since people cannot say they don't understand it—they are accounts that are part of our socially distributed knowledge of what "everyone knows"—the inquiry can be cut short.

Clearly, then, a single account will stand for a wide collection of events, and the efficacy of such accounts depends upon a set of shared background expectations.

In interacting with others, the socialized person learns a repertoire of background expectations that are appropriate for a variety of others. Hence the "normal" individual will change his account for different role others. A wife may respond sympathetically to her depressed husband because his favorite football team lost a championship game, but such an account for depression will appear bizarre when offered to one's inquiring boss. Thus background expectancies are the means not only for the honoring, but also for the nonhonoring of accounts. When the millionaire accounts for his depression by saying he is a failure, others will be puzzled since "everyone knows" that millionaires are not failures. The incapacity to invoke situationally appropriate accounts, i.e., accounts that are anchored to the background expectations of the situation, will often be taken as a sign of mental illness.[38] There are grounds then for conceptualizing normal individuals as "not stupid" rather than "not ill." [39] The person who is labeled ill has been behaving

---

[36] John Selden, *Table Talk*, 1696, quoted in Harry Johnson, *Sociology*, New York: Harcourt, Brace and Co., 1960, p. 552n.

[37] The term is borrowed from Harold Garfinkel. Besides the footnote references to Garfinkel already cited, see his *Studies in Ethnomethodology*, Englewood Cliffs, N. J.: Prentice-Hall, 1968. For an original discussion on how the meaning of an account depends upon background expectancies and a methodology for its study, see Harvey Sacks, *The Search for Help*, unpublished doctoral dissertation, University of California, Berkeley, 1966.

[38] On how background expectations are used to determine whether a person is judged criminal or sick see the neglected essay by Vilhelm Aubert and Sheldon L. Messinger, "The Criminal and the Sick," *Inquiry*, 1 (Autumn, 1958), pp. 137–160.

[39] This formulation is persistently (and we believe rightly) argued in the various writings of Ernest Becker. See especially *The Revolution in Psychiatry*, N. Y.: The Free Press of Glencoe, 1964; and his essay "Mills' Social Psychology and the Great Historical Convergence on the Problem of Alienation," in *The New Sociology*, edited by Irving L. Horowitz, N. Y.: Oxford University Press, 1964, pp. 108–133.

"stupidly" in terms of his culture and society: he offers accounts not situationally appropriate according to culturally defined background expectations.[40]

Often an account can be discredited by the appearance of the person offering an account. When a girl accounts for her late return from a date by saying the movie was overlong—that no untoward event occurred and that she still retains virgin status—her mother may discredit the account by noting the daughter's flushed appearance. Since individuals are aware that appearances may serve to credit or discredit accounts, efforts are understandably made to control these appearances through a vast repertoire of "impression management" activities.[41]

When an account is not honored it will be regarded as either *illegitimate* or *unreasonable*. An account is treated as *illegitimate* when the gravity of the event exceeds that of the account or when it is offered in a circle where its vocabulary of motives is unacceptable. As illustration of the former we may note that accidentally allowing a pet turtle to drown may be forgiven, but accidentally allowing the baby to drown with the same degree of oversight may not so easily be excused. As illustration of the latter, male prostitutes may successfully demonstrate their masculinity within the subculture of persons who regularly resort to homosexual acts by insisting that they are never fellators, but such a defense is not likely in heterosexual circles to lift from them the label of "queer." [42]

An account is deemed *unreasonable* when the stated grounds for action cannot be "normalized" in terms of the background expectancies of what "everybody knows." Hence when a secretary explained that she placed her arm in a lighted oven because voices had commanded her to do so in punishment for her evil nature, the account was held to be grounds for commitment to an asylum.[43] In general those who persist in giving unreasonable accounts for questioned actions are likely to be labelled as mentally ill. Or, to put this point another way, unreasonable accounts are one of the sure indices by which the mentally ill are apprehended. Conversely, those persons labeled as mentally ill may relieve themselves of the worst consequences of that label by recognizing before their psychiatrists the truth value of the label, by reconstructing their past to explain how they came to deviate from normal patterns, and by gradually coming to give acceptable accounts for their behavior.[44]

Beyond illegitimacy and unreasonableness are special types of situations in which accounts may not be acceptable. One such type involves the incorrect invocation of "commitment" or "attachment" [45] in account situations where one or the other, but only the correct one, is permitted. By commitment we refer to that

---

[40] In the case of schizophrenics, it has been noted that they are individuals who construct overly elaborate accounts, i.e., accounts that are perceived as being elaborately constructed. These accounts, it appears, take the form of "building up" the possibilities of a situation that others find improbable. Thus the paranoid husband accounts for his frenzied state by relating that his wife went shopping—and, to him, going shopping constitutes the most opportune occasion to rendezvous secretly with a lover. In response to the inquirer, the paranoid asks: "If you wanted to meet a lover, wouldn't you tell your spouse you're going shopping?" For a general discussion, see Becker, *The Revolution in Psychiatry, op. cit.*

[41] Erving Goffman, *Presentation of Self in Everyday Life,* University of Edinburgh, 1956.

[42] Albert J. Reiss, Jr., "The Social Integration of Queers and Peers," in *The Other Side, op. cit.,* pp. 181–210.

[43] Marguerite Sechehaye, *Autobiography of a Schizophrenic Girl,* New York: Grune and Stratton, 1951.

[44] See Thomas Scheff, *Being Mentally Ill,* Chicago: Aldine Press, 1966. See also Erving Goffman, *Asylums, op. cit.*

[45] These terms are adapted from Erving Goffman, *Behavior in Public Places,* New York: The Free Press of Glencoe, 1963, p. 36n, and *Encounters, op. cit.,* pp. 105 ff.

role orientation in which one has through investiture become liable and responsible for certain actions. By attachment we refer to the sense of vesting one's feelings and identity in a role. Certain statuses, especially those dealing with distasteful activities or acts that are condemned except when performed by licensed practitioners, are typically expected to invest their incumbents with only commitment and not with attachment. Hangmen who, when questioned about their occupation, profess to be emotionally attracted to killing, are not likely to have their account honored. Indeed, distasteful tasks are often imputed to have a clandestine but impermissible allure, and so those who regularly perform them are often on their guard to assert their commitment, but not their attachment, to the task.

Organizations systematically provide accounts for their members in a variety of situations. The rules of bureaucracy, for instance, make available accounts for actions taken toward clients—actions which, from the viewpoint of the client, are untoward.[46] Again, these accounts "work" because of a set of background expectations. Thus when people say they must perform a particular action because it is a rule of the organization, the account is regarded as at least reasonable, since "everyone knows" that people follow rules. Of course, the gravity of the event may discredit such accounts, as the trials of Nazi war criminals dramatically illustrate.[47]

Under certain situations behavior that would ordinarily require an account is normalized without interruption or any call for an account. Typically such situations are social conversations in which the values to be obtained by the total encounter supersede those which would otherwise require excuses or justifications. Two values that may override the requirement of accounts are *sociability* and *information*.

In the case of *sociability* the desire that the interactional circle be uninterrupted by any event that might break it calls for each interactant to weigh carefully whether or not the calling for an account might disrupt the entire engagement. When the gathering is a convivial one not dedicated to significant matters—that is, matters that have a proactive life beyond the engagement itself—the participants may overlook errors, inept statements, lies, or discrepancies in the statements of others. Parties often call for such behavior but are vulnerable to disruption by one who violates the unwritten rule of not questioning another too closely. In unserious situations in which strangers are privileged to interact as a primary group without future rights of similar interaction—such as in bars—the interactants may construct elaborate and self-contradictory biographies without fear of being called to account.[48]

In some engagements the interactants seek to obtain *information* from the speaker which is incidental to his main point but which might be withheld if any of the speaker's statements were called into account. Among the Japanese, for example, the significant item in a conversation may be circumscribed by a verbal wall of trivia and superfluous speech. To interrupt a speaker by calling for an

[46] The theme is widely explored in the literature on formal organizations. For an early and perhaps still the clearest statement of the theme, see Robert K. Merton's widely reprinted "Bureaucratic Structure and Personality," available in *Complex Organizations*, edited by Amitai Etzioni, New York: Holt, Rinehart and Winston, 1962, pp. 48–60.

[47] For a literary illustration, see the play by Peter Weiss, *The Investigation*, New York: Atheneum Books, 1967.

[48] See Sherri Cavan, *Liquor License*, Chicago: Aldine Press, 1966, pp. 79–87.

account might halt the conversation altogether or detour the speaker away from disclosing the particularly valued pieces of information.[49] Among adolescent boys in American society engaged in a "bull session" it is usually inappropriate to challenge a speaker describing his sexual exploits since, no matter how embellished and exaggerated the account might be, it permits the hearers to glean knowledge about sex—ordinarily withheld from them in the regular channels of education— with impunity. Calling for an account in the midst of such disclosures, especially when the account would require a discussion of the speaker's morality, might cut off the hearers from obtaining precisely that kind of information which is in no other way available to them.[50]

So far we have discussed accounts in terms of their content, but it should be pointed out that accounts also differ in form or style. Indeed, as we will now suggest, the style of an account will have bearing on its honoring or dishonoring.

Linguistic Styles and Accounts

We may distinguish five linguistic styles that frame the manner in which an account will be given and often indicate the social circle in which it will be most appropriately employed. These five styles, which in practice often shade into one another and are not unambiguously separated in ordinary life, are the *intimate, casual, consultative, formal,* and *frozen* styles.[51] These styles, as we shall see, are ordered on a scale of decreasing social intimacy.[52]

The *intimate* style is the socially sanctioned linguistic form employed among persons who share a deep, intense and personal relationship. The group within which it is employed is usually a dyad—lovers, a married pair, or very close friends. The group can be larger but not much larger, and when it reaches four or five it is strained to its limits. The verbal style employs single sounds or words, and jargon, to communicate whole ideas. An account given in this form may be illustrated by the situation in which a husband, lying beside his wife in bed, caresses her but receives no endearing response. His wife utters the single word, "pooped." By this term the husband understands that the account given in response to his unverbalized question, "Why don't you make love to me? After all I am your husband. You have wifely duties!" is "I realize that under ordinary circumstances I should and indeed would respond to your love making, but tonight I am too exhausted for that kind of activity. Do not take it to mean that I have lost affection for you, or that I take my wifely duties lightly."

The *casual* style is used among peers, in-group members and insiders. It is a style employed by those for whom the social distance is greater than that among intimates but is still within the boundaries of a primary relationship. Typically it employs ellipses, i.e., omissions, and slang. In casual style certain background information is taken for granted among the interactants and may be merely alluded

---

[49] Edward T. Hall, *The Hidden Dimension,* Garden City: Doubleday, 1966, pp. 139–144.

[50] When a boy is interrupted by a call for an account in the midst of his own recounting of sexual exploits he may simply relapse into uncommunicative silence, change the subject, or withdraw from the group. To prevent any of these, and to aid in the continuity of the original story, the other members of the audience may urge the speaker to continue as before, assure him of their interest and support, and sharply reprove or perhaps ostracize from the group the person who called for the account.

[51] We have adapted these styles from Martin Joos, *The Five Clocks,* New York: Harbinger Books, 1961.

[52] Each of these linguistic styles is associated with distinctive physical distances between the interactants. For a discussion of this point see Hall, *op. cit.,* pp. 116–122.

to in order to give an account. Thus among those who are regular users of hallu-cinogenic drugs, the question "Why were you running about naked in the park?" might be answered, "I was 'on.'" The hearer will then know that the speaker was under the influence of a familiar drug and was engaged in an activity that is common in response to taking that drug.

While each style differs from that to which it is juxtaposed by degree, the difference between any two styles—skipping an interval on the aforementioned social intimacy scale—is one of kind. Thus intimate and casual styles differ only in degree from one another and suggest a slight but significant difference in social distance among the interactants, but the *consultative* style differs in kind from the intimate. Consultative style is that verbal form ordinarily employed when the amount of knowledge available to one of the interactants is unknown or problematic to the others. Typically in such an interaction the speaker supplies background information which he is unsure the hearer possesses, and the hearer continuously participates by means of linguistic signs and gestures which indicate that he understands what is said or that he requires more background information. In offering accounts in this form there is a definite element of "objectivity," i.e., of non-subjective and technical terms. The individual giving an account relies on reference to things and ideas outside the intimate and personal realm. In response to the question, "Why are you smoking marijuana? Don't you know that it's dangerous?," the individual might reply, "I smoke marijuana because everybody who's read the LaGuardia Report knows that it's not habit-forming." But a casual response might be simply, "Don't be square."

Formal style is employed when the group is too large for informal co-participation to be a continuous part of the interaction. Typically it is suited to occasions when an actor addresses an audience greater than six. Listeners must then wait their turn to respond, or, if they interject comments, know that this will be an untoward event, requiring some kind of re-structuring of the situation. Speaker and audience are in an active and a passive role, respectively, and, if the group is large enough, may be obligated to speak or remain silent according to pre-established codes of procedure. Formal style may also be employed when speaker and auditor are in rigidly defined statuses. Such situations occur in bureaucratic organizations between persons in hierarchically differentiated statuses, or in the courtroom, in the interaction between judge and defendant.

Frozen style is an extreme form of formal style employed among those who are simultaneously required to interact and yet remain social strangers. Typically interaction in the frozen style occurs among those between whom an irremovable barrier exists. The barrier may be of a material or a social nature, or both. Thus pilots communicate to air scanners in a control tower in the same lingual style as prisoners of war to their captors or telephone operators to angered clients. Often the frozen accounts offered are tutored, memorized or written down in advance, and they may be applicable to a variety of situations. Thus the prisoner of war reiterates his name, rank and serial number to all questions and refers his interrogators to the Geneva Convention. The pilot replies to questions about his aberrant flight pattern, coming from the anonymous control tower. with a smooth flow of technical jargon quoted from his handbook on flying. The telephone operator refuses to become flustered or angered by the outraged demands and accusations of the caller unable to reach his party, and quotes from memory the rules of telephone conduct required of the situation.

In summary, then, accounts are presented in a variety of idioms. The idiomatic form of an account is expected to be socially suited to the circle into which it is introduced, according to norms of culture, subculture, and situation. The acceptance or refusal of an offered account in part depends on the appropriateness of the idiom employed. Failure to employ the proper linguistic style often results in a dishonoring of the account or calls for further accounts. Sometimes the situation results in requirements of compound accounting wherein an individual, having failed to employ idiomatic propriety in his first account, is required not only to re-account for his original untoward act but also to present an account for the unacceptable language of his first account. Note that idiomatic errors on the part of a person giving an account provide an unusual opportunity for the hearer to dishonor or punish the speaker if he so wishes. Thus even if the content of the tendered account is such as to excuse or justify the act, a hearer who wishes to discredit the speaker may "trip him up" by shifting the subject away from the matter originally at hand and onto the form of the account given. Typical situations of this kind arise when persons of inferior status provide substantially acceptable accounts for their allegedly untoward behavior to their inquiring superiors but employ idiomatically unacceptable or condemnable form. Thus school children who excuse their fighting with others by not only reporting that they were acting in self-defense but also, and in the process, by using profanity may still be punished for linguistic impropriety, even if they are let off for their original defalcation.[53]

Strategies for Avoiding Accounts

The vulnerability of actors to questions concerning their conduct varies with the situation and the status of the actors. Where hierarchies of authority govern the social situation, the institutionalized office may eliminate the necessity of an account, or even prevent the question from arising. Military officers are thus shielded from accountability to their subordinates. Where culture distance and hierarchy are combined—as in the case of slaveholders vis-à-vis their new imported slaves—those enjoying the superior status are privileged to leave their subordinates in a perplexed and frightened state.[54]

Besides the invulnerability to giving accounts arising from the status and position of the actors are the strategies that can prevent their announcement. We may refer to these strategies as meta-accounts. Three such strategies are prominent: *mystification, referral,* and *identity switching.*[55]

When the strategy of *mystification* is employed an actor admits that he is not meeting the expectations of another, but follows this by pointing out that, although there are reasons for his unexpected actions, he cannot tell the inquirer what they are. In its simplest sense the actor says "It's a long story," and leaves it

[53] Besides the five linguistic styles discussed, we may note that accounts may be usefully distinguished in the manner of their *delivery*. For a cogent typology see Robert E. Pittenger, *et al., The First Five Minutes,* Ithaca, New York: Paul Martineau, 1960, p. 255.

[54] Another kind of invulnerability arises in those situations in which physical presence is tantamount to task performance. Students in a classroom, parishioners in a church, and soldiers at a drill may be counted as "present"—their very visibility being all that is required for routine performance—although they might be "away" in the vicarious sense of day-dreaming, musing on other matters, or relaxing into a reverie.

[55] For these terms, in the context of strategies for avoiding accounts, we are indebted to Gregory Stone.

at that. Such accounts are most likely to be honored under circumstances which would normally hinder an elaborate account, as when students have a chance meeting while rushing off to scheduled classes.

More complicated versions of mystification are those that suggest that *alter* is not aware of certain facts—facts that are secret—which, if known, would explain the untoward action. Typically this is the response of the charismatic leader to his followers or the expert to his naive assistant. Thus does Jesus sometimes mystify his disciples and Sherlock Holmes his Dr. Watson. Finally, as already mentioned, certain statuses suggest mystification: in addition to charismatic leaders and experts at occult or little-understood arts are all those statuses characterized by specialized information including (but not limited to) doctors, lawyers, and spies.

Using the strategy of *referral*, the individual says, "I know I'm not meeting your expectations but if you wish to know why, please see. . . ." Typically referral is a strategy available to the sick and the subordinate. Illness, especially mental illness, allows the sick person to refer inquiries about his behavior to his doctor or psychiatrist. Subordinates may avoid giving accounts by designating superiors as the appropriate persons to be questioned. A special example of group referral is that which arises when accounts for the behavior of a whole people are avoided by sending the interrogator to the experts. Thus juvenile delinquents can refer inquiries to social workers, Hopi Indians to anthropologists, and unwed Negro mothers to the Moynihan Report.

In *identity switching*, *ego* indicates to *alter* that he is not playing the role that *alter* believes he is playing. This is a way of saying to *alter*, "You do not know who I am." This technique is readily available since all individuals possess a multiplicity of identities. Consider the following example.[56] A working-class Mexican husband comes home from an evening of philandering. His wife suspects this and says, "Where were you?" He responds with: "None of your business, you're a wife." Here the husband is assuming that it is not the wife's job to pry into the affairs of her husband. She replies, "What kind of a father are you?" What the woman does here is to suggest that she is not a wife, but a mother—who is looking out for the welfare of the children. To this the husband replies: "I'm a man— and you're a woman." In other words, he is suggesting that, in this status of man, there are things that a woman just doesn't understand. We note in this example that the status of persons not only affects the honoring and non-honoring of accounts, but also determines who can call for an account and who can avoid it. Again it should be pointed out that the normal features of such interaction depend upon the actors sharing a common set of background expectancies.

Negotiating Identities and Accounts

As our discussion of identity-switching emphasizes, accounts always occur between persons in roles—between husband and wife, doctor and patient, teacher and student, and so on. A normative structure governs the nature and types of communication between the interactants, including whether and in what manner accounts may be required and given, honored or discredited.

---

56 For this illustration we are again indebted to Gregory Stone. The illustration itself is derived from Oscar Lewis' *The Children of Sanchez, op. cit.*

Accounts, as suggested, presuppose an identifiable speaker and audience. The particular identities of the interactants must often be established as part of the encounter in which the account is presented.[57] In other words, people generate role identities for one another in social situations. In an account-giving situation, to cast *alter* in a particular role is to confer upon him the privilege of honoring a particular kind of account, the kind suitable to the role identity conferred and assumed for at least the period of the account. To assume an identity is to don the mantle appropriate to the account to be offered. Identity assumption and "alter-casting"[58] are prerequisites to the presentation of accounts, since the identities thus established interactionally "set" the social stage on which the drama of the account is to be played out.

The identities of speaker and audience will be negotiated as part of the encounter. Each of the interactants has a stake in the negotiations since the outcomes of the engagement will often depend on these pre-established identities. In competitive or bargaining situations[59] the interactants will each seek to maximize gains or minimize losses, and part of the strategy involved will be to assume and accept advantageous identities, refusing those roles that are disadvantageous to the situation. *Every account is a manifestation of the underlying negotiation of identities.*[60]

The most elementary form of identification is that of human and fellow human negotiated by the immediate perceptions of strangers who engage in abrupt and involuntary engagements. Thus once two objects on a street collide with one another and mutually perceive one another to be humans, an apology in the form of an excuse, or mutually paired excuses, will suffice. Those persons not privileged with full or accurate perception—the blind, myopic, or blindfolded—are not in a position to ascertain immediately whether the object with which they have collided is eligible to call for an account and to deserve an apology. In overcompensating for their inability to negotiate immediately such elementary identities, the persons so handicapped may indiscriminately offer apologies to everyone and everything with which they collide—doormen and doors, street-walkers and street signs. On the other hand, their identification errors are forgiven as soon as their handicap is recognized.

Some objects are ambiguously defined with respect to their deserving of accounts. Animals are an example. House pets, especially dogs and cats, are sometimes imputed to possess human attributes and are thus eligible for apologies and excuses when they are trodden upon by their masters. But insects and large beasts —ants and elephants, for example—do not appear to be normally eligible for accounts even when they are trodden upon by unwary (Occidental) humans.

However, there are instances wherein the anthropomorphosis of the human self is more difficult to negotiate than that of a dog. Racial minorities in caste societies often insist to no avail on the priority of their identity as "human beings"

[57] For an excellent discussion of this point as well as an insightful analysis of the concept of identity, see Anselm L. Strauss, *Mirror and Masks*, New York: The Free Press of Glencoe, 1959.
[58] The concept of "alter-casting" is developed by Eugene A. Weinstein and Paul Deutsch-berger, "Tasks, Bargains, and Identities in Social Interaction," *Social Forces*, V. 42 (May, 1964), pp. 451–456.
[59] See the brilliant discussion by Thomas C. Schelling, *The Strategy of Conflict*, New York: Galaxy Books, 1963, pp. 21–52.
[60] The terms "identities" and "roles" may be used as synonymous in that roles are identities mobilized in a specific situation; whereas role is alway situationally specific, identities are trans-situational.

over their identification as members of a racial group.[61] Indeed the "Negro human-being" role choice dilemma is but one instance of a particular form of strategy in the negotiation of identities. The strategy involves the competition between ego and alter over particularistic versus universalistic role identities. In any encounter in which a disagreement is potential or has already occurred, or in any situation in which an account is to be offered, the particularistic or universalistic identity of the interactants might dictate the manner and outcome of the account situation. Each participant will strive for the advantageous identity. A Negro psychoanalyst with considerable experience in Europe and North Africa has shown how the form of address—either consultative or deprecatingly casual—and the tone used, are opening moves in the doctor's designation of his patient as European or Negro: [62]

> Twenty European patients, one after another, came in: "Please sit down . . . Why do you wish to consult me?" Then comes a Negro or an Arab. "Sit here, boy. . . ."

And, as the psychoanalyst points out, the identity imputed to the patient might be accepted or rejected. To reject the particularistic identity in favor of a universalistic one, the Negro patient might reply, "I am in no sense your boy, Monsieur" [63] and the negotiations for identities begin again or get detoured in an argument.

In an account situation there is a further complication. Once identities have been established and an account offered, the individual has committed himself to an identity and thus seemingly assumed the assets and liabilities of that role for the duration of the encounter. If he accepts the identity as permanent and unchangeable, however, he may have limited his range of subsequent accounts. And if he wishes to shift accounts to one appropriate to another identity he may also need to account for the switch in identities. Thus, in the face of a pejorative particularistic identity, a Negro might wish to establish his claim to a positive universalistic one devoid of the pejorative contents of the imputed one. However, once this new universalistic identity has been established, the Negro might wish to shift back to the particularistic one, if there are positive qualities to be gained thereby, qualities utterly lost by an unqualified acceptance of the universalistic identity.[64] But the switch might require an account itself.

Identity switching has retroactive dangers, since it casts doubt on the attachment the claimant had to his prior identity, and his attachment may have been a crucial element in the acceptability of his first account. On the other hand, the hearer of an account may have a vested interest in accepting the entire range of accounts and may thus accommodate or even facilitate the switch in identities. Thus the hearer may "rationalize" the prior commitment, or reinterpret its mean-

---

[61] "An unconscious desire to be white, coupled with feelings of revulsion toward the Negro masses, may produce an assimilationist pattern of behavior at the purely personal level. Assimilation is in this sense a means of escape, a form of flight from 'the problem.' It involves a denial of one's racial identity which may be disguised by such sentiments as 'I'm not a Negro but a human being'—as if the two were mutually exclusive. This denial is accompanied by a contrived absence of race consciousness and a belittling of caste barriers. By minimizing the color line, the assimilationist loses touch with the realities of Negro life." Robert A. Bone, *The Negro Novel in America*, New Haven: Yale University Press, 1965, p. 4.

[62] Frantz Fanon, *Black Skin, White Masks*, New York: Grove Press, 1967, p. 32.

[63] *Ibid.*, p. 33.

[64] Fanon, *ibid.*, provides one of the most graphic examples of this phenomenon. For a socio-literary treatment, see St. Clair Drake, "Hide My Face—On Pan-Africanism and Negritude," in Herbert Hill, editor, *Soon One Morning*, New York: Alfred Knopf, 1963, pp. 77–105.

ing so that the speaker may carry off subsequent accounts.[65] Another strategy available to a hearer is to engage in alter-casting for purposes of facilitating or frustrating an account. The fact that individuals have multiple identities makes them both capable of strategic identity change and vulnerable to involuntary identity imputations.

In ordinary life, accounts are usually "phased." [66] One account generates the question which gives rise to another; the new account requires re-negotiation of identities; the identities necessitate excuses or justifications, improvisation and alter-casting; another account is given; another question arises, and so on. The following interview between a Soviet social worker and his client, a young woman, nicely illustrates this phenomenon.[67]

A girl of about nineteen years of age enters the social worker's office and sits down sighing audibly. The interview begins on a note of *mystification* which ends abruptly when the girl establishes her identity—abandoned wife.

> "What are you sighing so sadly for?" I asked. "Are you in trouble?" Lyuba raised her prim little head with a jerk, sighed pianissimo and smiled piteously.
> "No . . . it's nothing much. I *was* in trouble, but it's all over now. . . ."
> "All over, and you are still sighing about it?" I questioned further. Lyuba gave a little shiver and looked at me. A flame of interest had leaped into her earnest brown eyes.
> "Would you like me to tell you all about it?"
> "Yes, do."
> "It's a long story."
> "Never mind. . . ."
> "My husband has left me."

The interview carries on in what must be regarded as an unsuccessful approach by the social worker. He establishes that Lyuba still loves her wayward husband, has lost faith in men, and is unwilling to take his advice to forget her first husband and remarry. The abandoned wife turns out to be an identity with which the worker has difficulty coping. He, therefore, alter-casts with telling effect in the following manner.

> "Tell me, Lyuba, are your parents alive?"
> "Yes, they are. Daddy and Mummy! They keep on telling me off for having got married."
> "Quite right too."
> "No, it's not. What's right about it?"
> "Of course, they're right. You're still a child and already married and divorced."
> "Well . . . what about it! What's that got to do with them?"
> "Aren't you living with them?"
> "I have a room of my own. My husband left me and went to live with his . . . and the room is mine now. And I earn two hundred rubles. And I'm not a child! How can you call me a child?"

Note that little bits of information provide the cues for altercasting, so that Lyuba's volunteering the fact of her parents' disapproval of her first marriage, provides the grounds for the social worker's recasting her in the child role.

---

[65] Schelling, *op. cit.*, p. 34.
[66] For a discussion on the "phasing" of encounters, see Strauss, *op. cit.*, p. 44 ff.
[67] The following is from A. S. Makarenko, *The Collective Family*, Garden City: Doubleday Anchor, 1967, pp. 230–232.

However this new identity is rejected by Lyuba by further evidentiary assertions: she supports herself and maintains her own residence. The child role has been miscast. Even the social worker gives up his attempt at switching Lyuba out from her role as abandoned wife. He writes: "Lyuba looked at me in angry surprise and I saw that she was quite serious about this game she played in life." Thus negotiations for identities—as in financial transactions—usually end with both parties coming to an agreeable settlement.

Conclusion

The sociologist has been slow to take as a serious subject of investigation what is perhaps the most distinctive feature of humans—talk. Here we are suggesting a concern with one type of talk: the study of what constitutes "acceptable utterances" [68] for untoward action. The sociological study of communications has relegated linguistic utterances to linguists and has generally mapped out non-verbal behavior as its distinctive domain. We are suggesting that a greater effort is needed to formulate theory that will integrate both verbal and non-verbal behavior.[69]

Perhaps the most immediate task for research in this area is to specify the background expectations that determine the range of alternative accounts deemed culturally appropriate to a variety of recurrent situations. We want to know how the actors take bits and pieces of words and appearances and put them together to produce a perceivedly normal (or abnormal) state of affairs. This kind of inquiry crucially involves a study of background expectations.[70] On the basis of such investigations, the analyst should be able to provide a set of instructions on "how to give an account" that would be taken by other actors as "normal." [71] These instructions would specify how different categories of statuses affect the honoring of an account, and what categories of statuses can use what kinds of accounts.

Future research on accounts may fruitfully take as a unit of analysis the *speech community*.[72] This unit is composed of human aggregates in frequent and regular interaction. By dint of their association sharers of a distinct body of verbal signs are set off from other speech communities. By speech community we do not refer

---

[68] The term is borrowed from Noam Chomsky, *Aspects of a Theory of Syntax*, Cambridge, Mass.: MIT Press, 1965, p. 10.

[69] To our knowledge the most persuasive argument for this need is made by Kenneth L. Pike, *Language in Relation to a Unified Theory of the Structure of Human Behavior*, Glendale: Summer Institute of Linguistics, 1954. A short, clear programmatic statement is found in Dell Hymes' "The Ethnography of Speaking," in Thomas Gladwin and William C. Sturtevant, editors, *Anthropology and Human Behavior*, Washington, D.C.: Anthropological Society of Washington, 1962, pp. 72–85. For an argument that stresses the analytic separation of the content of talk from the forms of talk, see the brief but lucid statement by Erving Goffman, "The Neglected Situation," in The Ethnography of Communications, edited by John Gumperz and Dell Hymes, *American Anthropologist*, 66 (December, 1964), Part 2, pp. 133–136.

[70] For the methodology of such studies sociologists may well investigate the anthropological technique of componential analysis, i.e., the study of contrast sets. The clearest statement of the method of componential analysis is that of Charles O. Frake, "The Ethnographic Study of Cognitive Systems," in *Anthropology and Human Behavior, op. cit.*, pp. 72–85. A related methodology is developed by Sacks in *The Search for Help, op. cit.*

[71] See Charles O. Frake, "How to Ask for a Drink in Subanun," in *The Ethnography of Communications, op. cit.*, pp. 127–132.

[72] The idea of a "speech community" is usefully developed by John J. Gumperz in "Speech Variation and the Study of Indian Civilization," in *Language in Culture and Society*, edited by Dell Hymes, N. Y.: Harper and Row, 1964, pp. 416–423; and "Linguistic and Social Interaction in Two Communities," in *Ethnography of Communications, op. cit.*, pp. 137–153.

to language communities, distinguished by being composed of users of formally different languages. Nor do we refer simply to dialect communities, composed of persons who employ a common spoken language which is a verbal variant of a more widely used written language.

Speech communities define for their members the appropriate lingual forms to be used amongst themselves. Such communities are located in the social structure of any society. They mark off segments of society from one another, and also distinguish different kinds of activities. Thus, the everyday language of lower-class teenage gangs differs sharply from that of the social workers who interview them, and the language by which a science teacher demonstrates to his students how to combine hydrogen and oxygen in order to produce water differs from the language employed by the same teacher to tell his inquisitive six-year-old son how babies are created. The types of accounts appropriate to each speech community differ in form and in content. The usage of particular speech norms in giving an account has consequences for the speaker depending upon the relationship between the form used and the speech community into which it is introduced.

A single individual may belong to several speech communities at the same time, or in the course of a lifetime. Some linguistic devices (such as teenage argot) are appropriate only to certain age groups and are discarded as one passes into another age grouping; others, such as the linguistic forms used by lawyers in the presence of judges, are appropriate to certain status sets and are consecutively employed and discarded as the individual moves into and out of interactions with his various status partners. Some individuals are dwellers in but a single speech community; they move in circles in which all employ the same verbal forms. The aged and enfeebled members of class or ethnic ghettos are an obvious example. Others are constant movers through differing speech communities, adeptly employing language forms suitable to the time and place they occupy. Social workers who face teenage delinquents, fellow workers, lawyers, judges, their own wives, and children, all in one day, are an example.

In concluding we may note that, since it is with respect to deviant behavior that we call for accounts, the study of deviance and the study of accounts are intrinsically related, and a clarification of accounts will constitute a clarification of deviant phenomena—to the extent that deviance is considered in an interactional framework.[73]

---

[73] We refer to the approach to deviance clearly summarized by Howard S. Becker, *The Outsiders,* New York: The Free Press of Glencoe, 1963, esp. pp. 1–18.

PART NINE

SOCIALIZATION AS A LIFE PROCESS

Encompassing, as it does, not only the emergence of selves, their maintenance, change, loss, and reformulation, but also similar formulations and transformations of motive, the literature on socialization is vast. In this section we cannot begin to cover the extensive amount of theory and research that falls under this rubric.[1] The best that we can hope to do here is sketch out the perspective that symbolic interactionists bring to the study of socialization processes.

Above all, *socialization is conceived as a lifelong process.* Symbolic interactionists eschew holistic applications of such folk dicta as "the child is father to the man" or "as the twig is bent, so grows the tree." Psychoanalytic writings have probably most often been called upon to justify or rationalize such gross assertions. Sewell's early attempt to give some empirical precision to these so-called "chamber-pot hypotheses" accounts, in no small part, for our scepticism in regard to the overriding importance of infantile experience upon the subsequent course of personal careers or biographies. Although various tendentious arguments have been directed at Sewell's research, while other social scientists have simply ignored it,[2] so far as we know the literature is devoid of empirical refutations.

This does not mean that symbolic interactionists may not offer some plausible arguments against the uncritical generalization of Sewell's findings and in favor of some consideration for the hypothesis that early childhood experience *may have*

---

[1] For a current review of the present state of theory and research on socialization, see John A. Clausen (ed.), *Socialization and Society* (Boston: Little, Brown, and Company, 1968). An extremely condensed review is presented in this section. See William H. Sewell, "Some Recent Developments in Socialization Theory and Research."

[2] Neither Inkeles nor Clausen, in their specific discussions of childhood socialization, mention Sewell (see John A. Clausen, ed., *op. cit.*, pp. 75–181), although Clausen gives Sewell part of a sentence in his discussion of "Socialization Theory and Research," *ibid.*, p. 50.

some consequence for later self-formulations. Sewell, in fact, admits this, but his reasoning is more technical (what some call methodological) than theoretical. The argument, for which no direct empirical data are available, would focus on the fact that the concept "personality" is too gross and crude to be implemented in socialization studies. Rather, the social psychologist should focus on *identity* or identities. Now, some identities are "stickier" than others. They are more difficult to shrug off or reformulate in later socialization. One might say they are highly institutionalized. Gender, or sex, is one such identity, and we have already suggested that, because of sex differences in early investitures and childhood drama, boys in our society (at least in that generation whose childhood occurred before World War II) may have a more difficult time becoming men than girls have becoming women. However, once adulthood is established, men have an easier time being men than women do being women.[3] This is because of a relatively distinctive and pervasive characteristic of the larger social organization— namely, in all societies we find sexual differentiations of roles. Consequently, the sexual differentiation of communication matrices within which socialization goes on must be carefully considered along with the formulation of institutionalized dimensions of the self. This argument is directly commensurate with Sewell's recommendations for further research at the end of his study of infant training practices.

More speculatively, we might consider another application of this perspective. Orthodox Freudians have often contrasted the seemingly "underdeveloped" feminine superego with the allegedly "stronger" development of the masculine superego. This difference is traced to presumed sexual differences in the resolution of the Oedipus complex. Castration threats, so the reasoning goes, are simply not as convincing to young girls as they are to young boys. Thus, sex differences in the resolution of the Oedipal situation are construed as a matter of genetic destiny or fate—without a penis, a young girl can scarcely be intimidated by castration threats, her tabooed attraction for her father is difficult to discourage, and superego formation is impeded.

Now, let us acknowledge that these Freudian *observations* may well be correct (particularly those made at the turn of the nineteenth century and in the early years of the twentieth), but that an alternative *explanation* is readily available. We have shown that those engaged in interpersonal relations tend to qualify one another's identities more along the axis of mood than the axis of value, while the opposite seems to be the case for those engaged in structural relations.[4] Up until recently in Western civilization, social structures were built for men,[5] while women had to rely most often on interpersonal relations as accessible sources of self-validation. Notions of superego as well as libidinal excess in personality assessment were, of course, obtained by psychoanalysts through content analysis of verbal statements—free association, the recounting of dreams, reports of personal difficulties, etc. Quite probably male accounts contained more value references

---

[3] See Gregory P. Stone, "Appearance and the Self," reprinted in Part Six of this volume.
[4] *Ibid.*
[5] By 1940, women had apparently participated in all occupations in the U.S. labor force, including that of garbage collector, but problems of equal sexual opportunity in the central institutional structure of the U.S.—occupations—persisted as of 1960. See Edward Gross, "Plus Ça   Change . . . ? The Sexual Structure of Occupations over Time," *Social Problems,* XVI (Fall, 1968), pp. 198–208. Gross says that changes in sexual participation in the labor force may well represent the maintenance of male hegemony over male occupations along with a male invasion of presumably female occupations!

than female accounts. Hence superego differences were inferred, and, because of the medical model employed,[6] explanations focused on physiological differences. Our explanation would merely contrast the exclusion of women from structural participation with the participation of men in the central social structures of society, consequently enhancing the saliency of value for men in their reviews of themselves and one another. Therefore, a sociological or, more specifically, a symbolic interactionist perspective would not view such socialization differences as physiological outcomes, but as conditioned by differential sexual participation in the larger social organization.

Symbolic interactionists, then, in their analyses of socialization have not focused upon the unique, biologically relevant experiences of that process, but upon the learning and modification of rules that culminate in meaningful human differentiation and the formulation of selves. Games readily lend themselves to such an analysis, for they are, in a sense, miniature models of society. This was understood and acted upon long ago by Jean Piaget, a Swiss psychologist, who devoted his life to the study of early socialization.

In the selection presented here, Piaget uses the game of marbles as an entering wedge into the study of socialization. Marbles, seemingly so simple and trivial in the eyes of adults, proves, upon closer examination, to be a highly complex enterprise. Its usefulness as an analogue of the larger society can be readily seen. First, any system of morality is, in fact, a system of rules, and marbles presents such a system. Second, the system is relatively self-contained, since only children participate in the game, and, unlike the larger society, rules are not passed down and enforced by adults, but by other, older children, ultimately apprehended by Piaget as *formal* parent surrogates. Third, and as a consequence, the game world of marbles can be interpreted as a separate world, a kind of sub-culture, or distinct universe of discourse. On these points, Piaget observes, Pierre Bovet, the psychologist, and Emile Durkheim, the sociologist, would agree. However, on the matter of socialization—the practice and consciousness of the rules—a divergency is noted.

Durkheim, in his early work *The Division of Labor in Society*,[7] asserted that society progresses from a condition of relative homogeneity to one of relative heterogeneity, with concomitant increases in size, physical density, and dynamic density. In the former *mechanically solidary society*, rules automatically constrain the members, and violations are repressively punished as violations against the society itself. Thus, the practice of rules is obligatory, and consciousness of them a kind of sacred affair charged with affect or passion. Such a condition is interpreted by Piaget as a manifestation of *heteronomous morality*—the source of rules is found in others whose expectations are unquestioned, and which therefore make one feel strong obligations to conform. Piaget notes that the child is actually prepared for such obligatory observance of rules by his parents before he enters the world of games: "even before language he becomes conscious of certain obligations." In the world of children's games, however, adult intervention

---

[6] See Erving Goffman, "The Medical Model and Mental Hospitalization," in his *Asylums* (New York: Doubleday Anchor Books, 1961). Of course, this is a basic argument leveled by Thomas S. Szasz against conventional psychiatry. See his *The Myth of Mental Illness* (New York: Paul B. Hoeber, Inc., 1961); also his article by the same name reprinted in Part Ten of this volume.

[7] See the article by Gregory P. Stone and Harvey A. Farberman, "On the Edge of Rapprochement: Was Durkheim Moving Toward the Perspective of Symbolic Interaction?" reprinted in Part Two of this volume.

is reduced to a minimum, and older children stand *in loco parentis* as socializing agents and enforcers. In the latter *organically solidary society*, rules emerge to regulate the relations of members to one another (as in the case of contracts) rather than to the society as a whole. Violators of such rules must merely make restitution to the offended parties. At least two consequences are implied. First, persons enter into the formulation of rules, as in the process of legislation. Second, persons are confronted with the objective conditions of choice. Such a state of affairs is interpreted by Piaget as a manifestation of *autonomous morality*.

We have here a kind of social recapitulation theory of socialization. The child's practice and consciousness of rules vary throughout his early development. Among younger children up to about the ages of five to eight years, rules constitute a sort of sacred reality. Thereafter, they are more often based on mutual agreement or cooperation. As societies "progress" from mechanical to organic solidarity, children "progress" from heteronomous to autonomous morality. Age, then, is seen as the fundamental differentiating variable in early socialization. There is a gradual disappearance of uncritical conformity as the child grows older.[8] In our view the presumption of relative social homogeneity within age-grades is now highly questionable, given sex differentiation, socio-economic differences in early socialization, and historical variation.

There remains the matter of the emergence of reason in the socialization of the child, and this is a matter to which Piaget devoted extensive time and effort in later works. However, even in this early effort, he was keenly aware of the problem. The sheer objective confrontation of man with choice does not explain how choices are reasonably made. Here, the initial effort to reconcile sociological and psychological perspectives is undertaken. Piaget draws upon Pierre Bovet's observation that "reason requires cooperation as the proliferation of the division of labor requires cooperative law, insofar as being rational consists in situating oneself so as to submit the individual to the universal." Mutual respect is seen, therefore, as the necessary condition of autonomy. The "norm of reciprocity in sympathy" replaces the norms of authority.

Marbles is not a team game, but a type of game that George H. Mead passes over quickly in his well-known attempt to explain the emergence of the self. Mead focuses on team games as analogues, since teams may be construed as models of societies or, better, communities. Prior to his participation in team games, however, the child must develop the capacity to communicate with universal symbols and play at the various roles of his community or social circle. The former is accomplished through the transformation of a conversation of gestures, such as that formed in the fighting and playing of dogs. In this case, although reference is consistently made to the behavior of other organisms, reference to the self is absent.[9] Vocal gestures, particularly as they are elaborated into

---

[8] Erving Goffman has provided what seems to us a more convincing explanation of this phenomenon, avoiding as it does the many pitfalls of recapitulation theories. He has shown how and speculated why careers in the enactment of *all roles* (not only those of children) begin woodenly and, over time, are characterized by variations and improvisations on the theme or role. See his "Role Distance," in Erving Goffman, *Encounters* (Indianapolis: Bobbs-Merrill Co., 1961), pp. 105–152.

[9] It seems to us that even plausible explanations of the transition from the conversations of gestures found among the other animals to the linguistic conversations found among human beings are not provided in Mead's work. First, it is simply not convincing to contrast nonvocal with vocal gestures. The other animals vocalize. Though ranges of vocal tones may be limited in many species, among some birds, for example, the ranges may approximate or transcend the human range. Moreover, recent research has demonstrated the significance of bird calls and

language, are eminently suited to this self-reference or indication. One receives his own vocal gesture in about the way it is received by the other. This facilitates the arousal of responses in the gesturing organism similar to those in the organism toward which the gesture is directed. All this is implied in language that mobilizes concerted activity and lends it a universal character: "Our symbols are universal. You cannot say anything that is absolutely particular." Language enables the mutual assumption of roles or attitudes.

In play, the young child assumes the roles that are established in his larger social world. By playing at such roles, or playing out the attitudes of separate others, the child can, metaphorically, get outside himself and formulate a reflected view of himself as distinct from but related to these individual others. The culmination of such play, however, is the establishment of aggregated selves diversely related to one another depending upon the relationship of these dramatized roles to one another in the larger social organization. Participation in team games is another matter. Here rules, comprising the logic of organization, define the relationships of team members. Team players must each generalize the organization of the entire team and play the game from the standpoint of this "generalized other," incorporating the attitudes of the team in the formulation of an organized and generalized self. In time the teams of childhood games are replaced by "concrete classes" or sub-groups, for example political parties, clubs, and corporations, eventually by "abstract classes" or classifications that function only more or less indirectly as social units. Such abstract classes are rather more inclusive than exclusive, and their generalization widens the horizons of self, the universe of discourse in which the self is situated, and the possibilities of thought or intelligence. Mead, therefore, in explicit contrast to James and Cooley, conceived the self as cognitive, arising out of participation in the communicative organization of society.

That Mead views cognition as social, and affective experience as not, reflects, perhaps more than anything else, the intellectual temper of the period in which he was working. Then the tendency was to place emotion in the context of bodily passion or unmediated impulse and oppose it to cerebration or mind. It is ironic that Mead, who contributed so much to resolving the mind-body controversy by placing mind unequivocally in social concert, left the emotions "behind" with the body. Though he failed, Cooley at least made the effort to establish the sociality of affect. Today, one of the leading systematizers of symbolic interaction asserts as an axiom: "Emotions, as well as thought and will, are learned in

---

their replication for the "adjustment" of young birds to "adult" flocks. In addition, we have already touched upon the importance of nonverbal symbols or appearance for early human socialization. Second, if one scrutinizes carefully the play of "socialized" dogs and permits himself some anthropomorphic license, he can usually detect what *seems* to be a working consensus on what *seem* to be the rules of play. Specifically, the infliction of injury *seems* "studiously" to be avoided, and, if injury is inflicted, the play will usually end. True, animal communication is severely circumscribed and confined to the spatial and temporal dimensions within which it occurs, while human communication typically transcends such limits because of the transforming character of universal symbolism, but perhaps we ought to give up the explanation of the latter as an evolutionary emergent of the former. It is enough to observe, as Mead does elsewhere, after the fashion of Sullivan and Cooley, that infants are born into ongoing conversations, universes of discourse, social circles, or societies, and that this fact *constrains* the great majority of them eventually to join the conversation in one way or another. In this sense, Helen Keller, in spite of severe trauma—early deafness and blindness—was constrained to join the larger conversation. Of course, not all traumatically affected infants are subjected to the same persevering constraints.

communication." [10] In short, man, his ideas, and his passions are creatures of history. So are children!

Stone views the explanation of early socialization as an enormously complicated enterprise. First, the study of socialization is profoundly affected by historical variations in social definitions of the child. This difficulty has been partially met by cross-cultural studies and by studies of "social class" differences within societies, but these studies feature synchronic contrasts and omit diachronic contrasts or matters of historical change. The tendency in the vast majority of socialization studies is to treat the historical situation in which the study has been conducted as pervasive in time, usually by not treating the historical situation at all. How do we arrive at generalizations about the socialization of the child in eras or places when and where there are no children, as in medieval France, or in the Harlem of the fifties?

> . . . "Man, Sonny, they ain't got no kids in Harlem. I ain't never seen any. I've seen some real small people actin' like kids. They were too small to be grown, and they might've looked like kids, but they don't have any kids in Harlem, because nobody has time for a childhood. Man, do you ever remember bein' a kid? Not me. Shit, kids are happy, kids laugh, kids are secure. They ain't scared-a nothin'. You ever been a kid, Sonny? Damn, you lucky. I ain't never been a kid, man. I don't know what happened, man, but I think I missed out on that childhood thing, because I don't ever recall bein' a kid." [11]

The answer can only be uncovered through more extensive historical research—a desideratum that will be difficult to realize, at a time when sociological technicians are preoccupied with ahistorical techniques in their research and in methods curricula.

Mead's concept of play is viewed as too gross a concept, particularly when it is used to depict a phase of socialization. Mead, of course, distinguished between playing and playing at, and he made observations *en passant* about the child as the mother's plaything. However, he focused on the matter of playing at roles as the relevant play form for the emergence of self. Stone prefers to describe this phase as childhood *drama,* recognizing that other play forms, such as tests of poise, may be distinguished from drama and also importantly enter into the socialization process. A second criticism is made of Mead's conception of play. Although he recognized that children play at roles that are not directly (although they may be mythically) viable in the child's larger community, Mead made no analytical distinction between such roles and those that are directly and immediately present and being enacted by others. Stone therefore distinguishes *fantastic drama* from *anticipatory drama.* In the former, the child plays at roles he cannot reasonably expect to assume or encounter in later life; in the latter, he plays at roles he can reasonably expect to assume or encounter in later life. The fact that boys in our society may more frequently engage in fantastic drama, while girls more frequently engage in anticipatory drama, may well bear on our earlier speculations about the significance of sex differences in earlier socialization. Yet, even this distinction must be employed with caution: One child's fantasy is often another child's reality.

Nor do the complications in the application of Mead's model end here. One can

---

[10] Hugh Dalziel Duncan, *Symbols in Society* (New York: Oxford University Press, 1968), p. 47.
[11] Claude Brown, *Manchild in the Promised Land* (New York: Signet Books, 1965), p. 295.

apply the concept of *awareness context,* developed by Glaser and Strauss,[12] to matters of play, even though they focus primarily on the question of knowledge of one another in interaction.[13] Stone raises the question of the knowledge the child has of the role he is playing. In the dramas of childhood he may, for various reasons, be ignorant of the role he is enacting, but be completely "open" about his performance—he simply doesn't know any better. This situation is not as much "closed" in terms of knowledge of one another as it is in terms of knowledge of oneself. "Pretense awareness" is a frequent though seldom studied context of childhood drama. Probably each of us can recall playing doctor or nurse for reasons other than the drama itself. The performance of such roles grants a license to the child. Adopting such roles, he is granted access to tabooed areas, in this case, of the body.

Investigations of early socialization ordinarily terminate with what we call adolescence in our society. The article by Cavan traces the socialization of young American middle-class children through adolescence from a somewhat different standpoint than that taken by Piaget, Mead, and Stone. While these latter were concerned, for the most part, with the learning of specific rules, the assumption of specific identities, and the enactment of specific roles, Cavan is concerned with the phase of early socialization that involves the incorporation of moral precepts or standards of conduct that transcend specified situations, identities, and roles. Her concern is with the way in which young children, pre-adolescents, and adolescents learn about the world in general and how to conduct themselves "properly" in that general world.

Clearly, the "world" is that of the American middle class, and Cavan examines books of etiquette for children, pre-adolescents, and teen-agers. Most such books are specifically addressed to teen-age girls. Thus, generalizations about the particulars of this phase of socialization must be carefully confined to the audiences of the books reviewed. Apparently, mothers mediate the choices of such books for youngsters up to the age of twelve, while teen-agers, usually girls, select their own guides to good conduct.

The etiquette books under consideration provide markedly different views of the world for pre-teens and teen-agers. For the former, an essentially benign and beneficent world is presented, and this world carries with it implications for conduct in general. If the young child is honest, fair, strong, and wise (one is reminded of Boy and Girl Scout codes), this good world is his. As children approach adolescence, the evils of the world are brought into focus, and young people are encouraged not to accept the world at face value. Indeed, the world is construed as masked, and teen-agers are enjoined to penetrate the masks of others while building masks for themselves. They are taught to "work the system"— covertly to exploit the overt world. Finally, considerable attention is given in these books to the proper control of oneself vis à vis space and the body—as has been pointed out in an earlier section of this volume—to matters of poise.[14]

Cavan's article bridges the gap between early and later socialization, for, as

---

[12] See Barney G. Glaser and Anselm L. Strauss, "Awareness Contexts and Social Interaction," reprinted in Part Five of this volume.

[13] For a fascinating discussion of this question, the student is strongly urged to consult Kurt H. Wolff (ed.), *The Sociology of Georg Simmel* (New York: The Free Press of Glencoe, 1964 edition), pp. 307–316.

[14] See Edward Gross and Gregory P. Stone, "Embarrassment and the Analysis of Role Requirements," reprinted in Part Three of this volume.

Sewell indicates, studies of adolescent socialization are most often subsumed under the rubric of later socialization. Sewell, in reviewing studies of socialization between the mid-fifties and mid-sixties of this century, notes the influence of psychoanalysis on such studies, and it is true that this influence relegated investigations of socialization to the domain of infancy and childhood, although *at least* two scholars working *from* and *out of* this perspective—Harry Stack Sullivan and Erik H. Erikson—have had much to say about adolescence. Other influences upon the study of socialization are found in psychological behaviorism, learning theory, social anthropology, and sociology, particularly symbolic interaction. These influences were drawn together in the 1940's and 1950's, and, although the focus continued for the most part on the socialization of infants and young children, new directions were definitely established. Sewell selects three, acknowledging that other writers might well emphasize alternatives.

First, the *role approach* to socialization has undergone considerable development. In this regard, Orville Brim is singled out as bringing together the apparently disparate approaches of symbolic interaction and structural functionalism. This merger of approaches is reflected in studies of role taking and identification among children, as well as the effects of social class and social structure, especially family power arrangements, on early socialization. Nowhere is the situational relevance of role explored.

Second, research on *later socialization* has burgeoned. This is imperative, for, as Sewell says, "If socialization is role learning . . . it follows that in any but the most static societies the individual cannot possibly be prepared for the complex roles that he will be called upon to play in . . . later life." Here Sewell reviews studies of adolescence, noting the possibility that a "youth culture" has developed in our society. He decries the lack of studies of socialization into marital roles— how men become husbands and women, wives. Deutscher's study of socialization into post-parental lives is assessed as a valuable contribution. Explorations of socialization into occupational roles are extensive. Beyond these researches, there has been considerable attention paid to the matter of socialization into institutionalized worlds—the assumption of the sick role, the world of the mental patient, that of the convict, and the world of the institutionalized aged. Among studies of how people become old, Sewell cites one by Raymond Payne that finds that older people increasingly rely on their adult children for assistance in how to become old. There is a larger principle involved here that David Riesman has somewhere labeled *retroactive socialization:* the young socialize the old, as children may often socialize parents. Little research has been accomplished on the phenomenon.

Finally, *methodological advances* are considered. Sewell points out that such advances are mostly in the area of measurement and not techniques of sampling. What he neglects in his criticism is the complete disregard of historical methods in the attempt to carry the study of socialization forward. As a matter of fact, of the more than one hundred studies cited in Sewell's review, only three—those by Bronfenbrenner; Bronson, Katten, and Livson; and Miller and Swanson—take historical change into account.

The remaining essays in this section build on and attempt to illustrate the theory and research reviewed by Sewell in his discussion of later socialization. They begin with Becker's general treatment of change and stability in adult life. Situations make for change; commitments, for stability. The implications of these conceptualizations are examined with reference to such institutions as the undergraduate college, the medical school, and prisons. Changing situations require adjustments and readjustments, and it is to the character of such situations that we must look to explain why people change. Roles and role performances are always situated, and others recognize a person by such performances, noting the changes that *seem* to occur "in" him. Actually, these observed changes "in" the person only require of that person a desire to participate in the situation. Thus, prisoners, pre-meds, and college students all surrender early models of adjustment to these varied institutional situations toward the end of their careers, as they prepare for release. Such adjustments and readjustments are not only personal affairs, they are often collective, as when persons enter and leave situations in "batches" (for example, college classes). In these cases more room for deviation from institutional expectations is permitted than is the case for single recruits. Stability may also be afforded by situations, particularly when they are stabilized in highly stable institutions. Ordinarily, however, commitments to situations provide such stability by "locking" people into them. Commitments are often built up over time by a process of accruing "side bets." That is to say, the person may have a stake in so many other situations—his family, his home, neighborhood groups—that his commitment to his work is greatly increased and his mobility potential diminished. Often stable situations themselves conduce to such commitments.

Travisano shows that adult change is not all of a piece. To us, any detailed summary of his effort would be redundant. Insights abound. He distinguishes between *alternations* and *conversions* in adult life by contrasting Jews who become Unitarians with those who become fundamental Christians—Hebrew Christians. His analysis of these changes is generalized to adult socialization in American society. Conversion is the more dramatic change in the eyes of most observers. This involves changes in *informing aspect* (the platform from which one views the world), in allegiances from one source of authority to another, and in universes of discourse. Conversions are ordinarily accompanied by emotional upset in oneself and those others whose universe of discourse is left behind. Indeed, those others may treat the one who converts as a traitor. Most of all, conversion involves a sudden and traumatic rupture in that sequence of identities that may be conceived as a career. In contrast, alternation provides a rather easily explained sequence of identities. Some alternations merely involve a transition from one linked identity to another (from fiancé to husband). Others represent *cumulative identity sequences* (from husband to father)—one does not lose an earlier identity through the assumption of a later one. Now, as we have said, identities may be classified in terms of their "stickiness": basic, general, and independent. Ordinarily conversion implies a change in general identity—hence the change in informing aspect. Yet, every alternation is incipiently a conversion. One of the crucial problems of contemporary society is the increasing antipathy to converts in all areas. This pressure against total belief and faith may well culminate in a world where, as many wags have put it, the bland lead the bland.

One would wish that Travisano had asked how other Jews regarded the alternation to Unitarianism. Although these people themselves viewed the transition as minimal, others may have had a different impression, and there may well have been important social psychological consequences for the assumption of the new (cumulative) identity. Carper and Becker show that the responses of others to a college student's choice of an occupational career is indeed fraught with varying degrees of difficulty, depending on the extent to which the choice meets broad cultural expectations, family expectations, and the expectations of others in the occupation. Students of mechanical engineering, physiology, and philosophy, in that order, encounter increasing difficulties in their choice of careers. These difficulties are complicated by the specificity of family desires and the power of the family to impose them, the age at which one makes the decision, and the nature of the occupational ideology.

At last, there is the matter of becoming old. Zena Blau shows that this is not at all a matter of simple chronology. Less than two thirds (59 per cent) of those seventy years of age and older thought of themselves as old rather than middle-aged. Indeed, it is suggested that changes in self-identification as "old" precede an awareness of other changes in the self, irrespective of such visible changes as graying hair and wrinkled skin. The same holds true for the conception that these people have of how others view them. These conceptions are linked in various ways to changes in other identities, such as work, membership in friendship groups, and marital status.

Socialization, then, is a lifelong process, occurring from the moment of birth to, in many cases, the moment of death.[15] Interestingly, different concepts and hypotheses have been formulated for the analysis of early and later socialization. Perhaps an exciting and fruitful direction for future research will entail the application of concepts and hypotheses developed from the study of early socialization to that of later socialization (the drama, play, and games of adulthood), and, as Becker has suggested, *vice versa*.

Suggested Readings

ARIES, PHILIPPE. *Centuries of Childhood.* (trans.) Robert Baldick. New York: Alfred A. Knopf, Inc., 1962.

BRIM, O. G., JR., and S. WHEELER. *Socialization after Childhood: Two Essays.* New York: John Wiley and Sons, 1966.

BROWN, CLAUDE. *Manchild in the Promised Land.* New York: The Macmillan Co., 1965.

CAIN, L. D., JR. "Life, Course, and Social Structure." (ed.) R. E. L. Faris, *Handbook of Modern Sociology.* Chicago: Rand McNally & Co., 1964, pp. 272–309.

CLAUSEN, JOHN. (ed.) *Socialization and Society.* Boston: Little, Brown and Co., 1968.

COLEMAN, J. S. *The Adolescent Society.* New York: The Free Press, 1961.

FOOTE, N. N., and LEONARD S. COTTRELL, JR. *Identity and Interpersonal Competence.* Chicago: University of Chicago Press, 1955.

HOFFMAN, M. L. and LOIS W. (eds.). *Review of Child Development Research.* (2 vols.) New York: Russell Sage Foundation, 1964.

RILEY, MATILDA W. "Socialization for the Middle and Later Years." (eds.) D. A. Goslein and D. C. Glasse. *Handbook of Socialization Theory and Research.* New York: Rand McNally & Co., 1968.

RITCHIE, OSCAR W., and MARVIN R. KOLLER. *Sociology of Childhood.* New York: Appleton-Century-Crofts, 1964.

WHITING, BEATRICE. *Six Cultures: Studies of Child Rearing.* New York: John Wiley & Sons, 1963.

ZIEGLER, EDWARD and IRVIN L. CHILD. "Socialization." (ed.) Gardner Lindzey and Elliot Aronson, *The Handbook of Social Psychology,* second edition. Reading, Mass.: Addison-Wesley Publishing Co., 1969, Volume III, pp. 450–589.

---

[15] On the preparation for death, see Barney G. Glaser and Anselm L. Strauss, *Awareness of Dying* (Chicago: Aldine Publishing Co., 1965).

52 Infant Training and the Personality of the Child

● WILLIAM H. SEWELL

In recent years a great deal has been written about the influence of child training on personality formation and development.[1] In particular, these writings have stressed the crucial role of infant discipline in character formation and personality adjustment. As Orlansky has pointed out, in general, writers of this conviction have taken as proved the genetically and biologically oriented psychoanalytic assumption that the specific channeling of infantile physiological urges by parents produces specific psychological constellations in the individual.[2] For the most part the evidence brought to bear on these assumptions by the psychoanalytic school has been based on clinical observations of adults, with subsequent reconstruction of training experiences as an infant, rather than on empirical studies of the relation between observed experiences of infancy and personality traits.[3] The danger in this procedure is that the reconstruction of infant experiences may be erroneous, and even if not there is no way of knowing that those who are clinically treated differ from the general population in the infant training they have undergone. The lack of attention to alternative hypotheses, to negative evidence, and to adequate statistical and experimental techniques and standards means in the final analysis that the psychoanalytic assumptions have not been adequately tested, much less scientifically established by the psychoanalytic group.

This has in no way deterred certain writers from ascribing the main features of the character structure and culture of whole societies to specific infant disciplines supposedly common in that society.[4] Even more serious, many pediatricians,

SOURCE: William H. Sewell, in the *American Journal of Sociology*, 58 (July, 1952–May, 1953), pp. 150–159. Reprinted by permission of The University of Chicago Press.

This paper was presented at the 111th annual meeting of the American Statistical Association at a session sponsored by the Committee on Statistics in the Social Sciences.

The writer wishes to acknowledge the financial assistance of the Wisconsin Agricultural Experiment Station and the University Research Committee, the computational assistance of the University Computing Service, and the statistical assistance of William L. Hansen.

[1] No attempt will be made here to review the literature. R. R. Sears has surveyed objective studies designed to test psychoanalytic theory in his *Survey of Objective Studies of Psychoanalytic Concepts* (New York: Social Science Research Council, 1943) and in his "Experimental Analysis of Psychoanalytic Phenomena" in J. McV. Hunt, *Personality and the Behavior Disorders* (New York: Ronald Press, 1944). The pertinent empirical studies are well summarized in an article by Harold Orlansky, "Infant Care and Personality," *Psychological Bulletin*, No. 46 (January, 1949), pp. 1–48. Since that time a significant empirical study has been published by John R. Thurston and Paul H. Mussen, "Infant Feeding Gratification and Adult Personality," *Journal of Personality*, XIX (June, 1951), 449–58. A. R. Lindesmith and A. L. Strauss have made a critical review of the literature on culture and personality in their "Critique of Culture-Personality Writings," *American Sociological Review*, XV (October, 1950), pp. 587–600.

[2] A more sociological position is outlined in a paper by Robert F. Winch, "The Study of Personality in the Family Setting," *Social Forces*, XXVIII (March, 1950), pp. 310–16.

[3] See Orlansky, *op. cit.*, pp. 1–2.

[4] See particularly the following: G. Gorer, *The American People* (1948); Erik H. Erikson, "Childhood and Tradition in Two American Tribes," in Clyde Kluckhohn and Henry A. Murray, *Personality in Nature, Society, and Culture* (New York: Alfred A. Knopf, 1948); and Weston LaBarre, "Some Observations on Character Structure in the Orient," *Psychiatry*, VIII (1945), pp. 319–42, and IX (1946), pp. 375–95.

clinical psychologists, family counselors, and other practitioners have accepted psychoanalytic theory on faith and have strongly advocated systems of infant care which they believe follow logically from the Freudian position. Thus they emphasize breast feeding, a prolonged period of nursing, gradual weaning, a self-demand nursing schedule, easy and late bowel and bladder training, frequent mothering, freedom from restraint, freedom from punishment, sleeping with the child, and so on. They have assumed that these practices will promote the growth of secure and unneurotic personalities.

Recently, critics of the psychoanalytic position have reviewed the empirical evidence from a number of studies, most of which were either not designed to test the influence of infant training on personality or were not adequate to test the relationship. Orlansky in his critical study of existing empirical research concluded that there are relatively few studies which systematically explore the relationship between infant discipline and personality, that the data available are of questionable value, but that the evidence permits a negative conclusion as to the effect of infant-training practices on personality.[5] Lindesmith and Strauss concluded from their study of the culture-personality literature that the effects of infant experience on personality are undemonstrated.[6] This was essentially the position to which the writer had come when this study was undertaken. Dissatisfaction with the scientific adequacy of the existing studies prompted me to obtain detailed data on various aspects of infant-training practices in a field study of social factors and personality adjustment which was begun in 1947.

The purpose of the present paper is to report the results of this study which bear directly on the relationship between the actual infant-training of a group of children and their personality adjustments and traits, as indicated by scores on pencil-and-paper and projective personality tests, ratings by teachers, and behavioral information gained from interviews with their mothers.

The Study Design

The data for this study consist of detailed information on the infant-training experiences of 162 farm children of old American stock and the results of their ratings on various personality measures. In the design of the study an attempt was made to approximate experimental conditions by the prior control of several factors believed to be associated with personality adjustment. Thus diverse cultural influences were eliminated by selecting only children of old American cultural backgrounds in a predominantly old American community. By selecting children from a single occupational group (farm children), occupational and socioeconomic influences were roughly controlled. Age was held constant by selecting only children in the age group of five to six. Personal-social experiences were in some measure controlled by the selection of children who had not yet been subject to the socializing effects of school. Only the children of unbroken and never broken unions were selected; consequently, disrupted family situations could not affect the findings. It was not possible to control other factors which might have influenced the results, because of the difficulty and costs of obtaining a large enough sample to permit the type of statistical treatment planned; but even this rough approach to experimental conditions should make feasible a much more

---

[5] *Op. cit.*, p. 2.
[6] *Op. cit.*, pp. 596–99.

rigorous and satisfactory testing of the relationship between infant-training and personality than has been possible to date.

The data on the infant-training practices which the children had undergone were obtained from a personal interview with the mother. The interview was conducted in the home of the child by a highly trained interviewer, using guided interviewing techniques. Great attention was given to the planning and execution of the field interviews, so that dependable data would be forthcoming from the mothers.[7] The interview actually covered many aspects of parent-child relations, family relations, community relations, and family structure, but particular attention was focused on the personal-social experiences of the child under study—especially in relation to the specific training he had undergone during infancy and early childhood and to his personal adjustments in the family situation.

The data from these interviews were coded and punched on IBM cards. Examination of the schedules and preliminary analysis indicated that adequate data were available on the following specific infant-training practices: manner of nursing, nursing schedule, weaning, bowel training and bladder training, punishment for toilet accidents, and sleep security. Included in this list are most of the practices to which major attention has been given in the literature. They were defined as shown in Table 1.

The personality data are of three types, (1) over-all ratings of personality adjustment based on scores on standardized and unstandardized personality tests of both the paper-and-pencil and the projective types; (2) scores or ratings on personality components derived from the personality adjustment tests; (3) personality behavioral manifestations, based on interviews with the mothers or on teachers' ratings of the child's behavior. These data were obtained from tests administered by a trained clinician, who tested the children early during their first year in school, from teachers' ratings of the child, and from information supplied by the mother in the course of the original interview.

The principal measures of personality used in the study were the California Test of Personality (Primary Form A), the Ford modification of the Haggerty-Olson-Wickman Behavior Rating Scale, the Wisconsin Test of Personality, and a General Adjustment Index developed from the interview data. The California Test of Personality is a widely used paper-and-pencil test for children of this age.[8] It consists of 96 items which are grouped under 12 components, 6 of which produce a self-adjustment score and the remaining 6 a social adjustment score. The 12 component indexes commonly have been used for trait or component analysis. The Ford modification of the Haggerty-Olson-Wickman Behavior Rating Scale consists of several of the more important ratings made by the child's teacher on

---

[7] For a full discussion of the field techniques and the factors covered in the interview see William H. Sewell, "Field Techniques in Social Psychological Study in a Rural Community," *American Sociological Review*, XIV (December, 1949), pp. 718–26.

[8] For a description of this test, including its standardization and a review of studies in which it has been used, see *California Test of Personality: Summary of Investigations No. 1* (Los Angeles, Calif.: California Test Bureau, 1947); and L. P. Thorpe, W. W. Clark, and E. W. Tiegs, *Manual of Direction: California Test of Personality—Primary Series* (Los Angeles: California Test Bureau, 1947). Although its validity is not established, this test has been widely used in sociological studies. It has recently been employed in a study of rural children in Ohio by A. R. Mangus. See especially his "Personality Adjustment of Rural and Urban Children," *American Sociological Review*, XIII (October, 1948), 566–75; see also Joseph Jacobson's articles on the validity of this test: "A Mutual Validation of Personality Tests," *Journal of Social Psychology*, XXII (1945), 195–202, and "The Relative Effectiveness of Paper and Pencil Tests, Interview and Ratings as Techniques for Personality Evaluation," *ibid.*, XXIII (1946), 35–54.

TABLE 1

Practices	No. of Cases	Definition
Manner of nursing:		
Bottle fed	43*	Exclusively bottle fed from birth to weaning
Breast fed	60	Exclusively breast fed from birth to weaning
Nursing schedule:		
Regular	110	Nursed on a regular time schedule
Self-demand	52	Nursed on a self-demand basis
Weaning:		
Abrupt	23	Child abruptly taken from bottle or breast feeding and shifted to other foods
Gradual	139	Child gradually shifted from bottle or breast feeding over to other foods
Bowel training:		
Early	95	Began before the child was 12 months old
Late	67	Began after the child was 12 months old
Bladder training:		
Early	80	Began before the child was 12 months old
Late	82	Began after the child was 12 months old
Punishment for toilet accidents:		
Punished	92	Physical or verbal punishment for bowel and bladder accidents
Not punished	70	No physical or verbal punishment for bowel and bladder accidents
Sleep security:		
Low	119	Slept alone during first year of life
High	43	Slept with mother during first year of life

* Fifty-nine cases are excluded from the analysis of this item because they experienced both bottle and breast feeding.

acceptance of authority, reaction to frustration, self-assertiveness, emotional responses, and school behavior.[9] The Wisconsin Test of Personality is a projective test which was developed by Mary Simpson for use on children in the age group six to ten.[10] It consists of 10 unstructured water-color pictures (similar to TAT cards) about which the child is asked to tell a story. This story is taken down verbatim by the clinician, and the resulting protocols are scored according to a "need-press" system in essentially the same fashion as the TAT. In this study the protocols were "blind-scored" by the author of the test. The General Adjustment Index is a crude rating constructed for the purposes of this study from data available from the interview with the mother. It consists of information on the child's nervous symptoms and emotional adjustments in the family situation. Subscores on nervous symptoms and emotional adjustments are available also from this in-

[9] See Mary Ford, *The Application of the Rorschach Test to Young Children* (Minneapolis: University of Minnesota Press, 1946). For a discussion of the scale see M. E. Haggerty, W. C. Olson, and E. K. Wickman, *Scales for the Study of Behavior Problems and Problem Tendencies in Children* (New York: World Book Co., 1930).

[10] This test has not been published. It was standardized on a sample of rural and urban Wisconsin children. The ten pictures were selected by item-analysis techniques from sixty pictures designed for this test.

dex, and the single behavioral items may be examined separately as personality behavior manifestations.

From the tests, their components, and the individual items, it is possible to extract a number of personality assessments for the children included in the study. These fall into the three groups shown in Table 2.

TABLE 2

General Adjustment Measures

Total adjustment score *	Personality adjustment rating
Social adjustment score *	(Wisconsin Test of Personality) †
Self-adjustment score *	Teachers' rating of child's adjustment ‡
	General adjustment index §

Components

Self-reliance *	Social skills *
Sense of personal worth *	Antisocial tendencies *
Sense of personal freedom *	Family relations *
Feeling of belonging *	School relations *
Withdrawing tendencies *	Community relations *
Nervous symptoms *	Nervous symptoms §
Social standards *	Emotional adjustment §

Behavior Manifestations

Aggression (total) §	Eating troubles §
Arguing §	Penuriousness §
Fighting §	Acceptance of authority ‡
Temper (extent) §	Self-assertiveness ‡
Temper (demonstration) §	Reaction to frustration ‡
Biting nails §	Emotional responses ‡
Sucking fingers—now §	School behavior ‡
Sucking fingers—baby §	Crying §
Stuttering §	Sleep disturbances §
Fears §	Cautiousness §
Learning to talk §	Cuddling §
Bashfulness §	Jealousy §
Feelings hurt §	Happiness §

* From California Test of Personality.
† From Wisconsin Test of Personality.
‡ From Ford modification of the Haggerty-Olson-Wickman Behavior Rating Scale.
§ From interview with child's mother.

Statistical Analysis

Because no great claim can be made for either the precision, the validity, or the reliability of any of the personality tests, indexes, or items and because the sample size is not great, no attempt is made in this study to use any of them as quantitative measures.[11] Rather, each is used only as a crude indicator. Thus, in the case

---

[11] It is not at all clear what the theoretical basis has been for most of the personality tests now in existence. Many have been developed to distinguish between "neurotic" and "normal" persons. To my knowledge, no test has been developed which takes adequate account of the adjustment of the individual in the social roles which he is expected to play in the particular social systems in which he functions. In my opinion, tests of this type are necessary to sociologically relevant studies of personality, but, lacking them, existing tests must be used.

of the tests and components, the child's score on each of the personality indexes was computed, an array of scores was cast for each measure, and two relative score groups of approximately equal size were established.[12] The only assumption made was that those who made scores or ratings in the top half of the distribution were better adjusted as a group than those who made scores which placed them in the lower half of the distribution. Likewise, responses on the individual behavioral items were classified simply as "Favorable" or "Unfavorable." The categories derived from this process were then punched on the IBM cards containing the infant-training data.

In the actual statistical analysis the association between each of the seven infant-training practices and each of the forty-six personality indicators was determined by applying the chi square test to the fourfold tables which were obtained by cross-sorting the training practice responses with the dichotomized personality variables. The chi square test is, of course, a crude test of significance but probably is as precise as the data justify. The level of significance set for this study is the 5 per cent level.

The Hypotheses

The data from the foregoing analysis make possible the testing of a number of pertinent hypotheses about the influence of infant training on personality adjustment. In fact, in the strictest sense, null hypotheses might be set up by making a separate hypothesis for the relationship between each training item and each personality item. However, to save space and avoid repetition, one general hypothesis concerning the relation of infant-training to personality adjustment and several specific hypotheses concerning the relation between particular training practices and personality adjustment were formulated. The general hypothesis, stated in the null form, is that *the personality adjustment and traits of children who have undergone varying infant-training experiences do not differ significantly from each other.* The specific null hypotheses covering each of the training practices are stated in the section on results, which follows.

Results

It will not be possible because of space limitations to present the several hundred fourfold tables upon which the analysis that follows was based. However, Table 3 contains in summary form all the significant relations that were found between training practices and the various indicators of personality adjustment employed in this study. A supplement to this paper has been prepared which gives all the fourfold tables used to test the hypotheses of the study. This has been filed with the American Documentation Institute and is available to anyone who wishes to examine the basic tables.[13]

On the basis of the results of the statistical tests, the first specific hypothesis that *the personality adjustments of the children who were breast fed do not differ sig-*

---

[12] It was not possible to follow this procedure with the Wisconsin Test of Personality. Consequently, only those children whose protocols indicated disturbed personalities were placed in the unfavorable group, and all others were classified as favorable.

[13] For the detailed tables, order Document 3623 from American Documentation Institute, 1719 N Street, N.W., Washington 6, D.C., remitting $1.00 for microfilm (images 1 inch high on standard 35-mm. motion-picture film) or $1.50 for photocopies (6 × 8 inches) readable without optical aid.

nificantly from those of the children who were bottle fed cannot be rejected. None of the forty-six possible chi squares is statistically significant.

Likewise, the second specific hypothesis that *the personality adjustments of the children who were fed on a self-demand nursing schedule do not differ significantly from those of the children who were fed on a regular schedule* cannot be rejected. On the basis of the statistical tests, only one association is significant (see Table 3). The children fed on a self-demand schedule during infancy have significantly lower feelings of belonging, according to their scores on this component of the California Test of Personality, than do those fed on a regular schedule. This is contrary to the relationship expected on the basis of the theory.

TABLE 3

Training Practice and Indexes	Indicators of Personality Adjustment	χ^2	P
Self-demand feeding schedule	Low feeling of belonging *	3.91	0.05
Gradual weaning	High feeling of belonging *	5.83	0.02
Gradual weaning	High social standards *	4.61	0.05
Late bowel training	Poor school relations *	4.51	0.05
Late bowel training	Good temper †	9.26	0.01
Late bowel training	Little nail biting †	4.32	0.05
Late bladder training	Little nail biting †	9.22	0.01
No punishment for toilet accidents	High social adjustment *	8.76	0.01
No punishment for toilet accidents	High social standards *	8.30	0.01
No punishment for toilet accidents	Good school relations *	6.74	0.01
High sleep security	Low self-adjustment *	4.67	0.05
High sleep security	Low personal freedom *	5.87	0.02
High sleep security	Poor family relations *	4.12	0.05
High sleep security	Sleep disturbances †	3.93	0.05
High infantile security	High personal freedom *	4.82	0.05
High infantile security	Good temper †	4.03	0.05
Favorable toilet training factor	Little nail biting †	6.71	0.01
Favorable feeding training factor	Poor family relations *	6.03	0.01

* From California Test of Personality.
† From interview with the child's mother.

The third specific hypothesis that *the personality adjustments and traits of the children who were weaned gradually do not differ significantly from those of the children who were weaned abruptly* cannot be rejected on the basis of the statistical evidence (see Table 3). Of the forty-six chi squares, only two are significant. The children who were weaned gradually make a more favorable showing on the social standards and feeling of belonging components of the California Test of Personality than do the children who were weaned abruptly. These results are in keeping with the prediction that one would make on the basis of the theory. However, there are no significant differences on any of the other measures.

The fourth specific hypothesis that *the personality adjustments and traits of the children whose induction to bowel training was late do not differ significantly from those of the children whose induction was early* likewise must not be rejected. Again only three of the possible chi squares are significant [14] (see Table 3). Children whose induction to bowel training was late made less favorable showing on the school relations component of the California Test of Personality, had better tempers, and were less likely to bite their nails than those whose induction was early. The latter two findings are in keeping with the theoretical predictions, but the first is not.

The fifth hypothesis that *the personality adjustments and traits of the children whose induction to bladder training was late do not differ significantly from those of the children whose induction was early* must not be rejected. There is only one significant chi square (see Table 3). Those with late bladder training were less likely to bite their nails than those with early bladder training. This association is in the expected direction.

The sixth hypothesis that *the personality adjustments and traits of the children who were not punished for toilet training accidents do not differ significantly from those of the children who were punished* must not be rejected (see Table 3). Only three of the chi squares are significant. Those who were not punished for toilet training accidents made better showings in the social adjustment, social standards, and school relations components of the California Test of Personality. These results are in keeping with the prediction that would be made on the basis of the writings about this training practice.

The seventh hypothesis that *the personality adjustments of the children who slept with their mothers during infancy do not differ significantly from those of the children who did not sleep with their mothers* must not be rejected (see Table 3). Four of the possible chi squares were significant. The children who slept with their mothers during infancy made significantly poorer showings on the self-adjustment, personal freedom, and family relations components of the California Test of Personality and suffered more sleep disturbances than did those who slept alone. The direction of these associations is contrary to what would be expected on the basis of the theory but are the most consistent results yet found in the study. Obviously, they contradict the claim of those who hold that this practice promotes secure childhood personalities.

Because it was not possible on the basis of the analysis to reject any of the specific null hypotheses concerning the association between training experiences and personality adjustments and traits, the general null hypothesis that *the personality adjustments and traits of the children who have undergone varying infant-training experiences do not differ significantly* cannot be rejected. However, before reaching this unequivocal conclusion, it was decided that some attempt should be made to determine the joint effects of the several infancy experiences on personality adjustment. Consequently, a crude index was developed to indicate degree of infantile security. This index was based on the simple assumption that the combined effects of the various training experiences which are believed to be favorable would produce a more favorable infancy than would the combined effects of those training experiences which are assumed to be unfavorable. In ar-

---

[14] Some readers may wonder exactly how many differences would have to be significant before the null hypothesis would be rejected. Unfortunately, there is no accepted standard for rejection of the null hypothesis in situations of this kind where there is probably some intercorrelation between the variables but where, in no sense, the forty-six personality indicators can be thought of as measures of the same thing. I have discussed my results with several mathematical statisticians, who agree that the null hypotheses of this study cannot be rejected on the basis of the statistical evidence, but none of them has been willing to set an unequivocal standard.

riving at the index scores, one point was given for each of the supposedly favorable infant-training experiences, and a total was computed. Following the procedure used throughout the study, the resulting distribution was approximately halved, to produce favorable and unfavorable categories, and forty-six fourfold tables were produced relating the infantile security index to the personality indicators. This made possible the testing of an eighth null hypothesis that *the personality adjustments and traits of the children whose infantile security index scores are favorable do not differ significantly from those of the children whose scores are unfavorable.* This hypothesis, too, must not be rejected on the basis of the statistical analysis (see Table 3). Of the forty-six possible chi squares, only two are significant. The children with more favorable scores had better tempers and a higher sense of personal freedom than did those whose scores were unfavorable on the index of infantile security. These relationships are in the expected direction, but the over-all results of this analysis provide no basis for the rejection of either the specific or the general hypothesis.

As one phase of the larger study of social factors and personality adjustment of which the present paper is a part, a factor analysis has been made of thirty-eight child-training practices, in order to isolate meaningful constellations of practices.[15] As a result of this analysis, six factors have been isolated, two of which contain items which are in the infant-training period; one on the toilet training complex and the other on the feeding training complex. Factor scores were derived for the children on these two factors, the distributions were again divided into favorable and unfavorable groups, and fourfold tables were produced relating these factors to all the personality measures. This made possible the further testing of the original general hypothesis and a ninth and tenth hypothesis dealing with the specific factors. Thus, the ninth hypothesis is that *the personality adjustments and traits of the children whose toilet training factor scores are favorable do not differ significantly from those of the children whose scores are unfavorable.* This hypothesis cannot be rejected. Actually, only one of the possible forty-six chi squares is significant; children whose toilet training factor scores are favorable are less likely to bite their nails than are those whose scores are unfavorable (see Table 3). Likewise, the tenth hypothesis that *the personality adjustments and traits of the children whose feeding training factor scores are favorable do not differ significantly from those of the children whose scores are unfavorable* cannot be rejected (see Table 3). Again, only one of the possible chi squares is significant; children whose feeding training scores are more favorable score lower on the family relations components of the California Test of Personality than do those whose feeding scores are less favorable. Again, the results of the testing of these two hypotheses in no way change the judgment that the general hypothesis of no significant relation between the infant training and the personality adjustments of the children studied must not be rejected.

---

[15] The factoring procedure was the modified multiple-group method of C. W. Harris and John Schmidt, Jr. See their article, "Further Application of the Principles of Direct Rotation in Factor Analysis," *Journal of Experimental Education*, XVIII (March, 1950), pp. 175–93. The computation of the factor scores was done by Lederman's shortened method as generalized by Karl J. Holzinger and Harry J. Harman, *Factor Analysis* (Chicago: University of Chicago Press, 1941), pp. 278–88.

Summary and Conclusions

On the basis of the results of this study, the general null hypothesis that the personality adjustments and traits of children who have undergone varying training experiences do not differ significantly cannot be rejected.[16] Of the 460 chi square tests, only 18 were significant at or beyond the 5 per cent level.[17] Of these, 11 were in the expected direction and 7 were in the opposite direction from that expected on the basis of psychoanalytic writings. Such practices as breast feeding, gradual weaning, demand schedule, and easy and late induction to bowel and bladder training, which have been so much emphasized in the psychoanalytic literature, were almost barren in terms of relation to personality adjustment as measured in this study.[18] Actually, these 6 factors produced only 11 significant chi squares out of a possible total of 276. Of these, 9 are in the direction which would be predicted on the basis of psychoanalytic writings and 2 are in the opposite direction. The practice which produced the largest number of significant chi squares was "slept with mother during first year of life." There were 4 significant chi squares, but all of them were in the opposite from the predicted direction. The two factor indexes and the index constructed to measure the cumulative effects of the infant-training practices produce even more meager results. Only 4 of a possible total of 138 chi squares were statistically significant; 3 were in the predicted and 1 in the opposite direction from that expected on the basis of psychoanalytic writings.

It is also interesting to observe that none of the training experiences was significantly related to any of the major tests of personality adjustment. The few significant relationships that were found tend to scatter widely among the various personality components and behavioral items; consequently, it cannot be held that any of the personality indexes or traits is consistently related to infant discipline.

Certainly, the results of this study cast serious doubts on the validity of the psychoanalytic claims regarding the importance of the infant disciplines and on the efficacy of prescriptions based on them. However, it should not be concluded that these results unequivocally refute the claim that infancy is an important period in the development of the individual's personality, or even that the particular training practices studied have a bearing on personality formation and adjustments. To establish the first point would demand both controlled experiments and the study of other aspects of infancy. To establish the second point would demand

---

[16] Some may raise question as to whether the association between the infant-training practices and the personality indicators would have been more marked if (1) more precise statistical measures had been used or (2) only the children who differed more markedly in their personality adjustments had been compared. Both these possibilities were tested and in no way improved the association. Means on the various personality tests and components were computed and tested for significance by the use of the critical ratio technique. Not only were the differences in means nonsignificant, but in all cases differences were extremely small and inconsistent in direction. Likewise, when only the children whose personality adjustment scores placed them in the extreme quartiles were compared, the results were no more significant than when the original dichotomous adjustment categories were used.

[17] It should be pointed out that there was no consistent trend in the direction of association (whether significant or not) between the infant-training items and the personality indicators. Of the 460 chi squares, 215 were in the predicted and 245 were in the opposite direction from that expected on the basis of psychoanalytic writings.

[18] The findings of the present study are in agreement with the more carefully designed empirical studies which Orlansky cites (op. cit., pp. 3–21) and with the recent study by Thurston and Mussen (op. cit., pp. 456–57).

the corroboration of the results of this study by many and better-designed studies of different culture and age groups.[19]

It is entirely possible that the significant and crucial matter is not the practices themselves but the whole personal-social situation in which they find their expression, including the attitudes and behavior of the mother.[20] This aspect of the mother-child relationship was purposely excluded from this paper. To a great extent it has escaped the net that was cast in the larger study of which this is a part and in other studies of infant training.[21] Much work must be done to devise techniques which will give at least crude measures of these qualitative aspects of the personal-social situation if the importance of infancy on personality formation and adjustment is to be assessed adequately. However, assumptions about the importance of the personal-social situation should be put to scientific test before any more unfounded personality theories and practices are built upon them.

Finally, a word is in order about the limitations of this study. First, it must be admitted that the controls employed, although better than in most studies of this type, were very crude; consequently, factors not accounted for may have affected the findings. Second, the data on training experiences, although gathered and treated with care, may be inadequate for reasons cited or unknown. Third, the measures of personality employed in the study are far from perfect in relation to either their validity or their reliability. Consequently, the possibility remains that the results may be different when the children are tested at later periods in their development and with more satisfactory measures.[22] But, despite these and other limitations, the results of this study are unequivocal for the sample covered, and their generality must be affirmed or denied by means of better-designed and executed empirical studies, not by dialectic.

---

[19] It may well be that the full effects of infant discipline will not become apparent until the children reach adulthood. However, Thurston and Mussen (*loc. cit.*) found no relationship between infant feeding ratifications and adult personality. The plan of the present research is to follow the children as far as possible throughout their development.

[20] This point has been suggested by several writers, including Erich Fromm. See his "Psychoanalytic Characterology and Its Application to the Understanding of Culture" in S. S. Sargent and M. W. Smith (eds.), *Culture and Personality* (New York: Viking Fund, 1949). However, I know of no scientific study of the personality adjustments of persons who have actually undergone the same infant-training experiences in varying personal-social contexts.

[21] Limited data are available on this point from the larger study. A paper is planned which will report the influence of parent-child relationships on childhood personality adjustments.

[22] The children will be tested again in 1952. It is hoped that, as they grow older, it will be possible to use more adequate means of assessing their personalities, first, because better tests are available for older children and adults and, second, because it is expected that more adequate tests will be developed as time goes on.

53   The Rules of the Game

● JEAN PIAGET

Children's games constitute the most admirable social institutions. The game of marbles, for instance, as played by boys, contains an extremely complex system of rules, that is to say, a code of laws, a jurisprudence of its own. Only the psychologist, whose profession obliges him to become familiar with this instance of common law, and to get at the implicit morality underlying it, is in a position to estimate the extraordinary wealth of these rules by the difficulty he experiences in mastering their details.

If we wish to gain any understanding of child morality, it is obviously with the analysis of such facts as these that we must begin. All morality consists in a system of rules, and the essence of all morality is to be sought for in the respect which the individual acquires for these rules. The reflective analysis of Kant, the sociology of Durkheim, or the individualistic psychology of Bovet all meet on this point. The doctrines begin to diverge only from the moment that it has to be explained how the mind comes to respect these rules. For our part, it will be in the domain of child psychology that we shall undertake the analysis of this "how."

Now, most of the moral rules which the child learns to respect he receives from adults, which means that he receives them after they have been fully elaborated, and often elaborated, not in relation to him and as they are needed, but once and for all and through an uninterrupted succession of earlier adult generations.

In the case of the very simplest social games, on the contrary, we are in the presence of rules which have been elaborated by the children alone. It is of no moment whether these games strike us as "moral" or not in their contents. As psychologists we must ourselves adopt the point of view, not of the adult conscience, but of child morality. Now, the rules of the game of marbles are handed down, just like so-called moral realities, from one generation to another, and are preserved solely by the respect that is felt for them by individuals. The sole difference is that the relations in this case are only those that exist between children. The little boys who are beginning to play are gradually trained by the older ones in respect for the law; and in any case they aspire from their hearts to the virtue, supremely characteristic of human dignity, which consists in making a correct use of the customary practices of a game. As to the older ones, it is in their power to alter the rules. If this is not "morality," then where does morality begin? At least, it is respect for rules, and it appertains to an enquiry like ours to begin with the study of facts of this order. Of course the phenomena relating to the game of marbles are not among the most primitive. Before playing with his equals, the child is influenced by his parents. He is subjected from his cradle to a multiplicity of regulations, and even before language he becomes conscious of certain obligations. These circumstances even exercise . . . an undeniable influence upon the way in which the rules of games are elaborated. But in the case of play institutions, adult intervention is at any rate reduced to the minimum. We are therefore

SOURCE: Jean Piaget, in his *The Moral Judgment of the Child* (Glencoe, Illinois: The Free Press, 1948), pp. 1–3, 95–103. Reprinted by permission of The Macmillan Company and Routledge & Kegan Paul. First published in 1932.

    With the collaboration of Mme V. J. Piaget, MM M. Lambercier and L. Martinez.

in the presence here of realities which, if not amongst the most elementary, should be classed nevertheless amongst the most spontaneous and the most instructive.

With regard to game rules there are two phenomena which it is particularly easy to study: first the *practice* of rules, *i.e.*, the way in which children of different ages effectively apply rules: second the *consciousness* of rules, i.e., the idea which children of different ages form of the character of these game rules, whether of something obligatory and sacred or of something subject to their own choice, whether of heteronomy or autonomy.

. . . Now, a method is just what we are looking for at present in order to enable us to pass from the study of the rules of games to the analysis of moral realities imposed upon the child by the adult. It is only from the point of view of the right method to adopt that we shall here shortly touch upon the vexed question of the individual and society.

One way of attacking the problem is to analyse and explain the rules objectively, taking account of their connection with social groups defined by their morphology. This is the method which Durkheim used, and no one would think of denying his contribution to the subject of the evolution of moral realities. The mere fact of individuals living in groups is sufficient to give rise to new features of obligation and regularity in their lives. The pressure of the group upon the individual would thus explain the appearance of this *sui generis* feeling which we call respect and which is the source of all religion and morality. For the group could not impose itself upon the individual without surrounding itself with a halo of sanctity and without arousing in the individual the feeling of moral obligation. A rule is therefore nothing but the condition for the existence of a social group; and if to the individual conscience rules seem to be charged with obligation, that is because communal life alters the very structure of consciousness by inculcating into it the feeling of respect.

It is a striking fact, in this connection, that even such ephemeral groupings as those formed by children's societies or created primarily for the purpose of play have their rules and that these rules command the respect of individual minds. It is also curious to note how stable these rules remain in their main features and in their spirit throughout successive generations, and to what degree of elaboration and stylization they attain.

But . . . rules, although their content continues to be the same, do not remain identical throughout the child's social development from the point of view of the kind of respect connected with them.

For very young children, a rule is a sacred reality because it is traditional; for the older ones it depends upon mutual agreement. Heteronomy and autonomy are the two poles of this evolution. Does Durkheim's method enable us to explain these facts?

No one has felt more deeply than Durkheim nor submitted to a more searching analysis the development and disappearance of obligatory conformity. In societies of a segmented type conformity is at its maximum: each social unit is a closed system, all the individuals are identical with each other except in the matter of age, and tradition leans with its full weight on the spirit of each. But as a society increases in size and density the barriers between its clans are broken down, local conformities are wiped out as a result of this fusion, and individuals can escape from their own people's supervision. And above all, the division of labour which comes as the necessary result of this increasing density differentiates the individuals from one another psychologically and gives rise to individualism and to the formation of personalities in the true sense. Individual heteronomy and autonomy would thus seem to be in direct correlation with the morphology and the functioning of the group as a whole.

Now, does this analysis apply to our children's societies? In many respects, undoubtedly, it does. There is certainly a resemblance between segmented or mechanical solidarity and the societies formed by children of 5 to 8. As in the organized clan so in these groups, temporarily formed and isolated in relation to each other, the individual does not count. Social life and individual life are one. Suggestion and imitation are all-powerful. All individuals are alike except for differences of prestige and age. The traditional rule is coercive and conformity is demanded of all.

As to the gradual disappearance of conformity as the child grows older, this too we could explain by some of the factors defined by Durkheim. To the increasing size and density of social groups and to the ensuing liberation of the individual we can compare the fact that our children, as they grow older, take part in an ever-increasing number of local traditions. The marble player of 10 or 12 will discover, for example, that there are other usages in existence besides those to which he is accustomed; he will make friends with children from other schools who will free him from his narrow conformity, and in this way a fusion will take place between clans which up till then had been more or less isolated. At the same time, the growing child detaches himself more and more from his family circle, and since at first he assimilates games to the duties laid down for him by adults, the more he escapes from family conformity, the greater change will his consciousness of rules undergo.

If, however, we are able to compare all these facts to the growth of societies in size and density, we can do so only from the point of view of the gradual diminution of the supervision exercised over individuals. In other words, the outstanding fact in the evolution of game rules is that the child is less and less dominated by the "older ones." There is little or no progressive division of labour among children; such differentiations as arise are psychological and not economic or political. If, therefore, children's societies do, in a sense, develop from the segmented to the more highly organized type, and if there is a correlative evolution from conformity to individualistic cooperation, or from heteronomy to autonomy, this process, though we may describe it in the objective terms of sociology, must be attributed first and foremost to the morphology and activity of the various age classes of the population.

In other words, the main factor in the obligatory conformity of very young children is nothing but respect for age—respect for older children, and, above all, respect for adults. And if, at a given moment, cooperation takes the place of constraint, or autonomy that of conformity, it is because the child, as he grows older, becomes progressively free from adult supervision. This [comes] out very clearly in the game of marbles. Children of 11 to 13 have no others above them in this game, since it is one that is only played in the lower school. But apart from this, the boy begins at this age to feel himself more and more on the same level as adolescents and to free himself inwardly from adult constraint. As a result, his moral consciousness undergoes . . . alterations. . . . There can be no doubt that this phenomenon is peculiar to our civilization and therefore falls under the Durkheimian scheme. In our societies the child of 13 escapes from the family circle and

comes in contact with an ever-increasing number of social circles which widen
his mental outlook. Whereas in so-called primitive communities, adolescence is
the age of initiation, therefore of the strongest moral constraint, and the individual,
as he grows older, becomes more and more dependent. But keeping in mind only
our societies of children, we see that cooperation constitutes the most deep-lying
social phenomenon, and that which has the surest psychological foundations. As
soon as the individual escapes from the domination of age, he tends towards cooperation as the normal form of social equilibrium.

In short, if, putting other considerations aside for the moment, we seek only to
find a working hypothesis, the methodological difficulty of Durkheimism seems to
be the following with regard to the different kinds of respect. Durkheim argues
as though differences from one age or from one generation to another were of no
account. He assumes homogeneous individuals and tries to find out what repercussion different modes of grouping would have upon their minds. All that he gets
at in this way is profoundly true, but it is incomplete. We have only to make the
impossible supposition of a society where everyone would be of the same age, of
a society formed by a single generation indefinitely prolonged, to realize the immense significance attaching to age relations and especially to the relations between adults and children. Would such a society ever have known anything of
obligatory conformity? Would it be acquainted with religion or at any rate with
the religions that taught transcendence? Would unilateral respect with all its repercussions upon the moral consciousness be observed in such a group as this?
We only wish to ask these questions. Whichever way they are answered, there
can be no doubt that cooperation and social constraint deserve to be far more
sharply contrasted than they usually are, the latter being perhaps nothing more
than the pressure of one generation upon the other, whereas the former constitutes the deepest and most important social relation that can go to the development of the norms of reason.

This influence exercised by age brings us to the second possible view of the psychology of rules, we mean that held by M. Bovet. Theoretically, and in his
method, M. Bovet recognizes only individuals. Only, instead of becoming involved, as others have been in a barren discussion on the limits of what is social
and what is individual, M. Bovet admits that respect, the feeling of obligation,
and the making of rules presuppose the interaction of at least two individuals.
On this point his method is parallel to Durkheim's and in no way opposed to it.
For the real conflict lies between those who want to explain the moral consciousness by means of purely individual processes (habit, biological adaptation, etc.)
and those who admit the necessity for an inter-individual factor. Once grant that
two individuals at least must be taken into account if a moral reality is to develop,
then it matters not whether you describe the facts objectively, as Durkheim did,
or at least tried to do, or whether you describe them in terms of consciousness.[1]
How, asks M. Bovet, does the sense of duty appear? Two conditions, he says, are
necessary, and their conjunction sufficient. The individual must receive a command from another individual; the obligatory rule is therefore psychologically
different from the individual habit or from what we have called the motor rule.
The individual receiving the command must accept it, i.e. must respect the person from whom it came. M. Bovet differs on this point from Kant, since he

---

[1] See R. Lacombe's conclusive remarks, *La Méthode sociologique de Durkheim*. Also d'Esser-
tier, *Psychologie et Sociologie*, Paris, Alcan, and many other contributions to the subject.

regards respect as a feeling directed to persons and not to the rule as such. It is not the obligatory character of the rule laid down by an individual that makes us respect this individual, it is the respect we feel for the individual that makes us regard as obligatory the rule that he lays down. The appearance of the sense of duty in a child thus admits of the simplest explanation, namely that he receives commands from older children (in play) and from adults (in life), and that he respects older children and parents.

. . . Our results completely confirm this view of the matter. Before the intervention of adults or of older children there are in the child's conduct certain rules that we have called motor rules. But they are not imperative, they do not constitute duties but only spontaneous regularities of behaviour. From the moment, however, that the child has received from his parents a system of commands, rules and, in general, the world order itself seem to him to be morally necessary. In this way, as soon as the little child encounters the example of older children at marbles, he accepts these suggestions and regards the new rules discovered in this way as sacred and obligatory.

But the problem which faces us and which M. Bovet has himself clearly formulated and discussed is how this morality of duty will allow for the appearance of the morality of goodness.

The problem is two-fold. In the first place, the primitive consciousness of duty is essentially heteronomous, since duty is nothing more than the acceptance of commands received from without. How then, asks M. Bovet, will the child come to distinguish a "good" from a "bad" respect, and, after having accepted without distinction everything that was laid down for him by his environment, how will he learn to make his choice and to establish a hierarchy of values? In language which exactly recalls that in which Durkheim describes the effect of increasing social density on the minds of the individuals, M. Bovet points here to the effect of conflicting influences and even of contradictory commands: the child pulled in several directions at once is forced to appeal to his reason in order to bring unity into the moral material. Already we have autonomy, but since reason does not create new duties and can only choose from among the orders received, this autonomy is still only relative. In the second place, alongside of the sense of duty we must, according to M. Bovet, distinguish a sense of goodness, a consciousness of something attractive and not merely obligatory, a consciousness that is fully autonomous. In contrast to Durkheim who, while he fully recognized this dualism of duty and good nevertheless tried to trace them both to the same efficient cause, viz. pressure of the group, M. Bovet leaves the question open, and does so intentionally.

It is at this point, so it seems to us, that the part played by mutual respect comes in. Without going outside M. Bovet's fertile hypothesis, according to which all the moral sentiments are rooted in the respect felt by individuals for each other, we can, nevertheless, distinguish different types of respect. It seems to us an undeniable fact that in the course of the child's mental development, unilateral respect or the respect felt by the small for the great plays an essential part: it is what makes the child accept all the commands transmitted to him by his parents and is thus the great factor of continuity between different generations. But it seems to us no less undeniable . . . that as the child grows in years the nature of his respect changes. In so far as individuals decide questions on an equal footing—no matter whether subjectively or objectively—the pressure they exercise upon each other becomes collateral. And the interventions of reason, so rightly noted by M. Bovet, for the purpose of explaining the autonomy now acquired by morality, are precisely the outcome of this progressive cooperation. Our earlier studies led us to the conclusion that the norms of reason, and in particular the important norm of reciprocity, the source of the logic of relations, can only develop in and through cooperation. Whether cooperation is an effect or a cause of reason, or both, reason requires cooperation in so far as being rational consists in "situating oneself" so as to submit the individual to the universal. Mutual respect therefore appears to us as the necessary condition of autonomy under its double aspect, intellectual and moral. From the intellectual point of view, it frees the child from the opinions that have been imposed upon him while it favours inner consistency and reciprocal control. Within the moral point of view, it replaces the norms of authority by that norm immanent in action and in consciousness themselves, the norm of reciprocity in sympathy.

In short, whether one takes up the point of view of Durkheim or of M. Bovet, it is necessary, in order to grasp the situation, to take account of two groups of social and moral facts—constraint and unilateral respect on the one hand, cooperation and mutual respect on the other. . . . Whether we describe the facts in the terms of social morphology or from the point of view of consciousness (and the two languages are, we repeat, parallel and not contradictory) it is impossible to reduce the effects of cooperation to those of constraint and unilateral respect.

54   Development of the Self Through Play and Games

● GEORGE HERBERT MEAD

The problem now presents itself as to how, in detail, a self arises. We have to note something of the background of its genesis. First of all there is the conversation of gestures between animals involving some sort of co-operative activity. There the beginning of the act of one is a stimulus to the other to respond in a certain way, while the beginning of this response becomes again a stimulus to the first to adjust his action to the oncoming response. Such is the preparation for the completed act, and ultimately it leads up to the conduct which is the outcome of this preparation. The conversation of gestures, however, does not carry with it the reference of the individual, the animal, the organism, to itself. It is not acting in a fashion which calls for a response from the form itself, although it is conduct with reference to the conduct of others. We have seen, however, that there are certain gestures that do affect the organism as they affect other organisms and may, therefore, arouse in the organism responses of the same character as aroused in the other. Here, then, we have a situation in which the individual may at least arouse responses in himself and reply to these responses, the condition being that the social stimuli have an effect on the individual which is like that which they have on the other. That, for example, is what is implied in language; otherwise

Gesture

SOURCE: George Herbert Mead, in his *Mind, Self, and Society* (Chicago: The University of Chicago Press, 1934), pp. 144–147; 149–173. Reprinted by permission of The University of Chicago Press.

language as significant symbol would disappear, since the individual would not get the meaning of that which he says.

The peculiar character possessed by our human social environment belongs to it by virtue of the peculiar character of human social activity; and that character, as we have seen, is to be found in the process of communication, and more particularly in the triadic relation on which the existence of meaning is based: the relation of the gesture of one organism to the adjustive response made to it by another organism, in its indicative capacity as pointing to the completion or resultant of the act it initiates (the meaning of the gesture being thus the response of the second organism to it as such, or as a gesture). What, as it were, takes the gesture out of the social act and isolates it as such—what makes it something more than just an early phase of an individual act—is the response of another organism, or of other organisms, to it. Such a response is its meaning, or gives it its meaning. The social situation and process of behavior are here presupposed by the acts of the individual organisms implicated therein. The gesture arises as a separable element in the social act, by virtue of the fact that it is selected out by the sensitivities of other organisms to it; it does not exist as a gesture merely in the experience of the single individual. The meaning of a gesture by one organism, to repeat, is found in the response of another organism to what would be the completion of the act of the first organism which that gesture initiates and indicates.

We sometimes speak as if a person could build up an entire argument in his mind, and then put it into words to convey it to someone else. Actually, our thinking always takes place by means of some sort of symbols. It is possible that one could have the meaning of "chair" in his experience without there being a symbol, but we would not be thinking about it in that case. We may sit down in a chair without thinking about what we are doing, that is, the approach to the chair is presumably already aroused in our experience, so that the meaning is there. But if one is thinking about the chair he must have some sort of a symbol for it. It may be the form of the chair, it may be the attitude that somebody else takes in sitting down, but it is more apt to be some language symbol that arouses this response. In a thought process there has to be some sort of a symbol that can refer to this meaning, that is, tend to call out this response, and also serve this purpose for other persons as well. It would not be a thought process if that were not the case.

Our symbols are all universal.[1] You cannot say anything that is absolutely particular; anything you say that has any meaning at all is universal. You are saying something that calls out a specific response in anybody else provided that the symbol exists for him in his experience as it does for you. . . .

What is essential to communication is that the symbol should arouse in one's self what it arouses in the other individual. It must have that sort of universality to any person who finds himself in the same situation. There is a possibility of

---

[1] Thinking proceeds in terms of or by means of universals. A universal may be interpreted behavioristically as simply the social act as a whole, involving the organization and interrelation of the attitudes of all the individuals implicated in the act, as controlling their overt responses. This organization of the different individual attitudes and interactions in a given social act, with reference to their interrelations as realized by the individuals themselves, is what we mean by a universal; and it determines what the actual overt responses of the individuals involved in the given social act will be, whether that act be concerned with a concrete project of some sort (such as the relation of physical and social means to ends desired) or with some purely abstract discussion, say the theory of relativity or the Platonic ideas.

language whenever a stimulus can affect the individual as it affects the other. With a blind person such as Helen Keller, it is a contact experience that could be given to another as it is given to herself. It is out of that sort of language that the mind of Helen Keller was built up. As she has recognized, it was not until she could get into communication with other persons through symbols which could arouse in herself the responses they arouse in other people that she could get what we term a mental content, or a self.

Another set of background factors in the genesis of the self is represented in the activities of play and the game. . . .

We find in children . . . invisible, imaginary companions which a good many children produce in their own experience. They organize in this way the responses which they call out in other persons and call out also in themselves. Of course, this playing with an imaginary companion is only a peculiarly interesting phase of ordinary play. Play in this sense, especially the stage which precedes the organized games, is a play at something. A child plays at being a mother, at being a teacher, at being a policeman; that is, it is taking different rôles, as we say. We have something that suggests this in what we call the play of animals: a cat will play with her kittens, and dogs play with each other. Two dogs playing with each other will attack and defend, in a process which if carried through would amount to an actual fight. There is a combination of responses which checks the depth of the bite. But we do not have in such a situation the dogs taking a definite rôle in the sense that a child deliberately takes the rôle of another. This tendency on the part of the children is what we are working with in the kindergarten where the rôles which the children assume are made the basis for training. When a child does assume a rôle he has in himself the stimuli which call out that particular response or group of responses. He may, of course, run away when he is chased, as the dog does, or he may turn around and strike back just as the dog does in his play. But that is not the same as playing at something. Children get together to "play Indian." This means that the child has a certain set of stimuli which call out in itself the responses that they would call out in others, and which answer to an Indian. In the play period the child utilizes his own responses to these stimuli which he makes use of in building a self. The response which he has a tendency to make to these stimuli organizes them. He plays that he is, for instance, offering himself something, and he buys it; he gives a letter to himself and takes it away; he addresses himself as a parent, as a teacher; he arrests himself as a policeman. He has a set of stimuli which call out in himself the sort of responses they call out in others. He takes this group of responses and organizes them into a certain whole. Such is the simplest form of being another to one's self. It involves a temporal situation. The child says something in one character and responds in another character, and then his responding in another character is a stimulus to himself in the first character, and so the conversation goes on. A certain organized structure arises in him and in his other which replies to it, and these carry on the conversation of gestures between themselves.

If we contrast play with the situation in an organized game, we note the essential difference that the child who plays in a game must be ready to take the attitude of everyone else involved in that game, and that these different rôles must have a definite relationship to each other. Taking a very simple game such as hide-and-seek, everyone with the exception of the one who is hiding is a person who is hunting. A child does not require more than the person who is hunted and

the one who is hunting. If a child is playing in the first sense he just goes on playing, but there is no basic organization gained. In that early stage he passes from
one rôle to another just as a whim takes him. But in a game where a number of
individuals are involved, then the child taking one rôle must be ready to take the
rôle of everyone else. If he gets in a ball nine he must have the responses of each
position involved in his own position. He must know what everyone else is going
to do in order to carry out his own play. He has to take all of these rôles. They do
not all have to be present in consciousness at the same time, but at some moments
he has to have three or four individuals present in his own attitude, such as the
one who is going to throw the ball, the one who is going to catch it, and so on.
These responses must be, in some degree, present in his own make-up. In the
game, then, there is a set of responses of such others so organized that the attitude
of one calls out the appropriate attitudes of the other.

This organization is put in the form of the rules of the game. Children take a
great interest in rules. They make rules on the spot in order to help themselves
out of difficulties. Part of the enjoyment of the game is to get these rules. Now,
the rules are the set of responses which a particular attitude calls out. You can
demand a certain response in others if you take a certain attitude. These responses
are all in yourself as well. There you get an organized set of such responses as
that to which I have referred, which is something more elaborate than the rôles
found in play. Here there is just a set of responses that follow on each other indefinitely. At such a stage we speak of a child as not yet having a fully developed
self. The child responds in a fairly intelligent fashion to the immediate stimuli
that come to him, but they are not organized. He does not organize his life as we
would like to have him do, namely, as a whole. There is just a set of responses of
the type of play. The child reacts to a certain stimulus, and the reaction is in himself that is called out in others, but he is not a whole self. In his game he has to
have an organization of these rôles; otherwise he cannot play the game. The game
represents the passage in the life of the child from taking the rôle of others in play
to the organized part that is essential to self-consciousness in the full sense of the
term.

Play, the Game, and the Generalized Other

We are speaking of the social conditions under which the self arises as an object. In addition to language we found two illustrations, one in play and the other
in the game, and I wish to summarize and expand my account on these points. I
have spoken of these from the point of view of children. . . . The fundamental
difference between the game and play is that in the latter the child must have the
attitude of all the others involved in that game. The attitudes of the other players
which the participant assumes organize into a sort of unit, and it is that organization which controls the response of the individual. The illustration used was of a
person playing baseball. Each one of his own acts is determined by his assumption of the action of the others who are playing the game. What he does is controlled by his being everyone else on that team, at least in so far as those attitudes
affect his own particular response. We get then an "other" which is an organization of the attitudes of those involved in the same process.

The organized community or social group which gives to the individual his
unity of self may be called "the generalized other." The attitude of the generalized

other is the attitude of the whole community.[2] Thus, for example, in the case of such a social group as a ball team, the team is the generalized other in so far as it enters—as an organized process or social activity—into the experience of any one of the individual members of it.

If the given human individual is to develop a self in the fullest sense, it is not sufficient for him merely to take the attitudes of other human individuals toward himself and toward one another within the human social process, and to bring that social process as a whole into his individual experience merely in these terms: he must also, in the same way that he takes the attitudes of other individuals toward himself and toward one another, take their attitudes toward the various phases or aspects of the common social activity or set of social undertakings in which, as members of an organized society or social group, they are all engaged; and he must then, by generalizing these individual attitudes of that organized society or social group itself, as a whole, act toward different social projects which at any given time it is carrying out, or toward the various larger phases of the general social process which constitutes its life and of which these projects are specific manifestations. This getting of the broad activities of any given social whole or organized society as such within the experiential field of any one of the individuals involved or included in that whole is, in other words, the essential basis and prerequisite of the fullest development of that individual's self: only in so far as he takes the attitudes of the organized social group to which he belongs toward the organized, co-operative social activity or set of such activities in which that group as such is engaged, does he develop a complete self or possess the sort of complete self he has developed. And on the other hand, the complex co-operative processes and activities and institutional functionings of organized human society are also possible only in so far as every individual involved in them or belonging to that society can take the general attitudes of all other such individuals with reference to these processes and activities and institutional functionings, and to the organized social whole of experiential relations and interactions thereby constituted—and can direct his own behavior accordingly.

It is in the form of the generalized other that the social process influences the behavior of the individuals involved in it and carrying it on, i.e., that the community exercises control over the conduct of its individual members; for it is in this form that the social process or community enters as a determining factor into the individual's thinking. In abstract thought the individual takes the attitude of the generalized other [3] toward himself, without reference to its expression in any

[2] It is possible for inanimate objects, no less than for other human organisms, to form parts of the generalized and organized—the completely socialized—other for any given human individual, in so far as he responds to such objects socially or in a social fashion (by means of the mechanism of thought, the internalized conversation of gestures). Any thing—any object or set of objects, whether animate or inanimate, human or animal, or merely physical—toward which he acts, or to which he responds, socially, is an element in what for him is the generalized other; by taking the attitudes of which toward himself he becomes conscious of himself as an object or individual, and thus develops a self or personality. Thus, for example, the cult, in its primitive form, is merely the social embodiment of the relation between the given social group or community and its physical environment—an organized social means, adopted by the individual members of that group or community, of entering into social relations with that environment, or (in a sense) of carrying on conversations with it; and in this way that environment becomes part of the total generalized other for each of the individual members of the given social group or community.

[3] We have said that the internal conversation of the individual with himself in terms of words or significant gestures—the conversation which constitutes the process or activity of thinking— is carried on by the individual from the standpoint of the "generalized other." And the more

particular other individuals; and in concrete thought he takes that attitude in so far as it is expressed in the attitudes toward his behavior of those other individuals with whom he is involved in the given social situation or act. But only by taking the attitude of the generalized other toward himself, in one or another of these ways, can he think at all; for only thus can thinking—or the internalized conversation of gestures which constitutes thinking—occur. And only through the taking by individuals of the attitude or attitudes of the generalized other toward themselves is the existence of a universe of discourse, as that system of common or social meanings which thinking presupposes at its context, rendered possible.

The self-conscious human individual, then, takes or assumes the organized social attitudes of the given social group or community (or of some one section thereof) to which he belongs, toward the social problems of various kinds which confront that group or community at any given time, and which arise in connection with the correspondingly different social projects or organized co-operative enterprises in which that group or community as such is engaged; and as an individual participant in these social projects or co-operative enterprises, he governs his own conduct accordingly. In politics, for example, the individual identifies himself with an entire political party and takes the organized attitudes of that entire party toward the rest of the given social community and toward the problems which confront the party within the given social situation; and he consequently reacts or responds in terms of the organized attitudes of the party as a whole. He thus enters into a special set of social relations with all the other individuals who belong to that political party; and in the same way he enters into various other special sets of social relations, with various other classes of individuals respectively, the individuals of each of these classes being the other members of some one of the particular organized subgroups (determined in socially functional terms) of which he himself is a member within the entire given society or social community. In the most highly developed, organized, and complicated human social communities—those evolved by civilized man—these various socially functional classes or subgroups of individuals to which any given individual belongs (and with the other individual members of which he thus enters into a special set of social relations) are of two kinds. Some of them are concrete social classes or subgroups, such as political parties, clubs, corporations, which are all actually functional social units, in terms of which their individual members are directly related to one another. The others are abstract social classes or subgroups, such as the class of debtors and the class of creditors, in terms of which their individual members are related to one another only more or less indirectly, and which only more or less indirectly function as social units, but which afford or represent unlimited possibilities for the widening and ramifying and enriching of the social relations among all the individual members of the given society as an organized and unified whole. The given individual's membership in several of these abstract

---

abstract that conversation is, the more abstract thinking happens to be, the further removed is the generalized other from any connection with particular individuals. It is especially in abstract thinking, that is to say, that the conversation involved is carried on by the individual with the generalized other, rather than with any particular individuals. Thus it is, for example, that abstract concepts are concepts stated in terms of the attitudes of the entire social group or community; they are stated on the basis of the individual's consciousness of the attitudes of the generalized other toward them, as a result of his taking these attitudes of the generalized other and then responding to them. And thus it is also that abstract propositions are stated in a form which anyone—any other intelligent individual—will accept.

social classes or subgroups makes possible his entrance into definite social relations (however indirect) with an almost infinite number of other individuals who also belong to or are included within one or another of these abstract social classes or subgroups cutting across functional lines of demarcation which divide different human social communities from one another, and including individual members from several (in some cases from all) such communities. Of these abstract social classes or subgroups of human individuals the one which is most inclusive and extensive is, of course, the one defined by the logical universe of discourse (or system of universally significant symbols) determined by the participation and communicative interaction of individuals; for all such classes or subgroups, it is the one which claims the largest number of individual members, and which enables the largest conceivable number of human individuals to enter into some sort of social relation, however indirect or abstract it may be, with one another—a relation arising from the universal functioning of gestures as significant symbols in the general human social process of communication.

I have pointed out, then, that there are two general stages in the full development of the self. At the first of these stages, the individual's self is constituted simply by an organization of the particular attitudes of other individuals toward himself and toward one another in the specific social acts in which he participates with them. But at the second stage in the full development of the individual's self that self is constituted not only by an organization of these particular individual attitudes, but also by an organization of the social attitudes of the generalized other or the social group as a whole to which he belongs. These social or group attitudes are brought within the individual's field of direct experience, and are included as elements in the structure or constitution of his self, in the same way that the attitudes of particular other individuals are; and the individual arrives at them, or succeeds in taking them, by means of further organizing, and then generalizing, the attitudes of particular other individuals in terms of their organized social bearings and implications. So the self reaches its full development by organizing these individual attitudes of others into the organized social or group attitudes, and by thus becoming an individual reflection of the general systematic pattern of social or group behavior in which it and the others are all involved—a pattern which enters as a whole into the individual's experience in terms of these organized group attitudes which, through the mechanism of his central nervous system, he takes toward himself, just as he takes the individual attitudes of others.

The game has a logic, so that such an organization of the self is rendered possible: there is a definite end to be obtained; the actions of the different individuals are all related to each other with reference to that end so that they do not conflict; one is not in conflict with himself in the attitude of another man on the team. If one has the attitude of the person throwing the ball he can also have the response of catching the ball. The two are related so that they further the purpose of the game itself. They are interrelated in a unitary, organic fashion. There is a definite unity, then, which is introduced into the organization of other selves when we reach such a stage as that of the game, as over against the situation of play where there is a simple succession of one rôle after another, a situation which is, of course, characteristic of the child's own personality. The child is one thing at one time and another at another, and what he is at one moment does not determine what he is at another. That is both the charm of childhood as well as its inadequacy. You cannot count on the child; you cannot assume that all the things he does are going to determine what he will do at any moment. He is not organized into a whole. The child has no definite character, no definite personality.

The game is then an illustration of the situation out of which an organized personality arises. In so far as the child does take the attitude of the other and allows that attitude of the other to determine the thing he is going to do with reference to a common end, he is becoming an organic member of society. He is taking over the morale of that society and is becoming an essential member of it. He belongs to it in so far as he does allow the attitude of the other that he takes to control his own immediate expression. What is involved here is some sort of an organized process. That which is expressed in terms of the game is, of course, being continually expressed in the social life of the child, but this wider process goes beyond the immediate experience of the child himself. The importance of the game is that it lies entirely inside of the child's own experience, and the importance of our modern type of education is that it is brought as far as possible within this realm. The different attitudes that a child assumes are so organized that they exercise a definite control over his response, as the attitudes in a game control his own immediate response. In the game we get an organized other, a generalized other, which is found in the nature of the child itself, and finds its expression in the immediate experience of the child. And it is that organized activity in the child's own nature controlling the particular response which gives unity, and which builds up his own self.

What goes on in the game goes on in the life of the child all the time. He is continually taking the attitudes of those about him, especially the rôles of those who in some sense control him and on whom he depends. He gets the function of the process in an abstract sort of a way at first. It goes over from the play into the game in a real sense. He has to play the game. The morale of the game takes hold of the child more than the larger morale of the whole community. The child passes into the game and the game expresses a social situation in which he can completely enter; its morale may have a greater hold on him than that of the family to which he belongs or the community in which he lives. There are all sorts of social organizations, some of which are fairly lasting, some temporary, into which the child is entering, and he is playing a sort of social game in them. It is a period in which he likes "to belong," and he gets into organizations which come into existence and pass out of existence. He becomes a something which can function in the organized whole, and thus tends to determine himself in his relationship with the group to which he belongs. That process is one which is a striking stage in the development of the child's morale. It constitutes him a self-conscious member of the community to which he belongs. . . .

Emphasis should be laid on the central position of thinking when considering the nature of the self. Self-consciousness, rather than affective experience with its motor accompaniments, provides the core and primary structure of the self, which is thus essentially a cognitive rather than an emotional phenomenon. The thinking or intellectual process—the internalization and inner dramatization, by the individual, of the external conversation of significant gestures which constitutes his chief mode of interaction with other individuals belonging to the same society— is the earliest experiential phase in the genesis and development of the self. Cooley and James, it is true, endeavor to find the basis of the self in reflexive affective experiences, i.e., experiences involving "self-feeling"; but the theory that the nature of the self is to be found in such experiences does not account for the origin of the self, or of the self-feeling which is supposed to characterize such experiences. The individual need not take the attitudes of others toward himself in these experiences, since these experiences merely in themselves do not necessitate his doing so, and unless he does so, he cannot develop a self; and he will not do so in these experiences unless his self has already originated otherwise, namely, in the way we have been describing. The essence of the self, as we have said, is cognitive: it lies in the internalized conversation of gestures which constitutes thinking, or in terms of which thought or reflection proceeds. And hence the origin and foundations of the self, like those of thinking, are social.

55   The Play of Little Children

● GREGORY P. STONE

Social psychologists have long recognized the significance of play for preparing young children to participate later on in adult society. But social psychology, when viewed against the backdrop of history, is very young. Furthermore, there is a disquieting tendency for many social science disciplines to lose their sense of history and develop what they conceive to be universal propositions based on observations made in quite spatially and temporally delimited milieux. This article is primarily designed to place the play of children in historical perspective and, then, to set forth some functions of contemporary child's play, reserving judgment about the universality of such functions. It is hoped that the very tentativeness with which such assertions are set forth will inspire the curiosity of others and encourage them to extend the spatial and temporal focus of their studies of childhood. Play, like other collective enterprises, is a collective representation: it re-presents the arrangements of the society and historical era in which it is carried on.

Historical Emergence of Children and Child's Play

In an extraordinary work (Ref. 1), Philippe Ariès asks the seemingly naive question: where do children come from? He is not, of course, concerned with the biological origins of infants, but with the historical origins of the social *identity*, "child." Although the classical Greek civilization (and those it influenced directly) had distinguished children socially from babes and adults if only as objects of aesthetic appreciation, children did not emerge as social entities in the subsequent history of Western civilization until the early seventeenth century.

FRANCE AS AN EARLY SOURCE OF CHILDREN

Prior to the seventeenth century there were babes and adults in Western civilization, but no in-betweens. Babes were swaddled; adults attired; children were, in fact, *homunculi*. There was no distinctive dress to differentiate them, and expectations directed toward them were not age-specific. The elaborate record of the life of Louis XIII kept by his doctor, Heroard (1: pp. 62–67, 100), amazes us today. The Dauphin was betrothed by his first birthday. At seventeen months, he

SOURCE: Gregory P. Stone, a revised version of his "The Play of Little Children," *Quest*, IV (April 1965), pp. 23–31.

was singing and playing the violin. By the age of two years, he was dancing various kinds of dances. At three and a half, he was reading, and he was writing at four. It must be emphasized here that the child, Louis, was not thought of as particularly brilliant. Such activities were merely expected of the little people we call children today. Nor was this seemingly precocious activity necessarily confined to children of royalty and aristocracy, although such intricate play forms were undoubtedly concentrated in that estate. Paintings of the period, as well as earlier paintings, show the children of commoners and peasants freely participating in what we think of today as adult settings, e.g., taverns and wine shops.

It is not as though there were no play at that time. Louis had his hobby horse, tops, and balls. Rather, play permeated all segments of the society. Ariès chides the contemporary historian Van Marle for his amazement upon discovering that the games played by grown-ups were no less childish than those played by children, retorting, "Of course not: they were the same" (1: p. 72). Festivals were another matrix of community-wide play in medieval Europe. Despite the fact, however, that play was general in the society, its unanticipated consequences were probably different for children and adults as they are today. Certainly some child's play provided young people with a vehicle for anticipatory socialization, permitting them to rehearse roles they would enact or encounter in later life, as in military play. Then as now, the play of children pulled them into the larger society. Adult play, on the other hand, undoubtedly released the players at times from everyday social demands and obligations. That adults and children played the same games makes such differences difficult to verify.

If play was general in the society of medieval Europe, attitudes toward play were not. In fifteenth and sixteenth century France, the Catholic clergy took a dim view of play, unless it followed the performance of work, and this view was subsequently adopted by police and other authorities. Yet, play could not be suppressed by such moralizers in a society where play was general in the population, and work did not have the significance it was to acquire with industrialization. The only enforceable suppression of play was accomplished in universities where clergy were recruited and trained, and there is evidence to suggest that this was not very effective. Possibly for this very reason, the Jesuits assimilated the play of the larger society in the seventeenth century. Play was redefined as educational and incorporated in college curricula (1: pp. 88–89). At the end of the eighteenth century, emerging nationalism provided a further legitimation of play. Play was conceived as a way of preparing young people for military service. The inclusion of play forms in military training programs is a frequent mode of legitimation. Thus, boxing or "prize-fighting" became legal in the United States in 1917 when it became an integral part of the U.S. Army's physical training program (14: p. 258).

As play acquired the approval of the moral custodians of seventeenth and eighteenth century French society, childhood also became established as a separate social identity in the human biography, and play became rather more of a childish thing. Ariès interprets this emergence of the child in the social morphology as one consequence of the rise of an entrepreneurial stratum in European society. As work moved to the center of social arrangements, play became increasingly relegated to childhood, and, *pari passu*, children were established as identifiable social beings. This may have been the case with France, but play and children were to have a more painful birth in the Protestant nations.

PLAY IN THE HISTORY OF ENGLAND AND AMERICA

Protestantism provided a religious justification for the tremendous expansion of work in the emerging industrial societies. Work was the key to the gates of the Protestant heaven: by your works are ye known. In contrast to the relegation of play to childhood in seventeenth and eighteenth century France, play had been generally suppressed in England by the end of the eighteenth century. In particular, the legislated inclosures of open areas deprived much of the population of play space. Play was further suppressed by legislation in English towns which, for example, forbade children from playing with tops in the streets or running races on the roads (7). When Wesley drew up the rules for his school at Kingswood, no time was set aside for play, because, in his view, "he who plays as a boy will play as a man" (7: p. 123).

In America, the status of play in the seventeenth and eighteenth century is less clear. We do know, of course, that child labor persisted in the United States into the twentieth century. Tocqueville thought that the Americans of his time were so wrapped up in work that they could not enjoy play: "Instead of these frivolous delights, they prefer those more serious and silent amusements which are like business and which do not drive business wholly out of their minds" (16: p. 221). On the other hand, Green has observed that play was smuggled into many areas of earlier American life in the guise of work, as in quilting parties and barn-raisings (5: p. 480), and, by the end of the nineteenth century, Bryce was impressed by the "brighter" life afforded the factory workers in New England through their "amusements than that of the clerks and shopkeepers of England" (2: p. 223). The picture is, at best, a confused one. Moreover, what seemed "serious and silent" to a Frenchman may well have seemed "bright" to an Englishman.

Probably, however, there was no overall moral consensus on the value of work and play. In a very careful study, Miyakawa has shown that there were sharp regional differences and, within regions, denominational differences (12). In nineteenth century Ohio, Presbyterians led a gayer life than Methodists, and, in Connecticut, the Congregationalists did not hesitate to dance and enjoy musical entertainment (12: p. 143). Even on the frontier, "at least some German, Swedish, and other continental settlers had occasional songfests, plays, dances, and music" (12: p. 143). Miyakawa's observations, given the relatively high social status of Presbyterian and Congregational denominations, permit the inference that play was looked upon with favor in the higher socio-economic strata of nineteenth century America. At this status level, as Veblen has shown (17), we find a leisure class straining to shed the trappings of work, and I would offer the general hypothesis that play is introduced into the bleak ages of any society by high status circles and spread throughout the society as a consequence of the emulation carried on by lower status circles and aggregates. Once this is accomplished, the moral "character" of the society is transformed. Yet, the mere emulation of play styles is not a sufficient explanation for the spread of play in society. It is a necessary condition.

Ariès may well be correct in his assertion that the emergence of an entrepreneurial stratum in France established the identity of child and cloaked that identity with distinctive play forms, but in England and America it is a very different matter. It required a *social movement against the excesses of capitalism*, in the Protestant countries, to release children from the bonds of work and confer the privileges of play. The movement had its inception in the reformist and revolutionary thought of the mid-nineteenth century and persisted until the twentieth. Indeed, Ritchie and Koller maintain that, for the United States, the "institutionalization of children's play and games is largely a twentieth century phenomenon" (13: p. 205). It is even possible that this institutionalization was not formally secured until the formulation of the Children's Charter of the 1930 White House Conference on Child Health and Protection which proclaimed: "With the young child, his work is his play and his play is his work" (13: p. 206).

IMPLICATIONS FOR THE SOCIAL PSYCHOLOGY OF PLAY

Children and child's play, then, emerged much later on the social scene in the Protestant than in the Catholic countries. As I have pointed out elsewhere, this difference persists today in contrasting Protestant and Catholic attitudes toward gaming or gambling (14: p. 257). Nevertheless, the fact remains that children and child's play have not always been with us, particularly as we know them today. Thus, when we speculate upon the social significance of child's play, we may well be developing hypotheses that have relevance only for a particular and relatively recent era of Western civilization. I have often wondered whether or not this is the best any social scientist can do—to dramatize effectively his own sociohistorical era. As Marx, Veblen, and Freud effectively dramatized the industrial era, so have Mills, Riesman, and Harry S. Sullivan effectively dramatized the era that Walter Rostow calls high mass consumption. This may well be the case because of the interaction between the social scientist and his subject matter. The very publication of social science theory and research alters the behavior it attempts to explain. For example, the incorporation of Keynesian economics into national fiscal policy introduced a political variable into business cycle theory, and nothing has altered sexual attitudes more than the dissemination of Freudian theory, with the result that contemporary psychoanalysts, such as Allen Wheelis, are confounded by the presence of disorders which defy explanation in classical Freudian terms.

Differentiation and Integration of the Child's Self Through Play

It is the task of society to make the lives of its members meaningful. This is accomplished by bringing little children into a meaningful communication with adults and one another, and, at the same time, by establishing their selves as objects so they can refer the other objects of their worlds to such established selves, thereby imbuing those worlds with significance (10). Play has a major part in the accomplishment of these tasks.

THE PLAY OF MOTHER AND CHILD

Meaning only exists in communication, and it is established when one's own symbols call out in the other about the same symbolic responses as they call out in himself. (Thus, this article can only be meaningful if readers respond to these words about the way that I have responded. Failing this, the article is nonsense!) This seems to be accomplished very early by the infant when it takes over the response patterns of the mothering one as its own. It may be that babbling is a kind of playing with noise, but we shall never know, for we cannot ask the babbler. Nevertheless, in the course of babbling, the infant may hit upon a word-like sound which is then *re*-presented by the mothering one as a word, together with an appropriate response pattern. "Baa," for example, may be re-presented as "ball" as the round object is grasped and held up before the babbling baby. In time, the infant takes over the response pattern: "ball" *means* grasping the round object.

Too, in this early stage of the development of meaning, the infant is often a plaything, while the mothering one is the player. In time, both the child and the mothering one are mutually players and playthings:

> As actions become possible for him and as words take on meanings, the child is increasingly able to respond to the play actions of his mother with play actions of his own. Thus, for example, he uses his hands to play "peek-a-boo" and "patty cake." (13: p. 202)

Such commonalty of responses establishes a rudimentary domestic universe of discourse which can serve as a base from which a vast social symbolism can be elaborated.

CHILD'S PLAY AS DRAMA

"Play" has several meanings, among which *drama* must be included, and drama is fundamental for the child's development of a conception of self as an object different from but related to other objects—the development of an *identity*. To establish a separate identity (many identities depend for their establishment and maintenance on counter-identities, e.g., man-woman, parent-child, teacher-student), the child must literally get outside himself and apprehend himself from some other perspective. Drama provides a prime vehicle for this. By taking the role of another, the child gains a reflected view of himself as different from but related to that other.[1] Thus, we find little children playing house, store, or school in which they perform the roles of parent, merchant, or teacher, gaining a reflected view of their own identities from the perspective of those identities whose roles they perform. Indeed, in playing house, it is difficult to recruit a child to play the role of child or baby. Such a role has no implication for the building of his own identity. A doll, therefore, is better suited to the role.

We may note an additional consequence of such drama. In the examples cited, the child prepares himself for the subsequent enactment of such roles in later life or for communication with those who will be performing such roles. Merton speaks of such drama as anticipatory socialization (11: pp. 384–386). However, not all childhood drama is of this anticipatory character. Many of the roles the child performs are fantastic, in the sense that the child can not reasonably be expected to enact or encounter such role performances in later life. I have in mind such identities as cowboy and Indian, creatures from outer space, or pirate. In much fantastic drama, incidentally, we can detect an additional function of child's play. Fantastic drama often serves to maintain and keep viable the past of the society—its myths, legends, villains, and heroes. This is also true of toys and other

---

[1] George H. Mead, from whom many of these ideas have been taken, refers to this phase as "play," but, as we have already shown, there are many varieties of play. Drama is the more precise term. (See 5: pp. 149–151 and 15: pp. 108–113.) See preceding article, "Development of the Self Through Play and Games."

items of the technology of child's play. As one example, the jousting tournament disappeared in the sixteenth century and was replaced by the quintain and the unhooking of a ring by a galloping horseman. The latter persists today in the merry-go-round. This function of child's play has inspired Ariès to remark that "children form the most conservative of human societies" (1: p. 68). But Ariès seems unnecessarily acerb. An argument can be made that the dramatization of Buck Rogers' space feats by those who were children in the early thirties prepared that generation for the space accomplishments of today. There are certainly many areas of creativity and anticipation of the future that are to be found in children's drama.

Fantastic drama seems more to characterize the play of male children in our society than that of female children (15: pp. 110–112). Thus, the dramatic play of children in our society may function more to prepare little girls for adulthood than little boys (3: p. 333). This observation, however, may not necessarily be confined to contemporary American society and its recent past. In discussing the dress of children in eighteenth century France, Ariès points out: "the attempt to distinguish children was generally confined to boys . . . *as if childhood separated girls from adult life less than it did boys*" (1: p. 58). It may well be that the drama of childhood makes it difficult for boys to establish an early well-founded conception of adult life and, consequently, hinders their assumption of an adult identity. In contrast, such drama may facilitate the transition of female children to adulthood. However, once boys do become men (in the social psychological sense), given the sexual arrangements of our society, they have a relatively easy time of it, while the problems of females begin when girls become women!

Children differ, too, according to their *knowledge* of the roles they perform in childhood drama. Although he was not always consistent, Mead presumed an "open awareness" of the roles performed in drama (4: pp. 673–674). There are at least two reasons why such an assumption can not be maintained. First, the details of the role performance may not be objectively accessible to the young actor. For example, a colleague, Duane Gibson of Michigan State University, noticed a boy and girl playing house in a front yard. The little girl was very busy sweeping up the play area, rearranging furniture, moving dishes about, and caring for baby dolls. The boy, on the other hand, would leave the play area on his tricycle, disappear to the back of the (real) house, remain for a brief while, reappear in the play area, and lie down in a feigned sleep. The little girl had a rather extensive knowledge of the mother role, but, for the boy, a father was one who disappeared, reappeared, and slept, *ad infinitum!* Second, nuances of the role performance may be deliberately concealed from children. We tend to conceal domestic difficulties from children, e.g., financial troubles. Should a child overhear such a discussion, we play it down, encouraging the child not to worry about it (13: p. 215).

There is an additional matter that any student of child's play ought to consider in his investigations. Not all childhood drama bears directly upon either fantasy or preparation for adult life. It is often employed as a means to satisfy tabooed curiosity. Probably most of us can recall playing "doctor" or "nurse," but such drama had little, if anything, to do with preparing ourselves for encountering or assuming such roles in later life. We have here a variant of what Glaser and Strauss call "pretense awareness . . . a modification of the open one: both interactants are fully aware but pretend not to be." (4: p. 670) This variant of childhood drama has seldom been studied, probably because it conjures up feelings of guilt, shame, or embarrassment in the investigator. However, Oscar Lewis has provided an excellent example:

> I was a devil when I was a kid. I used to play with boys all the time, doing things I shouldn't, see? We would play prostitutes or doctor. I would put a pillow over my belly and they would examine me as though I were pregnant. The boys would be my husband and the dolls the babies. We would tie a rag around the doll's waist saying that was its navel. Then the doctor would come and cut the strip of cloth with a piece of glass and say, "All right, the baby is ready. What's missing now is the *mama*." So then they would pull my *panties* all the way down and look at my belly but without touching me, and say that now I was all right.
>
> Then the boys would get hold of me and begin fooling around and dancing dirty with me, rubbing it in, and then I would dance by myself and sing. One day I went under the house, and this boy came along and grabbed me. I asked what he was doing and he said, "You had a child with Guillo González. Now have one of mine. It's easy." We were making believe I was a prostitute, and I would say, "Ay, I can't because I'm not well, and when I'm not well I don't go with anybody." My mother was upstairs all the while, watching through a crack and laughing. She came down below, still laughing, and said to me, "So you want to be a whore, do you?" But then she gave me a spanking and I didn't play that any more. (9: p. 576)

Here we have the conversion of what might be called both anticipatory and fantastic dramas into the calculus of children's curiosity. Both dramas have clear implications for socialization, but there is a double *entendre* present in the play.

Finally, in this discussion of childhood drama, we ought to acknowledge that one child's fantasy is another child's reality. The probability that the roles children enact in their dramas will be assumed or encountered in adult life is very much restricted by their position in the various orders of stratification—income, prestige, and accessibility to political office—their rural or urban residence, their "race" or ethnicity, or their sex. It is, in short, anticipatory for the boy to play the role of baseball player, but not for the girl.

We have very few empirical studies of childhood play and, particularly, drama. When we do conduct them, then, we ought to realize the complex nature of drama. Is it anticipatory or fantastic? Is knowledge of the dramatized role accessible to the young performer? What is the meaning of the drama in the child world? Is it probable that the actor will, in later life, enact or encounter the role performance that he is dramatizing? Above all, how is recruitment into the adult roles that the drama of childhood represents organized by larger social arrangements? When such questions are answered, we will have far better knowledge of precisely how childhood drama provides children with identities, casting them in the character of meaningful objects.

Obviously, as Mead insisted (10: pp. 151–164), drama is not a sufficient source of identity, for it provides the young actor with many parts and scripts, and these are often unrelated. The development of an integrated self requires the playing of team games in which one can generalize the related team positions and adapt his own behavior to the generalized expectations of the entire team. Such games occur later in childhood and are beyond the scope of this article. However, one final form of play found in early childhood will be considered here, namely, tests of poise.

CHILDISH TESTS OF POISE

It is not enough only to establish an identity for one's self; it must be established for others at the same time. Identities are *announced* by those who appropriate them and *placed* by others. Identities must always be validated in this
manner to have reality in social interaction. Usually such announcements are silent, accomplished by clothing, the posturing of the body, painting of the face,
sculpting of the hair, the manipulation of props, or the physical location of the
self on the scene of action. For these reasons, child's play demands costume and
body control, and it is facilitated by props and equipment (toys) appropriate to
the drama. Moreover, as Huizinga has remarked, play spaces are usually clearly
marked off (8), and one's location within them communicates to other players
and on-lookers the part he is playing. Thus, child's play demands the assembly,
arrangement, and control of spaces, props, equipment, clothing, and bodies, as
well as other elements. If crucial elements are missing, if they become disarranged, or if control over them is lost, the play is spoiled, and the drama can not
be carried off. Loss of control over these elements is literally embarrassing and
may be equated to loss of poise (6).

We know that much of the drama of childhood replicates the interaction of the
larger society in which it occurs. Indeed, it is almost trite to observe that society
is drama. In everyday interaction, we must always announce to others who we
are and be poised or prepared for the upcoming communication. This requires
the assembly, arrangement, and control of a host of objects and demands considerable skill, for the staging of social interaction is an intricate affair, a highly complex juggling and balancing act.

Much childhood play takes the form of deliberately perpetrating loss of poise
with the unintended but highly important consequence of preparing the child for
the maintenance of self-control in later life. Thus, everywhere we find little children spinning about inducing dizziness, pushing and tripping one another, dis-
arranging clothing, teasing, playing pranks, or bringing play to a sudden halt by
depriving the players of some crucial item ("I'm going to take my ball and go
home"). Indeed, a technology has developed to facilitate such play and is found
in playgrounds, amusement parks, and carnivals.

All this is well known, but I have the distinct impression that such play is
viewed almost exclusively as contributing to body control or motor efficiency.
Playful tests of poise reach out beyond the body to include clothing and grooming. Pranks can be perpetrated by disturbing any element essential to the staging
process—furniture, equipment, locations, and a host of other objects and arrangements.[2] The analysis of such play, then, ought to take into account the development of body control and coordination, but the emphasis ought to be on its symbolic significance in relation to the other elements of staging essential to the silent
definition of situations in everyday life.

Conclusions

This article has placed the play of little children in the context of social symbolism. It has shown how playing with children, childhood drama, and childish

---

[2] My colleague, Edward Gross, and I have isolated about fifty of these "elements" as we pursue the study of staging prompted by our earlier study of embarrassment (6).

pranks function to prepare little children for their meaningful participation in adult society. Such play, however, is not always functional. Some childhood drama may militate against later social participation because of its relative inappropriateness, and I suppose some pranks may be so severe as to have unforeseen traumatic effects. In any case, the play of little children demands extensive scientific investigation. However, any propositions formulated as a consequence of such research may not have universal validity. Both children and child's play, like all other social phenomena, are creatures of history.

References

1. Ariès, Philippe. *Centuries of Childhood*. Translated by Robert Baldick, New York: Alfred A. Knopf, Inc., 1962.
2. Bryce, James. *Social Institutions of the United States*. New York: Grosset and Dunlap, 1891.
3. Erikson, Erik H., "Sex Differences in the Play Configurations of American Pre-Adolescents," in Margaret Mead and Martha Wolfenstein (eds.). *Childhood in Contemporary Cultures*. Chicago: The University of Chicago Press, Phoenix Edition, 1963, pp. 324–341.
4. Glaser, Barney G. and Anselm L. Strauss, "Awareness Contexts and Social Interaction," *American Sociological Review*, XXIX (October, 1964), pp. 669–679.
5. Green, Arnold. *Sociology*. New York: McGraw-Hill Book Co., Inc., 1956.
6. Gross, Edward and Gregory P. Stone, "Embarrassment and the Analysis of Role Requirements," *American Journal of Sociology*, LXX (July, 1964), pp. 1–15.
7. Hammond, J. L. and Barbara Hammond. *The Bleak Age*. Middlesex, England: Penguin Books, 1947.
8. Huizinga, Jan. *Homo Ludens: A Study of the Play Element in Culture*. London: Routledge and Kegan Paul, Ltd., 1949.
9. Oscar Lewis. *La Vida*. New York: Vintage Books, 1968.
10. Mead, George Herbert. *Mind, Self, and Society*. Chicago: University of Chicago Press, 1934.
11. Merton, Robert K. *Social Theory and Social Structure*. Glencoe, Illinois: The Free Press, 1957.
12. Miyakawa, T. Scott. *Protestants and Pioneers*. Chicago: University of Chicago Press, 1964.
13. Ritchie, Oscar W. and Marvin R. Koller. *Sociology of Childhood*. New York: Appleton-Century-Crofts, 1964.
14. Stone, Gregory P., "American Sports: Play and Display," in Eric Larrabee and Rolf Meyersohn (eds.), *Mass Leisure*. Glencoe, Illinois: The Free Press, 1958, pp. 253–264.
15. ———, "Appearance and the Self," in Arnold M. Rose (ed.), *Human Behavior and Social Processes*. Boston: Houghton-Mifflin Co., 1962, pp. 86–118.
16. Tocqueville, Alexis de. *Democracy in America*, II. Translated by Henry Reeves. New York: Alfred A. Knopf, Inc., 1946.
17. Veblen, Thorstein. *The Theory of the Leisure Class*. New York: Modern Library, Inc., 1934.

56　The Etiquette of Youth

● SHERRI CAVAN

In general, the basic problem addressed by the process of socialization is what the participants in a particular social world must both know and do if they are not only to be accorded *bona fide* membership in that social world, but also become active participants in its maintenance.[1] The distinction between childhood socialization and adult socialization has, however, been a distinction which has dealt more with the age differences of those participants who are being socialized than with any differences in problems of socialization as it takes place with respect to children and adults.[2] Thus, for example, Brimm, in writing on personality development as role learning, states that the aim of socialization is that of: [3]

> . . . producing individuals equipped to meet the variety of demands placed upon them by life in a society. Socialization is successful to the extent that it prepares individuals to perform adequately the many roles that will be expected of them in the normal course of their careers throughout society.

Within this formulation, the process of childhood socialization is the introduction of the child to those roles which he will be expected to perform as an adult. The basis of the socialization career of the child, as it is thus presented by Brimm, is the learning of the specific complexes of activity which constitutes social roles.

While it is undeniable that the child, as a child, does learn at least the fragments of many adult roles, it is questionable whether this in fact is the *primary* product of childhood socialization. Brimm's statement of the process of socialization is analagous to a Byzantium-like portrayal of children; children are miniature versions of adults, equipped with that array of socially sanctioned behavioral regularities which are taken for granted in adults.

But it would seem that childhood socialization, as distinct from adult socialization, addresses a problem prior to that of teaching specific role complexes—the problem of transforming newly born organisms into what will be accepted in the society as the basic model of a human being.

In terms of socialization as role learning, the advantage the army recruit and the medical student have over the child is that they are already more or less ade-

---

SOURCE: Sherri Cavan, "The Etiquette of Youth." Original paper prepared especially for this volume.

---

[1] See, for example, P. Berger and T. Luckman, *The Social Construction of Reality*, Garden City, N.Y.: Doubleday and Co., 1966, pp. 119–135; and T. Shibutani, *Society and Personality*, Englewood Cliffs, N.J.; Prentice-Hall, 1961, pp. 472–475.

[2] Although the terms "primary" and "secondary" socialization are sometimes employed in the literature, by and large, the referents of these terms are no different than the referent of "childhood" and "adult" socialization.

[3] O. Brimm, "Personality Development as Role Learning," in I. Iscoe and H. W. Stevenson (eds.), *Personality Development in Children*, University of Texas Press, 1960, p. 138. This seems to be G. H. Mead's general position as well, when he speaks (albeit loosely) of the child learning "to take the role of the other." (Cf. *Mind, Self and Society*, University of Chicago Press, 1959, pp. 135–222.) However, at times it is unclear whether Mead is employing "role" as it is more customarily employed in contemporary American sociology—as a complex of behavior associated with some specifiable position in social life—or whether he is employing it in a much more general sense—as a diffuse attitude or orientation to the situation on the part of the actor.

quately programmed human beings; the army and the medical school need only worry about turning them into soldiers and doctors. While this role transformation may necessitate altering certain characteristics of their humanness, it is only an alteration and not a creation.

In effect, the problem faced by parents and other agents of childhood socialization is somewhat different than the problem faced by the army and the medical school. The raw material which the former has to work with is, although more pliable, less refined: in its original state it indiscriminately makes noise, demands, and waste matter and has no deference whatsoever for any ongoing social world. Thus the problem of childhood socialization is basically the problem of channelizing the newly born infants' gross activities into modes of conduct which are, at a minimum, harmonious with the social world into which they have been born. But, beyond this, if that social world itself is to remain a viable world, it is not enough that those who populate it are merely inoffensive. They must somehow become responsible members. That is, they must also be trusted to take an active part in the maintenance of the normal features of the social order.

Both of these general problems of childhood socialization are evidenced in the following excerpt from a turn of the century etiquette book: [4]

> Nothing is more unkind than to allow a child to do as he pleases, for, as surely as he lives, he must learn sooner or later to yield to authority and to exercise self-control. The earlier the training begins, the earlier it will be. The child creeping about the room soon knows that the gentle, but firm "NO!" when spoken by the mother means that he must not touch the bit of bric-a-brac within reach. And even this lesson will stand him in good stead later on.
>
> The basic principle of home government must be love enforced by firmness. A punishment should seldom be threatened, but if promised, must be given. The time for threat and punishment is not in public. In the parlor, on the train, or boat, it is the height of ill-breeding to make a scene and to threaten a whipping, or a punishment of any kind. Were the child properly trained in private, parents and beholders would be spared the humiliating spectacle that too often confronts them in visiting and traveling.

To be trustworthy and responsible is not merely a matter of having learned specified social roles that are to be enacted at particular times and in certain social situations. It may ultimately include such role learning. But by and large, to be accorded the status of a trustworthy and responsible member of a social world is contingent upon having learned much more general modes of conduct which are expected along with any role-specific courses of action, crosscut a great number of social situations, and are mostly without temporal limitations. Thus, while there are specific behavioral expectations associated with the positions of mother, janitor, customer, or physician, there are also more general expectations, such as civility, deference, and respect, which are independent of any specific social position, are applicable to all participants of the social occasion, and provide the basic guidelines within which more specific interactions can be carried on.

A major problem of childhood socialization would appear to be the teaching of these general norms of social behavior that are taken for granted in the variety of social situations in which specific roles are enacted.

In middle-class American society, short of crises such as emergencies and disasters, there are few situations where the general rules of etiquette are not treated

[4] Marion Harland and Virginia Van De Water, *Everyday Etiquette,* Indianapolis, Ind.: The Bobbs-Merrill Co., 1905, pp. 262–263.

as applicable criteria for the evaluation of behavior in general. Such rules of etiquette in essence incorporate many of the general expectations of social conduct which crosscut the situational norms of the society and the particular roles that are enacted in those situations.

In effect, the justification of the codification of rules of etiquette is characteristically made on the basis of the ubiquitous effects of proper general conduct in social life. Thus, in the introductory remarks in books of etiquette, statements such as the following are typical:

> The world has fully recognized the fact that life's jostle and jar must of necessity be lessened if daily living is to be easy and pleasant. Upon this fact social regulations have founded and fashioned themselves. The rudeness which jostles, the selfishness which jars, whether against people or principles or opinions, are the first things ruled out and labeled "bad manners" when society formulates a code.

> There are other offenses which receive the same label, although the offenders are neither selfish nor rude. They simply are ignorant of small social requirements, and all unwittingly, their words and acts cause friction with the smooth running system of society.[5]

> To be loved is the instinctive desire of every human heart. To be respected, to be honored, to be successful, is the universal ambition. The ever constant desire of all is to be happy. This never varying instinct lies at the foundation of every action; it is the constantly propelling force in our every effort.

> To be happy, we strive for the acquisition of wealth, for position and place, for social and political distinction. And when all is obtained, the real enjoyment in its possession comes from the thousand little courtesies that are exchanged beween individuals—pleasant words and kindly acts, which the poor may enjoy as well as the rich.[6]

> It is hard to say why the word "etiquette" is so inevitably considered merely a synonym of the word "correct," as though it were no more than the fixed answer to a sum in arithmetic. In fact, it might be well to pull the word "correct" out by the roots and substitute "common sense." In short, I wish that those whose minds are focused on precise obedience to every precept would instead ask themselves, "What is the purpose of this rule? Does it help to make life pleasanter? Does it make the social machinery run more smoothly? Does it add to beauty? Is it essential to the code of good taste or to ethics?" If it serves any of these purposes, it is a rule to be cherished; but if it serves no helpful purpose, it is certainly not worth taking seriously.[7]

While etiquette books rarely cover all of the general expectations of sanctioned conduct, such as the proper distance or the proper spacial location for conversants,[8] and while all appropriate rules of etiquette are not actualized in all situations at all times, these books can serve at least as a partial codification of the precepts of befitting modes of general conduct.

Examining contemporary American etiquette books written specifically for young children, pre-adolescents, and adolescents, my concern with reference to the general problem of childhood socialization focuses on two questions:

---

[5] The New York Society of Self-Culture, *Correct Social Usage*, 5th revised edition, New York: 1906, p. 9.
[6] T. Hill, *Never Give a Lady a Restive Horse: A 19th Century Handbook of Etiquette*, Berkeley: Diablo Press, 1967, p. 9.
[7] Emily Post, *Etiquette: The Blue Book of Social Usage*, New York: Funk & Wagnalls Co., 1955, p. 1.
[8] Cf. E. T. Hall, *The Silent Language*, Primer Books, 1961, and Robert Sommer, "Studies in Personal Space," *Sociometry*, v. 22 (1959), pp. 247–261.

1. What is the implicit world view or *Weltanschauung* which characterizes the social world inhabited by each age group, and what are the implications of the *Weltanschauung* for the modes of behavior which are legitimately expected of each age group?

2. Given the rules for proper and fitting conduct for each age group, what can be said about the nature of trust and responsibility each cohort has for the on-going interactional system?

The nine manners and etiquette books used in the following analysis represent about a third of the manners and etiquette books in the Children's Section of the San Francisco Public Library. Rather than being representative, they are merely indicative of the collection. The specific selections were made with the help of the Librarian of the Children's Section on the basis of the frequency of their circulation.[9]

Of the total collection of such books available to the children of San Francisco, by far the greatest proportion is addressed specifically to teen-age girls,[10] although there are some addressed to adolescents of both sexes. Of the total of 32 books in the collection, there were only two which were addressed to young children between the ages of four and eight. According to the librarian, while mothers mediate between the etiquette books and both young children (ages 4–8) and pre-adolescents (ages 8–12), adolescents (those 13–18) almost always obtain the books themselves.

The Weltanschauung of Childhood and Adolescence

The social world presented to the young child is a basically good world, which is in fact as it appears to be. Gradually, as the child approaches adolescence, not only do the number of social evils in the world increase, but the relationship between what the world appears to be and what it is in fact alters. Thus, while the young child is assured that behind every good act is a good person with a good intention, the adolescent is cautioned not to accept the world at its face value. For the young child, *persona* and person are identical; for the adolescent this may or may not be the case.

The world view presented to the young child is virtually a utopia, wherein nothing exists but goodness and truth. To fit into this world, the child need be only honest, fair, strong, and wise.[11] And, if he is honest, fair, strong, and wise, the implication is that the world will be his.[12]

If you are honest and promise to do something, others will trust you. They will share things with you, tell you secrets, lend you money and help you to do many of the things you want to do.

---

9 The distribution of books employed in the following analysis is as follows:
   Young children (ages 4–8), two books addressed to both males and females.
   Pre-adolescents (ages 8–12), one book addressed to males and females; one to females.
   Adolescents (ages 13–18), two books addressed to males and females; three addressed to females.
10 This is not surprising in view of the definition of woman as the expressive leader in American society. Cf. T. Parsons and R. F. Bales, *Family Socialization and Interaction Process*, Glencoe, Ill.: The Free Press, 1960, pp. 39–131, and J. Sirjamaki, "Cultural Configurations in the American Family," in N. W. Bell and E. F. Vogel (eds.), *The Family*, Glencoe, Ill.: The Free Press, 1960, pp. 295–304.
11 M. Leaf, *How to Behave and Why*, Philadelphia, J. B. Lippincott Co., 1946, p. 10.
12 Ibid., p. 12.

Evil is at most a transitory phenomenon, which may be eradicated if one learns the proper behavior. Thus the young child is told: [13]

> Look out for the person who pretends to be your friend but doesn't want you to like anyone else. That isn't a friend—it's a selfish person who is trying to own you and hasn't *learned* to share to be happy.

The pre-adolescent is also warned of jealousy. For him, "Jealousy is public enemy no. 1. Beware!" [14] The implication is that there are other evils. One must beware also of strange people on the streets who may be dangerous [15] as well as acquaintances who may be mean.[16] At the same time, by pre-adolescence one must be cautious of signs of evil in himself. But even though it is hard to be a good sport, and one is naturally disappointed when someone else wins,[17] one can still *learn* to be virtuous.[18]

By adolescence, the transitory character of evil has disappeared. To the social sin of selfishness is added hostility, while the goal is no longer the practice and learning of virtue, but the masking of vice.

> Everybody is basically selfish and hostile to some degree; everybody is covering up something. What's more, *pretend* that you like someone, and strangely enough, often you will.[19]

> Don't show your scorn of dominoes, even if you would rather play rummy. It will not hurt you to *look as if* you were having a good time when you are not, and it will make things jollier for you and everybody else.[20]

Where the sanctioned world of the young child and pre-adolescent is populated by loving parents and friends,[21] the world of the adolescent is populated by *personae*, masks behind which one may or may not find an exact duplicate of the presented front.

The adolescent is admonished:

> At a class or school dance, try to regard your partners as outside acquaintances, not just fellow students. Be aware of their different personalities. You may find that some of them have sides they have not shown in the classroom.[22]

> The first thing people judge you by is your appearance. If what they see gives them a favorable impression, they are more interested in knowing the *you* behind it.[23]

> When a boy takes the girl he loves home for the weekend to meet his parents . . . she should not take it for granted that his parents will understand what a fine girl she is. She must show them.[24]

---

[13] M. Leaf, *Manners Can Be Fun*, Philadelphia: J. B. Lippincott, 1958, p. 32 (emphasis added).
[14] B. Bryant, *Future Perfect*, Indianapolis: Bobbs-Merrill, 1957, p. 147.
[15] T. Lee, *Manners to Grow On*, Garden City, N.Y.: Doubleday & Co., 1955, p. 62.
[16] *Future Perfect*, op. cit., p. 142.
[17] *Manners to Grow On*, op. cit., pp. 15–16.
[18] Ibid., p 16.; *Future Perfect*, op. cit., p. 151.
[19] J. Jackson (H. L. Crounse), *Guide to Dating*, Englewood Cliffs, N.J.: Prentice-Hall, 1955, p. 16 (emphasis added).
[20] E. Boykin, *This Way, Please*, New York: Macmillan, 1958, pp. 190–191 (emphasis added).
[21] Cf. *How to Behave and Why*, op. cit.; *Manners Can Be Fun*, op. cit.; *Future Perfect*, op. cit.
[22] *This Way, Please*, op. cit., p. 167.
[23] Ibid., p. 15 (emphasis in the original).
[24] *Guide to Dating*, op. cit., p. 117.

Furthermore, the adolescent listens to his parents' opinion, not because of filial devotion, but because, "They have inside information on what lies at the other end of the stretch." [25]

The proper mode of behavior outlined for each age group varies according to the way in which the world has been defined for them.[26] In the world of the young child and the pre-adolescent, where everything is as it appears, good sportsmanship is the only mode of behavior necessary. In such a world, merit can be rewarded because it can be recognized. But by adolescence, the key words become "impression management"—the expression, during interaction, of what the actor wishes to convey to those in his presence.[27] Irrespective of how deserving the adolescent is, the world does not grant an automatic pay-off; he must engage in active work to be assured of his just rewards.

Thus, while the young child and pre-adolescent need only be pleasant and considerate for people to appreciate them, the adolescent must engage in "an earnest effort to portray one's real self. . . ." [28] While the pre-adolescent need only be attentive to the ongoing interaction to join in successfully,[29] the adolescent is counseled to prepare in advance.

> Make a mental note every time you hear a good gag or punch line and spike them into your conversation.[30]

> A girl who is weak in carrying on good conversation might plan comments in advance, taking care to slip them in at opportune moments.[31]

The theme of impression management is part of a larger theme which is presented to the adolescent: that of "working the system." [32] The adolescent is expected to be able to utilize, for his own personal gains, the legitimate activities of social life.

For the young child and the pre-adolescent, friends, games, activities, school, are presented as having intrinsic value. They are good in and of themselves. For the adolescent, to this intrinsic value is added another dimension: things may be good in and of themselves, but they may also be good because they can be used. For the young child and the pre-adolescent, it is simply fun to be a host; [33] for the adolescent, hosting can be useful: [34]

---

[25] Ibid., p. 109.
[26] "The fact of belonging to the same class, and that of belonging to the same generation or age group, have this in common, that both endow the individuals sharing in them with a common location in the social and historical process, and thereby limit them to a specific range of potential experience, predisposing them for certain characteristic modes of thought and experience and a characteristic type of historically relevant action. Any given location, then, excludes a large number of possible modes of thought, experience, feeling, and action, and restricts the range of self-expression open to the individual to certain circumscribed possibilities." K. Mannheim, "The Sociological Problems of Generations," in *Essays in the Sociology of Knowledge*, P. Kecskemeti (ed.), Routledge and Kegan Paul, Ltd., 1959, p. 291. See also Y. Cohen, *Social Structure and Personality*, Holt, Rinehart and Winston, 1961, pp. 310–311.
[27] Cf. E. Goffman, *The Presentation of Self in Everyday Life*, University of Edinburgh, Monograph No. 2, 1958.
[28] *Guide to Dating*, op. cit., p. 21.
[29] *Future Perfect*, op. cit., p. 18.
[30] B. Betz, *Your Manners Are Showing*, New York: Grosset & Dunlap, 1946, p. 81.
[31] *Guide to Dating*, op. cit., p. 29.
[32] Cf. E. Goffman, "The Underlife of a Public Institution," in *Asylums*, Anchor Books, 1961, pp. 210–214.
[33] Cf. *Manners Can Be Fun; Manners to Grow On*.
[34] *Guide to Dating*, op. cit., p. 25.

Entertaining in the home offers a good opportunity for one to show her qualities . . . as hostess, a girl is very much the center of attention. . . . By organizing games and stunts, she has every opportunity of showing qualities of leadership
and finesse. Boys are attracted to girls who are fine hostesses.

And, last but not least in the ways to attract a boy is the party method. It's
simple and *appears to be so undesigning.*[35]

For the young child and pre-adolescent, introductions merely occur as a natural
part of the ever-widening social world; for the adolescent, the structure of the introduction can be used to make oneself available to the opposite sex.

If you are anxious to meet a certain person of the opposite sex, never be bashful
about asking a mutual friend to make the introduction. It may be a boy or girl you
pass every day on the way to school, but a proper introduction is the accepted way
of breaking the ice.[36]

Even though the boy may be in one of your classes at school, you might well
arrange to have a mutual friend introduce you. The motive behind the introduction
does not have to be obvious. . . . The friend could stop the boy on some pretense
or other . . . and then very casually turn and introduce you.[37]

Similarly the pre-adolescent is recommended to join the activities and organizations around him so that he may become acquainted with the world around him
and come to appreciate that world.

Know how the members of the Junior Civic League elect their officers, and you
will know how the people of the United States elect their president. Join the choral
club . . . "Serenade" becomes more real to a girl when she knows how Schubert
came to compose it.[38]

But the adolescent is told to take part in the activities and organizations around
him because, "In these groups she can plan things to say and do which will win the
respect of other members." [39]

In one sense, then, the process of childhood socialization may be characterized
as a gradual initiation into both the overt and the covert social world, where, by
adolescence, the American youth is presented with most of the ordinarily unspoken secrets of the world and with many of the methods by which the overt world
can be covertly used to his own advantage.

The main difference between the *Weltanschauung* and its concomitant modes
of behavior in early childhood and adolescence appears to be not so much a contradiction as an addition of a further dimension of social life—that of the self-
interest of the actor.[40]

At least in middle class American society, the young child, and, to a great extent, the pre-adolescent, appear to be defined more as objects than as acting sub-

---

[35] B. Bryant, *Miss Behavior*, Indianapolis: Bobbs-Merrill, 1960, p. 43 (emphasis added).

[36] *Your Manners Are Showing*, op. cit., p. 9.

[37] *Guide to Dating*, op. cit., p. 5.

[38] *Future Perfect*, op. cit., p. 140.

[39] *Guide to Dating*, op. cit., p. 196.

[40] The concern with self-interest would appear to be one important implication of what Hsu
has called the American core value: self-reliance. "Under this ideal every individual is his own
master, in control of his own destiny, and will advance and regress in society only according
to his own effort." F. L. K. Hsu, *Psychological Anthropology*, Homewood, Ill.: Dorsey Press,
1961, p. 218.

jects, while the change between childhood and adolescence appears to rest upon the legitimation of the child's possession of a self,[41] and its corresponding range of self-interests.

The Nature of Non-Adult Trust and Responsibility

Since social life is not a random, fortuitous sequence of actions and events, the child, who eventually is to become a fully accountable person, must learn the general rules which account for and generate social order. As Hebb has written:

> The effects of moral education, and training in the rules of courtesy, and the compulsion to dress, talk, and act as others do, adds up to ensuring that the individual member of society will not act in a way that is a provocation to others—will not, that is, be a source of strong emotional disturbance, except in highly ritualized circumstances approved by society. . . . The problem of moral education, from this point of view, is not simply to produce a stable individual, but to produce an individual that will (1) be stable in the existing environment and (2) contribute to its protective uniformity.[42]

While the infant, the non-person, the organism without powers of self-control, may be expected only to be relatively unobtrusive within the system, by the time he is four or five years old, the social world gradually begins to grant the child *bona fide* membership, and from then on he is gradually held responsible for the general rules of proper social behavior.[43]

As the child begins to enter into the ongoing society as a participating member rather than as merely an object, these rules of social organization have the character of what he can be held accountable for: what kinds of social rights he is expected to respect and what kinds of social obligations he must meet. These are the responsibilities he has for the ongoing interactional system—the features that must be taken into account by each individual participant if successful social interaction is to ensue.

By the time the child enters adolescence, he is accountable for both knowing and respecting the ecological boundaries of other participants in the system, as well as his own. The characterization of "childish" behavior, as opposed to adult or mature behavior, revolves primarily around the notion that the child does not have a complete sense of other people's privacy, or of the limits of his own individual area. Children are pictured as intruding and protruding at will.

Actually, by the time the young child is four or five years old, he is expected to learn at least that the boundaries of others' physical space exist and that they are something to be respected. He is admonished that,

---

[41] I. H. Josselyn also notes a change in conception of self and world between childhood and adolescence, but the implication in her statement is that the change is a direct result of the psychological and physiological changes of puberty rather than any change of expectations applicable to childhood and adolescence. Cf. her "The Older Adolescent," in E. Ginzberg (ed.), *Values and Ideals of American Youth*, Columbia University Press, 1961, pp. 27–36.

[42] D. O. Hebb, "The Mammal and His Environment," in T. Newcomb and E. Hartley (eds.), *Readings in Social Psychology*, 3rd edition, Holt, 1958, p. 341.

[43] On the extent to which children and adolescents actively participate in the ongoing social order in America, see R. Barker and H. Wright, *Midwest and Its Children*, Evanston, Ill.: Row, Peterson and Co., 1955, pp. 99–122; and R. Barker and L. Barker, "Behavior Units for the Comparative Study of Culture," in B. Kaplan (eds.), *Studying Personality Cross-Culturally*, Evanston, Ill.: Row, Peterson and Co., 1961, pp. 457–478.

> SNOOPERS walk right into rooms where other people are when the doors are closed. If they knocked first and asked if they might come in, people would not call them SNOOPERS.[44]

> This is a TOUCHER. Wherever he goes he touches. He never thinks whether he should or not—Maybe it's because he hasn't any head—he is all hands.[45]

So the young child is yet to learn that each person, himself included, has besides a delimited physical space, a personal space which is also to be respected.

By the time the child is 10 or 12 years old, he is expected to be fully responsible for the maintenance of both the physical and personal space of himself and others. To the specific injunctions against intruding into others' physical area and possessions [46] are added injunctions against intruding into others' activities and biographies as well.

From pre-adolescence on, the child is told that he must not "dip into" others' conversations,[47] look over their shoulders,[48] nor stare directly at them.[49]

He is cautioned that, while he should show interest in his friends, he must not trespass into specified regions of their biographies.[50]

> Be careful not to overdo the interest to the point of asking such questions as "How much money does your father make?" or "Are your parents divorced?" Be understanding and interested in any personal details which friends may tell you, but always let such information come from them.[51]

> Asking people questions is one way of getting them to talk about things that interest them. But unless you want to be avoided, don't ask prying questions that others may not want to answer—questions that are too curious or too personal.[52]

Although the pre-adolescent is warned only of the requirement of respecting the physical and personal space of others, the adolescent has the right to expect others to respect his own personal space: "If others pry, meet it with a pleasant, smiling gaze, and calmly change the subject." [53]

Besides being held accountable for not intruding into the territories of others, by pre-adolescence, the child is expected not to protrude from his own personal space. The pre-adolescent is told not to engage publicly in the "little repulsive habits of children" such as "picking your nose or ears, yawning, scratching your head or body, putting your fingers in your mouth, using a toothpick in public" [54] and the adolescent is presented with the rule: [55]

---

[44] *Manners Can Be Fun,* op. cit., p. 40.
[45] Ibid.
[46] Cf. O. R. Landers, *Modern Etiquette for Young People,* New York: Greenberg, 1936, pp. 84–85.
[47] *Manners to Grow On,* op. cit., p. 36; *This Way, Please,* op. cit., p. 83; *Modern Etiquette for Young People,* op. cit., p. 51.
[48] *This Way, Please,* op. cit., p. 20.
[49] Ibid., p. 83.
[50] Cf. G. Simmels' statement on discretion in *The Sociology of Georg Simmel,* K. Wolfe (ed.), The Free Press, 1950, pp. 320–321: "Discretion consists by no means only in the respect for the secret of others, for his specific will to conceal this or that from us, but in staying away from the knowledge of all that the other does not expressly reveal to us. It does not refer to anything particular which we are not permitted to know, but to a quite natural general reserve in regard to the total personality."
[51] *Manners to Grow On,* op. cit., pp. 11–12.
·[52] *This Way, Please,* op. cit., pp. 86–87.
[53] *Modern Etiquette for Young People,* op. cit., p. 54.
[54] *Future Perfect,* op. cit., pp. 75–76.
[55] *This Way, Please,* op. cit., p. 20.

Do nothing in company that calls attention to the body or its functions. . . . If and when you must blow your nose, get out your handkerchief inconspicuously and do it as quietly as possible without making the act more noticeable by apologizing for it, unless you have had to stop in the midst of speaking. Follow the same practice when you are forced to sneeze or cough.

In addition, both pre-adolescent and adolescent are expected to contain their psychological space in public situations. The categorical rule is not to protrude one's moods or problems.[56]

Moods, both good and blue, are something we all have, but don't let your blue ones spoil your fun or your friendships. Never sulk when in a mood. It is better to stay to yourself if you think you might be unpleasant. . . . A blue mood soon passes, and then you can emerge your cheerful self again, ready to enjoy your friends and have them enjoy you.[57]

In the same way that you refrain from using nail file and toothpick in the presence of others, be able to keep your personal difficulties, troubles, and complaints to yourself as far as you possibly can.[58]

Learning the territorial rights of others and his own personal boundaries, the child is also expected gradually to learn the rules which govern social relationships. He is expected to learn the rules of proper social involvement.

Just as the very young child is only minimally introduced to the rules of territoriality, so is he minimally introduced to the rules of social relationships. In fact, the young child's encounters with the ongoing social system are defined merely in terms of the acknowledgment of the presence of others. He is expected to say, "How do you do" when being introduced to others and "Good day" if he already has been introduced.[59] Beyond this he has no other social obligations.

By pre-adolescence the child's responsibility for interaction is greatly increased. While the young child is expected to know only the proper response to an introduction, the pre-adolescent is expected to know the proper procedures for effecting introductions. The pre-adolescent is held accountable for knowing the general form of social presentations and the differential hierarchy they are to embody, as well as knowing under what circumstances introductions must occur. The pre-adolescent is told,

Never let a person wait around while you chat on and on to someone he doesn't know. Don't introduce people who (sic) you meet very briefly, such as the person who stops just long enough to say a cheery hello . . .[60]

For the pre-adolescent there are no restrictions on who may be introduced to whom, but the adolescent is warned that, since an introduction has implications for future involvements between the parties, care must be exercised not to bring together people who would be incompatible. The adolescent is cautioned,

You have a certain responsibility when you introduce people. Do not go out of your way to introduce two who are not likely to care about knowing each other.[61]

---

[56] This may be contrasted with D. Matza's characterization of the Bohemia of youth, where the expression of moods forms an integral part of the culture. Cf. "Subterranean Traditions of Youth," *The Annals*, v. 338 (1961), pp. 102–118, especially p. 113.

[57] *Manners to Grow On*, op. cit., p. 14.

[58] *Modern Etiquette for Young People*, op. cit., p. 63.

[59] *Manners Can Be Fun*, op. cit., pp. 8–12.

[60] *Manners to Grow On*, op. cit., p. 9.

[61] *This Way, Please*, op. cit., p. 67.

In a similar manner, while the pre-adolescent's inclusion into interaction must be mediated by a third person, by adolescence one may properly include oneself, providing that (1) the setting is one where the presence of the participants imply a mutual knowledge of some third person or institution, such as wedding receptions, houseparties, or school playgrounds; and (2) one is certain that the other will be receptive to the proffered sociability.[62]

The general topic of social involvement and obligation, which is absent from the expectations for the behavior of the young child, is only touched upon in pre-adolescence.[63] The pre-adolescent is merely cautioned not to become overinvolved with others to the point of mutual utilization of private property [64] and to be careful about becoming committed to a negative position by stating that position in writing.[65]

In adolescence, social involvement and commitment become a major theme.[66] Not only is the adolescent told that the loaning and borrowing of physical objects leads to social obligations which may be undesirable, but that gifts and favors as well may result in such undesirable obligations.[67]

At the same time, the adolescent is admonished not to invest too much of himself in any particular relationship, and, primarily, in relationships with the other sex. The girl is advised not to show her eagerness when asked for a date,[68] and that:

> It is better for a girl to make the mistake of seeming to have too little rather than too much affection, unless she is sure that the boy has at least as much as she.[69]

In contrast to the problem of becoming overly involved in a relationship is the problem of handling someone else's overinvolvement. The adolescent is cautioned that one cannot simply tell the other that he or she is investing too much in a relationship, but instead must engage in a series of tactical social maneuvers which signify to the other that he is exhibiting an improper degree of involvement, yet provide the other the opportunity to save face in the situation.

The adolescent girl is told that she must take particular care in turning down a date so that she does not hurt the boy's feelings,[70] and the boy is informed that,[71]

> If she is already booked, don't take it as an insult, try again in a few days. If you don't succeed in landing some sort of a date after trying three or four times, then I suggest finding a new phone number. Chances are she's only brushing you off the nice way.

Boys are expected to offer the same face-saving opportunity to the girls. The boy is expected to "naturally have sense and consideration to break off a serious

---

[62] Cf. ibid., pp. 68, 234; *Miss Behavior*, op. cit., p. 148.
[63] Cf. E. Goffman, *Encounters*, The Bobbs-Merrill Co., 1961, pp. 39–40: "It is not only possible for participants to become involved in the encounter in progress, but it is also defined as obligatory that they sustain this involvement in given measure; too much is one kind of delict; too little, another." The exuberance of youth would appear to make only the former problematic.
[64] *Manners to Grow On*, op. cit., pp. 14, 35.
[65] Ibid., p. 26; *Future Perfect*, op. cit., p. 180.
[66] Simmel, in his essay "The Metropolis and Mental Life," treats the problem of social involvement and commitment under the concept of "reserve." Cf. Simmel, op. cit., pp. 414–418.
[67] *Guide to Dating*, op. cit., pp. 72–73.
[68] *Miss Behavior*, op. cit., p. 169.
[69] *Modern Etiquette for Young People*, op. cit., p. 94.
[70] *Guide to Dating*, op. cit., p. 10.
[71] *Your Manners Are Showing*, op. cit., p. 92.

romance with a girl, if need be, in a manner which will be the least damaging to her." [72] He is expected to "avoid giving a girl the feeling of being 'dropped.' " [73]

Thus the granting of a self to the child in adolescence certifies him as someone who can be expected to be a trustworthy and responsible member of the everyday social world. [74] All those who have been given the right to lay claim to a self are obligated both to keep that self in a proper state of social repair and to show the proper social care for the selves of other participants in the system. [75] The duty of social responsibility becomes, in effect, a concomitant duty to one's self as well as to others.

Conclusion

The focus of the present paper has been the content of childhood socialization in contemporary middle-class American society. Addressing the expectations about behavior contained in children's etiquette books for various ages, I have attempted to trace out the changing conception of the nature of the child as he moves through childhood, pre-adolescence, and adolescence. The specific concern has been the way the child and the world he is presented is socially defined for each age group, and the kinds of trust and responsibility demanded of each age group.

The basis of the present paper has been the assumption that the problem of childhood socialization is essentially different from the problem of adult socialization in that, in the process of childhood socialization, some form of a basic, efficacious self must be established in the new recruit, whereas in adult socialization, the concern is the development of some particular variety of that basic form.

To speak of the participants of social life as having a "formal self" as a prerequisite to having a particular variety of social self is essentially to speak of the social certification that members' general capacity for trust and responsibility can henceforth be taken for granted. At least as it is evidenced in middle-class American society, once a child has come to understand that both good and evil are normal features of the everyday world; that appearances may be deceiving; that merit is not always automatically rewarded; and that the arrangements of the social system merely set the conditions for individual action, rather than specifying what individual action must necessarily be, he has in effect been introduced into the world as it is known to the adult members. Concomitant with his entrance into the adult world of everyday life are the obligations for maintaining the sanctioned features of that world—its spacial allocations, its social relationships, and the variety of social selves that can be created and sustained therein.

---

[72] *Guide to Dating*, op. cit., p. 172.

[73] *This Way, Please*, op. cit., p. 104.

[74] For a general discussion of the problem of social responsibility and the identifiability of group members, see Simmel, op. cit., p. 374.

[75] Cf. E. Goffman, "On Face Work," *Psychiatry*, 18 (1955), pp. 213–231: "The combination of the rule of self-respect and the rule of considerateness is that the person tends to conduct himself during an encounter so as to maintain both his own face and the face of other participants." (See p. 215).

For a further discussion of this general problem, see also Edward Gross and Gregory P. Stone, "Embarrassment and the Analysis of Role Requirements," *American Journal of Sociology*, 70 (1964), pp. 1–15, reprinted in Part Three of this volume.

57 Some Recent Developments in Socialization Theory and Research

● WILLIAM H. SEWELL

The scientific study of socialization—the processes by which individuals selectively acquire the skills, knowledge, attitudes, values, and motives current in the groups of which they are or will become members—is of rather recent origin, despite the fact that throughout human history man has been concerned with the question of how the human animal is transmuted into a human being. The earliest contributions to the field came mainly from philosophers, psychologists, and sociologists who were intrigued with the problem but who had little other than their own insights and observations upon which to base their explanations. With the development of experimental psychology, interest in the scientific study of child development began both in Europe and America. This fact, coupled with the growth of public interest in child-rearing, gave rise to the establishment of a number of child-welfare research stations and child-study centers in the United States, especially after 1920.[1] These centers instituted descriptive and experimental studies which were carried out by educators, pediatricians, and home economists—usually under the leadership of a psychologist. For a number of years they have provided a great flow of detailed information on characteristics of children, particularly their mental and physical growth. But until relatively recently they have given comparatively little emphasis to emotional and social aspects of development. The field of child development has continued to prosper, and many contributions to current socialization research have come from those who are professionally identified with this field.

Much of the more recent work on socialization, however, has other sources of intellectual stimulation and support; probably the first and foremost of these has been the psychoanalytic movement. Psychoanalytic theory made its way into American psychology and was used increasingly in the study of personality and child psychology.[2] Freud's theories on the importance of the early life experiences for subsequent personality structure was and continues to be a major force in socialization theory and research. A second force of great importance was the development of behavior theory in psychology and particularly the elaboration of theories of social learning. The psychologists brought to the field of socialization not only a rather substantial body of empirically based theories to be tested but also a rich tradition of experimental method which was to supply much-needed rigor to investigations in the field. A third major force was social anthropology which, as a result of many years of careful ethnographic research in primitive societies, had clearly documented the role of socialization as a mechanism of culture trans-

SOURCE: William H. Sewell, from *The Annals of the American Academy of Political and Social Science*, 349 (September 1963); pp. 163–181.

The writer wishes to thank William H. Sewell, III, Ellen W. Sewell, Vimal P. Shah, and Renee Bash for bibliographical assistance.

[1] For an authoritative statement of the history by one of the leading participants in this development, see Lawrence K. Frank, "The Beginnings of Child Development and Family Life Education in the Twentieth Century," *Merrill-Palmer Quarterly*, Vol. 8 (October 1962), pp. 1–28.
[2] Kurt Lewin, Henry A. Murray, John Dollard, Neil Miller, O. Hobart Mowrer, and Robert Sears, to mention some of the well-known leaders in the field, helped to give the psychoanalytic view academic respectability by conducting research in part guided by psychoanalytic theories and by integrating various psychoanalytic views with behavior theory.

mission and suggested that culturally determined child-rearing systems might help explain "national character" or "modal personality." A fourth force, but not one of great strength until quite recently, has been sociology, with its emphasis on the importance of social structure in the development of human behavior—stressing particularly the family, the school, the community, primary groups, voluntary associations, and the social-class structure.

The convergence of these forces, in the early forties to the mid-fifties, with the older developmental emphasis has resulted in a tremendous outpouring of speculative writing, theoretical essays, research articles, and monographs on socialization, most of which have focused on the intellectual, emotional, and social development of the young child.[3] Socialization has come to be one of the principal areas of convergence between psychologists, anthropologists, and sociologists. It also constitutes an important area of specialization in the rapidly developing field of social psychology.

Before attempting to discuss developments in the field of socialization during the past five years, it will be useful to indicate briefly some of the major concerns and emphases current in the ten or fifteen years preceding this period. Irwin L. Child in his comprehensive summary of theory and research in the field of socialization, published in 1954, gives primary attention to the antecedents of specific systems of behavior.[4] The systems most emphasized were oral, anal, excretory, sexual, and aggressive behavior and, to a lesser extent, dependence, achievement, affection, and fear. These systems, especially the first five, are derived mainly from psychoanalytic theory. The antecedent variables emphasized in relation to this set of consequent variables were primary disciplines for handling sex, excretory, and oral drives—that is, various aspects of feeding and weaning, toilet-training, and punishment practices. These all deal with the stages of psychosexual development thought by Freud to be so crucial in their effect on later personality. Other matters treated in the review included the relation between: age at socialization and dependence and achievement orientation; discontinuity in socialization and psychological conflict; techniques of reward and punishment and anxiety, fear, guilt, and identification; and social class and child-rearing practices. The conclusion reached by Child after reviewing approximately one hundred such studies was: [5]

> Systematic research on socialization guided by the interpretive inferences of clinicians and ethnographers, has already succeeded in identifying a number of variables that appear to be of importance as influences on the later behavior of the individual who is socialized. A considerable body of tentative knowledge has been developed about these influences . . . every finding cited in this chapter is necessarily subject to some kind of explanation other than the one presented here. . . . In short, the existing body of research findings, while impressive as a whole, is not very solid in detail.

---

[3] Fortunately, there are currently several bibliographical aids to this literature, including: *Child Development Abstracts and Bibliography* published by The Society for Research on Child Development, *Psychological Abstracts* published by the American Psychological Association, *Sociological Abstracts* published by Sociological Abstracts, Inc., and the *Annual Review of Psychology* published by Annual Reviews, Inc., at Stanford, California. A valuable source on current research is *Research Relating to Children: Studies in Progress* published periodically by the U. S. Children's Bureau in Washington, D.C.
[4] Irwin L. Child, "Socialization," in Gardner Lindzey (ed.), *Handbook of Social Psychology* (Cambridge, Mass.: Addison-Wesley, 1954), pp. 655–692.
[5] *Ibid.*, p. 685.

A more critical observer would perhaps have concluded by this time or possibly a few years later that socialization research guided by the psychoanalytic approach had been quite barren in terms of its empirical findings. In any event, there seems little doubt that the psychoanalytic approach dominated the study of socialization and to a marked extent inhibited other approaches. The study of the modes by which parents and other socialization agents deal with the needs not so directly derivable from libidinal drives was relatively neglected. Moreover, the influence of social structure variables on either socialization practices or subsequent behavior was largely overlooked or was limited largely to the differences in the way the social classes handled infant-training. There was considerable neglect of problems of role-learning. Finally, many of the studies suffered from small and poorly designed samples, inadequate data-gathering techniques, rather loose handling of data analysis, and a tendency to make generalizations well beyond the limits supportable by their data.

The Role Approach

The developments in theory and research on socialization during the past five years that the writer finds interesting and thinks are important inevitably consist of personal selections; another observer with another orientation might well stress quite other developments or might not even see the trends which to this observer seem clear. What is intended here is not an inclusive review of the literature on the topic of socialization, in the tradition of the annual reviews on child development produced in psychology or education, but, rather, a statement of a few new directions in socialization research with only passing notice to the older traditions in the field. This will, of course, mean that certain important aspects of socialization research will not be covered. Three of these areas which will not be considered are animal socialization, the traditional child-development fields such as growth and maturation, language development, perceptual development, learning, and cognitive development, and the cross-cultural studies of socialization in the personality and cultural tradition.[6] Cross-cultural studies will be treated in another paper in this series dealing with culture and personality.

What, then, are the important new developments in socialization theory and research in the past five years? The one which seems most striking to this observer is the extent to which socialization research and thinking has been influenced by social-role and social-systems theory. While the study of social-role has a long and honored past in sociology and a more recent past in psychology and anthropology, its influence on socialization research has been comparatively recent. Possibly in part because of the rather disappointing empirical results of the studies guided by psychoanalytic thinking in the prior period, in part due to developments in sociological theory, social psychologists working in the field of socialization have shown a greatly renewed interest in role theory as a link between social structure and behavior. Some credit for this renewed interest must go to a hardy

---

[6] Authoritative reviews on all but the first and last of these topics will be found in Harold W. Stevenson (ed.), *Child Psychology: The Sixty-Second Yearbook of the National Society for the Study of Education* (Chicago: University of Chicago Press, 1963). For other coverage, see John C. Wright and Jerome Kagan (ed.), "Basic Cognitive Processes in Children," *Monographs of the Society for Research in Child Development*, Vol. 28 (1963); and J. P. Scott, "The Process of Primary Socialization in Canine and Human Infants," *Monographs of the Society for Research in Child Development*, Vol. 28 (1963).

group of sociologists trained at the University of Chicago, who kept the torch of symbolic-interaction theory burning for more than three decades after it had been handed to them by George Herbert Mead, its principal proponent.[7] Credit also goes to Talcott Parsons who has given impetus to the recent development of role theory. His interest arose naturally out of his attempts to produce a conceptual scheme for the analysis of the structure and process of social systems, focusing on the system of institutionalized roles.[8] His position is further elaborated in his writings on family structure and the socialization of the child, which presents a detailed analysis of the child's internalization of roles as he passes through various stages of psychosexual development and integration into the family system.[9] Because this work was written well before the period to be covered in this paper, and because Parsons' writings are likely to be well known to most readers, no attempt will be made to summarize his complex argument here other than to point out that he places great stress on psychoanalytic ideas of developmental crises.

More recently, a theory of socialization stressing role-learning has been elaborated by Orville G. Brim, Jr.[10] He draws heavily on interactionist ideas but also emphasizes the social-system context. Socialization is defined as a process of learning by which an individual is prepared to meet the requirements that society has set for his behavior in a variety of social situations. These requirements always attach to one or another of the positions or statuses in either the larger society or some smaller social system. The required behavior—including habits, beliefs, attitudes, and motives—in a given position is considered to be an individual's prescribed role, and the requirements themselves are the role prescriptions. Thus, there are sets of reciprocal requirements regulating the behavior of individuals toward each other depending on their positions in the system. One learns these reciprocal requirements from interacting with others in a variety of social situations and by gradually developing the ability to take the role of the other. His knowledge of these social situations, his ability to discharge successfully his role in each situation, and his motivation to perform up to the level which the situation requires are all variables explaining individual differences in behavior. The social structure regulates to a large degree the child's exposure to various aspects of the culture and, consequently, what he will learn. The absence of certain positions in the social structure will result in deficiencies in the child's socialization to the roles these positions represent. Any particular role relationship will vary with the particular culture or subculture in which it takes place and, of course, with the personal characteristics of the specific individuals occupying given statuses, with whom the child interacts. Variations in the culture and in the characteristics of the socializing agent will result in variations in child-rearing practices, leading to personality differences. Brim also discusses the importance of anticipatory

---

[7] Among those strongly identified with the interactionist tradition are Herbert Blumer, Leonard S. Cottrell, Jr., Robert E. L. Faris, Everett C. Hughes, Alfred Lindesmith, Anselm L. Strauss, Arnold Rose, Ralph Turner, Neil Gross, Tamotsu Shibutani, and Erving Goffman.

[8] Talcott Parsons, *The Social System* (Glencoe: The Free Press, 1951).

[9] Talcott Parsons and Robert F. Bales, *Family, Socialization and Interaction Process* (Glencoe: The Free Press, 1955).

[10] The most complete statement of his position yet published is his "Personality Development as Role-Learning," in Ira Iscoe and Harold Stevenson, *Personality Development in Children* (Austin: University of Texas Press, 1960), pp. 127–159. Other sources are his "The Parent-Child Relation as Social System I, Parent and Child Roles," *Child Development*, Vol. 28 (September 1957), pp. 343–346; and Orville G. Brim, Jr., David C. Glass, David E. Lavin, Norman Goodman, *Personality and Decision Process* (Stanford: Stanford University Press, 1962).

socialization, the crucial role of language in the socialization process, the importance of role playing in the learning of roles, and the development of the conception of self.

This approach suggests at least some different orientations to familiar problems, including greater attention to the ways in which parents teach the child to be aware of different roles, the influence of the parents' perception of the social structure on what they pass on to the child, the areas of differentiation in social structure which parents ignore or insist that the child learn, the modalities used in communicating with the child, the nature of the interaction of the child with significant persons in the social structure, the influence of the personal qualities of the socializing agents, the influence of the sex of the socializing agent and the sex of the child on what is learned, the effect of the absence of certain role models on role learning, the ways socialization processes are influenced by family structures —not only the age, sex, and size characteristics but also other less apparent aspects such as the power differential between generations and the instrumental-expressive relations between the sexes—the ways in which social systems other than the family affect the socialization processes, the consistency in the performance of the individual across roles, and the extent to which socialization is oriented toward future roles. These are some of the many concerns suggested by a social role-social systems approach to socialization.[11]

It would be gratifying if it could be reported that much systematic empirical work had been done on these and related problems arising out of recent developments in role and social-systems theory. This is not entirely true. Some good beginnings have been made, and a number of studies guided by these ideas are now under way. In fact, relatively few studies of socialization now completely ignore role and social structure variables.

ROLE-LEARNING AMONG CHILDREN

There are a number of studies which have emphasized social role-learning in children. These include Brim's study of sex role-learning within two-child families in which he set forth general propositions describing role-learning in terms of interaction with others, including taking the role of the other. From these propositions he derived the hypotheses that children who have a sibling of the opposite sex will have more personality traits of the opposite sex than will children whose sibling is of the same sex and that the effect will be greater for younger than for older siblings.[12] The results of the analysis confirmed both hypotheses. Another important study using the role and social-structure idea is Elder's research on parental power legitimation in which he found that adolescents are more likely to use their parents as role models if the parents explain their rules when asked to do so and that the attractiveness of parents as role models is less among both au-

11 For recent discussions of the interactionist position, see Frederick Elkin, *The Child and Society* (New York: Random House, 1960), and Tamotsu Shibutani, *Society and Personality* (Englewood Cliffs, N. J.: Prentice-Hall, 1961). See also Arnold Rose, "A Systematic Summary of Symbolic Interaction Theory," in Arnold Rose (ed.), *Human Behavior and Social Processes* (Boston: Houghton Mifflin, 1962), pp. 3–19; Anselm L. Strauss (ed.), *The Social Psychology of George Herbert Mead* (Chicago: University of Chicago Press, 1956); and George Herbert Mead, *Mind, Self and Society* (Chicago: University of Chicago Press, 1934).

12 Orville G. Brim, Jr., "Family Structure and Sex Role Learning by Children: A Further Analysis of Helen Koch's Data," *Sociometry*, Vol. 21 (September 1958), pp. 343–364.

13 Glen H. Elder, Jr., "Parental Power Legitimation and its Effects on the Adolescent," *Sociometry*, Vol. 26 (March 1963), pp. 50–65.

tocratic and permissive parents than among democratic parents.[13] Also relevant is
the McCords' study of the effects of parental role models.[14] They found that the
influence of a criminal father on the criminality of the son is dependent on the explicit values of the parents and the affectional and control structure of the family
system. Maccoby's studies of the learning of social roles are also pertinent.[15] She
describes the process by which children learn roles through role-taking in childhood and tests hypotheses about the influence of the parental model on the child's
tendency to be a rule enforcer in activities involving peers. She found that if the
mother had been generally restrictive in her dealings with the child in early childhood her boy would tend to be a rule enforcer; for girls the relationship did not
hold, but punishment was related to rule-enforcement behavior. Mussen and
Distler jointly and Mussen individually have investigated the effects of the father-
son relationships on the development of attitudes appropriate to the male role and
have found that the fathers who carry out both nurturing and controlling functions, and do so with warmth and rewards, are likely to be effective role models
for their sons.[16] Lynn and Sawrey report on the differential effects of the absence
of the father on the role behavior of children, finding, among other things, that
father-absent children showed poorer peer adjustment.[17] They also exhibited a
higher degree of dependence, pseudo maturity, and idealization of the father.
Hoffman's investigation of the relationship between the father's role in the family and the peer-group adjustments of the child concludes that, if the father is the
primary agent of control, the children will become assertive and aggressive.[18]
Other studies of social role-learning emphasizing social-systems variables include:
Hartley's studies of the sex-role concepts of children and of sex-role pressure in the
socialization of the male child,[19] the study by the McCords and Thurber on the
effects of paternal absence on the role behavior of male children,[20] Stotland and
Hillmer's experimental study of identification and self-esteem,[21] and the study by
Hoffman and associates of the effects of the child's experiences on his school role.[22]

---

[14] William McCord and Joan McCord, "Effects of Parental Role Model on Criminality," *Journal of Social Issues*, Vol. 14 (1958), pp. 66–75.

[15] Eleanor E. Maccoby, "Role-Taking in Childhood and its Consequences for Social Learning," *Child Development*, Vol. 30 (June 1959), pp. 239–252; and "The Taking of Adult Roles
in Middle Childhood," *Journal of Abnormal and Social Psychology*, Vol. 63 (November 1961),
pp. 493–503.

[16] Paul H. Mussen and Luther Distler, "Masculinity, Identity, and Father-Son Relationships,"
Journal of Abnormal and Social Psychology, Vol. 59 (November 1959), pp. 350–356; and
Paul H. Mussen, "Some Antecedents and Consequences of Masculine Sex Typing in Adolescent
Boys," *Psychological Monographs*, Vol. 75 (1961), pp. 1–24.

[17] David B. Lynn and William L. Sawrey, "The Effects of Father-Absence on Norwegian
Boys and Girls," *Journal of Abnormal and Social Psychology*, Vol. 59 (September 1959),
pp. 258–262.

[18] Louis W. Hoffman, "The Father's Role in the Family and the Child's Peer-Group Adjustment," *Merrill-Palmer Quarterly*, Vol. 7 (April 1961), pp. 97–105.

[19] Ruth E. Hartley, "Sex-Role Among Elementary School-Age Girls," *Marriage and Family
Living*, Vol. 21 (February 1959), pp. 59–64; "Sex Role Pressure and the Socialization of the
Male Child," *Psychological Reports*, Vol. 5 (September 1959), pp. 457–468; "Children's Con-
ceptions of Male and Female Roles," *Merrill-Palmer Quarterly*, Vol. 6 (January 1960), pp. 83–
91; "Some Implications of Current Changes in Sex Role Patterns," *Merrill-Palmer Quarterly*,
Vol. 6 (April 1960), pp. 153–164.

[20] Joan McCord, William McCord, and Emily Thurber, "Some Effects of Paternal Absence on
Male Children," *Journal of Abnormal and Social Psychology*, Vol. 64 (May 1962), pp. 361–
369.

[21] Ezra Stotland and Max L. Hillmer, Jr., "Identification, Authoritarian Defensiveness, and
Self-Esteem," *Journal of Abnormal and Social Psychology*, Vol. 64 (May 1962), pp. 334–342.

[22] Lois W. Hoffman, Sidney Rosen, and Ronald Lippitt, "Parental Coerciveness, Child Autonomy, and Child's Role at School," *Sociometry*, Vol. 23 (March 1960), pp. 15–22.

It should be noted also that Winch has elaborated and is currently testing a series of interesting hypotheses about identification which rely heavily on the learning of social roles in the context of the family system.[23] Lynn's paper in which he uses a social-systems approach to develop a theory of sex differences in identification development and in which he reviews data relevant to his formulation should also be mentioned.[24] Whiting has presented a theory of resource mediation and learning by identification which has grown out of his research at Harvard over the past ten years.[25] Finally, Slater has published a critique on Parsons' theory of differentiation in the nuclear family,[26] and Bronfenbrenner has made a critical analysis of Freud's and Parsons' theories of identification.[27]

SOCIAL CLASS

Studies of social class and socialization also reflect the trend toward social-system and social-role approaches. Studies recently reviewed by Bronfenbrenner [28] and by Sewell [29] indicate that the earlier emphasis on social-class differences was mainly on specific child-rearing practices. All of these studies emphasized social-class differences in toilet-training and weaning and a limited number of other specific infant-care techniques. Moreover, their findings were often inconsistent and contrary. Bronfenbrenner was able to discern differential trends in the training practices of lower- and middle-class mothers which he felt indicated that any previous gap between the classes was narrowing. Sewell in his review of the literature on social class and childhood personality found that most of the earlier studies had concentrated on general measures of adjustment or on constellations of neurotic symptoms rather than on more meaningful personality variables. What empirical evidence there was did not support the popular notion that middle-class children are more neurotic or less adjusted than lower-class children.

During the past five years, studies of social class and socialization have had, for the most part, a different emphasis. They have been concerned with such things a differences in the quality of family relationships, patterns of affection and authority, conceptions of parenthood, parents' expectations for the child, and other aspects of parent-child relationships. Kohn's studies of social class in relation to parental values, authority, and the allocation of parental responsibilities are good illustrations of the trend.[30] In these studies, he finds that middle-class parents em-

[23] Robert F. Winch, *Identification and Its Familial Determinants* (Indianapolis: Bobbs-Merrill, 1962).

[24] David B. Lynn, "Sex Differences in Identification Development," *Sociometry*, Vol. 24 (December 1961), pp. 372–384.

[25] John W. M. Whiting, "Resource Mediation and Learning by Identification," in Iscoe and Stevenson, *op. cit.*, pp. 112–126.

[26] Philip E. Slater, "Parental Role Differentiation," *American Journal of Sociology*, Vol. 67 (November 1961), pp. 296–308.

[27] Urie Bronfenbrenner, "Freudian Theories of Identification and their Derivatives," *Child Development*, Vol. 31 (March 1960), pp. 15–40.

[28] Urie Bronfenbrenner, "Socialization and Social Class through Time and Space," in Eleanor Maccoby, Theodore Newcomb, and Eugene Hartley (eds.), *Readings in Social Psychology* (New York: Henry Holt and Co., 1958), pp. 400–425; and "The Changing American Child—A Speculative Analysis," *Journal of Social Issues*, Vol. 17 (1961), pp. 6–18.

[29] William H. Sewell, "Social Class and Childhood Personality," *Sociometry*, Vol. 24 (December 1961), pp. 340–356.

[30] Melvin L. Kohn, "Social Class and Parental Values," *American Journal of Sociology*, Vol. 64 (January 1959), pp. 337–351; and "Social Class and the Exercise of Parental Authority,"

phasize internalized standards of conduct, including honesty and self-control, while working-class parents stress respectability, including obedience, neatness, and cleanliness. Responses to misbehaviors also differ: middle-class parents respond to misbehavior in terms of the child's intent and take into account his motives and feelings, while lower-class parents focus on the child's actions and respond according to their perception of the seriousness of the act. He also finds that working-class mothers expect the father to constrain and punish the child to a more marked extent than do middle-class mothers. Bronson and associates have been concerned with patterns of affection and authority in two generations and find that, in the middle class, parental patterns have not been as rigidly defined as in the lower-class family.[31] They also report that shifts are taking place over time in the companionship and authority relationship of working-class mothers with companionship being more emphasized than formerly. They also find that working-class mothers have always exercised more authority than middle-class mothers but that middle-class mothers are taking on more of the authority function in recent years. Rosen's work should be mentioned because it shows that independence training, achievement motive, and achievement values are all positively correlated with the social-class position of the child's family.[32] Middle-class parents in their child-rearing put pressure on their children to succeed, teach their children to believe in success, and create conditions making success possible. The Miller and Swanson studies of social class and personality are important in that they not only examined social-class differences in child-training but further differentiated their subjects by whether or not they came from families in the bureaucratic or entrepreneurial settings and related these variables to their ways of resolving conflict and to their mechanisms of defense.[33] Numerous predictions were made about how social class and the nature of the setting either singly or in combination would influence child-rearing and subsequent styles of coping with conflict. Some of these hypotheses were partially confirmed and others were not. There is not space to discuss their rather diverse findings, but at least they have suggested some promising dimensions for consideration in research on socialization. Other recent studies of social class and socialization which reflect some of the trends already noted may be mentioned. These include the work of Tuma and Livson on socioeconomic status and attitudes toward authority,[34] Kantor and associates on social class and maternal attitude toward the child,[35] the research of Burchinal and associates on the personality adjustment of children from various

---

American Sociological Review, Vol. 24 (June 1959), pp. 352–366; and Melvin L. Kohn and Eleanor E. Carroll, "Social Class and the Allocation of Parental Responsibilities," *Sociometry,* Vol. 23 (December 1960), pp. 372–392.

[31] Wanda C. Bronson, Edith S. Katten, and Norman Livson, "Patterns of Authority and Affection in Two Generations," *Journal of Abnormal and Social Psychology,* Vol. 58 (March 1959), pp. 143–152.

[32] Bernard C. Rosen, "Race, Ethnicity, and the Achievement Syndrome," *American Sociological Review,* Vol. 24 (February 1959), pp. 47–60; and "Family Structure and Achievement Motivation," *American Sociological Review,* Vol. 26 (August 1961), pp. 574–585.

[33] Daniel R. Miller and Guy E. Swanson, *The Changing American Parent* (New York: John Wiley and Sons, 1958); and *Inner Conflict and Defense* (New York: Henry Holt and Co., 1960).

[34] Elias Tuma and Norman Livson, "Family Socioeconomic Status and Adolescent Attitudes to Authority," *Child Development,* Vol. 31 (June 1960), pp. 387–399.

[35] Mildred B. Kantor, John C. Glidewell, Ivan N. Mensh, Herbert R. Domke, and Margaret C. L. Gildea, "Socioeconomic Level and Maternal Attitudes toward Parent-Child Relationships," *Human Organization,* Vol. 16 (Winter 1958), pp. 44–48.

social classes,[36] the study by Sewell and Haller on factors in the relationship between social status and childhood personality,[37] and the study by Boek and associates on social class and child-care practices.[38]

SOCIAL STRUCTURE

Recently a number of studies have appeared in which family-structure variables are examined in relation to socialization outcomes in children. One of these is Strodtbeck's study of the influence of family interaction in Jewish and Italian families on their sons' achievement values.[39] Using power as his antecedent variable, he found a negative correlation between father's power in the family and the achievement-value score of the son. Since he also found that Italian fathers tended to be more powerful than Jewish fathers and that Jewish boys tended to have higher achievement values than Italian boys, he uses this finding as a possible explanation of the higher social mobility of Jews. Rosen and D'Andrade, in an observational study designed to examine the origins of achievement motivation, found that boys high in n Achievement tended to be independent of their fathers in problem-solving situations but tended not to be independent of their mothers.[40] Both mothers and fathers of boys high in n Achievement tended to display more warmth than did parents of boys low in n Achievement. Straus, in a study of conjugal power structure, found that autonomic families—families in which husband and wife are roughly equal in power—produced sons with higher achievement values, lower anxiety, and lower rejection of parents than families in which either parent was dominant or in which the parents were in conflict.[41] Differences between the types of families on a fourth dimension—the boys' school grades—were in the same direction but not significant. In a study of structural variations in child-rearing, Elder found that lower-class, less-educated, and Catholic parents, and parents with large families, tended to be more authoritarian in their relationship with their adolescent children than middle-class, well-educated, and Protestant parents, and parents with small families.[42] Adolescents subjected to either extremely authoritarian child-rearing patterns or to extremely permissive patterns tended to feel their parents were less fair and tended to feel more rejected by their parents than those adolescents subjected to democratic patterns of child-rearing.

[36] Lee G. Burchinal, Bruce Gardiner, and Glen R. Hawkes, "Children's Personality Adjustment and the Socioeconomic Status of their Families," *Journal of Genetic Psychology*, Vol. 92 (June 1958), pp. 144–159; and Lee G. Burchinal, "Social Status, Measured Intelligence, Achievement, and Personality Adjustment of Rural Iowa Girls," *Sociometry*, Vol. 22 (March 1959), pp. 75–80.
[37] William H. Sewell and Archie O. Haller, Jr., "Factors in the Relationship Between Social Status and the Personality Adjustment of the Child," *American Sociological Review*, Vol. 24 (August 1959), pp. 511–520.
[38] Walter E. Boek, Marvin B. Sussman, and Alfred Yankauer, "Social Class and Child Care Practices," *Marriage and Family Living*, Vol. 20 (August 1958), pp. 326–333.
[39] Fred L. Strodtbeck, "Family Interaction, Values, and Achievement," in David C. McClelland, Alfred L. Baldwin, Urie Bronfenbrenner, and Fred L. Strodtbeck, *Talent and Society* (New York: D. Van Nostrand Co., 1958), pp. 135–194.
[40] Bernard C. Rosen and Roy D'Andrade, "The Psychological Origins of Achievement Motivation," *Sociometry*, Vol. 22 (September 1959), pp. 185–218. See also the references in footnote 32.
[41] Murray A. Straus, "Conjugal Power Structure and Adolescent Personality," *Marriage and Family Living*, Vol. 24 (February 1962), pp. 17–25.
[42] Glen H. Elder, Jr., "Structural Variations in the Child Rearing Relationship," *Sociometry*, Vol. 25 (September 1962), pp. 241–262.

Other studies of the influence of social structure on socialization outcomes include Becker's study of the effect of family-structure variables on the teacher-pupil relationship,[43] Yarrow's study of child-rearing in families of working and non-working mothers,[44] the study by Lippitt and Gold of classroom social structure as it relates to school performance, social adjustment, and self-conception of children,[45] Cohen's,[46] Miller's,[47] and the Matza and Sykes [48] studies of various aspects of social structure in relation to juvenile delinquency, Schachter's study of the effect of birth order on affiliative behavior,[49] Sears' follow-up study of the effects of early socialization on aggression in middle childhood,[50] Peck's study of family patterns and adolescent personality,[51] the Peck and Havighurst study of character development in Prairie City,[52] and Koch's article on siblings' attitudes toward each other and toward their parents.[53] Finally, Yarrow's review of studies of maternal deprivation should be mentioned.[54]

This, of course, is by no means a complete list of the studies which in part or in whole reflect the trend toward consideration of social-system and social-role variables (a number of the studies cited throughout this review would be equally good examples, especially those cited in connection with adolescence and socialization to occupational roles); nor would it be correct to infer that all these studies have been guided exclusively by social-system or social-role ideas—several of them have had their central inspiration from other theories. Nevertheless, all of them to a considerable degree reflect the increasing emphasis on social-role and social-systems variables.

---

[43] Howard S. Becker, "Social Class and Teacher-Pupil Relationships," in Edwin R. Carr and Blanie E. Mercer (eds.), *Education and the Social Order* (New York: Rinehart and Co., Inc., 1957), pp. 273–285.

[44] Marian Radke Yarrow, Phyllis Scott, Louise DeLeeuw, and Christine Heinig, "Child-rearing in Families of Working and Nonworking Mothers," *Sociometry*, Vol. 25 (June 1962), pp. 122–140; and Lois W. Hoffman, "Effect of Maternal Employment on the Child," *Child Development*, Vol. 32 (March 1961), pp. 167–197.

[45] Ronald Lippitt and Martin Gold, "Classroom Social Structure as a Mental Health Problem," *Journal of Social Issues*, Vol. 15 (1959), pp. 40–49.

[46] Albert K. Cohen, *Delinquent Boys* (Glencoe, Illinois: Free Press, 1955).

[47] Walter Miller, "Lower-Class Culture as a Generating Milieu of Gang Delinquency," *Journal of Social Issues*, Vol. 14 (1958), pp. 5–19.

[48] David Matza and Gresham Sykes, "Juvenile Delinquency and Subterranean Values," *American Sociological Review*, Vol. 26 (October 1961), pp. 712–719.

[49] Stanley Schachter, *The Psychology of Affiliation* (Stanford, California: Stanford University Press, 1959).

[50] Robert R. Sears, "Relation of Early Socialization Experiences to Aggression in Middle Childhood," *Journal of Abnormal and Social Psychology*, Vol. 63 (November 1961), pp. 466–492.

[51] Robert F. Peck, "Family Patterns Correlated with Adolescent Personality Structure," *Journal of Social and Abnormal Psychology*, Vol. 57 (November 1958), pp. 347–350.

[52] Robert F. Peck and Robert J. Havighurst, *The Psychology of Character Development* (New York: Wiley, 1960). See also Robert R. Sears, "The Growth of Conscience," in Iscoe and Stevenson, *op. cit.*, pp. 92–111.

[53] Helen L. Koch, "The Relation of Certain Formal Attributes of Siblings to Attitudes Held Toward Each Other and Toward Their Parents," *Monographs of the Society for Research in Child Development*, Vol. 25 (1960), pp. 1–124.

[54] Leon J. Yarrow, "Maternal Deprivation: Toward an Empirical and Conceptual Reevaluation," *Psychological Bulletin*, Vol. 58 (November 1961), pp. 459–490; and "Research in Dimensions of Early Maternal Care," *Merrill-Palmer Quarterly*, Vol. 9 (April 1963), pp. 101–114; and Lawrence Castler, "Maternal Deprivation: A Critical Review of the Literature," *Monographs of the Society for Research in Child Development*, Vol. 26 (1961), pp. 1–64. For reviews of research on other aspects of infancy, see William Kessen, "Research in the Psychological Development of Children," *ibid.*, pp. 83–94; and B. M. Foss (ed.), *The Determinants of Human Behavior* (New York: Wiley, 1961).

Later Socialization

A second recent development in socialization thinking and research has been the increased interest in socialization in periods other than childhood.[55] This interest is closely related to the development of a role-theory approach and flows directly from it. Thus, if socialization is role learning—in the sense that it refers to the process by which the individual acquires the skills, knowledge, attitudes, values, and motives necessary for performance of social roles—it follows that in any but the most static societies the individual cannot possibly be prepared during childhood for the complex roles that he will be called upon to play at later periods in his life. This is not to deny the fundamental importance of childhood socialization but only to assert that role-learning is a continuous process throughout life and that the individual must not only learn new roles and abandon old ones as he passes through various status sequences in his life cycle but that he will also have to learn new roles as he experiences social mobility and as disruptive changes take place in the society.

Perhaps the most direct evidence of the trend toward greater concern for later socialization is indicated by the increased attention given in recent years to adolescent socialization. Although the social psychology of adolescence has long been a concern of social scientists, it is only recently that much attention has been given to this period as one in which important socialization processes take place. Role theory and social-systems analysis are evident in much of present-day work in this field. Parsons' article on the school class as a social system is the classic statement on the manner in which first teachers and then peers become increasingly important as agents of socialization, while parents and family diminish in influence as the child passes through the school system and finds his place in society. This occurs in part through selection mechanisms that operate in the school and peer social systems.[56] Although authorities have debated the question of whether or not there is a distinctive youth culture, there seems to be no disagreement with the notion that the adolescent period is one in which some childhood habits and roles must be abandoned while new roles appropriate to sex and age must be learned or that the school and peer groups are the most important socialization agencies at this time.[57] Coleman's study of adolescents in ten high schools in the Chicago area not only is the most complete empirical study of adolescent values available but also clearly documents the extent to which peers rather than parents become the important reference figures for high-school youth.[58] Jones, using data

[55] This emphasis was highlighted in a recent Social Science Research Council conference on socialization throughout the life cycle (May 17–19, 1963). The preliminary papers presented included the following: Orville G. Brim, Jr., "Socialization Through the Life Cycle"; Murray A. Straus, "Childhood Socialization"; Charles E. Bidwell, "Pre-Adult Socialization"; Irving Rosow, "Forms and Functions of Adult Socialization"; Yonina Talmon, "Comparative Analysis of Adult Socialization"; Howard S. Becker, "Personal Change in Adult Life," reprinted in Part Nine of this volume.

[56] Talcott Parsons, "The School Class as a Social System: Some of Its Functions in American Society," *Harvard Educational Review*, Vol. 29 (Fall 1959), pp. 297–318.

[57] Robert R. Bell, "The Adolescent Subculture," in Robert R. Bell (ed.), *The Sociology of Education* (Homewood, Ill.: The Dorsey Press, 1962), pp. 106–109; Ernest A. Smith, *American Youth Culture: Group Life in Teen Age Society* (Glencoe: Free Press, 1962); and Edgar Z. Friedenberg, *The Vanishing Adolescent* (New York: Dell Laurel Editions, 1962).

[58] James S. Coleman, *The Adolescent Society* (Glencoe: The Free Press, 1962). See also Richard L. Simpson, "The School, the Peer Group, and Adolescent Development," *Journal of Educational Psychology*, Vol. 32 (September 1958), pp. 37–41; and James S. Coleman, "Academic Achievement and the Structure of Competition," *Harvard Educational Review*, Vol. 29

from the California Growth Study, shows that the school and the peer group, in their collaboration to promote their common goals, are powerful and pervasive forces in the socialization of the adolescent. Her studies also indicate how these forces differentially influence youth from varying social backgrounds.[59] A study by Bronfenbrenner, Devereux, and Suci describes the relations between parental and adolescent behavior, taking into account sex of child, sex of parent, level of parental power, and the socioeconomic position of the family. They examined various aspects of parent-child relationships, such as "perceived parental power," "adolescent competence," "expressive rejection," "affection," and "affiliative companionship," and found that girls receive more affection, praise, and companionship; by contrast, boys are subjected to more physical punishment and achievement demands. In general, both extremes of either affection or discipline were deleterious for all children; girls were especially susceptible to the detrimental influence of overprotection; boys to the ill effects of insufficient parental discipline and support.[60] This study has been replicated in Germany with basically similar results. Wilson has shown that the social climate of the high school has a decisive influence on the level of educational aspirations of boys from various social classes.[61] Harris has summarized evidence on the part that work plays in the socialization of adolescents, showing its importance to the development of responsibility, self-development, and a favorable self-image.[62] A study by Straus has shown the widespread concern of parents with providing meaningful work role-learning experiences for their adolescent sons.[63] The effect that socialization in lower-class and slum sub-cultures has on delinquent behavior has been the subject of considerable research interest but is most completely documented in the work of Cloward and Ohlin.[64] Bandura and Waters have studied the relation between child-training and adolescent aggression.[65] Reiss has examined the educational norms of normal and delinquent adolescents in relation to their positions in the

(Fall 1959); pp. 330–351; Robert D. Hess, "The Adolescent: His Society," *Review of Educational Research,* Vol. 30 (February 1960), pp. 5–12.

[59] Mary C. Jones, "A Study of Socialization Patterns at the High School Level," *Journal of Genetic Psychology,* Vol. 93 (1958), pp. 87–111.

[60] Urie Bronfenbrenner, "Toward a Theoretical Model for the Analysis of Parent-Child Relationships in a Social Context," in John C. Glidewell, *Parental Attitudes and Child Behavior* (Illinois: Charles C. Thomas, 1961), pp. 90–109; E. C. Devereux, Urie Bronfenbrenner, and G. J. Suci, "Patterns of Parent Behavior in the United States of America and the Federal Republic of Germany: A Cross-National Comparison," *International Social Science Journal,* Vol. 14 (Unesco: Reprint, 1963), pp. 1–20.

[61] Alan B. Wilson, "Residential Segregation of Social Classes and Aspiration of High School Boys," *American Sociological Review,* Vol. 24 (December 1959), pp. 836–845. For evidence on peer-group influences, see Archie O. Haller and C. E. Butterworth, "Peer Influences on Levels of Occupational and Educational Aspirations," *Social Forces,* Vol. 38 (May 1960), pp. 287–295.

[62] Dale B. Harris, "Work and the Adolescent Transition to Maturity," *Teachers College Record,* Vol. 63 (March 1961), pp. 146–153.

[63] Murray A. Straus, "Work Roles and Financial Responsibility in the Socialization of Farm, Fringe, and Town Boys," *Rural Sociology,* Vol. 27 (September 1962), pp. 257–274.

[64] Richard A. Cloward and Lloyd E. Ohlin, *Delinquency and Opportunity* (Glencoe: The Free Press, 1960). See also: Albert K. Cohen and James F. Short, Jr., "Research in Delinquent Subcultures," *Journal of Social Issues,* Vol. 14 (1958), pp. 20–37; Walter B. Miller, "Lower Class Culture as a Generating Milieu of Gang Delinquency," *Journal of Social Issues,* Vol. 14 (1958), pp. 5–19; Albert J. Reiss, Jr., and Albert Lewis Rhodes, "The Distribution of Juvenile Delinquency in the Social Class Structure," *American Sociological Review,* Vol. 26 (October 1961), pp. 653–661.

[65] Albert Bandura and Richard H. Waters, *Adolescent Aggression* (New York: Ronald Press, 1959).

social structure.[66] Rosenberg has assessed the influence of consonance or dissonance in religious affiliation on self-esteem and psychosomatic symptoms in adolescence.[67] Many other studies could be mentioned, but this sampling and some
of the studies cited in the previous section illustrate the wide range of concerns
and offer evidence of the stress currently being placed on adolescent socialization.

When attention shifts from adolescent to adult socialization, there is no comparable body of knowledge. Even on the descriptive level, what is known on adult
socialization is rather scant—especially in comparison with what is known on childhood and adolescence. Practically no good research on socialization into the marital role exists—despite the fact that numerous books on marriage and family contain "insightful advice" on adjustment to the marriage partner. There is some
research on family life education indicating some dimensions of the problem of
adult role-learning and suggesting some of the techniques that have been most
successful in getting parents to modify old or to adopt new child-rearing practices.[68] Some good beginnings have been made in recent years in the study of
socialization to occupational roles. These studies grow out of a long tradition of
research on careers by sociologists.[69] Becker and his colleagues have provided the
most complete study yet available on socialization to a professional role in their
research on the medical student.[70] Their study shows how the social selection
process operates to determine who will enter medical school and documents the
ways in which the students' perspectives change as they progress through the
years of training until they finally emerge from medical school with appropriate
skills and a sense of identity with their profession but with still unresolved dilemmas on a number of issues crucial to their future role as doctors. Lortie, in
his study of lawyers, finds that the most important phase of socialization for the
practice of law is the sorting and sifting process, which takes place during the first
year or so after completion of law school and determines the position the attorney
will occupy in the system of legal work.[71] It is probably not necessary to do more
than mention the many studies of socialization to different occupational roles that
have been done in the past five years to indicate the wide scope of interest in occupational socialization. Corwin has studied role conception and identity in nursing,[72] Westby has investigated the socialization of the symphony musician,[73] Tay-

[66] Albert J. Reiss, "Are Educational Norms and Goals of Conforming, Truant, and Delinquent
Adolescents Influenced by Group Position in American Society," Journal of Negro Education,
Vol. 28 (Summer 1959), pp. 309–333. See also his "Social Integration of Queers and Peers,"
Social Problems, Vol. 9 (January 1961), pp. 103–120.

[67] Morris Rosenberg, "The Dissonant Religious Context and Emotional Disturbance," American Journal of Sociology, Vol. 68 (July 1962), pp. 1–10.

[68] Orville G. Brim, Jr., Education for Child Rearing (New York: Russell Sage Foundation,
1959).

[69] A good deal of this interest has been stimulated by Everett C. Hughes, who has long been
interested in the part occupational roles play in the lives of men. See his Men and Their Work
(Glencoe: Free Press, 1958) for his writings on several occupational roles.

[70] Howard S. Becker, Everett C. Hughes, Blanche Geer, and Anselm L. Strauss, Boys in
White: Student Culture in Medical School (Chicago: University of Chicago Press, 1961); and
Howard S. Becker and Blanche Geer, "The Fate of Idealism in Medical School," American
Sociological Review, Vol. 23 (February 1958), pp. 50–56. See also Samuel W. Bloom, "The
Process of Becoming a Physician," THE ANNALS, Vol. 346 (March 1963), pp. 77–87; and
Anselm L. Strauss, Mirrors and Masks (Glencoe: Free Press, 1959).

[71] Dan C. Lortie, "Laymen to Lawmen: Law School, Careers, and Professional Socialization,"
Harvard Educational Review, Vol. 29 (Fall 1959), pp. 352–369.

[72] Ronald G. Corwin, "Role Conceptions and Career Aspiration: A Study of Identity in Nursing," Sociological Quarterly (April 1961), pp. 69–86; and Hans O. Mauksch, "Becoming a
Nurse: A Selective View," THE ANNALS, Vol. 346 (March 1963), pp. 88–89.

[73] David L. Westby, "The Career Experience of the Symphony Musician," Social Forces, Vol.
38 (March 1960), pp. 223–229.

lor and Pellegrin have studied the professionalization of the life-insurance salesman,[74] the Simpsons have examined the process by which the psychiatric attendant acquires an identity with his work,[75] Eulau and associates have investigated the political socialization of legislators,[76] and Braude has studied the ways in which the rabbi comes to develop an acceptable professional identity.[77] This list could be expanded to cover other professional and semiprofessional roles, but it would not include studies of socialization to skilled trades or to the many semiskilled and unskilled jobs that make up a large proportion of the occupational roles in society. Strangely enough, these occupations for the most part have escaped the recent concerns of sociologists.[78]

Work on other aspects of adult socialization has been quite limited and is mainly directed at socialization to old-age roles and to new statuses in institutional settings. Numerous articles and books have been published on the problems of adjustment to old age and the adjustments of patients and inmates to hospitals, mental institutions, prisons, and homes for the aged. There is no need to consider most of this work in this review because, for the most part, it does not employ a socialization approach. A notable exception is Goffman's book on the social situation of mental patients and other inmates.[79] Deutscher reports an interesting study on the ways in which parents prepare themselves for what he calls postparental life.[80] This is the stage in the family cycle following the marriage and departure of children from the parental home. He shows that anticipatory socialization through playing at the postparental role in situations analogous to it and by developing attitudes favorable to the anticipated role makes this a much less traumatic period than most writers on the family had expected. Cavan's article on role adjustment in old age is provocative.[81] She attempts to show how old persons can develop adequate self-conceptions at various stages of old age such as retirement, widowhood, and grandparenthood through participation in groups which permit and encourage them to play roles having group support and approval and thus to reformulate their self-conceptions in relation to their new statuses. A promising theory has been advanced by Cummings and associates which holds that aging is primarily a process of disengagement in which the individual participates in a process of mutual withdrawal with others in his social system.[82]

[74] M. Lee Taylor and Ronald J. Pellegrin, "Professionalization, Its Functions and Dysfunctions for the Life Insurance Occupation," *Social Forces*, Vol. 38 (December 1960), pp. 110–114. .

[75] Richard L. Simpson and Ida H. Simpson, "The Psychiatric Attendant: Development of an Occupational Self-Image in a Low Status Occupation," *American Sociological Review*, Vol. 24 (June 1959), pp. 389–392.

[76] Heinz Eulau, William Buchanan, LeRoy Ferguson, and John C. Wahlke, "The Political Socialization of American State Legislators," *Midwest Journal of Political Science*, Vol. 3 (May 1959), pp. 188–206.

[77] Lee Braude, "Professional Autonomy and the Role of the Layman," *Social Forces*, Vol. 39 (May 1961), pp. 297–301.

[78] The strong sense of identity with the occupational role that characterizes professionals is clearly not shared by industrial workers. For evidence on this point, compare Charles E. Bidwell, "The Young Professional in the Army: A Study of Occupational Identity," *American Sociological Review*, Vol. 26 (June 1961), pp. 360–372; and Robert Dubin, "Industrial Workers' Worlds: A Study of the Central Life Interests of Industrial Workers," in Rose, *op. cit.*, pp. 247–266.

[79] Erving Goffman, *Asylums* (New York: Doubleday and Co., 1961).

[80] Irwin Deutscher, "Socialization for Postparental Life," in Rose, *op. cit.*, pp. 506–525.

[81] Ruth S. Cavan, "Self and Role in Adjustment During Old Age," in Rose, *op. cit.*, 526–536.

[82] Elaine Cummings, Lois R. Dean, David Newell, and Isabel McCaffrey, "Disengagement— A Tentative Theory of Ageing," *Sociometry*, Vol. 23 (March 1960), pp. 15–21; and Elaine Cummings and William E. Henry, *Growing Old: The Process of Disengagement* (New York: Basic Books, 1961).

From research thus far completed, it appears that this process begins in later middle age with a shift in self-perception which reflects the beginning of anticipatory
socialization to aged roles. This shift is accompanied by a restriction on amount
and variety of interactions undertaken and on the quality of interaction with others. Finally, a self-centered and idiosyncratic set of behaviors comes to characterize the aged. Much more research needs to be done to test this formulation, but
at least it appears to offer some possibilities as a guide for future research in adult
socialization. Parsons argues in a recent essay that the process of disengagement
implies an increased capacity for disinterested judgment and that society should
take this capacity into account in making a positive redefinition of the aged role.[83]
Payne, in a study of the process of aging, finds that old people, when faced with
important decisions, turn to middle-aged adults for value support and information. He argues that this constitutes a role reversal whereby adult children become agents of socialization for their aged parents.[84] Other relevant writings
bearing on the problem of adult socialization are Streib's article on family patterns in retirement,[85] Thompson's study of preretirement and adjustment,[86] and
Talmon's study of retirement in a planned society.[87] There are also some suggestions on socialization to the sick role.[88] Litman, has made a study of the process
by which the self-conceptions are modified immediately after crippling accidents
or illnesses, as the individual passes through a long period of rehabilitation and finally learns roles appropriate for one with his handicaps.[89] Perhaps the best example of the study of socialization in an institutional context is Wheeler's study of
the complex processes by which the reformatory inmate is socialized to the role
of prisoner and then resocialized as he moves out of the correctional community.[90]
Other studies could be mentioned, but these are perhaps sufficient to show that
some attention is being given to adult socialization. Obviously, research is only
now beginning to come to grips with such key issues as the following: the extent
to which socialization to adult roles differs from socialization in childhood (does
later socialization involve primarily the learning of quite specific skills and values
as contrasted to childhood socialization, which is concerned more with the control
of primary drives and the internalization of general values and attitudes?); the
kinds of techniques which are useful in the socialization of adults; the possible
limitations placed on later socialization by the lasting effects of early socialization;

[83] Talcott Parsons, "Toward A Healthy Maturity," *Journal of Health and Human Behavior*,
Vol. 1 (Fall 1960), pp. 163–173.
[84] Raymond Payne, "Some Theoretical Approaches to the Sociology of Ageing," *Social Forces*,
Vol. 38 (May 1960), pp. 359–362.
[85] Gordon Streib, "Family Patterns and Retirement," *Journal of Social Issues*, Vol. 14 (1958),
pp. 46–60. See also Gordon F. Streib, Wayne E. Thompson, and Edward A. Suchman, "The
Cornell Study of Occupational Retirement," *ibid.*, pp. 3–17.
[86] Wayne E. Thompson, "Pre-Retirement Anticipation and Adjustment in Retirement," *Journal
of Social Issues*, Vol. 14 (1958), pp. 35–45.
[87] Yonina Talmon, "Ageing in Israel: A Planned Society," *American Journal of Sociology*, Vol.
67 (November 1961), pp. 284–295.
[88] See particularly David Mechanic and Edmund H. Volkart, "Stress, Illness Behavior, and the
Sick Role," *American Sociological Review*, Vol. 26 (February 1961), pp. 51–58; and David
Mechanic, "The Concept of Illness Behavior," *Journal of Chronic Diseases*, Vol. 15 (February
1962), pp. 189–194. A comprehensive statement is found in Talcott Parsons, *The Social System* (Glencoe: The Free Press, 1951), pp. 439–447.
[89] Theodore J. Litman, "Self Conception and Physical Rehabilitation," in Rose, *op. cit.*,
pp. 550–574.
[90] Stanton Wheeler, "Socialization in Correctional Communities," *American Sociological Review*, Vol. 26 (October 1961), pp. 697–712.

the influence of the differing interactional structure of various groups on the adult socialization processes; the extent to which there is anticipatory socialization for later stages in the life cycle; the factors preventing some individuals from responding to adult socialization; and the manner in which the individual learns to cope with conflicting role demands. Future work must give attention to these and related problems before we will know much about adult socialization on other than a descriptive level.

Methodological Advances

The third important recent trend in socialization work, and one which is not necessarily related to the two developments previously discussed, is toward increased sophistication in the design and execution of research. This trend is reflected in the growing concern about methodological matters shown by research workers in the field. This is evidenced by the recent publication of a handbook on methods of research sponsored by the Committee on Child Development of the National Academy of Sciences-National Research Council.[91] About half of the chapters in the compendium deal with matters directly relevant to socialization research, including interviewing, projective techniques, attitude and value measurement, the assessment of motivation and affect, the appraisal of personality characteristics, the study of children's groups, the study of interpersonal behavior, anthropological techniques, the measurement of family-life variables, and laboratory experimental methods. All are written by experts and reflect the strides made in the development of research methods in recent years. This methodological concern is also demonstrated by the amount of effort workers in the field are devoting to the development and testing of research instruments. A listing of this work would require more space than can be allotted, but some excellent examples can be given. One of the most widely used tools is the Parent Attitude Research Instrument, developed by Schaefer and Bell, which in its factor-analyzed version produces three factors: authoritarian control, hostility-rejection, and democratic attitude toward child-rearing.[92] Another instrument developed by Williams, called the PALS (parental authority-love statements), purports to evaluate the parents' behavior and attitudes from the child's point of view.[93] Calogeras has related TAT (thematic apperception test) responses to questionnaire and interview responses and finds that they produce comparable intrafamilial attitude scores.[94] Milton has factor analyzed the intercorrelation among child-rearing variables and finds stable factors including: strictness, adjustment, warmth, responsible child-training orientation, aggression, and punitiveness.[95] Straus has developed a questionnaire for assessing family interaction.[96] Bell has published a critical paper on

[91] Paul Mussen (ed.), *Handbook of Research Methods in Child Development* (New York: Wiley, 1960).

[92] Earl S. Schaefer and Richard Q. Bell, "Development of a Parental Attitude Research Instrument," *Child Development*, Vol. 29 (June 1958), pp. 339–362.

[93] Walter C. Williams, "The PALS Tests: A Technique for Children to Evaluate Both Parents," *Journal of Consulting Psychology*, Vol. 22 (December 1958), pp. 487–495.

[94] Roy C. Calogeras, "Some Relationships between Fantasy and Self-report Behavior," *Genetic Psychology Monographs*, Vol. 58 (November 1958), pp. 273–325.

[95] George A. Milton, "A Factor Analytic Study of Child-Rearing Behaviors," *Child Development*, Vol. 29 (June 1958), pp. 381–392.

[96] Murray A. Straus, *Family Interaction Schedule* (Minneapolis: Minnesota Family Study Center, 1963).

the methodological problem of retrospective parental attitude questionnaires.[97] Lesser has demonstrated that aggressive responses on the TAT are convertible to Guttman scales.[98] Sarason's group has produced evidence on the validity of the Test Anxiety Scale for Children.[99] Schaefer has developed circumplex models for material behavior and for the emotional and social behavior of the child.[100] He uses love-hostility and autonomy-control as the bipolar dimension in the maternal behavior model and love-hostility and extroversion-introversion in the model for the child. The models seem to be related to each other on the love-hostility dimension. Maccoby, in a thoughtful article, has discussed the choice of variables in socialization research, pointing out that standard variables employed in laboratory studies—or for that matter in various theories—undergo a great deal of modification in real-life situations and that subtle differences in the definition of a variable can affect the nature of the behavior predicted from it.[101] She further argues that the same socialization practice may well have different effects in different cultural situations.

Experiments are less common in socialization research than in some areas of child development or social psychology, but there are examples, among the studies reviewed, of both laboratory experiments and experiments in the family setting.[102] Most studies of socialization depend either on observational, questionnaire, or interviewing techniques for their data, but it is only fair to say that much less attention is paid to sampling than to data-gathering and data-analysis techniques.[103] A notable exception is Elder's study which had a large and well-designed sample, permitting controlled analysis.[104]

Increasingly, students of socialization are coming to the realization that studies in a social-systems context require much more complicated designs than the "single variable approach," which was so common formerly. This has led to a more careful choice of variables to conform to the theory guiding the research. The Straus study previously cited is a good example of this.[105] Using conjugal power

[97] Richard Q. Bell, "Retrospective Attitude Studies of Parent-child Relations," *Child Development*, Vol. 29 (June 1958), pp. 323–338.

[98] Gerald S. Lesser, "Application of Guttman's Scaling Method to Aggressive Fantasy in Children," *Educational and Psychological Measurement*, Vol. 18 (Autumn 1958), pp. 543–551.

[99] Seymour B. Sarason, Kenneth Davidson, Frederick F. Lighthall, and Richard R. Waite, "Rorschach Behavior and Performance of High and Low Anxious Children," *Child Development*, Vol. 29 (June 1958), pp. 277–286, and "Classroom Observations of High and Low Anxious Children," *ibid.*, pp. 287–296; and Charlotte Fox, Kenneth Davidson, Frederick F. Lighthall, Richard R. Waite, and Seymour B. Sarason, "Human Figure Drawings of High and Low Anxious Children," *ibid.*, pp. 297–302; and Irving Sarnoff, Frederick F. Lighthall, Richard R. Waite, Kenneth Davidson, and Seymour B. Sarason, "A Cross-cultural Study of Anxiety among American and English School Children," *Journal of Educational Psychology*, Vol. 49 (March 1958), pp. 129–136.

[100] Earl S. Schaefer, "Converging Conceptual Models for Maternal Behavior and for Child Behavior," in John C. Glidewell (ed.), *Parental Attitudes and Child Behavior* (Illinois: Charles C. Thomas, 1961), pp. 124–146.

[101] Eleanor E. Maccoby, "The Choice of Variables in the Study of Socialization," *Sociometry*, Vol. 24 (December 1961), pp. 357–371.

[102] For examples, see: Schachter, *op. cit.*, Strodtbeck, *op. cit.*, and Rosen and D'Andrade, *op. cit.*

[103] For a critique of questionnaire and interview techniques and a suggested program emphasizing observational techniques, see Marion R. Yarrow, "Problems in Parent-Child Research," *Child Development*, Vol. 34 (July 1963), pp. 215–226.

[104] Glen H. Elder, Jr., "Parental Power Legitimation and Its Effect on the Adolescent," *Sociometry*, Vol. 26 (March 1963), pp. 50–65.

[105] Murray A. Straus, "Conjugal Power Structure and Adolescent Personality," *Marriage and Family Living*, Vol. 24 (February 1962), pp. 17–25.

as his independent variable, he classified families into four types on the basis of distribution of power between the parents and related these types to his dependent variables, which were four adolescent personality attributes chosen to correspond with Parsons' "functional imperatives." Previously formulated hypotheses were then tested by appropriate statistical procedures. Another interesting observation is that there are now a few studies that have a programmatic and interdisciplinary character rarely found in socialization research in the past. One of the best examples is the work of the Cornell group on the relationship between authority and affection in the family and leadership and responsibility in children.[106] When a preliminary study came up with puzzling results, they reanalyzed their data, introducing more controls. They found curvilinear relationships with different optimal levels for the sexes. A theoretical model was constructed which accounted for the parent-child relationships. This has since been tested on German as well as American samples and is being revised as new empirical data indicate the need for modification. Although not all studies come up to the standards of these last two, many of those reviewed are equally well designed. Finally, a word should be said about the generalization made by the authors of recent studies. While to this reviewer there still seems to be a tendency to overgeneralize the results from limited studies, this is much less true today than in preceding periods. Socialization research cannot be said to be as rigorous as that in some other branches of social psychology, but it is becoming increasingly respectable.

58   Personal Change in Adult Life

● HOWARD S. BECKER

People often exhibit marked change—in their attitudes, beliefs, behavior and style of interaction—as they move through youth and adulthood. Many social scientists, and others interested in explaining human behavior, think that human beings are governed by deep and relatively unchanging components of the personality or self, so that important changes at late stages in the life cycle are viewed as anomalies that need to be explained away. They may trace the roots of behavior to personality components formed in early childhood—needs, defenses, identifications, and the like—and interpret change in adulthood as simply a variation on an already established theme. Or they may, more sociologically, see the sources of everyday behavior in values established in the society, inculcated in the young during childhood, and maintained thereafter by constraints built into major communal institutions. Like the personality theorists, those who use values as

SOURCE: Howard S. Becker, in *Sociometry*, 27 (March 1964), pp. 40–53. Reprinted by permission of the American Sociological Association.

    A slightly different version of this paper was presented at the Social Science Research Council Conference on Socialization Through the Life Cycle, New York, May 17, 1963. I wish to thank Orville G. Brim, Jr., Blanche Geer, and Anselm L. Strauss for their comments on an earlier draft.

106 For the references, see footnote 60.

a major explanatory variable see change in adulthood as essentially superficial, a new expression of an unchanging underlying system of values. In either case, the scientist wishes to concern himself with basic processes that will explain lasting trends in individual behavior.

Both these approaches err by taking for granted that the only way we can arrive at generalized explanations of human behavior is by finding some unchanging components in the self or personality. They err as well in making the prior assumption that human beings are essentially unchanging, that changes which affect only such "superficial" phenomena as behavior without affecting deeper components of the person are trivial and unimportant.

There are good reasons to deny these assumptions. Brim, for instance, has persuasively argued that there are no "deep" personality characteristics, traits of character which persist across any and all situations and social roles.[1] In any case, it is clearly a useful strategy to explore the theoretical possibilities opened up by considering what might be true if we look in other directions for generalizeable explanations of human behavior.

A good many studies are now available which suggest that an appropriate area in which further explanations might be sought is that of social structure and its patterned effects on human experience. Two of these seem of special importance, and I devote most of what I have to say to them. The process of *situational adjustment*, in which individuals take on the characteristics required by the situations they participate in, provides an entering wedge into the problem of change. It shows us one example of an explanation which can deal with superficial and immediate changes in behavior and at the same time allow us to make generalized theories about the processes involved. The process of *commitment*, in which externally unrelated interests of the person become linked in such a way as to constrain future behavior, suggests an approach to the problem of personal stability in the face of changing situations. Before dealing with these processes, however, I will consider a problem of definition which reveals a further influence of social structure, this time an influence on the very terms in which problems of socialization are cast.

The Eye of the Beholder

Many of the changes alleged to take place in adults do not take place at all. Or, rather, a change occurs but an optical illusion causes the outside observer to see it as a change quite different in kind and magnitude from what it really is. The observer (a layman or a social scientist looking at the phenomenon from a layman's point of view), through a semantic transformation, turns an observable change into something quite different.

Take, for example, the commonly asserted proposition that the professional education of physicians stifles their native idealism and turns it into a profound professional cynicism.[2] Educated laymen believe this, and scientific studies have been

---

[1] Orville G. Brim, Jr., "Personality as Role-Learning," in Ira Iscoe and Harold Stevenson, editors, *Personality Development in Children*, Austin: University of Texas Press, 1960, pp. 127–59.
[2] This problem is discussed at greater length in Howard S. Becker and Blanche Geer, "The Fate of Idealism in Medical School," *American Sociological Review*, 23 (Feb., 1958), pp. 50–56, and in Howard S. Becker, Blanche Geer, Everett C. Hughes, and Anselm L. Strauss, *Boys in White: Student Culture in Medical School*, Chicago: University of Chicago Press, 1961, pp. 419–33.

carried out to test the proposition.[3] Observed changes in the behavior of fledgling physicians attest to its truth. Doctors are in fact inclined to speak with little reverence of the human body; they appear to be and probably are to a large extent unmoved in the emotional way a layman would be by human death; their standards are not as high as the layman thinks they ought to be, their desire for wealth stronger than it ought to be.

People describe these changes with reference to an unanalyzed conception of idealism and cynicism. It would not be unfair to describe the conception as the perspective of a disgruntled patient, who feels that the doctor he has to deal with is thinking about other things than the patient's welfare. The perspective of the disgruntled patient itself draws on some very general lay conceptions which suggest that those who deal with the unpleasant and the unclean—in this case, with death and disease—must of necessity be cynical, since "normal people" prefer what is pleasant and clean and find the unclean repulsive.

It is typically the case in service occupations, however, that the practitioners who perform the service have a perspective quite different from the clients, patients or customers for whom they perform it.[4] They understand the techniques used by professionals, the reasons for their use in one case and not in another, the contingencies of the work situation and of work careers which affect a man's judgment and behavior, and the occupational ethos and culture which guide him. The client understands nothing of this. In an effort to make sense of his experience with those who serve him, he may resort to the folk notions I have already mentioned, reasoning that people who constantly deal with what decent people avoid may be contaminated: some of the dirt rubs off. The client is never sure that the practitioner has his best interests at heart and tends to suspect the worst.

But why should we assess and evaluate the change that takes place in the doctor as he goes through professional school from the point of view of his patient? Suppose we look at it instead from the characteristic perspective of the medical profession. If we do this, we find (as we would find if we studied the views of almost any occupation toward the institutions which train people for entrance into them) that medical schools are typically regarded as too idealistic. They train students to practice in ways that are not "practical," suited to an ideal world but not to the world we live in. They teach students to order more laboratory tests than patients will pay for, to ignore the patient's requests for "new" drugs or "popular" treatments,[5] but do not teach students what to do when the waiting room holds more patients than can be seen during one's office hours. Similarly, people often complain of schools of education that they train prospective teachers in techniques that are not adapted to the situation the teacher will really have to deal with; they idealistically assume that the teacher can accomplish ends which in fact cannot be gained in the situations she will face. They do not tell the teacher how to teach a fifteen-year-old fifth grader, nor do they tell her what to do when she discovers a pupil carrying a switchblade knife.

---

[3] See Leonard D. Eron, "Effect of Medical Education on Medical Students," *Journal of Medical Education*, 10 (Oct., 1955), pp. 559–66; and Richard Christie and Robert K. Merton, "Procedures for the Sociological Study of the Values Climate of Medical Schools," *ibid.*, 33 (1958), Part II, pp. 125–53.

[4] See, for a discussion of this point, Howard S. Becker, *Outsiders: Studies in the Sociology of Deviance*, New York: The Free Press, 1963, pp. 82 ff.; and Everett C. Hughes, *Men and their Work*, New York: The Free Press, 1958, *passim*.

[5] See Eliot Freidson, *Patients' Views of Medical Practice*, New York: Russell Sage Foundation, 1961, pp. 200–202.

It is a paradox. In one view, professional training makes physicians less ideal-istic, in the other, more idealistic. Where does the truth lie? I have already noted that many of the changes seen as signs of increasing cynicism in the young physi-cian do in fact take place. It can equally be demonstrated that the changes which make him seem too idealistic also take place. The medical students we studied at the University of Kansas expected, when they graduated, to practice in ways that would be regarded as hopelessly idealistic by many, if not most, medical practi-tioners. They proposed to see no more than 20 patients a day; they proposed never to treat a disease without having first made a firm diagnosis. These briefs, incul-cated by a demanding faculty, are just the opposite of the cynicism supposed to af-flict the new physician.[6]

The lesson we should learn from this is that personality changes are often pres-ent only in the eye of the beholder. Changes do take place in people, but the un-informed outsider interprets the change wrongly. Just as doctors acquire new perspectives and ideas as a result of their medical training, any adult may acquire new perspectives and ideas. But it would be a mistake to assume that these changes represent the kind of fundamental changes suggested by such polar terms as "idealism" and "cynicism." We learn less by studying the students who are al-leged to have lost their idealism than we do by studying those who claim they have become cynical.

Even so, adults do change. But we must make sure, not only by our own obser-vation but also by careful analysis of the terms we use to describe what we see, that the changes we try to explain do in fact take place. Parenthetically, an inter-esting possibility of transferring concepts from the study of adults to the study of socialization of children lies in defining the character of the changes that take place as children develop. Is it too farfetched to say that the definitions ordinarily used are excessively parochial in that they are all arrived at from the adult point of view? What would our theories look like if we made a greater effort to capture the child's point of view? What does he think is happening to him? How does his conception of the process differ from that of the adults who bring him up and those who study his growing up?

Situational Adjustment

One of the most common mechanisms in the development of the person in adult-hood is the process of situational adjustment. This is a very gross conception, which requires analytic elaboration it has not yet received. But the major out-lines are clear. The person, as he moves in and out of a variety of social situa-tions, learns the requirements of continuing in each situation and of success in it. If he has a strong desire to continue, the ability to assess accurately what is re-quired, and can deliver the required performance, the individual turns himself into the kind of person the situation demands.

Broadly considered, this is much the same as Brim's notion of learning adult roles. One learns to be a doctor or a policeman, learns the definitions of the sta-tuses involved and the appropriate behavior with respect to them. But the notion of situational adjustment is more flexible than that of adult role learning. It allows us to deal with smaller units and make a finer analysis. We construct the process of learning an adult role by analyzing sequences of smaller and more numerous

---

[6] Becker, et al., Boys in White, op. cit., pp. 426–428.

situational adjustments. We should have in our minds the picture of a person try-ing to meet the expectations he encounters in immediate face-to-face situations: doing well in today's chemistry class, managing to be poised and mature on to-night's date, surmounting the small crises of the moment. Sequences and combina-tions of small units of adjustment produce the larger units of role learning.

If we view situational adjustment as a major process of personal development, we must look to the character of the situation for the explanation of why people change as they do. We ask what there is in the situation that requires the person to act in a certain way or to hold certain beliefs. We do not ask what there is in him that requires the action or belief. All we need to know of the person is that for some reason or another he desires to continue his participation in the situation or to do well in it. From this we can deduce that he will do what he can to do what is necessary in that situation. Our further analysis must adjust itself to the character of the situation.

Thus, for example, in our present study of college undergraduates,[7] we find that they typically share a strong desire to get high grades. Students work very hard to get grades and consider them very important, both for their immediate conse-quences and as indicators of their own personal ability and worth. We need not look very deeply into the student to see the reason for his emphasis on grades. The social structure of the campus coerces students to believe that grades are im-portant because, in fact, they are important. You cannot join a fraternity or soror-ity if your grades do not meet a certain minimum standard. You cannot compete for high office in important campus organizations if your grades are not high enough. As many as one-fourth of the students may not be able to remain in school if they do not raise their grades in the next semester. For those who are failing, low grades do not simply mean blocked access to the highest campus hon-ors. Low grades, for these unfortunates, mean that every available moment must be spent studying, that the time the average student spends dating, playing, drink-ing beer or generally goofing off must be given over to the constant effort to stay in school. Grades are the currency with which the economy of campus social life operates. Only the well-to-do can afford the luxuries; the poor work as hard as they can to eke out a marginal existence.

The perspectives a person acquires as a result of situational adjustments are no more stable than the situation itself or his participation in it. Situations occur in institutions: stable institutions provide stable situations in which little change takes place. When the institutions themselves change, the situations they provide for their participants shift and necessitate development of new patterns of belief and action. When, for instance, a university decides to up-grade its academic pro-gram and begins to require more and different kinds of work from its students, they must adjust to the new contingencies with which the change confronts them.

Similarly, if an individual moves in and out of given situations, is a transient rather than a long-term participant, his perspectives will shift with his movement. Wheeler has shown that prisoners become more "prisonized" the longer they are in prison; they are more likely to make decisions on the basis of criminal than of law-abiding values. But he has also shown that if you analyze prisoners' responses by time still to be served, they become more law-abiding the nearer they approach

[7] Statements about college students are based on preliminary analysis of the data collected in a study of undergraduates at the University of Kansas, in which I collaborated with Blanche Geer and Everett C. Hughes. A monograph reporting our findings is in preparation. The study was supported by the Carnegie Corporation of New York.

release.[8] This may be interpreted as a situational shift. The prisoner is frequently sorry that he has been caught and is in a mood to give up crime; he tends to respect law-abiding values. But when he enters prison he enters an institution which, in its lower reaches, is dominated by men wedded to criminal values. Studies of prisons have shown that the most influential prisoners tend to have stable criminal orientations and that inmate society is dominated by these perspectives.[9] In order to "make out" in the prison, the new inmate discovers that he must make his peace with this criminally oriented social structure, and he does. As he approaches release, however, he realizes that he is going back into a world dominated by people who respect the law and that the criminal values which stand him in such good stead in prison society will not work as well outside. He thereupon begins to shed the criminal values appropriate to the prison and renew his attachment to the law-abiding values of the outside world.

We discovered the same process in the medical school, where students gave up a naive idealistic approach to the problems of medicine for an approach that was specifically oriented toward getting through school. As they approached the end of their schooling, they relinquished their attachment to these school-specific values and once more returned to their concern with problems that would arise in the outer world, albeit with a new and more professional approach than they would have been capable of before.

We find a similar change in college students, when we observe them in the Spring of their last college year. They look back over the four years of school and wonder why they have not spent their time better, wonder if college has been what they wanted. This concern reflects their preoccupation, while in school, with the pursuit of values that are valuable primarily within the confines of the collegiate community: grades, office in campus organizations, and the like. (Even though they justify their pursuit of these ends in part on the basis of their utility in the outside world, students are not sure that the pursuit of other ends, less valued on the campus, might not have even more usefulness for the future.) Now that they are leaving for the adult community, in which other things will be valuable, they find it hard to understand their past concerns as they try, retrospectively, to assess the experience they have just been through.

Situational adjustment is very frequently not an individual process at all, but a collective one. That is, we are not confronted with one person undergoing change, but with an entire cohort, a "class" of people, who enter the institution and go through its socializing program together. This is most clearly the case in those institutions which typically deal with "batches" of people.[10] Schools are perhaps the best example, taking in a class of students each year or semester who typically go through the entire training program as a unit, leaving together at the end of their training.

But situational adjustment may have a collective character even where people are not processed in groups. The individual enters the institution alone, or with a small group, but joins a larger group there already, who stand ready to tell him

---

[8] Stanton Wheeler, "Socialization in Correctional Communities," *American Sociological Review,* 26 (Oct., 1961), pp. 697–712.

[9] See Donald R. Cressey, editor, *The Prison: Studies in Institutional Organization and Change,* New York: Holt, Rinehart and Winston, 1961; and Richard A. Cloward, *et al., Theoretical Studies in Social Organization of the Prison,* New York: Social Science Research Council, 1960.

[10] See Erving Goffman's use of this idea in *Asylums: Essays on the Social Situation of Mental Patients and Other Inmates,* Garden City: Doubleday and Company, Inc., 1961, pp. 6 and *passim.*

how it is and what he should do, and he will be followed by others for whom he will perform the same good turn.[11] In institutions where people are acted upon in groups by socializing agents, much of the change that takes place—the motivation for it and the perceived desirability of different modes of change—cannot be traced to the predilections of the individual. It is, instead, a function of the interpretive response made by the entire group, the consensus the group reaches with respect to its problems.

The guidelines for our analysis can be found in Sumner's analysis of the development of folkways.[12] A group finds itself sharing a common situation and common problems. Various members of the group experiment with possible solutions to those problems and report their experiences to their fellows. In the course of their collective discussion, the members of the group arrive at a definition of the situation, its problems and possibilities, and develop consensus as to the most appropriate and efficient ways of behaving. This consensus thenceforth constrains the activities of individual members of the group, who will probably act on it, given the opportunity.

The collective character of socialization processes has a profound effect on their consequences. Because the solutions the group reaches have, for the individual being socialized, the character of "what everyone knows to be true," he tends to accept them. Random variation in responses that might arise from differences in prior experiences is drastically reduced. Medical students, for instance, began their training with a variety of perspectives on how one ought to approach academic assignments. The pressure generated by their inability to handle the tremendous amount of work given them in the first year anatomy course forced them to adopt collectively one of the many possible solutions to the problem, that of orienting their studying to learning what the faculty was likely to ask about on examinations. (Where the situation does not coerce a completely collective response, variation due to differences in background and experience remains. Irwin and Cressey [13] argue that the behavior of prisoners, both in prison and after release, varies depending on whether the convict was previously a member of the criminal underworld.)

In addition, where the response to problematic situations is collective, members of the group involved develop group loyalties that become part of the environment they must adjust to. Industrial workers are taught by their colleagues to restrict production in order that an entire work group may not be held to the higher production standard one or two people might be able to manage.[14] Medical students, similarly, find that they will only make it harder for others, and eventually for themselves, if they work too hard and "produce" too much.[15]

---

[11] See Anselm L. Strauss, *Mirrors and Masks: The Search for Identity*, New York: The Free Press, 1959; and Howard S. Becker and Anselm L. Strauss, "Careers, Personality and Adult Socialization," *American Journal of Sociology*, 62 (Nov., 1956), pp. 253–63.

[12] William Graham Sumner, *Folkways*, Boston: Ginn and Co., 1907. See also Albert K. Cohen, *Delinquent Boys: The Culture of a Gang*, New York: The Free Press, 1955; and Richard A. Cloward and Lloyd E. Ohlin, *Delinquency and Opportunity: A Theory of Delinquent Gangs*, New York: The Free Press, 1960.

[13] John Irwin and Donald R. Cressey, "Thieves, Convicts and the Inmate Culture," *Social Problems*, 10 (Fall, 1962), pp. 142–55. See also Howard S. Becker and Blanche Geer, "Latent Culture: A Note on the Theory of Latent Social Roles," *Administrative Science Quarterly*, 5 (Sept., 1960), pp. 304–13.

[14] Donald Roy, "Quota Restriction and Goldbricking in a Machine Shop," *American Journal of Sociology*, 57 (Mar., 1952), pp. 427–42.

[15] Becker, *et al.*, *Boys in White*, pp. 297–312.

One major consequence of the collective character of situational adjustment, a result of the factors just mentioned, is that the group being socialized is able to deviate much more from the standards set by those doing the socializing than would be possible for an individual. Where an individual might feel that his deviant response was idiosyncratic, and thus be open to persuasion to change it, the member of a group knows that there are many who think and act just as he does and is therefore more resistant to pressure and propaganda. A person being socialized alone, likewise, is freer to change his ways than one who is constrained by his loyalties to fellow trainees.

If we use situational adjustment as an explanation for changes in persons during adulthood, the most interesting cases for analysis are the negative cases, those instances in which people do not adjust appropriately to the norms implicit or explicit in the situation. For not everyone adjusts to the kind of major situational forces I have been discussing. Some prison inmates never take on criminal values; some college students fail to adopt campus values and therefore do not put forth their full effort in the pursuit of grades. In large part, cases in which it appears that people are not adjusting to situational pressures are cases in which closer analysis reveals that the situation is actually not the same for everyone involved in the institution. A job in the library may effectively remove the prisoner from the control of more criminally oriented prisoners; *his* situation does not constrain him to adopt criminal values. The political rewards owed a student's living group may require a campus organization to give him an office his grade point average would otherwise make it difficult for him to attain.

More generally, it is often the case that subgroups in an institution will often have somewhat different life situations. College, for instance, is clearly one thing for men, another for women; one thing for members of fraternities and sororities, another for independents. We only rarely find an institution as monolithic as the medical school, in which the environment is, especially during the first two years, exactly alike for everyone. So we must make sure that we have discovered the effective environment of those whose personal development we want to understand.

Even after removing the variation in personal change due to variation in the situation, we will find a few cases in which people sturdily resist situational pressures. Here we can expect to find a corresponding weakness in the desire to remain in the situation or to do well in it, or a determination to remain in the situation only on one's terms or as long as one can get what one wants out of it. Many institutions have enough leeway built into them for a clever and determined operator to survive without much adjustment.

Commitment

The process of situational adjustment allows us to account for the changes people undergo as they move through various situations in their adult life. But we also know that people exhibit some consistency as they move from situation to situation. Their behavior is not infinitely mutable, they are not infinitely flexible. How can we account for the consistency we observe?

Social scientists have increasingly turned to the concept of commitment for an explanation of personal consistency in situations which offer conflicting directives. The term has been used to describe a great variety of social-psychological mechanisms, such a variety that it has no stable meaning. Nevertheless, I think we can isolate at least one process referred to by the term commitment, a process which will help explain a great deal of behavioral consistency.[16]

Briefly, we say a person is committed when we observe him pursuing a consistent line of activity in a sequence of varied situations. Consistent activity persists over time. Further, even though the actor may engage in a variety of disparate acts, he sees them as essentially consistent; from his point of view they serve him in pursuit of the same goal. Finally, it is a distinguishing mark of commitment that the actor rejects other situationally feasible alternatives, choosing from among the available courses of action that which best suits his purpose. In so doing, he often ignores the principle of situational adjustment, pursuing his consistent line of activity in the face of a short-term loss.

The process of commitment consists in the linking of previously extraneous and irrelevant lines of action and sets of rewards to a particular line of action under study. If, for instance, a person refuses to change jobs, even though the new job would offer him a higher salary and better working conditions, we should suspect that his decision is a result of commitment, that other sets of rewards than income and working conditions have become attached to his present job so that it would be too painful for him to change. He may have a large pension at stake, which he will lose if he moves; he may dread the cost of making new friends and learning to get along with new working associates; he may feel that he will get a reputation for being flighty and erratic if he leaves his present job. In each instance, formerly extraneous interests have become linked to keeping his present job. I have elsewhere described this process metaphorically as the making of side-bets.

> The committed person has acted in such a way as to involve other interests of his, originally extraneous to the action he is engaged in, directly in that action. By his own actions . . . he has staked something of value to him, something originally unrelated to his present line of action, on being consistent in his present behavior. The consequences of inconsistency will be so expensive that inconsistency . . . is no longer a feasible alternative.[17]

A person may make side-bets producing commitments consciously and deliberately or he may acquire them or have them made for him almost without his knowledge, becoming aware that he is committed only when he faces a difficult decision. Side-bets and commitments of the latter type, made by default, arise from the operation of generalized cultural expectations, from the operation of impersonal bureaucratic arrangements, from the process of individual adjustment to social positions, and through the need to save face.

One way of looking at the process of becoming an adult is to view it as a process of gradually acquiring, through the operation of all these mechanisms, a variety of commitments which constrain one to follow a consistent pattern of behavior in many areas of life. Choosing an occupation, getting a job, starting a family—all these may be seen as events which produce lasting commitments and constrain the person's behavior. Careful study might show that the operation of the process of commitment accounts for the well-known fact that juvenile delinquents seldom become adult criminals, but rather turn into respectable, conventional, law-abiding lower-class citizens. It may be that the erratic behavior of the juvenile

---

[16] Howard S. Becker, "Notes on the Concept of Commitment," *American Journal of Sociology*, 66 (July, 1960), pp. 32–40.

[17] *Ibid.*, p. 35.

delinquent is erratic precisely because the boy has not yet taken any actions which commit him more or less permanently to a given line of endeavor.

Viewing commitment as a set of side-bets encourages us to inquire into the kind of currency with which bets are made in the situation under analysis. What things are valuable enough to make side-bets that matter with? What kinds of counters are used in the game under analysis? Very little research has been done on this problem, but I suspect that erratic behavior and "random" change in adult life result from situations which do not permit people to become committed because they deny to them the means, the chips with which to make side-bets of any importance.

Members of medical faculties complain, for instance, that students' behavior toward patients is erratic. They do not exhibit the continued interest in or devotion to the patient's welfare supposed to characterize the practicing physician. They leave the hospital at five o'clock, even though a patient assigned to them is in critical condition. Their interest in a surgical patient disappears when the academic schedule sends them to a medical ward and a new set of student duties. The reason for students' lack of interest and devotion becomes clear when we consider their frequent complaint that they are not allowed to exercise medical responsibility, to make crucial decisions or carry out important procedures. Their behavior toward patients can be less constrained than that of a practicing physician precisely because they are never allowed to be in a position where they can make a mistake that matters. No patient's life or welfare depends on them; they need not persist in any particular pattern of activity since deviation costs nothing.[18]

The condition of being unable to make important side-bets and thus commit oneself may be more widespread than we think. Indeed, it may well be that the age at which it becomes possible to make lasting and important side-bets is gradually inching up. People cannot become committed to a consistent line of activity until later in life. As divorce becomes more frequent, for instance, the ability to make a lasting commitment by getting married becomes increasingly rare. In studying the possibilities of commitment afforded by social structures, we discover some of the limits to consistent behavior in adult life.

(It might be useful to apply similar concepts in studies of child socialization. It is likely, for instance, that children can seldom commit themselves. Our society, particularly, does not give them the means with which to make substantial side-bets, nor does it think it appropriate for children to make committing side-bets. We view childhood and youth as a time when a person can make mistakes that do not count. Therefore, we would expect children's behavior to be flexible and changeable, as in fact it seems to be.)

Situational adjustment and commitment are closely related, but by no means identical, processes. Situational adjustment produces change; the person shifts his behavior with each shift in the situation. Commitment produces stability; the person subordinates immediate situational interests to goals that lie outside the situation. But a stable situation can evoke a well-adjusted pattern of behavior which itself becomes valuable to the person, one of the counters that has meaning in the game he is playing. He can become committed to preserving the adjustment.

We find another such complementary relationship between the two when we

---

18 Becker, et al., Boys in White, op. cit., pp. 254–73.

consider the length of time one is conventionally expected to spend in a situation, either by oneself or by others, and the degree to which the present situation is seen as having definite connections to important situations anticipated at some later stage of development. If one sees that his present situation is temporary and that later situations will demand something different, the process of adjustment will promote change. If one thinks of the present situation as likely to go on for a long time, he may resist what appear to him temporary situational changes because the strength of the adjustment has committed him to maintaining it. This relationship requires a fuller analysis than I have given it here.

Conclusion

The processes we have considered indicate that social structure creates the conditions for both change and stability in adult life. The structural characteristics of institutions and organizations provide the framework of the situations in which experience dictates the expediency of change. Similarly, they provide the counters with which side-bets can be made and the links between lines of activity out of which commitment grows. Together, they enable us to arrive at general explanations of personal development in adult life without requiring us to posit unvarying characteristics of the person, either elements of personality or of "value structure."

A structural explanation of personal change has important implications for attempts to deliberately mold human behavior. In particular, it suggests that we need not try to develop deep and lasting interests, be they values or personality traits, in order to produce the behavior we want. It is enough to create situations which will coerce people into behaving as we want them to and then to create the conditions under which other rewards will become linked to continuing this behavior. A final medical example will make the point. We can agree, perhaps, that surgeons ought not to operate unless there is a real need to do so; the problem of "unnecessary surgery" has received a great deal of attention both within and outside the medical profession. We might achieve our end by inculcating this rule as a basic value during medical training; or we might use personality tests to select as surgeons only those men whose own needs would lead them to exercise caution. In fact, this problem is approaching solution through a structural innovation: the hospital tissue committee, which examines all tissue removed at surgery and disciplines those surgeons who too frequently remove healthy tissue. Surgeons, whatever their values or personalities, soon learn to be careful when faced with the alternative of exposure or discipline.

59 Alternation and Conversion as Qualitatively Different Transformations

● RICHARD V. TRAVISANO

Kenneth Burke has suggested that every man is a poet. Peter Berger suggests an artist. Ernest Becker suggests a dramatist. They each are concerned with how the individual rationalizes his life; rationalizes, not in the psychological sense of propaganda to conceal "real" motives, but in Weber's sense of legitimizing behavior. Legitimation socializes behavior, and proceeds by labeling behavior with socially understandable categories. This view of human conduct argues that what a man does often has little meaning, rhyme, or reason, until the individual gets busy making autobiographical use of his already completed actions. As Berger has pointed out, we constantly remake our own biographies, and our interpretations and revisions are rarely integrated and consistent: [1]

> . . . Most of us do not set out deliberately to paint a grand portrait of our-selves. Rather we stumble like drunkards over the sprawling canvas of our self-conception, throwing a little paint here, erasing some lines there, never really stopping to obtain a view of the likeness we have produced. . . .

This perspective, then, sees man as an artist who more or less blunders into his biographical materials and then must work them into his story one way or another. From this perspective we wish to distinguish two different kinds of personal transformation.

Constancy and Change

Certainly, as Anselm Strauss has said, "The awareness of constancy of identity . . . is in the eye of the beholder rather than 'in' the behavior itself." [2] The corollary of this statement is that *change* in identity is also in the eye of the beholder. But who *is* this beholder? He is the self-reflective actor, the actor's others, the generalized others, the sociological observer. As identities are retained, discarded, transformed, or assumed, one or more of these observers will note that a change has, or is, taking place. It is they who say how great that change is. Strauss, then, is saying that such permanence as our personal histories have is defined through the give and take of interaction within shared universes of discourse. [3] We add that, as permanence is rationalized into the confusion of contrary

SOURCE: Richard V. Travisano, "Alternation and Conversion as Qualitatively Different Transformations," Original paper prepared especially for this volume.

The formulations in this paper are the outcome of a study the writer did for a Master's thesis. This study was concerned with Jews who had become fundamental Christians and Jews who had become members of a Unitarian Society. Through this work the writer became interested in general conceptualizations about identity change. See Richard V. Travisano, "Alternation and Conversion in Jewish Identities" (unpublished M.A. thesis, Department of Sociology, University of Minnesota, 1967).

[1] Peter L. Berger, *Invitation to Sociology* (Garden City, N.Y.: Anchor Doubleday, 1963), p. 61.

[2] Anselm Strauss, *Mirrors and Masks* (Glencoe, Ill.: The Free Press, 1959), p. 147.

[3] "Universe of discourse" is used in Mead's sense of "a system of common or social meanings." It "is constituted by a group of individuals carrying on and participating in a common social process of experience." See George Herbert Mead, *Mind, Self and Society* (Chicago, Ill.: University of Chicago Press, 1934), pp. 89–90. Peter Berger uses the term "meaning system," to

actions and meaning that make up a life, so also is change. Our task, then, as Nelson Foote has put it, is to apprehend the categories of identity and motive employed by the persons we study.[4]

Peter Berger has succinctly portrayed the flux of life and the ubiquity of personal transformations in it. For him values have become "relativized" in modern society. "Traditional societies assign definite and permanent identities to their members," whereas "In modern society identity itself is uncertain and in flux."[5] He argues that our unprecedented rates of geographical mobility and travel, along with the enormous amount of information available through our mass media "imply at least potentially the awareness that one's own culture, including its basic values, is relative in space and time."[6]

To continue in Berger's words:[7]

> Social mobility . . . augments this relativizing effect. Wherever industrialism occurs, a new dynamism is injected into the social system. Masses of people begin to change their social position, in groups or as individuals. And usually this change is in an "upward" direction. With this movement an individual's biography often involves a considerable journey not only through a variety of social groups but through the intellectual universes that are, so to speak, attached to these groups. Thus the Baptist mail clerk who used to read the *Reader's Digest* becomes an Episcopalian junior executive who reads *The New Yorker*, or the faculty wife whose husband becomes department chairman may graduate from the best-seller list to Proust or Kafka.

Berger then points out that each viewpoint available to modern man carries with it its own slant on some aspect of reality and that,[8]

> . . . the more fully elaborated meaning systems [such as Freudianism or Communism] . . . can provide a total interpretation of reality, within which will be included an interpretation of the alternate systems and of the ways of passing from one system to another.

In reference to these "fully elaborated meaning systems," Berger states:[9]

> Instead of speaking of conversion (a term with religiously charged connotations) we would prefer to use the more neutral term of "alternation" to describe this phenomenon. The intellectual situation just described brings with it the possibility that an individual may alternate back and forth between logically contradictory meaning systems. Each time, the meaning system he enters provides him with an interpretation of his existence and of his world, including in this interpretation an explanation of the meaning system he has abandoned.

It is plain enough that Berger is offering a broad sociological explanation for the prevalence of identity changes in our times (i.e., our society assigns us no definite permanent identity while at the same time exposing us to many alternative universes of discourse). Also, he prefers the term "alternation" to the term

---

denote the same idea. (See Berger, *op. cit.*) We shall use "universe of discourse" for two reasons: first, the word "system" implies integration and universes of discourse contain inconsistencies; second, the term "universe of discourse" emphasizes that meanings are established and exist in symbolic interaction.

[4] Nelson Foote, "Identification as the Basis for a Theory of Motivation," *American Sociological Review*, XVL (1951), p. 18. Reprinted in Part Eight of this volume.

[5] Berger, *op. cit.*, p. 48.

[6] *Ibid.*, p. 49.

[7] *Ibid.*, pp. 49–50.

[8] *Ibid.*, p. 51. The writer prefers the term "total (i.e., closed and all explaining) universes of discourse" to Berger's "fully elaborated meaning systems." Also see footnote 3 above.

[9] *Ibid.*, pp. 51–52.

"conversion." There are, however, certain points to be considered if we are to get at the nature of these transformations.

To begin with, when Berger talks about alternation to "fully elaborated meaning systems" he is referring to what is called conversion in the narrowest everyday sense. These are the most radically reorganizing changes of everyday life: Christian college students become atheists; Jews become fundamental Christians; communists become Catholics. Berger claims that ". . . an individual may alternate back and forth between contradictory meaning systems." This does not seem true. There are contradictions throughout our meanings, but it is the socially recognized and sanctioned contradictions that are central in what we recognize as antithetic universes of discourse. In addition, adoption of antithetic universes of discourse involves a complete reinterpretation and reorganization of life or autobiography. Kenneth Burke insists that conversion involves a change in the "informing aspect" of character.[10] That a person could change quickly back and forth in this respect seems quite unlikely. Experience does leave its mark. As Strauss writes, "one . . . misconception about conversion is that when a person becomes partly converted and then is 'lost' he returns to his previous identity. . . ." [11] Surely the point holds for complete conversion as well as for partial conversion. *One can't go home again.* The black sheep who return to the fold are somehow different from those who never left. Do not the angels rejoice more when one sinner repents? This is not to say that less than totally disruptive transformations do not occur. Middle-class youth, after all, will have their fling before they settle down into the world of meaning in which they were raised. While the break with middle-class respectability may be a conversion for such people, settling back into it is no conversion backwards. It is simply "learning the ropes." The fact is that genuine change back and forth between antithetic total universes of discourse is a rare possibility.

In his definition of alternation, Berger ignores many identity changes which do not involve total universes of discourse. Thus he neglects his own example of the Baptist mail clerk who used to read the *Reader's Digest*, who becomes an Episcopalian junior executive who reads *The New Yorker*. What of this fellow? Do all Baptist organization men undergo total and disruptive reorientations of their lives in becoming Episcopalians? Do they all make the difficult move from one total universe of discourse to another? Certainly not! But surely such a move is a change in perspective, in identity, and in situation. Berger has discussed different kinds of changes, but has grouped them all together under the general term "alternation." We will propose that important and useful distinctions between transformations can and should be made.

Alternation and Conversion as Different Identity Changes

IDENTITY

To discuss and distinguish transformations we shall utilize the concept of identity. It seems best, moreover, to limit our notion of identity by a concise behaviorally objectified definition. Thus, we may follow Stone, who writes: [12]

---

[10] Kenneth Burke, *Permanence and Change* (rev. ed.; Los Altos, Cal.: Hermes Publications, 1954), p. 77.
[11] Strauss, *op. cit.*, p. 123.
[12] Gregory P. Stone, "Appearance and the Self" in Arnold Rose (ed.), *Human Behavior and Social Processes* (Boston: Houghton Mifflin Co., 1962), p. 93. Also reprinted in Part Six in

Almost all writers using the term imply that identity establishes *what* and *where* the person is in social terms. It is not a substitute word for "self." Instead, when one has identity, he is *situated*—that is, cast in the shape of a social object by the acknowledgement of his participation or membership in social relations. One's identity is established when others *place* him as a social object by assigning him the same words of identity that he appropriates for himself or *announces*. . . .

Identity, then, is a placed or validated announcement. One announces that he is some particular social object; others read his cue and respond in kind, saying by their behavior, that he indeed is what he claims. This "coincidence of placements and announcements" gives one the feeling that he embodies what he has announced himself as, that is, gives him an experiential sense of felt identity. But note Stone's phrase: "when one has identity, he is situated . . ." This acknowledges the fact that people must establish identities for *both* themselves *and* others if an interaction is to proceed in any meaningful manner.

ROLE

Every social interaction proceeds in terms of some definition of the situation, and placing people in identities is an important part of that definition.[13] The importance of identities in this regard indicates the crucial nature of the concept. "Role" is a conceptualization of social probabilities. It is impossible to delineate a role completely because a single role demands many different actions in different situations. But "identity" *is* a signal *in interaction* for the mobilization of specific role expectations. Identities are, so to speak, the labels or names on the scripts of various situationally specified programs of behavior which make up the abstract totalities we call roles. Identities tell people what to do and expect during a given interaction. We use the plural because the specified behavior that an identity mobilizes usually depends on the identities of the others in the interaction. A sociologist acts like a sociologist. But what this means depends on where he is interacting—in the classroom, in the office, at home, or wherever else the identity might be relevant.[14] This is nothing new, but it is important because it emphasizes the interactional specificity of role as compared to identity, and the experiential reality of being a thing (say a sociologist) in a specific interaction, as compared to the non-experiential contemplation of being the same thing in general. Identities alone, of course, do not define situations. But we shall bypass, perhaps arbitrarily, a full consideration of the elements and process of situation definition, and simply state that the establishment of identities is usually an important part of the process.[15]

---

this volume. We might add that even in the best available study of identity, the author, for some mysterious reason, refuses to define the central concept. See Strauss, *op. cit.*, p. 13.

[13] On this point see Foote, *op. cit.*, p. 18. Also Strauss, *op. cit.*, p. 43; Erving Goffman, *The Presentation of Self in Everyday Life* (Garden City, N.Y.: Doubleday Anchor, 1959), p. 13; and the plays of Luigi Pirandello, especially *Enrico IV* and *Six Characters in Search of an Author*.

[14] Identities vary in relevance. Practically anyone, six years old or older, could validate the identity "president of the United States." But a six year old child could not validate the identity, "stock broker," as the child has no notion of what a stock broker is, and, more importantly, because the identity, "stock broker," cannot be a meaningful part of the interaction between the man and the child.

[15] Although identities usually play an important part in defining situations, situations often indicate identities, or at least severely limit the range of identities, that can be utilized. When one takes the rostrum before an assembly of dutifully registered students, one has to be a professor.

All this clearly has implications for our discussion of transformation. In the flux of life, it is the changes which get named that are dwelled upon, and the changes dwelled upon that get named. What, then, is the import of these considerations for an analysis of identity change? To establish a new identity, a new announcement must be recurrently made and validated.[16] But one does not take on only an abstract property called an identity, one takes on new definitions of situations and new situated behavior. This may be relatively easy (as when a husband becomes a father) or difficult (as when a wife becomes a divorcee). This relative ease or difficulty depends on how far afield one goes; that is, on whether a new identity is irrelevant, related, or opposed to old ones; on whether old relationshsips are unchanged, transformed, or destroyed. And it is on the interactional contingencies which make for relative ease or difficulty that our distinction between conversion and alternation rests. Complete disruption signals conversion while anything less signals alternation. Summary statements from the research which led to this paper will exemplify the differences in these transformation processes.

Hebrew Christians and Jewish Unitarians: Converts and Alternators

The differences between a Jew becoming a fundamental Christian (a process of conversion) and a Jew becoming a member of a Unitarian Society (a process of alternation) are simply enormous. The "average" Hebrew Christian (the subjects' term for themselves) is about 23 years old at the time of his *conversion*. He is likely to be unsettled in occupation and life style. He very likely had a usual Jewish upbringing, religiously and "culturally," but he is quite unlikely to be a synagogue member at the time of his conversion. If he does hold membership, it will be dropped. His conversion causes serious consternation among his relatives and friends. He is viewed as an apostate, a traitor, and heavy pressure is brought to bear against him. His change changes his life as his conversion and new identity become his central concern. He is quite likely to become a missionary worker by vocation or, at least, to adopt proselytizing as a very serious avocation. He loves to tell the story of his salvation and is, by this and other means, constantly trying to weave together the broken threads of his biography. The Hebrew Christian very definitely identifies himself as a Jew. He has not abandoned his Jewish identity but has transformed it into a Hebrew Christian one. This affords continuity from the past to the demanding new role of "born-again-believer," and it also affords an argument to meet the multitude of challenges that such a drastic change elicits. After all, who can argue with the basic logic of a statement made by one of my respondents:

> I was born a Jew, and now I have accepted the promised Messiah of Israel who came in fulfillment of the Scriptures. Christ came to the Jews. The first Christians were Jews. As a Hebrew Christian I am a completed Jew.

---

[16] Of course, the establishing of identities does not always follow the sequence we have indicated. Sometimes a person will be placed before, or differently, than he announces. He may then acknowledge the placement, or he may deny or ignore it and announce another identity. Such placement before or without announcement sometimes results in identity forcing, i.e., a person is forced to take on an identity which is strange to him or which he would rather avoid. Such identity forcing is much utilized by evangelists of all kinds, from students of Stephen Potter to emulators of Elmer Gantry.

But the focus of the Hebrew Christian identity is fundamental Christianity. The Hebrew Christian is, so to speak, more Christian than Jewish. He probably knows, and spends time with, other Hebrew Christians,[17] but he attends a gentile Christian church and has mostly gentile Christian friends and associates. The Hebrew Christian identity is viable enough, but only in the limited circle of fundamental Christianity.[18] The wider world rejects the Hebrew Christian as logically impossible, or regards him with a suspicious eye. Against the position of this wider world, his old others, and his old self, the Hebrew Christian is always arguing.

The "average" Jewish Unitarian is about 32 years old at the time of his *alternation*. He is settled in occupation and life style. He is likely to have had the usual Jewish upbringing, religiously and "culturally," and there is about a 50 per cent chance that he is a member of a synagogue. If he is a member, he is most likely to retain membership concurrently with Unitarian Society membership. The Jew who joins a Unitarian Society does not feel he has made any significant change. He does not think of himself as a "Jewish Unitarian," and he may not even think of himself as a "Unitarian." One may just be a member of a Unitarian Society, one does not have to accept a new label as definitive of self, and most Jewish Unitarians do not.[19] The Jewish Unitarian usually encounters little or no resistance from family or friends. His change does not change his life but actually can be understood as one of the possibilities in an already established and settled life style or program. Being solid middle- or upper-middle class, "liberal," "humanistic," and usually limited in formal ties to the Jewish community, he finds out about the Unitarian Society from friends or some other source; investigates; and joins. He may attend meetings (they are usually not called "services") regularly, or he may never attend, simply giving monetary support to what he feels is a good organization with good aims. If you ask whether he still considers himself a Jew, he will answer, "Yes, of course," but will consider your question strange and unnecessary. If pressed on this matter, he will suspect you are defining him as an apostate and will greatly resent your labeling his Unitarian Society membership in a way which neither he nor any of his associates, old or new, do. An example from an interview will serve well here. After a series of questions which began with the phrase, "Since you became a Unitarian," a subject exclaimed:

> One thing that bothers me is your phrases. I would say I'm Jewish, and you keep identifying me as a Unitarian. I'm Jewish. There is a Unitarian Society in [another city] where they have candles and robes and crap like that. If that were the case here, you wouldn't be interviewing me.

Clearly, we have in these examples, very different kinds of change. The Hebrew Christian has broken with his past, the Jewish Unitarian has not. The Hebrew Christian has completely reorganized his life, the Jewish Unitarian has not. In short, the Hebrew Christian has a new principle of organization for his action and

---

[17] Glick reports a small sect of Hebrew Christians who had organized their own Hebrew Christian Church and who defined themselves as separate and different from gentile Christians. There was no similar phenomenon where the writer conducted his study. See Ira O. Glick, "The Hebrew Christians: A Marginal Religious Group," in Marshall Sklare (ed.), *The Jews* (Glencoe, Ill.: The Free Press, 1958), pp. 415–431.

[18] Gentile fundamental Christians, it should be noted, are very sensitive to a "holier than thou" attitude in the Hebrew Christian's much-voiced claim that the first Christians were Jews. They often complain about it.

[19] In personal conversation Gladys Stone reports a similar finding among Japanese-Americans. They are Buddhist and Christian concurrently, but don't think of either identity as definitive of self.

autobiography, while the Jewish Unitarian has simply extended his old programs in one of many permissible directions. Symptomatically, the Jewish Unitarian identity is seldom or never central to an interaction, while the Hebrew Christian identity is very often central, and, when it is not, it is usually threatening. We propose to call these distinctly different kinds of change *conversion* and *alternation*.

CONVERSION AND ALTERNATION DISTINGUISHED

Conversions are drastic changes in life. Such changes require a change in the "informing aspect" of one's life or biography. Moreover, there must be a negation (often specifically forbidden) of some former identity. Conversion is signaled by a radical reorganization of identity, meaning, and life. The convert is recognizable by his piety. As William James observed, "To say a man is 'converted' means . . . that religious ideas, previously peripheral in his consciousness, now take a central place, and that religious aims form the habitual centre of his energy." [20] James unnecessarily limited his statement to religious transformations. Of course it is more widely applicable. Kenneth Burke purposely chose an unusual nonreligious example in discussing piety:

> . . . If a man who is a criminal lets the criminal trait in him serve as the informing aspect of his character, piously taking unto him all other traits and habits that he feels should go with his criminality, the criminal deterioration which the moralist with another point of view might discover in him is the very opposite of deterioration as regards the tests of piety. It is *integration*, guided by a scrupulous sense of the appropriate which, once we dismiss our personal locus of judgment, would seem to bear the marks of great conscientiousness. [21]

Conversion, then, involves a change in *informing aspect*. Given the social basis of meanings, such a change implies a change of allegiance from one source of authority to another. [22] Translating into symbolic interactionist terms, we may say that a conversion involves the adoption of a pervasive identity [23] which rests on a change (at least in emphasis) from one universe of discourse to another. Such universes of discourse are, of course, the properties of social groups or authorities. (After all, what is an authority, if not a legislator and guardian of meanings?) We may also note that conversion often involves a period of emotional upset and indecision during which the individual may become severely depressed or confused and may experience emotionally induced somatic upsets. As for the convert's former associates, they are usually disturbed by the convert's new identity and allegiances and may well treat him as a traitor.

[20] William James, *The Varieties of Religious Experiences* (New York: Modern Library, 1929), p. 193. Since James talks about ideas "previously peripheral," we should note that some changes which are called conversions in everyday interaction are not conversions in our sense. Many religious "conversions" do not meet our criterion of a change in universe of discourse. While individuals who "get religion," or "get filled with the Spirit," may experience a period of intense emotional upset and indecision, they are not switching to a new authority or universe of discourse when that "religion" or "Spirit" belongs to their established universe of discourse. Such adoption of the "true believer" identity, whether it is for the first time in an individual's life or is a "regeneration" after a period of "backsliding," is not a conversion in our terminology. On this very point see Kurt and Gladys Engel Lang, *Collective Dynamics* (New York: Thomas Y. Crowell Co., 1961), pp. 154–155.
[21] Burke, *op. cit.*, p. 77.
[22] On the point that conversion involves a change in allegiance, see Lang and Lang, *op. cit.*, p. 157, and Strauss, *op. cit.*, p. 123.
[23] By "pervasive identity" we mean an identity which is made central to many, if not most, interactions.

Finally, we must defend our use of the term "conversion" for this kind of transformation. It is, of course, the traditional term, but Berger suggests "alternation" to escape the religious connotations of "conversion." Yet, given the nature of conversion as distinguished from other changes, the religious connotation is just what is needed. By applying the "religious" word to secular areas (examples are communism, psychoanalysis, and science as an enterprise), social thinkers have gained insight into activities in these areas. Such elucidation through juxtaposition of meanings foreign to each other Kenneth Burke has called "perspective by incongruity." In fact, Burke quite correctly sees conversion itself as a process of perspective by incongruity.[24] "Conversion," then, is an apt word for these changes.

As we saw in our Jewish Unitarian example, there are identity changes which are not so drastic as those we have called conversions. These we propose to call "alternations." These are relatively easily accomplished changes of life which do not involve a radical change in universe of discourse and informing aspect, but which are a part of or grow out of existing programs of behavior. A Baptist mail clerk becomes an Episcopalian junior executive; a high school student becomes a college boy; a husband becomes a father; a professor becomes department chairman. To say such changes are easily accomplished, of course, does not mean that everyone makes them with no trouble whatsoever. Adjustments to college or to fatherhood, for example, are often quite painful and pervasive. But these changes and their attendant problems are provided for in established universes of discourse. The actor is only learning well a new part of a world he was always committed to, with the help of his established others. In conversion, a whole new world is entered, and the old world is transformed through reinterpretation. The father sees his bachelorhood as youthful fun; the convert sees his as debauchery.

Alternations and conversions, then, are different kinds of identity change. Alternations are transitions to identities which are prescribed or at least permitted within the person's established universes of discourse. Conversions are transitions to identities which are proscribed within the person's established universes of discourse, and which exist in universes of discourse that negate these formerly established ones. The ideal typical conversion can be thought of as the embracing of a negative identity.[25] The person becomes something which was specifically prohibited. Thus we might think of a continuum (but infinite gradations are neither implied nor denied at this point). On one side we have the most easily accomplished alternations. One joins a conservation club or perhaps frequents a different bar. Little change is noticed by most of the person's others.[26] There is no trauma. There is little reflection on the part of the actor either before or after. There is no important change in universe of discourse. On the other side we have the most radical of conversions. The person goes through a period of intense

---

[24] Burke, *op. cit.*, pp. 69–163, especially pp. 69–70 and p. 154.

[25] The concept of negative identity is found in Erik H. Erickson's "The Problem of Ego Identity," *Journal of the American Psychoanalytic Association*, IV, No. 1 (1956), pp. 58–121. Essentially the same idea is expressed in the concept of "anti-model" as found in Roy G. Francis, "The Anti-Model as a Theoretical Concept," *The Sociological Quarterly*, IV (Fall, 1963), pp. 197–205.

[26] We are assuming that the person is already a conservationist, or that the person is not a bar "regular." We say *most* of the person's others notice little change because the breaking of even very casual relationships can stir comment from those involved. A friend reports that ending an eighteen-month absence from a bar he had formerly frequented brought him warm welcomes from old associates and the feeling that he was "home." He adds that his return gives these associates the feeling that things are "right," a conviction which they apparently lacked because of his absence.

"inner struggle." There is great trauma. The actor reflects at great length on his change. The actor and all his others see his change as monumental and he is identified by himself and others as a new or different person. The actor has a new universe of discourse which negates the values and meanings of his old ones by exposing the "fallacies" of their assumptions and reasoning. The actor has great involvement with his new identity and perspective.[27] This ideal is approached and reached in Jews who become fundamental Christians, in young intellectuals who become communists, in communists who become monks, and in psychoanalysis.[28]

Identities and Alternations

In this paper we have delimited conversion much more closely than alternation. But since we have designated alternations as the usual changes in life and since we have posited that our lives are riddled with change, the reader might well expect that alternations bear much closer attention than we have given them so far. This indeed is true, and in this final section we shall address some of the problems that will face future thinking and research in what, as shall be seen, is a very difficult area.

We used as examples of alternation: a Baptist mail clerk becoming an Episcopalian junior executive; a high school student becoming a college boy; a husband becoming a father; and a professor becoming a department chairman. Our first two examples involve identities which negate old ones in a fully anticipated way. One identity grows "naturally" out of another. Such changes cause little disruption in the lives of those involved. We may call such linked identities *identity sequences*.[29] Such sequences may involve changes which are somewhat compul-

---

[27] Accuracy is sacrificed here for a simple definition. The actor does not always consider what is happening to him. Especially where new identities grow out of old ones (i.e., husband to father), the person may well find himself in a new identity before he knows it, and then may grieve for his former situation and identity.

[28] For a delightful fictional account of a career from intellectual-to-communist-to-monk see Nigel Dennis, *Cards of Identity* (New York: Meridian Books, 1960), pp. 255–285. For an equally excellent explication of psychoanalysis as a conversion process see Burke, *op. cit.*, pp. 125–129.

[29] I am indebted to Gregory P. Stone for the concept "identity sequence." Stone also makes some useful distinctions between what he calls "identity sets," categorizing relationships between identities as *formal, modal,* and *contingent.* Formal sets include identities which are formally or legally linked—the president of the United States must be thirty-five years old and must be an American citizen. Modal sets are not formally or legally linked, but if a person has one identity in such a set there is a high probability that he will have others—the president is most probably a man. In contingent sets, given one identity, it is neither probable nor required that a person have the other identities involved; but one must be cognizant of them to understand the person's behavior—John F. Kennedy was a Catholic, Muhammad Ali is a Muslim. The terms, "identity set" and "identity sequence" will remind the reader of Merton's similar terms, "status-set" and "status-sequence." Stone prefers his own terms to Merton's because, while every status is an identity, every identity is not a status (e.g., most nicknames).

We may note that Merton also distinguishes "role-sets." What this term indicates, in Merton's own terms, is that a person has many different roles to play within a given status. His example is the medical student, who is a student to his teachers, but something else to fellow students, nurses, medical technicians, etc. Actually, the student is a student in all these situations. It is the behavior and meaning of the identity "medical student" which varies situationally. The identity mobilizes different situationally specified role behavior in different situations. As mentioned earlier in this paper the term "role" rests on the conceptualization of all these possible behaviors. Perhaps "role-set" might be a useful term to adopt since the word "set" reminds one of the situationally specific character of behavior in a way that the word "role" does not. See Robert K. Merton, *Social Theory and Social Structure* (Glencoe, Ill.: The Free Press, 1957), pp. 368–371.

sory (graduate student to Ph.D. or "flunkie") or are a matter of choice or fate (high school student to college boy). Our last two examples, husband to father and professor to department chairman, involve identities which do not replace, but rather are added to, established identities. Again, this happens in an expected way with one identity arising "naturally" out of the other. And again such changes are easily accomplished. We may call these related identities *cumulative identity sequences*. As with non-cumulative identity sequences, changes may be somewhat compulsory (expectant father to husband) or open to choice or chance (spouse to parent). We should also note that some identity sequences are more casual and less insistent than these we have considered. "Liberal," "humanitarian" Jews become Unitarians; nature lovers become conservationists or birdwatchers. These changes are logical; they are extensions or addenda to formerly established programs; they are cumulative identity sequences. But they *are* casual and almost strictly a matter of choice or chance. Relative insistence in identity sequences seems to be *at least in part* dependent on the fact that some sequences (like husband-to-father) are related to formal structure and thus carry relatively binding commitments. For example, a young man may become a casual or frequent dater, a girl-chaser, or an out-and-out rake. He can maintain such an identity for some time. But, once engaged, he is caught in the fiancé-to-spouse (noncumulative) sequence; and, once married, the spouse-to-parent cumulative sequence begins to press. One senses the difference in commitment between the fiancé-to-spouse and spouse-to-parent sequences; the difference between proposing membership in a legally established structure and actually holding membership. When one is betrothed, one is a long way down a "betrayal funnel," [30] yet it clearly is easier to break off an engagement than, once married, to decide against having children.

Having attempted some delineation of the identity linkages that alternation gets people involved in, we may turn to a consideration of the pervasiveness of different identities and identity linkages in interaction.

Identities can be pervasive in two ways: they can be relevant in many situations, and they can be central to interaction. As we have noted, identity is trans-situational while role is situationally specified, and these situationally specific expectations of course mean that the meaning of an identity varies with situation. Some identities are relevant to more situations than others. By relevant we mean that the identity is an important part of the situation. One can be a father at home or at a PTA meeting, but one can't be a father at a faculty meeting. One can leave a faculty meeting early because one is a father who must take a child to the dentist, but in this case the identity is invoked as a motive to legitimate the termination of interaction.[31]

The centrality of an identity is a question of how many situations it can be dominant in. What we need, then, is some classification of identities according to how they usually operate in interaction. Banton has suggested a classification of roles, in terms of their currency in interaction, which is useful to our purpose

---

[30] On "betrayal funnels" see Erving Goffman, *Asylums* (Garden City, N.Y.: Doubleday Anchor, 1961), p. 140.

[31] Stone has discussed how value and mood are differentially relevant to structural and interpersonal interaction respectively. We can see a similar relationship in the case of identities. A secretary is expected to be a worker first and a woman second. But if, when under fire, she bursts into tears, she is making her womanhood foremost in the interaction. If her boss buys this, he is reduced to being a "man helping a woman in distress" and will sheepishly offer her a tissue. See Stone, *op. cit.*, pp. 96–100.

here.[32] In a review of Banton's work, Stone has suggested that identity, not role, was the concept needed, as it is identities, not roles, that persist across situations. Bearing identity in mind, then, let us quote from Stone: [33]

> . . . Banton asks us to distinguish at least three different kinds of role, classified, one might say, in terms of their "stickiness"—the number of situations with reference to which their performance is expected. *Basic roles*, like sex, are usually ascribed and seldom "shaken off." *General roles*, like priest, are not ascribed, but, nevertheless, extend through a variety of situations. *Independent roles*, like golfer, are relatively easy to take up or put down.

We may follow Stone's suggestion and change these concepts to basic, general, and independent identities. Now, as Banton realizes, these distinctions are not hard and fast; but they are at least modal, and they are based on the way identities function in interaction. Basic identities, like sex and age, function most often to help set the ground rules for interaction in terms of language and demeanor. "Basic," then, is an apt description. They are neither central nor secondary to an interaction, rather they are woven throughout it generally without much ado. General and independent identities are more difficult to distinguish. The identity, golfer, certainly is easier to take up and put down than the identity, priest, but it does extend through a variety of situations. One can be a golfer not only on the course, but in the clubhouse, at business luncheons, at cocktail parties, in sporting goods shops, etc. The difference between golfer and priest, however, is the insistence of the priestly identity. Others expect this identity to inform the whole man—he wears a uniform—and so it takes on the quality of a basic identity, i.e., it determines the language and demeanor trans-situationally. It is not a basic identity, however, because it tends to be central to interaction; it is the identity around which the interaction turns. Still, the distinction between general and independent identities is basically sound, and we can see a connection with our concept of identity sequence. Insistent identity sequences, like fiancé-to-husband-to-father, are usually general identities. More casual identity sequences, like nature-lover-to-conservationist-to-birdwatcher, are usually independent identities. Changes in independent identities cause little disruption and are alternations. Changes in general identities can cause much more disruption (one thinks of divorce or of leaving the priesthood) but these also are usually alternations.[34] Changes in basic identities are, of course, seldom made.[35]

Thus far, we have distinguished differences in how identities are linked and

---

[32] Michael Banton, *Roles: An Introduction to the Study of Social Relations* (New York: Basic Books, 1965).

[33] Gregory P. Stone, Review of *Roles: An Introduction to the Study of Social Relations*, by Michael Banton, *American Sociological Review*, XXXI (December, 1966), p. 899.

[34] We say changes in general identities are "usually" alternations because such changes can be conversions. Of course, identity alone does not explain conversion. The keystone of conversion, as we have noted, is a change in "informing aspect." Sometimes (as with monks, nuns, and Black Muslims) converts take a new name to lead their new life with. Just as often, however, converts retain their old identity (as the Hebrew Christian retains the identity "Jew") but build new roles around it. Any transformation, of course, involves continuity, as the paradox of permanence and change is the key to personal life.

[35] Stone, in his review of Banton, points out that modern society has a whole technology (e.g., cosmetics) for changing age. But there are obvious limits to this technology. Besides, one always knows what his age really is, and others are always trying to find out. Where basic identities are really changed, as in sex change operations, society and social psychology are faced with interesting, but perplexing, problems. For a most informative report on the social psychological issues attending a sex change see Harold Garfinkel, *Studies in Ethnomethodology* (Englewood Cliffs, N.J.: Prentice-Hall, 1967), pp. 116–187.

differences in how identities pervade interaction, and we have noted that adoptions of the kinds of identities we have been speaking of are usually alternations. More careful delineation of these issues awaits future work and research. But where, finally, do conversions come in?

CONVERSION AND UBIQUITY

Conversion means a change in informing aspect. When a person converts, his new identity has, from his new perspective, fantastic generality. Converts, as is well known, make their new identity central to almost all interactions. Actually, a conversion may not be merely a *change* in informing aspect but a *discovery* of one. This is the lure of a total universe of discourse. In a life of multiple alternations demanding constant autobiographical revision, most of us, as Berger notes, "do not set out deliberately to paint a grand portrait of ourselves." [36] Yet this is precisely what converts do. Total universes of discourse offer nothing less than the possibility of organizing and explaining an entire life on a single principle. Conversion, then, involves the ubiquitous utilization of an identity.[37]

Now, the adoption of even independent identities often looks something like conversion. We all know zealous golfers, fishermen, or whatever. Every alternation has the incipience of conversion,[38] which is to say that identities can be insisted upon in situations where they are irrelevant. But independent identities

---

[36] Berger, *op. cit.*, p. 61.

[37] This ubiquity, of course, lies in the total universe of discourse in whose terms the identity is defined. It is the total universe of discourse which enables the convert to define almost every situation in his own terms, make every event part of one grand portrait of life. The identities involved in conversions are usually *general* in Banton's terms. They are sometimes *basic* and this raises some very special problems, as changes are called for in what are unquestioned and supposedly unchangeable grounds of interaction. Garfinkel has dealt with this issue insightfully (see footnote 35). The aforementioned Hebrew Christians had, in these terms, taken the general identity "Jew" and transformed it by becoming "completed Jews" who accepted the promised Messiah of Israel. Thus they entered an evangelical (total) universe of discourse which enabled them to utilize ubiquitously their now transformed Jewishness. Being Jewish is a problem in this society. One has to come to terms with it as others can never leave it alone. Some Jews will claim that being Jewish makes no difference one way or the other and some gentiles will agree. But this claim is belied by the frequency of the question, "By the way, are you Jewish?" The Hebrew Christians have come to terms in the most logical way possible in this Christian society. The bother for them is that only other fundamental Christians appreciate their position.

[38] I am indebted to Gregory Stone for this insightful observation. We should note here that while every alternation has the incipience of conversion, the reverse is not true. Conversions cannot be played as alternations in interaction. An example will serve well. One of the writer's informants proved to be a case of what might be called "incomplete conversion." Living far from home with a gentile husband, this subject went along with her husband's suggestion that she become a Christian for the sake of their children. She met a Hebrew Christian woman and attended some social meetings at a nearby mission. In less than a year she joined her husband's church and was baptized. Her story is that simple, and because of the simplicity she was caught in the tensions of trying to maintain conflicting identities. Having embraced Christianity without any "soul-searching" she did not feel certain that she was a Christian, or that she wanted to be one. She feels she may have made a mistake. She knows the line, "The Hebrew Christian is the true complete Jew who has accepted the promised Messiah of Israel," but it means nothing to her. Her family berates her displays of Jewishness and so the only identity she really knows goes unvalidated. One of her final statements to the writer was a display of her Jewishness through an explanation of her predicament in terms of fate or chance, which stands in contradistinction to the fundamental Christian belief in God's direction of His peoples' lives. She said, with a sad smile, "I don't know. Nothing seems to be right for me. I guess I haven't got the mahzel, that's luck in Jewish." This is the outcome of making a change with little thought as if it were an alternation, and finding that the change is socially defined as a drastic one and thus demands a conversion to make it workable.

lack the total universe of discourse which would make them ubiquitous. This is why they are independent. They don't threaten to spill into, and flood out every interaction. And this is what our middle class society prefers. We don't like identity without moderation. We don't like identities to be too general. Outside of ethnic communities, one sees no widow's weeds.

Ours, then, is an age of alternation, but not an age of conversion. Although we complain about the lack of focus and direction in our lives (a lack of informing aspect), we are very suspect of converts, who are people with just such focus and direction. While work (in the face of a consumption society) continues to be our most important focus, we insist that the job be left at the office. We insist that the work identity not be too general. The few people we allow informing aspects and ubiquitous identities to are those closely circumscribed by structure (like priests) or by exclusion (like artists). And we are upset when they are too rabid,[39] like Oral Roberts, or when they aren't devout enough, like the Dutch Catholic hierarchy. The clergy seem to be our official "true believers," and we want no others.[40] We look askance at the many who flock to Oral Roberts, who listen religiously to right wing radio programs, who follow the gospel of Timothy Leary. And we simply do not believe Muhammad Ali. But our dislike for converts does not mean that we don't need them. As Kai Erickson has shown, to know "what one is," one needs examples of "what one isn't" handy for comparison.[41]

60 Adjustments to Conflicting Expectations in the Development of Identification with an Occupation

● JAMES W. CARPER AND HOWARD S. BECKER

Three sets of group expectations [1] influence the development of an individual's social-psychological identification with an occupation: generalized cultural expectations current in the society, specific expectations of the family, and expectations of the occupational group. Cultural expectations direct men in our society to have an occupation, to have one at an appropriate age, and to achieve success in this chosen field. Families elaborate these generalized expectations, setting specific criteria for satisfactory achievement. As the individual becomes involved in and identified with an occupation, he becomes responsive to the particular expectations of his occupational group.

SOURCE: James W. Carper and Howard S. Becker, in *Social Forces*, XXXVI (October 1957), pp. 51–56.

This paper is based on work done while the authors were Ford Foundation postdoctoral fellows at the University of Illinois. We wish to thank the Committee on the Ford Grant of the University of Illinois which also provided funds for clerical assistance. Blanche Geer, Gregory Stone, and Anselm Strauss gave us valuable comments on earlier versions of this paper.

[39] We must note the word "rabid." Anyone who is greatly enthused about something, be it God, birds, or baseball, we label a mad dog.
[40] Perhaps symptomatically for an age of alternation, the Catholic clergy seems to be defecting in greater numbers of late, or at least such defections are getting better press.
[41] Kai T. Erickson, *Wayward Puritans* (New York: John Wiley and Sons, 1966).

[1] These three sets of group expectations function clearly in the development of occupational identity in the professions we have studied. Because of particular requirements and conditions of training other group expectations might be important in other occupations.

In this paper we explore the problems of adjustment which may appear where these three sets of expectations present contradictions and incompatibilities. We base our discussion on interviews carried on with graduate students in three departments in a large state university and gathered in the course of a study of the development of identification with an occupation.[2] All male students of American origin were studied in the mechanical engineering (22) and philosophy departments (11), and a 50 percent random sample of students in the physiology department (18). The interviews were tape recorded, and ranged in length from one-half to two hours. Students at all levels of graduate work from the first year to those about to receive their Ph.D. were included. The same areas of interest were covered in all interviews, but the form in which questions were put to elicit material varied.

Of the three groups, the engineers exhibited few problems in the assumption of their occupational roles, while the philosophers and physiologists, in varying degrees and ways, did. We first present short descriptions of the problems of adjustment and solutions to these which are characteristic of each group, and follow this with a more general discussion which attempts to set up a model in whose terms the forces and processes involved can be analyzed fruitfully.

Engineers

Any problems of adjustment faced by the engineering student in graduate school are solved by the feeling of success he has already achieved, or sees as being just around the corner. He has viewed himself as an engineer since receiving his Bachelor's degree and probably before that time; the knowledge that he can at any time get a highly-paid job supports this view. He comes to graduate school only to broaden the avenues of success already available to him by acquiring more knowledge. At an early age, during his undergraduate training, he has clearly met the formal expectation that he have a profession and it becomes more and more clear that success within this profession can easily be had.

The young engineer has few problems meeting his family's expectations. Most come from the families of skilled workmen; a few have fathers in farming, engineering, business, or small trades. Most indicate that their families wanted them to enter an occupation of higher prestige than the father's, but did not insist on any particular occupation. The choice of engineering met these expectations by placing them (potentially or actually) in positions in industry which can be understood by their parents as positions of prestige and high economic return. All report their parents happy with the choice, some pointing out that their fathers had worked in industrial organizations with engineers, had looked up to them, and thus have a clear image of the worth of this position. In one case where there was some doubt on this point, the interviewee felt that the growing

[2] Other aspects of the study are reported in Howard S. Becker and James W. Carper, "The Development of Identification with an Occupation," *American Journal of Sociology*, 61 (January 1956), pp. 289–98, and "The Elements of Identification with an Occupation," *American Sociological Review*, 21 (June 1956), pp. 341–48. They contain further details on the students interviewed as well as more detailed discussions of the characteristics of the occupational identities of the three groups and the processes through which they develop. It should be noted that these students attended a large state university which may recruit from lower levels in the class structure; for this reason, it is possible and even likely that there are important differences between them and students in the same fields at other kinds of universities.

professionalization of engineering would allow him to satisfy his family's more specific desire that he become a "professional man."

The fact that engineers take their place in a rapidly expanding industrial system, and that there are a number of alternative routes upward for them in industry—sales, production, design, management—means that the professional ideology fostering this feeling of inevitable success has some basis in fact. It is, in consequence, extremely effective in minimizing potential conflict over occupational choice.

Physiologists

Of the 18 physiology students 14 had at some time wanted a medical degree, but found it either impossible to get accepted into medical school or the pace is too difficult to continue. This desire, if not originally fostered by parents, is steadfastly maintained by them, and the failure to get into medicine is a failure to meet specific parental expectations. These families tend to be of a kind that can present their desires in a way the individual must take account of, being stable well-knit families in which the fathers play strong male roles; they are not so culturally foreign as to allow the sons to discount their understanding of the occupational world.

All the students who have failed at medicine must find another life's work. Those whose early ambitions carry them as far as applying to medical school are slow to accept this and turn to physiology as a stop-gap measure. This allows them to mark time while making further efforts to enter medical school and yet study something that will be of use in the medical career for which they still strive. As this becomes increasingly unrealistic and they find themselves in need of an alternate career, they turn to physiology (to which they are already partially committed). Because they are still sensitive to their families' specific desires that they achieve social success through a medical career, they find it necessary to justify their new careers, and do this in various ways. They point out, both to themselves and their parents, that they will "still be doctors," albeit Ph.D.'s rather than M.D.'s, and will work in close association with medical men, perhaps teaching in a medical school.

More importantly, they may choose among the alternative careers available to a physiologist in such a way as most nearly to meet their parents' expectations. For example, some consider careers in commercial research because these pay well, hoping thus to approximate the income their parents expected them to achieve as physicians. In fact, the positions they will probably achieve in the academic or research worlds carry more prestige than the positions of their predominantly lower-middle class parents; but the position of physiologist does not seem as good to the parents as that of the M.D., because it is not as easily understood. The parents' own experiences with doctors are more real to them than all of the son's references to Nobel Prize winners and famous professors, none of which convince them that physiology is really as good a thing for their boy.

By the time this problem arises, many have come to accept wholeheartedly the profession's ideology, which spells out in detail the reasons for considering physiology superior to medicine; failing to meet family expectations, they fall back on this ideology as a way of denying the validity of their parents' claims.

Philosophers

Graduate study of philosophy does not represent an occupational commitment for the student, but rather acceptance of a way of life which bars commitment to any specific set of tasks or any particular set of organizational positions. He wishes to remain free to broaden himself intellectually in whatever directions he thinks appropriate, not fully admitting or realizing that he is preparing for a life in academia. To specialize, to have an occupational commitment, is something to be avoided; to strive for success by the standards of society at large is no virtue and may even be conceived as "immoral." These students do not, at this point, feel any compulsion to respond to generalized expectations that they have an occupation, since they accept the view that by the standards of "normal" society they are deviant.

Viewing a Ph.D. degree as the best way to realize these broad intellectual interests, they are forced, on finishing undergraduate work, to choose a specialty. The choice of philosophy makes it apparent for the first time that they are not going to meet the expectations of their parents for, though none of the families had any very specific expectations for their sons' futures, they now realize that they did not want them to become philosophers. Before this choice is made the family is able to explain away their concern over their sons' shifting from subject to subject in terms of a more or less legitimate period of youthful exploration. Once it is made, however, the disparity between the perspectives of parents and child are brought into clear focus.

But by this time the student is of an age where parental expectations are easily discounted, more easily because these students tend to come from families whose desires can be ignored with equanimity. In every case but one, the students came from homes where the parents were foreign-born or divorced, where one parent was dead or the father did not play a strong masculine role; there was no functioning group capable of presenting cultural imperatives forcefully. Their parents do not understand what it means to be a philosopher, but this makes little difference and produces few problems of adjustment because there is no effective power to enforce family disapproval.

The study of philosophy represents a definite rejection of conventional occupational expectations buttressed by the ideology current among their fellow students, both in philosophy and other fields in which they have contacts. This ideology specifies the importance of free, wide-ranging intellectual activity, not tied to any specific academic discipline, and finds support both historically and in current academic life.

Discussion

In what follows we present a model of the interaction between family and occupational expectations in the development of an individual's occupational identity. Our case material does not provide proof that the relations discussed are correctly stated,[3] but the model has been built by trying to take account of the several orders of things described in our interviews.

A set of generalized cultural expectations about the relation of an adult male to the work world operates in our society. Occupation is one of the major

---

[3] We are now undertaking more definitive tests, based on an analysis of questionnaire data from a much larger sample, of the propositions stated in this and earlier reports on the research.

determinants of social-class position and in other ways as well is one of the important criteria by which individuals are socially identified. At a given age (which varies in different parts of the society) a man is expected to have assumed (or committed himself to the training necessary to assume) a particular occupational role. Such adult responsibilities as marriage require him to have made arrangements guaranteeing the financial independence necessary for adulthood by making such an occupational commitment. With increasing age he is expected to behave "sensibly" and stick with such a choice once made, thus demonstrating his maturity and avoiding the loss of time and training involved in an occupational change. Finally, it is generally expected (although this expectation is no doubt violated more frequently than the others) that he will be "successful" (whatever that may mean) at his chosen work and that this success will aid in social-class mobility. Our society confronts adult males with the necessity of satisfying or otherwise adjusting to this set of generalized expectations.

These cultural expectations are probably presented most forcefully to the young individual in the form of specific expectations of his family, which translate such general dicta into specific and strong imperatives, backed by the family's sanctioning power. These family expectations tend to be specific statements of the more general mobility theme, directing the person to achieve mobility in a particular way, through success in one or a few kinds of occupations. To the degree that these expectations can be met only in one or a few ways, the individual feels his chances of failure to be greater and thus feels under greater pressure.

Families may differ in the specificity of their aspirations for their children and thus in the number of potential mobility routes they see as possibilities.[4] Those with specific notions begin grooming the child for the chosen profession at an early age, focusing attention on their desires through frequent references to the profession, to relatives and acquaintances in it, and so on. Such focusing constrains the child's choice, causing it to be made earlier. Constraint of this kind may be ineffective if the family lacks the authority to enforce its decisions on the child. If a son considers his family well-informed about the occupational world, it will have greater authority than one whose perspectives are regarded as limited and unrealistic. If, for example, the father or some other close relative or family friend is a member of the desired profession, the family will be regarded as knowledgeable and its desires will of necessity be taken seriously. Equally, if the child chooses a well-known profession (as the engineering student does) he may agree that, by virtue of general public knowledge, his family is well informed.

In the same way, a family's authority will likely vary with the degree to which it conforms to socially defined patterns of family organization. A family in which the parents are foreign born, poverty stricken, or socially nonconforming may find the son able, through reference to these characteristics, to discount their desires for his future. Similarly, families in which the parents are separated, in which one parent is dead, or in which the father does not play a dominant male role, are not in a position to use the father's traditional sanctioning power in affecting the son's career choices.

---

[4] In a study in which parents were asked what information they would consider important about a potential son-in-law, respondents from the lower socio-economic strata mentioned, among other items, whether he had a job and whether he was a good provider, while middle-stratum respondents were more concerned about his specific occupation. The study is reported in William H. Form and Gregory P. Stone, "Urbanism, Anonymity, and Status Symbolism," *American Journal of Sociology*, LXII (March 1957), 512.

Families with expectations of a more general kind allow the youth a much freer range in choosing a career and also allow him to postpone any choice until a later date. He can experiment longer and try out more possibilities, as did the philosophy students in our study. When the choice is finally made, however, it may turn out to be incompatible with the family's implicit expectations; they may have felt, as the philosophers' parents apparently did, that anything their son wanted to do was all right until they found out how far afield he had drifted. But in such cases conflict and the discovery of incompatibility are postponed till a relatively late date.

One of the consequences of such postponement is that by the time difficulties arise the person may be well on the way to commitment to an occupation. Once so committed, he acquires the option of viewing the situation from the perspective of the occupational group, and thus of becoming relatively less sensitive to his family's desires. The philosophers' parents do not realize their sons' deviant aspirations until the sons are well indoctrinated with an intellectual ideology which makes the ultimate break with family easy and painless.

It is not always necessary or possible for an individual to make use of occupational group perspectives in this way. In the first place, the person who has successfully met parental expectations, as have the engineering students, has no need for an alternative perspective with which to dismiss those expectations. He has no need for answers to parental criticism, for there is no criticism. In the second place, a person who has committed himself to something his family wanted and failed at it (as have those physiologists who intended to become physicians), finds himself unable to make use of occupational perspectives readily since he himself shares the view of his parents. Still trying to please them and thereby himself, he cannot so easily write off their desires from his new occupational point of view.

Approaching the problem in a different way, let us note that some occupations require very early commitment, while others can be entered later in one's career. One cannot easily decide to become a doctor at the age of 25; 15 or 16 is nearer the proper age to make such a choice. But the decision to become a philosopher can be made at 25 with little difficulty. When an occupation requiring early commitment is chosen, it is typically chosen by the family and individual together; it is not a step that an adolescent makes alone. Such choices may be unrealistic from the point of view of the young man involved. He tends to know less of the realities of the profession he has chosen than a man who makes his choice after he has had more opportunity to explore and observe the work world. This early uninformed choice, in its turn, increases the possibility that he will not be able to meet successfully the problems of his chosen career or that he will find he does not like it after all and would prefer something else. In either case, he will fail to meet his family's expectations and provoke conflict with them.

When the son chooses his father's occupation, the choice is also made early, but is much more likely to be made realistically. As Hall pointed out, the boy from a medical family chooses a career about which he knows a good deal at an early age.[5] Further, he will probably be given systematic encouragement and effective assistance in pursuing this career. If tension arises, it is likely to be over the son's failure to take advantage of this assistance, either through his failure to meet professional standards or his discovery that there is something he likes better.

---

[5] Oswald Hall, "The Stages of a Medical Career," *American Journal of Sociology*, 53 (March 1949), pp. 327–37.

As previously noted, the occupational groups to which these young men become committed have characteristic professional ideologies which specify the kinds of relations proper between members of the occupation and between them and persons who do not belong to the occupational group. These ideologies function to keep people in the occupation despite tensions produced by incompatible family expectations. Anticipating future difficulties and knotty questions which families are likely to raise, they provide models for action and ready answers to objections. For instance, the philosophers acquire a set of conceptions of the intellectual which explains why he must ignore the pressure of a "middle-class family" and indeed the pressure of a middle-class culture to settle down to a specific occupation. Similarly, the young physiologist learns to believe that his profession is really superior to that of the physician, to believe that, as one of our interviewees put it, "we write the music that the doctor plays" (that is, do the research without which medical diagnosis and treatment would not be possible). This ideology warns them that questions will be raised by the uninformed and provides the answers which make remaining in the profession a reasonable thing.

Such occupational ideologies will become working guides for action only when the person feels them legitimate, ordinarily only when he finds some kind of socially based support for them. Such support can be found in a variety of ways. The physiologists find it in a close-knit clique organization of student life, in which older students continuously indoctrinate younger ones in the same way they are themselves indoctrinated by their professors. They find support in the opinions of those above them in the graduate school and occupational hierarchy. The engineers find their support for an ideology of rapid and inevitable success in their experiences in the work world; the actions and statements of employers, present and potential, bear out the predictions of the ideology. The philosophers find their support in participation in an abstract intellectual "world," an amorphous grouping of those with similar cultural and intellectual interests which finds its concrete expressions in the writings and other productions of its members.

Under what circumstances does one rather than another source of such socially based support become prominent for a given group? Apparently this depends on who else understands one's career problems, and the degree of understanding and sympathy on the part of others whose opinion is considered important. Both the engineers and physiologists consider it important that their parents understand the character of their careers. But the engineer's career, essentially that of an industrial executive, is often discussed and portrayed in popular culture; since parents can be counted on, because of this, to understand, no support is needed from elsewhere. The physiologist, on the other hand, has embarked on a career whose inner workings and peculiar successes and failures are incomprehensible to his parents; if he is to meet successfully the problems his career creates in his relations with them he must find support, as he does, in an actual functioning group of colleagues. The philosopher, like the engineer, does not require such well-organized colleague support because, in his case, the ideology is self-confirming to a very great degree. It formally dismisses the necessity for worrying about parents' expectations on the grounds that they simply do not understand; when their actions bear out this prediction the philosopher is able to turn to the intellectual world freely, unencumbered by worry over his family's feelings.

Conclusion

It is often assumed that problems of adjustment are inevitably present for persons involved in important steps of their life career: adolescence, marriage, the choice of an occupation, and so on. Because our society is so heterogeneous and lacking in specific rules directing behavior at these points of crisis, the individual is said to be faced with conflicting expectations. Choice between these expectations is viewed as problematic and productive of problems of adjustment.

Our analysis indicates that conflict does not necessarily occur in assuming an occupational identity. When conflict does occur it centers around disparities between parental and occupational expectations. The following elements are importantly involved in the process: the specificity of family desires and the power of the family to make these felt, the character of the commitment and the time at which it is required by particular occupations, the nature of the occupational ideology and the kinds of social support for it, and the timing of appearance of incompatibilities between family and occupational expectations. It is the relationship among these that determines whether or not conflict and the necessity of adjustment will occur.

61   Changes in Status and Age Identification

● ZENA SMITH BLAU

The conceptions individuals have of themselves as young, middle-aged, or old are, of course, related to their actual age. People in their sixties are certainly more likely than people in their thirties to think of themselves as old. But the variations in age identification between persons in the same age group and the similarities between those whose actual age differs indicate that chronological age is only a limiting condition and does not fully explain the changes in age identification that occur in the course of the individual's life span.

In this paper two topics will be discussed: first, the relative influence of chronological age and age identification on other aspects of the self-image of older persons, and second, some of the social factors that hasten or forestall changes in age identification among older people.

A representative sample of 468 people 60 years old and over in Elmira, New York, were asked: "How do you think of yourself as far as age goes—middle-aged, elderly, old, or what?" Fully 60 per cent of the respondents considered themselves middle-aged, 38 per cent described themselves as old, elderly, or used an equivalent euphemism, and 2 per cent gave no answer to the question.

Of course, the likelihood that people consider themselves old rather than

SOURCE: Zena Smith Blau, in *American Sociological Review*, XXI (April 1956), pp. 198–203. Reprinted by permission of the American Sociological Association.

Paper read at the annual meeting of the American Sociological Society, September, 1955. The data presented in this paper are part of a series of studies in social gerontology being conducted by the Department of Sociology and Anthropology at Cornell University under the direction of M. Barron, J. Dean, B. Kutner, G. Streib, and E. Suchman, aided by grants from the Rockefeller and Lilly Foundations. I wish to express my gratitude to all concerned for the use of these data.

middle-aged steadily increases as they grow older. Under 65, only 18 per cent define themselves as old, between 65 and 70, 37 per cent do so, but in the age group of 70 and over this proportion rises to 59 per cent. Old age is, after all, something more than a state of mind, since the aging process is marked by objective physical and behavioral changes. Although these changes usually occur gradually and, therefore, do not immediately intrude upon the consciousness of the individual, one might expect that they become increasingly apparent to him and his associates as the years pass and thus finally bring about identification with old people. Indeed, when asked "How much have you changed in the past 10 or 15 years— would you say hardly at all, somewhat or a good deal?" less than a fifth of those under 70, compared to a third of those who are 70 or over, feel that they have changed "a good deal." (See Table 1.)

TABLE 1   Per Cent Who Perceive "A Good Deal" of Change in Self by Age Identification and Age

| | Age Identification | | |
Age	Middle-aged	Old	Total
Under 70	15 (206)	42 (31)	18 * (273)
70 and over	22 (73)	40 (88)	33 * (175)

* This difference is significant on the .01 level. Numbers in parentheses in all tables are the numbers of cases on which percentages are based.

However, if age identification is held constant, this relationship between chronological age and perceived change in oneself tends to disappear. These findings suggest that while objective changes mark the aging process, a shift in age identification is a crucial intervening variable for perceiving them. Not all older people, but only those who have shifted their age identification are likely to perceive these changes in themselves.[1] It seems that neither the knowledge of their years, nor even their white hair and wrinkles, induce older people to perceive that they have changed. As Proust writes: [2]

> It does us no good to know that the years go by, that youth gives way to old age, that the most stable thrones and fortunes crumble, that fame is ephemeral—our way of forming a conception—and so to speak, taking a photograph of this moving universe, hurried along by time, seeks on the contrary to make it stand still.

And so, to borrow Proust's metaphor, it is the conception of himself as old, and not the weight of his years as such, that constrains the older person to relinquish the photograph and reluctantly to substitute the mirror.

A similar phenomenon can be observed in respect to the older person's beliefs about the image his significant others have of him. The older people are, the more frequently do they answer affirmatively when asked, "Do you think that the peo-

[1] Although it is not known whether the shift in age identification or the perception of changes in self occurs first, there is some indirect evidence on this point. It was shown in the text that the relationship between chronological age and perception of changes in the self disappears when age identification is held constant. But if perceived change in self is held constant, the relationship between age and age identification persists. This suggests that a shift in age identification precedes and produces an increased awareness of changes in the self, and not vice-versa. For a discussion of this method of inferring the direction of influence between two variables see Peter M. Blau, "Determining the Dependent Variable in Certain Correlations," *Public Opinion Quarterly*, 19 (Spring, 1955), pp. 100–105.

[2] Marcel Proust, *Remembrance of Things Past*, New York: Random House, 1927, Vol. 2, p. 1063.

ple you see and care most about think of you as an old man (woman)?" Only about one eighth of those under 70, but a third of those who are 70 and over feel that their close associates consider them old. (See Table 2.) This relationship, however, also tends to disappear if the age identification of respondents is controlled. In other words, regardless of their actual age, people come to believe that *others* consider them old only if they consider *themselves* old.[3]

TABLE 2   *Per Cent Saying That Significant Others Consider Them Old by Age Identification and Age*

	Age Identification		
Age	Middle-aged	Old	Total
Under 70	7 (206)	45 (31)	13 * (276)
70 and over	14 (73)	50 (88)	32 * (187)

* This difference is significant on the .01 level.

In sum, various mental states that characterize older people and distinguish them from others are actually precipitated by shifts in age identification from middle-aged to old. The important question consequently becomes: What are the social conditions that hasten or forestall such shifts in age identification? The rest of the discussion will be devoted to an examination of this question.

In youth and middle-age, the loss of one social status is generally accompanied by entry into another. For example, the status of student is relinquished for a position in the occupational structure, or the young woman may give up her career to become a wife and mother. In contrast, retirement and widowhood, the two major status changes that typically occur in old age, designate the permanent loss of two crucially important social roles and the activities and relationships that define them.[4] It could be expected that these changes in social status of older persons are responsible for shifts in age identification among them, but the data only partly confirm this expectation.

Retirants, at each age level, do indeed consider themselves old more frequently than those who are still employed, but the widowed are not significantly different from the married in this respect. Under 70, less than a fifth of the employed, but more than a third of the retirants identify themselves as old. Among those who are 70 and over, 14 per cent of the employed, but fully two thirds of the retired, regard themselves as old. (See Table 3.) In contrast, at each age level, widowed people consider themselves old hardly more often than those who are still married. (See Table 4.)

The remark of a retirant suggests one of the reasons why retirement predisposes the older person to define himself as old.

> When did I start to feel old? Why, when I stopped working. I was always real proud that I'd come to Chicago and got a job and supported myself. Then when I couldn't work anymore, why I wasn't good for anything.[5]

[3] If, instead of controlling age identification, the beliefs respondents hold about the attitudes of their significant others are controlled, the relationship between age and age identification remains, which indicates that the sequence suggested in the text is the correct one.

[4] For a brief but suggestive discussion of this point see Talcott Parsons, "Age and Sex in the Social Structure of the United States," *American Sociological Review,* 7 (October, 1942), pp. 604–616.

[5] From an interview in William H. Harlan, "Isolation and Conduct in Later Life," Ph.D. dissertation, University of Chicago, 1950.

TABLE 3   *Per Cent Identified as Old by Age and Employment Status*

| Employment | Age | | |
Status	Under 70	70 and Over	Total
Employed	18 (136)	41 (37)	24 (170)
Retired	37 (41)	67 (57)	57 (93)

All differences are significant on the .05 level.

TABLE 4   *Per Cent Identified as Old by Age and Marital Status*

| Marital | Age | | |
Status	Under 70	70 and Over	Total
Married	22 (160)	55 (65)	33 (218)
Widowed	26 (81)	60 (99)	46 (173)

Retirement is a *social* pattern which implies an invidious judgment on the part of others in the society about the lack of fitness of old people to perform a culturally significant role, whereas the death of the marital partner, being a natural event, and not a socially induced one, does not have such implications in our culture. Thus, the retired individual, but not the widowed one, has reason to believe that he is socially defined as old.

Furthermore, retirement removes the individual from a social peer group and thereby disrupts the informal relations developed on the job. The death of the marital partner, on the other hand, disrupts a single, albeit a very significant, social relationship.[6] In other words, the hypothesis is suggested that loss of membership in a peer *group* has more pronounced effects on the self-image of older people than the loss of an intimate interpersonal relationship, and that this helps to explain the differential effect of retirement and widowhood on age identification.

This hypothesis can be tested by determining whether membership in a friendship clique is, indeed, more significant for age identification than relationships with individual friends.

Respondents were asked three questions about their social participation: "How many really close friends do you have here in town that you occasionally talk over confidential matters with?" "Now think of the friend that you know best here in town—how often do you get to see that friend?" and "Would you say you go around with a certain bunch of close friends who visit back and forth in each other's homes?"

Neither the number of friendships nor the frequency of contact with the closest friend is significantly related to age identification. But older people who belong to a friendship clique consider themselves old significantly less often than those who do not participate in such a group. Only 29 per cent of the members, in contrast to 41 per cent of the non-members, regard themselves as old. (See Table 5.) However, this relationship may be a spurious one, since, as they grow older, people tend to participate less in friendship groups, and they also are more likely to think of themselves as old.

[6] Of course, under some conditions, widowhood may also have a detrimental effect on group memberships of the individual. For example, the surviving marital partner may drop out of those friendship groups in which the marital couple had participated jointly, or discontinue membership in "auxiliary" organizations, that is, where participation of the wife is contingent on that of her husband.

TABLE 5   *Per Cent Identified as Old by Age and Membership
in a Friendship Group*

Friendship Group	Age		
	Under 70	70 and Over	Total
Member	20 (115)	49 (53)	29 * (168)
Non-member	24 (164)	63 (136)	41 * (300)

* This difference is significant on the .05 level.

Indeed, when age is controlled, the relationship between clique membership and age identification disappears among those who are under 70. The vast majority under 70 still define themselves as middle-aged whether or not they belong to a friendship group. But among people who are 70 and over clique membership makes a considerable difference for age identification. Only half of those who participate in a friendship group, but nearly two thirds of the others consider themselves old.

The fact that participation in a friendship clique makes no difference for age identification in the younger group only *appears* to refute the hypothesis that group memberships are more effective in forestalling old age than single relationships. Actually, this hypothesis helps to explain why participation in a friendship clique is less important in the younger than in the older age group. People under 70 are likely to have alternative group memberships. For example, since a majority of the men in this age group are still employed, they participate in work groups and other occupational groups. Younger women, as well, participate more in clubs and organizations than those who are older. Thus, it makes little difference whether or not they also participate in a friendship group as such. But after 70, when participation in these other social groups is the exception rather than the rule, the person's position in a friendship group becomes more important in forestalling a shift in age identification.

Similarly, the belief that his close associates consider him old is influenced by the individual's participation in a social peer group, but not by the number of friends he has. Regardless of their age, those who belong to such a group less often hold this belief than those who do not. (See Table 6.) Indeed, among people 70 and over, two-thirds of the clique members, compared to less than half of the others, deny that their associates consider them old.

These indications that participation in a social group more effectively forestalls the psychological changes that mark old age than participation in a number of dyadic relationships can be explained by the emergent properties that characterize social groups. Studies of various types of small groups by Roethlisberger and

TABLE 6   *Per Cent Denying That Significant Others Consider Them Old
by Age and Membership in a Friendship Group*

Friendship Group	Age		
	Under 70	70 and Over	Total
Member	87 (115)	64 * (53)	80 † (168)
Non-member	73 (164)	45 * (135)	60 † (300)

* This difference is significant on the .05 level.
† This difference is significant on the .01 level.

Dickson, Whyte, Homans and Bales,[7] show that recurrent interaction between individuals tends to fix the role of each member relative to the others in the group. The images and expectations that arise among the group members tend to persist and to influence their subsequent behavior toward one another. The stability of the network of relationships within a group of friends or co-workers prevents mutual awareness of gradual alterations that take place in each of the participants, particularly if these changes in the person do not interfere with his ability to share in the activities of the group. Consequently, the recurrent gatherings of the same people lend a sense of continuity to the life of each participant. An incongruous but revealing manifestation of this feeling of immutability provided by the groups is the practice of people who have grown old together to continue to refer to themselves as "the boys" or "the girls."

Participation in a friendship group does, indeed, serve to postpone shifts in age identification, and this provides support for the hypothesis that loss of the work group is one of the reasons why retirement influences the age identification of older persons more than widowhood. Further clarification of these relationships can be achieved by simultaneously comparing the relative impact of widowhood and retirement on age identification among those who do and do not participate in a friendship group.

Table 7 shows the relationship between friendship group, marital status, and age identification. Among those who are part of a friendship group, widowed people consider themselves old, hardly more often than married ones—34 per cent as against 29 per cent, a difference of only 5 per cent. However, among those who are not clique members, the widowed define themselves as old considerably more often than the married—51 per cent as against 35 per cent, a difference of 16 per cent. The death of the marital partner, even though it is a natural event, is more likely to precipitate "old age," if the elderly person does not participate in a friendship group.

TABLE 7   *Per Cent Identified as Old by Membership*
in a Friendship Group and Marital Status

Marital Status	Friendship Group		
	Member	*Non-member*	*Total*
Married	29 (85)	35 * (133)	33 (218)
Widowed	34 (53)	51 * (121)	46 (174)
Difference	5	16	

* This difference, as well as that between proportions among totals, is significant on the .05 level.

Membership in a friendship clique has similar implications for age identification following retirement. (See Table 8.) Among those who do not belong to a friendship group, nearly two-thirds of the retired, compared to only a quarter of the employed, consider themselves old, a difference of 37 per cent. Loss of employment status makes less difference if people are members of a friendship group:

[7] See F. J. Roethlisberger and William J. Dickson, *Management and the Worker*, Cambridge: Harvard University Press, 1930; William F. Whyte, *Street Corner Society*, Chicago: University of Chicago Press, 1943; George C. Homans, *The Human Group*, New York: Harcourt Brace and Company, 1950; and Robert F. Bales, *et al.*, "Channels of Communication in Small Groups," *American Sociological Review*, 16 (August, 1951), pp. 461–468.

42 per cent of the retired and 21 per cent of the employed feel that they are old—
a difference of 21 per cent. Thus, either change in social status is less likely to

TABLE 8   *Per Cent Identified as Old by Membership
in a Friendship Group and Employment Status*

Employment Status	Friendship Group		
	Member	*Non-member*	*Total*
Employed	21 (66)	25 * (104)	24 (170)
Retired	42 (24)	62 * (69)	57 (93)
Difference	21	37	

* This difference, as well as that between proportions among totals, is significant on the .01 level.

produce identification with the "old" if the older person maintains his position in
a group of peers. However, the friendship group is less effective in preventing
the consequences of retirement than those of widowhood. Among those who have
a group of friends, twice as many of the retired as of the employed consider themselves old, but hardly any more of the widowed than of the married do so.

Thus, the data that support one of the two explanatory hypotheses advanced to
account for the finding that retirement influences the age identification of older
people more than widowhood, furnish indirect evidence for the other one as well.
Group memberships are indeed more effective than even intimate dyadic relations
in postponing identification with the old, but this factor alone does not account
for the differential effects of retirement and widowhood on age identification.
Loss of employment status, as a socially induced event, implies a judgment on the
part of others that an individual is old, and this is an additional reason why it influences his age identification more than does widowhood, which, as a natural
event, is devoid of such a social judgment in our culture.

To summarize: The socio-psychological and physical aging processes can be
analytically distinguished. Age identification rather than actual age constrains older
people to recognize changes in themselves and to perceive that the attitudes of
others toward them have changed. Analysis revealed that of the two major
changes in social status that commonly occur in old age—retirement and widowhood—only retirement appears to hasten the onset of old age. Two hypotheses
were advanced to explain this difference: one, retirement implies a social judgment that the person has become old, whereas widowhood, because it comes about
through a natural event, does not have this implication for the older person; two,
retirement has more serious consequences for age identification because it removes the individual from a significant peer group, whereas death of the spouse
directly disrupts only a single, albeit a highly significant, relationship. The finding that participation in a friendship group serves to forestall a shift in age identification, but that the number of close friends and the frequency of contact with
one's closest friend do not, provides support for the second hypothesis. However,
the fact that participation in a friendship group appears to be less effective in retarding shifts in age identification among the retired than among the widowed indicates that the loss of the work group only partially explains the greater influence
that retirement exerts on age identification. It, therefore, furnishes inferential evidence for the first hypothesis that the cultural evaluation implied by retirement,
but not by widowhood, tends to force the person to recognize that he is socially
defined as old.

PART TEN

THE MAKING AND BREAKING OF DEVIANTS

The making and breaking of deviants takes us into the politics of reality. A massified, egalitarian, common denominator society must protect itself against all forms of behavioral extremism, for most extremism may be construed as based on an alien moral alternative. Such extremism implies willfulness, responsibility, and choice, and therefore is dangerous politically to those in power. One unobtrusive and fairly routine technique for rendering such moral opposition politically harmless is to assert that it is not rooted in a moral alternative at all, but rather in a medical pathology. When extremism is construed as being grounded in pathology, rather than morality, it is relieved of responsibility and dutifully placed under medical surveillance.

Conversion of political problems into medical problems has great currency. Political adversaries invariably are cast as somewhat sick. For example, there is wide agreement that Hitler was crazy, that De Gaulle is senile, Castro mad, Goldwater unstable, and Johnson egomaniacal. And the mere fact that Mr. Nixon was known to have visited some doctor who might have had something to do with psychotherapy was enough to lead one self-righteous guardian of the public interest to reveal all to the national news media. What better way to attempt to neutralize moral-political opposition, and the implied power struggle, than by reducing it to medical pathology?

Definition of what is or is not behaviorally extreme ultimately is left in the hands of a curious coalition of judges, psychiatrists, policemen, social investigators, welfare workers, and secondary school teachers. Together, they are involved in the creation and protection of those meanings, values, sentiments, and rules which constitute and broadly define the bounds of permissible behavior and reality. Moreover, this coalition of reality makers has power. Although the source of its power derives from social traditions and legal rules, the consequences of its power, more often than not, result in the restriction of someone's liberty.

From the viewpoint of a behavioral extremist, such as Seymour Krim, the narrow reality legislated and enforced by this coalition works to constrain, and condemn, anyone who pursues his art and being to the very furthest perimeter of reality. The behavioral pioneer is captured and jailed by the judgments and definitions of people whose conception of normality and sanity is "conditioned by inherited prejudice, fear, questionable middle-class assumptions of the purposes of life, a policeman's narrow idea of freedom, and dollar hard AMA notions of responsibility and expediency."

One may be less than a behavioral pioneer himself, and still pause for thought as he reads Krim's reaction to a psychiatrist who describes Greenwich Village as a "psychotic community." For one realizes, along with Krim, that "insanity and psychosis can no longer be respected as meaningful definitions—but are used by limited individuals in positions of social power to describe ways of behaving and thinking that are alien, threatening, and *obscure* to them."

Implicit in Krim's literary excursion is the profound insight that deviance is a matter of judgment, not a matter of fact. Deviance does not inhere in an act but is conferred upon it—and conferred by those who are "incapable of appreciating the rich, subtle and unconventional reality of the independent thinker and artist." Within the past five to ten years, however, social scientists have come to realize that to continue to speak in literary terms about madness, in legal terms about insanity, or in medical terms about mental illness, is to perpetuate a set of beliefs which misses the essentially normative, communicative nature of behavioral extremism.

Indeed, Szasz opens the assault on the myth of mental illness by distinguishing between the brain and the mind. While the brain may *succumb* to disease, the mind may *develop* problems in living. One is passive, the other active. An individual does not decide to have a disease, but he may decide to have a "mental illness." Moreover, the relationship between the brain and the mind is not reversible. A diseased brain may cause illness which leads to problems in living, but problems in living do not imply a diseased brain. The notion of problems in living therefore shifts the focus from organic deterioration to sociological dis-order, from inquiry in medical etiology to inquiry in deviant behavior.

How, then, do we come to the decision that someone's behavior is deviant? If someone says he is Napoleon, we would consider this symptomatic of disturbance only if we did not believe him. Such a declaration, for example, at a masquerade party would hardly upset anyone. The credibility of a piece of behavior stands or falls on whether *we judge* it plausible or not. *Our* judgment, however, implies a set of social, ethical, and legal rules that define, for us, the limits of credible behavior and reality. Statements or behavior that deviate from our standards of credibility are likely to be labeled symptomatic of mental malady. We are therefore in the position of defining deviation from social, ethical, and legal rules in medical terms. This inconsistency points again to what may be called the politics of reality, for sooner or later some specialist in psychotherapeutics is retained to confirm our judgment of someone else's deviation.

If a court hires a psychiatrist to determine whether or not a criminal is insane, it is a sure bet that the psychiatrist will not question the sanity of the men who formulated the social, ethical, and legal rules against which the criminal is being judged. The unstated question is, who has the *power* to legislate reality? People who specialize in the adjudication of reality quite naturally are committed to a particular conception of reality which usually takes into account what they consider to be society's conception. Needless to say, what society's conception of reality may be is open to debate. If the boundaries of reality are somewhat vague, they are not so vague as to prevent us from judging some people as having stepped beyond them. Somewhere, sometime, somehow, all of us have inched beyond the permissible perimeter, and have gone off limits—but, very few have been caught. As Scheff notes, on the one hand, there is a multiplicity of sources that generate behavior deviant enough to be judged dis-ordered. On the other, there is enough evidence to suggest that not all behavior that breaks rules *is judged* deviant. This leads to the proposition that most rule breaking is somehow ignored, disguised, rationalized, handled, or denied, and is therefore of transitory significance. The question is, then, how does rule-breaking behavior, most of which is transitory, become stabilized and categorically deviant? Scheff's answer is that the rule breaker is stigmatized by his audience as disturbed and placed into a deviant status. Thus placed, the deviant proceeds to play out the expected role.

The placement of a person into a deviant status can be seen in Lemert's brilliant essay on paranoia. The major point can be summed up in the now current phrase *paranoids have real enemies*. As with Szasz and Scheff, Lemert places the problem of paranoia squarely within an interactive communications matrix, and challenges the notion that paranoia is the unfolding of a pathology located in the individual. Paranoia is not a disease, or a symptom of a disease. More often than not, it is an individual's behavioral *response* to alternations in norms, values, or attitudes. The onset of stress between an actor and his circle usually is associated with some real status loss for the actor, such as death of a loved one, business failure, or divorce. In *response*, the actor may become gruff, abrupt, and generally offensive. At this initial stage, however, he is not marked as a deviant, but rather as someone who is difficult to get along with. After repeated interaction, or upon receiving additional damaging information about the actor, the *circle* begins to *re-orient* its appraisal, and *sees* the actor as someone with whom it is best not to get involved. At this point, the process of excluding the actor begins in earnest. The contention, then, is that the paranoid mobilizes a real, as opposed to a fabricated, social circle that reacts against him in a covert and conspiratorial manner. In sum, paranoia is seen as an *interaction* that implies reciprocal posturing on the part of both actor and audience.

After a person has been labeled mentally ill, the next step usually is to hospitalize and transform him into a patient. In a provocative essay on "The Moral Career of the Mental Patient," Goffman analyzes the effect of being tagged mentally ill, and *treated* as such within the institutional setting of a mental hospital. Often the individual's closest kin or friend brings him to a psychiatrist where the proposed stay at the hospital is described in less than realistic terms. The police escort, which eventually arrives, is chummy and solicitous, and the "admissions suite," where the patient is welcomed, is more hospitable than hospital—in all, it is as though no one was being put away. When the stark reality of it all comes clear, the patient feels conned, betrayed, and rather skeptical of those around him. Abandoned and confined, he becomes demoralized and withdrawn.

Confronted with isolation, humiliation, stark living circumstances, and the imposition of an unacceptable view of himself, the patient begins to construct a more favorable image of his past, present, and future. Either he proceeds to magnify appealing qualities of himself and his past, or he claims that he is not responsible for his current plight. Presumably the function of such agreeable image building is to counter the unacceptable image the patient is compelled to accept. Obviously the patient cannot legitimate his own preferred image, since all staff personnel have access to his case history, which focuses on his aberrant behavior, and thus know what the "real facts" are. Staff generally punctures the altered image of self and situation in accordance with the belief that the patient should be compelled to "face reality." Since information on patients is communicated freely and widely among all echelons of the staff, the patient is faced with a social environment mobilized completely to deny his own more agreeable conception of himself.

Constant moral review of who he is combined with fairly frequent rises and falls in the hierarchy of living arrangements eventually convinces the patient that it makes no sense whatever to stake a claim on a particular conception of self, since, chances are, it will be discredited. The patient, then, becomes rather apathetic and/or cosmopolitan in his commitment to an image of himself. He gives up in the effort to maintain control over the process of self-construction and submits to the environment and those in control of it. Adoption of the self they present to him becomes a more efficient way of coping with a fundamentally demoralizing situation. Genuine commitment to an agreeable image of self is replaced by a functional, amoral detachment. One begins to give off *impressions* of a self rather than a self that is wholly credible to him.

While the giving off of impressions may satisfy the staff, it presents even greater problems for the patient. As Messinger *et al.* contend, the patient does not want to *act* normal; he wants to *be* normal. Moreover, the patient is never quite sure whether the normal act he is putting on is representative of who he actually is. Is the presentation merely a "constructed object," or a "natural self"? Indeed, the connection between the real self and the character presented becomes ambiguous. Furthermore, in the desire to enhance the presentation of his constructed self, the patient develops a manipulative attitude; he uses everything and everybody to make the best presentation possible. Under constant pressure to appear normal, the patient becomes anxious and alienated and never quite establishes a clear-cut commitment to a genuine presentation of self.

It would appear that this outcome is a result of the very procedures that McHugh recommends for obtaining radical changes in behavior. Dissociating an individual from familiar networks of interaction, which support old values; placing him in a situation where he has no control over the flow of events and cannot even associate them in any meaningful way; stripping him down to his bare malleable essence, and resocializing him into a more acceptable product, results precisely in functional, amoral detachment. While this unsavory outcome may not be preferred by society, it may well be, in some perverse sense, demanded by society.

As Erikson notes, a fair amount of research exists that supports the idea that most agents and agencies engaged in social control and rehabilitation do more to perpetuate deviance than to eliminate it. Outcasts are brought together, stripped of integrity, learn the dangers of genuine commitment to self (and often the tricks of each other's trade), and sent back out. Subject to constant scrutiny (perhaps harassment) by control agencies, and widely recognized as bad risks, they cannot reclaim full citizenship. Unable to function successfully in a conventional sense, they still meet the demands of society in an unconventional sense. As Erikson claims, they help maintain the boundaries of permissible behavior and reality by serving as anti-models—as living examples of that which is impermissible. As we might expect, without sin there would be no church.

Suggested Readings

BECKER, HOWARD S. *Outsiders*. New York: The Free Press of Glencoe, 1963.

BELKNAP, IVAN, and JOHN G. STEINLE. *The Community and Its Hospitals*. New York: Syracuse University Press, 1963.

DURKHEIM, EMILE. *Suicide*. (trans.) John A. Spaulding and George Simpson. New York: The Free Press of Glencoe, 1951.

ERIKSON, KAI T. *The Wayward Puritan*. New York: Wiley, 1966.

FRIEDSON, ELLIOT. *The Hospital in Modern Society*. New York: The Free Press of Glencoe, 1963.

GOFFMAN, ERVING. *Asylums*. New York: Doubleday Anchor Book, 1961.

GOLDHAMER, HERBERT, and A. W. MARSHALL. *Psychosis and Civilization*. New York: The Free Press of Glencoe, 1953.

ROSE, ARNOLD M. (ed.). *Mental Health and Mental Disorder*. New York: Norton, 1955.

ROSEN, GEORGE. *Madness in Society*. Chicago: The University of Chicago Press, 1968.

RUBINGTON, EARL, and MARTIN S. WEINBERG (eds.). *Deviance: The Interactionist Perspective*. New York: The Macmillan Co., 1968.

SCHEFF, THOMAS J. *Being Mentally Ill: A Sociological Theory*. Chicago: Aldine Publishing Co., 1966.

SPITZER, STEPHAN P. and NORMAN K. DENZIN (eds.). *The Mental Patient: Studies in the Sociology of Deviance*. New York: McGraw-Hill Co., 1968.

SZASZ, THOMAS. *The Myth of Mental Illness*. New York: Hoeber-Harper, 1964.

62 The Insanity Bit

● SEYMOUR KRIM

I

Until this time of complete blast-off in seemingly every department of human life, the idea of insanity was thought of as the most dreadful thing that could happen to a person. Little was actually known about it and the mind conjured up pictures of Bedlam, ninnies walking around in a stupor, a living death that lasted until the poor damned soul's body expired and peace tucked him or her away for eternal keeps. But in this era of monumental need to re-think and re-define almost every former presumption about existence--which has inspired a bombing way of looking at what once were considered the most unbudgeable rocks of reality—the locked door of insanity has been shaken loose and shall yet be hurled wide open. Until one day the prisoners of this definition will walk beside us sharing only the insane plight of mortality itself, which makes quiet madmen of us all.

Every American family has its "psychotic" cousin or uncle; every friend has wept, prayed, hoped (and finally slid into indifference) for another friend sweating it out in insulin or electric-shock behind the grey walls (public institution) or beyond the clipped roses (private sanitarium). Although my brother, Herbert J. Krim, was institutionalized when I was barely in my 20's—and I co-signed the certificate for a pre-frontal lobotomy which ended with his death by hemorrhage on the operating table at Rockland State Hospital—I still had the conventional ideas about insanity that are shared by all "responsible" readers of *The New York Times.* It is true that as a serious writer I had inherited a great tradition of complete independence and honesty to my actual experience, regardless of what I was supposed to feel; but this was sabotaged by my youth, my ignorance, and an inability to separate my own personal life from a responsibility to question the clichés of experience to their ultimate depth. Like most American writers, from would-be's to celebrities, I was intensely preoccupied by my acutely painful and highly exaggerated subjective image—the Jewish cross, looks, sex, masculinity, a swarm of fears and devices for concealment that were secondary to my decent abilities and serious obligations as a writer intent on telling the truth. In other words: I was too narcissistically and masturbatorially stuck on myself to appreciate the horrible waste of my brother Herbert's death; and with the snotty sense of superiority usually felt by the young American writer, I thought *I* would be forever immune to the judgments of a society which I loftily ignored, or nose-thumbed, without ever coming to grips with on the actual mat of life. Like every creative type of my generation whom I met in my 20's, I was positive I was sanctified, protected by my "genius," my flair, my overwhelming ambition.

I was as wrong as you can be and still live to tell about it. In the summer of

SOURCE: Seymour Krim, in his *Views of a Nearsighted Cannoneer* (New York: E. P. Dutton & Co., Inc., 1961), pp. 112–129. Copyright, 1968, 1961 by Seymour Krim. Reprinted by permission of E. P. Dutton & Co., Inc.

1955, when I was 33, the thousand unacknowledged human (not literary) pressures in my being exploded. I ran barefooted in the streets, spat at members of my family, exposed myself, was almost bodily thrown out of the house of a Nobel Prize-winning author, and believed God had ordained me to act out every conceivable human impulse without an ounce of hypocritical caution. I know today that my instinct was sound, but my reasoning was self-deceptive. It was not God who ordained me, but I who ordained God for my own understandable human purposes. I needed an excuse to force some sort of balance between my bulging inner life and my timid outer behaviour, and I chose the greatest and most comforting symbol of them all. He was my lance and my shield as I tore through the New York streets acting out the bitter rot of a world-full of frustrations that my human nature could no longer lock up. I was finally cornered on the 14th floor of the St. Regis Hotel by two frightened friends and another brother; and with the aid of handcuffs seriously-humorously clipped on by a couple of bobbies I was led off to Bellevue, convinced all along that I was right. I tolerated those who took me away with the kindly condescension of a fake Jesus.

From Bellevue I was soon transferred to a private laughing academy in Westchester and given insulin-shock treatments. No deep attempt was made to diagnose my "case"—except the superficial and inaccurate judgment that I had "hallucinated." Factually, this was not true; I did not have visual images of people or objects which were not there; I merely believed, with the beautiful relief of absolute justice which the soul of man finds when life becomes unbearable, that God had given me the right and the duty to do everything openly that I had secretly fantasied for years. But this distinction was not gone into by my judges and indifferent captors. They did not have the time, the patience, or even the interest because work in a flip-factory is determined by mathematics: you must find a common denominator of categorization and treatment in order to handle the battalions of miscellaneous humanity that are marched past your desk with high trumpets blowing in their minds.

Like all the other patients, I was considered beyond reasoning with and was treated like a child; not brutally, but efficiently, firmly and patronizingly. In the eyes of this enclosed world I had relinquished my rights as an adult human being. The causes for my explosion were not even superficially examined, nor was the cheek-pinching house psychiatrist—with a fresh flower in the button hole of his fresh daily suit—truly equipped to cope with it even if he had tried, which he did not. Private sanitariums and state institutions, I realized much later, were isolation chambers rather than hospitals in the usual sense; mechanical "cures" such as the one I underwent in a setup of unchallenged authority, like the Army or a humanitarian prison, slowly brought 75 per cent of the inmates down to a more temporarily modest view of reality. Within nine or ten weeks I too came down, humbled, ashamed, willing to stand up before the class and repeat the middle-class credo of limited expressiveness and the meaning of a dollar in order to get my discharge.

In three months' time I was out, shaken, completely alone, living in a cheap Broadway hotel-room (having been ashamed to go back to Greenwich Village) and going to a conventional Ph.D. psychologist (I had been to three medically-trained therapists in the preceding decade) as a sop to both my conscience and family. I had broken beyond the bounds of "reality"—a shorthand word which is used by the average psychiatrist for want of the more truthfully complex approach that must eventually accommodate our beings' increasing flights into higher altitudes—and come back to the position I was in before. But once again the causes that had flung me into my own sky continued to eat me up. Sexually unconfident, I went to whores, ate my meals alone, and forced myself to write a few pieces in that loneliest of places, a tiny blank hotel-room in the middle of nowhere. For the first time in my life the incentive to live, the isolation and frustration of my existence, grew dim; while the psychologist smiled and smoked his pipe —and did the well-adjusted, tweed, urbane act behind his tastefully battered desk as he ladled out platitudes—I was saving up the sleeping bombs, and when I had enough to do the trick I burned the letters I had received through the years from the several men and women I had loved, destroyed my journal of 15 years' standing, and one carefully chosen night went to a hotel in Newark, N. J.

My plan was to take the pills and slowly conk out in the full bathtub, ultimately drowning like Thomas Heggen; if one missed the other would work. I splurged on a beautiful death-room in a modernistic hotel, one that included a bathroom with the biggest tub in the house. But it was too small to fit my long body. The idea of not being able to drown and of surviving the pills afterwards, perhaps to become a burden or an invalid, began to scar what seemed like a paradise of suicide. I went instead to a Polish bar in downtown Newark, vaguely seeking the eternal anodynes of snatch and booze while I mentally played with my fate.

I found the booze and saw a coarse, ignorant Polish girl do such a life-giving, saucy, raucous folk-dance (on the small dance-floor to the right of the bar) that I broke into loving sobs like prayers over my drink. The sun of life blazed from her into my grateful heart. I went back to the beautiful hotel-room, poured the pills down the toilet, and went to sleep. The next morning I returned to Manhattan a chastened man, shaking my head at how close I had come to non-being.

When I told my tale to Mr. Pipe, my psychologist, he speedily hustled me off to a legitimate head-doctor who doped me until a private ambulance came. Very much in my right and one and only mind but too paralyzed by drugs to move, I was once again taken on the long ride—this time to another hedge-trimmed bin in Long Island. I was helpless to protest, mainly because of the shame and guilt I felt for even contemplating suicide. Obviously I was not crazy, mad, psychotic, out of my mind, schizophrenic, paranoiac. I was simply a tormented man-kid who had never steeled himself to face the facts of life—who didn't know what it meant to have principles and live by them come grief or joy—and who thought that human worth and true independence comes as easily as it does in the movies we were all emotionally faked on. As a sputtering fiction-writer and fairly active literary critic, I had had occasional peaks of maturity and illumination; but as a man I was self-deceptive, self-indulgent, crying inwardly for the pleasures of a college-boy even while in my imagination I saw myself as another Ibsen or Dreiser. Ah, the extraordinary mismating of thoughts in the mind of the modern American literary romantic, as fantastic and truly unbelievable a stew of unrelated dreams as have ever been dreamt, believe me!

Once again I was on the human assembly-line: electric shock clubbed my good brain into needless unconsciousness (and I walked to my several executions like a brave little chappie instead of questioning them) and unquestioned Old Testament authority ruled our little club. Good-natured, but mostly cowlike and uneducated male orderlies carried out the orders from above; and apart from the mechanical treatment and the unimaginative grind of occupational therapy, each patient was left completely on his or her bewildered own, a sad and farcical sight when one considered the $125 per week that their frightened families were paying.

I saw now that nine-tenths of the people I was quartered with were not "insane" by any of the standards a normally intelligent person would use: the majority had lost confidence in their own ability to survive in the world outside, or their families were *afraid* of them and had palmed them off on "experts," but positively no serious effort was being made to equip them to become free and independent adults. This was their birthright—beyond country and society, indeed an almost religious obligation—but they were palliated with pills or jolted with shock, their often honest rage echoed back to them as a sign of their "illness." Some of them must have been "sick," you say. I answer: Who can not be conceived as such in a world so complex ("The truth is there is a truth on every side"—Richard Eberhart) that each group has its own method for judging manners, behaviour, ideas, and finally the worth of human values? What was more important was that I, a person from a hip milieu and with a completely opposite set of values, could see their so-called sickness with the human sensibility that an immersion in literature and experience had given me—rather than as a clinical manifestation. When I later recognized the objective provinciality of many psychiatrists in precisely the humanistic areas that could cover the actions of the majority of the inmates without finding it "psychotic," I realized that the independent thinker and artist today must learn to be resolute towards a subtle, socially powerful god-father who often drips paternalism: namely, the newly-enthroned psychiatric minority that has elevated itself to a dangerous position of "authority" in the crucial issues of mind, personality, and sanity.

I now began to fight persistently—but still with shakiness—for my release; my life was my own: it did not belong to the clichés of the salesman-aggressive, well-barbered, Jewish-refugee (my brother, my enemy!) house psychiatrist or to my smiling, betweeded nonentity of a psychologist, who paid me diplomatically inscrutable visits like a Japanese ambassador. Even if I had been or if there were such a reality as a "raving maniac"—which, perhaps childishly, I implore the over-imaginative, zeitgeist-vulnerable reader to believe is an impossible conception today—I would and should have fought for my release. What the institution-spared layman does not realize is that a sensitive and multiple-reacting human being remains the same everywhere, including a sanitarium, and such an environment can duplicate the injustice or vulgarity which drove your person there in the first place. By this I mean that a mental hospital is not an asylum or a sanctuary in the old-fashioned sense: it is just a roped-off side-street of modern existence, rife with as many contradictions, half-truths and lousy architecture as life itself.

Both of the sanitariums I was in were comparable to Grossinger's, in that they took in only financially comfortable, conventionally middle-class, non-intellectual people. By every human standard my being there was life's sarcastic answer to whatever romantic ideas I had about justice. Since the age of 19 I had deliberately led an existence of experimentation, pursuit of truth, bohemianism, and non-commercialism: fate's punishment for my green naivete was for me to recover my supposed mental health in this atmosphere of uncriticizable authority, air-conditioned by just the whiffs of truth that are perfumed and bland, and based on a pillar of middle-class propriety with the cut-throat reality of money underneath. Could I accept my former life, which had produced some good work, as a lie to myself—which the house-psychiatrist wanted me to do (in effect) in his one psychotherapeutic pass at me (he left me alone after this)? I could not and never would: not only for myself but for the great principles and accomplishments of others, both living and dead, which had been my guide throughout my adult life. I might fail—but why go on having an identity at all if in a crisis you will throw away not only your past years, but the moral achievements of rare souls who have shared in your emotional and intellectual experience and whose own contributions to existence are also at stake?

When I heard this second house-psychiatrist literally equate sanity with the current clichés of adjustment and describe Greenwich Village as a "psychotic community," I saw with sudden clarity that *insanity* and *psychosis* can no longer be respected as meaningful definitions—but are used by limited individuals in positions of social power to describe ways of behaving and thinking that are alien, threatening, and *obscure* to them. (A year later when I took a psychiatrist friend of mine to the San Remo, she told me with a straight face that it reminded her of the "admission ward in Bellevue," where she had interned. This was her analogy on the basis of accurate but limited experience, that increasing chasm which separates intelligent people from understanding each other. I realized with a sense of almost incommunicable hopelessness that the gap between her and the well-known poet with whom I had had a beer at the Remo two weeks before was tremendous, and that between these two poles of intelligence the neutral person—who could see the logic of each—was being mashed up with doubt and conflict. The poet was at home, or at least the heat was off, there; while the psychiatrist felt alien and had made a contemptuous psycho-sociological generalization. There was little bond of shared values and therefore genuine communication between both of these intelligent and honest human beings, each of whom contributed to my life.)

To finish with my four months in the sanitarium: I argued and reasoned for the basic right to the insecurity of freedom, and finally a good friend did the dirty in-fighting of getting me out. Had I to do it over again, I believe I would now have the guts to threaten such an institution or psychologist with a law suit, ugly as such a procedure can be to a person already vulnerable with the hash-marks of one legally defined "psychotic episode" and the contemplation of the criminal act of suicide. But I had been—as so many of Jack Kerouac's subterraneans are when faced with the machinery of official society—milk and sawdust when, in such situations, you must be iron and stone in spite of your own frailty. It is not that the present-day authorities of mental life want to railroad anyone, as in your Grade C horror movie; it is merely that as one grows older it becomes clear that there are almost irremediable differences between people in the total outlook towards life.

Mine had hardened as a result of my experiences, and I realized it was better to die out in the world if need be than be deprived of the necessity to confront existence because of the cheap authority of a lock and key. The majority of people who stay in mental institutions for any length of time do not want to return to the uncertain conditions outside the walls: which in our time spells out to emotionally anarchic, multi-dimensional, brain-trying, anxiety-loaded, and—O hear me mortality, from the Year One!—ultimate and divine life.

II

I returned downtown—to the very Village that I heard the psychiatrist place deep in Freudian Hell, with that pious over-extension of terminology which reveals a limited private morality behind the use of so-called scientific language—and tried to tenderly pick up the threads of my former social life. I saw that my closest and most brilliant friends did not really understand, or were afraid to understand, the contemporary insanity bit. Almost all of them had been soul-whirled by psychotherapy at some time, and each had the particularly contemporary fear of insanity which has become the psychological H-bomb of city life; in theory they may have granted that insanity was no longer the uniform horror it seems to the inexperienced imagination—like a spook in the night—but centuries of inherited fear, plus the daily crises of 1950's living, made them emotionally cautious about seeing my experience as merely an *extension* of their own.

One, a poet-philosopher whom I admire, clapped me on the back and said with some literary awe that I had "returned from the dead, like Lazarus." This struck me as greatly melodramatic, untruthful, and saddening because intellectuals and especially artists should be the very people to understand that insanity today is a matter of definition, not fact; that there can no longer be a fixed criterion, just as there is no longer a reality like that described by Allen Ginsberg in "Howl" (an exciting achievement), where he sees "the best minds of my generation destroyed by madness."

I believe this is lurid sentimentality. Ginsberg may have seen the most gifted people of his generation destroyed by an *interpretation* of madness, which is a much more real threat in a time of such infinite, moon-voyaging extension to experience that the validly felt act is often fearfully jailed in a windowless cell of definition by hard-pressed authorities, whose very moral axis is in danger of toppling. Madness today is a literary word; insanity is a dated legal conception as rigid as an Ibsen play; and "psychosis," the antiseptic modern word that sends chills down the ravines of my friends' minds, has become so weakened (despite its impressive white-jacketed look) by narrow-minded, square, and fast-slipping ideological preconceptions that it must be held at arm's length, like a dead rat, for any cool understanding. When this is done, I believe you will see that the word and the state of mind it tries to fix are subject to the gravest questioning; much of which centers around the amount of freedom either permitted to human expression or, more important, what it must take for itself to live in this time when such *unfamiliar* demands are made on the being. Norms crack when they can no longer fight back the content that spills over cookie-mold conceptions of "sane" behavior —and they must be elasticized to stretch around the new bundle of life.

Two weeks before I was back walking down 8th Street a gratefully free neurotic, I had been thought of in the minds of compassionate but uninformed friends as a fairly wild-eyed psychotic. The mere fact that I had been in a sanitarium had pulled a curtain of emotional blindness down over my friends' vision; and yet I was the same person I had been when I entered the happy-house. The unexamined fear of an "insanity" which no longer exists as a framed picture conventionalizes the very people who should view this now only *symbolic* word with clear, unafraid, and severely skeptical eyes. I had not been among "the dead"—unless killing time looking at "Gunsmoke" and Jackie Gleason on TV, playing bridge, and reading Tolstoy and Nathanael West is considered death. I had not been "destroyed by madness," Mr. Ginsberg!—in fact, the act of incarceration made me realize how significant (indeed indelible) individual freedom is, and thus helped brick-and-mortar my point of view rather than destroy it. When I was once again semi-knit into a way of life in my new Village home, I discovered that other writers and intellectuals whom I knew had also undergone the sanitarium or mental-hospital holiday, but had kept mum because of indecision as to how frankly one should confess such a stigma.

I understood their practical caution, but discovered that they lived in a sewer-light of guilt, fear and throat-gagging anxiety, instead of openly and articulately coping with the monster of doubt. "Do you think I'm sane?" is the question I ultimately began to hear from these brilliant people (one scarred tribesman to another!) who had been intimidated into denying the worth of their most pregnant ideas, the very ones that create *new concrete standards of sanity* or *sense* in a time that has emotionally, if not yet officially, out-lived the abstractions of the past. For myself—although uncertain as to how expressive I should be, even with the very intellectuals I had always considered my brothers in a completely free inquiry into every nook and cranny of life—the problem was suddenly answered when a gifted young writer told a charming hostess I had just met that I had been in "two insane asylums."

I was pierced and hurt, not because I actually considered my supposed nuttiness a yellow badge of dishonor, but because the writer in question had ducked out from under his own experience (which I instinctively knew included some of the crises which had launched me upon the streets like a human missile) and pretended such melodrama was foreign to him. I was appalled because I thought that of all people my fellow highbrow writers should be the first to understand and concede the universal nature of the blows that had felled me in the eyes of official society. But I was wrong. There are spikes on the truth which are so close to the slashed heart of contemporary mortality that men and women will lie and refuse acknowledgment, even when it is necessary to the survival of others, they forfeit their humanhood and final worth to life by doing this, but even in the small band of the avant-garde the pursuit of the truth is given up with that weak excuse: "a practical sense of reality."

After this turncoat put-down by a member of my own club, so to speak, there was no longer any issue for myself. I could not live with the squirming burden of secretiveness because my personal history had become public gossip in the small Village group I traveled with. After snake-bitten laughter at my own romantically cultivated simple-mindedness in thinking my fall would be taken with the hip sophistication I had truly expected, I was glad I had become a stooge or victim; because I basically knew that I had played a juicy part in a contemporary American morality play that is going to do standing-room nightly until its implications are understood. We live in what for the imaginative person are truly hallucinated times, because there is more life on every side—and the possibility of conceiving this surplus in a dizzying multitude of ways—than our inheritance and equipment enables us to deal with. My type and perhaps your type of person only *acted out* what other less passionate people feel, but do not express. A "breakdown" such as mine can therefore be learned from:

The first thing one can see is that the isolating of a person saves his or her friends and family from being embarrassed (trivial as this seems, it is a nasty factor in institutionalization), perhaps hurt, and theoretically stops the "sick" person from doing something irreparable while in the grip of the furies. Seen this way, the enforced shackling of an individual seems sad but reasonable. But contemporary adults, however disturbed (often with justice!), are not children; there is doubt in my mind whether we have any right, other than blunt self-interest, to impose our so-called humanitarian wishes on another to the degree where we jail them in order to save them. I must illustrate this with my own case. When I was considered out of my mind during my original upward thrust into the sheer ecstasy of 100 per cent uninhibitedness, I was aware of the "daringness" of my every move; it represented at heart an existential *choice* rather than a mindless discharge. It could not be tolerated by society, and I was punished for it, but my "cure" was ultimately a chastisement, *not a medical healing process.* In my own exhibitionistic and self-dramatizing way, when I flipped, I was nevertheless instinctively rebelling against a fact which I think is objectively true in our society and time: and that is the lack of alignment between an immense inner world and an outer one which has not yet legalized, or officially recognized, the forms that can tolerate the flood of communication from the mind to the stage of action.

Traditionally, it was always taught that the artistic person could work out his or her intense private life by expressing it on the easel or typewriter. In faded theory this seems reasonable, but with the billionaire's wealth of potential human experience both fore, aft, and sideways in the world today, it is abnormal not to want to participate more Elizabethanly in this over-abundant life. The hunchbacked joy the artist once may have had in poring over the objects of his interest, and then putting the extract into his work, can no longer be honestly sufficient to the most human hearts today. There has arisen an overwhelming need for the highly imaginative spirit (based on the recognition that the mere mind of man can no longer lock up the volume of its experience) to forge a bridge so that the bursting galaxy of this inner world can be received in actual public life. But there is such a time-lag between our literally amazing subjective life—which has conceptions of a powerful altitude equal to the heaven-exploring freedom of privacy—and the mummery of outer behavior, that when the contemporary imaginator expresses his genuine thoughts in public he often feels that he has exposed himself beyond redemption. Room has not yet been made by those who dominate social power for the natural outward show of the acrobatic thinking that ceaselessly swings in the surrealistic minds of our most acute contemporaries. Put crudely but simply, a bookish notion of what constitutes "normality" in this supremely a-normal age drives the liveliest American sensibilities back into the dungeon of self—creating pressures which must maim the soul one way or another—rather than understanding that the great need today is for imagination to come gloriously out in the open and shrink the light-years that separate the mind from external life. (Trying to fill this need is, hands-down, one of the significant accomplishments of the beats—in my opinion—no matter what defensive moralists say; the raw junk that they have peddled occasionally under a Kotex flag of liberation is a different matter, which doesn't rightly fit in here.)

It was trying to close this distance between Me and Thou, between the mind and externality, that I was instinctively attempting when I cut loose with my natural suffocating self in 1955 upon the taboo grounds of outer life. I could stand unfulfilled desire no longer. Thus it is my conviction today that ideals of social behavior must squat down and broaden to the point where they can both absorb and see the necessity for "aberrations" that were once, squarely and Teddy

Rooseveltianly, regarded as pathological. The imagination of living human beings, not dead gods, must be openly embodied if there is to be some rational connection between what people actually are and what they are permitted to show. But as with every significant change in meaning, such acts of expressiveness will cost blood before they will be tolerated and understood by psychiatrists, sociologists, the law, police, and all other instruments of social force. Ironically, it is the very "psychotics" in institutions who have unwittingly done the most to initiate a bigger and more imaginative conception of what constitutes *meaningful* behavior. By dealing with people imprisoned in this category, the most perceptive laymen and psychiatrists are beginning to see symbolic meanings where before they saw flat irrationality, because their approach was literal (as if anyone who had the imagination to go "mad" would be stuffy enough to act in prose!). It is then borne in upon them, out of common sense and humility, that a much more expanded conception of what is "sane" is a prerequisite to doing justice to the real emotional state of human beings today; not the abstract theorems of a clean Euclidian conception, but the real, harsh, multiple, often twisted, on-again, off-again mishmash of the so-called normal mind. One can say without pretense that the pioneering "psychotic" is the human poet of the future; and the most imaginative, least tradition-bound psychiatrists are now playing the role of New Critics, learning to closely read the difficult and unexpected meanings of what formerly were thought of as obscure—in fact, off-limits—warpings of humanity.

III

In my own case I was brought face-to-face because of my trial by shock (both electric and the human aftermath) with a crucial reality which I had long dodged. It can be put approximately this way: A serious artist-type must in the present environment, as always—clichés have a way of becoming profundities when you have to live them!—literally fight for survival if he or she is going to embody the high traditions that originally made the hot pursuit of truth through art the greatest kick in their lives. But to follow this ideal today is tougher than perhaps it has ever been before; and there are specific reasons why. Foremost is the increasing loss of position for the poet (the artist incarnate) as "the unacknowledged legislator of the race" in a period when the terrifying bigness of society makes the average person resort to more immediate and practical oracles (psychiatrists, sociologists, chemists) than to the kind of imaginative truth that the artist can give. Secondly, the artist-type in our mass society is no longer "priveleged" in any way, if indeed he ever was; by this I mean that the laws and shibboleths of the huge democratic tribe judge him as severely as they do the shoemaker next door. Whatever pampering the serious artist once received has become a laugh in our time, when everyone is hustling on approximately the same level for success, lovers, status, money, headlines, thrills, security—for everything.

The emergence of an emotionally mutinous democracy has upset the old categories and cast us all into the boiling sea of naked existence, without the props of class, or profession, or the certainty about one's worth as judged by the seemingly clear-cut hierarchies of the past. While, in my opinion, this should be sizzlingly beautiful to every true artist-type, because it is adventurous in the highest conceivable and most mortally dangerous sense, it is also full of the most sinking fears and doubts. For example: can the intelligent writer, painter or composer—the individual with a view of life all his own, which he believes to be true—be indifferent to the prevailing social climate and risk everything by sticking to a viewpoint which will bring him into conflict with the most *normal* (shared by the most people) human emotions in a mass society? (Tag him with the label of "insanity," estrangement from the tempting pie of regular-guy and regular-gal American experience, bring him the isolating fate of being misunderstood even by the "enlightened," and regarded as a personal challenge by others who have made an uneasy truce.)

This is a very serious problem and entails a bigger threat than in the past. Since the artist-type can no longer be realistically considered as being "outside" our definition of society or human nature—and must in this country above all others be seen within the circle of a mass-democratic humanity, for that is where his final strength probably lies—his defections will be judged by those in positions of social power as fluky aberrations *no different from anyone else's*. He will be judged and penalized by the same standards; and in a majority of cases, from what I have seen, his will and stamina are broken (or rationalized into loose harness) and his point of view changed. Frankly, for the artist-type in our environment there is no longer any solid ground whatever under his feet—anything solid he possesses must be won from air and shaped by fanatical resoluteness. For all is open to question today, is a gamble, and has none of the "official" security of the acknowledged professions or even any semblance of unity within his own field. It is for such reasons that the genuine artist-thinker is in such an unenviable and peculiar position in America right now. He is of society and yet, by instinct and inheritance, apart from it: therefore he has to clarify his position in his own mind to a menthol-sharp degree if he wants to survive with intactness, because, as I've tried to show, he will be crushed subtly or conclusively unless he separates his eternal role in society from the onrush of personal doubt that every human being worth the name lives with today.

I learned as a result of my far-out public exhibition, and the manhandling that followed, to distrust the definitions of crude social authority as they pertained to myself and my friends, who share a generally akin point of view and are all either professionals or semi-professionals in the arts and intellectual life. We can not be skimmed off the top and bracketed as thinly as I had been diagnosed at Bellevue; and the psychiatrists who impatiently felt for the bumps within my head, while presumably competent at a human-machine level, are not as a group sensitive, informed or sympathetic enough with my purposes in life to be of help. In fact, in a basic way they must be my defining opposition in history (daily life) while my friends beyond time (the ideal)—if that doesn't read too pretentiously. It was a sharp revelation for me to learn this as a result of my on-your-hands-and-knees, boy! defeat with authority. As I confessed before, like so many confused young Americans puttering around in the arts, I had phonily pumped into my serious intentions the gassiest dreams of what struggle for ideas truly is, of false and sentimentalized views of authority (both bowing before it and blow-hard defiance), and in general acted more like a Hollywood caricature of a "genius" than a person with the ballbreaking desire to uphold the immortal flame of art in his smallish hand.

I found after I had been handcuffed, ambulanced, doped, needled, marched in formation and given a leather belt to make as if I were in my dotage rather than the prime of life, that I *had* to disagree basically and deliberately with the cowardly normal notion of what constitutes insanity because it is only by *the assertion of the individual spirit that we can change definitions of reality that are already insecure and losing their hold on the conceptual imagination.* In other words, if a majority of people agree that what was once confidently called insanity no longer exists in its traditional sense, can not truthfully be a determining measurement in a time like this where each good person in the reaches of his mind is often an amateur lunatic by older slogans of "rationality," then the enslavement of the word and meaning are broken. Not only was I forced to this simple attitude because my human spirit refused the reduction of my total self to only one exaggerated aspect of it—namely the pathological label—I saw in both sanitariums no consistency in what was thought of as "sick."

In short, I could no longer afford to think of contemporary insanity as an exact objective phenomenon, like thunder or cancer, but rather as an interpretation of human thought and behavior conditioned by inherited prejudices, fear, questionable middle-class assumptions of the purpose of life, a policeman's narrow idea of freedom, and dollar-hard AMA notions of responsibility and *expediency* ("1. Apt and suitable to the end in view; as, an expedient solution; hence, advantageous. 2. Conducive to special advantage rather than to what is universally right."— Web. New Colleg. Dict.). No longer could I see any true authority or finality in a conception that could be too conveniently tailored to fit the situation. I knew then that anyone who dares the intellectual conventions of this local time must be prepared to have "psychotic" or any of its variants—paranoid, schizophrenic, even the mild psychopathic!—thrown at them. The pathological interpretation of human nature has become a style in our period (overemphasized by the junior science of psychiatry) and has come to mirror the fears, anxieties and values of those currently in positions of social authority more often than the person who is being gutted. Within the iron maiden of this fashion—which undeniably hurts, right down to the roots of the soul—the independent person and the artist-type have no choice but to trust implicitly what they see with their intellect and imagination; for when the climate changes, only the individual vision will stand secure upon its God-given legs of having had faith in actual experience.

I therefore believe that the fear and even the actual living through of much that used to be called "insanity" is almost an emotional necessity for every truly feeling, reacting, totally human person in America at this time—*until* he or she passes through the soul-crippling (not healing) judgment of such language and comes out of the fire at the point where other words and hence different conceptions are created from the wounds. The psychiatric vocabulary and definitions, which once seemed such a liberating instrument for modern man, have unwittingly woven a tight and ironically strangling noose around the neck of the brain; contemporary men and women—especially intellectuals—tremblingly judge themselves and others in the black light of psychopathology and shrink human nature to the size of their own fears instead of giving it the liberty of their greatest dreams. But we can be grateful that the human soul is so constructed that it ultimately bursts concepts once held as true out of its terrible need to live and creates the world anew just in order to breathe in it. One final thought: should any readers see this article as an effort at self-justification they are right, as far as they go; but they should remember that it is only out of the self and its experience (even if I have failed here) that new light has ever been cast on the perpetual burden of making life ever more *possible* at its most crucial level.

63 The Myth of Mental Illness

● THOMAS S. SZASZ

My aim in this essay is to raise the question "Is there such a thing as mental illness?" and to argue that there is not. Since the notion of mental illness is extremely widely used nowadays, inquiry into the ways in which this term is employed would seem to be especially indicated. Mental illness, of course, is not literally a "thing"—or physical object—and hence it can "exist" only in the same sort of way in which other theoretical concepts exist. Yet, familiar theories are in the habit of posing, sooner or later—at least to those who come to believe in them—as "objective truths" (or "facts"). During certain historical periods, explanatory conceptions such as deities, witches, and microorganisms appeared not only as theories but as self-evident *causes* of a vast number of events. I submit that today mental illness is widely regarded in a somewhat similar fashion, that is, as the cause of innumerable diverse happenings. As an antidote to the complacent use of the notion of mental illness—whether as a self-evident phenomenon, theory, or cause—let us ask this question: What is meant when it is asserted that someone is mentally ill?

In what follows I shall describe briefly the main uses to which the concept of mental illness has been put. I shall argue that this notion has outlived whatever usefulness it might have had and that it now functions merely as a convenient myth.

Mental Illness as a Sign of Brain Disease

The notion of mental illness derives its main support from such phenomena as syphilis of the brain or delirious conditions—intoxications, for instance—in which persons are known to manifest various peculiarities or disorders of thinking and behavior. Correctly speaking, however, these are diseases of the brain, not of the mind. According to one school of thought, *all* so-called mental illness is of this type. The assumption is made that some neurological defect, perhaps a very subtle one, will ultimately be found for all the disorders of thinking and behavior. Many contemporary psychiatrists, physicians, and other scientists hold this view. This position implies that people *cannot* have troubles—expressed in what are *now called* "mental illnesses"—because of differences in personal needs, opinions, social aspirations, values, and so on. *All problems in living* are attributed to physicochemical processes which in due time will be discovered by medical research.

"Mental illnesses" are thus regarded as basically no different than all other diseases (that is, of the body). The only difference, in this view, between mental and bodily diseases is that the former, affecting the brain, manifest themselves by means of mental symptoms; whereas the latter, affecting other organ systems (for example, the skin, liver, etc.), manifest themselves by means of symptoms referable to those parts of the body. This view rests on and expresses what are, in my opinion, two fundamental errors.

SOURCE: Thomas S. Szasz, in the *American Psychologist*, XV (February 1960), pp. 113–118. Copyright 1960 by the American Psychological Association and reproduced by permission.

In the first place, what central nervous system symptoms would correspond to a skin eruption or a fracture? It would *not* be some emotion or complex bit of behavior. Rather, it would be blindness or a paralysis of some part of the body. The crux of the matter is that a disease of the brain, analogous to a disease of the skin or bone, is a neurological defect, and not a problem in living. For example, a *defect* in a person's visual field may be satisfactorily explained by correlating it with certain definite lesions in the nervous system. On the other hand, a person's *belief*—whether this be a belief in Christianity, in Communism, or in the idea that his internal organs are "rotting" and that his body is, in fact, already "dead"— cannot be explained by a defect or disease of the nervous system. Explanations of this sort of occurrence—assuming that one is interested in the belief itself and does not regard it simply as a "symptom" or expression of something else that is *more interesting*—must be sought along different lines.

The second error in regarding complex psychosocial behavior, consisting of communications about ourselves and the world about us, as mere symptoms of neurological functioning is *epistemological*. In other words, it is an error pertaining not to any mistakes in observation or reasoning, as such, but rather to the way in which we organize and express our knowledge. In the present case, the error lies in making a symmetrical dualism between mental and physical (or bodily) symptoms, a dualism which is merely a habit of speech and to which no known observations can be found to correspond. Let us see if this is so. In medical practice, when we speak of physical disturbances, we mean either signs (for example, a fever) or symptoms (for example, pain). We speak of mental symptoms, on the other hand, when we refer to a patient's *communications about himself, others, and the world about him.* He might state that he is Napoleon or that he is being persecuted by the Communists. These would be considered mental symptoms *only* if the observer believed that the patient was *not* Napoleon or that he was *not* being persecuted by the Communists. This makes it apparent that the statement that "X is a mental symptom" involves rendering a judgment. The judgment entails, moreover, a covert comparison or matching of the patient's ideas, concepts, or beliefs with those of the observer and the society in which they live. The notion of mental symptom is therefore inextricably tied to the *social* (including *ethical*) *context* in which it is made in much the same way as the notion of bodily symptom is tied to an *anatomical* and *genetic context* (Szasz, 1957a, 1957b).

To sum up what has been said thus far: I have tried to show that for those who regard mental symptoms as signs of brain disease, the concept of mental illness is unnecessary and misleading. For what they mean is that people so labeled suffer from diseases of the brain; and, if that is what they mean, it would seem better for the sake of clarity to say that and not something else.

Mental Illness as a Name for Problems in Living

The term "mental illness" is widely used to describe something which is very different than a disease of the brain. Many people today take it for granted that living is an arduous process. Its hardship for modern man, moreover, derives not so much from a struggle for biological survival as from the stresses and strains inherent in the social intercourse of complex human personalities. In this context, the notion of mental illness is used to identify or describe some feature of an individual's so-called personality. Mental illness—as a deformity of the personality, so to speak—is then regarded as the *cause* of the human disharmony. It is implicit in this view that social intercourse between people is regarded as something *inherently harmonious*, its disturbance being due solely to the presence of "mental illness" in many people. This is obviously fallacious reasoning, for it makes the abstraction "mental illness" into a *cause*, even though this abstraction was created in the first place to serve only as a shorthand expression for certain types of human behavior. It now becomes necessary to ask: "What kinds of behavior are regarded as indicative of mental illness, and by whom?"

The concept of illness, whether bodily or mental, implies *deviation from some clearly defined norm*. In the case of physical illness, the norm is the structural and functional integrity of the human body. Thus, although the desirability of physical health, as such, is an ethical value, what health *is* can be stated in anatomical and physiological terms. What is the norm deviation from which is regarded as mental illness? This question cannot be easily answered. But whatever this norm might be, we can be certain of only one thing: namely, that it is a norm that must be stated in terms of *psychosocial, ethical,* and *legal* concepts. For example, notions such as "excessive repression" or "acting out an unconscious impulse" illustrate the use of psychological concepts for judging (so-called) mental health and illness. The idea that chronic hostility, vengefulness, or divorce are indicative of mental illness would be illustrations of the use of ethical norms (that is, the desirability of love, kindness, and a stable marriage relationship). Finally, the widespread psychiatric opinion that only a mentally ill person would commit homicide illustrates the use of a legal concept as a norm of mental health. The norm from which deviation is measured whenever one speaks of a mental illness is a *psychosocial and ethical one*. Yet, the remedy is sought in terms of *medical* measures which—it is hoped and assumed—are free from wide differences of ethical value. The definition of the disorder and the terms in which its remedy are sought are therefore at serious odds with one another. The practical significance of this covert conflict between the alleged nature of the defect and the remedy can hardly be exaggerated.

Having identified the norms used to measure deviations in cases of mental illness, we will now turn to the question: "Who defines the norms and hence the deviation?" Two basic answers may be offered: (*a*) It may be the person himself (that is, the patient) who decides that he deviates from a norm. For example, an artist may believe that he suffers from a work inhibition; and he may implement this conclusion by seeking help *for* himself from a psychotherapist. (*b*) It may be someone other than the patient who decides that the latter is deviant (for example, relatives, physicians, legal authorities, society generally, etc.). In such a case a psychiatrist may be hired by others to do something *to* the patient in order to correct the deviation.

These considerations underscore the importance of asking the question "Whose agent is the psychiatrist?" and of giving a candid answer to it (Szasz, 1956, 1958). The psychiatrist (psychologist or nonmedical psychotherapist), it now develops, may be the agent of the patient, of the relatives, of the school, of the military services, of a business organization, of a court of law, and so forth. In speaking of the psychiatrist as the agent of these persons or organizations, it is not implied that his values concerning norms, or his ideas and aims concerning the proper nature of remedial action, need to coincide exactly with those of his employer. For example, a patient in individual psychotherapy may believe that his salvation lies in a new marriage; his psychotherapist need not share this hypothesis. As the patient's agent, however, he must abstain from bringing social or legal force to bear on the patient which would prevent him from putting his beliefs into action. If his *contract* is with the patient, the psychiatrist (psychotherapist) may disagree with him or stop his treatment; but he cannot engage others to obstruct the patient's aspirations. Similarly, if a psychiatrist is engaged by a court to determine the sanity of a criminal, he need not fully share the legal authorities' values and intentions in regard to the criminal and the means available for dealing with him. But the psychiatrist is expressly barred from stating, for example, that it is not the criminal who is "insane" but the men who wrote the law on the basis of which the very actions that are being judged are regarded as "criminal." Such an opinion could be voiced, of course, but not in a courtroom, and not by a psychiatrist who makes it his practice to assist the court in performing its daily work.

To recapitulate: In actual contemporary social usage, the finding of a mental illness is made by establishing a deviance in behavior from certain psychosocial, ethical, or legal norms. The judgment may be made, as in medicine, by the patient, the physician (psychiatrist), or others. Remedial action, finally, tends to be sought in a therapeutic—or covertly medical—framework, thus creating a situation in which *psychosocial, ethical,* and/or *legal deviations* are claimed to be correctible by (so-called) *medical action.* Since medical action is designed to correct only medical deviations, it seems logically absurd to expect that it will help solve problems whose very existence had been defined and established on nonmedical grounds. I think that these considerations may be fruitfully applied to the present use of tranquilizers and, more generally, to what might be expected of drugs of whatever type in regard to the amelioration or solution of problems in human living.

The Role of Ethics in Psychiatry

Anything that people *do*—in contrast to things that *happen* to them (Peters, 1958)—takes place in a context of value. In this broad sense, no human activity is devoid of ethical implications. When the values underlying certain activities are widely shared, those who participate in their pursuit may lose sight of them altogether. The discipline of medicine, both as a pure science (for example, research) and as a technology (for example, therapy), contains many ethical considerations and judgments. Unfortunately, these are often denied, minimized, or merely kept out of focus; for the ideal of the medical profession as well as of the people whom it serves seems to be having a system of medicine (allegedly) free of ethical value. This sentimental notion is expressed by such things as the doctor's willingness to treat and help patients irrespective of their religious or political beliefs, whether they are rich or poor, etc. While there may be some grounds for this belief—albeit it is a view that is not impressively true even in these regards—the fact remains that ethical considerations encompass a vast range of human affairs. By making the practice of medicine neutral in regard to some specific issues of value need not, and cannot, mean that it can be kept free from all such values. The practice of medicine is intimately tied to ethics; and the first thing that we must do, it seems to me, is to try to make this clear and explicit. I shall let this matter rest here, for it does not concern us specifically in this essay. Lest there be any vagueness, however, about how or where ethics and medicine meet, let me remind the reader of such issues as birth control, abortion, suicide, and euthanasia as only a few of the major areas of current ethicomedical controversy.

Psychiatry, I submit, is very much more intimately tied to problems of ethics than is medicine. I use the word "psychiatry" here to refer to that contemporary discipline which is concerned with *problems in living* (and not with diseases of the brain, which are problems for neurology). Problems in human relations can be analyzed, interpreted, and given meaning only within given social and ethical contexts. Accordingly, it *does* make a difference—arguments to the contrary not-withstanding—what the psychiatrist's socioethical orientations happen to be; for these will influence his ideas on what is wrong with the patient, what deserves comment or interpretation, in what possible directions change might be desirable, and so forth. Even in medicine proper, these factors play a role, as for instance, in the divergent orientations which physicians, depending on their religious affilia-tions, have toward such things as birth control and therapeutic abortion. Can anyone really believe that a psychotherapist's ideas concerning religious belief, slavery, or other similar issues play no role in his practical work? If they do make a difference, what are we to infer from it? Does it not seem reasonable that we ought to have different psychiatric therapies—each expressly recognized for the ethical positions which they embody—for, say, Catholics and Jews, religious per-sons and agnostics, democrats and communists, white supremacists and Negroes, and so on? Indeed, if we look at how psychiatry is actually practiced today (especially in the United States), we find that people do seek psychiatric help in accordance with their social status and ethical beliefs (Hollingshead & Redlich, 1958). This should really not surprise us more than being told that practicing Catholics rarely frequent birth control clinics.

The foregoing position which holds that contemporary psychotherapists deal with problems in living, rather than with mental illnesses and their cures, stands in opposition to a currently prevalent claim, according to which mental illness is just as "real" and "objective" as bodily illness. This is a confusing claim since it is never known exactly what is meant by such words as "real" and "objective." I suspect, however, that what is intended by the proponents of this view is to create the idea in the popular mind that mental illness is some sort of disease entity, like an infection or a malignancy. If this were true, one could *catch* or *get* a "mental illness," one might *have* or *harbor* it, one might *transmit* it to others, and finally one could get rid of it. In my opinion, there is not a shred of evidence to support this idea. To the contrary, all the evidence is the other way and supports the view that what people now call mental illnesses are for the most part *communications* expressing unacceptable ideas, often framed, moreover, in an unusual idiom. The scope of this essay allows me to do no more than mention this alternative theoreti-cal approach to this problem (Szasz, 1957c).

This is not the place to consider in detail the similarities and differences between bodily and mental illnesses. It shall suffice for use here to emphasize only one im-portant difference between them: namely, that whereas bodily disease refers to public, physicochemical occurrences, the notion of mental illness is used to codify relatively more private, sociopsychological happenings of which the observer (diagnostician) forms a part. In other words, the psychiatrist does not stand *apart* from what he observes, but is, in Harry Stack Sullivan's apt words, a "participant observer." This means that he is *committed* to some picture of what he considers reality—and to what he thinks society considers reality—and he observes and judges the patient's behavior in the light of these considerations. This touches on our earlier observation that the notion of mental symptom itself implies a comparison between observer and observed, psychiatrist and patient. This is so obvious that I may be charged with belaboring trivialities. Let me therefore say once more that my aim in presenting this argument was expressly to criticize and counter a prevailing contemporary tendency to deny the moral aspects of psychiatry (and psychotherapy) and to substitute for them allegedly value-free medical considerations. Psychotherapy, for example, is being widely practiced as though it entailed nothing other than restoring the patient from a state of mental sickness to one of mental health. While it is generally accepted that mental illness has something to do with man's social (or interpersonal) relations, it is paradoxically maintained that problems of values (that is, of ethics) do not arise in this process.[1] Yet, in one sense, much of psychotherapy may revolve around nothing other than the elucidation and weighing of goals and values—many of which may be mutually contradictory—and the means whereby they might best be harmonized, realized, or relinquished.

The diversity of human values and the methods by means of which they may be realized is so vast, and many of them remain so unacknowledged, that they cannot fail but lead to conflicts in human relations. Indeed, to say that human relations at all levels—from mother to child, through husband and wife, to nation and nation—are fraught with stress, strain, and disharmony is, once again, making the obvious explicit. Yet, what may be obvious may be also poorly understood. This I think is the case here. For it seems to me that—at least in our scientific theories of behavior—we have failed to *accept* the simple fact that human relations are inherently fraught with difficulties and that to make them even relatively harmonious requires much patience and hard work. I submit that the idea of mental illness is now being put to work to obscure certain difficulties which at present may be inherent—not that they need be unmodifiable—in the social intercourse of persons. If this is true, the concept functions as a disguise; for instead of calling attention to conflicting human needs, aspirations, and values, the notion of mental illness provides an amoral and impersonal "thing" (an "illness") as an explanation for *problems in living* (Szasz, 1959). We may recall in this connection that not so long ago it was devils and witches who were held responsible for men's problems in social living. The belief in mental illness, as something other than man's trouble in getting along with his fellow man, is the proper heir to the belief in demonology and witchcraft. Mental illness exists or is "real" in exactly the same sense in which witches existed or were "real."

Choice, Responsibility, and Psychiatry

While I have argued that mental illnesses do not exist, I obviously did not imply that the social and psychological occurrences to which this label is currently being attached also do not exist. Like the personal and social troubles which people had

---

[1] Freud went so far as to say that: "I consider ethics to be taken for granted. Actually I have never done a mean thing" (Jones, 1957, p. 247). This surely is a strange thing to say for someone who has studied man as a social being as closely as did Freud. I mention it here to show how the notion of "illness" (in the case of psychoanalysis, "psychopathology," or "mental illness") was used by Freud—and by most of his followers—as a means for classifying certain forms of human behavior as falling within the scope of medicine, and hence (by *fiat*) outside that of ethics!

in the Middle Ages, they are real enough. It is the labels we give them that concerns us and, having labelled them, what we do about them. While I cannot go into the ramified implications of this problem here, it is worth noting that a demonologic conception of problems in living gave rise to therapy along theological lines. Today, a belief in mental illness implies—nay, requires—therapy along medical or psychotherapeutic lines.

What is implied in the line of thought set forth here is something quite different. I do not intend to offer a new conception of "psychiatric illness" nor a new form of "therapy." My aim is more modest and yet also more ambitious. It is to suggest that the phenomena now called mental illnesses be looked at afresh and more simply, that they be removed from the category of illnesses, and that they be regarded as the expressions of man's struggle with the problem of *how* he should live. The last mentioned problem is obviously a vast one, its enormity reflecting not only man's inability to cope with his environment, but even more his increasing self-reflectiveness.

By problems in living, then, I refer to that truly explosive chain reaction which began with man's fall from divine grace by partaking of the fruit of the tree of knowledge. Man's awareness of himself and of the world about him seems to be a steadily expanding one, bringing in its wake an ever larger *burden of understanding* (an expression borrowed from Susanne Langer, 1953). *This burden, then, is to be expected and must not be misinterpreted.* Our only *rational* means for lightening it is *more understanding*, and appropriate *action* based on such understanding. The main alternative lies in acting as though the burden were not what in fact we perceive it to be and taking refuge in an outmoded theological view of man. In the latter view, man does not fashion his life and much of his world about him, but merely lives out his fate in a world created by superior beings. This may logically lead to pleading nonresponsibility in the face of seemingly unfathomable problems and difficulties. Yet, if man fails to take increasing responsibility for his actions, individually as well as collectively, it seems unlikely that some higher power or being would assume this task and carry this burden for him. Moreover, this seems hardly the proper time in human history for obscuring the issue of man's responsibility for his actions by hiding it behind the skirt of an all-explaining conception of mental illness.

Conclusions

I have tried to show that the notion of mental illness has outlived whatever usefulness it might have had and that it now functions merely as a convenient myth. As such, it is a true heir to religious myths in general, and to the belief in witchcraft in particular; the role of all these belief-systems was to act as *social tranquilizers*, thus encouraging the hope that mastery of certain specific problems may be achieved by means of substitutive (symbolic-magical) operations. The notion of mental illness thus serves mainly to obscure the everyday fact that life for most people is a continuous struggle, not for biological survival, but for a "place in the sun," "peace of mind," or some other human value. For man aware of himself and of the world about him, once the needs for preserving the body (and perhaps the race) are more or less satisfied, the problem arises as to what he should do with himself. Sustained adherence to the myth of mental illness allows people to avoid facing this problem, believing that mental health, conceived as the absence of mental illness, automatically insures the making of right and safe choices in one's conduct of life. But the facts are all the other way. It is the making of good choices in life that others regard, retrospectively, as good mental health!

The myth of mental illness encourages us, moreover, to believe in its logical corollary: that social intercourse would be harmonious, satisfying, and the secure basis of a "good life" were it not for the disrupting influences of mental illness or "psychopathology." The potentiality for universal human happiness, in this form at least, seems to me but another example of the I-wish-it-were-true type of fantasy. I do believe that human happiness or well-being on a hitherto unimaginably large scale, and not just for a select few, is possible. This goal could be achieved, however, only at the cost of many men, and not just a few being willing and able to tackle their personal, social, and ethical conflicts. This means having the courage and integrity to forego waging battles on false fronts, finding solutions for substitute problems—for instance, fighting the battle of stomach acid and chronic fatigue instead of facing up to a marital conflict.

Our adversaries are not demons, witches, fate, or mental illness. We have no enemy whom we can fight, exorcise, or dispel by "cure." What we do have are *problems in living*—whether these be biologic, economic, political, or sociopsychological. In this essay I was concerned only with problems belonging in the last mentioned category, and within this group mainly with those pertaining to moral values. The field to which modern psychiatry addresses itself is vast, and I made no effort to encompass it all. My argument was limited to the proposition that mental illness is a myth, whose function it is to disguise and thus render more palatable the bitter pill of moral conflicts in human relations.

References

HOLLINGSHEAD, A. B., AND F. C. REDLICH. *Social class and mental illness.* New York: Wiley, 1958.

JONES, E. *The life and work of Sigmund Freud.* Vol. III. New York: Basic Books, 1957.

LANGER, S. K. *Philosophy in a new key.* New York: Mentor Books, 1953.

PETERS, R. S. *The concept of motivation.* London: Routledge & Kegan Paul, 1958.

SZASZ, T. S. Malingering: "Diagnosis" or social condemnation? *AMA Arch Neurol. Psychiat.,* 1956, 76, 432–443.

SZASZ, T. S. *Pain and pleasure: A study of bodily feelings.* New York: Basic Books, 1957. (a)

SZASZ, T. S. The problem of psychiatric nosology: A contribution to a situational analysis of psychiatric operations. *Amer. J. Psychiat.,* 1957, 114, 405–413. (b)

SZASZ, T. S. On the theory of psychoanalytic treatment. *Int. J. Psycho-Anal.,* 1957, 38, 166–182. (c)

SZASZ, T. S. Psychiatry, ethics and the criminal law. *Columbia Law Rev.,* 1958, 58, 183–198.

SZASZ, T. S. Moral conflict and psychiatry. *Yale Rev.,* 1959, in press.

64 Mental Illness as Residual Deviance

● THOMAS J. SCHEFF

The Origins of Residual Rule-Breaking

It is customary in psychiatric research to seek a single generic source or at best a small number of sources for mental illness. The redefinition of psychiatric symptoms as residual deviance immediately suggests, however, that there should be an unlimited number of sources of deviance. The first proposition is therefore:

1. *Residual rule-breaking arises from fundamentally diverse sources.* Four distinct types of sources will be discussed here: organic, psychological, external stress, and volitional acts of innovation or defiance. The organic and psychological origins of residual rule-breaking are widely noted and will not be discussed at length here. It has been demonstrated repeatedly that particular cases of mental disorder had their origin in genetic, bio-chemical or physiological conditions. Psychological sources are also frequently indicated: peculiarity of upbringing and training have been reported often, particularly in the psychoanalytic literature. The great majority of precise and systematic studies of causation of mental disorder have been limited to either organic or psychological sources.

It is widely granted, however, that psychiatric symptoms can also arise from external stress: from drug ingestion, the sustained fear and hardship of combat, and from deprivation of food, sleep, and even sensory experience. Excerpts from reports on the consequences of stress will illustrate the rule-breaking behavior that is generated by this less familiar source.

Physicians have long known that toxic substances can cause psychotic-like symptoms, when ingested in appropriate doses. Recently a wide variety of substances have been the subject of experimentation in producing "model psychoses." Drugs such as mescaline and LSD–25, particularly, have been described as producing fairly close replicas of psychiatric symptoms, such as visual hallucinations, loss of orientation to space and time, interference with thought processes, etc. Here is an excerpt from a report by a person who had taken LSD–25, who was a qualified psychologist: [1]

> One concomitant of LSD that I shared with other subjects was distortion of the time sense. The subjective clock appeared to race. This was observed even at 25 milligrams in counting 60 seconds. My tapping rate was also speeded up. On the larger dose (½ gram) my time sense was displaced by hours. I thought the afternoon was well spent when it was only 1:00 P.M. I could look at my watch and realize the error, but I continued to be disoriented in time. The time sense depends on the way time is "filled," and I was probably responding to the quickened tempo of experience.
>
> This was, in fact, my overwhelming impression of LSD. Beginning with the physiological sensations (lightheadedness, excitement) I was shortly flooded by a

---

SOURCE: Thomas J. Scheff, in his *Being Mentally Ill* (Chicago: Aldine Publishing Company, 1966), pp. 31–54. Copyright © 1966 by Thomas J. Scheff.

[1] C. C. Bennett, "The Drugs and I," in L. Uhr and J. G. Miller (eds.), *Drugs and Behavior* (New York: Wiley, 1960), pp. 606–607.

montage of ideas, images, and feelings that seemed to thrust themselves upon me unbidden. I had glimpses of very bright thoughts, like a fleeting insight into the psychotic process, which I wanted to write down. . . . But they pushed each other aside. Once gone, they could not be recaptured because the parade of new images could not be stopped.

The time disorientation described is a familiar psychiatric symptom, as is the ideational "pressure," which is usually described as a feature of manic excitement.

Combat psychosis and psychiatric symptoms arising from starvation have been repeatedly described in the psychiatric literature. Psychotic symptoms resulting from sleeplessness are less familiar. One instance will be used to illustrate this reaction. Brauchi and West reported the symptoms of two participants in a radio marathon, which required them to talk alternately every thirty minutes.[2] After 168 hours, one of the contestants felt that he and his opponent belonged to a secret club of nonsleepers. He accused his girl-friend of kissing an observer, even though she was with him at the time. He felt he was being punished, had transient auditory and visual hallucinations and became suggestible, he and his opponent exhibiting a period of *folie à deux* when the delusions and hallucinations of the one were accepted by the other. He showed persistence of his psychotic symptoms, with delusions about secret agents, and felt that he was responsible for the Israeli-Egyptian conflict. His reactions contain many elements which psychiatrists would describe as paranoid and depressive features.

There have been a number of recent studies which show that deprivation of sensory stimulation can cause hallucinations and other symptoms. In one such study Heron reported on subjects who were cut off from sensations:[3]

> Male college students were paid to lie 24 hours a day on a comfortable bed in a lighted semi-soundproof cubicle . . . wearing translucent goggles which admitted diffuse light but prevented pattern vision. Except when eating or at toilet, they wore cotton gloves and cardboard cuffs . . . in order to limit tactile perceptions.

The subjects stayed from two to three days. Twenty-five of the 29 subjects reported hallucinations, which usually were initially simple, and became progressively more complex over time. Three of the subjects believed their visions to be real:

> One man thought that he saw things coming at him and showed head withdrawal quite consistently when this happened; a second was convinced that we were projecting pictures on his goggles by some sort of movie camera; a third felt that someone else was in the cubicle with him.[4]

Merely monotonous environments, as in long-distance driving or flying, are now thought to be capable of generating symptoms. The following excerpt is taken from a series on psychiatric symptoms in military aviation:[5]

> A pilot was flying a bomber at 40,000 feet and had been continuing straight and level for about an hour. There was a haze over the ground which prevented a proper view and rendered the horizon indistinct. The other member of the crew

---

[2] J. T. Brauchi and L. J. West, "Sleep Deprivation," *Journal of the American Medical Association,* 171 (1959), p. 11.

[3] W. Heron, "Cognitive and Physiological Effects of Perceptual Isolation," in P. Solomon *et al.* (eds.), *Sensory Deprivation* (Cambridge, Mass.: Harvard University Press, 1961), p. 8.

[4] *Ibid.,* p. 17.

[5] A. M. H. Bennett, "Sensory Deprivation in Aviation," in Solomon, *op. cit.,* p. 166.

was sitting in a separate place out of the pilot's view, and the two men did not talk to each other. Suddenly the pilot felt detached from his surroundings and then had the strong impression that the aircraft had one wing down and was turning. Without consulting his instruments he corrected the attitude, but the aircraft went to a spiral dive because it had in fact been flying straight and level. The pilot was very lucky to recover from the spiral dive, and when he landed the airframe was found to be distorted [from the stress caused by the dive].

On examining the pilot, no psychiatric abnormality was found. . . . As the man had no wish to give up flying and was in fact physically and mentally fit, he was offered an explanation of the phenomenon and was reassured. He returned to flying duties.

In this case, the symptoms (depersonalization and spatial disorientation) occurring as they did in a real-life situation, could easily have resulted in a fatal accident. In laboratory studies of model psychoses, the consequences are usually easily controlled. Particularly relevant to this discussion is the role of reassurance of the subject by the experimenter, after the experiment is over.

In all of the laboratory studies (as in this last case as well), the persons who have had "psychotic" experiences are reassured; they are told, for example, that the experiences they had were solely due to the situation that they were placed in, and that anyone else placed in such a situation would experience similar sensations. In other words, the implications of the rule-breaking for the rule-breaker's social status and self-conception are *denied*. Suppose, however, for purposes of argument, that a diabolical experiment were performed in which subjects, after having exhibited the psychotic symptoms under stress, were "labeled." That is, they were told that the symptoms were not a normal reaction, but a reliable indication of deep-seated psychological disorder in their personality. Suppose, in fact, that such labeling were continued in their ordinary lives. Would such a labeling process stabilize rule-breaking which would have otherwise been transitory? . . .

Returning to the consideration of origins, rule-breaking finally can be seen as a volitional act of innovation or rebellion. Two examples from art history illustrate the deliberate breaking of residual rules. It is reported that the early reactions of the critics and the public to the paintings of the French impressionists was one of disbelief and dismay; the colors, particularly, were thought to be so unreal as to be evidence of madness. It is ironic that in the ensuing struggle, the Impressionists and their followers effected some changes in the color norms of the public. Today we accept the colors of the Impressionists (as in Pepsi-Cola ads) without a second glance.

The Dada movement provides an example of an art movement deliberately conceived to violate, and thereby reject, existing standards of taste and value. The jewel-encrusted book of Dada, which was to contain the greatest treasures of contemporary civilization, was found to be filled with toilet-paper, grass, and similar materials. A typical *objet d'art* produced by Dadaism was a fur-lined teacup. A climactic event in the movement was the Dada Exposition given at the Berlin Opera House. All of the celebrities of the German art world and dignitaries of the Weimar Republic were invited to attend the opening night. The first item of the evening was a poetry-reading contest, in which there were fourteen contestants. Since the fourteen read their poems simultaneously, the evening soon ended in a riot.

The examples of residual rule-breaking given here are not presented as scientifically impeccable instances of this type of behavior. There are many problems connected with reliability in these areas, particularly with the material on behavior resulting from drug ingestion, and sleep and sensory deprivation. Much of this material is simply clinical or autobiographical impressions of single, isolated instances. In the studies that have been conducted, insufficient attention is usually paid to research design, systematic techniques of data collection, and devices to guard against experimenter or subject bias.

Of the many questions of a more general nature that are posed by these examples, one of the more interesting is: are the "model psychoses" produced by drugs, or food, sleep, or sensory deprivation actually identical to "natural" psychoses, or, on the other hand, are the similarities only superficial, masking fundamental differences between the laboratory and the natural rule-breaking? The opinions of researchers are split on this issue. Many investigators state that model and real psychoses are basically the same. According to a recent report, in the autobiographical, clinical, and experimental accounts of sensory deprivation, Bleuler's cardinal symptoms of schizophrenia frequently appear: disturbances of associations, disharmony of affect, autism, ambivalence, disruption of secondary thought processes accompanied by regression to primary processes, impairment of reality-testing capacity, distortion of body image, depersonalization, delusions, and hallucinations.[6] Other researchers, however, insist that there are fundamental differences between experimental and genuine psychoses.

The controversy over model psychoses provides evidence of a basic difficulty in the scientific study of mental disorder. Although there is an enormous literature on the description of psychiatric symptoms, at this writing, scientifically respectable descriptions of the major psychiatric symptoms, that is to say, descriptions which have been shown to be precise, reliable, and valid, do not exist.[7] It is not only that studies which demonstrate the precision, reliability, and validity of measures of symptomatic behavior have not been made, but that the very basis of such studies, operational definitions of psychiatric symptoms, have yet to be formulated. In physical medicine, there are instruments that yield easily verified, repeatable measures of disease symptoms; the thermometer used in detecting the presence of fever is an obvious example. The analogous instruments in psychiatric medicine, questionnaires, behavior rating scales, etc., which yield verifiable measures of the presence of some symptom pattern (paranoid ideation, for example) have yet to be found, tested, and agreed upon.

In the absence of scientifically acceptable evidence, we can only rely on our own assessment of the evidence, in conjunction with our appraisal of the conflicting opinions of the psychiatric investigators. In this case, there is at present no conclusive answer, but the weight of evidence seems to be that there is some likelihood that the model psychoses are not basically dissimilar to ordinary psychoses. Therefore it appears that the first proposition, that there are many diverse sources of residual rule-breaking, is supported by available knowledge.

---

[6] N. Rosenzweig, "Sensory Deprivation and Schizophrenia: Some Clinical and Theoretical Similarities," *American Journal of Psychiatry*, 116 (1959), p. 326.

[7] W. A. Scott, "Research Definitions of Mental Health and Mental Illness," *Psychological Bulletin*, 55 (January, 1958), pp. 29–45.

Prevalence

The second proposition concerns the prevalence of residual rule-breaking in entire and ostensibly normal populations. This prevalence is roughly analogous to what medical epidemiologists call the "total" or "true" prevalence of mental symptoms.

2. Relative to the rate of treated mental illness, the rate of unrecorded residual rule-breaking is extremely high. There is evidence that gross violations of rules are often not noticed or, if noticed, rationalized as eccentricity. Apparently, many persons who are extremely withdrawn, or who "fly off the handle" for extended periods of time, who imagine fantastic events, or who hear voices or see visions, are not labeled as insane either by themselves or others.[8] Their rule-breaking, rather, is unrecognized, ignored, or rationalized. This pattern of inattention and rationalization will be called "denial."[9]

In addition to the kind of evidence cited above there are a number of epidemiological studies of total prevalence. There are numerous problems in interpreting the results of these studies; the major difficulty is that the definition of mental disorder is different in each study, as are the methods used to screen cases. These studies represent, however, the best available information and can be used to estimate total prevalence.

A convenient summary of findings is presented in Plunkett and Gordon.[10] These authors compare the methods and populations used in eleven field studies, and list rates of total prevalence (in percentage) as 1.7, 3.6, 4.5, 4.7, 5.3, 6.1, 10.9, 13.8, 23.2, 23.3, and 33.3.

Since the Plunkett and Gordon review was published two elaborate studies of symptom prevalence have appeared, one in Manhattan, the other in Nova Scotia.[11] In the Midtown Manhattan study it is reported that 80 per cent of the sample currently had at least one psychiatric symptom. Probably more comparable to the earlier studies is their rating of "impaired because of psychiatric illness," which was applied to 23.4 per cent of the population. In the Stirling County studies, the estimate of current prevalence is 57 per cent, with 20 per cent classified as "Psychiatric Disorder with Significant Impairment."

How do these total rates compare with the rates of treated mental disorder? One of the studies cited by Plunkett and Gordon, the Baltimore study reported by Pasamanick, is useful in this regard since it includes both treated and untreated rates.[12] As compared with the untreated rate of 10.9 per cent, the rate of treatment in state, VA, and private hospitals of Baltimore residents was 0.5 per cent.[13] That is, for every mental patient there were approximately 20 untreated persons located

---

[8] See, for example, J. A. Clausen and M. R. Yarrow, "Paths to the Mental Hospital," *Journal of Social Issues,* 11 (December, 1955), pp. 25–32; A. B. Hollingshead and F. C. Redlich, *Social Class and Mental Illness* (New York: Wiley, 1958), pp. 172–176; and E. and J. Cumming, *Closed Ranks* (Cambridge, Mass.: Harvard University Press, 1957), pp. 92–103.

[9] The term "denial" is used in the same sense as in Cumming and Cumming, *ibid.,* Chapter VII.

[10] R. J. Plunkett and J. E. Gordon, *Epidemiology and Mental Illness* (New York: Basic Books, 1960).

[11] L. Srole *et al., Mental Health in the Metropolis* (New York: McGraw-Hill, 1962); D. C. Leighton *et al., The Character of Danger* (New York: Basic Books, 1963).

[12] B. Pasamanick, "A Survey of Mental Disease in an Urban Population: IV. An Approach to Total Prevalence Rates," *Archives of General Psychiatry,* 5 (August, 1961), pp. 151–155.

[13] *Ibid.,* p. 153.

by the survey. It is possible that the treated rate is too low, however, since patients treated by private physicians were not included. Judging from another study, the New Haven study of treated prevalence, the number of patients treated in private practice is small in comparison with those hospitalized: over 70 per cent of the patients located in that study were hospitalized even though extensive case-finding techniques were employed. The overall treated prevalence in the New Haven study was reported as 0.8 per cent, a figure that is in good agreement with my estimate of 0.7 per cent for the Baltimore study.[14] If we accept 0.8 per cent as an estimate of the upper limit of treated prevalence for the Pasamanick study, the ratio of treated to untreated patients is 1 : 14. That is, for every patient we should expect to find 14 untreated cases in the community.

One interpretation of this finding is that the untreated patients in the community represent those with less severe disorders, while patients with severe impairments all fall into the treated group. Some of the findings in the Pasamanick study point in this direction. Of the untreated patients, about half are classified as psychoneurotic. Of the psychoneurotics, in turn, about half again are classified as suffering from minimal impairment. At least a fourth of the untreated group, then, involved very mild disorders.[15]

The evidence from the group diagnosed as psychotic does not support this interpretation, however. Almost all of the persons diagnosed as psychotic were judged to have severe impairment; yet half of the diagnoses of psychosis occurred in the untreated group. In other words, according to this study, there were as many untreated as treated cases of psychoses.[16]

In the Manhattan study, a direct comparison by age group was made between the most deviant group (those classified as "incapacitated") and persons actually receiving psychiatric treatment. The results for the groups of younger age (twenty to forty years) is similar to that in the Pasamanick study: treated prevalence is roughly 0.6 per cent, and the proportion classified as "incapacitated" is about 1.5 per cent. In the older age group, however, the ratio of treated to treatable changes abruptly. The treated prevalence is about 0.5 per cent, but 4 per cent are designated as "incapacitated" in the population. In the older group, therefore, the ratio of treatable to treated [17] is about 8 : 1.

Once again, because of lack of complete comparability between studies, conflicting results, and inadequate research designs, the evidence regarding prevalence is not conclusive. The existing weight of evidence appears, however, very strongly to support Proposition 2.

The Duration and Consequences of Residual Rule-Breaking

In most epidemiological research, it is frequently assumed that treated prevalence is an excellent index of total prevalence. The community studies discussed above, however, suggest that the majority of cases of "mental illness" never receive medical attention. This finding has great significance for a crucial question about residual deviance: given a typical instance of residual rule-breaking, what is its expected course and consequences? Or, to put the same question in medical lan-

---

14 Hollingshead and Redlich, *op. cit.*, p. 199.
15 Pasamanick, *op. cit.*, pp. 153–154.
16 *Ibid.*
17 Srole, *loc. cit.*

guage, what is the prognosis for a case in which psychiatric signs and symptoms are evident?

The usual working hypothesis for physicians confronted with a sign or symptom is that of progressive development as the inner logic of disease unfolds. The medical framework thus leads one to expect that unless medical intervention occurs, the signs and symptoms of disease are usually harbingers of further, and more serious, consequences for the individual showing the symptoms. This is not to say, of course, that physicians think of all symptoms as being parts of a progressive disease pattern; witness the concept of the "benign" condition. The point is that the imagery which the medical model calls up tends to predispose the physician toward expecting that symptoms are but initial signs of further illness.

The finding that the great majority of persons displaying psychiatric symptoms go untreated leads to the third proposition:

3. *Most residual rule-breaking is "denied" and is of transitory significance.* The enormously high rates of total prevalence suggest that most residual rule-breaking is unrecognized or rationalized away. For this type of rule-breaking, which is amorphous and uncrystallized, Lemert used the term "primary deviation." [18] Balint describes similar behavior as "the unorganized phase of illness." [19] Although Balint assumes that patients in this phase ultimately "settle down" to an "organized illness," other outcomes are possible. A person in this stage may "organize" his deviance in other than illness terms, e.g., as eccentricity or genius, or the rule-breaking may terminate when situational stress is removed.

The experience of battlefield psychiatrists can be interpreted to support the hypothesis that residual rule-breaking is usually transitory. Glass reports that combat neurosis is often self-terminating if the soldier is kept with his unit and given only the most superficial medical attention. [20] Descriptions of child behavior can be interpreted in the same way. According to these reports, most children go through periods in which at least several of the following kinds of rule-breaking may occur: temper tantrums, head banging, scratching, pinching, biting, fantasy playmates or pets, illusory physical complaints, and fears of sounds, shapes, colors, persons, animals, darkness, weather, ghosts, and so on. [21] In the vast majority of instances, however, these behavior patterns do not become stable.

There are, of course, conditions which do fit the model of a progressively unfolding disease. In the case of a patient exhibiting psychiatric symptoms because of general paresis, the early signs and symptoms appear to be good, though not perfect, indicators of later more serious deterioration of both physical health and social behavior. Conditions that have been demonstrated to be of this type are relatively rare, however. Paresis, which was once a major category of mental disease, accounts today for only a very minor proportion of mental patients under treatment. Proposition 3 would appear to fit the great majority of mental patients, in whom external stress such as family conflict, fatigue, drugs and similar factors are often encountered.

---

[18] E. M. Lemert, *Social Pathology* (New York: McGraw-Hill, 1951), chap. 4.

[19] M. Balint, *The Doctor, His Patient, and the Illness* (New York: International Universities Press, 1957), p. 18.

[20] A. J. Glass, "Psychotherapy in the Combat Zone," in *Symposium on Stress* (Washington, D.C.: Army Medical Service Graduate School, 1953). *Cf.* A. Kardiner and H. Spiegal, *War Stress and Neurotic Illness* (New York: Hoeber, 1947), Chapters III–IV.

[21] F. L. Ilg and L. B. Ames, *Child Behavior* (New York: Dell, 1960), pp. 138–188.

Of the first three propositions, the last is both the most crucial for the theory as a whole and the least well supported by existing evidence. It is not a matter of there being great amounts of negative evidence, showing that psychiatric symptoms are reliable indicators of subsequent disease, but that there is little evidence of any kind concerning development of symptoms over time. There are a number of analogies in the history of physical medicine, however, which are suggestive. For example, until the late 1940's, histoplasmosis was thought to be a rare tropical disease, with a uniformly fatal outcome.[22] Recently, however, it has been discovered that it is widely prevalent, and with fatal outcome or even impairment extremely unusual. It is conceivable that most "mental illnesses" may prove to follow the same pattern, when adequate longitudinal studies of cases in normal populations have been made.

If residual rule-breaking is highly prevalent among ostensibly "normal" persons and is usually transitory, as suggested by the last two propositions, what accounts for the small percentage of residual rule-breakers who go on to deviant careers? To put the question another way, under what conditions is residual rule-breaking stabilized? The conventional hypothesis is that the answer lies in the rule-breaker himself. The hypothesis suggested here is that the most important single factor (but not the only factor) in the stabilization of residual rule-breaking is the societal reaction. Residual rule-breaking may be stabilized if it is defined to be evidence of mental illness, and/or the rule-breaker is placed in a deviant status, and begins to play the role of the mentally ill.

65 Paranoia and the Dynamics of Exclusion

● EDWIN M. LEMERT

One of the few generalizations about psychotic behavior which sociologists have been able to make with a modicum of agreement and assurance is that such behavior is a result or manifestation of a disorder in communication between the individual and society. The generalization, of course, is a large one, and, while it can be illustrated easily with case history materials, the need for its conceptual refinement and detailing of the process by which disruption of communication occurs in the dynamics of mental disorder has for some time been apparent. Among the more carefully reasoned attacks upon this problem is Cameron's formulation of the paranoid pseudocommunity (1).

---

[22] J. Schwartz and G. L. Baum, "The History of Histoplasmosis," *New England Journal of Medicine*, 256 (1957), pp. 253–258.

SOURCE: Edwin M. Lemert, in *Sociometry*, XXV (March 1962), pp. 2–20. Reprinted by permission of the American Sociological Association and the author.

The research for this paper was in part supported by a grant from the California State Department of Mental Hygiene, arranged with the assistance of Dr. W. A. Oliver, Associate Superintendent of Napa State Hospital, who also helped as a critical consultant and made the facilities of the hospital available.

In essence, the conception of the paranoid pseudocommunity can be stated as follows:

Paranoid persons are those whose inadequate social learning leads them in situations of unusual stress to incompetent social reactions. Out of the fragments of the social behavior of others the paranoid person symbolically organizes a pseudocommunity whose functions he perceives as focused on him. His reactions to this *supposed community* of response which he sees loaded with threat to himself bring him into open conflict with the actual community and lead to his temporary or permanent isolation from its affairs. The "real" community, which is unable to share in his attitudes and reactions, takes action through forcible restraint or retaliation *after* the paranoid person "bursts into defensive or vengeful activity." [1]

That the community to which the paranoid reacts is "pseudo" or without existential reality is made unequivocal by Cameron when he says:

> As he (the paranoid person) begins attributing to others the attitudes which he has towards himself, he unintentionally organizes these others into a functional community, a group unified in their supposed reactions, attitudes and plans with respect to him. He in this way organizes individuals, some of whom are actual persons and some only inferred or imagined, into a whole which satisfies for the time being his immediate need for explanation but which brings no assurance with it, and usually serves to increase his tensions. The community he forms not only fails to correspond to any organization shared by others but actually contradicts this consensus. More than this, the actions ascribed by him to its personnel are not actually performed or maintained by them; *they are united in no common undertaking against him* (1). (Italics ours.)

The general insightfulness of Cameron's analysis cannot be gainsaid and the usefulness of some of his concepts is easily granted. Yet a serious question must be raised, based upon empirical inquiry, as to whether in actuality the insidious qualities of the community to which the paranoid reacts are pseudo or a symbolic fabrication. There is an alternative point of view, which is the burden of this paper, namely that, while the paranoid person reacts differentially to his social environment, it is also true that "others" react differentially to him and this reaction commonly if not typically involves covertly organized action and conspiratorial behavior in a very real sense. A further extension of our thesis is that these differential reactions are reciprocals of one another, being interwoven and concatenated at each and all phases of a process of exclusion which arises in a special kind of relationship. Delusions and associated behavior must be understood in a context of exclusion which attenuates this relationship and disrupts communication.

By thus shifting the clinical spotlight away from the individual to a relationship and a process, we make an explicit break with the conception of paranoia as a disease, a state, a condition, or a syndrome of symptoms. Furthermore, we find it unnecessary to postulate trauma of early childhood or arrested psychosexual development to account for the main features of paranoia—although we grant that these and other factors may condition its expression.

This conception of paranoia is neither simple *a priori* theory nor is it a proprietary product of sociology. There is a substantial body of writings and empirical researches in psychiatry and psychology which question the sufficiency of the

---

[1] In a subsequent article Cameron (2) modified his original conception, but not of the social aspects of paranoia, which mainly concern us.

individual as primary datum for the study of paranoia. Tyhurst, for example, concludes from his survey of this literature that reliance upon intrapsychic mechanisms and the "isolated organism" have been among the chief obstacles to fruitful discoveries about this disorder (18). Significantly, as Milner points out, the more complete the investigation of the cases the more frequently do unendurable external circumstance make their appearance (13). More precisely, a number of studies have ended with the conclusions that external circumstances—changes in norms and values, displacement, strange environments, isolation, and linguistic separation—may create a paranoid disposition in the absence of any special character structure (15). The recognition of paranoid reactions in elderly persons, alcoholics, and the deaf adds to the data generally consistent with our thesis. The finding that displaced persons who withstood a high degree of stress during war and captivity subsequently developed paranoid reactions when they were isolated in a foreign environment commands special attention among data requiring explanation in other than organic or psychodynamic terms (7, 10).

From what has been said thus far, it should be clear that our formulation and analysis will deal primarily with what Tyhurst (18) calls paranoid patterns of behavior rather than with a clinical entity in the classical Kraepelinian sense. Paranoid reactions, paranoid states, paranoid personality disturbances, as well as the seldom-diagnosed "true paranoia," which are found superimposed or associated with a wide variety of individual behavior or "symptoms," all provide a body of data for study so long as they assume priority over other behavior in meaningful social interaction. The elements of behavior upon which paranoid diagnoses are based—delusions, hostility, aggressiveness, suspicion, envy, stubbornness, jealousy, and ideas of reference—are readily comprehended and to some extent empathized by others as social reactions, in contrast to the bizarre, manneristic behavior of schizophrenia or the tempo and affect changes stressed in manic-depressive diagnoses. It is for this reason that paranoia suggests, more than any other forms of mental disorder, the possibility of fruitful sociological analysis.

Data and Procedure

The first tentative conclusions which are presented here were drawn from a study of factors influencing decisions to commit mentally disordered persons to hospitals, undertaken with the cooperation of the Los Angeles County Department of Health in 1952. This included interviews by means of schedules with members of 44 families in Los Angeles County who were active petitioners in commitment proceedings and the study of 35 case records of public health officer commitments. In 16 of the former cases and in 7 of the latter, paranoid symptoms were conspicuously present. In these cases family members and others had plainly accepted or "normalized" paranoid behavior, in some instances longstanding, until other kinds of behavior or exigencies led to critical judgments that "there was something wrong" with the person in question, and, later, that hospitalization was necessary. Furthermore, these critical judgments seemed to signal changes in the family attitudes and behavior towards the affected persons which could be interpreted as contributing in different ways to the form and intensity of the paranoid symptoms.

In 1958 a more refined and hypothesis-directed study was made of eight cases of persons with prominent paranoid characteristics. Four of these had been admitted to the state hospital at Napa, California, where they were diagnosed as paranoid schizophrenic. Two other cases were located and investigated with the assistance of the district attorney in Martinez, California. One of the persons had previously been committed to a California state hospital, and the other had been held on an insanity petition but was freed after a jury trial. Added to these was one so-called "White House case," which had involved threats to a President of the United States, resulting in the person's commitment to St. Elizabeth's Hospital in Washington, D.C. A final case was that of a professional person with a history of chronic job difficulties, who was designated and regarded by his associates as "brash," "queer," "irritating," "hypercritical," and "thoroughly unlikeable."

In a very rough way the cases made up a continuum ranging from one with very elaborate delusions, through those in which fact and misinterpretation were difficult to separate, down to the last case, which comes closer to what some would call paranoid personality disturbance. A requirement for the selection of the cases was that there be no history or evidence of hallucinations and also that the persons be intellectually unimpaired. Seven of the cases were of males, five of whom were over 40 years of age. Three of the persons had been involved in repeated litigations. One man published a small, independent paper devoted to exposures of psychiatry and mental hospitals. Five of the men had been or were associated with organizations, as follows: a small-town high school, a government research bureau, an association of agricultural producers, a university, and a contracting business.

The investigations of the cases were as exhaustive as it was possible to make them, reaching relatives, work associates, employers, attorneys, police, physicians, public officials and any others who played significant roles in the lives of the persons involved. As many as 200 hours each were given to collecting data on some of the cases. Written materials, legal documents, publications and psychiatric histories were studied in addition to the interview data. Our procedure in the large was to adopt an interactional perspective which sensitized us to sociologically relevant behavior underlying or associated with the more apparent and formal contexts of mental disorder. In particular we were concerned to establish the order in which delusions and social exclusion occur and to determine whether exclusion takes conspiratorial form.

The Relevant Behavior

In another paper (8) we have shown that psychotic symptoms as described in formal psychiatry are not relevant bases for predictions about changes in social status and social participation of persons in whom they appear. Apathy, hallucinations, hyperactivity, mood swings, tics, tremors, functional paralysis or tachychardias have no intrinsic social meanings. By the same token, neither do such imputed attributes as "lack of insight," "social incompetence," or "defective role-taking ability" favored by some sociologists as generic starting points for the analysis of mental disorders. Rather, it is behavior which puts strain on social relationships that leads to status changes: informal or formal exclusion from groups, definition as a "crank," or adjudication as insane and commitment to a mental hospital (8). This is true even where the grandiose and highly bizarre delusions of paranoia are present. Definition of the socially stressful aspects of this disorder is a minimum essential, if we are to account for its frequent occurrence in partially compensated or benign form in society, as well as account for its more familiar presence as an official psychiatric problem in a hospital setting.

It is necessary, however, to go beyond these elementary observations to make it pre-eminently clear that strain is an emergent product of a relationship in which the behaviors of two or more persons are relevant factors, and in which the strain is felt both by ego and *alter* or *alters*. The paranoid relationship includes reciprocating behaviors with attached emotions and meanings which, to be fully understood, must be described cubistically from at least two of its perspectives. On one hand the behavior of the individual must be seen from the perspective of others or that of a group, and conversely the behavior of others must be seen from the perspective of the involved individual.

From the vantage of others the individual in the paranoid relationship shows:

1. A disregard for the values and norms of the primary group, revealed by giving priority to verbally definable values over those which are implicit, a lack of loyalty in return for confidences, and victimizing and intimidating persons in positions of weakness.
2. A disregard for the implicit structure of groups, revealed by presuming to privileges not accorded him, and the threat or actual resort to formal means for achieving his goals.

The second items have a higher degree of relevancy than the first in an analysis of exclusion. Stated more simply, they mean that, to the group, the individual is an ambiguous figure whose behavior is uncertain, whose loyalty can't be counted on. In short, he is a person who can't be trusted because he threatens to expose informal power structures. This, we believe, is the essential reason for the frequently encountered idea that the paranoid person is "dangerous" (4).

If we adopt the perceptual set of ego and see others or groups through his eyes, the following aspects of their behavior become relevant:

1. the spurious quality of the interaction between others and himself or between others interacting in his presence;
2. the overt avoidance of himself by others;
3. the structured exclusion of himself from interaction.

The items we have described thus far—playing fast and loose with the primary group values by the individual, and his exclusion from interaction—do not alone generate and maintain paranoia. It is additionally necessary that they emerge in an interdependent relationship which requires trust for its fulfillment. The relationship is a type in which the goals of the individual can be reached only through cooperation from particular others, and in which the ends held by others are realizable if cooperation is forthcoming from ego. This is deduced from the general proposition that cooperation rests upon perceived trust, which in turn is a function of communication (11). When communication is disrupted by exclusion, there is a lack of mutually perceived trust and the relationship becomes dilapidated or paranoid. We will now consider the process of exclusion by which this kind of relationship develops.

The Generic Process of Exclusion

The paranoid process begins with persistent interpersonal difficulties between the individual and his family, or his work associates and superiors, or neighbors, or other persons in the community. These frequently or even typically arise out of bona fide or recognizable issues centering upon some actual or threatened loss of status for the individual. This is related to such things as the death of relatives, loss of a position, loss of professional certification, failure to be promoted, age and physiological life cycle changes, mutilations, and changes in family and marital relationships. The status changes are distinguished by the fact that they leave no alternative acceptable to the individual, from whence comes their "intolerable" or "unendurable" quality. For example: the man trained to be a teacher who loses his certificate, which means he can never teach; or the man of 50 years of age who is faced with loss of a promotion which is a regular order of upward mobility in an organization, who knows that he can't "start over"; or the wife undergoing hysterectomy, which mutilates her image as a woman.

In cases where no dramatic status loss can be discovered, a series of failures often is present, failures which may have been accepted or adjusted to, but with progressive tension as each new status situation is entered. The unendurability of the current status loss, which may appear unimportant to others, is a function of an intensified commitment, in some cases born of an awareness that there is a quota placed on failures in our society. Under some such circumstances, failures have followed the person, and his reputation as a "difficult person" has preceded him. This means that he often has the status of a stranger on trial in each new group he enters, and that the groups or organizations willing to take a chance on him are marginal from the standpoint of their probable tolerance for his actions.

The behavior of the individual—arrogance, insults, presumption of privilege and exploitation of weaknesses in others—initially has a segmented or checkered pattern in that it is confined to status-committing interactions. Outside of these, the person's behavior may be quite acceptable—courteous, considerate, kind, even indulgent. Likewise, other persons and members of groups vary considerably in their tolerance for the relevant behavior, depending on the extent to which it threatens individual and organizational values, impedes functions, or sets in motion embarrassing sequences of social actions. In the early generic period, tolerance by others for the individual's aggressive behavior generally speaking is broad, and it is very likely to be interpreted as a variation of normal behavior, particularly in the absence of biographical knowledge of the person. At most, people observe that "there is something odd about him," or "he must be upset," or "he is just ornery," or "I don't quite understand him" (3).

At some point in the chain of interactions, a new configuration takes place in perceptions others have of the individual, with shifts in figure-ground relations. The individual, as we have already indicated, is an ambiguous figure, comparable to textbook figures of stairs or outlined cubes which reverse themselves when studied intently. From a normal variant the person becomes "unreliable," "untrustworthy," "dangerous," or someone with whom others "do not wish to be involved." An illustration nicely apropos of this came out in the reaction of the head of a music department in a university when he granted an interview to a man who had worked for years on a theory to compose music mathematically:

When he asked to be placed on the staff so that he could use the electronic computers of the University *I shifted my ground* . . . when I offered an objection to his theory, he became disturbed, so I changed my reaction to "yes and no."

As is clear from this, once the perceptual reorientation takes place, either as the outcome of continuous interaction or through the receipt of biographical information, interaction changes qualitatively. In our words, it becomes *spurious*, distinguished by patronizing, evasion, "humoring," guiding conversation onto selected topics, underreaction, and silence, all calculated either to prevent intense interaction or to protect individual and group values by restricting access to them. When the interaction is between two or more persons in the individual's presence it is cued by a whole repertoire of subtle expressive signs which are meaningful only to them.

The net effects of spurious interaction are to:

1. stop the flow of information to ego;
2. create a discrepancy between expressed ideas and affect among those with whom he interacts;
3. make the situation or the group image an ambiguous one for ego, much as he is for others.

Needless to say this kind of spurious interaction is one of the most difficult for an adult in our society to cope with, because it complicates or makes decisions impossible for him and also because it is morally invidious.[2]

The process from inclusion to exclusion is by no means an even one. Both individuals and members of groups change their perceptions and reactions, and vacillation is common, depending upon the interplay of values, anxieties and guilt on both sides. Members of an excluding group may decide they have been unfair and seek to bring the individual back into their confidence. This overture may be rejected or used by ego as a means of further attack. We have also found that ego may capitulate, sometimes abjectly, to others and seek group re-entry, only to be rejected. In some cases compromises are struck and a partial reintegration of ego into informal social relations is achieved. The direction which informal exclusion takes depends upon ego's reactions, the degree of communication between his interactors, the composition and structure of the informal groups, and the perceptions of "key others" at points of interaction which directly affect ego's status.

Organizational Crisis and Formal Exclusion

Thus far we have discussed exclusion as an informal process. Informal exclusion may take place but leave ego's formal status in an organization intact. So long as this status is preserved and rewards are sufficient to validate it on his terms, an uneasy peace between him and others may prevail. Yet ego's social isolation and his strong commitments make him an unpredictable factor; furthermore the rate of change and internal power struggles, especially in large and complex organizations, means that preconditions of stability may be short lived.

Organizational crises involving a paranoid relationship arise in several ways. The individual may act in ways which arouse intolerable anxieties in others, who demand that "something be done." Again, by going to higher authority or making

---

[2] The interaction in some ways is similar to that used with children, particularly the "*enfant terrible.*" The function of language in such interaction was studied by Sapir (16) years ago.

appeals outside the organization, he may set in motion procedures which leave those in power no other choice than to take action. In some situations ego remains relatively quiescent and does not openly attack the organization. Action against him is set off by growing anxieties or calculated motives of associates—in some cases his immediate superiors. Finally, regular organizational procedures incidental to promotion, retirement or reassignment may precipitate the crisis.

Assuming a critical situation in which the conflict between the individual and members of the organization leads to action to formally exclude him, several possibilities exist. One is the transfer of ego from one department, branch or division of the organization to another, a device frequently resorted to in the armed services or in large corporations. This requires that the individual be persuaded to make the change and that some department will accept him. While this may be accomplished in different ways, not infrequently artifice, withholding information, bribery, or thinly disguised threats figure conspicuously among the means by which the transfer is brought about. Needless to say, there is a limit to which transfers can be employed as a solution to the problem, contingent upon the size of the organization and the previous diffusion of knowledge about the transferee.

Solution number two we call encapsulation, which, in brief, is a reorganization and redefinition of ego's status. This has the effect of isolating him from the organization and making him directly responsible to one or two superiors who act as his intermediators. The change is often made palatable to ego by enhancing some of the material rewards of his status. He may be nominally promoted or "kicked upstairs," given a larger office, or a separate secretary, or relieved of onerous duties. Sometimes a special status is created for him.

This type of solution often works because it is a kind of formal recognition by the organization of ego's intense commitment to his status and in part a victory for him over his enemies. It bypasses them and puts him into direct communication with higher authority who may communicate with him in a more direct manner. It also relieves his associates of further need to connive against him. This solution is sometimes used to dispose of troublesome corporation executives, high-ranking military officers, and academic *personae non gratae* in universities.

A third variety of solutions to the problem of paranoia in an organization is outright discharge, forced resignation or non-renewal of appointment. Finally, there may be an organized move to have the individual in the paranoid relationship placed on sick leave, or to compel him to take psychiatric treatment. The extreme expression of this is pressure (as on the family) or direct action to have the person committed to a mental hospital.

The order of the enumerated solutions to the paranoid problem in a rough way reflects the amount of risk associated with the alternatives, both as to the probabilities of failure and of damaging repercussions to the organization. Generally, organizations seem to show a good deal of resistance to making or carrying out decisions which require expulsion of the individual or forcing hospitalization, regardless of his mental condition. One reason for this is that the person may have power within the organization, based upon his position, or monopolized skills and information,[3] and unless there is a strong coalition against him the general conservatism of administrative judgments will run in his favor. Herman

---

[3] For a systematic analysis of the organizational difficulties in removing an "unpromotable" person from a position see (9).

Wouk's novel of *The Caine Mutiny* dramatizes some of the difficulties of cashiering a person from a position of power in an essentially conservative military organization. An extreme of this conservatism is illustrated by one case in which we found a department head retained in his position in an organization even though he was actively hallucinating as well as expressing paranoid delusions.[4] Another factor working on the individual's side is that discharge of a person in a position of power reflects unfavorably upon those who placed him there. Ingroup solidarity of administrators may be involved, and the methods of the opposition may create sympathy for ego at higher levels.

Even when the person is almost totally excluded and informally isolated within an organization, he may have power outside. This weighs heavily when the external power can be invoked in some way, or when it automatically leads to raising questions as to the internal workings of the organization. This touches upon the more salient reason for reluctance to eject an uncooperative and retaliatory person, even when he is relatively unimportant to the organization. We refer to a kind of negative power derived from the vulnerability of organizations to unfavorable publicity and exposure of their private lives that are likely if the crisis proceeds to formal hearings, case review or litigation. This is an imminent possibility where paranoia exists. If hospital commitment is attempted, there is a possibility that a jury trial will be demanded, which will force leaders of the organization to defend their actions. If the crisis turns into a legal contest of this sort, it is not easy to prove insanity, and there may be damage suits. Even if the facts heavily support the petitioners, such contests can only throw unfavorable light upon the organization.

The Conspiratorial Nature of Exclusion

A conclusion from the foregoing is that organizational vulnerability as well as anticipations of retaliations from the paranoid person lay a functional basis for conspiracy among those seeking to contain or oust him. Probabilities are strong that a coalition will appear within the organization, integrated by a common commitment to oppose the paranoid person. This, the exclusionist group, demands loyalty, solidarity and secrecy from its members; it acts in accord with a common scheme and in varying degrees utilizes techniques of manipulation and misrepresentation.

Conspiracy in rudimentary form can be detected in informal exclusion apart from an organizational crisis. This was illustrated in an office research team in which staff members huddled around a water cooler to discuss the unwanted associate. They also used office telephones to arrange coffee breaks without him and employed symbolic cues in his presence, such as humming the Dragnet theme song when he approached the group. An office rule against extraneous conversation was introduced with the collusion of supervisors, ostensibly for everyone, actually to restrict the behavior of the isolated worker. In another case an interview schedule designed by a researcher was changed at a conference arranged without him. When he sought an explanation at a subsequent conference, his associates pretended to have no knowledge of the changes.

Conspiratorial behavior comes into sharpest focus during organizational crises in which the exclusionists who initiate action become an embattled group. There

---

[4] One of the cases in the first study.

is a concerted effort to gain consensus for this view, to solidify the group and to halt close interaction with those unwilling to completely join the coalition. Efforts are also made to neutralize those who remain uncommitted but who can't be kept ignorant of the plans afoot. Thus an external appearance of unanimity is given even if it doesn't exist.

Much of the behavior of the group at this time is strategic in nature, with determined calculations as to "what we will do if he does this or that." In one of our cases, a member on a board of trustees spoke of the "game being played" with the person in controversy with them. Planned action may be carried to the length of agreeing upon the exact words to be used when confronted or challenged by the paranoid individual. Above all there is continuous, precise communication among exclusionists, exemplified in one case by mutual exchanging of copies of all letters sent and received from ego.

Concern about secrecy in such groups is revealed by such things as carefully closing doors and lowering of voices when ego is brought under discussion. Meeting places and times may be varied from normal procedures; documents may be filed in unusual places and certain telephones may not be used during a paranoid crisis.

The visibility of the individual's behavior is greatly magnified during this period; often he is the main topic of conversation among the exclusionists, while rumors of the difficulties spread to other groups, which in some cases may be drawn into the controversy. At a certain juncture steps are taken to keep the members of the ingroup continually informed of the individual's movements and, if possible, of his plans. In effect, if not in form, this amounts to spying. Members of one embattled group, for example, hired an outside person unknown to their accuser to take notes on a speech he delivered to enlist a community organization on his side. In another case, a person having an office opening onto that of a department head was persuaded to act as an informant for the nucleus of persons working to depose the head from his position of authority. This group also seriously debated placing an all-night watch in front of their perceived malefactor's house.

Concomitant with the magnified visibility of the paranoid individual come distortions of his image, most pronounced in the inner coterie of exclusionists. His size, physical strength, cunning, and anecdotes of his outrages are exaggerated, with a central thematic emphasis on the fact that he is dangerous. Some individuals give cause for such beliefs in that previously they have engaged in violence or threats, others do not. One encounters characteristic contradictions in interviews on this point, such as: "No, he has never struck anyone around here—just fought with the policemen at the State Capitol," or "No, I am not afraid of him, but one of these days he will explode."

It can be said parenthetically that the alleged dangerousness of paranoid persons storied in fiction and drama has never been systematically demonstrated. As a matter of fact, the only substantial data on this, from a study of delayed admissions, largely paranoid, to a mental hospital in Norway, disclosed that "neither the paranoiacs nor the paranoids have been dangerous, and most not particularly troublesome" (14). Our interpretation of this, as suggested earlier, is that the imputed dangerousness of the paranoid individual does not come from physical fear but from the organizational threat he presents and the need to justify collective action against him.

However, this is not entirely tactical behavior—as is demonstrated by anxieties and tensions which mount among those in the coalition during the more critical phases of their interaction. Participants may develop fears quite analogous to those of classic conspirators. One leader in such a group spoke of the period of the paranoid crisis as a "week of terror," during which he was wracked with insomnia and "had to take his stomach pills." Projection was revealed by a trustee who, during a school crisis occasioned by discharge of an aggressive teacher, stated that he "watched his shadows," and "wondered if all would be well when he returned home at night." Such tensional states, working along with a kind of closure of communication within the group, are both a cause and an effect of amplified group interaction which distorts or symbolically rearranges the image of the person against whom they act.

Once the battle is won by the exclusionists, their version of the individual as dangerous becomes a crystallized rationale for official action. At this point misrepresentation becomes part of a more deliberate manipulation of ego. Gross misstatements, most frequently called "pretexts," become justifiable ways of getting his cooperation, for example, to get him to submit to psychiatric examination or detention preliminary to hospital commitment. This aspect of the process has been effectively detailed by Goffman, with his concept of a "betrayal funnel" through which a patient enters a hospital (5). We need not elaborate on this, other than to confirm its occurrence in the exclusion process, complicated in our cases by legal strictures and the ubiquitous risk of litigation.

The Growth of Delusion

The general idea that the paranoid person symbolically fabricates the conspiracy against him is in our estimation incorrect or incomplete. Nor can we agree that he lacks insight, as is so frequently claimed. To the contrary, many paranoid persons properly realize that they are being isolated and excluded by conceived interaction, or that they are being manipulated. However, they are at a loss to estimate accurately or realistically the dimensions and form of the coalition arrayed against them.

As channels of communication are closed to the paranoid person, he has no means of getting feedback on consequences of his behavior, which is essential for correcting his interpretations of the social relationships and organization which he must rely on to define his status and give him identity. He can only read overt behavior without the informal context. Although he may properly infer that people are organized against him, he can only use confrontation or formal inquisitorial procedures to try to prove this. The paranoid person must provoke strong feelings in order to receive any kind of meaningful communication from others—hence his accusations, his bluntness, his insults. Ordinarily this is non-deliberate; nevertheless, in one complex case we found the person consciously provoking discussions to get readings from others on his behavior. This man said of himself: 'Some people would describe me as very perceptive, others would describe me as very imperceptive."

The need for communication and the identity which goes with it does a good deal to explain the preference of paranoid persons for formal, legalistic, written communications, and the care with which many of them preserve records of their contracts with others. In some ways the resort to litigation is best interpreted as the effort of the individual to compel selected others to interact directly with him as equals, to engineer a situation in which evasion is impossible. The fact that the person is seldom satisfied with the outcome of his letters, his petitions, complaints and writs testifies to their function as devices for establishing contact and interaction with others, as well as "setting the record straight." The wide professional tolerance of lawyers for aggressive behavior in court and the nature of Anglo-Saxon legal institutions, which grew out of a revolt against conspiratorial or star-chamber justice, mean that the individual will be heard. Furthermore his charges must be answered; otherwise he wins by default. Sometimes he wins small victories, even if he loses the big ones. He may earn grudging respect as an adversary, and sometimes shares a kind of legal camaraderie with others in the courts. He gains an identity through notoriety.

Reinforcement of Delusion

The accepted psychiatric view is that prognosis for paranoia is poor, that recoveries from "true" paranoia are rare, with the implication that the individual's delusions more or less express an unalterable pathological condition. Granting that the individual's needs and dispositions and his self-imposed isolation are significant factors in perpetuating his delusional reactions, nevertheless there is an important social context of delusions through which they are reinforced or strengthened. This context is readily identifiable in the fixed ideas and institutionalized procedures of protective, custodial, and treatment organizations in our society. They stand out in sharpest relief where paranoid persons have come into contact with law enforcement agencies or have been hospitalized. The cumulative and interlocking impacts of such agencies work strongly to nurture and sustain the massive sense of injustice and need for identity which underlie the delusions and aggressive behavior of the paranoid individual.

Police in most communities have a well-defined concept of cranks, as they call them, although the exact criteria by which persons are so judged are not clear. Their patience is short with such persons: in some cases they investigate their original complaints and if they conclude that the person in question is a crank they tend to ignore him thereafter. His letters may be thrown away unanswered, or phone calls answered with patronizing reassurance or vague promises to take steps which never materialize.

Like the police, offices of district attorneys are frequently forced to deal with persons they refer to as cranks or soreheads. Some offices delegate a special deputy to handle these cases, quaintly referred to in one office as the "insane deputy." Some deputies say they can spot letters of cranks immediately, which means that they are unanswered or discarded. However, family or neighborhood quarrels offer almost insoluble difficulties in this respect, because often it is impossible to determine which of two parties is delusional. In one office some complainants are called "fifty-fifty," which is jargon meaning that it is impossible to say whether they are mentally stable. If one person seems to be persistently causing trouble, deputies may threaten to have him investigated, which, however, is seldom if ever done.

Both police and district attorney staffs operate continuously in situations in which their actions can have damaging legal or political repercussions. They tend to be tightly ingrouped and their initial reaction to outsiders or strangers is one of suspicion or distrust until they are proved harmless or friendly. Many of their office procedures and general manner reflect this—such as carefully recording in a log book names, time, and reason for calling of those who seek official interviews. In some instances a complainant is actually investigated before any business will be transacted with him.

When the paranoid person goes beyond local police and courts to seek redress through appeals to state or national authorities, he may meet with polite evasion, perfunctory treatment of his case or formalized distrust. Letters to administrative people may beget replies up to a certain point, but thereafter they are ignored. If letters to a highly placed authority carry threats, they may lead to an investigation by security agencies, motivated by the knowledge that assassinations are not unknown in American life. Sometimes redress is sought in legislatures, where private bills may be introduced, bills which by their nature can only be empty gestures.

In general, the contacts which the delusional person makes with formal organizations frequently disclose the same elements of shallow response, evasion, or distrust which played a part in the generic process of exclusion. They become part of a selective or selected pattern of interaction which creates a social environment of uncertainty and ambiguity for the individual. They do little to correct and much to confirm his suspicion, distrust and delusional interpretations. Moreover, even the environment of treatment agencies may contribute to the furtherance of paranoid delusion, as Stanton and Schwartz have shown in their comments on communication within the mental hospital. They speak pointedly of the "pathology of communication" brought about by staff practices of ignoring explicit meanings in statements or actions of patients and reacting to inferred or imputed meanings, thereby creating a type of environment in which "the paranoid feels quite at home" (17).

Some paranoid or paranoid-like persons become well known locally or even throughout larger areas to some organizations. Persons and groups in the community are found to assume a characteristic stance towards such people—a stance of expectancy and preparedness. In one such case, police continually checked the whereabouts of the man and, when the governor came to speak on the courthouse steps, two officers were assigned the special task of watching the man as he stood in the crowd. Later, whenever he went to the state capitol, a number of state police were delegated to accompany him when he attended committee hearings or sought interviews with state officials.[5] The notoriety this man acquired because of his reputed great strength in tossing officers around like tenpins was an obvious source of pleasure to him, despite the implications of distrust conveyed by their presence.

It is arguable that occupying the role of the mistrusted person becomes a way of life for these paranoids, providing them with an identity not otherwise possible. Their volatile contentions with public officials, their issuance of writings, publications, litigations in *persona propria*, their overriding tendency to contest issues which other people dismiss as unimportant or as "too much bother" become a central theme for their lives, without which they would probably deteriorate.

If paranoia becomes a way of life for some people, it is also true that the difficult person with grandiose and persecutory ideas may fulfill certain marginal

---

[5] This technique in even more systematic form is sometimes used in protecting the President of the United States in "White House cases."

functions in organizations and communities. One is his scapegoat function, being made the subject of humorous by-play or conjectural gossip as people "wonder what he will be up to next." In his scapegoat role, the person may help integrate primary groups within larger organizations by directing aggressions and blame towards him and thus strengthening feelings of homogeneity and consensus of group members.

There are also instances in which the broad, grapeshot charges and accusations of the paranoid person function to articulate dissatisfactions of those who fear openly to criticize the leadership of the community, organization, or state, or of the informal power structures within these. Sometimes the paranoid person is the only one who openly espouses values of inarticulate and politically unrepresented segments of the population (12). The "plots" which attract the paranoid person's attention—dope rings, international communism, monopolistic "interests," popery, Jewry, or "psychopoliticians"—often reflect the vague and ill-formed fears and concerns of peripheral groups, which tend to validate his self-chosen role as a "protector." At times in organizational power plays and community conflicts his role may even be put to canny use by more representative groups as a means of embarrassing their opposition.

The Larger Socio-cultural Context

Our comments draw to a close on the same polemic note with which they were begun, namely, that members of communities and organizations do unite in common effort against the paranoid person prior to or apart from any vindictive behavior on his part. The paranoid community is real rather than pseudo in that it is composed of reciprocal relationships and processes whose net results are informal and formal exclusion and attenuated communication.

The dynamics of exclusion of the paranoid person are made understandable in larger perspective by recognizing that decision making in American social organization is carried out in small, informal groups through casual and often subtle male interaction. Entree into such groups is ordinarily treated as a privilege rather than a right, and this privilege tends to be jealously guarded. Crucial decisions, including those to eject persons or to reorganize their status in larger formal organizations, are made secretly. The legal concept of "privileged communication" in part is a formal recognition of the necessity for making secret decisions within organizations.

Added to this is the emphasis placed upon conformity in our organization-oriented society and the growing tendency of organization elites to rely upon direct power for their purposes. This is commonly exercised to isolate and neutralize groups and individuals who oppose their policies both inside and outside of the organization. Formal structures may be manipulated or deliberately reorganized so that resistant groups and individuals are denied or removed from access to power or the available means to promote their deviant goals and values. One of the most readily effective ways of doing this is to interrupt, delay, or stop the flow of information.

It is the necessity to rationalize and justify such procedures on a democratic basis which leads to concealment of certain actions, misrepresentation of their underlying meaning, and even the resort to unethical or illegal means. The difficulty of securing sociological knowledge about these techniques, which we might call the "controls behind the controls," and the denials by those who use them that they exist are logical consequences of the perceived threat such knowledge and admissions become to informal power structures. The epiphenomena of power thus become a kind of shadowy world of our culture, inviting conjecture and condemnation.

Concluding Comment

We have been concerned with a process of social exclusion and with the ways in which it contributes to the development of paranoid patterns of behavior. While the data emphasize the organizational forms of exclusion, we nevertheless believe that these are expressions of a generic process whose correlates will emerge from the study of paranoia in the family and other groups. The differential responses of the individual to the exigencies of organized exclusion are significant in the development of paranoid reactions only insofar as they partially determine the "intolerable" or "unendurable" quality of the status changes confronting him. Idiosyncratic life history factors of the sort stressed in more conventional psychiatric analyses may be involved, but equally important in our estimation are those which inhere in the status changes themselves, age being one of the more salient of these. In either case, once situational intolerability appears, the stage is set for the interactional process we have described.

Our cases, it will be noted, were all people who remained undeteriorated, in contact with others and carrying on militant activities oriented towards recognizable social values and institutions. Generalized suspiciousness in public places and unprovoked aggression against strangers were absent from their experiences. These facts, plus the relative absence of "true paranoia" among mental-hospital populations, leads us to conclude that the "pseudo-community" associated with random aggression (in Cameron's sense) is a sequel rather than an integral part of paranoid patterns. They are likely products of deterioration and fragmentation of personality appearing, when and if they do, in the paranoid person after long or intense periods of stress and complete social isolation.

References

1. Cameron, N., "The Paranoid Pseudocommunity," *American Journal of Sociology*, 1943, 46, 33–38.
2. Cameron, N., "The Paranoid Pseudocommunity Revisited," *American Journal of Sociology*, 1959, 65, 52–58.
3. Cumming, E., and J. Cumming, *Closed Ranks*, Cambridge, Mass.: Harvard University Press, 1957, Ch. VI.
4. Dentler, R. A., and K. T. Erikson, "The Functions of Deviance in Groups," *Social Problems*, 1959, 7, 102.
5. Goffman, E., "The Moral Career of the Mental Patient," *Psychiatry*, 1959, 22, 127 ff.
6. Jaco, E. G., "Attitudes Toward, and Incidence of Mental Disorder: A Research Note," *Southwestern Social Science Quarterly*, June, 1957, p. 34.
7. Kine, F. F., "Aliens' Paranoid Reaction," *Journal of Mental Science*, 1951, 98, 589–594.
8. Lemert, E., "Legal Commitment and Social Control," *Sociology and Social Research*, 1946, 30, 370–378.
9. Levenson, B., "Bureaucratic Succession," in *Complex Organizations*, A. Etzioni, (ed.), New York: Holt, Rinehart and Winston, 1961, 362–395.

10. Listivan, I., "Paranoid States: Social and Cultural Aspects," *Medical Journal of Australia*, 1956, 776–778.
11. Loomis, J. L., "Communications, The Development of Trust, and Cooperative Behavior," *Human Relations*, 1959, 12, 305–315.
12. Marmor, J., "Science, Health and Group Opposition" (mimeographed paper), 1958.
13. Milner, K. O., "The Environment as a Factor in the Etiology of Criminal Paranoia," *Journal of Mental Science*, 1949, 95, 124–132.
14. Ödegard, Ö., "A Clinical Study of Delayed Admissions to a Mental Hospital," *Mental Hygiene*, 1958, 42, 66–77.
15. Pederson, S., "Psychological Reactions to Extreme Social Displacement (Refugee Neuroses)," *Psychoanalytic Review*, 1946, 36, 344–354.
16. Sapir, E., "Abnormal Types of Speech in Nootka," *Canada Department of Mines, Memoir 62*, 1915, No. 5.
17. Stanton, A. H., and M. S. Schwartz, *The Mental Hospital*, New York: Basic Books, 1954, 200–210.
18. Tyhurst, J. S., "Paranoid Patterns," in A. H. Leighton, J. A. Clausen, and R. Wilson (eds.), *Exploration in Social Psychiatry*, New York: Basic Books, 1957, Ch. II.

66   The Moral Career of the Mental Patient

● ERVING GOFFMAN

Traditionally the term *career* has been reserved for those who expect to enjoy the rises laid out within a respectable profession. The term is coming to be used, however, in a broadened sense to refer to any social strand of any person's course through life. The perspective of natural history is taken: unique outcomes are neglected in favor of such changes over time as are basic and common to the members of a social category, although occurring independently to each of them. Such a career is not a thing that can be brilliant or disappointing; it can no more be a success than a failure. In this light, I want to consider the mental patient.

One value of the concept of career is its two-sidedness. One side is linked to internal matters held dearly and closely, such as image of self and felt identity; the other side concerns official position, jural relations, and style of life, and is part of a publicly accessible institutional complex. The concept of career, then, allows one to move back and forth between the personal and the public, between the self and its significant society, without having to rely overly for data upon what the person says he thinks he imagines himself to be.

This paper, then, is an exercise in the institutional approach to the study of self. The main concern will be with the *moral* aspects of career—that is, the regular sequence of changes that career entails in the person's self and in his framework of imagery for judging himself and others.[1]

SOURCE: Erving Goffman, in *Psychiatry* (1959) 22: pp. 123–142. Reprinted by special permission of The William Alanson White Psychiatric Foundation, Inc., copyright holder.

[1] Material on moral career can be found in early social anthropological work on ceremonies of status transition, and in classic social psychological descriptions of those spectacular changes in one's view of self that can accompany participation in social movements and sects. Recently new kinds of relevant data have been suggested by psychiatric interest in the problem of "identity" and sociological studies of work careers and "adult socialization."

The category "mental patient" itself will be understood in one strictly socio-logical sense. In this perspective, the psychiatric view of a person becomes sig-nificant only in so far as this view itself alters his social fate—an alteration which seems to become fundamental in our society when, and only when, the person is put through the process of hospitalization.[2] I therefore exclude certain neigh-boring categories: the undiscovered candidates who would be judged "sick" by psychiatric standards but who never come to be viewed as such by themselves or others, although they may cause everyone a great deal of trouble;[3] the office patient whom a psychiatrist feels he can handle with drugs or shock on the out-side; the mental client who engages in psychotherapeutic relationships. And I include anyone, however robust in temperament, who somehow gets caught up in the heavy machinery of mental-hospital servicing. In this way the effects of being treated as a mental patient can be kept quite distinct from the effects upon a person's life of traits a clinician would view as psychopathological.[4] Persons who become mental-hospital patients vary widely in the kind and degree of ill-ness that a psychiatrist would impute to them, and in the attributes by which lay-men would describe them. But once started on the way, they are confronted by some importantly similar circumstances and respond to these in some im-portantly similar ways. Since these similarities do not come from mental illness, they would seem to occur in spite of it. It is thus a tribute to the power of social forces that the uniform status of mental patient cannot only assure an aggregate of persons a common fate and eventually, because of this, a common character, but that this social reworking can be done upon what is perhaps the most obsti-nate diversity of human materials that can be brought together by society. Here there lacks only the frequent forming of a protective group life by ex-patients to illustrate in full the classic cycle of response by which deviant subgroupings are psychodynamically formed in society.

This general sociological perspective is heavily reinforced by one key finding of sociologically oriented students in mental-hospital research. As has been re-peatedly shown in the study of non-literate societies, the awesomeness, distaste-fulness, and barbarity of a foreign culture can decrease to the degree that the student becomes familiar with the point of view to life that is taken by his sub-jects. Similarly, the student of mental hospitals can discover that the craziness or "sick behavior" claimed for the mental patient is by and large a product of the

---

[2] This point has recently been made by Elaine and John Cumming, *Closed Ranks* (Cambridge: Commonwealth Fund, Harvard University Press, 1957), pp. 101–2: *"Clinical experience sup-ports the impression that many people define mental illness as 'that condition for which a per-son is treated in a mental hospital.'. . . Mental illness, it seems, is a condition which afflicts people who must go to a mental institution, but until they go almost anything they do is nor-mal."* Leila Deasy has pointed out to me the correspondence here with the situation in white-collar crime. Of those who are detected in this activity, only the ones who do not manage to avoid going to prison find themselves accorded the social role of the criminal.

[3] Case records in mental hospitals are just now coming to be exploited to show the incredible amount of trouble a person may cause for himself and others before anyone begins to think about him psychiatrically, let alone take psychiatric action against him. See John A. Clausen and Marian Radke Yarrow, "Paths to the Mental Hospital," *Journal of Social Issues,* XI (1955), pp. 25–32; August B. Hollingshead and Frederick C. Redlich, *Social Class and Mental Illness* (New York: Wiley, 1958), pp. 173–74.

[4] An illustration of how this perspective may be taken to all forms of deviancy may be found in Edwin Lemert, *Social Pathology* (New York: McGraw-Hill, 1951), see especially pp. 74–76. A specific application to mental defectives may be found in Stewart E. Perry, "Some Theoretic Problems of Mental Deficiency and Their Action Implications," *Psychiatry,* XVII (1954), pp. 45–73, see especially pp. 67–68.

claimant's social distance from the situation that the patient is in, and is not primarily a product of mental illness. Whatever the refinements of the various patients' psychiatric diagnoses, and whatever the special ways in which social life on the "inside" is unique, the researcher can find that he is participating in a community not significantly different from any other he has studied. Of course, while restricting himself to the off-ward grounds community of paroled patients, he may feel, as some patients do, that life in the locked wards is bizarre; and while on a locked admissions or convalescent ward, he may feel that chronic "back" wards are socially crazy places. But he need only move his sphere of sympathetic participation to the "worst" ward in the hospital, and this, too, can come into social focus as a place with a livable and continuously meaningful social world. This in no way denies that he will find a minority in any ward or patient group that continues to seem quite beyond the capacity to follow rules of social organization, or that the orderly fulfillment of normative expectations in patient society is partly made possible by strategic measures that have somehow come to be institutionalized in mental hospitals.

The career of the mental patient falls popularly and naturalistically into three main phases: the period prior to entering the hospital, which I shall call the pre-patient phase; the period in the hospital, the inpatient phase; the period after discharge from the hospital, should this occur, namely, the ex-patient phase.[5] This paper will deal only with the first two phases.

The Prepatient Phase

A relatively small group of prepatients come into the mental hospital willingly, because of their own idea of what will be good for them, or because of whole-hearted agreement with the relevant members of their family. Presumably these recruits have found themselves acting in a way which is evidence to them that they are losing their minds or losing control of themselves. This view of oneself would seem to be one of the most pervasively threatening things that can happen to the self in our society, especially since it is likely to occur at a time when the person is in any case sufficiently troubled to exhibit the kind of symptom which he himself can see. As Sullivan described it,[6]

> What we discover in the self-system of a person undergoing schizophrenic change or schizophrenic processes, is then, in its simplest form, an extremely fear-marked puzzlement, consisting of the use of rather generalized and anything but exquisitely refined referential processes in an attempt to cope with what is essentially a failure at being human—a failure at being anything that one could respect as worth being.

Coupled with the person's disintegrative re-evaluation of himself will be the new, almost equally pervasive circumstance of attempting to conceal from others what he takes to be the new fundamental facts about himself, and attempting to discover whether others, too, have discovered them.[7] Here I want to stress that perception of losing one's mind is based on culturally derived and socially

---

[5] This simple picture is complicated by the somewhat special experience of roughly a third of ex-patients—namely, readmission to the hospital, this being the recidivist or "repatient" phase.
[6] Harry Stack Sullivan, *Clinical Studies in Psychiatry*, edited by Helen Swick Perry, Mary Ladd Gawel, and Martha Gibbon (New York: Norton, 1956), pp. 184–85.
[7] This moral experience can be contrasted with that of a person learning to become a marihuana addict, whose discovery that he can be "high" and still "op" effectively without being detected apparently leads to a new level of use. See Howard S. Becker, "Marihuana Use and Social Control," *Social Problems*, III (1955), pp. 35–41; see especially pp. 40–41.

engrained stereotypes as to the significance of symptoms such as hearing voices, losing temporal and spatial orientation, and sensing that one is being followed, and that many of the most spectacular and convincing of these symptoms in some instances psychiatrically signify merely a temporary emotional upset in a stressful situation, however terrifying to the person at the time. Similarly, the anxiety consequent upon this perception of oneself, and the strategies devised to reduce this anxiety, are not a product of abnormal psychology, but would be exhibited by any person socialized into our culture who came to conceive of himself as someone losing his mind. Interestingly, subcultures in American society apparently differ in the amount of ready imagery and encouragement they supply for such self-views, leading to differential rates of *self*-referral; the capacity to take this disintegrative view of oneself without psychiatric prompting seems to be one of the questionable cultural privileges of the upper classes.[8]

For the person who has come to see himself—with whatever justification—as mentally unbalanced, entrance to the mental hospital can sometimes bring relief, perhaps in part because of the sudden transformation in the structure of his basic social situation; instead of being to himself a questionable person trying to maintain a role as a full one, he can become an officially questioned person known to himself to be not so questionable as that. In other cases, hospitalization can make matters worse for the willing patient, confirming by the objective situation what has theretofore been a matter of the private experience of self.

Once the willing prepatient enters the hospital, he may go through the same routine of experiences as do those who enter unwillingly. In any case, it is the latter that I mainly want to consider, since in America at present these are by far the more numerous kind.[9] Their approach to the institution takes one of three classic forms: they come because they have been implored by their family or threatened with the abrogation of family ties unless they go "willingly"; they come by force under police escort; they come under misapprehension purposely induced by others, this last restricted mainly to youthful prepatients.

The prepatient's career may be seen in terms of an extrusory model; he starts out with relationships and rights, and ends up, at the beginning of his hospital stay, with hardly any of either. The moral aspects of this career, then, typically begin with the experience of abandonment, disloyalty, and embitterment. This is the case even though to others it may be obvious that he was in need of treatment, and even though in the hospital he may soon come to agree.

The case histories of most mental patients document offenses against some arrangement for face-to-face living—a domestic establishment, a work place, a semi-public organization such as a church or store, a public region such as a street or park. Often there is also a record of some *complainant*, some figure who takes that action against the offender which eventually leads to his hospitalization. This may not be the person who makes the first move, but it is the person who makes what turns out to be the first effective move. Here is the *social* beginning of the patient's career, regardless of where one might locate the psychological beginning of his mental illness.

---

[8] See Hollingshead and Redlich, *op. cit.*, p. 187, Table B, where relative frequency is given of self-referral by social class grouping.

[9] The distinction employed here between willing and unwilling patients cuts across the legal one of voluntary and committed, since some persons who are glad to come to the mental hospital may be legally committed, and of those who come only because of strong familial pressure, some may sign themselves in as voluntary patients.

The kinds of offenses which lead to hospitalization are felt to differ in nature from those which lead to other extrusory consequences—to imprisonment, divorce, loss of job, disownment, regional exile, non-institutional psychiatric treatment, and so forth. But little seems known about these differentiating factors; and when one studies actual commitments, alternate outcomes frequently appear to have been possible. It seems true, moreover, that for every offense that leads to an effective complaint, there are many psychiatrically similar ones that never do. No action is taken; or action is taken which leads to other extrusory outcomes; or ineffective action is taken, leading to the mere pacifying or putting off of the person who complains. Thus, as Clausen and Yarrow have nicely shown, even offenders who are eventually hospitalized are likely to have had a long series of ineffective actions taken against them.[10]

Separating those offenses which could have been used as grounds for hospitalizing the offender from those that are so used, one finds a vast number of what students of occupation call career contingencies.[11] Some of these contingencies in the mental patient's career have been suggested, if not explored, such as socioeconomic status, visibility of the offense, proximity to a mental hospital, amount of treatment facilities available, community regard for the type of treatment given in available hospitals, and so on.[12] For information about other contingencies one must rely on atrocity tales: a psychotic man is tolerated by his wife until she finds herself a boy friend, or by his adult children until they move from a house to an apartment; an alcoholic is sent to a mental hospital because the jail is full, and a drug addict because he declines to avail himself of psychiatric treatment on the outside; a rebellious adolescent daughter can no longer be managed at home because she now threatens to have an open affair with an unsuitable companion; and so on. Correspondingly there is an equally important set of contingencies causing the person to by-pass this fate. And should the person enter the hospital, still another set of contingencies will help determine when he is to obtain a discharge—such as the desire of his family for his return, the availability of a "manageable" job, and so on. The society's official view is that inmates of mental hospitals are there primarily because they are suffering from mental illness. However, in the degree that the "mentally ill" outside hospitals numerically approach or surpass those inside hospitals, one could say that mental patients distinctively suffer not from mental illness, but from contingencies.

Career contingencies occur in conjunction with a second feature of the prepatient's career—the circuit of agents—and agencies—that participate fatefully in his passage from civilian to patient status.[13] Here is an instance of that increasingly important class of social system whose elements are agents and agencies which are brought into systemic connection through having to take up and send on the same persons. Some of these agent roles will be cited now, with the

---

[10] Clausen and Yarrow, *op. cit.*

[11] An explicit application of this notion to the field of mental health may be found in Edwin Lemert, "Legal Commitment and Social Control," *Sociology and Social Research,* XXX (1946), pp. 370–78.

[12] For example, Jerome K. Meyers and Leslie Schaffer, "Social Stratification and Psychiatric Practice: A Study of an Outpatient Clinic," *American Sociological Review,* XIX (1954), pp. 307–10; Lemert, *op. cit.,* pp. 402–3; *Patients in Mental Institutions, 1941* (Washington, D.C.: Department of Commerce, Bureau of the Census, 1941), p. 2.

[13] For one circuit of agents and its bearing on career contingencies, see Oswald Hall, "The Stages of a Medical Career," *American Journal of Sociology,* LIII (1948), pp. 327–36.

understanding that in any concrete circuit a role may be filled more than once, and that the same person may fill more than one of them.

First is the *next-of-relation*—the person whom the prepatient sees as the most available of those upon whom he should be able to depend most in times of trouble, in this instance the last to doubt his sanity and the first to have done everything to save him from the fate which, it transpires, he has been approaching. The patient's next-of-relation is usually his next of kin; the special term is introduced because he need not be. Second is the *complainant*, the person who retrospectively appears to have started the person on his way to the hospital. Third are the *mediators*—the sequence of agents and agencies to which the prepatient is referred and through which he is relayed and processed on his way to the hospital. Here are included police, clergy, general medical practitioners, office psychiatrists, personnel in public clinics, lawyers, social service workers, schoolteachers, and so on. One of these agents will have the legal mandate to sanction commitment and will exercise it, and so those agents who precede him in the process will be involved in something whose outcome is not yet settled. When the mediators retire from the scene, the prepatient has become an inpatient, and the significant agent has become the hospital administrator.

While the complainant usually takes action in a lay capacity as a citizen, an employer, a neighbor, or a kinsman, mediators tend to be specialists and differ from those they serve in significant ways. They have experience in handling trouble, and some professional distance from what they handle. Except in the case of policemen, and perhaps some clergy, they tend to be more psychiatrically oriented than the lay public, and will see the need for treatment at times when the public does not.[14]

An interesting feature of these roles is the functional effects of their interdigitation. For example, the feelings of the patient will be influenced by whether or not the person who fills the role of complainant also has the role of next-of-relation—an embarrassing combination more prevalent, apparently, in the higher classes than in the lower.[15] Some of these emergent effects will be considered now.[16]

In the prepatient's progress from home to the hospital he may participate as a third person in what he may come to experience as a kind of alienative coalition. His next-of-relation presses him into coming to "talk things over" with a medical practitioner, an office psychiatrist, or some other counselor. Disinclination on his part may be met by threatening him with desertion, disownment, or other legal action, or by stressing the joint and exploratory nature of the interview. But typically the next-of-relation will have set the interview up, in the sense of selecting the professional, arranging for time, telling the professional something about the case, and so on. This move effectively tends to establish the next-of-relation as the responsible person to whom pertinent findings can be divulged, while effectively establishing the other as the patient. The prepatient often goes to the interview with the understanding that he is going as an equal of someone

---

[14] See Cumming and Cumming, *op. cit.*, p. 92.

[15] Hollingshead and Redlich, *op. cit.*, p. 187.

[16] For an analysis of some of these circuit implications for the inpatient, see Leila Deasy and Olive W. Quinn, "The Wife of the Mental Patient and the Hospital Psychiatrist," *Journal of Social Issues*, XI (1955), pp. 49–60. An interesting illustration of this kind of analysis may also be found in Alan G. Gowman, "Blindness and the Role of the Companion," *Social Problems*, IV (1956), pp. 68–75. A general statement may be found in Robert Merton, "The Role Set: Problems in Sociological Theory," *British Journal of Sociology*, VIII (1957), pp. 106–20.

who is so bound together with him that a third person could not come between them in fundamental matters; this, after all, is one way in which close relationships are defined in our society. Upon arrival at the office the prepatient suddenly finds that he and his next-of-relation have not been accorded the same roles, and apparently that a prior understanding between the professional and the next-of-relation has been put in operation against him. In the extreme but common case, the professional first sees the prepatient alone, in the role of examiner and diagnostician, and then sees the next-of-relation alone, in the role of adviser, while carefully avoiding talking things over seriously with them both together.[17] And even in those non-consultative cases where public officials must forcibly extract a person from a family that wants to tolerate him, the next-of-relation is likely to be induced to "go along" with the official action, so that even here the prepatient may feel that an alienative coalition has been formed against him.

The moral experience of being third man in such a coalition is likely to embitter the prepatient, especially since his troubles have already probably led to some estrangement from his next-of-relation. After he enters the hospital, continued visits by his next-of-relation can give the patient the "insight" that his own best interests were being served. But the initial visits may temporarily strengthen his feeling of abandonment; he is likely to beg his visitor to get him out or at least to get him more privileges and to sympathize with the monstrousness of his plight—to which the visitor ordinarily can respond only by trying to maintain a hopeful note, by not "hearing" the requests, or by assuring the patient that the medical authorities know about these things and are doing what is medically best. The visitor then nonchalantly goes back into a world that the patient has learned is incredibly thick with freedom and privileges, causing the patient to feel that his next-of-relation is merely adding a pious gloss to a clear case of traitorous desertion.

The depth to which the patient may feel betrayed by his next-of-relation seems to be increased by the fact that another witnesses his betrayal—a factor which is apparently significant in many three-party situations. An offended person may well act forbearantly and accommodatively toward an offender when the two are alone, choosing peace ahead of justice. The presence of a witness, however, seems to add something to the implication of the offense. For then it is beyond the power of the offended and offender to forget about, erase, or suppress what has happened; the offense has become a public social fact.[18] When the witness is a mental health commission, as is sometimes the case, the witnessed betrayal can verge on a "degradation ceremony." [19] In such circumstances, the offended patient may feel that some kind of extensive reparative action is required before witnesses, if his honor and social weight are to be restored.

Two other aspects of sensed betrayal should be mentioned. First, those who suggest the possibility of another's entering a mental hospital are not likely to provide a realistic picture of how in fact it may strike him when he arrives. Often he is told that he will get required medical treatment and a rest, and may

---

[17] I have one case record of a man who claims he thought *he* was taking his wife to see the psychiatrist, not realizing until too late that his wife had made the arrangements.
[18] A paraphrase from Kurt Riezler, "Comment on the Social Psychology of Shame," *American Journal of Sociology,* XLVIII (1943), p. 458.
[19] See Harold Garfinkel, "Conditions of Successful Degradation Ceremonies," *American Journal of Sociology,* LXI (1956), pp. 420–24.

well be out in a few months or so. In some cases they may thus be concealing what they know, but I think, in general, they will be telling what they see as the truth. For here there is quite relevant difference between patients and mediating professionals; mediators, more so than the public at large, may conceive of mental hospitals as short-term medical establishments where required rest and attention can be voluntarily obtained, and not as places of coerced exile. When the prepatient finally arrives he is likely to learn quite quickly, quite differently. He then finds that the information given him about life in the hospital has had the effect of his having put up less resistance to entering than he now sees he would have put up had he known the facts. Whatever the intentions of those who participated in his transition from person to patient, he may sense they have in effect "conned" him into his present predicament.

I am suggesting that the prepatient starts out with at least a portion of the rights, liberties, and satisfactions of the civilian and ends up on a psychiatric ward stripped of almost everything. The question here is how this stripping is managed. This is the second aspect of betrayal I want to consider.

As the prepatient may see it, the circuit of significant figures can function as a kind of betrayal funnel. Passage from person to patient may be effected through a series of linked stages, each managed by a different agent. While each stage tends to bring a sharp decrease in adult free status, each agent may try to maintain the fiction that no further decrease will occur. He may even manage to turn the prepatient over to the next agent while sustaining this note. Further, through words, cues, and gestures, the prepatient is implicitly asked by the current agent to join with him in sustaining a running line of polite small talk that tactfully avoids the administrative facts of the situation, becoming, with each stage, progressively more at odds with the facts. The spouse would rather not have to cry to get the prepatient to visit a psychiatrist; psychiatrists would rather not have a scene when the prepatient learns that he and his spouse are being seen separately and in different ways; the police infrequently bring a prepatient to the hospital in a strait jacket, finding it much easier all around to give him a cigarette, some kindly words, and freedom to relax in the back seat of the patrol car; and finally, the admitting psychiatrist finds he can do his work better in the relative quiet and luxury of the "admission suite" where, as an incidental consequence, the notion can survive that a mental hospital is indeed a comforting place. If the prepatient heeds all of these implied requests and is reasonably decent about the whole thing, he can travel the whole circuit from home to hospital without forcing anyone to look directly at what is happening or to deal with the raw emotion that his situation might well cause him to express. His showing consideration for those who are moving him toward the hospital allows them to show consideration for him, with the joint result that these interactions can be sustained with some of the protective harmony characteristic of ordinary face-to-face dealings. But should the new patient cast his mind back over the sequence of steps leading to hospitalization, he may feel that everyone's current comfort was being busily sustained while his long-range welfare was being undermined. This realization may constitute a moral experience that further separates him for the time from the people on the outside.[20]

---

[20] Concentration-camp practices provide a good example of the function of the betrayal funnel in inducing co-operation and reducing struggle and fuss, although here the mediators could not be said to be acting in the best interests of the inmates. Police picking up persons from their homes would sometimes joke good-naturedly and offer to wait while coffee was being served.

I would now like to look at the circuit of career agents from the point of view of the agents themselves. Mediators in the person's transition from civil to patient status—as well as his keepers, once he is in the hospital—have an interest in establishing a responsible next-of-relation as the patient's deputy or guardian; should there be no obvious candidate for the role, someone may be sought out and pressed into it. Thus while a person is gradually being transformed into a patient, a next-of-relation is gradually being transformed into a guardian. With a guardian on the scene, the whole transition process can be kept tidy. He is likely to be familiar with the prepatient's civil involvements and business, and can tie up loose ends that might otherwise be left to entangle the hospital. Some of the prepatient's abrogated civil rights can be transferred to him, thus helping to sustain the legal fiction that while the prepatient does not actually have his rights he somehow actually has not lost them.

Inpatients commonly sense, at least for a time, that hospitalization is a massive unjust deprivation, and sometimes succeed in convincing a few persons on the outside that this is the case. It often turns out to be useful, then, for those identified with inflicting these deprivations, however justifiably, to be able to point to the co-operation and agreement of someone whose relationship to the patient places him above suspicion, firmly defining him as the person most likely to have the patient's personal interest at heart. If the guardian is satisfied with what is happening to the new inpatient, the world ought to be.[21]

Now it would seem that the greater the legitimate personal stake one party has in another, the better he can take the role of guardian to the other. But the structural arrangements in society which lead to the acknowledged merging of two persons' interests lead to additional consequences. For the person to whom the patient turns for help—for protection against such threats as involuntary commitment—is just the person to whom the mediators and hospital administrators logically turn for authorization. It is understandable, then, that some patients will come to sense, at least for a time, that the closeness of a relationship tells nothing of its trustworthiness.

There are still other functional effects emerging from this complement of roles. If and when the next-of-relation appeals to mediators for help in the trouble he is having with the prepatient, hospitalization may not, in fact, be in his mind. He may not even perceive the prepatient as mentally sick, or, if he does, he may not consistently hold to this view.[22] It is the circuit of mediators, with their greater psychiatric sophistication and their belief in the medical character of mental hospitals, that will often define the situation for the next-of-relation, assuring him that hospitalization is a possible solution and a good one, that

---

Gas chambers were fitted out like delousing rooms, and victims taking off their clothes were told to note where they were leaving them. The sick, aged, weak, or insane who were selected for extermination were sometimes driven away in Red Cross ambulances to camps referred to by terms such as "observation hospital." See David Boder, *I Did Not Interview the Dead* (Urbana: University of Illinois Press, 1949), p. 81; and Elie A. Cohen, *Human Behavior in the Concentration Camp* (London: Jonathan Cape, 1954), pp. 32, 37, 107.

21 Interviews collected by the Clausen group at NIMH suggest that when a wife comes to be a guardian, the responsibility may disrupt previous distance from in-laws, leading either to a new supportive coalition with them or to a marked withdrawal from them.

22 For an analysis of these non-psychiatric kinds of perception, see Marian Radke Yarrow, Charlotte Green Schwartz, Harriet S. Murphy, and Leila Deasy, "The Psychological Meaning of Mental Illness in the Family," *Journal of Social Issues,* XI (1955), pp. 12–24; Charlotte Green Schwartz, "Perspectives on Deviance—Wives' Definitions of their Husbands' Mental Illness," *Psychiatry,* XX (1957), pp. 275–91.

it involves no betrayal, but is rather a medical action taken in the best interests of the prepatient. Here the next-of-relation may learn that doing his duty to the prepatient may cause the prepatient to distrust and even hate him for the time. But the fact that this course of action may have had to be pointed out and prescribed by professionals, and be defined by them as a moral duty, relieves the next-of-relation of some of the guilt he may feel.[23] It is a poignant fact that an adult son or daughter may be pressed into the role of mediator, so that the hostility that might otherwise be directed against the spouse is passed on to the child.[24]

Once the prepatient is in the hospital, the same guilt-carrying function may become a significant part of the staff's job in regard to the next-of-relation.[25] These reasons for feeling that he himself has not betrayed the patient, even though the patient may then think so, can later provide the next-of-relation with a defensible line to take when visiting the patient in the hospital and a basis for hoping that the relationship can be re-established after its hospital moratorium. And of course this position, when sensed by the patient, can provide him with excuses for the next-of-relation, when and if he comes to look for them.[26]

Thus while the next-of-relation can perform important functions for the mediators and hospital administrators, they in turn can perform important functions for him. One finds, then, an emergent unintended exchange or reciprocation of functions, these functions themselves being often unintended.

The final point I want to consider about the prepatient's moral career is its peculiarly retroactive character. Until a person actually arrives at the hospital there usually seems no way of knowing for sure that he is destined to do so, given the determinative role of career contingencies. And until the point of hospitalization is reached, he or others may not conceive of him as a person who is becoming a mental patient. However, since he will be held against his will in the hospital, his next-of-relation and the hospital staff will be in great need of a rationale for the hardships they are sponsoring. The medical elements of the staff will also need evidence that they are still in the trade they were trained for. These problems are eased, no doubt unintentionally, by the case-history construction that is placed on the patient's past life, this having the effect of demonstrating that all along he had been becoming sick, that he finally became very sick, and that if he had not been hospitalized much worse things would have happened to him—all of which, of course, may be true. Incidentally, if the patient wants to make sense out of his stay in the hospital, and, as already suggested, keep alive the possibility of once again conceiving of his next-of-relation

---

[23] This guilt-carrying function is found, of course, in other role complexes. Thus, when a middle-class couple engages in the process of legal separation or divorce, each of their lawyers usually takes the position that his job is to acquaint his client with all of the potential claims and rights, pressing his client into demanding these, in spite of any nicety of feelings about the rights and honorableness of the ex-partner. The client, in all good faith, can then say to self and to the ex-partner that the demands are being made only because the lawyer insists it is best to do so.

[24] Recorded in the Clausen data.

[25] This point is made by Cumming and Cumming, *op. cit.*, p. 129.

[26] There is an interesting contrast here with the moral career of the tuberculosis patient. I am told by Julius Roth that tuberculous patients are likely to come to the hospital willingly, agreeing with their next-of-relation about treatment. Later in their hospital career, when they learn how long they yet have to stay and how depriving and irrational some of the hospital rulings are, they may seek to leave, be advised against this by the staff and by relatives, and only then begin to feel betrayed.

as a decent, well-meaning person, then he, too, will have reason to believe some of this psychiatric work-up of his past.

Here is a very ticklish point for the sociology of careers. An important aspect of every career is the view the person constructs when he looks backward over his progress; in a sense, however, the whole of the prepatient career derives from this reconstruction. The fact of having had a prepatient career, starting with an effective complaint, becomes an important part of the mental patient's orientation, but this part can begin to be played only after hospitalization proves that what he had been having, but no longer has, is a career as a prepatient.

The Inpatient Phase

The last step in the prepatient's career can involve his realization—justified or not—that he has been deserted by society and turned out of relationships by those closest to him. Interestingly enough, the patient, especially a first admission, may manage to keep himself from coming to the end of this trail, even though in fact he is now in a locked mental-hospital ward. On entering the hospital, he may very strongly feel the desire not to be known to anyone as a person who could possibly be reduced to these present circumstances, or as a person who conducted himself in the way he did prior to commitment. Consequently, he may avoid talking to anyone, may stay by himself when possible, and may even be "out of contact" or "manic" so as to avoid ratifying any interaction that presses a politely reciprocal role upon him and opens him up to what he has become in the eyes of others. When the next-of-relation makes an effort to visit, he may be rejected by mutism, or by the patient's refusal to enter the visiting room, these strategies sometimes suggesting that the patient still clings to a remnant of relatedness to those who made up his past, and is protecting this remnant from the final destructiveness of dealing with the new people that they have become.[27]

Usually the patient comes to give up this taxing effort at anonymity, at not-hereness, and begins to present himself for conventional social interaction to the hospital community. Thereafter he withdraws only in special ways—by always using his nickname, by signing his contribution to the patient weekly with his initial only, or by using the innocuous "cover" address tactfully provided by some hospitals; or he withdraws only at special times, when, say, a flock of nursing students makes a passing tour of the ward, or when, paroled to the hospital grounds, he suddenly sees he is about to cross the path of a civilian he happens to know from home. Sometimes this making of oneself available is called "settling down" by the attendants. It marks a new stand openly taken and supported by the patient, and resembles the "coming-out" process that occurs in other groupings.[28]

27 The inmate's initial strategy of holding himself aloof from ratifying contact may partly account for the relative lack of group formation among inmates in public mental hospitals, a connection that has been suggested to me by William R. Smith. The desire to avoid personal bonds that would give licence to the asking of biographical questions could also be a factor. In mental hospitals, of course, as in prisoner camps, the staff may consciously break up incipient group formation in order to avoid collective rebellious action and other ward disturbances.
28 A comparable coming out occurs in the homosexual world, when a person finally comes frankly to present himself to a "gay" gathering not as a tourist but as someone who is "available." See Evelyn Hooker, "A Preliminary Analysis of Group Behavior of Homosexuals," *Journal of Psychology*, XLII (1956), pp. 217–25; see especially p. 221. A good fictionalized treatment may be found in James Baldwin's *Giovanni's Room* (New York: Dial, 1956), pp. 41–57. A familiar instance of the coming-out process is no doubt to be found among prepubertal

Once the prepatient begins to settle down, the main outlines of his fate tend to follow those of a whole class of segregated establishments—jails, concentration camps, monasteries, work camps, and so on—in which the inmate spends the whole round of life on the grounds, and marches through his regimented day in the immediate company of a group of persons of his own institutional status.

Like the neophyte in many of these total institutions, the new inpatient finds himself cleanly stripped of many of his accustomed affirmations, satisfactions, and defenses, and is subjected to a rather full set of mortifying experiences: restriction of free movement, communal living, diffuse authority of a whole echelon of people, and so on. Here one begins to learn about the limited extent to which a conception of oneself can be sustained when the usual setting of supports for it are suddenly removed.

While undergoing these humbling moral experiences, the inpatient learns to orient himself in terms of the "ward system." [29] In public mental hospitals this usually consists of a series of graded living arrangements built around wards, administrative units called services, and parole statuses. The "worst" level often involves nothing but wooden benches to sit on, some quite indifferent food, and a small piece of room to sleep in. The "best" level may involve a room of one's own, ground and town privileges, contacts with staff that are relatively undamaging, and what is seen as good food and ample recreational facilities. For disobeying the pervasive house rules, the inmate will receive stringent punishments expressed in terms of loss of privileges; for obedience he will eventually be allowed to reacquire some of the minor satisfactions he took for granted on the outside.

The institutionalization of these radically different levels of living throws light on the implications for self of social settings. And this in turn affirms that the self arises not merely out of its possessor's interactions with significant others, but also out of the arrangements that are evolved in an organization for its members.

These are some settings that the person easily discounts as an expression or extension of him. When a tourist goes slumming, he may take pleasure in the situation not because it is a reflection of him but because it so assuredly is not. There are other settings, such as living rooms, which the person manages on his own and employs to influence in a favorable direction other persons' views of him. And there are still other settings, such as a work place, which express the employee's occupational status, but over which he has no final control, this being exerted, however tactfully, by his employer. Mental hospitals provide an extreme instance of this latter possibility. And this is due not merely to their uniquely degraded living levels, but also to the unique way in which significance for self is made explicit to the patient, piercingly, persistently, and thoroughly. Once lodged on a given ward, the patient is firmly instructed that the restrictions and deprivations he encounters are not due to such blind forces as tradition or economy—and hence dissociable from self—but are intentional parts of his treatment, part of his need at the time, and therefore an expression of the state that his self has fallen to. Having every reason to initiate requests for better

children at the moment one of these actors sidles *back* into a room that had been left in an angered huff and injured *amour propre*. The phrase itself presumably derives from a *rite-de-passage* ceremony once arranged by upper-class mothers for their daughters. Interestingly enough, in large mental hospitals the patient sometimes symbolizes a complete coming out by his first active participation in the hospital-wide patient dance.

[29] A good description of the ward system may be found in Ivan Belknap, *Human Problems of a State Mental Hospital* (New York: McGraw-Hill, 1956), ch. ix, especially p. 164.

conditions, he is told that when the staff feel he is "able to manage" or will be "comfortable with" a higher ward level, then appropriate action will be taken. In short, assignment to a given ward is presented not as a reward or punishment, but as an expression of his general level of social functioning, his status as a person. Given the fact that the worst ward levels provide a round of life that inpatients with organic brain damage can easily manage, and that these quite limited human beings are present to prove it, one can appreciate some of the mirroring effects of the hospital.[30]

The ward system, then, is an extreme instance of how the physical facts of an establishment can be explicitly employed to frame the conception a person takes of himself. In addition, the official psychiatric mandate of mental hospitals gives rise to even more direct, even more blatant, attacks upon the inmate's views of himself. The more "medical" and the more progressive a mental hospital is— the more it attempts to be therapeutic and not merely custodial—the more he may be confronted by high-ranking staff arguing that his past has been a failure, that the cause of this has been within himself, that his attitude to life is wrong, and that if he wants to be a person he will have to change his way of dealing with people and his conceptions of himself. Often the moral value of these verbal assaults will be brought home to him by requiring him to practice taking this psychiatric view of himself in arranged confessional periods, whether in private sessions or group psychotherapy.

Now a general point may be made about the moral career of inpatients which has bearing on many moral careers. Given the stage that any person has reached in a career, one typically finds that he constructs an image of his life course— past, present, and future—which selects, abstracts, and distorts in such a way as to provide him with a view of himself that he can usefully expound in current situations. Quite generally, the person's line concerning self defensively brings him into appropriate alignment with the basic values of his society, and so may be called an apologia. If the person can manage to present a view of his current situation which shows the operation of favorable personal qualities in the past and a favorable destiny awaiting him, it may be called a success story. If the facts of a person's past and present are extremely dismal, then about the best he can do is to show that he is not responsible for what has become of him, and the term sad tale is appropriate. Interestingly enough, the more the person's past forces him out of apparent alignment with central moral values, the more often he seems compelled to tell his sad tale in any company in which he finds himself. Perhaps he partly responds to the need he feels in others of not having their sense of proper life courses affronted. In any case, it is among convicts, "winos," and prostitutes that one seems to obtain sad tales the most readily.[31] It is the vicissitudes of the mental patient's sad tale that I want to consider now.

---

[30] Here is one way in which mental hospitals can be worse than concentration camps and prisons as places in which to "do" time; in the latter, self-insulation from the symbolic implications of the settings may be easier. In fact, self-insulation from hospital settings may be so difficult that patients have to employ devices for this which staff interpret as psychotic symptoms.

[31] In regard to convicts, see Anthony Heckstall-Smith, *Eighteen Months* (London: Allan Wingate, 1954), pp. 52–53. For "winos" see the discussion in Howard G. Bain, "A Sociological Analysis of the Chicago Skid-Row Lifeway" (Unpublished M.A. thesis, Department of Sociology, University of Chicago, September 1950), especially "The Rationale of the Skid-Row Drinking Group," pp. 141–46. Bain's neglected thesis is a useful source of material on moral careers.

In the mental hospital, the setting and the house rules press home to the patient that he is, after all, a mental case who has suffered some kind of social collapse on the outside, having failed in some over-all way, and that here he is of little social weight, being hardly capable of acting like a full-fledged person at all. These humiliations are likely to be most keenly felt by middle-class patients, since their previous condition of life little immunizes them against such affronts, but all patients feel some downgrading. Just as any normal member of his outside subculture would do, the patient often responds to this situation by attempting to assert a sad tale proving that he is not "sick," that the "little trouble" he did get into was really somebody else's fault, that his past life course had some honor and rectitude, and that the hospital is therefore unjust in forcing the status of mental patient upon him. This self-respecting tendency is heavily institutionalized within the patient society where opening social contacts typically involve the participants' volunteering information about their current ward location and length of stay so far, but not the reasons for their stay—such interaction being conducted in the manner of small talk on the outside.[32] With greater familiarity, each patient usually volunteers relatively acceptable reasons for his hospitalization, at the same time accepting without open immediate question the lines offered by other patients. Such stories as the following are given and overtly accepted.

> I was going to night school to get a M.A. degree, and holding down a job in addition, and the load got too much for me.

> The others here are sick mentally but I'm suffering from a bad nervous system and that is what is giving me these phobias.

> I got here by mistake because of a diabetes diagnosis, and I'll leave in a couple of days. [The patient had been in seven weeks.]

> I failed as a child, and later with my wife I reached out for dependency.

> My trouble is that I can't work. That's what I'm in for. I had two jobs with a good home and all the money I wanted.[33]

Apparently one of the occupational hazards of prostitution is that clients and other professional contacts sometimes persist in expressing sympathy by asking for a defensible dramatic explanation for the fall from grace. In having to bother to have a sad tale ready, perhaps the prostitute is more to be pitied than damned. Good examples of prostitute sad tales may be found in Henry Mayhew, *London Labour and the London Poor*, Vol. IV, *Those That Will Not Work* (London: Charles Griffin and Co., 1862), pp. 210–72. For a contemporary source, see *Women of the Streets*, edited by C. H. Rolph (London: Secker and Warburg, 1955), especially p. 6: "*Almost always, however, after a few comments on the police, the girl would begin to explain how it was that she was in the life, usually in terms of self-justification. . . .*" Lately, of course, the psychological expert has helped out the profession in the construction of wholly remarkable sad tales. See, for example, Harold Greenwald, *The Call Girl* (New York: Ballantine Books, 1958).

[32] A similar self-protecting rule has been observed in prisons. Thus, Alfred Hassler, *Diary of a Self-Made Convict* (Chicago: Regnery, 1954), p. 76, in describing a conversation with a fellow prisoner: "*He didn't say much about why he was sentenced, and I didn't ask him, that being the accepted behavior in prison.*" A novelistic version for the mental hospital may be found in J. Kerkhoff, *How Thin the Veil: A Newspaperman's Story of His Own Mental Crackup and Recovery* (New York: Greenberg, 1952), p. 27.

[33] From the writer's field notes of informal interaction with patients, transcribed as nearly verbatim as he was able.

The patient sometimes reinforces these stories by an optimistic definition of his occupational status. A man who managed to obtain an audition as a radio announcer styles himself a radio announcer; another who worked for some months as a copy boy and was then given a job as a reporter on a large trade journal, but fired after three weeks, defines himself as a reporter.

A whole social role in the patient community may be constructed on the basis of these reciprocally sustained fictions. For these face-to-face niceties tend to be qualified by behind-the-back gossip that comes only a degree closer to the "objective" facts. Here, of course, one can see a classic social function of informal networks of equals: they serve as one another's audience for self-supporting tales—tales that are somewhat more solid than pure fantasy and somewhat thinner than the facts.

But the patient's apologia is called forth in a unique setting, for few settings could be so destructive of self-stories except, of course, those stories already constructed along psychiatric lines. And this destructiveness rests on more than the official sheet of paper which attests that the patient is of unsound mind, a danger to himself and others—an attestation, incidentally, which seems to cut deeply into the patient's pride, and into the possibility of his having any.

Certainly the degrading conditions of the hospital setting belie many of the self-stories that are presented by patients, and the very fact of being in the mental hospital is evidence against these tales. And of course there is not always sufficient patient solidarity to prevent patient discrediting patient, just as there is not always a sufficient number of "professionalized" attendants to prevent attendant discrediting patient. As one patient informant repeatedly suggested to a fellow patient:

If you're so smart, how come you got your ass in here?

The mental-hospital setting, however, is more treacherous still. Staff have much to gain through discreditings of the patient's story—whatever the felt reason for such discreditings. If the custodial faction in the hospital is to succeed in managing his daily round without complaint or trouble from him, then it will prove useful to be able to point out to him that the claims about himself upon which he rationalizes his demands are false, that he is not what he is claiming to be, and that in fact he is a failure as a person. If the psychiatric faction is to impress upon him its views about his personal make-up, then they must be able to show in detail how their version of his past and their version of his character hold up much better than his own.[34] If both the custodial and psychiatric factions are to get him to co-operate in the various psychiatric treatments, then it will prove useful to disabuse him of his views of their purposes, and cause him to appreciate that they know what they are doing, and are doing what is best for him. In brief, the difficulties caused by a patient are closely tied to his version of what has been happening to him, and if co-operation is to be secured,

[34] The process of examining a person psychiatrically and then altering or reducing his status in consequence is known in hospital and prison parlance as bugging, the assumption being that once you come to the attention of the testers you either will automatically be labeled crazy or the process of testing itself will make you crazy. Thus psychiatric staff are sometimes seen not as discovering whether you are sick, but as making you sick; and "Don't bug me, man" can mean, "Don't pester me to the point where I'll get upset." Sheldon Messinger has suggested to me that this meaning of bugging is related to the other colloquial meaning, of wiring a room with a secret microphone to collect information usable for discrediting the speaker.

it helps if this version is discredited. The patient must "insightfully" come to take, or affect to take, the hospital's view of himself.

The staff also have ideal means—in addition to the mirroring effect of the setting—for denying the inmate's rationalizations. Current psychiatric doctrine defines mental disorder as something that can have its roots in the patient's earliest years, show its signs throughout the course of his life, and invade almost every sector of his current activity. No segment of his past or present need be defined, then, as beyond the jurisdiction and mandate of psychiatric assessment. Mental hospitals bureaucratically institutionalize this extremely wide mandate by formally basing their treatment of the patient upon his diagnosis and hence upon the psychiatric view of his past.

The case record is an important expression of this mandate. This dossier is apparently not regularly used, however, to record occasions when the patient showed capacity to cope honorably and effectively with difficult life situations. Nor is the case record typically used to provide a rough average or sampling of his past conduct. One of its purposes is to show the ways in which the patient is "sick" and the reasons why it was right to commit him and is right currently to keep him committed; and this is done by extracting from his whole life course a list of those incidents that have or might have had "symptomatic" significance.[35] The misadventures of his parents or siblings that might suggest a "taint" may be cited. Early acts in which the patient appeared to have shown bad judgment or emotional disturbance will be recorded. Occasions when he acted in a way which the layman would consider immoral, sexually perverted, weak-willed, childish, ill-considered, impulsive, and crazy may be described. Misbehaviors which someone saw as the last straw, as cause for immediate action, are likely to be reported in detail. In addition, the record will describe his state on arrival at the hospital—and this is not likely to be a time of tranquillity and ease for him. The record may also report the false line taken by the patient in answering embarrassing questions, showing him as someone who makes claims that are obviously contrary to the facts:

> Claims she lives with oldest daughter or with sisters only when sick and in need of care; otherwise with husband, he himself says not for twelve years.

> Contrary to the reports from the personnel, he says he no longer bangs on the floor or cries in the morning.

> . . . conceals fact that she had her organs removed, claims she is still menstruating.

> At first she denied having had premarital sexual experience, but when asked about Jim she said she had forgotten about it 'cause it had been unpleasant.[36]

Where contrary facts are not known by the recorder, their presence is often left scrupulously an open question:

---

[35] While many kinds of organization maintain records of their members, in almost all of these some socially significant attributes can only be included indirectly, being officially irrelevant. But since mental hospitals have a legitimate claim to deal with the "whole" person, they need officially recognize no limits to what they consider relevant, a sociologically interesting licence. It is an odd historical fact that persons concerned with promoting civil liberties in other areas of life tend to favor giving the psychiatrist complete discretionary power over the patient. Apparently it is felt that the more power possessed by medically qualified administrators and therapists, the better the interests of the patients will be served. Patients, to my knowledge, have not been polled on this matter.

[36] Verbatim transcriptions of hospital case-record material.

The patient denied any heterosexual experiences nor could one trick her into admitting that she had ever been pregnant or into any kind of sexual indulgence, denying masturbation as well.

Even with considerable pressure she was unwilling to engage in any projection of paranoid mechanisms.

No psychotic content could be elicited at this time.[37]

And if in no more factual way, discrediting statements often appear in descriptions given of the patient's general social manner in the hospital:

When interviewed, he was bland, apparently self-assured, and sprinkles highsounding generalizations freely throughout his verbal productions.

Armed with a rather neat appearance and natty little Hitlerian mustache this 45 year old man who has spent the last five or more years of his life in the hospital, is making a very successful hospital adjustment living within the role of a rather gay liver and jim-dandy type of fellow who is not only quite superior to his fellow patients in intellectual respects but who is also quite a man with women. His speech is sprayed with many multi-syllabled words which he generally uses in good context, but if he talks long enough on any subject it soon becomes apparent that he is so completely lost in this verbal diarrhea as to make what he says almost completely worthless.[38]

The events recorded in the case history are, then, just the sort that a layman would consider scandalous, defamatory, and discrediting. I think it is fair to say that all levels of mental-hospital staff fail, in general, to deal with this material with the moral neutrality claimed for medical statements and psychiatric diagnosis, but instead participate, by intonation and gesture if by no other means, in the lay reaction to these acts. This will occur in staff-patient encounters as well as in staff encounters at which no patient is present.

In some mental hospitals, access to the case record is technically restricted to medical and higher nursing levels, but even here informal access or relayed information is often available to lower staff levels.[39] In addition, ward personnel are felt to have a right to know those aspects of the patient's past conduct which, embedded in the reputation he develops, purportedly make it possible to manage him with greater benefit to himself and less risk to others. Further, all staff levels typically have access to the nursing notes kept on the ward, which chart the daily course of each patient's disease, and hence his conduct, providing for the near present the sort of information the case record supplies for his past.

I think that most of the information gathered in case records is quite true, although it might seem also to be true that almost anyone's life course could yield up enough denigrating facts to provide grounds for the record's justification of

---

[37] Verbatim transcriptions of hospital case-record material.
[38] Verbatim transcriptions of hospital case-record material.
[39] However, some mental hospitals do have a "hot file" of selected records which can be taken out only by special permission. These may be records of patients who work as administration-office messengers and might otherwise snatch glances at their own files; of inmates who had elite status in the environing community; and of inmates who may take legal action against the hospital and hence have a special reason to maneuver access to their records. Some hospitals even have a "hot-hot file," kept in the superintendent's office. In addition, the patient's professional title, especially if it is a medical one, is sometimes purposely omitted from his file card. All of these exceptions to the general rule for handling information show, of course, the institution's realization of some of the implications of keeping mental-hospital records. For a further example, see Harold Taxel, "Authority Structure in a Mental Hospital Ward" (Unpublished M.A. thesis, Department of Sociology, University of Chicago, 1953), pp. 11–12.

commitment. In any case, I am not concerned here with questioning the desirability of maintaining case records, or the motives of staff in keeping them. The point is that, these facts about him being true, the patient is certainly not relieved from the normal cultural pressure to conceal them, and is perhaps all the more threatened by knowing that they are neatly available, and that he has no control over who gets to learn them.[40] A manly looking youth who responds to military induction by running away from the barracks and hiding himself in a hotel-room clothes closet, to be found there, crying, by his mother; a woman who travels from Utah to Washington to warn the President of impending doom; a man who disrobes before three young girls; a boy who locks his sister out of the house, striking out two of her teeth when she tries to come back in through the window—each of these persons has done something he will have very obvious reason to conceal from others, and very good reason to tell lies about.

The formal and informal patterns of communication linking staff members tend to amplify the disclosive work done by the case record. A discreditable act that the patient performs during one part of the day's routine in one part of the hospital community is likely to be reported back to those who supervise other areas of his life where he implicitly takes the stand that he is not the sort of person who could act that way.

Of significance here, as in some other social establishments, is the increasingly common practice of all-level staff conferences, where staff air their views of patients and develop collective agreement concerning the line that the patient is trying to take and the line that should be taken to him. A patient who develops a "personal" relation with an attendant, or manages to make an attendant anxious by eloquent and persistent accusations of malpractice, can be put back into his place by means of the staff meeting, where the attendant is given warning or assurance that the patient is "sick." Since the differential image of himself that a person usually meets from those of various levels around him comes here to be unified behind the scenes into a common approach, the patient may find himself faced with a kind of collusion against him—albeit one sincerely thought to be for his own ultimate welfare.

In addition, the formal transfer of the patient from one ward or service to another is likely to be accompanied by an informal description of his characteristics, this being felt to facilitate the work of the employee who is newly responsible for him.

---

[40] This is the problem of "information control" that many groups suffer from in varying degrees. See Goffman, "Discrepant Roles," in *The Presentation of Self in Everyday Life* (New York: Anchor Books, 1959), ch. iv, pp. 141–166. A suggestion of this problem in relation to case records in prisons is given by James Peck in his story, "The Ship that Never Hit Port," in *Prison Etiquette*, edited by Holley Cantine and Dachine Rainer (Bearsville, N.Y.: Retort Press, 1950), p. 66:

The hacks of course hold all the aces in dealing with any prisoner because they can always write him up for inevitable punishment. Every infraction of the rules is noted in the prisoner's jacket, a folder which records all the details of the man's life before and during imprisonment. There are general reports written by the work detail screw, the cell block screw, or some other screw who may have overheard a conversation. Tales pumped from stoolpigeons are also included.

Any letter which interests the authorities goes into the jacket. The mail censor may make a photostatic copy of a prisoner's entire letter, or merely copy a passage. Or he may pass the letter on to the warden. Often an inmate called out by the warden or parole officer is confronted with something he wrote so long ago he had forgot all about it. It might be about his personal life or his political views—a fragment of thought that the prison authorities felt was dangerous and filed for later use.

Finally, at the most informal of levels, the lunchtime and coffee-break small talk of staff often turns upon the latest doings of the patient, the gossip level of any social establishment being here intensified by the assumption that everything about him is in some way the proper business of the hospital employee. Theoretically there seems to be no reason why such gossip should not build up the subject instead of tear him down, unless one claims that talk about those not present will always tend to be critical in order to maintain the integrity and prestige of the circle in which the talking occurs. And so, even when the impulse of the speakers seems kindly and generous, the implication of their talk is typically that the patient is not a complete person. For example, a conscientious group therapist, sympathetic with patients, once admitted to his coffee companions:

> I've had about three group disrupters, one man in particular—a lawyer [*sotto voce*] James Wilson—very bright—who just made things miserable for me, but I would always tell him to get on the stage and do something. Well, I was getting desperate and then I bumped into his therapist, who said that right now behind the man's bluff and front he needed the group very much and that it probably meant more to him than anything else he was getting out of the hospital—he just needed the support. Well, that made me feel altogether different about him. He's out now.

In general, then, mental hospitals systematically provide for circulation about each patient the kind of information that the patient is likely to try to hide. And in various degrees of detail this information is used daily to puncture his claims. At the admission and diagnostic conferences, he will be asked questions to which he must give wrong answers in order to maintain his self-respect, and then the true answer may be shot back at him. An attendant whom he tells a version of his past and his reason for being in the hospital may smile disbelievingly, or say, "That's not the way I heard it," in line with the practical psychiatry of bringing the patient down to reality. When he accosts a physician or nurse on the ward and presents his claims for more privileges or for discharge, this may be countered by a question which he cannot answer truthfully without calling up a time in his past when he acted disgracefully. When he gives his view of his situation during group psychotherapy, the therapist, taking the role of interrogator, may attempt to disabuse him of his face-saving interpretations and encourage an interpretation suggesting that it is he himself who is to blame and who must change. When he claims to staff or fellow patients that he is well and has never been really sick, someone may give him graphic details of how, only one month ago, he was prancing around like a girl, or claiming that he was God, or declining to talk or eat, or putting gum in his hair.

Each time the staff deflates the patient's claims, his sense of what a person ought to be and the rules of peer-group social intercourse press him to reconstruct his stories; and each time he does this, the custodial and psychiatric interests of the staff may lead them to discredit these tales again.

Behind these verbally instigated ups and downs of the self is an institutional base that rocks just as precariously. Contrary to popular opinion, the "ward system" insures a great amount of internal social mobility in mental hospitals, especially during the inmate's first year. During that time he is likely to have altered his service once, his ward three or four times, and his parole status several times; and he is likely to have experienced moves in bad as well as good directions. Each of these moves involves a very drastic alteration in level of living

and in available materials out of which to build a self-confirming round of activities, an alteration equivalent in scope, say, to a move up or down a class in the
wider class system. Moreover, fellow inmates with whom he has partially
identified himself will similarly be moving, but in different directions and at
different rates, thus reflecting feelings of social change to the person even when
he does not experience them directly.

As previously implied, the doctrines of psychiatry can reinforce the social
fluctuations of the ward system. Thus there is a current psychiatric view that the
ward system is a kind of social hothouse in which patients start as social infants
and end up, within the year, on convalescent wards as resocialized adults. This
view adds considerably to the weight and pride that staff can attach to their
work, and necessitates a certain amount of blindness, especially at higher staff
levels, to other ways of viewing the ward system, such as a method for disciplining unruly persons through punishment and reward. In any case, this resocialization perspective tends to overstress the extent to which those on the worst wards
are incapable of socialized conduct and the extent to which those on the best
wards are ready and willing to play the social game. Because the ward system is
something more than a resocialization chamber, inmates find many reasons for
"messing up" or getting into trouble, and many occasions, then, for demotion to
less privileged ward positions. These demotions may be officially interpreted as
psychiatric relapses or moral backsliding, thus protecting the resocialization view
of the hospital; these interpretations, by implication, translate a mere infraction
of rules and consequent demotion into a fundamental expression of the status of
the culprit's self. Correspondingly, promotions, which may come about because
of ward population pressure, the need for a "working patient," or for other psychiatrically irrelevant reasons, may be built up into something claimed to be
profoundly expressive of the patient's whole self. The patient himself may be
expected by staff to make a personal effort to "get well," in something less than a
year, and hence may be constantly reminded to think in terms of the self's success
and failure.[41]

In such contexts inmates can discover that deflations in moral status are not so
bad as they had imagined. After all, infractions which lead to these demotions
cannot be accompanied by legal sanctions or by reduction to the status of mental
patient, since these conditions already prevail. Further, no past or current
delict seems to be horrendous enough in itself to excommunicate a patient from
the patient community, and hence failures at right living lose some of their
stigmatizing meaning.[42] And finally, in accepting the hospital's version of his fall
from grace, the patient can set himself up in the business of "straightening up,"
and make claims of sympathy, privileges, and indulgence from the staff in order to
foster this.

Learning to live under conditions of imminent exposure and wide fluctuation
in regard, with little control over the granting or withholding of this regard, is an
important step in the socialization of the patient, a step that tells something
important about what it is like to be an inmate in a mental hospital. Having one's
past mistakes and present progress under constant moral review seems to make for
a special adaptation consisting of a less than moral attitude to ego ideals. One's
shortcomings and successes become too central and fluctuating an issue in life to

[41] For this and other suggestions, I am indebted to Charlotte Green Schwartz.
[42] See "The Underlife of a Public Institution," in Erving Goffman, *Asylums* (New York:
Doubleday-Anchor, 1961).

allow the usual commitment of concern for other persons' views of them. It is not very practicable to try to sustain solid claims about oneself. The inmate tends to learn that degradations and reconstructions of the self need not be given too much weight, at the same time learning that staff and inmates are ready to view an inflation or deflation of a self with some indifference. He learns that a defensible picture of self can be seen as something outside oneself that can be constructed, lost, and rebuilt, all with great speed and some equanimity. He learns about the viability of taking up a standpoint—and hence a self—that is outside the one which the hospital can give and take away from him.

The setting, then, seems to engender a kind of cosmopolitan sophistication, a kind of civic apathy. In this unserious yet oddly exaggerated moral context, building up a self or having it destroyed becomes something of a shameless game, and learning to view this process as a game seems to make for some demoralization, the game being such a fundamental one. In the hospital, then, the inmate can learn that the self is not a fortress, but rather a small open city; he can become weary of having to show pleasure when held by troops of his own, and weary of having to show displeasure when held by the enemy. Once he learns what it is like to be defined by society as not having a viable self, this threatening definition —the threat that helps attach people to the self society accords them—is weakened. The patient seems to gain a new plateau when he learns that he can survive while acting in a way that society sees as destructive of him.

A few illustrations of this moral loosening and moral fatigue might be given. In state mental hospitals currently a kind of "marriage moratorium" appears to be accepted by patients and more or less condoned by staff. Some informal peer-group pressure may be brought against a patient who "plays around" with more than one hospital partner at a time, but little negative sanction seems to be attached to taking up, in a temporarily steady way, with a member of the opposite sex, even though both partners are known to be married, to have children, and even to be regularly visited by these outsiders. In short, there is licence in mental hospitals to begin courting all over again, with the understanding, however, that nothing very permanent or serious can come of this. Like shipboard or vacation romances, these entanglements attest to the way in which the hospital is cut off from the outside community, becoming a world of its own, operated for the benefit of its own citizens. And certainly this moratorium is an expression of the alienation and hostility that patients feel for those on the outside to whom they were closely related. But, in addition, one has evidence of the loosening effects of living in a world within a world, under conditions which make it difficult to give full seriousness to either of them.

The second illustration concerns the ward system. On the worst ward level, discreditings seem to occur the most frequently, in part because of lack of facilities, in part through the mockery and sarcasm that seem to be the occupational norm of social control for the attendants and nurses who administer these places. At the same time, the paucity of equipment and rights means that not much self can be built up. The patient finds himself constantly toppled, therefore, but with very little distance to fall. A kind of jaunty gallows humor seems to develop in some of these wards, with considerable freedom to stand up to the staff and return insult for insult. While these patients can be punished, they cannot, for example, be easily slighted, for they are accorded as a matter of course few of the niceties that people must enjoy before they can suffer subtle abuse. Like prostitutes in connection with sex, inmates on these wards have very little reputation or rights to lose and can therefore take certain liberties. As the person moves up the ward system, he can manage more and more to avoid incidents which discredit his claim to be a human being, and acquire more and more of the varied ingredients of self-respect; yet when eventually he does get toppled—and he does—there is a much farther distance to fall. For instance, the privileged patient lives in a world wider than the ward, containing recreation workers who, on request, can dole out cake, cards, table-tennis balls, tickets to the movies, and writing materials. But in the absence of the social control of payment which is typically exerted by a recipient on the outside, the patient runs the risk that even a warmhearted functionary may, on occasion, tell him to wait until she has finished an informal chat, or teasingly ask why he wants what he has asked for, or respond with a dead pause and a cold look of appraisal.

Moving up and down the ward system means, then, not only a shift in self-constructive equipment, a shift in reflected status, but also a change in the calculus of risks. Appreciation of risks to his self-conception is part of everyone's moral experience, but an appreciation that a given risk level is itself merely a social arrangement is a rarer kind of experience, and one that seems to help to disenchant the person who undergoes it.

A third instance of moral loosening has to do with the conditions that are often associated with the release of the inpatient. Often he leaves under the supervision and jurisdiction of his next-of-relation or of a specially selected and specially watchful employer. If he misbehaves while under their auspices, they can quickly obtain his readmission. He therefore finds himself under the special power of persons who ordinarily would not have this kind of power over him, and about whom, moreover, he may have had prior cause to feel quite bitter. In order to get out of the hospital, however, he may conceal his displeasure in this arrangement, and, at least until safely off the hospital rolls, act out a willingness to accept this kind of custody. These discharge proceedings, then, provide a built-in lesson in overtly taking a role without the usual covert commitments, and seem further to separate the person from the worlds that others take seriously.

The moral career of a person of a given social category involves a standard sequence of changes in his way of conceiving of selves, including, importantly, his own. These half-buried lines of development can be followed by studying his moral experiences—that is, happenings which mark a turning point in the way in which the person views the world—although the particularities of this view may be difficult to establish. And note can be taken of overt tacks or strategies—that is, stands that he effectively takes before specifiable others, whatever the hidden and variable nature of his inward attachments to these presentations. By taking note of moral experiences and overt personal stands, one can obtain a relatively objective tracing of relatively subjective matters.

Each moral career, and behind this, each self, occurs within the confines of an institutional system, whether a social establishment such as a mental hospital or a complex of personal and professional relationships. The self, then, can be seen as something that resides in the arrangements prevailing in a social system for its members. The self in this sense is not a property of the person to whom it is attributed, but dwells rather in the pattern of social control that is exerted in connection with the person by himself and those around him. This special kind of institutional arrangement does not so much support the self as constitute it.

In this paper, two of these institutional arrangements have been considered, by pointing to what happens to the person when these rulings are weakened. The first concerns the felt loyalty of his next-of-relation. The prepatient's self is described as a function of the way in which three roles are related, arising and declining in the kinds of affiliation that occur between the next-of-relation and the mediators. The second concerns the protection required by the person for the version of himself which he presents to others, and the way in which the withdrawal of this protection can form a systematic, if unintended, aspect of the working of an establishment. I want to stress that these are only two kinds of institutional rulings from which a self emerges for the participant; others, not considered in this paper, are equally important.

In the usual cycle of adult socialization one expects to find alienation and mortification followed by a new set of beliefs about the world and a new way of conceiving of selves. In the case of the mental-hospital patient, this rebirth does sometimes occur, taking the form of a strong belief in the psychiatric perspective, or, briefly at least, a devotion to the social cause of better treatment for mental patients. The moral career of the mental patient has unique interest, however; it can illustrate the possibility that in casting off the raiments of the old self—or in having this cover torn away—the person need not seek a new robe and a new audience before which to cower. Instead he can learn, at least for a time, to practise before all groups the amoral arts of shamelessness.

67 Life as Theater: Some Notes on the Dramaturgic Approach to Social Reality

● SHELDON E. MESSINGER with HAROLD SAMPSON
and ROBERT D. TOWNE

The aim of this paper is to raise some questions about the uses of the "dramaturgic approach"[1] to social experience, a mode of analysis finding increasing use in social-psychological circles. In particular, we wish to inquire into and comment upon the nature of the actor's[2] perspective in everyday life, as this is sometimes assumed to appear to the dramaturgic analyst.

To this end, we shall describe a perspective on the world and the self within it, a perspective that renders life a kind of "theater" in which a "show" is "staged." Someone viewing self and world from within this perspective will be said to be

SOURCE: Sheldon E. Messinger, Harold Sampson and Robert D. Towne, in *Sociometry*, XXV (September 1962), pp. 98–110. Reprinted by permission of the American Sociological Association.

We should like to thank Aaron Cicourel, Fred Davis, and Leo F. Schnore for critical comment on earlier versions of this paper. We are indebted to several unpublished papers by Harold Garfinkel for a number of the views expressed. And we owe a special debt to Erving Goffman, for his patience in the face of "constructive criticism."

[1] This phrase is used by Erving Goffman in (4). Reference (6) is a revised and enlarged edition of the same work. Our criticism, as well as appreciation, of the "dramaturgic approach" are directed primarily at Goffman's work as its foremost exponent.
[2] When used in an unqualified way, we intend the term "actor" to refer to that "Anybody" whose "action" is the subject of the dramaturgic analyst's analytic efforts. "Anybody" need not be a stage actor.

"on." In order to show the incompatibility of this perspective with the view that persons in everyday life seem to consider "natural," we shall present some observations by and about mental patients taken from a recently completed study.[3] Finally, we shall suggest that the perspective of persons who are "on" is akin or identical to the view seemingly attributed by the dramaturgic analyst to his subjects, that is, to persons plying their routine rounds of daily activities. We shall hold that this seeming attribution is a misreading of dramaturgic analysis, if a misreading against which the dramaturgic analyst has not sufficiently guarded.

I

A reported comment by Sammy Davis, Jr. first suggested our usage of the term "to be on." Remarking on the hazards of fame, he said, "As soon as I go out the front door of my house in the morning, I'm on, Daddy, I'm on." [4] And further, "But when I'm with the group I can relax. We trust each other" (12). Drawing on his experience in the theater, Davis seems to be saying that there are times when, although "off-stage," he feels "on-stage." He contrasts this perspective on self and other with another associated with "relaxation" and "trust."

Seeing that someone who has been "on-stage" may find the same experience in everyday life, we can appreciate that those who have never crossed the boards may attain the same perspective, even though they may have no consistent name for it. Thus Bernard Wolfe tells us that, seldom out of sight of a white audience, "Negroes in our culture spend most of their lives 'on' . . . Every Negro is to some extent a performer." At other times, "relaxing among themselves," Negroes will "mock the 'type' personalities they are obliged to assume when they're 'on'" (11, p. 202). We may expect, perhaps, that the members of any oppressed group will have similar experiences.

But there seems no reason to confine these experiences to the oppressed. It would seem that adolescents at graduation ceremonies, as well as buying drinks at bars, and clerks taken for store owners, as well as those mistaken for customers, share with Norman Mailer's "hip" the need to "come on strong" (8). And we can see that a person may be rendered "on" when he has no prior reason to believe that this will be his fate. Thus, the plight of one "put on" by joking if sadistic friends, and the person suddenly made aware of a *gaffe* by another's inability to be tactful (3, 5).

All of these situations point up the fact that under some circumstances in everyday life the actor becomes, is, or is made *aware* of an actual or potential discrepancy between his "real" and his "projected" selves, between his "self" and his "character." [5] He may greet this sensed discrepancy with joy or anxiety; presumably he usually finds himself somewhere between these affective poles. However this may be, insofar as he *consciously* orients himself to narrow, sustain, or widen this discrepancy and thereby achieves a sense of "playing a role" or "man-

---

[3] The study was carried out by the California Department of Mental Hygiene and partially supported by Grant 3M-9124 from the National Institute of Mental Health. The study, carried out by the authors and others, consisted in observing and frequently interviewing the members of 17 families in which the wife was hospitalized for "schizophrenia." A description of the study group and of study procedures may be found in (10).

[4] The context of his remarks is Davis' discussion of a group of intimates of which he is a member—known as the "Clan" by some, the "Rat Pack" by others—and the relations between this group and the "public."

[5] Perhaps the best description of the variety of these situations is found in Goffman (5).

aging a character," he is "on" in the sense intended here. It may be inferred that it is during such periods, if his projection is a joint enterprise, that the actor *experiences* the constraints of "dramaturgic loyalty," "discipline," and "circumspection" (6, pp. 212–228); although, as we shall try to make clear later, it may *not* be inferred that when the actor fails to experience these constraints they have ceased to operate. It is at these other times, however, when the actor is not "on," that we shall refer to his perspective as "natural." At these other times persons tell us that their conduct appears to them as "spontaneous."

II

We may be better able to appreciate the difference between being "on" and being "natural"—and the difference this difference makes—if we turn to the experiences of a class of persons who must cope with it for a relatively long period of time. Entertainers would seem to be such a class, as Davis' statement suggests. Davis' statement also suggests, however, that a relatively well supported hiatus exists for entertainers between occasions of being "on" and "natural." There are those before whom one is "on," like the "public," and those with whom one is "natural," like the "group." These worlds may on occasion touch or even overlap, but presumably the boundaries usually remain clear.[6] What we seek is a class of persons who have difficulty creating or sustaining such a hiatus. For them, presumably, the incompatibilities of being "on" and being "natural," should such incompatibilities exist, will be magnified. Mental patients are such a class of persons.

There can be little doubt that mental patients are in a situation productive of being "on." Bereft of membership in the group of reasonable men, they are forced to address the task of restoring their "character," of becoming "sane persons" again. It does not take mental patients long to discover that, as they lost their "sanity" in the eyes of others through what they did and said, so may they regain it. Under these conditions, we might expect mental patients to be "on" without reserve, that for them, truly, life becomes a theater.[7] There is some truth in this: mental patients are "on" at times and feel under pressure to be "on" even more often. But, given their motives to be "on" and the pressure they are under, it is perhaps more remarkable that mental patients cannot sustain this perspective without experiencing severe anxiety and discomfort. From this, as from other experiences of mental patients, we may learn something of importance about everyday life.[8]

We can get at this experience by considering more closely some aspects of the perspective of being "on." Let us consider that, when one is "on," activities come to be regarded as "performances," other persons as an "audience," and the world

[6] Jonathan Winters, an entertainer, provides us with an example of the breakdown of these boundaries. Of a period in his life when he experienced a "crack-up" he says, "I was 'on' all the time, always playing the part—in parks, restaurants, whenever [*sic*] I went—and I couldn't get 'off.' Well, I got 'off.' I look around now and think how much I have to be thankful for. And there's no use throwing myself on the floor because once in a while something bugs me" (13, p. 32). Stories about stage actors who carry their "parts" home, as well as audience members who take "character" for "reality," are common, if the events they point to infrequent.
[7] Goffman has something like this in mind when he remarks that the mental patient "can learn, at least for a time, to practice before all groups the amoral arts of shamelessness" (7, "The Moral Career of the Mental Patient," p. 169). Reprinted in this volume.
[8] The whole remarkable series of papers by Goffman on mental patients and their keepers provides an example of what we may learn about everyday life from them (7).

around as a series of "scenes" and "props." Let us also consider how this view conflicts with what mental patients consider "natural."

Like others who are "on," the mental patient comes to regard his own activities as potential "performances," as potential means of creating and sustaining a "character" for the benefit of others. At times, he uses them this way. Unlike some who are "on," however, the mental patient faces a dilemma. The "show" he experiences himself as "staging" concerns a fundamental matter, a matter that, as he sees it, should not and should not need to be "staged"; namely, his "normality." This is not only an aspect of self that he wants others to again take for granted. This he might indeed accomplish through a judicious "performance." More important, "normality" is an aspect of self the mental patient *himself* profoundly desires to take for granted again. And regarding his activities as "performances" interferes with this crucial aim.

Thus, a patient may enact a "normal character," succeed in "taking in" the audience, and retrospectively discover that he has, in the process, left himself more unconvinced than ever about the "reality" of his "normality."

> Mr. Yale [9] told the interviewer that a nurse had remarked to him that his wife was much "improved." As a mark of "improvement" the nurse cited the fact that Mrs. Yale was playing "Scrabble" (a word game) a great deal. The next day, after some hesitance about confidentiality, Mrs. Yale confided to the interviewer that she and her friends had recently taken to playing "Scrabble" as a means of impressing the staff with their ability to think clearly and be sociable. During the balance of the interview, Mrs. Yale expressed a great deal of concern over whether she was "really" better or had merely misled personnel.

Or, anticipating this sort of conflict, a patient may pointedly avoid "performing."

> Mrs. White said that, if she decided to, she could easily get out of the hospital: she realized that she had come to learn what one was "supposed to say and do" to accomplish this. However, she added, *to* do these things was to deny one's "own self" and what "one felt."

Finally, what the patient has been saying and doing may be defined by an authoritative other *as* "performing," thereby provoking the conflict.

> Mrs. Quinn said that when Dr. X suggested that she was "painting the picture too rosy," she realized that she had been trying to impress hospital staff just to get out of the hospital, and this frightened her.

We are led to see, then, that the mental patient is not satisfied to *appear* "normal," he strives to *be* "normal." Paradoxically, this means, in part, that he wants to "appear normal" to *himself* Striving to "appear normal" for others—"putting on a show of normality"—interferes with this objective.

It may also be noted that the mental patient addresses others as a potential "audience." The hospital, self-defined as a place of "observation," is obviously conducive to this effect. Others, the patient learns, are "witnesses" of as well as "participants" in his activities. With this a matter of awareness—and, moreover, assumed by the patient to be a matter of awareness for the other—it becomes difficult for a patient to have a relationship in which the impression the other receives of his "illness" or lack of it is not relevant.

---

[9] This, as the other patients' and relatives' names we have used, is fictitious. We have, however, consistently used the same names for identical patients and relatives throughout the several papers we have published or are publishing.

During hospitalization patients tend to construe all situations as, potentially, "test" situations in which their "sanity" is being assessed. Thus, many patients make a particular point of knowing the day, month, year, and season, anticipating that "requests for information" will in fact be "orientation examinations." And others, not appreciating how seldom hospital personnel have a chance to become familiar with "the record," consider what are in fact requests for information (like, "how many children do you have?") as further tests. The perspective, in a few cases, tends to become omnipresent: thus, Mrs. Karr believed throughout her hospitalization that several of the "patients" were "spies" who collected information for the hospital and were only feigning illness. And, of course, there is little reason to believe that regarding others as an "audience" ends with release from the hospital. So for a time during the post-hospital period several patients responded to the greeting "How are you?" by launching a description of their mental health or by inquiring into the interviewers' motives for asking such a "question." Information received from patients' relatives suggests that this kind of response was not confined to the interview situation.

These kinds of responses suggest that, within his perspective, the patient consciously follows a kind of "script" in which his primary appearance is that of a "suspect person." In part, it is the others who have these "suspicions" and the patient must disabuse them of these. This is to be accomplished by "watching" one's own "reactions" and by fitting them to the model of a "normal person," also included in the "script." As well, the patient attempts to restrict the actions of others toward him to those which may appropriately be directed to a "normal person."

But, again, the patient's appearance before others is only part of a weighty problem. Not only must he fashion a "normal character" for others and attempt to induce them to provide the social conditions under which he can carry this off, he must do these things while remaining the most critical "audience" of his own "show." Viewing his own activities from "inside," the mental patient finds that he must work with "reactions" which *he* perceives as contrived and controlled. And for him, as for his other "audiences," a critical aspect of "normality" is that "reactions" are just that: they appear "spontaneous." More is at stake, then, than "putting on" a creditable "performance" for an "audience"; indeed, doing so would seem to undermine the most important "show" of all.

Finally, let us note that the mental patient tends to view things as potential "props." That is, "things," including persons and places ("scenes"), tend to be appreciated directly for the information they potentially and actually convey about the self, for their communicative value in creating, sustaining, or disrupting a "character."

Thus some patients, as well as some sociologists, recognize that the limited expressive materials afforded by the hospital insure that many activities will almost certainly "look crazy." And patients feel under constant pressure to remain aware of the communicative value of their own affective expressions.

> Mrs. Vick said, "Life is a pretense. I have to pretend every day that I'm here. That I'm gay and happy in order to stay out of the isolation ward. So I laugh and pretend to be gay."

Other persons, too, may be regarded as "props" to be maneuvered in the interests of the "show" at hand. Thus patients frequently demand that relatives visibly express affection and need for them on the ward. Such expressions were correctly perceived by patients as important to personnel in establishing the patients' "return to normality."

The problem with this view of "things" is that the patient reinforces his own uncertainty as to what is "real" and what is "mere appearance." Thus, the effort to appear "gay" seems to make patients wonder if all "gayness" isn't "mere appearance"; and prearrangements with relatives seem to make patients more uncertain about just what their relatives "really" feel toward them, as well as how they "really" feel toward their relatives. Indeed, this seems to be the core problem with being "on" in regard to fundamental matters: not only can the patient no longer trust others but, most devastating of all, he can no longer trust himself. He is, for a while, anxiously uncertain as to whether the "normal character" he projects *is* his "self." And the more he appears to himself as "acting"—the more single-mindedly he strives for "effect"—the more uncertain he seems to become.

The foregoing may be summarized in this way. The mental patient is under pressure to experience the world, with his self at its center, in a "technical" way. Like the stage actor contemplating the cloak-over-self he will don for his audience, so the mental patient comes to address his own character. Instead of a "natural" phenomenon, flowing from and reflecting the self, the mental patient's character comes to appear to him as a "constructed object,"[10] as a "function" of manipulated activities and contrived scenes, of the assessments of an audience and the standards they invoke, and of the nature and availability of props.[11] The connection between self and character becomes a questionable, undependable matter. Or, to use another figure, this connection becomes a matter of wit and stagecraft, of the contingencies of "staging a show." An intrinsic link is shattered.

III

We have said that, for a while, the mental patient is "on." It remains to note that this perspective bears a remarkable resemblance to the perspective that the dramaturgic analyst seems to attribute to the individual in everyday life, whatever the mental status of the latter. Thus, the dramaturgic analyst conceives the individual as a "performer" whose activities function to create the "appearance" of a "self"—a "character"—for an "audience." In the process of maintaining or changing his "character" for others, the individual manipulates things as "props." Others are related to the individual in terms of their "parts" in putting a "show" together, of witnessing it, of sustaining it, or of disrupting it. Places become "scenes" which are fitted or unfitted for the creation of "character" at hand. The outcome of interest to the analyst is the "effective" creation of a "character" which, by "taking in" the "audience" or failing to do so, will permit the individual to continue a rewarding line of activity or to avoid an unrewarding one, or which will result in his being "discredited." Finally, the dramaturgic analyst seems to make mental patients of us all, for he conceives the individual as "staging" *fundamental* qualities: aspects of self taken for granted *with* intimate others.[12]

---

[10] Harold Garfinkel has used this term—and "assembled object"—in a similar way, but in another connection, in his unpublished work.

[11] Compare Goffman's view of the "self" in (6), especially pp. 252–253, in (2), "The Moral Career . . . ," pp. 168–169, and in (3), p. 271.

[12] Consider Goffman's statement to the effect that "when we observe a young American middle-class girl playing dumb for the benefit of her boy friend, we are ready to point to items of guile

This vision of the world is for a time, as we have tried to show, a core aspect of the mental patient's perspective. Finding himself in the eyes of others either a doubtful person or a thoroughly discredited one, he may consciously undertake to fashion an image of "normality." Insofar as this is the case, he will "act" with full awareness; he will see himself as "acting"; he will be "on."

Now we must ask, is the dramaturgic analyst asserting that individuals are "on" in everyday life, routinely and as a matter of course? Is he suggesting that ordinarily, say among family and friends, the individual views "life as theater"? If so, what shall we make of the fact that the mental patient experiences being "on" as an *interruption* of his "normal" perspective and as a source of anxiety and alienation? How shall we account for the patient's intense desire to get "off"?

We wish to suggest that no paradox is involved. In viewing "life as theater," the dramaturgic analyst does not present us with a model of the actor's consciousness; *he is not suggesting that this is the way his subjects understand the world.* Instead, the dramaturgic analyst invokes the theatrical model as a device, a tool, to permit *him* to focus attention on the consequences of the actor's activities for others' perceptions of the actor. The dramaturgic analyst finds this important because, according to *his* theory of social stability and change, others' "impressions" determine the ways they will act toward the actor. Thus, whether the actor self-consciously takes account of these "impressions" or not, whether or not he is even aware that he is creating an "impression," such "impressions" are demonstrably relevant to the fate of such interaction as the actor enters.

In one sense, then, the actor's "perspective," that is, the actor's view of what he is doing, is not relevant to the dramaturgic analyst. For whatever the actor believes he is doing, so long as he is engaged in interaction, the analyst finds and focusses on the "impression" the actor is making on others. The analyst's "frame of reference," his rules for converting the actor's motions into conduct (1), are given by the theatrical simile. This frame of reference, these rules, may be quite different than those used by the actor to understand his own behavior.[13] This feature of dramaturgic analysis seems to be frequently misunderstood, even by its appreciators.[14] At least in part, this seems to be due to a lack of explicitness, if not a lack of clarity,[15] on the part of those using the dramaturgic framework.

In another sense, however, the actor's perspective is quite relevant to the dramaturgic analyst. As a social-psychologist, the dramaturgic analyst is little interested in documenting what "everybody knows." Instead he wants to get at

---

and contrivance in her behavior. But like herself and her boy friend, we accept as an unperformed fact that this performer *is* a young American middle-class girl. But surely here we neglect the greater part of the performance. . . . The unthinking ease with which performers consistently carry off such standard-maintaining routines does not deny that a performance has occurred, merely that the participants have been aware of it" (6, pp. 74–75).

13 In this respect, if in no other, the dramaturgic analyst's approach resembles that of the psychoanalytic psychiatrist. The psychoanalyst, too, is professionally engaged in attributing meanings to the behavior of individuals which are variant from the individuals' understandings of their own behavior.

14 For example, Don Martindale (9, pp. 61–72) discusses Goffman's work as if it were a representation of the growing amorality of urban individuals. We are explicitly disagreeing with this interpretation and would hold that the dramaturgic approach is applicable to the analysis of moral conduct in any age. We agree with Martindale, however, that the growing amorality of urban individuals may help account for the emergence of the dramaturgic perspective.

15 Surely it does little to clarify matters to suggest that "the *object* of a performer is to sustain a particular definition of the situation, this representing, as it were, his claim as to what reality is" (6, p. 85, italics added). "Performer" here refers to a person in everyday life carrying out his routine projects of action, *not* to someone who is "on."

how everybody knows what they know, at "hidden" effects or *latent* functions of interaction. The theatrical simile, like any of the similes invoked by the drama- turgic analyst, is revealing precisely insofar as it clarifies a latent function. More- over, it seems to do so only when the actor is "unconscious" of the "impressive" effects of his activities, that is, only insofar as the actor "takes for granted" or "takes notice of without seeing" these effects. This may be appreciated by con- sidering what a dramaturgic analysis of a theatrical performance might be.

A dramaturgic analysis of a theatrical performance would presumably *not* focus on how stage actors manage to bring a play "to life" for an audience. An analysis in these terms would be merely a technical analysis of the business at hand as the principles and the audience define this business. It would produce a manual of stage directions. In order to produce an account of interest to the dramaturgic analyst, what would have to be considered is how stage actors manage to keep the audience continually convinced that the play they are witnessing *is a play*. Such an analysis might point out, for example, that, by altering the segments of time within which events can "really" be accomplished, actors provide the audi- ence with a sense of "play" as distinguished from "reality." It might document the gestures actors employ on stage which *interrupt* the audience member's sense of emerging character, which remind the audience that "character" and actor are not the same. It might note that returning for bows after the curtain has fallen not only services actors' egos, but also functions to remind the audience that there *is* someone "behind" the "appearance" they have been attending, for example, that the "appearance" of the dead man was "merely an appearance." Such an analysis might inquire as to which members of the audience, children under cer- tain ages, for example, cannot retain the sense of the play *as* a play. And more. In general, a dramaturgic analysis of a theatrical performance would ask, what are the relations between the world in which the attitude of "play acting" prevails and that in which the attitude of "daily life" or "fundamental reality" obtains? What are the social devices whereby these worlds are kept distinct, and under what circumstances does this distinction collapse?

It should be noted that, insofar as the above is correct, the dramaturgic analyst seeks to describe the ways in which "impressions" are created, sustained, and ruptured under the condition that the actor is "unconscious" or only dimly "con- scious" that this is a part of the business he is in. The other "models" used by the dramaturgic analyst reveal the same feature. Thus, the "con man" instructs us how, in everyday life, without being explicitly aware of it, those who do not conceive themselves as "con men" may sustain another's conception of themselves as "trustworthy" in the face of events which might lead him to conceive them quite differently. And persons who attach television aerials to their houses but do not own sets, those who put exotic travel labels on luggage that gets no fur- ther than the front door, in brief, those who *intentionally* misrepresent their quali- ties, thereby taking on a "character" for the audience to which they feel they have no "real" claim, are interesting to the dramaturgic analyst, not in themselves, but as persons who furnish "clear-cut evidence of the impressive function of pre- sumably instrumental objects" and acts (6, p. 67).

Indeed, it does not seem too much to say that the power of dramaturgic analysis lies *in* the discrepancy between the perspective of the actor and that of the analyst. It is through this discrepancy that the analyst is able to elucidate matters that are beyond the immediate awareness of his subjects. It is when this discrepancy exists, when, for example, the actor provides "impressions" without being aware that he is doing so, that the theatrical simile is most revealing. What it reveals is this: the ways in which interactants *manage*, that is, *produce through their own activities*, that which they "take for granted" is "out there, really." Since the dramaturgic analyst aims to explore the conditions of constancy and change in others' impressions of actors as "being" what they claim, the theatrical simile seems exquisitely suited to his purpose. It focusses attention on that *aspect* of interaction of central interest to the analyst; affecting others' perceptions is the principal business of those in the theater. In the theater, creating appearances is regarded as a *task;* thus the analyst can more easily consider what individuals in everyday life *do* to create and sustain the realities they honor, even though they are not entirely aware of their doings. In the theater, the "expressive" and "impressive" functions of activity are *separated;* therefore the analyst can consider in isolation that function of interaction so central to his theory of social stability and change.

All this adds up to pointing out some of the ways in which the theatrical simile is a simile, not a homology. It is a simile, a frame of reference, invoked by the analyst to segregate and permit him to analyze *one* of the multiple functions of interaction: its "impressive" function. The purpose is facilitated *because* this function is segregated in the theater; in daily life, this function is a concretely inextricable part of a larger complex.

It is also worth noting that this frame of reference enables the analyst to himself abandon, if only for a while, the perspective of everyday life; it enables or forces him to *stop* taking for granted what his subjects *do* take for granted, thereby permitting him to talk *about* these matters. In this way, the perspective stands ready, as does the anthropologist's "tribe," to furnish a lens through which "what everybody knows" can be rendered problematic. We may then ask what we do that stabilizes Grar.d Central Station as a place for people with destinations, and not a place to live, subway cars as objects for travel, not for sleeping, a hotel lounge as a place to meet people in, a library for reading, a fire escape for survival, and more (7, p. 182).

But, as with any model, so the theatrical one has limits which, if not observed, pose dangers to analysis. The analyst and his readers run the risk of considering the dramaturgic framework to represent his subjects' model of the world. Because "impression management" is critical in the *analyst's* scheme of things, because in any situation it is this dimension that *he* attends to, he may leave the impression that this is the way things "are" as his subjects see things—or at least that, if they could be brought to be honest for a bit, they would see and admit that this is the case. There is, of course, no justification for this. Indeed, within the dramaturgic framework one must address in all seriousness the subjects' view of self and world; this is, after all, the topic of analysis. On the other hand, there is no justification for overlooking the impressive function of daily activities in an analysis of human conduct. Adding the dramaturgic perspective to the social-psychological tool kit should go some way toward preventing this.

Second, if we are correct in asserting that the dramaturgic analyst does **not** present "life as theater" as his subjects' view of the world, then we must ask after the relation between his subjects' view and "life as theater." The dramaturgic analyst does not claim that the actor is aware of the impressive functions of his activities; indeed, he seems to claim that, to the extent that the actor is aware of these functions, he becomes alienated from interaction and, moreover, from himself (5). We concur with this view and have presented some observations by and about mental patients to help warrant it. But, although in the dramaturgic vision the actor does not attend to the impressive effects of his activities *as* impressive effects, he nonetheless exhibits a remarkable ability to produce the right effect at just the right time, or, short of this, to correct for the errors he and his teammates may make. How is this accomplished? More pointedly, what is the relation between the *actor's* model of the world and the *dramaturgic analyst's* model? Is the actor merely the outcome of a dynamicized set of "organizational principles" which shove and haul him about without his awareness? Anyone committed to an understanding of everyday life and of the "actor's world" must cope with such a question. The dramaturgic analyst is self-admittedly so committed.

Finally, the theatrical simile may encourage the analyst to forget another important aspect of any everyday actor's communications: the actor is communicating *about* himself, and this constrains the attitude he may take toward the qualities he projects.

The stage actor's obligations do not ordinarily include a belief that the character he projects be a "presentation of self." It is an "Anybody" that the stage actor presents, if a particular one: an other-than-himself. His task, as usually defined, is to employ whatever means will facilitate the "coming alive" of the character for the audience. This leaves the actor free, or relatively so, to select an attitude toward the character he plays. He may, for example, conceive that getting "inside" the character will aid the accomplishment of his task; he may conceive that this is not necessary, taking a "classical" stance rather than a "method" one. So long as he convinces the audience that the character he portrays is a plausible one, his obligations are fulfilled. It is presumably only "method" actors, however, who succeed in experiencing the characters they are projecting as their selves, however temporarily.

The everyday actor's obligations, at least so far as fundamental qualities are concerned, do not leave him free to select an attitude toward the character he communicates. He does not, finally, experience life as theater. He does not expect the curtain to ring down, returning what came before to the realm of make-believe. He is constrained to *be* what he claims, and mental patients suggest that these constraints operate "inside" the individual as well as "on" him. Indeed, his need to believe in himself seems even stronger than his need to be certain that others entertain a particular view of him. He is in the grip of an ethic, and he violates this ethic so long as he is "on."

The basic task joined by mental patients would seem to be the locating and fixing of the reality of themselves. In this, they differ from stage actors; they cannot remain "on" with impunity. And in this, mental patients represent us all.

Bibliography

1. Burke, K. *A Grammar of Motives.* Englewood Cliffs, N.J.: Prentice-Hall, 1952.
2. Goffman, E. "Cooling the Mark Out: Some Aspects of Adaptation to Failure," *Psychiatry*, 1952, 25, 451–463.
3. Goffman, E. "Embarrassment and Social Organization," *The American Journal of Sociology*, 1956, 62, 264–271.
4. Goffman, E. *The Presentation of Self in Everyday Life.* Edinburgh: University of Edinburgh Social Sciences Research Centre, 1956.

5. Goffman, E. "Alienation from Interaction," *Human Relations,* 1957, 10, 47–60.
6. Goffman, E. *The Presentation of Self in Everyday Life.* Garden City, New York: Doubleday, 1959.
7. Goffman, E. *Asylums.* New York: Doubleday, 1961.
8. Mailer, N. *Advertisements for Myself.* New York: The New American Library of World Literature, 1960.
9. Martindale, D. *American Society.* New York: D. Van Nostrand, 1960.
10. Sampson, H., S. L. Messinger, and R. D. Towne. "The Mental Hospital and Marital Family Ties," *Social Problems,* 1961, 9, 141–155.
11. Wolfe, B. "Ecstatic in Blackface: The Negro as a Song-and-Dance Man," *Modern Review,* 1950, 111, 196–208.
12. *Life Magazine.* December 22, 1958, 45, p. 116.
13. *San Francisco Chronicle.* January 24, 1961, p. 32.

68   Social Disintegration as a Requisite of Resocialization

● PETER MC HUGH

One needn't go very far to discover that attempts to rehabilitate deviants fail to change the person at least as often as they succeed. Cressy, Bloch and Geis, Korn and McCorkle, and Clausen, among others, estimate that recidivism among criminals, drug addicts, and the mentally ill varies from 50 percent up to nearly 100 percent.[1] Bloch and Geis state that "An analysis of imprisoned men and the recognition that approximately 65 percent—almost two-thirds—return to prison indicate the futility of many of our present procedures."[2] Regardless of the amount of activity meant to foster it, changed behavior remains an unmet aim of rehabilitation.

There are several reasons for this state of affairs, and I shall mention two here. First, in regard to the administrative procedures of rehabilitating organizations, they operate in an environment marked by goals that are either contradictory in themselves or antithetical to the concrete practices that could produce changed behavior. This situation of deterrence and punishment versus rehabilitation has been commented upon any number of times and is not surprising to those familiar with penal and psychiatric organizations. The second reason is of a different order and much less often cited: the nature of social theorizing, perhaps especially sociological theorizing, has tended to emphasize stable social structures, with attendant concentration on orderly interaction attuned to the overall norms and values of the larger society. However apt this perspective may be in depicting the whole panorama of social life, deviance and the like have been discussed

SOURCE: Peter McHugh, in *Social Forces,* XLIV (March 1966), pp. 355–363.
    Revision of paper given at the annual meeting of the American Sociological Society, Montreal, Canada, 1964.

[1] Edwin H. Sutherland and Donald R. Cressey, *Criminology* (6th ed.; New York: J. B. Lippincott Co., 1960), p. 591; Herbert A. Bloch and Gilbert Geis, *Man, Crime and Society* (New York: Random House, 1962), p. 575; Richard R. Korn and Lloyd W. McCorkle, *Criminology and Penology* (New York: Henry Holt Co., 1959); John A. Clausen, "Mental Disorders," in Robert K. Merton and Robert A. Nisbet (eds.), *Contemporary Social Problems* (New York: Harcourt, Brace & Co.), p. 209.
[2] Bloch & Geis, *loc. cit.*

primarily as curious contrasts, over and against our abiding interest in order. Consequently, we tend to use the ideas we have developed to explain order in our attempts to account for rehabilitation, on the assumption that bringing men back to a legitimate social life is the same kind of activity as the routine constraints on men who are already part of the legitimate social order. To give a single example, note how we transplant into rehabilitation our ideas of socialization and learning, ideas that originally explained how neophytes become conforming members of their cultures and in so doing perpetrate society that had existed before their arrival. Yet if rehabilitation requires unlearning, a phenomenon which is not ubiquitous in the socialization of children, typical theories of socialization will not suffice. They will not suffice because they do not cover the very important elements of unlearning and radically changed behavior which are part and parcel of the process of rehabilitation.

To put it another way, the toilers in deviant rehabilitation can tell us why it does not occur. But, unfortunately, we cannot in the telling learn much about how it could occur, perhaps because our views of a stable social order do not help us to understand the radical changes in behavior which characterize rehabilitation. For a *theory* of radical change and rehabilitation, as opposed to the administrative practices which must be orderly to put rehabilitation into effect, some ideas stressing disorder and disintegration may be fruitful.

It will be the burden of this paper to delineate some ideas about disintegration as the social condition which precedes rehabilitation. In so doing, we shall investigate the difference between ordinary socialization and resocialization; the differential effects on resocialization of social organization and disintegration; and the actual empirical operations for inducing rehabilitation in concrete organizations. Sources will be of several kinds. Research in criminology and penology will be utilized to depict the failure of current practices, followed by a review of alienation and anomie and their possibilities as conditions of disintegration and rehabilitation. Running throughout will be references to industrialization, which, surprisingly, is an actual case of existent radical change in natural systems. It is a case strikingly similar to changes which are now only hopes in rehabilitating organizations.

First, however, I shall list basic premises and conclusions—some very obvious —in order to clarify what follows:

1. Rehabilitation requires radical rather than ordinary changes in behavior.
2. Radical change requires changes in values.
3. Socially organized relationships tend to reinforce old values, or to only gradually diminish their efficacy in guiding behavior.
4. Disintegrated social relationships tend to eradicate rather than simply diminish the efficacy of values in guiding behavior.
5. Therefore, social disintegration can be one phase of radically changed behavior.
6. Social disintegration occurs when group activity is random and interpersonal sanctions are either ineffective or nonexistent.
7. In a situation of resource monopoly, disintegration can be operationalized as follows:

   A. Activity can be made random by scheduling each activity according to a table of random numbers.

B. Interpersonal sanctions can be made ineffective by a continuous turnover of individual interactants (random group composition).

These conditions will be treated as necessary but insufficient requisites of radical individual change. They would be required as one stage of rehabilitation, but would not automatically lead to changes because they would have to be followed by the well-known, typical forms of social learning.

The Meaning of Radical Change and Socialization

We probably should begin by indicating what is meant by radical change. Simply put, radical change will be treated as the substitution of one set of value orientations for another. Here we make the usual distinction between specific norms of low generality and overarching values of high generality.[3] The values of a group are shared by all its members and therefore give them a common identity over and above their particular roles, and against the coexistence of other groups. Norms, on the other hand, are specifications of value for different positions within the group, varying according to the statuses to which they apply. Radical change according to this view is a change in the values which bind a whole collectivity to certain kinds of behavior, and must remain distinct from ordinary change exemplified by shifts in role norms—shifts which are simply different modes of interaction, not indicators of any change in the characteristic goals of the whole group as a solidary unit. The difference is one between transformation of (radical change) and transformation in (ordinary change).[4] Similarly, radical change occurs rapidly: for individuals, a change in values within a single lifetime, for societies, a change in one or two generations. The term radical implies revolutionary rather than evolutionary change when time is the basis of measurement.

The other major concept to be used in this analysis is socialization. Obviously, the process of value change must be completed through some kind of social learning. However, since we are trying to describe radical change in the same person rather than continuity between generations, we are directed toward a particular kind of learning quite different from the ordinary kind: resocialization. Resocialization is unlike plain socialization because in resocialization the person adopts values which are contradictory to the old ones binding the collectivity. As resocialization requires us to handle the notion of contradiction, it is different from plain socialization, which entails "merely" the successive expansion of learned norms and values upon a congruent base. To this degree, resocialization involves distinctive processes of interaction and social organization, i.e., desocialization. It is suggested that, since radical change requires a change in values, plain socialization will be ineffective because it cannot handle the contradiction which must occur under that condition. I shall now offer evidence for this assertion.

---

[3] Clyde Kluckhohn *et al.*, "Values and Value Orientations in the Theory of Action" in Talcott Parsons and Edward A. Shils (eds.), *Toward a General Theory of Action* (Cambridge: Harvard University Press, 1951), pp. 388–483; Neil J. Smelser, *Theory of Collective Behavior* (New York: The Free Press of Glencoe, 1963), p. 114 ff. Richard Christie and Robert K. Merton indicate that values can be tested, diminishing the old argument that whatever one makes of values conceptually, they cannot be fruitful empirically. "Procedure for the Sociological Study of the Value Climate of Medical Schools," *Journal of Medical Education*, 33 (October 1958), pp. 125–153.

[4] Talcott Parsons, Edward A. Shils, Kaspar D. Naegele and Jesse Pitts (eds.), *Theories of Society* (New York: The Free Press of Glencoe, 1961), Vol. 2, p. 1214.

Plain Socialization Cannot Produce Radical Change

When conflict exists between groups, social control must be exerted either through complete monopoly of resources (cultural, social, biological and physical), or through appeals to legitimate authority.[5] (The latter requires no monopoly and no coercion, since legitimacy makes the agency of control congruent with the values of the controlled group.) Thus, where values conflict the agencies of control must either monopolize the perquisites of behavior or convert the deviant group to a new set of legitimizing norms. For example, psychiatric treatment cannot be successful to the degree it requires the cooperation of the prisoner, because the authority of the therapist is illegitimate from the point of view of the deviant, and therefore fails to elicit his cooperation. Evidence for this is the exclusively middle-class clientele of psychoanalytic therapy as well as the failure of such treatment in prisons—the successfully treated middle-class group imbues the therapist with legitimacy to begin with, prisoners do not.[6] Due to differences in the reference group values of prisoners and therapists, cost exceeds reward to the extent that prisoners choose any alternative to treatment. The values of therapist and prisoner are so divergent that for one to adopt those of the other would require contradiction of the original set (a resocializing situation) rather than mere elaboration upon it (a plain socializing situation).

Similar conditions exist in colonial administrations. Although there is a practical monopoly of armed force in these societies, there is neither total monopoly of resources nor legitimacy, resulting in "Messianism which is inimical to economic growth."[7] Messianism maintains the traditional features of the system in much the same way that inmate subcultures maintain their values. The following is taken from a work describing the inability of central governments in some emerging societies to induce participation in industrial activities:[8]

> Those in the subsistence sector have not had their commitments to institutions eroded very greatly. Consequently a frontal attack on any one of these institutions is likely to be perceived as an attack on all of them. Moreover, because the sentiments in support of the institution remain intact, such a procedure is likely to evoke a strong response, one that is strong enough in most cases probably to cause the central government to give up the programme. The institution in question, having been successfully defended, is thus apt to emerge from the contest not weaker than it was before but stronger.

One could accurately substitute inmate subcultures here and leave the description of process as is. Without legitimacy or monopoly, plain socialization is nothing more than moral suasion, because the social organization of the target group supports, may even require, the efficacy of old values. The attributes of ordinary socialization, in which cumulative behavioral additions develop upon a congruent base, cannot be applied to situations in which radical changes in behavior are either expected or required. Since we are talking of *value*, something which per-

[5] H. H. Gerth and C. Wright Mills (trans. and ed.), *Max Weber: Essays in Sociology* (New York: Oxford University Press, 1946), p. 78 ff.

[6] Hans H. Strupp, "Psychotherapy," *Annual Review of Psychology*, 13 (1962), pp. 445–478; David Abrahamson, "Evaluation of the Treatment of Criminals," in Paul H. Hoch (ed.), *Failures in Psychiatric Treatment* (New York: Grune & Stratton, 1948), pp. 58–77.

[7] Everett E. Hagen, *On the Theory of Social Change* (Homewood, Illinois: The Dorsey Press, 1962), p. 411.

[8] Terence K. Hopkins, "On Economic Planning in Tropical Africa," *Co-existence*, 1 (May 1964), p. 87.

vades the activity of the group in many spheres, the contradiction between new and old cannot be eliminated by lower-level status separation or priority, because the value is operant in all statuses. Instead, for radical change to occur, resocialization must occur. Rather than adding the new to the old—plain socialization—the old must first be eliminated—desocialization. The question remains how desocialization operates as the first step in the process of resocialization.

Desocialization

On the face of it, the most promising examples of desocialization are depicted in the literature devoted to anomie, alienation, disruption, disorganization, and the like, as well as in several discussions of rapid industrialization, because they depict behavior which is quite different from, and often antithetical to, the behavior occurring when the system was integrated. Some studies of Africa indicate that the mobility, urbanism, and corporate organization of work in a transitional society increase the scale of interaction and communication in a way that disrupts the extended family and paves the way for free-floating individualism. The works of Schein, Biderman and others concerning American prisoners in Chinese camps suggest that certain disruptions of prisoner relationships will foster collaboration or withdrawal, behavior which requires an important change in the soldier's reference group. A laboratory study which violates expectations between subject and experimenter produces innovation, powerlessness and meaninglessness in subjects whose attitude scale scores in no way forecast these behaviors before violation. Dornbusch discovers that a military academy must destroy the symbolic accoutrements of earlier systems of interaction before its own rather different norms can be effective in guiding cadet behavior. Hagen depicts a point at which industrialization includes "withdrawal of status respect," meaning the old relationships disappear into limbo before what he calls "creative innovation," e.g., the introduction of new behavior, can appear.[9]

On the other hand, the penological works devoted to deviant rehabilitation are unanimous in suggesting that criminal behavior is not so much rehabilitated as reinforced; that these efforts are more likely to disrupt the staff than change inmates; and that there is something about custodial organizations which inhibits rehabilitation. Clemmer talks of "prisonization," which is actually a continuing socialization to the values of the inmate subculture—plain socialization in our terms. Sykes describes the sustaining congruence between prison roles and criminal norms. Cressy reports that the requirements of custody and rehabilitation are exclusive to the extent that staff must enlist the cooperation of inmates and thereby becomes "corrupted," e.g., acts to reinforce the prisoner relationships which are supposed to be changing.[10]

[9] Godfrey Wilson and Monica Wilson, *The Analysis of Social Change* (Cambridge, England: Cambridge University Press, 1955); George A. Theodorson, "Acceptance of Industrialization and its Consequences for the Social Patterns of Non-Western Societies," *American Sociological Review*, 18 (October 1953), pp. 477–484; Edgar H. Schein, "Interpersonal Communication, Group Solidarity, and Social Influence," *Sociometry*, 23 (June 1960), pp. 148–161 (the ideas in this paper are clearly similar to Schein's, exemplified by his topic heading in the cited paper: "Creating Influenceability through Social Alienation"); Peter McHugh, *Order and Disorder in Social Time and Space*, unpublished Ph.D. dissertation, Northwestern University, 1962; Sanford M. Dornbusch, "The Military Academy as an Assimilating Institution," *Social Forces*, 34 (July 1956), pp. 316–321; Hagen, *op. cit.*, pp. 186–200.

[10] Donald Clemmer, *The Prison Community* (Boston: Christopher Press, 1940); Gresham M. Sykes, *The Society of Captives: A Study of a Maximum Security Prison* (Princeton, New Jer-

These studies indicate that the twenty-four-hour control of force in prisons fails to induce radical change in prisoner behavior, while in a developing society such changes do occur. Perhaps the difference is due to the absence of desocialization in the prison case, an absence which obviates resocialization; and perhaps the absence of desocialization is attributable to the absence of social disintegration. It may be that the new values which would mobilize conforming behavior are not effectively socialized because the *organized* relationships in the inmate social system serve as the vehicles for expression of old values. To the degree that continuing relationships reinforce the old values, the old values can be discontinued only by discontinuing the relationships. In other language, the interactional *skills* or norms specified by new values may in fact be absorbed, but the *commitment* which must precede the valued use of these skills is in no way redirected. In the industrializing situation, on the other hand, the disruption of previous relationships makes possible the development of a new (industrial) commitment, upon which base the learning of skills may proceed. One observes that the depletion of previous relations through withdrawal of status respect never occurs in prison.[11]

The import of this examination is that social disintegration disrupts the ongoing relationships which are the vehicles of values at the level of interaction. If one assumes that values influence interaction, there is no inherent reason to deny the influence of interaction upon values. Anomie, as a terminal or chaotic state, could be so only if values were disrupted in that state. The suggestion here is that disintegration of interaction can eradicate values and thereby desocialize those who undergo the disintegration.

The next question involves just what happens in this process of disintegration. How can alienation from the antecedent social order be programmed? What operations will produce it?

Operant Disintegration

Disintegration consists of two parts: (1) normatively meaningless events, a dislocation of the cohort's sequence of activity; and (2) subverted interpersonal relationships, the social isolation of individuals. The first discoordinates the activities of the group, the second makes its sanctions ineffective.[12] We shall take up normatively meaningless events first.

I. NORMATIVELY MEANINGLESS EVENTS

Normatively meaningless events refers primarily to disruption of the routine activity of the cohort rather than to the interaction of its members. Obvious ex-

---

sey: Princeton University Press, 1958); Donald R. Cressey, "Contradictory Directives in Correctional Group Therapy Programs," *Federal Probation*, 18 (June 1954), pp. 20–26.

[11] Hagen, *op. cit.*, p. 186.

[12] Dislocation of sequence alone would not work, since this lack could become "socially shared" in a cohesive group of inmates, thereby increasing their solidarity. Schein, Thibaut and Kelley, Sykes and others note this as one of the "problems" in rehabilitation of various kinds. Purely situational adversity probably binds the membership more closely, something Goffman refers to when he writes of an institutional underlife. Subverted interpersonal relations should prevent such an adaptation, however, because it would obviate the development of solidarity. See Schein, *op. cit.*; Sykes, *op. cit.*; John W. Thibaut and Harold H. Kelley, *The Social Psychology of Groups* (New York: John Wiley & Sons, 1959), pp. 169–187; Erving Goffman, *Asylums* (New York: Doubleday & Co.), pp. 207–225.

amples are sleeping, eating, work and recreation. Operant meaninglessness would involve the following steps in scheduling activities:

A. List all such activity
B. Assign a number to each activity
C. Organize these activities by consulting a table of random numbers
D. Randomize the completion of each activity

Such a procedure would deconstitute social organization by making it unpredictable to the member in the follow ways:

A. The person's assumption that he can affect events is destroyed. That the actor must be able to perceive and actualize his own efficacy in affecting his environment has been suggested as a necessary concomitant of continued normatively governed behavior, i.e., the concomitant of behavior which is not anomic.[13] To the degree this assumption is both necessary and absent, disintegration must occur. Randomized routines are external social conditions which correspond to and induce the social psychological state of powerlessness in that the actor's participation does not result in order or in any other conceived state of affairs.

B. The coordination or consistency of events through chronological time disappears. In Schutz's language, the actor's assumption of "et cetera"—that future events are expected to be comparable to past events—serves to connect discrete occurrences, and so makes it possible for behavior to proceed through recognition of the similarity between events.[14] Insofar as events are not temporally coordinated, they become incomparable and therefore perceptually meaningless as phenomenal foci of norms.

C. Time perspective becomes indeterminate. Since sequential events are one measure of time, a random sequence should disorganize this perspective. Cohen, Farber, and the Cosers, among others, suggest that an indeterminate end to a deprived situation makes its effects all the more drastic.[15] Thus, besides the uncoordinated temporal sequence of events, one can expect the very uncertainty of randomness as a time measure to increment the disintegration.

It is suggested that these characteristics—one referring to the actor's direct relation to events, the others to his perception of the relations between events themselves—are descriptive of Leites' and others' characteristics of depersonalization: things become "questionable instead of valid," "value judgments cease to be self-evident," "alternative courses of action lead to an identical result," and the actor becomes "tabula rasa as to previous conceptions of the meaningful life." [16] In the language of this paper, the person and his behavior come to be valueless, uninfluenced by previous goals or standards, because they are not encapsulated in an environment which meets his standards of minimal clarity.

[13] Alfred Schutz, "Common-Sense and Scientific Understandings of Human Action," *Philosophy and Phenomenological Research*, 14 (September 1953); Thibaut and Kelley, *op. cit.*, p. 180 ff.

[14] Lewis A. Coser and Rose Laub Coser, "Time Perspective and Social Structure," in Alvin E. Gouldner and Helen P. Gouldner (eds.), *Modern Sociology* (New York: Harcourt, Brace & World, 1963), pp. 638–647.

[15] E. A. Cohen, *Human Behavior in the Concentration Camp* (New York: W. W. Norton Co., 1953), p. 128; Maurice L. Farber, "Suffering and Time Perspective of the Prisoner," *Authority and Frustration: Studies in Topological and Vector Psychology* (Ames: University of Iowa Studies in Child Welfare, 20), pp. 153–227; Coser and Coser, *op. cit.*

[16] Nathan Leites, "Trends in Affectlessness," in Clyde Kluckhohn and Henry A. Murray (eds.), *Personality in Nature, Society and Culture* (2d ed.; New York: Alfred A. Knopf, 1953), pp. 620–622.

II. SUBVERTED INTERPERSONAL RELATIONSHIPS

The ruination of a system of interpersonal relations would have to (1) inhibit the continuation of pre-existing relationships and (2) prevent shared adaptation by members of the old system to new conditions. If the former did not occur, the system would continue unaffected. If the latter did not occur, the old system would continue as the old system but with new characteristics, i.e., the change would be dialectical, rather than radical.

Compressing the views of functionalists, and oversimplifying their works as well, we can assert that a system of viable social interaction requires reciprocal exchange between persons; complementary roles; and a unit structure which maintains values, adapts to external conditions, reaches some unit goals, and solidifies the positions of sub-units toward one another.[17] Much sociological writing expends a good deal of energy depicting these features, but when it comes to assessing the attributes of a failing interaction system, ideas are sparse— (a reflection of theorizing restricted to order mentioned above). Failure is usually attributed to the absence or reversal of one or another of the characteristics of order already in the accounting scheme, but not to any special condition which is independent of them.[18] The problem with such self-contained, logically closed arrays is that they do not specify the operations through which extreme change and/or failure are generated once the system is in motion, either at the system level or at some lower level. So-called "conflict" theories are seldom more helpful, since they usually begin with the assumption of some "incompatible differences of objective," when for our purposes these are just the differences which must be produced to induce failure.[19] And, of course, social conflict is not social disintegration, because a system can maintain a social order forever in the face of both internal and external conflict (prisons and some colonial societies are good examples of this). We are thus left with literature that describes organization and disintegration, but which does not link the two by depicting an explicit relation between them which could be used to induce disintegration.

Assuming an on-going system will tend to adapt to externally imposed conditions and thereby obviate radical change as opposed to ordinary change—most penology can be read in this light—the generating mechanism of interpersonal behavior must reveal the way to disintegration. It remains to discover those mechanisms and to construct conditions which will prevent their realization. What, we must ask, are the prior conditions which allow interaction to proceed and the system to continue? How can these conditions be transformed, disintegrated, dis-equilibrated? And how can this occur in situations where conflict is an important system-maintenance device, as is the case with inmate subcultures in prisons?

Let me suggest that one of the binding features of any interaction system is constancy between partners (individual propinquity), and that lack of constancy

[17] Works often consulted for their lists of necessary functions are Talcott Parsons, *The Social System* (Glencoe, Illinois: The Free Press, 1951), pp. 26–36; and Marion J. Levy, *The Structure of Society* (Princeton, New Jersey: Princeton University Press, 1952), pp. 149–197.
[18] Homans suggests that less frequent interaction between members tends to disintegrate the system, but Schein depicts situations where frequency remains about the same but disintegration appears. George C. Homans, *The Human Group* (New York: Harcourt, Brace & Co., 1950), p. 361; and Schein, *op. cit.*
[19] Rolf Dahrendorf, *Class and Class Conflict in Industrial Society* (Stanford: Stanford University Press, 1959), p. 135.

prevents the erection of integrated interpersonal relationships. Let me further suggest that absence of individual propinquity can exist in conjoint activity, so that disintegration is a problem that remains sociological and is the obverse of purely physical isolation. A combination of absence of propinquity and conjoint activity resides in a continuous turnover in group composition: individuals randomly thrown into contact with other individuals, even in the playing of roles and while engaged in concerted activity, making them all strangers face-to-face. Under these circumstances, they should be unable to conceive of themselves as members of one group or another, or as capable of maintaining interaction with a particular set of others. Because the assignment of individuals to the loci of interaction can be controlled, a total institution need not rely upon cooperation from those holding deviant values. And constancy or lack of it is a parameter of action which is conceptually independent of the theories of social organization summarized above.

A basis for asserting that random assignment of individuals is a generating mechanism for subverted interpersonal relationships can be found in the works of Blau, Homans, and Jones and Thibaut.[20] These studies indicate that the beginnings of interaction and group activity depend upon conjoint behavior between *particular* others—individuals qua individuals—if any sustained relations are to develop. In fact, the idea of increased scale in number and kind of interacting partners during industrialization is the societal counterpart of changing group composition. Interaction with multitudes of qualitatively dissimilar others induces secondary relationships between members of the system, tending first to disintegrate and then to reorient their actions and values.

These studies indicate that the *early* stage of an interaction must include a relationship between persons instead of roles, or persons in roles, because roles are only skeletal guidelines to behavior and must be fleshed out through the "informal" and "personal" attributes of those who play them if interaction is to continue. Blau suggests that interaction is particularly vulnerable to failure here, because its attraction for each member is accompanied by fear of rejection.[21] In sociological terms, the actor is faced with normative ambiguity in his expectations, since he cannot know whether his acts will be deemed appropriate by the strange other and he therefore is unsure about the response the other will emit. Further, when more than two actors are involved, competition for attraction develops which deflects solidary coalitions. We can suggest that this is a stage of pre-group individualism in which the orientation of one person to another is not completed by a substantive agreement that expectations are reciprocal or complementary. Neither consensus nor dissensus exists as a group property, and in fact the aggregate of persons does not comprise a group at all. Continuous turnover should— if the above correctly distinguishes between person and group as the difference between initial and succeeding stages of interaction—keep the interaction always concerned with the potential failure of impression management and never a *fait accompli*. In his defensive reactions while competing for attraction, therefore,

---

[20] Peter Blau, "A Theory of Social Integration," *American Journal of Sociology*, 65 (May 1960), pp. 545–556; Edward E. Jones and John W. Thibaut, "Interaction Goals as Bases of Inference in Interpersonal Perception," in Renato Tagiuri and Luigi Petrullo (eds.), *Person Perception and Interpersonal Behavior* (Stanford: Stanford University Press, 1958), pp. 151–178; George Homans, "Social Behavior as Exchange," *American Journal of Sociology*, 63 (May 1958), pp. 597–606.

[21] Blau, *op. cit.*, p. 549.

the individual would remain socially isolated in the presence of others similarly situated, and a following stage of group cohesion would not emerge. Since reciprocity, or exchange, does not develop, disintegration must occur to the extent that reciprocity is a necessary characteristic of order.[22]

There is a final consequence related to random completion of activity and interpersonal subversion. Much small group work has conceived member satisfaction as a product of instrumental accomplishment of the task. Other works depict the way dissatisfaction develops and blame is assigned when tasks are not completed.[23] Blame is, interestingly, often ascribed to *persons* rather than situations, because situations are too abstract to be punished as a symbolic affirmation of norms. From this, we can suggest that as activities are continually begun but never finished, dissatisfaction will be personified and thereby amplify interpersonal subversion. All members of the cohort would, in effect, occupy failure roles, and these roles would be unpredictable enough in location and intensity that a stratification toward leadership would be unlikely, reinforcing the disintegrating effects of random routines and subverted interpersonal relationships.

Summary

Radical change, the complete transformation of behavior, must stem from comparable transformations of value if this latter concept has any utility for social science. The failure of deviant rehabilitation on the one hand, and the Messianism of colonial societies on the other, informs us that moral suasion and monopoly of force in the context of different values do not result in radical change. To the degree these circumstances represent the conditions of ordinary socialization, one must look elsewhere for an explanation of radical change. Studies of anomie and studies of the proliferation of societal scale suggest that the polar changes in behavior which mark them are uninfluenced by old values, and we may infer that anomie or disintegration serves to erase that influence and desocialize those facing such conditions. The operant meaning of desocialization and disintegration, a meaning which can be used as a specification of radical change as well as a program for the inducement of such change, involves randomization of activity and subversion of interpersonal relationships, assuming that activity and interaction are the behavioral vehicles of values. As operations, they produce suspicious encounters between strangers and meaningless links between events, phenomena which, we suggest, vitiate the efficacy of the values of the group, the system, or the society.

It should be stressed that disintegration is not proposed as a sure resocializer, but rather only as a precedent for resocialization. It is meant only to provide a way of conceiving the fission of values which makes new fusions possible, not inevitable.

And it is probably unnecessary to cite the proximity of these ideas to what has been called brainwashing and all the ethical problems these matters entail.

---

[22] Alvin W. Gouldner, "The Norm of Reciprocity: A Preliminary Statement," *American Sociological Review*, 25 (April 1960), pp. 161–178.

[23] Fritz Heider, "Social Perception and Phenomenal Causality," *Psychological Review* (1944), pp. 358–374; Gustav Ichheisiser, "Misunderstandings in Human Relations: A Study in False Social Perception," *American Journal of Sociology*, 55 (September 1945), Part 2.

69   The Sociology of Deviance

● KAI T. ERIKSON

It is common practice in sociology to picture deviant behavior as an alien element in society. Deviance is considered a vagrant form of human activity which has somehow broken away from the more orderly currents of social life and needs to be controlled. And since it is generally understood that this sort of aberration could only occur if something were wrong within the organization of society itself, deviant behavior is described almost as if it were leakage from machinery in poor condition: it is an incidental result of disorder and anomie, a symptom of internal breakdown.

The purpose of the following remarks will be to review this conventional outlook and to argue that it provides too narrow a framework for many kinds of sociological research. Deviation, we will suggest, recalling Durkheim's classic statement on the subject, can often be understood as a normal product of stable institutions, an important resource which is guarded and preserved by forces found in all human organizations.[1]

I

According to current theory, deviant behavior is most likely to occur when the sanctions governing conduct in any given social setting seem to be contradictory [2] —as would be the case, for example, if the work rules posted by a company required one course of action from its employees and the longer-range policies of the company required quite another. Any situation marked by this kind of ambiguity, of course, can pose a serious dilemma for the individual: if he is careful to observe one set of demands imposed upon him, he runs the immediate risk of violating some other, and thus may find himself caught in a deviant stance no matter how earnestly he tries to avoid it. In this limited sense, deviance can be viewed as a "normal" social response to "abnormal" social circumstances, and we are therefore invited to assume that every act of deviation results from some imbalance within the social order—a condition of strain, anomie, or alienation.

This approach to the study of deviant behavior has generated a good deal of useful research, but it has at least one serious drawback for investigators who share an interest in what is known as "social problems." The "anomie" theory (if we may use that convenient label for a moment) is designated to account for all behavior which varies in some technical way from the norms of the community, whether or not that behavior is considered a problem by anyone else. For

SOURCE: Kai T. Erikson, in Edward C. McDonagh and Jon E. Simpson (eds.), *Social Problems: Persistent Challenges* (New York: Holt, Rinehart, and Winston, Inc., 1965), pp. 457–464.

A revised version of a paper, "Notes on the Sociology of Deviance," which first appeared in *Social Problems*, vol. 9, no. 4 (Spring 1962), pp. 307–314. Reprinted with the permission of the author and publisher.

[1] Emile Durkheim, *The Rules of Sociological Method* (translated by S. A. Solovay and J. H. Meuller), Glencoe: The Free Press, 1958.

[2] The best known statements of this general position, of course, are by Robert K. Merton and Talcott Parsons. Merton, *Social Theory and Social Structure* (revised edition), Glencoe: The Free Press, 1957; and Parsons, *The Social System*, Glencoe: The Free Press, 1951.

example, the bank teller who becomes a slave to routine and the armed bandit who relieves him of the day's receipts both register as deviants according to the logic of this scheme, since each is deviating in his own way from the ideal standards of the culture. Yet the most important difference between these men is one that the "anomie" theory cannot easily take into account: the bank teller, no matter how desperate his private needs, does not ordinarily create any concern in the rest of the community, while the bandit triggers the whole machinery of social control into vigorous action. In short, the "anomie" theory may help us appreciate the various ways in which people respond to conditions of strain, but it does not help us differentiate between those people who infringe the letter of the norm without attracting any notice and those who excite so much alarm that they earn a deviant reputation in society and are committed to special institutions like prisons and hospitals.

II

From a sociological standpoint, deviance can be defined as conduct which is generally thought to require the attention of social control agencies—that is, conduct about which "something should be done." Deviance is not a property *inherent in* certain forms of behavior; it is a property *conferred upon* these forms by the audiences which directly or indirectly witness them. The critical variable in the study of deviance, then, is the social audience rather than the individual actor, since it is the audience which eventually determines whether or not any episode of behavior or any class of episodes is labelled deviant.

This definition may seem a little indirect, but it has the advantage of bringing a neglected sociological issue into proper focus. When a community acts to control the behavior of one of its members, it is engaged in a very intricate process of selection. After all, even the worst miscreant in society conforms most of the time, if only in the sense that he uses the correct spoon at mealtime, takes good care of his mother, or in a thousand other ways respects the ordinary conventions of his group; and if the community elects to bring sanctions against him for the occasions when he does misbehave, it is responding to a few deviant details set within a vast array of entirely acceptable conduct. Thus it happens that a moment of deviation may become the measure of a person's position in society. He may be jailed or hospitalized, certified as a full-time deviant, despite the fact that only a fraction of his behavior was in any way unusual or dangerous. The community has picked a few scattered particles out of the stream of behavior and has decided that they reflect what kind of person he "really" is.

The screening device which sifts these telling details out of the person's over-all performance, then, is a very important instrument of social control. We know very little about the properties of this screen, but we do know that it takes many factors into account which are not directly related to the deviant act itself: it is sensitive to the suspect's social class, his past record as an offender, the amount of remorse he manages to convey, and many similar concerns which take hold in the shifting moods of the community. This may not be so obvious when the screen is dealing with extreme forms of deviance like serious crimes, but in the day by day filtering processes which take place throughout the community this feature is easily observable. Some men who drink too much are called alcoholics and others are not, some men who act oddly are committed to hospitals and others are not, some men who have no visible means of support are hauled into court and others are not—and the difference between those who earn a deviant label and those who go their way in peace depends almost entirely on the way in which the community sifts out and codes the many details of behavior to which it is witness. In this respect, the community screen may be a more relevant subject for sociological research than the actual behavior which is filtered through it.

Once the problem is phrased in this way we can ask: how does a community decide what forms of conduct should be singled out for this kind of attention? The conventional answer to this question, of course, is that society sets up the machinery of control in order to protect itself against the "harmful" effects of deviation, in much the same way that an organism mobilizes its resources to combat an invasion of germs. Yet this simple view of the matter has not always proven to be a very productive one. In the first place, as Durkheim and Mead pointed out some years ago, it is by no means clear that all acts considered deviant in a culture are in fact (or even in principle) harmful to group life.[3] In the second place, it is gradually becoming more evident to sociologists engaged in this area of research that deviant behavior can play an important part in keeping the social order intact.

This raises a number of interesting questions for sociology.

III

In recent years, sociological theory has become more and more concerned with the concept "social system"—an organization of society's component parts into a form which sustains internal equilibrium, resists change, and is boundary-maintaining. In its most abstract form, the "system" concept describes a highly complex network of relations, but the scheme is generally used by sociologists to draw attention to those forces in the social order which promote a high level of uniformity among human actors and a high degree of symmetry within human institutions. The main organizational drift of a system, then, is seen as centripetal: it acts to draw the behavior of actors toward those centers in social space where the core values of the group are figuratively located, bringing them within range of basic norms. Any conduct which is neither attracted toward this nerve center by the rewards of conformity nor compelled toward it by other social pressures is considered "out of control," which is to say, deviant.

This basic model has provided the theme for most contemporary thinking about deviation, and as a result little attention has been given to the notion that systems operate to maintain boundaries. To say that a system maintains boundaries is to say that it controls the fluctuation of its constituent parts so that the whole retains a defined range of activity, a unique pattern of constancy and stability, within the larger environment.[4] Because the range of human behavior is potentially so wide, social groups maintain boundaries in the sense that they try to limit the flow of behavior within their domain so that it circulates within a defined cultural territory. Boundaries, then, are an important point of reference for persons participating in any system. A people may define its boundaries by referring to a geographical location, a set of honored traditions, a particular religious or political viewpoint, an occupational specialty, a common language, or just some local way

[3] Emile Durkheim, *The Division of Labor in Society* (translated by George Simpson), Glencoe: The Free Press, 1952; and George Herbert Mead, "The Psychology of Punitive Justice," *American Journal of Sociology*, 23 (1918), pp. 577–602.
[4] Cf. Talcott Parsons, *The Social System, op. cit.*

of doing things; but in any case, members of the group have some idea about the contours of the niche they occupy in social space. They know where the group begins and ends as a special entity; they know what kinds of experience "belong" within these precincts and what kinds do not.

For all its apparent abstractness, a social system is organized around the movements of persons joined together in regular social relations. The only material found in a system for marking boundaries, then, is the behavior of its participants; and the kinds of behavior which best perform this function are often deviant, since they represent the most extreme variety of conduct to be found within the experience of the group. In this sense, transactions taking place between deviant persons on the one side and agencies of control on the other are boundary-maintaining mechanisms. They mark the outside limits of the area within which the norm has jurisdiction, and in this way assert how much diversity and variability can be contained within the system before it begins to lose its distinct structure, its cultural integrity.

A social norm is rarely expressed as a firm rule or official code. It is an abstract synthesis of the many separate times a community has stated its sentiments on a given kind of issue. Thus the norm has a history much like that of an article of common law: it is an accumulation of decisions made by the community over a long period of time which gradually gathers enough moral eminence to serve as a precedent for future decisions. And like an article of common law, the norm retains its validity only if it is regularly used as a basis for judgment. Each time the group censures some act of deviation, then, it sharpens the authority of the violated norm and declares again where the boundaries of the group are located.

It is important to notice that these transactions between deviant persons and agents of control have always attracted a good deal of attention in this and other cultures. In our own past, both the trial and punishment of deviant offenders took place in the public market and gave the crowd a chance to participate in a direct, active way. Today we no longer parade deviants in the town square or expose them to the carnival atmosphere of Tyburn, but it is interesting to note that the "reform" which brought about this change in penal policy coincided almost precisely with the development of newspapers as media of public information. Perhaps this is no more than an accident of history, but it is nevertheless true that newspapers (and now radio and television) offer its readers the same kind of entertainment once supplied by public hangings or the use of stocks and pillories. An enormous amount of modern "news" is devoted to reports about deviant behavior and its punishment: indeed the largest-circulation newspaper in the United States prints very little else. Yet how do we explain what makes these items "newsworthy" or why they command the great attention they do? Perhaps they satisfy a number of psychological perversities among the mass audience, as commentators sometimes point out, but at the same time they constitute our main source of information about the normative contours of society. In a figurative sense, at least, morality and immorality meet at the public scaffold, and it is during this meeting that the community declares where the line between them should be drawn.

People who gather together into communities need to be able to describe and anticipate those areas of experience which lie outside the immediate compass of the group—the unseen dangers which in any culture and in any age seem to threaten its security. Traditional folklore depicting demons, devils, witches, and evil spirits may be one way to give form to these otherwise formless dangers, but the visible deviant is another kind of reminder. As a trespasser against the group norms, he represents those forces which lie outside the group's boundaries: he informs us, as it were, what evil looks like, what shapes the devil can assume. And in doing so, he shows us the difference between the inside of the group and the outside. It may well be that without this ongoing drama at the outer edges of group space, the community would have no inner sense of identity and cohesion, no sense of the contrasts which set it off as a special place in the larger world.

Thus deviance cannot be simply dismissed as behavior which *disrupts* stability in society, but may itself be, in controlled quantities, an important condition for *preserving* stability.

IV

This raises a delicate theoretical issue. If we grant that deviant forms of behavior are often beneficial to society in general, can we then assume that societies are organized in such a way as to promote this resource? Can we assume, in other words, that forces operate within the social order to recruit deviant actors and commit them to deviant forms of activity? Sociology has not yet developed a conceptual language in which this sort of question can be discussed with any ease, but one observation can be made which gives the question an interesting perspective—namely, that deviant activities often seem to derive support from the very agencies designed to suppress them. Indeed, the institutions devised by society for discouraging deviant behavior are often so poorly equipped for that task that we might well ask why this is considered their "real" function at all.

It is by now a thoroughly familiar argument that many of the institutions built to inhibit deviation actually operate in such a way as to perpetuate it. For one thing, prisons, hospitals, and similar agencies of control provide aid and shelter to large numbers of deviant persons, sometimes enhancing their survival chances in the world as a whole. But beyond this, such institutions gather marginal people into tightly segregated groups, give them an opportunity to teach one another the skills and attitudes of a deviant career, and often provoke them into employing these skills by reinforcing their sense of alienation from the rest of society.[5] It should be pointed out, furthermore, that this process is found not only in the institutions which actually confine the deviant, but throughout the general community as well.

The community's decision to bring deviant sanctions against an individual is not a simple act of censure. It is a sharp rite of transition, at once moving him out of his normal position in society and transferring him into a distant deviant role.[6] The ceremonies which accomplish this change of status, ordinarily, have three related phases. They provide a formal *confrontation* between the deviant suspect and representatives of his community (as in the criminal trial or

---

[5] For a good description of this process in the modern prison, see Gresham Sykes, *The Society of Captives*, Princeton: Princeton University Press, 1958. For views of two different types of mental hospital settings, see Erving Goffman, "The Characteristics of Total Institutions," *Symposium on Preventive and Social Psychiatry*, Washington, D.C.: Walter Reed Army Institute of Research, 1957; and Kai T. Erikson, "Patient Role and Social Uncertainty: A Dilemma of the Mentally Ill," *Psychiatry*, 20 (1957), pp. 263–74.

[6] Parsons, *op. cit.*, has provided the classical description of how this role transfer works in the case of medical patients.

psychiatric case conference); they announce some *judgment* about the nature of his deviancy (a verdict or diagnosis, for example); and they perform an act of social *placement*, assigning him to a special role (like that of prisoner or patient) which redefines his position in society. These ceremonies tend to be events of wide public interest and usually take place in a dramatic, ritualized setting.[7] Perhaps the most obvious example of a commitment ceremony is the criminal trial, with its elaborate formality and ritual trappings, but more modest equivalents can be found everywhere that procedures are set up to judge whether someone is deviant or not.

Now an important feature of these ceremonies in our own culture is that they are almost irreversible. Most provisional roles conferred by society—like those of the student or conscripted soldier, for example—include some kind of terminal ceremony to mark the individual's movement back out of the role once its temporary advantages have been exhausted. But the roles allotted to the deviant seldom make allowance for this type of passage. He is ushered into the deviant position by a decisive and often dramatic ceremony, yet is retired from it with hardly a word of public notice. And as a result, the deviant often returns home with no proper license to resume a normal life in the community. Nothing has happened to cancel out the stigmas imposed upon him by earlier commitment ceremonies; from a formal point of view, the original verdict or diagnosis is still in effect. It should not be surprising, then, that the members of the community seem reluctant to accept the returning deviant on an entirely equal footing. In a very real sense, they do not know who he is.

A circularity is thus set into motion which has all the earmarks of a "self-fulfilling prophecy," to use Merton's fine phrase. On the one hand, it seems obvious that the community's reluctance to accept the deviant back helps reduce whatever chance he might otherwise have for a successful readjustment. Yet on the other hand, everyday experience seems to show that this reluctance is entirely reasonable, for it is a well-known and highly publicized fact that large numbers of ex-convicts return to criminal activity and that many discharged mental patients suffer later breakdowns. The common assumption that deviants cannot often be cured or reformed, then, may be based on a faulty premise, but this assumption is stated so frequently and with such conviction that it often creates the facts which later "prove" it to be correct. If the returning deviant has to face the community's apprehensions often enough, it is understandable that he too may begin to wonder whether he has graduated from the deviant role—and respond to the uncertainty by resuming deviant activity. In some respects, this may be the only way for the individual and his community to agree what kind of person he really is, for it often happens that the community is only able to perceive his "true colors" when he lapses momentarily into some form of deviant performance.

Moreover, this prophecy is found in the official policies of even the most advanced agencies of control. Police departments could not operate with any real effectiveness if they did not regard ex-convicts as an almost permanent population of offenders, a pool from which to draw suspects; and psychiatric hospitals could not do a responsible job in the community if they were not alert to the fact that ex-patients are highly susceptible to relapse. Thus the prophecy gains currency at many levels within the social order, not only in the poorly informed

---

[7] Cf. Harold Garfinkel, "Successful Degradation Ceremonies," *American Journal of Sociology*, 61 (1956), pp. 420–24.

opinions of the community at large, but in the best-informed theories of most control agencies as well.

In one form or another, this problem has been known in Western culture for many hundreds of years, and the single fact that this is so becomes a highly significant one for sociology. If the culture has supported a steady flow of deviant behavior throughout long periods of historical evolution, then the rules which apply to any form of functionalist thinking would suggest that strong forces must be at work to keep this flow intact—and this because it contributes in some important way to the survival of the system as a whole. This may not be reason enough to assert that deviant behavior is "functional," in any of the many senses of that term, but it should make us wary of the assumption that human communities are organized in such a way as to prevent deviance from occurring.[8]

This in turn might suggest that our present models of society, with their emphasis on the harmony and equilibrium of social life, do a one-sided job of representing the situation. Perhaps two different and often competing currents are found in any well-functioning system: those forces which promote a high overall degree of conformity among its members, and those forces which encourage some degree of diversity so that actors can be deployed throughout social space to patrol the system's boundaries. These different gravitational pulls in the social system set up a constant tension of opposites, outlining the area within which human life, with all its contradiction and variety, takes place. Perhaps this is what Aldous Huxley had in mind when he wrote: [9]

> Now tidiness is undeniably good—but a good of which it is easily possible to have too much and at too high a price . . . The good life can only be lived in a society in which tidiness is preached and practised, but not too fanatically, and where efficiency is always haloed, as it were, by a tolerated margin of mess.

V

These brief remarks are no more than a prelude to further thinking and research, and in the remaining paragraphs we will try to indicate some of the directions this line of reasoning might take.

In the first place, the paper has indirectly addressed itself to one of the oldest problems in sociology. It is all very well for an investigator to conclude that something called a "system" has certain "requirements" in respect to its participants, but the major problem for research is to ask how these needs are imposed upon the people who eventually satisfy them. Ordinarily, the fact that deviant behavior is not evenly distributed throughout the social structure is explained by declaring that something called "anomie" or "disorganization" prevails at certain sensitive points. Deviance leaks out through defects in the social structure; it occurs when the system *fails* to impose its needs on human actors. But if we consider the possibility that even the best-organized collectivity needs to produce occasional episodes of deviation for the sake of its own stability, we are engaged in quite another order of inquiry. Perhaps the coherence of some social groupings

---

[8] Albert K. Cohen, for example, speaking for sociologists in general, seems to take the question for granted: "It would seem that the control of deviant behavior is, by definition, a culture goal." In "The Study of Social Disorganization and Deviant Behavior," Merton *et al.*, editors, *Sociology Today*. New York: Basic Books, 1959, p. 465.

[9] Aldous Huxley, *Prisons: The "Carceri" Etchings by G. B. Piranesi*. London: The Trianon Press, 1949.

is maintained only when a few juvenile offenders are enlisted to balance the conformity of an adult majority; perhaps communities can only retain a sense of their own territorial identity if they keep up an ongoing dialogue with deviants who mark and publicize the outer limits of group space; perhaps some families can remain intact only if one of its members becomes a visible deviant to serve as a focus for the rest.[10] If these suppositions prove useful, we should try to learn how a social system appoints certain of its members to deviant roles and how it encourages them to spend a period of service testing the group's boundaries. This is not to suggest that a system necessarily creates the crises which impel people into deviant activity but that it deploys these resources in a patterned, organized way.

In the second place, it is evident that cultures vary in the way they regulate deviant traffic moving back and forth from their outer boundaries. We might begin with the observation, for example, that many features of the traffic pattern in our own culture seem to have a marked Puritan cast: a defined portion of the population, largely drawn from young adult groups and from the lower economic classes, is stabilized in deviant roles and often expected to remain there indefinitely. The logic which prevails in many of our formal agencies of control and in the public attitudes which sustain them sometimes seem to echo earlier Puritan theories about predestination, reprobation, and the nature of sin. Be this as it may, different traffic patterns are found in other parts of the world which offer an interesting contrast. There are societies in which deviance is considered a natural mode of behavior for the young, a pursuit which they are expected to abandon once they move through defined ceremonies into adulthood. There are societies which give license to large groups of people to engage in deviant behavior during certain seasons or on certain days of the year. And there are societies which form special groups whose stated business it is to act in ways contrary to the normal expectations of the culture. Each of these patterns regulates deviant traffic differently, yet each of them provides some institutional means for a person to give up a deviant career without any kind of permanent stigma. In either of these cases, the person's momentary commitment to deviant styles of behavior is easily reversed—when the group promotes him to manhood, declares a period of festival to be over, or permits him to give up the insignia which marked his membership in a band of "contraries." Perhaps the most interesting problem here from the point of view of pure research is to see whether these various patterns are functionally equivalent in any meaningful way. Perhaps the most interesting problem for those of us who lean over into the applied areas of the field, however, is to ask whether we have anything to learn from those cultures which permit re-entry into normal social life for persons who have spent a period of time in the deviant ranks and no longer have any special need to remain there.

---

[10] Cf. Robert A. Dentler and Kai T. Erikson, "The Functions of Deviance in Groups," *Social Problems*, 7 (1959), pp. 98–107.

APPENDIX

Hans J. Eysenck's article supports the view that therapies based on traditional approaches to "behavioral extremism" are virtually ineffective. It is proposed, however, that something akin to operant-conditioning or behavior modification be substituted. At the present time, we cannot endorse this approach. Rather than offer a full-scale critique, or delete sections incommensurate with our view, we have included the entire article, in the form of an appendix, and urge the reader to mull it over. For additional summary material on "behavior modification," the reader may consult:

Leonard P. Ullman and Leonard Krazner. *A Psychological Approach to Abnormal Behavior* (Englewood Cliffs, N.J.: Prentice Hall, Inc., 1969).

Case Studies in Behavior Modification, edited by Ullman and Krazner (New York: Holt, Rinehart and Winston, 1966).

The Effects of Psychotherapy

● HANS J. EYSENCK

In theory, the study of the effects of psychotherapy should be similar in methodology and experimental treatment to the study of the effects of any other therapeutic agent about which definite theories are held. In actual practice this is not so. An emotional feeling of considerable intensity has grown up in this field which makes many people regard the very questioning of its effectiveness as an attack on psychotherapy; as Teuber and Powers (1953) point out; "To some of the counselors, the whole control group idea . . . seemed slightly blasphemous, as if we were attempting a statistical test of the efficacy of prayer . . ." When the writer (1952) published a short paper summarizing the available evidence and concluding that there was little support for those who believed in the efficacy of psychotherapy, reactions ranged all the way from Sanford's (1953) opinion that "the only wise course with respect to such a challenge is to ignore it," to Meehl (1955) who said: "I cannot agree with those who consider this a foolish question or who feel little need to meet such challenges." The considerable argument aroused by this paper (Luborsky, 1954; De Charms *et al.*, 1954; Rosenzweig, 1954; Eysenck, 1954, 1955) seems to have arisen from the conviction, well put by Shoben (1956), that "the conclusive evidence of therapeutic effectiveness must come not from argument, but from relevant and rigorous research." This chapter is an attempt to review the literature, much of which has appeared since the writer's previous review was published, in order to discover whether any new light has been thrown on this thorny problem.

To judge by their writings, some advocates of psychotherapy appear to take an attitude similar to that adopted by Galen, the father of modern medicine, in his advocacy of the wondrous powers of Samian clay: "All who drink this remedy recover in a short time, except those whom it does not help, who all die and have no relief from any other medicine. Therefore it is obvious that it fails only in incurable cases." There are three main differences between Galen's hypothesis and that maintained by modern psychotherapists. In the first place, we have the question of *definition*. There is no disagreement about the nature of Samian clay, but as regards psychotherapy, *quot homines, tot sententiae*. In the second place there is the question of the *criterion of cure*. In Galen's case this was survival, which is easy to observe; in the case of psychotherapy, the criterion itself is in doubt, and its measurement fraught with difficulties. In the third place there is the *time factor*. Those who partook of Galen's remedy "recovered in a short time," so that the effects were easily observed; psychotherapy, particularly that of the psychoanalytic type, may go on for as many as twenty years or more, so that considerable difficulties arise in allocating responsibility for any recovery. We will now take up these points in detail, before turning to an examination of the evidence.

SOURCE: Hans J. Eysenck, Chapter 18 of *Handbook of Abnormal Psychology*, edited by Hans J. Eysenck, © Pitman Medical Publishing Co. 1960, Basic Books, Inc., Publishers, New York, 1961, pp. 697–725.

Definition of Psychotherapy

Raimy (1950) has characterized the confusion existing with respect to the nature of psychotherapy by defining it as, "an unidentified technique applied to unspecified problems with unpredictable outcomes. For this technique we recommend rigorous training." When we turn to definitions offered in a more serious vein, we find considerable divergences. Perhaps the most inclusive definition is one given by Levine (1948) to whom "psychotherapy means therapy by psychological means . . . it means treatment applied directly to the 'mind,' by which we mean not a separate entity, but the functioning of the person as a human being. Psychotherapy includes the direct treatment of one person, as a person, by another. It includes also the indirect treatment of one person by another, through the intermediary of other persons or situations . . . in general, psychotherapy can be defined as the provision by the physician of new life experiences which can influence a patient in the direction of health." Similar but rather briefer is Rosanoff's (1957) definition: "Psychotherapy . . . consists in the employment of mental factors in the treatment of disease," and that of Jaspers (1918): "Psychotherapie heissen alle die Behandlungs-methoden, die auf die Seele oder den Körper mit Mitteln wirken, die über die Seele führen." (As evidence of the inclusiveness of these definitions we may quote the fact that Jasper expressly mentions "gymnastics" as one of the methods of psychotherapy!) English and Finch (1954) may also be quoted here: "Psychotherapy may be defined as the art and science of treating mental and emotional disorders and diseases through changing ideas and emotions to bring about a more favourable psychic equilibrium . . . Almost any method utilised to alleviate or remove the results of emotional conflict and improve psychic adjustment may be termed psychotherapy."

Rather more restrictive and less all-inclusive are Curran and Partridge (1955), who say that: "Psychotherapy aims at relieving symptoms of psychic origin by adjusting the attitudes that have led to their development . . . The treatment proceeds by stages which are often referred to as *explanation, suggestion, persuasion* and *reeducation*." Shoben (1953) is a little more specific still. "Psychotherapy is a certain kind of social relationship between two persons who hold periodic conversations in pursuit of certain goals: namely, the lessening of emotional discomfort and the alteration of various other aspects of client behaviour . . . Therapy proceeds by virtue of communication and the therapist-patient relationship towards the goal of alleviating symptoms and increasing the patient's affective comfort and social utility."

Most restrictive of all are certain psychoanalysts and other members of specific schools who would restrict the use of the term to procedures practised by members of their particular school. Psychotherapy would then be defined in terms of a particular theoretical system giving rise to specific methods of procedure, such as the employment of transference and counter-transference, catharsis, ego-strengthening, and so forth. Hathaway (1951) has well contrasted this narrow conception with the very broad ones quoted at the beginning of this section—

> With the intention of arriving at a working definition of the term psychotherapy, at least two extremes in connotation may help in orientation. The first extreme is illustrated by those few psychoanalysts who affirm that there is only one type of psychotherapy, namely, psychoanalytic therapy, and that any other approach is a

covering up or ameliorative procedure not properly so considered. Although the most brash proponents of such an extreme concept of psychotherapy are probably psychoanalytic in persuasion, there are here and there other therapists who hold analogously restricted views. At the other extreme, psychotherapy becomes almost any predominantly psychological procedure, personal or environmental, that is assumed to be contributory to mental hygiene or personal adjustment. With this broader definition, better living conditions, better food, and the like, all become psychotherapeutic procedures in so far as they have psychological implications. One might then cite a music program in a clinic or hospital as an example of psychotherapy and the staff musician as a psychotherapist. Neither of these extreme positions is here accepted as particularly useful . . . The former connotation restricts progress by encouraging doctrinal and isolated positions antipathetic to new ideas. It inhibits active experimentation by persons who might not accept the tenets of the particular procedures defined as psychotherapy. The latter is so broad as to constitute almost a statement of the general principle that simply healthy living is therapeutic.

A decision on a definition in view of these wide divergencies must obviously be arbitrary. We shall here adopt the middle-of-the-road position not dissimilar to that defined by Winder (1957), according to which a treatment is labelled "psychotherapy" when the following conditions are fulfilled—

1. There is an interpersonal relationship of a prolonged kind between two or more people.
2. One of the participants has had special experience and/or has received special training in the handling of human relationships.
3. One or more of the participants have entered the relationship because of a felt dissatisfaction with their emotional and/or interpersonal adjustment.
4. The methods used are of a psychological nature, i.e., involve such mechanisms as explanation, suggestion, persuasion, and so forth.
5. The procedure of the therapist is based upon some formal theory regarding mental disorder in general, and the specific disorder of the patient in particular.
6. The aim of the process is the amelioration of the difficulties which cause the patient to seek the help of the therapist.

Having thus defined psychotherapy in general, we may add that it may be useful in many circumstances to specify different types of psychotherapy in terms of the particular theory adopted by the therapist. This may be done most simply by adopting a system of subscripts so that psychotherapy$_{PA}$ denotes psychotherapy carried out according to the dictates of the psychoanalytic method. Psychotherapy$_{CR}$ would denote non-directive psychotherapy carried out according to the theories of Carl Rogers. Psychotherapy$_E$ would denote eclectic psychotherapy based on the rather less formalized theories which currently pass as "orthodox" in psychiatric circles. Further types of psychotherapy can be distinguished, but there is little point in attempting any complete listing here. The device of indicating types of psychotherapy by the initials of the originators will retain its usefulness as long as there are sufficient letters of the alphabet to go round.

This question of definition does not, of course, settle the very difficult problem of whether the different methods we have distinguished by subscripts do *in fact* differ from each other in practice, nor does a definition tell us what does actually happen during treatment. Many attempts have been made to answer these questions, but the evidence is still so fragmentary, anecdotal and uncoordinated that a review of it at this point would serve little useful purpose (Ellis, 1955). It is impossible therefore to say whether the different types of therapy are in fact differentiated from each other in terms of the actual procedures adopted, or whether individual differences between the therapists of the same persuasion are as great or greater than those between therapists of different persuasions. (For studies of therapeutic procedures, cf. Matarazzo, 1956; Saslow, *et al.*, 1955; Moustakas, *et al.*, 1955; Sommer, *et al.*, 1955; Danskin, 1955; Bordin, 1955; Eldred, *et al.*, 1954; Grossman, 1952; Rogers, 1951, 1942; Harway, *et al.*, 1955; Rausch, *et al.*, 1956.)

Measurement of Outcome

When the method of psychotherapy has been applied to a group of patients, we obviously must have some measure to determine the initial status as well as the final status of the group. Many discussions of this problem have been reported by Zubin (1953), Knight (1941), Thorne (1952), Greenhill (1955), Watson, *et al.* (1951, 1952), and Miles, *et al.* (1951). In addition there are discussions in the books by Rogers and Dymond (1953) and by Mowrer (1953). We may summarize rather briefly in the following paragraphs the possible measures of outcome which may be used.

INTROSPECTIVE REPORTS

It is the patient who seeks our aid, and, obviously, his own judgment of any changes that have taken place is important. This may be obtained by interview, in the form of a freely written essay, by answers to a questionnaire, by means of Q-sorts, through a set of attitude endorsements, or in many similar ways (Lipkin, 1954; Murray, *et al.*, 1954; Dollard, *et al.*, 1953; Gallagher, 1953). It is obvious that the more objective the method used, the more trustworthy will the results be. Thus a questionnaire would be preferable to an essay. It need hardly be emphasized that, in making use of formal instruments, technical competence regarding their construction and evaluation is required. This point is mentioned only because so many experimenters have failed to take into account obvious technical difficulties arising from the method of research adopted. Thus many workers have made considerable use of Q-sorts without heeding the warning given by Cronbach and Gleser (1954) in their review of this method: "It is imperative to discourage students of personality and social psychology from copying Stephenson's designs as he presents them . . . We fear that Stephenson's book (1953) may misdirect much research effort."

RATING

Many of the difficulties of which the patient complains are a kind which can be observed by outsiders. Irritability, social clumsiness, hyperemotionality and other behaviour patterns can be rated by outside observers, and such observations should always supplement the patient's own report. Ratings can be formal or informal, and may be made by psychiatrists, social workers or the patient's family, friends or workmates. Again, it need hardly be said that these ratings are more

valuable the more systematic they are, and the more they pay attention to the
rules laid down by psychologists on the basis of the very large body of experimental work in this field (Eysenck, 1953). If possible, the reliability of such
ratings should be established, and it should not need to be emphasized that those
judges who are emotionally concerned with the particular direction of change
should never be the only ones to give a rating on a particular patient. (This
refers more particularly to the psychiatrist in charge of the patient, who must
always be suspected of favouring the positive outcome compared with a negative
one.) Sociometric measures are of value and may be listed here, as they appear
to be essentially similar in their nature to ratings (Neuburger and Schauer, 1953;
Rosenburg, 1954; Parloff, *et al.*, 1954). Rating methods are discussed in Chapter
I in some detail.

PERSONALITY TESTS

This is not the place to discuss the wide variety of personality tests which may
be administered to the patient in order to test specific hypotheses regarding a
change that has taken place; many such tests are described in other chapters of
this book. It may be necessary, however, to insist that it is useless to administer
a test whose reliability and validity is either low or unknown. The writer has
reviewed elsewhere the literature bearing on the reliability and validity of the
so-called "projective techniques" (Eysenck, 1958), and the conclusion arrived at
in that review was that these had failed to establish their value in any of the fields
in which they had been used. Thus projective techniques should not be used as
evidence to establish the outcome of psychotherapy, because any changes which
might occur in the test would not be capable of interpretation. Few personality
tests are characterized by a high degree of reliability and validity, but tests such
as those of level of aspiration, suggestibility, and conditionability, do enable the
research worker to test specific hypotheses and arrive at interpretations of his
results which have a solid experimental foundation.

PHYSIOLOGICAL MEASURES

In view of the close relationship between the autonomic system and emotion,
and in view also of the predominantly emotional character of so many neurotic
complaints, it seems desirable that the possibility of psychological changes should
not be disregarded. Much of the relevant work has been reviewed in another
chapter of this book and little will, therefore, be said here about it (Shagass and
Malmo, 1954; Thetford, 1948; Di Mascio, *et al.*, 1955; Boyd, *et al.*, 1954; Bixenstine,
1955; Coleman, *et al.*, 1956).

EXPERIMENTAL INVESTIGATIONS

The most useful type of study, in our view, is that which is specifically designed
to test a clear-cut hypothesis, and it will often be found that, in order to test such
a hypothesis, a special experimental set-up will have to be elaborated. Thus we
may hypothesize that psychotherapy of a certain type applied to a certain group
will lead to an increase in frustration tolerance. In order to test this hypothesis
it will be necessary to define frustration tolerance experimentally, and to design
the experiment in such a way that psychotherapy is included as the independent

variable. Little has been found in the literature to suggest that this method of research, in our view much the most preferable, has been used much by research workers.

SOCIAL ACTION EFFECTS

It is sometimes possible to assess the effects of treatment by reference to certain actions taken by society in relation to the patients who are being treated. Thus, for instance, certification presents us with an example of social action which can be given a numerical value and treated statistically. In the same way, we may consider the effect of psychotherapy on psychopathic behaviour, and a record of court appearances may be of relevance in assessing the value of the therapy. Here again, considerable experience and knowledge are required to evaluate the many factors liable to mislead the investigator and invalidate his conclusions; it must be assumed that the investigator is competent in such lines of research.

Each of the six methods outlined above has its own advantages and disadvantages. It may be a counsel of perfection to suggest that in any worthwhile investigation more than one method should be used and that, preferably, all six methods should be included. The necessity for this, is highlighted in an experiment by Kogan, et al., (1953), who used three reliable measures of the effectiveness of therapy (client evaluation, case reader movement rating, and distress relief quotient shifts), only to find negligible correlations between them. As Meehl (1955) points out "such a fact should make us cautious about single 'criteria' used in the evaluation of therapeutic outcome."

One other point may require to be stressed. The effects of psychotherapy, as of most other experimental manipulations of human beings, are presumably multidimensional, and consequently research should be concerned with shifts in more than one direction. The usual habit of simply rating people as "improved" or "not improved" entirely neglects to pay attention to the important and obvious fact that "improvement" is not a unidimensional concept. Under treatment a man may lose his depression, but start beating his wife; is this to be rated as "improved" or "not improved"? It is clear that research must become much more analytic before we can find out very much about the effects of psychotherapy. Further, this belief implies that progress will become much more rapid when hypotheses regarding change become more specific. It is almost impossible to prove or disprove vague and general talk about "improvement"; specific statements are much more valuable scientifically as well as easier to investigate experimentally.

GENERAL METHODOLOGY

We have now defined what we mean by psychotherapy, and have indicated the kind of measures which might be used with advantage to study the effects of therapy. What kind of design is appropriate for studies of this kind? Hunt (1952) and Watson (1952) have considered this problem, as have Greenhill (1955), Thorne (1952), Zubin (1953) and many others. A paper by Campbell (1957) which discusses the problem from a more general point of view is perhaps the most useful. A set of minimum requirements is stated by Meehl (1955) as follows: "The minimum standard for an adequate outcome study obviously includes (a) a control group, (b) pre- and post-therapy evaluation procedures which are either 'objective' or, if judgmental, are uncontaminated, (c) follow-up of both groups, preferably repeated so that exacerbation and remission rates can be estimated and the curves extrapolated." Meehl goes on to say: "I am saddened to report that perusal of over two hundred journal articles and a dozen books reveals one paper approximating these desiderata (relaxing requirements by forgetting follow-up but insisting upon controls does not change this figure)."

It would not be so necessary to insist on the need for a control group when studying the effects of psychotherapy, were it not for the fact that practically all the studies in the field have neglected to provide such a group. The one or two exceptions to this will be discussed below, but by and large it is depressing to report that this absolutely essential minimum requirement has not been met by ninety-nine out of a hundred studies in this field. It would probably be an idle exercise of ingenuity to try and describe the various possible ways in which control groups could and ought to be used; it is doubtful in any case whether much could be added to the very complete discussion given by Campbell (1957). It may be more useful to consider one or two of the reasons why control groups are so noticeably lacking in this field.

The reason most frequently given is that the effects of psychotherapy are so clear-cut and obvious that no reasonable person could doubt its effectiveness. In answer we may perhaps quote Meehl (1955)—

> The history of the healing arts furnishes ample grounds for skepticism as to our nonsystematic "clinical" observations. Most of my older relatives had all their teeth extracted because it was "known" in the 1920s that the clearing up of occult focal infections improved arthritis and other disorders. No doubt the physicians who treated our ancestors by venesection had "observed" many "cures" in longitudinal study of their patients. Like all therapists, I personally experience an utter inability not to believe I effect results in individual cases; but as a psychologist I know it is foolish to take this conviction at face value. In order to bring about the needed research, it will probably be necessary for therapists and administrators to get really clear on this point. Our daily therapeutic experiences, which (on good days!) make it hard for us to take Eysenck seriously, can be explained within a crude statistical model of the patient-therapist population that assigns very little specific "power" to therapeutic intervention. If the majority of neurotics are in "unstable equilibrium" and hence tend to improve under moderately favorable régimes, those who are in therapy while improving will be talking about their current actions and feelings in the sessions. Client and therapist will naturally attribute changes to the therapy. Furthermore, neurosis often shows cyclical fluctuations, and upswing terminators will be perceived as "successful," since therapists do not automatically find out when cases relapse or enter therapy with someone else.

Another argument is the ethical one, to the effect that we are not entitled to withhold therapy from patients in need who might benefit from it. There are several answers to this point. In the first place, the benefits are merely putative, and consequently nothing is being withheld which is known to be of assistance to the patient. The argument assumes that we have already proved what is in fact the point at issue. In the second place it is a universal practice in medicine, whenever a new method of treatment is put forward, that this new method must receive clinical trials, *including a control group not treated by means of the new method.* If this is ethically admissible in the whole of medicine, even when the most serious disorders are involved and where the *a priori* probability of effectiveness in favour of the new cure may be rather high, then it is difficult to see why a different set of ethical ideals should apply in psychiatry where disorders are rather less serious and where, as we shall see, the evidence regarding the efficacy of the treatment proposed tends on the whole to be singularly negative. In the third place it is quite untrue that psychotherapy would have to be withdrawn from certain people in order to provide a control group. Of all those who are said to be able to benefit from psychotherapy only a very small number have in fact received it. In the United States, at least, there is a high correlation between the income of the patient and the choice of therapy; middle-class patients by and large get psychotherapy, working-class patients, physical treatment. It would be very easy indeed to get together large groups of patients who would not in the normal way obtain psychotherapy, and to form an experimental and control group from these patients. If this were done the outcome would not be that psychotherapy was withheld from people who might otherwise benefit from it, because of the experiment; rather, the experiment would be instrumental in bringing psychotherapy to people who would not otherwise have received it. The Cambridge-Somerville Youth Study reviewed below illustrates what can be done along these lines.

A fourth argument which is sometimes put forward relates to the great difficulty in diagnosing psychiatric patients, and the difficulty in assessing the severity of illness. This, it is said, makes impossible the appropriate matching of the experimental and control groups, and thus invalidates the experimental design. This argument, which tends to be put forward by the more sophisticated psychotherapists, is clearly erroneous in that it implies that matching is an essential part of the control-group technique. It certainly is a useful adjunct, where it can be carried out with reasonable reliability, but the essential nature of the control group method implies nothing more than the random allocation of subjects to the experimental and the control groups. When this is done the appropriate statistical formulae for the assessing of sampling errors will enable us to judge the significance of any differences due to the action of the experimental variable.

One further point should be mentioned. It is sometimes believed that if an experimental and a control group are selected on an appropriate system of random allocation or matched allocation, and if the experimental group is provided with psychotherapy while the control group is not, then any superiority of the experimental group over the control group must be due to the effects of psychotherapy. Such a result, it might then be claimed, would establish the validity of the theoretical system lying at the basis of the psychotherapeutic procedure. Nothing could be further from the truth. The experimental and the control group are differentiated in terms of a large number of variables, any one of which might be responsible for any differences that might be observed. Among the procedures to which the usual experimental group would be subjected, but which might not be experienced by the control group, are the following—

1. physical examination and the medical treatment of all sorts of minor illnesses, etc;
2. long period of rest in hospital, clinic or other institution;
3. manipulation of the environment on the part of the doctor, including attempts to change the attitudes of family, employers, etc. (Klumpner, 1955);
4. more regular and better balanced food in hospital compared with previous existence (cf. the paper by Watson and Camney, 1954, on the effects of nutritional replacement on neurotic disorders).

This list could be extended almost *ad infinitum,* and will be seen that either more than one control group would be required in order to control for these different hypothetical causal agents, or the specification of the hypothetical causal agent in psychotherapy would have to be much more precise than it usually is, so that a single group could be provided which would take care of all the possible causal agents except the one specified by the hypothesis. Thus if we were to test the hypothesis that interpretation of Oedipus material is a necessary part of psychotherapy, then our control group would have to receive an equal number of therapeutic sessions with an experienced therapist who refrained from giving any interpretation of Oedipus material, but in all other ways duplicated the treatment design of the experimental group. Thus, even if the very rough-and-ready studies summarized below had indicated some degree of effectiveness of psychotherapy, the interpretation of this finding would have been completely open. What we would have gained would have been an indication that research into the distinguishing features of psychotherapeutic treatment might be worthwhile and might, if accompanied by the formulation of more specific hypotheses, lead to greater understanding. On no account could such a result have been interpreted as unequivocal support for the beliefs of psychotherapists.

We have now discussed in sufficient detail the general logic of work in this field; we must next turn to the actual investigations which have been reported. This will be done in three sections, beginning with those investigations which have used a control group, going on to those investigations on adult patients which failed to use a control group, and terminating with investigations of children in which no control group was used. In the final section the findings will be summarized and the conclusions which we believe can be drawn from these studies will be indicated.

Studies Using a Control Group

THE CAMBRIDGE-SOMERVILLE YOUTH STUDY

Pride of place in any discussion of experiments on the effects of psychotherapy must undoubtedly go to the Cambridge-Somerville Youth Study. It is the only experiment known to us which made use of a properly chosen control group, which used large enough numbers of cases to make the results statistically convincing, which carried on both treatment and follow-up over a sufficiently long period to make the results meaningful, which used objective methods of acknowledged social significance to assess the final outcome, and which investigated the process of therapy itself in an unbiased and properly controlled fashion. In all these ways the study can serve as an example by which to judge the deficiencies of other work to be reviewed in this chapter.

The aim of the programme has been summed up as follows by Teuber and Powers (1953): "For approximately eight years, from 1937–1945, this large-scale treatment effort was directed at the prevention of delinquency, by guidance, counseling and therapy, in a group of over six hundred underprivileged boys . . . By setting up a control group, and by keeping unusually detailed records, the Study made provision for quantitive measurement of the effects of therapy, and for systematic attempts at an objective description of the therapeutic relationships."

The first step in the programme consisted of the selection of subjects from among underprivileged boys aged between 6 and 10 whose names had been obtained from welfare workers as being "likely to become delinquent." A list of six hundred and fifty boys having been obtained, the boys were individually matched in pairs on variables such as age, intelligence quotient, school grade, delinquency rating and ethnic and socioeconomic background. The decision as to which boy in each pair should be assigned to the treatment group (T) and which to the untreated control group (C) was made by the toss of a coin. In this way two equal groups of three hundred and twenty-five boys were obtained whose chances of delinquency as far as could be ascertained were very nearly equal.

As soon as a boy had been selected as a member of the treatment group he was assigned to one of the counsellors employed by the Study and treatment was begun. Details of this treatment are given in the book by Powers and Witmer (1951) and little will be said about it here except to mention that both adherents of the psychoanalytic school and followers of Carl Roger's non-directive approach participated in the treatment programme. "Regardless of the individual counselor's predilection all treatment consisted of individual, face-to-face contacts. These individual relationships between counselors and boys thus served as the independent variable; they represented 'treatment' . . . they were restricted to the treatment group and consistently withheld from the control group."

The follow-up extended from the end of the treatment period in 1945, when treatment had lasted for between two and eight years in individual cases, to 1948 when the outcome was evaluated. Powers (1949) gives an interesting discussion of the results which would have been reported had no control group been present. Speaking of the treatment group he points out that—

1. "There are seventy T boys who are now well past the age of 17, whose careers have been closely followed and who, as boys under 12, appeared to the predictors to be more likely than not to develop delinquent careers . . . after these boys had been through the treatment program, not more than one third (twenty-three boys) committed serious repeated delinquent acts, while thirty-one of them proved not to be delinquent at all."

2. "There are one hundred and sixty-three T boys who, when under 12, were rated . . . as probable delinquents." Of these only 14.1 per cent committed delinquent acts which led to their admission to a correctional institution. This rate seems a surprisingly low one in view of the fact that the study, it was believed, included practically all the boys in the two cities participating in the study, with a combined population of 213,000, who showed early signs of future delinquency.

3. The counsellors, during the middle period of the program were asked on several different occasions to list all T boys who were thought to have "substantially benefited" by their contact with the study. About two thirds of the boys were so listed, and about half of these were reported by the counselors as having been "outstanding" in respect of benefit received.

4. Of the boys themselves more than half (62 per cent) stated that the study had been of value to them. Many of them declared that "they help me to keep out of trouble," and this seems to have been a majority view. Powers concludes: "By such evidence at least, we might reasonably conclude that the study had been successful in preventing delinquency. Many illustrative cases could be

given to 'prove' the point in the traditional manner. But the evaluation, though of the customary type, is inconclusive."

The picture changes dramatically when the control group is brought into the picture. The total number of court appearances from the beginning of treatment was recorded, and it was found that ninety-six *T* boys and ninety-two *C* boys were involved, the number of offences being two hundred and sixty-four for the *T* group and two hundred and eighteen for the *C* group. A similar picture is given by the number of appearances before the Court Prevention Bureau. Here we find that forty-nine *T* boys and forty-nine *C* boys appeared on one occasion and sixty-five *T* boys and fifty-two *C* boys two or three times. Teuber and Powers comment as follows—

> Such an outcome of the delinquency prevention program of the Study appears to be not only negative, but paradoxical. Instead of confirming the expectation that the treatment group would be less delinquent than the matched control group, there is a slight difference in favour of the control group. This apparent advantage of the control group may be offset, however, by other factors which more detailed statistics seem to reveal. There is a slightly greater incidence of serious recidivism . . . in the control group, and a rating of all offenses according to "seriousness" likewise shows a slight advantage of the treatment cases over the controls; there is a tendency on the part of the controls to commit a proportionately greater number of the more serious offenses. None of these trends, however, are as yet significant. Unless further developments change the picture . . . the direct comparison between *T* and *C* groups fails to show that the major hypothesis can be sustained; treatment did not . . . reduce the incidence of adjudged delinquency in the treatment group.

It is not surprising that the authors, in contrasting this negative outcome of the control investigation with the enthusiastic beliefs of the counselors, conclude that "quantitative indices . . . are better than professions of faith bolstered by the therapist's prestige and the skillful use of the illustrative case."

The reactions of the therapists themselves are of some interest. In a detailed study of the therapist-boy relationship it was found that a number of therapists completely misinterpreted the attitudes and feelings of the boys towards themselves and that it was precisely these therapists who "considered their counseling relations as a highly effective tool in producing changes in their charges." Altogether the attitude of the therapists themselves appeared worthy of comment—

> To some of the counselors, the whole control group idea . . . seemed slightly blasphemous, . . . they insisted that the relationships established had their value in themselves, irrespective of their possible effects on the boys' behavior, and they were not perturbed when seemingly negative results of the delinquency prevention program became known. Other counselors reacted differently; they felt that research was superfluous, since all the necessary rules of conduct in therapy were already known. When they were informed of the outcome of the Study, they reacted in a characteristic fashion: those who were analytically trained and oriented asserted that the results would have been positive, had analytic principles been applied by all staff members, consistently, throughout the course of the treatment period. Conversely, those counselors, who were followers of Carl Rogers' non-directive approach averred that a systematic use of non-directive methods would have produced more definite success.

The reader may feel that, while the study failed in providing any evidence in favour of the hypothesis that treatment of the kind administered prevented delinquency, this treatment may have had many other important and desirable results. This, of course, is not impossible, but we would like to quote one final paragraph from Teuber and Powers: "We submit . . . that the data yield one definite conclusion: that the burden of proof is on anyone who claims specific results for a given form of therapy. It is admittedly difficult to provide for expensive control settings. . . . But the objective evaluation of therapeutic processes is of such importance that similar studies, in many areas of therapy, are indicated."

THE BRILL-BEEBE STUDY

The data to be considered next come from *A Follow-up Study of War Neuroses* by Brill and Beebe (1955), which is essentially a statistical analysis of data collected during and after the war in connection with soldiers discharged from the army for neurotic disorders or returned to the army as cured. The book from which the data are taken is a rather monumental account of a very large number of analyses carried out in great detail. Much of what is said in this book is relevant to the interpretation of the data to be quoted, but it would take us too far afield to go into any detail. Let it merely be said that the combination of background experience characterizing the two authors—one of whom is a well-known psychiatrist, the other an eminent statistician—gives the book and its conclusions a unique authority and an enviable absence of the all too frequent faults of analysis usually encountered in this field.

The data relevant to this chapter come from two sources. The first relates to the improvement experienced after separation from the service by men suffering with mild or moderate neuroses at the time of separation from the service. Some of the men experienced a breakdown in combat, others outside the combat zone and before reaching it (Z/I zone). These two groups were in turn subdivided into those who received treatment after their separation from the army and those who did not. The results of the analysis are shown in Table 1. It will be seen

TABLE 1 *Percentage of Men with Mild or Moderate Neuroses of Separation Who Improved After Separation from Service, by Location at Breakdown, and by Treatment Since Separation* (Quoted by permission of Brill and Beebe (1955) and the V.A.)

Treatment since separation	Early Z/I breakdown		Breakdown in combat	
	Number of men	*Percentage improved*	*Number of men*	*Percentage improved*
None	82	65	58	62
Some	44	57	42	55
Total	126	62	100	59

that, if anything, those who received treatment improved less than those who received no treatment. The authors summarize their findings in the following words: "Given an individual who broke down in service and who was still ill with a neurosis on discharge, any change in his condition after discharge seems to be related more to sociologic factors than anything else. What his military experience was, *what treatment he had,* and how sick he had been, seemed to make no difference. It is the poorly educated, unskilled individual of limited intelligence who was not well-adjusted before entering the service, and who was more liable to have had marital difficulty after discharge, who is least apt to improve and most apt to get worse. The overall tendency for the entire sample was to improve." We need only add that the special care taken in the follow-up study reported in this volume makes criticism of the conclusions rather less admissible than is usually the case with studies of a purely actuarial nature, and that the authors must be congratulated on the very careful work done by them to render follow-ups psychologically meaningful as well as statistically comparable. This makes the conclusion that there was no difference in remission of neuroses between those who did and those who did not receive psychiatric treatment all the more interesting.

The other type of comparison made in this book is with respect to soldiers treated in service. Table 2 shows the mean service period in months following

TABLE 2   *Type of Psychiatric Treatment at First Breakdown in Military Service and Subsequent Length of Service*

(Quoted by permission of Brill and Beebe (1955) and the V.A.)

Type of psychiatric treatment	Number of cases [1]	Mean months of service (including time in hospital) following first breakdown
None	165	8.6
Rest and sedation	150	11.0
Individual therapy	265	10.7
Hospital routine	328	8.4
Total	908	9.5

[1] Count of cases is slightly inflated since some men receive more than one form of treatment.

first breakdown, analysed by type of psychiatric treatment received. "Men who received individual therapy served somewhat longer, on the average, than men who received routine hospital care, or men who received essentially no psychiatric treatment. Men who received only rest and sedation also served longer than these two groups. *The differences, however, are remarkably small.*" A similar conclusion seems appropriate to the results reported in the next Table 3 showing

TABLE 3   *Type of Psychiatric Treatment at First Breakdown in Service and Return to Duty*

(Quoted by permission of Brill and Beebe (1955) and the V.A.)

Treatment	*Per cent returned to duty*
Essentially no treatment	56
Rest and sedation only	68
Individual therapy	62
Hospital routine	48
Total	57

the percentage of casualties returned to duty. Here again "rest and sedation only" appears slightly superior to individual therapy, with "essentially no treatment" very close behind.

The authors find it necessary to correct the overall figures because they found that "individual therapy was given more often to combat than to non-combat cases, to men with a more adequate preservice personality (who were more apt to be in combat), and to those whose illness seemed most severe." The following summary may illustrate the results of a complex method of making the samples statistically comparable—

Although the present study provides no real basis for assessing the effects of the several forms of treatment, it was considered worthwhile to undertake a single controlled comparison of the several types of treatment. These treatment groups were established—

A—Not more than rest and sedation.

B—Individual therapy.

C—Hospital routine.

Matching was done on the basis of the following characteristics, so that the confounding of choice of treatment with characteristics of the patient might be minimized—

Major area of precipitating stress.

Preservice personality and impairment.

Severity of breakdown.

The three matched treatment groups (A, B, and C) were then compared as to health and separation and condition at follow-up with essentially negative findings. It therefore appears doubtful that there was any difference in the effectiveness of the three gross types of treatment.

In drawing conclusions from these results it may be advisable to keep in mind the warning given by the authors of the report under review: "An *ex post facto* study of different treatments is naturally hazardous; the experimentalist requires an element of physical randomization in the allocation of treatments before he is usually willing to associate differences in outcome with differential effectiveness of therapies. Here the categories of treatment are quite broad and pay little regard to intensity, but in view of the limited resources available for treatment in the military situation only a rough classification is possible." Provided that these possible sources of error are borne in mind and also that it is remembered that war neuroses may differ in many ways from civilian neuroses, the outcome of the two studies just summarized gives a reasonably clear and consistent answer to the question of the effectiveness of therapy after breakdown within the army, and after separation from the army. No evidence of such effectiveness can be found, and the main results of this comparatively well controlled and competently analysed study in so far as effectiveness of psychotherapy is concerned, must be considered to be completely negative.

THE BARRON-LEARY STUDY

In this experiment one hundred and fifty psychoneurotic patients, all drawn from the same clinic population, were tested with the Minnesota Multiphasic Personality Inventory before and after an interval of time during which some of them received psychotherapy, and some of them did not. (Barron and Leary, 1955). "All one hundred and fifty patients had applied for psychotherapy in the psychiatric clinic in which the study was conducted, and all of them had been accepted for treatment; a group of twenty-three cases, however, had to be placed on a waiting list until the hospital facilities became available, and they waited some six months before beginning treatment. Of those who received psycho- therapy immediately, eighty-five received group therapy, and forty-two received individual therapy; they included only those patients treated for a minimum of three months during the period of time covered by the study. The aim of the study (was) to discover what changes, if any, occurred in M.M.P.I. profiles of patients who received psychotherapy, and to compare these changes with whatever changes may be observed in the M.M.P.I. profiles of patients who during the same period of time remained untreated."

The psychotherapists carrying out the treatment included psychiatrists, social workers and psychologists; all therapists had at least three years of post-doctoral or post-graduate training and experience. The general orientation was psychoanalytic. Individual treatment consisted largely of ego-orientated psychotherapy on a once-a-week basis, whereas group therapy laid somewhat greater stress on current interpersonal relations.

The experimental and control groups were found to be quite comparable with one another in diagnosis, prognosis, severity of initial condition, age, sex and education. The interval between the initial state and terminal state was 7.00 months for non-treatment group, 8.23 months for the individual therapy group and 8.63 months for the group-therapy group. The differences between these means fell short of significance, although it will be noted that the time interval for the non-treatment group was noticeably shorter than that for the other two groups, thus making a positive outcome of the study more likely.

None of the patients were so ill as to require hospitalization, and most were diagnosed as suffering from psychosomatic neuroses, obsessive or schizoid characters, phobias, anxiety neuroses and occasional psychopathic or hysterical disorders.

In the two psychotherapy groups significant decreases occurred in the Depression, Hysteria, Hypochondriasis and Lie scores of the M.M.P.I., whether individual or group. With group psychotherapy there was a significant decrease in the Paranoia and Psychasthenia scores as well. With both forms of therapy, there was "a significant rise in the Ego-strength scores. Finally, for the individual psychotherapy patients there is also a significant rise in the K scale."

Patients of the control group, i.e. those not receiving any treatment, also had fewer complaints on second testing. "On the neurotic triad (D,Ps,Hy) the average decrease is slightly greater for the controls than for the group therapy patients. There is a significant increase in scores on Es, which would suggest that at the end of the waiting period the patients are somewhat more amenable to psychotherapy than at the beginning of that period."

We see, then, that changes in the treatment and non-treatment groups occur in very much the same fashion and in the same direction. The question arises whether the changes in the treatment group are significantly greater than those in the untreated group. The answer is that none of the differences on the psychiatric scales approach significance although in the twenty-four comparisons made altogether one would have expected one difference at least to have been significant by chance. Such a significant difference is in fact found, but it occurs in connection with the K scale. This is not a psychiatric scale and the meaning of the difference is obscure; the authors do not attempt to interpret it. They conclude that "for the most part . . . the changes tended to be in the same direction for treatment and non-treatment groups, and of about equal magnitude." In so far as we can regard the M.M.P.I. as a reasonable measure of psychiatric status this study would appear to indicate a complete failure of psychotherapy to produce any effects whatever.

Barron and Leary add a rather curious argument. They question whether the patients on the waiting list should really be thought of as "untreated." "In a sense, of course, simply having committed oneself to participating in psychotherapy, and having had a reciprocal commitment from a clinic to afford psychotherapy, even though not immediately, represent a breaking of the neurotic circle. A force for change has already been introduced. In addition, the initial interview and the psychological testing may themselves be therapeutic events." It is, of course, possible that filling in a questionnaire and registering at a hospital may have therapeutic functions. The authors do not really give any reasons for assuming that these events were responsible for the change in the untreated group, and in any case this would not detract from the main conclusion, namely that psychotherapy adds nothing to the total situation.

It should always be possible in studies of this kind to invent *ad hoc* hypotheses to account for the improvement of the untreated group; this does not appear to be a worthwhile procedure. What is required, clearly, is a method for *investigating* the factors which are believed to be responsible for the improvement, and which will tell us whether, in fact, these do or do not exert an influence. If the complex and lengthy procedure of psychotherapy cannot be shown to have any effect it does not seem likely to the present writer that filling in a questionnaire, or registering at a hospital, are likely to be so much more powerful in effecting a change.

THE ROGERS AND DYMOND STUDY

This study has been reported in book form under the title *Psychotherapy and Personality Change* (Rogers and Dymond, 1954). Since it is the only one of the studies reviewed here which reports a positive outcome, and since it has been widely quoted and discussed in this connection, a review of this book obviously cannot be omitted here; the faults of the experimental design are such, however, that on the grounds of merit alone it is doubtful whether it should have been included.

The authors claim that: "This is the first thoroughly objective study of outcomes of psychotherapy in which adequate controls have been utilized. . . . We can, with a reasonable degree of assurance, sort out those changes which occur as concomitants of psychotherapy from those which occur as a result of other factors." The "objective" methods used to assess outcome are counsellor judgments, behaviour ratings by friends, questionnaires and attitude scales, T.A.T. responses and Q-Sorts. These were applied to the subjects of the experiment according to a design illustrated in Fig. 13.—

> It will be discerned that there is a therapy, or experimental, group and a control group. A portion of the therapy group is set apart as the own-control group in which there is a sixty-day wait period, preceded and followed by the administration of the research tests, before therapy starts. This group is also matched in the so-called "wait group" of the controls. The rationale of the design is that, through the own-control group, we can control for personality factors and motivation for therapy. This is accomplished by comparing changes made during the wait and the therapy periods. The no-therapy control group provides a more precise control for the passage of time and the effects of repeated administration of the tests. If change occurs in the therapy and follow-up period which is greater than the change in the waiting period of the own-control group, or in the equivalent period for the control group, then we would have strong evidence that therapy produces change which is not accounted for on other grounds.

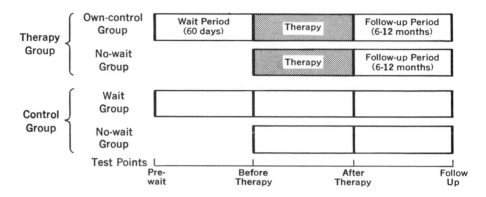

FIGURE 13. ARRANGEMENT OF EXPERIMENT BY ROGERS
AND DYMOND (1954)
(*Quoted by permission of Univ. of Chicago Press*)

The therapy group consisted of twenty-nine clients whose disorders appeared to have been of a rather mild nature. The own-control group was formed by asking half of these clients to defer their therapy for sixty days. The equivalent control group was made up of twenty-three normal volunteers rather poorly matched for sex, age and social economic status with the patients.

The main criticism to be made of this arrangement is that contrary to the belief of the writers of the book, *no proper control group is in fact provided.* It is difficult to see what purpose the so-called normal control group serves. No one has, to our knowledge, advanced the hypothesis that a group of normal people not subjected to any kind of psychotherapeutic or other manipulation should change in the direction of greater integration and better mental health. The counter-hypothesis against which controls are necessary in research on the effects of psychotherapy is that spontaneous remission occurs among patients to an extent which equals the alleged effects of therapy; to this counter-hypothesis a normal control group is irrelevant.

When we come to the so-called "own-control" group it must be admitted that the logic of the design is much less susceptible to criticism *provided that the time-intervals of the waiting period and the therapy period are equal.* This is an absolutely essential proviso because the counter-hypothesis specifies that spontaneous remission would be a monotonic function of time; in other words, the longer the period of waiting, the greater the amount of spontaneous remission. If the so-called therapy period is appreciable longer than the waiting period, then we would expect on the spontaneous-remission hypothesis that more such remissions would occur in the therapy period than in the waiting period *irrespective of therapy,* so that it would be impossible to ascribe any difference in outcome between the two periods to therapy. The comparison between the waiting period and the follow-up period with respect to outcome is only meaningful if the two periods did not differ in any other variable, such as time, which is relevant to outcome. Unfortunately, it is only too obvious from what the authors say that the therapy period was in no way equated with the wait period, but was probably appreciably longer. As the authors themselves admit: "The own-control plan controls motivation for therapy and, indeed, for most of the factors listed above *except passage of time* and environmental influences." The authors do not seem to realize that this admission is sufficient by itself to make the data incapable of throwing any light on the effects of psychotherapy. So far from being able "with a reasonable degree of assurance to sort out those changes which occur as con- comitants of psychotherapy from those which occur as a result of other factors," they have designed the experiment in such a manner as to make it quite certain that the theory of therapeutic effectiveness and the main counter-thesis are con- founded in the effects to such an extent as to make interpretation of the results impossible.

In principle no more need be said about this study, but nevertheless some of the results are interesting enough to make it desirable to say a few words about the measures used to assess the effects of therapy. Nearly all of these, it will have been noticed, are verbal in nature, calling for Q-Sorts, questionnaire responses, and other types of verbal behaviour. Even if the design of the experiment had been acceptable, verbal behaviour of this type would not be acceptable as the only evidence of improvement. There is ample evidence, from the work of Thorn- dike (1935), Taffel (1955), Verplanck (1955), Greenspoon (1950), Wickes (1956), Salzinger (1957), and others, that verbal responses can very easily be conditioned to indications of approval or disapproval on the part of the examiner or therapist. It requires no more than a simple nod of the head, or a repetition of the magic syllables "uh-huh" or "hmm, hmm," to produce remarkably extensive and consistent changes in verbal behaviour. It does not follow that these verbal behaviour changes are in any sense accompanied by psychological changes more directly relevant to the process of therapy. Thus we have here another alternative hypothesis which is disregarded by Rogers and Dymond in their account, although it would again have been better able than their own to account for the actual findings. Some data are in fact provided which strongly support this alternative hypothesis. "It was found that there was no significant difference between the pre-therapy and post-therapy behaviour of our clients, on the average, according to their friends' observations. . . . When the clients' ratings of their own be- haviour were compared with the ratings by their friends, it was discovered that our clients consistently rated themselves less favourably than did their friends; but this discrepancy steadily diminished, so that by the follow-up point their perception agreed much more closely with that of their friends." What appears to happen, therefore, is that there is no observable change in the behaviour of the clients, but that they become conditioned through therapy to make different responses on the purely semantic level to questions regarding their behaviour.

It is not suggested that the data prove this alternative hypothesis. We do not feel that this research was organized or analysed in a manner which makes it possible to draw any definite conclusions and we merely want to draw attention to possibilities which do not appear to have been considered by the authors. Many other such counter-hypotheses could be advanced, and would have to be eliminated before one could even begin to take the results very seriously. What strikes one most about this work is not so much its failure to be conclusive, or even the obvious faults in design and execution; it is rather that the writers ap- pear to pride themselves on the methodological advances of their work over previous studies (among which there are such excellent prototypes of research as the Cambridge-Somerville Youth Study), and that reviewers appear to have re- garded this as a major contribution without appearing to realize the crippling defects of design of the study. It would appear almost as if reviewers singled out studies giving positive results with respect to the effects of psychotherapy, while neglecting those with negative outcomes, irrespective of the quality of the work reported.

THE BARENDREGT STUDY

In 1961 J. T. Barendregt of the University of Amsterdam published an important follow-up study of three groups of patients. These were derived from a number of subjects who were tested psychologically when they applied for psychotherapy at the Institute for Psychoanalysis in Amsterdam. After about 2½ years the patients were tested a second time. Of these patients 47 (Group A) had been given psychoanalysis; 79 patients (Group P) had been given psychotherapy, other than psychoanalysis, and not at the Institute for Psychoanalysis; 74 patients (Group C) did not have any form of psychotherapy or any therapeutic contact with psychiatrists. The essential design of the experiment is concerned with the comparison of the changes which occurred in these three groups, and it is obviously important to know why patients were assigned to these groups. "Patients were classified in Group P for various reasons. The decision in favour of psychotherapy for a number of patients was made for practical reasons (mainly financial), when psychoanalysis would actually have been more desirable. . . . For some of the patients in Group C psychoanalysis or psychotherapy was advised but impracticable. Moreover, patients for whom psychoanalysis had been indicated and who were put on a waiting list, were included in the control group if they were still waiting at the time of the second psychological examination." Barendregt considers the possibility that selection may have vitiated the effects of any comparison between the groups but concludes "The classification of the patients on the basis of the psychiatric examination had little relationship to the criteria set up in the experiment. Therefore, it seems unlikely that the psychiatric classification could be used to predict a possible change in the criteria set up. However, it is possible."

The following criteria were used in this study.

1. Self rating of a sense of well-being.
2. Wechsler-Bellevue Intelligence Test (Verbal Scale).
3. Neuroticism Questionnaire.
4. Score on a Lie Scale.
5. An Introversion-Extraversion Questionnaire.
6. Thematic Apperception Test, scored according to two different methods.
7. Rorschach Test.

The following hypothesis was set up:

"Groups A and P would show more positive changes than Group C, any difference between A and P should come out in favour of A. From this general hypothesis eight predictions were derived." First prediction: "The A and the P group will show a greater difference on the ratings (of well-being) in the positive direction than Group C." The figures refute this prediction; there were no differences among the groups. Second prediction: "There will be a greater difference in I.Q. in a positive direction for groups A and P than for Group C. . . . The second prediction was refuted as the differences between the groups are far from significant." Third prediction: The patients' neuroticism score was predicted to improve more for Groups A and P than for Group C; this prediction "was confirmed to the extent that Group A shows a significant sharper drop than Groups P and C." Fifth prediction: It was anticipated that the treatment groups would show an increase in extraversion greater than the control group. The differences were not significant, and if anything Group A showed a trend in the opposite direction. The sixth and seventh predictions related to the Thematic Apperception Test. On the whole these do not show a differential improvement between the groups. Eighth prediction: this relates to changes on the Rorschach Test. Slight differences in the predicted direction were found but these are of doubtful significance.

On the whole the results of this study give very little evidence in favour of the therapeutic usefulness of psychoanalysis or psychotherapy. The positive outcome of one or two predictions relates in the main to effects which are far from central; thus it is not the patient's sense of well-being or his neuroticism which is affected but rather his score on the Lie Scale, i.e. a score, the meaning of which is very difficult to ascertain. Barendregt concludes that "All the same this study is felt to have been useful. For one thing, the patients' opinion of feeling better after some time of psychotherapy has proved to be of little meaning in favour of psychotherapy. For another, the present study has shown two ways which may possibly lead to compelling evidence of the usefulness of psychotherapy. However, such evidence has not been arrived at by this investigation."

THE LAZARUS STUDY

A. A. Lazarus is a student of J. Wolpe who originated one form of behaviour therapy, a method of treatment based on the laws of modern learning theory and conditioning techniques. The actual methods used by behaviour therapists are discussed at some greater length below, in connection with Wolpe's own work. Lazarus (1961) was concerned with the comparative study of psychotherapy and behaviour therapy. His sample consisted of 35 middle class, urban, white South Africans who were suffering phobic disorders. The basic experimental design was to compare behaviour therapy administered in groups with more conventional methods of group therapy based on "dynamic" principles. The method of behaviour therapy used was that of "interpretation." The same therapist (the investigator) conducted all the therapeutic groups. Throughout the experiment, pairs of phobic patients were matched in terms of sex, age and the nature and objective severity of the phobic disorders. A coin was tossed to decide whether a given member of each matched pair would be treated by desensitization therapy or by group interpretation. Group desensitization was applied to 18 patients; group interpretation was applied to 9 patients, and 8 patients were treated by group interpretation plus relaxation.

One month after therapy had terminated the acrophobic and claustrophobic patients who claimed to have recovered from their phobias were required to undergo stress tolerance tests (climbing to the third landing of a fire escape, etc., or remaining in a very small cubicle with the window shut). Altogether two main criteria were used in assessing therapeutic results. There were 13 recoveries and 5 failures in desensitization, and 2 recoveries and 15 failures for other forms of treatment. The resulting chi square test of significance was significant at the $P < .01$ level.

The 15 patients who had derived no apparent benefit from the interpretation procedures were treated by means of desensitization. Ten recovered from their phobias after a mean of 10.1 group desensitization sessions, as compared with a mean of 20.4 sessions which were necessary for effective group desensitization when only this procedure was employed. A plausible interpretation for this is given by Lazarus.

This study suffers from certain difficulties; it would clearly have been preferable if a different therapist had been employed for the purpose of running the interpretation type of treatment. The possibility always exists that a given therapist has preferences which influence the adequacy of particular treatments attempted by him, and while it is very unlikely that such influences could account for the very large difference obtained, nevertheless this is a point which should be considered in future researches. In spite of this criticism the writer would suggest that this study is of historic significance as being probably the first really convincing and methodologically adequate comparison of two different methods of therapy.

THE ANKER AND WALSH STUDY

This study by Anker and Walsh (1961, 1964) constitutes another comparison between traditional methods of treatment and methods based on modern learning theory. The orthodox type of treatment was by means of group psychotherapy. The experimental treatment, based on learning theory, incorporated an activity programme designed to promote a certain type of social organization which, it was hoped, would lead to behaviour alteration through the extinction of interpersonal avoidance responses.

Two other variables were also used in what was essentially a 2 x 2 x 2 factorial design which resulted in 8 distinct "treatment" groups. The effectiveness of group therapy was evaluated by contrast with a comparable group not receiving group therapy, the effectiveness of the learning theory type of treatment by contrast with a comparable group not in the special activity programme, and the effectiveness of heterogeneity of the group by contrast with a comparable homogeneous group. Because the patients' original level of behavioural adjustment could influence the degree of change in adjustment the data were adjusted for this fact by covariance.

Eight groups having the same level of pathology, as measured by Lorr's multidimensional scale for rating psychiatric patients, were established from a total population of 134 male schizophrenic patients. The principal dependent variable, behavioural adjustment, was measured by a special scale, and ancillary measures of group cohesiveness and social choice were also taken. The study continued for one year, with measures taken every six weeks. The results of the study were relatively clear-cut. The activity variable, based on learning theory, produced significant and consistent results in the predicted (desirable) direction. Group psychotherapy produced relatively minor positive results and the group structure variable produced none. None of the interactions were significant. Anker (1964) concludes his discussion by saying that: "The implications of this study for the use of this kind of activity programme involving non-professional personnel in the treatment of chronic psychiatric patients are positive and compelling." This conclusion does not seem to us to exaggerate the value of this experiment which from the methodological point of view seems to be the first really adequate evaluation of behaviour changes in schizophrenic patients as a consequence of the application of different methods of treatment. It will be noted that this study, like the one by Lazarus quoted above, gives highly significant results in comparing two types of treatment; the clear-cut nature of the results undoubtedly reflects in part the excellent quality of the experimental design. It is important to stress that it is apparently not impossible to demonstrate experimentally and statistically the modification of behaviour patterns as a consequence of methods of treatment. The inconclusive results so frequently reported have sometimes been interpreted as demonstrating the difficulty, if not the impossibility of the task attempted. The results of Lazarus' and of Anker's and Walsh's work demonstrate that methods of treatment which are based on adequate theoretical considerations can be shown to be effective when included in a proper experimental design and furnished with appropriate control data.

THE LANG AND LAZOVIK STUDY

This experiment in some ways resembles the Lazarus study referred to above but deals with a rather different type of population and does not make use of two types of treatment. Lang and Lazovik (1964) set out to test Wolpe's systematic desensitization therapy for phobic reactions (Wolpe 1958, 1961). Lang and Lazovik studied a total of 24 subjects all of whom were college students and none of whom showed any evidence of severe emotional disturbance. They were selected on the basis of a classroom questionnaire on which they rated their fear of non-poisonous snakes as "intense." Subjects were also interviewed by the two authors and filled in a special fear survey schedule (F.S.S.). A direct assessment of each subject's avoidance behaviour was obtained by confronting him with a non-poisonous snake in a glass case; his behaviour was observed and he was asked to rate his anxiety on a 10 point fear thermometer. The degree of anxiety was also rated on a 3 point scale by the experimenter. Subjects were randomly placed in one of two experimental or one of two control groups. This was done so that the different parts of the experimental treatment could be experimentally separated. The experimental treatment consisted of two sequential parts, training and desensitization proper. The training procedures required five sessions of about 45 minutes each, during which an anxiety hierarchy was constructed, consisting of a series of twenty sections involving the phobic object graded from most to least frightening. Each subject was then trained in deep muscle relaxation, was introduced to hypnosis and an effort was made to teach him to visualize vividly hypnotic scenes. Following this training there were 11 sessions of systematic desensitization in which the subject was hypnotised, and instructed to relax deeply. Items from the anxiety hierarchy were then presented as scenes which the subject was told to visualize clearly, the less frightening scenes being presented first. When the subject could experience these without anxiety, items further along in the hierarchy were administered until the subject reported no distress while experiencing the maximum "dose" or phobic stimulation.

"The basic plan of the study is described in Table 4. It consisted of two experimental and two control groups. The sub-groups were created so that the effects of repeating the avoidance test, pre-therapy training, and desensitization itself could be separately evaluated. Thus, the experimental groups E-1 and E-2 both experienced the laboratory analogue of a desensitization therapy already

TABLE 4   *The Design of the Experiment, Showing the Times at Which Ss Were Evaluated (the snake avoidance test, experimenter's rating, fear thermometer, and taped interview)*

Group					
E-1	test 1	training	test 2	desensitization	test 3
E-2	—	training	test 2	desensitization	test 3
C-1	test 1	—	test 2	—	test 3
C-2	—	—	test 2	—	test 3

described. However, Ss assigned to E-1 were administered the avoidance test before the training period, prior to desensitization, and again at the end of the experiment. E-2 Ss, on the other hand, were tested before desensitization and after, but did not participate in the initial evaluation. The control Ss did not participate in desensitization, but the C-1 and C-2 groups were evaluated at the same time as their opposite numbers in the experimental series. All available Ss were seen and evaluated six months after the termination of therapy."

The results of the experiment are quite significant and demonstrate the importance of the type of behaviour therapy used. It was demonstrated that the experimental analogue of desensitization therapy effectively reduces phobic behaviour. Both subjective rating of fear and overt avoidance behavior were modified, and gains were maintained or increased at the six-month follow-up. The results of objective measures were in turn supported by extensive interview material. "Close questioning could not persuade any of the experimental Ss that a desire to please the E had been a significant factor in their change. Furthermore, in none of these interviews was there any evidence that other symptoms appeared to replace the phobic behavior.

"The fact that no significant change was associated with the pre-therapy training argues that hypnosis and general muscle relaxation were not in themselves vehicles of change. . . . Clearly, the responsibility for the reduction in phobic behavior must be assigned to the desensitization process itself. This is evidenced not only by the difference between experimental and control Ss but also by the relationship within the experimental groups between degree of change and the number of hierarchy items successfully completed. . . . The present experiment also reveals an interesting connection between changes in overt avoidance behavior and the S's verbal report. The relationship between these two dimensions is generally positive. However, even when precisely the same event is being evaluated, it is sometimes surprisingly low (Test 3 avoidance scale and fear thermometer $r = + .40$). Furthermore, initial changes in phobic behavior seem to occur in either one dimension or the other, rather than in both simultaneously. Most frequently subjective report lags behind overt behavior. Thus avoidance test scores differentiated between experimental and control Ss immediately following the experiment, but it was not until the follow-up interview that the subjective scales yielded the same finding. It will be interesting to observe in future studies if this pattern continues, and to what extent it is characteristic of any reduction in phobic behavior, or simply a function of the desensitization technique.

"But of greatest interest are the implications of the present research for traditional theories of clinical practice. The findings suggest the following important conclusions: (a) It is not necessary to explore with a subject the factors contributing to the learning of a phobia or its 'unconscious meaning' in order to eliminate the fear behavior; (b) The form of treatment employed here does not lead to symptom substitution or create new disturbances of behavior; (c) In reducing phobic behavior it is not necessary to change basic attitudes, values, or attempt to modify the 'personality as a whole.' The unlearning of phobic behavior appears to be analogous to the elimination of other responses from a subject's behavior repertoire."

The results of this experiment are in good agreement with the more clinical type of study reported by Lazarus and the report by Wolpe (1961) which lacked a control group in demonstrating the effectiveness of behavior therapy as applied to phobic disorders. It is unlikely to be an accident that the only three experiments giving clear-cut evidence of therapeutic usefulness in this chapter are all characterised by two features; (a) an adequate experimental design and (b) an adequate theoretical foundation for the type of treatment chosen. The implication of these facts need hardly be emphasized.

THE LOVIBOND STUDY

Lovibond (1963a, 1963b) has published two papers in which he compared different methods of treating enuresis. The methods used all employed the "bell and blanket" method of treatment [1] but Lovibond made certain important changes in this method. In the first of these papers he suggested that (a) conditioning treatment of enuresis followed the avoidance rather than the classical conditioning model and (b) the conditioned stimulus is provided by the pattern of stimulation arising from the micturition response and not by bladder distension stimulation. He suggested an implication for practice, namely that the response to the noxious stimulus should provide escape from stimulus in order to facilitate the development of the required avoidance response. He accordingly constructed a modified auditory apparatus which he called the "twin signal" apparatus. This presents two auditory stimuli; the first of these is provided by a 240V warning signal similar to a modern car hooter and considerably attenuated. This stimulus lasts for a little less than one second and is followed by an interval of silence of about one minute. After this period an ordinary buzzer operates continuously until it is switched off. The duration of the hooter was chosen to be slightly longer than the latency plus the duration of the response of sphincter contraction. Thus this response would appear to provide escape from the noxious stimulus and should become conditioned to the preceding stimuli arising from sphincter relaxation.

The twin signal apparatus was compared with the orthodox Mowrer type of apparatus and also with Crosby's method. Lovibond was able to show that the medium number of reinforcements required for arrest of the bed wetting was 14.5 with the twin signal apparatus, 20 with the Crosby apparatus and 30.5 with the Mowrer apparatus. There were no differences between the three instruments in the rate of extinction of the acquired response (relapse).

In his second study Lovibond attached the problem of relapse, and suggested that intermittent reinforcement might be of value in retarding the tendency towards relapse in aversion therapy. An animal experiment demonstrating the value of this technique was followed by a field investigation of the conditioning

---

[1] In this method the child sleeps on a special pad imbedded in which are electrodes which are connected to a battery and a buzzer. Urination provides a contact between the electrodes, thus completing the circuit, causing the buzzer to sound and the child to wake up. In this situation the buzzer is the UCS, the enlargement of the bladder prior to urination the CS and waking up the response.

treatment of enuresis. It was found that intermittent reinforcement did not re-
tard acquisition of the required response, i.e. waking up in time to avoid bed wetting, and produced less relapse than did 100% reinforcement. The comparable
figures given by Lovibond show that with the Mowrer apparatus 17.5 stimuli were
required to arrest the bed wetting in 34 subjects, out of whom 15 relapsed during
the period of between 3 to 12 months after cessation of treatment. An equal
number of subjects treated by means of the twin signal apparatus show a 19% relapse rate having required 13.5 stimulations to arrest the bed wetting. Sixteen
subjects treated on the twin signal apparatus with intermittent reinforcement
needed 14 stimuli to arrest bed wetting and showed no relapses during the 3 to
12 months period following cessation of treatment. During the first 3 months
after cessation of treatment these three groups showed respectively 20%, 25%, and
6% relapse rates. Thus during the first year (which includes practically all the relapses likely to happen) we find that complete reinforcement produces 35% of
relapse for the Mowrer apparatus, 44% for the twin signal apparatus, whereas intermittent reinforcement only produces 6%. Thus on both accounts Lovibond's
theories regarding the effectiveness of a particular technique of behaviour therapy
as supplied to enuresis have been verified.

THE GLIEDMAN STUDY

This experiment reported by Gliedman *et al.* (1958) is one of a series of reports
on the effects of placebos on psychiatric cases. Of particular interest in this connection is the comparison between placebos and psychotherapy. The design is
adequate for the required comparison, which disclosed that symptom reduction
was approximately equal for the two methods of treatment. The authors unfortunately failed to provide a "no treatment" group for comparison; it is by no
means clear that their interpretation of the results in terms of placebo effects
is actually correct; it is just as reasonable to hypothesize that they are dealing
throughout with spontaneous remission influenced either by placebos or psychotherapy. While the study thus does have a control group in its design it may
be doubted whether this was the most effective control group for the purpose.

THE WALKER AND KELLY STUDY

Walker and Kelly (1960) compared 44 male schizophrenic patients who received short term psychotherapy with a control group of 38 patients who did not.
Basing their judgements on symptom improvement, ward behaviour, discharge
from hospital and post-hospital adjustment after 90 days they found no differences
in improvement. Only one significant result appeared, namely that more control
patients than therapy patients were discharged within six months of admission.
This study fails to disprove the null hypothesis and does not show any effects of
psychotherapy.

An interesting comment is made by Strupp in his review of this experiment
(1962). He says "Studies of this kind are frequently cited as 'evidence' for the
alleged effectiveness of psychotherapy. Yet, while critics excoriate therapists for
their failure to do better research they quickly seize upon manifestly defective
studies as welcome ammunition." This comment indicates a misunderstanding of
the point at issue. The contention of critics is that psychotherapists have failed
to demonstrate the effectiveness of psychotherapy. This criticism can only be

countered by a properly designed experiment showing the effectiveness of psychotherapy in suitably arranged follow-up studies. Strupp and other apologists
for psychotherapy suggest that the failure to show positive results is due entirely
to faulty criteria, faulty designs and other errors of technique. This may be so,
and certainly most of the data published by psychotherapists are not of a high
technical standard as far as experimental design and statistical treatment are
concerned. However, this does not prove that if these faults were eradicated
then the hypothetical effects of psychotherapy would become obvious. There is
nothing in all these arguments to suggest that the null hypothesis is not an appropriate one to maintain, i.e. that there are in fact no observable effects of
psychotherapy. Only positive proof can alter this situation. The fact that the
adherents of behaviour therapy have been able to demonstrate highly significant
effects of their chosen technique as compared with psychotherapy, suggests that
even if psychotherapists should finally improve their techniques sufficiently, results might still remain insignificant.

Studies without Control Groups

PSYCHOTHERAPY WITH ADULTS

The experiments reviewed so far have illustrated the absolute necessity of including a control group in any experiment designed to test the efficacy of psychotherapy. When looking at the large body of studies without such control
groups we cannot, in the nature of the case, draw any very definite conclusions.
What we can do, however, is to try and provide a kind of base-line with which to
compare the results of treatment, a base-line which is derived from the best available estimate of remission in the absence of psychotherapy. Our efforts along
these lines will, of course, suffer from certain obvious defects. The matching of
cases is difficult enough when the same investigator selects the treatment and
control groups; it becomes almost impossibly complex when all we have to go
on is the usually very inadequate account given in a written report. The severity
of the illness and the standards of recovery are not usually discussed in sufficient
detail to make exact comparisons possible. Data on duration of treatment and
the length of follow-up are not usually given in sufficient detail to enable the
reader to form an accurate judgement of the time intervals involved. When all
these difficulties are added to those usually implied in any actuarial comparison,
it will be realized that not too much faith should be placed in the results of the
comparisons here given, particularly if the results should differ from those of the
better-controlled studies reported earlier.

Three attempts are worth mentioning in this connection as giving us some help
in finding the requisite base-line. The first study to be quoted is a rather indirect
one by Shepherd and Gruenberg (1957) in which they attempt to estimate the
duration of neurotic illnesses not treated by psychotherapy by reference to the
general rule stating that *the prevalence of an illness in a population is equal to
the product of its incidence and duration.* They quote figures relating to both incidence and prevalence from the Health Insurance Plan of Greater New York
(H.I.P.)—

From these data age-specific curves are plotted [in Fig. 14] for cases reported as
receiving a service in any one year and for cases receiving a service for psychoneu-

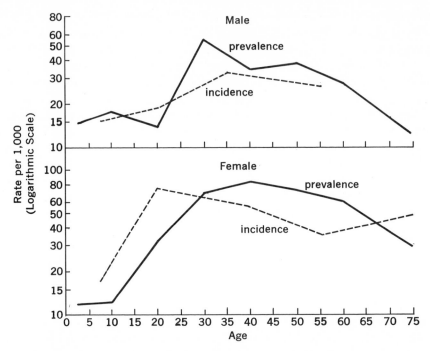

FIGURE 14. AVERAGE ANNUAL PREVALENCE OF PSYCHONEUROSES IN
1948–1951 AND INCIDENCE OF NEW CASES IN 1951, FOR ENROLLEES IN H.I.P.

The prevalence curves reflect the average annual experience over the
years 1948–1951 of all H.I.P. enrollees with twelve months of coverage in
any one of those calendar years. There was a total of 60,302 person-years
of exposure over this period; 2,714 of these person-years were characterized
by the existence of one or more services related to mental illness.

The new case curves show the experience in 1951 of 6,643 enrollees who
had entered H.I.P. by January 15, 1948, were still in the Plan on December
31, 1951, and had not received service related to psychoneurosis in 1948,
1949, and 1950.

(*Quoted by permission of Shepherd and Gruenberg, 1957*)

rotic illness *for the first time* from H.I.P. in 1951, having been H.I.P. enrollees for
at least three previous years without having a service for a psychoneurotic illness.
While it is recognized that these are not direct estimates of momentary prevalence
nor direct measures of the date of onset, they are superior to most of the other
data available in that they are from a large population and that both measures derive from the same data. Because the reports stem from many different physicians
trained in many different schools and practicing in diverse groups, it is not possible to know just what criteria were being used to make and record these diagnoses.
They undoubtedly varied widely. However, whether from accident or from consistency, both the "prevalence" curve and the "incidence" curve are similar to those
obtained from other sources of data.

It will be noticed in Fig. 14 that the incidence and prevalence curves are not
only of the same shape, but are very close to one another, running almost parallel—

From this it may be concluded that the variations in prevalence are due, predominantly, to variations in incidence, since apparently the average duration of the

neuroses reported in this population does not vary equally with age . . . since the prevalence curve here is only slightly higher than the incidence curve, it follows that the average duration of these illnesses is of between one and two years.

The authors sum up their study as follows—

> While it is well known that neurotic illnesses can occur at any age and exhibit extremely long courses as well as very brief courses, the available data are remarkably consistent in suggesting that neurotic illnesses are most characteristic of early adult life, that there is a rising incidence and prevalence during the twenties and thirties, a parallel rising prevalence continuing into the forties, and then a rapid decline in prevalence of recognized neuroses. From these data it is perfectly clear that, in the mass, neuroses must have a limited course even if untreated; in fact, the best available data would suggest an average duration between one and two years.

As a very rough-and-ready estimate of our base-line, therefore, we appear to have a figure suggesting that neurotic disorders will tend to remit spontaneously over a period of two years or so. The calculations are rather indirect, and we must next turn to two rather more direct studies.

The first of these is an evaluation by Landis (1938) who begins his discussion by pointing out that—

> . . . before any sort of measurement can be made, it is necessary to establish a base-line and a common unit of measure. The only unit of measure available is the report made by the physician stating that the patient has recovered, is much improved, is improved or unimproved. This unit is probably as satisfactory as any type of human subjective judgement, partaking of both the good and bad points of such judgements.

For a unit Landis suggests "that of expressing therapeutic results in terms of the number of patients recovered or improved per hundred cases admitted to the hospital." As an alternative, he suggests "the statement of therapeutic outcome for some given group of patients during some stated interval of time."

Landis realized quite clearly that in order to evaluate the effectiveness of any form of therapy, data from a control group of non-treated patients would be required in order to compare the effects of therapy with the spontaneous remission rate. In the absence of anything better, he used the amelioration rate in state mental hospitals for patients diagnosed under the heading of "neuroses." As he points out—

> There are several objections to the use of the consolidated amelioration rate . . . of the . . . state hospitals . . . as a base rate for spontaneous recovery. The fact that psychoneurotic cases are not usually committed to state hospitals unless in a very bad condition; the relatively small number of voluntary patients in the group; the fact that such patients do get some degree of psychotherapy especially in the reception hospitals; and the probably quite different economic, educational, and social status of the State Hospital group compared to the patients reported from each of the other hospitals—all argue against the acceptance of [this] figure . . . as a truly satisfactory base line, but in the absence of any better figure this must serve.

Actually the various figures quoted by Landis agree very well. The percentage of neurotic patients discharged annually as recovered or improved from New York state hospitals is seventy (for the years 1925–1934); for the United States as a whole it is sixty-eight (for the years 1926–1933). The percentage of neurotics discharged as recovered or improved within one year of admission is sixty-six for the United States (1933) and sixty-eight for New York (1914). The consolidated amelioration rate of New York state hospitals, 1917–1934, is 72 per cent. As this is the figure chosen by Landis, we may accept it in preference to the other very similar ones quoted. By and large, we may thus say that of severe neurotics receiving in the main custodial care, and very little, if any, psychotherapy, over two-thirds recovered or improved to a considerable extent: "Although this is not, strictly speaking, a basic figure for 'spontaneous' recovery, still any therapeutic method must show an appreciably greater size than this to be seriously considered."

Another estimate of the required base-line is furnished by Denker (1946). Here is a description of his procedure—

> Five hundred consecutive disability claims due to psychoneurosis, treated by general practitioners throughout the country, and not by accredited specialists of sanatoria, were reviewed. All types of neurosis were included, and no attempt made to differentiate the neurasthenic, anxiety, compulsive, hysteric, or other states, but the greatest care was taken to eliminate the true psychotic or organic lesions which in the early stages of illness so often simulate neurosis. These cases were taken consecutively from the files of the Equitable Life Assurance Society of the United States, were from all parts of the country, and all had been ill of a neurosis for at least three months before claims were submitted. They, therefore, could be fairly called "severe," since they had been totally disabled for at least a three months' period, and rendered unable to carry on with any "occupation for remuneration or profit" for at least that time.
>
> These patients were regularly seen and treated by their own physicians with sedatives, tonics, suggestion, and reassurance, but in no case was any attempt made at anything but this most superficial type of "psychotherapy" which has always been the stock-in-trade of the general practitioner. Repeated statements, every three months or so by their physicians, as well as independent investigations by the insurance company, confirmed the fact that these people actually were not engaged in productive work during the period of their illness. During their disablement, these cases received disability benefits. . . . It is appreciated that this fact of disability income may have actually prolonged the total period of disability and acted as a barrier to incentive for recovery. One would, therefore, not expect the therapeutic results in such a group of cases to be as favourable as in other groups where the economic factor might act as an important spur in helping the sick patient adjust to his neurotic conflict and illness.

The cases were all followed up for at least a five-year period, and often as long as ten years after the period of disability had begun. The criteria of "recovery" used by Denker were as follows: (*a*) return to work, and ability to carry on well in economic adjustments for at least a five-year period; (*b*) complaint of no further or only very slight difficulties; (*c*) making of successful social adjustments. Using these criteria, which are very similar to those usually used by psychiatrists, Denker found that 45 per cent of the patients recovered after one year, another 27 per cent after two years, making 72 per cent in all. Another 10 per cent, 5 per cent, and 4 per cent recovered during the third, fourth, and fifth years, respectively, making a total of 90 per cent recoveries after five years.

The recovery of the patients in Denker's sample as a function of time is plotted in Figure 15. An exponential curve has been fitted to these data. The formula for this curve is—

$$X = 100(1 - 10^{-0.00435N})$$

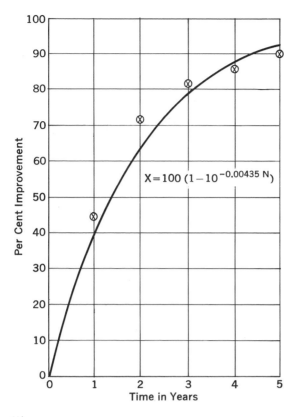

FIGURE 15. IMPROVEMENT SHOWN BY FIVE HUNDRED SEVERE NEUROTICS, NOT RECEIVING PSYCHOTHERAPY, AFTER BETWEEN ONE AND FIVE YEARS

In the formula, X denotes the proportional improvement while N denotes the number of weeks lapsing from the beginning of the experiment.

where X stands for the amount of improvement achieved in per cent and N for the number of weeks elapsed. While the exact values in this formula should not be taken too seriously, its general form is of course that of the typical learning curve with which psychologists are familiar. It will be seen later that many other data are in good agreement with the generalization embodied in this formula.

The Landis and Denker studies supplement each other in a variety of ways. The patients Landis is discussing were largely working-class; those reported on by Denker almost entirely middle-class. The criterion of recovery in the Landis study was probably more lenient, that of the Denker study less lenient than the criteria usually applied by psychotherapists to their own cases. In spite of these differences the recovery figures for the two samples are not too dissimilar. If we take a period of about two years for each base-line estimate, which appears to be a reasonable figure in view of the fact that psychotherapy does not usually last very much longer than two years and may sometimes last less, we may conclude with some confidence that about two-thirds of severe neurotics show recovery or considerable improvement, without the benefit of systematic psychotherapy, after a lapse of two years from the time that their disorder is notified, or they are hospitalized. These figures are less optimistic than those given by Shepherd and Gruenberg who seem to suggest 100 per cent remission after two years; this is probably because the severity of their cases appears to have been rather less than that of those studied by Landis and Denker. When we bear in mind the different methods used by these two investigators and the very divergent samples studied, we cannot but conclude that the estimates of the rate of spontaneous remission are sufficiently similar to enable us to form a very rough-and-ready guess as to the facts of the case.[2]

We must now turn to the effects of psychotherapeutic treatment. The results of nineteen studies reported in the literature, covering over seven thousand cases, and dealing with both psychoanalytic and eclectic types of treatment, are quoted in detail in Table 5. An attempt has been made to report results under the four headings: (a) cured, or much improved; (b) improved; (c) slightly improved; (d) not improved, died, discontinued treatment, etc. It was usually easy to reduce additional categories given by some writers to these basic four; some writers give only two or three categories, and in those cases it was, of course, impossible to subdivide further, and the figures for combined categories are given. A slight degree of subjectivity inevitably enters into this procedure, but it is doubtful if it has caused much distortion. A somewhat greater degree of subjectivity is probably implied in the writer's judgement as to which disorders and diagnoses should be considered to fall under the heading of "neuroses." Schizophrenic, manic-depressive, and paranoid states have been excluded; organ neuroses, psychopathic states, and character disturbances have been included. The number of cases where there was genuine doubt is probably too small to make much change in the final figures, regardless of how they are allocated.

Further details regarding the method of arriving at these various figures are given by Eysenck (1952). The overall figures show that patients treated by means of psychoanalysis improved to the extent of 44 per cent; patients treated eclectically improved to the extent of 64 per cent. These figures may be compared with our base-line estimate of spontaneous remission of 72 per cent. There thus appears to be an inverse correlation between recovery and psychotherapy; the more psychotherapy, the smaller the recovery rate. The difference between eclectic treatment and no psychotherapy is probably too small to be of any significance when we bear in mind the very rough and ready methods used in arriving at these figures. As regards the psychoanalytic results we have classed those who stopped treatment together with those who have not improved. This appears to be reasonable because a patient who fails to finish his treatment, and has not improved, is surely a therapeutic failure. If we class these cases separately and deal only with the percentage of completed treatments which are successful, we find that a percentage of successful treatments of patients who finished their course must be put at approximately 66 per cent, thus bringing these figures in line with those for eclectic treatment and no psychotherapy at all.

The results have been summarized by the writer as follows (Eysenck 1952)—

> In general, certain conclusions are possible from these data. They fail to prove that psychotherapy, Freudian or otherwise, facilitates the recovery of neurotic

---

[2] It may be of interest in this connection to recall some historical comments by Bockover (1956), who points out that "early American mental hospitals recognized the importance of psychologic and social influences in what was called 'moral treatment' of the mentally ill." He points out that Worcester State Hospital showed a recovery and improvement rate of 60 per cent between 1833 and 1846, and Bloomingdale Hospital one of 65 per cent between 1821 and 1844. For the Worcester State Hospital it is claimed that between 1833 and 1946, 50 per cent of patients had no relapse.

TABLE 5   *Summary of Reports of the Results of Psychotherapy*

	N	Cured; much im- proved	Im- proved	Slightly im- proved	Not im- proved; died; left treat- ment	Per cent cured; much im- proved; im- proved
(A) Psychoanalytic						
1. Fenichel [1920–1930]	484	104	84	99	197	39
2. Kessel and Hyman [1933]	34	16	5	4	9	62
3. Jones [1926–1936]	59	20	8	28	3	47
4. Alexander [1932–1937]	141	28	42	23	48	50
5. Knight [1941]	42	8	20	7	7	67
All cases	760		335		425	44
(B) Eclectic						
1. Huddleson [1927]	200	19	74	80	27	46
2. Matz [1929]	775	10	310	310	145	41
3. Maudsley Hospital Report [1931]	1,721	288	900		533	69
4. Maudsley Hospital Report [1935]	1,711	371	765		575	64
5. Neustatter [1935]	46	9	14	8	15	50
6. Luff and Garrod [1935]	500	140	135	26	199	55
7. Luff and Garrod [1935]	210	38	84	54	34	68
8. Ross [1936]	1,089	547	306		236	77
9. Yaskin [1936]	100	29	29		42	58
10. Curran [1937]	83		51		32	61
11. Masserman and Carmichael [1938]	50	7	20	5	18	54
12. Carmichael and Masserman [1939]	77	16	25	14	22	53
13. Schilder [1939]	35	11	11	6	7	63
14. Hamilton and Wall [1941]	100	32	34	17	17	66
15. Hamilton et al. [1942]	100	48	5	17	32	51
16. Landis [1938]	119	40	47		32	73
17. Institute Med. Psychol. (quoted Neustatter)	270	58	132	55	25	70
18. Wilder [1945]	54	3	24	16	11	50
19. Miles et al. [1951]	54	13	18	13	9	58
All cases	7,293		4,661		2,632	64

patients. They show that roughly two-thirds of a group of neurotic patients will recover or improve to a marked extent within about two years of the onset of their illness, whether they are treated by means of psychotherapy or not. This figure appears to be remarkably stable from one investigation to another, regardless of type of patient treated, standard of recovery employed, or method of therapy used. From the point of view of the neurotic, these figures are encouraging; from the point of view of the psychotherapist, they can hardly be called very favourable to his claims. The figures quoted do not necessarily disprove the possibility of therapeutic effectiveness. There are obvious shortcomings in any actuarial comparison and these shortcomings are particularly serious when there is so little agreement among psychiatrists relating even to the most fundamental concepts and definitions. Definite proof would require a special investigation, carefully planned and methodologically more adequate than these *ad hoc* comparisons.

PSYCHOTHERAPY WITH CHILDREN

Our review here will follow very closely that published by Levitt (1957), who has summarized a large number of published and unpublished studies and arranged them in tables patterned on that published by the writer in connection with adults. Levitt also used as the "unit of measurement" the evaluation of the degree of improvement of the patient by the clinicians concerned: "Individuals listed as 'much improved, improved, partially improved, successful, partially successful, adjusted, partially adjusted, satisfactory,' etc., will be grouped under the general heading of improved. The unimproved cases were found in groupings like 'slightly improved, unimproved, unadjusted, failure, worse,' etc."

For various good reasons Levitt refused to use the discharge rate of children's wards in state hospitals as a base-line for evaluating the effects of psychotherapy. Instead he made use of a rather different group of children—

> A common phenomenon of the child guidance clinic is the patient who is accepted for treatment, but who voluntarily breaks off the clinic relationship without ever being treated. In institutions where the service load is heavy and the waiting period between acceptance and onset of treatment may range up to six months, this group of patients is often quite large. Theoretically, they have the characteristics of an adequate control group. So far as is known, they are similar to treated groups in every respect except for the factor of treatment itself. Nevertheless, the use of this type of group as a control is not common in follow-up evaluations of the efficacy of treatment. Three studies report follow-up data on such groups. Of these, the data of Morris and Soroker (1953) are not suitable for the purposes of this paper. Of their seventy-two cases, at least eleven had treatment elsewhere between the last formal contact with the clinic and the point of evaluation, while an indeterminate number had problems too minor to warrant clinic treatment. The samples in the remaining two studies appear satisfactory as sources of baseline data. Witmer and Keller (1942) appraised their group eight to thirteen years after clinic treatment, and reported that 78 per cent were improved. In the Lehrman study (1949), a one-year follow-up interval found 70 per cent improved. The overall rate of improvement for one hundred and sixty cases in both reports is 72.5 per cent. This figure will be used as the baseline for evaluating the results of treatment of children.

It is, as will be noted, identical with that used by the writer with adults.

As regards the results of psychotherapy, Levitt, like Eysenck, rejects a number of studies for various reasons, such as peculiar or inadequate presentation of data, or because results for children and adults were inseparable. The remaining studies cover an age range from pre-school to 21 years at the time of the original clinic contact. However, very few patients were over 18 years at that time, and not many were over 17. At a rough estimate Levitt states that the median age would be about 10 years.

The data are presented in the form of two tables, the first stating the results at the close of psychotherapy. Table 6 shows that the average percentage of im-

TABLE 6   *Summary of Results of Psychotherapy with Children at Close*
(Quoted from Levitt (1957) by permission of the Editor, "J. Cons. Psychol.")

Study	N	Much improved		Partially improved		Unimproved		Per cent improved
Cohen, Marion, *et al.*	100	13	18		12	8	3	80.7
Hubbard, Ruth M., *et al.*	57	16	18		42	26	1	73.0
Irgens, Effie M.	70	12	29		19	10		85.7
Reid, J. H., *et al.*	250	54	82		46	68		72.8
Lehrman, L. J., *et al.*	196	76		52		68		65.3
La More, Mary T.	50	15		18		17		66.0
Christianson, Eva, *et al.*	126	25		54		47		62.7
Witmer, Helen L., *et al.*	290	75		154		61		79.0
Barbour, R. F.	814	207		398		209		74.3
Newell, N. W.	72	26		31		15		79.2
Lee, P. R., *et al.*	196	93		61		42		78.6
Brown, Marjorie	27	5		11		11		59.3
Carpenter, Jean A.	31	13		8		10		67.7
Canaday, Louise J.	23	2		9		12		47.8
Burlingham, Susan	75	35		22		18		76.0
Albright, Sue, *et al.*	80	31		21		28		65.0
Maas, H. S., *et al.*	522	225				297		43.1
Cunningham, J. M., *et al.*	420	251				169		59.8
All cases	3,399	1,174		1,105		1,120		67.05
Per cent	100.00	34.54		32.51		32.95		

provement, i.e. the combined percentages in the much improved and partially improved categories is 67.05 at close. "As in the case of Eysenck's data, there is a considerable amount of consistency, considering the interstudy differences in methodology, definition, etc."

Table 7 gives the results of follow-up evaluations, and in this table the follow-up interval is given as a range of years. The average percentage of improvement in the follow-up studies is given as 78.22 per cent. Two further studies are quoted by Levitt as combining close and follow-up evaluation and are given in Table 8. The percentage of improvement for these studies is 73.98, roughly intermediate between the averages of the other two tables. Levitt points out that "the discrepancy between results at close and at follow-up suggests that time is a factor in improvement," and he quotes Denker's study in support of the generalization that "the rate of improvement as a function of time . . . is negatively accelerating." He then goes on to present a rank-order correlation between estimated median follow-up interval and percentage of improvement in the seventeen studies in Table 7, which turns out to be 0.48 and is statistically significant. Plotting the amount of improvement against time shows that "the curve is more or less the same as that of Denker's data, negatively accelerating with most of the

TABLE 7   *Summary of Results of Psychotherapy with Children at Follow-up*

(Quoted from Levitt (1957) by permission of the Editor, "J. Cons. Psychol.")

Study	Interval in years	N	Much improved		Partially improved	Unimproved		Per cent improved
Lee, P. R., et al.	1–5	197	49	55	39	38	16	72.6
Brown, Jane L.	2	33	8	11	7	6	1	78.8
Cohen, Marion, et al.	2–3	57	25	17	6	6	3	84.2
Witmer, Helen L.[1]	1–10	366	81	78	106	101		72.4
Irgens, Effie M.	2–3	70	21	30	13	6		91.4
Walcott, Esther	5–8	17	7		3	4	3	58.8
Lehrman, L. J., et al.	1	196	99		46	51		74.0
Morris, D. P., et al.	16–27	34	22		11	1		97.1
Barbour, R. F.	1–20	705	358		225	122		82.7
Bronner, Augusta F.	5–18	650	355		181	114		82.5
Maberly, A., et al.	3–15	484	111		264	109		77.5
Fenton, N., et al.	1–4	732	179		398	155		78.8
Cunningham, J. M., et al.	5	359	228		80	51		85.8
Gollander, Barbara	1–2	25	6		12	7		72.0
Moses, Jane	1–2	25	10		6	9		64.0
Maas, H. S., et al.	½–1½	191	82			109		42.9
Healy, W., et al.	1–20	78	71			7		91.0
Per cent	4.8[2]	4,219	1,712		1,588	919		78.22
All cases		100.00	40.58		37.64	21.78		

[1] Data based on thirteen studies originally reported in Witmer, Helen L., et al., 1935; results of eight of these are included here.

[2] Estimated average follow-up interval per case.

TABLE 8   *Summary of Results of Psychotherapy with Children Based on Combined Close-Follow-up Evaluation*

(Quoted from Levitt (1957) by permission of the Editor, "J. Cons. Psychol.")

Study	Interval in years	N	Much improved		Partially improved		Unimproved		Per cent improved
Jacobsen, Virginia	1–10	339	94		81	76	42	46	74.04
Johnson, Lillian J., et al.	1–10	30		9	13		8		73.33
All cases	5.5[1]	369	103		170		96		73.98
Per cent		100.00	27.91		46.07		26.02		

[1] Estimated average follow-up interval per case.

improvement accomplished by 2½ years. . . . This analysis suggests that improvement is in part a function of time, but the mechanisms involved remain purely speculative. Future comparisons of the results of psychotherapy should properly take this factor into consideration."

Levitt discusses certain features of his data at some length and finally comes to the conclusion that "the therapeutic eclecticism, the number of subjects, the results, and the conclusions of this paper are markedly similar to that of Eysenck's study. Two-thirds of the patients examined at close and about three-quarters seen in follow-up have improved. Approximately the same percentages of improvement are found for comparable groups of untreated children. . . . It now appears that Eysenck's conclusion concerning the data for adult psychotherapy is applicable to children as well; the results do not support the hypothesis that recovery from neurotic disorder is facilitated by psychotherapy."

In evaluation of Levitt's study it should perhaps be said that his control groups are less well chosen than might ideally be desired. Patients who voluntarily break off the clinic relationship while still on the waiting list are perhaps likely to be suffering from less severe and disabling disorders than those who persevere. If that were so then we would expect this group to have a higher spontaneous rating of remission than those who remain. As Levitt points out, it is not known that there are in fact any such differences between the groups, but the possibility cannot be disregarded and ought certainly to be investigated. The fact that although there have been over sixty years of psychotherapeutic work with children Levitt failed to discover in the literature a single properly controlled study, or a single investigation providing unambiguous evidence regarding a base-line figure for untreated groups, is perhaps the most eloquent testimony for the failure of clinical psychologists and psychiatrists to take seriously their task of appraising the effects of the methods they use.

Levitt's original study was supported by the results of a long range follow-up study at the Institute for Juvenile Research in Chicago, one of the largest community child guidance clinics in the United States. Treated groups were compared with defector controls from the same clinic population on 26 variables, and no differences were found.

The criticism made above of the use of defector groups has also been repeated by Eisenberg and Gruenberg (1961), Heinicke (1960) and Hood-Williams (1960). Levitt (1960) replied to this criticism and showed that data from several studies suggest that defectors are not in fact a biased control group and that the criticisms made on these grounds are therefore not as damaging as was at first thought.

Another criticism which has been made relates to the failure to distinguish among diagnostic categories, thus possibly obfuscating an evaluation of outcome. Levitt (1963) carried out an analysis on 22 evaluation studies grouped by type of disorder. "The results of this second review of evaluation of outcome of therapy with children are similar to those of the earlier review and like those earlier findings, do not differ markedly from results obtained with defector cases. And again, the inescapable conclusion is that available evaluation studies do not furnish a reasonable basis for the hypothesis that psychotherapy facilitates recovery from emotional illness in children. Apart from this global inference, the data suggest that there is merit in Eisenberg's contention that comparisons of treated and defector cases should be made within diagnostic categories. It appears that the improvement rate with psychotherapy is lowest for cases of delinquency and antisocial acting-out, and highest for identifiable behavioural symptoms, like enuresis and school phobia. However, until the required comparisons are actually made, it would be incautious to conclude that therapy is more or less successful with any diagnostic group. It is perfectly possible that the spontaneous remission rate, as indicated by appropriate defector control groups, is also lower for the delinquents and higher for the special symptoms, and that the differences which are found . . . simply reflect these facts.

THE WOLPE STUDY

As Winder (1957) has pointed out—

In psychotherapy, it is assumed that the therapist adopts a set of ground rules which guide his behavior. Although the limiting case is probably never achieved, the ideal therapist's contribution would be completely deliberate. This is not to say that therapy cannot be effective if done intuitively, nor that the therapist can be a disinterested administrator of doses of this and that. It is to say that the ideal therapist would provide whatever is essential to therapy (warmth, empathic emotion arousal, intellectual understanding, nonjudgemental understanding, rewards, and punishments, etc.) on the basis of reason and knowledge. The next step is obviously the investigation of the effects of defined techniques, when used with particular kinds of patients, within particular contexts.

This view is also shared by Shoben, when he writes—

> No matter how eclectic the counselor's manner of approach to a diagnostic judgement, it seems inevitable that he make use of some theory. Indeed, "clinical intuition" seems to represent in part this kind of utilization of theory when it has been sufficiently well practiced to occur with great rapidity. Certainly, one rarely encounters "intuitive" behavior of this kind in counselors without considerable training and experience. If this point holds in any significant degree, and if one recalls the finding of Holtzmann and Sells (1954) that clinicians were consistently wrong in their predictions, but that they agreed remarkably well among themselves in their errors, then one can hardly escape the suspicion that something must be amiss in available theories typically employed by clinicians. Even though the situation may have been one where actuarial methods were more appropriate, the agreement in errors hints at some common stereotypes among counselors, rather than at useful theoretical constructs.

As regards the usual process of psychotherapy, some doubt has been thrown on the existence of marked differences in practice deriving from differences in theory by Fiedler (1950, 1951, 1953) whose investigations have emphasized the role of experience as opposed to that of theoretical preconception. Strupp (1955) has come to similar conclusions regarding experience as a predominant determinant. Certainly the differences between "psychoanalysis" and "psychoanalytic orientated psychotherapy" appear to be vanishing. This seems to be tacitly admitted by Alexander (1953) whose contribution is summarized by Meehl (1955) as follows: "He has been making a very convincing case to the effect that the two products are not 'essentially different,' so long as both are (a) mainly uncovering rather than supportive and (b) based on adequate dynamic formulations. It almost looks as though Alexander shares with his more orthodox colleagues the need to keep a monopoly on the prestigeful term 'psychoanalyst,' in spite of the steady breakdown, both in theory and practice, of the distinction it once really made." Certainly psychologists working in mental hospitals will have found it more and more difficult to distinguish in actual practice between adherents of different schools and different theories, and to a very real degree, therefore, it might be said that our device of distinguishing between different schools by appropriate subscripts may be a task of supererogation.

There is one outstanding exception to this general rule, and that is the kind of therapy which derives its theoretical justification not from psychoanalysis but from learning theory, and which may suitably be labelled psychotherapy$_{LT}$. A long discussion of what is implied in this has been given by the writer elsewhere (Eysenck, 1959), and several chapters in this book are concerned with an elaboration of the principles involved. Here we shall only take note of this novel departure in order to introduce the work of Wolpe (1952, 1954, 1958) who is probably the outstanding exponent of this point of view, and who has published figures on the therapeutic successes of his method and compared them with published figures of the success of psychoanalysis in similar cases. Briefly, Wolpe bases his therapy on the following hypothesis: "When fundamental psychotherapeutic effects are obtained in neuroses—no matter by what therapist—these effects are nearly always really a consequence of the occurrence of reciprocal inhibition of neurotic anxiety responses, i.e. the complete or partial suppression of the anxiety responses as a consequence of the simultaneous evocation of other responses physiologically antagonistic to anxiety." In his view, "neurotic behaviour is persistent unadaptive learned behaviour in which anxiety is almost always prominent and which is acquired in anxiety-generating situations. By 'anxiety' is meant the autonomic response pattern or patterns that are characteristically part of the given organism's response to noxious stimulation, and the term is applied irrespective of the duration of the autonomic responses or of what has led to them. Anxiety response is unadaptive when it is evoked in circumstances in which there is objectively no threat."

This theory differs radically from the psychoanalytic and has given rise to methods of treatment which also differ profoundly from those usually classified under psychotherapy. Wolpe has reported on a total of one hundred and twenty-two patients treated by him, making use in his report of five criteria originally suggested by Knight (1951): "symptomatic improvement, increased productiveness, improved adjustment and pleasure in sex, improved interpersonal relationships, and ability to handle ordinary psychological conflicts and reasonable reality stresses." In addition, the patient's score on Willoughby's questionnaire is compared with his score at the beginning of treatment, and no patient is regarded as greatly benefited unless his score has dropped markedly, preferably to 20 or less.

Wolpe compared the total results of his investigations with reported results from two large psychoanalytic institutions involving almost four hundred cases. He reports that 90 per cent of his patients were either apparently cured or much improved, and only about 60 per cent of those cases treated by psychoanalysis. "If the favourable results of the present series are, to the extent of 60 per cent, regarded as due to the non-specific reciprocal inhibition that would occur in any kind of interview situation, the additional 30 per cent of good results appear to be attributable to the special measures for obtaining reciprocal inhibition described above. Furthermore, the small average number of interviews needed (four-fifths of the patients had thirty interviews or less) suggests that the use of these special measures early in treatment greatly accelerates the improvement of those patients who would have responded to the nonspecific factor alone." Several replications have been carried out of Wolpe's work such as the study by Lazarus (1963), and Wolpe himself has extended his treatment to larger numbers of cases. Much of this work will be found in Experiments in Behavior Therapy (Eysenck, 1964) and in the pages of the new journal "Behavior Research and Therapy" (Pergamon Press) which was founded specifically to report experiments and researches in the field of behaviour therapy.

It is, of course, impossible to accept either Wolpe's theory or his figures without question. As regards the theory, he appears to be concerned almost exclusively with dysthymic disorders and to disregard hysterics and psychopaths. There may, as the writer has suggested (Eysenck, 1957), be other methods in addition to that of reciprocal inhibition which may lead to extinction of the faulty emotional habits which constitute the neurotic disorder. As regards the published figures it would clearly have been more satisfactory if a control group had been included in the experimental design; the difficulties of using published figures as a control have been pointed out earlier in this chapter. This criticism cannot detract from the very great importance of Wolpe's work. By using the standards of recovery advocated and widely used by psychoanalysts, he has obviated the main criticism that might have been brought against him, namely that of using a more lenient criterion than the psychoanalysts. By publishing a number of his cases in considerable detail he has made it possible for the reader to judge whether the type of patient treated by him is comparable to the type of patient who usually has recourse to psychoanalytic treatment. All in all, criticism of the weaknesses of his paper would come badly from those whose theories have never been submitted to a more rigorous and well-designed test. Of all the hundreds of papers and books examined the writer has found this to be the only one to give positive evidence in favour of one specified type of psychotherapy. Obviously a repetition of the work is urgently required, preferably with two or more control groups to duplicate psychoanalytic treatment, eclectic treatment, non-psychiatric medical treatment, non-directive treatment and no treatment at all. The fact that Wolpe's treatment is so firmly anchored in a very definite theoretical framework which governs the therapeutic procedures much more directly than is usually the case, makes a test of his hypothesis very much easier than would be a similar test of the Freudian or Jungian theory. The considerable difference in approach between Wolpe and the majority of psychiatrists suggests that it may be advisable not to discard our subscripts to the term "psychotherapy" yet.

One study has recently appeared under the authorship of Cooper (1963) which is relevant here. It purports to compare the effects of behaviour therapy and orthodox psychotherapy. Indeed this study might be thought to belong in the previous section dealing with "Studies Using a Control Group" were it not for the fact that the comparison group used was not in fact a proper control group. Cooper was able to locate 30 patients who had been treated by means of behaviour therapy at the Maudsley Hospital and for whom a one-year follow-up was possible. As far as possible, control cases were located from the files in such a way that they should be similar to the experimental group in age, sex, symptom duration before treatment and severity of symptom. In spite of the large number of patients treated during the years involved, only 16 control cases were found.

Results were a slightly better outcome for the behaviour therapy cases. There were 10 phobic cases in each of the two groups, and at the end of treatment the ratio of improved to unimproved was 9 : 1 for behaviour therapy and 5 : 5 for the controls; this difference just fails to reach the usually accepted level of significance.

The results of this study, while interesting, should not be taken too seriously for two reasons. In the first place, the two groups are not strictly comparable, as referral for behaviour therapy during the years in question was frequently on the basis of using it as a last resort and after everything else had failed; this would necessarily bias the outcome against behaviour therapy. Secondly, the psychologists who carried out behaviour therapy were only just beginning to experiment with the techniques, and had not received any satisfactory form of training in these methods (which indeed at the time were only in the process of being worked out). Results achieved by them therefore are not representative of what well trained behaviour therapists like Wolpe or Lazarus would be able to achieve at the present time.

THE LAKIN PHILLIPS STUDY

Somewhat analogous to the Wolpe Studies in the adult field is the Phillips (1957) study in the child behaviour field. Like Wolpe, Phillips declines to use methods based on psychoanalytic theories and puts forward his own "interference" theory, based on modern learning theory. Again, like Wolpe, he applies this theory to actual clinical cases and compares the outcome and the duration of his treatment with psychoanalytic treatment. It might be thought that his study would deserve to be regarded as coming under our heading of "Studies Using a Control Group"; it is included here because it did not contain an *untreated* control group, and because the psychoanalytically treated sample which constitutes his control was selected by the therapists according to different principles from those covering Phillips' own selection.

The theory involved may best be summed up in the author's own words—

Very briefly considered, interference theory constitutes the viewpoint that behavior—pathological or otherwise—is a result of various *assertions* made by the individual about himself or about his relationship with others. The person chooses now one kind of behavior, now another, depending on what kind of behavior seems likely to bring (from the environment) confirmation of his assertions. Certain behavior possibilities "interfere" with each other, that is, the person cannot do both at the same time. However, since possible behavior is always selected by a person on the basis of its appropriateness to the environment, the whole process with which we are concerned goes on "in the open." Depth views which regard the mental life of people as having a kind of deep-going reservoir from which diabolical forces spring, are entirely anathema to the present viewpoint. The depth view is essentially untestable—an elementary, too elementaristic view, one that cannot meet the complexity of problems that we contrive in the laboratory, see in the nursery school, or meet daily in a myriad of practical situations.

The results of comparing an assertion-structured therapy with psychoanalytic therapy are given in Table 8. Before turning to this table, it should be noted that the number of interviews required by Phillips' method was less than half that required by psychoanalytic methods, a difference which was highly significant statistically. Introducing Table 9, Phillips writes as follows—

Existing follow-up research on psychotherapy deals almost exclusively with the outcomes of treatment among patients who completed (or nearly completed) therapy. Interest here is shown in the *total problem:* that is, in tracing the *efficiency* with which therapy is brought to the patients, and the *effectiveness* it was judged to have by both patient and therapist on a follow-up basis. This manner of proceeding can give us a more complete picture of the observed value of psychotherapy.

In order to do this, three groups are compared here as to their effectiveness and efficiency; a group treated by the depth-oriented, psychoanalytically-derived methods; a group treated by the assertion-structured therapy method (representing the viewpoint of this book); and a hypothetical group illustrating what one might expect under near-optimum conditions in out-patient, parent-child treatment.

As Phillips points out, "the results shown [in Table 9] suggest strongly that there are real differences in the effectiveness and efficiency of out-patient, parent-child psychotherapy, when assertion-structured therapy and psychoanalytic-derived depth methods are compared." Particularly striking, in looking at the figures for psychoanalytic therapy, is that of all those applying for therapy, only 25 per cent (forty-five out of one hundred and ninety) were actually accepted for

TABLE 9   *Comparing the Efficiency and Effectiveness of Hypothetical (Ideal) Therapy, Assertion-Structured Therapy, and Depth-Oriented Therapy*
(Quoted by permission from Phillips, 1957)

	1	2	3	4	5	6	7
	Number applying for therapy	*Number treated from among applicants*	*Number refused treatment by clinicians*	*Number who themselves refuse treatment*	*Number completing 3 or more interviews*	*Number benefited by 3 or more interviews*	*Percentage of original applicants benefited*
Hypothetical group	100	90	5	5	90	90	81
Assertion structured therapy	59	53	—	6	53	51	86.4
Psychoanalytic depth-oriented therapy	190	45	103	42	45	21[1] (patients' rating) 33[1] (therapists' rating)	11.05[1] (patients' rating) 17.3[1] (therapists' rating)

[1] Therapists' ratings were available for all forty-five patients who completed three or more interviews. Only twenty-seven of these forty-five patients returned questionnaires rating their therapy experience; the twenty-one who rated themselves as having improved somewhat supplied the figures used here.

therapy; over half of all applications were refused treatment by clinicians! "This seems like an enormously large figure and one that is not reflected in the subjective writings and appraisals of clinicians when they report on or discuss therapeutic success and failure."

Phillips has here drawn attention to a fact which is obviously important in evaluating the respective successes of different types of therapy, but which is hardly ever mentioned in the literature. Psychoanalysts are usually very selective in accepting cases for treatment, and unless the proportion of cases accepted for treatment out of the total number of the cases applying for treatment is known, it is impossible to compare the results of psychoanalytic treatment with some other treatment (or no treatment at all) where no such selection has taken place. There is a certain amount of knowledge and agreement as to good and bad prognostic signs in neurotic and psychotic disorders, and by a suitable selection of cases for treatment, it should be easy to beat the "no treatment" or "other treatment" groups not using such a process of selection. It is somewhat puzzling to the writer, in view of these considerations, that no superiority of psychoanalytic methods over others has in fact been demonstrated. Many reasons can be adduced for this; thus it might be that the total effect of psychoanalytic treatment is actually negative, thus cancelling out the effects of selection, or it might be that our principles of selection and prognosis are less valid than is commonly thought. However that might be, this is a point which should be borne in mind in all future studies.

If we disregard these considerations and concentrate on the number of patients completing three or more interviews, we find that fifty-one out of fifty-three are benefited by assertion-structure therapy, but only twenty-one out of forty-five are so benefited by psychoanalytic therapy. These figures are significantly different from each other and suggest strongly the superiority of the non-psychoanalytic method.

It is difficult not to agree with Phillips in his summing up—

> One may produce certain arguments against interpreting these results as being in any way adverse so far as psychoanalytic depth-derived, parent-child, out-patient treatment cases are concerned. One might say that the methods used are not "true psychoanalysis" of children. However, the record of "true" psychoanalysis of children is hardly better, if as good: witness the work of Klein and Anna Freud. The argument for depth-derived practices cannot be bolstered on the basis of probable value latent in unstudied and unreported upon therapeutic results of psychoanalysis of children. The hard reality here is that, first, there are no convincing results of a follow-up nature that can be used to support psychoanalytically derived (or "true" psychoanalysis) treatment of children; and, second, that the results that do exist fail to support any very hopeful view regarding the effectiveness and efficiency of depth-derived, parent-child, out-patient psychotherapy.

THE ALBERT ELLIS STUDY

A third study comparing psychoanalytic and other types of psychotherapy is reported by Ellis (1957). He himself has used, on his patients, psychoanalytic psychotherapy of the orthodox kind; psychoanalytically oriented psychotherapy; and finally what he calls "rational psychotherapy"—

> The main emphasis of the therapist who employs rational techniques is on analysing the client's current problems—especially his negative feelings of anger, depression, anxiety and guilt—and concretely showing him that these emotions arise, not from past events or external situations, but from his present irrational attitudes toward, or illogical fears about, these events and situations. . . . Where, in psychoanalytic techniques, considerable time is spent on showing the patient how he originally *became* neurotic, in rational analysis much more emphasis is placed on how he is *sustaining* his disturbance by *still* believing the nonsense, or illogical ideas, which first led him to feel and act in an aberrated fashion.

Two groups, closely matched as to diagnosis, age, sex and education were formed, each consisting of seventy-eight cases. The first group consisted of individuals treated with rational techniques over an average period of twenty-six sessions; the second group consisted of seventy-eight patients treated with psychoanalytically oriented techniques over an average of thirty-five sessions. In addition, there was a group of sixteen patients treated by orthodox psychoanalysis, and having an average of ninety-three sessions. Ellis himself treated all the patients in these three groups, and rated them soon after each case had been closed, in terms of whether he or she had made (a) little or no progress while being seen; (b) some distinct improvement; or (c) considerable improvement.

Ellis found "that therapeutic results appear to be best for clients treated with rational analysis and poorest for those treated with orthodox analysis . . . significantly more clients treated with rational analysis showed considerable improvement and significantly fewer showed little or no improvement than clients treated with the other two techniques." The actual proportions of cases showing distinct or considerable improvement were 90 per cent for rational psychotherapy, 63 per cent for psychoanalytically oriented psychotherapy, and 50 per cent for orthodox psychoanalysis. These figures should be seen in the light of the fact that orthodox psychoanalysis was carried on for three times as many sessions as rational psychotherapy. Ellis concludes: "While the obtained data of the study do not offer incontrovertible proof of the superiority of the technique of rational psychotherapy, they strongly indicate that neither orthodox nor liberal psychoanalytic procedures may be the very last word in effective technique."

Without the use of a non-treated control group it is difficult to say whether the patients treated by rational psychotherapy did better than those treated psychoanalytically because rational psychotherapy had a positive effect, or because psychoanalytic therapy had a negative effect. The former appears to be the more likely hypothesis, when taken in conjunction with data previously quoted, although the other hypothesis may not be altogether absurd. Ellis does not attempt to derive his rational psychotherapy from learning theory, but this should not be impossible. There are obvious similarities, as well as differences, in the approaches of Ellis, Phillips, and Wolpe, and it is to be hoped that properly controlled studies will soon be initiated to test the specific hypotheses of these authors, and compare the resuts of their methods of treatment.

Discussion, Summary and Conclusions

In this concluding section we will first of all state very briefly the main conclusions which may be drawn from the researchers outlined above, and will then go on to discuss certain theoretical points to which these conclusions are relevant. The qualifications to which the conclusions are subject have been fully stated in the text and will not be repeated. Nor will it be emphasized again that these conclusions are simply a summary of the existing literature and may have to be changed when further more adequate research is reported.

It appears that eight major conclusions can be derived from the literature—

1. When untreated neurotic control groups are compared with experimental groups of neurotic patients treated by means of psychotherapy, both groups recover to approximately the same extent.

2. When soldiers who have suffered a neurotic breakdown and have not received psychotherapy are compared with soldiers who have received psychotherapy, the chance of the two groups returning to duty are approximately equal.

3. When neurotic soldiers are separated from the Service, their chances of recovery are not affected by their receiving or not receiving psychotherapy.

4. Civilian neurotics who are treated by psychotherapy recover or improve to approximately the same extent as similar neurotics receiving no psychotherapy.

5. Children suffering from emotional disorders and treated by psychotherapy recover or improve to approximately the same extent as similar children not receiving psychotherapy.

6. Neurotic patients treated by means of psychotherapeutic procedures based on learning theory, improve significantly more quickly than do patients treated by means of psychoanalytic or eclectic psychotherapy, or not treated by psychotherapy at all.

7. Neurotic patients treated by psychoanalytic psychotherapy do not improve more quickly than patients treated by means of eclectic psychotherapy, and may improve less quickly when account is taken of the large proportion of patients breaking off treatment.

8. With the single exception of the psychotherapeutic methods based on learning theory, results of published research with military and civilian neurotics, and with both adults and children, suggest that the therapeutic effects of psychotherapy are small or non-existent, and do not in any demonstrable way add to the non-specific effects of routine medical treatment, or to such events as occur in the patients' everyday experience.

These conclusions go a little beyond those which resulted from the writer's original survey of the literature which was published in 1952. The conclusion then was simply that published research failed to disprove the null-hypothesis with respect to psychotherapeutic effectiveness. The additional studies which have come to hand since, particularly those making use of a control group, have been so uniformly negative in their outcome that a somewhat stronger conclusion appears warranted. Methodologically, of course, it is impossible to prove that any treatment has no effect whatsoever, and no such conclusion is implied. The results do show that whatever effects psychotherapy may have are likely to be extremely small; if they were large as compared with the effects of non-specific treatments and events it seems reasonable to suppose that some effects would have been found in the studies quoted. It is possible, of course, that effects were looked for in the wrong quarter; psychotherapy may affect personality traits and behaviour patterns other than those relevant to psychiatric improvement as ordinarily understood. In the absence of specific hypotheses and experimental research there is no fruitful way of discussing such a possibility. The writer must admit to being somewhat surprised at the uniformly negative results issuing from all this work. In advancing his rather challenging conclusion in the 1952 report, the main motive was one of stimulating better and more worthwhile research in this important but somewhat neglected field; there was an underlying belief that while results to date had not disproved the null-hypothesis, improved methods of research would undoubtedly do so. Such a belief does not seem to be tenable any longer in this easy optimistic form, and it rather seems that psychologists and psychiatrists will have to acknowledge the fact that current psychotherapeutic procedures have not lived up to the hopes which greeted their emergence fifty years ago.

Clearly the matter cannot be left there. It will be necessary in the first place to account for the fact that so many therapists and so many patients believe quite firmly in the efficacy of psychotherapy; this is an undoubted fact which appears to be in contradiction to our conclusion and requires explanation. In the second place it will be necessary to examine the consequences of our conclusions, in so far as they are relevant to psychological theories of neurotic disorder and breakdown; quite clearly the failure of a commonly held belief to be supported by the facts must have some repercussion on widely-held theories which have given rise to such beliefs.

To take the first point first we may perhaps take a clue from Meehl (1955). In a quotation already given he pointed out that therapeutic experiences could be explained within a crude statistical model which assigns very little specific power to therapeutic intervention. If the majority of neurotics tend to improve under moderately favourable external circumstances anyway, those who are under therapy while improving will be talking about their current actions and feelings in the sessions, and client and therapist will naturally attribute any changes to the therapy. Meehl goes on like this—

How will such a statistical system be experienced by therapists? Very much as therapy admittedly appears to its candid practitioners. The best cases are types which seem most likely to improve anyhow. Sometimes there are temporal associations between improvement and interview events of the kind considered important, at other times such covariation is disconcertingly lacking. The therapist gradually conceptualizes the client, but there seems to be no clear-cut connection between the client's learning of this conceptualization and outcome . . . The therapist is like a Skinner-box rat on a schedule of intermittent reinforcement, which generates habits notoriously resistive to extinction. A sprinkling of even 5 or 10 per cent of "specific cures," cases whose shift towards recovery would not have occurred without intervention, could combine with the life-cures and the (unimproved) upswing terminators to yield the experiences therapists actually have in their daily work.

With this statement of the model the present writer would wholeheartedly agree, except that he can find no evidence for the "sprinkling of even 5 or 10 per cent specific cures." The fact that improvement is taking place in the whole group of patients all the time in conformity with the formula given previously will produce sufficient reinforcement for the growth of very strong beliefs in the efficacy of therapy, prayer, shock treatment, confession, or whatever else may in point of time be associated with the improvement which is taking place anyway. The fact that so many different types of treatment of neurotic disorders and so many different theories regarding neurotic disorders have found enthusiastic adherents among both therapists and patients thus finds an adequate explanation in terms of this hypothesis which is fully in conformity with the teaching of modern learning theories.

The psychoanalytic view, which is probably much the most widely accepted of all, would seem to generate certain very definite conclusions. Among these would be the following: (1) neurotic disorders have complex roots in early childhood experiences; (2) such neuroses are not self-limiting but relatively permanent; (3) they do not become extinguished in the ordinary way but require definite psychotherapy; (4) such psychotherapy requires the uncovering of the roots which lie at the base of the neurotic disorder; (5) only psychoanalysis, as a method based on Freudian theory, can carry this task to successful conclusion.

The facts summarized in this chapter contradict, in a fairly conclusive manner, all these statements.[3] We have found that neurotic disorders tend to be self-limiting, that psychonalysis is no more successful than any other method, and that in fact all methods of psychotherapy fail to improve on the recovery rate obtained through ordinary life experiences and non-specific treatment. What is even more conclusive, we have found that there is strong evidence to suggest that short methods of treatment based on an alternative hypothesis are significantly more successful in treating neurotic disorders than is psychotherapy of the psychoanalytic type. This alternative method is based on a point of view which regards neurotic disorders as conditioned responses or learnt habits which are non-adaptive, but which are persistent because they are constantly receiving reinforcement. Like all other habits they are subject to extinction according to rules elab-

---

[3] It is interesting that Jaspers (1948), perhaps the most sophisticated and knowledgeable of modern psychiatrists, has no doubt in his own mind that, as far as therapeutic success is concerned, psychiatrists and psychoanalysts are decidedly inferior to all sorts of quacks and "headshrinkers." "Es ist selbstverständlich dass den grössten Erfolg nicht Nervenärzte, sonder—in früheren Zieten—Schamanen, Priester und Sektenstifter, Wundermänner, Beichtväter und Seelenführer gehabt haben." He specifically quotes Ignatius Loyola, Yoga, Lourdes, and "die Gemütskurbewegung in Amerika."

orated by modern learning theory and sufficiently well understood to make possible deductions which can be tested experimentally. All the facts summarized in this chapter fall in line with this alternative hypothesis, and there are none which contradict it. It would appear advisable, therefore, to discard the psychoanalytic model, which both on the theoretical and practical plain fails to be useful in mediating verifiable predictions, and to adopt, provisionally at least, the learning theory model which, to date, appears to be much more promising theoretically and also with regard to application. Much further evidence is available to reinforce this suggestion and will be found in other chapters of this book; all we can say in conclusion is that such work as had been done on the effects of psychotherapy not only fails to contradict, but lends strong support to this general conclusion.

The more fair-minded psychoanalysts do not appear on the whole to oppose this denial of therapeutic usefulness or theoretical and experimental appropriateness of their model and method. Glover (1955) specifically renounces therapeutic effects, and has the following to say about psychoanalytic research (Glover, 1952, as summarized by Saslow, 1954)—

> The possibility that the psychoanalysts, who gave the impetus to the enormous enrichment of psychological understanding of the last decades, will save the general situation is made to seem rather remote by the picture of psychoanalytic research presented by Glover. His address before the International Psycho-Analytical Congress on research methods in psychoanalysis is based on his own long clinical experience and his observations as Director of Research of the London Institute of Psycho-Analysis for sixteen years. He believes there has been an increasing tendency by psychoanalysts not to apply to their data such scientific controls as are available. He described vividly how hearsay evidence becomes attested conclusion (given an analyst with seniority, enthusiasm or plain dogmatism); how a student whose professional career depends on overcoming "resistance" to the satisfaction of his training analyst can hardly be expected to defend his own scientific integrity against his analyst's theories and practice; so that inherent in the training situation is a tendency to perpetuate error; how, no matter how ideal their own analysis, individual analysts tend to show at meetings and elsewhere their own conflicts and "favorite pathological mechanisms"; how these three factors lead to the stereotyped proceedings of the Psycho-Analytical Association; and how peculiarly susceptible to fashion, "canalized no doubt through a hierarchy of transferences and counter-transferences" are psychoanalytic groups. He has the impression that present-day psychoanalytic teaching preserves many of the disadvantages of mid-Victorian pedagogy and few of its advantages, and that the deficiencies of such authoritarian spoon-feeding are not remedied, as is often thought, by the candidate's training analysis. He believes it is time these issues were faced, and that a first task of psychoanalysts is to settle down to the arduous task of defining terms, verifying criteria, and developing reliable statistics. His portrayal of the association between lack of scientific productivity and the psychoanalytic training procedure is that of a self-reinforcing system with tremendous internal resistance to change.

If this be true, and it is difficult to disagree with Glover on these points, then the task of those desirous of advancing to a truly scientific study of psychotherapy will be made much more difficult than need be by the opposition of practitioners more interested in the preservation of the *status quo* than in new theories, new methods, and scientific advance generally.

References

Albright, S., and Gambrell, H. "Personality traits as criteria for the psychiatric treatment of adolescents." *Smith Coll. Stud. Soc. Wk.*, 1938, 9, 1–26.

Alexander, F. *Five Year Report of the Chicago Institute for Psycho-analysis,* 1932–1937.

Alexander, F. "Current views on psychotherapy." *Psychiatry,* 1953, 16, 111–123.

Anker, J. M. "Behavior modification in chronic schizophrenia." In H. J. Eysenck (Ed.), *Experiments in behaviour therapy.* Oxford: Pergamon Press, 1964.

Anker, J. M., and Walsh, R. O. "Group psychotherapy, a special activity program and group structure in the treatment of chronic schizophrenia." *J. Consult. Psychol.,* 1961, 25, 476–481.

Barbour, R. F. "Selected surveys prepared for the inter-clinic conference." In J. F. Davidson (Ed.), *Follow-up on child guidance cases 49–59.* Ninth Child Guidance Inter-Clinic Conference, London, 1951.

Barendregt, J. T. "A psychological investigation of the effects of psychoanalysis and psychotherapy." In J. T. Barendregt (Ed.), *Res. in psychodiadnostics.* Paris: Mouton, 1961.

Barron, F. and Leary, T. F. "Changes in psychoneurotic patients with and without psychotherapy." *J. Cons. Psychol.,* 1955, 19, 239–245.

Bixenstine, V. E. "A case study of the use of palmar sweating as a measure of psychological tension." *J. Abnorm. (Soc.) Psychol.,* 1955, 50, 138–143.

Bockover, J. G. "Moral treatment in American psychiatry." *J. Nerv. Ment. Dis.,* 1956, 124, 107–194.

Bordin, E. S. "Ambiguity as a therapeutic variable." *J. Cons. Psychol.,* 1955, 19, 9–15.

Boyd, R. V., and Di Mascio, G. "Social behavior and autonomic physiology. A sociophysiologic study." *J. Nerv. Ment. Dis.,* 1954, 120, 207–212.

Brill, N. Q., and Beebe, G. W. "A follow-up study of war neuroses," Washington, *V.A. Medical Monograph,* 1955.

Bronner, A. F. "Treatment and what happened afterward." *Amer. J. Orthopsychiat.,* 1944, 14, 28–35.

Brown, J. L. "The follow-up procedure of an intermittent child guidance clinic," Unpubl. Master's Thesis (1931), quoted by Levitt.

Brown, M. "Adolescents treatable by a family agency." *Smith Coll. Stud. Soc. Wk.,* 1947, 18, 37–67.

Burlington, S. "A quantitative analysis of psychiatric social treatment carried out in seventy-five cases at the Institute for Juvenile Research," Unpubl. Master's Thesis (1931), quoted by Levitt.

Campbell, D. T. "Factors relevant to the validity of experiments in social settings." *Psychol. Bull.,* 1957, 54, 297–312.

Canaday, L. J. "A way of predicting the probable outcome of treatment of young children who run away," Unpubl. Master's Thesis (1940), quoted by Levitt.

Carmichael, H. T., and Masserman, T. H. "Results of treatment in a psychiatric outpatients' department." *J. Amer. Ment. Ass'n,* 1939, 113, 2,292–2,298.

Carpenter, J. A. "Some factors relating to the method and outcome of case-work treatment with the adolescent girl when the girl herself is the focus of treatment," Unpubl. Master's Thesis (1939), quoted by Levitt.

Christianson, E., Gates, M., and Coleman, F. A. "Survey of the intake of a mental hygiene clinic with special reference to the outcome of treatment." *Smith Coll. Stud. Soc. Wk.,* 1943, 5, 211–212.

Cohen, M., and Davis, E. "Factors related to the outcome of treatment in a child guidance clinic." *Smith Coll. Stud. Soc. Wk.,* 1934, 5, 212–214.

Cooper, J. E. "A study of behaviour therapy in thirty psychiatric patients." *Lancet,* 1963 Feb. 23, 411–415.

Cronbach, L. J., and Gleser, G. C. Review: "The study of behavior," *Psychometrika,* 1957, 19, 327–330.

Cunningham, J. M., et al. "A follow-up study of children seen in a psychiatric clinic for children." Paper read at Amer. Orthopsychiat. Ass'n, Chicago (1955), quoted by Levitt.

Curran, D. "The problem of assessing psychiatric treatment." *Lancet,* 1937, II, 1,005–1,009.

Curran, D., and Partridge, M. *Psychological medicine* (London, Livingstone, 1955).

Danskin, D. E. "Roles played by counselors in their interviews." *J. Cons. Psychol.,* 1955, 2, 22–27.

De Charmes, R., Levy, J., and Wertheimer, M. "A note on attempted evaluations of psychotherapy." *J. Clin. Psychol.,* 1954, 10, 233–235.

Dittman, A. T. "The interpersonal process in psychotherapy: department of a research method." *J. Abnorm. (Soc.) Psychol.,* 1952, 47, 236–244.

Dollard, J., Auld, F., and White, A. *Steps in Psychotherapy* (New York, Macmillan, 1953).

Eisenberg, L., and Gruenberg, E. M. "The current status of secondary prevention in child psychiatry." *Amer. J. Orthopsychiat.* 1961, 31, 355–367.

Eldred, S. H. et al. "A procedure for the systematic analysis of psychotherapeutic interviews." *Psychiatry,* 1954, 17, 337–346.

Ellis, A. "New approaches to psychotherapy techniques," *J. Clin. Psychol.,* 1955, 11, 208–260.

Ellis, A. "Outcome of employing three techniques of psychotherapy." *J. Clin. Psychol.,* 1957, 13, 344–350.

Ellis, A. "Rational psychotherapy." In H. J. Eysenck (Ed.), *Experiments in behavior therapy.* Oxford: Pergamon Press, 1964.

English, O. S., and Finch, S. M. *Introduction to psychiatry* (New York and London, Norton, 1954).

Eysenck, H. J. "The effects of psychotherapy: an evaluation." *J. Cons. Psychol.,* 1952, 16, 319–324.

Eysenck, H. J. *The structure of human personality* (London, Methuen, 1953).

Eysenck, H. J. "A reply to Luborsky's note." *Brit. J. Psychol.,* 1954, 45, 132–133.

Eysenck, H. J. "The effects of psychotherapy: a reply." *J. Abnorm. (Soc.) Psychol.,* 1955, 50, 147–148.

Eysenck, H. J. *The dynamics of anxiety and hysteria* (London, Routledge & Kegan Paul, 1957).

Eysenck, H. J. "Personality tests: 1950–1955." In *Recent advances in psychiatry* (London, Churchill, 1958).

Eysenck, H. J. (Ed.) *Behaviour therapy and the neuroses* (London, Pergamon Press, 1959).

Eysenck, H. J. (Ed.) *Experiments in behaviour therapy* (Oxford, Pergamon Press, 1964).

Fenichel, O. *Ten years of the Berlin Psychoanalysis Institute,* 1920–1930.

Fenton, N., and Wallace, R. "Child guidance in California communities." *J. Juv. Res.,* 1938, 22, 43–60.

Fiedler, F. E. "A comparison of therapeutic relationships in psychoanalytic, non-directive, and Adlerian therapy." *J. Cons. Psychol.,* 1950, 14, 436–445.

Fiedler, F. E. "The concept of the ideal therapeutic relationship." *J. Cons. Psychol.,* 1950, 14, 239–245.

Fiedler, F. E. "Factor analyses of psychoanalytic non-directive, and Adlerian therapeutic relationships." *J. Cons. Psychol.,* 1951, 15, 32–38.

Fiedler, F. E. "Quantitative studies on the role of therapists' feelings toward their patients." In H. Mowrer (Ed.), *Psychotherapy: theory and research,* pp. 296–315 (New York, Ronald Press, 1953).

Gallagher, J. J. "M.M.P.I. changes concomitant with client-entered therapy." *J. Cons. Psychol.*, 1953, 17, 234–338.

Gallagher, J. J. "Manifest anxiety changes concomitant with client-entered therapy." *J. Cons. Psychol.*, 1953, 17, 443–446.

Gliedman, L. H., Nash, E. H., Imber, S. D., Stone, A. R., and Franks, J. D. "Reduction symptoms by pharmacologically inert substances and by short term psychotherapy." *A.M.A. Arch. Neurol. Psychiat.*, 1958, 79, 345–555.

Glover, E. "Research methods in psycho-analysis." *Int. J. Psycho-Anal.*, 1952, 33, 403–409.

Glover, E. *The technique of psychoanalysis* (London, Bailliere, 1955).

Gollander, B. "A study of overinhibited and unsocialized aggressive children: III. Later adjustment," Unpubl. Master's Thesis (1944), quoted by Levitt.

Greenhill, M. H., et al. "Evaluation in mental health." *Hlth. Serv. Publ. No. 413* (Washington, U.S. Gov't Printing Off. 1955).

Greenspoon, J. In J. Dollard and N. G. Miller (Eds.). *Personality and psychotherapy* (New York, McGraw-Hill, 1950).

Grossman, D. "An experimental investigation of a psychotherapeutic technique." *J. Cons. Psychol.*, 1952, 16, 325–331.

Hamilton, D. M., Vanney, I. H., and Wall, T. H. "Hospital treatment of patients with psychoneurotic disorder." *Amer. J. Psychiat.*, 1942, 99, 243–247.

Hamilton, D. M., and Wall, T. H. "Hospital treatment of patients with psychoneurotic disorder." *Amer. J. Psychiat.*, 1941, 98, 551–557.

Harway, V. I., Dittmann, A. T., Raush, H. L., Bordin, E. S. and Rigler, D. "The measurement of depth of interpretation." *J. Cons. Psychol.*, 1955, 19, 247–253.

Hathaway, S. R. "Clinical methods: Psychotherapy," *Annual Rev. Psychol.*, 1951, 2, 259–280.

Healy, V., Bronner, G. F., Baylor, E. G., and Murphy, J. P. *Reconstructing behavior in youth: a study of problem children in foster families* (New York, Knopf, 1929).

Heinicke, C. M. "Research on psychotherapy with children: a review and suggestions for further study." *Amer. J. Orthopsychiat.*, 1960, 30, 483–493.

Holtzman, V. V., and Sells, G. B. "Prediction of flying success by clinical analysis of test protocols." *J. Abnorm. (Soc.) Psychol.*, 1954, 99, 485–490.

Hood-Williams, J. "The results of psychotherapy with children: a revelation." *J. Consult. Psychol.*, 1960, 24, 84–88.

Hubbard, R. M., and Adams, C. F. "Factors affecting the success of child guidance treatment." *Amer. J. Orthopsychiat.*, 1936, 6, 81–102.

Huddleson, J. H. "Psychotherapy in two hundred cases of psychoneurosis." *Milt. Surg.*, 1927, 60, 161–170.

Hunt, J. McV. "Toward an integrated program of research on psychotherapy." *J. Cons. Psychol.*, 1952, 16, 233–246.

Irgens, E. M. "Must parents' attitudes become modified in order to bring about adjustment in problem children?" *Smith Coll. Stud. Soc. Wk.*, 1936, 7, 17–45.

Jacobsen, V. "Influential factors in the outcome of treatment of school phobia." *Smith Coll. Stud. Soc. Wk.*, 1948, 18, 181–202.

Jaspers, K. *Allgemeine psychopathologie* (Berlin, Springer, 1913, 1948).

Johnson, L., and Reid, J. N. "An evaluation of ten years work with emotionally disturbed children." *Ryther Child Cent. Monogr. IV* (1947), quoted by Levitt.

Jones, E. *Decannual Report of the London Clinic of Psychoanalysis*, 1926–1936.

Jones, M. C. "The elimination of children's fear." *J. Exper. Psychol.*, 1924, 7, 382–390.

Kessel, L., and Hyman, H. T. "The value of psychoanalysis as a therapeutic procedure." *J. Amer. Med. Ass'n*, 1933, 101, 1,612–1,615.

Klumpner, G. H. "Army psychiatry in Korea following the cease fire agreement." *Amer. J. Psychiat.*, 1955, 112, 260–269.

Knight, R. P. "Evaluation of the results of psychoanalytic therapy." *Amer. J. Psychiat.*, 1941, 98, 434–446.

Kogan, L. S., Hunt, J. McV., and Bartelime, P. *A follow-up study of the results of social casework* (New York, Family Ass'n, of Amer. 1953).

La More, M. T. "An evaluation of a state hospital child guidance clinic," *Smith Coll. Stud. Soc. Wk.*, 1941, 12, 137–164.

Landis, C. "Statistical evaluation of psychotherapeutic methods." In S. E. Himie (Ed.), *Concepts and problems of psychotherapy* (London, Heinemann, 1938).

Lang, P. J., and Lazovik, A. D. "The experimental desensitization of a phobia." In H. J. Eysenck (Ed.), *Experiments in behaviour therapy* (Oxford, Pergamon Press, 1964).

Lazarus, A. A. "Group therapy of phobia disorders by systematic desensitization." *J. abnor. soc. Psychol.*, 1961, 63, 504–510.

Lazarus, A. A. "The results of behavior therapy in 126 cases of severe neurosis." *Beh. Res. Ther.*, 1963, 1, 69–79.

Lee, P. R., and Kenworthy, M. G. *Mental hygiene and social work* (New York, Commonwealth Fund 1929).

Lehrman, L. J., Sirluck, H., Black, B. J., and Glick, S. J. "Success and failure of treatment of children in the child guidance clinics of the Jewish Branch of Guardians, New York City." *Jewish Bd. Guard. Res. Monogr.*, No. 1 (1949).

Levine, M. *Psychotherapy in medical practice* (New York, Macmillan, 1948).

Levitt, E. E. "The results of psychotherapy with children: an evaluation." *J. Cons. Psychol.*, 1957, 21, 189–196.

Levitt, E. E. "A comparison of 'remainders' and 'defectors' among child clinic patients." *J. Consult. Psychol.*, 1957, 21, 314.

Levitt, E. E. "Reply to Hood-Williams." *J. Consult. Psychol.*, 1960, 24, 89–91.

Levitt, E. E. "Psychotherapy with children: a further evaluation." *Beh. Res. Ther.*, 1963, 1, 45–51.

Levitt, E. E., Beiser, H. R., and Robertson, R. E. "A follow-up evaluation of cases treated at a community child guidance clinic." *Amer. J. Orthopsychiat.*, 1939, 29, 337–347.

Lipkin, S. "Clients' feelings and attitudes in relations to the outcome of client-centered therapy." *Psychol. Monogr.*, 1954, 68.

Lovibond, S. H. "The mechanism of conditioning treatment of enuresis." *Beh. Res. Ther.*, 1963a, 1, 17–22.

Lovibond, S. H. "Intermittent reinforcement in behaviour therapy." *Beh. Res. Ther.*, 1963b, 1, 127–132.

Luborsky, L. "A note on Eysenck's article 'The effects of psychotherapy, an evaluation.'" *Brit. J. Psychol.*, 1954, 45, 129–131.

Luff, M. C., and Garrod, M. "The after-results of psychotherapy in five hundred adult cases." *Brit. Med. J.*, 1935, 2, 54–59.

Maas, H. S., et al. "Socio-cultural factors in psychiatric-clinic services for children." *Smith Coll. Stud. Soc. Wk.*, 1955, 25, 1–90.

Maberly, G., and Sturge, B. "After-results of child guidance." *Brit. Med. J.*, 1939, 1, 1,130–1,134.

Masserman, T. H., and Carmichael, H. T. "Diagnosis and prognosis in psychiatry." *J. Ment. Sci.*, 1938, 84, 893–946.

Matarazzo, J. D., et al. "The interaction chromograph as an instrument for objective measurement of interaction patterns during interviews." *J. Psychol.*, 1956, 41, 347–367.

Matz, P. B. "Outcome of hospital treatment of ex-service patients with nervous and mental disease in the U.S. Veteran's Bureau." *U.S. Vet. Bur. Med. Bull.*, 1929, 5, 829–842.

Meehl, P. E. "Psychotherapy." *Annual Rev. Psychol.*, 1955, 6, 357–378.

Miles, H., Barrabee, E. L., and Finesinger, J. E. "Evaluation of psychotherapy." *Psychosom. Med.*, 1951, 13, 83–105.

Morris, D. P., and Soroker, E. "A follow-up study of a guidance clinic visiting list." *Ment. Hyg.*, N.Y. 1953, 37, 84–88.

Morris, D. P., Soroker, E., and Burress, G. "Follow-up studies of shy, withdrawn children: I. Evaluation of later adjustment." *Amer. J. Orthopsychiat.*, 1954, 24, 743–754.

Moses, J. "A study of overinhibited and unsocialized aggressive children: Part IV. The later adjustment of unsocialized aggressive children," Unpubl. Master's Thesis (1944), quoted by Levitt.

Moustakas, C. E., and Schalock, H. D. "An analysis of therapist-child interaction in child therapy." *Child Developm.*, 1955, 26, 143–157.

Mowrer, H., *Psychotherapy: theory and research* (New York, Ronald Press, 1953).

Murray, E. J., Auld, F., and White, A. M. "A psychotherapy case showing progress but no decrease in the discomfort relief quotient." *J. Cons. Psychol*, 1955, 18, 349–353.

Neustatter, W. L. "The results of fifty cases treated by psychotherapy." *Lancet*, 1935, 1, 796–799.

Newburger, H. M. "The effect of group therapy upon certain aspects of the behavior and attitudes of institutionalized delinquents," Unpubl. Ph.D. Thesis, New York, 1952.

Newell, N. W. "The methods of child guidance adapted to a public school system." *Ment. Hyg.*, N.Y. 1934, 18, 362–373.

Parloff, M. B., Kelman, W. C., and Franks, J. "Comfort, effectiveness, and self-awareness as criteria of improvement in psychotherapy." *Amer. J. Psychiat.*, 1954, 110, 343–351.

Phillips, E. L. *Psychotherapy: a modern theory and practice* (London, Staples, 1957).

Powers, E. "An experiment in prevention of delinquency." *Ann. Amer. Acad. Pol. Soc. Science*, 1949, 77–88.

Powers, E., and Witmer, H. *An experiment in the prevention of delinquency* (New York, Columbia Univ. Press, 1951).

Rainy, V. (Ed.) *Training in clinical psychology* (New York, Prentice-Hall 1950).

Raush, H. L., et al. "A dimensional analysis of depth of interpretation." *J. Cons. Psychol.*, 1956, 20, 43–48.

Reid, J. H., and Hagan, H. R. *Residential treatment of emotionally disturbed children* (New York, Child Welfare League of America, 1952).

Roger, C. A. *Counseling and psychotherapy* (New York, Houghton Mifflin, 1942).

Rogers, C. R. (Ed.) *Client centered therapy* (New York, Houghton Mifflin, 1954).

Rogers, C., and Dymond, R. *Psychotherapy and Personality Change* (Chicago, Univ. of Chicago Press, 1954).

Rosanoff, A. J. *Manual of psychiatry* (New York, John Wiley & Sons, Inc., 1947).

Rosenberg, S. "The relationship of certain personality factors to prognosis in psychotherapy." *J. Clin. Psychol.*, 1954, 10, 341–345.

Rosenzweig, S. "A transvaluation of psychotherapy: a reply to Hans Eysenck." *J. Abnorm. (Soc.) Psychol.*, 1954, 49, 298–304.

Ross, T. A. *An enquiry into prognosis in the neuroses* (London, Cambridge Univ. Press, 1936).

Salzinger, K. "An experimental approach to the interview." *Resumes des communications,* XVth International Congress of Psychology.

Sanford, N. "Clinical methods: Psychotherapy." *Annual Rev. Psychol.*, 1953, 4, 317–342.

Saslow, G. "Psychotherapy." *Annual Rev. Psychol.*, 1954, 5, 311–336.

Saslow, G., et al. "The stability of interaction chronograph patterns in psychiatric interviews." *J. Cons. Psychol.*, 1955, 19, 417–430.

Schilder, P. "Results and problems of group psychotherapy in severe neuroses." *Ment. Hyg.*, N.Y. 1939, 23, 87–98.

Shagass, C., and Malmo, R. M. "Psychodynamic themes and localised muscular tension during psychotherapy." *Psychosom. Med.*, 1954, 16, 295–314.

Shepherd, M., and Gruenberg, E. M. "The age for neuroses." *Millbank Mem. F. Quart. Bull.*, 1957, 35, 258–265.

Shoben, E. J. "Some observations on psychotherapy and the learning process." In O. H. Mowrer (Ed.), *Psychotherapy, theory and research* (New York, Ronald Press, 1953).

Shoben, E. J. "Counseling." *Annual Rev. Psychol.*, 1956, 7, 147–172.

Sommer, G. R., Maxo, B., and Lehner, G. F. "An empirical investigation of therapeutic 'listening.'" *J. Clin. Psychol.*, 1955, 11, 132–136.

Stephenson, W. *The study of behavior* (Chicago, Univ. of Chicago Press, 1953).

Strupp, H. H. "An objective comparison of Rogerian and psychoanalytic techniques." *J. Cons. Psychol.*, 1955, 19, 1–7.

Strupp, H. H. "Psychotherapy." In *Amer. Rev. Psychol.*, 1960, 13, 445–478.

Taffel, C. "Anxiety and the conditioning of verbal behavior." *J. Abnorm. (Soc.) Psychol.*, 1955, 51, 496–501.

Teuber, N. L., and Powers, E. "Evaluating therapy in a delinquency prevention program." *Proc. Ass'n, Res. Nerv. Ment. Dis.*, 31, 138–147 (Baltimore, Williams & Wilkins, 1953).

Thetford, W. N. "The measurement of physiological response to frustration before and after nondirective psychotherapy." *Amer. Psychologist*, 1948, 3, 278.

Thorndike, E. L. *The psychology of wants, interests, and attitudes* (New York, Appleton-Century, 1935).

Thorne, F. C. "Rules of evidence in the evaluation of the effects of psychotherapy." *J. Clin. Psychol.*, 1952, 8, 38–41.

Verplanck, W. S. "The control of the content of conversation: reinforcement of statement of opinion." *J. Abnorm. (Soc.) Psychol.*, 1955, 51, 668–676.

Walcott, G. "A study of the present adjustment made by solitary children who had withdrawn into an imaginary world," Unpubl. Master's Thesis (1931), quoted by Levitt.

Walker, R. G., and Kelley, F. E. "Short term psychotherapy with hospitalized schizophrenic patients." *Act. Psychiat. Neurol. Scand.*, 1960, 35, 34–56.

Watson, G., and Comrey, A. L. "Nutritional replacement for mental illness." *J. Psychol.*, 1954, 38, 251–264.

Watson, J. B., and Raynor, R. "Conditioned emotional reactions." *J. Exp. Psychol.*, 1928, 3, 1–4.

Watson, R. I. "Research design and methodology in evaluating the results of psychotherapy." *J. Clin. Psychol.*, 1952, 8, 29–33.

Watson, R. I., and Mensh, I. N. "The evaluation of the effects of psychotherapy: I. Sources of material." *J. Psychol.*, 1951, 32, 259–273.

Watson, R. I., Mensh, I. N., and Gildea, E. F. "The evaluation of the effects of psychotherapy: III. Research design." *J. Psychol.*, 1951, 32, 293–308.

Wickes, T. G. "Examiners' influence on a testing situation." *J. Cons. Psychol.*, 1956, 20, 23–26.

Wilder, J. "Facts and figures on psychotherapy." *J. Clin. Psychopath.*, 1945, 7, 311–347.

Winder, C. L. "Psychotherapy." *Annual Rev. Psychol.*, 1957, 8, 309–330.

Witmer, H. L. "A comparison of treatment results in various types of child guidance clinics." *Amer. J. Ortho-psychiat.*, 1935, 5, 351–360.

Witmer, H. L., et al. "The later adjustment of problem children." *Smith Coll. Stud. Soc. Wk.*, 1935, 6, 1–98.

Witmer, H. L., et al. "The outcome of treatment in a child guidance clinic: a comparison and an evaluation." *Smith Coll. Stud. Soc. Wk.*, 1933, 3, 339–399.

Witmer, H. L., & Keller, J. "Outgrowing childhood problems: a study in the value of child guidance treatment." *Smith Coll. Stud. Soc. Wk.*, 1942, 13, 74–90.

Wolpe, J. "Experimental neuroses as learned behaviour." *Brit. J. Psychol.*, 1952, 43, 243–268.

Wolpe, J. "Learning versus lesions as the basis of neurotic behavior." *Amer. J. Psychiat.,* 1956, 112, 923–931.

Wolpe, J. "Objective psychotherapy of the neuroses." *S. Afr. Med. J.,* 1952, 26, 825–829.

Wolpe, J. *Psychotherapy by reciprocal inhibition* (California, Stanford Univ. Press, 1958).

Wolpe, J. "Reciprocal inhibition as the main basis of psychotherapeutic effects." *A.M.A. Arch. Neurol. Psychiat.,* 1954, 72, 205–226.

Wolpe, J. "The systematic desensitization treatment of neuroses." *J. Nerv. Ment. Dis.,* 1961, 132, 189–203.

Yaskin, J. C. "The psychoneuroses and neuroses. A review of a hundred cases with special reference to treatment and results." *Amer. J. Psychiat.,* 1936, 93, 107–125.

Zubin, J. "Evaluation of therapeutic outcome in mental disorders." *J. Nerv. Ment. Dis.,* 1953, 117, 95–111.

Author Index

Alexander, F., 754
Alexander, Samuel, 125
Allport, Floyd H., 2
Allport, G. W., 48
Anker, J. M., 738, 739
Ardrey, Robert, 190
Arendt, Hannah, 30
Ariès, Philippe, 545, 546, 547, 550
Aristotle, 327

Back, Kurt W., 358
Bacon, Sir Francis, 137
Bagley, W. C., 166, 168, 169, 170, 172
Baldwin, James M., 70, 325
Bales, Robert F., 300, 349, 618
Balint, M., 651
Ball, Donald W., 18, 152, 196, 312
Bandura, Albert, 577
Banton, Michael, 604
Barendregt, J. T., 736, 737
Barker, R. G., 300
Barron, F., 731, 732
Bates, Alan P., 78
Becker, Ernest, 16, 90, 95, 594
Becker, Howard S., 18, 19, 79, 260, 460,
    462, 518n., 519, 574, 578, 583, 606
Beebe, G. W., 729
Bell, Richard Q., 581
Bellah, Robert, 24
Bendix, Reinhard, 30
Bennett, David J., 151, 190
Bennett, Judith D., 151, 190
Bentham, Jeremy, 327
Berger, Peter, 594, 595, 596, 601, 605
Bergson, Henri, 119
Berkeley, Bishop, 38
Berreman, Gerald D., 241, 246, 247
Biblarz, Arturo, 437, 438, 442
Biderman, A. D., 703
Bierstadt, Robert, 261
Bixenstine, V. E., 722

Blake, Judith, 350
Blau, Peter, 707
Blau, Zena Smith, 520, 613
Bleuler, E., 648
Block, Herbert A., 699
Blumer, Herbert, 1, 28, 70, 72, 209, 277,
    279, 282, 295, 458
Boas, Franz, 83
Boehm, Max, 260
Boek, Walter E., 574
Bordin, E. S., 721
Bovet, Pierre, 513, 514, 532, 535, 536,
    537
Bowen, Elizabeth, 229
Boyd, R. V., 722
Braroe, Niels Winther, 210, 240
Brauchi, J. T., 646
Braude, Lee, 579
Brill, N. Q., 729
Brim, Orville, 518, 554, 569, 570, 584,
    586
Bronfenbrenner, Urie, 518, 572, 577
Bronson, Wanda C., 573
Bruner, Jerome, 77
Bryce, James, 547
Burchinal, Lee G., 574
Burgess, Ernest W., 8, 293, 348
Burke, Kenneth, 11, 78–79, 368, 401,
    403, 484, 488, 594, 596, 600, 601
Bury, J. B., 24

Calogeros, Roy C., 581
Calvin, A. D., 410
Cameron, N., 652, 653
Campbell, Donald T., 451, 458, 772, 724
Cantril, H., 481
Carnap, Rudolf, 123, 139
Carper, James W., 519, 606
Cassirer, Ernest, 80, 81
Cavan, Ruth S., 517, 579
Cavan, Sherri, 554

Chang Tung-Sun, 91, 92, 121
Child, Irwin, 567
Clark, Alexander L., 350
Clausen, John A., 671, 699
Clemmer, Donald, 703
Clifford, W. L., 304
Cloward, Richard A., 577
Cohen, Albert K., 575
Cohen, E. A., 705
Cohen, Morris, 25
Coleman, F. A., 722
Coleman, James S., 576
Collingwood, R. G., 31, 32
Comte, Auguste, 22, 24
Confucius, 132, 136, 137
Cooley, Charles Horton, 13, 18, 55, 63,
    70, 71, 75, 76, 77, 370, 371, 372, 377,
    395, 398, 402, 404, 406, 409, 415,
    419, 435, 489, 515
Cooper, J. E., 756
Cooper, Joseph, 415, 416, 417, 436
Copernicus, 89
Corwin, Ronald G., 578
Coser, Lewis, 11, 30, 31, 705
Coser, Rose Laub, 705
Cottrell, Leonard S., Jr., 17, 18, 63, 78,
    82, 293, 295, 300, 419, 421
Crawford, Meredith, 99
Cressey, Donald R., 81, 699, 703
Cronbach, L. J., 721
Crutchfield, R. S., 69
Cummings, Elaine, 579
Cunnington, C. Willet, 229
Curran, D., 719

Dahrendorf, Ralf, 23, 30, 36, 37
D'Andrade, Ray, 574
Danskin, D. E., 721
Darwin, Charles, 17, 37, 55, 56, 126,
    310, 321
Davis, Fred, 341, 345–46
Davis, Kingsley, 21, 23, 350
De Charmes, R., 718
Denzin, Norman K., 416, 417, 447
Desmonde, William H., 16, 17, 55
Deutsch, Morton, 78
Deutschberger, Paul, 327
Deutscher, Irwin, 518, 579
Devereux, E. C., 577

Dewey, John, 5, 16, 17, 26, 43–54, 55,
    69, 70, 71, 75, 77, 100, 107, 350, 352,
    402, 435, 467, 468, 471, 473, 484
Dick, Harry B., 78
Dickson, William J., 618
Di Mascio, G., 722
Dinitz, Simon, 78
Distler, Luther, 571
Dobriner, William, 264
Dollard, John, 39, 431, 721
Donohue, George, 437, 438, 442
Dornbusch, Sanford M., 78, 415, 416,
    417, 419, 437, 438, 439, 442, 443,
    445, 446, 447, 703
Durkheim, Emile, 21, 24, 26, 32, 33, 38,
    90, 100–112, 229, 273, 280, 352, 353,
    354, 513, 532, 533, 534, 535, 536, 711
Dymond, Rosalind, 64, 82, 296, 421,
    721, 727, 735

Eberhart, Richard, 629
Einstein, Albert, 89
Eisenberg, L., 753
El-Shabazz, 12
Elder, Glen H., Jr., 570, 582
Eldred, S. H., 721
Ellis, A., 721, 759, 760
Emerson, Ralph Waldo, 50
Engels, Frederick, 142
English, O. S., 719
Erikson, Erik H., 398, 518
Erickson, Kai, T., 606, 626, 709
Eulau, Heinz, 579
Eysenck, Hans J., 717, 718, 722, 748,
    750, 752, 755

Farber, Maurice L., 705
Farberman, Harvey A., 90, 100
Faris, Ellsworth, 70, 71, 72, 75, 76, 300
Fiedler, F. E., 754
Finch, S. M., 719
Foote, Nelson N., 18, 70, 79, 278, 300,
    319, 468, 469, 480, 595
Form, William, 261, 263
Fortes, Meyer, 207, 208, 213
Frank, Waldo, 54
Freidman, Neil, 457
Freud, Sigmund, 5, 13, 14, 16, 33, 34,

39, 42, 63, 80, 320, 321, 327, 479, 484, 548, 566, 567
Fromm, Erich, 322

Gallagher, J. J., 721
Gallagher, Ruth, 78
Gantt, W. H., 98
Garfinkel, Harold, 151, 280, 354
Garretson, Wynona, 78
Geis, Gilbert, 699
Gibbs, Jack F., 350
Gibson, Duane, 550
Ginsberg, Allen, 631, 632
Glaser, Barney G., 264, 265, 279, 280, 517, 550
Glaser, Daniel, 81
Glass, A. J., 651
Gleser, G. C., 721
Gliedman, L. H., 742
Glover, E., 763
Goffman, Erving, 19, 79, 151, 177, 179, 186, 190, 200, 203, 210, 211, 241, 246, 247, 248, 259, 329, 341, 342–44, 455, 457, 579, 626, 662, 664
Gold, Martin, 575
Gold, Raymond L., 458
Gordon, J. E., 649
Gorer, Geoffrey, 407
Gough, Harrison G., 296
Gouldner, Alvin W., 12, 24, 212, 264, 265
Green, Arnold, 547
Greenhill, M. H., 721, 723
Greenspoon, J., 735
Groos, Karl, 325
Gross, Edward, 174, 349
Gross, Neal, 75, 150, 151, 297, 298, 348, 349, 350, 435
Grossman, D., 721
Gruenberg, E. M., 743, 747, 753
Guthrie, E. R., 15

Hall, Oswald, 611
Hall, Robert T., 191
Haller, Archie O., Jr., 574
Hallowell, A. I., 99
Harris, Dale B., 577
Hartley, Eugene L., 77
Hartley, Ruth E., 571

Harway, V. I., 721
Hathaway, S. R., 719
Havighurst, Robert J., 575
Hebb, D. O., 561
Heider, Fritz, 298, 300
Heinicke, C. M., 753
Heron, W., 646
Hess, Robert, 320
Hilgard, E. R., 65
Hill, Reuben, 358
Hillmer, Max L., 571
Hobbes, Thomas, 13, 31, 37, 38
Hobhouse, L., 43
Hoffman, Louis W., 571
Hollingshead, A. B., 641
Holtzman, Wayne H., 420
Homans, George C., 38, 618, 707
Hood-Williams, J., 753
Hook, Sidney, 53
Hu Shih, Dr., 132, 137
Hughes, Everett C., 19, 79
Hughes, Langston, 90, 92, 210, 237
Huizinga, J., 409
Hume, David, 44
Hunt, J. McV., 723
Hurlburt, Julia Knaff, 81
Hyman, H., 76

Irwin, John, 589

James, William, 42, 43, 53, 54, 70, 100, 106, 107, 108, 110, 184, 369, 370, 372, 373, 486, 515, 600
Jaspers, K., 719
Jensen, A. R., 432
Jones, Edward E., 707
Jones, Mary C., 576

Kallen, Horace, 53
Kant, Immanuel, 1, 123, 137, 138, 532
Kantor, Mildred B., 573
Kardiner, Abram, 34
Kecskemeti, Paul, 33
Keller, Helen, 539
Kelley, H. H., 76
Kelly, F. E., 742
Kerouac, Jack, 630
Kitt, Alice S., 76
Klapp, Orrin E., 348, 349, 363, 365

Kluckhohn, Clyde, 19, 81
Knight, Frank H., 326
Knight, R. P., 721, 755
Koch, Helen L., 575
Kogan, L. S., 723
Kohler, W., 165
Kohn, Melvin L., 572
Koller, Marvin R., 548
Komarovsky, Mirra, 76
Korn, Richard R., 699
Kretch, D., 69
Krim, Seymour, 622, 626
Kuhn, Manford H., 14, 18, 19, 70, 415, 416, 417, 424, 447, 448

Laing, Ronald, 280, 355, 356, 357, 358, 364
Landis, C., 745, 747, 748
Lang, P. J., 739
Langer, Suzanne, 149, 371, 643
LaPiere, Richard T., 299
Lazarus, A. A., 737, 738, 739, 741, 755, 757
Lazovik, A. D., 739
Leary, Timothy F., 606, 731, 732
Lee, A. Russell, 92, 280, 355, 365
Leites, Nathan, 705
Lemert, Edwin M., 81, 626, 651, 652
Lenzen, V. F., 125
Lesser, Gerald S., 582
Levine, M., 719
Levitt, E. E., 750, 751, 752, 753
Lewin, Kurt, 56, 69
Lewis, Oscar, 494, 551
Lindesmith, Alfred R., 66, 72, 405, 460, 461, 481, 482, 522
Linton, Ralph, 35, 75, 235, 415, 434, 435
Lipkin, S., 721
Lippitt, Ronald, 575
Lipps, Theodor, 305, 306, 311, 312
Litman, Theodore J., 580
Little, Malcolm, 12
Livson, Norman, 518, 573
Locke, John, 45
Lockwood, David, 24, 30
Lopara, Helena Znaniecki, 156
Lortie, Dan C., 578

Lovibond, S. H., 741, 742
Luborsky, L., 718
Lundberg, George, 481
Lyman, Stanford M., 18, 208, 211, 214, 469, 489
Lymes, Russell, 233
Lynd, Helen, 401, 402
Lynn, David B., 571, 572

McCall, George, 90, 93
Maccoby, Eleanor E., 77, 571, 582
McCord, Joan, 571
McCord, William, 571
McCorkle, Lloyd W., 699
McDougall, William, 14
MacEachern, Alexander, 75, 297, 349
McHugh, Peter, 626, 699
MacIver, Robert M., 147
McKee, John P., 78
McPartland, Thomas S., 78, 425, 429
Malcolm X, 12
Malik, El-Haij, 12
Malinowski, Bronislaw, 21, 22, 148, 149, 158
Malmo, R. M., 722
Mangus, A. R., 78
Mannheim, Karl, 8, 53, 91, 92, 106, 122, 140, 261
Maranell, Gary M., 78
Marx, Karl, 548
Maslow, Abraham H., 78, 80
Mason, Ward S., 75, 297, 349
Matarazzo, J. D., 721
Matza, David, 575
Mead, George Herbert, 2, 8, 14, 16, 17, 43, 53, 54, 55, 56, 57, 58, 59, 60, 61, 62, 63, 65, 69, 71, 72, 73, 75, 76, 77, 80, 90, 94, 106, 108, 109, 110, 111, 112, 174, 207, 209, 229, 230, 231, 279, 282–93, 294, 295, 341–42, 350, 352, 361, 362, 365, 370, 371, 372, 383, 395, 396, 397, 398, 399, 402, 404, 405, 408, 409, 412, 415, 416, 418, 419, 420, 421, 434, 435, 436, 437, 438, 439, 440, 447, 448, 453, 474, 482, 483, 514, 515, 516, 517, 537, 551, 569, 711
Mead, Margaret, 5–6
Meehl, P. E., 723, 724, 754, 761

Merton, Robert K., 11, 21, 76, 148, 260, 261, 262, 265, 436, 549, 714
Messinger, Sheldon E., 624, 689
Meyerson, Emile, 134
Michener, James, 486
Miller, Daniel R., 573
Miller, Walter, 575
Mills, C. Wright, 15, 16, 17, 29, 30, 31, 42, 263, 468, 470, 472, 482, 548
Milner, K. O., 654
Milton, George A., 581
Miyakawa, T. Scott, 547
Miyamoto, S. Frank, 78, 277, 293, 415, 416, 417, 419, 437, 438, 439, 442, 443, 445, 446, 447
Molière, 23
Moore, Barrington, Jr., 29, 30
Moreno, J. L., 75
Morris, Charles W., 55
Morris, Richard T., 350
Moustakas, C. E., 721
Mowrer, H., 721, 741, 742
Mulford, Harold A., Jr., 81
Mullaby, Patrick, 61
Mumford, Lewis, 54
Murphy, A. E., 54
Murray, E. J., 721
Mussen, Paul H., 571
Myrdal, Gunnar, 364, 431

Nardini, William, 81
Nass, Gilbert D., 81
Neuberger, H. M., 722
Newcomb, Theodore M., 69, 72, 76, 77, 296, 297, 300, 351, 355, 358, 359, 362, 364, 365
Newton, Sir Isaac, 89
Nietzsche, Friedrich, 310
Nisbet, Robert, 23

Ohlin, Lloyd E., 577
Orlansky, Harold, 521, 522
Orwell, George, 227, 228

Pao Hsi Shih, 132
Pareto, Vilfredo, 124, 138
Park, Robert E., 293, 348, 360, 401, 462
Parloff, M. B., 722
Parsons, Talcott, 3, 11, 12, 21, 22, 23, 26–27, 31, 32, 33, 35, 75, 286, 350, 449, 478, 569, 572, 576, 580, 583
Partridge, M., 719
Pasamanick, B., 650
Pavlov, Ivan, 15, 95, 97
Payne, Raymond, 518, 580
Peck, Robert F., 575
Peirce, Charles, 53, 54, 100, 107
Pellegrin, Ronald J., 579
Peters, R. S., 18
Petrullo, Luigi, 77
Phillips, E. Lakin, 757, 758, 759
Phillipson, H., 280, 355, 365
Piaget, Jean, 81, 373, 411, 412, 513, 514, 517, 532
Plant, James, 322
Plato, 26, 32, 128, 160, 327
Plunkett, R. J., 649
Powers, E., 718, 726, 727, 729
Prescott, Daniel, 321
Prothro, E. T., 432
Proust, Marcel, 614
Ptolemy, 89

Quarantelli, E. L., 415, 416, 417, 436
Quelch, H., 142

Radcliffe-Brown, A. R., 21
Rainy, V., 719
Raush, H. L., 721
Reckless, Walter C., 81
Redlich, F. C., 641
Reeder, Lee, 437, 438, 439, 442, 445, 446
Reiss, Albert J., 577
Renouvier, Charles Bernard, 107
Richards, J. A., 136
Riesman, David, 13, 263, 518, 548
Riley, John W., 349
Riley, Matilda W., 349
Ritchie, Oscar W., 548
Roberts, Oral, 606
Roethlisberger, F. J., 617
Roger, Carl A., 81, 720, 721, 727
Rogers, Carol, 77
Rogler, Lloyd H., 78
Rosanoff, A. J., 719
Rose, Arnold M., 75, 76, 82, 241, 437
Rose, Edward, 483

Rosen, Bernard C., 573, 574
Rosenberg, Morris, 578
Rosenberg, S., 768
Rosenzweig, Saul, 718
Ross, Edward Alsworth, 14, 71
Rostow, Walter, 548
Rousseau, Jean-Jacques, 38
Roy, Donald, 341, 345–46
Russell, Bertrand, 54, 107, 108, 128, 139

Saint-Simon, Henri, 24
Salzinger, K., 735
Sampson, Harold, 689
Sandburg, Carl, 13
Sapir, Edward, 8, 9, 78, 80, 81
Sarason, Seymour B., 582
Sarbin, Theodore R., 19, 75
Saslow, G., 721, 763
Sawrey, William L., 571
Schachter, Stanley, 575
Schaefer, Earl S., 581, 582
Scheff, Thomas J., 18, 280, 348, 623, 645
Schein, Edgar H., 703
Scheler, Max, 18, 303, 317, 318, 352
Schelling, Thomas C., 189, 352, 353, 354
Schiller, F. C. S., 107
Schurz, Carl, 54
Schutz, Alfred, 22, 26, 312, 352, 354,
    705
Schwartz, M. S., 664
Scott, Marvin B., 11, 12, 18, 21, 208,
    211, 214, 469, 489
Sears, Robert R., 575
Sewell, William H., 511, 512, 518, 521,
    572, 574
Sharp, Paul F., 248
Sheperd, M., 743, 747
Sherif, M., 76, 481
Sheriffs, Alex C., 78
Sherrington, Charles, 95
Shibutani, Tamotsu, 72, 75, 76, 80, 449,
    450
Shils, Edward A., 350
Shoben, E. J., 718, 719, 754
Simmel, George, 13, 278, 300, 312, 315,
    456, 493
Simmons, J. L., 90, 93
Simpson, Ida H., 579
Simpson, Mary, 524

Simpson, Richard L., 579
Slater, Philip E., 299, 349, 572
Solomon, Leonard, 78
Sommer, G. R., 721
Spencer, Herbert, 12, 22, 44, 309, 310
Spengler, Oswald, 123, 134
Stanley, Julian C., 451, 458
Stanton, A. H., 664
Stein, Edith, 411
Stein, Gertrude, 29
Stephenson, W., 721
Stewart, Robert L., 78
Stone, Gregory P., 79, 90, 100, 150, 151,
    174, 209, 227, 250, 262, 263, 266,
    371, 372, 394, 453, 454, 516, 517,
    545, 596, 597, 604
Stotland, Ezra, 571
Stouffer, Samuel, 76
Straus, Murray A., 577, 581, 582
Strauss, Anselm L., 66, 72, 178, 279,
    280, 329, 336, 405, 481, 517, 522,
    550, 594, 596
Streib, Gordon, 580
Strodtbeck, Fred L., 574
Strupp, H. H., 742, 754
Stryker, Sheldon, 18, 78, 355, 356, 361,
    362, 364, 365, 436
Stycos, J. Mayone, 358
Suci, G. J., 577
Sullivan, Harry Stack, 8, 14, 16, 63, 65,
    76, 78, 79, 80, 82, 322, 368, 371, 372,
    386, 395, 398, 404, 411, 412, 518, 548,
    641, 669
Sumner, William Graham, 589
Sun, see Chang Tung Sun
Swanson, Guy E., 518, 573
Sykes, Gresham M., 263, 264, 265, 575,
    703
Szasz, Thomas S., 622, 623, 637, 638,
    639, 641, 642

Taffel, C., 735
Tagiuri, Renato, 77
Talmon, Yonina, 580
Tarde, Gabriel, 57
Taylor, M. Lee, 578–79
Teuber, N. L., 718, 720, 729
Thetford, W. N., 722
Thibaut, John W., 707

Thielbar, Gerald, 211, 259
Thomas, Dorothy Swaine, 148, 154
Thomas, William I., 8, 43, 70, 75, 147, 148, 154, 162, 163, 293
Thompson, Wayne E., 580
Thorndike, E. L., 735
Thorne, F. C., 721
Thurber, Emily, 571
Toby, Jackson, 76
Toby, Marcia L., 349
Tocqueville, Alexis de, 547
Tönnies, Ferdinand, 13, 261
Towne, Robert D., 689
Travisano, Richard V., 519, 594
Tugwell, Rexford, 54
Tuma, Elia S., 573
Turner, Ralph H., 19, 75, 76
Tyhurst, J. S., 654
Tylor, E. B., 22

Uexküll, Jakob von, 95

Veblen, Thorstein, 4, 54, 235, 547, 548
Verplanck, W. S., 735
Videbeck, Richard, 78

Waisanen, Carl, 78
Waisanen, Fred, 78, 429
Walker, R. G., 742
Wallace, Henry A., 54
Wallas, Graham, 43
Waller, Willard, 150, 162
Walsh, R. O., 738, 739
Ward, Lester F., 43
Waters, Richard H., 577
Watson, G. H., 721, 723
Watson, J. B., 721, 723
Watson, R. I., 271, 723

Weber, Max, 22, 25, 29, 474, 478, 594
Weinstein, Eugene A., 327
West, L. J., 646
Westby, David L., 578
Wheeler, Stanton, 580
Wheelis, Allen, 548
White, Leslie, 95, 98
Whitehead, Alfred North, 55, 124
Whiting, John W. M., 572
Whorf, Benjamin Lee, 8, 14, 15, 19, 40, 78, 80, 81, 90, 92, 112, 149, 160, 192
Whyte, William F., 618
Wickes, T. G., 735
Williams, Walter C., 581
Wilson, Alan B., 577
Winch, Robert F., 572
Winder, C. L., 720, 753
Wirth, Louis, 2, 3, 5, 348, 400
Witmer, H., 727
Wittgenstein, Ludwig, 21
Wolfe, Bernard, 690
Wolpe, J., 737, 739, 741, 753, 754, 755, 756, 757
Wright, H. F., 300
Wrong, Dennis H., 13, 14, 15, 28, 29
Wundt, W., 56

Yang, C. N., 92
Yarrow, Leon J., 575
Yarrow, Marian Radke, 575, 671
Young, E. F., 48
Young, Kimball, 70, 71

Zettergerg, Hans, 36
Zimmerman, Carle, 261
Znaniecki, Florian, 3, 147, 148, 156, 157, 158
Zubin, J., 721, 723

Subject Index

Accounts, 469, 489–509
  excuses, 491
  and identities, 504
  justifications, 491
  taken-for-granted, 496
  typical, 469
Act, 284, 293–300
  dispositional qualities, 277
  motivated, 468
  social, 94, 294
Action, 25, 59n.
  joint, 288
Actors, 192
Adornment, 225
Age, 235, 613–19
Agreement, 280
Altercasting, 327–36
Ambivalence, 320
Anomie, 709
Anxiety, 389
Appearance, 176n.
  and self, 394–414
  universe of, 229
Appreciation, 301
Audience, 323
Awareness, 279, 336, 517

Background
  expectations, 497
  phenomena, 116
  understanding, 354
Behavior
  document, 152
  motivated, 482
Biological Individualism, 43
Boundaries, 69, 711; see also
  territories, 215
  of situations, 208

Career
  contingencies, 671

moral aspects, 667
Categories, 25, 123
Causality, 133
Character, 694
  types, 13
Children, 521–31, 532–37, 545–53
  identity of, 545
  morality of, 532
  play of, 545
Choice, 642
Circumstances, 209, 235, 250
Clothing, 184
Cognition, 28
Collective
  consciousness, 352
  misrepresentation, 209
  representation, 101, 109, 150
Commitment, 584, 590–93
Communication, 2–5, 9, 17, 112
Competence, 321
Comprehension, 301
Conflict, 32
Conformity, 33–35, 38
Consensus, 8, 348
Constraint, 33
Constructs
  common sense, 28
  first order, 26
  sensitizing, 455
Contamination, 221
Contents, 122
Co-orientation, 296, 348–65
  ABX Model, 350
Cosmology
  Catholic, 134
  Chinese, 132
Cosmopolitans, 211, 259
Cultural history, 123

Darwinism, 31
Delusion, 662, 663

Derivations, 138
Designation, 90
Desocialization, 703
Determinacy, 18–19, 72
Deviance, 34, 709
Dialectic, 32
Dichotomies
  mentalistic-culturological, 147
  mind-body, 57
Drama
  anticipatory, 516
  fantastic, 549
Dramaturgy, 19
Drive, 39
Dualism, 56
Duration, 192, 194
Dynamic assessment, 150

Eclecticism, 6–7
Economics, 37
Embarrassment, 151, 174, 175, 187
Environment, 56
Epistemology, 143–44
Equilibrium, 28
Equipment, 183
Ethics, 640
Ethnomethodology, 148
Events, 704
Exclusion, 657
  background, 497
  complementarity of, 35
Experiments, 456
Explanations, 491
Extremism, 622

Feeling
  about, 278
  common, 278, 307
  fellow, 303, 307
Felt-valve, 469
Form, 313
  invariant properties, 277
Formulation, 113
  of ideas, 117
  of reality, 107
Freedom, 61
Functionalism, 21

Game, 411, 513, 539
  con, 210, 244

rules of, 532
team, 515
Gazeline, 181n.
"Generalized-other," 17, 61, 420, 421,
  540
Gestures, 17, 58
Grammar, 113
  Greek, 7, 19, 127
Guilt, 13, 14, 33

Habit, 42n., 46–50
  formation of, 33
Historicist, 29
Humanistic coefficient, 147, 156

"I," 14, 17, 18, 28, 60, 61
Id, 34
Identification, 468, 484
  and age, 606
  emotional, 278, 311
  and occupation, 613
  "of," 18
  and status, 613
  "with," 18
Identity, 6, 7, 67, 176–77, 398, 512, 545
  alternation of, 519, 594–96, 600
  appropriation of, 469
  change of, 594
  constancy of, 594
  conversion of, 519, 594–96, 600
  counter, 175n.
  documents, 178
  logic, 128
  negotiation of, 469, 603
  relicit, 179
  reserve, 179
  sequences of, 519, 603

Ideology, 91
  particular, 140, 141
  total, 140–41
Imitation, 71
Impulse, 50–57
Indeterminacy, 18–19, 72
Individualism, 42
Infant training, 521
Inner-direction, 34
"Inner-forum," 60, 62
In-patient, 677

Insanity, 626, 630
Insulation, 223
Intelligence, 50
Intention, 14
Interaction, 45–46
    visual, 300
Internalization, 13, 33
Interpersonal theory, 19, 79–80
Interpretation, 28, 277, 285
Intersubjectivity, 352
Introspection, 57
    method of, 52
Invasion, 200

Knowledge
    forms of, 122
    interpretive, 123
    theory of, 121–23

Labeling, 148
Laissez-faire, 42–43
Language, 59
    emotive, 120
Learning, 33
Legitimization, 199
Leviathan, 31
Linguistic
    collusion, 224
    context, 159
Living
    problems in, 637
Localism-cosmopolitanism, 264–75
"Locals," 211, 259
    Aristotelian, 5–8
    correlative, 127, 130, 135–36
    formal, 114
    mathematical, 128
    natural, 112–15
    properties, 118
    of sentiment, 124
Love, 278, 319

Manipulation, 225
"Mark," 210
Marxism, 122, 136, 139–40
Materialism, 134
"Me," 17, 18, 28, 60, 373
Meaning, 1, 3, 9, 42, 90
    consensual, 387

Measurement of
    actual response of others, 421
    generalized-other, 421, 443
    perceived response of others, 421
    self-conception, 421, 425
Mental illness, 637, 645
Metaphors, 2, 9, 100
    mechanistic, 101
Metaphysics, 122, 139
Method
    Life-history, 642
    participant observation, 459
    survey, 458
Mind, 59, 107
Modifiers, 192
Morality, 51; see also Children
    autonomous, 514
    heteronomous, 513
Motivation, 17, 70, 467–509; see also
    Motives
Motives, 34–39, 149n., 467, 471, 473,
    474; see also Motivation
    avowal of, 472
    function of, 468, 469
    imputations of, 472
    vocabularies of, 468

Names, 178
Neurosis, 33
Norms, 639
    performance, 151, 186
Nouns, 118

Objectivism, 26–28
Objects, 287
Occupational psychosis, 5
Omenism, 132
Order
    conceptual, 125
    Hobbesian, 30
Organism, 56–60
Overintegrated, 30, 37
Oversocialized, 28, 30, 37

Panel design, 416
Paradox of substance, 11, 175n.
Paranoia, 623, 652
Parataxic, 80
    distortion, 14

Passing, 237
Penetration, 225–26
Person perception, 76–77
Personal
    identity, 376
    life, 148
    meaning, 2
    poise, 180
Personal consistency, 590
Personality, 28, 35
Phenomenology, 22
Play, 408, 515, 539
    as drama, 549
    history of, 547
    social psychology, 548
Poise, 151, 175–76t.
    tests of, 551
Pollyanna fallacy, 24, 121
Power, 623
Pragmatism, 17, 53, 106
Pre-patient, 669
Private selves, 74
Processes, 7
    empathic, 17, 18, 63
    interpretive, 25
Progression, 192, 194
Props, 182, 192
Prototaxic, 80
Psychiatry, 640
Psychoanalysis, 34, 39, 41
Psychologistic fallacy, 9, 15
Psychology
    associationist, 57
    behaviorism, 41, 57
    dramaturgical, 78
    gestalt, 15, 41
    instinct, 17, 42
    social behaviorism, 21, 57
Psychosis, 630
Psychotherapy, 717–70
    with adults, 742
    with children, 751
    definition of, 719
    results of, 749
Public, 74

Rationality, 51
Reactivity, 97
Reality, 3, 6–7, 107

    negotiated, 448
    politics of, 89
Realization, 280
Relativity
    principle of, 118
Rebellion, 38
Reference group, 19, 36, 76
    relationship, 260
Referential language, 126
Reflexivity, 60
Regulative, 33
Relationism, 140, 143
Relational proposition, 127
Relativism, 140, 143
Relevance, 1–9
Residues, 138
Responsibility, 642
Revolution, 32
Rhetoric, 8, 9, 152
Ritual, 172
Role, 19, 37, 165, 175, 397
    adjunct, 179
    definition of, 208
    distance, 14, 246
    dominant, 179
    expectations, 75
    learning, 570
    performance, 75
    playing, 75
    requirements, 176
    segregation, 246
    taking, 68, 352
    theory, 19, 75–76
Routine grounds, 151
Rule-breaking, 645

Sarcasm, 278, 312
Scene, 191
Self-conception, 420, 441
Selective inattention, 389
Self, 17–19, 53n., 65, 367–414
    as antecedent, 73
    and appearance, 394, 414
    conception, 66
    as consequent, 173
    as illusion, 387
    as knower, 377
    as object, 383
    and other, 67

Self (*cont.*)
  as sentiment, 377
  theory, 77
Sex, 231
Sign, 98
Significant other, 415
Situated conduct, 149
Situation, 17, 68, 149, 209,
    235, 250
  context of, 148, 158
  definition of, 147–48, 150, 164
  elements of, 151
  historical, 30
  typical, 468
Situational
  adjustment, 584, 586
  determination, 143
Social
  contract, 31
  Darwinism, 17, 34, 42
  factors, 35
  facts, 12, 103
  interaction, 285
  knowledge, 125
  "Me," 374
  norms, 3
  object, 93–94, 99
  pragmatism, 108–10
  reality, 29
  self, 42*n.*
  space, 260
  status, 250
  structure, 584
  survey, 458
Socialization, 6
  adolescent, 566
  adult, 583–93
  anticipatory, 412
  childhood, 566
  fantastic, 412
  later, 576
  methodological advances, 581
  plain, 702
  radical, 702
  and social class, 572
  and social structure, 574
  theoretical development of, 566
Sociological
  dispositional qualities, 298

epistemology, 104
Sociology of knowledge, 122, 126, 143
Space, 224
Spaces, 180
Staging, 151
Structural
  differentiation, 24
  functionalism, 11
  relationships, 399
Subject-predicate preposition, 127
Substance, 128, 132–33
Superego, 33, 34
Symbol, 98, 148, 208, 538
Symbolic
  interaction, 70
  relativity, 160
  representations, 25
Symbolization, 99
Symbols, 59, 109
Sympathy, 18

Taken-for-granted
  logic, 80
  rules, 151
Tautology, 12
Territory, 214–26
  encroachment, 220
  types of, 215–20
Time, 120, 175
Titles, 178
Trained incapacities, 4
Transcendental interpretation, 141*n.*
Transformations, 12, 148
Triangulation, 450
Truth, 106
Turf, 223
Twenty Statements Test (TST), 415,
    425

Understanding, 26, 122, 280
Universality, 5, 8
Utilitarianism, 37

Validity, 3–9, 451
Value, 14, 48–49, 145, 469
Variable analysis, 212
Variables, 1, 7, 25, 209
Verbs, 118

Vienna school, 139
Violation, 220
Violence, 32
Vulgar Marxism, 37

Working consensus, 151, 210, 241

Youth
  etiquette of, 554

A B C D E F G H I J   5 4 3 2 1 7 0